THE COMPLETE RECORD
OF
GLOUCESTER CITY AFC
1883 TO 2009

Compiled by Timothy RD Clark
in collaboration with
Rob Kujawa

ISBN 978-0-9557425-1-4

Published by
TigerTimbo Publications,
2 Rosemary Close,
Abbeydale,
Gloucester GL4 5TL

Email: tigertimbo@hotmail.co.uk

© Timothy RD Clark 2009

Printed and Bound by
Inky Little Fingers,
Unit A3,
Churcham Business Park,
Churcham,
Gloucester GL2 8AX

Tel: 01452 751139
Email: helpdesk@inkylittlefingers.co.uk

Website: www.inkylittlefingers.co.uk

Cover design by Daniel Hunston

Dedicated to
Sidney Walter Clark
1912-2004
Winifred Edna Clark
1915-2008
"Gratitude is the heart's memory"

FOREWORD
By Dave Phillips
Chairman of Gloucester City Association Football Club

One can only stand back and admire the labour of love that has gone into producing such a comprehensive statistical guide of the playing history of Gloucester City Association Football Club.
Such an accolade is richly deserved by its author, Tim Clark, for having taken on such a mammoth task. An effort of the highest order!

The fact that the very early days have been researched so comprehensively, from an era when reporting of matches was less accurate and efficient, is something in itself. Even today with the world-wide web at our fingertips, reporting inaccuracies abound in the general media, with only the keen observance of the trained eye likely to spot an error here or there. If an error goes undetected it can quite mistakenly become fact! There is no fear of that happening while Tim Clark is on duty! There are inevitably a few gaps that even the most diligent research has failed to uncover, but given half a clue and the hunt for the truth will be on again for those missing snippets of information! (For instance, it has never been authenticated at what game the first ever City match day programme was produced, but the oldest known is referenced)

Tim Clark, quite rightly, always refers to himself as a 'statistician' and declines quite vigorously, the use of the word 'historian'. I would never wish to argue the point with him, but there is, between the lines and amongst all those statistics, the history of the club. Unspoken, yes indeed, but the history is still there.

I have been statistically aware from quite a young age, through obtaining a copy of the 'Wisden' Almanac, which led me to a love (or an obsession) with cricket and its statistics, which in a curious way, led me to delve beneath the figures to uncover the rich history of many a good, bad or indifferent performance! I can fully appreciate how statistics provide an understanding of our heritage and what we will be leaving for discovery by generations yet to come.
It is a measurement of the past in terms of achievement, upon which we can build during our time of influence, so that others yet to come may create new targets towards which to strive.

Before history-making beckoned at Farnborough on Saturday 2nd May 2009, we were the longest continuous club member in the Southern Football League, which in itself says something. Is there anyone still around who can remember anything of the pre-Southern League days? My first memories are from 1957, when the club was based at Nine Elms Road - now a housing development; on to Horton Road in 1964 - also now a housing development; then the move to Meadow Park in 1986. Three floodings later - culminating in the Great Flood of July 2007 - has led to a period of exile, firstly at The New Lawn, Nailsworth for 2007/08, and to the Corinium Stadium in Cirencester since.
In that time-line alone there is a lot of history. What of the playing arrangements pre Nine Elms Road? Well, they are all documented for sure, and Tim has researched and catalogued the lot!

In terms of appearances it has intrigued me to re-call that the record still stands with Stan Myers at 413. In 126 years of the Club's history to date, it is an amazingly low figure, especially when you read from other clubs that 'X' has just passed 600 appearances, or 'Y' has just retired after 743 games, etc. Without Tim's assiduous work, we would be unaware that in the next year or two, that record may well be broken! This depends on the form and fitness of two current players each with over 300 appearances, and one other nearing the 300 mark. Even so, it is not impossible to believe that Stan's current record, which has stood for a good few years now, may be broken more than once in the short to medium term!

Tim's enthusiasm for his subject is astounding and I will quote one example. This happened during the last season when we played a Quarter-Final of the Southern League Cup at Bridgwater Town. For personal reasons, our then regular goalkeeper, Kevin Sawyer could not play, and thus, making his debut for us that night, was one Stuart Jones. It was quickly passed on to me that Stuart was the 1,886th player to have turned out for Gloucester City. (That figure has since increased, by the way). It was perhaps not vitally important for me to know that fact at that time, but there was great delight in knowing that there was someone like Tim noting it all the same!

There are a lot of football clubs with a more successful history to their name, but there are not so many with such a well documented statistical history. We must all thank Tim Clark for his great devotion and success in achieving something for us all to enjoy. I know that it will be much appreciated.

Dave Phillips
25 May 2009

By Tim Harris
Former General Manager, Manager, Assistant Manager and Player of Gloucester City Association Football Club

A fabulous book, that will be enjoyed by Players, Managers and Fans up and down the country and around parts of the world. A must for any fan who follows the statistical side of football, also a must for all the players that have pulled on the shirt of *Gloucester City AFC* .

Many Non – League Football Fans are truly dedicated, very committed to the cause of their club and the efforts of Tim Clark, his endless hours of research has culminated to produce a remarkable record of 126 years of statistics.

The first time I looked into all the hard work and time that Tim has put in the production of The Complete Record, I was amazed and hooked into looking at my various times spent at the club going back to 1978 when as a youngster I was privileged to pull on the jersey for my local Semi – Professional club. The memories of games played and managed came flooding back good times and like all football not so good times!

To finish this book in the season of promotion to The Blue Square League under extreme difficulties with losing our Meadow Park home was a magnificent achievement and a fitting way to end the history and statistics of Gloucester City AFC up to season ending 2009.

Tim Harris
5 July 2009

By Phil Warren
Chairman of Gloucester City Supporters' Trust

As Chair of the Supporters Trust I take particular pleasure in welcoming this mighty tome of Gloucester City records : statistical data, photographs and documents from down the years. The author is a man of military ancestry and he has his facts and figures all brassed up and jangling. Assiduous research has seen him criss-crossing the county, plundering the press archive and plumbing the Internet. He has interviewed an army of former players to catch up that last statistical detail and has produced an astonishing, burgeoning volume, with rank upon rank of records.

Tim will be quick to assert that he has not done it unaided, and will pay tribute in his preface to all those who have assisted him, not least our very good, mutual friend, Robert Kujawa. That having been said, Tim has been on a mission, trawling the record offices and tenaciously following up leads to build his material. This is a breathtaking endeavour by any standard, especially so considering the history that unfolds of a brave footballing minnow, so often swimming against the tide. It is unsurprising that you can find not dissimilar accounts of the histories of the country's major clubs but astonishing that Gloucester City has a supporter who would go to the lengths that Tim Clark has to compile his wonderful record.

The satisfaction for Tim is doubtless in a job excellently done, but I know it has been a joy to him to forensically track down information unknown to anyone else and, but for his endeavour, vulnerable to the risk of being lost for ever. An arresting example of this, for me concerns my second club : Tottenham Hotspur. I have seen Spurs play against Gloucester City on two occasions and knew of the most famous game in 1952. But I knew nothing of a further fixture, way before my time, circa 1930, the details of which Tim's remarkable detective work has uncovered when it must have been all but lost.

I hope this foreword does not offend, but I am not a statistics man. I do not generally deal in empirical evidence, but in anecdote and memory and the passion of the game. This book nonetheless serves me very well. In a way I care less how the statistics fall out than for the way in which the memories build up – of the players, the matchday moments, the vital relegation and promotion occasions, the ref's decisions even.

My perspective is that I come as any reader to any book, to bring the pages alive. Tim will argue fervently that he is not a historian, not a teller of stories. However, he provides me with the answers to questions the answers to which provide the pegs for me to hang my stories on. I could not answer for certain, for instance, without Tim's assurance as to who were the two players who, on successive Saturdays at Longlevens, scored four and five goals respectively. Now at last I can tell you, and then resurrect the stories from the games on that old mudpatch of a pitch at Nine Elms.

Tim Clark would firmly refute that this book is a history. Indeed, he has it as "a complete record". My pleasure, and yours perhaps, may come not only in the information he conveys so diligently but in re-creating the narrative by putting the flesh on the bone : by exploring the data and the pictures, re-writing the stories that have been stored in the memory.

This record must be a source of great pride to those who are named in it as representing the club. What a thrill to have one's name listed as having worn the black and yellow, or else the red and white or even the black and white strips that the club has favoured down the years. Tim's research has revealed that many of these men have been heroes both on and off the pitch.

I am proud to have watched so many of them. I am also proud of the many good friends whom I have made at the five home grounds the club has had in my time, and amongst whom I have travelled to all parts of the country to so many memorable games. This club has been blessed by good and kind people. Take for instance those who serve with me on the Board of the Trust. At this moment in our history we are celebrating the great success of the promotion season 2008-2009, but we are simultaneously in the midst of a struggle to find a home and secure the club's future. A book like this deserves a second volume. The club must go on.

Many a time I exchanged a half-time pleasantry with Tim Clark before going off to get a cup of tea. I never dreamed that Tim was working on the project now fulfilled in this wonderful book, which is as joyous an investment for me as I could want to make in terms of a football book, and I have read a good many. Thank you, Tim, for all your application to this task and may you take the greatest pride in its publication. You certainly deserve to.

I recall that the wives of Sultan Shariar only lasted one night because he cut off their heads at dawn, until his new wife, Sheherezade, had an idea. If she could get the sultan interested in a new story just before dawn each day, he would not cut off her head because he would want to hear the end of the story. So begins the tale of the Thousand and One Nights.

I think this fine new book by Tim Clark has at least a thousand and one tales in it. Delving into this kaleidoscope of records brings up one memory after another for me and I shall be forever grateful for it. May Gloucester City Football Club be preserved, like Sheherezade, and may Tim add regularly to his record hereafter.

Phil Warren
8 July 2009

INTRODUCTIONS

"Tiger, Tiger, Burning Bright"

The Complete Record is probably a misnomer as it is virtually impossible to find everything about Gloucester City Association Football Club but this is as good an effort as can be mustered. To list all the players who donned the shirt of Gloucester, Gloucester YMCA and Gloucester City was a Herculean task of the first water. The amount of hours, days, months, years I spent on this project does not bear thinking about. I am confident I have found most of the players who are the 'purveyors of our dreams'.

It had always been a desire of mine to get in one publication the player records of all those individuals who had worn the Gloucester shirt in anger i.e competitive games season by season. I had been collecting information on and off for thirty plus years but it was my fortuitous early voluntary retirement of five years ago that allowed me the opportunity to spend more time on this project. It goes without saying that this was a labour of love and it is coincidental that it falls between two significant club anniversaries, the 125th Anniversary of the formation of a Gloucester Association Football Club in 2008 and the 100th Anniversary of the current club in 2010. We can thank Colin Timbrell, The Gloucestershire FA Historian for unearthing this double celebration. To this can I add the 50th Anniversary of my watching Gloucester City for the first time at Longlevens commencing Good Friday 27 March 1959 and no matter where I was domiciled remained a fan ever since.

The meeting with Rob Kujawa, the Club Historian, opened up an Aladdin's cave of information. I know this is blasphemous but when I met Rob I thought I had gone to heaven and met God! Thank goodness there are people like him who have had the foresight to save so much memorabilia about our beloved club. I was able to incorporate incalculable information from his valuable collection and feel it right his name should be associated with this work. I believe I am sharing his dream also.

To support a team like Gloucester City Football Club has to be a most difficult decision to make in a City totally dominated by a Rugby Club that has been one of the most supreme exponents of 'egg chasing' since its inception in 1873. Ten years later, on Monday, 5 March 1883, a group of gentlemen gathered at a well attended meeting to consider the advisability of forming a club under Association rules in Gloucester. The present club is directly descended from this point.

It is oft times said to me that Gloucester is a rugby town. I am not totally convinced. Sure, Gloucester has a major national rugby team, which the City should be justly proud of, but if Gloucester had a major national football team I know which would get the greatest audience. This is the dream. It came true at Wigan! Football is as popular a sport in Gloucester as anywhere else in the country and this needs to be emphasised. However, if Gloucester could have as successful a football club as the rugby team what a boost this would be for the City of Gloucester and therefore should be encouraged. 'The Tigers' elevation to The Football Conference could be just the start.

I hear and read sometimes that history is not important. They miss the point. John Sherman, a US Senator (for it is he) in a speech in 1890 said "The best prophet of the future, is the past". This rings very true in the case of football clubs. A club's present and the dreams of its future are all inspired by its past. A club's past affords good food for thought. If it was successful, it inspires them to work for the achievement of greater success. If it was not so successful, it helps them to draw lessons for the future, avoid the committing of mistakes made by the ancestors and to build up a present and a future that makes up for the past and wash off the dark periods in its history. So there!

This book is not a history but a statistical record of the First XI only. I have listed a season by season record followed by team, player's and officials records. Although the club was formed in 1883 there appears to be little record of teams between 1883 to 1889 apart from one match in 1883/1884, one in 1884/1885 and a couple of matches in 1886 that get a mention in one or two booklets. I have provided the league tables (of which one or two do not add up) and dates of matches with goalscorers and attendances (where possible). Also included are friendlies which are no doubt incomplete but are of interest nonetheless. For each player I have provided the following information: name, favoured playing position, date and place of birth and death (where possible), competitive record season by season, club record (where possible), international record (where possible) and any brief notes of interest. Keeping track of other clubs played for is a nightmare but, again, is of interest albeit incomplete.

Bearing in mind we are dealing with non-league players a massive amount of information is missing during the amateur years particularly pre First World War and during the YMCA years 1913 to 1925 and a fair amount from 1925 to 1935. This information may be lost forever. Therefore many appearances and goalscorers figures are distorted prior to 1935 as a lot of the line-ups are culled from match reports only and, as you may be aware, scorers and providers and players who have had an excellent or poor game get prominence. Post 1935 we are a little luckier as the Club became semi-professional and therefore the coverage was a lot better. It's quite possible that missing line-ups may be lurking in the local papers of those teams visited. Who knows? No doubt in the fullness of time this may be sorted out. I suppose we should be grateful for what we have thus far.

It is highly unlikely that this publication is error free. I take full responsibility. It is incumbent on a statistician, apart from having a beard, to accept sometimes he can be wrong. An amazing amount of stuff was sifted through just to get what we have now. I have used my discretion with surnames on occasions. As a rule if a player had the same surname and played in a similar position from one season to the next then I have assumed he is the same individual. It may be that a player is duplicated because initials sometimes changed from game to game in the announcements of team line-ups in the newspaper. I have also committed the heinous crime of making educated guesses with some line ups where it may appear obvious viewing line ups either side of fixtures. These players are indicated (?). It is possible I may have missed quite a lot but I hope I have captured as much as I could.

I hope you enjoy perusing this publication. If nothing else it introduces you to players who should not be forgotten and who paved the way to where we are today. Hopefully it gives you a feel of Gloucester City AFC and is a permanent record of the club we all love. It is my intention to continue keeping records of the Club so if anyone can add anything that would enhance these records for me and for future statisticians of the Club I would be most grateful as it will help to keep as best a comprehensive record of Gloucester City AFC as we can muster and rebuild records that may have been lost in the catastrophic fire of the Clubs office in 1946. Please write to me via the publishers address at the front of this book.

Love, Light and Peace,
Timothy RD Clark
September 2009

ROB KUJAWA
Gloucester City AFC Club Historian

In 1966 England won the World Cup and my Gloucester City love affair began. By the mid 1980's I had started collecting newspaper reports, teams and memorabilia with the aim of writing the history of the Club. Nearly thirty years later a start had been made but the project had stalled, therefore when I was introduced to Tim Clark and he told me that he wanted to write the history of the Club it was my pleasure to make my collection of City information available to him.

Like all Gloucester City supporters, I look forward to having my copy of the Complete Record of Gloucester City at hand so that we can remind ourselves of all the good times and those that are so not good! Well done Tim on completing such a project.

Rob Kujawa
July 2009

ACKNOWLEDGEMENTS

First of all can I express my thanks to Gloucester City AFC for endorsing this project. I was absolutely delighted that Dave Phillips, Tim Harris and Phil Warren agreed to write forewords for me as this lends this book some gravitas.

The biggest frustration of being a football statistician are the many times that one of your enquiries is not replied to despite sending stamped addressed envelopes so therefore I am indebted to those who did. Even e-mails are ignored. I know....unbelievable!!

Many thanks to the Gloucester Record Office in Alvin Street for allowing me so many hours searching through the old Citizens and Gloucester Journals but also The Gloucestershire Chronicles, The Tewkesbury Register, The Dursley, Berkeley & Sharpness Gazette & Wotton-Under-Edge Advertiser and The Gloucester Standard & Gloucestershire News. I would also like to thank Cheltenham Reference Library for allowing me access to The Gloucestershire Echo, the Stroud Reference Library with The Stroud News & Gloucester County Advertiser and Stroud Journal, Cinderford Reference Library with The Dean Forest Mercury and Gloucester Reference Library for the more current Citizens.

A special mention must be given to Rob Kujawa, the Club Historian and former Assistant Secretary of the club and current Secretary of The Supporters Trust, who trusted me by allowing me access to his archives. Without his collection this book would have been bereft of valuable information and I am proud to add his name as collaborator. To this can I add Neil Phelps, whose photographs are second to none and his enthusiasm for the club a wonder to behold, his website testament to this. His stats from 1988-89 were invaluable and his help in almost acting as a proof reader and amending information was of invaluable help to me. To Phil Gough, who lives and breathes Gloucester City, I thank him for those many Friday afternoon meetings at my house adding and amending much information of players from the 1960s on. His memory defies comprehension.

A special thanks to Phil Warren, Chairman of the Supporters Trust for his co-operation and enthusiasm for this project who patiently answered my e-mail queries pointing me in many good directions and who wrote such kind things in my first effort which raised nearly £600 for The Supporters' Trust. We are fortunate to have such a man at the helm of The Supporters Trust.

An invaluable help was Colin Timbrell, Historian, Gloucestershire Football Association who since 1994 has furnished me with much valued information about Gloucester City football answering every single query I threw his way.

The Internet has been a vital tool especially in finding some of the full names of players and birth dates and death dates. Club sites have been tremendously helpful. I would especially like to thank my elder brother, Ian Clark, who ploughed through various Census Returns and other genealogical sites looking for birth years/death years and places of pre WW1 players and for contributing other 'brilliant' suggestions. I also brought him out of retirement with his draughtsman skills to plot the home venues of the various Gloucester clubs with the collaboration of Russell Shortland, Sleaford, Lincolnshire.

I am indebted to Paul Godfrey, Secretary of Cheltenham Town Football Club who was more than helpful with regard to players who had connections with both our clubs. We may have our rivalries but we are united in that common denominator that transcends rivalry – the love of football. To Shaun Wetson, Secretary of Gloucester City Football Club who waded in with information on current players for which I thank him and to Mike Dunstan, Press Officer and Editor of the official match day programme who contributed much needed advice.

I wish to thank the following current and ex-players and relations for their contribution and interest no matter how large or small – Larry Cowley (brother of Edgar Cowley); Dave Collins; the late Tom Rutherford; Margaret Millar (widow of Dusty Millar); Trevor Hurcombe (son in law of the late Albert Shelley); Gus Stow; Frank Tredgett; Terry Foote; Rob Coldray; Lloyd Smith (son of the late Archie Smith); Dick Etheridge; Adam Parker (distant relation of Reginald and Grahame Parker); Stan Myers; Michael Noakes; Lee Smith; Reg and Doug Perks (sons of the late Harry Perks); Alan Lloyd MBE; Kevin Willetts; Rob Simpson; Tim Harris; Ron Coltman MBE; Adie Harris; Nick Delves; Des Edwards (son of George Edwards); Adie Tandy; Sandra Proudfoot (daughter of Archie Proudfoot); Fred Gittings; Colin Anderson (son of Bob Anderson); Ken Blackburn; Dave Lewis; Jamie Vittles; Keith Mortimer; Brian Ballinger and Doug Foxwell.

Others who have pitched in and to whom I am most grateful no matter how large or small - Mr. J. Veale, General Secretary of The Western League who provided me with information during the formative years of my research in 1974; Gordon Pointer; Tony Gaze; Monty Taynton; Lionel Waite (former groundsman at Horton Road Stadium); John Davies; Jerry Dwyer; John Phillips; R.J. Pearce (Frome Town FC); Heather Cook (Forest Green Rovers FC); Dave Rey; David Allan (Cowdenbeath FC); David Woods (statistician with regards to football in the Bristol area); Steve Turk; Simon Drake ('Drakey'); Robbie Green; Dave Hatton; Les Lewis (Broadwell Amateur FC); Neil Harvey (Cambridge City FC); Gordon Spragg; Phil Tustain and Martyn Ellis.

To Laurence Felton and staff at Inky Little Fingers I thank them for their advice which has been invaluable to the production of this book. I must also mention, as I did in 'The Pioneers' booklet, Jon Barnes of Gingerjonny Publications and author of 'The Who's Who of Grantham Town Football Club' who initially gave me some interesting tips in the ways of publishing.

Finally, I also have to thank my wife, Christine for her patience and permission to pursue this project after I had completed all my domestic chores! My two boys, Paul and Simon (both loyal T-Enders) for encouraging me to take on such a task and who provided suggestions for the interior of the book – and spending my money!

By the same statistician

The Pioneers: Gloucester City Association Football Club 1883-1914 – League Football Statistics (TigerTimbo Publications, £6.49 inc. p&p) – all profits go to The Supporters Trust.

About the statistician

When I was born peace broke out! That was in Münster, Germany 1946. My 45 year working life consisted of Bookshop Assistant, Civil Servant and British Telecom Engineer to get to what I really wanted to do – collate football stats – and get it in print! My education was sporadic including dropping out from Open University! I have a wonderful wife, Christine, who bore me three smashing boys, Paul, Jason (deceased) and Simon. That's it really!

THE CLUB'S STORY IN BRIEF

1883 to 1886 – Gloucester - Original club formed 5 March 1883 and disbanded sometime in 1886 or 1887.
1889 to 1901 – Gloucester – Re-formed 10 September 1889 and disbanded in 1901.
1902 to 1904 – Gloucester City – Re-formed 1902 and disbanded in 1904
1906 to 1910 – Gloucester City – Amalgamated with the Saint Michael's club of Hempsted in 1906 and disbanded in 1910.
1910 to 1925 – Gloucester YMCA – YMCA club formed in 1910.
1925 to date   - Gloucester City – Merged with the YMCA club in 1925 and re-named Gloucester City.

During this entire period (1883 to date) all these clubs had two things in common – player links with each reincarnation of the Club and the desire to represent the City as the senior club. From 1935 Gloucester City became semi-professional.

SIGNIFICANT CHANGES

1895-1896 Goal average introduced
1966-1967 Substitutes introduced
1976-1977 Goal difference introduced
1982-1983 3 points for a win introduced

SPONSORS OF COMPETITIONS

League
1987-1988 to 1995-1996 Beazer Homes sponsored Southern League
1996-1997 to 2005-2006 Dr. Martens sponsored Southern League
2006-2007 to 2008-2009 British Gas Business sponsored Southern League

FA Cup
1994-1995 to 1997-1998 Littlewoods sponsored FA Cup
1998-1999 to 2005-2006 AXA sponsored FA Cup
2006-2007 to date   Eon sponsored FA Cup

FA Trophy
1991-1992 to 1993-1994 Vauxhall sponsored FA trophy
1994-1995 to 2006-2007 Umbro sponsored FA Trophy
2007-2008 to date   Carlsberg sponsored FA Trophy

Southern League Cup
1984-1985 to 1986-1987 Bill Dellow sponsored Southern League Cup
1987-1988 to 1989-1990 Westgate Insurance sponsored Southern League Cup
1990-1991   Larchimage sponsored Southern League Cup
1991-1992 to 1992-1993 Barclays Commercial Services sponsored Southern League Cup
1993-1994 to 2004-2005 Dr. Martens sponsored Southern League Cup
2005-2006 to 2007-2008 Errea sponsored Southern League Cup
2008-2009 to 2008-2009 GX Soccer sponsored Southern League Cup

Major Gloucester City Association Football Club Websites

www.gloucestercityafc.com

www.tigerroar.co.uk

www.t-ender.co.uk

Please Note:
Every effort was made to obtain copyright permission for using photographs and cartoons contained within this publication. Photographs and cartoons were obtained from official programmes, handbooks, individual collections etc. particularly Rob Kujawa's collection so clear copyright was not established.
The publisher would be pleased to hear from those whose copyright has been unintentionally infringed so as to avoid any further misuse in subsequent publications.
The publisher will not accept any responsibility for accuracy of content. Every effort was made to ensure accuracy.
The quality of some of the illustrations are not perfect but I feel it necessary to include.

CONTENTS

Throughout the book there are two themes. They are programme designs through the years and players who broke club records.

GLOUCESTER CITY AFC HONOURS BOARD

1897-1898 Gloucester & District League Division 1 Champions
1898-1899 Mid Gloucestershire League Champions
1899-1900 Gloucester & District League Division 1 Champions
1899-1900 Mid Gloucestershire League Champions
1900-1901 Mid Gloucestershire League Champions
1902-1903 Gloucestershire FA Junior Challenge Cup Winners
1903-1904 Gloucester & District League Division 1 Champions
1906-1907 Cheltenham & District League Division 1 Champions
1907-1908 North Gloucestershire League Division 1 Champions
1908-1909 North Gloucestershire League Division 1 Champions
1931-1932 Gloucestershire FA Northern Senior Amateur Cup Winners
1933-1934 Gloucestershire Northern Senior League Champions
1935-1936 Birmingham Combination Tillotson Shield Winners
1937-1938 Gloucestershire FA Northern Senior Professional Cup Winners
1949-1950 Gloucestershire FA Northern Senior Professional Cup Winners
1950-1951 Gloucestershire FA Northern Senior Professional Cup Winners
1952-1953 Gloucestershire FA Northern Senior Professional Cup Winners
1954-1955 Gloucestershire FA Northern Senior Professional Cup Winners
1955-1956 Southern League Cup Winners
1955-1956 Gloucestershire FA Northern Senior Professional Cup Winners
1957-1958 Gloucestershire FA Northern Senior Professional Cup Winners
1965-1966 Gloucestershire FA Northern Senior Professional Cup Winners
1968-1969 Southern League Merit Cup Winners
1968-1969 Gloucestershire FA Northern Senior Professional Cup Winners
1970-1971 Gloucestershire FA Northern Senior Professional Cup Winners
1974-1975 Gloucestershire FA Northern Senior Professional Cup Winners
1978-1979 Gloucestershire FA Northern Senior Professional Cup Winners
1979-1980 Gloucestershire FA Northern Senior Professional Cup Winners
1981-1982 Gloucestershire FA Northern Senior Professional Cup Winners
1982-1983 Gloucestershire FA Northern Senior Professional Cup Winners
1983-1984 Gloucestershire FA Northern Senior Professional Cup Winners
1988-1989 Southern League Midland Division Champions
1990-1991 Gloucestershire FA Northern Senior Professional Cup Winners
1992-1993 Gloucestershire FA Northern Senior Professional Cup Winners
2008-2009 Southern League Premier Division Play Off Winners

THE ANNOUNCEMENT OF THE FORMATION OF THE FIRST
GLOUCESTER ASSOCIATION FOOTBALL CLUB

GLOUCESTER JOURNAL, SATURDAY, MARCH 10, 1883.

GLOUCESTER ASSOCIATION FOOTBALL CLUB.—A meeting of association players was held on Monday to consider the advisability of forming a club under association rules. The meeting was well attended, and a resolution was passed that a club should be formed, and the election of officers was forthwith proceeded with. Mr. W. H. Clarke, British School, was appointed secretary. Already the club has enrolled 25 members.

THE OLDEST TEAM PHOTOGRAPH
This photograph hung on the study wall of former captain, Walter Sessions

1889

G. Robins   G. Speck   Speck   King   Clemenshaw

                                         F. Fielding   King

           C. F. Poole   W. Sessions   C. M. Henderson

A. Beaven   Mathews

SEASON BY SEASON

(All teams are 1 to 11 as published in any source that was used. If fixture in *italics* the game was expunged. If (?) next to player this was an educated guess)

SEASON 1883-1884
(Home Ground: Budding's Field)

The first Gloucester Club was formed in March 1883 so one could presume that this was the first active season commencing perhaps in the October although no record can be found to substantiate this. There is mention in The Rothmans Yearbook 1999-2000 in the Cheltenham Town section that 'a scratch team representing Cheltenham played a match against Gloucester in 1884.' Given our close proximity, surely it would have been this season and therefore is the oldest recorded match in Gloucester's history.

SEASON 1884-1885
(Home Ground: Budding's Field)

A book entitled 'Bristol Rovers – The Definitive History 1883-2003' by Stephen Byrne and Mike Jay there is reference to a Gloucester team playing Eastville Rovers in 1884-1885, date and result unknown.

SEASON 1885-1886
(Home Ground: Budding's Field)

There were unsubstantiated newspaper reports that following a friendly defeat at Eastville Rovers on 2 January 1886 there was reference to their first Gloucestershire FA Junior Cup win at Budding's Field which would imply another match in the next round. However, it would seem the club disbanded from 'inanition and lack of public support'.

SEASON 1889-1890
(Home Ground: Budding's Field)

Date: Saturday 26/10/1889
Result: **GLOUCESTER 10 CLIFTON ASSOCIATION RESERVES 0**
Competition: Gloucestershire FA Junior Challenge Cup 1st Round
Teamsheet: Cooke, Brereton, Bonnor, Ely, Grimley, Sessions, Wade, Perkins, Hockin, Poole, Fielding
Scorers: Perkins (2), Wade (4), Hockin, Grimley, -----, -----

Date: Saturday 09/11/1889
Result: **GLOUCESTER 8 OLD BOYS QUEEN ELIZABETH HOSPITAL BRISTOL 1**
Competition: Gloucestershire FA Junior Challenge Cup 2nd Round
Teamsheet: Cooke, Brereton, Gardner, Vickery, Higginson, Johnson, Chadborn, Wade, Henderson, Poole, Fielding
Scorers: Henderson (4), Poole (3), Fielding

Date: Saturday 23/11/1889
Result: **WARMLEY RESERVES 3 GLOUCESTER 2**
Competition: Gloucestershire FA Junior Challenge Cup Semi-Final
Teamsheet: Cooke, Gardner, Bonnor, Higginson, Vickery, Macfarlane, Perkins, Wade, Henderson, Poole, Fielding
Scorers: Wade, Fielding

Appearances – GR Bonnor 2, Rev. HL Brereton 2, WH Chadborn 1, AB Cooke 3, WAS Ely 1, FB Fielding 3, A Gardner 2, HF Grimley 1, CM Henderson 2, S Higginson 2, HV Hockin 1, AE Johnson 1, Rev. AB Macfarlane 1, GB Perkins 2, CF Poole 3, Walter Sessions 1, WH Vickery 2, Rev. RD Wade 3.
Scorers – Rev. RD Wade 5, CM Henderson 4, CF Poole 3, FB Fielding 2, GB Perkins 2, HF Grimley 1, HV Hockin 1.

SEASON 1890-1891
(Home Ground: Budding's Field)

There were no competitive fixtures played this season. 20 friendlies or Challenge Matches were played instead.

SEASON 1891-1892
(Home Ground: Budding's Field)

Date: Saturday 30/01/1892
Result: **GLOUCESTER 3 SAINT GEORGE 4**
Competition: Gloucestershire FA Senior Challenge Cup 1st Round
Teamsheet: Speck, Scott, Sampson, Johnson, Sessions, Matthews, Perkins, Robins, Powell, Stout, Sherwood
Scorers: Robins, Perkins, Powell

Appearances – AE Johnson 1, AA Matthews 1, GB Perkins 1, JOT Powell 1, HT Robins 1, TG Sampson 1, HH Scott 1, Walter Sessions 1, HG Sherwood 1, G Speck 1, PW Stout 1.
Scorers - GB Perkins 1, JOT Powell 1, HT Robins 1.

SEASON 1892-1893
(Home Ground: Budding's Field)

Date: Saturday 28/01/1893
Result: **CLIFTON 1 GLOUCESTER 6**
Competition: Gloucestershire FA Senior Challenge Cup 1st Round
Teamsheet: Speck, Cragg, Green, Harvey, Scott, Somerville, Robins, Sherwood, Fielding, Jones, Gardner
Scorers: Sherwood (2), Fielding (3), -----

Date: Saturday 25/02/1893
Result: **GLOUCESTER 5 BEDMINSTER 0**
Competition: Gloucestershire FA Senior Challenge Cup Semi-Final
Teamsheet: Speck, Cragg, Green, Harvey, Scott, Somerville, Sherwood, Robins, Sessions, Stout, Fielding
Scorers: Fielding, Sessions (2), Robins (2)
Attendance: 2000

Date: Saturday 01/04/1893
Result: **WARMLEY 4 GLOUCESTER 1**
Competition: Gloucestershire FA Senior Challenge Cup Final
Teamsheet: Speck, Cragg, Green, Somerville, Scott, Harvey, Fielding, Stout, Sessions, Sherwood, Robins
Scorer: Sessions
Attendance: 3000-4000
Note: Played at Bedminster

Appearances – AC Cragg 3, FB Fielding 3, WT Gardner 1, RN Green 3, Rev. JH Harvey 3, HW Jones 1, HT Robins 3, HH Scott 3, Wilfred Sessions 2, HG Sherwood 3, JL Somerville 3, G Speck 3, PW Stout 2.
Scorers - FB Fielding 4, Wilfred Sessions 3, HT Robins 2, HG Sherwood 2.

SEASON 1893-1894

(Home Ground: Budding's Field)

Date: Saturday 30/09/1893
Result: **BEDMINSTER 3 GLOUCESTER 2**
Competition: Bristol & District League Division 1
Teamsheet: Kent, Somerville, Green, Harvey, Scott, Clark, Matthews, Robins, FB Fielding, Sherwood, PW Stout
Scorers: PW Stout, FB Fielding
Attendance: 1500

Date: Saturday 14/10/1893
Result: **EASTVILLE ROVERS 5 GLOUCESTER 2**
Competition: Bristol & District League Division 1
Teamsheet: Kent, Somerville, Green, Scott, Harvey, Pennington, Robins, Sherwood, PW Stout, AF Fielding, FB Fielding
Scorers: PW Stout, Robins
Attendance: 200-300

Date: Saturday 28/10/1893
Result: **SAINT GEORGE 0 GLOUCESTER 3**
Competition: Bristol & District League Division 1
Teamsheet: Kent, Somerville, Green, Cragg, Scott, Harvey, Robins, Stebbing, FB Fielding, Sherwood, PW Stout
Scorer: PW Stout (3)

Date: Saturday 04/11/1893
Result: **GLOUCESTER 1 STAPLE HILL 1**
Competition: Bristol & District League Division 1
Teamsheet: Kent, Somerville, Green, Cragg, Scott, Harvey, Robins, Stebbing, FB Fielding, Wilfred Sessions, PW Stout
Scorer: Stebbing

Date: Saturday 11/11/1893
Result: **GLOUCESTER 3 EASTVILLE ROVERS 0**
Competition: Bristol & District League Division 1
Teamsheet: Kent, Somerville, Green, Cragg, Scott, Harvey, Robins, Stebbing, FB Fielding, Sherwood, PW Stout
Scorers: Sherwood, Robins, PW Stout
Attendance: 700
Note: Played at Kingsholm Rugby Ground

Date: Saturday 18/11/1893
Result: **GLOUCESTER 2 CLEVEDON 1**
Competition: Bristol & District League Division 1
Teamsheet: Kent, Somerville, Green, FM Stout, Scott, Cragg, Robins, Stebbing, FB Fielding, Sherwood, PW Stout
Scorers: Sherwood, Stebbing

Date: Saturday 02/12/1893
Result: **GLOUCESTER 2 CLIFTON 0**
Competition: Bristol & District League Division 1
Teamsheet: Kent, Somerville, Cragg, FM Stout, Scott, Harvey, Robins, Matthews, FB Fielding, Sherwood, PW Stout
Scorers: Sherwood, Matthews

Date: Saturday 16/12/1893
Result: **GLOUCESTER 1 TROWBRIDGE TOWN 3**
Competition: Bristol & District League Division1
Teamsheet: Kent, Somerville, Green, FM Stout, Scott, Cragg, Robins, Harvey, FB Fielding, Sherwood, PW Stout
Scorer: PW Stout

Date: Saturday 23/12/1893
Result: **MANGOTSFIELD 3 GLOUCESTER 1**
Competition: Bristol & District League Division 1
Teamsheet: Kent, Morris, Scott, Cragg, Walter Sessions, Johnson, Robins, FM Stout, Jessop, Sherwood, FB Fielding
Scorer: Jessop

Date: Saturday 13/01/1894
Result: **GLOUCESTER 0 WARMLEY 3**
Competition: Bristol & District League Division 1
Teamsheet: Kent, Somerville, Fowler, Walter Sessions, Scott, FM Stout, PW Stout, FB Fielding, Cragg, Robins, Sherwood
Attendance: 400

Date: Saturday 20/01/1894
Result: **TROWBRIDGE TOWN 8 GLOUCESTER 2**
Competition: Bristol & District League Division 1
Teamsheet: Kent, Cragg, Fowler, FM Stout, Scott, Clark, Matthews, Robins, AF Fielding, Sherwood, FB Fielding
Scorer: FB Fielding (2)

Date: Saturday 27/01/1894
Result: **GLOUCESTER 8 CLIFTON 0**
Competition: Gloucestershire FA Senior Challenge Cup 1st Round
Teamsheet: Kent, Somerville, Norrington, Walter Sessions, Scott, FM Stout, FB Fielding, PW Stout, Wilfred Sessions, Cragg, Sherwood
Scorers: Sherwood, Wilfred Sessions (2), PW Stout (2), Walter Sessions (2), FB Fielding

Date: Saturday 10/02/1894
Result: **WARMLEY 2 GLOUCESTER 0**
Competition: Bristol & District League Division 1
Teamsheet: Kent, Somerville, Norrington, Cragg, Scott, FM Stout, Matthews, Robins, Sherwood, AF Fielding, PM Stout
Attendance: 600

Date: Saturday 17/02/1894
Result: **GLOUCESTER 4 MANGOTSFIELD 2**
Competition: Bristol & District League Division 1
Teamsheet: Kent, Somerville, Cragg, FM Stout, Scott, Hoitt, PW Stout, AF Fielding, FB Fielding, Matthews, Robins
Scorer: FB Fielding (4)

Date: Saturday 24/02/1894
Result: **GLOUCESTER 0 EASTVILLE ROVERS 1**
Competition: Gloucestershire FA Senior Challenge Cup Semi-Final
Teamsheet: Kent, Somerville, Cragg, Walter Sessions, Scott, FM Stout, Sherwood, Hoitt, FB Fielding, Snell, PW Stout
Attendance: 1000

Date: Saturday 17/03/1894
Result: **CLIFTON 6 GLOUCESTER 2**
Competition: Bristol & District League Division 1
Teamsheet: -----, Somerville (?), -----, -----, Hoitt (?), FM Stout (?), Sherwood (?), -----, FB Fielding (?), PW Stout (?), -----
Scorers: -----, -----

Date: Saturday 24/03/1894
Result: **STAPLE HILL 3 GLOUCESTER 1**
Competition: Bristol & District League Division 1
Teamsheet: Robins, Somerville, Tadman, FM Stout, Hoitt, Ward, Matthews, Mason, FB Fielding, PW Stout, Sherwood
Scorer: PW Stout (pen)

Date: Monday 26/03/1894
Result: **GLOUCESTER 1 SAINT GEORGE 2**
Competition: Bristol & District League Division 1
Teamsheet: Kent, Somerville, Tadman, FM Stout, Hoitt, Cragg, FB Fielding, PW Stout, Powell, Sherwood, Matthews
Scorer: Powell

Date: Saturday 31/03/1894
Result: **GLOUCESTER 5 BEDMINSTER 2**
Competition: Bristol & District League Division 1
Teamsheet: Robins, Somerville, Tadman, FM Stout, Hoitt, JT Stout, Matthews, Ward, Mason, FB Fielding, PW Stout
Scorers: Matthews, PW Stout, FM Stout, FB Fielding, Somerville
Attendance: Half-dozen!

Date: ?
Result: **CLEVEDON 1 GLOUCESTER 0**
Competition: Bristol & District League Division 1
Teamsheet: -----, -----, -----, -----, -----, -----, -----, -----, -----, -----, -----

Appearances – T Clark 2, AC Cragg 14, AF Fielding 4, FB Fielding 18, HO Fowler 2, RN Green 7, Rev. JH Harvey 7, AC Hoitt 6, A Jessop 1, AE Johnson 1, SJF Kent 16, AM Mason 2, WG Matthews 8, FM Morris 1, CH Norrington 2, ? Pennington 1, JOT Powell 1, HT Robins 15, HH Scott 15, Walter Sessions 4, Wilfred Sessions 2, HG Sherwood 16, ES Snell 1, JL Somerville 17, EF Stebbing 4, FM Stout 14, JT Stout 1, PW Stout 18, ETS Tadman 3, GS Ward 2.
Scorers – PW Stout 10, FB Fielding 9, HG Sherwood 4, WG Matthews 2, Walter Sessions 2, Wilfred Sessions 2, EF Stebbing 2, A Jessop 1, JOT Powell 1, HT Robins 1, JL Somerville 1, FM Stout 1.

BRISTOL & DISTRICT LEAGUE DIVISION 1

POS	CLUB	P	W	D	L	F	A	PTS
1	WARMLEY	18	12	5	1	32	13	27*
2	SAINT GEORGE (Bristol)	18	10	6	2	39	23	26
3	TROWBRIDGE TOWN	18	9	4	5	54	33	22
4	BEDMINSTER	18	9	2	7	41	36	20
5	CLEVEDON	18	7	5	6	34	41	19
6	CLIFTON	18	6	4	8	37	30	16
7	STAPLE HILL	18	5	5	8	23	33	15
8	**GLOUCESTER**	**18**	**6**	**1**	**11**	**32**	**45**	**13**
9	EASTVILLE ROVERS	18	5	2	11	30	39	12
10	MANGOTSFIELD	18	2	4	12	19	48	8
		180	71	38	71	341	341	178

* Two points deducted for misconduct.

SEASON 1894-1895
(Home Ground: Budding's Field)

Date: Saturday 06/10/1894
Result: **GLOUCESTER 4 CLIFTON 3**
Competition: Bristol & District League Division 1
Teamsheet: Speck, Fowler, Vaughan, Cragg, Pitt, FM Stout, AF Fielding, Sherwood, PW Stout, FB Fielding, Snell
Scorers: Sherwood, PW Stout (2, 1 pen), FB Fielding

Date: Saturday 20/10/1894
Result: **GLOUCESTER 1 EASTVILLE ROVERS 2**
Competition: Bristol & District League Division 1
Teamsheet: Speck, Vaughan, Tadman, FM Stout, Pitt, Cragg, FB Fielding, Turner, PW Stout, Sherwood, AF Fielding
Scorer: Sherwood

Date: Saturday 27/10/1894
Result: **CLIFTON 4 GLOUCESTER 3**
Competition: Bristol & District League Division 1
Teamsheet: Speck, Goodwin, Tadman, Cragg, Pitt, FM Stout, FB Fielding, Sherwood, PW Stout, Robins, AF Fielding
Scorers: PW Stout (2), FB Fielding

Date: Saturday 03/11/1894
Result: **GLOUCESTER 10 CLEVEDON 0**
Competition: Bristol & District League Division 1
Teamsheet: Speck, Goodwin, Tadman, Pitt, Wade-Smith, Cragg, FB Fielding, AF Fielding, PW Stout, Matthews, Robins
Scorers: PW Stout (5), AF Fielding (3), FB Fielding (2)

Date: Saturday 17/11/1894
Result: **GLOUCESTER 1 SAINT GEORGE 2**
Competition: Bristol & District League Division 1
Teamsheet: Speck, Fowler, Tadman, FM Stout, Wade-Smith, Cragg, AF Fielding, FB Fielding, PW Stout, "Bedman", Sherwood
Scorer: Sherwood

Date: Saturday 24/11/1894
Result: **MANGOTSFIELD 1 GLOUCESTER 1**
Competition: Bristol & District League Division 1
Teamsheet: Speck, Burt, Tadman, FM Stout, Wade-Smith, Parker, AF Fielding, FB Fielding, PW Stout, Cragg, Sherwood
Scorer: PW Stout

Date: Saturday 01/12/1894
Result: **GLOUCESTER 2 TROWBRIDGE TOWN 3**
Competition: Bristol & District League Division 1
Teamsheet: Speck, Tadman, Mansfield, Parker, Wade-Smith, FM Stout, AF Fielding, Robins, FB Fielding, Sherwood, Cragg
Scorers: FB Fielding, Sherwood

Date: Saturday 08/12/1894
Result: **GLOUCESTER 2 SWINDON WANDERERS 0**
Competition: Bristol & District League Division 1
Teamsheet: Speck, Tadman, Cragg, Parker, Wade-Smith, FM Stout, Sherwood, Snell, PW Stout, AF Fielding, FB Fielding
Scorers: Snell, PW Stout

Date: Saturday 15/12/1894
Result: **STAPLE HILL 2 GLOUCESTER 0**
Competition: Bristol & District League Division 1
Teamsheet: Speck (?), Fowler, ------, -----, FM Stout (?), Cragg, Sherwood (?), Robins, PW Stout, AF Fielding (?), FB Fielding (?)

Date: Saturday 22/12/1894
Result: **HEREFORD THISTLE 6 GLOUCESTER 6**
Competition: Bristol & District League Division 1
Teamsheet: Speck, Fowler, Goodwin, Morris, FM Stout, Cragg, AF Fielding, Robins, FB Fielding, Sherwood, Clutterbuck
Scorers: Sherwood (3), AF Fielding, FB Fielding, Cragg

Date: Saturday 26/01/1895
Result: **GLOUCESTER ? SAINT PAUL'S ?**
Competition: Gloucestershire FA Senior Challenge Cup 1st Round
Teamsheet: Speck, Fowler, Tadman, Wade-Smith, Taylor, FM Stout, Sherwood, Snell, PW Stout, AF Fielding, FB Fielding
Scorer: -----
Note: Gloucester won

Date: Saturday 23/02/1895
Result: **GLOUCESTER 4 MANGOTSFIELD 2**
Competition: Gloucestershire FA Senior Challenge Cup Semi-Final
Teamsheet: Speck (?), -----, Tadman (?), Wade-Smith (?), -----, FM Stout (?), Sherwood (?), -----, PW Stout (?), AF Fielding (?), FB Fielding (?)
Scorers: -----, -----, -----, -----

Date: Saturday 02/03/1895
Result: **GLOUCESTER 3 BEDMINSTER 0**
Competition: Bristol & District League Division 1
Teamsheet: Speck, Tadman, Vaughan, FM Stout, Wade-Smith, Cragg, FB Fielding, AF Fielding, PW Stout, Sherwood, Clutterbuck
Scorers: FB Fielding (2), -----

Date: Saturday 09/03/1895
Result: **SAINT GEORGE 3 GLOUCESTER 1**
Competition: Bristol & District League Division 1
Teamsheet: Speck, Goodwin, Tadman, Cragg, Wade-Smith, FM Stout, Matthews, Clutterbuck, Sherwood, AF Fielding, FB Fielding
Scorer: -----

Date: Saturday 16/03/1895
Result: **EASTVILLE ROVERS 3 GLOUCESTER 5**
Competition: Bristol & District League Division 1
Teamsheet: Speck, Goodwin, Tadman (?), Cragg (?), Wade-Smith, FM Stout (?), -----, AF Fielding (?), PW Stout, Sherwood, FB Fielding
Scorers: FB Fielding, PW Stout (4)

Date: Saturday 23/03/1895
Result: **GLOUCESTER 3 WARMLEY 2**
Competition: Bristol & District League Division 1
Teamsheet: Speck, Fowler, Tadman, FM Stout, Wade-Smith, Cragg, Sherwood, Morris, PW Stout, AF Fielding, FB Fielding
Scorers: AF Fielding, Morris, FB Fielding

Date: Monday 25/03/1895
Result: **GLOUCESTER 2 STAPLE HILL 2**
Competition: Bristol & District League Division 1
Teamsheet: Speck, Fowler, Carter, Cragg, Wade-Smith, Morris, FM Stout, Sherwood, PW Stout, AF Fielding, FB Fielding
Scorers: AF Fielding, -----

Date: Saturday 30/03/1895
Result: **CLEVEDON 2 GLOUCESTER 5**
Competition: Bristol & District League Division 1
Teamsheet: Speck, Fowler, Tadman, Morris, Cragg, Wade-Smith, AF Fielding, Pettey, FB Fielding, Radford, Sherwood
Scorers: -----, -----, -----, -----, -----

Date: Saturday 06/04/1895
Result: **BEDMINSTER 3 GLOUCESTER 5**
Competition: Bristol & District League Division 1
Teamsheet: Robins, Morris, Fowler, Cragg, Wade-Smith, FM Stout, Sherwood, Clutterbuck, PW Stout, AF Fielding, FB Fielding
Scorers: Sherwood, FB Fielding, PW Stout (3, 1 pen)

1893-4

J. T. Stout Matthews Somerville Hoitt Kent Cragg F. M. Stout Robins
(Hon. Sec.)
Matthews Sherwood Fielding P. W. Stout Powell Tadman
(Capt.) *(Hon. Treas.)*

Champions Gloucester and District League 1897-8
Left to Right (Standing) : W. L. Badham, S. Harris, G. Speck, J. G. Washbourn
(Sitting) : H. Porter, J. A. Oakey, W. H. Hicks (*Captain*), A. F. Fielding, F. B. Fielding
(Front) : A. L. Lane, H. G. Sherwood, H. W. Arkell

Date: Monday 08/04/1895
Result: **WARMLEY 7 GLOUCESTER 0**
Competition: Bristol & District League Division 1
Teamsheet: Speck (?), -----, Fowler (?), Cragg (?), Wade-Smith (?), FM Stout (?), Sherwood (?), AF Fielding (?), PW Stout (?), FB Fielding (?), Robins

Date: Sunday 14/04/1895
Result: **SAINT GEORGE 4 GLOUCESTER 3**
Competition: Gloucestershire FA Senior Challenge Cup Final
Teamsheet: Speck, Fowler, Tadman, Cragg, Wade-Smith, FM Stout, Sherwood, Powell, PW Stout, AF Fielding, FB Fielding
Scorers: PW Stout (2), FB Fielding
Note: Played at Kingswood

Date: Saturday 20/04/1895
Result: **TROWBRIDGE TOWN 0 GLOUCESTER 4**
Competition: Bristol & District League Division 1
Teamsheet: Speck, Fowler, Barnard, FM Stout, Wade-Smith, Pitt, AF Fielding, Frith, FB Fielding, Radford, Robins
Scorers: FB Fielding (2), Robins (2)

Date: ?
Result: **GLOUCESTER 0 HEREFORD THISTLE 4**
Competition: Bristol & District League Division 1
Teamsheet: -----, -----, -----, -----, -----, -----, -----, -----, -----, -----, -----

Date: ?
Result: **GLOUCESTER 4 MANGOTSFIELD 2**
Competition: Bristol & District League Division 1
Teamsheet: -----, -----, -----, -----, -----, -----, -----, -----, -----, -----, -----
Scorers: -----, -----, -----, -----

Date: ?
Result: **SWINDON WANDERERS 2 GLOUCESTER 2**
Competition: Bristol & District League Division 1
Teamsheet: -----, -----, -----, -----, -----, -----, -----, -----, -----, -----, -----
Scorers: -----, -----

Appearances – H Barnard 1, W "Bedman" 1, ? Burt 1, LH Carter 1, GC Clutterbuck 4, AC Cragg 18, AF Fielding 21, FB Fielding 22, RC Fowler 11, AP Frith 1, AE Goodwin 5, ? Mansfield 1, WG Matthews 2, FM Morris 5, JM Parker 3, C Pettey 1, WT Pitt 5, JOT Powell 1, J Radford 2, HT Robins 8, HG Sherwood 20, ES Snell 3, G Speck 20, FM Stout 19, PW Stout 17, ETS Tadman 15, ? Taylor 1, EL Turner 1, CG Vaughan 3, Rev. M Wade-Smith 16.
Scorers – PW Stout 20, FB Fielding 14, HG Sherwood 8, AF Fielding 6, HT Robins 2, AC Cragg 1, FM Morris 1, ES Snell 1.

BRISTOL & DISTRICT LEAGUE DIVISION 1

POS	CLUB	P	W	D	L	F	A	PTS
1	HEREFORD THISTLE	22	18	3	1	93	22	39
2	SAINT GEORGE (Bristol)	22	18	3	1	76	21	39
3	WARMLEY	22	14	2	6	74	30	30
4	STAPLE HILL	22	11	4	7	56	38	26
5	**GLOUCESTER**	**22**	**10**	**4**	**8**	**64**	**54**	**24**
6	EASTVILLE ROVERS	22	10	4	8	46	40	24
7	TROWBRIDGE TOWN	22	9	4	9	68	48	22
8	CLIFTON	22	8	2	12	47	55	18
9	BEDMINSTER	22	7	0	15	39	73	14
10	SWINDON WANDERERS	22	5	3	14	40	63	13
11	MANGOTSFIELD	22	5	2	15	22	68	12
12	CLEVEDON	22	1	1	20	23	136	3
		264	116	32	116	648	648	264

SEASON 1895-1896
(Home Ground: Avenue Road Ground, Tuffley Avenue)

Date: Saturday 28/09/1895
Result: **GLOUCESTER 3 SAINT PAUL'S 3**
Competition: Western League Division 1
Teamsheet: Speck, Goodwin, Fowler, Scott, Wade-Smith, Spence, FB Fielding, AF Fielding, Green, Sherwood, Clutterbuck
Scorers: Green (2), Sherwood

Date: Saturday 05/10/1895
Result: **TROWBRIDGE TOWN 3 GLOUCESTER 1**
Competition: Western League Division 1
Teamsheet: Robins, Goodwin, Fowler, Scott, Wade-Smith, Spence, FB Fielding, AF Fielding, Green, Radford, Clutterbuck
Scorer: FB Fielding

Date: Saturday 19/10/1895
Result: **GLOUCESTER 1 TROWBRIDGE TOWN 8**
Competition: Western League Division 1
Teamsheet: Speck, Goodwin, Green, Scott, Wade-Smith, Spence, AF Fielding, FB Fielding, Harris, Sherwood, Clutterbuck
Scorer: FB Fielding

Date: Saturday 26/10/1895
Result: **GLOUCESTER 2 SAINT GEORGE 0**
Competition: Western League Division 1
Teamsheet: Speck, Cragg, Tadman, Scott, Wade-Smith, Clutterbuck, AF Fielding, FB Fielding, Harris, Sherwood, Franklin
Scorers: FB Fielding, Harris

Date: Saturday 02/11/1895
Result: **STAPLE HILL 3 GLOUCESTER 1**
Competition: Western League Division 1
Teamsheet: Speck, Cragg, Tadman, Scott, Wade-Smith, Pitt, AF Fielding, FB Fielding, Harris (?), Pettey, Clutterbuck
Scorer: FB Fielding

Date: Saturday 09/11/1895
Result: **EASTVILLE ROVERS 1 GLOUCESTER 2**
Competition: Western League Division 1
Teamsheet: Speck, Tadman, Cragg, Spence, Scott, Wade-Smith, AF Fielding, FB Fielding, Harris, Frith, Robins
Scorers: FB Fielding, own goal.

Date: Saturday 23/11/1895
Result: GLOUCESTER 0 CARDIFF 2
Competition: Western League Division 1
Teamsheet: Speck, Cragg, Tadman, Scott, Wade-Smith, Spence, AF Fielding, FB Fielding, Harris, Sherwood, Clutterbuck
Note: Originally League game. Cardiff withdrew

Date: Saturday 30/11/1895
Result: **CLIFTON 2 GLOUCESTER 6**
Competition: Western League Division 1
Teamsheet: Speck, Cragg, Tadman, Spence, Scott, Wade-Smith, AF Fielding, FB Fielding, Snell, -----, Clutterbuck
Scorers: FB Fielding, Clutterbuck, -----, -----, -----, -----

Date: Saturday 07/12/1895
Result: **WARMLEY 2 GLOUCESTER 1**
Competition: Western League Division 1
Teamsheet: Speck, Frith, Tadman, Spence, Scott, Carely, AF Fielding, FB Fielding, Harris, -----, Robins
Scorer: FB Fielding

Date: Saturday 14/12/1895
Result: **GLOUCESTER 4 MANGOTSFIELD 0**
Competition: Western League Division 1
Teamsheet: Speck, Tadman, Frith, Scott, Wade-Smith, Spence, FB Fielding, AF Fielding, Sherwood, Cragg, Clutterbuck
Scorers: Clutterbuck (2), Sherwood, FB Fielding

Date: Saturday 21/12/1895
Result: **BEDMINSTER 0 GLOUCESTER 0**
Competition: Western League Division 1
Teamsheet: Speck, Tadman, Frith, Fowler, Scott, Spence, AF Fielding, FB Fielding, Sherwood, Cragg, Clutterbuck
Attendance: 1000

Date: Saturday 04/01/1896
Result: **SAINT PAUL'S 0 GLOUCESTER 1**
Competition: Western League Division 1
Teamsheet: Speck, Frith, Cragg, Spence, Scott, Morris, AF Fielding, FB Fielding, Sherwood, Pearce, -----
Scorer: -----

Date: Saturday 18/01/1896
Result: **GLOUCESTER 1 CLIFTON 2**
Competition: Western League Division 1
Teamsheet: Speck, Tadman, Frith, Spence, Scott, White, AF Fielding, James, FB Fielding, Clutterbuck, Franklin
Scorer: FB Fielding

Date: Saturday 01/02/1896
Result: **GLOUCESTER 2 EASTVILLE ROVERS 3**
Competition: Western League Division 1
Teamsheet: Speck, Frith, Fowler, Spence, Scott, Clutterbuck, AF Fielding, FB Fielding, Harris, Cragg, Sherwood
Scorer: FB Fielding (2)

Date: Saturday 08/02/1896
Result: **GLOUCESTER 0 STAPLE HILL 2**
Competition: Western League Division 1
Teamsheet: Speck, Tadman, Frith, Fowler, Spence, Hicks, AF Fielding, FB Fielding, Sherwood, Cragg, James

Date: Saturday 15/02/1896
Result: **SAINT GEORGE 5 GLOUCESTER 0**
Competition: Western League Division 1
Teamsheet: Speck, Frith, Tadman, Spence, Mackay, Hicks, AF Fielding, FB Fielding, Jessop, -----, James

Date: Saturday 22/02/1896
Result: **SWINDON WANDERERS 3 GLOUCESTER 2**
Competition: Western League Division 1
Teamsheet: -----, -----, -----, -----, -----, -----, -----, -----, -----, Pettey, -----
Scorers: own goal, Pettey

Date: Saturday 29/02/1896
Result: **MANGOTSFIELD 1 GLOUCESTER 1**
Competition: Gloucestershire FA Senior Challenge Cup 1st Round
Teamsheet: -----, -----, -----, -----, -----, -----, -----, -----, -----, -----, -----
Scorer: -----
Note: Replay scheduled for 18 March. Gloucester withdrew from Cup. This may have been because of the small-pox epidemic in Gloucester.

Date: Saturday 07/03/1896
Result: **MANGOTSFIELD 0 GLOUCESTER 1**
Competition: Western League Division 1
Teamsheet: Speck, -----, -----, -----, -----, -----, AF Fielding, -----, Sherwood, -----
Scorer: Sherwood
Note: Only 10 men played

Date: Saturday 14/03/1896
Result: **GLOUCESTER 1 WARMLEY 4**
Competition: Western League Division 1
Teamsheet: Speck, Tadman, Frith, Pitt, Hicks, Oakey, Daniells, AF Fielding, FB Fielding, Jessop, Porter
Scorer: Daniells

Date: Saturday 28/03/1896
Result: **GLOUCESTER – BEDMINSTER –**
Competition: Western League Division 1
Note: Unplayed match due to small-pox epidemic in Gloucester. It was resolved that the game should be considered a draw and each club given one point

Date: Saturday 25/04/1896
Result: **GLOUCESTER – SWINDON WANDERERS –**
Competition: Western League Division 1
Note: Unplayed match due to small-pox epidemic in Gloucester. It was resolved that the game should be considered a draw and each club given one point

Appearances – F Carely 1, GC Clutterbuck 11, AC Cragg 10, H Daniells 1, AF Fielding 18, FB Fielding 17, RC Fowler 5, J Franklin 2, AP Frith 10, AE Goodman 3, HD Green 3, H Harris 7, WH Hicks 3, ET James 3, GL Jessop 2, ? Mackay 1, FM Morris 1, JA Oakey 1, F Pearce 1, C Pettey 2, WT Pitt 2, HT Porter 1, J Radford 1, HT Robins 3, HH Scott 14, HG Sherwood 10, ES Snell 1, G Speck 17, A Spence 14, ETS Tadman 12, Rev. M Wade-Smith 9, CF White 1.
Scorers - FB Fielding 11, GC Clutterbuck 3, HG Sherwood 3, HD Green 2, H Daniells 1, H Harris 1, C Pettey 1, own goals 2.

WESTERN LEAGUE DIVISION 1

POS	CLUB	P	W	D	L	F	A	PTS
1	WARMLEY	20	16	3	1	65	13	35
2	EASTVILLE ROVERS	20	14	1	5	57	22	29
3	STAPLE HILL	20	13	3	4	48	19	29
4	TROWBRIDGE TOWN	20	13	1	6	50	31	27
5	SAINT GEORGE (Bristol)	20	10	4	6	47	38	24
6	CLIFTON	20	8	3	9	44	50	17*
7	**GLOUCESTER +**	**20**	**6**	**4**	**10**	**29**	**42**	**16**
8	BEDMINSTER	20	6	2	12	36	41	14
9	SWINDON WANDERERS	20	4	4	12	22	57	12
10	MANGOTSFIELD	20	3	3	14	17	54	9
11	SAINT PAUL'S	20	2	2	16	12	60	6
12	CARDIFF							
		220	95	30	95	427	427	218

Cardiff withdrew. All scores were expunged from records.
*Two points deducted for misconduct.
+ Gloucester v Bedminster and Gloucester v Swindon Wanderers unplayed. It was resolved that the games should be considered drawn and each club given one point.

SEASON 1896-1897
(Home Ground: Co-operative Field, India Road – ground share with the Post Office Club)

No competitive games were played this season. 15 friendlies or challenge games were played.

SEASON 1897-1898
(Home Ground: Budding's Field)

Date: Saturday 25/09/1897
Result: **ROSS KYRLE 0 GLOUCESTER 3**
Competition: Gloucester & District League Division 1
Teamsheet: -----, -----, -----, -----, -----, -----, -----, Stephens, -----, Arkell, -----
Scorers: Arkell (2), Stephens

Date: Saturday 02/10/1897
Result: **TEWKESBURY ABBEY 2 GLOUCESTER 0**
Competition: Gloucester & District League Division 1
Teamsheet: Speck, -----, -----, -----, -----, -----, -----, -----, -----, -----, -----

Date: Saturday 13/11/1897
Result: **CAVENDISH HOUSE 0 GLOUCESTER 1**
Competition: Gloucester & District League Division 1
Teamsheet: Speck (?), -----, -----, -----, -----, -----, -----, -----,Porter, -----, -----
Scorer: Porter

Date: Saturday 20/11/1897
Result: **PRICE WALKERS 0 GLOUCESTER 1**
Competition: Gloucester & District League Division 1
Teamsheet: Speck, -----, -----, -----, -----, -----, -----, Porter (?), -----, Lane
Scorer: Lane

Date: Saturday 27/11/1897
Result: **GLOUCESTER 4 ROSS TOWN 1**
Competition: Gloucester & District League Division 1
Teamsheet: Speck, Hicks, Harris, Brown, AF Fielding, Oakey, FB Fielding, Sherwood, Porter, Stephens, Lane
Scorers: Sherwood, Porter (2), FB Fielding

Date: Saturday 04/12/1897
Result: **GLOUCESTER 5 TEWKESBURY ABBEY 0**
Competition: Gloucester & District League Division 1
Teamsheet: Speck, -----, -----, -----, AF Fielding, -----, FB Fielding (?), Sherwood, Porter, -----, -----
Scorers: AF Fielding, Sherwood (3), Porter

Date: Saturday 15/01/1898
Result: **ROSS TOWN 2 GLOUCESTER 4**
Competition: Gloucester & District League Division 1
Teamsheet: Speck (?), -----, -----, -----, -----, -----, FB Fielding, -----, Porter, -----, -----
Scorers: Porter (3), FB Fielding

Date: Saturday 22/01/1898
Result: **GLOUCESTER 2 CAVENDISH HOUSE 1**
Competition: Gloucester & District League Division 1
Teamsheet: Speck, Hicks, Harris, Brown, Oakey, Washbourne, Lane, Saunders, Porter, Arkell, Gardner
Scorers: Saunders, Porter

Date: Friday 04/02/1898
Result: **GLOUCESTER 8 PRICE WALKERS 0**
Competition: Gloucester & District League Division 1
Teamsheet: Speck, Hicks, Harris, Brown, AF Fielding, Oakey, FB Fielding, Arkell, Sherwood, Porter, Pettey
Scorers: AF Fielding (2), Porter (2), FB Fielding (3), Oakey

Date: Saturday 09/04/1898
Result: **GLOUCESTER 1 ROSS KYRLE 1**
Competition: Gloucester & District League Division 1
Teamsheet: -----, -----, -----, -----, -----, -----, -----, -----, Sherwood, -----, -----
Scorer: Sherwood

Appearances – HW Arkell 4, WA Brown 3, AF Fielding 3, FB Fielding 4, WT Gardner 1, SS Harris 3, WH Hicks 3, LA Lane 2, JA Oakey 3, C Pettey 1, HT Porter 7, G Saunders 1, HG Sherwood 4, G Speck 8, AJ Stephens 2, JG Washbourne 1.
Scorers – HT Porter 10, FB Fielding 5, HG Sherwood 5, AF Fielding 3, HW Arkell 2, LA Lane 1, JA Oakey 1, G Saunders 1, AJ Stephens 1.

GLOUCESTER & DISTRICT LEAGUE DIVISION 1

POS	CLUB	P	W	D	L	F	A	PTS
1	**GLOUCESTER**	**10**	**8**	**1**	**1**	**33**	**7**	**17**
2	ROSS TOWN	10	7	0	3	24	10	14
3	ROSS KYRLE	10	5	1	4	19	22	11
4	PRICE WALKERS	10	3	1	6	9	23	7
5	TEWKESBURY ABBEY	10	3	0	7	10	18	6
6	CAVENDISH HOUSE (Cheltenham)	10	2	1	7	10	26	5
		60	28	4	28	105	106	60

SEASON 1898-1899
(Home Ground: Avenue Road Ground, Tuffley Avenue)

Date: Saturday 08/10/1898
Result: **GLOUCESTER 6 LEDBURY VICTORIA 0**
Competition: Gloucester & District League Division 1
Teamsheet: Speck, Harris, Hicks, Guy, AF Fielding, H Lane, Porter, BH Lane, LA Lane, Sherwood, Arkell
Scorers: LA Lane (3), Guy, AF Fielding, Porter

Date: Saturday 15/10/1898
Result: **GLOUCESTER 5 CHALFORD 0**
Competition: Mid Gloucestershire League
Teamsheet: Robins, Hicks, Arkell, H Lane, AF Fielding, Guy, Porter, BH Lane, LA Lane, Sherwood, FB Fielding
Scorers: FB Fielding (2), Sherwood, Porter, LA Lane

Date: Saturday 22/10/1898
Result: **GLOUCESTER 2 EBLEY 0**
Competition: Gloucester & District League Division 1
Teamsheet: Speck, Arkell, Harris, H Lane, AF Fielding, Oakey, FB Fielding, Sherwood, LA Lane, BH Lane, Porter
Scorers: AF Fielding, Arkell

Date: Saturday 29/10/1898
Result: **TEWKESBURY ABBEY 1 GLOUCESTER 1**
Competition: Gloucester & District League Division 1
Teamsheet: Speck, Hicks, Harris, Oakey, AF Fielding, H Lane, Arkell, Sherwood, LA Lane, BH Lane, Porter
Scorer: Porter

Date: Saturday 12/11/1898
Result: **ROSS TOWN 2 GLOUCESTER 1**
Competition: Gloucester & District League Division 1
Teamsheet: -----, -----, -----, -----, -----, -----, Arkell, -----, -----, -----, -----
Scorer: Arkell

Date: Saturday 19/11/1898
Result: GLOUCESTER 3 WOTTON-UNDER-EDGE 0
Competition: Mid Gloucestershire League
Teamsheet: -----, -----, -----, -----, -----, -----, Arkell (?), -----, -----, -----, -----
Scorers: -----, -----, -----
Note: Originally League game. Wotton-Under-Edge withdrew

Date: Saturday 10/12/1898
Result: **GLOUCESTER 7 TEWKESBURY ABBEY 1**
Competition: Gloucester & District League Division 1
Teamsheet: Speck, -----, -----, -----, AF Fielding, -----, Arkell, Sherwood, LA Lane, -----, Porter
Scorers: Porter, Sherwood (3), AF Fielding, Arkell, LA Lane

Date: Saturday 17/12/1898
Result: **GLOUCESTER 1 CHELTENHAM TOWN 1**
Competition: Gloucester & District League Division 1
Teamsheet: -----, -----, -----, -----, -----, -----, -----, -----, -----, -----, -----
Scorer: -----

[10]

Date: Saturday 24/12/1898
Result: **EBLEY 0 GLOUCESTER 0**
Competition: Mid Gloucestershire League
Teamsheet: -----, -----, -----, -----, -----, -----, -----, -----, -----, -----, -----

Date: Saturday 07/01/1899
Result: **GLOUCESTER 1 ROSS TOWN 1**
Competition: Gloucester & District League Division 1
Teamsheet: Speck, Arkell, Harris, Oakey, AF Fielding, H Lane, BH Lane, Sherwood, LA Lane, Porter, Long
Scorer: Sherwood

Date: Saturday 14/01/1899
Result: **BRISTOL AMATEURS 5 GLOUCESTER 0**
Competition: Gloucestershire FA Senior Challenge Cup 1st Round
Teamsheet: Speck, Frith, Arkell, Harris, AF Fielding, Oakey, BH Lane, Porter, LA Lane, Sherwood, Long

Date: Saturday 28/01/1899
Result: **LEDBURY VICTORIA 0 GLOUCESTER 0**
Competition: Gloucester & District League Division 1
Teamsheet: Speck (?), -----, Arkell (?), Harris (?), -----, Oakey (?), -----, AF Fielding (?), LA Lane (?), Sherwood (?), Porter (?)

Date: Saturday 18/02/1899
Result: **EBLEY 0 GLOUCESTER 5**
Competition: Gloucester & District League Division 1
Teamsheet: Speck, Arkell, Harris, Sly, Oakey, H Lane, Rust, AF Fielding, LA Lane, Sherwood, Porter
Scorers: Sherwood (2), own goal, Rust, Porter

Date: Saturday 25/02/1899
Result: **GLOUCESTER 1 ROSS KYRLE 3**
Competition: Gloucester & District League Division 1
Teamsheet: Speck, Arkell, Harris, Sly, Oakey, H Lane, Rust, AF Fielding, LA Lane, Sherwood, Porter
Scorer: AF Fielding

Date: Saturday 11/03/1899
Result: **GLOUCESTER 0 BRIMSCOMBE 1**
Competition: Mid Gloucestershire League
Teamsheet: Speck, Arkell, Harris, Sly, Oakey, H Lane, Rust, AF Fielding, LA Lane, Long, Porter

Date: Saturday 18/03/1899
Result: **ROSS KYRLE 0 GLOUCESTER 3**
Competition: Gloucester & District League Division 1
Teamsheet: Speck, Arkell, Harris, Sly, Oakey, H Lane, AF Fielding, Rust, LA Lane, Sherwood, Porter
Scorers: own goals (2), Rust

Date: Saturday 01/04/1899
Result: **CHELTENHAM TOWN 0 GLOUCESTER 2**
Competition: Gloucester & District League Division 1
Teamsheet: Speck, Arkell (?), Harris (?), LA Lane (?), Oakey (?), Sly, AF Fielding, Rust, Sherwood, Long, Porter
Scorers: Porter, Rust

Date: Saturday 08/04/1899
Result: **GLOUCESTER 3 EBLEY 0**
Competition: Mid Gloucestershire League
Teamsheet: Speck, Arkell, Harris, LA Lane, Oakey, Sly, Porter, AF Fielding, Sherwood, Rust, Stock
Scorers: AF Fielding, Sherwood, Rust

Date: Saturday 15/04/1899
Result: **CHALFORD 0 GLOUCESTER 6**
Competition: Mid Gloucestershire League
Teamsheet: Speck (?), Arkell (?), Harris (?), -----, Oakey (?), Sly (?), Rust, Sherwood (?), AF Fielding (?), Sherwood (?), Porter (?)
Scorers: -----, -----, -----, -----, -----, -----

Date: Saturday 22/04/1899
Result: **BRIMSCOMBE 1 GLOUCESTER 3**
Competition: Mid Gloucestershire League
Teamsheet: Speck, Harris, Arkell, H Lane, Oakey, Sly, Long, Rust, Sherwood, AF Fielding, Porter
Scorers: AF Fielding (2), Sherwood

Appearances – HW Arkell 18, AF Fielding 16, FB Fielding 2, AP Frith 1, B Guy 2, SS Harris 14, WH Hicks 3, BH Lane 6, H Lane 10, LA Lane 14, W Long 5, JA Oakey 13, HT Porter 16, HT Robins 1, FT Rust 8, HG Sherwood 15, RR Sly 8, G Speck 15, JW Stock 1.
Scorers – HG Sherwood 9, AF Fielding 7, HT Porter 6, LA Lane 5, FT Rust 4, HW Arkell 3, FB Fielding 2, B Guy 1, own goals 3.

GLOUCESTER & DISTRICT LEAGUE DIVISION 1

POS	CLUB	P	W	D	L	F	A	PTS
1	ROSS KYRLE	12	10	0	2	32	13	20
2	**GLOUCESTER**	**12**	**6**	**4**	**2**	**30**	**9**	**16**
3	ROSS TOWN	12	5	2	5	23	19	12
4	LEDBURY VICTORIA	12	4	3	5	14	19	11
5	TEWKESBURY ABBEY	12	3	3	6	12	28	9
6	EBLEY	12	3	2	7	19	22	8
7	CHELTENHAM TOWN	12	2	4	6	13	33	8
		84	33	18	33	143	143	84

MID GLOUCESTERSHIRE LEAGUE

POS	CLUB	P	W	D	L	F	A	PTS
1	**GLOUCESTER**	**6**	**4**	**1**	**1**	**17**	**2**	**9**
2	EBLEY	6	3	2	1	13	9	8
3	BRIMSCOMBE	6	2	0	4	12	14	4
4	CHALFORD	6	1	1	4	7	24	3
5	WOTTON-UNDER-EDGE							
		24	10	4	10	49	49	24

Wotton-under-Edge withdrew from league.

SEASON 1899-1900

(Home Ground: Avenue Road Ground, Tuffley Avenue)

Date: Saturday 07/10/1899
Result: **FOREST GREEN ROVERS 1 GLOUCESTER 6**
Competition: Mid Gloucestershire League
Teamsheet: Hallett, Arkell, Keys, Lane, Oakey, Sly, Stock, Rust, Porter, Sherwood, Long
Scorers: Sherwood (3), Porter (2), Rust

Date: Saturday 21/10/1899
Result: **TEWKESBURY ABBEY 1 GLOUCESTER 1**
Competition: Gloucestershire FA Junior Challenge Cup 1st Round
Teamsheet: Hallett, Keys, Langley-Smith, Lane, Robotham, Sly, Rust, Stock, Carpenter, Hart, Merry
Scorer: Carpenter

Date: Saturday 28/10/1899
Result: **GLOUCESTER 8 CHALFORD 1**
Competition: Mid Gloucestershire League
Teamsheet: Hallett, Arkell, Pinnegar, Oakey, Keys, Sly, Stock, Rust, Porter, Hart (?), Long
Scorers: Long (2), Porter (2), Stock, Arkell, Rust, Oakey

Date: Saturday 11/11/1899
Result: **GLOUCESTER 0 TEWKESBURY ABBEY 1**
Competition: Gloucestershire FA Junior Challenge Cup 1st Round Replay
Teamsheet: Hallett, Arkell (?), Langley-Smith, Keys, Robotham, Sly, Rust, Stock, Porter, Hart, Merry

Date: Saturday 18/11/1899
Result: **GLOUCESTER 4 ROSS TOWN 1**
Competition: Gloucester & District League Division 1
Teamsheet: Hallett, Arkell, -----, Sly, Fielding, Keys (?), -----, Rust, Hart, Stock (?), Porter
Scorers: Arkell, Fielding, Hart, Porter

Date: Saturday 25/11/1899
Result: **GLOUCESTER 2 CHELTENHAM TOWN 1**
Competition: Gloucester & District League Division 1
Teamsheet: Hallett, Arkell, Pinnegar, Sly, Fielding, Keys, Stock, Rust, Porter, Llewellyn, Long
Scorers: Llewellyn, Porter

Date: Saturday 02/12/1899
Result: **GLOUCESTER 2 TEWKESBURY ABBEY 2**
Competition: Gloucester & District League Division 1
Teamsheet: Hallett, Arkell, Pinnegar, Sly, Fielding, Keys, Long, Shaw, Porter, Rust, Sherwood
Scorers: Sherwood, Porter

Date: Saturday 09/12/1899
Result: **ROSS KYRLE 1 GLOUCESTER 2**
Competition: Gloucester & District League Division 1
Teamsheet: Hallett, Arkell, Pinnegar, Lane, Keys, Sly, Wakefield, Shaw, Fielding, Rust, Porter
Scorers: Lane, Shaw

Date: Saturday 06/01/1900
Result: **GLOUCESTER 7 STONEHOUSE 4**
Competition: Mid Gloucestershire League
Teamsheet: Hallett (?), Arkell (?), Pinnegar (?), Keys (?), -----, Sly, Shaw (?), -----, Porter, Rust (?), -----
Scorers: -----, -----, -----, -----, -----, -----, -----

Date: Saturday 13/01/1900
Result: **GLOUCESTER 10 FOREST GREEN ROVERS 0**
Competition: Mid Gloucestershire League
Teamsheet: Hallett, Arkell, Pinnegar, Keys, Long, Sly, Shaw, Hart, Porter, Rust, Stock
Scorers: Shaw (5), Rust (2), Hart, Sly, Long

Date: Saturday 20/01/1900
Result: **GLOUCESTER 6 ROSS KYRLE 0**
Competition: Gloucester & District League Division 1
Teamsheet: Hallett, Arkell, Pinnegar, Sly, Fielding, Keys, Stock, Rust, Rich, Shaw, Porter
Scorers: Shaw (2), Fielding (pen), Porter, Keys, Rust

Date: Saturday 27/01/1900
Result: **STAPLE HILL 3 GLOUCESTER 1**
Competition: Gloucestershire FA Senior Challenge Cup 1st Round
Teamsheet: Hallett (?), Arkell (?), Pinnegar (?), Sly, Fielding (?), Keys (?), Stock (?), Rust (?), -----, Shaw (?), Porter
Scorer: -----

Date: Saturday 24/02/1900
Result: **CHELTENHAM TOWN 3 GLOUCESTER 3**
Competition: Gloucester & District League Division 1
Teamsheet: Hallett, Arkell, Pinnegar, Sly, Morley, Keys, Stock, Rust, Fielding, Shaw, Porter
Scorers: Porter (2), Shaw

Date: Saturday 03/03/1900
Result: **GLOUCESTER 3 ROSS TOWN 2**
Competition: Gloucester & District League Division 1
Teamsheet: Hallett, Arkell, Pinnegar, Nicholls, Keys, Sly, Stock, Rust, Hart, Shaw, Porter
Scorers: Rust, Porter, Shaw
Note: Played at Kingsholm Rugby Ground

Date: Saturday 10/03/1900
Result: **LEDBURY VICTORIA 1 GLOUCESTER 2**
Competition: Gloucester & District League Division 1
Teamsheet: Hallett (?), Arkell (?), -----, -----, Keys (?), Sly, Stock (?), Rust (?), -----, -----, Porter
Scorers: -----, -----

Date: Saturday 17/03/1900
Result: **EBLEY 1 GLOUCESTER 2**
Competition: Mid Gloucestershire League
Teamsheet: Hallett, Arkell, Arnold, Keys, Oakey, Sly, Porter, May, Fielding, Rust, Stock
Scorers: May, Rust

Date: Saturday 24/03/1900
Result: **TEWKESBURY ABBEY 0 GLOUCESTER 2**
Competition: Gloucester & District League Division 1
Teamsheet: Hallett (?), Arkell (?), Arnold (?), -----, Keys (?), Sly, Wakefield, May (?), Rust (?), Shaw, Porter
Scorers: Shaw, Wakefield

Date: Saturday 31/03/1900
Result: **BRIMSCOMBE 2 GLOUCESTER 5**
Competition: Mid Gloucestershire League
Teamsheet: Hallett, Arnold, Arkell, Sly, Keys, Fielding, Wakefield, Shaw, Porter, Rust, May
Scorers: Sly, Rust, Shaw, Keys (pen), May

Date: Wednesday 04/04/1900
Result: **GLOUCESTER 7 EBLEY 4**
Competition: Mid Gloucestershire League
Teamsheet: Hallett (?), -----, Arkell (?), Sly, Keys, Fielding, Wakefield, Shaw, Porter, Rust, May
Scorers: Fielding (3), Shaw (3), Rust

Date: Saturday 07/04/1900
Result: **STONEHOUSE 0 GLOUCESTER 3**
Competition: Mid Gloucestershire League
Teamsheet: Hallett, Arkell, Pinnegar, Fielding, Keys, Sly, Wakefield, Shaw, Porter, Rust, May
Scorers: Shaw (2), May

Date: Saturday 14/04/1900
Result: **CHALFORD 0 GLOUCESTER 1**
Competition: Mid Gloucestershire League
Teamsheet: Hallett, -----, -----, -----, -----, Sly, Wakefield, -----, Porter, -----, May
Scorer: Porter

Appearances – HW Arkell 19, GR Arnold 3, ? Carpenter 1, AF Fielding 11, F Hallett 21, WJ Hart 6, GEH Keys 20, H Lane 3, ? Langley-Smith 2, W Llewellyn 1, W Long 5, E May 6, W Merry 2, RF Morley 1, H Nicholls 1, JA Oakey 3, FJ Pinnegar 11, HT Porter 20, ST Rich 1, ? Robotham 2, FT Rust 20, W Shaw 13, HG Sherwood 2, RR Sly 21, JW Stock 12, J Wakefield 8.
Scorers – W Shaw 17, HT Porter 12, FT Rust 9, AF Fielding 5, HG Sherwood 4, W Long 3, E May 3, HW Arkell 2, WJ Hart 2, GEH Keys 2, RR Sly 2, ? Carpenter 1, H Lane 1, W Llewellyn 1, JA Oakey 1, JW Stock 1, J Wakefield 1.

GLOUCESTER & DISTRICT LEAGUE DIVISION 1

POS	CLUB	P	W	D	L	F	A	PTS
1	**GLOUCESTER**	9	7	2	0	26	11	16
2	TEWKESBURY ABBEY	9	3	3	3	8	12	9
3	LEDBURY VICTORIA+	6	4	1	1	11	7	7*
4	CHELTENHAM TOWN	8	1	5	2	16	13	7
5	ROSS TOWN	10	3	2	5	15	17	6*
6	ROSS KYRLE	10	1	1	8	13	30	3
		52	19	14	19	89	90	48

* Two points deducted for playing ineligible players.
+ Ledbury Victoria notified their resignation from the League after 6 matches. Results stayed.
  Ross Kyrle v Tewkesbury Abbey not played although recorded as played. Tewkesbury Abbey awarded 2 points.

MID GLOUCESTERSHIRE LEAGUE

POS	CLUB	P	W	D	L	F	A	PTS
1	**GLOUCESTER +**	9	9	0	0	49	13	18
2	EBLEY	10	7	0	3	30	13	14
3	BRIMSCOMBE +	9	3	2	4	17	22	8
4	CHALFORD	10	3	2	5	10	17	8
5	STONEHOUSE	10	1	3	6	16	30	5
6	FOREST GREEN ROVERS	10	2	1	7	9	36	5
		58	25	8	25	131	131	58

+ Brimscombe were down to play on 21/04/1900 but were unable to raise a team. They expressed themselves willing to forfeit the two points.

SEASON BY SEASON

SEASON 1900-1901
(Home Ground: Avenue Road Ground, Tuffley Avenue)

Date: Saturday 27/10/1900
Result: **CHELTENHAM TRAINING COLLEGE 3 GLOUCESTER 1**
Competition: Gloucester & District League Division 1
Teamsheet: Willetts, Arkell, Pinnegar, Axford, Keys, Fielding, Wakefield, Shaw, Mason, FT Rust, Porter
Scorer: Porter

Date: Saturday 03/11/1900
Result: **TEWKESBURY ABBEY 4 GLOUCESTER 1**
Competition: Gloucester & District League Division 1
Teamsheet: Willetts, Arkell (?), -----, Axford (?), Fielding (?), -----, Wakefield (?), Shaw (?), Mason, FT Rust (?), Porter
Scorer: Porter

Date: Saturday 17/11/1900
Result: **GLOUCESTER 5 BRIMSCOMBE 1**
Competition: Mid Gloucestershire League
Teamsheet: Willetts, Arkell, Arnold, Crawley, Fielding, Axford, Mason, Shaw, Wakefield, FT Rust, Porter
Scorers: FT Rust (3), Shaw, Mason

Date: Saturday 24/11/1900
Result: **GLOUCESTER 6 ROSS TOWN 0**
Competition: Gloucester & District League Division 1
Teamsheet: Willetts, Arkell, Arnold, Fielding, Axford, Crawley, Wakefield, Mason, Porter, Shaw, Wilson
Scorers: Shaw, Wakefield (2), Wilson, -----, -----

Date: Saturday 01/12/1900
Result: **CHELTENHAM TOWN 1 GLOUCESTER 0**
Competition: Gloucester & District League Division 1
Teamsheet: Willetts, Arkell, Arnold, Fielding, Crawley, Axford, Mason, FT Rust, Wakefield, Wilson, Porter

Date: Saturday 08/12/1900
Result: **ROSELEIGH 3 GLOUCESTER 2**
Competition: Gloucester & District League Division 1
Teamsheet: Stafford, Washbourne, Arkell, James, Crawley, Axford, Mason, Smith, Wakefield, Wilson, Porter
Scorers: Porter, Wilson

Date: Saturday 15/12/1900
Result: **FOREST GREEN ROVERS 1 GLOUCESTER 4**
Competition: Mid Gloucestershire League
Teamsheet: -----, -----, -----, -----, -----, -----, -----, -----, -----, -----, -----
Scorers: -----, -----, -----, -----

Date: Saturday 22/12/1900
Result: **WOODCHESTER 1 GLOUCESTER 2**
Competition: Mid Gloucestershire League
Teamsheet: -----, -----, -----, -----, -----, -----, -----, -----, -----, -----, -----
Scorers: -----, -----

Date: Saturday 05/01/1901
Result: **CHALFORD 0 GLOUCESTER 2**
Competition: Mid Gloucestershire League
Teamsheet: Willetts, Lambe, Arnold, Crawley, Fielding, Axford, Wilson, Porter, Wakefield, Shaw, Mason
Scorers: -----, -----

Date: Saturday 19/01/1901
Result: **GLOUCESTER 0 CHELTENHAM TOWN 2**
Competition: Gloucester & District League Division 1
Teamsheet: Willetts, Lambe, Lane, Crawley, Fielding, Axford, Mason, Shaw, Wakefield, Porter, Wilson
Note: Played at Budding's Field

Date: Saturday 09/02/1901
Result: **GLOUCESTER 1 CHELTENHAM TRAINING COLLEGE 0**
Competition: Gloucester & District League Division 1
Teamsheet: Willetts, Fielding, Arkell, Crawley, Griffiths, Axford, Wakefield, Mason, Shaw, Porter, Wilson
Scorer: Wakefield
Note: Abandoned at half-time ground unfit. Score stands

Date: Saturday 09/03/1901
Result: **GLOUCESTER 1 TEWKESBURY ABBEY 5**
Competition: Gloucester & District League Division 1
Teamsheet: Willetts (?), -----, Arkell (?), -----, -----, -----, -----, Mason, -----, -----, Wilson (?)
Scorer: -----

Date: Saturday 16/03/1901
Result: **ROSS TOWN 0 GLOUCESTER 0**
Competition: Gloucester & District League Division 1
Teamsheet: Willetts, -----, Arkell, -----, -----, -----, -----, -----, -----, -----, Wilson

Date: Saturday 23/03/1901
Result: **GLOUCESTER – ROSELEIGH –**
Competition: Gloucester & District League Division 1
Note: Unplayed match. Roseleigh had withdrawn from League. Win accorded to Gloucester

Date: Saturday 30/03/1901
Result: **BRIMSCOMBE 0 GLOUCESTER 6**
Competition: Mid Gloucestershire League
Teamsheet: Willetts, Arkell, Fielding, Crawley, Griffiths, Axford, Mason, Shaw, Wakefield, FT Rust, Porter
Scorers: Wakefield, Shaw (2), -----, -----, Fielding

Date: Saturday 06/04/1901
Result: **GLOUCESTER 9 CHALFORD 0**
Competition: Mid Gloucestershire League
Teamsheet: Willetts, Arkell, James, Crawley, Griffiths, Axford, FT Rust, Mason, Wakefield, Porter
Scorers: Mason (4), Griffiths (2), Wakefield (2), FT Rust
Note: Only 10 players used

Date: Saturday 13/04/1901
Result: **EBLEY 0 GLOUCESTER 2**
Competition: Mid Gloucestershire League
Teamsheet: Willetts, -----, -----, Axford (?), Crawley (?), -----, -----, FT Rust, Mason, Wakefield (?), Porter (?)
Scorer: Mason (2)

Date: Thursday 18/04/1901
Result: **GLOUCESTER 5 EBLEY 0**
Competition: Mid Gloucestershire League
Teamsheet: Willetts, Lane, Pinnegar, Axford, Crawley, Shaw, Mason, Porter, Wakefield, FT Rust, Wilson
Scorers: Shaw (3), FT Rust, Mason

Date: Saturday 20/04/1901
Result: **GLOUCESTER 5 FOREST GREEN ROVERS 0**
Competition: Mid Gloucestershire League
Teamsheet: Willetts, Arkell, Pinnegar, Crawley, Keys, Axford, Porter, Mason, Shaw, FT Rust, Wilson
Scorers: Shaw (2), Mason, FT Rust, Crawley

Date: Saturday 27/04/1901
Result: **GLOUCESTER 2 WOODCHESTER 0**
Competition: Mid Gloucestershire League
Teamsheet: Willetts, Fielding, Pinnegar, TH Rust, Axford, Wilson, Hart, Shaw, Mason, FT Rust, Porter
Scorers: Shaw, FT Rust

Appearances – HW Arkell 12, GR Arnold 4, TE Axford 15, FR Crawley 12, AF Fielding 10, DE Griffiths 3, WJ Hart 1, A James 2, GEH Keys 2, WH Lambe 2, H Lane 2, W Mason 16, FJ Pinnegar 4, HT Porter 15, FT Rust 10, TH Rust 1, W Shaw 11, ? Smith 1, ? Stafford 1, J Wakefield 13, JG Washbourne 1, W Willetts 16, C Wilson 11.
Scorers – W Shaw 10, W Mason 9, FT Rust 7, J Wakefield 6, HT Porter 3, DE Griffiths 2, C Wilson 2, FR Crawley 1, AF Fielding 1.

GLOUCESTER & DISTRICT LEAGUE DIVISION 1

POS	CLUB	P	W	D	L	F	A	PTS
1	TEWKESBURY ABBEY *	10	8	2	0	23	5	18
2	CHELTENHAM TOWN *	10	6	2	2	20	7	14
3	CHELTENHAM TRAINING COLLEGE *+	10	6	1	3	18	9	13
4	**GLOUCESTER *+**	10	3	1	6	12	18	7
5	ROSS TOWN	10	2	1	7	9	32	5
6	ROSELEIGH	10	1	1	8	5	16	3
		60	26	8	26	87	87	60

* These Clubs had two points awarded as the result of Roseleigh's withdrawal from the Division. In this table the matches have been reckoned as played and won by four teams.
+ The return fixture between these Clubs was abandoned at half-time owing to the state of the ground. The Training College subsequently conceded Gloucester two points.

1900-1901 – MID GLOUCESTERSHIRE LEAGUE

POS	CLUB	P	W	D	L	F	A	PTS
1	**GLOUCESTER**	10	10	0	0	43	3	20
2	BRIMSCOMBE	9	4	3	2	24	18	11
3	CHALFORD	10	4	2	4	15	20	10
4	FOREST GREEN ROVERS	6	3	1	2	13	15	7
5	WOODCHESTER	8	1	1	6	7	23	3
6	EBLEY	9	0	2	7	6	28	2
7	WYCLIFFE COLLEGE							
		52	22	9	21	108	107	53

Wycliffe College withdrew from league. Table as at 3 May 1901 in The Stroud News.

SEASON 1902-1903
(Home Ground: Budding's Field)

Date: Saturday 01/11/1902
Result: **GLOUCESTER CITY 1 ROSS TOWN 1**
Competition: Gloucester & District League Division 1
Teamsheet: Willetts, Arkell, Davy, Else, Eddowes, Sly, Wakefield, Parker, Rust, AF Fielding, Romans
Scorer: Parker

Date: Saturday 15/11/1902
Result: **SAINT ANNE'S 2 GLOUCESTER CITY 3**
Competition: Gloucestershire FA Junior Challenge Cup 3rd Round
Teamsheet: Willetts, Davy, Arkell, Crawley, Eddowes, Sly, Wakefield, Parker, Rust, AF Fielding, Romans
Scorers: Romans (2), Rust

Date: Saturday 13/12/1902
Result: **GLOUCESTER CITY 1 BOURTON ROVERS 1**
Competition: Gloucestershire FA Junior Challenge Cup Semi-Final
Teamsheet: Willetts, Davy, Arkell, Crawley, Eddowes, Sly, Wakefield, Parker, Rust, AF Fielding, Romans
Scorer: Rust

[15]

Date: Saturday 20/12/1902
Result: **BOURTON ROVERS 0 GLOUCESTER CITY 1**
Competition: Gloucestershire FA Junior Challenge Cup Semi-Final Replay
Teamsheet: Willetts, Davy, Arkell, Crawley, Eddowes, Sly, Wakefield, Fowler, Rust, AF Fielding, Romans
Scorer: Rust (pen)

Date: Friday 26/12/1902
Result: **WARMLEY 1 GLOUCESTER CITY 3**
Competition: Gloucestershire FA Junior Challenge Cup Final
Teamsheet: Willetts, Davy, Arkell, Crawley, Eddowes, Sly, Wakefield, Parker, Rust, AF Fielding, Romans
Scorers: Romans (2), Parker
Attendance: 1000

Date: Saturday 03/01/1903
Result: **GLOUCESTER CITY 1 CHELTENHAM TOWN 3**
Competition: Gloucester & District League Division 1
Teamsheet: Willetts, Davy, Arkell, Crawley, Eddowes, Sly, Wakefield, Parker, Rust, AF Fielding, Romans
Scorer: Parker

Date: Saturday 07/02/1903
Result: **CHELTENHAM TOWN 6 GLOUCESTER CITY 1**
Competition: Gloucester & District League Division 1
Teamsheet: Hawkins, Parker, Arkell, Crawley, Eddowes, Sly, Fowler, Wakefield, Rust, AF Fielding, Romans
Scorer: Parker

Date: Saturday 21/02/1903
Result: **GLOUCESTER CITY 1 BOURTON ROVERS 1**
Competition: Gloucester & District League Division 1
Teamsheet: Willetts, Dee, Arkell, Crawley, Eddowes, Sly, Fowler, Parker, Rust, Griffiths, Richardson
Scorer: -----

Date: Saturday 28/02/1903
Result: **ROSS TOWN 2 GLOUCESTER CITY 1**
Competition: Gloucester & District League Division 1
Teamsheet: Willetts, Vinson, Arkell, Crawley, Eddowes, Sly, Richardson, Parker, Rust, AF Fielding, Fowler
Scorer: Parker

Date: Saturday 14/03/1903
Result: **GLOUCESTER CITY 3 TEWKESBURY ABBEY 1**
Competition: Gloucester & District League Division 1
Teamsheet: Willetts, Vinson, Arkell, Crawley, Eddowes, Sly, Fowler, Parker, Rust, AF Fielding, Romans
Scorers: Rust, Sly, Parker

Date: Saturday 21/03/1903
Result: **BOURTON ROVERS 1 GLOUCESTER CITY 1**
Competition: Gloucester & District League Division 1
Teamsheet: Willetts, Vinson, Arkell, Crawley, Peckover, Sly, Richardson, Fowler, Rust, SJ Fielding, Romans
Scorer: Rust (pen)

Date: Saturday 28/03/1903
Result: **TEWKESBURY ABBEY 1 GLOUCESTER CITY 1**
Competition: Gloucester & District League Division 1
Teamsheet: Willetts, -----, Arkell, -----, -----, -----, -----, -----, Rust, -----, -----
Scorer: Rust

Appearances – HW Arkell 12, FR Crawley 10, EF Davy 6, WH Dee 1, CFB Eddowes 10, SO Else 1, AF Fielding 9, SJ Fielding 1, GW Fowler 6, DE Griffiths 1, J Hawkins 1, A Parker 9, L Peckover 1, HL Richardson 3, FCJ Romans 9, FT Rust 12, RR Sly 11, WD Vinson 3, J Wakefield 7, W Willetts 11.
Scorers – A Parker 6, FT Rust 6, FCJ Romans 4, RR Sly 1.

GLOUCESTER & DISTRICT LEAGUE DIVISION 1

POS	CLUB	P	W	D	L	F	A	PTS
1	CHELTENHAM TOWN	8	7	1	0	24	5	15
2	TEWKESBURY ABBEY	8	4	2	2	14	9	10
3	**GLOUCESTER CITY**	8	1	4	3	10	16	6
4	ROSS TOWN	8	2	1	5	11	15	5
5	BOURTON ROVERS	8	1	2	5	8	22	4
		40	15	10	15	67	67	40

SEASON 1903-1904
(Home Ground: Budding's Field)

Date: Saturday 24/10/1903
Result: **MIDLAND & SOUTH WESTERN JUNCTION RAILWAY 1 GLOUCESTER CITY 6**
Competition: Gloucester & District League Division 1
Teamsheet: Willetts, Davy, Lamb, Crawley, Eddowes, TH Rust, Wakefield, Arnold, Parker, FT Rust, Fielding
Scorers: FT Rust (5), Arnold

Date: Saturday 07/11/1903
Result: **GLOUCESTER CITY 2 CHELTENHAM TOWN 0**
Competition: Gloucester & District League Division 1
Teamsheet: Willetts, Davy, Arkell, Crawley, Eddowes, TH Rust, Fielding, FT Rust, Parker, Arnold, Wakefield
Scorer: FT Rust (2)

Date: Saturday 14/11/1903
Result: **KINGSWOOD ROVERS 1 GLOUCESTER CITY 0**
Competition: Gloucestershire FA Junior Challenge Cup 1st Round
Teamsheet: Willetts (?), Davy (?), Arkell (?), Crawley (?), Eddowes (?), -----, Fielding (?), FT Rust (?), Parker (?), -----, Wakefield (?)

Date: Saturday 28/11/1903
Result: GLOUCESTER CITY 3 SAINT MICHAEL'S 4
Competition: Gloucester & District League Division 1
Teamsheet: Willetts, Davy, Arkell, TH Rust, Eddowes, Crawley, Fielding, FT Rust, Parker, Keys, Wakefield
Scorers: Parker, FT Rust, TH Rust

Date: Saturday 23/01/1904
Result: GLOUCESTER CITY 4 CIRENCESTER TOWN 1
Competition: Gloucester & District League Division 1
Teamsheet: Murray, Trueman, Davy, Crawley, Eddowes, TH Rust, Wakefield, Keys, Parker, FT Rust, Fielding
Scorers: Fielding, Parker, FT Rust, own goal

Date: Saturday 06/02/1904
Result: GLOUCESTER CITY 2 BOURTON ROVERS 1
Competition: Gloucester & District League Division 1
Teamsheet: -----, Davy (?), -----, Crawley (?), Eddowes (?), TH Rust (?), Wakefield (?), Boonavalle, Parker, FT Rust (?), Fielding (?)
Scorers: Parker, Boonavalle

Date: Thursday 25/02/1904
Result: TEWKESBURY TOWN 1 GLOUCESTER CITY 2
Competition: Gloucester & District League Division 1
Teamsheet: Hoare, Davy, Eddowes, Crawley, TH Rust, Sly, Wakefield, Trueman, Parker, FT Rust, Fielding
Scorers: Wakefield, FT Rust

Date: Saturday 27/02/1904
Result: CHELTENHAM TOWN 1 GLOUCESTER CITY 5
Competition: Gloucester & District League Division 1
Teamsheet: Hoare (?), Davy (?), Eddowes (?), Crawley, -----, Sly (?), Wakefield, Trueman, Parker (?), FT Rust, -----
Scorers: Crawley, FT Rust (2), Trueman, Wakefield

Date: Thursday 03/03/1904
Result: GLOUCESTER CITY 3 MIDLAND & SOUTH WESTERN JUNCTION RAILWAY 1
Competition: Gloucester & District League Division 1
Teamsheet: Hoare, Eddowes, Davy, Sly, TH Rust, Crawley (?), Richardson, FT Rust, Parker, Trueman, Wakefield
Scorers: FT Rust (2), Parker

Date: Saturday 05/03/1904
Result: GLOUCESTER CITY 1 TEWKESBURY TOWN 1
Competition: Gloucester & District League Division 1
Teamsheet: Jones, Davy, Eddowes, Sly, TH Rust, Crawley, Fielding, FT Rust, Parker, Trueman, Wakefield
Scorer: FT Rust (pen)

Date: Saturday 12/03/1904
Result: SAINT MICHAEL'S 1 GLOUCESTER CITY 0
Competition: Gloucester & District League Division 1
Teamsheet: Jones, Eddowes, Davy, Sly, TH Rust, Crawley, Fielding, FT Rust, Parker, Richardson, Wakefield

Date: Saturday 19/03/1904
Result: CIRENCESTER TOWN 0 GLOUCESTER CITY 6
Competition: Gloucester & District League Division 1
Teamsheet: -----, -----, -----, -----, TH Rust (?), -----, -----, -----, Parker (?), -----, Wakefield (?)
Scorers: -----, -----, -----, -----, -----, -----

Date: Thursday 24/03/1904
Result: BOURTON ROVERS 0 GLOUCESTER CITY 3
Competition: Gloucester & District League Division 1
Teamsheet: -----, -----, -----, -----, TH Rust, -----, -----, Lewis, Parker, -----, Wakefield
Scorers: Lewis, Parker, Wakefield

Appearances – HW Arkell 3, GR Arnold 2, FR Crawley 11, EF Davy 11, CFB Eddowes 11, AF Fielding 9, AS Hoare 3, W Jones 2, GEH Keys 2, A Lamb 1, C Murray 1, A Parker 11, HL Richardson 2, FT Rust 11, TH Rust 10, RR Sly 5, T Trueman 5, J Wakefield 12, W Willetts 4.
Scorers – FT Rust 15, A Parker 3, J Wakefield 2, GR Arnold 1, FR Crawley 1, AF Fielding 1, TH Rust 1, T Trueman 1.

GLOUCESTER & DISTRICT LEAGUE DIVISION 1

POS	CLUB	P	W	D	L	F	A	PTS
1	**GLOUCESTER CITY**	**12**	**9**	**1**	**2**	**37**	**12**	**19**
2	SAINT MICHAEL'S	11	7	2	2	24	15	16
3	TEWKESBURY TOWN	10	6	3	1	23	8	15
4	MIDLAND & SOUTH WESTERN JUNCTION RAILWAY	9	4	1	4	15	16	9
5	CHELTENHAM TOWN	11	3	0	8	12	24	6
6	CIRENCESTER TOWN	10	1	2	7	6	31	4
7	BOURTON ROVERS	9	1	1	7	6	17	1*
		72	31	10	31	123	123	70

* Two points deducted for playing an ineligible man.
The Citizen of 26 March 1904 would indicate this as possible Final Table as winners of cups and medals announced.

SEASON 1906-1907
(Home Ground: Budding's Field)

Date: Saturday 22/09/1906
Result: BOURTON ROVERS 0 GLOUCESTER CITY 4
Competition: Gloucester & District League Division 1
Teamsheet: Willetts, Dee, Quixley, Harris, AH Smith, Boughton, Crouch, H Smith, Rust, Niblett, W Smith
Scorers: -----, -----, -----, -----
Note: Originally League game. Bourton Rovers withdrew

Date: Saturday 06/10/1906
Result: **GLOUCESTER CITY 3 TEWKESBURY TOWN 2**
Competition: Cheltenham & District League Division 1
Teamsheet: Willetts, Keeping, Quixley, Hill, AH Smith, Boughton, Davy, Haddon, Niblett, W Smith, Baldwin
Scorers: W Smith (2, 1 pen), Niblett

Date: Saturday 03/11/1906
Result: **GLOUCESTER CITY 6 TEWKESBURY TOWN 1**
Competition: Gloucester & District League Division 1
Teamsheet: Willetts, Taylor, Quixley, GA Vinson, Boughton, AH Smith, Crouch, Haddon, Squier, Kent, W Smith
Scorers: Haddon, Boughton, Squier (2), Kent, Crouch

Date: Saturday 17/11/1906
Result: **CHELTENHAM TOWN 2 GLOUCESTER CITY 4**
Competition: Gloucestershire FA Junior Challenge Cup 1st Round
Teamsheet: Willetts, Davy, Quixley, GA Vinson, Boughton, AH Smith, Niblett, H Smith, Squier, Haddon, Baldwin
Scorers: Squier, H Smith, Baldwin, own goal

Date: Saturday 24/11/1906
Result: **SAINT PAUL'S UNITED 3 GLOUCESTER CITY 1**
Competition: Gloucester & District League Division 1
Teamsheet: Willetts, Dee, Quixley, GA Vinson, Boughton, AH Smith, Niblett, H Smith, Squier, Haddon, Baldwin
Scorer: -----

Date: Saturday 01/12/1906
Result: **KINGSWOOD ROVERS 0 GLOUCESTER CITY 2**
Competition: Gloucestershire FA Junior Challenge Cup Semi-Final
Teamsheet: Willetts, Taylor, Quixley, GA Vinson, Boughton, AH Smith, Niblett, Haddon, Squier, H Smith, Baldwin
Scorers: Baldwin, Haddon

Date: Saturday 08/12/1906
Result: **GLOUCESTER CITY 6 CHELTENHAM TOWN 1**
Competition: Gloucester & District League Division 1
Teamsheet: Willetts, Taylor, Quixley, GA Vinson, Boughton, AH Smith, Haddon, H Smith, Squier, A Carter, Baldwin
Scorers: Squier, H Smith (2), Baldwin (2), Haddon

Date: Saturday 15/12/1906
Result: **TEWKESBURY TOWN 0 GLOUCESTER CITY 1**
Competition: Cheltenham & District League Division 1
Teamsheet: Willetts, WD Vinson, Quixley, GA Vinson, Boughton, AH Smith, Haddon, Baldwin, Squier, H Smith, W Smith
Scorer: Squier

Date: Wednesday 26/12/1906
Result: **WARMLEY AMATEURS 5 GLOUCESTER CITY 0**
Competition: Gloucestershire FA Junior Challenge Cup Final
Teamsheet: Willetts, Davey, Quixley, GA Vinson, Boughton, AH Smith, Haddon, H Smith, Nicholls, W Smith, Baldwin

Date: Saturday 29/12/1906
Result: **GLOUCESTER CITY 6 WINCHCOMBE TOWN 0**
Competition: Cheltenham & District League Division 1
Teamsheet: Willetts, Davy, Quixley, GA Vinson, Boughton, Bain, Harris, Bland, Nicholls, OJA Carter, Baldwin
Scorers: Bland (4), Baldwin, Nicholls

Date: Saturday 05/01/1907
Result: **CHELTENHAM TOWN 0 GLOUCESTER CITY 1**
Competition: Cheltenham & District League Division 1
Teamsheet: Willetts, WD Vinson, Davy, GA Vinson, AH Smith, Quixley, W Smith, Bland, Nicholls, Boughton, Baldwin
Scorer: Bland

Date; Saturday 02/02/1907
Result: **GLOUCESTER CITY 3 CHELTENHAM TOWN 2**
Competition: Cheltenham & District League Division 1
Teamsheet: Willetts, WD Vinson, Quixley, GA Vinson, Boughton, AH Smith, Haddon, H Smith, Baldwin, AJ Carter, W Smith
Scorers: AJ Carter (2), H Smith

Date: Saturday 09/02/1907
Result: **WINCHCOMBE TOWN 1 GLOUCESTER CITY 1**
Competition: Cheltenham & District League Division 1
Teamsheet: Willetts, WD Vinson, Quixley, GA Vinson, Boughton, AH Smith, Haddon, H Smith, Squier, Baldwin, W Smith
Scorer: Squier

Date: Saturday 23/02/1907
Result: **CHELTENHAM TOWN 1 GLOUCESTER CITY 4**
Competition: Gloucester & District League Division 1
Teamsheet: Willetts, Davy, Quixley, GA Vinson, Boughton, AH Smith, Haddon, H Smith, Squier, Baldwin, W Smith
Scorers: Squier (2), Baldwin (2)

Date: Saturday 02/03/1907
Result: **TEWKESBURY TOWN 1 GLOUCESTER CITY 2**
Competition: Gloucester & District League Division 1
Teamsheet: Willetts, Davy, Quixley, GA Vinson, Boughton, AH Smith, Haddon, H Smith, Squier, Baldwin, W Smith
Scorer: Squier (2)

Date: Saturday 09/03/1907
Result: **GLOUCESTER CITY 0 SAINT PAUL'S UNITED 1**
Competition: Gloucester & District League Division 1
Teamsheet: Willetts, Davy, Quixley, GA Vinson, AH Smith, Kent, Haddon, H Smith, Squier, Baldwin, W Smith

Date: Saturday 23/03/1907
Result: **GLOUCESTER CITY 2 SAINT PAUL'S UNITED 0**
Competition: Cheltenham & District League Division 1
Teamsheet: Willetts, Davy, Quixley, GA Vinson, Boughton, AH Smith, Haddon, AJ Carter, Squier, Kent, W Smith
Scorer: Squier (2)

GLOUCESTER CITY 1906-1907

GLOUCESTER CITY (WINNERS).

Back row.—G. A. Vinson, E. F. Davy, B. Boughton, W. Willetts, A. H. Smith, F. E. Quixley.

Front row.—C. H. Haddon, H. Smith, A. Carter, A. E. Kent, W. Smith.

**Winners of the North Gloucestershire League Cup and Medals—1st Division
Season 1907-8**
Left to Right (Standing) : F. E. TAYLOR (*Committee*), A. V. BOUGHTON, N. SQUIER,
O. J. A. CARTER (*Committee*), W. C. VICKERY, F. E. QUIXLEY, C. M. WIGGIN
(*Assistant Hon. Secretary*)
(Sitting) : E. W. HUNT (*Committee*), W. G. REYNOLDS (*Committee*), C. H. HADDON,
A. H. SMITH, E. F. DAVY (*Captain*), A. J. CARTER, G. A. VINSON, J. E. PALMER
(*Hon. Secretary*), J. DAVY (*Committee*)
(Front) : O. J. LUCAS, A. E. KENT

This photograph was on a commercial postcard of the day. Could they be lined up in their positions?

Date: Saturday 06/04/1907
Result: **SAINT PAUL'S UNITED 1 GLOUCESTER CITY 3**
Competition: Cheltenham & District League Division 1
Teamsheet: Willetts, Davy, Quixley, GA Vinson, Boughton, Bain, H Smith, AJ Carter, AH Smith, Kent, W Smith
Scorers: Kent, AJ Carter, -----

Appearances – C Bain 2, JM Baldwin 13, AE Bland 2, AV Boughton 16, AJ Carter 4, OJA Carter 1, FEA Crouch 2, EF Davy 9, FW Dee 2, CH Haddon 13, BG Harris 2, J Hill 1, AS Keeping 1, AE Kent 4, WD Niblett 5, Wilfred Nicholls 2, FGE Quixley 17, FT Rust 1, AH Smith 16, H Smith 12, W Smith 12, N Squier 11, FE Taylor 3, GA Vinson 15, WD Vinson 4, W Willetts 18.
Scorers – N Squier 12, JM Baldwin 7, AE Bland 5, H Smith 4, AJ Carter 3, CH Haddon 3, AE Kent 2, W Smith 2, AV Boughton 1, FEA Crouch 1, WD Niblett 1, Wilfred Nicholls 1, own goal 1.

GLOUCESTER & DISTRICT LEAGUE DIVISION 1

POS	CLUB	P	W	D	L	F	A	PTS
1	SAINT PAUL'S UNITED	6	3	3	0	10	5	9
2	**GLOUCESTER CITY**	6	4	0	2	19	8	8
3	CHELTENHAM TOWN	6	1	2	3	7	18	4
4	TEWKESBURY TOWN	6	1	1	4	8	13	3
5	BOURTON ROVERS							
		24	9	6	9	44	44	24

Bourton Rovers withdrew during season. All records expunged.
One score is missing Saint Paul's United v Cheltenham Town although it is known to have ended in a draw as it was reported Gloucester City missed out on the Championship by one point.

CHELTENHAM & DISTRICT LEAGUE DIVISION 1

POS	CLUB	P	W	D	L	F	A	PTS
1	**GLOUCESTER CITY**	8	7	1	0	20	6	15
2	SAINT PAUL'S UNITED	5	1	1	3	6	9	3
3	WINCHCOMBE TOWN	4	1	1	2	2	10	3
4	CHELTENHAM TOWN	4	1	0	3	5	6	2
5	TEWKESBURY TOWN	3	0	1	2	3	5	1
		24	10	4	10	36	36	24

Table incomplete. No table in either The Citizen or The Gloucestershire Echo. Based only on results I could find.

SEASON 1907-1908
(Home Ground: Budding's Field)

Date: Saturday 12/10/1907
Result: **SHARPNESS 3 GLOUCESTER CITY 6**
Competitition: North Gloucestershire League Division 1
Teamsheet: Blake, Davy, WD Vinson, GA Vinson, Boughton, Hill, Lucas, Turner, Squier, Carter, Kent
Scorers: Turner (3), Squier (2, 1 pen), Kent

Date: Saturday 26/10/1907
Result: **STROUD 1 GLOUCESTER CITY 10**
Competition: North Gloucestershire League Division 1
Teamsheet: Blake, Davy, Quixley, GA Vinson, Boughton, Smith, Lucas, Turner, Squier, Carter, Kent
Scorers: Carter (3, 1 pen), Lucas (2), Turner (4), GA Vinson

Date: Saturday 02/11/1907
Result: **GLOUCESTER CITY 4 TEWKESBURY TOWN 0**
Competition: North Gloucestershire League Division 1
Teamsheet: Blake, Davy, Quixley, GA Vinson, Boughton, Smith, Lucas, Turner, Squier, Carter, Kent
Scorers: Squier (2), Carter (2)

Date: Saturday 16/11/1907
Result: **CLEVEDON 5 GLOUCESTER CITY 1**
Competition: English Amateur Cup Semi-Final Qualifying Round
Teamsheet: Blake, Davy, Quixley, GA Vinson, Boughton, Smith, Lucas, Turner, Squier, Carter, Kent
Scorer: Kent

Date: Saturday 23/11/1907
Result: **GLOUCESTER CITY 10 STROUD 0**
Competition: North Gloucestershire League Division 1
Teamsheet: Blake, Davy, Quixley, GA Vinson, Boughton, Smith, Lucas, Turner, Squier, Carter, Kent
Scorers: Turner (5), Squier (4), Carter

Date: Saturday 30/11/1907
Result: **GLOUCESTER CITY 10 LINDEN OLD BOYS 1**
Competition: North Gloucestershire League Division 1
Teamsheet: Blake, Davy, Quixley, GA Vinson, Boughton, Smith, Lucas, Carter, Squier, Turner, Kent
Scorers: Carter, Squier (4), Turner (5)

Date: Saturday 25/01/1908
Result: **GLOUCESTER CITY 1 MIDLAND & SOUTH WESTERN JUNCTION RAILWAY 2**
Competition: North Gloucestershire League Division 1
Teamsheet: Vickery, Davy, Quixley, GA Vinson, Boughton, Smith, Kent, Carter, Squier, Haddon, Bottomley
Scorer: -----

Date: Saturday 01/02/1908
Result: **GLOUCESTER CITY 1 WARMLEY AMATEURS 1**
Competition: Gloucestershire FA Intermediate Challenge Cup 2nd Round
Teamsheet: Vickery, Davy, Quixley, GA Vinson, Boughton, Smith, Kent, Carter, Squier, Haddon, Bottomley
Scorer: -----

Date: Saturday 08/02/1908
Result: **WARMLEY AMATEURS 2 GLOUCESTER CITY 0**
Competition: Gloucestershire FA Intermediate Challenge Cup 2nd Round Replay
Teamsheet: Vickery, Davy, Parker, GA Vinson, Boughton, Smith, Haddon, Lucas, Squier, Carter, Kent

Date: Saturday 15/02/1908
Result: **TEWKESBURY TOWN 1 GLOUCESTER CITY 1**
Competition: North Gloucestershire League Division 1
Teamsheet: Vickery, Davy, Quixley, GA Vinson, Smith, Hill, Kent, Lucas, Squier, Carter, Bottomley
Scorer: Davy

Date: Saturday 22/02/1908
Result: **LINDEN OLD BOYS 0 GLOUCESTER CITY 4**
Competition: North Gloucestershire League Division 1
Teamsheet: Vickery, Davy, Quixley, GA Vinson, Boughton, Smith, Haddon, Lucas, Squier, Carter, Kent
Scorers: Kent (2), Smith, Squier

Date: Saturday 29/02/1908
Result: **GLOUCESTER CITY 1 SHARPNESS 1**
Competition: North Gloucestershire League Division 1
Teamsheet: Vickery, Davy, Quixley, GA Vinson, Boughton, Smith, Haddon, Lucas, Squier, Carter, Kent
Scorer: Lucas

Date: Saturday 07/03/1908
Result: **CHELTENHAM TOWN 0 GLOUCESTER CITY 3**
Competition: North Gloucestershire League Division 1
Teamsheet: Vickery, Davy, Quixley, GA Vinson, Boughton, Jill, Hale, Haydon, Smith, Carter, Kent
Scorers: Hill, Carter (2)

Date: Saturday 14/03/1908
Result: **SAINT PAUL'S UNITED 1 GLOUCESTER CITY 3**
Competition: North Gloucestershire League Division 1
Teamsheet: Vickery, Davy, Quixley, GA Vinson, Boughton, Smith, Squier, Lucas, Hale, Carter, Kent
Scorers: Squier (2), Smith

Date: Wednesday 18/03/1908
Result: **GLOUCESTER CITY 2 CHELTENHAM TOWN 1**
Competition: North Gloucestershire League Division 1
Teamsheet: Vickery, Davy, Quixley, GA Vinson, Boughton, Smith, Haddon, Squier, Lucas, Carter, Kent
Scorers: Kent, Haddon

Date: Saturday 28/03/1908
Result: **MIDLAND & SOUTH WESTERN JUNCTION RAILWAY 1 GLOUCESTER CITY 4**
Competition: North Gloucestershire League Division 1
Teamsheet: Vickery, Davy, Quixley, GA Vinson, Boughton, Smith, Haddon, Squier, Lucas, Carter, kent
Scorers: Squier, Lucas, -----, -----

Date: Saturday 11/04/1908
Result: **GLOUCESTER CITY 3 SAINT PAUL'S UNITED 1**
Competition: North Gloucestershire League Division 1
Teamsheet: Vickery, Davy, -----, GA Vinson, Boughton, -----, -----, -----, Lucas, Carter, Kent
Scorers: Davy, Lucas, Carter
Note: Played at Barnwood

Appearances – WT Blake 6, F Bottomley 3, AV Boughton 16, AJ Carter 17, EF Davy 17, CH Haddon 7, HW Hale 2, AL Haydon 1, J Hill 3, AE Kent 17, OJ Lucas 14, RM Parker 1, FGE Quixley 14, AH Smith 15, N Squier 15, R Turner 6, WC Vickery 11, GA Vinson 17, WD Vinson 1.
Scorers – R Turner 17, N Squier 16, AJ Carter 10, AE Kent 5, OJ Lucas 5, EF Davy 2, AH Smith 2, CH Haddon 1, J Hill 1, GA Vinson 1.

NORTH GLOUCESTERSHIRE LEAGUE DIVISION 1

POS	CLUB	P	W	D	L	F	A	PTS
1	**GLOUCESTER CITY**	**14**	**12**	**1**	**1**	**61**	**13**	**25**
2	STROUD	14	8	2	4	31	35	18
3	SHARPNESS	14	7	3	4	47	27	17
4	MIDLAND & SOUTH WESTERN JUNCTION RAILWAY	14	7	2	5	28	24	16
5	SAINT PAUL'S UNITED	14	4	4	6	24	23	12
6	TEWKESBURY TOWN	14	5	2	7	23	31	12
7	CHELTENHAM TOWN	14	3	2	9	11	30	8
8	LINDEN OLD BOYS	14	2	2	10	17	59	4
		112	48	18	46	242	242	112

SEASON 1908-1909
(Home Ground: Budding's Field)

Date: Saturday 03/10/1908
Result: **GLOUCESTER CITY 3 MIDLAND & SOUTH WESTERN JUNCTION RAILWAY 1**
Competition: North Gloucestershire League Division 1
Teamsheet: Vickery, Quixley, Taylor, GA Vinson, Boughton, AH Smith, Haddon, Simpson, Watts, Carter, Kent
Scorers: Kent, Watts (2)

Date: Saturday 14/11/1908
Result: **STROUD 0 GLOUCESTER CITY 0**
Competition: North Gloucestershire League Division 1
Teamsheet: Vickery, WD Vinson, Quixley, GA Vinson, AH Smith, Hill, Simpson, Watts, Squier, Kent, W Smith

Date: Saturday 21/11/1908
Result: **MIDLAND & SOUTH WESTERN JUNCTION RAILWAY 1 GLOUCESTER CITY 1**
Competition: North Gloucestershire League Division 1
Teamsheet: Vickery, WD Vinson, Quixley, GA Vinson, AH Smith, Hill, Kent, Watts, Squier, Carter, W Smith
Scorer: Squier (pen)

Date: Saturday 28/11/1908
Result: **HEREFORD CITY 4 GLOUCESTER CITY 2**
Competition: English Amateur Cup 4th Round
Teamsheet: Vickery, WD Vinson, Quixley, GA Vinson, AH Smith, Hill, Kent, Watts, Squier, Carter, W Smith
Scorer: W Smith (2)

Date: Saturday 05/12/1908
Result: **SAINT PAUL'S UNITED 3 GLOUCESTER CITY 4**
Competition: North Gloucestershire League Division 1
Teamsheet: Vickery, WD Vinson, Parker, GA Vinson, AH Smith, Hill, Kent, Carter, Jarman, Watts, W Smith
Scorers: Jarman (3), -----

Date: Saturday 12/12/1908
Result: **GLOUCESTER CITY 2 STROUD 0**
Competition: North Gloucestershire League Division 1
Teamsheet: Vickery, WD Vinson, Quixley, GA Vinson, AH Smith, Hill, Kent, Carter, Jarman, Watts, W Smith
Scorers: Carter, Jarman

Date: Saturday 19/12/1908
Result: **GLOUCESTER CITY 3 CHELTENHAM TOWN 2**
Competition: North Gloucestershire League Division 1
Teamsheet: Vickery, Quixley, WD Vinson, GA Vinson, AH Smith, Hill, Kent, Watts, Jarman, Carter, W Smith
Scorers: Jarman (2), Carter

Date: Saturday 02/01/1909
Result: **GLOUCESTER CITY 6 DURSLEY 0**
Competition: North Gloucestershire League Division 1
Teamsheet: Vickery, WD Vinson, Quixley, GA Vinson, AH Smith, Hill, Cook, Carter, Jarman, Butler, W Smith
Scorers: Hill, Carter, Jarman (2), W Smith (2)

Date: Saturday 23/01/1909
Result: **DURSLEY 1 GLOUCESTER CITY 4**
Competition: North Gloucestershire League Division 1
Teamsheet: Vickery, WD Vinson, Quixley, GA Vinson, AH Smith, Hill, Simpson, Watts, Jarman, Kent, W Smith
Scorers: Watts (2, 1 pen), W Smith (2)

Date: Saturday 30/01/1909
Result: **GLOUCESTER CITY 6 SAINT PAUL'S UNITED 0**
Competition: North Gloucestershire League Division 1
Teamsheet: Vickery, WD Vinson, Quixley, GA Vinson, AH Smith, Hill, Squier, Watts, Jarman, W Smith, Kent
Scorers: W Smith (2), Kent, Jarman (2), Watts

Date: Saturday 06/02/1909
Result: **WARMLEY AMATEURS 2 GLOUCESTER CITY 0**
Competition: Gloucestershire FA Intermediate Challenge Cup 2nd Round
Teamsheet: Vickery, WD Vinson, Quixley, GA Vinson, AH Smith, Hill, Cook, Watts, Jarman, W Smith, Kent

Date: Saturday 20/02/1909
Result: **SHARPNESS 2 GLOUCESTER CITY 2**
Competition: North Gloucestershire League Division 1
Teamsheet: Vickery, WD Vinson, Quixley, GA Vinson, AH Smith, Hill, Kent, W Smith, Jarman, Watts, Simpson
Scorer: Jarman (2)

Date: Saturday 27/02/1909
Result: **GLOUCESTER CITY 3 TEWKESBURY TOWN 0**
Competition: North Gloucestershire League Division 1
Teamsheet: Vickery, WD Vinson, Quixley, GA Vinson, AH Smith, Hill, Simpson, Watts, Jarman, W Smith, Kent
Scorers: W Smith, Jarman, Watts

Date: Saturday 13/03/1909
Result: **TEWKESBURY TOWN 0 GLOUCESTER CITY 3**
Competition: North Gloucestershire League Division 1
Teamsheet: Vickery, WD Vinson, Quixley, GA Vinson, AH Smith, Hill, Simpson, Watts, Jarman, W Smith, Kent
Scorers: W Smith, Simpson, Jarman

Date: Wednesday 17/03/1909
Result: **GLOUCESTER CITY 8 SHARPNESS 0**
Competition: North Gloucestershire League Division 1
Teamsheet: Vickery, WD Vinson, Quixley, GA Vinson, AH Smith, Hill, Simpson, Watts, Jarman, Squier, Kent
Scorers: Simpson, Jarman (3), Squier (2), Watts, Kent

Date: Saturday 20/03/1909
Result: **CHELTENHAM TOWN 0 GLOUCESTER CITY 3**
Competition: North Gloucestershire League Division 1
Teamsheet: Vickery, WD Vinson, Quixley, GA Vinson, AH Smith, Hill, Simpson, Squier, Jarman, Watts, Kent
Scorers: own goal, Squier (2)

Appearances – AV Boughton 1, L Butler 1, AJ Carter 7, S Cook 2, CH Haddon 1, J Hill 15, WA Jarman 12, AE Kent 15, RM Parker 1, FGE Quixley 15, E Simpson 8, AH Smith 16, W Smith 13, N Squier 6, FE Taylor 1, WC Vickery 16, GA Vinson 16, WD Vinson 15, A Watts 15.
Scorers – WA Jarman 17, W Smith 10, A Watts 7, N Squier 5, AJ Carter 3, AE Kent 3, E Simpson 2, J Hill 1, own goal 1.

SEASON BY SEASON

NORTH GLOUCESTERSHIRE LEAGUE DIVISION 1

POS	CLUB	P	W	D	L	F	A	PTS
1	**GLOUCESTER CITY**	**14**	**11**	**3**	**0**	**48**	**10**	**25**
2	STROUD	12	7	3	2	37	21	17
3	SHARPNESS	12	6	5	1	43	31	17
4	TEWKESBURY TOWN	14	7	3	4	33	25	17
5	CHELTENHAM TOWN	14	3	4	7	25	33	10
6	DURSLEY	13	2	3	8	24	41	7
7	SAINT PAUL'S UNITED	14	3	1	10	22	45	7
8	MIDLAND & SOUTH WESTERN JUNCTION RAILWAY	13	2	2	9	22	52	6
		106	41	24	41	254	258	106

To early April 1909 only. Some fixtures missing. Could not find in The Citizen.

SEASON 1909-1910
(Home Ground: Budding's Field)

Date: Saturday 25/09/1909
Result: **GLOUCESTER CITY 3 WINCHCOMBE TOWN 2**
Competition: Cheltenham & District League Division 1
Teamsheet: WC Vickery, Ingles, Taylor, Vinson, AH Smith, Hill, Bland, Haynes, Jarman, AJ Carter, Kent
Scorers: Bland, Jarman, Haynes

Date: Saturday 09/10/1909
Result: **GLOUCESTER CITY 2 EVESHAM UNITED 2**
Competition: Cheltenham & District League Division 1
Teamsheet: WC Vickery, Eldridge, Ingles, Vinson, Watts, Hill, Bathurst, Bland, Jarman, W Smith, Kent
Scorers: own goal, Watts

Date: Saturday 16/10/1909
Result: **GLOUCESTER CITY 2 CHELTENHAM TOWN 1**
Competition: North Gloucestershire League Division 1
Teamsheet: WC Vickery, Ingles, Eldridge, Vinson, Watts, Hill, Cook, Bathurst, Jarman, W Smith, Kent
Scorers: Jarman, W Smith

Date: Saturday 23/10/1909
Result: **STROUD 2 GLOUCESTER CITY 5**
Competition: English Amateur Cup 2nd Round
Teamsheet: WC Vickery, Eldridge, Ingles, Hill, AH Smith, Vinson, Kent, W Smith, Jarman, Watts, Cook
Scorers: Jarman, Cook, W Smith (2), own goal

Date: Saturday 06/11/1909
Result: **SWINDON AMATEURS 2 GLOUCESTER CITY 2**
Competition: English Amateur Cup 3rd Round
Teamsheet: WC Vickery, Eldridge, Ingles, Vinson, Watts, AH Smith, Cook, Squier, Jarman, W Smith, Kent
Scorers: Squier, Jarman

Date: Saturday 13/11/1909
Result: **GLOUCESTER CITY 3 SWINDON AMATEURS 2**
Competition: English Amateur Cup 3rd Round Replay
Teamsheet: WC Vickery, Ingles, AH Smith, Vinson, Watts, Hill, Cook, Squier, Jarman, W Smith, Kent
Scorers: Kent (2), Cook

Date: Saturday 20/11/1909
Result: **TEWKESBURY TOWN 2 GLOUCESTER CITY 4**
Competition: Cheltenham & District League Division 1
Teamsheet: WC Vickery, Ingles, Eldridge, Vinson, AH Smith, Hill, Cook, Squier, Watts, W Smith, Kent
Scorers: Squier (3), Kent

Date: Saturday 27/11/1909
Result: **HEREFORD CITY 4 GLOUCESTER CITY 1**
Competition: English Amateur Cup 4th Round
Teamsheet: WC Vickery, Ingles, AH Smith, Vinson, Watts, Hill, Cook, Bathurst, Jarman, W Smith, Kent
Scorer: Jarman

Date: Saturday 11/12/1909
Result: **CHELTENHAM TOWN 2 GLOUCESTER CITY 1**
Competition: North Gloucestershire League Division 1
Teamsheet: WC Vickery, Carleton, Ingles, Vinson, Watts, Hill, Jarman, Benbow, Squier, W Smith, Cook
Scorer: own goal

Date: Saturday 18/12/1909
Result: **GLOUCESTER CITY 2 TEWKESBURY TOWN 2**
Competition: Cheltenham & District League Division 1
Teamsheet: WC Vickery, Ingles, Carleton, Vinson, Quixley, Hill, Haydon, Watts, Jarman, W Smith, Kent
Scorers: Watts, Haydon

Date: Saturday 01/01/1910
Result: **GLOUCESTER CITY 2 WARMLEY ATHLETIC 0**
Competition: Gloucestershire FA Intermediate Challenge Cup 1st Round
Teamsheet: WC Vickery, Quixley, Carleton, Vinson, AH Smith, Hill, C Carter, W Smith, Jarman, Parsons, Ingles
Scorer: Parsons (2)

Date: Saturday 08/01/1910
Result: **GLOUCESTER CITY 2 STROUD 2**
Competition: North Gloucestershire League Division 1
Teamsheet: WC Vickery, Ingles, Carleton, Vinson, AH Smith, Hill, Barnes, Parsons, Jarman, W Smith, C Carter
Scorers: W Smith, Jarman

[24]

Date: Saturday 15/01/1910
Result: **BRIMSCOMBE 3 GLOUCESTER CITY 0**
Competition: North Gloucestershire League Division 1
Teamsheet: WC Vickery, Ingles, Vinson, AH Smith, Hill, Kent, Watts, Jarman, W Smith, Parsons
Note: Only 10 players used

Date: Saturday 22/01/1910
Result: **TEWKESBURY TOWN 2 GLOUCESTER CITY 4**
Competition: North Gloucestershire League Division 1
Teamsheet: WC Vickery, Carleton, Ingles, Vinson, Watts, CG Carter, Cook, Parsons, Jarman, W Smith, Kent
Scorers: Cook, own goal, W Smith, CG Carter

Date: Saturday 29/01/1910
Result: **SHARPNESS 2 GLOUCESTER CITY 1**
Competition: North Gloucestershire League Division 1
Teamsheet: WC Vickery, Ingles, Carleton, Vinson, Quixley, Williams, Kent, Watts, Jarman, AH Smith, W Smith
Scorer: Williams
Note: City had 2 points deducted for playing an ineligible man and the goal scored disallowed

Date: Saturday 05/02/1910
Result: **GLOUCESTER CITY 2 BRISTOL AMATEURS 4**
Competition: Gloucestershire FA Intermediate Challenge Cup 2nd Round
Teamsheet: WC Vickery, Carleton, Ingles, Vinson, Watts, CG Carter, Cook, Parsons, Jarman, W Smith, Kent
Scorers: Jarman, Parsons

Date: Thursday 10/02/1910
Result: **GLOUCESTER CITY 5 TEWKESBURY TOWN 2**
Competition: North Gloucestershire League Division 1
Teamsheet: WC Vickery, Carleton, Ingles, Vinson, Watts, CG Carter, Cook, Durrett, Jarman, W Smith, Kent
Scorers: Durrett (2), Ingles, CG Carter (pen), Kent

Date: Saturday 12/02/1910
Result: **STROUD 4 GLOUCESTER CITY 2**
Competition: North Gloucestershire League Division 1
Teamsheet: WC Vickery, Carleton, Ingles, Vinson, Watts, CG Carter, Cook, AH Smith, Jarman, W Smith, Kent
Scorers: W Smith, CG Carter

Date: Thursday 24/02/1910
Result: **CHELTENHAM TOWN 2 GLOUCESTER CITY 1**
Competition: Cheltenham & District League Division 1
Teamsheet: WC Vickery, Ingles, Vinson, Watts, CG Carter, Cook, AH Smith, Jarman, W Smith, Kent
Scorer: W Smith
Note: Only 10 players used

Date: Thursday 03/03/1910
Result: **GLOUCESTER CITY 3 SHARPNESS 3**
Competition: North Gloucestershire League Division 1
Teamsheet: Brace, Ingles (?), CG Carter (?), Vinson (?), Watts (?), Hill (?), Cook, AH Smith (?), Jarman, W Smith (?), Kent
Scorers: Jarman, Cook (2)
Note: Played at Gloucester Old Boys Ground, Denmark Road

Date: Saturday 05/03/1910
Result: **GLOUCESTER CITY 5 SAINT PAUL'S UNITED 1**
Competition: North Gloucestershire League Division 1
Teamsheet: WC Vickery, Ingles, CG Carter, Vinson, AH Smith, Hill, Cook, Watts, Jarman, W Smith, Kent
Scorers: AH Smith, Jarman (2, 1 pen), Cook, Ingles

Date: Sunday 13/03/1910
Result: **EVESHAM UNITED 3 GLOUCESTER CITY 0**
Competition: Cheltenham & District League Division 1
Teamsheet: WC Vickery, Carleton, Vinson, AH Smith, CG Carter, Cook, Watts, Jarman, W Smith, Kent
Note: Only 10 players used

Date: Saturday 26/03/1910
Result: **GLOUCESTER CITY 3 CHELTENHAM TOWN 3**
Competition: Cheltenham & District League Division 1
Teamsheet: Brace, Carleton, Ingles, Vinson, Watts, Acton, AH Smith, Jarman, W Smith, Kent, Parsons
Scorers: Jarman (2), Kent

Date: Monday 28/03/1910
Result: **GLOUCESTER CITY 1 BRIMSCOMBE 1**
Competition: North Gloucestershire League Division 1
Teamsheet: Brace, Ingles, Trueman, Vinson, AH Smith, CG Carter, Davoll, Kent, Watts, W Smith, Parsons
Scorer: AH Smith

Date: Saturday 23/04/1910
Result: **SAINT PAUL'S UNITED 1 GLOUCESTER CITY 1**
Competitions: North Gloucestershire League Division 1/Cheltenham & District League Division 1
Teamsheet: WC Vickery, Ingles, Carleton, TF Vickery, Quixley, Hill, Brown, Taylor, Cook, Parsons, C Carter
Scorer: Parsons
Note: Permission was given to use this fixture to count for both leagues. Played 35 minutes each way

Date: ?
Result: **WINCHCOMBE TOWN 1 GLOUCESTER CITY 1**
Competition: Cheltenham & District League Division 1
Teamsheet: -----, -----, -----, -----, -----, -----, -----, -----, -----, -----, -----
Scorer: -----

Appearances – ? Acton 1, C Barnes 1, LW Bathurst 3, LJ Benbow 1, AE Bland 2, GB Brace 3, CE Brown 1, LA Carleton 12, AJ Carter 1, C Carter 3, CG Carter 9, S Cook 16, HGH Davoll 1, C Durrett 1, JG Eldridge 5, AL Haydon 1, F Haynes 1, J Hill 15, W Ingles 23, WA Jarman 22, AE Kent 21, JT Parsons 8, FGE Quixley 4, AH Smith 17, W Smith 23, N Squier 4, FE Taylor 2, ? Trueman 1, TF Vickery 1, WC Vickery 22, GA Vinson 24, A Watts 21, ? Williams 1.
Scorers – WA Jarman 12, W Smith 7, AE Kent 5, S Cook 6, JT Parsons 4, N Squier 4, CG Carter 3, C Durrett 2, W Ingles 2, AH Smith 2, A Watts 2, AE Bland 1, AL Haydon 1, F Haynes 1, own goals 4.

[25]

NORTH GLOUCESTERSHIRE LEAGUE DIVISION 1

POS	CLUB	P	W	D	L	F	A	PTS
1	SHARPNESS	12	8	3	1	45	14	19
2	BRIMSCOMBE	12	7	2	3	29	24	16
3	TEWKESBURY TOWN	12	6	1	5	28	28	13
4	**GLOUCESTER CITY**	**12**	**4**	**4**	**4**	**26**	**24**	**10***
5	CHELTENHAM TOWN	12	3	3	6	16	19	9
6	SAINT PAUL'S UNITED	12	2	5	5	14	24	9
7	STROUD	12	2	2	8	20	46	6
		84	32	20	32	178	179	82

*Two points deducted for playing ineligible man v Sharpness and the goal scored by them disallowed.

CHELTENHAM AND DISTRICT LEAGUE DIVISION 1

POS	CLUB	P	W	D	L	F	A	PTS
1	CHELTENHAM TOWN	7	3	3	1	12	11	9
2	**GLOUCESTER CITY**	**9**	**2**	**5**	**2**	**17**	**18**	**9**
3	SAINT PAUL'S UNITED	7	2	3	2	11	7	7
4	TEWKESBURY TOWN	6	2	2	2	8	12	6
5	EVESHAM UNITED	4	2	1	1	9	6	5
6	WINCHCOMBE TOWN	3	0	0	3	3	6	0
		36	11	14	11	60	60	36

Table incomplete. No table in either The Citizen or The Gloucestershire Echo. Based only on results I could find.

In 1910, the Gloucester YMCA Football Club was formed and initially participated in the local Gloucester Thursday League until 1913 when entered the more competitive North Gloucestershire League.

SEASON 1913-1914
(Home Ground: Llanthony, Hempsted)

Date: Saturday 04/10/1913
Result: **GLOUCESTER YMCA 1 MITCHELDEAN 1**
Competition: North Gloucestershire League Division 2
Teamsheet: Davoll, Macfarlane, Bretherton, Corbett, Shadgett, Mills, Danks, Searles, Jones, Allen, Parsons
Scorer: -----

Date: Saturday 18/10/1913
Result: **WESTGATE 2 GLOUCESTER YMCA 1**
Competition: North Gloucestershire League Division 2
Teamsheet: Davoll, Macfarlane, Bretherton, Durrett, Shadgett, Mills, Danks, Searles, Jones, Dudbridge, Parsons
Scorer: -----

Date: Saturday 01/11/1913
Result: **GLOUCESTER YMCA 0 LONGHOPE UNITED 3**
Competition: North Gloucestershire League Division 2
Teamsheet: Davoll, Macfarlane, Bretherton, Bygrave, Shadgett, Mills, Danks, Allen, Jones, Dudbridge, Parsons

Date: Saturday 08/11/1913
Result: **GLOUCESTER YMCA 0 MINSTERWORTH 5**
Competition: North Gloucestershire League Division 2
Teamsheet: Rhodes, Macfarlane, Bretherton, Shadgett, Durrett, Lane, Mills, Allen, Jones, Dudbridge, Parsons

Date: Saturday 29/11/1913
Result: **NEWNHAM EXCELSIOR 2 GLOUCESTER YMCA 0**
Competition: North Gloucestershire League Division 2
Teamsheet: -----, -----, -----, -----, -----, -----, -----, -----, -----, -----, -----

Date: Saturday 20/12/1913
Result: **TUFFLEY & WHADDON 4 GLOUCESTER YMCA 0**
Competition: North Gloucestershire League Division 2
Teamsheet: -----, -----, -----, -----, -----, -----, -----, -----, -----, -----, -----

Date: Saturday 24/01/1914
Result: **GLOUCESTER YMCA 1 TUFFLEY & WHADDON 5**
Competition: North Gloucestershire League Division 2
Teamsheet: Davoll, Macfarlane, Bretherton, Lane, Shadgett, Mills, Danks, Allen, Jones, Parsons, Dudbridge
Scorer: -----

Date: Saturday 07/02/1914
Result: *MITCHELDEAN 2 GLOUCESTER YMCA 0*
Competition: North Gloucestershire League Division 2
Teamsheet: Davoll, Macfarlane, Bretherton, Lane, Shadgett, Mills, Danks, Allen, Jones, Parsons, Dudbridge
Note: Originally League game. Due to an irregularity made null and void and ordered to be replayed 18/04/1914

Date: Saturday 21/02/1914
Result: **MINSTERWORTH 2 GLOUCESTER YMCA 0**
Competition: North Gloucestershire League Division 2
Teamsheet: Davoll, Lane, Bretherton, Merrett, Shadgett, Mills, Danks, Allen, Sides, Parsons, Dudbridge

Date: Saturday 07/03/1914
Result: **LONGHOPE UNITED ? GLOUCESTER YMCA ?**
Competition: North Gloucestershire League Division 2
Teamsheet: Davoll, Macfarlane, Bretherton, Shadgett, Sides, Lane, Danks, Allen, Jones, Barrett, Mills

For the two World Wars many Gloucester City/YMCA players either volunteered or were conscripted and a few made the ultimate sacrifice. Private Archibald Barrett of the Army Cyclist Corps and 2nd Lieutenant Ernest Danks of the Royal Flying Corps were two such men. Private Barrett was killed in 1916 and is buried at the Merville Communal Cemetery in France. 2nd Lieutenant Danks died in 1921 as a result of injuries sustained in World War 1 and is buried at St Philip and James in Hucclecote, Gloucester

FOR THE FALLEN
They shall not grow old, as we that are left grow old.
Age shall not weary them, nor the years condemn.
At the going down of the sun and in the morning
We will remember them.
Laurence Binyon. 1914

1914 –1918
Private Archibald BARRETT, Army Cyclist Corps
2nd Corporal Archibald BLAND, Australian Engineers
Lieutenant Reginald DANKS, Royal Flying Corps
Corporal Henry DAVOLL, Duke of Cornwall's Light Infantry
Staff Quartermaster Sergeant Martin LEWIS, Canadian Army Pay Corps
Lieutenant Herbert PEARCE, Royal Gloucestershire Hussars
Private Oliver LUCAS, Devonshire Regiment
Lance Corporal John MACFARLANE, Royal West Kent Regiment
2nd Lieutenant Ronald TURNER, Essex Regiment

1939-1945
Frederick FIGGURES, Civilian
Driver Ernest FOOTE, Royal Army Service Corps
Able Seaman Thomas McNEILL, Merchant Navy
Private Wilfred SHAW, Argyll & Sutherland Highlanders

Date: Saturday 14/03/1914
Result: **GLOUCESTER YMCA 4 WESTGATE 0**
Competition: North Gloucestershire League Division 2
Teamsheet: Davoll, -----, -----, Shadgett, -----, -----, Danks, -----, Jones, -----, -----
Scorers: Danks, Shadgett, Jones, Davoll (pen)

Date: Saturday 28/03/1914
Result: **GLOUCESTER YMCA 2 NEWNHAM EXCELSIOR 0**
Competition: North Gloucestershire League Division 2
Teamsheet: -----, -----, -----, -----, -----, -----, -----, -----, -----, -----, -----
Scorers: -----, -----

Date: Saturday 18/04/1914
Result: **MITCHELDEAN ? GLOUCESTER YMCA ?**
Competition: North Gloucestershire League Division 2
Teamsheet: -----, -----, -----, -----, -----, -----, -----, -----, -----, -----, -----
Note: Played at Minsterworth

Appearances – EE Allen 7, AM Barrett 1, CA Bretherton 8, P Bygrave 1, F Corbett 1, ER Danks 8, HGH Davoll 8, LF Dudbridge 6, C Durrett 2, EJ Jones 8, JB Lane 5, JM Macfarlane 7, JH Merrett 1, FL Mills 8, JT Parsons 7, JH Rhodes 1, HE Searles 2, JB Shadgett 9, C Sides 2.
Scorers – ER Danks 1, HGH Davoll 1, EJ Jones 1, JB Shadgett 1.

NORTH GLOUCESTERSHIRE LEAGUE DIVISION 2

POS	CLUB	P	W	D	L	F	A	PTS
1	TUFFLEY & WHADDON	12	10	1	1	52	11	21
2	WESTGATE	12	6	3	3	35	18	15
3	LONGHOPE UNITED	12	4	5	3	31	23	13
4	MITCHELDEAN	11	4	4	3	18	12	12
5	MINSTERWORTH	12	2	5	5	18	20	9
6	NEWNHAM EXCELSIOR	12	2	3	7	18	57	7
7	**GLOUCESTER YMCA**	**11**	**1**	**3**	**7**	**11**	**30**	**5**
8	HATHERLEY UNITED							
		82	29	24	29	183	171	82

Hatherley United having applied to withdraw from the competition their record is eliminated.
Gloucester YMCA agreed to play Mitcheldean on 18 April 1914. Cannot find result in The Citizen.

SEASON 1919-1920
(Home Ground: Llanthony, Hempsted)

Only friendlies played this season. 20 fixtures found.

SEASON 1920-1921
(Home Ground: Llanthony, Hempsted)

Only friendlies played this season. 8 fixtures found.

SEASON 1921-1922
(Home Ground: Llanthony, Hempsted)

Date: Saturday 21/09/1921
Result: **WOODCHESTER 'A' 4 GLOUCESTER YMCA 1**
Competition: North Gloucestershire League Division 2
Teamsheet: -----, Salt, -----, Colley, -----, -----, -----, -----, -----, -----, -----
Scorer: -----

Date: Saturday 22/10/1921
Result: **GLOUCESTER YMCA ? WESTBURY UNITED ?**
Competition: North Gloucestershire Minor Cup 1st Round
Teamsheet: -----, Salt (?), -----, -----, -----, -----, -----, -----, -----, -----, -----
Note: Gloucester YMCA won

Date: Saturday 05/11/1921
Result: **GLOUCESTER YMCA 5 BRIMSCOMBE 'A' 0**
Competition: North Gloucestershire League Division 2
Teamsheet: Woodcock, Salt, Ford, Hall, Tomlinson, Beddis, Goddard, Woodger, Wells, Jarman, Mullins
Scorers: Mullins (2), Jarman (2), Wells

Date: Saturday 12/11/1921
Result: **WOODMANCOTE 4 GLOUCESTER YMCA 7**
Competition: North Gloucestershire Minor Cup 2nd Round
Teamsheet (from): Woodcock, Salt, Ford, Watson, Tomlinson, Bretherton, Goddard, Woodger, Beddis, Hall, Mullins, Jones
Scorers: Woodger (4), Jones, Hall, Mullins

Date: Saturday 19/11/1921
Result: **SHARPNESS 'A' 3 GLOUCESTER YMCA 3**
Competition: North Gloucestershire League Division 2
Teamsheet: -----, -----, -----, Hall (?), Tomlinson, -----, -----, -----, -----, Jarman, -----
Scorers: Tomlinson (2), Jarman

Date: Saturday 26/11/1921
Result: **GLOUCESTER YMCA 0 FOREST GREEN ROVERS RESERVES 3**
Competition: North Gloucestershire League Division 2
Teamsheet: -----, -----, -----, Hall, -----, -----, -----, -----, -----, -----, -----

Date: Saturday 03/12/1921
Result: **ASHTON-UNDER-HILL 3 GLOUCESTER YMCA 1**
Competition: North Gloucestershire Minor Cup 3rd Round
Teamsheet: -----, -----, -----, -----, -----, -----, -----, Price, -----, -----, -----
Scorer: Price

Date: Saturday 10/12/1921
Result: **GLOUCESTER YMCA 5 WOODCHESTER 'A' 2**
Competition: North Gloucestershire League Division 2
Teamsheet: -----, -----, -----, -----, -----, -----, Goddard, Price, -----, Jarman, Mullins
Scorers: Jarman (2), Mullins, Goddard

Date: Saturday 31/12/1921
Result: **GLOUCESTER YMCA 4 BERKELEY TOWN 3**
Competition: North Gloucestershire League Division 2
Teamsheet: -----, -----, -----, -----, Hall, Tomlinson, -----, -----, -----, -----, Jarman, -----
Scorers: Jarman (2), Hall, Tomlinson

Date: Saturday 07/01/1922
Result: **BRIMSCOMBE 'A' 1 GLOUCESTER YMCA 3**
Competition: North Gloucestershire League Division 2
Teamsheet: -----, -----, -----, -----, Tomlinson (?), -----, -----, Clarke, -----, Jarman, -----
Scorers: Jarman (2), Clarke

Date: Saturday 21/01/1922
Result: **BERKELEY TOWN 6 GLOUCESTER YMCA 2**
Competition: North Gloucestershire League Division 2
Teamsheet: -----, -----, -----, -----, Tomlinson, -----, -----, James, -----, -----, -----
Scorers: Tomlinson, James

Date: Saturday 18/02/1922
Result: **FOREST GREEN ROVERS RESERVES 5 GLOUCESTER YMCA 1**
Competition: North Gloucestershire League Division 2
Teamsheet: -----, -----, -----, -----, Tomlinson (?), -----, James, Woodger, Bassett, Surman, -----
Scorer: Bassett

Date: Saturday 04/03/1922
Result: **GLOUCESTER YMCA 3 SYNWELL ROVERS 4**
Competition: North Gloucestershire League Division 2
Teamsheet: Woodcock, Ford, Jones, Watson, Tomlinson, Corlett, Morgan, Woodger, Jarman, Surman, Beddis
Scorers: Surman (2), Beddis

Date: Saturday 25/03/1922
Result: **MITCHELDEAN 1 GLOUCESTER YMCA 1**
Competition: North Gloucestershire League Division 2
Teamsheet: Clarke, -----, -----, -----, Tomlinson, -----, -----, -----, -----, Jarman, -----
Scorer: Tomlinson (pen)

Date: Saturday 01/04/1922
Result: **GLOUCESTER YMCA 2 SHARPNESS 'A' 3**
Competition: North Gloucestershire League Division 2
Teamsheet: -----, -----, -----, -----, Tomlinson (?), -----, -----, -----, Jarman, Clarke, -----
Scorers: Clarke, Jarman

Date: Saturday 08/04/1922
Result: **GLOUCESTER YMCA 8 MITCHELDEAN 1**
Competition: North Gloucestershire League Division 2
Teamsheet: -----, -----, Ford, -----, Tomlinson, -----, -----, Dawes, Surman, -----, Beddis
Scorers: Surman (4), Beddis, Tomlinson, Dawes, Ford

Date: Monday 17/04/1922
Result: **SYNWELL ROVERS 2 GLOUCESTER YMCA 1**
Competition: North Gloucestershire League Division 2
Teamsheet: -----, -----, -----, -----, -----, -----, -----, -----, -----, -----, -----
Scorer: -----

Appearances – FA Bassett 1, LA Beddis 4, CA Bretherton 1, VP Clarke 3, J Colley 1, WA Corlett 1, ? Dawes 1, LS Ford 4, N Goddard 3, TG Hall 5, H James 2, W Jarman 8, R Jones 2, H Morgan 1, F Mullins 3, J Price 2, H Salt 4, G Surman 3, SC Tomlinson 11, G Watson 2, F Wells 1, V Woodcock 3, WE Woodger 4.
Scorers – W Jarman 10, G Surman 6, SC Tomlinson 6, F Mullins 4, WE Woodger 4, LA Beddis 2, VP Clarke 2, TG Hall 2, J Price 2, FA Bassett 1, ? Dawes 1, LS Ford 1, G Goddard 1, H James 1, R Jones 1, F Wells 1.

NORTH GLOUCESTERSHIRE LEAGUE DIVISION 2

POS	CLUB	P	W	D	L	F	A	PTS
1	FOREST GREEN ROVERS RESERVES	13	10	1	2	46	19	21
2	BERKELEY TOWN	12	9	0	3	41	16	18
3	SHARPNESS 'A'	14	7	4	3	29	26	18
4	SYNWELL ROVERS	12	7	1	4	39	13	15
5	**GLOUCESTER YMCA**	**14**	**5**	**2**	**7**	**39**	**38**	**12**
6	WOODCHESTER 'A'	14	3	5	6	25	40	11
7	MITCHELDEAN	14	2	2	10	27	66	6
8	BRIMSCOMBE 'A'	13	2	1	10	17	40	5
		106	45	16	45	263	258	106

To late April 1922 only.

SEASON 1922-1923
(Home Ground: Llanthony, Hempsted)

Date: Saturday 16/09/1922
Result: **GLOUCESTER YMCA 5 DURSLEY TOWN 1**
Competition: Gloucestershire Northern Senior League
Teamsheet: Eamer, Watson, R Jones, Corlett, Tomlinson, Beddis, Malpass, Doel, Surman, Watkins, Mullins
Scorers: Surman (3), Watkins (2)

Date: Saturday 23/09/1922
Result: **GLOUCESTER YMCA 2 DURSLEY ROVERS 4**
Competition: Gloucestershire Northern Senior League
Teamsheet: Eamer, Watson, R Jones, Corlett, Tomlinson, Beddis, Moreton, Abbott, Surman, Watkins, Doel
Scorer: Tomlinson (2)

Date: Saturday 07/10/1922
Result: **CINDERFORD TOWN 0 GLOUCESTER YMCA 0**
Competition: Gloucestershire Northern Senior League
Teamsheet: Eamer, F Stone, Jarman, Beddis, Tomlinson, Corlett, Norcott, Malpass, Surman, Doel, Watkins

Date: Saturday 21/10/1922
Result: **WINCHCOMBE UNITED ? GLOUCESTER YMCA ?**
Competition: Gloucestershire FA Northern Senior Amateur Cup 1st Round
Teamsheet: -----, -----, -----, -----, Tomlinson (?), -----, Norcott (?), -----, Surman (?), -----, -----
Note: Gloucester YMCA drew

Date: Saturday 28/10/1922
Result: **GLOUCESTER YMCA 4 WINCHCOMBE UNITED 1**
Competition: Gloucestershire FA Northern Senior Amateur Cup 1st Round Replay
Teamsheet: -----, -----, -----, -----, Tomlinson, -----, Norcott, -----, Surman, -----, -----
Scorers: Norcott (2), Surman, Tomlinson

Date: Saturday 04/11/1922
Result: **GLOUCESTER YMCA 3 WOODCHESTER 2**
Competition: Gloucestershire Northern Senior League
Teamsheet: -----, -----, -----, -----, -----, -----, Norcott, -----, Surman (?), Doel, Watkins
Scorers: Norcott (2), Doel

Date: Saturday 11/11/1922
Result: **TEWKESBURY TOWN 3 GLOUCESTER YMCA 1**
Competition: Gloucestershire FA Northern Senior Amateur Cup 2nd Round
Teamsheet: -----, -----, -----, -----, -----, -----, -----, -----, Surman, -----, -----
Scorer: Surman

Date: Saturday 18/11/1922
Result: **WOODCHESTER 4 GLOUCESTER YMCA 1**
Competition: Gloucestershire Northern Senior League
Teamsheet: -----, -----, -----, -----, Tomlinson, -----, -----, -----, Surman (?), -----, -----
Scorer: Tomlinson

Date: Saturday 25/11/1922
Result: **GLOUCESTER YMCA 2 STONEHOUSE 4**
Competition: Gloucestershire Northern Senior League
Teamsheet: -----, -----, -----, -----, -----, -----, Norcott, -----, Surman, -----, -----
Scorers: Surman, Norcott

Date: Saturday 02/12/1922
Result: **GLOUCESTER YMCA 2 CHALFORD 2**
Competition: Gloucestershire Northern Senior League
Teamsheet: -----, -----, -----, -----, -----, -----, Norcott (?), -----, Surman, -----, -----
Scorer: Surman (2)

Date: Saturday 09/12/1922
Result: **CHELTENHAM TOWN 2 GLOUCESTER YMCA 1**
Competition: Gloucestershire Northern Senior League
Teamsheet: Eamer, R Jones, Thonger, Goddard, Tomlinson, Beddis, Malpass, Norcott, Jarman, Surman, Watkins
Scorer: Surman

Date: Saturday 23/12/1922
Result: **KINGSWOOD 3 GLOUCESTER YMCA 1**
Competition: Gloucestershire Northern Senior League
Teamsheet: Eamer, R Jones, Browning, James, Beddis, Goodman, H Stone, Watkins, Surman, Thorburn, Norcott
Scorer: Beddis

Date: Tuesday 26/12/1922
Result: **GLOUCESTER YMCA 1 BROADWELL AMATEURS 2**
Competition: Gloucestershire Northern Senior League
Teamsheet: Eamer, R Jones, -----, James, Devereux, Goodman, Beddis, Watkins, Surman, Thorburn, Norcott
Scorer: Thorburn

Date: Saturday 30/12/1922
Result: **GLOUCESTER YMCA 2 CHELTENHAM TOWN 3**
Competition: Gloucestershire Northern Senior League
Teamsheet: Eamer, Thonger, R Jones, Beddis, Tomlinson, Goodman, Norcott, Surman, Thorburn, Watkins, Ward
Scorers: Watkins, Norcott

Date: Saturday 06/01/1923
Result: **STONEHOUSE 8 GLOUCESTER YMCA 1**
Competition: Gloucestershire Northern Senior League
Teamsheet: Eamer, -----, -----, -----, -----, -----, Norcott (?), -----, -----, Watkins, -----
Scorer: Watkins

Date: Saturday 13/01/1923
Result: **CHALFORD 4 GLOUCESTER YMCA 1**
Competition: Gloucestershire Northern Senior League
Teamsheet: Eamer (?), -----, -----, -----, -----, -----, Norcott, -----, -----, -----, -----
Scorer: Norcott

Date: Saturday 20/01/1923
Result: **GLOUCESTER YMCA 0 KING'S STANLEY 0**
Competition: Gloucestershire Northern Senior League
Teamsheet: Eamer, -----, -----, -----, -----, -----, -----, -----, -----, -----, -----

Date: Saturday 27/01/1923
Result: **BRIMSCOMBE 14 GLOUCESTER YMCA 0**
Competition: Gloucestershire Northern Senior League
Teamsheet: -----, -----, -----, -----, -----, -----, -----, -----, -----, -----, -----

Date: Saturday 03/02/1923
Result: **GLOUCESTER YMCA 0 BRIMSCOMBE 3**
Competition: Gloucestershire Northern Senior League
Teamsheet: -----, -----, -----, -----, -----, -----, -----, -----, -----, -----, -----

Date: Saturday 10/02/1923
Result: **KING'S STANLEY 1 GLOUCESTER YMCA 3**
Competition: Gloucestershire Northern Senior League
Teamsheet: Clarke, -----, -----, -----, Tomlinson, -----, Norcott, -----, Surman, -----, -----
Scorers: Tomlinson, Norcott, Surman

Date: Saturday 17/02/1923
Result: **WICKWAR 6 GLOUCESTER YMCA 0**
Competition: Gloucestershire Northern Senior League
Teamsheet: -----, -----, -----, -----, -----, -----, Norcott (?), -----, Surman (?), -----, -----

Date: Saturday 24/02/1923
Result: **WOTTON-UNDER-EDGE 4 GLOUCESTER YMCA 3**
Competition: Gloucestershire Northern Senior League
Teamsheet: Eamer, -----, -----, -----, -----, -----, Norcott, -----, Surman, -----, -----
Scorers: Surman (2), Norcott

Date: Saturday 03/03/1923
Result: **GLOUCESTER YMCA 1 KINGSWOOD 3**
Competition: Gloucestershire Northern Senior League
Teamsheet: -----, -----, -----, -----, Tomlinson, -----, -----, -----, -----, -----, -----
Scorer: Tomlinson

Date: Saturday 10/03/1923
Result: **DURSLEY ROVERS 8 GLOUCESTER YMCA 0**
Competition: Gloucestershire Northern Senior League
Teamsheet: -----, -----, -----, -----, -----, -----, -----, -----, -----, -----, -----

Date: Saturday 17/03/1923
Result: **GLOUCESTER YMCA 1 SHARPNESS 2**
Competition: Gloucestershire Northern Senior League
Teamsheet: Eamer, -----, -----, -----, -----, -----, Norcott, -----, -----, -----, -----
Scorer: Norcott

Date: Saturday 24/03/1923
Result: **GLOUCESTER YMCA 3 WOTTON-UNDER-EDGE 2**
Competition: Gloucestershire Northern Senior League
Teamsheet: -----, -----, -----, -----, -----, -----, Norcott, -----, Surman, -----, -----
Scorers: Norcott (2), Surman

Date: Saturday 31/03/1923
Result: **GLOUCESTER YMCA 2 WICKWAR 3**
Competition: Gloucestershire Northern Senior League
Teamsheet: -----, -----, -----, -----, -----, -----, -----, Heyden, Surman, -----, -----
Scorers: Heyden, Surman

Date: Tuesday 03/04/1923
Result: **GLOUCESTER YMCA 1 FOREST GREEN ROVERS 4**
Competition: Gloucestershire Northern Senior League
Teamsheet: -----, -----, -----, -----, Tomlinson, -----, -----, -----, Surman (?), -----, -----
Scorer: Tomlinson

Date: Saturday 07/04/1923
Result: **GLOUCESTER YMCA 2 CINDERFORD TOWN 1**
Competition: Gloucestershire Northern Senior League
Teamsheet: -----, -----, -----, -----, -----, -----, -----, -----, A Jones, Surman, -----
Scorers: A Jones, Surman

Date: Saturday 14/04/1923
Result: **DURSLEY TOWN 5 GLOUCESTER YMCA 1**
Competition: Gloucestershire Northern Senior League
Teamsheet: -----, -----, -----, -----, -----, -----, -----, -----, -----, -----, -----
Scorer: -----

Date: Saturday 21/04/1923
Result: **SHARPNESS ? GLOUCESTER YMCA ?**
Competition: Gloucestershire Northern Senior League
Teamsheet: -----, -----, -----, -----, -----, -----, -----, -----, -----, -----, -----
Note: Gloucester YMCA lost

Date: ?
Result: **FOREST GREEN ROVERS ? GLOUCESTER YMCA ?**
Competition: Gloucestershire Northern Senior League
Teamsheet: -----, -----, -----, -----, -----, -----, -----, -----, -----, -----, -----
Note: Gloucester YMCA lost

Date: ?
Result: **BROADWELL AMATEURS ? GLOUCESTER YMCA ?**
Competition: Gloucestershire Northern Senior League
Teamsheet: -----, -----, -----, -----, -----, -----, -----, -----, -----, -----, -----
Note: Gloucester YMCA lost

Appearances – RE Abbott 1, LA Beddis 7, W Browning 1, VP Clarke 1, WA Corlett 3, G Devereux 1, HE Doel 4, A Eamer 12, N Goddard 1, A Goodman 3, ? Heyden 1, H James 2, W Jarman 2, Rev. A Jones 1, R Jones 6, AS Malpass 3, JE Moreton 1, F Mullins 1, TS Norcott 17, F Stone 1, H Stone 1, G Surman 21, T Thonger 2, H Thorburn 3, SC Tomlinson 11, A Ward 1, L Watkins 9, G Watson 2.
Scorers – G Surman 15, TS Norcott 12, SC Tomlinson 7, L Watkins 4, LA Beddis 1, HE Doel 1, ? Heyden 1, Rev. A Jones 1, H Thorburn 1.

GLOUCESTERSHIRE NORTHERN SENIOR LEAGUE

POS	CLUB	P	W	D	L	F	A	PTS
1	BRIMSCOMBE	30	23	4	3	102	31	50
2	DURSLEY ROVERS	30	21	2	7	73	45	44
3	STONEHOUSE	30	18	5	7	102	47	41
4	FOREST GREEN ROVERS	30	18	5	7	79	35	41
5	SHARPNESS	30	17	6	7	93	51	40
6	BROADWELL AMATEURS	30	18	4	8	90	62	40
7	CHALFORD	30	15	5	10	73	57	35
8	CHELTENHAM TOWN	30	15	3	12	59	71	33
9	WICKWAR	30	13	4	13	59	51	30
10	WOODCHESTER	30	11	7	12	65	52	29
11	DURSLEY TOWN	30	12	2	16	64	58	26
12	CINDERFORD TOWN	30	7	7	16	49	80	21
13	WOTTON-UNDER-EDGE	30	7	3	20	43	103	17
14	GLOUCESTER YMCA	30	5	3	22	43	112	13
15	KINGSWOOD	30	4	3	23	46	111	11
16	KING'S STANLEY	30	2	5	23	30	104	9
		480	206	68	206	1070	1070	480

SEASON 1923-1924
(Home Ground: Llanthony, Hempsted)

Date: Saturday 08/09/1923
Result: **GLOUCESTER YMCA 1 FOREST GREEN ROVERS 1**
Competition: Gloucestershire Northern Senior League
Teamsheet: -----, -----, -----, -----, -----, -----, -----, -----, Surman, -----, -----
Scorer: Surman

Date: Saturday 15/09/1923
Result: **BRIMSCOMBE 2 GLOUCESTER YMCA 0**
Competition: Gloucestershire Northern Senior League
Teamsheet: Eamer, Hardman, Bayliss, Dainty, Hamer, Corlett, AS Malpass, Tomlinson, Surman, Dix, Beddis

Date: Saturday 22/09/1923
Result: **WOODCHESTER 2 GLOUCESTER YMCA 0**
Competition: Gloucestershire Northern Senior League
Teamsheet: Eamer, Banks, Bayliss, Hardman, Hamer, Corlett, Dainty, Dix, Surman, Beddis, JL Malpass

Date: Saturday 29/09/1923
Result: **GLOUCESTER YMCA 0 SHARPNESS 5**
Competition: Gloucestershire Northern Senior League
Teamsheet: -----, -----, -----, -----, -----, -----, -----, -----, -----, -----, -----

Date: Saturday 06/10/1923
Result: **WOTTON-UNDER-EDGE 2 GLOUCESTER YMCA 0**
Competition: Gloucestershire Northern Senior League
Teamsheet: -----, -----, -----, -----, -----, -----, -----, -----, -----, -----, -----

Date: Saturday 13/10/1923
Result: **CINDERFORD TOWN 2 GLOUCESTER YMCA 0**
Competition: Gloucestershire Northern Senior League
Teamsheet: -----, -----, -----, -----, -----, -----, -----, -----, -----, -----, -----

Date: Saturday 20/10/1923
Result: **CHELTENHAM TOWN 1 GLOUCESTER YMCA 1**
Competition: Gloucestershire FA Northern Senior Amateur Cup 1st Round
Teamsheet: Eamer, Hardman, Bayliss, Banks, Tomlinson, Hamer, Corlett, Dix, Jarman, Surman, Bayliss, Beddis
Scorer: Surman

Date: Saturday 27/10/1923
Result: **GLOUCESTER YMCA 0 CHELTENHAM TOWN 4**
Competition: Gloucestershire FA Northern Senior Amateur Cup 1st Round Replay
Teamsheet: Eamer, Thonger, Hardman, Tomlinson, Hamer, Corlett, AS Malpass, Dix, Surman, Beddis, A Jones

Date: Saturday 03/11/1923
Result: **GLOUCESTER YMCA 1 KINGSWOOD 1**
Competition: Gloucestershire Northern Senior League
Teamsheet: Eamer (?), -----, -----, Tomlinson (?), -----, -----, -----, -----, Surman (?), -----, -----
Scorer: -----

Date: Saturday 10/11/1923
Result: **GLOUCESTER YMCA 0 CINDERFORD TOWN 3**
Competition: Gloucestershire Northern Senior League
Teamsheet: Eamer, -----, -----, Tomlinson, -----, -----, -----, -----, -----, Surman, -----

Date: Saturday 17/11/1923
Result: **CHALFORD 3 GLOUCESTER YMCA 0**
Competition: Gloucestershire Northern Senior League
Teamsheet: -----, -----, -----, -----, -----, -----, -----, -----, Tomlinson (?), -----, -----, -----

Date: Saturday 24/11/1923
Result: **GLOUCESTER YMCA 0 CHALFORD 0**
Competition: Gloucestershire Northern Senior League
Teamsheet: -----, Banks, -----, -----, Hamer, -----, -----, Tomlinson, -----, -----, -----

Date: Saturday 01/12/1923
Result: **GLOUCESTER YMCA 2 WOODCHESTER 3**
Competition: Gloucestershire Northern Senior League
Teamsheet: Eamer, Banks, Hamer (?), -----, -----, Corlett, Allen, -----, Fletcher, -----, Beddis
Scorers: Fletcher, Beddis

Date: Saturday 15/12/1923
Result: **GLOUCESTER YMCA 0 DURSLEY TOWN 1**
Competition: Gloucestershire Northern Senior League
Teamsheet: Eamer, Banks, Hamer, -----, -----, Corlett, Allen (?), -----, -----, -----, Beddis (?)

Date: Saturday 22/12/1923
Result: **GLOUCESTER YMCA 1 CHELTENHAM TOWN 1**
Competition: Gloucestershire Northern Senior League
Teamsheet: Masters, Banks, Hamer, Tomlinson, Corlett, JL Malpass, Allen, Ford, Collins, Surman, Beddis
Scorer: Collins

Date: Saturday 29/12/1923
Result: **GLOUCESTER YMCA 4 BROADWELL AMATEURS 2**
Competition: Gloucestershire Northern Senior League
Teamsheet: -----, Banks, Hamer, Tomlinson, Ford, Corlett, Allen (?), Dix, Surman, Collins (?), Beddis
Scorers: Surman (2), Corlett, Beddis

Date: Saturday 05/01/1924
Result: **CHELTENHAM TOWN 4 GLOUCESTER YMCA 3**
Competition: Gloucestershire Northern Senior League
Teamsheet: Eamer, Hamer, Banks, Tomlinson, Ford, JL Malpass, Allen, Dix, Surman, Collins, Hodges
Scorers: Collins (2, 1 pen), Surman

Date: Saturday 19/01/1924
Result: **TEWKESBURY TOWN 6 GLOUCESTER YMCA 2**
Competition: Gloucestershire Northern Senior League
Teamsheet: Eamer, -----, -----, Murdock, Ford (?), JL Malpass, -----, Dix (?), Surman, Collins (?), -----
Scorers: Surman, Murdock (pen)

Date: Saturday 02/02/1924
Result: **GLOUCESTER YMCA 3 STONEHOUSE 0**
Competition: Gloucestershire Northern Senior League
Teamsheet: Eamer, -----, -----, -----, Ford, -----, -----, Dix, -----, Collins, -----
Scorers: Dix, Collins, Ford

Date: Saturday 16/02/1924
Result: **BROADWELL AMATEURS 4 GLOUCESTER YMCA 4**
Competition: Gloucestershire Northern Senior League
Teamsheet: -----, -----, -----, -----, -----, -----, -----, Dix (?), -----, -----, Beddis
Scorers: Beddis (2), -----, -----

Date: Saturday 23/02/1924
Result: **KINGSWOOD 2 GLOUCESTER YMCA 1**
Competition: Gloucestershire Northern Senior League
Teamsheet: -----, Banks, -----, -----, -----, -----, -----, Dix, Surman, -----, Beddis
Scorer: Beddis

Date: Saturday 01/03/1924
Result: **FOREST GREEN ROVERS 8 GLOUCESTER YMCA 0**
Competition: Gloucestershire Northern Senior League
Teamsheet: Eamer, Hamer, Ward, Hopewell, Dix, Murdock, Surman (?), -----, Beddis (?)
Note: Only 9 players turned up. Two missed the train

Date: Saturday 08/03/1924
Result: **GLOUCESTER YMCA 1 DURSLEY ROVERS 5**
Competition: Gloucestershire Northern Senior League
Teamsheet: Eamer, Hamer, Banks, Ford, Fearis, Ward, Hopewell, Dix, Murdock, Surman, Beddis
Scorer: Surman

Date: Saturday 15/03/1924
Result: **SHARPNESS 2 GLOUCESTER YMCA 0**
Competition: Gloucestershire Northern Senior League
Teamsheet: Eamer, Hamer, Banks, Ford (?), Fearis, Ward, -----, Surman (?), Pitt, Murdock, -----

Date: Saturday 22/03/1924
Result: **GLOUCESTER YMCA 2 WOTTON-UNDER-EDGE 1**
Competition: Gloucestershire Northern Senior League
Teamsheet: Eamer (?), -----, -----, -----, Ford, JL Malpass, -----, Surman, Pitt, Murdock, -----
Scorers: Murdock, Pitt

Date: Saturday 29/03/1924
Result: **WICKWAR 1 GLOUCESTER YMCA 1**
Competition: Gloucestershire Northern Senior League
Teamsheet: Eamer, -----, -----, -----, Ford, JL Malpass (?), -----, Surman, Pitt (?), Tomlinson, -----
Scorer: Surman

Date: Saturday 05/04/1924
Result: **GLOUCESTER YMCA 5 WICKWAR 0**
Competition: Gloucestershire Northern Senior League
Teamsheet: Eamer, Banks, Hamer, Murdock, Surman, JL Malpass, Tomlinson, Dix, Pitt, Ford, Beddis
Scorers: Dix (3), Pitt (2)

Date: Saturday 12/04/1924
Result: **DURSLEY ROVERS 2 GLOUCESTER YMCA 1**
Competition: Gloucestershire Northern Senior League
Teamsheet: Eamer (?), -----, -----, Murdock (?), -----, -----, -----, -----, Pitt (?), -----, Beddis (?)
Scorer: -----

Date: Saturday 19/04/1924
Result: **DURSLEY TOWN 3 GLOUCESTER YMCA 3**
Competition: Gloucestershire Northern Senior League
Teamsheet: Eamer, -----, -----, -----, -----, -----, -----, -----, Murdock, Pitt, Beddis
Scorers: Pitt, Beddis, Murdock

Date: Monday 21/04/1924
Result: **GLOUCESTER YMCA 0 BRIMSCOMBE 2**
Competition: Gloucestershire Northern Senior League
Teamsheet: Eamer, Hamer, -----, Crump, -----, -----, -----, Dix, -----, Pitt (?), Beddis

Date: Thursday 24/04/1924
Result: **STONEHOUSE 0 GLOUCESTER YMCA 2**
Competition: Gloucestershire Northern Senior League
Teamsheet: -----, -----, -----, -----, Fearis, -----, -----, -----, Pitt, Surman, -----
Scorers: Surman (pen), Pitt

Date: ?
Result: **GLOUCESTER YMCA 3 TEWKESBURY TOWN 6**
Competition: Gloucestershire Northern Senior League
Teamsheet: -----, -----, -----, -----, -----, -----, -----, -----, -----, -----, -----
Scorers: -----, -----, -----

Appearances – EE Allen 5, H Banks 12, F Bayliss 3, LA Beddis 15, AF Collins 5, WA Corlett 7, LO Crump 1, GE Dainty 2, W Dix 14, A Eamer 20, EN Fearis 3, ? Fletcher 1, LS Ford 10, SC Hamer 15, A Hardman 4, K Hodges 1, R Hopewell 2, W Jarman 1, Rev. A Jones 1, AS Malpass 2, JL Malpass 7, R Masters 1, AFT Murdock 8, AG Pitt 8, G Surman 20, T Thonger 1, SC Tomlinson 12, L Ward 3.
Scorers – G Surman 10, AG Pitt 5, LA Beddis 4, AF Collins 4, W Dix 4, AFT Murdock 3, WA Corlett 1, ? Fletcher 1, LS Ford 1.

GLOUCESTERSHIRE NORTHERN SENIOR LEAGUE

POS	CLUB	P	W	D	L	F	A	PTS
1	SHARPNESS	30	24	2	4	90	34	50
2	DURSLEY ROVERS	30	19	6	5	81	42	44
3	BRIMSCOMBE	30	19	5	6	84	38	43
4	BROADWELL AMATEURS	30	17	5	8	116	53	39
5	STONEHOUSE	30	18	1	11	71	54	37
6	FOREST GREEN ROVERS	30	14	7	9	71	47	35
7	TEWKESBURY TOWN	30	14	5	11	61	47	33
8	CINDERFORD TOWN	30	13	3	14	82	76	29
9	CHALFORD	30	11	7	12	53	50	29
10	WOODCHESTER	30	11	6	13	53	61	28
11	WOTTON-UNDER-EDGE	30	12	3	15	56	78	27
12	CHELTENHAM TOWN	30	9	7	14	74	94	25
13	DURSLEY TOWN	30	7	5	18	36	72	19
14	**GLOUCESTER YMCA**	**30**	**5**	**7**	**18**	**40**	**74**	**17**
15	KINGSWOOD	30	7	2	21	46	104	16
16	WICKWAR	30	3	3	24	26	116	9
		480	203	74	203	1040	1040	480

SEASON 1924-1925
(Home Ground: Llanthony, Hempsted)

Date: Saturday 06/09/1924
Result: **CHALFORD ? GLOUCESTER YMCA ?**
Competition: Gloucestershire Northern Senior League
Teamsheet: Eamer, Banks, Hamer, Crump, W Ford, Malpass, Murdock, Heyden, Pitt, Surman, Beddis

Date: Saturday 13/09/1924
Result: **GLOUCESTER YMCA ? SHARPNESS ?**
Competition: Gloucestershire Northern Senior League
Teamsheet: Eamer, Hamer, Banks, Malpass, W Ford, Murdock, -----, Dix, Kirton, Pitt, Heyden

Date: Saturday 20/09/1924
Result: **BERKELEY TOWN 4 GLOUCESTER YMCA 3**
Competition: Gloucestershire Northern Senior League
Teamsheet: Eamer, Hamer, Banks, Malpass, W Ford, Murdock, Dix, Pitt, Heyden, Beddis, -----
Scorers: -----, -----, -----

Date: Saturday 27/09/1924
Result: **GLOUCESTER YMCA 0 WOTTON-UNDER-EDGE 4**
Competition: Gloucestershire Northern Senior League
Teamsheet: Eamer (?), Hamer (?), -----, -----, W Ford (?), Murdock (?), Dix (?), -----, Pitt (?), Beddis (?), -----

Date: Saturday 04/10/1924
Result: **STONEHOUSE 5 GLOUCESTER YMCA 1**
Competition: Gloucestershire Northern Senior League
Teamsheet: Eamer, Hamer, LS Ford, Crump, W Ford, Ward, Murdock, Dix, Pitt, Beddis, -----
Scorer: -----

Date: Saturday 11/10/1924
Result: **CINDERFORD TOWN 2 GLOUCESTER YMCA 2**
Competition: Gloucestershire Northern Senior League
Teamsheet: -----, -----, -----, -----, -----, -----, -----, Dix, Pitt (?), -----, -----
Scorer: Dix (2)

Date: Saturday 18/10/1924
Result: **GLOUCESTER YMCA 5 KINGSWOOD 2**
Competition: Gloucestershire Northern Senior League
Teamsheet: -----, -----, -----, -----, Surman, Butler, -----, Dix, Pitt, -----, Bayliss
Scorers: Dix, Pitt (3), Bayliss

Date: Saturday 25/10/1924
Result: **GLOUCESTER YMCA 3 BRIMSCOMBE 4**
Competition: Gloucestershire Northern Senior League
Teamsheet: -----, -----, -----, -----, -----, -----, -----, -----, Pitt, -----, -----
Scorer: Pitt (3)

Date: Saturday 01/11/1924
Result: **GLOUCESTER YMCA ? CINDERFORD TOWN ?**
Competition: Gloucestershire Northern Senior League
Teamsheet: -----, -----, -----, -----, -----, -----, -----, Pitt (?), -----, -----

Date: Saturday 08/11/1924
Result: **TEWKESBURY TOWN 3 GLOUCESTER YMCA 0**
Competition: Gloucestershire Northern Senior League
Teamsheet: Eamer, Hamer, LS Ford, Malpass, Surman, Butler, Richards, Dix, Pitt, Murdock, Bayliss

Date: Saturday 15/11/1924
Result: **WOTTON-UNDER-EDGE 2 GLOUCESTER YMCA 1**
Competition: Gloucestershire Northern Senior League
Teamsheet: Eamer, Hamer, Murdock, Malpass, Surman, LS Ford, Richards, Dix, Pitt, Butler, Bayliss
Scorer: -----

Date: Saturday 22/11/1924
Result: **GLOUCESTER YMCA 4 BERKELEY TOWN 0**
Competition: Gloucestershire Northern Senior League
Teamsheet: Eamer, Hamer, Murdock, Malpass, Surman, Butler, Richards, Dix, Pitt, LS Ford, Bayliss
Scorers: Eamer (2), Dix, Butler (pen)

Date: Saturday 29/11/1924
Result: **GLOUCESTER YMCA 1 CHALFORD 2**
Competition: Gloucestershire Northern Senior League
Teamsheet: -----, -----, -----, -----, -----, -----, -----, -----, -----, -----, -----
Scorer: -----

Date: Saturday 06/12/1924
Result: **GLOUCESTER YMCA 1 STONEHOUSE 2**
Competition: Gloucestershire Northern Senior League
Teamsheet: -----, -----, -----, -----, -----, -----, -----, -----, -----, -----, -----
Scorer: -----

Date: Saturday 20/12/1924
Result: **CHELTENHAM TOWN 1 GLOUCESTER YMCA 1**
Competition: Gloucestershire Northern Senior League
Teamsheet: -----, -----, -----, -----, -----, -----, -----, -----, -----, Beddis, -----
Scorer: Beddis

Date: Saturday 27/12/1924
Result: **GLOUCESTER YMCA 2 BROADWELL AMATEURS 4**
Competition: Gloucestershire Northern Senior League
Teamsheet: -----, -----, -----, -----, -----, -----, -----, -----, -----, -----, -----
Scorers: -----, -----

Date: Saturday 03/01/1925
Result: **CADBURY'S ATHLETIC 4 GLOUCESTER YMCA 1**
Competition: Gloucestershire Northern Senior League
Teamsheet: -----, -----, -----, -----, -----, -----, -----, -----, -----, -----, -----
Scorer: -----

Date: Saturday 10/01/1925
Result: **BRIMSCOMBE 7 GLOUCESTER YMCA 1**
Competition: Gloucestershire FA Northern Senior Amateur Cup 1st Round
Teamsheet: -----, -----, -----, -----, -----, -----, -----, -----, -----, -----, -----
Scorer: -----

SEASON BY SEASON

Date: Saturday 17/01/1925
Result: **GLOUCESTER YMCA 1 TEWKESBURY TOWN 1**
Competition: Gloucestershire Northern Senior League
Teamsheet: -----, -----, -----, -----, -----, -----, -----, Dix, -----, -----, -----
Scorer: Dix

Date: Saturday 24/01/1925
Result: **GLOUCESTER YMCA ? CADBURY'S ATHLETIC ?**
Competition: Gloucestershire Northern Senior League
Teamsheet: -----, -----, -----, -----, -----, -----, -----, Dix (?), -----, -----, -----

Date: Saturday 14/02/1925
Result: **DURSLEY ROVERS 3 GLOUCESTER YMCA 1**
Competition: Gloucestershire Northern Senior League
Teamsheet: -----, -----, -----, -----, Tomlinson, Butler, -----, Dix, -----, -----, Beddis
Scorer: Butler (pen)

Date: Saturday 07/03/1925
Result: **SHARPNESS 5 GLOUCESTER YMCA 0**
Competition: Gloucestershire Northern Senior League
Teamsheet: -----, -----, -----, -----, -----, -----, -----, -----, -----, -----, -----

Date: Saturday 14/03/1925
Result: **DURSLEY TOWN 5 GLOUCESTER YMCA 1**
Competition: Gloucestershire Northern Senior League
Teamsheet: -----, -----, -----, -----, -----, -----, -----, -----, -----, -----, -----
Scorer: (centre forward)

Date: Saturday 21/03/1925
Result: **KINGSWOOD 3 GLOUCESTER YMCA 0**
Competition: Gloucestershire Northern Senior League
Teamsheet: -----, -----, -----, -----, -----, -----, -----, -----, -----, -----, -----

Date: Saturday 28/03/1925
Result: **GLOUCESTER YMCA 2 DURSLEY ROVERS 2**
Competition: Gloucestershire Northern Senior League
Teamsheet: -----, -----, -----, -----, -----, -----, -----, -----, -----, -----, -----
Scorers: -----, -----

Date: Monday 13/04/1925
Result: **GLOUCESTER YMCA 1 WOODCHESTER 1**
Competition: Gloucestershire Northern Senior League
Teamsheet: -----, -----, -----, -----, -----, -----, -----, -----, -----, -----, -----
Scorer: -----

Date: Tuesday 14/04/1925
Result: **WOODCHESTER 2 GLOUCESTER YMCA 2**
Competition: Gloucestershire Northern Senior League
Teamsheet: -----, -----, -----, -----, -----, -----, -----, -----, -----, -----, -----
Scorers: -----, -----

Date: Monday 20/04/1925
Result: **GLOUCESTER YMCA 2 CHELTENHAM TOWN 1**
Competition: Gloucestershire Northern Senior League
Teamsheet: Allen, LS Ford, Hamer, Malpass, Tomlinson, Murdock, Bailey, Banks, Surman, Butler, Dean
Scorers: Surman (2)

Date: Saturday 25/04/1925
Result: **GLOUCESTER YMCA ? DURSLEY TOWN ?**
Competition: Gloucestershire Northern Senior League
Teamsheet (from): Allen, Hamer, LS Ford, Malpass, Tomlinson, Murdock, Dean, Surman, Butler, Bailey, Banks, Dix, Heyden

Date: ?
Result: **BRIMSCOMBE ? GLOUCESTER YMCA ?**
Competition: Gloucestershire Northern Senior League
Teamsheet: -----, -----, -----, -----, -----, -----, -----, -----, -----, -----, -----

Date: ?
Result: **BROADWELL AMATEURS ? GLOUCESTER YMCA ?**
Competition: Gloucestershire Northern Senior League
Teamsheet: -----, -----, -----, -----, -----, -----, -----, -----, -----, -----, -----

Appearances – E Allen 2, F Bailey 2, H Banks 5, F Bayliss 4, LA Beddis 6, A Butler 7, LO Crump 2, C Dean 2, W Dix 14, A Eamer 8, LS Ford 6, W Ford 5, SC Hamer 10, H Heyden 5, J Kirton 1, JL Malpass 8, AFT Murdock 10, AG Pitt 12, C Richards 3, G Surman 7, SC Tomlinson 3, L Ward 1.
Scorers – AG Pitt 6, W Dix 5, A Butler 2, A Eamer 2, G Surman 2, F Bayliss 1, LA Beddis 1.

RECORD BREAKER

Sam Hamer
Most Seasons Played (jointly) - 12

[37]

SEASON BY SEASON

GLOUCESTERSHIRE NORTHERN SENIOR LEAGUE

POS	CLUB	P	W	D	L	F	A	PTS
1	BROADWELL AMATEURS	30	22	6	2	85	30	50
2	SHARPNESS	30	20	5	5	77	32	45
3	DURSLEY TOWN	30	16	5	9	73	46	37
4	CHALFORD	30	13	11	6	70	51	37
5	STONEHOUSE	30	16	3	11	82	49	35
6	WOODCHESTER	30	12	10	8	72	47	34
7	CADBURY'S ATHLETIC	30	13	7	10	68	46	33
8	BRIMSCOMBE	30	14	5	11	68	53	33
9	DURSLEY ROVERS	30	13	6	11	62	66	32
10	TEWKESBURY TOWN	30	10	10	10	49	51	30
11	CHELTENHAM TOWN	30	8	10	12	54	56	26
12	KINGSWOOD	30	9	4	17	48	87	22
13	WOTTON-UNDER-EDGE	30	10	1	19	42	92	21
14	CINDERFORD TOWN	30	6	6	18	36	74	18
15	**GLOUCESTER YMCA**	**30**	**4**	**8**	**18**	**38**	**75**	**16**
16	BERKELEY TOWN	30	5	6	19	36	74	16
		480	191	103	186	960	929	485

SEASON 1925-1926

(Home Ground: Avenue Road Ground, Tuffley Avenue)

Date: Saturday 05/09/1925
Result: **GLOUCESTER CITY 2 SHARPNESS 1**
Competition: Gloucestershire Northern Senior League
Teamsheet: Browning, Hamer, Banks, Tomlinson, Alder, Dainty, Edwards, Ringrose, Perks, Kirton, Bailey
Scorers: Perks, Kirton
Attendance: 300

Date: Saturday 12/09/1925
Result: **DURSLEY ROVERS 4 GLOUCESTER CITY 2**
Competition: Gloucestershire Northern Senior League
Teamsheet: Browning, Hamer, Banks, Tomlinson, Alder, Dainty, Edwards, Ringrose, Kirton, Perks, Bailey
Scorers: Edwards, Kirton

Date: Thursday 17/09/1925
Result: **CHELTENHAM TOWN 1 GLOUCESTER CITY 1**
Competition: Gloucestershire Northern Senior League
Teamsheet: Browning, Hamer, Banks, Tomlinson, Alder, Dainty, Edwards, Ringrose, Tucker, Perks, Murdin
Scorer: Edwards

Date: Saturday 19/09/1925
Result: **GLOUCESTER CITY 2 STONEHOUSE 0**
Competition: Gloucestershire Northern Senior League
Teamsheet: Browning, Hamer, Banks, Tomlinson, Alder, Dainty, Edwards, Ringrose, Tucker, Perks, Murdin
Scorer: Ringrose (2)

Date: Saturday 26/09/1925
Result: **GLOUCESTER CITY 4 CAM MILLS 0**
Competition: Gloucestershire Northern Senior League
Teamsheet: Browning, Hamer, Banks, Tomlinson, Alder, Dainty, Edwards, Ringrose, Perks, Tucker, Murdin
Scorers: Tucker, Ringrose, Perks, Edwards

Date: Saturday 03/10/1925
Result: **GLOUCESTER CITY 2 BROADWELL AMATEURS 0**
Competition: Gloucestershire Northern Senior League
Teamsheet: Browning, Hamer, Banks, Tomlinson, Alder, Dainty, Edwards, Ringrose, Perks, Tucker, Murdin
Scorers: Alder, Edwards
Attendance: 700

Date: Saturday 17/10/1925
Result: **BRIMSCOMBE 3 GLOUCESTER CITY 4**
Competition: Gloucestershire Northern Senior League
Teamsheet: Browning, Hamer, Banks, Tomlinson, Alder, Dainty, Edwards, Ringrose, Perks, Tucker, Murdin
Scorers: Edwards, Tucker, own goal, Ringrose

Date: Saturday 31/10/1925
Result: **GLOUCESTER CITY 0 DURSLEY ROVERS 2**
Competition: Gloucestershire Northern Senior League
Teamsheet: Browning, Hamer, Banks, Dainty, Alder, Tucker, Edwards, Ringrose, Perks, Burton, Murdin

Date: Saturday 07/11/1925
Result: **TEWKESBURY TOWN 1 GLOUCESTER CITY 3**
Competition: Gloucestershire Northern Senior League
Teamsheet: Browning, Hamer, Banks, Tomlinson, Alder, Dainty, Edwards, Murdock, Perks, Surman, Murdin
Scorers: Surman, Murdock, Perks

Date: Saturday 21/11/1925
Result: **CINDERFORD TOWN 2 GLOUCESTER CITY 4**
Competition: Gloucestershire Northern Senior League
Teamsheet: Summers, Hamer, Banks, Tomlinson, Alder, Dainty, Edwards, Ringrose, Mills, Burton, Tucker
Scorers: Edwards, Ringrose, Alder, Burton

[38]

Date: Saturday 28/11/1925
Result: **DURSLEY TOWN 3 GLOUCESTER CITY 5**
Competition: Gloucestershire Northern Senior League
Teamsheet: Browning, Hamer, Banks, Tomlinson, Alder, Dainty, Edwards, Ringrose, Perks, Tucker, Burton
Scorers: Perks (3), Tucker (2)

Date: Saturday 12/12/1925
Result: **SHARPNESS 4 GLOUCESTER CITY 1**
Competition: Gloucestershire FA Northern Senior Amateur Cup 2nd Round
Teamsheet: Browning, Hamer, Bayliss, Tomlinson, Alder, Dainty, Edwards, Ringrose, Perks, Collins, Murdin
Scorer: Murdin

Date: Saturday 19/12/1925
Result: **STONEHOUSE 2 GLOUCESTER CITY 2**
Competition: Gloucestershire Northern Senior League
Teamsheet: Browning, Hamer, Bayliss, Tomlinson, Alder, Dainty, Edwards, Perks, Burton, Tucker, Murdin
Scorers: Tucker, -----

Date: Saturday 26/12/1925
Result: **WOODCHESTER 2 GLOUCESTER CITY 4**
Competition: Gloucestershire Northern Senior League
Teamsheet: Browning, Hamer, Ford, Dainty, Alder, Ayland, Malpass, Edwards, Perks, Tucker, Burton
Scorers: Tucker (2), Edwards, Perks

Date: Saturday 09/01/1926
Result: **CHALFORD 1 GLOUCESTER CITY 1**
Competition: Gloucestershire Northern Senior League
Teamsheet: Browning, Hamer, Bayliss, Tomlinson, Tucker, Dainty, Malpass, Edwards, Perks, Ringrose, Burton
Scorer: Perks

Date: Saturday 16/01/1926
Result: **GLOUCESTER CITY 2 DURSLEY TOWN 2**
Competition: Gloucestershire Northern Senior League
Teamsheet: Browning, Hamer, Bayliss, Tomlinson, Alder, Dainty, Edwards, Ringrose, Perks, Tucker, Burton
Scorers: Burton, Ringrose

Date: Saturday 23/01/1926
Result: **GLOUCESTER CITY 4 KINGSWOOD 1**
Competition: Gloucestershire Northern Senior League
Teamsheet: Browning, Hamer, Bayliss, Tomlinson, Alder, Dainty, Edwards, Ringrose, Perks, Tucker, Burton
Scorers: Tucker (2), Edwards (2)

Date: Saturday 30/01/1926
Result: **CAM MILLS 1 GLOUCESTER CITY 5**
Competition: Gloucestershire Northern Senior League
Teamsheet: Browning, Hamer, Bayliss, Tomlinson, Alder, Murdock, Edwards, Ringrose, Perks, Tucker, Burton
Scorers: Perks (3), Burton (2)

Date: Saturday 06/02/1926
Result: **SHARPNESS 5 GLOUCESTER CITY 1**
Competition: Gloucestershire Northern Senior League
Teamsheet: Browning, Hamer, Bayliss, Tomlinson, Alder, Murdock, Edwards, Ringrose, Perks, Tucker, Burton
Scorer: Perks

Date: Saturday 20/02/1926
Result: **CADBURY'S ATHLETIC 2 GLOUCESTER CITY 5**
Competition: Gloucestershire Northern Senior League
Teamsheet: Browning, Hamer, Ford, Tomlinson, Alder, Murdock, Edwards, Ringrose, Perks, Tucker, Burton
Scorers: Perks, Tucker (2), Edwards, Alder

Date: Saturday 27/02/1926
Result: **GLOUCESTER CITY 7 WOTTON-UNDER-EDGE 0**
Competition: Gloucestershire Northern Senior League
Teamsheet: Browning, Hamer, Ford, Tomlinson, Alder, Murdock, Edwards, Ringrose, Perks, Tucker, Burton
Scorers: Perks (3), Ringrose (2), Burton, Alder

Date: Saturday 06/03/1926
Result: **GLOUCESTER CITY 4 CHELTENHAM TOWN 2**
Competition: Gloucestershire Northern Senior League
Teamsheet: Browning, Hamer, Bayliss, Tomlinson, Alder, Dainty, Edwards, Ringrose, Burton, Murdock, Ayland
Scorers: Ringrose (2), Edwards (pen), Murdock

Date: Saturday 13/03/1926
Result: **GLOUCESTER CITY 6 CADBURY'S ATHLETIC 1**
Competition: Gloucestershire Northern Senior League
Teamsheet: Browning, Hamer, Ford, Bayliss, Alder, Murdock, Edwards, Tomlinson, Perks, Tucker, Burton
Scorers: Edwards (2, 1 pen), Ford, Perks (2), Murdock

Date: Saturday 20/03/1926
Result: **BROADWELL AMATEURS 2 GLOUCESTER CITY 4**
Competition: Gloucestershire Northern Senior League
Teamsheet: Browning, Hamer, Bayliss, Tomlinson, Alder, Murdock, Edwards, Ringrose, Perks, Tucker, Burton
Scorer: Edwards (4, 1 pen)

Date: Saturday 27/03/1926
Result: **KINGSWOOD 3 GLOUCESTER CITY 3**
Competition: Gloucestershire Northern Senior League
Teamsheet: Browning, Hamer, Bayliss, Tomlinson, Murdock, Dainty, Edwards, Malpass, Perks, Ringrose, Tucker
Scorers: -----, -----, -----

Date: Saturday 03/04/1926
Result: **WOTTON-UNDER-EDGE 1 GLOUCESTER CITY 6**
Competition: Gloucestershire Northern Senior League
Teamsheet: Browning, Hamer, Bayliss, Tomlinson, Alder, Murdock, Edwards, Ringrose, Perks, Tucker, Burton
Scorers: Ringrose, Edwards (4, 1 pen), Alder

Date: Monday 05/04/1926
Result: **GLOUCESTER CITY 8 WOODCHESTER 1**
Competition: Gloucestershire Northern Senior League
Teamsheet: Browning, Hamer, Bayliss, Tomlinson, Alder, Murdock, Malpass, Ringrose, Perks, Tucker, Burton
Scorers: Perks, Tucker (4), Ringrose (2), Malpass
Attendance: 800

Date: Tuesday 06/04/1926
Result: **GLOUCESTER CITY 5 CHALFORD 0**
Competition: Gloucestershire Northern Senior League
Teamsheet: Browning, Hamer, Bayliss, Tomlinson, Alder, Murdock, Edwards, Ringrose, Perks, Tucker, Burton
Scorers: Edwards (2), Perks (2), Ringrose
Attendance: 1200

Date; Saturday 10/04/1926
Result: **GLOUCESTER CITY 6 CINDERFORD TOWN 1**
Competition: Gloucestershire Northern Senior League
Teamsheet: Browning, Hamer, Bayliss, Tomlinson, Alder, Murdock, Edwards, Ringrose, Perks, Tucker, Burton
Scorers: Ringrose (3), Edwards (2), Tucker
Attendance: 1000

Date: Thursday 15/04/1926
Result: **GLOUCESTER CITY 1 BRIMSCOMBE 0**
Competition: Gloucestershire Northern Senior League
Teamsheet: Browning, Hamer, Bayliss, Tomlinson, Alder, Murdock, Edwards, Ringrose, Perks, Tucker, Burton
Scorer: Perks

Date: Thursday 22/04/1926
Result: **GLOUCESTER CITY 1 TEWKESBURY TOWN 1**
Competition: Gloucestershire Northern Senior League
Teamsheet: Browning, Hamer, Maysey, Tomlinson, Alder, Murdock, Richards, Edwards, Perks, Ringrose, Tucker
Scorer: -----

Appearances – S Alder 29, AFL Ayland 2, F Bailey 2, H Banks 10, F Bayliss 15, HC Browning 30, JT Burton 20, AF Collins 1, GE Dainty 19, G Edwards 30, LS Ford 4, SC Hamer 31, J Kirton 2, M Malpass 4, CH Maysey 1, ? Mills 1, JH Murdin 9, AFT Murdock 15, RH Perks 29, C Richards 1, S Ringrose 27, L Summers 1, G Surman 1, SC Tomlinson 29, CH Tucker 25.

Scorers – G Edwards 24, RH Perks 19, S Ringrose 17, CH Tucker 15, S Alder 5, JT Burton 5, AFT Murdock 3, J Kirton 2, LS Ford 1, JL Malpass 1, JH Murdin 1, G Surman 1, own goal 1.

GLOUCESTERSHIRE NORTHERN SENIOR LEAGUE

POS	CLUB	P	W	D	L	F	A	PTS
1	SHARPNESS	30	23	3	4	109	42	49
2	**GLOUCESTER CITY**	30	21	6	3	104	45	48
3	CHALFORD	30	19	8	3	77	33	46
4	CAM MILLS	30	17	6	7	84	64	38*
5	BROADWELL AMATEURS	30	17	3	10	77	38	37
6	BRIMSCOMBE	30	14	4	12	83	68	32
7	DURSLEY ROVERS	30	14	4	12	82	77	32
8	STONEHOUSE	30	14	1	15	69	69	29
9	TEWKESBURY TOWN	30	11	6	13	62	62	28
10	CHELTENHAM TOWN	30	10	6	14	80	81	26
11	WOODCHESTER	30	9	8	13	76	104	26
12	DURSLEY TOWN	30	7	8	15	52	90	22
13	CADBURY'S ATHLETIC	30	8	4	18	76	79	20
14	CINDERFORD TOWN	30	8	4	18	68	102	20
15	KINGSWOOD	30	5	3	22	63	132	13
16	WOTTON-UNDER-EDGE	30	4	4	22	42	129	12
		480	201	78	201	1204	1215	478

* Two points deducted for playing ineligible man.

SEASON 1926-1927
(Home Ground: Avenue Road Ground, Tuffley Avenue)

It would appear Gloucester City played two first teams this season hence two games on the same day on occasions

Date: Saturday 04/09/1926
Result: **CAM MILLS 5 GLOUCESTER CITY 0**
Competition: Gloucestershire Northern Senior League
Teamsheet: L Gibson, -----, -----, -----, -----, -----, -----, -----, -----, -----, -----
Attendance: 300

Date: Saturday 11/09/1926
Result: **GLOUCESTER CITY 8 WOODCHESTER 2**
Competition: Gloucestershire Northern Senior League
Teamsheet: L Gibson, Clarke, W Ford, Tomlinson, Perrins, Roche, Burton, Day, Tucker, Stone, AF Collins
Scorers: Day, Stone (5), Burton, AF Collins
Attendance: 300

Lemuel Archibald Beddis
Gloucester YMCA/Gloucester City Secretary-Manager 1919-1931

GLOUCESTER CITY 1925-1926
(Photograph courtesy of Des Edwards, son of George Edwards)

A. Murdin.   J. Harris.   R. Parker.   F. Taylor.   A. H. Smith.   W. Ingles.   C. Maysey.
W. J. Courtice.   A. Billingham.   J. Price.   A. Ayland.   S. Hamer.   H. Browning.   F. Bayliss.   L. Ford.   J. Baker.   A. Burton.   G. H. Bishop (Vice-Chairman).
W. Rea   L. A. Beddis   A. Wybrow (Chairman).   A. Burton.   C. Tucker.   S. Alder (Capt.)   G. Dainty.   S. Ringrose (Vice-Capt.)   R. Skevington   F. Speck
(Trainer)   (Hon. Sec.)   W. Stokes.   G. Edwards.   S. Tomlinson.   (Treasurer)   (Trainer)

[41]

1926 to 1928
George Edwards was club captain during this period and appeared both in goal and as a winger as these two photographs testify
(Photographs courtesy of Des Edwards)

28 April 1928
Gloucester City v Tottenham Hotspur Reserves in a friendly at Sutgrove Park which ended 3-3. George Edwards is the goalkeeper
(Photographs courtesy of Des Edwards)

[42]

GLOUCESTER CITY v. DURSLEY TOWN.

"By TEEK."

GLOUCESTER CITY v. BRISTOL CITY RESERVES.

By "TEEK."

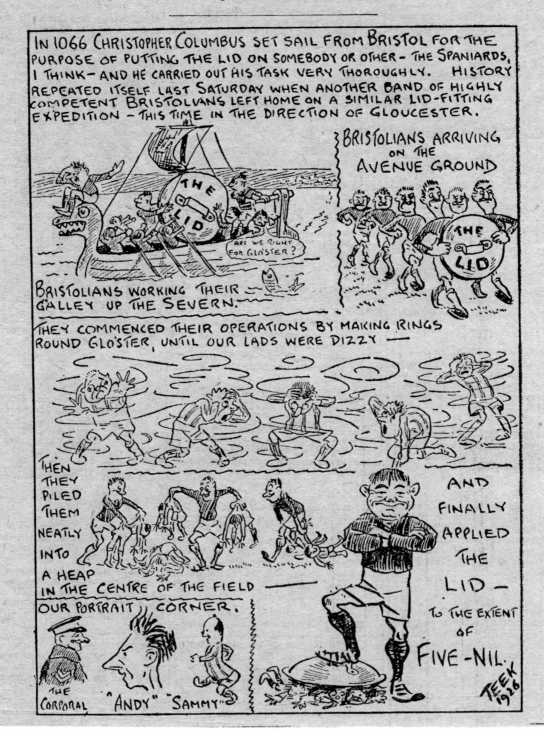

IN 1066 CHRISTOPHER COLUMBUS SET SAIL FROM BRISTOL FOR THE PURPOSE OF PUTTING THE LID ON SOMEBODY OR OTHER - THE SPANIARDS, I THINK - AND HE CARRIED OUT HIS TASK VERY THOROUGHLY. HISTORY REPEATED ITSELF LAST SATURDAY WHEN ANOTHER BAND OF HIGHLY COMPETENT BRISTOLIANS LEFT HOME ON A SIMILAR LID-FITTING EXPEDITION - THIS TIME IN THE DIRECTION OF GLOUCESTER.

BRISTOLIANS ARRIVING ON THE AVENUE GROUND

ARF WE RIGHT FOR GLO'STER?

THE LID

BRISTOLIANS WORKING THEIR GALLEY UP THE SEVERN.

THEY COMMENCED THEIR OPERATIONS BY MAKING RINGS ROUND GLO'STER, UNTIL OUR LADS WERE DIZZY —

THEN THEY PILED THEM NEATLY INTO A HEAP IN THE CENTRE OF THE FIELD —

AND FINALLY APPLIED THE LID — TO THE EXTENT OF FIVE-NIL.

OUR PORTRAIT CORNER.

THE CORPORAL "ANDY" "SAMMY"

TEEK 1926

SEASON BY SEASON

Date: Saturday 11/09/1926
Result: **WELTON ROVERS 7 GLOUCESTER CITY 2**
Competition: Bristol Charity League
Teamsheet: Browning, Hamer, Williams, -----, Alder, Murdock, Perks, Edwards, Ringrose, Marler, Turner
Scorers: Ringrose, Perks

Date: Saturday 18/09/1926
Result: **GLOUCESTER CITY 1 CHELTENHAM TOWN 2**
Competition: Gloucestershire Northern Senior League
Teamsheet: L Gibson, Dainty, Roche, Eamer, Tucker, Doel, Burton, Beddis, Turner, AF Collins, Murdin
Scorer: AF Collins

Date: Thursday 23/09/1926
Result: **GLOUCESTER CITY 0 TEWKESBURY TOWN 1**
Competition: Gloucestershire Northern Senior League
Teamsheet: L Gibson, Williams, Roche, Dainty, Tucker, Doel, Edwards, Eamer, Aubrey, AF Collins, Turner

Date: Saturday 25/09/1926
Result: **WOTTON-UNDER-EDGE 4 GLOUCESTER CITY 2**
Competition: Gloucestershire Northern Senior League
Teamsheet: L Gibson, Speck, Roche, Dainty, Perrin, Doel, Ayland, Day, Aubrey, AF Collins, Turner
Scorers: -----, -----

Date: Saturday 02/10/1926
Result: **GLOUCESTER CITY 3 CADBURY'S ATHLETIC 3**
Competition: Gloucestershire Northern Senior League
Teamsheet: L Gibson, D Collins, Roche, Ayland, Tomlinson, Doel, Eamer, Day, Surman, Aubrey, AF Collins
Scorers: Eamer, Day, Surman

Date: Saturday 09/10/1926
Result: **KINGSWOOD 3 GLOUCESTER CITY 2**
Competition: Gloucestershire Northern Senior League
Teamsheet: L Gibson, D Collins, Roche, Dainty, Tucker, Doel, Eamer, Day, Aubrey, Surman, AF Collins
Scorers: -----, -----

Date: Saturday 09/10/1926
Result: **KINGSWOOD 3 GLOUCESTER CITY 1**
Competition: English Amateur Cup 1st Qualifying Round
Teamsheet: Browning, Hamer, Williams, Perrins, Alder, Murdock, Edwards, Ringrose, Perks, Marler, Turner
Scorer: Perks

Date: Saturday 16/10/1926
Result: **BRIMSCOMBE 1 GLOUCESTER CITY 1**
Competition: Gloucestershire Northern Senior League
Teamsheet: L Gibson, Banks, Roche, Dainty, Surman, Doel, Richards, Aubrey, Tucker, Perrin, AF Collins
Scorer: -----

Date: Saturday 23/10/1926
Result: **CINDERFORD TOWN 5 GLOUCESTER CITY 3**
Competition: Gloucestershire Northern Senior League
Teamsheet: L Gibson, Banks, Roche, Tomlinson, Surman, Doel, Richards, Aubrey, Tucker, Dainty, AF Collins
Scorers: -----, -----, -----

Date: Saturday 30/10/1926
Result: **GLOUCESTER CITY 2 DURSLEY ROVERS 0**
Competition: Gloucestershire Northern Senior League
Teamsheet: L Gibson, Banks, Roche, Ayland, Tomlinson, Doel, Richards, Surman, Aubrey, Tucker, AF Collins
Scorer: Surman (2)

Date: Saturday 06/11/1926
Result: **BROADWELL AMATEURS 5 GLOUCESTER CITY 0**
Competition: Gloucestershire Northern Senior League
Teamsheet: L Gibson, D Collins, Roche, Ayland, Tomlinson, Doel, Richards, Surman, Aubrey, Tucker, AJ Gibson

Date: Saturday 20/11/1926
Result: **GLOUCESTER CITY 1 WELTON ROVERS 3**
Competition: Bristol Charity League
Teamsheet: Browning, Hamer, Williams, Tomlinson, Alder, Murdock, Burton, Edwards, Perks, Tucker, AF Collins
Scorer: Perks

Date: Saturday 27/11/1926
Result: **DURSLEY ROVERS 4 GLOUCESTER CITY 3**
Competition: Gloucestershire Northern Senior League
Teamsheet: L Gibson, Gent, Roche, Dainty, HF Kibble, Doel, Perrins, Ringrose, Aubrey, AJ Gibson, Tucker
Scorers: Doel, Aubrey, Perrins

Date: Saturday 04/12/1926
Result: **GLOUCESTER CITY 6 WOTTON-UNDER-EDGE 1**
Competition: Gloucestershire Northern Senior League
Teamsheet: Surman, Alder, Banks, Aubrey, HF Kibble, Bampton, Perks, Ringrose, Perrins, DL Kibble, AF Collins
Scorers: Ringrose, AF Collins, Perks (2), DL Kibble, HF Kibble

Date; Saturday 11/12/1926
Result: **GLOUCESTER CITY 13 FAIRFORD TOWN 0**
Competition: Gloucestershire FA Northern Senior Amateur Cup 1st Round
Teamsheet: Browning, Hamer, Williams, Tomlinson, Alder, Murdock, Edwards, Ringrose, Perks, Marler, AF Collins
Scorers: Perks (7), Marler (5), AF Collins

Date: Sunday 26/12/1926
Result: **CHALFORD 6 GLOUCESTER CITY 1**
Competition: Gloucestershire Northern Senior League
Teamsheet: L Gibson, Roche, Banks, Aubrey, HF Kibble, Dainty, Richards, Day, Perks, AJ Gibson, AF Collins
Scorer: -----

[45]

Date: Monday 27/12/1926
Result: **RADSTOCK TOWN 5 GLOUCESTER CITY 2**
Competition: Bristol Charity League
Teamsheet: Browning, Hamer, Williams, Aubrey, Alder, Murdock, Burton, Edwards, Perks, Tucker, DL Kibble
Scorers: Aubrey, Burton

Date: Saturday 01/01/1927
Result: **TEWKESBURY TOWN 5 GLOUCESTER CITY 1**
Competition: Gloucestershire Northern Senior League
Teamsheet: L Gibson, Banks, Roche, Dainty, HF Kibble, Doel, -----, Aubrey, AJ Gibson, Surman, AF Collins
Scorer: -----

Date: Saturday 01/01/1927
Result: **GLOUCESTER CITY 6 SUNNINGEND 0**
Competition: Gloucestershire FA Northern Senior Amateur Cup 2nd Round
Teamsheet: Browning, Perrins, Williams, Tomlinson, Alder, Murdock, Tucker, Ringrose, Perks, DL Kibble, Edwards
Scorers: Perks (3), Ringrose (2), Tucker

Date: Saturday 08/01/1927
Result: **GLOUCESTER CITY 3 KINGSWOOD 3**
Competition: Gloucestershire Northern Senior League
Teamsheet: L Gibson, Perrins (?), -----, -----, HF Kibble, -----, Burton, -----, -----, -----, -----
Scorer: Burton (3)

Date: Saturday 15/01/1927
Result: **CADBURY'S ATHLETIC 7 GLOUCESTER CITY 2**
Competition: Gloucestershire Northern Senior League
Teamsheet: L Gibson, Perrins, Banks, Dainty, HF Kibble, Doel, Ricks, May, Roche, AJ Gibson, Burton
Scorers: -----, -----

Date: Saturday 22/01/1927
Result: **GLOUCESTER CITY 4 BROADWELL AMATEURS 2**
Competition: Gloucestershire FA Northern Senior Amateur Cup 3rd Round
Teamsheet: Browning, Hamer, Williams, Tomlinson, Alder, Murdock, Edwards, Ringrose, Perks, Marler, DL Kibble
Scorers: Marler, Perks (2), Edwards

Date: Saturday 29/01/1927
Result: **CHELTENHAM TOWN 4 GLOUCESTER CITY 1**
Competition: Gloucestershire Northern Senior League
Teamsheet: L Gibson, L Ford, Banks, Dainty, HF Kibble, Doel, Richards, Aubrey, AJ Gibson, Surman, AF Collins
Scorer: Banks

Date: Saturday 05/02/1927
Result: **FOREST GREEN ROVERS 1 GLOUCESTER CITY 7**
Competition: Gloucestershire Northern Senior League
Teamsheet: L Gibson, L Ford, Banks, Dainty, HF Kibble, Maysey, Burton, Aubrey, Surman, Doel, Roche
Scorers: -----, -----, -----, -----, -----, -----, -----

Date: Saturday 05/02/1927
Result: **GLOUCESTER CITY 3 FROME TOWN 3**
Competition: Bristol Charity League
Teamsheet: Browning, Hamer, Williams, Tomlinson, Alder, Murdock, Edwards, Ringrose, Perks, Marler, DL Kibble
Scorers: Perks, Ringrose, Marler

Date: Saturday 12/02/1927
Result: **SHARPNESS 6 GLOUCESTER CITY 2**
Competition: Gloucestershire FA Northern Senior Amateur Cup Semi-Final
Teamsheet: Browning, Hamer, Williams, Tomlinson, Alder, Murdock, Edwards, Ringrose, Perks, Marler, DL Kibble
Scorers: -----, -----

Date: Saturday 19/02/1927
Result: **STONEHOUSE 7 GLOUCESTER CITY 0**
Competition: Gloucestershire Northern Senior League
Teamsheet: L Gibson, L Ford, Maysey, Dainty, HF Kibble, Doel, AJ Gibson, Aubrey, May, Surman, Roche

Date: Saturday 26/02/1927
Result: **GLOUCESTER CITY 2 BRIMSCOMBE 3**
Competition: Gloucestershire Northern Senior League
Teamsheet: L Gibson, Banks, Maysey, Aubrey, Tomlinson, DL Kibble, Burton, Alder, Perks, L Ford, Roche
Scorers: Perks, Burton

Date: Saturday 12/03/1927
Result: **GLOUCESTER CITY 0 CAM MILLS 0**
Competition: Gloucestershire Northern Senior League
Teamsheet: L Gibson, Hamer, Banks, Edwards, Alder, Tomlinson, Aubrey, Tucker, Perks, Marler, Burton
Note: Played at Co-operative Field, India Road

Date: Saturday 26/03/1927 (3pm)
Result: **GLOUCESTER CITY 0 FOREST GREEN ROVERS 4**
Competition: Gloucestershire Northern Senior League
Teamsheet: Browning, Hamer, Williams, Dainty, Alder, Murdock, Edwards, Ringrose, Perks, Marler, AF Collins

Date: Saturday 26/03/1927 (5pm)
Result: **GLOUCESTER CITY 6 CHALFORD 0**
Competition: Gloucestershire Northern Senior League
Teamsheet: L Gibson, Banks, Maysey, Doel, HF Kibble, Tucker, AJ Gibson, Aubrey, L Ford, Roche, Burton
Scorers: -----, -----, -----, -----, -----, -----

Date: Saturday 02/04/1927
Result: **GLOUCESTER CITY 3 BROADWELL AMATEURS 3**
Competition: Gloucestershire Northern Senior League
Teamsheet: Surman, Maysey, Banks, Dainty, Tomlinson, Speck, Burton, AJ Gibson, Perks, Roche, AF Collins
Scorers: AF Collins, own goal, Perks

Date: Saturday 09/04/1927
Result: **GLOUCESTER CITY 2 PAULTON ROVERS 1**
Competition: Bristol Charity League
Teamsheet: Browning, Hamer, Williams, Edwards, Tomlinson, Aubrey, Tucker, Monks, Perks, Marler, Burton
Scorers: Monks, Perks

Date: Monday 11/04/1927
Result: **GLOUCESTER CITY 2 CINDERFORD TOWN 4**
Competition: Gloucestershire Northern Senior League
Teamsheet: -----, Hamer (?), Williams (?), Edwards (?), Tomlinson (?), -----, Tucker (?), -----, Perks (?), Marler (?), Burton (?)
Scorers: -----, -----

Date: Thursday 14/04/1927
Result: **WOODCHESTER 4 GLOUCESTER CITY 7**
Competition: Gloucestershire Northern Senior League
Teamsheet: L Gibson, Hamer, Williams, L Ford, Tomlinson, Tucker, Burton, Edwards, Perks, Marler, DL Kibble
Scorers: -----, -----, -----, -----, -----, -----, -----

Date: Saturday 16/04/1927
Result: **SHARPNESS 4 GLOUCESTER CITY 2**
Competition: Gloucestershire Northern Senior League
Teamsheet: Edwards, Hamer, Williams, Tomlinson, Alder, Doel, Burton, Tucker, Monks, AF Collins
Scorers: Tucker, AF Collins
Note: Only 10 players used

Date: Monday 18/04/1927
Result: **GLOUCESTER CITY 1 RADSTOCK TOWN 2**
Competition: Bristol Charity League
Teamsheet: -----, Hamer, -----, Doel, Alder, -----, Burton, Tucker, -----, Monks, Edwards (?)
Scorer: Monks

Date: Saturday 23/04/1927
Result: **GLOUCESTER CITY 5 TROWBRIDGE TOWN 4**
Competition: Bristol Charity League
Teamsheet: Browning, Hamer, Roche, Doel, Alder, Monks, Burton, Tucker, Perks, Marler, Edwards
Scorers: Marler (2), Perks (3, 1 pen)

Date: Tuesday 03/05/1927
Result: **TROWBRIDGE TOWN 5 GLOUCESTER CITY 0**
Competition: Bristol Charity League
Teamsheet: Edwards, -----, -----, -----, -----, -----, -----, -----, -----, -----, -----

Date; Saturday 07/05/1927
Result: **PAULTON ROVERS 1 GLOUCESTER CITY 1**
Competition: Bristol Charity League
Teamsheet: -----, -----, -----, -----, -----, -----, -----, -----, -----, -----, -----
Scorer: -----

Date: ?
Result: **GLOUCESTER CITY 2 SHARPNESS 4**
Competition: Gloucestershire Northern Senior League
Teamsheet: -----, -----, -----, -----, -----, -----, -----, -----, -----, -----, -----
Scorers: -----, -----

Date: ?
Result: **GLOUCESTER CITY 3 STONEHOUSE 2**
Competition: Gloucestershire Northern Senior League
Teamsheet: -----, -----, -----, -----, -----, -----, -----, -----, -----, -----, -----
Scorers: -----, -----, -----

Appearances – S Alder 17, R Aubrey 20, AFL Ayland 3, G Bampton 1, H Banks 13, LA Beddis 1, HC Browning 13, JT Burton 17, W Clarke 1, AF Collins 18, D Collins 3, GE Dainty 15, J Day 5, HE Doel 19, A Eamer 4, G Edwards 19, LS Ford 7, W Ford 1, A Gent 1, AJ Gibson 9, L Gibson 23, SC Hamer 17, DL Kibble 9, HF Kibble 11, LA Marler 13, R May 3, CH Maysey 5, E Monks 5, JH Murdin 1, AFT Murdock 10, RH Perks 19, J Perrins 9, C Richards 6, B Ricks 1, S Ringrose 10, S Roche 20, AF Speck 2, W Stone 1, G Surman 13, SC Tomlinson 18, CH Tucker 22, E Turner 5, S Williams 16.
Scorers – RH Perks 18, LA Marler 9, AF Collins 7, JT Burton 6, S Ringrose 6, W Stone 5, R Aubrey 2, J Day 2, R May 2, E Monks 2, G Surman 2, CH Tucker 2, S Alder 1, H Banks 1, HE Doel 1, A Eamer 1, G Edwards 1, DL Kibble 1, HF Kibble 1, J Perrins 1, own goal 1.

SEASON BY SEASON

GLOUCESTERSHIRE NORTHERN SENIOR LEAGUE

POS	CLUB	P	W	D	L	F	A	PTS
1	SHARPNESS	30	26	2	2	138	34	54
2	FOREST GREEN ROVERS	30	24	2	4	95	44	50
3	CHELTENHAM TOWN	30	22	5	3	110	46	49
4	TEWKESBURY TOWN	30	17	4	9	108	65	38
5	BRIMSCOMBE	30	14	5	11	86	83	33
6	CHALFORD	30	16	1	13	88	69	31*
7	BROADWELL AMATEURS	30	11	9	10	84	74	31
8	STONEHOUSE	30	14	2	14	103	80	30
9	CAM MILLS	30	12	3	15	85	84	27
10	CADBURY'S ATHLETIC	30	11	4	15	89	95	26
11	CINDERFORD TOWN	30	9	3	18	71	97	21
12	WOODCHESTER	30	9	3	18	75	111	21
13	GLOUCESTER CITY	30	7	5	18	64	98	17*
14	DURSLEY ROVERS	30	5	6	19	65	106	16
15	KINGSWOOD	30	6	4	20	62	128	16
16	WOTTON-UNDER-EDGE	30	7	2	21	61	170	16
		480	210	60	210	1384	1384	476

* Two points deducted for playing ineligible players.

BRISTOL CHARITY LEAGUE

POS	CLUB	P	W	D	L	F	A	PTS
1	WELTON ROVERS	10	7	3	0	38	11	17
2	RADSTOCK TOWN	10	7	1	2	29	15	15
3	FROME TOWN	9	3	4	2	15	19	10
4	GLOUCESTER CITY	10	2	3	5	20	34	7
5	TROWBRIDGE TOWN	9	2	1	6	20	30	5
6	PAULTON ROVERS	10	0	4	6	12	23	4
		58	21	16	21	134	132	58

Table as at 7 May 1927.

SEASON 1927-1928
(Home Ground: Sutgrove Park, Calton Road/Stroud Road)

Date: Saturday 10/09/1927
Result: **GLOUCESTER CITY 1 VINEY HILL 5**
Competition: Gloucestershire Northern Senior League
Teamsheet: Bourton, Dyke, S Alder, HF Kibble, Monks, Doel, Edwards, Tingle, Beale, Marler, Mace
Scorer: Tingle

Date: Thursday 15/09/1927
Result: **GLOUCESTER CITY 1 CHELTENHAM TOWN 2**
Competition: Gloucestershire Northern Senior League
Teamsheet: Edwards, Maysey, S Alder, HF Kibble, Monks, Doel, Stephens, Tingle, Marler, Tucker, DL Kibble
Scorer: Tucker

Date: Saturday 24/09/1927
Result: **CHELTENHAM TOWN 5 GLOUCESTER CITY 4**
Competition: Gloucestershire Northern Senior League
Teamsheet: Bourton, Tanner, Bayliss, Monks, HF Kibble, Tucker, Stephens, Edwards, Tingle, Marler, DL Kibble
Scorers: Stephens, Bayliss, Edwards, Marler

Date: Thursday 29/09/1927
Result: **GLOUCESTER CITY 1 BRISTOL CITY RESERVES 4**
Competition: Bristol Charity League
Teamsheet: Bourton, Bayliss (?), Williams, -----, HF Kibble, Murdock, Edwards, Tucker, Tingle, Stephens, DL Kibble
Scorer: Edwards (pen)

Date: Saturday 01/10/1927
Result: **CAM MILLS 1 GLOUCESTER CITY 10**
Competition: Gloucestershire Northern Senior League
Teamsheet: Bourton, Bayliss, Maysey, Tucker, HF Kibble, Doel, Edwards, Monks, Tingle, Marler, Stephens
Scorers: Monks (3), Marler (2), Edwards (2), Stephens (2), Tingle

Date: Saturday 08/10/1927
Result: **GLOUCESTER CITY 4 SNEYD PARK 2**
Competition: English Amateur Cup 1st Qualifying Round
Teamsheet: Bourton, Williams, Bridges, -----, HF Kibble, -----, Edwards, Monks, Stephens, Marler, DL Kibble
Scorers: Edwards (2), DL Kibble, Stephens

Date: Saturday 15/10/1927
Result: **CHEPSTOW TOWN 4 GLOUCESTER CITY 1**
Competition: Gloucestershire Northern Senior League
Teamsheet: Bourton (?), Williams (?), Bridges (?), -----, HF Kibble (?), -----, Edwards (?), Monks (?), Stephens (?), Marler (?), DL Kibble (?)
Scorer: -----

Date: Saturday 22/10/1927
Result: **GLOUCESTER CITY 1 SAINT PHILIPS ATHLETIC 2**
Competition: English Amateur Cup 2nd Qualifying Round
Teamsheet: Bourton, Bridges, Williams, Tingle, HF Kibble, Tucker, Edwards, Monks, Stephens, Marler, DL Kibble
Scorer: Williams

Date: Saturday 05/11/1927
Result: **GLOUCESTER CITY 6 SHARPNESS 2**
Competition: Gloucestershire Northern Senior League
Teamsheet: Edwards, Hamer, Bayliss, Tucker, HF Kibble, Aubrey, Stephens, Monks, Tingle, DL Kibble, Tucker
Scorers: Tucker (3), Tingle (2), DL Kibble

Date: Saturday 26/11/1927
Result: **BRISTOL CITY RESERVES 11 GLOUCESTER CITY 0**
Competition: Bristol Charity League
Teamsheet: Edwards, Hamer, Williams, S Alder, HF Kibble, Doel, -----, Monks (?), -----, DL Kibble (?), Tucker (?)

Date: Saturday 10/12/1927
Result: **GLOUCESTER CITY 5 BROADWELL AMATEURS 0**
Competition: Gloucestershire Northern Senior League
Teamsheet: Edwards, Hamer, Bridges, S Alder, Brain, Goddard, Murdock, Monks, Bayliss, DL Kibble, Tucker
Scorers: Tucker (3), DL Kibble, Goddard

Date: Saturday 17/12/1927
Result: **GLOUCESTER CITY 2 CHELTENHAM TOWN 1**
Competition: Bristol Charity League
Teamsheet: Edwards (?), Hamer (?), -----, S Alder (?), Brain (?), Goddard, -----, Monks, -----, DL Kibble, Tucker
Scorers: Monks, DL Kibble

Date: Saturday 24/12/1927
Result: **GLOUCESTER CITY 5 TEWKESBURY TOWN 1**
Competition: Gloucestershire Northern Senior League
Teamsheet: Edwards, Hamer, Williams, S Alder, Brain, Murdock, -----, Monks, Tingle, DL Kibble, -----
Scorers: Monks (3), Tingle, own goal

Date: Saturday 07/01/1928
Result: **SHARPNESS 4 GLOUCESTER CITY 2**
Competition: Gloucestershire FA Northern Senior Amateur Cup 1st Round
Teamsheet: Edwards, Hamer, HF Kibble, S Alder, Brain, Doel, Murdock, Goddard, Tingle, Monks, DL Kibble
Scorers: Murdock, Tingle

Date: Saturday 21/01/1928
Result: **GLOUCESTER CITY 1 CHEPSTOW TOWN 0**
Competition: Gloucestershire Northern Senior League
Teamsheet: Edwards, Hamer, Ford, S Alder, Brain, Murdock, Bayliss, Goddard, Tucker, Marler, Skipp
Scorer: Tucker

Date: Saturday 04/02/1928
Result: **VINEY HILL 1 GLOUCESTER CITY 0**
Competition: Gloucestershire Northern Senior League
Teamsheet: Edwards, Hamer, Ford, S Alder, Brain, Murdock, Goddard, Aubrey, Ringrose, Tucker, Bayliss

Date: Saturday 11/02/1928
Result: **BROADWELL AMATEURS 1 GLOUCESTER CITY 4**
Competition: Gloucestershire Northern Senior League
Teamsheet: Edwards, Hamer, S Alder, Doel, Brain, Murdock, Goddard, Aubrey, Ringrose, Jackson, Bayliss
Scorers: -----, -----, -----, -----

Date: Saturday 18/02/1928
Result: **CINDERFORD TOWN 1 GLOUCESTER CITY 3**
Competition: Gloucestershire Northern Senior League
Teamsheet: Edwards, Hamer, S Alder, Doel, Brain, Murdock, Goddard, Aubrey, Jackson, -----, Bayliss
Scorers: -----, -----, -----

Date: Saturday 25/02/1928
Result: **GLOUCESTER CITY 1 CINDERFORD TOWN 1**
Competition: Gloucestershire Northern Senior League
Teamsheet: Edwards, Hamer, S Alder, Doel, Brain, Murdock, Goddard, Aubrey, Jackson, Bayliss, DL Kibble
Scorer: -----

Date: Saturday 10/03/1928
Result: **SHARPNESS 3 GLOUCESTER CITY 2**
Competition: Gloucestershire Northern Senior League
Teamsheet: Edwards, Hamer, S Alder, Doel, Brain, Murdock, Goddard, Aubrey, Jackson, Bayliss, DL Kibble
Scorer: Jackson (2)

Date: Saturday 24/03/1928
Result: **CADBURY'S ATHLETIC 1 GLOUCESTER CITY 6**
Competition: Gloucestershire Northern Senior League
Teamsheet: Edwards, Hamer, S Alder, Murdock, Brain, Doel, Aubrey, Goddard, Jackson, -----, DL Kibble
Scorers: -----, -----, -----, -----, -----, -----

Date: Saturday 31/03/1928
Result: **GLOUCESTER CITY 2 CAM MILLS 3**
Competition: Gloucestershire Northern Senior League
Teamsheet: Edwards, Hamer, -----, Doel, Brain, Murdock, Goddard, Aubrey, Jackson, Marler, DL Kibble
Scorers: -----, -----

Date: Friday 06/04/1928
Result: **CLEVEDON 3 GLOUCESTER CITY 2**
Competition: Bristol Charity League
Teamsheet: -----, -----, -----, -----, -----, -----, -----, Aubrey (?), Jackson (?), Marler (?), DL Kibble (?)
Scorers: -----, -----

Date: Saturday 07/04/1928
Result: **GLOUCESTER CITY 4 CADBURY'S ATHLETIC 0**
Competition: Gloucestershire Northern Senior League
Teamsheet: -----, -----, -----, -----, -----, -----, -----, Aubrey, Jackson, Marler, DL Kibble
Scorers: DL Kibble, Marler (2), Aubrey

Date: Monday 09/04/1928
Result: **GLOUCESTER CITY 2 SHARPNESS 1**
Competition: Bristol Charity League
Teamsheet: -----, -----, -----, -----, -----, -----, Monks, Jackson, Ringrose, DL Kibble (?)
Scorers: Monks, Ringrose

Date: Tuesday 10/04/1928
Result: **GLOUCESTER CITY 3 CLEVEDON 1**
Competition: Bristol Charity League
Teamsheet: Bourton, S Alder, -----, Doel, HF Kibble, Murdock, Goddard, Ringrose, Jackson, DL Kibble, Green
Scorers: Jackson (2), Murdock

Date: Thursday 12/04/1928
Result: **TEWKESBURY TOWN 2 GLOUCESTER CITY 0**
Competition: Gloucestershire Northern Senior League
Teamsheet: -----, -----, -----, -----, -----, -----, -----, -----, -----, -----, -----

Date: Wednesday 18/04/1928
Result: **CHELTENHAM TOWN 4 GLOUCESTER CITY 1**
Competition: Bristol Charity League
Teamsheet: -----, -----, -----, -----, -----, -----, -----, -----, -----, Marler, -----
Scorer: Marler

Date: Saturday 21/04/1928
Result: **GLOUCESTER CITY 1 WELTON ROVERS 3**
Competition: Bristol Charity League
Teamsheet: Edwards, Hamer, S Alder, Doel, PK Alder, Murdock, Goddard, Ringrose, -----, Marler, Green
Scorer: Marler

Date: Thursday 26/04/1928
Result: **SHARPNESS ? GLOUCESTER CITY ?**
Competition: Bristol Charity League
Teamsheet: -----, Hamer (?), S Alder (?), Doel (?), PK Alder (?), Murdock (?), Goddard (?), -----, Ringrose (?), Marler (?), -----

Date: Saturday 05/05/1928
Result: **WELTON ROVERS ? GLOUCESTER CITY ?**
Competition: Bristol Charity League
Teamsheet: Bourton, S Alder, Hamer, Doel, PK Alder, Murdock, Goddard, Brain, Ringrose, Marler, Monks

Appearances – PK Alder 3, S Alder 19, R Aubrey 9, F Bayliss 11, W Beale 1, HC Bourton 9, W Brain 14, S Bridges 4, HE Doel 15, JG Dyke 1, G Edwards 23, LS Ford 3, N Goddard 17, H Green 2, SC Hamer 18, R Jackson 9, DL Kibble 19, HF Kibble 12, A Mace 1, LA Marler 15, CH Maysey 2, E Monks 17, AFT Murdock 17, S Ringrose 7, R Skipp 2, EJ Stephens 8, WG Tanner 1, HC Tingle 9, CH Tucker 12, S Williams 6.
Scorers – CH Tucker 8, HC Tingle 6, E Monks 5, G Edwards 4, R Jackson 4, DL Kibble 4, EJ Stephens 4, LA Marler 3, AFT Murdock 2, F Bayliss 1, G Goddard 1, S Ringrose 1, S Williams 1, own goal 1.

GLOUCESTERSHIRE NORTHERN SENIOR LEAGUE

POS	CLUB	P	W	D	L	F	A	PTS
1	SHARPNESS	18	13	3	2	81	36	29
2	CHELTENHAM TOWN	18	11	2	5	85	52	24
3	CHEPSTOW TOWN	18	11	0	7	59	39	22
4	VINEY HILL	18	9	4	5	58	39	22
5	**GLOUCESTER CITY**	18	9	1	8	54	32	19
6	TEWKESBURY TOWN	18	8	1	9	52	57	17
7	CINDERFORD TOWN	18	7	2	9	54	57	16
8	BROADWELL AMATEURS	18	5	4	9	41	57	14
9	CADBURY'S ATHLETIC	18	4	1	13	27	87	9
10	CAM MILLS	18	4	0	14	43	98	8
		180	81	18	81	554	554	180

BRISTOL CHARITY LEAGUE

POS	CLUB	P	W	D	L	F	A	PTS
1	BRISTOL CITY RESERVES	10	9	0	1	67	11	18
2	WELTON ROVERS	10	9	0	1	53	20	18
3	CLEVEDON	10	3	1	6	26	44	7
4	SHARPNESS	10	2	2	6	25	36	6
5	**GLOUCESTER CITY**	10	3	0	7	16	40	6
6	CHELTENHAM TOWN	10	2	1	7	24	60	5
		60	28	4	28	211	211	60

Championship Play-off: Welton Rovers 0 Bristol City Reserves 4

SEASON 1928-1929
(Home Ground: Sutgrove Park, Calton Road/Stroud Road)

Date: Saturday 01/09/1928
Result: **GLOUCESTER CITY 2 CHELTENHAM TOWN 1**
Competition: FA Cup Extra Preliminary Round
Teamsheet: Edwards, Hamer, S Alder, Doel, PK Alder, AFT Murdock, Gough, Tingle, Tucker, Marler, AF Collins
Scorers: Tucker, S Alder (pen)

Date: Saturday 15/09/1928
Result: **SPENCER MOULTON 1 GLOUCESTER CITY 0**
Competition: FA Cup Preliminary Round
Teamsheet: Edwards, Hamer, S Alder, Doel, PK Alder, AFT Murdock, Gough, Marler, Tingle, Tucker, AF Collins

Date: Saturday 06/10/1928
Result: **CHALFORD 2 GLOUCESTER CITY 3**
Competition: English Amateur Cup 1st Qualifying Round
Teamsheet: Edwards, Hamer, Quick, Doel, PK Alder, AFT Murdock (?), Radford, Gough, Tucker, Tingle, Marler
Scorers: Marler (2), Tingle

Date: Saturday 20/10/1928
Result: **HANHAM ATHLETIC 4 GLOUCESTER CITY 2**
Competition: English Amateur Cup 2nd Qualifying Round
Teamsheet: Edwards, Hamer, Parker, Doel, PK Alder, AFT Murdock, Goodman, Marler, Tucker, AF Collins, Tingle
Scorers: -----, -----

Date: Saturday 27/10/1928
Result: **GLOUCESTER CITY 3 VINEY HILL 0**
Competition: Gloucestershire Northern Senior League
Teamsheet: Edwards, Hamer, PK Alder, Doel, Kibble, AFT Murdock, Radford, Marler, Apperley, Carter, Tingle
Scorers: -----, -----, -----

Date: Saturday 03/11/1928
Result: **FOREST GREEN ROVERS 1 GLOUCESTER CITY 0**
Competition: Gloucestershire Northern Senior League
Teamsheet: Edwards, Hamer, Round, Dainty, PK Alder, AFT Murdock, Doel, Marler, Apperley, Carter, Tingle

Date: Saturday 10/11/1928
Result: **GLOUCESTER CITY 3 LISTER'S WORKS 0**
Competition: Gloucestershire Northern Senior League
Teamsheet: Edwards, Hamer, PK Alder, Dean, AFT Murdock, Tucker, Doel, Marler, Apperley, Carter, Tingle
Scorers: -----, -----, -----

Date: Saturday 17/11/1928
Result: **GLOUCESTER CITY 1 WOODCHESTER 4**
Competition: Gloucestershire Northern Senior League
Teamsheet: White, Hamer, S Alder, Dean, AFT Murdock, Dainty, Doel, Marler, Apperley, Carter, Tingle
Scorer: -----

Date: Saturday 24/11/1928
Result: **CINDERFORD TOWN 1 GLOUCESTER CITY 0**
Competition: Gloucestershire Northern Senior League
Teamsheet: Edwards, PK Alder, Goodman, AFT Murdock, Hamer, Tucker, Doel, Marler, Apperley, Carter, Tingle

Date: Saturday 01/12/1928
Result: **BREAM AMATEURS 1 GLOUCESTER CITY 2**
Competition: Gloucestershire Northern Senior League
Teamsheet: Edwards (?), PK Alder (?), -----, AFT Murdock (?), Hamer (?), Tucker (?), Doel (?), Marler (?), Apperley (?), Carter (?), Tingle (?)
Scorers: -----, -----

Date: Saturday 08/12/1928
Result: **GLOUCESTER CITY 0 CHEPSTOW TOWN 2**
Competition: Gloucestershire FA Northern Senior Amateur Cup 1st Round
Teamsheet (from): Edwards, S Alder, PK Alder, AFT Murdock, Hamer, Tucker, Doel, Marler, Tingle, Carter, Dainty, Apperley, Kerslake, AF Collins

Date: Saturday 15/12/1928
Result: **GLOUCESTER CITY 3 CHEPSTOW TOWN 1**
Competition: Gloucestershire Northern Senior League
Teamsheet: Edwards, Hamer, S Alder, Dainty, PK Alder, AFT Murdock, Doel, Carter, Lewis, Apperley, AF Collins
Scorers: Apperley, Lewis, S Alder (pen)

Date: Saturday 29/12/1928
Result: **BROADWELL AMATEURS 8 GLOUCESTER CITY 0**
Competition: Gloucestershire Northern Senior League
Teamsheet: Edwards, Hamer, S Alder, Dainty, PK Alder, AFT Murdock, Doel, Tucker, Apperley, Lewis, AF Collins

Date: Saturday 05/01/1929
Result: **GLOUCESTER CITY 4 BRIMSCOMBE 0**
Competition: Gloucestershire Northern Senior League
Teamsheet: Edwards, Hamer, S Alder, -----, PK Alder, AFT Murdock (?), Doel, Ringrose, Apperley, Tucker (?), AF Collins
Scorers: AF Collins (2), PK Alder, Apperley

Date: Saturday 19/01/1929
Result: **SHARPNESS 7 GLOUCESTER CITY 2**
Competition: Gloucestershire Northern Senior League
Teamsheet: Edwards, Hamer, S Alder, Ford, PK Alder, AFT Murdock, Doel, Marler, Apperley, Tucker, AF Collins
Scorers: -----, -----

Date: Saturday 26/01/1929
Result: **BRIMSCOMBE 0 GLOUCESTER CITY 1**
Competition: Gloucestershire Northern Senior League
Teamsheet: Edwards, Hamer, S Alder, -----, PK Alder, AFT Murdock, Doel, Marler, Turner, Ford, Vick
Scorer: Turner

Date: Saturday 02/02/1929
Result: **GLOUCESTER CITY 2 CINDERFORD TOWN 1**
Competition: Gloucestershire Northern Senior League
Teamsheet: Edwards, Hamer, S Alder, Ford, PK Alder, AFT Murdock, -----, Ringrose, -----, Marler, -----
Scorers: S Alder (pen), Marler

Date: Saturday 09/02/1929
Result: **CHELTENHAM TOWN 3 GLOUCESTER CITY 1**
Competition: Gloucestershire Northern Senior League
Teamsheet: Edwards, Hamer, S Alder, AFT Murdock, PK Alder, Kerslake, Davidson, Ringrose, Apperley, Collins
Scorer: Marler

Date: Saturday 23/02/1929
Result: **TEWKESBURY TOWN 3 GLOUCESTER CITY 2**
Competition: Gloucestershire Northern Senior League
Teamsheet: Edwards, -----, S Alder (?), -----, -----, -----, -----, Ringrose, -----, Apperley
Scorers: Apperley, Ringrose
Note: Only 10 players used

Date: Saturday 02/03/1929
Result: **GLOUCESTER CITY 1 TEWKESBURY TOWN 3**
Competition: Gloucestershire Northern Senior League
Teamsheet: Edwards, Hamer, S Alder, AFT Murdock, PK Alder, Kerslake, Davidson, Ringrose, Apperley, Marler, Tingle
Scorer: Marler

Date: Saturday 09/03/1929
Result: **LISTER'S WORKS 1 GLOUCESTER CITY 0**
Competition: Gloucestershire Northern Senior League
Teamsheet: -----, Hamer (?), -----, AFT Murdock (?), PK Alder (?), Kerslake (?), Davidson (?), -----, Apperley (?), Marler (?), Tingle (?)

Date: Saturday 16/03/1929
Result: **WOODCHESTER 4 GLOUCESTER CITY 3**
Competition: Gloucestershire Northern Senior League
Teamsheet: Browning, Hamer, Tingle, AFT Murdock, PK Alder, Kerslake, Davidson, Edwards, Apperley, Marler, Ayland
Scorers: -----, -----, -----

Date: Tuesday 02/04/1929
Result: **GLOUCESTER CITY 1 BREAM AMATEURS 0**
Competition: Gloucestershire Northern Senior League
Teamsheet: -----, -----, -----, -----, -----, -----, -----, -----, -----, -----, -----
Scorer: -----

Date: Saturday 06/04/1929
Result: **CHEPSTOW TOWN 3 GLOUCESTER CITY 2**
Competition: Gloucestershire Northern Senior League
Teamsheet: -----, -----, -----, -----, -----, -----, -----, -----, -----, -----, -----
Scorers: -----, -----

Date: Thursday 11/04/1929
Result: **GLOUCESTER CITY 0 SHARPNESS 0**
Competition: Gloucestershire Northern Senior League
Teamsheet: -----, -----, -----, -----, -----, -----, -----, -----, -----, -----, -----

Date: Saturday 13/04/1929
Result: **GLOUCESTER CITY 1 BROADWELL AMATEURS 2**
Competition: Gloucestershire Northern Senior League
Teamsheet: Browning, Hamer, Parker, AFT Murdock, PK Alder, Kerslake, Davidson, Edwards, Ringrose, Marler, Apperley
Scorer: Marler

Date: Thursday 18/04/1929
Result: **GLOUCESTER CITY 3 CHELTENHAM TOWN 3**
Competition: Gloucestershire Northern Senior League
Teamsheet: Browning, Parker, Hamer, -----, -----, -----, Davidson, Edwards, Ringrose, -----, -----
Scorers: Davidson, Ringrose, Edwards

Date: Tuesday 23/04/1929
Result: **VINEY HILL 8 GLOUCESTER CITY 0**
Competition: Gloucestershire Northern Senior League
Teamsheet: Browning (?), Parker (?), Hamer (?), -----, -----, -----, Edwards (?), Ringrose (?), -----, -----, -----

Date: Saturday 27/04/1929
Result: **GLOUCESTER CITY 3 FOREST GREEN ROVERS 3**
Competition: Gloucestershire Northern Senior League
Teamsheet: Browning, Ford, Parker, Hamer, PK Alder, GAS Murdock, Edwards, Ringrose, AFT Murdock, Apperley, Tingle
Scorers: Ringrose, Ford, Apperley

Appearances – PK Alder 22, S Alder 13, G Apperley 18, AFL Ayland 1, HC Browning 5, C Carter 8, AF Collins 9, GE Dainty 5, H Davidson 6, C Dean 2, HE Doel 16, G Edwards 24, LS Ford 4, A Goodman 2, N Gough 3, SC Hamer 25, A Kerslake 6, HF Kibble 1, WH Lewis 2, LA Marler 19, AFT Murdock 24, GAS Murdock 1, GW Parker 5, S Quick 1, S Radford 2, S Ringrose 9, S Round 1, HC Tingle 15, CH Tucker 11, E Turner 1, ? Vick 1, G White 1.
Scorers – LA Marler 6, G Apperley 4, S Alder 3, S Ringrose 3, AF Collins 2, PK Alder 1, H Davidson 1, G Edwards 1, LS Ford 1, W Lewis 1, HC Tingle 1, CH Tucker 1, E Turner 1.

GLOUCESTERSHIRE NORTHERN SENIOR LEAGUE

POS	CLUB	P	W	D	L	F	A	PTS
1	CHELTENHAM TOWN	24	19	4	1	107	36	42
2	VINEY HILL	24	16	3	5	91	41	35
3	BROADWELL AMATEURS	24	15	4	5	74	51	34
4	TEWKESBURY TOWN	24	13	4	7	71	49	30
5	SHARPNESS	24	13	2	9	85	61	28
6	CINDERFORD TOWN	24	10	5	9	55	57	25
7	LISTER'S WORKS (Dursley)	24	9	4	11	61	63	22
8	FOREST GREEN ROVERS	24	9	4	11	50	60	22
9	**GLOUCESTER CITY**	**24**	**8**	**3**	**13**	**38**	**57**	**19**
10	BRIMSCOMBE	24	8	2	14	64	84	18
11	CHEPSTOW TOWN	24	8	1	15	60	72	17
12	BREAM AMATEURS	24	4	4	16	39	83	12
13	WOODCHESTER	24	4	0	20	34	115	8
		312	136	40	136	829	829	312

SEASON BY SEASON

SEASON 1929-1930
(Home Ground: Sutgrove Park, Calton Road/Stroud Road)

Date: Saturday 14/09/1929
Result: **GLOUCESTER CITY 1 BRIMSCOMBE 0**
Competition: Gloucestershire Northern Senior League
Teamsheet: Edwards, PK Alder, Parker, Dudfield, Lee, AFT Murdock, Ayland, Ringrose, Taylor, Marler, Mander
Scorer: PK Alder (pen)

Date: Saturday 21/09/1929
Result: **BREAM AMATEURS 0 GLOUCESTER CITY 2**
Competition: Gloucestershire Northern Senior League
Teamsheet: Edwards, PK Alder, Parker, Dainty, AFT Murdock, Dudfield, Ayland, Hickman, Taylor, Marler, Applin
Scorers: -----, -----

Date: Saturday 05/10/1929
Result: **CHEPSTOW TOWN 1 GLOUCESTER CITY 1**
Competition: Gloucestershire Northern Senior League
Teamsheet: Edwards, Mander, Parker, Lee, PK Alder, AFT Murdock, Ayland, Hickman, Taylor, Marler, Applin
Scorer: own goal

Date: Saturday 12/10/1929
Result: **GLOUCESTER CITY 4 BRISTOL SAINT GEORGE 3**
Competition: English Amateur Cup 1st Qualifying Round
Teamsheet: Edwards, Mander, Parker, Lee, PK Alder, AFT Murdock, Ayland, Hickman, Taylor, Marler, Applin
Scorers: Taylor (2), Marler, Applin

Date: Saturday 26/10/1929
Result: **GLOUCESTER CITY 2 BRISTOL SAINT PHILIPS 0** (aet)
Competition: English Amateur Cup 2nd Qualifying Round
Teamsheet: Edwards, Mander, Parker, Lee, PK Alder, AFT Murdock, Ayland, Hickman, Taylor, Marler, Applin
Scorers: Taylor, Hickman

Date: Saturday 02/11/1929
Result: **GLOUCESTER CITY 0 LISTER'S WORKS 1**
Competition: Gloucestershire Northern Senior League
Teamsheet: Edwards, Mander, Parker, Lee, PK Alder, AFT Murdock, Ayland, Hickman, Taylor, Wayman, Applin

Date: Saturday 09/11/1929
Result: **KEYNSHAM TOWN 3 GLOUCESTER CITY 1**
Competition: English Amateur Cup 3rd Qualifying Round
Teamsheet: Edwards, Mander, Parker, Lee (?), PK Alder, AFT Murdock (?), Ayland, Hickman, Taylor, Marler, Applin
Scorer: Marler

Date: Saturday 16/11/1929
Result: **LISTER'S WORKS 3 GLOUCESTER CITY 0**
Competition: Gloucestershire Northern Senior League
Teamsheet: Edwards, Mander, Parker, Lee, PK Alder, AFT Murdock, Ayland, Taylor, Spragg, Marler, Wayman

Date: Saturday 30/11/1929
Result: **CINDERFORD TOWN 0 GLOUCESTER CITY 0**
Competition: Gloucestershire Northern Senior League
Teamsheet: Dudfield, Mander, S Alder, Lee, PK Alder, AFT Murdock, Wayman, Ayland, Taylor, Marler, Applin

Date: Saturday 07/12/1929
Result: **WOODCHESTER 3 GLOUCESTER CITY 4**
Competition: Gloucestershire FA Northern Senior Amateur Cup 1st Round
Teamsheet: Dudfield, Mander, Parker, Lee, PK Alder, AFT Murdock, Ayland, Hickman, Dainty, Marler, Applin
Scorers: PK Alder (pen), Ayland, AFT Murdock, Applin

Date: Saturday 14/12/1929
Result: **BRIMSCOMBE 2 GLOUCESTER CITY 2**
Competition: Gloucestershire Northern Senior League
Teamsheet: Dudfield, S Alder, Parker (?), Lee (?), PK Alder (?), AFT Murdock, Ayland, Hickman, Taylor, Bowker, Applin
Scorers: own goal, Applin

Date: Saturday 21/12/1929
Result: **TEWKESBURY TOWN 3 GLOUCESTER CITY 1**
Competition: Gloucestershire Northern Senior League
Teamsheet: Dudfield, Mander, Parker, Lee, PK Alder, AFT Murdock, Ayland, Hickman, Taylor, Storer, Applin
Scorer: -----

Date: Saturday 28/12/1929
Result: **GLOUCESTER CITY 4 SHARPNESS 2**
Competition: Gloucestershire Northern Senior League
Teamsheet: Dudfield, Parker, Mander, Lee, PK Alder, AFT Murdock, Ayland, Ford, Taylor, Wayman, Applin
Scorers: Taylor (3), AFT Murdock

Date: Saturday 04/01/1930
Result: **EASTINGTON 2 GLOUCESTER CITY 2**
Competition: Gloucestershire FA Northern Senior Amateur Cup 2nd Round
Teamsheet: Dudfield, Mander, Foote, Storer, PK Alder, AFT Murdock, Bowker, Hickman, Taylor, Marler, Applin
Scorer: Taylor (2)

Date: Saturday 11/01/1930
Result: **GLOUCESTER CITY 5 EASTINGTON 1**
Competition: Gloucestershire FA Northern Senior Amateur Cup 2nd Round Replay
Teamsheet: Dudfield, Mander, Parker, Edwards, PK Alder, AFT Murdock, Bowker, Hickman, Taylor, Marler, Applin
Scorers: Hickman (2), Taylor, Applin, Marler

Date: Saturday 18/01/1930
Result: **FOREST GREEN ROVERS 3 GLOUCESTER CITY 2**
Competition: Gloucestershire Northern Senior League
Teamsheet: Dudfield, Mander, Parker, Ayland, PK Alder, AFT Murdock, Harrison, Hickman, Taylor, Marler, Applin
Scorer: Marler (2)

Date: Saturday 25/01/1930
Result: **GLOUCESTER CITY 3 LECKHAMPTON 1**
Competition: Gloucestershire FA Northern Senior Amateur Cup 3rd Round
Teamsheet: Dudfield (?), Mander (?), Parker, Ayland, PK Alder (?), AFT Murdock (?), Harrison, -----, Taylor, Marler (?), Applin
Scorers: Taylor, Applin (2)

Date: Saturday 01/02/1930
Result: **GLOUCESTER CITY 3 CINDERFORD TOWN 1**
Competition: Gloucestershire Northern Senior League
Teamsheet: Dudfield, Mander, Parker, GAS Murdock, PK Alder, AFT Murdock, Harrison, Bowker, Taylor, Marler, Applin
Scorers: Marler, Taylor (2)

Date: Saturday 08/02/1930
Result: **CHELTENHAM TOWN 7 GLOUCESTER CITY 2**
Competition: Gloucestershire Northern Senior League
Teamsheet: Dudfield, Mander, S Alder, GAS Murdock, AFT Murdock, Ayland, Harrison, Hickman, Taylor, Marler, Applin
Scorers: S Alder, -----

Date: Saturday 15/02/1930
Result: **GLOUCESTER CITY 1 BROADWELL AMATEURS 2**
Competition: Gloucestershire Northern Senior League
Teamsheet: Dudfield, Mander, Sadler, GAS Murdock, PK Alder, AFT Murdock, Harrison, Bowker, Taylor, Smith, Applin
Scorer: Taylor

Date: Saturday 22/02/1930
Result: **LISTER'S WORKS 3 GLOUCESTER CITY 4**
Competition: Gloucestershire FA Northern Senior Amateur Cup Semi-Final
Teamsheet: Dudfield, Mander, Parker, GAS Murdock, PK Alder, AFT Murdock, Harrison, Hickman, Taylor, Marler, Applin
Scorers: own goal, Taylor (2), Harrison
Note: Played at Stonehouse

Date: Saturday 01/03/1930
Result: **SHARPNESS 2 GLOUCESTER CITY 5**
Competition: Gloucestershire Northern Senior League
Teamsheet: Dudfield, Mander, Parker, GAS Murdock, PK Alder, AFT Murdock, Harrison, Hickman, Taylor, Marler, Applin
Scorers: -----, -----, -----, -----, -----

Date: Saturday 08/03/1930
Result: **GLOUCESTER CITY 2 CHEPSTOW TOWN 2**
Competition: Gloucestershire Northern Senior League
Teamsheet: Dudfield (?), Mander (?), -----, GAS Murdock (?), PK Alder, AFT Murdock (?), Harrison, Hickman, Taylor (?), Marler (?), Applin (?)
Scorers: -----, -----

Date: Saturday 22/03/1930
Result: **BROADWELL AMATEURS 1 GLOUCESTER CITY 0**
Competition: Gloucestershire Northern Senior League
Teamsheet: Dudfield, Mander, S Alder, GAS Murdock, PK Alder, AFT Murdock, Ayland, Hickman, Taylor, Marler, Applin

Date: Saturday 05/04/1930
Result: **VINEY HILL 2 GLOUCESTER CITY 2**
Competition: Gloucestershire Northern Senior League
Teamsheet: Dudfield, Mander, Parker, GAS Murdock, PK Alder, AFT Murdock, Ayland, Harrison, Taylor, Marler, Applin
Scorer: Taylor (2)

Date: Saturday 12/04/1930
Result: **CHELTENHAM TOWN 0 GLOUCESTER CITY 0**
Competition: Gloucestershire FA Northern Senior Amateur Cup Final
Teamsheet: Dudfield, Mander, Parker, GAS Murdock, PK Alder, AFT Murdock, Harrison, Applin, Taylor, LA Marler, S Alder
Attendance: 1440
Note: Played at Tewkesbury

Date: Tuesday 15/04/1930
Result: **GLOUCESTER CITY 2 VINEY HILL 2**
Competition: Gloucestershire Northern Senior League
Teamsheet: Dudfield, Mander, Parker, GAS Murdock, PK Alder, AFT Murdock, Harrison, Smith, Taylor, Marler, Ayland
Scorers: Marler, own goal

Date: Saturday 19/04/1930
Result: **GLOUCESTER CITY 6 BREAM AMATEURS 1**
Competition: Gloucestershire Northern Senior League
Teamsheet: Dudfield, Hamer, Parker, GAS Murdock, PK Alder, AFT Murdock, Ayland, Hickman, Taylor, Marler, Applin
Scorers: own goals (2), Marler (2), Taylor, Applin

Date: Tuesday 22/04/1930
Result: **GLOUCESTER CITY 0 FOREST GREEN ROVERS 0**
Competition: Gloucestershire Northern Senior League
Teamsheet (from): Dudfield, Mander, Parker, GAS Murdock, PK Alder, AFT Murdock, Harrison, Hickman, Applin, Taylor, Marler, S Alder, Ayland, Dee, Smith

Date: Thursday 24/04/1930
Result: **GLOUCESTER CITY 0 CHELTENHAM TOWN 0**
Competition: Gloucestershire Northern Senior League
Teamsheet (from): AFT Murdock, Townsend, Hamer, Parker, PK Alder, Smith, Stirland, Grist, Harrison, Hickman, Taylor, Bishop, Evans, Marler, Applin, Roche
Note: Mostly reserves played as Cup match fixture two days later

[54]

GLOUCESTER CITY 1928-1929
(Photograph courtesy of Des Edwards)

GLOUCESTER CITY 1929-1930

Back row players in suits behind kitted players – unknown, unknown, unknown, W.Taylor(?), unknown
Middle row kitted players – Norman Mander, Harold Hickman, Andy Murdock, James Dudfield, Jock Murdock, Leslie Marler
Front row kitted players – Dick Harrison, Ollie Wayman(?), Percy Alder (Capt), Grahame Parker, George Applin
Seated next to Harrison is Lemuel Beddis (Secretary-Manager)

CITY v. TOWN IN CUP FINAL AT TEWKESBURY

The final of the Senior Cup, between Gloucester and Cheltenham, at Tewkesbury on Saturday, resulted in a goalless draw. LEFT : Geil (Cheltenham) fails to intercept a pass from Taylor (Gloucester), which is being taken by Marler. The members of the Gloucester team are (left to right) : P. Alder, D. Harrison, G. Applin, J. Murdock, J. Dudfield, W. Taylor, A. Murdock, L. Marler, N. Mander, S. Alder and G. Parker.

RECORD BREAKER

Jerry Causon
Most Goals In All Matches – 195
Most Goals In League Matches – 152
Most Goals In Cup Matches – 43
Most Hat-Tricks - 25

Date: Saturday 26/04/1930
Result: **CHELTENHAM TOWN 2 GLOUCESTER CITY 1**
Competition: Gloucestershire FA Northern Senior Amateur Cup Final Replay
Teamsheet: Dudfield, Mander, Parker, GAS Murdock, PK Alder, AFT Murdock, Harrison, Marler, Taylor, Applin, S Alder
Scorer: Taylor
Note: Played at Cirencester

Date: Thursday 01/05/1930
Result: **GLOUCESTER CITY 2 TEWKESBURY TOWN 2**
Competition: Gloucestershire Northern Senior League
Teamsheet: Dudfield, Mander, S Alder, Dainty, PK Alder, AFT Murdock, Harrison, Parker, Taylor, Marler, Applin
Scorers: Parker, Marler

Appearances – PK Alder 31, S Alder 8, G Applin 29, AFL Ayland 21, C Bishop 1, A Bowker 5, GE Dainty 3, F Dee 1, J Dudfield 25, G Edwards 9, T Evans 1, SB Foote 1, LS Ford 1, N Grist 1, SC Hamer 2, WR Harrison 16, HC Hickman 20, E Lee 12, NV Mander 28, LA Marler 27, AFT Murdock 32, GAS Murdock 13, GW Parker 26, S Ringrose 1, S Roche 1, O Sadler 1, L Smith 4, W Spragg 1, AV Stirland 1, G Storer 2, W Taylor 30, T Townsend 1, OF Wayman 4.
Scorers – W Taylor 19, LA Marler 10, G Applin 7, H Hickman 3, PK Alder 2, AFT Murdock 2, S Alder 1, AFL Ayland 1, WR Harrison 1, GW Parker 1, own goals 6.

GLOUCESTERSHIRE NORTHERN SENIOR LEAGUE

POS	CLUB	P	W	D	L	F	A	PTS
1	VINEY HILL	22	16	4	2	79	39	36
2	CHELTENHAM TOWN	22	14	5	3	99	36	33
3	TEWKESBURY TOWN	22	10	5	7	58	44	25
4	CHEPSTOW TOWN	22	10	5	7	69	62	25
5	**GLOUCESTER CITY**	**22**	**6**	**9**	**7**	**38**	**39**	**21**
6	LISTER'S WORKS (Dursley)	22	10	1	11	56	64	21
7	FOREST GREEN ROVERS	22	8	5	9	48	62	21
8	CINDERFORD TOWN	22	9	2	11	49	53	20
9	BROADWELL AMATEURS	22	7	3	12	39	52	17
10	SHARPNESS	22	7	2	13	54	66	16
11	BRIMSCOMBE	22	6	3	13	46	81	15
12	BREAM AMATEURS	22	5	4	13	35	72	14
		264	108	48	108	670	670	264

SEASON 1930-1931
(Home Ground: Sutgrove Park, Calton Road/Stroud Road)

Date: Saturday 06/09/1930
Result: **GLOUCESTER CITY 4 BREAM AMATEURS 0**
Competition: Gloucestershire Northern Senior League
Teamsheet: Dudfield, Hamer, Mander, GAS Murdock, Davies, AFT Murdock, Harrison, Farnell, Tingle, Marler, Applin
Scorers: Marler, GAS Murdock, Applin, -----

Date: Saturday 13/09/1930
Result: GLOUCESTER CITY 3 BROADWELL AMATEURS 0
Competition: Gloucestershire Northern Senior League
Teamsheet: Dudfield, Hamer, Mander, GAS Murdock, Artus, Tingle, Harrison, Dee, Berry, Marler, Applin
Scorers: Harrison, Marler, Dee
Note: Originally League game. Broadwell Amateurs withdrew

Date: Saturday 20/09/1930
Result: **CHEPSTOW TOWN 5 GLOUCESTER CITY 1**
Competition: Gloucestershire Northern Senior League
Teamsheet: Dudfield, Hamer, Mander, AFT Murdock, GAS Murdock, Tingle, Harrison, Artus, Dee, Marler, Applin
Scorer: Harrison

Date: Saturday 27/09/1930
Result: **VINEY HILL 4 GLOUCESTER CITY 1**
Competition: Gloucestershire Northern Senior League
Teamsheet: Dudfield, Mander, Dainty, GAS Murdock, Hamer, AFT Murdock, Harrison, Artus, Causon, Marler, Applin
Scorer: Causon

Date: Saturday 18/10/1930
Result: **TEWKESBURY TOWN 5 GLOUCESTER CITY 2**
Competition: Gloucestershire Northern Senior League
Teamsheet: Dudfield, Hamer (?), Mander, GAS Murdock (?), -----, AFT Murdock (?), Harrison (?), Artus (?), Causon, Marler (?), Applin
Scorer: Causon (2)

Date: Saturday 25/10/1930
Result: **GLOUCESTER CITY 0 WESTON-SUPER-MARE 0** (aet)
Competition: English Amateur Cup 1st Qualifying Round
Teamsheet: Dudfield, Hamer, Mander, GAS Murdock, Fellows, AFT Murdock, Harrison, Artus, Causon, Marler, Applin

Date: Saturday 01/11/1930
Result: **WESTON-SUPER-MARE 1 GLOUCESTER CITY 0**
Competition: English Amateur Cup 1st Qualifying Round Replay
Teamsheet: Dudfield, Hamer, Mander, GAS Murdock, Roche, AFT Murdock, Harrison, Artus, Causon, Kerslake, Applin

Date: Saturday 22/11/1930
Result: **LISTER'S WORKS 3 GLOUCESTER CITY 3**
Competition: Gloucestershire Northern Senior League
Teamsheet: Dudfield, Mander, Hamer, GAS Murdock, AFT Murdock, Marler, Harrison, Causon, Taylor, Blackhouse, Applin
Scorers: AFT Murdock, Causon (2)

SEASON BY SEASON

Date: Saturday 29/11/1930
Result: **CHELTENHAM TOWN 2 GLOUCESTER CITY 3**
Competition: Gloucestershire Northern Senior League
Teamsheet: Dudfield, Hamer, Mander, Eamer, GAS Murdock, AFT Murdock, Harrison, Causon, Taylor, Blackhouse, Artus
Scorers: Taylor (2), Blackhouse

Date: Saturday 06/12/1930
Result: **GLOUCESTER CITY 8 RODBOROUGH OLD BOYS 1**
Competition: Gloucestershire FA Northern Senior Amateur Cup 1st Round
Teamsheet: Dudfield, Hamer, Mander, GAS Murdock, AFT Murdock, Kerslake, Harrison, Causon, Taylor, Blackhouse, Butler
Scorers: Taylor (3), Blackhouse (4), Causon

Date: Saturday 13/12/1930
Result: **SHARPNESS 3 GLOUCESTER CITY 4**
Competition: Gloucestershire Northern Senior League
Teamsheet: Dudfield, Hamer, Mander, GAS Murdock, AFT Murdock, Butler, Harrison, Causon, Taylor, Blackhouse, Applin
Scorers: Causon (3), Taylor

Date: Saturday 20/12/1930
Result: **GLOUCESTER CITY 5 CAM MILLS 3**
Competition: Gloucestershire Northern Senior League
Teamsheet: Dudfield, Hamer, Mander, Stephens, H Whitney, AFT Murdock, Marler, Causon, Taylor, Blackhouse, Applin
Scorers: Taylor (3), Blackhouse, Stephens

Date: Saturday 27/12/1930
Result: **BREAM AMATEURS 1 GLOUCESTER CITY 4**
Competition: Gloucestershire Northern Senior League
Teamsheet: Dudfield (?), Hamer (?), Mander (?), -----, H Whitney (?), AFT Murdock (?), Marler (?), Causon, Taylor, Blackhouse (?), -----
Scorers: Taylor (2), Causon (2)

Date: Saturday 03/01/1931
Result: **GLOUCESTER CITY 3 CIRENCESTER TOWN 0**
Competition: Gloucestershire FA Northern Senior Aamateur Cup 2nd Round
Teamsheet: Dudfield, Hamer, Mander, GAS Murdock, H Whitney, AFT Murdock, Harrison, Marler, Taylor, Causon, Blackhouse
Scorers: Blackhouse, Taylor, Causon

Date: Saturday 10/01/1931
Result: **FOREST GREEN ROVERS 1 GLOUCESTER CITY 2**
Competition: Gloucestershire Northern Senior League
Teamsheet: Dudfield, Hamer, Mander, GAS Murdock, H Whitney, AFT Murdock, Harrison, Marler, Taylor, Causon, Blackhouse
Scorers: Causon, H Whitney

Date: Saturday 17/01/1931
Result: **GLOUCESTER CITY 1 CINDERFORD TOWN 0**
Competition: Gloucestershire Northern Senior League
Teamsheet: Dudfield, Hamer, Mander, GAS Murdock, H Whitney, AFT Murdock, Marler, Causon, Taylor, Blackhouse, Hartshorne
Scorer: H Whitney

Date: Saturday 24/01/1931
Result: **GLOUCESTER CITY 2 CHELTENHAM TOWN 3**
Competition: Gloucestershire FA Northern Senior Amateur Cup 3rd Round
Teamsheet: Dudfield, Hamer, Mander, GAS Murdock, H Whitney, AFT Murdock, Harrison, Causon, Taylor, Blackhouse, Applin
Scorer: Causon (2)

Date: Saturday 31/01/1931
*Result: **BROADWELL AMATEURS 0 GLOUCESTER CITY 1***
Competition: Gloucestershire Northern Senior League
Teamsheet: Dudfield, Hamer, Mander, GAS Murdock, H Whitney, AFT Murdock, Grist, Causon, Dee, W Whitney, Applin
Scorer: Causon
Note: Originally League game. Broadwell Amateurs withdrew

Date: Saturday 07/02/1931
Result: **GLOUCESTER CITY 3 LISTER'S WORKS 1**
Competition: Gloucestershire Northern Senior League
Teamsheet: Simpson, Hamer, Mander, GAS Murdock, H Whitney, AFT Murdock, Hartshorne, Marler, Taylor, Causon, Blackhouse
Scorers: Causon, Taylor, Marler

Date: Saturday 14/02/1931
Result: **GLOUCESTER CITY 6 SHARPNESS 3**
Competition: Gloucestershire Northern Senior League
Teamsheet: Dudfield, Hamer, Mander, GAS Murdock, H Whitney, AFT Murdock, Hartshorne, Marler, Taylor, Causon, Blackhouse
Scorers: H Whitney, Taylor (3), Marler, Causon

Date: Saturday 21/02/1931
Result: **CAM MILLS 2 GLOUCESTER CITY 5**
Competition: Gloucestershire Northern Senior League
Teamsheet: Dudfield, Hamer, Mander, GAS Murdock, H Whitney, AFT Murdock, Hartshorne, Marler, Taylor, Causon, Blackhouse
Scorers: Marler, Causon (2), Hartshorne, H Whitney

Date: Saturday 28/02/1931
Result: **CINDERFORD TOWN 1 GLOUCESTER CITY 3**
Competition: Gloucestershire Northern Senior League
Teamsheet: Dudfield, Hamer, Mander, GAS Murdock, H Whitney, AFT Murdock, Hartshorne, Marler, Taylor, Causon, Blackhouse
Scorers: GAS Murdock, Causon, Blackhouse

Date: Saturday 07/03/1931
Result: **GLOUCESTER CITY 2 TEWKESBURY TOWN 2**
Competition: Gloucestershire Northern Senior League
Teamsheet: Dudfield, Hamer, Mander, GAS Murdock (?), H Whitney (?), Eamer, Hartshorne, Marler (?), Taylor, Causon, Blackhouse
Scorers: Causon, Blackhouse

Date: Saturday 14/03/1931
Result: **GLOUCESTER CITY 5 CHEPSTOW TOWN 3**
Competition: Gloucestershire Northern Senior League
Teamsheet: Dudfield, Mander, WF Whitney, GAS Murdock, H Whitney, AFT Murdock, Hartshorne, Marler, Smith, Causon, Blackhouse
Scorers: Smith (3), Causon, Blackhouse

Date: Saturday 21/03/1931
Result: **GLOUCESTER CITY 3 BRIMSCOMBE 4**
Competition: Gloucestershire Northern Senior League
Teamsheet: Dudfield, Mander, WF Whitney, GAS Murdock, H Whitney, AFT Murdock, Harrison, Hartshorne, Smith, Causon, Marler
Scorers: Causon, WF Whitney, Harrison

Date: Saturday 28/03/1931
Result: **BRIMSCOMBE 5 GLOUCESTER CITY 4**
Competition: Gloucestershire Northern Senior League
Teamsheet: Dudfield, Hamer, Mander, GAS Murdock, AFT Murdock, Marler, Blackhouse, Dee, Taylor, Causon, Harrison
Scorers: Causon (2), Taylor (2)

Date: Saturday 04/04/1931
Result: **GLOUCESTER CITY 2 VINEY HILL 0**
Competition: Gloucestershire Northern Senior League
Teamsheet: Dudfield, Hamer, Mander, H Whitney, AFT Murdock, Marler, Hartshorne, Dee, Taylor, Causon, Harrison
Scorers: Taylor, -----

Date: Tuesday 07/04/1931
Result: **GLOUCESTER CITY 0 FOREST GREEN ROVERS 2**
Competition: Gloucestershire Northern Senior League
Teamsheet: Browning, Hamer, Mander, GAS Murdock, AFT Murdock, Parker, Hartshorne, Causon, Taylor, Marler, Harrison

Date: Saturday 11/04/1931
Result: **GLOUCESTER CITY 0 CHELTENHAM TOWN 0**
Competition: Gloucestershire Northern Senior League
Teamsheet: Dudfield, Hamer, Mander, Marler, AFT Murdock, GAS Murdock, Finch, Hickman, Taylor, Causon, Harrison

Appearances – G Applin 12, CJ Artus 7, J Berry 1, J Blackhouse 17, HC Browning 1, J Butler 2, WJ Causon 27, G Dainty 1, E Davies 1, F Dee 5, J Dudfield 27, A Eamer 2, E Farnell 1, D Fellows 1, R Finch 1, N Grist 1, SC Hamer 27, WR Harrison 19, C Hartshorne 10, HC Hickman 1, A Kerslake 2, NV Mander 29, LA Marler 23, AFT Murdock 27, GAS Murdock 25, GW Parker 1, S Roche 1, ? Simpson 1, F Smith 2, EJ Stephens 1, W Taylor 19, HC Tingle 3, H Whitney 15, WF Whitney 3.
Scorers – WJ Causon 26, W Taylor 19, J Blackhouse 10, LA Marler 5, H Whitney 4, WR Harrison 3, F Smith 3, GAS Murdock 2, G Applin 1, F Dee 1, C Hartshorne 1, AFT Murdock 1, EJ Stephens 1, WF Whitney 1.

GLOUCESTERSHIRE NORTHERN SENIOR LEAGUE

POS	CLUB	P	W	D	L	F	A	PTS
1	BRIMSCOMBE	22	19	2	1	114	45	40
2	CHELTENHAM TOWN	22	18	1	3	99	32	37
3	TEWKESBURY TOWN	22	14	2	6	82	40	30
4	**GLOUCESTER CITY**	**22**	**13**	**3**	**6**	**63**	**50**	**29**
5	CHEPSTOW TOWN	22	11	2	9	68	60	24
6	VINEY HILL	22	10	3	9	59	55	23
7	LISTER'S WORKS (Dursley)	22	8	3	11	66	74	19
8	BREAM AMATEURS	22	7	4	11	38	99	18
9	CINDERFORD TOWN	22	5	4	13	44	70	14
10	FOREST GREEN ROVERS	22	3	7	12	34	50	13
11	CAM MILLS	22	5	2	15	56	88	12
12	SHARPNESS	22	2	1	19	28	88	5
13	BROADWELL AMATEURS							
		264	115	34	115	751	751	264

Broadwell Amateurs withdrew after 13 games. All records expunged.

SEASON 1931-1932
(Home Ground: Sutgrove Park, Calton Road/Stroud Road)

Date: Saturday 05/09/1931
Result: **GLOUCESTER CITY 3 KEYNSHAM TOWN 3**
Competition: FA Cup Extra Preliminary Round
Teamsheet: Jones, Hamer, Cook, H Whitney, Brinkworth, AFT Murdock, Dowle, Hartshorne, Causon, Marler, Morris
Scorers: -----, -----, -----

Date: Wednesday 09/09/1931
Result: **CHELTENHAM TOWN 3 GLOUCESTER CITY 1**
Competition: Gloucestershire Northern Senior League
Teamsheet: Jones, Hamer, Cook, H Whitney, Brinkworth, AFT Murdock, Dowle, Hartshorne, Causon, Marler, Morris
Scorer: -----

Date: Thursday 10/09/1931
Result: **KEYNSHAM TOWN 5 GLOUCESTER CITY 1**
Competition: FA Cup Extra Preliminary Round Replay
Teamsheet: Jones, Hamer, Cook, H Whitney, Brinkworth, AFT Murdock, Dowle, F Smith, Causon, Mann, Morris
Scorer: Causon

Date: Saturday 12/09/1931
Result: **BRISTOL CITY 'A' 5 GLOUCESTER CITY 3**
Competition: Bristol Charity League
Teamsheet: Jones, Hamer, Cook, H Whitney, Brinkworth, AFT Murdock, Dowle, -----, Causon, Marler, Morris
Scorers: Causon (2), -----

Date: Thursday 17/09/1931
Result: **GLOUCESTER CITY 5 CHELTENHAM TOWN 2**
Competition: Bristol Charity League
Teamsheet: Dudfield, Hamer, Cook, H Whitney, SG Smith, AFT Murdock, Dowle, Drew, Causon, Marler, Morris
Scorers: Drew (2), Causon, Dowle, Morris

Date: Saturday 19/09/1931
Result: **GLOUCESTER CITY 3 CHALFORD 3**
Competition: Gloucestershire Northern Senior League
Teamsheet: Dudfield, Hamer, Cook, Marler, Brinkworth, Mander, Dowle, Hartshorne, Morris, Causon, Applin
Scorers: Morris, Brinkworth, Hartshorne

Date: Saturday 03/10/1931
Result: **CAM MILLS 1 GLOUCESTER CITY 3**
Competition: Gloucestershire Northern Senior League
Teamsheet: -----, Hamer (?), Cook (?), Brinkworth (?), -----, -----, Dowle (?), Hartshorne (?), Causon, Marler, Applin (?)
Scorers: Marler (2), Causon

Date: Saturday 10/10/1931
Result: **LISTER'S WORKS 4 GLOUCESTER CITY 2**
Competition: English Amateur Cup 1st Qualifying Round
Teamsheet: Jones, Hamer, Cook, Brinkworth, H Whitney, Dovey, Dowle, Hartshorne, Causon, Marler, Applin
Scorers: Applin, Causon

Date: Saturday 17/10/1931
Result: **GLOUCESTER CITY 4 POPE'S HILL 1**
Competition: Gloucestershire Northern Senior League
Teamsheet: Jones, Hamer, Cook, H Whitney, Brinkworth, Applin, Dowle, Hartshorne, Causon, Marler, Dovey
Scorers: Marler, Causon (3)
Note: AFT Murdock's Benefit Match

Date: Saturday 24/10/1931
Result: **TEWKESBURY TOWN 4 GLOUCESTER CITY 3**
Competition: Gloucestershire Northern Senior League
Teamsheet: Jones, Hamer, Cook, Brinkworth, H Whitney, Dovey, Dowle, F Smith, Causon, Hartshorne, Applin
Scorers: Causon (2), F Smith

Date: Saturday 31/10/1931
Result: **STONEHOUSE 4 GLOUCESTER CITY 3**
Competition: Gloucestershire Northern Senior League
Teamsheet: Jones, Cook, Foote, Brinkworth, H Whitney, Marler, Dowle, Hartshorne, Causon, F Smith, Applin
Scorers: -----, -----, -----

Date: Saturday 07/11/1931
Result: **GLOUCESTER CITY 3 BRIMSCOMBE 3**
Competition: Gloucestershire Northern Senior League
Teamsheet: Jones, WF Whitney, Cook, Sinkinson, H Whitney, Marler, Dowle, Hartshorne, Causon, F Smith, Applin
Scorers: Hartshorne, Applin, Dowle

Date: Saturday 14/11/1931
Result: VINEY HILL 2 GLOUCESTER CITY 5
Competition: Gloucestershire Northern Senior League
Teamsheet: Jones, Meehan, Cook, Sinkinson, Brinkworth, H Whitney, Dowle, Hartshorne, Causon, Marler, Applin
Scorers: Causon (3), Hartshorne, Marler
Note: Originally League game. Viney Hill suspended

Date: Saturday 21/11/1931
Result: **CINDERFORD TOWN 3 GLOUCESTER CITY 2**
Competition: Gloucestershire Northern Senior League
Teamsheet: Jones, WF Whitney, Cook, Sinkinson, H Whitney, Marler, Dowle, Hartshorne, Causon, F Smith, Applin
Scorers: Dowle, -----

Date: Saturday 28/11/1931
Result: **GLOUCESTER CITY 8 FOREST GREEN ROVERS 0**
Competition: Gloucestershire Northern Senior League
Teamsheet: Jones, Cook, WF Whitney, Brinkworth, H Whitney, Sinkinson, Dowle, Hartshorne, Causon, F Smith, Applin
Scorers: Causon (6), Hartshorne, Applin

Date: Saturday 05/12/1931
Result: **GLOUCESTER CITY 1 BRISTOL CITY 'A' 3**
Competition: Bristol Charity League
Teamsheet: Jones, WF Whitney, Cook, Brinkworth, H Whitney, Marler, Dowle, F Smith, Causon, Drew, Applin
Scorer: Drew

Date: Saturday 12/12/1931
Result: **BRISTOL SAINT GEORGE 3 GLOUCESTER CITY 2**
Competition: Bristol Charity League
Teamsheet: Jones, WF Whitney, Cook, Brinkworth, H Whitney, Sinkinson, Dowle, F Smith, Causon, Drew, Applin
Scorer: Drew (2, 1 pen)

Date: Saturday 26/12/1931
Result: **BREAM AMATEURS 0 GLOUCESTER CITY 1**
Competition: Gloucestershire Northern Senior League
Teamsheet: Jones, Cook (?), WF Whitney (?), -----, Drew, Sinkinson (?), Dowle (?), Hartshorne (?), Causon (?), F Smith (?), Applin (?)
Scorer: Drew

Date: Saturday 02/01/1932
Result: **GLOUCESTER CITY 6 ELLWOOD 3**
Competition: Gloucestershire FA Northern Senior Amateur Cup 1st Round
Teamsheet: Jones, Cook, WF Whitney, H Whitney, Drew, Sinkinson, Dowle, Hartshorne, Causon, F Smith, Applin
Scorers: Causon (4), Applin, Hartshorne

Date: Saturday 16/01/1932
Result: **BRISTOL ROVERS RESERVES 11 GLOUCESTER CITY 1**
Competition: Bristol Charity League
Teamsheet: Jones, Cook, WF Whitney, Brinkworth, Drew, Sinkinson, Dowle, Hartshorne, Causon, F Smith, Applin
Scorer: -----

Date: Saturday 23/01/1932
Result: **FOREST GREEN ROVERS 2 GLOUCESTER CITY 1**
Competition: Gloucestershire Northern Senior League
Teamsheet: Jones, Cook, WF Whitney, Brinkworth, AFT Murdock, Sinkinson, Mansfield, Hartshorne, Causon, F Smith, Applin
Scorer: -----

Date: Saturday 30/01/1932
Result: **CHEPSTOW TOWN 0 GLOUCESTER CITY 5**
Competition: Gloucestershire FA Northern Senior Amateur Cup 2nd Round
Teamsheet: Jones, WF Whitney, Cook, Brinkworth, Meek, AFT Murdock, Dowle, Hartshorne, Causon, Drew, Applin
Scorers: Drew, own goal, Causon, Hartshorne, Dowle

Date: Sunday 07/02/1932
Result: **GLOUCESTER CITY 3 CHEPSTOW TOWN 2**
Competition: Gloucestershire Northern Senior League
Teamsheet: Jones, Cook, WF Whitney, Brinkworth, Meek, AFT Murdock, Dowle, Hartshorne, Causon, Drew, Applin
Scorers: -----, -----, -----

Date: Sunday 14/02/1932
Result: **CHEPSTOW TOWN 4 GLOUCESTER CITY 3**
Competition: Gloucestershire Northern Senior League
Teamsheet: Jones, Cook, WF Whitney, Brinkworth, Meek, AFT Murdock, Dowle, Drew, Sinkinson, Applin, Morris
Scorers: Applin (2), Dowle

Date: Saturday 27/02/1932
Result: **POPE'S HILL 1 GLOUCESTER CITY 4**
Competition: Gloucestershire Northern Senior League
Teamsheet: Jones, Hamer, WF Whitney, Brinkworth, Meek, AFT Murdock, Dowle, Drew, F Smith, Hartshorne, Applin
Scorers: Applin, Drew (3, 1 pen)

Date: Saturday 05/03/1932
Result: **CHELTENHAM TOWN 1 GLOUCESTER CITY 2**
Competition: Gloucestershire FA Northern Senior Amateur Cup Semi-Final
Teamsheet: Jones, Hamer, WF Whitney, Brinkworth, Meek, AFT Murdock, Dowle, Hartshorne, Causon, Drew, Applin
Scorers: Applin, -----
Note: Played at Tewkesbury

Date: Saturday 12/03/1932
Result: **GLOUCESTER CITY 3 STONEHOUSE 4**
Competition: Gloucestershire Northern Senior League
Teamsheet: Jones, Hamer, WF Whitney, Sinkinson, Meek, AFT Murdock, Dowle, Hartshorne, Causon, F Smith, Applin
Scorers: Causon (2), Sinkinson

Date: Saturday 19/03/1932
Result: **GLOUCESTER CITY 1 CINDERFORD TOWN 0**
Competition: Gloucestershire Northern Senior League
Teamsheet: Jones, Hamer, Cook, Brinkworth, Meek, AFT Murdock, Dowle, Drew, Causon, Hartshorne, Applin
Scorer: Causon

Date: Saturday 26/03/1932
Result: **GLOUCESTER CITY 4 TEWKESBURY TOWN 4**
Competition: Gloucestershire Northern Senior League
Teamsheet: Jones, WF Whitney, Hamer, Sinkinson, Meek, AFT Murdock, Dowle, Drew, Dee, Hartshorne, Applin
Scorers: Dee (2), Applin, -----

Date: Tuesday 29/03/1932
Result: **GLOUCESTER CITY 0 BREAM AMATEURS 0**
Competition: Gloucestershire Northern Senior League
Teamsheet: Jones (?), Hamer (?), WF Whitney (?), -----, Meek (?), AFT Murdock (?), Dowle (?), Drew (?), -----, Hartshorne (?), Applin (?)

Date: Saturday 02/04/1932
Result: **CHALFORD 1 GLOUCESTER CITY 2**
Competition: Gloucestershire Northern Senior League
Teamsheet: Jones, Hamer, WF Whitney, Brinkworth, Meek, AFT Murdock, Dowle, Drew, Causon, Hartshorne, Applin
Scorers: Meek, Drew

Date: Saturday 09/04/1932
Result: **GLOUCESTER CITY 2 BRISTOL ROVERS RESERVES 1**
Competition: Bristol Charity League
Teamsheet: Jones, Hamer, WF Whitney, Brinkworth, Meek, AFT Murdock, Dowle, Drew, Causon, Hartshorne, Applin
Scorers: Drew, Causon

Date; Saturday 16/04/1932
Result: **LISTER'S WORKS 2 GLOUCESTER CITY 8**
Competition: Gloucestershire FA Northern Senior Amateur Cup Final
Teamsheet: Jones, Hamer, WF Whitney, Brinkworth, Meek, AFT Murdock, Dowle, Hartshorne, Causon, Drew, Applin
Scorers: Applin, Causon (3), Dowle, Drew (2), Hartshorne

Date: Monday 18/04/1932
Result: **GLOUCESTER CITY 2 CAM MILLS 0**
Competition: Gloucestershire Northern Senior League
Teamsheet: Jones, Hamer, WF Whitney, Brinkworth, Meek, AFT Murdock, Dowle, Hartshorne, Causon, Drew, Applin
Scorers: Causon, Applin

Date: Wednesday 20/04/1932
Result: **CHELTENHAM TOWN 4 GLOUCESTER CITY 1**
Competition: Bristol Charity League
Teamsheet: Jones, Cook, Foote, Brinkworth, Meek, AFT Murdock, Finch, Atherton, Dee, Meadows, Applin
Scorer: Atherton

Date: Thursday 21/04/1932
Result: **GLOUCESTER CITY 1 CHELTENHAM TOWN 1**
Competition: Gloucestershire Northern Senior League
Teamsheet: Jones, Cook, WF Whitney, Brinkworth, H Whitney, Sinkinson, Dowle, Hartshorne, Causon, Drew, Applin
Scorer: Drew

Date: Saturday 23/04/1932
Result: **BATH CITY RESERVES 2 GLOUCESTER CITY 0**
Competition: Bristol Charity League
Teamsheet: Jones, Hamer, WF Whitney, Brinkworth, Meek, F Smith, Dowle, Hartshorne, Causon, Drew, Applin

Date: Saturday 30/04/1932
Result: **GLOUCESTER CITY 3 BATH CITY RESERVES 1**
Competition: Bristol Charity League
Teamsheet: Jones, Hamer, WF Whitney, Brinkworth, Meek, GAS Murdock, Dowle, F Smith, Causon, Drew, Applin
Scorers: -----, -----, -----

Date: Saturday 07/05/1932
Result: **GLOUCESTER CITY 0 BRISTOL SAINT GEORGE 3**
Competition: Bristol Charity League
Teamsheet: Jones, WF Whitney, Hamer, AFT Murdock, Meek, Brinkworth, Dowle, Hartshorne, Causon, Dee, Applin

Date: ?
Result: **BRIMSCOMBE 4 GLOUCESTER CITY 3**
Competition: Gloucestershire Northern Senior League
Teamsheet: -----, -----, -----, -----, -----, -----, -----, -----, -----, -----, -----
Scorers: -----, -----, -----

Appearances – G Applin 33, F Atherton 1, A Brinkworth 30, WJ Causon 33, C Cook 26, J Dee 3, WE Dovey 3, C Dowle 36, EW Drew 20, J Dudfield 2, R Finch 1, SB Foote 2, SC Hamer 23, C Hartshorne 30, H Jones 35, NV Mander 1, EW Mann 1, C Mansfield 1, LA Marler 13, DIK Meadows 1, J Meehan 1, W Meek 17, L Morris 7, AFT Murdock 20, GAS Murdock 1, AE Sinkinson 12, F Smith 15, SG Smith 1, H Whitney 16, WF Whitney 24.
Scorers – WJ Causon 33, EW Drew 15, G Applin 11, C Hartshorne 7, C Dowle 6, LA Marler 4, J Dee 2, L Morris 2, F Atherton 1, A Brinkworth 1, W Meek 1, AE Sinkinson 1, F Smith 1.

GLOUCESTERSHIRE NORTHERN SENIOR LEAGUE

POS	CLUB	P	W	D	L	F	A	PTS
1	CHEPSTOW TOWN	22	16	4	2	79	34	36
2	CHELTENHAM TOWN	22	16	1	5	103	35	33
3	CINDERFORD TOWN	22	12	2	8	65	56	26
4	STONEHOUSE	22	11	4	7	46	41	26
5	BRIMSCOMBE	22	10	3	9	56	68	23
6	GLOUCESTER CITY	22	9	5	8	57	45	21*
7	TEWKESBURY TOWN	22	7	6	9	54	51	20
8	BREAM AMATEURS	22	9	2	11	45	51	20
9	FOREST GREEN ROVERS	22	8	3	11	47	77	19
10	CHALFORD	22	8	2	12	66	64	18
11	POPE'S HILL	22	6	3	13	42	63	15
12	CAM MILLS	22	1	3	18	42	118	5
13	VINEY HILL							
		264	113	38	113	702	703	262

* Two points and one goal deducted for playing ineligible men.
Viney Hill, suspended by the league

BRISTOL CHARITY LEAGUE

POS	CLUB	P	W	D	L	F	A	PTS
1	BRISTOL CITY 'A'	10	8	1	1	33	17	17
2	BRISTOL ROVERS RESERVES	10	5	2	3	37	20	12
3	BATH CITY RESERVES	10	4	3	3	16	12	11
4	BRISTOL SAINT GEORGE	10	4	2	4	28	30	10
5	GLOUCESTER CITY	10	3	0	7	18	35	6
6	CHELTENHAM TOWN	10	2	0	8	20	38	4
		60	26	8	26	152	152	60

Season 1932-1933
(Home Ground: Sutgrove Park, Calton Road/Stroud Road)

Date: Saturday 03/09/1932
Result: **GLOUCESTER CITY 1 BRISTOL SAINT GEORGE 2**
Competition: Bristol Charity League
Teamsheet: Birch, Hamer, Whitney, Whiston, AFT Murdock, Atherton, Applin, Dee, Causon, Drew, Cox
Scorer: Dee

Date: Saturday 10/09/1932
Result: **BRISTOL CITY 'A' 7 GLOUCESTER CITY 0**
Competition: Bristol Charity League
Teamsheet: Birch, Hamer, Whitney, Brinkworth, AFT Murdock, Whiston, Dee, Smith, Causon, Drew, Applin

Date: Saturday 17/09/1932
Result: **GLOUCESTER CITY 3 BRISTOL CITY 'A' 2**
Competition: Bristol Charity League
Teamsheet: Birch, Hamer, Whitney, Brinkworth, Meek, AFT Murdock, Birt, Hartshorne, Causon, Drew, Applin
Scorers: Applin, Drew (2)

Date: Saturday 24/09/1932
Result: **GLOUCESTER CITY 2 CHELTENHAM TOWN RESERVES 3**
Competition: Gloucestershire Northern Senior League
Teamsheet: Birch, Hamer, Cook, Brinkworth, Meek, AFT Murdock, Birt, Hartshorne, Causon, Drew, Applin
Scorers: Drew, Causon

Date: Monday 26/09/1932
Result: **FOREST GREEN ROVERS 3 GLOUCESTER CITY 2**
Competition: Gloucestershire Northern Senior League
Teamsheet: Birch (?), Hamer (?), -----, -----, Meek (?), AFT Murdock (?), Birt (?), -----, Causon (?), Drew (?), Applin (?)
Scorers: -----, -----

Date: Saturday 01/10/1932
Result: **LISTER'S WORKS 3 GLOUCESTER CITY 6**
Competition: Gloucestershire Northern Senior League
Teamsheet: Birch, Hamer, Branigan, Whiston, Meek, AFT Murdock, Birt, Hickman, Causon, Drew, Applin
Scorers: -----, -----, -----, -----, -----, -----

Date: Saturday 08/10/1932
Result: **WESLEY RANGERS 3 GLOUCESTER CITY 0**
Competition: English Amateur Cup 1st Qualifying Round
Teamsheet: Birch, Hamer, Brinkworth, Whiston, Meek, AFT Murdock, Birt, Hickman, Causon, Drew, Applin

Date: Saturday 15/10/1932
Result: **GLOUCESTER CITY 2 BATH CITY RESERVES 0**
Competition: Bristol Charity League
Teamsheet: Birch, Hamer, Meek, Whiston, Drew, AFT Murdock, Applin, Hartshorne, Jackson, Causon, Birt
Scorer: Jackson (2)

Date: Saturday 22/10/1932
Result: **BRISTOL SAINT GEORGE 6 GLOUCESTER CITY 1**
Competition: Bristol Charity League
Teamsheet: Jones, Hamer, Meek, Brinkworth, Drew, AFT Murdock, Birt, Hartshorne, Smith, Wayman, Applin
Scorer: Applin

Date: Saturday 29/10/1932
Result: **GLOUCESTER CITY 3 TEWKESBURY TOWN 1**
Competition: Gloucestershire Northern Senior League
Teamsheet: Jones, Hamer, Meek, Brinkworth, Drew, AFT Murdock, Birt, Hartshorne, Wayman, Causon, Applin
Scorers: Causon (2), Hartshorne

Date: Saturday 05/11/1932
Result: **CINDERFORD TOWN 3 GLOUCESTER CITY 4**
Competition: Gloucestershire Northern Senior League
Teamsheet: Birch, Hamer, Cook, Whiston, Drew, AFT Murdock, Birt, Hartshorne, Hurcum, Causon, Applin
Scorers: Causon, Drew (2, 1 pen), Birt

Date: Saturday 12/11/1932
Result: **STONEHOUSE 0 GLOUCESTER CITY 2**
Competition: Gloucestershire Northern Senior League
Teamsheet: Birch, Hamer, Meek, Brinkworth, Drew, AFT Murdock, Birt, Hartshorne, Hurcum, Causon, Whiston
Scorers: Causon, Drew

Date: Saturday 19/11/1932
Result: **GLOUCESTER CITY 8 CHALFORD 4**
Competition: Gloucestershire Northern Senior League
Teamsheet: Birch, Hamer, Meek, Brinkworth, Drew, AFT Murdock, Birt, Hartshorne, Hurcum, Causon, Whiston
Scorers: Whiston, Hurcum (2), Drew, Causon (3), own goal

Date: Saturday 26/11/1932
Result: **POPE'S HILL 2 GLOUCESTER CITY 3**
Competition: Gloucestershire Northern Senior League
Teamsheet: Birch, Hamer, Meek, Brinkworth, Drew, AFT Murdock, Birt, Hartshorne, Hurcum, Causon, Applin
Scorer: Causon (3)

Date: Saturday 03/12/1932
Result: **DURSLEY TOWN 2 GLOUCESTER CITY 5**
Competition: Gloucestershire FA Northern Senior Amateur Cup 1st Round
Teamsheet: Birch, Hamer, Meek, Brinkworth, Drew, AFT Murdock, Birt, Hartshorne, Hurcum, Causon, Applin
Scorers: Drew, Causon (2), Hartshorne (2)

Date: Saturday 10/12/1932
Result: **GLOUCESTER CITY 3 BRIMSCOMBE 1**
Competition: Gloucestershire Northern Senior League
Teamsheet: Birch, Hamer, Meek, Brinkworth, Drew, AFT Murdock, Birt, Hartshorne, Hurcum, Causon, Applin
Scorers: Drew (2), -----

Date: Saturday 24/12/1932
Result: **GLOUCESTER CITY 2 POPE'S HILL 0**
Competition: Gloucestershire Northern Senior League
Teamsheet: Birch, AFT Murdock, Griffiths, Atherton, Drew, W Mann, Birt, E Mann, Dee, Causon, Applin
Scorers: Causon, Dee

Date: Saturday 31/12/1932
Result: **GLOUCESTER CITY 0 CHEPSTOW TOWN 2**
Competition: Gloucestershire Northern Senior League
Teamsheet: Birch, Hamer, Meek, Brinkworth, Drew, AFT Murdock, Birt, Hartshorne, Chadd, Causon, Applin

Date: Saturday 07/01/1933
Result: **CIRENCESTER TOWN 1 GLOUCESTER CITY 4**
Competition: Gloucestershire FA Northern Senior Amateur Cup 2nd Round
Teamsheet: Birch, Hamer, Bayliss, Smith, Drew, AFT Murdock, Birt, Hartshorne, Dee, Causon, Applin
Scorers: Causon (2), Drew, Birt

Date: Saturday 14/01/1933
Result: **BLAKENEY 1 GLOUCESTER CITY 5**
Competition: Gloucestershire Northern Senior League
Teamsheet: Birch, Hamer, Meek, Smith, Drew, AFT Murdock, Birt, Hartshorne, Hickman, Causon, Applin
Scorers: Hartshorne, Causon (3), Hickman

Date: Saturday 21/01/1933
Result: **CHALFORD 2 GLOUCESTER CITY 4**
Competition: Gloucestershire Northern Senior League
Teamsheet: Birch, Hamer, Atherton, Smith, Drew, AFT Murdock, Birt, Hartshorne, Causon, Hickman, Applin
Scorers: Drew, Causon (2), AFT Murdock

Date: Saturday 28/01/1933
Result: **GLOUCESTER CITY 8 LISTER'S WORKS 0**
Competition: Gloucestershire Northern Senior League
Teamsheet: Birch, Hamer, Foote, Smith, Drew, AFT Murdock, Birt, Chadd, Causon, Hickman, Applin
Scorers: Causon (4), Chadd (3), Drew (pen)
Note: Played at Bon Marche Ground, Estcourt Road

Date: Saturday 04/02/1933
Result: **GLOUCESTER CITY 4 STONEHOUSE 1**
Competition: Gloucestershire FA Northern Senior Amateur Cup 3rd Round
Teamsheet: Birch, Hamer, Bayliss, Smith, Drew, AFT Murdock, Birt, Dee, Causon, Hickman, Applin
Scorers: Applin, Hickman, Dee, Causon
Note: Played at Bon Marche Ground, Estcourt Road

Date: Saturday 11/02/1933
Result: **GLOUCESTER CITY 2 STONEHOUSE 0**
Competition: Gloucestershire Northern Senior League
Teamsheet: Birch, Hamer, Foote, Smith, Drew, AFT Murdock, Birt, Brinkworth, Causon, Hickman, Applin
Scorers: Drew, Causon

Date: Saturday 18/02/1933
Result: **CHEPSTOW TOWN 0 GLOUCESTER CITY 2**
Competition: Gloucestershire Northern Senior League
Teamsheet: Birch, Hamer, Foote, Brinkworth, AFT Murdock, Atherton, Birt, Hartshorne, Causon, Hickman, Applin
Scorers: Hartshorne, Hickman

Date: Saturday 04/03/1933
Result: **FOREST GREEN ROVERS 1 GLOUCESTER CITY 5**
Competition: Gloucestershire FA Northern Senior Amateur Cup Semi-Final
Teamsheet: Birch, Hamer, Foote, Smith, Drew, AFT Murdock, Birt, Hartshorne, Causon, Chadd, Applin
Scorers: Causon (2), Chadd (2), Birt
Note: Played at Stonehouse

Date: Saturday 11/03/1933
Result: **BREAM AMATEURS 0 GLOUCESTER CITY 3**
Competition: Gloucestershire Northern Senior League
Teamsheet: Birch, Hamer, Foote, Smith, Drew, AFT Murdock, Birt, Hartshorne, Causon, Hickman, Applin
Scorers: Hartshorne, Birt, Hamer

Date: Saturday 25/03/1933
Result: **GLOUCESTER CITY 1 BRISTOL ROVERS RESERVES 5**
Competition: Bristol Charity League
Teamsheet: Birch, Hamer, Wilson, Smith, Harris, AFT Murdock, Birt, Drew, Causon, Hickman, Applin
Scorer: Causon

Date: Saturday 01/04/1933
Result: **GLOUCESTER CITY 1 BLAKENEY 0**
Competition: Gloucestershire Northern Senior League
Teamsheet: Birch, Wilson, Foote, Smith, Drew, AFT Murdock, Birt, Hartshorne, Causon, Hickman, Applin
Scorer: -----

Date: Saturday 08/04/1933
Result: **CHELTENHAM TOWN 3 GLOUCESTER CITY 1**
Competition: Gloucestershire FA Northern Senior Amateur Cup Final
Teamsheet: Birch, Hamer, Foote, Smith, Drew, AFT Murdock, Birt, Hickman, Causon, Chadd, Applin
Scorer: Applin
Attendance: 2000
Note: Played at Cam

SEASON BY SEASON

Date: Monday 10/04/1933
Result: **BRIMSCOMBE 0 GLOUCESTER CITY 1**
Competition: Gloucestershire Northern Senior League
Teamsheet: Birch (?), Hamer (?), Foote (?), Smith (?), Drew (?), AFT Murdock (?), Birt (?), Hickman (?), Causon (?), Chadd (?), Applin (?)
Scorer: -----

Date: Saturday 15/04/1933
Result: **GLOUCESTER CITY 3 BREAM AMATEURS 0**
Competition: Gloucestershire Northern Senior League
Teamsheet: Birch, Hamer, Foote, Smith, Drew, AFT Murdock, Birt, Hickman, Causon, Chadd, Applin
Scorers: Drew, Causon, Chadd

Date: Tuesday 18/04/1933
Result: **GLOUCESTER CITY 1 FOREST GREEN ROVERS 1**
Competition: Gloucestershire Northern Senior League
Teamsheet: Birch, Hamer, Foote, Smith, Drew, AFT Murdock, Birt, Hickman, Causon, Chadd, Applin
Scorer: Causon

Date: Wednesday 19/04/1933
Result: **BRISTOL ROVERS RESERVES 7 GLOUCESTER CITY 2**
Competition: Bristol Charity League
Teamsheet: -----, -----, -----, -----, -----, -----, -----, Dee, -----, -----, Applin
Scorers: Dee, Applin

Date: Thursday 20/04/1933
Result: **TEWKESBURY TOWN 0 GLOUCESTER CITY 4**
Competition: Gloucestershire Northern Senior League
Teamsheet: -----, -----, -----, -----, -----, -----, -----, -----, -----, -----, Applin (?)
Scorers: -----, -----, -----, -----

Date: Saturday 22/04/1933
Result: **GLOUCESTER CITY 4 CINDERFORD TOWN 1**
Competition: Gloucestershire Northern Senior League
Teamsheet: Birch, W Murdock, Foote, Smith, Drew, AFT Murdock, Birt, Chadd, Causon, Yeates, Applin
Scorers: Causon (3), -----

Date: Wednesday 26/04/1933
Result: **CHELTENHAM TOWN RESERVES 5 GLOUCESTER CITY 1**
Competition: Gloucestershire Northern Senior League
Teamsheet: Birch, Hamer, AFT Murdock, Smith, Drew, Hartshorne, Dowle, Dee, Causon, Chadd, Applin
Scorer: Smith

Date: Saturday 06/05/1933
Result: **BATH CITY RESERVES 7 GLOUCESTER CITY 2**
Competition: Bristol Charity League
Teamsheet: -----, -----, -----, -----, -----, -----, -----, -----, -----, -----, -----
Scorers: -----, -----

Appearances – G Applin 35, F Atherton 3, F Bayliss 2, A Birch 33, J Birt 32, J Branigan 1, A Brinkworth 14, WJ Causon 34, RT Chadd 9, C Cook 2, C Cox 1, F Dee 7, C Dowle 1, EW Drew 34, SB Foote 11, W Griffiths 1, SC Hamer 32, WAH Harris 1, C Hartshorne 20, HC Hickman 15, G Hurcum 8, RT Jackson 1, H Jones 2, EW Mann 1, W Mann 1, W Meek 15, AFT Murdock 35, W Murdock 1, OF Wayman 2, R Whiston 8, WF Whitney 3, M Wilson 2, W Yeates 1.
Scorers – WJ Causon 35, EW Drew 15, RT Chadd 6, C Hartshorne 6, G Applin 5, J Birt 4, F Dee 4, HC Hickman 3, RT Jackson 2, SC Hamer 1, AFT Murdock 1, F Smith 1, R Whiston 1, own goal 1.

GLOUCESTERSHIRE NORTHERN SENIOR LEAGUE

POS	CLUB	P	W	D	L	F	A	PTS
1	CHELTENHAM TOWN RESERVES	24	21	2	1	102	35	44
2	**GLOUCESTER CITY**	**24**	**19**	**1**	**4**	**74**	**32**	**39**
3	CHEPSTOW TOWN	24	15	3	6	87	44	33
4	CINDERFORD TOWN	24	11	4	9	56	50	26
5	FOREST GREEN ROVERS	24	11	3	10	55	62	25
6	CHALFORD	24	10	4	10	55	69	24
7	STONEHOUSE	24	8	6	10	53	61	22
8	BRIMSCOMBE	24	7	6	11	55	66	20
9	BREAM AMATEURS	24	7	5	12	47	65	19
10	TEWKESBURY TOWN	24	8	1	15	47	69	17
11	LISTER'S WORKS (Dursley)	24	6	5	13	61	90	17
12	BLAKENEY	24	5	4	15	54	78	14
13	POPE'S HILL	24	3	6	15	38	63	12
		312	131	50	131	784	784	312

BRISTOL CHARITY LEAGUE

POS	CLUB	P	W	D	L	F	A	PTS
1	BRISTOL ROVERS RESERVES	8	6	0	2	31	15	12
2	BRISTOL SAINT GEORGE	8	4	1	3	19	24	9
3	BATH CITY RESERVES	8	4	0	4	24	18	8
4	BRISTOL CITY 'A'	8	3	1	4	22	15	7
5	**GLOUCESTER CITY**	**8**	**2**	**0**	**6**	**12**	**36**	**4**
		40	19	2	19	108	108	40

[65]

SEASON 1933-1934

(Home Ground: Bon Marche Ground, Estcourt Road)

Date: Saturday 26/08/1933
Result: LISTER'S WORKS 8 GLOUCESTER CITY 3
Competition: Gloucestershire Northern Senior League
Teamsheet: Saunders, Hamer, Whitney, -----, Drew, -----, -----, Yeates, -----, -----, Mann, W Jones
Scorers: Yeates, Mann (2)
Note: Originally League game. Due to an irregularity made null and void and replayed 24/03/1934

Date: Saturday 02/09/1933
Result: **GLOUCESTER CITY 4 LISTER'S WORKS 2**
Competition: Gloucestershire Northern Senior League
Teamsheet: Saunders, Hamer, Whitney, Hartshorne, Easter, Newlands, Dowle, Birt, Drew, Applin, W Jones
Scorers: Dowle (2), Applin, -----

Date: Saturday 09/09/1933
Result: **GLOUCESTER CITY 2 STONEHOUSE 0**
Competition: Gloucestershire Northern Senior League
Teamsheet: Saunders, Hamer, Whitney, F Smith, Drew, Murdock, Dowle, Hartshorne, Malpass, Applin, W Jones
Scorers: W Jones, Hartshorne

Date: Monday 11/09/1933
Result: **CHELTENHAM TOWN RESERVES 5 GLOUCESTER CITY 2**
Competition: Bristol Charity League
Teamsheet: Saunders, Hamer, Whitney, Newling, Drew, Wayman, Dowle, Hartshorne, Applin, Malpass, W Jones
Scorers: Malpass (2)

Date: Saturday 16/09/1933
Result: **BRISTOL CITY 'A' 4 GLOUCESTER CITY 2**
Competition: Bristol Charity League
Teamsheet: Saunders, Whitney (?), Easter, Hartshorne (?), Newling, -----, Dowle, Malpass (?), Causon, Applin, W Jones
Scorers: Applin, Causon

Date: Saturday 23/09/1933
Result: **GLOUCESTER CITY 1 BLAKENEY 2**
Competition: Gloucestershire Northern Senior League
Teamsheet: Saunders, Whitney, Easter, F Smith, Hartshorne, Murdock, Dowle, Applin, Causon, Malpass, W Jones
Scorer: Dowle

Date: Saturday 30/09/1933
Result: **BRISTOL SAINT GEORGE 5 GLOUCESTER CITY 2**
Competition: Bristol Charity League
Teamsheet: Saunders, Anderson, Whitney, F Smith, Murdock, Wayman, Dowle, Hartshorne, Causon, Applin, W Jones
Scorers: Causon, Wayman

Date: Saturday 07/10/1933
Result: **GLOUCESTER CITY 8 STONEHOUSE 0**
Competition: English Amateur Cup 1st Qualifying Round
Teamsheet: Saunders, Wayman, Whitney, F Smith, Hartshorne, Murdock, Dowle, Dee, Causon, Applin, W Jones
Scorers: Dee (3), Causon (3), W Jones (2, 1 pen)

Date: Saturday 14/10/1933
Result: **FOREST GREEN ROVERS 2 GLOUCESTER CITY 3**
Competition: Gloucestershire Northern Senior League
Teamsheet: Saunders, Wayman, Whitney, F Smith, Drew, Anderson, Dowle, Hartshorne, Causon, Applin, W Jones
Scorers: Applin, Hartshorne, Causon

Date: Saturday 21/10/1933
Result: **GLOUCESTER CITY 4 CHALFORD 2**
Competition: English Amateur Cup 2nd Qualifying Round
Teamsheet: Saunders, Wayman, Whitney, F Smith, Drew, Murdock, Dowle, Hartshorne, Causon, Applin, W Jones
Scorers: W Jones (pen), Causon (2), Drew

Date: Saturday 28/10/1933
Result: **BRIMSCOMBE 2 GLOUCESTER CITY 4**
Competition: Gloucestershire Northern Senior League
Teamsheet: Saunders, Wayman, Whitney, F Smith, Drew, Murdock, Dowle, C Jones, Causon, Applin, W Jones
Scorers: Applin, C Jones, Dowle, Causon

Date: Saturday 04/11/1933
Result: **GLOUCESTER CITY 5 BRISTOL SAINT PANCRAS 4**
Competition: English Amateur Cup 3rd Qualifying Round
Teamsheet: Saunders, Wayman, Whitney, F Smith, Drew, Murdock, Dowle, Dee, Causon, Applin, W Jones
Scorer: Causon (5)

Date: Saturday 11/11/1933
Result: **GLOUCESTER CITY 1 BROADWELL AMATEURS 3**
Competition: Gloucestershire Northern Senior League
Teamsheet: Saunders, Wayman, Whitney, F Smith, Drew, Murdock, Dowle, Hartshorne, Causon, Applin, W Jones
Scorer: Drew

Date: Saturday 18/11/1933
Result: **KEYNSHAM TOWN 3 GLOUCESTER CITY 1**
Competition: Englsih Amateur Cup 4th Qualifying Round
Teamsheet: Saunders, Wayman, Whitney, F Smith, Drew, Murdock, Dowle, Hartshorne, Causon, Applin, W Jones
Scorer: Causon

Date: Saturday 25/11/1933
Result: **GLOUCESTER CITY 4 CINDERFORD TOWN 2**
Competition: Gloucestershire Northern Senior League
Teamsheet: Saunders, -----, Wayman (?), F Smith, Drew (?), Murdock (?), Dowle, Hartshorne (?), Causon, Applin, W Jones
Scorers: Causon (3), W Jones

Date: Saturday 02/12/1933
Result: **GLOUCESTER CITY 3 POPE'S HILL 0**
Competition: Gloucestershire FA Northern Senior Amateur Cup 1st Round
Teamsheet: Saunders, Hamer, Wayman, F Smith, Drew, Murdock, Dowle, Hartshorne, Causon, Applin, W Jones
Scorers: Hartshorne, Drew (2)

Date: Saturday 09/12/1933
Result: **GLOUCESTER CITY 1 BRISTOL ROVERS RESERVES 5**
Competition: Bristol Charity League
Teamsheet: Saunders, Hamer, Wayman, Hartshorne, Drew, Anderson, Dowle, Dee, Causon, Applin, W Jones
Scorer: W Jones

Date: Saturday 16/12/1933
Result: **STONEHOUSE 2 GLOUCESTER CITY 1**
Competition: Gloucestershire Northern Senior League
Teamsheet: Saunders, Easter, Hamer (?), Anderson (?), Murdock, Drew (?), Dowle (?), Hartshorne (?), Causon (?), Applin (?), W Jones
Scorer: -----

Date: Saturday 23/12/1933
Result: **GLOUCESTER CITY 3 TEWKESBURY TOWN 1**
Competition: Gloucestershire Northern Senior League
Teamsheet: Saunders, Hamer, Foote, Anderson, Drew, Wayman, Dowle, Hartshorne, Causon, Applin, W Jones
Scorer: Causon (3)

Date: Tuesday 26/12/1933
Result: **GLOUCESTER CITY 3 WESTON-SUPER-MARE 4**
Competition: Bristol Charity League
Teamsheet: Gibson, Hamer (?), Foote (?), Wayman (?), Drew, Murdock, Louch, Stoles, Bevan, Applin (?), W Jones
Scorers: Bevan, Stoles, Drew

Date: Saturday 30/12/1933
Result: **GLOUCESTER CITY 3 FOREST GREEN ROVERS 1**
Competition: Gloucestershire Northern Senior League
Teamsheet: Saunders, Hamer, Foote, F Smith, Drew, Wayman, Birt, Hartshorne, Causon, Applin, W Jones
Scorers: Causon (2), Hartshorne

Date: Saturday 06/01/1934
Result: **GLOUCESTER CITY 1 CINDERFORD TOWN 2**
Competition: Gloucestershire FA Northern Senior Amateur Cup 2nd Round
Teamsheet: Saunders, Hamer, Wayman, F Smith, Drew, Murdock, Birt, Hartshorne, Causon, Applin, W Jones
Scorer: Hartshorne

Date: Saturday 13/01/1934
Result: **BLAKENEY 1 GLOUCESTER CITY 5**
Competition: Gloucestershire Northern Senior League
Teamsheet: Saunders, Hamer, Wayman, Anderson, Drew, Murdock, Harrison, Hartshorne, Causon, Dee, W Jones
Scorers: Harrison, Dee, Causon, W Jones, Drew

Date: Saturday 20/01/1934
Result: **GLOUCESTER CITY 1 LEDBURY TOWN 1**
Competition: Gloucestershire Northern Senior League
Teamsheet: Saunders, Hamer, Wayman, Anderson, Drew, Murdock, Harrison, Hartshorne, Causon, F Smith, W Jones
Scorer: Drew (pen)

Date: Saturday 27/01/1934
Result: **BROADWELL AMATEURS 0 GLOUCESTER CITY 1**
Competition: Gloucestershire Northern Senior League
Teamsheet: Saunders, Hamer, Wayman, Anderson, Drew, Murdock, Harrison, Hartshorne, Causon, F Smith, W Jones
Scorer: Causon

Date: Saturday 03/02/1934
Result: **LEDBURY TOWN 1 GLOUCESTER CITY 6**
Competition: Gloucestershire Northern Senior League
Teamsheet: Saunders, Hamer, Wayman, Anderson, Murdock, Hartshorne, Dowle, Dee, Causon, Applin, W Jones
Scorers: Causon (3), Dee (2), Dowle

Date: Saturday 10/02/1934
Result: **GLOUCESTER CITY 3 BRIMSCOMBE 0**
Competition: Gloucestershire Northern Senior League
Teamsheet: Saunders, Hamer, Atherton, Anderson, Murdock, Hartshorne, Dee, Drew, Causon, Applin, Dowle
Scorers: Dee (2), Murdock

Date: Saturday 17/02/1934
Result: **TEWKESBURY TOWN 0 GLOUCESTER CITY 4**
Competition: Gloucestershire Northern Senior League
Teamsheet: Saunders, Hamer, Anderson, F Smith, Drew, Murdock, Dowle, Dee, Causon, W Jones, Harrison
Scorers: Dee, Drew, Causon, W Jones

Date: Saturday 24/02/1934
Result: **CHELTENHAM TOWN RESERVES 3 GLOUCESTER CITY 2**
Competition: Gloucestershire Northern Senior League
Teamsheet: Saunders, Hamer, Anderson, F Smith, Drew, Murdock, Dowle, Hartshorne, Causon, Dee, Harrison
Scorers: Dowle, Causon

Date: Saturday 03/03/1934
Result: **BREAM AMATEURS 2 GLOUCESTER CITY 2**
Competition: Gloucestershire Northern Senior League
Teamsheet: Saunders, Hamer, Anderson, F Smith, Hartshorne, Murdock, Dowle, Dee, Causon, W Jones, Kirby
Scorers: Murdock, Causon

Date: Saturday 10/03/1934
Result: **GLOUCESTER CITY 3 CHELTENHAM TOWN RESERVES 0**
Competition: Gloucestershire Northern Senior League
Teamsheet: Saunders, Hamer, Anderson, F Smith, Drew, Murdock, Dowle, Hartshorne, Causon, Barnes, W Jones
Scorers: Causon (2), Murdock

Date: Saturday 17/03/1934
Result: **GLOUCESTER CITY 3 CINDERFORD TOWN 1**
Competition: Gloucestershire Northern Senior League
Teamsheet: Saunders, Hamer, Anderson, F Smith, Drew, Murdock, Applin, Hartshorne, Causon, Barnes, W Jones
Scorers: Causon, W Jones (2)

Date: Saturday 24/03/1934
Result: **LISTER'S WORKS 1 GLOUCESTER CITY 3**
Competition: Gloucestershire Northern Senior League
Teamsheet: Taylor, Hamer, Anderson, F Smith, Drew, Murdock, Dowle, Hartshorne, Causon, Barnes, W Jones
Scorers: W Jones, -----, Drew

Date: Sunday 30/03/1934
Result: **GLOUCESTER CITY 2 BATH CITY RESERVES 2**
Competition: Bristol Charity League
Teamsheet: Saunders, Hamer, Anderson, Foote, Drew, Murdock, Harrison, Hartshorne, Causon, Wayman, W Jones
Scorers: Causon, Hartshorne
Attendance: 2000

Date: Saturday 31/03/1934
Result: **CHALFORD 0 GLOUCESTER CITY 1**
Competition: Gloucestershire Northern Senior League
Teamsheet: Taylor, Hamer, Wayman, F Smith, Drew, Murdock, Applin, Dee, Causon, Hartshorne, W Jones
Scorer: Drew (pen)

Date: Monday 02/04/1934
Result: **BATH CITY RESERVES 2 GLOUCESTER CITY 1**
Competition: Bristol Charity League
Teamsheet: Griffiths, Hamer, Anderson, SB Foote, F Smith, Drew, Harrison, Yeates, Causon, Hartshorne, W Jones
Scorer: Yeates

Date: Saturday 07/04/1934
Result: **CHEPSTOW TOWN 0 GLOUCESTER CITY 0**
Competition: Gloucestershire Northern Senior League
Teamsheet: Taylor, Hamer, Anderson, F Smith, Drew, Murdock, Dowle, Hartshorne, Causon, Louch, W Jones

Date: Wednesday 11/04/1934
Result: **GLOUCESTER CITY 7 CHEPSTOW TOWN 0**
Competition: Gloucestershire Northern Senior League
Teamsheet: Griffiths, Hamer, Anderson, F Smith, Drew, Yeates, Dowle, Hartshorne, Causon, Louch, W Jones
Scorers: Louch (2), Causon (4), Hartshorne

Date: Saturday 14/04/1934
Result: **GLOUCESTER CITY 4 BREAM AMATEURS 0**
Competition: Gloucestershire Northern Senior League
Teamsheet: Taylor, Hamer, Anderson, F Smith, Drew, Murdock, Dowle, Hartshorne, Causon, Louch, W Jones
Scorers: W Jones, F Smith, Hartshorne, Dowle

Date: Monday 16/04/1934
Result: **GLOUCESTER CITY 3 CHELTENHAM TOWN RESERVES 2**
Competition: Bristol Charity League
Teamsheet: Griffiths, Hamer, Anderson, F Smith, Drew, Murdock, Louch, Hartshorne, Hayes, Causon, W Jones
Scorers: Hayes, W Jones, Causon

Date: Saturday 21/04/1934
Result: **BRISTOL ROVERS RESERVES 6 GLOUCESTER CITY 0**
Competition: Bristol Charity League
Teamsheet: Birch, Hamer, Anderson, F Smith, Drew, Murdock, Louch, Hartshorne, Causon, Yeates, W Jones

Date: Monday 23/04/1934
Result: **GLOUCESTER CITY 1 CHALFORD 1**
Competition: Gloucestershire Northern Senior League
Teamsheet: Saunders, Hamer, Anderson, F Smith, Drew, Murdock, Louch, Hartshorne, Causon, Yeates, W Jones
Scorer: Louch

Date: Thursday 26/04/1934
Result: **GLOUCESTER CITY 4 BRISTOL CITY 'A' 0**
Competition: Bristol Charity League
Teamsheet: Birch, Hamer, Anderson, F Smith, Drew, Murdock, Louch, Hartshorne, Causon, Hayes, W Jones
Scorers: Causon (3), Louch

Date: Saturday 28/04/1934
Result: **GLOUCESTER CITY 12 BRISTOL SAINT GEORGE 1**
Competition: Bristol Charity League
Teamsheet: Birch, Hamer, Anderson, F Smith, Drew, Murdock, Dowle, Yeates, Causon, Hartshorne, W Jones
Scorers: Causon (3), Dowle, Yeates (3), Hartshorne, W Jones (2), Drew, Anderson (pen)

Date: Saturday 05/05/1934
Result: **WESTON-SUPER-MARE 5 GLOUCESTER CITY 1**
Competition: Bristol Charity League
Teamsheet: Saunders, Hamer, Anderson, F Smith, Drew, Newman, Louch, Causon, Applin, Yeates, W Jones
Scorer: Causon

Appearances – D Anderson 27, G Applin 26, F Atherton 1, WB Barnes 3, J Bevan 1, A Birch 3, J Birt 3, WJ Causon 40, F Dee 10, C Dowle 29, EW Drew 39, G Easter 4, SB Foote 5, L Gibson 1, W Griffiths 3, SC Hamer 34, WR Harrison 7, C Hartshorne 39, GE Hayes 2, C Jones 1, W Jones 43, AT Kirby 1, LA Louch 9, OR Malpass 4, EW Mann 1, AFT Murdock 34, ? Newlands 1, ? Newman 1, VH Newling 2, G Saunders 34, F Smith 33, AW Stoles 1, L Taylor 4, OF Wayman 22, WF Whitney 14, W Yeates 7.
Scorers – WJ Causon 47, W Jones 15, EW Drew 11, F Dee 9, C Hartshorne 9, C Dowle 8, W Yeates 5, G Applin 4, LA Louch 4, AFT Murdock 3, OR Malpass 2, EW Mann 2, D Anderson 1, J Bevan 1, WR Harrison 1, GE Hayes 1, C Jones 1, F Smith 1, AW Stoles 1, OF Wayman 1.

GLOUCESTERSHIRE NORTHERN SENIOR LEAGUE

POS	CLUB	P	W	D	L	F	A	PTS
1	**GLOUCESTER CITY**	**26**	**18**	**4**	**4**	**72**	**27**	**40**
2	CHELTENHAM TOWN RESERVES	26	19	0	7	81	35	38
3	BROADWELL AMATEURS	26	15	5	6	84	44	35
4	BLAKENEY	26	14	4	8	78	60	32
5	LEDBURY TOWN	26	13	6	7	58	53	32
6	CINDERFORD TOWN	26	13	2	11	71	47	28
7	CHALFORD	26	12	4	10	73	65	28
8	STONEHOUSE	26	12	3	11	49	49	27
9	CHEPSTOW TOWN	26	8	8	10	70	81	24
10	LISTER'S WORKS (Dursley)	26	7	5	14	77	92	19
11	FOREST GREEN ROVERS	26	7	3	16	50	83	17
12	TEWKESBURY TOWN	26	6	5	15	49	84	17
13	BRIMSCOMBE	26	6	3	17	54	94	15
14	BREAM AMATEURS	26	6	2	18	42	94	14
		364	156	54	154	908	908	366

BRISTOL CHARITY LEAGUE

POS	CLUB	P	W	D	L	F	A	PTS
1	BRISTOL ROVERS RESERVES	12	11	1	0	58	12	23
2	WESTON-SUPER-MARE	12	6	3	3	31	21	15
3	BATH CITY RESERVES	12	6	2	4	30	28	14
4	CHELTENHAM TOWN RESERVES	12	5	2	5	30	34	12
5	**GLOUCESTER CITY**	**12**	**3**	**1**	**8**	**32**	**39**	**7**
6	BRISTOL CITY 'A'	12	3	1	8	22	31	7
7	BRISTOL SAINT GEORGE	12	2	2	8	21	59	6
		84	36	12	36	224	224	84

SEASON 1934-1935
(Home Ground: Bon Marche Ground, Estcourt Road)

Date: Saturday 25/08/1934
Result: **ELLWOOD 0 GLOUCESTER CITY 3**
Competition: Gloucestershire Northern Senior League
Teamsheet: Saunders, Hamer, Anderson, Murdock, Drew, Hartshorne, Louch, McKenzie, Causon, Henderson, W Jones
Scorers: McKenzie (2), Causon

Date: Saturday 01/09/1934
Result: **GLOUCESTER CITY 2 BATH CITY RESERVES 4**
Competition: Bristol Charity League
Teamsheet: Saunders, Hamer, Anderson, Mills, Drew, F Smith, Hartshorne, McKenzie, Causon, Henderson, W Jones
Scorers: Causon, Henderson

Date: Thursday 06/09/1934
Result: **BRIMSCOMBE 2 GLOUCESTER CITY 3**
Competition: Gloucestershire Northern Senior League
Teamsheet: Saunders (?), Hamer (?), Anderson (?), F Smith (?), Drew (?), Leach, Hartshorne, McKenzie (?), Causon, Henderson (?), W Jones
Scorers: W Jones, Causon, Hartshorne

Date: Saturday 08/09/1934
Result: **WESTON-SUPER-MARE 1 GLOUCESTER CITY 2**
Competition: Bristol Charity League
Teamsheet: Birch, Hamer, Anderson, F Smith, Drew, Murdock, Hartshorne, McKenzie, Causon, Henderson, W Jones
Scorers: Causon, McKenzie

Date: Thursday 13/09/1934
Result: **TEWKESBURY TOWN 2 GLOUCESTER CITY 3**
Competition: Gloucestershire Northern Senior League
Teamsheet: Saunders, Hamer, Anderson, F Smith, Drew, Murdock, C Jones, Hartshorne, Causon, McKenzie, W Jones
Scorers: Drew, Causon, McKenzie

Date: Saturday 15/09/1934
Result: **BRISTOL SAINT GEORGE 0 GLOUCESTER CITY 3**
Competition: Bristol Charity League
Teamsheet: Saunders, Hamer, Anderson, F Smith, Drew, Murdock, C Jones, McKenzie, Causon, Henderson, W Jones
Scorers: W Jones, C Jones, Causon

[69]

Date: Saturday 22/09/1934
Result: **GLOUCESTER CITY 4 CHALFORD 1**
Competition: Gloucestershire Northern Senior League
Teamsheet: Saunders, Hamer, Anderson, F Smith, Drew, Leach, C Jones, McKenzie, Causon, Hartshorne, W Jones
Scorers: W Jones, Causon (2), Drew

Date: Saturday 29/09/1934
Result: **GLOUCESTER CITY 5 HIGHBEECH 0**
Competition: Gloucestershire Northern Senior League
Teamsheet: Saunders, Hamer, Anderson, F Smith, Drew, Murdock, C Jones, Dee, Causon, Henderson, W Jones
Scorers: Causon (3), Drew, Henderson

Date: Saturday 06/10/1934
Result: **MOUNT HILL ENTERPRISE 3 GLOUCESTER CITY 4**
Competition: English Amateur Cup 1st Qualifying Round
Teamsheet: Saunders, Hamer, Anderson, F Smith, Drew, Hartshorne, Evans, McKenzie, C Jones, Henderson, W Jones
Scorers: McKenzie (2), Drew, Henderson

Date: Saturday 13/10/1934
Result: **CHEPSTOW TOWN 2 GLOUCESTER CITY 5**
Competition: Gloucestershire Northern Senior League
Teamsheet: Saunders, Hamer, Anderson, F Smith, Drew, Hartshorne, C Jones, McKenzie, Causon, Henderson, W Jones
Scorers: Anderson (4), Drew

Date: Saturday 20/10/1934
Result: **GLOUCESTER CITY 7 BRISTOL SAINT GEORGE 2**
Competition: English Amateur Cup 2nd Qualifying Round
Teamsheet: Saunders, Hamer, Anderson, F Smith, Drew, Murdock, C Jones, McKenzie, Causon, Henderson, W Jones
Scorers: McKenzie, Causon, Henderson, W Jones, -----, -----, -----

Date: Saturday 27/10/1934
Result: **BROADWELL AMATEURS 1 GLOUCESTER CITY 2**
Competition: Gloucestershire Northern Senior League
Teamsheet: Saunders, Hamer, Anderson, F Smith, Drew, Murdock, Hartshorne, McKenzie, Causon, Henderson, Stoles
Scorers: Causon, Henderson

Date: Saturday 03/11/1934
Result: **GLOUCESTER CITY 2 SAINT PHILIPS MARSH ADULT SCHOOL 2** (aet)
Competition: English Amateur Cup 3rd Qualifying Round
Teamsheet: Saunders, Hamer, Anderson, F Smith, Drew, Murdock, Hartshorne, McKenzie, Causon, Henderson, Applin
Scorers: Hartshorne, Causon

Date: Saturday 10/11/1934
Result: **SAINT PHILIPS MARSH ADULT SCHOOL 3 GLOUCESTER CITY 3** (aet)
Competition: English Amateur Cup 3rd Qualifying Round Replay
Teamsheet: Saunders, Hamer, Anderson, F Smith, Drew, Murdock, Hartshorne, McKenzie, Causon, Henderson, Spaight
Scorers: Causon (2), Murdock

Date: Thursday 15/11/1934
Result: **SAINT PHILIPS MARSH ADULT SCHOOL 3 GLOUCESTER CITY 4**
Competition: English Amateur Cup 3rd Qualifying Round 2nd Replay
Teamsheet: Saunders, Foote, Anderson, Stoodley, Drew, Murdock, McKenzie, Hartshorne, Causon, Henderson, Spaight
Scorers: -----, -----, -----, -----
Note: Played at Dursley

Date: Saturday 17/11/1934
Result: **GLOUCESTER CITY 5 CLEVEDON 2**
Competition: English Amateur Cup 4th Qualifying Round
Teamsheet: Saunders, Foote, Anderson, F Smith, Drew, Murdock, McKenzie, Hartshorne, Causon, Henderson, Spaight
Scorers: Spaight, Drew, Murdock, McKenzie, Henderson

Date: Saturday 24/11/1934
Result: **GLOUCESTER CITY 7 LEDBURY TOWN 1**
Competition: Gloucestershire Northern Senior League
Teamsheet: Saunders, Foote, Anderson, F Smith, Drew, Murdock, Hartshorne, McKenzie, Causon, Henderson, Spaight
Scorers: Causon (2), Drew (2), Henderson (3)

Date: Saturday 01/12/1934
Result: **BRISTOL ROVERS 'A' 3 GLOUCESTER CITY 1**
Competition: Bristol Charity League
Teamsheet: Saunders, Foote, Anderson, F Smith, Drew, Murdock, McKenzie, Hartshorne, Causon, Henderson, Spaight
Scorer: Spaight

Date: Saturday 08/12/1934
Result: **GLOUCESTER CITY 2 BRISTOL ROVERS 'A' 4**
Competition: Bristol Charity League
Teamsheet: Saunders, Barnes, Anderson, F Smith, Drew, Murdock, McKenzie, Hartshorne, Causon, FG Smith, Spaight
Scorers: -----, -----

Date: Saturday 15/12/1934
Result: **CHELTENHAM TOWN RESERVES 5 GLOUCESTER CITY 2**
Competition: Bristol Charity League
Teamsheet (from): Saunders, Neale, Anderson, F Smith, Drew, Murdock, McKenzie, Hartshorne, Causon, Henderson, Spaight, FG Smith, W Jones
Scorers: McKenzie, Causon

Date: Saturday 22/12/1934
Result: **GLOUCESTER CITY 5 BROADWELL AMATEURS 0**
Competition: Gloucestershire Northern Senior League
Teamsheet: Saunders, Leach, Anderson, F Smith, Drew, Murdock, Stoles, McKenzie, Causon, Henderson, Spaight
Scorers: Causon (3), Henderson, Stoles

Date: Thursday 27/12/1934
Result: **GLOUCESTER CITY 6 WESTON-SUPER-MARE 2**
Competition: Bristol Charity League
Teamsheet: Saunders, Leach, Anderson, Dee, Cook, Foote, Stoles, McKenzie, Causon, Henderson, Spaight
Scorers: Henderson (3), Causon (2), Spaight

Date: Saturday 29/12/1934
Result: **GLOUCESTER CITY 4 TEWKESBURY TOWN 0**
Competition: Gloucestershire Northern Senior League
Teamsheet: Saunders, Leach, Anderson, F Smith, Drew, Murdock, Hartshorne, McKenzie, Causon, Henderson, Spaight
Scorers: McKenzie, Causon (2), Henderson

Date: Saturday 05/01/1935
Result: **GLOUCESTER CITY 9 TEWKESBURY TOWN 0**
Competition: Gloucestershire FA Northern Senior Amateur Cup 2nd Round
Teamsheet: Saunders, Foote, Anderson, F Smith, Drew, Murdock, FG Smith, McKenzie, Causon, Henderson, Spaight
Scorers: Henderson (2), Spaight (2), Drew, Causon (4, 1 pen)

Date: Saturday 12/01/1935
Result: **GLOUCESTER CITY 0 FROME TOWN 3**
Competition: English Amateur Cup 1st Round
Teamsheet: Saunders, Leach, Anderson, F Smith, Drew, Murdock, McKenzie, FG Smith, Causon, Henderson, Spaight
Attendance: 2500

Date: Saturday 19/01/1935
Result: **STONEHOUSE 3 GLOUCESTER CITY 0**
Competition: Gloucestershire Northern Senior League
Teamsheet: Saunders, Foote, Anderson, F Smith, Drew, Murdock, McKenzie, FG Smith, Causon, Henderson, Spaight

Date: Saturday 26/01/1935
Result: **WOODCHESTER 1 GLOUCESTER CITY 8**
Competition: Gloucestershire Northern Senior League
Teamsheet: Saunders, Foote, Anderson, F Smith, Drew, Murdock, McKenzie, Hartshorne, Causon, Henderson, Spaight
Scorers: Causon (5), Drew, Henderson, McKenzie

Date: Saturday 26/01/1935
Result: **GLOUCESTER CITY 2 BRISTOL SAINT GEORGE 2**
Competition: Bristol Charity League
Teamsheet: Griffiths, Short, Barnett, Yeates, Kilminster, Coley, Stoles, FG Smith, C Jones, Louch, Roberts
Scorers: Stoles, Kilminster
Note: Two matches on same day presumably due to fixture congestion. Reserves played this game but still counted as a first team match

Date: Saturday 02/02/1935
Result: **CAM MILLS 1 GLOUCESTER CITY 3**
Competition: Gloucestershire FA Northern Senior Amateur Cup 3rd Round
Teamsheet: Saunders, Foote, Anderson, F Smith, Drew, Murdock, Hartshorne, McKenzie, Causon, Stoles, Henderson
Scorers: McKenzie, Stoles, Causon

Date: Saturday 09/02/1935
Result: **GLOUCESTER CITY 4 BLAKENEY 2**
Competition: Gloucestershire Northern Senior League
Teamsheet: Saunders, Foote, Anderson, F Smith, Kilminster, Murdock, McKenzie, Haines, Causon, Henderson, Stoles
Scorers: Henderson (2), Haines, Causon

Date: Saturday 16/02/1935
Result: **CHELTENHAM TOWN 3 GLOUCESTER CITY 1**
Competition: Gloucestershire FA Northern Senior Amateur Cup Semi-Final
Teamsheet: Saunders, Foote, Anderson, F Smith, Drew, Murdock, Hartshorne, Haines, McKenzie, Henderson, Stoles
Scorer: Drew

Date: Saturday 23/02/1935
Result: **BLAKENEY 4 GLOUCESTER CITY 6**
Competition: Gloucestershire Northern Senior League
Teamsheet: Saunders, Foote, Anderson, Kilminster, Drew, Murdock, McKenzie, Haines, Causon, Henderson, Stoles
Scorers: Causon (5), McKenzie

Date: Saturday 02/03/1935
Result: **BRISTOL CITY 'A' 6 GLOUCESTER CITY 3**
Competition: Bristol Charity League
Teamsheet: Saunders, -----, Cannock, Drew (?), Kilminster, Murdock (?), McKenzie (?), Haines, Causon, AL Smith, Stoles
Scorers: Causon, Haines, Stoles

Date: Saturday 09/03/1935
Result: **GLOUCESTER CITY 2 BRISTOL CITY 'A' 1**
Competition: Bristol Charity League
Teamsheet: Saunders, Murdock, Anderson, F Smith, Drew, FG Smith, McKenzie, AL Smith, Causon, Henderson, Haines
Scorers: Drew (pen), Causon

Date: Saturday 16/03/1935
Result: **BATH CITY RESERVES 5 GLOUCESTER CITY 1**
Competition: Bristol Charity League
Teamsheet: Saunders, Murdock, Anderson, F Smith, Drew, Foote, McKenzie, Haines, Causon, AL Smith, Henderson
Scorer: Causon

Date: Saturday 23/03/1935
Result: **CINDERFORD TOWN 1 GLOUCESTER CITY 2**
Competition: Gloucestershire Northern Senior League
Teamsheet: Saunders, Murdock, Anderson, F Smith, Drew, Kilminster, Stoles, Haines, Hartshorne, McKenzie, Henderson
Scorers: Haines, Drew

Date: Monday 25/03/1935
Result: **CHELTENHAM TOWN RESERVES 1 GLOUCESTER CITY 2**
Competition: Gloucestershire Northern Senior League
Teamsheet: Saunders, Murdock, Anderson, F Smith, Drew, Kilminster, Stoles, Hartshorne, Haines, McKenzie, Henderson
Scorers: Drew, Stoles

Date: Saturday 30/03/1935
Result: **GLOUCESTER CITY 1 WOODCHESTER 1**
Competition: Gloucestershire Northern Senior League
Teamsheet: Saunders, Murdock, Anderson, F Smith, Drew, Kilminster, Stoles, Hartshorne, Haines, McKenzie, Henderson
Scorer: -----

Date: Saturday 06/04/1935
Result: **CHALFORD 0 GLOUCESTER CITY 3**
Competition: Gloucestershire Northern Senior League
Teamsheet: Saunders, Short, Anderson, Foote, Drew, Murdock, Sherman, Haines, Hartshorne, McKenzie, Grundy
Scorers: Hartshorne (3)

Date: Saturday 13/04/1935
Result: **GLOUCESTER CITY 3 CINDERFORD TOWN 0**
Competition: Gloucestershire Northern Senior League
Teamsheet: Saunders, Murdock, Anderson, F Smith, Drew, Kilminster, McKenzie, Haines, Sherman, Grundy, Stoles
Scorers: own goal, Drew (pen), Haines

Date: Tuesday 16/04/1935
Result: **GLOUCESTER CITY 6 BRIMSCOMBE 0**
Competition: Gloucestershire Northern Senior League
Teamsheet: Saunders, Murdock, Griffiths, F Smith, Drew, Kilminster, Stoles, Haines, Causon, McKenzie, Grundy
Scorers: Drew (pen), Haines (2), Causon (3)

Date: Wednesday 17/04/1935
Result: **GLOUCESTER CITY 3 CHEPSTOW TOWN 1**
Competition: Gloucestershire Northern Senior League
Teamsheet: Saunders, Griffiths, Anderson, Murdock, Drew, Kilminster, Stoles, Haines, Causon, McKenzie, Grundy
Scorers: McKenzie, Causon, Haines

Date: Friday 19/04/1935
Result: **GLOUCESTER CITY 5 CHELTENHAM TOWN RESERVES 1**
Competition: Gloucestershire Northern Senior League
Teamsheet: Saunders, Murdock, Anderson, F Smith, Drew, Kilminster, McKenzie, Hartshorne, Causon, Henderson, Grundy
Scorers: McKenzie (2), Henderson (2), Hartshorne
Attendance: 2500

Date: Saturday 20/04/1935
Result: **GLOUCESTER CITY 2 ELLWOOD 0**
Competition: Gloucestershire Northern Senior League
Teamsheet: Saunders (?), Murdock (?), Anderson (?), F Smith (?), Drew (?), Kilminster (?), McKenzie (?), Hartshorne, Causon (?), Henderson (?), Grundy
Scorers: Grundy, Hartshorne

Date: Tuesday 23/04/1935
Result: **BREAM AMATEURS 2 GLOUCESTER CITY 0**
Competition: Gloucestershire Northern Senior League
Teamsheet (from): Saunders, Griffiths, Murdock, Anderson, Drew, Kilminster, Foote, Stoles, Hartshorne, Causon, McKenzie, Yeates, Featherstone, Henderson, Grundy

Date: Thursday 25/04/1935
Result: **GLOUCESTER CITY 2 CHELTENHAM TOWN RESERVES 2**
Competition: Bristol Charity League
Teamsheet (from): Saunders, Griffiths, Murdock, Anderson, Drew, Kilminster, Foote, Stoles, Hartshorne, Causon, McKenzie, Yeates, Featherstone, Henderson, Grundy
Scorers: -----, -----

Date: Saturday 27/04/1935
Result: **GLOUCESTER CITY 1 STONEHOUSE 2**
Competition: Gloucestershire Northern Senior League
Teamsheet (from): Saunders, Murdock, Anderson, Hartshorne, Drew, Kilminster, Stoles, McKenzie, Causon, Haines, Henderson, Griffiths, Foote
Scorer: -----

Date: Monday 29/04/1935
Result: **GLOUCESTER CITY 3 BREAM AMATEURS 1**
Competition: Gloucestershire Northern Senior League
Teamsheet (from): Saunders, Foote, Griffiths, F Smith, Leach, Kilminster, Stoles, McKenzie, Haines, Featherstone, Henderson, Grundy, Anderson
Scorers: Henderson, Haines, McKenzie

Date: Thursday 02/05/1935
Result: **LEDBURY TOWN 2 GLOUCESTER CITY 2**
Competition: Gloucestershire Northern Senior League
Teamsheet (from): Saunders, Griffiths, Anderson, Leach, Drew, Kilminster, McKenzie, Haines, Causon, Henderson, Stoles, Hartshorne
Scorer: McKenzie (2)

Date: ?
Result: **HIGHBEECH 2 GLOUCESTER CITY 0**
Competition: Gloucestershire Northern Senior League
Teamsheet: -----, -----, -----, -----, -----, -----, -----, -----, -----, -----, -----

Appearances – D Anderson 47, G Applin 1, WJ Barnett 2, A Birch 1, J Cannock 1, WJ Causon 39, V Coley 1, HJ Cook 1, J Dee 2, EW Drew 46, WS Evans 1, R Featherstone 3, SB Foote 18, W Griffiths 10, WJ Grundy 10, A Haines 17, SC Hamer 14, C Hartshorne 32, VJD Henderson 42, C Jones 8, W Jones 12, E Kilminster 18, H Leach 8, LA Louch 2, JD McKenzie 48, R Mills 1, GAS Murdock 41, F Neale 1, R Roberts 1, G Saunders 49, R Sherman 2, J Short 2, AL Smith 3, F Smith 38, FG Smith 7, W Spaight 14, AW Stoles 21, ? Stoodley 1, W Yeates 4.
Scorers – WJ Causon 49, VJD Henderson 22, JD McKenzie 19, EW Drew 16, A Haines 8, C Hartshorne 7, W Spaight 5, AW Stoles 5, D Anderson 4, W Jones 4, W Griffiths 2, GAS Murdock 2, C Jones 1, WJ Grundy 1, E Kilminster 1, own goal 1.

5 October 1935

OPENING OF GLOUCESTER CITY'S NEW STAND

Section of the big crowd at the Gloucester City-Market Harborough match at Cheltenham-road, when the club's new stand was opened by the City Member.

Winners Tillotson Cup, Birmingham Combination Non-League Club Trophy.
Season 1935-6.

W. Rea   W. Harris   G. Saunders   A. V. Stirland   W. Peart   A. Smith   M. S. Hukin
(Trainer)   *(Chairman)*   *(Secretary)*
M. Edwards   R. Powell   G. Shelley   E. Drew   R. Cox   W. Langley   H. Leach

Harold Leach, Bob Cox and Archie Smith in the mid-1930s
(Photograph courtesy of Lloyd Smith, Archie's son)

GLOUCESTER CITY 1935-1936
(Photograph courtesy of Trevor Hurcombe, son in law of Albert Shelley)

Back Row – J Price (Assistant Trainer), AFT Murdock (Assistant Trainer), J Avery (Assistant Trainer), W Griffiths (Committee), R Oakey (Committee), A Hayward (Committee), L Weston, V Bishop (Committee), L Bennett (Committee), Counc. H Bishop

Middle Row – IW Gwatkin, RW Frith (Committee), SB Foote, FE Taylor, J Connor, WAH Harris, G Saunders, AV Stirland (Chairman), WC Peart, AL Smith, MS Hukin (Hon.Sec.), LA Beddis (Hon.Treasurer), S Ball (Committee)

Front Row – H Clissold, W Rea (Trainer), GH Buckmaster (Committee), M Edwards, RT Powell, EW Drew (Captain), WH Langley, H Leach, E Greening (Committee), E Kilminster

Front – A Shelley, RD Cox

SEASON BY SEASON

GLOUCESTERSHIRE NORTHERN SENIOR LEAGUE

POS	CLUB	P	W	D	L	F	A	PTS
1	STONEHOUSE	28	22	3	3	93	43	47
2	**GLOUCESTER CITY**	**28**	**22**	**2**	**4**	**92**	**36**	**46**
3	CHELTENHAM TOWN RESERVES	28	16	7	5	87	51	37*
4	BLAKENEY	28	16	3	9	93	52	35
5	CINDERFORD TOWN	28	16	2	10	88	35	34
6	CHALFORD	28	11	7	10	56	67	29
7	ELLWOOD	28	10	7	11	71	54	27
8	LEDBURY TOWN	28	11	5	12	83	87	25*
9	CHEPSTOW TOWN	28	11	2	15	66	82	24
10	HIGHBEECH	28	9	6	13	41	64	24
11	BROADWELL AMATEURS	28	9	3	16	37	61	21
12	BREAM AMATEURS	28	9	3	16	48	80	21
13	WOODCHESTER	28	8	5	15	49	86	21
14	TEWKESBURY TOWN	28	6	4	18	43	96	16
15	BRIMSCOMBE	28	3	3	22	42	95	9
		420	179	62	179	989	989	416

* Two points deducted for playing ineligible men.

BRISTOL CHARITY LEAGUE

POS	CLUB	P	W	D	L	F	A	PTS
1	BRISTOL CITY 'A'	12	9	1	2	43	17	19
2	BATH CITY RESERVES	12	8	3	1	30	12	19
3	BRISTOL ROVERS 'A'	12	7	1	4	38	27	15
4	CHELTENHAM TOWN RESERVES	12	4	3	5	27	24	11
5	**GLOUCESTER CITY**	**12**	**4**	**2**	**6**	**28**	**35**	**10**
6	WESTON-SUPER-MARE	12	3	0	9	17	39	6
7	BRISTOL SAINT GEORGE	12	1	2	9	15	44	4
		84	36	12	36	198	198	84

SEASON 1935-1936

(Home Ground: The Ground, Cheltenham Road, Longlevens)

Date: Saturday 31/08/1935
Result: **CHELTENHAM TOWN 0 GLOUCESTER CITY 3**
Competition: Birmingham Combination
Teamsheet: Saunders, Langley, Cox, Leach, Drew, Anderson, Stoles, AL Smith, Shelley, Henderson, Maisey
Scorers: AL Smith, Stoles, Leach
Attendance: 3000

Date: Saturday 14/09/1935
Result: **EVESHAM TOWN 1 GLOUCESTER CITY 4**
Competition: Birmingham Combination
Teamsheet: Saunders, Langley, Cox, O'Brien, Drew, Wise, Watson, Leach, Shelley, AL Smith, Jones
Scorers: Watson, AL Smith, Leach, Shelley

Date: Saturday 21/09/1935
Result: **HALESOWEN TOWN 1 GLOUCESTER CITY 4**
Competition: Birmingham Combination
Teamsheet: Saunders, Langley, Cox, O'Brien, Drew, Leach, Stoles, Figgures, Shelley, AL Smith, Jones
Scorers: Shelley (2), Drew, Jones

Date: Saturday 28/09/1935
Result: **WALSALL RESERVES 1 GLOUCESTER CITY 0**
Competition: Birmingham Combination
Teamsheet: Saunders, Langley, Cox, O'Brien, Drew, Leach, Watson, Stoles, Shelley, AL Smith, Jones

Date: Saturday 05/10/1935
Result: GLOUCESTER CITY 7 MARKET HARBOROUGH 1
Competition: Birmingham Combination
Teamsheet: Saunders, Langley, Cox, O'Brien, Drew, Leach, Watson, Stoles, Shelley, AL Smith, Jones
Scorers: Stoles, AL Smith (2), Watson (2), Shelley (2)
Attendance: 1500
Note: Originally League game. Market Harborough withdrew

Date: Saturday 12/10/1935
Result: **GLOUCESTER CITY 6 REDDITCH TOWN 2**
Competition: Birmingham Combination
Teamsheet: Saunders, Langley, Cox, O'Brien, Drew, Leach, Watson, Stoles, Shelley, AL Smith, Jones
Scorers: AL Smith (2), Shelley (3), Watson
Attendance: 1000

Date: Saturday 26/10/1935
Result: **GLOUCESTER CITY 1 WEST BROMWICH ALBION 'A' 2**
Competition: Birmingham Combination
Teamsheet: Saunders, Langley, Cox, O'Brien, Drew, Leach, Watson, Stoles, Shelley, AL Smith, Jones
Scorer: Jones
Attendance: 2281

Date: Saturday 02/11/1935
Result: **GLOUCESTER CITY 4 DARLASTON 2**
Competition: Birmingham Combination
Teamsheet: Saunders, Langley, Cox, O'Brien, Drew, Leach, Watson, Stoles, Shelley, AL Smith, Jones
Scorers: Shelley, AL Smith (3, 1 pen)

Date: Saturday 09/11/1935
Result: **BIRMINGHAM TRAMS 1 GLOUCESTER CITY 1**
Competition: Birmingham Combination
Teamsheet: Saunders, Langley, Cox, O'Brien, Drew, Leach, Gwatkin, Stoles, Shelley, AL Smith, Jones
Scorer: Jones

Date: Saturday 16/11/1935
Result: **BOURNEVILLE ATHLETIC 1 GLOUCESTER CITY 1**
Competition: Birmingham Combination
Teamsheet: Saunders, Langley, Cox, O'Brien, Drew, Stoles, Watson, Watkins, Shelley, AL Smith, Jones
Scorer: Shelley

Date: Saturday 23/11/1935
Result: **GLOUCESTER CITY 1 BIRMINGHAM 'A' 1**
Competition: Birmingham Senior Cup 1st Round
Teamsheet: Saunders, Langley, Cox, O'Brien, Drew, Leach, Stoles, Harris, Shelley, AL Smith, Anderson
Scorer: Harris
Attendance: 1400

Date: Thursday 28/11/1935
Result: **LEAMINGTON TOWN 1 GLOUCESTER CITY 2**
Competition: Birmingham Combination
Teamsheet: Saunders, Langley, Cox, O'Brien, Drew, Leach, AL Smith, Alden, Shelley, Harris, Jones
Scorers: Shelley, Alden
Attendance: 1000

Date: Saturday 30/11/1935?
Result: **BIRMINGHAM 'A' ? GLOUCESTER CITY ?**
Competition: Birmingham Senior Cup 1st Round Replay
Teamsheet: Saunders (?), Langley (?), Cox (?), O'Brien (?), Drew (?), Leach (?), Stoles (?), Harris (?), Shelley (?), AL Smith (?), Jones (?)
Note: Gloucester City lost

Date: Saturday 07/12/1935
Result: **GLOUCESTER CITY 2 BROMSGROVE ROVERS 1**
Competition: Birmingham Combination
Teamsheet: Saunders, Langley, Cox, O'Brien, Drew, Leach, Stoles, Harris, Shelley, AL Smith, Jones
Scorers: Harris, Shelley
Attendance: 1000

Date: Saturday 14/12/1935
Result: **GLOUCESTER CITY 4 TAMWORTH 2**
Competition: Birmingham Combination
Teamsheet: Saunders, Langley, Cox, O'Brien, Drew, Leach, AL Smith, Alden, Shelley, Causon, Harris
Scorers: AL Smith, Shelley (2 pens), Causon

Date: Saturday 21/12/1935
Result: **WOLVERHAMPTON WANDERERS 'A' 2 GLOUCESTER CITY 1**
Competition: Birmingham Combination
Teamsheet: Saunders, Langley, Cox, O'Brien, Drew, S Smith, Chambers, AL Smith, Shelley, Causon, Jones
Scorer: own goal

Date: Thursday 26/12/1935
Result: **GLOUCESTER CITY 4 ATHERSTONE TOWN 2**
Competition: Birmingham Combination
Teamsheet: Saunders, Langley, Cox, O'Brien, Drew, Leach, Watson, AL Smith, Shelley, Causon, Harris
Scorer: Shelley (4)

Date: Saturday 28/12/1935
Result: **ASTON VILLA 'A' 2 GLOUCESTER CITY 1**
Competition: Birmingham Combination
Teamsheet: Saunders, Langley, Cox, O'Brien, Drew, Leach, Chambers, Watson, Shelley, Causon, Harris
Scorer: -----

Date: Saturday 04/01/1936
Result: **GLOUCESTER CITY 2 CHELTENHAM TOWN 2**
Competition: Birmingham Combination
Teamsheet: Saunders, Langley, Cox, O'Brien, Drew, Leach, Alden, AL Smith, Causon, Harris, Jones
Scorers: Drew, AL Smith

Date: Saturday 11/01/1936
Result: **SHIRLEY TOWN 3 GLOUCESTER CITY 0**
Competition: Birmingham Combination
Teamsheet: Saunders, Langley, Cox, O'Brien, Drew, Leach, Watson, AL Smith, Harris, Chambers, Jones

Date: Saturday 18/01/1936
Result: **GLOUCESTER CITY 5 EVESHAM TOWN 0**
Competition: Birmingham Combination
Teamsheet: Saunders, Langley, Cox, F Smith, Drew, Leach, Watson, Causon, Shelley, AL Smith, Harris
Scorers: Causon, Shelley, AL Smith, Watson

Date: Saturday 25/01/1936
Result: **GLOUCESTER CITY 5 HALESOWEN TOWN 2**
Competition: Birmingham Combination
Teamsheet: Saunders, Langley, Cox, O'Brien, Drew, Leach, Watson, Causon, Shelley, Norris, Harris
Scorers: Norris, Harris, Shelley, Drew (2)

Date: Saturday 08/02/1936
Result: **BROMSGROVE ROVERS 1 GLOUCESTER CITY 4**
Competition: Birmingham Combination
Teamsheet: Saunders, Langley, Cox, O'Brien, Drew, Leach, Causon, Anderson, Shelley, AL Smith, Harris
Scorers: Anderson, Harris (2), Shelley

Date: Saturday 15/02/1936
Result: **REDDITCH TOWN 2 GLOUCESTER CITY 2**
Competition: Birmingham Combination
Teamsheet: Saunders, Langley, Cox, O'Brien, Drew, Leach, Anderson, Causon, Shelley, AL Smith, Harris
Scorers: Shelley, Anderson
Attendance: 600

Date: Saturday 22/02/1936
Result: **GLOUCESTER CITY 5 HINCKLEY ATHLETIC 1**
Competition: Birmingham Combination
Teamsheet: Saunders, Langley, Cox, O'Brien, Drew, Leach, Causon, AL Smith, Shelley, Anderson, Harris
Scorers: AL Smith (2), Shelley (2), Causon

Date: Saturday 29/02/1936
Result: **GLOUCESTER CITY 2 WEST BROMWICH ALBION 'A' 3**
Competition: Birmingham Combination
Teamsheet: Saunders, Langley, Cox, O'Brien, Drew, Leach, Causon, AL Smith, Shelley, Anderson, Harris
Scorer: Shelley (2)

Date: Saturday 07/03/1936
Result: **DARLASTON 1 GLOUCESTER CITY 1**
Competition: Birmingham Combination
Teamsheet: Saunders, Langley, Cox, Anderson, Drew, Leach, Angrove, AL Smith, Shelley, Causon, Jones
Scorer: Angrove

Date: Saturday 14/03/1936
Result: **GLOUCESTER CITY 2 BIRMINGHAM TRAMS 0**
Competition: Birmingham Combination
Teamsheet: Saunders, Langley, Cox, Anderson, Drew, Leach, Angrove, AL Smith, Shelley, Harris, Hopkins
Scorers: Drew, AL Smith

Date: Saturday 21/03/1936
Result: **GLOUCESTER CITY 4 BOURNEVILLE ATHLETIC 3**
Competition: Birmingham Combination
Teamsheet: Saunders, Langley, Cox, O'Brien, Drew, Leach, Angrove, AL Smith, Shelley, Harris, Hopkins
Scorers: Harris (2), Shelley, Leach

Date: Saturday 28/03/1936
Result: **GLOUCESTER CITY 3 BANBURY SPENCER 6**
Competition: Birmingham Combination
Teamsheet: Saunders, Langley, Cox, Norris, Drew, Leach, Causon, AL Smith, Shelley, Harris, Hopkins
Scorers: Hopkins, Harris, AL Smith
Attendance: 2500

Date: Saturday 04/04/1936
Result: **GLOUCESTER CITY 3 LEAMINGTON TOWN 0**
Competition: Birmingham Combination
Teamsheet: Saunders, Langley, Cox, F Smith, Drew, Leach, Norris, Causon, Shelley, AL Smith, Hopkins
Scorers: Leach, Shelley, Hopkins

Date: Saturday 11/04/1936
Result: **HINCKLEY ATHLETIC 2 GLOUCESTER CITY 2**
Competition: Birmingham Combination
Teamsheet: Saunders, Langley, Cox, O'Brien, Drew, Leach, Causon, AL Smith, Shelley, Harris, Hopkins
Scorer: Hopkins (2)

Date: Monday 13/04/1936
Result: **TAMWORTH 2 GLOUCESTER CITY 3**
Competition: Birmingham Combination
Teamsheet: Saunders, Langley, Peart, O'Brien, Drew, Leach, Causon, AL Smith, Shelley, Harris, Hopkins
Scorers: Shelley (2), own goal
Attendance: 3800

Date: Tuesday 14/04/1936
Result: **GLOUCESTER CITY 6 SHIRLEY TOWN 3**
Competition: Birmingham Combination
Teamsheet: Saunders, Langley, Peart, O'Brien, Drew, Leach, Causon, AL Smith, Shelley, Harris, Hopkins
Scorers: Shelley (3), Drew (2), -----

Date: Saturday 18/04/1936
Result: **GLOUCESTER CITY 3 WOLVERHAMPTON WANDERERS 'A' 0**
Competition: Birmingham Combination
Teamsheet: Saunders, Langley, Cox, O'Brien, Drew, Leach, Causon, AL Smith, Shelley, Harris, Hopkins
Scorers: Harris, Hopkins, AL Smith

Date: Thursday 23/04/1936
Result: **BANBURY SPENCER 7 GLOUCESTER CITY 2**
Competition: Birmingham Combination
Teamsheet: Saunders, Langley, Cox, O'Brien, Drew, Leach, Causon, AL Smith, Shelley, Harris, Hopkins
Scorers: Causon, AL Smith

Date: Saturday 25/04/1936
Result: **ATHERSTONE TOWN 0 GLOUCESTER CITY 2**
Competition: Birmingham Combination
Teamsheet: Saunders, Langley, Cox, O'Brien, Drew, Grey, Griffiths, AL Smith, Shelley, Leach, Hopkins
Scorers: AL Smith, Shelley

Date: Thursday 30/04/1936
Result: **GLOUCESTER CITY 0 WALSALL RESERVES 1**
Competition: Birmingham Combination
Teamsheet: Saunders, Langley, Cox, O'Brien, Peart, Powell, AL Smith, Leach, Shelley, Drew, Hopkins

Date: Saturday 02/05/1936
Result: **GLOUCESTER CITY 5 ASTON VILLA 'A' 2**
Competition: Birmingham Combination
Teamsheet: Saunders, Langley, Cox, Powell, Peart, Leach, AL Smith, Edwards, Shelley, Drew, Harris
Scorers: AL Smith, Edwards (2), Shelley (2)
Attendance: 2600

Appearances – E Alden 3, D Anderson 8, E Angrove 3, WJ Causon 19, T Chambers 3, RD Cox 37, EW Drew 39, M Edwards 1, FWG Figgures 1, ? Grey 1, W Griffiths 1, IW Gwatkin 1, WAH Harris 24, VJD Henderson 1, ? Hopkins 11, W Jones 16, HW Langley 39, H Leach 37, J Maisey 1, WH Norris 3, P O'Brien 32, WC Peart 4, RT Powell 2, G Saunders 39, A Shelley 37, AL Smith 37, F Smith 2, SG Smith 1, AW Stoles 12, H Watkins 1, GS Watson 12, SR Wise 1.
Scorers – A Shelley 36, AL Smith 20, WAH Harris 10, EW Drew 7, ? Hopkins 5, GS Watson 5, WJ Causon 4, H Leach 4, W Jones 3, D Anderson 2, M Edwards 2, AW Stoles 2, E Alden 1, E Angrove 1, WH Norris 1, own goals 2.

BIRMINGHAM COMBINATION

POS	CLUB	P	W	D	L	F	A	PTS
1	ASTON VILLA 'A'	36	25	3	8	126	54	53
2	WEST BROMWICH ALBION 'A'	36	25	3	8	119	71	53
3	WOLVERHAMPTON WANDERERS 'A'	36	23	4	9	99	58	50
4	**GLOUCESTER CITY**	**36**	**21**	**6**	**9**	**99**	**62**	**48**
5	TAMWORTH	36	22	2	12	113	65	46
6	WALSALL RESERVES	36	21	3	12	98	57	45
7	CHELTENHAM TOWN RESERVES	36	19	6	11	79	61	44
8	DARLASTON	36	16	8	12	86	70	40
9	BANBURY SPENCER	36	16	5	15	88	90	37
10	BIRMINGHAM TRAMS	36	13	9	14	66	64	35
11	SHIRLEY TOWN	36	14	4	18	86	94	32
12	HALESOWEN TOWN	36	14	3	19	88	115	31
13	EVESHAM TOWN	36	13	5	18	78	107	31
14	LEAMINGTON TOWN	36	12	6	18	65	84	30
15	ATHERSTONE TOWN	36	10	7	19	82	93	27
16	BROMSGROVE ROVERS	36	9	7	20	65	100	25
17	REDDITCH TOWN	36	8	8	20	66	108	24
18	HINCKLEY ATHLETIC	36	9	5	22	60	133	23
19	BOURNEVILLE ATHLETIC	36	2	6	28	50	127	10
20	MARKET HARBOROUGH							
		684	292	100	292	1613	1613	684

Market Harborough withdrew December 1935. All records expunged.
West Bromwich Albion 'A' played all their games away.
Gloucester City won the Tillotson Shield for being the highest placed non-league club in the Birmingham Combination

SEASON 1936-1937
(Home Ground: The Ground, Cheltenham Road, Longlevens)

Date: Saturday 29/08/1936
Result: **GLOUCESTER CITY 4 SHIRLEY TOWN 3**
Competition: Birmingham Combination
Teamsheet: Saunders, Langley, SG Smith, Norris, Peart, Drew, Russell, AL Smith, Shelley, T Mayo, Middlecote
Scorers: T Mayo (2), Shelley, Russell

Date: Tuesday 01/09/1936
Result: **GLOUCESTER CITY 0 BIRMINGHAM TRAMS 1**
Competition: Birmimgham Combination
Teamsheet: Saunders, Langley, Cox, Leach, Peart, Drew, Gwatkin, Causon, Shelley, T Mayo, Middlecote

Date: Saturday 05/09/1936
Result: **GLOUCESTER CITY 4 HINCKLEY ATHLETIC 1**
Competition: Birmingham Combination
Teamsheet: Saunders, Langley, Cox, Norris, Peart, Leach, Russell, Edwards, Shelley, T Mayo, Middlecote
Scorers: -----, -----, -----, -----

Date: Wednesday 09/09/1936
Result: **BIRMINGHAM 'A' 2 GLOUCESTER CITY 2**
Competition: Birmingham Combination
Teamsheet: Saunders, Langley, Peart, Leach, Norris, Connor, Russell, Edwards, Shelley, T Mayo, Middlecote
Scorers: T Mayo, Shelley

Date: Saturday 12/09/1936
Result: **CHELTENHAM TOWN 3 GLOUCESTER CITY 2**
Competition: Gloucestershire FA Northern Senior Professional Cup Final
Teamsheet: Saunders, Langley, Cox, Norris, Peart, Leach, Russell, Drew, Shelley, T Mayo, Middlecote
Scorers: T Mayo, Drew

Date: Saturday 19/09/1936
Result: **GLOUCESTER CITY 3 REDDITCH TOWN 1**
Competition: Birmingham Combination
Teamsheet: Saunders, Langley, Cox, Norris, Peart, Leach, Russell, Hartshorne, Drew, Edwards, Middlecote
Scorers: -----, -----, -----

Date: Saturday 26/09/1936
Result: **GLOUCESTER CITY 2 DARLASTON 2**
Competition: Birmingham Combination
Teamsheet: Saunders, Peart, Cox, Norris, Drew, Leach, Russell, Hartshorne, Shelley, Edwards, Middlecote
Scorers: -----, -----

Date: Saturday 03/10/1936
Result: **WALSALL RESERVES 5 GLOUCESTER CITY 1**
Competition: Birmingham Combination
Teamsheet: Saunders, Langley, Cox, Norris, Drew, Peart, Russell, Hartshorne, Shelley, Leach, Middlecote
Scorer: -----

Date: Saturday 10/10/1936
Result: **WOLVERHAMPTON WANDERERS 'A' 1 GLOUCESTER CITY 3**
Competition: Birmingham Combination
Teamsheet: Saunders, Langley, Peart, Norris, Drew, Leach, Russell, Edwards, Shelley, T Mayo, Middlecote
Scorers: -----, -----, -----

Date: Saturday 17/10/1936
Result: **GLOUCESTER CITY 3 BANBURY SPENCER 4**
Competition: Birmingham Combination
Teamsheet: Saunders, Langley, Peart, Norris, Drew, Leach, Russell, AL Smith, Shelley, T Mayo, Middlecote
Scorers: -----, -----, -----

Date: Saturday 24/10/1936
Result: **BOURNEVILLE ATHLETIC 0 GLOUCESTER CITY 4**
Competition: Birmingham Combination
Teamsheet: Saunders, Langley, Cox, Norris, Peart, Leach, Russell, Drew, AL Smith, T Mayo, Middlecote
Scorers: -----, -----, -----, -----

Date: Saturday 07/11/1936
Result: **GLOUCESTER CITY 6 BROMSGROVE ROVERS 0**
Competition: Birmingham Combination
Teamsheet: Saunders, Langley, Cox, Norris, Peart, Leach, Harris, Drew, Shelley, T Mayo, Middlecote
Scorers: T Mayo, Shelley (2), Drew (3)

Date: Saturday 14/11/1936
Result: **WEST BROMWICH ALBION 'A' 2 GLOUCESTER CITY 1**
Competition: Birmingham Combination
Teamsheet: Saunders, Langley, Cox, Norris, Peart, Connor, Russell, Drew, Shelley, T Mayo, Harris
Scorer: Shelley
Attendance: 1200

Date: Saturday 21/11/1936
Result: **HALESOWEN TOWN 1 GLOUCESTER CITY 4**
Competition: Birmingham Combination
Teamsheet: Saunders, Langley, Cox, Griffiths, Peart, Harris, Russell, Drew, Shelley, Causon, Weston
Scorers: Drew, Causon, Shelley, Russell

Date: Saturday 28/11/1936
Result: **GLOUCESTER CITY 2 BOURNEVILLE ATHLETIC 0**
Competition: Birmingham Combination
Teamsheet: Saunders, Langley, Cox, Drew, Peart, Harris, Russell, Edwards, Shelley, Hutchins, Weston
Scorers: Shelley, Russell

Date: Saturday 12/12/1936
Result: **SHIRLEY TOWN 1 GLOUCESTER CITY 3**
Competition: Birmingham Combination
Teamsheet: Saunders, Langley, Cox, Drew, Peart, Murdock, Goodall, Russell, AL Smith, Edwards, WH Mayo
Scorers: Edwards, WH Mayo, AL Smith

Date: Saturday 19/12/1936
Result: **BIRMINGHAM TRAMS 2 GLOUCESTER CITY 1**
Competition: Birmingham Combination
Teamsheet: Saunders, Langley, Cox, Drew, Peart, Murdock, Goodall, Russell, AL Smith, Edwards, WH Mayo
Scorer: AL Smith

Date: Saturday 02/01/1937
Result: **HINCKLEY ATHLETIC 4 GLOUCESTER CITY 1**
Competition: Birmingham Combination
Teamsheet: Saunders, Langley, Peart, Murdock, Drew, Gothing, Gwatkin, Russell, AL Smith, T Mayo, WH Mayo
Scorer: AL Smith

Date: Saturday 09/01/1937
Result: **GLOUCESTER CITY 2 BIRMINGHAM 'A' 1**
Competition: Birmingham Combination
Teamsheet: Saunders, Langley, Cox, Norris, Peart, Weston, Russell, Drew, AL Smith, T Mayo, WH Mayo
Scorers: T Mayo, Drew

Date: Saturday 16/01/1937
Result: **ATHERSTONE TOWN 2 GLOUCESTER CITY 0**
Competition: Birmingham Combination
Teamsheet: Saunders, Langley, Murdock, Norris, Drew, Morgan, Russell, Hartshorne, Edwards, T Mayo, WH Mayo
Attendance: 500

Date: Saturday 23/01/1937
Result: **EVESHAM TOWN 3 GLOUCESTER CITY 0**
Competition: Birmingham Combination
Teamsheet: Saunders, Langley, Cox, Murdock, Norris, Connor, Meadows, Russell, Edwards, T Mayo, WH Mayo

Date: Thursday 28/01/1937
Result: **GLOUCESTER CITY 0 ASTON VILLA 'A' 1**
Competition: Birmingham Combination
Teamsheet: Saunders, Langley, Cox, Murdock, Peart, Connor, Russell, Norris, Edwards, Drew, WH Mayo

Date: Saturday 30/01/1937
Result: **REDDITCH TOWN 2 GLOUCESTER CITY 1**
Competition: Birmingham Combination
Teamsheet: Manners, Langley, Cox, Murdock, Peart, Connor, Russell, Norris, Edwards, Drew, WH Mayo
Scorer: WH Mayo

Date: Saturday 06/02/1937
Result: **GLOUCESTER CITY 1 TAMWORTH 3**
Competition: Birmingham Combination
Teamsheet: Manners, Langley, Cox, Norris, Drew, Connor, Edwards, Comer, Merrie, Harris, WH Mayo
Scorer: Merrie

Date: Saturday 13/02/1937
Result: **DARLASTON 5 GLOUCESTER CITY 0**
Competition: Birmingham Combination
Teamsheet: Manners, Langley, Cox, Norris, Drew, Connor, Edwards, Harding, Haile, Moore, WH Mayo

Date: Saturday 27/02/1937
Result: **GLOUCESTER CITY 1 WOLVERHAMPTON WANDERERS 'A' 1**
Competition: Birmingham Combination
Teamsheet: Saunders, Langley, Cox, Murdock, Peart, Drew, Edwards, Comer, Merrie, AL Smith, Russell
Scorer: Merrie

Date: Saturday 06/03/1937
Result: **BANBURY SPENCER 3 GLOUCESTER CITY 2**
Competition: Birmingham Combination
Teamsheet: Saunders, Langley, Cox, Murdock, Peart, Drew, Edwards, Comer, Merrie, AL Smith, Russell
Scorers: AL Smith, Merrie

Date: Saturday 13/03/1937
Result: **GLOUCESTER CITY 1 LEAMINGTON TOWN 3**
Competition: Birmingham Combination
Teamsheet: Saunders, Langley, Cox, Murdock, Peart, Drew, Russell, Comer, Merrie, Hartshorne, Connor
Scorer: Russell

Date: Saturday 20/03/1937
Result: **ASTON VILLA 'A' 4 GLOUCESTER CITY 1**
Competition: Birmingham Combination
Teamsheet: Saunders, Langley, Cox, Murdock, Peart, Drew, Edwards, Comer, Merrie, Hartshorne, Russell
Scorer: Edwards

Date: Friday 26/03/1937
Result: **GLOUCESTER CITY 1 CHELTENHAM TOWN RESERVES 4**
Competition: Birmingham Combination
Teamsheet: Saunders, Langley, Cox, Murdock, Drew, Haile, Gwatkin, Comer, Merrie, Hartshorne, Jones
Scorer: Gwatkin
Attendance: 2000

Date: Saturday 27/03/1937
Result: **BROMSGROVE ROVERS 5 GLOUCESTER CITY 2**
Competition: Birmingham Combination
Teamsheet: Saunders, Langley, Cox, Murdock, Haile, Weston, Gwatkin, Comer, AL Smith, Merrie, Russell
Scorers: Cox, Haile
Attendance: 300

Date: Monday 29/03/1937
Result: **CHELTENHAM TOWN RESERVES 1 GLOUCESTER CITY 1**
Competition: Birmingham Combination
Teamsheet: Saunders, Langley, Cox, Haile, Drew, Connor, Gwatkin, Taylor, AL Smith, Hartshorne, Middlecote
Scorer: AL Smith

Date: Saturday 03/04/1937
Result: **GLOUCESTER CITY 0 WEST BROMWICH ALBION 'A' 0**
Competition: Birmingham Combination
Teamsheet: Saunders, Peart, Cox, Murdock, Drew, Connor, Gwatkin, Comer, AL Smith, Merrie, Middlecote

Date: Saturday 10/04/1937
Result: **GLOUCESTER CITY 4 HALESOWEN TOWN 0**
Competition: Birmingham Combination
Teamsheet: Saunders, Peart, Cox, Murdock, Drew, Connor, Gwatkin, Russell, AL Smith, Merrie, Middlecote
Scorers: Merrie, Middlecote, -----, -----

Date: Saturday 17/04/1937
Result: **LEAMINGTON TOWN 2 GLOUCESTER CITY 2**
Competition: Birmingham Combination
Teamsheet: Saunders, Peart, Cox, Murdock, Drew, Connor, Gwatkin, Russell, AL Smith, Merrie, Middlecote
Scorers: AL Smith, Peart (pen)

Date: Saturday 24/04/1937
Result: **GLOUCESTER CITY 3 ATHERSTONE TOWN 0**
Competition: Birmingham Combination
Teamsheet: Saunders, Langley, Cox, Hartshorne, Peart, Connor, Gwatkin, Russell, AL Smith, Merrie, Middlecote
Scorers: Merrie, AL Smith (2)
Attendance: 700-800

Date: Wednesday 28/04/1937
Result: **GLOUCESTER CITY 2 EVESHAM TOWN 0**
Competition: Birmingham Combination
Teamsheet: Saunders, Peart, Cox, Norris, Drew, Connor, Gwatkin, Meadows, Langley, Merrie, Middlecote
Scorers: Drew, Middlecote

Date: Thursday 29/04/1937
Result: **GLOUCESTER CITY 0 WALSALL RESERVES 1**
Competition: Birmingham Combination
Teamsheet: Saunders, Langley, Peart, Connor, Drew, Cox, Gwatkin, Russell, Edwards, Merrie, Middlecote

Date: Saturday 01/05/1937
Result: **TAMWORTH 10 GLOUCESTER CITY 1**
Competition: Birmingham Combination
Teamsheet: Saunders, Langley, Cox, Hartshorne, Drew, Connor, Gwatkin, Russell, Edwards, AL Smith, Middlecote
Scorer: -----

Appearances – WJ Causon 2, WC Comer 9, J Connor 16, RD Cox 34, EW Drew 35, M Edwards 18, J Goodall 2, F Gothing 1, W Griffiths 1, IW Gwatkin 12, F Haile 4, ? Harding 1, WAH Harris 5, C Hartshorne 11, ? Hutchins 1, W Jones 2, HW Langley 36, H Leach 11, ? Manners 3, T Mayo 14, WH Mayo 10, W Meadows 2, AB Merrie 13, ? Middlecote 20, ? Moore 1, D Morgan 1, GAS Murdock 17, WH Norris 20, WC Peart 31, K Russell 31, G Saunders 36, A Shelley 13, AL Smith 16, SG Smith 1, ? Taylor 1, L Weston 4.
Scorers – AL Smith 8, EH Drew 7, A Shelley 7, T Mayo 6, AB Merrie 5, K Russell 4, M Edwards 2, WH Mayo 2, ? Middlecote 2, WJ Causon 1, RD Cox 1, IW Gwatkin 1, F Haile 1, WC Peart 1.

BIRMINGHAM COMBINATION

POS	CLUB	P	W	D	L	F	A	PTS
1	WALSALL RESERVES	38	29	2	7	144	50	60
2	WEST BROMWICH ALBION 'A'	38	27	5	6	110	43	59
3	BANBURY SPENCER	38	22	5	11	96	88	49
4	WOLVERHAMPTON WANDERERS 'A'	38	20	7	11	105	58	47
5	TAMWORTH	38	21	5	12	124	85	47
6	ASTON VILLA 'A'	38	20	6	12	85	55	46
7	CHELTENHAM TOWN RESERVES	38	18	10	10	99	63	46
8	BIRMINGHAM TRAMS	38	19	6	13	100	83	44
9	DARLASTON	38	19	5	14	102	59	43
10	SHIRLEY TOWN	38	17	6	15	99	83	40
11	REDDITCH TOWN	38	15	6	17	87	96	36
12	**GLOUCESTER CITY**	**38**	**13**	**6**	**19**	**69**	**81**	**32**
13	HALESOWEN TOWN	38	13	5	20	69	88	31
14	EVESHAM TOWN	38	12	7	19	76	113	31
15	ATHERSTONE TOWN	38	12	5	21	85	127	29
16	BIRMINGHAM 'A'	38	11	5	22	63	83	27
17	BROMSGROVE ROVERS	38	10	6	22	61	135	26
18	HINCKLEY ATHLETIC	38	10	4	24	73	146	24
19	LEAMINGTON TOWN	38	9	5	24	44	88	23
20	BOURNEVILLE ATHLETIC	38	8	4	26	63	130	20
		760	325	110	325	1754	1754	760

SEASON 1937-1938
(Home Ground: The Ground, Cheltenham Road, Longlevens)

Date: Saturday 28/08/1937
Result: **GLOUCESTER CITY 4 BIRMINGHAM 'A' 1**
Competition: Birmingham Combination
Teamsheet: Saunders, Langley, Peart, Dyer, Drew, Leach, Gwatkin, Hartshorne, Weaver, McNeill, Middlecote
Scorer: Weaver (4)
Attendance: 800

Date: Monday 30/08/1937
Result: **BIRMINGHAM TRAMS 3 GLOUCESTER CITY 1**
Competition: Birmingham Combination
Teamsheet: Saunders, Langley, Leach, Dyer, Drew, Murdock, Gwatkin, Hartshorne, Taylor, McNeill, Middlecote
Scorer: Hartshorne

Date: Thursday 09/09/1937
Result: **GLOUCESTER CITY 8 BROMSGROVE ROVERS 2**
Competition: Birmingham Combination
Teamsheet: Saunders, Langley, Peart, Norris, Drew, Leach, Gwatkin, Stoles, Weaver, McNeill, Payne
Scorers: Gwatkin, Weaver (4), Drew, Payne (2)

Date: Saturday 11/09/1937
Result: **CHELTENHAM TOWN 2 GLOUCESTER CITY 3**
Competition: Gloucestershire FA Northern Senior Professional Cup Final
Teamsheet: Saunders, Langley, Murdock, Hartshorne, Drew, Leach, Gwatkin, Stoles, Weaver, McNeill, Payne
Scorer: Weaver (3)

Date: Saturday 18/09/1937
Result: **GLOUCESTER CITY 4 BRISTOL SAINT GEORGE 1**
Competition: FA Cup Preliminary Round
Teamsheet: Saunders, Langley, Peart, Weston, Drew, Leach, Gwatkin, Hartshorne, Weaver, McNeill, Payne
Scorer: Weaver (4)
Attendance: 800

[81]

Date: Thursday 23/09/1937
Result: **GLOUCESTER CITY 3 WALSALL RESERVES 4**
Competition: Birmingham Combination
Teamsheet: Saunders, Langley, Peart, Norris, Drew, Leach, Gwatkin, Edwards, Weaver, McNeill, Payne
Scorers: Weaver (2), Edwards

Date: Saturday 02/10/1937
Result: **GLOUCESTER CITY 5 BRISTOL SAINT PHILIP'S 0**
Competition: FA Cup 1st Qualifying Round
Teamsheet: Saunders, Langley, Peart, Norris, Drew, Leach, Meadows, Gwatkin, Weaver, McNeill, Payne
Scorers: Payne, Weaver (3), McNeill

Date: Saturday 09/10/1937
Result: **GLOUCESTER CITY 2 ASTON VILLA 'A' 6**
Competition: Birmingham Combination
Teamsheet: Saunders, Langley, Peart, Norris, Drew, Leach, Gwatkin, Edwards, Weaver, McNeill, Payne
Scorers: Edwards, Weaver
Attendance: 2500

Date: Saturday 16/10/1937
Result: **GLOUCESTER CITY 0 LOVELLS ATHLETIC 1**
Competition: FA Cup 2nd Qualifying Round
Teamsheet: Saunders, Langley, Peart, Norris, Drew, Leach, Gwatkin, Kirby, Weaver, McNeill, Payne
Attendance: 1300

Date: Saturday 30/10/1937
Result: **TAMWORTH 2 GLOUCESTER CITY 2**
Competition: Birmingham Combination
Teamsheet: Saunders, Langley, Peart, Leach, Drew, Weston, Gwatkin, Edwards, Weaver, McNeil, Payne
Scorers: Gwatkin, McNeill

Date: Saturday 06/11/1937
Result: **GLOUCESTER CITY 2 HALESOWEN TOWN 2**
Competition: Birmingham Combination
Teamsheet: Saunders, Langley, Peart, Leach, Drew, Weston, Gwatkin, Edwards, Weaver, McNeill, Payne
Scorer: Weaver (2)

Date: Saturday 13/11/1937
Result: **REDDITCH TOWN 1 GLOUCESTER CITY 2**
Competition: Birmingham Combination
Teamsheet: Saunders, Langley, Peart, Leach, Drew, Gribble, Gwatkin, Edwards, Weaver, McNeill, Johnson
Scorers: Edwards, Gwatkin

Date: Saturday 20/11/1937
Result: **GLOUCESTER CITY 4 ATHERSTONE TOWN 0**
Competition: Birmingham Combination
Teamsheet: Saunders, Langley, Peart, Weston, Leach, Gribble, Gwatkin, Edwards, Weaver, McNeill, Rickelton
Scorers: Weaver (2), McNeill, Rickelton

Date: Saturday 27/11/1937
Result: **GLOUCESTER CITY 6 HINCKLEY ATHLETIC 0**
Competition: Birmingham Combination
Teamsheet: Saunders, Langley, Peart, Gribble, Leach, Weston, Gwatkin, Drew, Weaver, McNeill, Rickelton
Scorers: Weaver (5), Drew

Date: Saturday 04/12/1937
Result: **GLOUCESTER CITY 2 WEST BROMWICH ALBION 'A' 5**
Competition: Birmingham Combination
Teamsheet: Saunders, Langley, Peart, Gribble, Leach, Drew, Gwatkin, Edwards, Weaver, McNeill, Rickelton
Scorers: Weaver, Peart (pen)

Date: Saturday 11/12/1937
Result: **GLOUCESTER CITY 3 BANBURY SPENCER 3**
Competition: Birmingham Combination
Teamsheet: Saunders, Langley, Peart, Gribble, Leach, Drew, Gwatkin, Kirby, Weaver, McNeill, Rickelton
Scorers: Weaver (2), Rickelton

Date: Saturday 18/12/1937
Result: **BANBURY SPENCER 2 GLOUCESTER CITY 1**
Competition: Birmingham Combination
Teamsheet: Brock, Langley, Peart, Gribble, Leach, Drew, Gwatkin, Edwards, Weaver, McNeill, Rickelton
Scorer: Peart (pen)

Date: Monday 27/12/1937
Result: **EVESHAM TOWN 2 GLOUCESTER CITY 0**
Competition: Birmingham Combination
Teamsheet: Saunders, Langley, Peart, Gribble, Leach, Drew, Gwatkin, Bromage, Weaver, McNeill, Rickelton

Date: Tuesday 28/12/1937
Result: **BIRMINGHAM 'A' 9 GLOUCESTER CITY 3**
Competition: Birmingham Combination
Teamsheet: Saunders, Langley, Anderson, Gribble, Leach, Weston, Gwatkin, Drew, Weaver, McNeill, Rickelton
Scorers: Weaver (2), McNeill

Date: Saturday 01/01/1938
Result: **WEST BROMWICH ALBION 'A' 5 GLOUCESTER CITY 3**
Competition: Birmingham Combination
Teamsheet: Saunders, Langley, Peart, Gribble, Neale, Murdock, Gwatkin, Drew, Weaver, McNeill, Kirby
Scorers: Drew, Weaver, Kirby

Date: Saturday 08/01/1938
Result: **HINCKLEY ATHLETIC 2 GLOUCESTER CITY 5**
Competition: Birmingham Combination
Teamsheet: Saunders, Langley, Peart, Gribble, Drew, Neale, Gwatkin, Hartshorne, Weaver, McNeill, Kirby
Scorers: Gwatkin, Weaver (3), Neale

Date: Saturday 15/01/1938
Result: **ATHERSTONE TOWN 1 GLOUCESTER CITY 0**
Competition: Birmingham Combination
Teamsheet: Saunders, Langley, Peart, Gribble, Drew, Neale, Gwatkin, Hartshorne, Weaver, McNeill, Kirby

Date: Saturday 22/01/1938
Result: **GLOUCESTER CITY 3 REDDITCH TOWN 4**
Competition: Birmingham Combination
Teamsheet: Saunders, Langley, Peart, Gribble, Drew, Leach, Gwatkin, Hartshorne, Weaver, Neale, McNeill
Scorers: Hartshorne, Neale, Drew

Date: Saturday 29/01/1938
Result: **HALESOWEN TOWN 5 GLOUCESTER CITY 4**
Competition: Birmingham Combination
Teamsheet: Saunders, Peart, Cox, Moule, Drew, Cale, Gwatkin, Hartshorne, Weaver, McNeill, Silvey
Scorers: Hartshorne (2), Weaver, Silvey

Date: Saturday 05/02/1938
Result: **GLOUCESTER CITY 1 TAMWORTH 5**
Competition: Birmingham Combination
Teamsheet: Saunders, Moule, Cox, McNeill, Peart, Neale, Gwatkin, Hartshorne, Weaver, Goodburn, Silvey
Scorer: Weaver
Attendance: 700

Date: Saturday 12/02/1938
Result: **SHIRLEY TOWN 0 GLOUCESTER CITY 0**
Competition: Birmingham Combination
Teamsheet: Neale, Langley, Cox, Weston, Drew, Connor, Gwatkin, Hartshorne, Edwards, McNeill, Silvey

Date: Saturday 19/02/1938
Result: **GLOUCESTER CITY 1 COVENTRY CITY 'A' 0**
Competition: Birmingham Combination
Teamsheet: Neale, Langley, Cox, McNeill, Drew, Connor, Gwatkin, Edwards, Weaver, Goodburn, Silvey
Scorer: Goodburn
Attendance: 800

Date: Saturday 26/02/1938
Result: **ASTON VILLA 'A' 4 GLOUCESTER CITY 2**
Competition: Birmingham Combination
Teamsheet: Neale, Langley, Cox, McNeill, Drew, Connor, Gwatkin, Hartshorne, Weaver, Goodburn, Silvey
Scorer: Weaver (2)

Date: Saturday 05/03/1938
Result: **BOURNEVILLE ATHLETIC 1 GLOUCESTER CITY 4**
Competition: Birmingham Combination
Teamsheet: Neale, Langley, Cox, Leach, Drew, Connor, Gwatkin, Hartshorne, Weaver, McNeill, Silvey
Scorer: Weaver (4)

Date: Saturday 12/03/1938
Result: **WOLVERHAMPTON WANDERERS 'A' 2 GLOUCESTER CITY 2**
Competition: Birmingham Combination
Teamsheet: Neale, Langley, Cox, Leach, Drew, Connor, Gwatkin, Hartshorne, Weaver, McNeill, Silvey
Scorer: Weaver (2)

Date: Saturday 19/03/1938
Result: **WALSALL RESERVES 2 GLOUCESTER CITY 4**
Competition: Birmingham Combination
Teamsheet: Neale, Langley, Cox, Connor, Drew, Leach, Gwatkin, Hartshorne, Weaver, McNeill, Silvey
Scorers: Gwatkin, Weaver (3)
Attendance: 1500

Date: Saturday 26/03/1938
Result: **GLOUCESTER CITY 1 DARLASTON 4**
Competition: Birmingham Combination
Teamsheet: Neale, Langley, Cox, McNeill, Leach, Connor, Gwatkin, Stoles, Weaver, Meadows, Silvey
Scorer: Weaver

Date: Saturday 02/04/1938
Result: **GLOUCESTER CITY 7 WOLVERHAMPTON WANDERERS 'A' 1**
Competition: Birmingham Combination
Teamsheet: Neale, Langley, Cox, Leach, Drew, Connor, Gwatkin, Stoles, Weaver, McNeill, Silvey
Scorers: Weaver (5), Gwatkin, Stoles
Attendance: 1000

Date: Saturday 09/04/1938
Result: **GLOUCESTER CITY 3 BIRMINGHAM TRAMS 2**
Competition: Birmingham Combination
Teamsheet: Neale, Leach, Cox, McNeill, Drew, Taylor, Gwatkin, Stoles, Weaver, Edwards, Silvey
Scorers: Weaver (2), Edwards

Date: Friday 15/04/1938
Result: **GLOUCESTER CITY 3 CHELTENHAM TOWN RESERVES 0**
Competition: Birmingham Combination
Teamsheet: Neale, Langley, Cox, Leach, Drew, Connor, Gwatkin, Stoles, Weaver, McNeill, Silvey
Scorers: Weaver (2), Drew
Attendance: 2000

SEASON BY SEASON

Date: Saturday 16/04/1938
Result: **BROMSGROVE ROVERS 2 GLOUCESTER CITY 2**
Competition: Birmingham Combination
Teamsheet: Brock, Langley, Cox, Leach, Drew, Connor, Gwatkin, Stoles, Weaver, McNeill, Silvey
Scorer: Drew (2)

Date: Monday 18/04/1938
Result: **CHELTENHAM TOWN RESERVES 0 GLOUCESTER CITY 0**
Competition: Birmingham Combination
Teamsheet: Brock, Langley, Cox, Leach, Drew, Connor, Gwatkin, Stoles, Weaver, McNeill, Silvey

Date: Tuesday 19/04/1938
Result: **GLOUCESTER CITY 3 SHIRLEY TOWN 0**
Competition: Birmingham Combination
Teamsheet: Brock, Langley, Cox, Leach, Drew, Connor, Meadows, Gwatkin, Weaver, Kirby, Payne
Scorers: Weaver (2), Drew (pen)

Date: Saturday 23/04/1938
Result: **GLOUCESTER CITY 1 EVESHAM TOWN 1**
Competition: Birmingham Combination
Teamsheet: Neale, Langley, Leach, Ayland, Drew, Connor, Gwatkin, Stoles, Weaver, McNeill, Payne
Scorer: McNeill

Date: Tuesday 26/04/1938
Result: **GLOUCESTER CITY 2 BOURNEVILLE ATHLETIC 0**
Competition: Birmingham Combination
Teamsheet: Neale, Langley, Cox, Leach, Drew, Connor, Gwatkin, Stoles, Weaver, McNeill, Bray
Scorer: Weaver (2)

Date: Saturday 30/04/1938
Result: **COVENTRY CITY 'A' 0 GLOUCESTER CITY 1**
Competition: Birmingham Combination
Teamsheet: Neale, Langley, Cox, Leach, Drew, Connor, Gwatkin, Stoles, Weaver, McNeill, Bray
Scorer: Weaver

Date: Saturday 07/05/1938
Result: **DARLASTON 3 GLOUCESTER CITY 0**
Competition: Birmingham Combination
Teamsheet: Neale, Langley, Cox, Leach, Drew, Connor, Gwatkin, Taylor, Stoles, McNeill, Bye
Attendance: 1500

Appearances – D Anderson 1, AFL Ayland 1, AJW Bray 2, JGG Brock 4, A Bromage 1, E Bye 1, ? Cale 1, J Connor 16, RD Cox 18, EW Drew 39, ? Dyer 2, M Edwards 11, ? Goodburn 3, ? Gribble 12, IW Gwatkin 42, C Hartshorne 14, ? Johnson 1, AT Kirby 6, HW Langley 39, H Leach 33, T McNeill 41, W Meadows 3, ? Middlecote 2, D Moule 2, GAS Murdock 3, J Neale 19, WH Norris 5, ? Payne 11, WC Peart 23, ? Rickelton 7, G Saunders 24, ? Silvey 14, AW Stoles 12, ? Taylor 3, RW Weaver 39, L Weston 7.
Scorers – RW Weaver 67, EW Drew 8, IW Gwatkin 6, T McNeill 5, M Edwards 4, C Hartshorne 4, ? Payne 3, J Neale 2, WC Peart 2, ? Rickelton 2, ? Goodburn 1, AT Kirby 1, ? Silvey 1, AW Stoles 1.

BIRMINGHAM COMBINATION

POS	CLUB	P	W	D	L	F	A	PTS
1	DARLASTON	38	31	2	5	135	34	64
2	ASTON VILLA 'A'	38	29	3	6	145	47	61
3	WEST BROMWICH ALBION 'A'	38	19	13	6	96	51	51
4	TAMWORTH	38	20	8	10	119	71	48
5	BIRMINGHAM 'A'	38	21	5	12	86	68	47
6	COVENTRY CITY 'A'	38	19	6	13	98	57	44
7	BANBURY SPENCER	38	19	6	13	105	68	44
8	WALSALL RESERVES	38	18	8	12	107	71	44
9	EVESHAM TOWN	38	18	5	15	75	89	41
10	SHIRLEY TOWN	38	17	6	15	81	82	40
11	BIRMINGHAM TRAMS	38	17	6	15	63	79	40
12	WOLVERHAMPTON WANDERERS 'A'	38	16	7	15	101	66	39
13	**GLOUCESTER CITY**	**38**	**15**	**8**	**15**	**96**	**85**	**38**
14	ATHERSTONE TOWN	38	13	10	15	77	104	36
15	CHELTENHAM TOWN RESERVES	38	11	11	16	67	97	33
16	REDDITCH TOWN	38	12	3	23	81	111	27
17	HALESOWEN TOWN	38	6	5	27	63	137	17
18	BROMSGROVE ROVERS	38	5	7	26	49	135	17
19	HINCKLEY ATHLETIC	38	6	3	29	49	144	15
20	BOURNEVILLE ATHLETIC	38	4	6	28	43	140	14
		760	316	128	316	1736	1736	760

SEASON 1938-1939
(Home Ground: The Ground, Cheltenham Road, Longlevens)

Date: Saturday 27/08/1938
Result: **GLOUCESTER CITY 0 TAMWORTH 0**
Competition: Birmingham Combination
Teamsheet: Neale, Plummer, Cox, Leach, Foote, Ellis, Gwatkin, Roy Davis, Weaver, Riley, DS Edwards
Attendance: 1000

[84]

An early programme 26 March 1937 v Cheltenham Town Reserves in the Birmingham Combination.

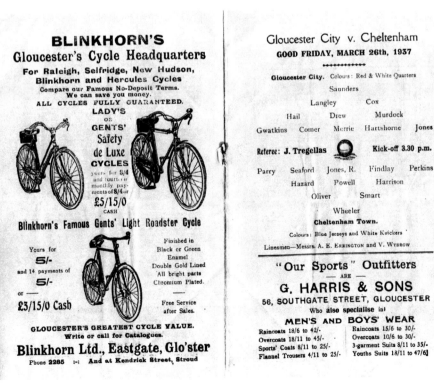

11 September 1937

MR. W. J. PEPWORTH, Chairman of the Northern Council of the Gloucestershire Football Association, presenting the Northern Professional Cup to the Gloucester City captain (Drew). Gloucester City surprisingly defeated Cheltenham Town's full Southern League side on the Whaddon-lane Ground to win the Cup.

15 October 1938

GLOUCESTER CITY'S CUP VICTORY: Above is a section of the crowd at Longlevens which saw Gloucester City defeat Aberdare 4—0. Below is Irdis Evans clearing from one of the many raids of the City forwards.

Date: Saturday 03/09/1938
Result: **GLOUCESTER CITY 2 WEST BROMWICH ALBION 'A' 0**
Competition: Birmingham Combination
Teamsheet: Brock, Plummer, Cox, Leach, Foote, Ellis, Gwatkin, Roy Davis, Weaver, Potter-Smith, DS Edwards
Scorer: Weaver (2)

Date: Thursday 08/09/1938
Result: **GLOUCESTER CITY 2 BROMSGROVE ROVERS 1**
Competition: Birmingham Combination
Teamsheet: Neale, Plummer, Cox, Leach, Foote, Ellis, Gwatkin, Roy Davis, Weaver, Potter-Smith, DS Edwards
Scorer: Weaver (2)

Date: Saturday 10/09/1938
Result: **GLOUCESTER CITY 0 CHELTENHAM TOWN 2**
Competition: Gloucestershire FA Northern Senior Professional Cup Final
Teamsheet: Neale, Plummer, Cox, Leach, Foote, Ellis, Gwatkin, Roy Davis, Weaver, Potter-Smith, DS Edwards
Attendance: 2000

Date: Thursday 15/09/1938
Result: **GLOUCESTER CITY 1 REDDITCH TOWN 1**
Competition: Birmingham Combination
Teamsheet: Brock, Plummer, Cox, Foote, Leach, Ellis, Gwatkin, Riley, Weaver, Roy Davis, DS Edwards
Scorer: Riley

Date: Saturday 17/09/1938
Result: **WALSALL RESERVES 2 GLOUCESTER CITY 1**
Competition: Birmingham Combination
Teamsheet: Brock, Plummer, Ellis, Foote, Leach, Potter-Smith, Gwatkin, Weaver, Riley, DS Edwards, Roy Davis
Scorer: Riley

Date: Saturday 24/09/1938
Result: **GLOUCESTER CITY 1 HINCKLEY ATHLETIC 1**
Competition: Birmingham Combination
Teamsheet: Brock, Plummer, Ellis, Foote, Leach, Potter-Smith, Gwatkin, Roy Davis, Riley, Weaver, DS Edwards
Scorer: Riley
Attendance: 1200

Date: Saturday 01/10/1938
Result: **GLOUCESTER CITY 1 CLEVEDON 1**
Competition: FA Cup 1st Qualifying Round
Teamsheet: Brock, Plummer, Ellis, Stoles, Leach, Potter-Smith, Gwatkin, Riley, Weaver, Foote, DS Edwards
Scorer: Weaver (pen)

Date: Wednesday 05/10/1938
Result: **CLEVEDON 1 GLOUCESTER CITY 3**
Competition: FA Cup 1st Qualifying Round Replay
Teamsheet: Brock, Plummer, Ellis, Birch, Leach, Potter-Smith, Gwatkin, Riley, Weaver, Roy Davis, DS Edwards
Scorers: Roy Davis, Potter-Smith, Riley

Date: Saturday 08/10/1938
Result: **GLOUCESTER CITY 0 WOLVERHAMPTON WANDERERS 'A' 3**
Competition: Birmingham Combination
Teamsheet: Brock, Plummer, Ellis, Stoles, Foote, Potter-Smith, Gwatkin, Roy Davis, Riley, Merrick, Wakeman

Date: Saturday 15/10/1938
Result: **GLOUCESTER CITY 4 ABERDARE 0**
Competition: FA Cup 2nd Qulaifying Round
Teamsheet: Neale, Plummer, Ellis, Foote, Leach, Potter-Smith, Gwatkin, Stoles, Weaver, Riley, DS Edwards
Scorers: Weaver (2), DS Edwards, Gwatkin

Date: Saturday 29/10/1938
Result: **GLOUCESTER CITY 1 BARRY 2**
Competition: FA Cup 3rd Qualifying Round
Teamsheet: Neale, Plummer, Ellis, Foote, Leach, Potter-Smith, Gwatkin, Stoles, Weaver, Riley, DS Edwards
Scorer: Weaver
Attendance: 2700

Date: Saturday 05/11/1938
Result: **GLOUCESTER CITY 1 ASTON VILLA 'A' 1**
Competition: Birmingham Combination
Teamsheet: Roy Davis, Ellis, Cox, Potter-Smith, Leach, Connor, Gwatkin, Stoles, Weaver, Riley, DS Edwards
Scorer: Weaver

Date: Saturday 12/11/1938
Result: **SOLIHULL TOWN 3 GLOUCESTER CITY 1**
Competition: Birmingham Combination
Teamsheet: Neale, Plummer, Ellis, Foote, Potter-Smith, Connor, Meadows, Gwatkin, Weaver, Stoles, DS Edwards
Scorer: Weaver

Date: Saturday 19/11/1938
Result: **BIRMINGHAM 'A' 2 GLOUCESTER CITY 2**
Competition: Birmingham Combination
Teamsheet: Neale, Plummer, Ellis, Roy Davis, Potter-Smith, Foote, Gwatkin, Stoles, Weaver, Riley, DS Edwards
Scorer: DS Edwards (2)

Date: Saturday 26/11/1938
Result: **DARLASTON 5 GLOUCESTER CITY 0**
Competition: Birmingham Combination
Teamsheet: Neale, Plummer, Ellis, Stoles, Potter-Smith, Foote, Meadows, Roy Davis, Weaver, Riley, Evans
Attendance: 2000

[87]

Date: Saturday 03/12/1938
Result: **GLOUCESTER CITY 6 ATHERSTONE TOWN 0**
Competition: Birmingham Combination
Teamsheet: Neale, Plummer, Ellis, Foote, Leach, Potter-Smith, Gwatkin, Dixon, Weaver, Riley, DS Edwards
Scorers: Gwatkin (2), Weaver (3), Riley

Date: Saturday 10/12/1938
Result: **COVENTRY CITY 'A' 1 GLOUCESTER CITY 1**
Competition: Birmingham Combination
Teamsheet: Neale, Plummer, Ellis, Foote, Leach, Potter-Smith, Gwatkin, Evans, Weaver, Riley, Roy Davis
Scorer: Plummer

Date: Saturday 17/12/1938
Result: **GLOUCESTER CITY 0 HALESOWEN TOWN 0**
Competition: Birmingham Combination
Teamsheet: Neale, Plummer, Ellis, Foote, Leach, Potter-Smith, Gwatkin, Evans, Weaver, Riley, Roy Davis

Date: Saturday 24/12/1938
Result: **WEST BROMWICH ALBION 'A' 2 GLOUCESTER CITY 2**
Competition: Birmingham Combination
Teamsheet: Neale, Plummer, Ellis, Stoles, Leach, Foote, Gwatkin, Evans, Weaver, Riley, DS Edwards
Scorer: DS Edwards (2)

Date: Monday 26/12/1938
Result: **NUNEATON BOROUGH 2 GLOUCESTER CITY 5**
Competition: Birmingham Combination
Teamsheet: Langley, Morefield, Ellis, Stoles, Leach, Foote, Gwatkin, Evans, Weaver, Riley, DS Edwards
Scorers: Weaver (3), Gwatkin, Evans

Date: Tuesday 27/12/1938
Result: **GLOUCESTER CITY 3 BANBURY SPENCER 2**
Competition: Birmingham Combination
Teamsheet: Neale, Morefield, Ellis, Foote, Leach, Stoles, Gwatkin, Evans, Weaver, Riley, DS Edwards
Scorers: DS Edwards, Riley, Weaver

Date: Saturday 31/12/1938
Result: **BROMSGROVE ROVERS 1 GLOUCESTER CITY 3**
Competition: Birmingham Combination
Teamsheet: Neale, Morefield, Ellis, Foote, Leach, Potter-Smith, Gwatkin, Evans, Weaver, Riley, DS Edwards
Scorers: Riley, Weaver, Gwatkin

Date: Saturday 07/01/1939
Result: **GLOUCESTER CITY 8 BOURNEVILLE ATHLETIC 1**
Competition: Birmingham Combination
Teamsheet: Neale, Morefield, Ellis, Plummer, Foote, Potter-Smith, Gwatkin, Evans, Weaver, Riley, DS Edwards
Scorers: Weaver (2), Gwatkin, Riley (2), Ellis, Evans, DS Edwards

Date: Saturday 14/01/1939
Result: **REDDITCH TOWN 2 GLOUCESTER CITY 2**
Competition: Birmingham Combination
Teamsheet: Neale, Plummer, Ellis, Foote, Leach, Potter-Smith, Morefield, Gwatkin, Weaver, Riley, DS Edwards
Scorers: Ellis, Gwatkin

Date: Saturday 21/01/1939
Result: **GLOUCESTER CITY 2 WALSALL RESERVES 1**
Competition: Birmingham Combination
Teamsheet: Neale, Plummer, Ellis, Foote, Leach, Potter-Smith, Gwatkin, Dixon, Weaver, Riley, DS Edwards
Scorers: Potter-Smith, Weaver
Attendance: 800

Date: Saturday 28/01/1939
Result: **HINCKLEY ATHLETIC 0 GLOUCESTER CITY 3**
Competition: Birmingham Combination
Teamsheet: Neale, Plummer, Ellis, Foote, Leach, Potter-Smith, Gwatkin, Stoles, Weaver, Riley, DS Edwards
Scorers: Gwatkin (2), Weaver

Date: Saturday 04/02/1939
Result: **BIRMINGHAM TRAMS 2 GLOUCESTER CITY 2**
Competition: Birmingham Combination
Teamsheet: Neale, Plummer, Ellis, Foote, Leach, Potter-Smith, Gwatkin, Roy Davis, Weaver, Riley, DS Edwards
Scorers: Gwatkin, Weaver

Date: Saturday 11/02/1939
Result: **WOLVERHAMPTON WANDERERS 'A' 2 GLOUCESTER CITY 2**
Competition: Birmingham Combination
Teamsheet: Neale, Plummer, Ellis, Foote, Leach, Potter-Smith, Gwatkin, Thompson, Weaver, Riley, DS Edwards
Scorer: Thompson (2)

Date: Saturday 18/02/1939
Result: **GLOUCESTER CITY 3 NUNEATON BOROUGH 2**
Competition: Birmingham Combination
Teamsheet: Neale, Plummer, Ellis, Foote, Leach, Potter-Smith, Gwatkin, Thompson, Weaver, G Edwards, DS Edwards
Scorers: Thompson, G Edwards, Weaver
Attendance: 1000

Date: Saturday 04/03/1939
Result: **BANBURY SPENCER 2 GLOUCESTER CITY 0**
Competition: Birmingham Combination
Teamsheet: Neale, Morefield, Ellis, Foote, Leach, Potter-Smith, Gwatkin, Thompson, Weaver, Riley, DS Edwards

Date: Saturday 11/03/1939
Result: **ASTON VILLA 'A' 7 GLOUCESTER CITY 1**
Competition: Birmingham Combination
Teamsheet: Sterry, Plummer, Ellis, Foote, Leach, Potter-Smith, Gwatkin, Thompson, Weaver, Riley, DS Edwards
Scorer: Riley

Date: Saturday 18/03/1939
Result: **GLOUCESTER CITY 3 SOLIHULL TOWN 0**
Competition: Birmingham Combination
Teamsheet: Langley, Plummer, Ellis, Foote, Leach, Potter-Smith, Gwatkin, Thompson, Riley, G Edwards, Weaver
Scorers: G Edwards, Gwatkin, Riley

Date: Saturday 25/03/1939
Result: **GLOUCESTER CITY 1 BIRMINGHAM 'A' 0**
Competition: Birmingham Combination
Teamsheet: Sterry, Langley, Ellis, Plummer, Leach, Foote, Gwatkin, Potter-Smith, Riley, G Edwards, Weaver
Scorer: Gwatkin

Date: Saturday 01/04/1939
Result: **GLOUCESTER CITY 2 DARLASTON 0**
Competition: Birmingham Combination
Teamsheet: Sterry, Morefield, Ellis, Plummer, Leach, Foote, Gwatkin, Gaughan, Riley, G Edwards, Weaver
Scorers: Gwatkin, Riley
Attendance: 1000

Date: Friday 07/04/1939
Result: **GLOUCESTER CITY 1 CHELTENHAM TOWN RESERVES 0**
Competition: Birmingham Combination
Teamsheet: Sterry, Langley, Ellis, Plummer, Leach, Foote, Gwatkin, Weaver, Riley, Roy Davis, Ron Davis
Scorer: Weaver
Attendance: 2000

Date: Saturday 08/04/1939
Result: **ATHERSTONE TOWN 4 GLOUCESTER CITY 3**
Competition: Birmingham Combination
Teamsheet: Sterry, Morefield, Ellis, Plummer, Leach, Foote, Gwatkin, Weaver, Riley, Roy Davis, Langley
Scorers: Weaver (2), Gwatkin

Date: Monday 10/04/1939
Result: **CHELTENHAM TOWN RESERVES 2 GLOUCESTER CITY 0**
Competition: Birmingham Combination
Teamsheet: Sterry, Morefield, Ellis, Plummer, Leach, Foote, Gwatkin, Weaver, Riley, Roy Davis, Ron Davis

Date: Saturday 15/04/1939
Result: **GLOUCESTER CITY 0 COVENTRY CITY 'A' 1**
Competition: Birmingham Combination
Teamsheet: Sterry, Morefield, Ellis, Plummer, Leach, Foote, Gwatkin, Weaver, Riley, Roy Davis, Griffiths

Date: Wednesday 19/04/1939
Result: **BOURNEVILLE ATHLETIC 2 GLOUCESTER CITY 2**
Competition: Birmingham Combination
Teamsheet: Sterry (?), -----, Ellis (?), Plummer (?), Leach (?), Foote (?), Gwatkin (?), Weaver, Riley (?), -----, Griffiths (?)
Scorers: Weaver (2)

Date: Saturday 22/04/1939
Result: **HALESOWEN TOWN 0 GLOUCESTER CITY 3**
Competition: Birmingham Combination
Teamsheet: Roy Davis, Ellis, Plummer, Foote, Leach, Potter-Smith, Gwatkin, Weaver, Riley, DS Edwards, Griffiths
Scorers: Riley, DS Edwards, Weaver (pen)

Date: Saturday 29/04/1939
Result: **TAMWORTH 5 GLOUCESTER CITY 0**
Competition: Birmingham Combination
Teamsheet: Sterry (?), Ellis (?), Plummer (?), Foote (?), Leach (?), Potter-Smith (?), Gwatkin (?), -----, Weaver (?), DS Edwards (?), Griffiths (?)

Date: Saturday 06/05/1939
Result: **GLOUCESTER CITY 3 BIRMINGHAM TRAMS 1**
Competition: Birmingham Combination
Teamsheet: Sterry, Plummer, Ellis, Foote, Leach, Potter-Smith, Gwatkin, Thompson, Weaver, Griffiths, DS Edwards
Scorer: Weaver (3)

Appearances – J Birch 1, JGG Brock 7, J Connor 2, RD Cox 6, Ron Davis 2, Roy Davis 20, ? Dixon 2, DS Edwards 31, G Edwards 4, BR Ellis 43, ? Evans 8, E Foote 41, P Gaughan 1, K Griffiths 5, IW Gwatkin 42, HW Langley 5, H Leach 38, W Meadows 2, ? Merrick 1, WJT Morefield 10, J Neale 22, AE Plummer 38, T Potter-Smith 32, J Riley 36, F Sterry 10, AW Stoles 12, P Thompson 6, ? Wakeman 1, RW Weaver 42.
Scorers – RW Weaver 33, IW Gwatkin 14, J Riley 13, DS Edwards 8, P Thompson 3, G Edwards 2, BR Ellis 2, ? Evans 2, T Potter-Smith 2, Roy Davis 1, AE Plummer 1.

RECORD BREAKER	**PROGRAMME**	**RECORD BREAKER**

Arthur Stoles	**1938-1939**	**Reg Weaver**
Youngest Goalscorer 15 years 349 days		Most Goals In One Season - 67

[89]

BIRMINGHAM COMBINATION

POS	CLUB	P	W	D	L	F	A	PTS
1	ASTON VILLA 'A'	38	26	8	4	130	38	60
2	WALSALL RESERVES	38	27	5	6	129	54	59
3	BIRMINGHAM 'A'	38	24	4	10	124	48	52
4	DARLASTON	38	26	0	12	120	52	52
5	TAMWORTH	38	22	7	9	112	64	51
6	WEST BROMWICH ALBION 'A'	38	22	5	11	101	52	49
7	WOLVERHAMPTON WANDERERS 'A'	38	22	4	12	101	63	48
8	**GLOUCESTER CITY**	**38**	**16**	**12**	**10**	**73**	**61**	**44**
9	COVENTRY CITY 'A'	38	20	3	15	112	86	43
10	BIRMINGHAM TRAMS	38	19	5	14	91	86	43
11	REDDITCH TOWN	38	14	9	15	74	74	37
12	CHELTENHAM TOWN RESERVES	38	17	1	20	91	110	35
13	SOLIHULL TOWN	38	14	4	20	68	83	32
14	BANBURY SPENCER	38	11	8	19	68	87	30
15	HINCKLEY ATHLETIC	38	9	10	19	77	116	28
16	HALESOWEN TOWN	38	8	7	23	77	137	23
17	NUNEATON BOROUGH	38	9	4	25	66	127	22
18	ATHERSTONE TOWN	38	9	2	27	74	170	20
19	BROMSGROVE ROVERS	38	6	6	26	62	128	18
20	BOURNEVILLE ATHLETIC	38	4	6	28	51	165	14
		760	325	110	325	1801	1801	760

SEASON 1939-1940

(Home Ground: The Ground, Cheltenham Road, Longlevens)

Date: Saturday 26/08/1939
Result: **BANBURY SPENCER 3 GLOUCESTER CITY 1**
Competition: Birmingham Combination
Teamsheet: Sterry, Durham, Ellis, Davis, Foote, Potter-Smith, Gwatkin, Stoles, Shelley, Griffiths, Parks
Scorer: Shelley (pen)

Date: Saturday 02/09/1939
Result: **GLOUCESTER CITY 0 TAMWORTH 1**
Competition: Birmingham Combination
Teamsheet: Sterry, Plummer, Ellis, Stoles, Leach, Foote, Gwatkin, Perkins, Shelley, Potter-Smith, Parks

Date: Saturday 11/11/1939
Result: **HEREFORD UNITED 5 GLOUCESTER CITY 3**
Competition: Southern League Wartime League Western Section
Teamsheet: Sterry, Langley, Ellis, Plummer, Leach, Foote, Beale, JM Landells, Davis, Hart, Glaister
Scorers: JM Landells, Beale, Hart

Date: Saturday 25/11/1939
Result: **BATH CITY 2 GLOUCESTER CITY 5**
Competition: Southern League Wartime League Western Section
Teamsheet: Bowles, Plummer, Ellis, McDonough, Foote, Potter-Smith, Gwatkin, JM Landells, Beale, Glaister, Parris
Scorers: Parris (2), Glaister, Beale (2)

Date: Saturday 16/12/1939
Result: **GLOUCESTER CITY 3 BATH CITY 1**
Competition: Southern League Wartime League Western Section
Teamsheet: Sterry, Leach, Ellis, McDonough, Foote, Potter-Smith, Gwatkin, JM Landells, Beale, Glaister, Parris
Scorers: Gwatkin, JM Landells, Potter-Smith

Date: Saturday 23/12/1939
Result: **GLOUCESTER CITY 3 LOVELLS ATHLETIC 7**
Competition: Southern League Wartime League Western Section
Teamsheet: Sterry, Leach, Ellis, McDonough, Foote, Potter-Smith (?), Gwatkin, JM Landells, Beale (?), Glaister, Parris
Scorers: -----, -----, -----

Date: Monday 25/12/1939
Result: **CHELTENHAM TOWN 5 GLOUCESTER CITY 0**
Competition: Southern League Wartime League Western Section
Teamsheet: Sterry, Leach (?) Ellis, McDonough (?), Foote, Potter-Smith, Gwatkin, JM Landells, Beale, Glaister, Parris (?)

Date: Tuesday 26/12/1939
Result: **GLOUCESTER CITY 0 CHELTENHAM TOWN 1**
Competition: Southern League Wartime League Western Section
Teamsheet: Sterry, Leach, Ellis, Dall, Foote, Within, Gwatkin, JM Landells, Beale, Glaister, Morefield

Date: Saturday 30/12/1939
Result: **GLOUCESTER CITY 2 WORCESTER CITY 3**
Competition: Southern League Wartime League Western Section
Teamsheet: Sterry, Payne, Ellis, McDonough, Leach, Foote, Gwatkin, JM Landells, Beale, Glaister, Parris
Scorer: Glaister (2)

Date: Saturday 06/01/1940
Result: **YEOVIL & PETTERS UNITED 2 GLOUCESTER CITY 3**
Competition: Southern League Wartime League Western Section
Teamsheet: Sterry, Leach, Ellis, McDonough, Foote, Payne, Gwatkin, JM Landells, Glaister, Farrelly, Parris
Scorers: Farrelly (2), Glaister

Date: Saturday 23/02/1940
Result: **BARRY 2 GLOUCESTER CITY 3**
Competition: Southern League Cup Western Section 2nd Round
Teamsheet: Sterry, Davis, Peart, McDonough, Foote, Leach, Gwatkin, JM Landells, Farrelly, Glaister, Parris
Scorers: Parris, Gwatkin, JM Landells

Date: Saturday 16/03/1940
Result: **WORCESTER CITY 9 GLOUCESTER CITY 3**
Competition: Southern League Wartime League Western Section
Teamsheet: Sterry, Jordan, Peart, McDonough, Leach, Davis, Gwatkin, JM Landells, Farrelly, Thompson, Parris
Scorers: Farrelly (2), -----
Attendance: 2000

Date: Friday 22/03/1940
Result: **GLOUCESTER CITY 0 CHELTENHAM TOWN 0**
Competition: Gloucestershire FA Northern Senior Professional Cup Final
Teamsheet: Sterry, Jordan, Peart, McDonough, Foote, Leach, Gwatkin, JM Landells, Farrelly, Thompson, Parris

Date: Saturday 23/03/1940
Result: **GLOUCESTER CITY 3 BARRY 2**
Competition: Southern League Wartime League Western Section
Teamsheet: Sterry, Jordan, Peart, McDonough, Foote, Leach, Gwatkin, Thompson, Farrelly, Parris, Davis
Scorers: Parris, Farrelly (2)

Date: Monday 25/03/1940
Result: **CHELTENHAM TOWN 2 GLOUCESTER CITY 1**
Competition: Gloucestershire FA Northern Senior Professional Cup Final Replay
Teamsheet: Sterry, Jordan, Peart, McDonough, Foote, Leach, Gwatkin, JM Landells, Farrelly, Thompson, Parris
Scorer: Gwatkin

Date: Saturday 30/03/1940
Result: **GLOUCESTER CITY 0 YEOVIL & PETTERS UNITED 1**
Competition: Southern League Wartime League Western Section
Teamsheet: Sterry, Jordan, Peart, McDonough, Leach, Davis, Gwatkin, Thompson, Edwards, Farrelly, Parris

Date: Saturday 06/04/1940
Result: **LOVELLS ATHLETIC 3 GLOUCESTER CITY 2**
Competition: Southern League Wartime League Western Section
Teamsheet: Sterry, Davis, Peart, McDonough, Foote, Leach, Gwatkin, JM Landells, Farrelly, Edwards, Parris
Scorers: JM Landells, -----

Date: Saturday 13/04/1940
Result: **BARRY 6 GLOUCESTER CITY 2**
Competition: Southern League Wartime League Western Section
Teamsheet: Sterry, Reeves, Peart, McDonough, Foote, Leach, Gwatkin, Sheeby, Farrelly, JM Landells, Parris
Scorers: Gwatkin, Parris

Date: Saturday 20/04/1940
Result: **GLOUCESTER CITY 6 HEREFORD UNITED 2**
Competition: Southern League Wartime League Western Section
Teamsheet: Sterry, Reeves, Peart, McDonough, Foote, Leach, Gwatkin, JM Landells, Farrelly, W Landells, Parris
Scorers: Gwatkin, Parris (2), Farrelly (2), JM Landells

Date: Saturday 27/04/1940
Result: **GLOUCESTER CITY 0 CHELTENHAM TOWN 0**
Competition: Southern League Cup Western Section Semi-Final
Teamsheet: Sterry, Plummer, Peart, McDonough, Lawrence, Pincot, Gwatkin, JM Landells, Farrelly, Carr, Parris

Date: Saturday 04/05/1940
Result: **CHELTENHAM TOWN 2 GLOUCESTER CITY 4**
Competition: Southern League Cup Western Section Semi-Final Replay
Teamsheet: Sterry, Plummer, Peart, JM Landells, Lawrence, Sneddon, Gwatkin, White, Farrelly, Parris, Parks
Scorers: Parris (2), Parks, Gwatkin

Date: Saturday 11/05/1940
Result: **WORCESTER CITY 6 GLOUCESTER CITY 0**
Competition: Southern League Cup Western Section Final 1st Leg
Teamsheet: Sterry, Plummer, Peart, McDonough, Sneddon, Davis, Gwatkin, JM Landells, Farrelly, Parris, Parks
Attendance: 2000

Date: Saturday 18/05/1940
Result: **GLOUCESTER CITY 0 WORCESTER CITY 0**
Competition: Southern League Cup Western Section Final 2nd Leg
Teamsheet: Sterry, Plummer, Peart, McDonough, Lawrence, Sneddon, Gwatkin, W Landells, JM Landells, Parris, Barrow

Appearances – ? Barrow 1, ? Beale 7, JC Bowles 1, LL Carr 1, ? Dall 1, Roy Davis 8, E Durham 1, G Edwards 2, BR Ellis 10, ? Farrelly 13, E Foote 17, G Glaister 9, K Griffiths 1, IW Gwatkin 22, JP Hart 1, ? Jordan 5, JM Landells 19, W Landells 2, HW Langley 1, RS Lawrence 3, H Leach 17, J McDonough 18, WJT Morefield 1, ? Parks 4, JE Parris 19, ? Payne 2, WC Peart 13, ? Perkins 1, F Pincot 1, AE Plummer 7, T Potter-Smith 6, J Reeves 2, ? Sheeby 1, A Shelley 2, WC Sneddon 3, F Sterry 22, AW Stoles 2, P Thompson 5, ? White 1, ? Within 1.
Scorers – JE Parris 10, ? Farrelly 8, IW Gwatkin 7, JM Landells 5, G Glaister 4, ? Beale 3, JP Hart 1, ? Parks 1, T Potter-Smith 1, A Shelley 1.

BIRMINGHAM COMBINATION

CLUB	P	W	D	L	F	A	PTS
GLOUCESTER CITY	2	0	0	2	1	4	0

When war was declared on September 3, all league football was suspended. The teams in this league were Aston Villa 'A', Atherstone Town, Banbury Spencer, Birmingham 'A', Birmingham Trams, Bromsgrove Rovers, Cheltenham Town Reserves, Coventry City 'A', Darlaston, **Gloucester City**, Halesowen Town, Hinckley Athletic, Nuneaton Borough, Redditch Town, Solihull Town, Stourbridge, Tamworth, Walsall Reserves, West Bromwich Albion 'A' and Wolverhampton Wanderers 'A'.

SOUTHERN LEAGUE – WARTIME LEAGUE WESTERN SECTION

POS	CLUB	P	W	D	L	F	A	PTS
1	LOVELLS ATHLETIC	14	11	1	2	53	22	23
2	WORCESTER CITY	14	9	2	3	55	30	20
3	HEREFORD UNITED	14	8	0	6	45	31	16
4	YEOVIL & PETTERS UNITED	14	7	2	5	30	24	16
5	**GLOUCESTER CITY**	**14**	**5**	**0**	**9**	**35**	**49**	**10**
6	BARRY	14	4	1	9	31	56	9
7	CHELTENHAM TOWN	13	3	2	8	21	38	8
8	BATH CITY	13	3	2	8	21	41	8
		110	50	10	50	291	291	110

After two months, wartime football was introduced and the Southern League resumed again, with a reduced number of clubs on November 4. This was the only season during the war that the Southern League operated.

SEASON 1940-1941
(Home Ground: The Ground, Cheltenham Road, Longlevens)

There were no competitive fixtures played this season. 33 friendly matches were played instead.

SEASON 1941-1942
(Home Ground: The Ground, Cheltenham Road, Longlevens)

All Gloucester City league games played at Longlevens

Date: Saturday 13/09/1941
Result: **GLOUCESTER CITY 14 ARMY 'K' 2**
Competition: Gloucester City Hurran Cup League
Teamsheet: Strickland, Davis, D Anderson, Baillie, Stevenson, McDonough, Stoles, K Griffiths, Parris, Wilkins, Hanson
Scorers: Parris (2), Hanson (2), K Griffiths (4), Wilkins (3), own goal, Stoles, -----

Date: Saturday 20/09/1941
Result: **GLOUCESTER CITY 2 ROYAL AIR FORCE 'A' 7**
Competition: Gloucester City Hurran Cup League
Teamsheet: Strickland, Davis, D Anderson, Cassidy, Stevenson, J Griffiths, Stoles, K Griffiths, Bevan, Abbott, Wilkins
Scorers: Davis, Wilkins

Date: Saturday 27/09/1941
Result: **GLOUCESTER CITY 2 ARMY 'L' 2**
Competition: Gloucester City Hurran Cup League
Teamsheet: Strickland, D Anderson, Davis, Baillie, Stevenson, McPherson, Stoles, K Griffiths, Delaney, Cassidy, Wilkins
Scorers: Davis (pen), Wilkins

Date: Saturday 04/10/1941
Result: **ROYAL AIR FORCE 'E' 0 GLOUCESTER CITY 4**
Competition: Godsman Cup 1st Round
Teamsheet: Strickland, D Anderson, Davis, Baillie, Stevenson, McPherson, Stoles, K Griffiths, Delaney, Cassidy, Wilkins
Scorers: Wilkins (2), McPherson (2)

Date: Saturday 11/10/1941
Result: **GLOUCESTER CITY 0 ARMY 'J' 3**
Competition: Gloucester City Hurran Cup League
Teamsheet: Strickland, D Anderson, Davis, Baillie, Stevenson, McPherson, Stoles, Cassidy, Fitzsimmons, K Griffiths, Frew

Date: Saturday 18/10/1941
Result: **GLOUCESTER CITY 7 ROYAL AIR FORCE 'C' 1**
Competition: Gloucester City Hurran Cup League
Teamsheet: Strickland, Davis, D Anderson, Baillie, Stevenson, McPherson, Stoles, ? Anderson, Fitzsimmons, K Griffiths, Wilkins
Scorers: D Anderson (pen), Fitzsimmons (4), K Griffiths, Wilkins

Date: Saturday 25/10/1941
Result: **GLOUCESTER CITY 8 ROYAL AIR FORCE 'B' 1**
Competition: Gloucester City Hurran Cup League
Teamsheet: Strickland, Davis, D Anderson, Baillie, Stevenson, McPherson, Stoles, ? Anderson, Fitzsimmons, K Griffiths, Wilkins
Scorers: Fitzsimmons (3), K Griffiths (3), ? Anderson, own goal

Date: Saturday 01/11/1941
Result: **GLOUCESTER CITY 12 ROTOL AFC 1**
Competition: Godsman Cup 2nd Round
Teamsheet: Strickland, Davis, D Anderson, Baillie, Stevenson, McPherson, Stoles, Jenkins, Fitzsimmons, K Griffiths, Wilkins
Scorers: K Griffiths (2), Jenkins (2), Wilkins (2), Stoles, Fitzsimmons (4), McPherson

Date: Saturday 08/11/1941
Result: **GLOUCESTER CITY 2 GLOUCESTER AERO 1**
Competition: Gloucester City Hurran Cup League
Teamsheet: Strickland, Davis, D Anderson, Baillie, Stevenson, McPherson, Stoles, Gill, Fitzsimmons, K Griffiths, Wilkins
Scorers: Wilkins, K Griffiths

Date: Saturday 15/11/1941
Result: **GLOUCESTER CITY 9 ROYAL AIR FORCE 'C' 2**
Competition: Gloucester City Hurran Cup League
Teamsheet: Strickland, Davis, D Anderson, Baillie, Stevenson, McPherson, Stoles, Jenkins, Batstone, K Griffiths, Wilkins
Scorers: Batstone (4), Stoles, Davis, K Griffiths, Wilkins, McPherson

Date: Saturday 29/11/1941
Result: **GLOUCESTER CITY 2 ROYAL AIR FORCE 'D' 0**
Competition: Gloucester City Hurran Cup League
Teamsheet: Strickland, Davis, D Anderson, Baillie, Stevenson, J Griffiths, Stoles, Jenkins, Fitzsimmons, K Griffiths, Wilkins
Scorers: Jenkins, K Griffiths

Date: Saturday 06/12/1941
Result: **GLOUCESTER CITY 12 ARMY 'G' 2**
Competition: Gloucester City Hurran Cup League
Teamsheet: Strickland, Davis, D Anderson, Baillie, Stevenson, Fitzsimmons, Stoles, K Griffiths, Starr, Jenkins, Wilkins
Scorers: Stoles, K Griffiths (2), Starr (6), Wilkins, Fitzsimmons (2)

Date: Saturday 13/12/1941
Result: **GLOUCESTER CITY 3 ROYAL AIR FORCE 'F' 3**
Competition: Gloucester City Hurran Cup League
Teamsheet: Strickland, Davis, D Anderson, Baillie, Stevenson, Fitzsimmons, Stoles, K Griffiths, Batstone, Starr, Wilkins
Scorers: Batstone, Stoles, Wilkins

Date: Saturday 20/12/1941
Result: **GLOUCESTER CITY 11 ROYAL AIR FORCE 'B' 1**
Competition: Gloucester City Hurran Cup League
Teamsheet: Strickland, Davis, D Anderson, Baillie, Stevenson, J Griffiths, Stoles, K Griffiths, Starr, Jenkins, Wilkins
Scorers: Starr (9), Wilkins, Jenkins

Date: Saturday 03/01/1942
Result: **GLOUCESTER CITY 2 ROYAL AIR FORCE 'E' 1**
Competition: Gloucester City Hurran Cup League
Teamsheet: Strickland, Bevan, D Anderson, Baillie, Stevenson, J Griffiths, Stoles, Davis, Starr, K Griffiths, Wilkins
Scorers: Starr (2)

Date: Saturday 10/01/1942
Result: **GLOUCESTER CITY 5 ROYAL AIR FORCE 'F' 6**
Competition: Godsman Cup Semi-Final
Teamsheet: Strickland, Davis, D Anderson, Baillie, Stevenson, J Griffiths, Stoles, K Griffiths, Starr, Jenkins, Wilkins
Scorers: Wilkins (3), Starr, Jenkins

Date: Saturday 31/01/1942
Result: **GLOUCESTER CITY 7 ARMY 'M' 1**
Competition: Gloucester City Hurran Cup League
Teamsheet: Strickland, Davis, D Anderson, Baillie, Stevenson, Rose, Stoles, K Griffiths, Batstone, Jenkins, Wilkins
Scorers: Batstone (3), Stoles (2), K Griffiths, Wilkins

Date: Saturday 07/02/1942
Result: **GLOUCESTER CITY 3 GLOUCESTER AERO 0**
Competition: Gloucester City Hurran Cup League
Teamsheet: Strickland, Davis, D Anderson, Bailiie, Stevenson, Leach, Stoles, K Griffiths, Batstone, Jenkins, Wilkins
Scorers: Batstone, Jenkins, Baillie

Date: Saturday 14/02/1942
Result: **GLOUCESTER CITY 6 ARMY 'M' 1**
Competition: Gloucester City Hurran Cup League
Teamsheet: Strickland, Davis, D Anderson, Stoles, Stevenson, W Griffiths, Selkirk, Cornelius, K Griffiths, Jenkins, Wilkins
Scorers: Cornelius (3), Jenkins (3)

Date: Saturday 21/02/1942
Result: **GLOUCESTER CITY 5 ROYAL AIR FORCE 'D' 2**
Competition: Gloucester City Hurran Cup League
Teamsheet: Strickland, Davis, D Anderson, Baillie, Stevenson, Stoles, Selkirk, K Griffiths, Batstone, Jenkins, Cornelius
Scorers: Batstone (3), Jenkins, Baillie (pen)

Date: Saturday 28/02/1942
Result: **GLOUCESTER CITY 16 ARMY 'G' 0**
Competition: Gloucester City Hurran Cup League
Teamsheet: Strickland, Davis, D Anderson, Stoles, Stevenson, Parris, Selkirk, K Griffiths, Batstone, Jenkins, Cornelius
Scorers: K Griffiths (4), Parris (2), Batstone (4), Jenkins (4), Selkirk, Cornelius

Date: Saturday 14/03/1942
Result: **GLOUCESTER CITY 2 ARMY 'J' 0**
Competition: Gloucester City Hurran Cup League
Teamsheet: Strickland, Davis, D Anderson, Stoles, Stevenson, Baillie, Wilkins, K Griffiths, Batstone, Parris, Jenkins
Scorers: K Griffiths, Parris

Date: Saturday 21/03/1942
Result: **GLOUCESTER CITY 4 ROYAL AIR FORCE 'A' 3**
Competition: Gloucester City Hurran Cup League
Teamsheet: Strickland, Gardner, D Anderson, Stoles, Stevenson, Baillie, K Griffiths, Thomas, Jenkins, Parris, Wilkins
Scorers: Parris (2), Wilkins (2)

Date: Saturday 28/03/1942
Result: **GLOUCESTER CITY 4 ROYAL AIR FORCE 'E' 3**
Competition: Gloucester City Hurran Cup League
Teamsheet: Strickland, Peart, D Anderson, Foote, Stevenson, Baillie, Stoles, K Griffiths, Fitzsimmons, Parris, Wilkins
Scorers: Parris (2), Fitzsimmons, Wilkins

Date: Saturday 04/04/1942
Result: **GLOUCESTER CITY 2 ARMY 'L' 3**
Competition: Gloucester City Hurran Cup League
Teamsheet: Strickland, Gainsboro, D Anderson, Carruthers, Stevenson, Baillie, Stoles, K Griffiths, Wilkins, Parris, Jenkins
Scorers: Wilkins, Jenkins

Date: Saturday 09/05/1942
Result: **GLOUCESTER CITY 9 ROYAL AIR FORCE 'F' 0**
Competition: Gloucester City Hurran Cup League
Teamsheet: Strickland, Wilkins, D Anderson, Stoles, Stevenson, Baillie, Bevan, K Griffiths, W Griffiths, Parris, Jenkins
Scorers: K Griffiths (3), Jenkins (4), W Griffiths, Parris

Date: ?
Result: **GLOUCESTER CITY ? ARMY 'K' ?**
Competition: Gloucester City Hurran Cup League
Teamsheet: -----, -----, -----, -----, -----, -----, -----, -----, -----, -----, -----
Note: Gloucester City lost

Appearances – F Abbott 1, ? Anderson 2, D Anderson 26, J Baillie 23, WD Basford 1, VF Batstone 7, J Bevan 3, ? Carruthers 1, ? Cassidy 4, ? Cornelius 3, Roy Davis 22, ? Delaney 2, ? Fitzsimmons 9, E Foote 1, ? Frew 1, ?? Gainsboro 1, ? Gardner 1, ? Gill 1, J Griffiths 5, K Griffiths 26, W Griffiths 2, AJ Hanson 1, ? Jenkins 15, H Leach 1, J McDonough 1, JC McPherson 8, JE Parris 7, WC Peart 1, ? Rose 1, ? Selkirk 3, F Starr 5, ? Stevenson 26, AW Stoles 26, W Strickland 26, ? Thomas 1, EWJ Wilkins 23.
Scorers – K Griffiths 24, EWJ Wilkins 23, ? Jenkins 19, F Starr 18, V Batstone 16, ? Fitzsimmons 14, JE Parris 10, AW Stoles 7, J Baillie 4, ? Cornelius 4, JC McPherson 4, Roy Davis 3, AJ Hanson 2, ? Anderson 1, D Anderson 1, W Griffiths 1, ? Selkirk 1, own goals 2.

GLOUCESTER CITY HURRAN CUP LEAGUE

POS	CLUB	P	W	D	L	F	A	PTS
1	ARMY 'L'	24						38
2	ROYAL AIR FORCE 'A'	24						38
3	**GLOUCESTER CITY**	24	18	2	4	132+	39+	36
	ARMY 'G'	24						
	ARMY 'J'	24						
	ARMY 'K'	24						
	ARMY 'M'	24						
	GLOUCESTER AERO	24						
	ROYAL AIR FORCE 'B'	24						
	ROYAL AIR FORCE 'C'	24						
	ROYAL AIR FORCE 'D'	24						
	ROYAL AIR FORCE 'E'	24						
	ROYAL AIR FORCE 'F'	24						
	ARMY 'H'							
	ROTOL AFC							

Only top three positions mentioned in The Citizen.
Army 'H' withdrew before season started. Army 'M' took over the fixtures of Rotol AFC January 1942.
All the Services teams had their results published under a nom-de-plume.

SEASON 1942-1943

(Home Ground: The Ground, Cheltenham Road, Longlevens)

All Gloucester City league games played at Longlevens

Date: Satrurday 12/09/1942
Result: **GLOUCESTER CITY 10 ROTOL AFC 1**
Competition: Gloucester City Hurran Cup League
Teamsheet: Strickland, Morgan, Anderson, O'Gorman, Stevenson, Tillion, Webb, Stoles, Burnett, Parris, Ball
Scorers: Stoles (2), Webb, Ball (2), Parris (3), Burnett (2)

Date: Saturday 19/09/1942
Result: **GLOUCESTER CITY 4 ARMY 'F' 0**
Competition: Gloucester City Hurran Cup League
Teamsheet: Strickland, Morgan, Anderson, O'Gorman, Stoles, Tillion, Webb, Jarrett, Ball, Parris, Reeves
Scorers: Parris (2), Ball (2)

Date: Saturday 03/10/1942
Result: **ROYAL AIR FORCE 'C' 3 GLOUCESTER CITY 3**
Competition: City Cup 2nd Round
Teamsheet: Strickland, Morgan, Anderson, O'Gorman, Reeves, Tillion, Webb, Stoles, Burnett, Parris, Ball
Scorers: Webb, Parris (pen), Burnett

Date: Saturday 24/10/1942
Result: **GLOUCESTER CITY 5 ROYAL AIR FORCE 'C' 4**
Competition: City Cup 2nd Round Replay
Teamsheet: Strickland, Morgan, Anderson, Rushforth, Stevenson, Tillion, Webb, Stoles, Burnett, Parris, Davis
Scorers: Burnett (2), Webb, Parris, Davis

Date: Saturday 07/11/1942
Result: **GLOUCESTER CITY ? ROYAL AIR FORCE 'B' ?**
Competition: Gloucester City Hurran Cup League
Teamsheet: Strickland, Davis, Anderson, O'Gorman, Stevenson, Tillion, Webb, Stoles, Burnett, Parris, Reeves
Scorer: -----
Note: Gloucester City won

Date: Saturday 14/11/1942
Result: **GLOUCESTER CITY 9 ARMY 'E' 1**
Competition: Gloucester City Hurran Cup League
Teamsheet: Strickland, Morgan, Anderson, O'Gorman, Stevenson, Tillion, Webb, Bevan, Burnett, Parris, Reeves
Scorers: Parris (4), Bevan, Reeves (2), Burnett, Webb

Date: Saturday 28/11/1942
Result: **GLOUCESTER CITY ? ROTOL AFC ?**
Competition: City Cup Semi-Final
Teamsheet: Strickland, Davis, Anderson, O'Gorman, Stevenson, Tillion, Webb, Stoles, Burnett, Parris, Reeves
Scorer: -----
Note: Gloucester City won

Either side of World War II Gloucester City celebrated two anniversaries – 6 years too late in either case!!
Within the Golden Jubilee booklet were sponsors who had associations with the club

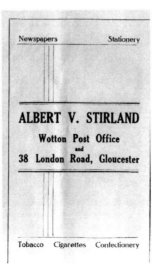

The Diamond Jubilee booklet included a History of the Club by Doug Hunt, Secretary-Manager

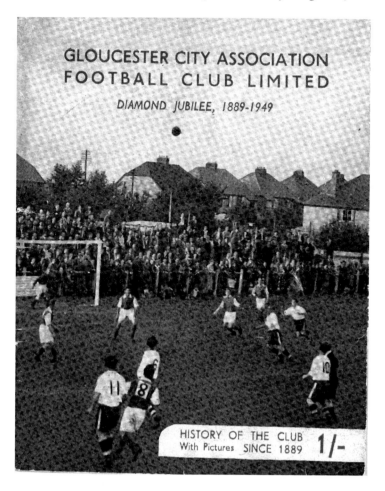

Douglas Hunt

Gloucester City
Association Football Club Limited

PRESIDENT :

Sir Leslie Boyce, K.B.E., J.P., M.A.

DIRECTORS :

A. Hurran (Chairman)
C. R. Stephens (Vice-Chairman)
F. A. Morris
A. V. Stirland
W. Rea
T. L. Lawrence

CLUB SECRETARY-MANAGER :

D. A. Hunt

HON. TREASURER :

A. A. Dunlop

Date: Saturday 05/12/1942
Result: **GLOUCESTER CITY 12 ROYAL AIR FORCE 'D' 3**
Competition: Gloucester City Hurran Cup League
Teamsheet: Strickland (?), Morgan, Anderson (?), Stoles, Stevenson (?), Tillion (?), Webb (?), Griffiths, Ball, Parris, Reeves
Scorers: Ball (4), Parris (3), Reeves (2), Griffiths (2), own goal

Date: Saturday 12/12/1942
Result: **GLOUCESTER CITY ? ROYAL AIR FORCE 'B' ?**
Competition: City Cup Final
Teamsheet: Strickland, Davis, Anderson, -----, Stevenson, Tillion, Webb, Stoles, Burnett, Parris, Reeves

Date: Saturday 19/12/1942
Result: **GLOUCESTER CITY 7 ARMY 'F' 2**
Competition: Gloucester City Hurran Cup League
Teamsheet: Strickland, Davis, Anderson, Rushforth, Reeves, Tillion, Webb, Stoles, Foote, Lawson, Wilkins
Scorers: Stoles, Foote (4), Rushforth, Lawson

Date: Saturday 02/01/1943
Result: **GLOUCESTER CITY 10 ARMY 'E' 1**
Competition: Gloucester City Hurran Cup League
Teamsheet: Strickland, Rushforth, Anderson, King, Stevenson, Reeves, Webb, Stoles, Burnett, Parris, Wilkins
Scorers: Webb (2), Burnett (3), Stoles, Reeves (2), Wilkins, -----

Date: Saturday 09/01/1943
Result: **GLOUCESTER CITY 3 ROYAL AIR FORCE 'A' 1**
Competition: Gloucester City Hurran Cup League
Teamsheet: Strickland, Davis, Anderson, King, Stevenson, Reeves, Webb, Stoles, Burnett, Parris, Wilkins
Scorers: Burnett, Parris, Webb

Date: Saturday 16/01/1943
Result: **GLOUCESTER CITY 8 ROTOL AFC 4**
Competition: Gloucester City Hurran Cup League
Teamsheet: Strickland, Rushforth, Anderson, King, Stevenson, Reeves, Webb, Stoles, Burnett, Parris, Wilkins
Scorers: Burnett (3), Wilkins, Parris (2, 1 pen), Webb (2)

Date: Saturday 30/01/1943
Result: **GLOUCESTER CITY 13 ROYAL AIR FORCE 'D' 1**
Competition: Godsman Cup 2nd Round
Teamsheet: Strickland, Davis, Anderson, King, Stevenson, Reeves, Webb, Stoles, Morris, Parris, Wilkins
Scorers: Webb (3), Parris (5), Morris (3), Wilkins, -----

Date: Saturday 13/02/1943
Result: **GLOUCESTER CITY 3 ROYAL AIR FORCE 'C' 4**
Competition: Gloucester City Hurran Cup League
Teamsheet: Strickland, Davis, Anderson, King, Stevenson, Reeves, Webb, Stoles, Morris, Parris, Wilkins
Scorers: Parris (2, 1 pen), own goal

Date: Saturday 27/02/1943
Result: **GLOUCESTER CITY 6 PIONEER CORPS 4**
Competition: Godsman Cup Semi-Final
Teamsheet: Strickland, Seaforth, Anderson, Davis, Stevenson, Reeves, Webb, Stoles, Burnett, Parris, Wilkins
Scorers: Wilkins (2), Webb, Parris (2, 1 pen), Burnett

Date: Saturday 20/03/1943
Result: **GLOUCESTER CITY 4 ROYAL AIR FORCE 'A' 2**
Competition: Gloucester City Hurran Cup League
Teamsheet: Strickland, Seward, Anderson, Davis, Stevenson, King, Webb, Stoles, Levey, Parris, Wilkins
Scorers: Parris (3, 1 pen), Levey

Date: Saturday 17/04/1943
Result: **GLOUCESTER CITY 1 ROYAL AIR FORCE 'B' 3**
Competition: Godsman Cup Final
Teamsheet: Strickland, Davis, Anderson, Seward, Stevenson, King, Webb, Stoles, Rushforth, Tillion, Reeves
Scorer: Rushforth

Date: Saturday 24/04/1943
Result: **GLOUCESTER CITY 8 ROYAL AIR FORCE 'B' 4**
Competition: Gloucester City Hurran Cup League
Teamsheet: Strickland, Davis, Anderson, Seward, Stevenson, King, Stoles, Twinning, Bolting, Parris (?), Reeves
Scorers: Bolting (4), Twinning (2), Stoles, Reeves

Date: Monday 26/04/1943
Result: **GLOUCESTER CITY ? ROYAL AIR FORCE 'D' ?**
Competition: Gloucester City Hurran Cup League
Teamsheet: Strickland (?), -----, Anderson (?), -----, Stevenson (?), King (?), Stoles (?), -----, -----, Parris (?), Reeves (?)

Date: Saturday 01/05/1943
Result: **GLOUCESTER CITY 2 ROYAL AIR FORCE 'C' 3**
Competition: Gloucester City Hurran Cup League
Teamsheet: Strickland, Seward, Anderson, Prout, King, Stevenson, Stoles, -----, -----, Parris, Reeves
Scorers: Prout, Parris

Appearances – D Anderson 21, NG Ball 4, J Bevan 1, ? Bolting 1, ? Burnett 11, Roy Davis 12, E Foote 1, K Griffiths 1, ? Jarrett 1, ? King 10, ? Lawson 1, ? Levey 1, ? Morgan 6, ? Morris 2, ? O'Gorman 6, JE Parris 19, ? Prout 1, J Reeves 18, ? Rushforth 5, ? Seaforth 1, SC Seward 4, ? Stevenson 18, AW Stoles 20, W Strickland 21, ? Tillion 11, ? Twinning 1, R Webb 18, EWJ Wilkins 8.
Scorers – JE Parris 30, ? Burnett 14, R Webb 13, NG Ball 8, J Reeves 7, AW Stoles 5, EWJ Wilkins 5, ? Bolting 4, E Foote 4, ? Morris 3, K Griffiths 2, ? Rushforth 2, ? Twinning 2, J Bevan 1, Roy Davis 1, ? Lawson 1, ? Levey 1, ? Prout 1, own goals 2.

GLOUCESTER CITY HURRAN CUP LEAGUE

POS	CLUB	P	W	D	L	F	A	PTS
1	ROYAL AIR FORCE 'C'	14						
2	**GLOUCESTER CITY**	14				80+	26+	
	ARMY 'E'	14						
	ARMY 'F'	14						
	ROTOL AFC	14						
	ROYAL AIR FORCE 'A'	14						
	ROYAL AIR FORCE 'B'	14						
	ROYAL AIR FORCE 'D'	14						

Only top two positions mentioned in The Citizen.
All the Services teams had their results published under a nom-de-plume.

SEASON 1946-1947
(Home Ground: The Ground, Cheltenham Road, Longlevens)

Date: Saturday 31/08/1946
Result: **COLCHESTER UNITED 2 GLOUCESTER CITY 3**
Competition: Southern League
Teamsheet: Clarke, Tweed, Bartlett, Elliott, Miller, Jennings, Bryant, Dean, Roy Davis, Griffiths, Hawkins
Scorers: Griffiths, Bryant (2)
Attendance: 6000

Date: Saturday 07/09/1946
Result: **GLOUCESTER CITY 2 CHELMSFORD CITY 1**
Competition: Southern League
Teamsheet: Clarke, Brown, Tweed, Elliott, Miller, Jennings, Bryant, Dean, Roy Davis, Griffiths, Hawkins
Scorers: Hawkins, Dean
Attendance: 3500-4000

Date: Wednesday 11/09/1946
Result: **MERTHYR TYDFIL 9 GLOUCESTER CITY 4**
Competition: Southern League
Teamsheet: Clarke, Brown, Tweed, Elliott, Miller, Jennings, Bryant, Dean, Roy Davis, Perrott, Hawkins
Scorers: Hawkins, Miller, Jennings, Dean
Attendance: 8500

Date: Saturday 14/09/1946
Result: **BARRY TOWN 3 GLOUCESTER CITY 1**
Competition: Southern League
Teamsheet: Clarke, Brown, Tweed, Elliott, Miller, Jennings, Bryant, Dean, Roy Davis, Griffiths, Hawkins
Scorer: Dean

Date: Saturday 21/09/1946
Result: **SAINT JOHN'S** (Weston-Super-Mare) **0 GLOUCESTER CITY 5**
Competition: FA Cup Preliminary Round
Teamsheet: Clarke, Tweed, Cox, Elliott, Miller, Jennings, Roy Davis, Dean, Cowley, Perrott, Donovan
Scorers: Miller, Dean (3), Cowley
Attendance: 500

Date: Saturday 28/09/1946
Result: **DARTFORD 7 GLOUCESTER CITY 2**
Competition: Southern League
Teamsheet: Clarke, Tweed, Cox, Elliott, Miller, Jennings, Roy Davis, Dean, Cowley, Perrott, Donovan
Scorers: Donovan, Dean

Date: Saturday 05/10/1946
Result: **BRISTOL SAINT PHILIPS 2 GLOUCESTER CITY 0**
Competition: FA Cup 1st Qualifying Round
Teamsheet: Clarke, Tweed, Brown, Elliott, Miller, Jennings, Roy Davis, Dean, Cole, Hawkins, Sweeting

Date: Saturday 12/10/1946
Result: **GLOUCESTER CITY 1 GRAVESEND & NORTHFLEET 6**
Competition: Southern League
Teamsheet: Clarke, Seward, Tweed, Elliott, Burley, Jennings, Cole, Dean, Miller, Hawkins, Sweeting
Scorer: Elliott
Attendance: 1500

Date: Saturday 26/10/1946
Result: **GLOUCESTER CITY 0 MERTHYR TYDFIL 8**
Competition: Southern League
Teamsheet: Ray Davis, Seward, Bartlett, Elliott, Miller, Jennings, Bryant, Dean, Cole, Harris, Sweeting
Attendance: 3000

Date: Saturday 02/11/1946
Result: **GLOUCESTER CITY 1 YEOVIL TOWN 3**
Competition: Southern League
Teamsheet: Ray Davis, Seward, Jennings, Elliott, Miller, Midwinter, Cowley, Edwards, Weaver, Dean, Roberts
Scorer: Edwards

Date: Thursday 07/11/1946
Result: **GLOUCESTER CITY 5 MILLWALL 4**
Competition: Southern League
Teamsheet: Burgess, Seward, Jennings, Elliott, Miller, Dean, Cowley, Edwards, Cole, Hawkins, Sweeting
Scorers: Cole (2), Edwards, Sweeting (2)

Date: Saturday 09/11/1946
Result: **GILLINGHAM 12 GLOUCESTER CITY 1**
Competition: Southern League
Teamsheet: Burgess, Seward, Jennings, Cowley, Miller, Dean, Campbell, Murray, Weaver, Hawkins, Sweeting
Scorer: Weaver
Attendance: 5000

Date: Saturday 16/11/1946
Result: **GLOUCESTER CITY 4 WORCESTER CITY 6**
Competition: Southern League Cup Group 2
Teamsheet: Burgess, Roy Davis, Bartlett, Elliott, Miller, Jennings, Hawkins, Dean, Weaver, Stenton, Stow
Scorers: Dean, Weaver (2), Miller (pen)

Date: Saturday 23/11/1946
Result: **GLOUCESTER CITY 2 GILLINGHAM 5**
Competition: Southern League
Teamsheet: Burgess, Roy Davis, Miller, Cowley, Elliott, Jennings, Edwards, Dean, Grace, Stenton, Stow
Scorers: Stow, Dean

Date: Monday 25/11/1946
Result: **MILLWALL 2 GLOUCESTER CITY 0**
Competition: Southern League
Teamsheet: Burgess, Roy Davis, Miller, Cowley, Elliott, Jennings, Edwards, Dean, Grace, Stenton, Stow

Date: Saturday 30/11/1946
Result: **CHELMSFORD CITY 4 GLOUCESTER CITY 2**
Competition: Southern League
Teamsheet: Burgess, Brown, Miller, Cowley, Seward, Jennings, Edwards, Dean, Grace, Stenton, Stow
Scorer: Dean (2)
Attendance: 4000

Date: Saturday 07/12/1946
Result: **BEDFORD TOWN 1 GLOUCESTER CITY 0**
Competition: Southern League
Teamsheet: Burgess, Brown, Miller, Cowley, Seward, Jennings, Cunnah, Dean, Grace, Stenton, Stow
Attendance: 1500

Date: Saturday 21/12/1946
Result: **BATH CITY 1 GLOUCESTER CITY 0**
Competition: Southern League
Teamsheet: Burgess, Brown, Miller, Cowley, Seward, Jennings, Stenton, Dean, Edwards, Roy Davis, Stow
Attendance: 1600

Date: Thursday 26/12/1946
Result: **GLOUCESTER CITY 1 CHELTENHAM TOWN 3**
Competition: Gloucestershire FA Northern Senior Professional Cup Final
Teamsheet: Burgess, Brown, Miller, Cowley, Seward, Jennings, Roy Davis, Dean, Edwards, Elliott, Midwinter
Scorer: Edwards
Attendance: 2000

Date: Saturday 28/12/1946
Result: **GLOUCESTER CITY 1 HEREFORD UNITED 2**
Competition: Southern League
Teamsheet: Burgess, Brown, Miller, Cowley, Seward, Jennings, Roy Davis, Dean, Edwards, Elliott, Midwinter
Scorer: Dean

Date: Saturday 04/01/1947
Result: **GLOUCESTER CITY 7 EXETER CITY RESERVES 3**
Competition: Southern League
Teamsheet: Burgess, Brown, Miller, Cowley, Seward, Jennings, Roy Davis, Dean, Grace, Stenton, Stow
Scorers: Dean (2), Stow (3), Roy Davis (2)

Date: Saturday 11/01/1947
Result: **GLOUCESTER CITY 1 BATH CITY 1**
Competition: Southern League
Teamsheet: Burgess, Brown, Miller, Cowley, Seward, Jennings, Roy Davis, Dean, Grace, Stenton, Stow
Scorer: Dean
Attendance: 800

Date: Saturday 18/01/1947
Result: **GRAVESEND & NORTHFLEET 0 GLOUCESTER CITY 3**
Competition: Southern League
Teamsheet: Burgess, Brown, Miller, Cowley, Seward, Jennings, Roy Davis, Dean, Sweeting, Stenton, Stow
Scorers: Dean, Stow, Sweeting
Attendance: 5000

Date: Thursday 23/01/1947
Result: **GLOUCESTER CITY 5 CHELTENHAM TOWN 1**
Competition: Southern League Cup Group 2
Teamsheet: Burgess, Brown, Miller, Cowley, Seward, Jennings, Roy Davis, Dean, Grace, Sweeting, Stow
Scorers: Roy Davis (4), Dean
Attendance: 800

Date: Saturday 25/01/1947
Result: **HEREFORD UNITED 2 GLOUCESTER CITY 0**
Competition: Southern League
Teamsheet: Burgess, Brown, Miller, Cowley, Seward, Jennings, Midwinter, Dean, Grace, Sweeting, Jones

Date: Thursday 06/02/1947
Result: **WORCESTER CITY 5 GLOUCESTER CITY 2**
Competition: Southern League Cup Group 2
Teamsheet: Burgess, Brown, Elliott, Cowley, Seward, Jennings, Roy Davis, Dean, Cole, Sweeting, Stow
Scorers: Roy Davis, Cole
Attendance: 600

Date: Saturday 08/02/1947
Result: **GLOUCESTER CITY 1 GUILDFORD CITY 3**
Competition: Southern League
Teamsheet: Burgess, Brown, Miller, Cowley, Seward, Jennings, Roy Davis, Stenton, Grace, Sweeting, Stow
Scorer: Roy Davis

Date: Saturday 22/02/1947
Result: **WORCESTER CITY 4 GLOUCESTER CITY 1**
Competition: Southern League
Teamsheet: Ray Davis, Brown, Miller, Cowley, Seward, Jennings, Roy Davis, Dean, Grace, Hawkins, Stow
Scorer: Stow

Date: Saturday 22/03/1947
Result: **GLOUCESTER CITY 2 BARRY TOWN 6**
Competition: Southern League
Teamsheet: Burgess, Brown, Miller, Cowley, Seward, Jennings, Roberts, Dean, Sweeting, Stenton, Stow
Scorers: Stow, Roberts

Date: Saturday 29/03/1947
Result: **GLOUCESTER CITY 3 BEDFORD TOWN 1**
Competition: Southern League
Teamsheet: Clarke, Brown, Miller, Cowley, Seward, Jennings, Stenton, Dean, Grace, Sweeting, Stow
Scorers: Miller (pen), Dean (pen), Grace

Date: Friday 04/04/1947
Result: **CHELTENHAM TOWN 3 GLOUCESTER CITY 1**
Competition: Southern League
Teamsheet: Burgess, Brown, Miller, Cowley, Seward, Jennings, Stenton, Dean Grace, Sweeting, Stow
Scorer: Dean
Attendance: 2500

Date: Saturday 05/04/1947
Result: **EXETER CITY RESERVES 5 GLOUCESTER CITY 1**
Competition: Southern League
Teamsheet: Burgess, Brown, Miller, Cowley, Seward, Jennings, Roberts, Dean, Sweeting, Stenton, Stow
Scorer: Stenton
Attendance: 2500

Date: Monday 07/04/1947
Result: **GLOUCESTER CITY 1 CHELTENHAM TOWN 2**
Competition: Southern League
Teamsheet: Burgess, Brown, Miller, Cowley, Seward, Jennings, Roberts, Dean, Sweeting, Stenton, Grace
Scorer: Miller (pen)

Date: Saturday 12/04/1947
Result: **GLOUCESTER CITY 3 DARTFORD 2**
Competition: Southern League
Teamsheet: Burgess, Brown, Miller, Cowley, Seward, Jennings, Farrell, Dean, Atkinson, Stenton, Grace
Scorers: Atkinson, Grace, Miller
Attendance: 1200

Date: Saturday 26/04/1947
Result: **YEOVIL TOWN 7 GLOUCESTER CITY 1**
Competition: Southern League
Teamsheet: Burgess, Brown, Miller, Cowley, Seward, Jennings, Farrell, Dean, Atkinson, Stenton, Sweeting
Scorer: Farrell

Date: Saturday 03/05/1947
Result: **GUILDFORD CITY 5 GLOUCESTER CITY 1**
Competition: Southern League
Teamsheet: Burgess, Brown, Miller, Cowley, Seward, Jennings, Farrell, Dean, Atkinson, Hawkins, Stow
Scorer: Atkinson

Date: Saturday 10/05/1947
Result: **GLOUCESTER CITY 4 WORCESTER CITY 1**
Competition: Southern League
Teamsheet: Burgess, Brown, Miller, Cowley, Seward, Jennings, Farrell, Grace, Atkinson, Hawkins, Stow
Scorers: Grace (2), Atkinson, Miller

Date: Saturday 31/05/1947
Result: **GLOUCESTER CITY 2 COLCHESTER UNITED 5**
Competition: Southern League
Teamsheet: Burgess, Brown, Miller, Cowley, Seward, Jennings, Stenton, Grace, Dean, Hawkins, Stow
Scorers: Stow, Grace

Appearances – ? Atkinson 4, FL Bartlett 3, WH Brown 27, W Bryant 5, RJ Burgess 26, D Burley 1, ? Campbell 1, R Clarke 9, W Cole 5, EM Cowley 30, RD Cox 2, ? Cunnah 1, Ray Davis 4, Roy Davis 19, CG Dean 36, J Donovan 2, DS Edwards 8, F Elliott 18, V Farrell 4, A Grace 16, K Griffiths 3, G Harris 1, D Hawkins 13, RC Jennings 38, C Jones 1, TH Midwinter 4, WV Miller 36, ? Murray 1, R Perrott 3, ? Roberts 4, SC Seward 28, EH Stenton 18, AC Stow 20, D Sweeting 16, GE Tweed 8, RW Weaver 3.
Scorers – CG Dean 19, Roy Davis 8, AC Stow 8, WV Miller 7, A Grace 5, ? Atkinson 3, W Cole 3, D Sweeting 3, RW Weaver 3, W Bryant 2, D Hawkins 2, EM Cowley 1, J Donovan 1, DS Edwards 1, F Elliott 1, V Farrell 1, K Griffiths 1, RC Jennings 1, TH Midwinter 1, ? Roberts 1, EH Stenton 1.

SEASON BY SEASON

SOUTHERN LEAGUE

POS	CLUB	P	W	D	L	F	A	PTS
1	GILLINGHAM	31	20	6	5	103	45	47*
2	GUILDFORD CITY	32	21	4	7	86	39	46
3	MERTHYR TYDFIL	31	21	2	8	104	37	45*
4	YEOVIL TOWN	32	19	6	7	100	49	44
5	CHELMSFORD CITY	31	17	3	11	90	62	38*
6	GRAVESEND & NORTHFLEET	32	17	4	11	82	58	38
7	BARRY TOWN	30	14	6	10	89	57	36*
8	COLCHESTER UNITED	31	15	4	12	65	60	35*
9	CHELTENHAM TOWN	31	14	3	14	68	75	32*
10	MILLWALL	24	8	5	11	59	57	29*
11	DARTFORD	32	10	5	17	71	100	25
12	BEDFORD TOWN	32	8	8	16	62	96	24
13	HEREFORD UNITED	32	8	7	17	37	85	23
14	WORCESTER CITY	31	8	5	18	55	90	22*
15	EXETER CITY RESERVES	32	10	2	20	69	126	22
16	BATH CITY	32	7	7	18	52	93	21
17	**GLOUCESTER CITY**	**32**	**8**	**1**	**23**	**57**	**120**	**17**
18	DAGENHAM							
		528	225	78	225	1249	1249	544

* Millwall, who played their strongest team were allowed to play all their matches mid-week. Because of a government ban on mid-week games, eight games were not played. A point was allowed for each game unplayed.
Dagenham withdrew just prior to the season starting.

SEASON 1947-1948
(Home Ground: The Ground, Cheltenham Road, Longlevens)

Date: Saturday 23/08/1947
Result: **GRAVESEND & NORTHFLEET 1 GLOUCESTER CITY 2**
Competition: Southern League
Teamsheet: Silcocks, Brown, Miller, Cowley, Shanks, Jennings, Gwatkin, Dean, Giles, Jones, Stow
Scorers: Gwatkin, Giles

Date: Saturday 30/08/1947
Result: **GLOUCESTER CITY 3 EXETER CITY RESERVES 1**
Competition: Southern League
Teamsheet: Silcocks, Brown, Miller, Cowley, Shanks, Jennings, Newcombe, Dean, Giles, Stow
Scorers: Stow, Jones, Giles
Attendance: 1700

Date: Thursday 04/09/1947
Result: **GLOUCESTER CITY 2 LOVELLS ATHLETIC 4**
Competition: Southern League
Teamsheet: Silcocks, Brown, Miller, Cowley, Shanks, Jennings, Gwatkin, Dean, Giles, Jones, Stow
Scorer: Dean (2)
Attendance: 2500

Date: Saturday 06/09/1947
Result: **COLCHESTER UNITED 8 GLOUCESTER CITY 0**
Competition: Southern League
Teamsheet: Silcocks, Brown, Miller, Cowley, Shanks, Jennings, Newcombe, Dean, Crowther, Jones, Stow

Date: Thursday 11/09/1947
Result: **GLOUCESTER CITY 1 WORCESTER CITY 2**
Competition: Southern League
Teamsheet: Davis, Clark, Brown, Cowley, Shanks, Jennings, Jones, Dean, Giles, Crowther, Stow
Scorer: Jones
Attendance: 3000

Date: Saturday 13/09/1947
Result: **CHELTENHAM TOWN 0 GLOUCESTER CITY 0**
Competition: Gloucestershire FA Northern Senior Professional Cup Final
Teamsheet: Silcocks, Clark, Brown, Cowley, Shanks, Jennings, Jones, Dean, Giles, Crowther, Stow
Attendance: 3000

Date: Thursday 18/09/1947
Result: **LOVELLS ATHLETIC 4 GLOUCESTER CITY 2**
Competition: Southern League
Teamsheet: Silcocks, Clark, Brown, Cowley, Shanks, Jennings, Jones, Dean, Giles, Crowther, Grace
Scorers: Dean, Jones

Date: Saturday 20/09/1947
Result: **GLOUCESTER CITY 3 HANHAM ATHLETIC 4**
Competition: FA Cup Preliminary Round
Teamsheet: Silcocks, Clark, Brown, Cowley, Seward, Jennings, Jones, Dean, Giles, Crowther, Grace
Scorers: -----, -----, Cowley

Date: Thursday 25/09/1947
Result: **WORCESTER CITY 4 GLOUCESTER CITY 2**
Competition: Southern League
Teamsheet: Silcocks, Brown, Watkins, Cowley, Shanks, Jennings, Jones, Dean, Grace, Giles, Stow
Scorer: Dean (2, 1 pen)
Attendance: 4000

Date: Saturday 27/09/1947
Result: **GLOUCESTER CITY 2 BARRY TOWN 2**
Competition: Southern League
Teamsheet: Silcocks, Brown, Miller, Cowley, Shanks, Jennings, Gwatkin, Dean, Giles, Jones, Grace
Scorers: Dean, Giles
Attendance: 1000

Date: Saturday 04/10/1947
Result: **BATH CITY 0 GLOUCESTER CITY 1**
Competition: Southern League
Teamsheet: Silcocks, Brown, Miller, Cowley, Shanks, Jennings, Gwatkin, Dean, Giles, Jones, Grace
Scorer: Giles
Attendance: 4000

Date: Saturday 11/10/1947
Result: **GLOUCESTER CITY 4 CHELMSFORD CITY 2**
Competition: Southern League
Teamsheet: Silcocks, Brown, Miller, Cowley, Shanks, Jennings, Gwatkin, Dean, Giles, Jones, Grace
Scorers: Gwatkin (2), Jones, Dean
Attendance: 1000

Date: Saturday 18/10/1947
Result: **YEOVIL TOWN 0 GLOUCESTER CITY 0**
Competition: Southern League
Teamsheet: Silcocks, Brown, Miller, Cowley, Shanks, Jennings, Gwatkin, Giles, Boonham, Jones, Grace

Date: Saturday 25/10/1947
Result: **GLOUCESTER CITY 2 GILLINGHAM 1**
Competition: Southern League
Teamsheet: Silcocks, Brown, Miller, Cowley, Shanks, Jennings, Gwatkin, Dean, Giles, Jones, Grace
Scorers: Giles, Jones
Attendance: 2000

Date: Saturday 08/11/1947
Result: **HEREFORD UNITED 4 GLOUCESTER CITY 1**
Competition: Southern League
Teamsheet: Miller, Brown, Jennings, Cowley, Shanks, Giles, Gwatkin, Dean, Boonham, Jones, Grace
Scorer: Boonham
Attendance: 3500

Date: Saturday 15/11/1947
Result: **GLOUCESTER CITY 3 TORQUAY UNITED RESERVES 0**
Competition: Southern League
Teamsheet: Silcocks, Brown, Watkins, Cowley, Shanks, Jennings, Miller, Dean, Giles, Jones, Grace
Scorers: Dean (pen), Jones, Giles
Attendance: 2000

Date: Saturday 22/11/1947
Result: **BEDFORD TOWN 0 GLOUCESTER CITY 6**
Competition: Southern League
Teamsheet: Silcocks, Brown, Watkins, Cowley, Shanks, Jennings, Miller, Dean, Giles, Jones, Grace
Scorers: Miller, Giles (3), Dean (2)

Date: Saturday 29/11/1947
Result: **GLOUCESTER CITY 0 YEOVIL TOWN 3**
Competition: Southern League
Teamsheet: Silcocks, Brown, Watkins, Cowley, Shanks, Jennings, Miller, Dean, Giles, Jones, Parris
Attendance: 1200

Date: Saturday 06/12/1947
Result: **EXETER CITY RESERVES 2 GLOUCESTER CITY 0**
Competition: Southern League
Teamsheet: Silcocks, Brown, Watkins, Cowley, Shanks, Jennings, Miller, Dean, Moscrop, Giles, Jones
Attendance: 3000

Date: Saturday 13/12/1947
Result: **GLOUCESTER CITY 4 WORCESTER CITY 2**
Competition: Southern League Cup Group 2
Teamsheet: Silcocks, Brown, Miller, Cowley, Fowler, Jennings, Bakker, Dean, Giles, Jones, Grace
Scorers: Giles, Bakker, Jones, Grace
Attendance: 1250

Date: Saturday 20/12/1947
Result: **MERTHYR TYDFIL 3 GLOUCESTER CITY 1**
Competition: Southern League
Teamsheet: Silcocks, Brown, Watkins, Cowley, Fowler, Jennings, Bakker, Dean, Giles, Jones, Grace
Scorer: Jennings

Date: Saturday 27/12/1947
Result: **GLOUCESTER CITY 1 GUILDFORD CITY 5**
Competition: Southern League
Teamsheet: Silcocks, Brown, Miller, Cowley, Fowler, Jennings, Bakker, Dean, Giles, Jones, Grace
Scorer: Dean
Attendance: 1200

Date: Saturday 03/01/1948
Result: **GUILDFORD CITY 2 GLOUCESTER CITY 0**
Competition: Southern League
Teamsheet: Silcocks, Brown, Watkins, Cowley, Shanks, Jennings, Bakker, Dean, Giles, Jones, Grace
Attendance: 3500

GLOUCESTER CITY A.F.C SOUTHERN LEAGUE TEAM 1946–47

| W. S. Blunn (Director) | W. Rea (Director) | W. V. Miller | W. H. Brown | R. J. Burgess | S. Seward | E. Cowley | R. Jennings | W. Roberts (Asst. Secretary and Treasurer) | A. V. Stirland (Director) |

| E. Stenton | A. Grace | C. G. Dean (Captain) | D. Hawkins | A. Stow | F. Howell (Trainer) |

(Photograph courtesy of Larry Cowley, brother of Edgar Cowley)

1947-1948

GLOUCESTER CITY SOUTHERN LEAGUE XI.—From left to right are F. Howells (trainer), Stowe, Shanks (captain), Silcocks, Cowley, Brown and Seward; front row: Giles, Jennings, Bakker, Jones and Watkins.

March 1947 – The Gloucester City curse!

Floods on the playing pitch of Gloucester City's ground at Longlevens caused the postponement of the Southern League match with Colchester to-day.

Gloucester City supporters at Mansfield for the FA Cup 1st Round 27 November 1948

Date: Saturday 10/01/1948
Result: **GLOUCESTER CITY 1 GRAVESEND & NORTHFLEET 3**
Competition: Southern League
Teamsheet: Silcocks, Brown, Watkins, Cowley, Shanks, Jennings, Bakker, Dean, Giles, Nutt, Jones
Scorer: Dean

Date: Saturday 17/01/1948
Result: **WORCESTER CITY 5 GLOUCESTER CITY 1**
Competition: Southern League Cup Group 2
Teamsheet: Silcocks, Brown, Watkins, Cowley, Shanks, Jennings, Bakker, Dean, Giles, Nutt, Jones
Scorer: Dean
Attendance: 3000

Date: Saturday 24/01/1948
Result: **GLOUCESTER CITY 1 MERTHYR TYDFIL 10**
Competition: Southern League Cup Group 2
Teamsheet: Silcocks, Brown, Stow, Cowley, Shanks, Jennings, Bakker, Dean, Giles, Nutt, Jones
Scorer: Dean
Attendance: 1200

Date: Saturday 31/01/1948
Result: **CHELMSFORD CITY 4 GLOUCESTER CITY 2**
Competition: Southern League
Teamsheet: Silcocks, Brown, Watkins, Jennings, Shanks, Crowther, Gwatkin, Giles, Cowley, Jones, Stow
Scorers: own goal, Cowley

Date: Saturday 07/02/1948
Result: **GLOUCESTER CITY 3 BATH CITY 1**
Competition: Southern League
Teamsheet: Silcocks, Brown, Watkins, Broadbent, Shanks, Jennings, Gwatkin, Giles, Cowley, Jones, Stow
Scorers: Giles, Jones, Cowley
Attendance: 1000

Date: Saturday 21/02/1948
Result: **GLOUCESTER CITY 1 BEDFORD TOWN 2**
Competition: Southern League
Teamsheet: Silcocks, Brown, Watkins, Broadbent, Shanks, Jennings, Newcombe, Giles, Cowley, Jones, Stow
Scorer: Stow (pen)

Date: Saturday 06/03/1948
Result: **GLOUCESTER CITY 1 DARTFORD 1**
Competition: Southern League
Teamsheet: Silcocks, Brown, Colenutt, Seward, Shanks, Jennings, Bakker, Giles, Cowley, Jones, Stow
Scorer: Cowley
Attendance: 1300

Date: Thursday 11/03/1948
Result: **GLOUCESTER CITY 2 MERTHYR TYDFIL 2**
Competition: Southern League
Teamsheet: Silcocks, Brown, Colenutt, Seward, Shanks, Jennings, Gwatkin, Cowley, Giles, Jones, Stow
Scorer: Stow (2)
Attendance: 1400

Date: Saturday 13/03/1948
Result: **GILLINGHAM 4 GLOUCESTER CITY 0**
Competition: Southern League
Teamsheet: Silcocks, Brown, Colenutt, Seward, Shanks, Jennings, Gwatkin, Cowley, Giles, Jones, Stow

Date: Saturday 20/03/1948
Result: **MERTHYR TYDFIL 7 GLOUCESTER CITY 1**
Competition: Southern League Cup Group 2
Teamsheet: Silcocks, Brown, Colenutt, Seward, Shanks, Jennings, Bakker, Cowley, Giles, Jones, Stow
Scorer: Jones

Date: Friday 26/03/1948
Result: **CHELTENHAM TOWN 1 GLOUCESTER CITY 0**
Competition: Southern League
Teamsheet: Silcocks, Brown, Colenutt, Seward, Shanks, Jennings, Bakker, Miller, Cowley, Jones, Stow
Attendance: 4000

Date: Saturday 27/03/1948
Result: **GLOUCESTER CITY 1 HEREFORD UNITED 3**
Competition: Southern League
Teamsheet: Silcocks, Brown, Colenutt, Cowley, Shanks, Jennings, Gwatkin, Seward, Miller, Giles, Stow
Scorer: Giles
Attendance: 1500

Date: Monday 29/03/1948
Result: **GLOUCESTER CITY 0 CHELTENHAM TOWN 0**
Competition: Southern League
Teamsheet: Silcocks, Brown, Colenutt, Cowley, Shanks, Seward, Bakker, Holland, Miller, Jones, Stow
Attendance: 1500-2000

Date: Saturday 03/04/1948
Result: **DARTFORD 1 GLOUCESTER CITY 0**
Competition: Southern League
Teamsheet: Silcocks, Brown, Clark, Seward, Shanks, Jennings, Bakker, Gwatkin, Cowley, Nutt, Stow

Date: Thursday 08/04/1948
Result: **GLOUCESTER CITY 3 HEREFORD UNITED 1**
Competition: Southern League Cup Group 2
Teamsheet: Silcocks, Brown, Clark, Seward, Shanks, Jennings, Bakker, Giles, Cowley, Watkins, Stow
Scorers: -----, Cowley (2)
Attendance: 1500

Date: Thursday 15/04/1948
Result: **GLOUCESTER CITY 1 CHELTENHAM TOWN 2**
Competition: Gloucestershire FA Northern Senior Professional Cup Final Replay
Teamsheet: Silcocks, Brown, Giles, Seward, Shanks, Jennings, Bakker, Jones, Cowley, Watkins, Stow
Scorer: Bakker
Attendance: 2556

Date: Saturday 17/04/1948
Result: **GLOUCESTER CITY 1 COLCHESTER UNITED 3**
Competition: Southern League
Teamsheet: Thomas, Brown, Clark, Seward, Shanks, Jennings, Bakker, Giles, Cowley, Holland, Stow
Scorer: Holland
Attendance: 2000

Date: Wednesday 21/04/1948
Result: **TORQUAY UNITED RESERVES 0 GLOUCESTER CITY 0**
Competition: Southern League
Teamsheet: Davies, Brown, Thomas, Seward, Shanks, Jennings, Bakker, Nutt, Cowley, Holland, Stow
Attendance: 1500

Date: Monday 26/04/1948
Result: **BARRY TOWN 5 GLOUCESTER CITY 0**
Competition: Southern League
Teamsheet: Burgess, Brown, Thomas, Seward, Shanks, Jennings, Gwatkin, Holland, Cowley, Parris, Stow

Date: Thursday 29/04/1948
Result: **HEREFORD UNITED 6 GLOUCESTER CITY 1**
Competition: Southern League Cup Group 2
Teamsheet: Burgess, Brown, Thomas, Seward, Stow, Jennings, Bakker, Nutt, Cowley, Roberts, Sayer
Scorer: Roberts

Appearances – J Bakker 17, G Boonham 2, S Broadbent 2, WH Brown 43, RJ Burgess 2, H Clark 7, JMW Colenutt 7, EM Cowley 42, ? Crowther 6, ? Davies 1, Ray Davis 1, CG Dean 25, H Fowler 3, AE Giles 36, A Grace 15, K Griffiths 1, IW Gwatkin 14, C Holland 4, RC Jennings 42, C Jones 36, WV Miller 19, RJ Moscrop 1, G Newcombe 3, ? Nutt 6, E Parris 2, ? Roberts 1, VT Sayer 1, SC Seward 15, R Shanks 38, L Silcocks 37, AC Stow 25, ? Thomas 4, ? Watkins 14.
Scorers – CG Dean 14, AE Giles 11, C Jones 9, EM Cowley 5, AC Stow 4, IW Gwatkin 3, J Bakker 2, G Boonham 1, A Grace 1, C Holland 1, RC Jennings 1, WV Miller 1, ? Roberts 1, own goal 1.

SOUTHERN LEAGUE

POS	CLUB	P	W	D	L	F	A	PTS
1	MERTHYR TYDFIL	34	23	7	4	84	38	53
2	GILLINGHAM	34	21	5	8	81	43	47
3	WORCESTER CITY	34	21	3	10	74	45	45
4	COLCHESTER UNITED	34	17	10	7	88	41	44
5	HEREFORD UNITED	34	16	10	8	77	53	42
6	LOVELLS ATHLETIC	34	17	6	11	74	50	40
7	EXETER CITY RESERVES	34	15	7	12	65	57	37
8	YEOVIL TOWN	34	12	11	11	56	50	35
9	CHELMSFORD CITY	34	14	7	13	62	58	35
10	CHELTENHAM TOWN	34	13	9	12	71	71	35
11	BATH CITY	34	12	8	14	55	62	32
12	BARRY TOWN	34	10	9	15	60	70	29
13	GRAVESEND & NORTHFLEET	34	11	6	17	52	81	28
14	GUILDFORD CITY	34	11	4	19	69	74	26
15	DARTFORD	34	10	6	18	35	62	26
16	**GLOUCESTER CITY**	**34**	**8**	**6**	**20**	**45**	**78**	**22**
17	TORQUAY UNITED RESERVES	34	6	9	19	43	95	21
18	BEDFORD TOWN	34	6	3	25	41	104	15
		612	243	126	243	1132	1132	612

SEASON 1948-1949
(Home Ground: The Ground, Cheltenham Rooad, Longlevens)

Date: Saturday 21/08/1948
Result: **GLOUCESTER CITY 2 GUILDFORD CITY 2**
Competition: Southern League
Teamsheet: Ward, Ash, Moore, Cowley, Bartlett, Lawson, Smith, Hunt, Boyd, Jenkins, Jones
Scorer: Hunt (2)
Attendance: 2500

Date: Saturday 28/08/1948
Result: **LOVELLS ATHLETIC 7 GLOUCESTER CITY 1**
Competition: Southern League
Teamsheet: Ward, Ash, Moore, Cowley, Bartlett, Stow, Tibbitts, Hunt, Bazeley, Jenkins, Jones
Scorer: Moore

Date: Thursday 02/09/1948
Result: **HEREFORD UNITED 3 GLOUCESTER CITY 2**
Competition: Southern League
Teamsheet: Cripps, Brown, Colenutt, Cowley, Bartlett, Moore, Tibbitts, Hunt, Stow, Jenkins, Jones
Scorers: Jenkins, Jones

Date: Saturday 04/09/1948
Result: **GLOUCESTER CITY 4 CINDERFORD TOWN 0**
Competition: FA Cup Extra Preliminary Round
Teamsheet: Cripps, Brown, Colenutt, Cowley, Bartlett, Moore, Tibbitts, Hunt, Stow, Jenkins, Jones
Scorers: Moore, Hunt, Jenkins (2)
Attendance: 3500

Date:Thursday 09/09/1948
Result: **WORCESTER CITY 4 GLOUCESTER CITY 2**
Competition: Southern League
Teamsheet: Cross, Brown, Colenutt, Cowley, Basford, Moore, Tibbitts, Lawson, Bazeley, Jenkins, Jones
Scorers: Moore, Tibbitts
Attendance:5000

Date: Saturday 11/09/1948
Result: **GLOUCESTER CITY 1 CHELTENHAM TOWN 1**
Competition: Gloucestershire FA Northern Senior Professional Cup Final
Teamsheet: Cross, Brown, Colenutt, Cowley, Bartlett, Moore, Tibbitts, Lawson, Hunt, Jenkins, Jones
Scorer: Jones
Attendance: 3000

Date: Thursday 16/09/1948
Result: **BATH CITY 3 GLOUCESTER CITY 2**
Competition: Southern League Cup 1st Round
Teamsheet: Cross, Brown, Colenutt, Cowley, Basford, Moore, Starling, Hunt, Lawson, Jenkins, Jones
Scorer: Hunt (2)

Date: Saturday 18/09/1948
Result: **GLOUCESTER CITY 5 BARNSTAPLE TOWN 2**
Competition: FA Cup Preliminary Round
Teamsheet: Cross, Basford, Colenutt, Cowley, Bartlett, Moore, Starling, Hunt, Stow, Jenkins, Jones
Scorers: Jenkins, Moore (2 pens), Hunt (2)
Attendance: 2000

Date: Thursday 23/09/1948
Result: **BEDFORD TOWN 2 GLOUCESTER CITY 2**
Competition: Southern League
Teamsheet: Cross, Basford, Colenutt, Hunt, Bartlett, Lawson, Starling, Jones, Stow, Jenkins, Roberts
Scorers: Stow, Jones

Date: Saturday 25/09/1948
Result: **DARTFORD 1 GLOUCESTER CITY 0**
Competition: Southern League
Teamsheet: Cross, Ash, Colenutt, Moore, Bartlett, Lawson, Harding, Hunt, Stow, Jenkins, Jones

Date: Thursday 30/09/1948
Result: **GLOUCESTER CITY 1 HEREFORD UNITED 3**
Competition: Worcestershire FA Senior Challenge Cup 1st Round
Teamsheet: Cross, Ash, Colenutt, Brown, Bartlett, Moore, Starling, Jenkins, Bazeley, Jones, Stow
Scorer: Stow
Attendance: 1500

Date: Saturday 02/10/1948
Result: **GLOUCESTER CITY 8 CLEVEDON 2**
Competition: FA Cup 1st Qualifying Round
Teamsheet: Cross, Ash, Colenutt, Cowley, Bartlett, Moore, Starling, Hunt, Bazeley, Jenkins, Jones
Scorers: Jenkins, Bazeley, Moore (pen), Jones (2), Hunt, own goal, Starling
Attendance: 2500

Date: Monday 04/10/1948
Result: **MERTHYR TYDFIL 1 GLOUCESTER CITY 0**
Competition: Southern League
Teamsheet: Cross, Ash, Colenutt, Cowley, Bartlett, Moore, Starling, Hunt, Bazeley, Jenkins, Jones

Date: Saturday 16/10/1948
Result: **GLASTONBURY 1 GLOUCESTER CITY 1**
Competition: FA Cup 2nd Qualifying Round
Teamsheet: Cross, Colenutt, Brown, Cowley, Bartlett, Moore, Starling, Hunt, Bazeley, Jenkins, Jones
Scorer: Bazeley
Attendance: 2000

Date: Saturday 23/10/1948
Result: **GLOUCESTER CITY 3 GLASTONBURY 1**
Competition: FA Cup 2nd Qualifying Round Replay
Teamsheet: Cross, Brown, Colenutt, Cowley, Bartlett, Moore, Starling, Hunt, Bazeley, Jenkins, Stow
Scorers: Bazeley, Hunt, Moore (pen)
Attendance: 3000

Date: Saturday 30/10/1948
Result: **GLOUCESTER CITY 4 STREET 1**
Competition: FA Cup 3rd Qualifying Round
Teamsheet: Cross, Brown, Colenutt, Cowley, Bartlett, Moore, Starling, Hunt, Bazeley, Jenkins, Jones
Scorers: Jenkins, Bazeley, Moore (pen), Starling
Attendance: 4500

Date: Saturday 06/11/1948
Result: **HASTINGS UNITED 3 GLOUCESTER CITY 2**
Competition: Southern League
Teamsheet: Cross, Basford, Colenutt, Cowley, Bartlett, Giles, Starling, Hunt, Bazeley, Jenkins, Jones
Scorers: Starling, Bazeley

Date: Saturday 13/11/1948
Result: **BATH CITY 2 GLOUCESTER CITY 3**
Competition: FA Cup 4th Qualifying Round
Teamsheet: Cross, Brown, Colenutt, Cowley, Bartlett, Moore, Starling, Hunt, Bazeley, Giles, Jones
Scorers: Jones, Bazeley, Giles
Attendance: 7095

Date: Saturday 20/11/1948
Result: **GLOUCESTER CITY 3 BEDFORD TOWN 1**
Competition: Southern League
Teamsheet: Cross, Brown, Colenutt, Cowley, Bartlett, Moore, Starling, Hunt, Bazeley, Giles, Jones
Scorers: Hunt (2), Starling
Attendance: 2500

Date: Saturday 27/11/1948
Result: **MANSFIELD TOWN 4 GLOUCESTER CITY 0**
Competition: FA Cup 1st Round
Teamsheet: Cross, Brown, Giles, Cowley, Bartlett, Moore, Starling, Hunt, Bazeley, Jenkins, Jones
Attendance: 11401

Date: Saturday 04/12/1948
Result: **GLOUCESTER CITY 2 KIDDERMINSTER HARRIERS 0**
Competition: Southern League
Teamsheet: Cross, Brown, Colenutt, Cowley, Bartlett, Moore, Starling, Hunt, Bazeley, Giles, Jones
Scorers: Moore, Jones
Attendance: 2000

Date: Saturday 11/12/1948
Result: **BATH CITY 0 GLOUCESTER CITY 1**
Competition: Southern League
Teamsheet: Cross, Brown, Colenutt, Cowley, Bartlett, Moore, Starling, Hunt, Bazeley, Hedge, Stow
Scorer: Stow
Attendance: 2006

Date: Saturday 18/12/1948
Result: **GLOUCESTER CITY 3 CHELMSFORD CITY 2**
Competition: Southern League
Teamsheet: Cross, Brown, Colenutt, Cowley, Bartlett, Moore, Starling, Hunt, Bazeley, Beattie, Stow
Scorers: Hunt, Starling, Bazeley
Attendance: 3000

Date: Saturday 25/12/1948
Result: **COLCHESTER UNITED 1 GLOUCESTER CITY 1**
Competition: Southern League
Teamsheet: Cross, Brown, Colenutt, Cowley, Bartlett, Moore, Starling, Jenkins, Bazeley, Beattie, Stow
Scorer: Jenkins
Attendance: 7000

Date: Saturday 01/01/1949
Result: **EXETER CITY RESERVES 1 GLOUCESTER CITY 2**
Competition: Southern League
Teamsheet: Cross, Brown, Colenutt, Cowley, Bartlett, Moore, Starling, Jenkins, Bazeley, Beattie, Stow
Scorers: Bazeley, Jenkins

Date: Saturday 08/01/1949
Result: **GLOUCESTER CITY 4 CHINGFORD TOWN 1**
Competition: Southern League
Teamsheet: Cross, Brown, Colenutt, Cowley, Bartlett, Moore, Starling, Jenkins, Bazeley, Beattie, Stow
Scorers: Bazeley, Stow, Beattie (2)

Date: Saturday 15/01/1949
Result: **GLOUCESTER CITY 1 GRAVESEND & NORTHFLEET 3**
Competition: Southern League
Teamsheet: Cross, Brown, Colenutt, Cowley, Bartlett, Moore, Starling, Hunt, Bazeley, Beattie, Stow
Scorer: own goal
Attendance: 2500

Date: Saturday 22/01/1949
Result: **GUILDFORD CITY 2 GLOUCESTER CITY 1**
Competition: Southern League
Teamsheet: Cross, Brown, Colenutt, Cowley, Bartlett, Moore, Starling, Hunt, Bazeley, Beattie, Stow
Scorer: Starling

Date: Saturday 29/01/1949
Result: **GLOUCESTER CITY 3 DARTFORD 2**
Competition: Southern League
Teamsheet: Cross, Brown, Colenutt, Cowley, Bartlett, Moore, Starling, Jenkins, Hunt, Beattie, Stow
Scorers: Beattie (2), Hunt
Attendance: 3000

Date: Thursday 03/02/1949
Result: **GLOUCESTER CITY 1 WORCESTER CITY 1**
Competition: Southern League
Teamsheet: Cross, Brown, Colenutt, Moore, Bartlett, Lawson, Starling, Jenkins, Hunt, Beattie, Stow
Scorer: Jenkins

Date: Thursday 10/02/1949
Result: **GLOUCESTER CITY 4 HEREFORD UNITED 2**
Competition: Southern League
Teamsheet: Cross, Brown, Colenutt, Moore, Bartlett, Lawson, Starling, Hunt, Beattie, Jenkins, Jones
Scorers: Moore (pen), Hunt, Jones (2)
Attendance: 2000

Date: Thursday 17/02/1949
Result: **GLOUCESTER CITY 2 TONBRIDGE 3**
Competition: Southern League
Teamsheet: Cross, Brown, Colenutt, Moore, Lawson, Bartlett, Starling, Beattie, Bazeley, Jenkins, Jones
Scorers: Bazeley, Jenkins

Date: Saturday 19/02/1949
Result: **TONBRIDGE 1 GLOUCESTER CITY 2**
Competition: Southern League
Teamsheet: Cross, Brown, Colenutt, Cowley, Bartlett, Moore, Starling, Hunt, Beattie, Jenkins, Jones
Scorer: Jones (2)

Date: Saturday 05/03/1949
Result: **GLOUCESTER CITY 1 LOVELLS ATHLETIC 2**
Competition: Southern League
Teamsheet: Cross, Brown, Colenutt, Cowley, Bartlett, Moore, Starling, Jenkins, Hunt, Beattie, Jones
Scorer: Hunt

Date: Saturday 12/03/1949
Result: **GLOUCESTER CITY 0 MERTHYR TYDFIL 3**
Competition: Southern League
Teamsheet: Cross, Brown, Colenutt, Cowley, Giles, Moore, Starling, Hunt, Bazeley, Jenkins, Jones
Attendance: 2500-3000

Date: Thursday 17/03/1949
Result: **GLOUCESTER CITY 4 HASTINGS UNITED 2**
Competition: Southern League
Teamsheet: King, Brown, Lawson, Cowley, Bartlett, Moore, Bakker, Hunt, Boyd, Beattie, Stow
Scorers: Boyd, Beattie (2), Hunt

Date: Saturday 19/03/1949
Result: **KIDDERMINSTER HARRIERS 4 GLOUCESTER CITY 3**
Competition: Southern League
Teamsheet: Cross, Brown, Colenutt, Cowley, Bartlett, Moore, Starling, Hunt, Jenkins, Beattie, Stow
Scorers: Stow, Hunt, Moore (pen)
Attendance: 2000

Date: Wednesday 23/03/1949
Result: **GRAVESEND & NORTHFLEET 3 GLOUCESTER CITY 2**
Competition: Southern League
Teamsheet: Cross, Brown, Lawson, Cowley, Bartlett, Moore, Bakker, Hunt, Jenkins, Beattie, Stow
Scorers: Bakker, Moore

Date: Saturday 26/03/1949
Result: **CHINGFORD TOWN 4 GLOUCESTER CITY 4**
Competition: Southern League
Teamsheet: King, Lawson, Colenutt, Cowley, Bartlett, Moore, Bakker, Hunt, Jenkins, Beattie, Stow
Scorers: Beattie, Hunt, Bakker, own goal

Date: Monday 28/03/1949
Result: **GILLINGHAM 4 GLOUCESTER CITY 1**
Competition: Southern League
Teamsheet: Cross, Giles, Colenutt, Hunt, Basford, Moore, Bakker, Beattie, Jenkins, Jones, Stow
Scorer: Stow
Attendance: 5000

Date: Thursday 31/03/1949
Result: **GLOUCESTER CITY 1 TORQUAY UNITED RESERVES 1**
Competition: Southern League
Teamsheet: King, Brown, Lawson, Cowley, Bartlett, Moore, Bakker, Hunt, Boyd, Beattie, Stow
Scorer: Boyd
Attendance: 2000

Date: Saturday 02/04/1949
Result: **GLOUCESTER CITY 0 GILLINGHAM 0**
Competition: Southern League
Teamsheet: King, Brown, Lawson, Cowley, Bartlett, Moore, Bakker, Hunt, Boyd, Beattie, Stow
Attendance: 3000

Date: Thursday 07/04/1949
Result: **GLOUCESTER CITY 2 YEOVIL TOWN 2**
Competition: Southern League
Teamsheet: King, Brown, Lawson, Cowley, Basford, Moore, Bakker, Hunt, Boyd, Beattie, Stow
Scorer: Boyd (2)
Attendance: 2300

Date: Saturday 09/04/1949
Result: **TORQUAY UNITED RESERVES 6 GLOUCESTER CITY 2**
Competition: Southern League
Teamsheet: King, Brown, Colenutt, Cowley, Basford, Moore, Starling, Jenkins, Boyd, Jones, Stow
Scorer: Boyd (2)

Date: Friday 15/04/1949
Result: **GLOUCESTER CITY 0 CHELTENHAM TOWN 0**
Competition: Southern League
Teamsheet: King, Lawson, Colenutt, Cowley, Giles, Moore, Starling, Hunt, Boyd, Beattie, Stow
Attendance: 5300

Date: Saturday 16/04/1949
Result: **GLOUCESTER CITY 4 BARRY TOWN 1**
Competition: Southern League
Teamsheet: King, Brown, Colenutt, Cowley, Giles, Moore, Starling, Hunt, Boyd, Beattie, Stow
Scorers: Hunt (2), Beattie, own goal
Attendance: 2300

Date: Monday 18/04/1949
Result: **CHELTENHAM TOWN 2 GLOUCESTER CITY 1**
Competition: Southern League
Teamsheet: King, Lawson, Colenutt, Cowley, Basford, Moore, Starling, Hunt, Boyd, Beattie, Stow
Scorer: Hunt
Attendance: 5000

Date: Saturday 23/04/1949
Result: **GLOUCESTER CITY 2 BATH CITY 5**
Competition: Southern League
Teamsheet: King, Brown, Colenutt, Cowley, Giles, Moore, Starling, Hunt, Jenkins, Beattie, Stow
Scorers: Hunt, Jenkins
Attendance: 2500

Date: Monday 25/04/1949
Result: **BARRY TOWN 4 GLOUCESTER CITY 1**
Competition: Southern League
Teamsheet: King, Brown, Lawson, Cowley, Basford, Moore, Bakker, Hunt, Jenkins, Beattie, Jones
Scorer: Hunt

Date: Wednesday 27/04/1949
Result: **CHELMSFORD CITY 7 GLOUCESTER CITY 1**
Competition: Southern League
Teamsheet: Cross, Lawson, Stow, Hunt, Basford, Moore, Starling, Beattie, Bazeley, Jenkins, Bakker
Scorer: Jenkins

Date: Saturday 30/04/1949
Result: **GLOUCESTER CITY 6 COLCHESTER UNITED 1**
Competition: Southern League
Teamsheet: Cross, Brown, Lawson, Cowley, Giles, Moore, Bakker, Hunt, Boyd, Jenkins, Stow
Scorers: Bakker (2), Hunt (2), Jenkins, Moore

Date: Thursday 05/05/1949
Result: **YEOVIL TOWN 5 GLOUCESTER CITY 1**
Competition: Southern League
Teamsheet: Cross, Brown, Colenutt, Cowley, Giles, Moore, Starling, Hunt, Boyd, Bakker (?), Stow
Scorer: Starling

Date: Saturday 07/05/1949
Result: **GLOUCESTER CITY 1 EXETER CITY RESERVES 1**
Competition: Southern League
Teamsheet: Cross, Brown, Colenutt, Cowley, Giles, Moore, Bakker, Hunt, Boyd, Beattie, Stow
Scorer: Boyd
Attendance: 2000

Date: Saturday 14/05/1949
Result: **CHELTENHAM TOWN 2 GLOUCESTER CITY 1**
Competition: Gloucestershire FA Northern Senior Professional Cup Final Replay
Teamsheet: Cross, Brown, Lawson, Cowley, Bartlett, Moore, Bakker, Hunt, Bazeley, Jenkins, Stow
Scorer: Bazeley
Attendance: 3000

Appearances – W Ash 6, J Bakker 13, FL Bartlett 39, WD Basford 11, S Bazeley 24, G Beattie 27, J Boyd 12, WH Brown 41, JMW Colenutt 42, EM Cowley 46, K Cripps 2, D Cross 39, AE Giles 13, ? Harding 1, ? Hedge 1, DA Hunt 47, M Jenkins 38, C Jones 28, H King 11, G Lawson 21, JWM Moore 52, ? Roberts 1, J Smith 1, L Starling 36, AC Stow 35, J Tibbitts 5, C Ward 2.

Scorers – DA Hunt 25, M Jenkins 13, JWM Moore 13, S Bazeley 11, C Jones 9, G Beattie 8, J Boyd 7, L Starling 7, AC Stow 5, J Bakker 4, AE Giles 1, J Tibbitts 1, own goals 4.

PROGRAMME

PROGRAMME

PROGRAMME

1947-1948

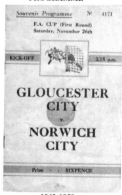

1949-1950

1946-1947

PROGRAMME FOR DIAMOND JUBILEE DINNER 13 OCTOBER 1949
(Courtesy of Frank Tredgett)

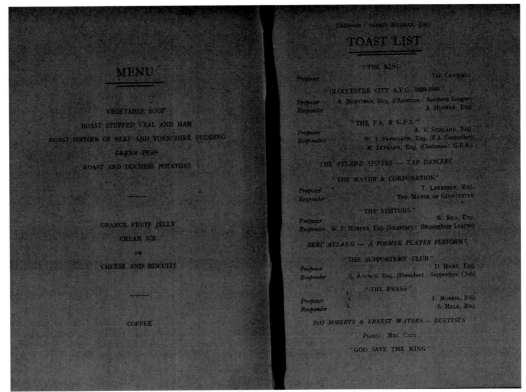

Glo'ster Soccer Club Celebrates Its Diamond Jubilee

TRIBUTES AT DINNER

FROM THE MAYOR, FROM THE NATIONAL AND COUNTY FOOTBALL ASSOCIATIONS AND OTHER SOCCER ORGANISATIONS, AND FROM LEADING CITIZENS, CONGRATULATIONS WERE SHOWERED UPON GLOUCESTER CITY A.F.C. WHEN, LAST EVENING, THE DINNER MARKING THE CLUB'S DIAMOND JUBILEE TOOK PLACE.

Its tables and walls gleaming with the club decorations of red and white, Mercers Hall accommodated a large gathering, which included, besides well-known civic and administrative soccer personalities, players past and present of Gloucester City and the Yeovil team, which the City defeated in a Southern League Cup match at Longlevens earlier in the evening.

Mr. A. Hurran, Chairman of the Directors of the City Club, presided, and was supported by among others, the Mayor of Gloucester (Councillor J. H. Edge), the Mayoress (Mrs. W. V. Eggleton), The City High Sheriff (Mr. E. W. Fry) and Mrs. Fry, the Deputy Mayor (Mr. W. J. Smith) and Mrs. Smith, Mrs. Hurran, Mr. W. J. Pepworth (Chairman of the Northern Council of the Glo'shire Football Association and F.A. Councillor Mr. R. Lethaby (Chairman, Glo'shire F.A.), Mr. A. Mortimer (Chairman of the Southern League), Mr. L. O. Need (Town Clerk), Mr. G. J. J. Robertson (Editor of "The Citizen"), Messrs. W. Rea, A. Stirland, F. A. Morris and C. R. Stephens (Directors) and Mrs. Rea, Mrs. Stephens, Mrs. Morris, Mr. A. A. Dunlop (Treasurer), Mr. Douglas Hunt (Secretary-Manager) and Mrs. Hunt, Messrs. S. Adcock (President) and L. A. Beddis (Chairman), Supporters Club, former directors, officials and players

Among apologies was one from the President, Sir Leslie Boyce, who wired congratulating the club on its diamond jubilee and hoping that they would go from strength to strength.

First congratulations came from Mr. A. Mortimer, who proposed "Gloucester City A.F.C. 1889—1949." In doing so, he remarked that when the hazards of the game, its ups and downs, were remembered, it must have been a very fine band of stalwarts to keep the club going over a 60 years span, and to place it in the position it occupied to-day.

"I know a little of the difficulties confronting all managements and boards of directors," continued Mr. Mortimer. "Everyone who takes part in such management, professional or amateur, does make an important contribution to the game. What is more, he puts in more than he takes out, and his sole reward is the knowledge that he is fostering a great sport."

Need Of Support

Emphasising the need that existed in every club still making its way for whole-hearted support, Mr. Mortimer stressed that civic authorities with a good football club in their midst possessed a profitable asset.

"I hear with very great pleasure that your local authority gives all the help it can to aid soccer in Gloucester," continued Mr. Mortimer.

From personal experience in watching seven City games, Mr. Mortimer praised the spirit of the club and its players and concluded by saying:

This afternoon your boys gave a brilliant performance. They beat Yeovil, the holders, on their merits. So some one else must win the League Cup this season and may it be Gloucester City. May they go a long way in the F.A. Cup also."

Tribute to the past, rather than prophecies for the future, emerged from the speech with which Mr. Hurran acknowledged the toast.

"More than once during the 60 years we have ceased to function for longer or shorter periods," he remarked. "Always a band of enthusiasts has come forward to renew the fight for soccer in Gloucester."

It had been hoped to see there two survivors of the first game on October 5, 1889, Mr. Chadborn and Mr. Frank Fielding, but as this was not possible, the Club sent grateful thanks to them for their services of 60 years ago.

Mr. Hurran also expressed gratitude to some of the notable personalities in club history. He spoke of the many anxieties experienced by the club in their anxiety to give the public the football it wanted and to gain the support that was needed.

Equal To Any

"We shall only receive that support if we produce good football, and I am proud of the fact that this year we have a team equal to any in the Southern League," he said.

"Are we going to be given that support now we deserve it? Where are we going to end?" One ambition I have had—for the City to be in the League and to be at Wembly."

"The Football Association and Gloucestershire Football Association" was proposed by Mr. Stirland. After referring to the admirable work of these controlling bodies of the game, Mr. Stirland remarked: "These occasions give the smaller fry an opportunity of expressing gratitude to those who, on their pinnacle, do everything for the game they possible can."

The first to respond to the toast, Mr. Pepworth, said that there were governments who would be very pleased to be able to say they had done their job as well as the F.A.

The fact that our soccer prestige on the Continent was higher than ever, was proved by the constant demand for missionary touring teams.

Pluck And Determination

At home no better example of pluck and determination could be supplied than that of Gloucester City.

"I have watched the fortunes of soccer in Gloucester for 50 out of the 60 years of your existence," revealed Mr. Pepworth, and the work of your pioneers has won everybody's admiration. I know some of the sacrifices made, and I take off my hat most reverently for what has been achieved.

"Gloucester's reputation for grit has penetrated far beyond the county . . . They say the F.A. Cup produces giant killers. Some day Gloucester may play the role of Jack. Why not this year?"

Mr. Lethaby outlined the activities of the G.F.A. to the gathering, and wished the club a very happy time in the future. "All your struggles are not over," he prophesied, "but I am sure you will meet them with courage equal to that shown in the past."

Toasting "The Mayor and Corporation" Mr. Stephens told the gathering that in all the club's dealing's with the civic authorities the latter had always been considerate and ready to meet them halfway.

The club hoped that help would be continued in the future, and that Gloucester City A.F.C. would, on their part, help to keep the City of Gloucester on the map.

Laughter greeted the remarks of the Mayor when, responding, he reminded the club that their ground was in the county. "Anything you may have achieved is largely due to the city; anything you have failed to do is due to the county," he joked.

Never Asked Corporation For Money

One line about both the soccer and rugby clubs was that they had never asked the Corporation for financial assistance.

"I am a realist," proceeded the Mayor. "I read week in and week out about the city's requirements —a city hall, a theatre, an open-air swimming pool, playing fields —and yet we have to face the fact that to-day there is, and will for a long time continue to be, a restriction on all public expenditure.

As a country to-day we cannot even afford to re-equip industry for its gigantic task in making both ends meet and securing an export trade that will at least enable us to maintain our present standard of life.

"If we cannot do that, it is obvious we cannot indulge large capital projects such as those I have named, desirable in themselves, but in these serious times absolutely impracticable.

"In my opinion there is not the remotest chance of this Government or the next giving sanction for many years to expenditure on these projects, or allowing the building permits for the work to be done.

"So let us realise that in the next few years we have to do things for ourselves instead of relying on the city or state to do things for us"

Support Of The Crowd

Many foolish things had been said about crowds who attended sports spectacles instead of playing games themselves.

In these modern times it was impossible to conduct either amateur or professional cricket or football, owing to high and rising costs, without the support of the crowd, and there was nothing to be ashamed of in soliciting their support.

At Longlevens he hoped the club would have increasing gates and increasing success.

The toast of "The Visitors" was aptly proposed by Mr. Rea, and the Town Clerk replied, alluding to the fact that the City ground was in the rural district. he said, "I hope the day will not be far distant when it will be on the right side of the Rubicon, if not the Horsebere brook."

Tribute to the invaluable work of the Supporters Club came from Mr. Hunt when he submitted that toast, and Mr. Adcock, replying, said the Supporters Club had striven very hard especially during the past six months to raise all money they could to put the club on its feet, and soccer on the map in Gloucester.

A happy understanding existed between the Supporters Club and the parent club, and there was general satisfaction at the manner in which the A.F.C. was being run.

He concluded with a plea for better public transport services to Longlevens matches.

The remaining toast was that of "The Press," honoured on the call of Mr. Morris, and responded to by Mr. S. Hale.

During the evening entertainment was provided by the Ayland Sisters (tap dancers), Bert Ayland (Gloucestershire comedian), and Dai Roberts and Ernest Waters (duettists). The pianist was Mrs. Cain.

22 October 1949

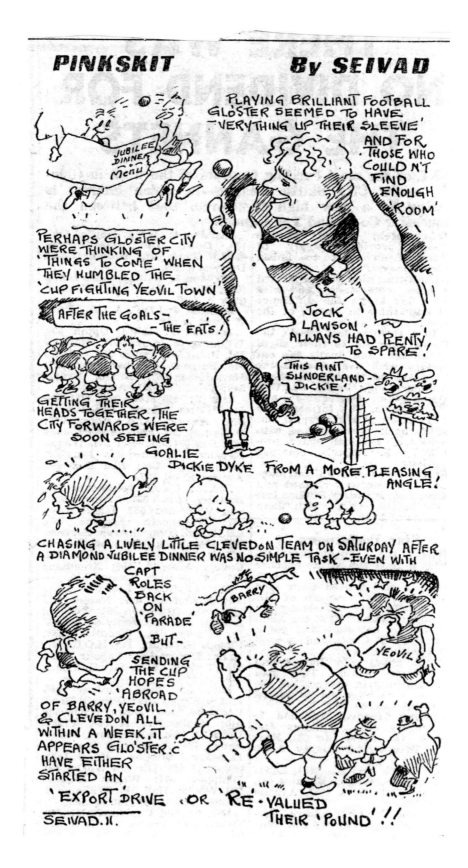

[114]

SOUTHERN LEAGUE

POS	CLUB	P	W	D	L	F	A	PTS
1	GILLINGHAM	42	26	10	6	104	48	62
2	CHELMSFORD CITY	42	27	7	8	115	64	61
3	MERTHYR TYDFIL	42	26	8	8	133	54	60
4	COLCHESTER UNITED	42	21	10	11	94	61	52
5	WORCESTER CITY	42	22	7	13	87	56	51
6	DARTFORD	42	21	9	12	73	53	51
7	GRAVESEND & NORTHFLEET	42	20	9	13	60	46	49
8	YEOVIL TOWN	42	19	9	14	90	53	47
9	CHELTENHAM TOWN	42	19	9	14	71	64	47
10	KIDDERMINSTER HARRIERS	42	19	6	17	77	94	44
11	EXETER CITY RESERVES	42	18	7	17	83	73	43
12	HEREFORD UNITED	42	17	6	19	83	84	40
13	BATH CITY	42	15	8	19	72	87	38
14	HASTINGS UNITED	42	14	10	18	69	93	38
15	TORQUAY UNITED RESERVES	42	15	7	20	73	93	37
16	LOVELLS ATHLETIC	42	14	8	20	73	74	36
17	GUILDFORD CITY	42	12	12	18	58	85	36
18	**GLOUCESTER CITY**	**42**	**12**	**10**	**20**	**78**	**100**	**34**
19	BARRY TOWN	42	12	10	20	55	95	34
20	TONBRIDGE	42	9	7	26	54	105	25
21	CHINGFORD TOWN	42	6	9	27	43	94	21
22	BEDFORD TOWN	42	5	8	29	32	101	18
		924	369	186	369	1677	1677	924

SEASON 1949-1950
(Home Ground: The Ground, Cheltenham Road, Longlevens)

Date: Saturday 20/08/1949
Result: **GUILDFORD CITY 1 GLOUCESTER CITY 2**
Competition: Southern League
Teamsheet: King, Roles, Colenutt, Cowley, Bartlett, Harvey, Newman, Haydon, Bazeley, Beattie, Buist
Scorers: Newman, Bazeley

Date: Thursday 25/08/1949
Result: **GLOUCESTER CITY 1 WORCESTER CITY 4**
Competition: Southern League
Teamsheet: King, Lawson, Colenutt, Cowley, Bartlett, Harvey, Newman, Haydon, Bazeley, Beattie, Buist
Scorer: Bazeley
Attendance: 4000

Date: Saturday 27/08/1949
Result: **GILLINGHAM 6 GLOUCESTER CITY 1**
Competition: Southern League
Teamsheet: Hatcher, Roles, Colenutt, Cowley, Bartlett, Harvey, Newman, Granville, Bazeley, Beattie, Buist
Scorer: Granville
Attendance: 10000

Date: Thursday 01/09/1949
Result: **GLOUCESTER CITY 2 COLCHESTER UNITED 3**
Competition: Southern League
Teamsheet: Hatcher, Lawson, Colenutt, Cowley, Bartlett, Lowe, Newman, Hunt, Boyd, Granville, Buist
Scorer: Boyd (2)
Attendance: 3500

Date: Saturday 03/09/1949
Result: **GLOUCESTER CITY 3 CHELMSFORD CITY 3**
Competition: Southern League
Teamsheet: Hatcher, Lawson, Roles, Cowley, Bartlett, Lowe, Newman, Hunt, Boyd, Granville, Buist
Scorers: Boyd, Hunt (pen), Buist
Attendance: 3500

Date: Saturday 10/09/1949
Result: **GLOUCESTER CITY 3 GRAVESEND & NORTHFLEET 2**
Competition: Southern League
Teamsheet: Hatcher, Roles, Lawson, Cowley, Bartlett, Lowe, Newman, Hunt, Boyd, Granville, Buist
Scorers: Boyd (2), Buist
Attendance: 3000

Date: Wednesday 14/09/1949
Result: **EXETER CITY RESERVES 5 GLOUCESTER CITY 4**
Competition: Southern League
Teamsheet: McAdam, Griffiths, Colenutt, Tredgett, Bartlett, Harvey, Starling, Hunt, Haydon, Granville, Buist
Scorers: Haydon (3), Hunt (pen)
Attendance: 3000

Date: Saturday 17/09/1949
Result: **WESTON-SUPER-MARE 2 GLOUCESTER CITY 3**
Competition: FA Cup Preliminary Round
Teamsheet: Hatcher, Roles, Lawson, Cowley, Bartlett, Lowe, Newman, Hunt, Boyd, Granville, Buist
Scorers: Newman, Hunt (pen), Boyd
Attendance: 2000

SEASON BY SEASON

Date: Thursday 22/09/1949
Result: **LOVELLS ATHLETIC 1 GLOUCESTER CITY 2**
Competition: Southern League
Teamsheet: King, Lawson, Colenutt, Cowley, Bartlett, Lowe, Newman, Hunt, Haydon, Granville, Buist
Scorers: Granville, Haydon

Date: Saturday 24/09/1949
Result: **WORCESTER CITY 2 GLOUCESTER CITY 3**
Competition: Southern League
Teamsheet: King, Roles, Lawson, Cowley, Bartlett, Lowe, Newman, Beattie, Boyd, Granville, Buist
Scorers: Beattie (2), Newman
Attendance: 4420

Date: Saturday 01/10/1949
Result: **BARRY TOWN 1 GLOUCESTER CITY 1**
Competition: FA Cup 1st Qualifying Round
Teamsheet: Hatcher, Roles, Lawson, Cowley, Bartlett, Lowe, Newman, Beattie, Boyd, Granville, Buist
Scorer: Newman
Attendance: 3000

Date: Saturday 08/10/1949
Result: **GLOUCESTER CITY 1 BARRY TOWN 0**
Competition: FA Cup 1st Qualifying Round Replay
Teamsheet: Hatcher, Roles, Lawson, Cowley, Bartlett, Lowe, Newman, Beattie, Boyd, Granville, Buist
Scorer: Granville
Attendance: 4900

Date: Thursday 13/10/1949
Result: **GLOUCESTER CITY 4 YEOVIL TOWN 0**
Competition: Southern League Cup Preliminary Round
Teamsheet: Hatcher, Lawson, Colenutt, Cowley, Tredgett, Lowe, Newman, Beattie, Boyd, Hunt, Buist
Scorers: Boyd, Beattie (2), Hunt
Attendance: 2500

Date: Saturday 15/10/1949
Result: **GLOUCESTER CITY 3 CLEVEDON 0**
Competition: FA Cup 2nd Qualifying Round
Teamsheet: Hatcher, Roles, Lawson, Cowley, Bartlett, Lowe, Newman, Beattie, Boyd, Granville, Buist
Scorers: Granville, Boyd, Beattie
Attendance: 4123

Date: Saturday 22/10/1949
Result: **BARRY TOWN 1 GLOUCESTER CITY 1**
Competition: Southern League
Teamsheet: Hatcher, Roles, Lawson, Cowley, Bartlett, Lowe, Newman, Beattie, Boyd, Granville, Buist
Scorer: Buist

Date: Thursday 27/10/1949
Result: **GLOUCESTER CITY 2 DARTFORD 2**
Competition: Southern League
Teamsheet: King, Lawson, Stow, Cowley, Tredgett, Lowe, Starling, Haydon, Bazeley, Hunt, Buist
Scorers: Hunt, Bazeley
Attendance: 1000

Date: Saturday 29/10/1949
Result: **LOVELLS ATHLETIC 0 GLOUCESTER CITY 3**
Competition: FA Cup 3rd Qualifying Round
Teamsheet: Hatcher, Roles, Lawson, Cowley, Bartlett, Lowe, Newman, Beattie, Boyd, Hunt, Buist
Scorers: Hunt, Beattie, Newman
Attendance: 2100

Date: Saturday 05/11/1949
Result: **MERTHYR TYDFIL 3 GLOUCESTER CITY 0**
Competition: Southern League
Teamsheet: Hatcher, Roles, Lawson, Tredgett, Bartlett, Lowe, Newman, Beattie, Boyd, Granville, Buist
Attendance: 5000

Date: Saturday 12/11/1949
Result: **BIDEFORD 1 GLOUCESTER CITY 1**
Competition: FA Cup 4th Qualifying Round
Teamsheet: Hatcher, Roles, Lawson, Cowley, Bartlett, Lowe, Newman, Beattie, Boyd, Hunt, Buist
Scorer: Beattie
Attendance: 5000

Date: Saturday 19/11/1949
Result: **GLOUCESTER CITY 3 BIDEFORD 1**
Competition: FA Cup 4th Qualifying Round Replay
Teamsheet: Hatcher, Roles, Lawson, Cowley, Bartlett, Lowe, Newman, Beattie, Boyd, Hunt, Buist
Scorer: Boyd (3)
Attendance: 6000

Date: Saturday 26/11/1949
Result: **GLOUCESTER CITY 2 NORWICH CITY 3**
Competition: FA Cup 1st Round
Teamsheet: Hatcher, Roles, Lawson, Cowley, Bartlett, Lowe, Newman, Beattie, Boyd, Hunt, Buist
Scorer: Hunt (2 pens)
Attendance: 9500

Date: Thursday 01/12/1949
Result: **GLOUCESTER CITY 1 TORQUAY UNITED RESERVES 2**
Competition: Southern League Cup 1st Round
Teamsheet: King, Lawson, Colenutt, Hunt, Tredgett, Lowe, Newman, Beattie, Boyd, Granville, Buist
Scorer: Beattie

Date: Saturday 03/12/1949
Result: **GLOUCESTER CITY 4 CHINGFORD TOWN 2**
Competition: Southern League
Teamsheet: Hatcher, Roles, Lawson, Cowley, Bartlett, Lowe, Newman, Beattie, Boyd, Hunt, Buist
Scorers: Beattie, Hunt, Cowley, Boyd
Attendance: 2500

Date: Saturday 10/12/1949
Result: **HEADINGTON UNITED 5 GLOUCESTER CITY 0**
Competition: Southern League
Teamsheet: Hatcher, Roles, Lawson, Cowley, Bartlett, Lowe, Newman, Beattie, Stow, Hunt, Buist

Date: Saturday 17/12/1949
Result: **CHELMSFORD CITY 4 GLOUCESTER CITY 0**
Competition: Southern League
Teamsheet: Hatcher, Roles, Lawson, Cowley, Farnen, Lowe, Newman, Beattie, Boyd, Haydon, Buist

Date: Saturday 24/12/1949
Result: **GLOUCESTER CITY 3 GILLINGHAM 1**
Competition: Southern League
Teamsheet: Hatcher, Roles, Lawson, Cowley, Farnen, Lowe, Newman, Beattie, Boyd, Haydon, Buist
Scorers: Newman, Beattie, Boyd

Date: Monday 26/12/1949
Result: **KIDDERMINSTER HARRIERS 3 GLOUCESTER CITY 0**
Competition: Southern League
Teamsheet: King, Roles, Lawson, Colenutt, Farnen, Tredgett, Newman, Beattie, Boyd, Hunt, Buist

Date: Tuesday 27/12/1949
Result: **GLOUCESTER CITY 1 KIDDERMINSTER HARRIERS 0**
Competition: Southern League
Teamsheet: Hatcher, Roles, Lawson, Cowley, Farnen, Lowe, Newman, Beattie, Boyd, Hunt, Buist
Scorer: Beattie
Attendance: 3400

Date: Saturday 31/12/1949
Result: **GLOUCESTER CITY 0 TORQUAY UNITED RESERVES 2**
Competition: Southern League
Teamsheet: Hatcher, Roles, Lawson, Cowley, Farnen, Lowe, Newman, Beattie, Boyd, Haydon, Buist
Attendance: 3500

Date: Saturday 07/01/1950
Result: **COLCHESTER UNITED 6 GLOUCESTER CITY 1**
Competition: Southern League
Teamsheet: Hatcher, Roles, Lawson, Cowley, Farnen, Lowe, Boyd, Beattie, Bazeley, Haydon, Buist
Scorer: Bazeley
Attendance: 10000

Date: Saturday 14/01/1950
Result: **GLOUCESTER CITY 4 HASTINGS UNITED 1**
Competition: Southern League
Teamsheet: Hatcher, Lawson, Roles, Cowley, Farnen, Lowe, Boyd, Hunt, Bazeley, Beattie, Buist
Scorers: Boyd, Hunt (2), Buist
Attendance: 3000

Date: Saturday 21/01/1950
Result: **BEDFORD TOWN 1 GLOUCESTER CITY 1**
Competition: Southern League
Teamsheet: Hatcher, Lawson, Roles, Cowley, Farnen, Lowe, Newman, Beattie, Bazeley, Jenkins, Buist
Scorer: Bazeley
Attendance: 3000

Date: Saturday 28/01/1950
Result: **GLOUCESTER CITY 2 WEYMOUTH 1**
Competition: Southern League
Teamsheet: Hatcher, Lawson, Roles, Cowley, Tredgett, Lowe, Newman, Beattie, Bazeley, Hunt, Stow
Scorers: Bazeley, Hunt
Attendance: 1949

Date: Saturday 04/02/1950
Result: **GLOUCESTER CITY 0 GUILDFORD CITY 1**
Competition: Southern League
Teamsheet: Hatcher, Lawson, Roles, Cowley, Farnen, Lowe, Newman, Beattie, Bazeley, Hunt, Buist
Attendance: 3000

Date: Saturday 11/02/1950
Result: **GRAVESEND & NORTHFLEET 3 GLOUCESTER CITY 3**
Competition: Southern League
Teamsheet: Hatcher, Lawson, Roles, Cowley, Farnen, Lowe, Boyd, Beattie, Bazeley, Hunt, Buist
Scorers: Lowe, Boyd, Beattie
Attendance: 2267

Date: Saturday 18/02/1950
Result: **TORQUAY UNITED RESERVES 2 GLOUCESTER CITY 1**
Competition: Southern League
Teamsheet: Hatcher, Lawson, Roles, Cowley, Farnen, Lowe, Boyd, Beattie, Bazeley, Hunt, Buist
Scorer: Hunt

Date: Saturday 25/02/1950
Result: **GLOUCESTER CITY 0 BARRY TOWN 0**
Competition: Southern League
Teamsheet: Hatcher, Lawson, Roles, Cowley, Farnen, Lowe, Newman, Beattie, Bazeley, Hunt, Buist

Date: Saturday 04/03/1950
Result: **BATH CITY 1 GLOUCESTER CITY 1**
Competition: Southern League
Teamsheet: King, Lawson, Roles, Cowley, Farnen, Lowe, Newman, Beattie, Boyd, Granville, Buist
Scorer: Newman
Attendance: 4000

Date: Saturday 11/03/1950
Result: **CHINGFORD TOWN 3 GLOUCESTER CITY 2**
Competition: Southern League
Teamsheet: King, Lawson, Roles, Cowley, Farnen, Lowe, Newman, Beattie, Boyd, Granville, Buist
Scorer: Buist (2)

Date: Thursday 16/03/1950
Result: **GLOUCESTER CITY 3 BEDFORD TOWN 2**
Competition: Southern League
Teamsheet: King, Lawson, Colenutt, Hunt, Farnen, Lowe, Bakker, Beattie, Boyd, Jenkins, Buist
Scorers: Hunt, Boyd, Buist
Attendance: 1200

Date: Thursday 23/03/1950
Result: **GLOUCESTER CITY 2 MERTHYR TYDFIL 5**
Competition: Southern League
Teamsheet: King, Lawson, Colenutt, Lowe, Tredgett, Farnen, Newman, Beattie, Boyd, Hunt, Buist
Scorers: Boyd, Buist

Date: Saturday 25/03/1950
Result: **HASTINGS UNITED 1 GLOUCESTER CITY 0**
Competition: Southern League
Teamsheet: King, Roles, Colenutt, Lawson, Farnen, Lowe, Boyd, Beattie, Hunt, Granville, Buist
Attendance: 4000

Date: Thursday 30/03/1950
Result: **GLOUCESTER CITY 2 BATH CITY 1**
Competition: Southern League
Teamsheet: King, Lawson, Colenutt, Tredgett, Farnen, Lowe, Newman, Hunt, Boyd, Beattie, Buist
Scorer: Newman (2)

Date: Saturday 01/04/1950
Result: **DARTFORD 2 GLOUCESTER CITY 1**
Competition: Southern League
Teamsheet: Hatcher, Roles, Colenutt, Hunt, Farnen, Lowe, Newman, Beattie, Boyd, Bazeley, Buist
Scorer: Newman

Date: Wednesday 05/04/1950
Result: **YEOVIL TOWN 3 GLOUCESTER CITY 0**
Competition: Southern League
Teamsheet: Summerhayes, Brown, Getgood, Leach, Bartlett, Cook, Buist, Granville, Jenkins, Haydon, Stow

Date: Friday 07/04/1950
Result: **GLOUCESTER CITY 2 CHELTENHAM TOWN 2**
Competition: Southern League
Teamsheet: Hatcher, Lawson, Roles, Cowley, Farnen, Lowe, Newman, Hunt, Stow, Beattie, Buist
Scorers: Stow, Newman
Attendance: 5500

Date: Saturday 08/04/1950
Result: **GLOUCESTER CITY 0 HEADINGTON UNITED 0**
Competition: Southern League
Teamsheet: Hatcher, Roles, Stow, Cowley, Farnen, Lowe, Newman, Beattie, Bazeley, Jenkins, Buist

Date: Monday 10/04/1950
Result: **CHELTENHAM TOWN 0 GLOUCESTER CITY 1**
Competition: Southern League
Teamsheet: Hatcher, Lawson, Stow, Hunt, Tredgett, Lowe, Starling, Beattie, Boyd, Bazeley, Buist
Scorer: Boyd
Attendance: 4000

Date: Thursday 13/04/1950
Result: **GLOUCESTER CITY 3 LOVELLS ATHLETIC 2**
Competition: Southern League
Teamsheet: King, Lawson, Stow, Cowley, Tredgett, Lowe, Starling, Beattie, Boyd, Jenkins, Buist
Scorers: Jenkins, Boyd, Beattie (pen)
Attendance: 2000

Date: Saturday 15/04/1950
Result: **TONBRIDGE 2 GLOUCESTER CITY 0**
Competition: Southern League
Teamsheet: Hatcher, Lawson, Roles, Tredgett, Bartlett, Farnen, Newman, Beattie, Boyd, Bazeley, Buist

Date: Thursday 20/04/1950
Result: **GLOUCESTER CITY 2 HEREFORD UNITED 3**
Competition: Southern League
Teamsheet: King, Lawson, Stow, Cowley, Tredgett, Hunt, Bakker, Beattie, Boyd, Jenkins, Buist
Scorers: Jenkins, Hunt
Attendance: 3000

Date: Saturday 22/04/1950
Result: **GLOUCESTER CITY 3 TONBRIDGE 3**
Competition: Southern League
Teamsheet: Hatcher, Lawson, Roles, Cowley, Bartlett, Hunt, Newman, Beattie, Boyd, Jenkins, Buist
Scorers: Newman, Buist, Hunt

Date: Wednesday 26/04/1950
Result: **WEYMOUTH 3 GLOUCESTER CITY 1**
Competition: Southern League
Teamsheet (from): Summerhayes, Brown, Colenutt, Stow, Hunt, Tredgett, Harvey, Bakker, Granville, Jenkins, Haydon, Buist
Scorer: Jenkins

Date: Thursday 27/04/1950
Result: **GLOUCESTER CITY 1 EXETER CITY RESERVES 1**
Competition: Southern League
Teamsheet: King, Lawson, Colenutt, Cowley, Bartlett, Farnen, Starling, Beattie, Boyd, Hunt, Buist
Scorer: Buist

Date: Saturday 29/04/1950
Result: **HEREFORD UNITED 2 GLOUCESTER CITY 0**
Competition: Southern League
Teamsheet: Hatcher, Lawson, Roles, Cowley, Bartlett, Tredgett, Newman, Beattie, Boyd, Jenkins, Buist

Date: Monday 01/05/1950
Result: **GLOUCESTER CITY 4 YEOVIL TOWN 0**
Competition: Southern League
Teamsheet: King, Lawson, Stow, Cowley, Tredgett, Jenkins, Starling, Beattie, Boyd, Haydon, Buist
Scorers: own goal, Boyd, Starling, Haydon
Attendance: 3000

Date: Saturday 06/05/1950
Result: **CHELTENHAM TOWN 1 GLOUCESTER CITY 1**
Competition: Gloucestershire FA Northern Senior Professional Cup Final
Teamsheet: King, Lawson, Stow, Cowley, Bartlett, Jenkins, Bakker, Beattie, Boyd, Hunt, Buist
Scorer: Boyd
Attendance: 4000

Date: Saturday 13/05/1950
Result: **GLOUCESTER CITY 2 CHELTENHAM TOWN 1**
Competition: Gloucestershire FA Northern Senior Professional Cup Final Replay
Teamsheet: King, Lawson, Stow, Cowley, Tredgett, Jenkins, Bakker, Haydon, Boyd, Hunt, Buist
Scorers: Bakker, Hunt
Attendance: 4115

Appearances – J Bakker 5, FL Bartlett 27, S Bazeley 16, G Beattie 48, J Boyd 43, WH Brown 3, JG Buist 57, JMW Colenutt 16, CI Cook 1, EM Cowley 45, AL Farnen 23, B Getgood 1, NT Granville 19, K Griffiths 1, F Harvey 5, C Hatcher 36, TJ Haydon 13, DA Hunt 36, M Jenkins 12, H King 19, G Lawson 51, H Leach 1, D Lowe 43, ? McAdam 1, J Newman 41, AJ Roles 39, L Starling 6, AC Stow 13, D Summerhayes 2, KF Tredgett 17.
Scorers – J Boyd 20, DA Hunt 17, G Beattie 13, J Newman 12, JG Buist 10, S Bazeley 6, TJ Haydon 5, NT Granville 4, M Jenkins 3, J Bakker 1, EM Cowley 1, D Lowe 1, L Starling 1, AC Stow 1, own goal 1.

SOUTHERN LEAGUE

POS	CLUB	P	W	D	L	F	A	PTS
1	MERTHYR TYDFIL	46	34	3	9	143	62	71
2	COLCHESTER UNITED	46	31	9	6	109	51	71
3	YEOVIL TOWN	46	29	7	10	104	45	65
4	CHELMSFORD CITY	46	26	9	11	121	64	61
5	GILLINGHAM	46	23	9	14	92	61	55
6	DARTFORD	46	20	9	17	70	65	49
7	WORCESTER CITY	46	21	7	18	85	80	49
8	GUILDFORD CITY	46	18	11	17	79	73	47
9	WEYMOUTH	46	19	9	18	79	82	47
10	BARRY TOWN	46	18	10	18	78	72	46
11	EXETER CITY RESERVES	46	16	14	16	73	83	46
12	LOVELLS ATHLETIC	46	17	10	19	86	78	44
13	TONBRIDGE	46	16	12	18	65	76	44
14	HASTINGS UNITED	46	17	8	21	92	140	42
15	GRAVESEND & NORTHFLEET	46	16	9	21	88	81	41
16	TORQUAY UNITED RESERVES	46	14	12	20	80	89	40
17	BATH CITY	46	16	7	23	61	78	39
18	**GLOUCESTER CITY**	**46**	**14**	**11**	**21**	**72**	**101**	**39**
19	HEREFORD UNITED	46	15	8	23	74	76	38
20	CHELTENHAM TOWN	46	13	11	22	75	96	37
21	HEADINGTON UNITED	46	15	7	24	72	97	37
22	BEDFORD TOWN	46	12	11	23	63	79	35
23	KIDDERMINSTER HARRIERS	46	12	11	23	64	108	35
24	CHINGFORD TOWN	46	10	6	30	63	151	26
		1104	442	220	442	1988	1988	1104

SEASON 1950-1951
(Home Ground: The Ground, Cheltenham Road, Longlevens)

Date: Saturday 19/08/1950
Result: **GLOUCESTER CITY 3 WORCESTER CITY 3**
Competition: Southern League
Teamsheet: King, Lawson, Peacock, Myers, Farnen, Canavan, Elliott, Beattie, Bury, Hunt, Buist
Scorers: Beattie (3)
Attendance: 3700

Date: Thursday 24/08/1950
Result: **BATH CITY 4 GLOUCESTER CITY 0**
Competition: Southern League
Teamsheet: King, Lawson, Colenutt, Myers, Tredgett, Canavan, Elliott, Haydon, Beattie, Bury, Buist
Attendance: 6000

Date: Saturday 26/08/1950
Result: **YEOVIL TOWN 1 GLOUCESTER CITY 0**
Competition: Southern League
Teamsheet: King, Lawson, Peacock, Myers, Tredgett, Canavan, Elliott, Haydon, Beattie, Bury, Buist
Attendance: 7000

Date: Thursday 31/08/1950
Result: GLOUCESTER CITY 8 CHINGFORD TOWN 1
Competitition: Southern League
Teamsheet: King, Lawson, Peacock, Myers, Tredgett, Canavan, Boyd, Haydon, Beattie, Bury, Buist
Scorers: Beattie (3), Haydon (2), Buist, Boyd, Bury
Attendance: 2800
Note: Originally League game. Chingford Town withdrew

Date: Saturday 02/09/1950
Result: **GLOUCESTER CITY 4 DARTFORD 1**
Competition: Southern League
Teamsheet: King, Lawson, Peacock, Canavan, Tredgett, Myers, Boyd, Haydon, Beattie, Bury, Buist
Scorers: Haydon, Boyd (2), Beattie
Attendance: 3000

Date: Thursday 07/09/1950
Result: **GLOUCESTER CITY 1 LOVELLS ATHLETIC 3**
Competition: Southern League
Teamsheet: King, Lawson, Peacock, Myers, Tredgett, Canavan, Boyd, Haydon, Jenkins, Bury, Buist
Scorer: Myers (pen)
Attendance: 4000

Date: Saturday 09/09/1950
Result: **HASTINGS UNITED 2 GLOUCESTER CITY 4**
Competition: Southern League
Teamsheet: King, Lawson, Peacock, Myers, Tredgett, Canavan, Boyd, Haydon, Hunt, Bury, Buist
Scorers: Hunt (2), Boyd, Canavan
Attendance: 3000

Date: Wednesday 13/09/1950
Result: **GRAVESEND & NORTHFLEET 1 GLOUCESTER CITY 1**
Competition: Southern League
Teamsheet: Pugsley, Lawson, Stow, Myers, Tredgett, Jenkins, Boyd, Haydon, Hunt, Bury, Buist
Scorer: Boyd
Attendance: 3876

Date: Saturday 16/09/1950
Result: **GLOUCESTER CITY 3 KETTERING TOWN 1**
Competition: Southern League
Teamsheet: King, Lawson, Peacock, Myers, Tredgett, Jenkins, Boyd, Haydon, Beattie, Bury, Buist
Scorers: Myers, Haydon, Beattie
Attendance: 4000

Date: Thursday 21/09/1950
Result: **GLOUCESTER CITY 1 CHELMSFORD CITY 0**
Competition: Southern League
Teamsheet: King, Lawson, Peacock, Myers, Tredgett, Jenkins, Boyd, Haydon, Beattie, Bury, Buist
Scorer: Beattie
Attendance: 3600

Date: Saturday 23/09/1950
Result: **HEREFORD UNITED 1 GLOUCESTER CITY 1**
Competition: Southern League
Teamsheet: King, Lawson, Peacock, Myers, Tredgett, Canavan, Boyd, Haydon, Beattie, Bury, Buist
Scorer: Myers (pen)
Attendance: 5000

Date: Wednesday 27/09/1950
Result: **GUILDFORD CITY 3 GLOUCESTER CITY 1**
Competition: Southern League
Teamsheet: Farmer, Lawson, Peacock, Myers, Tredgett, Jenkins, Elliott, Haydon, Boyd, Bury, Buist
Scorer: Haydon

Date: Saturday 30/09/1950
Result: **TORQUAY UNITED RESERVES 3 GLOUCESTER CITY 0**
Competition: Southern League
Teamsheet: King, Lawson, Peacock, Myers, Tredgett, Canavan, Elliott, Haydon, Boyd, Bury, Buist

Date: Thursday 05/10/1950
Result: **GLOUCESTER CITY 3 LLANELLY 1**
Competition: Southern League
Teamsheet: King, Lawson, Peacock, Myers, Tredgett, Canavan, Elliott, Haydon, Boyd, Bury, Buist
Scorers: Boyd, Buist, Haydon
Attendance: 2800

Date: Saturday 07/10/1950
Result: **KETTERING TOWN 2 GLOUCESTER CITY 3**
Competition: Southern League
Teamsheet: King, Lawson, Peacock, Myers, Tredgett, Canavan, Boyd, Haydon, Jenkins, Bury, Buist
Scorers: Buist, Tredgett, Boyd

Date: Saturday 14/10/1950
Result: **GLOUCESTER CITY 7 GRAVESEND & NORTHFLEET 0**
Competition: Southern League
Teamsheet: King, Lawson, Peacock, Myers, Tredgett, Canavan, Boyd, Haydon, Jenkins, Bury, Buist
Scorers: Bury, Jenkins (3), Myers (pen), Buist, Haydon
Attendance: 3000

Date: Saturday 21/10/1950
Result: **TONBRIDGE 0 GLOUCESTER CITY 0**
Competition: Southern League
Teamsheet: King, Lawson, Peacock, Myers, Tredgett, Canavan, Boyd, Haydon, Jenkins, Bury, Buist
Attendance: 3000

Date: Saturday 28/10/1950
Result: **GLOUCESTER CITY 1 TORQUAY UNITED RESERVES 1**
Competition: Southern League
Teamsheet: King, Lawson, Peacock, Myers, Tredgett, Canavan, Boyd, Haydon, Jenkins, Bury, Buist
Scorer: Haydon
Attendance: 3500

Date: Saturday 04/11/1950
Result: **WEYMOUTH 4 GLOUCESTER CITY 2**
Competition: Southern League
Teamsheet: King, Lawson, Peacock, Myers, Tredgett, Canavan, Boyd, Haydon, Jenkins, Bury, Buist
Scorers: Jenkins (2)
Attendance: 3928

Date: Saturday 11/11/1950
Result: **GLOUCESTER CITY 2 SALISBURY 1**
Competition: FA Cup 4th Qualifying Round
Teamsheet: King, Lawson, Peacock, Myers, Farnen, Canavan, Boyd, Haydon, Jenkins, Bury, Buist
Scorers: Buist, Myers (pen)
Attendance: 6289

Date: Saturday 18/11/1950
Result: **GLOUCESTER CITY 3 BATH CITY 2**
Competition: Southern League Cup Preliminary Round
Teamsheet: King, Lawson, Peacock, Myers, Tredgett, Canavan, Boyd, Haydon, Jenkins, Evans, Buist
Scorers: Myers (pen), Haydon, Boyd
Attendance: 2000-3000

Date: Saturday 25/11/1950
Result: **BRISTOL CITY 4 GLOUCESTER CITY 0**
Competition: FA Cup 1st Round
Teamsheet: King, Lawson, Peacock, Myers, Tredgett, Canavan, Boyd, Haydon, Jenkins, Bury, Buist
Attendance: 17058

Date: Saturday 02/12/1950
Result: **GLOUCESTER CITY 0 BATH CITY 1**
Competition: Southern League
Teamsheet: King, Lawson, Peacock, Myers, Tredgett, Canavan, Boyd, Jenkins, Hunt, Bury, Buist
Attendance: 3500

Date: Saturday 09/12/1950
Result: **BARRY TOWN 2 GLOUCESTER CITY 3**
Competition: Southern League
Teamsheet: King, Lawson, Peacock, Myers, Tredgett, Canavan, Boyd, Jenkins, Stow, Bury, Buist
Scorers: Jenkins, Stow (2)
Attendance: 500

Date: Saturday 23/12/1950
Result: **GLOUCESTER CITY 2 BARRY TOWN 0**
Competition: Southern League
Teamsheet: King, Lawson, Peacock, Myers, Tredgett, Canavan, Robertson, Jenkins, Stow, Bury, Buist
Scorers: Jenkins, Stow

Date: Monday 25/12/1950
Result: **GLOUCESTER CITY 3 KIDDERMINSTER HARRIERS 1**
Competition: Southern League
Teamsheet: King, Lawson, Colenutt, Myers, Tredgett, Canavan, Robertson, Haydon, Stow, Bury, Buist
Scorers: Robertson, Haydon (2)

Date: Tuesday 26/12/1950
Result: **KIDDERMINSTER HARRIERS 0 GLOUCESTER CITY 0**
Competition: Southern League
Teamsheet: King, Lawson, Stow, Myers, Tredgett, Canavan, Robertson, Haydon, Jenkins, Bury, Buist

Date: Saturday 30/12/1950
Result: **CHELMSFORD CITY 4 GLOUCESTER CITY 2**
Competition: Southern League
Teamsheet: King, Lawson, Peacock, Myers, Tredgett, Canavan, Robertson, Haydon, Stow, Bury, Buist
Scorers: Robertson, Stow

Date: Saturday 13/01/1951
Result: **GLOUCESTER CITY 1 EXETER CITY RESERVES 2**
Competition: Southern League
Teamsheet: King, Lawson, Peacock, Myers, Tredgett, Canavan, Robertson, Haydon, Stow, Bury, Buist
Scorer: Robertson

Date: Saturday 20/01/1951
Result: **EXETER CITY RESERVES 0 GLOUCESTER CITY 0**
Competition: Southern League
Teamsheet: King, Lawson, Peacock, Myers, Tredgett, Canavan, Robertson, Haydon, Jenkins, Bury, Buist

Date: Saturday 27/01/1951
Result: **WORCESTER CITY 1 GLOUCESTER CITY 0**
Competition: Southern League
Teamsheet: King, Lawson, Peacock, Myers, Tredgett, Canavan, Robertson, Haydon, Jenkins, Bury, Buist
Attendance: 2677

Date: Saturday 03/02/1951
Result: **GLOUCESTER CITY 2 YEOVIL TOWN 0**
Competition: Southern League
Teamsheet: King, Lawson, Peacock, Myers, Tredgett, Canavan, Bury, Haydon, Robertson, Jenkins, Buist
Scorers: Robertson, Bury

Date: Saturday 10/02/1951
Result: **DARTFORD 4 GLOUCESTER CITY 2**
Competition: Southern League
Teamsheet: King, Lawson, Peacock, Myers, Tredgett, Canavan, Nicholls, Haydon, Robertson, Jenkins, Buist
Scorer: Robertson (2)

Date: Saturday 24/02/1951
Result: **HEADINGTON UNITED 2 GLOUCESTER CITY 0**
Competition: Southern League
Teamsheet: King, Lawson, Peacock, Myers, Tredgett, Jones, Nicholls, Haydon, Robertson, Jenkins, Buist

Date: Saturday 03/03/1951
Result: **GLOUCESTER CITY 4 HEREFORD UNITED 1**
Competition: Southern League
Teamsheet: King, Lawson, Peacock, Cowley, Tredgett, Jones, Myers, Jenkins, Robertson, Canavan, Buist
Scorers: Robertson (2), Canavan (2)

Date: Wednesday 07/03/1951
Result: **TORQUAY UNITED RESERVES 4 GLOUCESTER CITY 1**
Competition: Southern League Cup 1st Round
Teamsheet: Farmer, Lawson, Peacock, Myers, Tredgett, Jones, Bury, Jenkins, Robertson, Canavan, Buist
Scorer: Robertson

Date: Saturday 17/03/1951
Result: **BEDFORD TOWN 1 GLOUCESTER CITY 1**
Competition: Southern League
Teamsheet: King, Lawson, Peacock, Cowley, Tredgett, Jenkins, Myers, Bury, Robertson, Hunt, Buist
Scorer: Myers

Date: Saturday 24/03/1951
Result: **MERTHYR TYDFIL 3 GLOUCESTER CITY 1**
Competition: Southern League
Teamsheet: King, Lawson, Peacock, Cowley, Tredgett, Jenkins, Myers, Bury, Robertson, Canavan, Buist
Scorer: Robertson

Date: Monday 26/03/1951
Result: **CHELTENHAM TOWN 4 GLOUCESTER CITY 3**
Competition: Southern League
Teamsheet: Brinsford, Lawson, Peacock, Cowley, Tredgett, Jenkins, Myers, Bury, Robertson, Hunt, Buist
Scorers: Hunt, Bury, Robertson

Date: Friday 30/03/1951
Result: **GLOUCESTER CITY 3 HASTINGS UNITED 1**
Competition: Southern League
Teamsheet: King, Lawson, Peacock, Cowley, Witt, Tredgett, Boseley, Jenkins, Robertson, Canavan, Buist
Scorers: Boseley (2), Canavan (pen)

Date: Saturday 31/03/1951
Result: **GLOUCESTER CITY 2 TONBRIDGE 2**
Competition: Southern League
Teamsheet (from): King, Lawson, Peacock, Colenutt, Cowley, Witt, Tredgett, Myers, Jenkins, Robertson, Bury, Buist
Scorer: Jenkins (2)

Date: Saturday 07/04/1951
Result: **GLOUCESTER CITY 2 MERTHYR TYDFIL 6**
Competition: Southern League
Teamsheet (from): King, Lawson, Peacock, Cowley, Myers, Witt, Tredgett, Boseley, Jenkins, Robertson, Canavan, Buist
Scorers: Canavan (pen), Jenkins

Date: Thursday 12/04/1951
Result: **GLOUCESTER CITY 4 GUILDFORD CITY 0**
Competition: Southern League
Teamsheet: King, Lawson, Peacock, Myers, Tredgett, Canavan, Bakker, Robertson, Stow, Jenkins, Buist
Scorers: Buist, Robertson, Jenkins, Stow
Attendance: 1500

Date: Saturday 14/04/1951
Result: **GLOUCESTER CITY 4 WEYMOUTH 0**
Competition: Southern League
Teamsheet: King, Lawson, Peacock, Myers, Tredgett, Canavan, Bakker, Robertson, Stow, Jenkins, Buist
Scorers: Roberston (2), Jenkins, Stow

Date: Monday 16/04/1951
Result: **WORCESTER CITY 3 GLOUCESTER CITY 0**
Competition: Worcestershire FA Senior Challenge Cup 2nd Round
Teamsheet: Pugsley, Lawson, Miller, Cowley, Jones, Lowe, Jenkins, Bury, Boseley, Nicholls, Buist

Date: Thursday 19/04/1951
Result: **GLOUCESTER CITY 2 HEADINGTON UNITED 0**
Competition: Southern League
Teamsheet: King, Lawson, Peacock, Myers, Tredgett, Canavan, Bakker, Robertson, Stow, Jenkins, Buist
Scorers: Jenkins, Canavan (pen)

Date: Saturday 21/04/1951
Result: **LOVELLS ATHLETIC 2 GLOUCESTER CITY 2**
Competition: Southern League
Teamsheet: King, Lawson, Peacock, Myers, Tredgett, Witt, Bakker, Canavan, Stow, Jenkins, Buist
Scorers: Bakker, Stow

Date: Thursday 26/04/1951
Result: **GLOUCESTER CITY 2 CHELTENHAM TOWN 0**
Competition: Gloucestershire FA Northern Senior Professional Cup Final
Teamsheet: King, Lawson, Peacock, Myers, Tredgett, Canavan, Bakker, Boseley, Stow, Jenkins, Buist
Scorers: Stow, Buist
Attendance: 4221

Date: Thursday 03/05/1951
Result: **GLOUCESTER CITY 0 CHELTENHAM TOWN 3**
Competition: Southern League
Teamsheet: King, Lawson, Peacock, Myers, Tredgett, Canavan, Bakker, Jenkins, Robertson, Bury, Buist
Attendance: 3000

Date: Saturday 05/05/1951
Result: **GLOUCESTER CITY 2 BEDFORD TOWN 2**
Competition: Southern League
Teamsheet: King, Lawson, Peacock, Myers, Tredgett, Canavan, Boseley, Hunt, Witt, Jenkins, Buist
Scorer: Witt (2)

Date: Tuesday 08/05/1951
Result: **LLANELLY 3 GLOUCESTER CITY 1**
Competition: Southern League
Teamsheet: King, Lawson, Peacock, Myers, Tredgett, Canavan, Bakker, Hunt, Bury, Jenkins, Buist
Scorer: Bakker

Appearances – J Bakker 7, G Beattie 8, LG Boseley 5, J Boyd 21, N Brinsford 1, JG Buist 50, J Bury 39, J Canavan 42, JMW Colenutt 3, EM Cowley 8, J Elliott 5, A Evans 2, ? Farmer 2, AL Farnen 2, TJ Haydon 30, DA Hunt 10, M Jenkins 39, R Jones 4, H King 47, G Lawson 51, D Lowe 1, WV Miller 1, S Myers 49, E Nicholls 3, G Peacock 46, DG Pugsley 2, J Robertson 22, AC Stow 12, KF Tredgett 47, D Witt 5.
Scorers – J Robertson 14, M Jenkins 13, TJ Haydon 11, G Beattie 9, J Boyd 8, JG Buist 7, S Myers 7, AC Stow 7, J Canavan 5, J Bury 4, DA Hunt 3, J Bakker 2, LG Boseley 2, D Witt 2, KF Tredgett 1.

SOUTHERN LEAGUE

POS	CLUB	P	W	D	L	F	A	PTS
1	MERTHYR TYDFIL	44	29	8	7	152	66	66
2	HEREFORD UNITED	44	27	7	10	110	69	61
3	GUILDFORD CITY	44	23	8	13	88	60	54
4	CHELMSFORD CITY	44	21	12	11	84	58	54
5	LLANELLY	44	19	13	12	89	73	51
6	CHELTENHAM TOWN	44	21	8	15	91	61	50
7	HEADINGTON UNITED	44	18	11	15	84	83	47
8	TORQUAY UNITED RESERVES	44	20	6	18	93	79	46
9	EXETER CITY RESERVES	44	16	12	16	90	94	44
10	WEYMOUTH	44	16	12	16	83	89	44
11	TONBRIDGE	44	16	12	16	79	87	44
12	**GLOUCESTER CITY**	**44**	**16**	**11**	**17**	**81**	**76**	**43**
13	YEOVIL TOWN	44	13	15	16	72	73	41
14	WORCESTER CITY	44	15	11	18	69	78	41
15	BATH CITY	44	15	10	19	66	73	40
16	DARTFORD	44	14	11	19	61	70	39
17	BEDFORD TOWN	44	15	9	20	64	94	39
18	GRAVESEND & NORTHFLEET	44	12	14	18	65	83	38
19	KETTERING TOWN	44	13	11	20	87	87	37
20	LOVELLS ATHLETIC	44	12	13	19	81	93	37
21	KIDDERMINSTER HARRIERS	44	13	9	22	58	103	35
22	BARRY TOWN	44	13	7	24	54	100	33
23	HASTINGS UNITED	44	11	6	27	91	143	28
24	CHINGFORD TOWN							
		1012	388	236	388	1892	1892	1012

Chingford Town withdrew in December after 18 matches due to financial difficulties. All scores were expunged from the records.

SEASON 1951-1952
(Home Ground: The Ground, Cheltenham Road, Longlevens)

Date: Saturday 18/08/1951
Result: **GLOUCESTER CITY 3 BARRY TOWN 1**
Competition: Southern League
Teamsheet: King, Lawson, Peacock, Myers, Witt, Canavan, Grubb, Wright, Robertson, Pullen, Buist
Scorers: Robertson, Wright, Myers
Attendance: 4500

Date: Thursday 23/08/1951
Result: **GLOUCESTER CITY 1 HEADINGTON UNITED 1**
Competition: Southern League
Teamsheet: King, Lawson, Peacock, Myers, Tredgett, Canavan, Grubb, Wright, Robertson, Pullen, Harper
Scorer: Canavan (pen)
Attendance: 3800

Date: Saturday 25/08/1951
Result: **DARTFORD 2 GLOUCESTER CITY 1**
Competition: Southern League
Teamsheet: King, Lawson, Peacock, Myers, Tredgett, Canavan, Hunt, Wright, Robertson, Pullen, Harper
Scorer: Harper
Attendance: 2500

Date: Monday 27/08/1951
Result: **BARRY TOWN 3 GLOUCESTER CITY 2**
Competition: Southern League Cup Qualifying Round 1st Leg
Teamsheet: King, Lawson, Peacock, Canavan, Tredgett, Myers, Wright, Jenkins, Robertson, Pullen, Buist
Scorers: Pullen, Jenkins
Attendance: 3500

Date: Saturday 01/09/1951
Result: **GLOUCESTER CITY 2 HEREFORD UNITED 1**
Competition: Southern League
Teamsheet: King, Lawson, Peacock, Myers, Tredgett, Canavan, Grubb, Wright, Robertson, Jenkins, Buist
Scorers: Roberston, Buist

Date: Thursday 06/09/1951
Result: **GLOUCESTER CITY 5 BARRY TOWN 3**
Competition: Southern League Cup Qualifying Round 2nd Leg
Teamsheet: Pugsley, Lawson, Peacock, Myers, Tredgett, Canavan, Grubb, Wright, Robertson, Pullen, Buist
Scorers: Robertson (3), Canavan (pen), Grubb
Attendance: 3000

Date: Saturday 08/09/1951
Result: **YEOVIL TOWN 3 GLOUCESTER CITY 1**
Competition: Southern League
Teamsheet: Pugsley, Lawson, Peacock, Myers, Tredgett, Canavan, Grubb, Wright, Robertson, Pullen, Buist
Scorer: Canavan

Date: Monday 10/09/1951
Result: **WORCESTER CITY 3 GLOUCESTER CITY 0**
Competition: Southern League
Teamsheet: Pugsley, Lawson, Peacock, Myers, Witt, Canavan, Grubb, Jenkins, Robertson, Pullen, Buist
Attendance: 4554

Date: Thursday 13/09/1951
Result: **GLOUCESTER CITY 2 LOVELLS ATHLETIC 0**
Competition: Southern League
Teamsheet: Pugsley, Lawson, Peacock, Myers, Witt, Canavan, Grubb, Wright, Robertson, Pullen, Buist
Scorers: Robertson, Buist
Attendance: 2400

Date: Monday 17/09/1951
Result: **GLOUCESTER CITY 1 LOVELLS ATHLETIC 3**
Competition: Southern League Cup 1st Round
Teamsheet: Pugsley, Lawson, Peacock, Myers, Canavan, Jenkins, Boseley, Hunt, Robertson, Pullen, Buist
Scorer: Peacock
Attendance: 1900

Date: Thursday 20/09/1951
Result: **GLOUCESTER CITY 1 WORCESTER CITY 3**
Competition: Southern League
Teamsheet: King, Lawson, Stow, Myers, Tredgett, Canavan, Grubb, Wright, Peacock, Pullen, Buist
Scorer: Lawson
Attendance: 3000

Date: Saturday 22/09/1951
Result: **BATH CITY 2 GLOUCESTER CITY 0**
Competition: Southern League
Teamsheet: Pugsley, Lawson, Peacock, Myers, Witt, Jenkins, Barnfield, Wright, Robertson, Pullen, Buist

Date: Saturday 29/09/1951
Result: **STONEHOUSE 1 GLOUCESTER CITY 2**
Competition: FA Cup 1st Qualifying Round
Teamsheet: Jepson, Lawson, Peacock, Myers, Witt, Canavan, Grubb, Robertson, Stow, Jenkins, Buist
Scorers: Stow, own goal
Attendance: 6000

Date: Saturday 06/10/1951
Result: **GLOUCESTER CITY 1 MERTHYR TYDFIL 0**
Competition: Southern League
Teamsheet: Jepson, Lawson, Peacock, Myers, Witt, Canavan, Grubb, Robertson, Stow, Jenkins, Buist
Scorer: Grubb
Attendance: 5000

Date: Saturday 13/10/1951
Result: **GLOUCESTER CITY 1 EBBW VALE 2**
Competition: FA Cup 2nd Qualifying Round
Teamsheet: Jepson, Lawson, Peacock, Myers, Witt, Canavan, Grubb, Wright, Robertson, Jenkins, Buist
Scorer: Jenkins
Attendance: 5000

Date: Saturday 20/10/1951
Result: **GLOUCESTER CITY 2 YEOVIL TOWN 0**
Competition: Southern League
Teamsheet: Jepson, Lawson, Peacock, Myers, Witt, Tredgett, Barnfield, Wright, Grubb, Jenkins, Buist
Scorer: Barnfield (2)
Attendance: 2800

Date: Saturday 27/10/1951
Result: **HEADINGTON UNITED 2 GLOUCESTER CITY 0**
Competition: Southern League
Teamsheet: Jepson, Lawson, Peacock, Myers, Witt, Tredgett, Barnfield, Wright, Boseley, Jenkins, Harper

Date: Saturday 03/11/1951
Result: **GUILDFORD CITY 4 GLOUCESTER CITY 1**
Competition: Southern League
Teamsheet: Pugsley, Peacock, Lawson, Jenkins, Witt, Myers, Stow, Grubb, Asher, Pullen, Barnfield
Scorer: Barnfield

Date: Saturday 10/11/1951
Result: **GLOUCESTER CITY 2 GRAVESEND & NORTHFLEET 1**
Competition: Southern League
Teamsheet: Jepson, Lawson, Peacock, Myers, Witt, Canavan, Barnfield, Grubb, Asher, Jenkins, Stow
Scorers: Jenkins, Asher

Date: Saturday 17/11/1951
Result: **TONBRIDGE 1 GLOUCESTER CITY 0**
Competition: Southern League
Teamsheet: Jepson, Lawson, Peacock, Myers, Witt, Canavan, Barnfield, Wright, Asher, Jenkins, Pullen

Date: Saturday 24/11/1951
Result: **GRAVESEND & NORTHFLEET 0 GLOUCESTER CITY 1**
Competition: Southern League
Teamsheet: Jepson, Lawson, Peacock, Myers, Witt, Canavan, Barnfield, Pullen, Asher, Jenkins, Buist
Scorer: Buist
Attendance: 1450

Date: Saturday 01/12/1951
Result: **LOVELLS ATHLETIC 2 GLOUCESTER CITY 2**
Competition: Southern League
Teamsheet: Jepson, Lawson, Peacock, Myers, Witt, Canavan, Barnfield, Pullen, Asher, Wright, Buist
Scorers: Barnfield, Buist

Date: Saturday 08/12/1951
Result: **GLOUCESTER CITY 2 KETTERING TOWN 0**
Competition: Southern League
Teamsheet: Jepson, Lawson, Peacock, Myers, Witt, Canavan, Barnfield, Wright, Asher, Jenkins, Buist
Scorers: Asher, Jenkins
Attendance: 1500

Date: Saturday 15/12/1951
Result: **GLOUCESTER CITY 4 EXETER CITY RESERVES 0**
Competition: Southern League
Teamsheet: Jepson, Lawson, Peacock, Myers, Witt, Canavan, Barnfield, Wright, Asher, Jenkins, Buist
Scorers: Asher (2), Jenkins (2)

Date: Tuesday 25/12/1951
Result: **GLOUCESTER CITY 0 KIDDERMINSTER HARRIERS 1**
Competition: Southern League
Teamsheet: Jepson, Lawson, Colenutt, Myers, Witt, Canavan, Grubb, Wright, Asher, Jenkins, Buist

Date: Wednesday 26/12/1951
Result: **KIDDERMINSTER HARRIERS 3 GLOUCESTER CITY 0**
Competition: Southern League
Teamsheet: Jepson, Lawson, Peacock, Myers, Witt, Canavan, Grubb, Wright, Asher, Jenkins, Buist
Attendance: 4140

Date: Saturday 05/01/1952
Result: **GLOUCESTER CITY 0 TONBRIDGE 0**
Competition: Southern League
Teamsheet: Jepson, Lawson, Peacock, Myers, Witt, Canavan, Grubb, Wright, Asher, Jenkins, Nicholls

Date: Saturday 12/01/1952
Result: **GLOUCESTER CITY 2 WEYMOUTH 1**
Competition: Southern League
Teamsheet: Jepson, Lawson, Peacock, Myers, Witt, Canavan, Grubb, Wright, Asher, Jenkins, Nicholls
Scorers: Nicholls, Asher

Date: Saturday 26/01/1952
Result: **GLOUCESTER CITY 4 HASTINGS UNITED 1**
Competition: Southern League
Teamsheet: Jepson, Lawson, Peacock, Myers, Witt, Canavan, Grubb, Wright, Asher, Jenkins, Buist
Scorers: Grubb (2), Canavan, Wright

[125]

Date: Saturday 02/02/1952
Result: **EXETER CITY RESERVES 4 GLOUCESTER CITY 2**
Competition: Southern League
Teamsheet: Jepson, Lawson, Peacock, Myers, Witt, Canavan, Grubb, Wright, Asher, Jenkins, Buist
Scorer: Asher (2)

Date: Saturday 09/02/1952
Result: **GLOUCESTER CITY 1 DARTFORD 1**
Competition: Southern League
Teamsheet: Jepson, Lawson, Peacock, Myers, Witt, Canavan, Grubb, Wright, Asher, Jenkins, Buist
Scorer: Grubb

Date: Saturday 16/02/1952
Result: **KETTERING TOWN 1 GLOUCESTER CITY 0**
Competition: Southern League
Teamsheet: Jepson, Lawson, Peacock, Myers, Witt, Canavan, Barnfield, Grubb, Asher, Boseley, Buist

Date: Saturday 23/02/1952
Result: **CHELMSFORD CITY 2 GLOUCESTER CITY 2**
Competition: Southern League
Teamsheet: Jepson, Lawson, Peacock, Myers, Witt, Jenkins, Grubb, Wright, Boseley, Pullen, Buist
Scorers: Pullen, Wright

Date: Saturday 01/03/1952
Result: **GLOUCESTER CITY 3 BEDFORD TOWN 1**
Competition: Southern League
Teamsheet: Jepson, Lawson, Peacock, Myers, Witt, Jenkins, Grubb, Wright, Boseley, Pullen, Buist
Scorers: Boseley (2), Grubb

Date: Saturday 08/03/1952
Result: **HASTINGS UNITED 1 GLOUCESTER CITY 2**
Competition: Southern League
Teamsheet: Jepson, Lawson, Peacock, Myers, Witt, Jenkins, Barnfield, Wright, Asher, Pullen, Buist
Scorers: Barnfield, Wright
Attendance: 500

Date: Saturday 15/03/1952
Result: **GLOUCESTER CITY 1 CHELMSFORD CITY 1**
Competition: Southern League
Teamsheet: Jepson, Lawson, Peacock, Myers, Tredgett, Jenkins, Barnfield, Wright, Asher, Pullen, Buist
Scorer: Wright

Date: Wednesday 19/03/1952
Result: **WEYMOUTH 1 GLOUCESTER CITY 1**
Competition: Southern League
Teamsheet: Jepson, Lawson, Peacock, Myers, Tredgett, Canavan, Barnfield, Wright, Asher, Jenkins, Stow
Scorer: Stow

Date: Saturday 22/03/1952
Result: **GLOUCESTER CITY 0 GUILDFORD CITY 0**
Competition: Southern League
Teamsheet: Jepson, Lawson, Peacock, Myers, Tredgett, Canavan, Barnfield, Wright, Asher, Jenkins, Buist

Date: Monday 24/03/1952
Result: **BARRY TOWN 4 GLOUCESTER CITY 0**
Competition: Southern League
Teamsheet: Jepson, Lawson, Miller, Myers, Tredgett, Canavan, Barnfield, Wright, Asher, Nicholls, Stow

Date: Thursday 27/03/1952
Result: **BEDFORD TOWN 0 GLOUCESTER CITY 4**
Competition: Southern League
Teamsheet: Jepson, Lawson, Colenutt, Myers, Tredgett, Canavan, Barnfield, Wright, Asher, Pullen, Stow
Scorers: Stow, Asher, Barnfield, Wright
Attendance: 4000

Date: Friday 11/04/1952
Result: **GLOUCESTER CITY 3 CHELTENHAM TOWN 0**
Competition: Southern League
Teamsheet: Jepson, Lawson, Peacock, Myers, Tredgett, Canavan, Barnfield, Wright, Asher, Pullen, Stow
Scorers: Pullen, Asher (2)
Attendance: 5000

Date: Saturday 12/04/1952
Result: **HEREFORD UNITED 2 GLOUCESTER CITY 1**
Competition: Southern League
Teamsheet: Jepson, Lawson, Peacock, Myers, Tredgett, Canavan, Barnfield, Wright, Asher, Pullen, Stow
Scorer: Asher

Date: Monday 14/04/1952
Result: **CHELTENHAM TOWN 0 GLOUCESTER CITY 4**
Competition: Southern League
Teamsheet: Jepson, Lawson, Peacock, Myers, Tredgett, Canavan, Barnfield, Wright, Asher, Pullen Colenutt
Scorers: Pullen (2), Canavan, Asher
Attendance: 3000

Date: Saturday 19/04/1952
Result: **GLOUCESTER CITY 2 LLANELLY 0**
Competition: Southern League
Teamsheet: Jepson, Lawson, Peacock, Myers, Tredgett, Canavan, Barnfield, Wright, Asher, Jenkins, Colenutt
Scorers: Canavan (pen), Jenkins

This is the Gloucester City line up prior to the FA Cup 1st Round tie on 25 November 1950 v Bristol City at Ashton Gate. Gloucester City lost 0-4. It was the biggest crowd a Gloucester City team played before – 17,058

(Photoraph courtesy of Frank Tredgett)

Back row – Fred Howell (trainer), Stan Myers, George Lawson, Frank Tredgett, Harold King, George Peacock, Jimmy Canavan.
Front row – Jack Boyd, Trevor Haydon, Mansell Jenkins, Doug Hunt (manager), Arthur Evans, Jimmy Buist, Jimmy Bury.

Longlevens 9 February 1952 v Dartford following the death of King George VI

(Photograph courtesy of Stan Myers)

Part of the invitation for the Gloucester City v Tottenham Hotspur friendly at Longlevens 27 October 1952 which City won 2-1 in front of record home attendance of 10,500
(Courtesy of Frank Tredgett)

Teams

Gloucester City

PLAYER/MANAGER J. G. BUIST
TRAINER · · F. HOWELLS

JEPSON

WILLIAMS   CRAWFORD

MYERS   TREDGETT   CANAVAN

WRIGHT   PULLEN
BARNFIELD   PRICE   HAINES

REFEREE: A. V. MARTIN, GLOUCESTER
LINESMEN: W. G. BAIRD
L. B. HARRIS

MEDLEY   DUQUEMIN   WALTERS
BAILEY   BENNETT

BURGESS   CLARKE   NICHOLSON

WILLIS   RAMSEY

DITCHBURN

TEAM MANAGER: A. ROWE

Tottenham Hotspur

MATCH COMMENCES 7.15 p.m.

Under Floodlight

TEAMS AND OFFICIALS WILL MEET
AT URCH'S RESTAURANT AT 9.30 p.m.
FOR DINNER.

*I take this opportunity of welcoming
the Tottenham Hotspur Players and
Officials and trust that they will enjoy
their visit to our City and also the
Match—I know that our players and
Officials will remember their visit with
pleasure.*

A. Hurran.

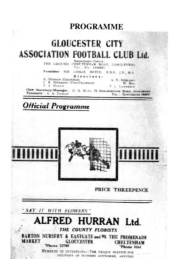

1950-1951

1950-1951

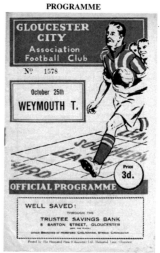

1952-1953

Date: Thursday 24/04/1952
Result: **CHELTENHAM TOWN 1 GLOUCESTER CITY 0**
Competition: Gloucestershire FA Northern Senior Professional Cup Final
Teamsheet: Jepson, Lawson, Stow, Myers, Tredgett, Canavan, Barnfield, Wright, Witt, Pullen, Colenutt
Attendance: 1500

Date: Monday 28/04/1952
Result: **MERTHYR TYDFIL 4 GLOUCESTER CITY 2**
Competition: Southern League
Teamsheet (from): Jepson, Lawson, Peacock, Myers, Tredgett, Canavan, Barnfield, Wright, Witt, Pullen, Stow, Colenutt
Scorers: Barnfield, Witt

Date: Thursday 01/05/1952
Result: **GLOUCESTER CITY 3 BATH CITY 0**
Competition: Southern League
Teamsheet (from): Jepson, Lawson, Peacock, Myers, Tredgett, Stow, Barnfield, Wright, Witt, Pullen, Colenutt, Nicholls
Scorers: Pullen (2), Barnfield

Date: Saturday 03/05/1952
Result: **LLANELLY 1 GLOUCESTER CITY 5**
Competition: Southern League
Teamsheet: King, Lawson, Colenutt, Myers, Tredgett, Stow, Barnfield, Wright, Witt, Pullen, Nicholls
Scorers: Witt (3), Pullen (2)

Appearances – SJ Asher 25, BR Barnfield 25, LG Boseley 5, JG Buist 29, J Canavan 38, JMW Colenutt 8, AJ Grubb 24, R Harper 3, DA Hunt 2, M Jenkins 30, A Jepson 34, H King 7, G Lawson 48, WV Miller 1, S Myers 48, E Nicholls 5, G Peacock 43, DG Pugsley 7, WE Pullen 27, J Robertson 14, AC Stow 14, KF Tredgett 22, D Witt 31, R Wright 40.
Scorers – SJ Asher 12, WE Pullen 9, BR Barnfield 8, M Jenkins 7, J Canavan 6, AJ Grubb 6, J Robertson 6, R Wright 6, JG Buist 4, D Witt 4, AC Stow 3, LG Boseley 2, R Harper 1, G Lawson 1, S Myers 1, E Nicholls 1, G Peacock, own goal 1.

SOUTHERN LEAGUE

POS	CLUB	P	W	D	L	F	A	PTS
1	MERTHYR TYDFIL	42	27	6	9	128	59	60
2	WEYMOUTH	42	22	13	7	81	42	57
3	KIDDERMINSTER HARRIERS	42	22	10	10	70	40	54
4	GUILDFORD CITY	42	18	16	8	66	47	52
5	HEREFORD UNITED	42	21	9	12	80	59	51
6	WORCESTER CITY	42	23	4	15	86	73	50
7	KETTERING TOWN	42	18	10	14	83	56	46
8	LOVELLS ATHLETIC	42	18	10	14	87	68	46
9	**GLOUCESTER CITY**	**42**	**19**	**8**	**15**	**68**	**55**	**46**
10	BATH CITY	42	19	6	17	75	67	44
11	HEADINGTON UNITED	42	16	11	15	55	53	43
12	BEDFORD TOWN	42	16	10	16	75	64	42
13	BARRY TOWN	42	18	6	18	84	89	42
14	CHELMSFORD CITY	42	15	10	17	67	80	40
15	DARTFORD	42	15	9	18	63	65	39
16	TONBRIDGE	42	15	6	21	63	86	36
17	YEOVIL TOWN	42	12	11	19	57	76	35
18	CHELTENHAM TOWN	42	15	4	23	59	86	34
19	EXETER CITY RESERVES	42	13	7	22	76	107	33
20	LLANELLY	42	13	6	23	70	111	32
21	GRAVESEND & NORTHFLEET	42	12	7	23	68	88	31
22	HASTINGS UNITED	42	3	5	34	41	131	11
		924	370	184	370	1602	1602	924

SEASON 1952-1953
(Home Ground: The Ground, Cheltenham Road, Longlevens)

Date: Saturday 23/08/1952
Result: **GLOUCESTER CITY 4 CHELMSFORD CITY 2**
Competition: Southern League
Teamsheet: James, MJW Williams, Crawford, Myers, Tredgett, Canavan, Barnfield, Wright, Price, Pullen, Buist
Scorers: Buist, Pullen (3)
Attendance: 3027

Date: Thursday 28/08/1952
Result: **GLOUCESTER CITY 4 LLANELLY 2**
Competition: Southern League
Teamsheet: James, MJW Williams, Crawford, Myers, Tredgett, Canavan, Barnfield, Wright, Price, Pullen, Buist
Scorers: Canavan (2 pens), Barnfield, Pullen
Attendance: 3537

Date: Saturday 30/08/1952
Result: **BEDFORD TOWN 5 GLOUCESTER CITY 1**
Competition: Southern League
Teamsheet: T Williams, MJW Williams, Crawford, Myers, Tredgett, Canavan, Barnfield, Haines, Price, Pullen, Buist
Scorer: Canavan (pen)

Date: Monday 01/09/1952
Result: **GLOUCESTER CITY 1 WORCESTER CITY 1**
Competition: Southern League
Teamsheet: T Williams, MJW Williams, Crawford, Myers, Tredgett, Canavan, Barnfield, Haines, Price, Pullen, Buist
Scorer: Barnfield

Date: Thursday 04/09/1952
Result: **GLOUCESTER CITY 2 CHELTENHAM TOWN 1**
Competition: Southern League Cup Qualifying Round 1st Leg
Teamsheet: T Williams, MJW Williams, Crawford, Myers, Tredgett, Canavan, Barnfield, Haines, Price, Pullen, Buist
Scorers: Pullen, Haines
Attendance: 4000

Date: Saturday 06/09/1952
Result: **BARRY TOWN 1 GLOUCESTER CITY 2**
Competition: Southern League
Teamsheet: T Williams, MJW Williams, Crawford, Myers, Tredgett, Canavan, Barnfield, Haines, Price, Molloy, Buist
Scorers: -----, -----

Date: Wednesday 10/09/1952
Result: **CHELTENHAM TOWN 1 GLOUCESTER CITY 1**
Competition: Southern League Cup Qualifying Round 2nd Leg
Teamsheet: T Williams, MJW Williams, Crawford, Myers, Tredgett, Canavan, Barnfield, Haines, Price, Molloy, Buist
Scorer: Price

Date: Saturday 13/09/1952
Result: **GLOUCESTER CITY 1 LLANELLY 1**
Competition: FA Cup Preliminary Round
Teamsheet: T Williams, MJW Williams, Crawford, Myers, Tredgett, Canavan, Barnfield, Haines, Price, Molloy, Buist
Scorer: Myers

Date: Tuesday 16/09/1952
Result: **LLANELLY 5 GLOUCESTER CITY 0**
Competition: FA Cup Preliminary Round Replay
Teamsheet: T Williams, MJW Williams, Crawford, Myers, Tredgett, Molloy, Barnfield, Haines, Price, Pullen, Buist
Attendance: 7000

Date: Thursday 18/09/1952
Result: **GLOUCESTER CITY 2 KIDDERMINSTER HARRIERS 0**
Competition: Southern League
Teamsheet: T Williams, MJW Williams, Crawford, Myers, Tredgett, Molloy, Barnfield, Wright, Price, Pullen, Haines
Scorers: Pullen, Price

Date: Saturday 20/09/1952
Result: **GLOUCESTER CITY 3 MERTHYR TYDFIL 1**
Competition: Southern League
Teamsheet: T Williams, MJW Williams, Crawford, Myers, Tredgett, Witt, Barnfield, Wright, Price, Pullen, Molloy
Scorers: Pullen, Price, Molloy

Date: Monday 22/09/1952
Result: **LLANELLY 3 GLOUCESTER CITY 1**
Competition: Southern League
Teamsheet: James, MJW Williams, Crawford, Myers, Tredgett, Witt, Barnfield, Wright, Price, Pullen, Molloy
Scorer: Pullen
Attendance: 6000

Date: Thursday 02/10/1952
Result: **LOVELLS ATHLETIC 3 GLOUCESTER CITY 1**
Competition: Southern League Cup 1st Round
Teamsheet: Jepson, MJW Williams, Crawford, Myers, Tredgett, Witt, Barnfield, Wright, Price, Pullen, Molloy
Scorer: Pullen

Date: Saturday 04/10/1952
Result: **GRAVESEND & NORTHFLEET 0 GLOUCESTER CITY 0**
Competition: Southern League
Teamsheet: Jepson, MJW Williams, Crawford, Myers, Tredgett, Witt, Barnfield, Wright, Price, Pullen, Haines
Attendance: 3282

Date: Saturday 11/10/1952
Result: **WEYMOUTH 1 GLOUCESTER CITY 3**
Competition: Southern League
Teamsheet: Jepson, MJW Williams, Crawford, Myers, Tredgett, Witt, Barnfield, Wright, Price, Etheridge, Haines
Scorers: Price (2), Wright
Attendance: 3773

Date: Saturday 18/10/1952
Result: **KIDDERMINSTER HARRIERS 3 GLOUCESTER CITY 0**
Competition: Southern League
Teamsheet: Jepson, Witt, Crawford, Myers, Tredgett, Canavan, Barnfield, Wright, Price, Pullen, Haines

Date: Saturday 25/10/1952
Result: **GLOUCESTER CITY 1 WEYMOUTH 1**
Competition: Southern League
Teamsheet: Jepson, Witt, Crawford, Myers, Tredgett, Canavan, Barnfield, Wright, Price, Pullen, Haines
Scorer: Wright
Attendance: 2300

Date: Saturday 01/11/1952
Result: **BATH CITY 4 GLOUCESTER CITY 0**
Competition: Southern League
Teamsheet: T Williams, Canavan, Crawford, Myers, Tredgett, Witt, Barnfield, Wright, Price, Pullen, Haines

Date: Saturday 08/11/1952
Result: **GLOUCESTER CITY 1 LOVELLS ATHLETIC 0**
Competition: Southern League
Teamsheet: Jepson, Canavan, Crawford, Myers, Tredgett, Witt, Barnfield, Wright, Price, Pullen, Haines
Scorer: Pullen

Date: Saturday 15/11/1952
Result: **GLOUCESTER CITY 2 TONBRIDGE 0**
Competition: Southern League
Teamsheet: Jepson, Canavan, Crawford, Myers, Tredgett, Witt, Barnfield, Wright, Price, Pullen, Haines
Scorers: Price, Wright

Date: Saturday 22/11/1952
Result: **GLOUCESTER CITY 3 DARTFORD 0**
Competition: Southern League
Teamsheet: Jepson, Witt, Crawford, Myers, Tredgett, Swankie, Barnfield, Wright, Price, Pullen, Haines
Scorers: Barnfield, Pullen, Price
Attendance: 1200

Date: Saturday 29/11/1952
Result: **GLOUCESTER CITY 0 YEOVIL TOWN 0**
Competition: Southern League
Teamsheet: Jepson, Witt, Crawford, Myers, Tredgett, Swankie, Barnfield, Wright, Price, Pullen, Haines

Date: Saturday 06/12/1952
Result: **KETTERING TOWN 3 GLOUCESTER CITY 0**
Competition: Southern League
Teamsheet: Jepson, Canavan, Crawford, Myers, Tredgett, Swankie, Barnfield, Wright, Price, Pullen, Haines

Date: Saturday 13/12/1952
Result: **GLOUCESTER CITY 1 HEADINGTON UNITED 7**
Competition: Southern League
Teamsheet: Jepson, Crawford, Proudfoot, Myers, Witt, Swankie, Barnfield, Etheridge, Price, Pullen, Molloy
Scorer: -----

Date: Saturday 20/12/1952
Result: **TONBRIDGE 5 GLOUCESTER CITY 3**
Competition: Southern League
Teamsheet: Jepson, MJW Williams, Crawford, Myers, Tredgett, Canavan, Friel, Wright, Price, Pullen, Molloy
Scorers: Friel (3)

Date: Thursday 25/12/1952
Result: **GLOUCESTER CITY 2 GUILDFORD CITY 1**
Competition: Southern League
Teamsheet: James, MJW Williams, Crawford, Myers, Tredgett, Canavan, Friel, Wright, Price, Pullen, Molloy
Scorers: Price, Pullen
Attendance: 1800

Date: Saturday 03/01/1953
Result: **DARTFORD 3 GLOUCESTER CITY 0**
Competition: Southern League
Teamsheet: Coltman, MJW Williams, Crawford, Myers, Tredgett, Canavan, Barnfield, Wright, Friel, Pullen, Molloy

Date: Saturday 10/01/1953
Result: **GLOUCESTER CITY 0 KETTERING TOWN 3**
Competition: Southern League
Teamsheet: Coltman, MJW Williams, Crawford, Myers, Tredgett, Canavan, Friel, Wright, Price, Pullen, Molloy

Date: Saturday 17/01/1953
Result: **YEOVIL TOWN 1 GLOUCESTER CITY 0**
Competition: Southern League
Teamsheet: Coltman, Proudfoot, Crawford, Myers, Tredgett, Canavan, Friel, Wright, Price, Swankie, Nicholls

Date: Saturday 14/02/1953
Result: **GLOUCESTER CITY 1 BATH CITY 0**
Competition: Southern League
Teamsheet: Coltman, Proudfoot, Crawford, Myers, Cook, Canavan, Barnfield, Haines, Friel, Swankie, Price
Scorer: Swankie

Date: Saturday 21/02/1953
Result: **GUILDFORD CITY 1 GLOUCESTER CITY 1**
Competition: Southern League
Teamsheet: Coltman, Proudfoot, Crawford, Myers, Cook, Swankie, Barnfield, Etheridge, Friel, Pullen, Haines
Scorer: Etheridge

Date: Saturday 28/02/1953
Result: **GLOUCESTER CITY 1 EXETER CITY RESERVES 0**
Competition: Southern League
Teamsheet: Coltman, Proudfoot, Crawford, Myers, Cook, Swankie, Barnfield, Etheridge, Friel, Pullen, Haines
Scorer: Friel

Date: Saturday 07/03/1953
Result: **HASTINGS UNITED 4 GLOUCESTER CITY 0**
Competition: Southern League
Teamsheet: Coltman, Proudfoot, Crawford, Myers, Cook, Swankie, Barnfield, Etheridge, Friel, Pullen, Haines

Date: Saturday 21/03/1953
Result: **MERTHYR TYDFIL 3 GLOUCESTER CITY 1**
Competition: Southern League
Teamsheet: Coltman, Proudfoot, Crawford, Myers, Tredgett, Canavan, Barnfield, Etheridge, Price, Pullen, Townsend
Scorer: -----

Date: Saturday 28/03/1953
Result: **GLOUCESTER CITY 1 HEREFORD UNITED 0**
Competition: Southern League
Teamsheet: Coltman, Proudfoot, Crawford, Myers, Tredgett, Canavan, Barnfield, Etheridge, Price, Pullen, Haines
Scorer: Pullen

Date: Friday 03/04/1953
Result: **GLOUCESTER CITY 1 CHELTENHAM TOWN 1**
Competition: Southern League
Teamsheet: Coltman, Proudfoot, Crawford, Myers, Tredgett, Canavan, Barnfield, Etheridge, Price, Pullen, Haines
Scorer: Pullen
Attendance: 3275

Date: Saturday 04/04/1953
Result: **HEREFORD UNITED 0 GLOUCESTER CITY 1**
Competition: Southern League
Teamsheet: Coltman, Proudfoot, Crawford, Myers, Tredgett, Canavan, Barnfield, Etheridge, Price, Pullen, Haines
Scorer: Haines
Attendance: 3000

Date: Monday 06/04/1953
Result: **CHELTENHAM TOWN 1 GLOUCESTER CITY 1**
Competition: Southern League
Teamsheet: Coltman, Proudfoot, Crawford, Myers, Tredgett, Canavan, Barnfield, Etheridge, Price, Pullen, Haines
Scorers: Canavan (pen)
Attendance: 2500

Date: Saturday 11/04/1953
Result: **GLOUCESTER CITY 1 BARRY TOWN 0**
Competition: Southern League
Teamsheet: Coltman, Proudfoot, Crawford, Myers, Tredgett, Canavan, Barnfield, Etheridge, Price, Pullen, Haines
Scorer: Pullen

Date: Monday 13/04/1953
Result: **GLOUCESTER CITY 0 HASTINGS UNITED 0**
Competition: Southern League
Teamsheet: Coltman, Proudfoot, Crawford, Myers, Clark, Canavan, Barnfield, Etheridge, Price, Pullen, Haines

Date: Tuesday 14/04/1953
Result: **LOVELLS ATHLETIC 1 GLOUCESTER CITY 2**
Competition: Southern League
Teamsheet: James, Proudfoot, Crawford, Myers, Tredgett, Canavan, Barnfield, Etheridge, Price, Pullen, Haines
Scorers: Haines, Barnfield

Date: Saturday 18/04/1953
Result: **GLOUCESTER CITY 1 BEDFORD TOWN 1**
Competition: Southern League
Teamsheet: Coltman, Proudfoot, Crawford, Myers, Tredgett, Canavan, Barnfield, Etheridge, Price, Pullen, Haines
Scorer: Pullen

Date: Monday 20/04/1953
Result: **WORCESTER CITY 3 GLOUCESTER CITY 0**
Competition: Southern League
Teamsheet: James, Proudfoot, Crawford, Myers, Tredgett, Canavan, Barnfield, Etheridge, Townsend, Pullen, Haines
Attendance: 2562

Date: Thursday 23/04/1953
Result: **GLOUCESTER CITY 1 CHELTENHAM TOWN 0**
Competition: Gloucestershire FA Northern Senior Professional Cup Final
Teamsheet: Coltman, Proudfoot, Crawford, Myers, Tredgett, Canavan, Barnfield, Etheridge, Townsend, Pullen, Haines
Scorer: Townsend
Attendance: 1457

Date: Saturday 25/04/1953
Result: **CHELMSFORD CITY 4 GLOUCESTER CITY 1**
Competition: Southern League
Teamsheet: Coltman, Proudfoot, Crawford, Myers, Tredgett, Canavan, Barnfield, Etheridge, Townsend, Pullen, Haines
Scorer: Pullen

Date: Tuesday 28/04/1953
Result: **GLOUCESTER CITY 3 GRAVESEND & NORTHFLEET 0**
Competition: Southern League
Teamsheet: Coltman, Proudfoot, Crawford, Myers, Tredgett, Swankie, Barnfield, Etheridge, Townsend, Pullen, Haines
Scorers: own goal, Haines, Pullen
Attendance: 1250

Date: Wednesday 29/04/1953
Result: **HEADINGTON UNITED 6 GLOUCESTER CITY 0**
Competition: Southern League
Teamsheet: Coltman, Proudfoot, Crawford, Myers, Tredgett, Swankie, Barnfield, Wright, Townsend, Pullen, Haines

Date: Saturday 02/05/1953
Result: **EXETER CITY RESERVES 5 GLOUCESTER CITY 0**
Competition: Southern League
Teamsheet: Coltman, Proudfoot, Crawford, Myers, Tredgett, Leach, Barnfield, Wright, Price, Haines, Townsend

Appearances – BR Barnfield 44, JG Buist 9, J Canavan 32, JD Clark 1, RL Coltman 20, ? Cook 4, M Crawford 48, RJ Etheridge 18, P Friel 9, MJ Haines 36, J James 6, A Jepson 12, J Leach 1, GW Molloy 13, S Myers 48, E Nicholls 1, P Price 39, AB Proudfoot 21, WE Pullen 41, RB Swankie 11, J Townsend 7, KF Tredgett 43, MJW Williams 19, T Williams 10, D Witt 13, R Wright 23.
Scorers – WE Pullen 18, P Price 8, BR Barnfield 4, J Canavan 4, P Friel 4, MJ Haines 4, RJ Etheridge 2, R Wright 2, JG Buist 1, GW Molloy 1, S Myers 1, RB Swankie 1, J Townsend 1, own goal 1.

SOUTHERN LEAGUE

POS	CLUB	P	W	D	L	F	A	PTS
1	HEADINGTON UNITED	42	23	12	7	93	50	58
2	MERTHYR TYDFIL	42	25	8	9	117	66	58
3	BEDFORD TOWN	42	24	8	10	91	61	56
4	KETTERING TOWN	42	23	8	11	88	50	54
5	BATH CITY	42	22	10	10	71	47	54
6	WORCESTER CITY	42	20	11	11	100	66	51
7	LLANELLY	42	21	9	12	95	72	51
8	BARRY TOWN	42	22	3	17	89	69	47
9	GRAVESEND & NORTHFLEET	42	19	7	16	83	76	45
10	**GLOUCESTER CITY**	**42**	**17**	**9**	**16**	**50**	**78**	**43**
11	GUILDFORD CITY	42	17	8	17	64	60	42
12	HASTINGS UNITED	42	18	5	19	75	66	41
13	CHELTENHAM TOWN	42	15	11	16	70	89	41
14	WEYMOUTH	42	15	10	17	70	75	40
15	HEREFORD UNITED	42	17	5	20	76	73	39
16	TONBRIDGE	42	12	9	21	62	88	33
17	LOVELLS ATHLETIC	42	12	8	22	68	81	32
18	YEOVIL TOWN	42	11	10	21	75	99	32
19	CHELMSFORD CITY	42	12	7	23	58	92	31
20	EXETER CITY RESERVES	42	13	4	25	69	94	30
21	KIDDERMINSTER HARRIERS	42	12	5	25	54	85	29
22	DARTFORD	42	6	5	31	40	121	17
		924	376	172	376	1658	1658	924

SEASON 1953-1954
(Home Ground: The Ground, Cheltenham Road, Longlevens)

Date: Thursday 20/08/1953
Result: **GLOUCESTER CITY 3 BEDFORD TOWN 1**
Competition: Southern League
Teamsheet: James, Proudfoot, McMillan, Myers, Tredgett, McCall, Barnfield, Ross, Millar, Perkins, Rutherford
Scorers: Millar (2), Perkins
Attendance: 3500

Date: Saturday 22/08/1953
Result: **GLOUCESTER CITY 1 HASTINGS UNITED 1**
Competition: Southern League
Teamsheet: Coltman, Proudfoot, McMillan, Myers, Tredgett, McCall, Barnfield, Ross, Millar, Perkins, Rutherford
Scorer: Millar

Date: Thursday 27/08/1953
Result: **GLOUCESTER CITY 2 WORCESTER CITY 1**
Competition: Southern League
Teamsheet: Coltman, Proudfoot, McMillan, Myers, Tredgett, Ross, Barnfield, Etheridge, Millar, Perkins, Rutherford
Scorers: Rutherford, Etheridge
Attendance: 3700

Date: Saturday 29/08/1953
Result: **BARRY TOWN 6 GLOUCESTER CITY 0**
Competition: Southern League
Teamsheet: Coltman, Proudfoot, McMillan, Myers, Tredgett, McCall, Barnfield, Ross, Millar, Perkins, Rutherford

Date: Thursday 03/09/1953
Result: **GLOUCESTER CITY 0 YEOVIL TOWN 0**
Competition: Southern League Cup Qualifying Round 1st Leg
Teamsheet: Coltman, Proudfoot, McMillan, Myers, Tredgett, McCall, Barnfield, Ross, Millar, Perkins, Rutherford
Attendance: 2500

Date: Saturday 05/09/1953
Result: **GLOUCESTER CITY 3 KETTERING TOWN 0**
Competition: Southern League
Teamsheet: Coltman, Proudfoot, McMillan, Myers, Tredgett, McCall, Barnfield, Ross, Millar, Perkins, Rutherford
Scorers: Millar (2), Barnfield

Date: Thursday 10/09/1953
Result: **YEOVIL TOWN 2 GLOUCESTER CITY 1**
Competition: Southern League Cup Qualifying Round 2nd Leg
Teamsheet: Coltman, Proudfoot, McMillan, Myers, Tredgett, McCall, Barnfield, Ross, Millar, Perkins, Rutherford
Scorers: own goal
Attendance: 5500

Date: Saturday 12/09/1953
Result: **HEADINGTON UNITED 2 GLOUCESTER CITY 0**
Competition: Southern League
Teamsheet: Coltman, Proudfoot, McMillan, Myers, Tredgett, McCall, Barnfield, Ross, Millar, Etheridge, Rutherford

Date: Monday 14/09/1953
Result: **WORCESTER CITY 5 GLOUCESTER CITY 2**
Competition: Southern League
Teamsheet: James, Proudfoot, McMillan, Myers, Tredgett, McCall, Barnfield, Ross, Millar, Etheridge, Rutherford
Scorers: Ross, Rutherford
Attendance: 5282

[133]

Date: Saturday 19/09/1953
Result: **GLOUCESTER CITY 1 MERTHYR TYDFIL 1**
Competition: Southern League
Teamsheet: James, Proudfoot, McMillan, Myers, Tredgett, McCall, Barnfield, Ross, Millar, Etheridge, Rutherford
Scorer: Millar

Date: Thursday 24/09/1953
Result: **GLOUCESTER CITY 2 YEOVIL TOWN 2**
Competition: Southern League
Teamsheet: Morton, Proudfoot, McMillan, Myers, Tredgett, McCall, Barnfield, Ross, Millar, Etheridge, Rutherford
Scorers: Rutherford, Ross

Date: Saturday 26/09/1953
Result: **GLOUCESTER CITY 2 CINDERFORD TOWN 1**
Competition: FA Cup 1st Qualifying Round
Teamsheet: Morton, Proudfoot, McMillan, Myers, Tredgett, McCall, Barnfield, Ross, Millar, Etheridge, Rutherford
Scorers: Millar, Rutherford

Date: Saturday 30/09/1953
Result: **TONBRIDGE 4 GLOUCESTER CITY 2**
Competition: Southern League
Teamsheet: Morton, Proudfoot, Clark, Myers, McCall, Ross, Barnfield, Perkins, Millar, Etheridge, Friel
Scorers: Barnfield, Millar
Attendance: 2054

Date: Saturday 03/10/1953
Result: **GLOUCESTER CITY 2 BATH CITY 5**
Competition: Southern League
Teamsheet: Morton, Proudfoot, Clark, Myers, McCall, Ross, Barnfield, Perkins, Millar, Etheridge, Friel
Scorer: Perkins (2)

Date: Saturday 10/10/1953
Result: **BARRY TOWN 2 GLOUCESTER CITY 1**
Competition: FA Cup 2nd Qualifying Round
Teamsheet: Morton, McMillan, Clark, Millar, Tredgett, McCall, Barnfield, Etheridge, Perkins, Rutherford, Buist
Scorer: -----

Date: Thursday 15/10/1953
Result: **GLOUCESTER CITY 1 KIDDERMINSTER HARRIERS 1**
Competition: Southern League
Teamsheet: Morton, Proudfoot, Clark, Myers, Tredgett, Ross, Barnfield, Etheridge, Perkins, Millar, Rutherford
Scorer: -----

Date: Saturday 17/10/1953
Result: **GUILDFORD CITY 1 GLOUCESTER CITY 4**
Competition: Southern League
Teamsheet: Morton, Proudfoot, Clark, Myers, Millar, Ross, Barnfield, Etheridge, Friel, Rutherford, Price
Scorers: Friel (2), Rutherford, Etheridge

Date: Monday 19/10/1953
Result: **GLOUCESTER CITY 1 CHELTENHAM TOWN 0**
Competition: Gloucestershire FA Northern Senior Professional Cup Semi-Final
Teamsheet: Morton, Proudfoot, Clark, Myers, Tredgett, Ross, Barnfield, Etheridge, Friel, Millar, Price
Scorer: Friel
Attendance: 2400

Date: Saturday 24/10/1953
Result: **GLOUCESTER CITY 3 DARTFORD 1**
Competition: Southern League
Teamsheet: Morton, Proudfoot, Clark, Myers, Tredgett, Ross, Barnfield, Etheridge, Friel, Millar, Rutherford
Scorers: Ross, Friel, Barnfield

Date: Saturday 31/10/1953
Result: **WEYMOUTH 2 GLOUCESTER CITY 1**
Competition: Southern League
Teamsheet: Morton, Proudfoot, Clark, Myers, Tredgett, Ross, Barnfield, Etheridge, Friel, Millar, Rutherford
Scorer: Etheridge
Attendance: 2964

Date: Thursday 12/11/1953
Result: **GLOUCESTER CITY 4 LLANELLY 1**
Competition: Southern League
Teamsheet: Morton, Proudfoot, Clark, Millar, Tredgett, Ross, Barnfield, Etheridge, Friel, Rutherford, Perkins
Scorers: Friel (3), Rutherford

Date: Saturday 14/11/1953
Result: **CHELMSFORD CITY 4 GLOUCESTER CITY 4**
Competition: Southern League
Teamsheet: Coltman, Proudfoot, Clark, Millar, Tredgett, Ross, Barnfield, Etheridge, Friel, Rutherford, Perkins
Scorers: Rutherford, Etheridge, Friel (2)

Date: Saturday 21/11/1953
Result: **GLOUCESTER CITY 0 GRAVESEND & NORTHFLEET 0**
Competition: Southern League
Teamsheet: Coltman, Proudfoot, Clark, Millar, Tredgett, Ross, Barnfield, Etheridge, Friel, Rutherford, Perkins

Date: Saturday 28/11/1953
Result: **LOVELLS ATHLETIC 0 GLOUCESTER CITY 0**
Competition: Southern League
Teamsheet: Coltman, Proudfoot, Clark, Millar, Tredgett, Ross, Barnfield, Etheridge, Friel, Rutherford, Price

Date: Saturday 05/12/1953
Result: **GLOUCESTER CITY 2 EXETER CITY RESERVES 1**
Competition: Southern League
Teamsheet: Coltman, Proudfoot, Clark, Millar, Tredgett, Ross, Barnfield, Etheridge, Friel, Rutherford, Price
Scorers: Ross, Rutherford

Date: Saturday 12/12/1953
Result: **BEDFORD TOWN 3 GLOUCESTER CITY 1**
Competition: Southern League
Teamsheet: Coltman, McMillan, Clark, Millar, Tredgett, Ross, Barnfield, Etheridge, Friel, Rutherford, Price
Scorer: Friel

Date: Saturday 19/12/1953
Result: **HASTINGS UNITED 4 GLOUCESTER CITY 0**
Competition: Southern League
Teamsheet: Coltman, McMillan, Clark, Millar, Tredgett, Ross, Barnfield, Friel, Proudfoot, Rutherford, Townsend
Attendance: 2999

Date: Friday 25/12/1953
Result: **GLOUCESTER CITY 1 HEREFORD UNITED 1**
Competition: Southern League
Teamsheet: Coltman, Proudfoot, Clark, Myers, Tredgett, McCall, Rutherford, Etheridge, Friel, Ross, Townsend
Scorer: -----

Date: Saturday 26/12/1953
Result: **HEREFORD UNITED 2 GLOUCESTER CITY 0**
Competition: Southern League
Teamsheet: Coltman, Proudfoot, Clark, Myers, Tredgett, McCall, Barnfield, Etheridge, Friel, Ross, Rutherford

Date: Saturday 16/01/1954
Result: **KETTERING TOWN 1 GLOUCESTER CITY 0**
Competition: Southern League
Teamsheet: Coltman, McMillan, Clark, Myers, Tredgett, McCall, Barnfield, Perkins, Millar, Ross, Rutherford

Date: Saturday 23/01/1954
Result: **GLOUCESTER CITY 2 HEADINGTON UNITED 1**
Competition: Southern League
Teamsheet: Coltman, McMillan, Clark, Myers, Tredgett, McCall, Barnfield, Perkins, Millar, Ross, Armit
Scorers: Ross, Armit

Date: Saturday 30/01/1954
Result: **YEOVIL TOWN 3 GLOUCESTER CITY 1**
Competition: Southern League
Teamsheet: Coltman, McMillan, Clark, Myers, Tredgett, McCall, Barnfield, Perkins, Millar, Ross, Morrison
Scorer: Morrison

Date: Saturday 06/02/1954
Result: **MERTHYR TYDFIL 4 GLOUCESTER CITY 1**
Competition: Southern League
Teamsheet: Coltman, McMillan, McCall, Myers, Tredgett, Etheridge, Barnfield, Morrison, Friel, Ross, Armit
Scorer: Friel

Date: Saturday 20/02/1954
Result: **BATH CITY 1 GLOUCESTER CITY 2**
Competition: Southern League
Teamsheet: Coltman, McMillan, Clark, Myers, Tredgett, McCall, Morrison, Rutherford, Millar, Etheridge, Armit
Scorers: -----, -----

Date: Saturday 27/02/1954
Result: **KIDDERMINSTER HARRIERS 1 GLOUCESTER CITY 1**
Competition: Southern League
Teamsheet: Coltman, McMillan, Clark, Myers, Tredgett, McCall, Morrison, Rutherford, Millar, Etheridge, Armit
Scorer: Rutherford

Date: Thursday 04/03/1954
Result: **GLOUCESTER CITY 2 TONBRIDGE 1**
Competition: Southern League
Teamsheet: Coltman, McMillan, Clark, Myers, Tredgett, McCall, Morrison, Rutherford, Millar, Etheridge, Armit
Scorers: Millar, Clark (pen)

Date: Saturday 06/03/1954
Result: **GLOUCESTER CITY 0 GUILDFORD CITY 0**
Competition: Southern League
Teamsheet: Coltman, McMillan, Clark, Myers, Tredgett, McCall, Morrison, Rutherford, Millar, Etheridge, Armit

Date: Saturday 13/03/1954
Result: **DARTFORD 2 GLOUCESTER CITY 5**
Competition: Southern League
Teamsheet: Coltman, McMillan, Clark, Myers, Tredgett, McCall, Barnfield, Rutherford, Millar, Etheridge, Armit
Scorers: Millar (2), Etheridge (2), Barnfield

Date: Saturday 20/03/1954
Result: **GLOUCESTER CITY 2 WEYMOUTH 1**
Competition: Southern League
Teamsheet: Coltman, McMillan, Clark, Myers, Tredgett, McCall, Barnfield, Rutherford, Millar, Morrison, Armit
Scorers: Clark (pen), Armit

Date: Saturday 27/03/1954
Result: **LLANELLY 2 GLOUCESTER CITY 0**
Competition: Southern League
Teamsheet: Coltman, McMillan, Clark, Myers, Tredgett, McCall, Barnfield, Perkins, Millar, Morrison, Armit

Date: Saturday 03/04/1954
Result: **GLOUCESTER CITY 1 CHELMSFORD CITY 1**
Competition: Southern League
Teamsheet: Coltman, McMillan, Clark, Myers, Tredgett, McCall, Perkins, Rutherford, Millar, Etheridge, Armit
Scorer: Clark (pen)

Date: Saturday 10/04/1954
Result: **GRAVESEND & NORTHFLEET 1 GLOUCESTER CITY 2**
Competition: Southern League
Teamsheet: Coltman, McMillan, Clark, Myers, Tredgett, McCall, Friel, Rutherford, Millar, Etheridge, Armit
Scorers: Clark (pen), Millar
Attendance: 1740

Date: Friday 16/04/1954
Result: **GLOUCESTER CITY 2 CHELTENHAM TOWN 4**
Competition: Southern League
Teamsheet: Coltman, McMillan, Clark, Myers, Tredgett, McCall, Friel, Rutherford, Millar, Etheridge, Armit
Scorers: Millar, Clark (pen)

Date: Saturday 17/04/1954
Result: **GLOUCESTER CITY 2 LOVELLS ATHLETIC 0**
Competition: Southern League
Teamsheet: Coltman, McMillan, Clark, Myers, Tredgett, McCall, Friel, Rutherford, Millar, Etheridge, Armit
Scorers: Etheridge, Armit

Date: Monday 19/04/1954
Result: **CHELTENHAM TOWN 0 GLOUCESTER CITY 4**
Competition: Southern League
Teamsheet: Coltman, McMillan, Clark, Myers, Tredgett, McCall, Friel, Rutherford, Millar, Etheridge, Armit
Scorers: Friel, Rutherford, Millar, Armit
Attendance: 2500

Date: Saturday 24/04/1954
Result: **EXETER CITY RESERVES 4 GLOUCESTER CITY 1**
Competition: Southern League
Teamsheet: Coltman, McMillan, Clark, Myers, Tredgett, McCall, Friel, Rutherford, Millar, Etheridge, Armit
Scorer: Millar

Date: Monday 26/04/1954
Result: **GLOUCESTER CITY 1 STONEHOUSE 2**
Competition: Gloucestershire FA Northern Senior Professional Cup Final
Teamsheet: James, McMillan, Clark, Myers, Tredgett, McCall, Friel, Rutherford, Millar, Etheridge, Armit
Scorer: Millar

Date: Thursday 29/04/1954
Result: **GLOUCESTER CITY 2 BARRY TOWN 1**
Competition: Southern League
Teamsheet: Morris, McMillan, Clark, Myers, Tredgett, McCall, Barnfield, Rutherford, Friel, Etheridge, Armit
Scorer: Friel

Appearances – PA Armit 17, BR Barnfield 36, JG Buist 1, JD Clark 35, RL Coltman 32, RJ Etheridge 36, P Friel 23, J James 4, J McCall 35, J McMillan 34, J Millar 44, J Morris 1, W Morrison 8, GD Morton 11, S Myers 40, J Perkins 19, P Price 5, AB Proudfoot 27, WB Ross 32, JDJ Rutherford 41, J Townsend 2, KF Tredgett 45.
Scorers – J Millar 16, P Friel 14, JDJ Rutherford 10, RJ Etheridge 7, JD Clark 5, WB Ross 5, PA Armit 4, BR Barnfield 4, J Perkins 3, W Morrison 1, own goal 1.

SOUTHERN LEAGUE

POS	CLUB	P	W	D	L	F	A	PTS
1	MERTHYR TYDFIL	42	27	8	7	98	55	62
2	HEADINGTON UNITED	42	22	9	11	68	43	53
3	YEOVIL TOWN	42	20	8	14	87	76	48
4	BATH CITY	42	17	12	13	73	67	46
5	KIDDERMINSTER HARRIERS	42	18	9	15	62	60	45
6	WEYMOUTH	42	18	8	16	83	72	44
7	BARRY TOWN	42	17	9	16	108	91	43
8	BEDFORD TOWN	42	19	5	18	80	84	43
9	**GLOUCESTER CITY**	**42**	**16**	**11**	**15**	**69**	**77**	**43**
10	HASTINGS UNITED	42	16	10	16	71	67	42
11	KETTERING TOWN	42	15	12	15	65	63	42
12	HEREFORD UNITED	42	16	9	17	64	62	41
13	LLANELLY	42	16	9	17	80	85	41
14	GUILDFORD CITY	42	15	11	16	56	60	41
15	GRAVESEND & NORTHFLEET	42	16	8	18	76	78	40
16	WORCESTER CITY	42	17	6	19	66	72	40
17	LOVELLS ATHLETIC	42	14	11	17	62	60	39
18	TONBRIDGE	42	15	9	18	85	91	39
19	CHELMSFORD CITY	42	14	10	18	67	71	38
20	EXETER CITY RESERVES	42	11	13	18	61	72	35
21	CHELTENHAM TOWN	42	11	12	19	56	83	34
22	DARTFORD	42	6	13	23	42	89	25
		924	356	212	356	1579	1578	924

Player's Pass 1954-1955
(Courtesy of Margaret Millar)

NOT TRANSFERABLE

Gloucester City A.F.C. Ltd.

Tel. 248951

•

SEASON, 1954-55

RULES

for the observance of Players

1—All professional players must attend at the football ground or such other place as the Directors may appoint every Tuesday and Thursday at 6.30 p.m. to undergo such training as the trainer shall order. Players attending late shall be deemed to be guilty of mis-conduct, and shall be dealt with by the Directors. This rule will be strictly enforced.

2—Players shall at all times obey the orders and instructions of the team manager and trainer.

3—Any Player who is ill or injured shall immediately notify the Trainer and must obey the Trainers orders. Such Player must immediately place himself under the care of the Club's Physician, Dr. Newman, Cheltenham Road, Gloucester In addition the necessary Medical Certificate and claim forms must be completed and handed to the Secretary within 24 hours failure can cause loss of pay.

4—Any Player desiring to be excused from Training shall give at least 48 hours notice to the Team Manager who shall place such application before the Directors for decision.

5—Any player absenting himself without leave shall be dealt with by the Directors.

6—All applications or complaints by the Players to the Directors shall be made in writing and forwarded to the Team Manager.

7—Any player misconducting himself in any way so as to interfere with his training or fitness for Play shall be dealt with by the Directors. Dancing is prohibited after Wednesday.

8—Players shall be provided with the necessary outfits for training and playing, such outfits being the property of the Club. Match jerseys must not be used for training purposes and players must see that their boots are kept in proper condition.

9—The trainer must report to the Team Manager all breaches of these rules.

10—Players wilfully dis-obeying any of the foregoing Rules shall be liable to immediate suspension without pay, or be fined at the discretion of the Directors.

All Players must be in their Homes or Lodgings not later than 11 p.m. after Wednesday.

By order of the Directors

HARRY FERRIER

Team Manager

This Players Pass is the property

of

GLOUCESTER CITY
23 August 1954
Prior to the match at Worcester

Back row (l to r) – Stan Myers, Jim Clark, Ron Coltman, Frank Tredgett, Joe Martin, Harry Ferrier
Front Row (l to r) Phil Friel, Jimmy Rutherford, Dusty Millar, Bob Etheridge, Bill Morrison

COACH TRIP c 1955
(Photograph courtesy of Margaret Millar)

[138]

SEASON 1954-1955

(Home Ground: The Ground, Cheltenham Road, Longlevens)

Date: Saturday 21/08/1954
Result: **GLOUCESTER CITY 3 CHELMSFORD CITY 0**
Competition: Southern League
Teamsheet: Coltman, Clark, Ferrier, Myers, Tredgett, Martin, Friel, JDJ Rutherford, Millar, RJ Etheridge, Morrison
Scorers: Millar (2), RJ Etheridge

Date: Monday 23/08/1954
Result: **WORCESTER CITY 1 GLOUCESTER CITY 1**
Competition: Southern League Cup Qualifying Round 1st Leg
Teamsheet: Coltman, Clark, Ferrier, Myers, Tredgett, Martin, Friel, JDJ Rutherford, Millar, RJ Etheridge, Morrison
Scorer: Millar
Attendance: 5553

Date: Saturday 28/08/1954
Result: **BATH CITY 1 GLOUCESTER CITY 1**
Competition: Southern League
Teamsheet: Coltman, Clark, Ferrier, Myers, Tredgett, Martin, Friel, JDJ Rutherford, Millar, RJ Etheridge, McLaughlin
Scorer: Millar

Date: Thursday 02/09/1954
Result: **GLOUCESTER CITY 3 WORCESTER CITY 1**
Competition: Southern League Cup Qualifying Round 2nd Leg
Teamsheet: Coltman, Clark, Ferrier, Myers, Tredgett, Martin, Friel, JDJ Rutherford, Millar, RJ Etheridge, McLaughlin
Scorers: Millar (2), J Rutherford

Date: Saturday 04/09/1954
Result: **GLOUCESTER CITY 1 HEREFORD UNITED 0**
Competition: Southern League
Teamsheet: Coltman, Clark, Ferrier, Myers, Tredgett, Martin, Friel, JDJ Rutherford, Millar, RJ Etheridge, McLaughlin
Scorer: Friel

Date: Saturday 11/09/1954
Result: **GLOUCESTER CITY 2 GUILDFORD CITY 0**
Competition: Southern League
Teamsheet: Coltman, Clark, Ferrier, Myers, Tredgett, Martin, Friel, JDJ Rutherford, Millar, RJ Etheridge, McLaughlin
Scorers: McLaughlin, RJ Etheridge

Date: Wednesday 15/09/1954
Result: **EXETER CITY RESERVES 2 GLOUCESTER CITY 3**
Competition: Southern League
Teamsheet: Coltman, Clark, Ferrier, Myers, Tredgett, McMillan, Friel, JDJ Rutherford, Millar, RJ Etheridge, McLaughlin
Scorers: Millar (2), RJ Etheridge

Date: Saturday 18/09/1954
Result: **TONBRIDGE 4 GLOUCESTER CITY 1**
Competition: Southern League
Teamsheet: Coltman, Clark, Ferrier, Myers, Tredgett, McMillan, Friel, JDJ Rutherford, Millar, RJ Etheridge, McLaughlin
Scorer: RJ Etheridge
Attendance: 3500

Date: Monday 20/09/1954
Result: **KETTERING TOWN 4 GLOUCESTER CITY 1**
Competition: Southern League
Teamsheet: Coltman, Clark, Ferrier, Myers, Tredgett, Proudfoot, Friel, RJ Etheridge, Millar, Moulsdale, McLaughlin
Scorer: RJ Etheridge
Attendance: 2000

Date: Thursday 25/09/1954
Result: **CINDERFORD TOWN 0 GLOUCESTER CITY 3**
Competition: FA Cup 1st Qualifying Round
Teamsheet: Coltman, Clark, Ferrier, Myers, Tredgett, Martin, Friel, JDJ Rutherford, Millar, RJ Etheridge, McLaughlin
Scorer: McLaughlin (3)
Attendance: 2600

Date: Monday 27/09/1954
Result: **GLOUCESTER CITY 2 DARTFORD 1**
Competition: Southern League
Teamsheet: Coltman, Clark, Ferrier, Myers, Tredgett, Cook, Barnfield, JDJ Rutherford, Friel, RJ Etheridge, McLaughlin
Scorer: McLaughlin (2)

Date: Saturday 02/10/1954
Result: **HASTINGS UNITED 0 GLOUCESTER CITY 0**
Competition: Southern League
Teamsheet: Coltman, Clark, Ferrier, Myers, Tredgett, Proudfoot, Barnfield, JDJ Rutherford, Friel, RJ Etheridge, McLaughlin

Date: Saturday 09/10/1954
Result: **BARRY TOWN 1 GLOUCESTER CITY 4**
Competition: FA Cup 2nd Qualifying Round
Teamsheet (from): Coltman, Clark, Ferrier, Myers, Tredgett, Proudfoot, Martin, Barnfield, JDJ Rutherford, Friel, RJ Etheridge, McLaughlin
Scorers: JDJ Rutherford, Friel (3)

Date: Thursday 14/10/1954
Result: **GLOUCESTER CITY 1 EXETER CITY RESERVES 1**
Competition: Southern League
Teamsheet: Coltman, Clark, Ferrier, Myers, Tredgett, Proudfoot, Barnfield, JDJ Rutherford, McLaughlin, RJ Etheridge, Flood
Scorer: RJ Etheridge
Attendance: 3000

Date: Saturday 16/10/1954
Result: **GLOUCESTER CITY 1 CHELTENHAM TOWN 1**
Competition: Southern League
Teamsheet: Coltman, Clark, Ferrier, Myers, Tredgett, Martin, Barnfield, JDJ Rutherford, RJ Etheridge, Moulsdale, McLaughlin
Scorer: RJ Etheridge

Date: Saturday 23/10/1954
Result: **GLOUCESTER CITY 0 MERTHYR TYDFIL 1**
Competition: FA Cup 3rd Qualifying Round
Teamsheet: Coltman, Clark, Ferrier, Myers, Tredgett, Martin, Barnfield, JDJ Rutherford, Friel, RJ Etheridge, Mclaughlin
Attendance: 5614

Date: Wednesday 27/10/1954
Result: **HEADINGTON UNITED 0 GLOUCESTER CITY 0**
Competition: Southern League Cup 1st Round
Teamsheet: Coltman, Clark, Ferrier, Myers, Tredgett, Proudfoot, Friel, JDJ Rutherford, T Rutherford, RJ Etheridge, McLaughlin

Date: Saturday 30/10/1954
Result: **GLOUCESTER CITY 4 BEDFORD TOWN 0**
Competition: Southern League
Teamsheet: Coltman, Clark, Ferrier, Myers, Tredgett, Proudfoot, Friel, JDJ Rutherford, T Rutherford, RJ Etheridge, McLaughlin
Scorers: McLaughlin (2), RJ Etheridge, T Rutherford

Date: Saturday 06/11/1954
Result: **GRAVESEND & NORTHFLEET 1 GLOUCESTER CITY 1**
Competition: Southern League
Teamsheet: Coltman, Clark, Ferrier, Myers, Tredgett, Proudfoot, Friel, JDJ Rutherford, T Rutherford, RJ Etheridge, McLaughlin
Scorer: own goal
Attendance: 1555

Date: Saturday 13/11/1954
Result: **GLOUCESTER CITY 5 BARRY TOWN 2**
Competition: Southern League
Teamsheet: Coltman, Clark, Ferrier, Myers, Tredgett, Proudfoot, Friel, JDJ Rutherford, T Rutherford, RJ Etheridge, McLaughlin
Scorers: T Rutherford (3), JDJ Rutherford, Ferrier

Date: Saturday 20/11/1954
Result: **HEREFORD UNITED 1 GLOUCESTER CITY 1**
Competition: Southern League
Teamsheet: Coltman, Clark, Ferrier, Myers, Tredgett, Proudfoot, Friel, JDJ Rutherford, T Rutherford, RJ Etheridge, Flood
Scorer: JDJ Rutherford

Date: Saturday 04/12/1954
Result: **YEOVIL TOWN 1 GLOUCESTER CITY 1**
Competition: Southern League
Teamsheet: Coltman, Clark, Ferrier, Myers, Tredgett, Proudfoot, Barnfield, Friel, T Rutherford, RJ Etheridge, McLaughlin
Scorer: RJ Etheridge

Date: Monday 06/12/1954
Result: **GLOUCESTER CITY 2 HEADINGTON UNITED 1**
Competition: Southern League Cup 1st Round Replay
Teamsheet: Coltman, Clark, Ferrier, Myers, Tredgett, Proudfoot, Barnfield, Friel, Gardiner, RJ Etheridge, McLaughlin
Scorers: Gardiner, Clark (pen)

Date: Saturday 11/12/1954
Result: **GLOUCESTER CITY 1 LLANELLY 1**
Competition: Southern League
Teamsheet: Coltman, Clark, Ferrier, Myers, Tredgett, Proudfoot, Barnfield, Friel, T Rutherford, RJ Etheridge, McLaughlin
Scorer: T Rutherford

Date: Tuesday 14/12/1954
Result: **GLOUCESTER CITY 4 KIDDERMINSTER HARRIERS 2**
Competition: Southern League
Teamsheet: Coltman, Clark, Ferrier, Myers, Tredgett, Proudfoot, Friel, T Rutherford, Gardiner, RJ Etheridge, Lawrence
Scorers: Lawrence, T Rutherford, Friel, own goal

Date: Saturday 18/12/1954
Result: **CHELMSFORD CITY 3 GLOUCESTER CITY 0**
Competition: Southern League
Teamsheet: Coltman, Clark, Ferrier, Myers, Tredgett, Proudfoot, Barnfield, Friel, T Rutherford, RJ Etheridge, Lawrence

Date: Saturday 25/12/1954
Result: **LOVELLS ATHLETIC 1 GLOUCESTER CITY 1**
Competition: Southern League
Teamsheet: Coltman, Clark, Ferrier, Myers, Tredgett, Coldray, Friel, RJ Etheridge, T Rutherford, Williamson, Lawrence
Scorer: T Rutherford

Date: Monday 27/12/1954
Result: **GLOUCESTER CITY 2 LOVELLS ATHLETIC 0**
Competition: Southern League
Teamsheet: Coltman, Clark, Ferrier, Myers, Tredgett, RJ Etheridge, Friel, T Rutherford, Gardiner, Williamson, Lawrence
Scorers: Williamson, Clark (pen)
Attendance: 3000

Date: Saturday 01/01/1955
Result: **GLOUCESTER CITY 1 BATH CITY 0**
Competition: Southern League
Teamsheet: Coltman, Clark, Ferrier, Myers, Tredgett, RJ Etheridge, Friel, JDJ Rutherford, T Rutherford, Williamson, Lawrence
Scorer: T Rutherford

Date: Saturday 08/01/1955
Result: **WORCESTER CITY 4 GLOUCESTER CITY 1**
Competition: Southern League
Teamsheet: Coltman, Clark, Ferrier, Myers, Tredgett, Coldray, Gardiner, JDJ Rutherford, Friel, RJ Etheridge, Williamson
Scorer: Williamson
Attendance: 3374

Date: Saturday 22/01/1955
Result: **GUILDFORD CITY 2 GLOUCESTER CITY 1**
Competition: Southern League
Teamsheet: Coltman, Clark, Ferrier, Myers, Tredgett, Coldray, Friel, JDJ Rutherford, T Rutherford, RJ Etheridge, Lawrence
Scorer: RJ Etheridge

Date: Saturday 29/01/1955
Result: **GLOUCESTER CITY 1 WORCESTER CITY 1**
Competition: Southern League
Teamsheet: Coltman, McMillan, Ferrier, Myers, Tredgett, Proudfoot, Friel, JDJ Rutherford, T Rutherford, RJ Etheridge, McLaughlin
Scorer: RJ Etheridge

Date: Saturday 05/02/1955
Result: **GLOUCESTER CITY 1 TONBRIDGE 1**
Competition: Southern League
Teamsheet: Coltman, Clark, Ferrier, Myers, Tredgett, Proudfoot, Friel, JDJ Rutherford, T Rutherford, RJ Etheridge, McLaughlin
Scorer: McLaughlin

Date: Saturday 12/02/1955
Result: **DARTFORD 3 GLOUCESTER CITY 1**
Competition: Southern League
Teamsheet: Coltman, Clark, Ferrier, Myers, Tredgett, Proudfoot, Friel, JDJ Rutherford, Coldray, RJ Etheridge, McLaughlin
Scorer: JDJ Rutherford

Date: Saturday 19/02/1955
Result: **GLOUCESTER CITY 2 HASTINGS UNITED 0**
Competition: Southern League
Teamsheet: Coltman, Clark, Ferrier, Myers, Tredgett, Proudfoot, Friel, JDJ Rutherford, Coldray, RJ Etheridge, Swankie
Scorer: JDJ Rutherford, Coldray

Date: Monday 21/02/1955
Result: **LOVELLS ATHLETIC 4 GLOUCESTER CITY 0**
Competition: Southern League Cup 2nd Round
Teamsheet: Coltman, Clark, Ferrier, Myers, Tredgett, Proudfoot, Friel, JDJ Rutherford, Coldray, RJ Etheridge, Swankie

Date: Saturday 26/02/1955
Result: **GLOUCESTER CITY 5 MERTHYR TYDFIL 0**
Competition: Southern League
Teamsheet: Coltman, Clark, Ferrier, Myers, Tredgett, Swankie, Friel, JDJ Rutherford, Coldray, RJ Etheridge, Lawrence
Scorers: Clark (pen), RJ Etheridge (2), Coldray (2)

Date: Saturday 05/03/1955
Result: **CHELTENHAM TOWN 3 GLOUCESTER CITY 3**
Competition: Southern League
Teamsheet: Coltman, Clark, Ferrier, Myers, Tredgett, Swankie, Friel, JDJ Rutherford, Coldray, RJ Etheridge, Lawrence
Scorers: RJ Etheridge (2), Clark (pen)

Date: Saturday 12/03/1955
Result: **GLOUCESTER CITY 1 GRAVESEND & NORTHFLEET 1**
Competition: Southern League
Teamsheet: Coltman, Clark, Ferrier, Myers, Tredgett, Swankie, Friel, JDJ Rutherford, Coldray, RJ Etheridge, Lawrence
Scorer: Coldray
Attendance: 2000

Date: Saturday 19/03/1955
Result: **BEDFORD TOWN 2 GLOUCESTER CITY 1**
Competition: Southern League
Teamsheet: Coltman, Clark, Ferrier, Myers, Tredgett, Swankie, Friel, JDJ Rutherford, Coldray, RJ Etheridge, Martin
Scorer: RJ Etheridge

Date: Saturday 26/03/1955
Result: **GLOUCESTER CITY 2 HEADINGTON UNITED 0**
Competition: Southern League
Teamsheet: Coltman, Clark, Ferrier, Myers, Tredgett, Swankie, Friel, JDJ Rutherford, Coldray, RJ Etheridge, Flood
Scorers: RJ Etheridge, Ferrier

Date: Thursday 31/03/1955
Result: **GLOUCESTER CITY 5 STONEHOUSE 0**
Competition: Gloucestershire FA Northern Senior Professional Cup Semi-Final
Teamsheet: Coltman, Clark, Ferrier, Myers, Tredgett, Swankie, Friel, JDJ Rutherford, Coldray, RJ Etheridge, Flood
Scorers: JDJ Rutherford (2), Coldray (3)

Date: Saturday 02/04/1955
Result: **BARRY TOWN 2 GLOUCESTER CITY 1**
Competition: Southern League
Teamsheet: Coltman, Clark, Ferrier, Myers, Tredgett, Swankie, Friel, JDJ Rutherford, Coldray, RJ Etheridge, Flood
Scorer: JDJ Rutherford

Date: Friday 08/04/1955
Result: **GLOUCESTER CITY 2 WEYMOUTH 1**
Competition: Southern League
Teamsheet: Coltman, Clark, Ferrier, Myers, Tredgett, Coldray, Friel, JDJ Rutherford, T Rutherford, RJ Etheridge, Flood
Scorers: Clark (pen), Coldray

Date: Saturday 09/04/1955
Result: **GLOUCESTER CITY 2 KETTERING TOWN 0**
Competition: Southern League
Teamsheet: Coltman, Clark, Ferrier, Myers, Tredgett, Coldray, Friel, JDJ Rutherford, T Rutherford, RJ Etheridge, Flood
Scorers: JDJ Rutherford, T Rutherford

Date: Monday 11/04/1955
Result: **WEYMOUTH 2 GLOUCESTER CITY 1**
Competition: Southern League
Teamsheet: Coltman, Clark, Ferrier, Myers, Tredgett, Coldray, Friel, JDJ Rutherford, T Rutherford, RJ Etheridge, Flood
Scorer: T Rutherford

Date: Saturday 16/04/1955
Result: **KIDDERMINSTER HARRIERS 3 GLOUCESTER CITY 1**
Competition: Southern League
Teamsheet: Coltman, Clark, Ferrier, Myers, Tredgett, Coldray, Friel, JDJ Rutherford, RF Etheridge, Swankie, T Rutherford
Scorer: Swankie

Date: Monday 18/04/1955
Result: **MERTHYR TYDFIL 4 GLOUCESTER CITY 0**
Competition: Southern League
Teamsheet: Coltman, Clark, Ferrier, Fordham, Tredgett, Coldray, Barnfield, Myers, Friel, JDJ Rutherford, T Rutherford

Date: Wednesday 20/04/1955
Result: **HEADINGTON UNITED 0 GLOUCESTER CITY 2**
Competition: Southern League
Teamsheet: Coltman, Clark, Ferrier, Fordham, Tredgett, Coldray, Barnfield, Myers, Friel, JDJ Rutherford, T Rutherford
Scorers: Barnfield, Myers

Date: Saturday 23/04/1955
Result: **GLOUCESTER CITY 0 YEOVIL TOWN 1**
Competition: Southern League
Teamsheet: Coltman, Clark, Ferrier, Fordham, Tredgett, Coldray, Barnfield, Myers, Friel, JDJ Rutherford, T Rutherford

Date: Saturday 30/04/1955
Result: **LLANELLY 3 GLOUCESTER CITY 1**
Competition: Southern League
Teamsheet: Coltman, Clark, Ferrier, Fordham, Tredgett, Coldray, Barnfield, Myers, Friel, JDJ Rutherford, T Rutherford
Scorer: Coldray

Date: Thursday 04/05/1955
Result: **CHELTENHAM TOWN 1 GLOUCESTER CITY 2**
Competition: Gloucestershire FA Northern Senior Professional Cup Final
Teamsheet: Coltman, McMillan, Clark, Fordham, Tredgett, Coldray, Barnfield, Myers, Friel, JDJ Rutherford, T Rutherford
Scorers: Friel, Myers
Attendance: 2321

Appearances – BR Barnfield 15, JD Clark 51, RA Coldray 22, RL Coltman 52, CI Cook 1, RF Etheridge 1, RJ Etheridge 46, H Ferrier 51, W Flood 8, R Fordham 5, P Friel 50, D Gardiner 4, M Lawrence 9, J Martin 11, JC McLaughlin 24, J McMillan 4, J Millar 10, W Morrison 2, RW Moulsdale 2, S Myers 52, AB Proudfoot 19, JDJ Rutherford 44, T Rutherford 24, RB Swankie 10, KF Tredgett 52, A Williamson 4.
Scorers – RJ Etheridge 17, JDJ Rutherford 10, T Rutherford 10, RA Coldray 9, J McLaughlin 9, J Millar 8, P Friel 6, JD Clark 5, H Ferrier 2, S Myers 2, A Williamson 2, BR Barnfield 1, D Gardiner 1, M Lawrence 1, RB Swankie 1, own goals 2.

SOUTHERN LEAGUE

POS	CLUB	P	W	D	L	F	A	PTS
1	YEOVIL TOWN	42	23	9	10	105	66	55
2	WEYMOUTH	42	24	7	11	105	84	55
3	HASTINGS UNITED	42	21	9	12	94	60	51
4	CHELTENHAM TOWN	42	21	8	13	85	72	50
5	GUILDFORD CITY	42	20	8	14	72	59	48
6	WORCESTER CITY	42	19	10	13	78	73	48
7	BARRY TOWN	42	16	15	11	82	87	47
8	**GLOUCESTER CITY**	**42**	**16**	**13**	**13**	**66**	**59**	**45**
9	BATH CITY	42	18	9	15	73	80	45
10	HEADINGTON UNITED	42	18	7	17	82	61	43
11	KIDDERMINSTER HARRIERS	42	18	7	17	84	87	43
12	MERTHYR TYDFIL	42	17	8	17	97	94	42
13	EXETER CITY RESERVES	42	19	4	19	67	78	42
14	LOVELLS ATHLETIC	42	15	11	16	71	68	41
15	KETTERING TOWN	42	15	11	16	70	70	41
16	HEREFORD UNITED	42	17	5	20	91	72	39
17	LLANELLY	42	16	7	19	78	81	39
18	BEDFORD TOWN	42	16	3	23	74	103	35
19	TONBRIDGE	42	11	8	23	68	93	30
20	DARTFORD	42	9	12	21	55	75	30
21	CHELMSFORD CITY	42	11	6	25	73	111	28
22	GRAVESEND & NORTHFLEET	42	9	9	24	62	98	27
		924	369	186	369	1732	1732	924

[144]

SEASON 1955-1956

(Home Ground: The Ground, Cheltenham Road, Longlevens)

Date: Saturday 20/08/1955
Result: **GLOUCESTER CITY 2 HEADINGTON UNITED 0**
Competition: Southern League
Teamsheet: Coltman, McMillan, Clark, Docker, Tredgett, Etheridge, Friel, JDJ Rutherford, Dunbar, Millar, Crichton
Scorers: Crichton, Millar

Date: Wednesday 24/08/1955
Result: **EXETER CITY RESERVES 0 GLOUCESTER CITY 0**
Competition: Southern League
Teamsheet: Coltman, McMillan, Clark, Docker, Tredgett, Myers, Friel, JDJ Rutherford, Dunbar, Millar, Crichton
Attendance: 2143

Date: Saturday 27/08/1955
Result: **DARTFORD 3 GLOUCESTER CITY 0**
Competition: Southern League
Teamsheet: Coltman, McMillan, Clark, Docker, Tredgett, Etheridge, Friel, JDJ Rutherford, Dunbar, Armstrong, Crichton

Date: Thursday 01/09/1955
Result: **GLOUCESTER CITY 1 KIDDERMINSTER HARRIERS 3**
Competition: Southern League Cup Qualifying Round 1st Leg
Teamsheet: Coltman, Clark, Ferrier, Docker, Coldray, Myers, Friel, JDJ Rutherford, Dunbar, Armstrong, Crichton
Scorer: Dunbar
Attendance: 2103

Date: Saturday 03/09/1955
Result: **GLOUCESTER CITY 4 KETTERING TOWN 3**
Competition: Southern League
Teamsheet: Coltman, Clark, Ferrier, Docker, Coldray, Myers, Friel, JDJ Rutherford, Dunbar, Armstrong, Crichton
Scorers: Myers, Friel (2), Crichton
Attendance: 2311

Date: Thursday 08/09/1955
Result: **KIDDERMINSTER HARRIERS 2 GLOUCESTER CITY 3**
Competition: Southern League Cup Qualifying Round 2nd Leg
Teamsheet: Coltman, Clark, Ferrier, Docker, Coldray, Myers, Friel, JDJ Rutherford, Dunbar, Millar, Crichton
Scorers: Millar, Crichton, JDJ Rutherford
Note: The first 16 teams progressed to the next round of the Southern League Cup

Date: Saturday 10/09/1955
Result: **CHELTENHAM TOWN 1 GLOUCESTER CITY 0**
Competition: Southern League
Teamsheet: Coltman, Clark, Ferrier, Docker, Coldray, Myers, Friel, JDJ Rutherford, Dunbar, Millar, Crichton
Attendance: 4004

Date: Wednesday 14/09/1955
Result: **GLOUCESTER CITY 2 EXETER CITY RESERVES 2**
Competition: Southern League
Teamsheet: Coltman, Clark, Ferrier, Docker, Coldray, Myers, Friel, JDJ Rutherford, Dunbar, T Rutherford, Crichton
Scorer: Dunbar (2)

Date: Saturday 17/09/1955
Result: **WORCESTER CITY 2 GLOUCESTER CITY 1**
Competition: Southern League
Teamsheet: Coltman, Clark, Ferrier, Docker, Coldray, Myers, Friel, JDJ Rutherford, Dunbar, Ireland, Crichton
Scorer: JDJ Rutherford
Attendance: 4767

Date: Saturday 24/09/1955
Result: **EBBW VALE 2 GLOUCESTER CITY 2**
Competition: FA Cup 1st Qualifying Round
Teamsheet: Coltman, McMillan, Ferrier, Docker, Coldray, Myers, Friel, JDJ Rutherford, Dunbar, Etheridge, Crichton
Scorers: Ferrier (pen), Crichton

Date: Wednesday 28/09/1955
Result: **GLOUCESTER CITY 4 EBBW VALE 1**
Competition: FA Cup 1st Qualifying Round Replay
Teamsheet: Coltman, McMillan, Ferrier, Docker, Coldray, Myers, Friel, JDJ Rutherford, Dunbar, Etheridge, Crichton
Scorers: JDJ Rutherford (2), Etheridge, Crichton
Attendance: 6000

Date: Saturday 01/10/1955
Result: **KIDDERMINSTER HARRIERS 2 GLOUCESTER CITY 0**
Competition: Southern League
Teamsheet: Coltman, McMillan, Ferrier, Docker, Coldray, Myers, Friel, JDJ Rutherford, Dunbar, Etheridge, Crichton

Date: Saturday 08/10/1955
Result: **BARRY TOWN 5 GLOUCESTER CITY 2**
Competition: FA Cup 2nd Qualifying Round
Teamsheet: Coltman, McMillan, Ferrier, Docker, Coldray, Myers, Friel, JDJ Rutherford, Millar, Etheridge, Crichton
Scorers: JDJ Rutherford, Ferrier (pen)

Date: Saturday 15/10/1955
Result: **GRAVESEND & NORTHFLEET 2 GLOUCESTER CITY 0**
Competition: Southern League
Teamsheet: Coltman, Clark, Ferrier, Docker, Tredgett, Myers, Friel, JDJ Rutherford, Millar, Ireland, Crichton
Attendance: 3284

[145]

Date: Wednesday 19/10/1955
Result: **GLOUCESTER CITY 2 WEYMOUTH 0**
Competition: Southern League
Teamsheet: Coltman, Clark, Ferrier, Docker, Tredgett, Myers, Friel, Etheridge, Dunbar, Ireland, Crichton
Scorers: Etheridge, Myers

Date: Saturday 22/10/1955
Result: **GLOUCESTER CITY 0 GUILDFORD CITY 1**
Competition: Southern League
Teamsheet: Coltman, Clark, Ferrier, Docker, Tredgett, Myers, Friel, Etheridge, Dunbar, Ireland, Crichton

Date: Saturday 29/10/1955
Result: **BEDFORD TOWN 1 GLOUCESTER CITY 1**
Competition: Southern League
Teamsheet: Coltman, McMillan, Clark, Myers, Tredgett, Fordham, Friel, Armstrong, Dunbar, Etheridge, Ireland
Scorer: own goal

Date: Saturday 05/11/1955
Result: **BARRY TOWN 0 GLOUCESTER CITY 3**
Competition: Southern League Cup 1st Round
Teamsheet: Coltman, Clark, Ferrier, Myers, Tredgett, Coldray, Friel, Armstrong, Dunbar, Ireland, Etheridge
Scorers: Etheridge, Ireland, Dunbar

Date: Saturday 12/11/1955
Result: **LLANELLY 2 GLOUCESTER CITY 0**
Competition: Southern League
Teamsheet: Coltman, Clark, Ferrier, Myers, Tredgett, Fordham, JDJ Rutherford, Armstrong, Dunbar, Ireland, Friel

Date: Saturday 26/11/1955
Result: **TONBRIDGE 2 GLOUCESTER CITY 1**
Competition: Southern League
Teamsheet: Coltman, Cook, Ferrier, Docker, Tredgett, Etheridge, Friel, Myers, Millar, Coldray, Crichton
Scorer: Ferrier (pen)

Date: Saturday 03/12/1955
Result: **GLOUCESTER CITY 2 BATH CITY 1**
Competition: Southern League
Teamsheet: Coltman, Clark, Ferrier, Docker, Tredgett, Etheridge, Friel, JDJ Rutherford, Dunbar, Beattie, Crichton
Scorers: Dunbar, Friel

Date: Saturday 10/12/1955
Result: **HEREFORD UNITED 3 GLOUCESTER CITY 3**
Competition: Southern League
Teamsheet: Coltman, Clark, Ferrier, Docker, Tredgett, Etheridge, Friel, JDJ Rutherford, Dunbar, Beattie, Crichton
Scorers: Docker, Dunbar, Friel

Date: Saturday 17/12/1955
Result: **HEADINGTON UNITED 0 GLOUCESTER CITY 2**
Competition: Southern League
Teamsheet: Coltman, Clark, Cook, Docker, Tredgett, Etheridge, Friel, JDJ Rutherford, Dunbar, Beattie, Crichton
Scorers: Beattie, Dunbar

Date: Saturday 24/12/1955
Result: **GLOUCESTER CITY 1 DARTFORD 2**
Competition: Southern League
Teamsheet: Coltman, Clark, Cook, Myers, Tredgett, Etheridge, Friel, JDJ Rutherford, Dunbar, Beattie, Crichton
Scorer: Crichton

Date: Monday 26/12/1955
Result: **MERTHYR TYDFIL 2 GLOUCESTER CITY 3**
Competition: Southern League
Teamsheet: Coltman, Clark, Cook, Docker, Tredgett, Myers, Friel, Etheridge, Dunbar, Beattie, Crichton
Scorers: Friel, Crichton, Etheridge

Date: Tuesday 27/12/1955
Result: **GLOUCESTER CITY 5 MERTHYR TYDFIL 1**
Competition: Southern League
Teamsheet: Coltman, Clark, Cook, Docker, Tredgett, Myers, Dunbar, Friel, Millar, Beattie, Crichton
Scorers: Beattie (2), Friel, Crichton, Millar

Date: Saturday 31/12/1955
Result: **KETTERING TOWN 1 GLOUCESTER CITY 1**
Competition: Southern League
Teamsheet: Coltman, Clark, Cook, Docker, Tredgett, Myers, Dunbar, Friel, Millar, Beattie, Crichton
Scorer: Millar

Date: Saturday 07/01/1956
Result: **GLOUCESTER CITY 3 CHELMSFORD CITY 2**
Competition: Southern League
Teamsheet: Coltman, Clark, Cook, Docker, Tredgett, Myers, Dunbar, Beattie, Friel, Etheridge, Crichton
Scorers: Friel, Crichton, Beattie

Date: Saturday 14/01/1956
Result: **GLOUCESTER CITY 4 CHELTENHAM TOWN 1**
Competition: Southern League
Teamsheet: Coltman, Clark, Cook, Docker, Tredgett, Myers, Dunbar, Beattie, Friel, Etheridge, Crichton
Scorers: Friel (3, 2 pens), Beattie
Attendance: 4000

Date: Saturday 21/01/1956
Result: **GLOUCESTER CITY 2 WORCESTER CITY 0**
Competition: Southern League
Teamsheet: Coltman, Clark, Cook, Docker, Tredgett, Myers, Dunbar, Beattie, Friel, Etheridge, Crichton
Scorers: Etheridge, Crichton

Date: Wednesday 25/01/1956
Result: **GLOUCESTER CITY 2 LLANELLY 2**
Competition: Southern League Cup 2nd Round
Teamsheet: Coltman, Clark, Cook, Docker, Tredgett, Myers, Dunbar, Beattie, Friel, Etheridge, Crichton
Scorer: Friel (2)

Date: Saturday 28/01/1956
Result: **YEOVIL TOWN 2 GLOUCESTER CITY 1**
Competition: Southern League
Teamsheet: Coltman, Clark, Cook, Docker, Tredgett, Myers, Dunbar, JDJ Rutherford, Friel, Etheridge, Crichton
Scorer: Myers

Date: Saturday 04/02/1956
Result: **CHELMSFORD CITY 2 GLOUCESTER CITY 0**
Competition: Southern League
Teamsheet: Coltman, Clark, Cook, Docker, Tredgett, Myers, Dunbar, JDJ Rutherford, Friel, Etheridge, Coldray

Date: Saturday 11/02/1956
Result: **GLOUCESTER CITY 1 KIDDERMINSTER HARRIERS 0**
Competition: Southern League
Teamsheet: Coltman, Clark, Cook, Docker, Tredgett, Myers, Dunbar, Beattie, Friel, Etheridge, Crichton
Scorer: Beattie

Date: Saturday 18/02/1956
Result: **WEYMOUTH 2 GLOUCESTER CITY 2**
Competition: Southern League
Teamsheet: Coltman, Clark, Cook, Docker, Tredgett, Myers, Dunbar, Beattie, Friel, Etheridge, Crichton
Scorers: Dunbar, Myers
Attendance: 2112

Date: Tuesday 21/02/1956
Result: **LLANELLY 1 GLOUCESTER CITY 2**
Competition: Southern League Cup 2nd Round Replay
Teamsheet: Coltman, Clark, Cook, Docker, Tredgett, Myers, Dunbar, Beattie, Friel, Etheridge, Crichton
Scorers: Friel, Etheridge

Date: Saturday 25/02/1956
Result: **GLOUCESTER CITY 3 GRAVESEND & NORTHFLEET 2**
Competition: Southern League
Teamsheet: Coltman, Clark, Cook, Docker, Tredgett, Myers, Dunbar, Beattie, Friel, Etheridge, Crichton
Scorers: Beattie, Dunbar, Friel
Attendance: 1800

Date: Saturday 03/03/1956
Result: **GUILDFORD CITY 1 GLOUCESTER CITY 0**
Competition: Southern League
Teamsheet: Coltman, Clark, Cook, Docker, Tredgett, Myers, Dunbar, Beattie, Friel, Etheridge, JDJ Rutherford

Date: Saturday 10/03/1956
Result: **GLOUCESTER CITY 1 BEDFORD TOWN 1**
Competition: Southern League
Teamsheet: Coltman, Clark, Cook, Docker, Tredgett, Myers, Dunbar, Armstrong, Beattie, Etheridge, JDJ Rutherford
Scorer: Dunbar

Date: Wednesday 14/03/1956
Result: **GLOUCESTER CITY 1 CHELMSFORD CITY 0**
Competition: Southern League Cup Semi-Final
Teamsheet: Coltman, Clark, Cook, Docker, Tredgett, Myers, Dunbar, Beattie, Friel, Etheridge, JDJ Rutherford
Scorer: -----

Date: Saturday 17/03/1956
Result: **HASTINGS UNITED 2 GLOUCESTER CITY 2**
Competition: Southern League
Teamsheet: Coltman, Clark, Cook, Docker, Coldray, Myers, Dunbar, Beattie, Friel, Etheridge, JDJ Rutherford
Scorers: Dunbar, Etheridge
Attendance: 4000

Date: Wednesday 21/03/1956
Result: **GLOUCESTER CITY 2 HASTINGS UNITED 1**
Competition: Southern League
Teamsheet: Coltman, Clark, Proudfoot, Docker, Tredgett, Myers, Dunbar, Beattie, Coldray, Etheridge, JDJ Rutherford
Scorers: Etheridge, Coldray

Date: Saturday 24/03/1956
Result: **GLOUCESTER CITY 2 LLANELLY 0**
Competition: Southern League
Teamsheet: Coltman, Clark, Proudfoot, Docker, Tredgett, Myers, Dunbar, Beattie, Coldray, Etheridge, JDJ Rutherford
Scorer: Coldray (2)

Date: Friday 30/03/1956
Result: **BARRY TOWN 2 GLOUCESTER CITY 3**
Competition: Southern League
Teamsheet: Coltman, Clark, Proudfoot, Myers, Tredgett, Coldray, Dunbar, Beattie, Friel, Etheridge, JDJ Rutherford
Scorers: Beattie, -----, -----

[147]

Date: Saturday 31/03/1956
Result: **LOVELLS ATHLETIC 3 GLOUCESTER CITY 2**
Competition: Southern League
Teamsheet: Coltman, Clark, Proudfoot, Myers, Tredgett, Coldray, Dunbar, Beattie, Friel, Etheridge, JDJ Rutherford
Scorers: Myers, Friel

Date: Monday 02/04/1956
Result: **GLOUCESTER CITY 4 BARRY TOWN 2**
Competition: Southern League
Teamsheet: Coltman, Clark, Proudfoot, Myers, Tredgett, Coldray, Dunbar, Beattie, Friel, Etheridge, JDJ Rutherford
Scorers: Beattie (2), Etheridge (2)

Date: Saturday 07/04/1956
Result: **GLOUCESTER CITY 1 TONBRIDGE 0**
Competition: Southern League
Teamsheet: Coltman, Clark, Proudfoot, Myers, Tredgett, Coldray, Dunbar, Beattie, Friel, Etheridge, JDJ Rutherford
Scorer: Friel

Date: Wednesday 11/04/1956
Result: **GLOUCESTER CITY 3 LOVELLS ATHLETIC 3**
Competition: Southern League
Teamsheet: Coltman, Clark, Proudfoot, Myers, Tredgett, Coldray, Dunbar, Beattie, Friel, Etheridge, JDJ Rutherford
Scorers: Beattie (2), Etheridge

Date: Saturday 14/04/1956
Result: **YEOVIL TOWN 4 GLOUCESTER CITY 1**
Competition: Southern League Cup Final 1st Leg
Teamsheet: Coltman, Clark, Proudfoot, Myers, Tredgett, Coldray, Dunbar, Beattie, Friel, Etheridge, JDJ Rutherford
Scorer: Beattie

Date: Saturday 21/04/1956
Result: **GLOUCESTER CITY 5 YEOVIL TOWN 1**
Competition: Southern League Cup Final 2nd Leg
Teamsheet: Coltman, Clark, Proudfoot, Myers, Tredgett, Etheridge, Dunbar, Friel, Coldray, Beattie, JDJ Rutherford
Scorers: JDJ Rutherford, Dunbar, Friel (pen), Coldray (2)

Date: Thursday 26/04/1956
Result: **GLOUCESTER CITY 3 HEREFORD UNITED 1**
Competition: Southern League
Teamsheet: Coltman, Clark, Cook, Proudfoot, Tredgett, Etheridge, Dunbar, Friel, Coldray, Beattie, JDJ Rutherford
Scorers: Coldray, JDJ Rutherford (2)

Date: Saturday 28/04/1956
Result: **GLOUCESTER CITY 2 YEOVIL TOWN 0**
Competition: Southern League
Teamsheet: Coltman, Clark, Proudfoot, Myers, Tredgett, Etheridge, Dunbar, Friel, Coldray, Beattie, JDJ Rutherford
Scorer: Coldray (2)

Date: Monday 30/04/1956
Result: **BATH CITY 3 GLOUCESTER CITY 1**
Competition: Southern League
Teamsheet: Coltman, Clark, Proudfoot, Myers, Tredgett, Etheridge, Dunbar, Friel, Coldray, Beattie, JDJ Rutherford
Scorer: Friel

Date: Saturday 02/05/1956
Result: **CHELTENHAM TOWN 3 GLOUCESTER CITY 3**
Competition: Gloucestershire FA Northern Senior Professional Cup Final
Teamsheet: Coltman, Clark, Proudfoot, Myers, Tredgett, Etheridge, Dunbar, Friel, Coldray, Beattie, JDJ Rutherford
Scorers: own goal, JDJ Rutherford, Friel
Attendance: 3000

Date: Thursday 07/05/1956
Result: **GLOUCESTER CITY 2 CHELTENHAM TOWN 0**
Competition: Gloucestershire FA Northern Senior Professional Cup Final Replay
Teamsheet: Coltman, Clark, Proudfoot, Docker, Tredgett, Myers, Dunbar, Friel, Coldray, Etheridge, JDJ Rutherford
Scorers: Coldray, Myers

Appearances – W Armstrong 7, G Beattie 32, JD Clark 50, RA Coldray 28, RL Coltman 55, CI Cook 21, J Crichton 33, A Docker 40, J Dunbar 52, RJ Etheridge 44, H Ferrier 18, R Fordham 2, R Ireland 7, J Millar 9, P Friel 52, J McMillan 8, S Myers 49, AB Proudfoot 14, JDJ Rutherford 39, T Rutherford 1, KF Tredgett 44.
Scorers – P Friel 19, G Beattie 13, J Dunbar 12, RJ Etheridge 11, J Crichton 10, RA Coldray 9, JDJ Rutherford 9, S Myers 6, J Millar 4, H Ferrier 3, A Docker 1, R Ireland 1, own goals 2.

PROGRAMME

1952-1953

PROGRAMME

1954-1955

Southern League Cup Winners 21 April 1956 v Yeovil Town

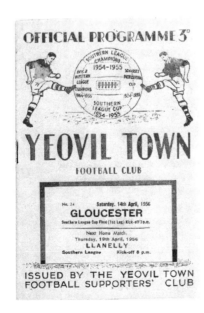

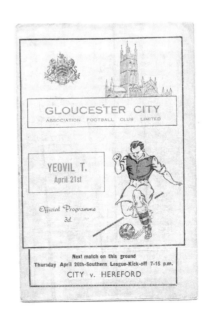

GLOUCESTER CITY SOUTHERN LEAGUE CUP WINNING TEAM 1956
(Photograph courtesy of Rob Coldray)

Back row - Stan Myers, Jackie Dunbar, Ron Coltman, Frank Tredgett, Rob Coldray
Middle row – Fred Howell (Trainer), Arthur Docker, Phil Friel, George Beattie, Jim Clark, Bobby Etheridge, Jimmy Rutherford, Archie Proudfoot, Harry Ferrier (Player-Manager)
Front row – Albert Stirland (Director), Tom Griffiths (Director), Alfred Hurran (Chairman), Albert Rea (Vice Chairman), C.R. Stephens (Director), Charles Warner (Director)

SOUTHERN LEAGUE

POS	CLUB	P	W	D	L	F	A	PTS
1	GUILDFORD CITY	42	26	8	8	74	34	60
2	CHELTENHAM TOWN	42	25	6	11	82	53	56
3	YEOVIL TOWN	42	23	9	10	98	55	55
4	BEDFORD TOWN	42	21	9	12	99	69	51
5	DARTFORD	42	20	9	13	78	62	49
6	WEYMOUTH	42	19	10	13	83	63	48
7	**GLOUCESTER CITY**	**42**	**19**	**9**	**14**	**72**	**60**	**47**
8	LOVELLS ATHLETIC	42	19	9	14	91	78	47
9	CHELMSFORD CITY	42	18	10	14	67	55	46
10	KETTERING TOWN	42	16	11	15	105	86	43
11	EXETER CITY RESERVES	42	17	9	16	75	76	43
12	GRAVESEND & NORTHFLEET	42	17	8	17	79	75	42
13	HEREFORD UNITED	42	17	7	18	90	90	41
14	HASTINGS UNITED	42	15	10	17	90	73	40
15	HEADINGTON UNITED	42	17	6	19	82	86	40
16	KIDDERMINSTER HARRIERS	42	14	7	21	86	108	35
17	LLANELLY	42	14	6	22	64	98	34
18	BARRY TOWN	42	11	11	20	91	108	33
19	WORCESTER CITY	42	12	9	21	66	83	33
20	TONBRIDGE	42	11	11	20	53	74	33
21	MERTHYR TYDFIL	42	7	10	25	52	127	24
22	BATH CITY	42	7	10	25	43	107	24
		924	365	194	365	1720	1720	924

SEASON 1956-1957
(Home Ground: The Ground, Cheltenham Road, Longlevens)

Date: Saturday 18/08/1956
Result: **BEDFORD TOWN 2 GLOUCESTER CITY 1**
Competition: Southern League
Teamsheet: Coltman, Clark, Cook, Docker, Tredgett, RJ Etheridge, Dunbar, Friel, Coldray, Bryceland, Rutherford
Scorer: Coldray

Date: Wednesday 22/08/1956
Result: **GLOUCESTER CITY 1 LLANELLY 0**
Competition: Southern League
Teamsheet: Coltman, Clark, Proudfoot, Docker, Tredgett, McKee, Friel, Bryceland, Coldray, Carruthers, Rutherford
Scorer: Carruthers

Date: Saturday 25/08/1956
Result: **GLOUCESTER CITY 4 CHELMSFORD CITY 0**
Competition: Southern League
Teamsheet: Coltman, Clark, Proudfoot, Docker, Tredgett, McKee, Friel, RJ Etheridge, Coldray, Bryceland, Rutherford
Scorers: RJ Etheridge, Coldray, Rutherford, Friel

Date: Monday 27/08/1956
Result: **GLOUCESTER CITY 4 WORCESTER CITY 1**
Competition: Southern League Cup Qualifying Round 1st Leg
Teamsheet: Coltman, Cook, Proudfoot, Docker, Tredgett, McKee, Friel, Bryceland, Coldray, RJ Etheridge, Rutherford
Scorers: Rutherford, Bryceland, RJ Etheridge (2)

Date: Saturday 01/09/1956
Result: **DARTFORD 3 GLOUCESTER CITY 3**
Competition: Southern League
Teamsheet: Coltman, Cook, Proudfoot, Docker, Tredgett, McKee, Friel, Bryceland, Coldray, RJ Etheridge, Rutherford
Scorers: Coldray (2), own goal

Date: Monday 03/09/1957
Result: **WORCESTER CITY 2 GLOUCESTER CITY 4**
Competition: Southern League Cup Qualifying Round 2nd Leg
Teamsheet: Coltman, Clark, Cook, Docker, Tredgett, McKee, Dunbar, Bryceland, Coldray, RJ Etheridge, Rutherford
Scorers: RJ Etheridge (2), Bryceland, Rutherford
Attendance: 3181

Date: Saturday 08/09/1956
Result: **GLOUCESTER CITY 3 MERTHYR TYDFIL 0**
Competition: Southern League
Teamsheet: Coltman, Clark, Cook, Docker, Tredgett, McKee, Friel, Bryceland, Coldray, RJ Etheridge, Rutherford
Scorers: Coldray, Docker, Bryceland

Date: Monday 10/09/1956
Result: **LLANELLY 0 GLOUCESTER CITY 3**
Competition: Southern League
Teamsheet: Coltman, Clark, Cook, Docker, Tredgett, McKee, Friel, Bryceland, Coldray, RJ Etheridge, Rutherford
Scorers: Coldray (2), Bryceland

Date: Saturday 15/09/1956
Result: **HEADINGTON UNITED 2 GLOUCESTER CITY 0**
Competition: Southern League
Teamsheet: Coltman, Clark, Cook, Docker, Tredgett, McKee, Dunbar, Carruthers, Coldray, Bryceland, Squires

[151]

SEASON BY SEASON

Date: Wednesday 19/09/1956
Result: **GLOUCESTER CITY 0 EXETER CITY RESERVES 1**
Competition: Southern League
Teamsheet: Coltman, Clark, Cook, RF Etheridge, Tredgett, McKee, Dunbar, Bryceland, Friel, Carruthers, Squires

Date: Saturday 22/09/1956
Result: **GLOUCESTER CITY 3 BARRY TOWN 1**
Competition: FA Cup 1st Qualifying Round
Teamsheet: Coltman, Clark, Cook, Docker, Tredgett, McKee, Dunbar, Rutherford, Coldray, Bryceland, Squires
Scorers: Rutherford, Coldray, Cook (pen)

Date: Wednesday 26/09/1956
Result: **GUILDFORD CITY 3 GLOUCESTER CITY 0**
Competition: Championship Game
Teamsheet: Coltman, Meek, Clark, RF Etheridge, Watson, McKee, Dunbar, Carruthers, Coldray, Bryceland, Squires
Note: Cup for winners of last seasons League and Cup in the Southern League

Date: Saturday 29/09/1956
Result: **LOVELLS ATHLETIC 5 GLOUCESTER CITY 1**
Competition: Southern League
Teamsheet: Coltman, Clark, Cook, RF Etheridge, Watson, McKee, Dunbar, Carruthers, Coldray, Bryceland, Weston
Scorer: Cook (pen)

Date: Saturday 06/10/1956
Result: **GLOUCESTER CITY 1 CHELTENHAM TOWN 2**
Competition: FA Cup 2nd Qualifying Round
Teamsheet: Coltman, Clark, Cook, Docker, Tredgett, McKee, Friel, Rutherford, Coldray, Bryceland, Weston
Scorer: Coldray
Attendance: 5500

Date: Saturday 13/10/1956
Result: **BARRY TOWN 1 GLOUCESTER CITY 2**
Competition: Southern League
Teamsheet: Coltman, Clark, Cook, Docker, Tredgett, McKee, Dunbar, Friel, Coldray, Bryceland, Rutherford
Scorers: Rutherford, Docker

Date: Saturday 20/10/1956
Result: **GLOUCESTER CITY 2 GUILDFORD CITY 0**
Competition: Southern League
Teamsheet: Coltman, Clark, Cook, Docker, Tredgett, McKee, Dunbar, Friel, Coldray, Bryceland, Rutherford
Scorers: Friel, Bryceland

Date: Saturday 27/10/1956
Result: **YEOVIL TOWN 5 GLOUCESTER CITY 1**
Competition: Southern League
Teamsheet: Coltman, Clark, Cook, Docker, Tredgett, McKee, Dunbar, Friel, RF Etheridge, Bryceland, Rutherford
Scorer: RF Etheridge

Date: Monday 29/10/1956
Result: **GLOUCESTER CITY 4 EXETER CITY RESERVES 1**
Competition: Southern League Cup 1st Round
Teamsheet: Coltman, Meek, Clark, Docker, Tredgett, McKee, Friel, Myers, RF Etheridge, Bryceland, Rutherford
Scorers: RF Etheridge, Myers (3)

Date: Saturday 03/11/1956
Result: **GLOUCESTER CITY 0 KETTERING TOWN 3**
Competition: Southern League
Teamsheet: Coltman, Meek, Clark, Docker, Tredgett, McKee, Coldray, Myers, RF Etheridge, Bryceland, Rutherford

Date: Saturday 10/11/1956
Result: **GRAVESEND & NORTHFLEET 0 GLOUCESTER CITY 0**
Competition: Southern League
Teamsheet: Coltman, Meek, Cook, Myers, Tredgett, McKee, Friel, Docker, RF Etheridge, Bryceland, Rutherford
Attendance: 3157

Date: Saturday 24/11/1956
Result: **BATH CITY 2 GLOUCESTER CITY 0**
Competition: Southern League
Teamsheet: Coltman, Meek, Cook, Myers, Tredgett, McKee, Friel, Docker, RF Etheridge, Bryceland, Rutherford

Date: Monday 26/11/1956
Result: **GLOUCESTER CITY 1 WEYMOUTH 2**
Competition: Southern League
Teamsheet: Coltman, Meek, Cook, Myers, Tredgett, McKee, Friel, Docker, RF Etheridge, Bryceland, Rutherford
Scorer: RF Etheridge

Date: Saturday 01/12/1956
Result: **KETTERING TOWN 4 GLOUCESTER CITY 0**
Competition: Southern League
Teamsheet: Teague, Meek, Cook, Myers, Tredgett, McKee, Dunbar, Docker, RF Etheridge, Bryceland, Rutherford

Date: Saturday 08/12/1956
Result: **MERTHYR TYDFIL 3 GLOUCESTER CITY 2**
Competition: Southern League
Teamsheet: Teague, Cook, Clark, Docker, Tredgett, McKee, Bryceland, RF Etheridge, Coldray, Myers, Weston
Scorers: Coldray, Docker (pen)

Date: Saturday 15/12/1956
Result: **GLOUCESTER CITY 2 BEDFORD TOWN 1**
Competition: Southern League
Teamsheet: Teague, Clark, Cook, Docker, Tredgett, Myers, Rutherford, Bryceland, Dunbar, McKee, Weston
Scorers: McKee, Weston

[152]

Date: Saturday 22/12/1956
Result: **CHELMSFORD CITY 1 GLOUCESTER CITY 4**
Competition: Southern League
Teamsheet: Teague, Cook, Clark, Docker, Tredgett, Myers, Rutherford, Bryceland, Dunbar, McKee, Weston
Scorer: Weston (4)

Date: Monday 24/12/1956
Result: **GLOUCESTER CITY 2 KIDDERMINSTER HARRIERS 1**
Competition: Southern League
Teamsheet: Teague, Cook, Clark, Docker, Tredgett, Myers, Rutherford, Bryceland, Dunbar, McKee, Weston
Scorers: Cook, Dunbar

Date: Saturday 05/01/1957
Result: **GLOUCESTER CITY 3 BATH CITY 0**
Competition: Southern League
Teamsheet: Teague, Clark, Cook, Docker, Tredgett, Myers, Friel, Rutherford, Dunbar, Bryceland, Weston
Scorers: Rutherford (2), Dunbar

Date: Saturday 12/01/1957
Result: **TONBRIDGE 2 GLOUCESTER CITY 2**
Competition: Southern League
Teamsheet: Teague, Cook, Clark, Docker, Tredgett, Myers, Friel, Rutherford, Dunbar, Bryceland, Weston
Scorers: Weston, Dunbar

Date: Monday 14/01/1957
Result: **GLOUCESTER CITY 0 HEREFORD UNITED 0**
Competition: Southern League Cup 2nd Round
Teamsheet: Teague, Cook, Clark, Docker, Tredgett, Myers, Friel, Rutherford, Dunbar, Bryceland, Weston

Date: Saturday 19/01/1957
Result: **GLOUCESTER CITY 2 HEADINGTON UNITED 0**
Competition: Southern League
Teamsheet: Teague, Meek, Cook, Docker, Tredgett, Myers, Friel, Bryceland, Dunbar, Coldray, Rutherford
Scorers: Myers, Dunbar

Date: Wednesday 23/01/1957
Result: **HEREFORD UNITED 4 GLOUCESTER CITY 0**
Competition: Southern League Cup 2nd Round Replay
Teamsheet: Teague, Meek, Cook, Docker, Tredgett, Myers, Dunbar, Rutherford, Coldray, Bryceland, Weston
Attendance: 2657

Date: Saturday 02/02/1957
Result: **WORCESTER CITY 5 GLOUCESTER CITY 3**
Competition: Southern League
Teamsheet: Coltman, Meek, Proudfoot, Docker, Tredgett, Myers, Friel, Bryceland, Dunbar, Coldray, Rutherford
Scorers: Dunbar (2), Docker
Attendance: 2446

Date: Saturday 09/02/1957
Result: **GLOUCESTER CITY 4 LOVELLS ATHLETIC 1**
Competition: Southern League
Teamsheet: Teague, Meek, Clark, Docker, Tredgett, Myers, Friel, Bryceland, Dunbar, Coldray, Weston
Scorers: Myers, Bryceland, Friel, Dunbar

Date: Saturday 16/02/1957
Result: **HEREFORD UNITED 8 GLOUCESTER CITY 0**
Competition: Southern League
Teamsheet: Teague, Meek, Clark, Docker, Tredgett, Myers, Friel, Bryceland, Dunbar, Coldray, Rutherford

Date: Saturday 23/02/1957
Result: **GLOUCESTER CITY 4 BARRY TOWN 1**
Competition: Southern League
Teamsheet: Teague, Meek, Proudfoot, Docker, Tredgett, Myers, Dunbar, Rutherford, RF Etheridge, Coldray, Weston
Scorers: Dunbar, Coldray (2), RF Etheridge

Date: Saturday 02/03/1957
Result: **GUILDFORD CITY 1 GLOUCESTER CITY 1**
Competition: Southern League
Teamsheet: Teague, Meek, Proudfoot, Docker, Tredgett, Myers, Friel, Rutherford, Dunbar, Coldray, Weston
Scorer: own goal

Date: Monday 04/03/1957
Result: **GLOUCESTER CITY 0 CHELTENHAM TOWN 1**
Competition: Gloucestershire FA Northern Senior Professional Cup Final
Teamsheet: Teague, Meek, Proudfoot, Docker, Tredgett, Myers, Rutherford, Friel, Dunbar, Coldray, Townsend
Attendance: 3000

Date: Saturday 09/03/1957
Result: **GLOUCESTER CITY 0 YEOVIL TOWN 2**
Competition: Southern League
Teamsheet: Teague, Meek, Proudfoot, Docker, Tredgett, Myers, Dunbar, Friel, RF Etheridge, Coldray, Townsend

Date: Saturday 16/03/1957
Result: **HASTINGS UNITED 1 GLOUCESTER CITY 1**
Competition: Southern League
Teamsheet: Teague, Meek, Proudfoot, Docker, Tredgett, Myers, Friel, Bryceland, Dunbar, Coldray, Weston
Scorer: Friel

Date: Monday 18/03/1957
Result: **GLOUCESTER CITY 2 HEREFORD UNITED 1**
Competition: Southern League
Teamsheet: Teague, Meek, Proudfoot, Docker, Tredgett, Myers, Friel, Bryceland, Dunbar, Coldray, Weston
Scorer: Coldray (2)

Date: Saturday 23/03/1957
Result: **GLOUCESTER CITY 3 GRAVESEND & NORTHFLEET 1**
Competition: Southern League
Teamsheet: Teague, Meek, Proudfoot, Docker, Tredgett, Carruthers, Friel, Myers, Dunbar, Coldray, Weston
Scorers: Carruthers, Dunbar (2)
Attendance: 2300

Date: Monday 25/03/1957
Result: **KIDDERMINSTER HARRIERS 0 GLOUCESTER CITY 1**
Competition: Southern League
Teamsheet: Teague, Meek, Proudfoot, Docker, Tredgett, Carruthers, Friel, Myers, Dunbar, Coldray, Weston
Scorer: Weston

Date: Saturday 30/03/1957
Result: **WEYMOUTH 1 GLOUCESTER CITY 2**
Competition: Southern League
Teamsheet: Teague, Meek, Proudfoot, Docker, Tredgett, Carruthers, Friel, Myers, Dunbar, Coldray, Weston
Scorer: Dunbar (2)

Date: Monday 01/04/1957
Result: **GLOUCESTER CITY 0 DARTFORD 1**
Competition: Southern League
Teamsheet: Teague, Clark, Proudfoot, Docker, Tredgett, Carruthers, Bryceland, Myers, Dunbar, Coldray, Weston

Date: Monday 08/04/1957
Result: **GLOUCESTER CITY 6 TONBRIDGE 1**
Competition: Southern League
Teamsheet: Teague, Clark, Proudfoot, Myers, Tredgett, Carruthers, Friel, Bryceland, Dunbar, Coldray, Weston
Scorers: Coldray (2), Bryceland (3), Dunbar

Date: Saturday 13/04/1957
Result: **GLOUCESTER CITY 3 WORCESTER CITY 3**
Competition: Southern League
Teamsheet: Teague, Meek, Proudfoot, Docker, Tredgett, Carruthers, Friel, Myers, Dunbar, Coldray, Weston
Scorers: -----, Coldray, Dunbar

Date: Friday 19/04/1957
Result: **GLOUCESTER CITY 1 CHELTENHAM TOWN 1**
Competition: Southern League
Teamsheet: Teague, Meek, Proudfoot, Docker, Tredgett, Carruthers, Friel, Myers, Coldray, Bryceland, Weston
Scorer: Myers

Date: Monday 22/04/1957
Result: **CHELTENHAM TOWN 2 GLOUCESTER CITY 0**
Competition: Southern League
Teamsheet: Teague, Clark, Proudfoot, Docker, Tredgett, Myers, Friel, Bryceland, Dunbar, Carruthers, Weston

Date: Saturday 27/04/1957
Result: **EXETER CITY RESERVES 2 GLOUCESTER CITY 2**
Competition: Southern League
Teamsheet: Teague, Clark, Proudfoot, Docker, Tredgett, Myers, Friel, Bryceland, Dunbar, Carruthers, Weston
Scorers: Bryceland, Dunbar

Date: Monday 29/04/1957
Result: **GLOUCESTER CITY 1 HASTINGS UNITED 3**
Competition: Southern League
Teamsheet: Teague, Clark, Proudfoot, Docker, Tredgett, Myers, Dunbar, Bryceland, RF Etheridge, Friel, Weston
Scorer: RF Etheridge

Appearances – S Bryceland 43, J Carruthers 14, JD Clark 31, RA Coldray 35, RL Coltman 23, CI Cook 27, A Docker 47, J Dunbar 37, RF Etheridge 14, RJ Etheridge 7, P Friel 37, FJ McKee 26, D Meek 23, S Myers 34, AB Proudfoot 21, JDJ Rutherford 32, ? Squires 4, WE Teague 28, J Townsend 2, KF Tredgett 49, S Watson 2, J Weston 25.
Scorers – RA Coldray 17, J Dunbar 15, S Bryceland 10, JDJ Rutherford 7, J Weston 7, S Myers 6, RF Etheridge 5, RJ Etheridge 5, A Docker 4, P Friel 4, CI Cook 3, J Carruthers 2, FJ McKee 1, own goals 2.

RECORD BREAKER

Stan Myers
Most Appearances In All Matches – 413
Most Appearances in League Matches – 354

RECORD BREAKER

Bobby Etheridge
Most Years Between First And Last Match Played – 23 years 14 days

SEASON BY SEASON

SOUTHERN LEAGUE

POS	CLUB	P	W	D	L	F	A	PTS
1	KETTERING TOWN	42	28	10	4	106	47	66
2	BEDFORD TOWN	42	25	8	9	89	52	58
3	WEYMOUTH	42	22	10	10	92	71	54
4	CHELTENHAM TOWN	42	19	15	8	73	46	53
5	GRAVESEND & NORTHFLEET	42	21	11	10	74	58	53
6	LOVELLS ATHLETIC	42	21	7	14	99	84	49
7	GUILDFORD CITY	42	18	11	13	68	49	47
8	HEREFORD UNITED	42	19	8	15	96	60	46
9	HEADINGTON UNITED	42	19	7	16	64	61	45
10	**GLOUCESTER CITY**	**42**	**18**	**8**	**16**	**74**	**72**	**44**
11	HASTINGS UNITED	42	17	9	16	70	58	43
12	WORCESTER CITY	42	16	10	16	81	80	42
13	DARTFORD	42	16	10	16	79	88	42
14	CHELMSFORD CITY	42	16	9	17	73	85	41
15	TONBRIDGE	42	14	12	16	74	65	40
16	YEOVIL TOWN	42	14	11	17	83	85	39
17	BATH CITY	42	15	8	19	56	78	38
18	EXETER CITY RESERVES	42	10	10	22	52	89	30
19	MERTHYR TYDFIL	42	9	11	22	72	95	29
20	BARRY TOWN	42	6	11	25	39	84	23
21	KIDDERMINSTER HARRIERS	42	7	10	25	60	83	20*
22	LLANELLY	42	5	8	29	39	123	18
		924	355	214	355	1613	1613	920

* Four points deducted for playing ineligible player

SEASON 1957-1958
(Home Ground: The Ground, Cheltenham Road, Longlevens)

Date: Saturday 24/08/1957
Result: **GLOUCESTER CITY 2 EXETER CITY RESERVES 0**
Competition: Southern League
Teamsheet: Coltman, Meek, May, Docker, Smith, Carruthers, Sloan, Johnson, McNiven, Gallagher, Knox
Scorers: Johnson, McNiven
Attendance: 3000

Date: Monday 26/08/1957
Result: **GLOUCESTER CITY 2 WORCESTER CITY 1**
Competition: Southern League
Teamsheet: Coltman, Meek, May, Docker, Smith, Carruthers, Sloan, Johnson, McNiven, Gallagher, Knox
Scorers: Johnson, McNiven
Attendance: 5000

Date: Saturday 31/08/1957
Result: **DARTFORD 4 GLOUCESTER CITY 2**
Competition: Southern League
Teamsheet: Coltman, Meek, May, Docker, Smith, Carruthers, Sloan, Johnson, Coldray, Gallagher, Knox
Scorer: Knox (2)

Date: Saturday 07/09/1957
Result: **CHELTENHAM TOWN 2 GLOUCESTER CITY 0**
Competition: Southern League Cup Qualifying Round 1st Leg
Teamsheet: Coltman, Meek, May, Docker, Smith, Rutherford, Sloan, Johnston, Dunbar, Gallagher, Knox

Date: Monday 09/09/1957
Result: **GLOUCESTER CITY 0 CHELTENHAM TOWN 2**
Competition: Southern League Cup Qualifying Round 2nd Leg
Teamsheet: Coltman, Meek, May, Docker, Smith, Carruthers, Sloan, Gallagher, Johnson, Coldray, Knox

Date: Saturday 14/09/1957
Result: **HASTINGS UNITED 1 GLOUCESTER CITY 1**
Competition: Southern League
Teamsheet: Coltman, Proudfoot, May, Etheridge, Smith, Carruthers, Dunbar, Myers, Johnson, Coldray, Weston
Scorer: Coldray

Date: Monday 16/09/1957
Result: **WORCESTER CITY 5 GLOUCESTER CITY 0**
Competition: Southern League
Teamsheet: Coltman, Proudfoot, May, Etheridge, Smith, Carruthers, Dunbar, Myers, Johnson, Coldray, Weston
Attendance: 4165

Date: Saturday 21/09/1957
Result: **CINDERFORD TOWN 2 GLOUCESTER CITY 1**
Competition: FA Cup 1st Qualifying Round
Teamsheet: Coltman, Proudfoot, Watson, Docker, Smith, Myers, Sloan, Coldray, Johnson, Weston, Knox
Scorer: Coldray
Attendance: 3000

Date: Thursday 26/09/1957
Result: **BATH CITY 2 GLOUCESTER CITY 1**
Competition: Southern League
Teamsheet: Teague, Myers, Proudfoot, Docker, Smith, Carruthers, Sloan, Johnson, Etheridge, Coldray, Weston
Scorer: Coldray

[155]

Date: Saturday 28/09/1957
Result: **MERTHYR TYDFIL 2 GLOUCESTER CITY 4**
Competition: Southern League
Teamsheet: Teague, Myers, Proudfoot, Etheridge, Smith, Carruthers, Dunbar, Sloan, Gallagher, Coldray, Weston
Scorers: Carruthers, Sloan (2), Weston

Date: Monday 30/09/1957
Result: **GLOUCESTER CITY 2 BARRY TOWN 0**
Competition: Southern League
Teamsheet: Teague, Myers, Proudfoot, Gallagher, Smith, Carruthers, Knox, Sloan, Etheridge, Coldray, Watson
Scorers: Carruthers, Etheridge

Date: Saturday 05/10/1957
Result: **BEDFORD TOWN 4 GLOUCESTER CITY 2**
Competition: Southern League
Teamsheet: Teague, Myers, Proudfoot, Gallagher, Smith, Carruthers, Knox, Johnston, Johnson, Coldray, Weston
Scorers: Johnston, Knox

Date: Monday 07/10/1957
Result: **GLOUCESTER CITY 1 WEYMOUTH 2**
Competition: Southern League
Teamsheet: Teague, Myers, Proudfoot, Gallagher, Smith, Carruthers, Knox, Johnston, Johnson, Coldray, Weston
Scorer: Smith

Date: Saturday 12/10/1957
Result: **GLOUCESTER CITY 0 YEOVIL TOWN 2**
Competition: Southern League
Teamsheet: Coltman, Meek, Proudfoot, Gallagher, Smith, Carruthers, Sloan, Johnston, Etheridge, Coldray, Johnson

Date: Saturday 19/10/1957
Result: **KIDDERMINSTER HARRIERS 1 GLOUCESTER CITY 1**
Competition: Southern League
Teamsheet: Coltman, Meek, Proudfoot, Docker, Gallagher, Carruthers, Knox, Sloan, Smith, Johnson, Weston
Scorer: Weston

Date: Saturday 26/10/1957
Result: **GLOUCESTER CITY 3 TONBRIDGE 0**
Competition: Southern League
Teamsheet: Coltman, Kimberley, Proudfoot, Docker, Smith, Carruthers, Sloan, Bell, Gallagher, Johnson, Weston
Scorers: Gallagher, Johnson (2)

Date: Saturday 02/11/1957
Result: **GLOUCESTER CITY 1 KETTERING TOWN 0**
Competition: Southern League
Teamsheet: Coltman, Kimberley, Proudfoot, Docker, Smith, Carruthers, Knox, Bell, Gallagher, Johnson, Weston
Scorer: Johnson

Date: Saturday 09/11/1957
Result: **GLOUCESTER CITY 4 CHELMSFORD CITY 1**
Competition: Southern League
Teamsheet: Coltman, Kimberley, Proudfoot, Docker, Smith, Carruthers, Knox, Johnston, Gallagher, Johnson, Weston
Scorers: Johnson (2), Johnston, Weston

Date: Wednesday 13/11/1957
Result: **GRAVESEND & NORTHFLEET 0 GLOUCESTER CITY 0**
Competition: Southern League
Teamsheet: Coltman, Kimberley, Proudfoot, Docker, Smith, Carruthers, Knox, Johnston, Gallagher, Johnston, Weston
Attendance: 2533

Date: Saturday 16/11/1957
Result: **HEADINGTON UNITED 3 GLOUCESTER CITY 1**
Competition: Southern League
Teamsheet: Coltman, Kimberley, Proudfoot, Docker, Smith, Carruthers, Knox, Johnston, Gallagher, Johnston, Weston
Scorer: Weston

Date: Saturday 23/11/1957
Result: **GLOUCESTER CITY 0 BATH CITY 5**
Competition: Southern League
Teamsheet: Coltman, Kimberley, Proudfoot, Docker, Smith, Carruthers, Johnson, Bell, Gallagher, Johnston, Weston

Date: Saturday 30/11/1957
Result: **BARRY TOWN 1 GLOUCESTER CITY 1**
Competition: Southern League
Teamsheet: Coltman, Kimberley, May, Gallagher, Smith, Carruthers, Sloan, Johnson, Etheridge, Coldray, Knox
Scorer: Coldray

Date: Saturday 14/12/1957
Result: **CHELTENHAM TOWN 4 GLOUCESTER CITY 0**
Competition: Southern League
Teamsheet: Coltman, Kimberley, May, Gallagher, Smith, Carruthers, Dunbar, Coldray, Johnson, Weston, Knox

Date: Saturday 21/12/1957
Result: **EXETER CITY RESERVES 2 GLOUCESTER CITY 1**
Competition: Southern League
Teamsheet: Coltman, Kimberley, May, Gallagher, Smith, Carruthers, Sloan, Johnson, Dunbar, Coldray, Weston
Scorer: Sloan

Date: Thursday 26/12/1957
Result: **GLOUCESTER CITY 7 POOLE TOWN 0**
Competition: Southern League
Teamsheet: Coltman, Kimberley, May, Gallagher, Smith, Carruthers, Sloan, Johnson, Dunbar, Coldray, Knox
Scorers: Carruthers, Dunbar, Johnson, Coldray (2), Knox (2)

Date: Saturday 28/12/1957
Result: **GLOUCESTER CITY 2 DARTFORD 0**
Competition: Southern League
Teamsheet: Coltman, Kimberley, May, Gallagher, Smith, Carruthers, Sloan, Johnson, Dunbar, Coldray, Knox
Scorers: Coldray, Knox

Date: Saturday 11/01/1958
Result: **WEYMOUTH 0 GLOUCESTER CITY 1**
Competition: Southern League
Teamsheet: Teague, Kimberley, May, Docker, Smith, Carruthers, Dunbar, Johnson, Gallagher, Coldray, Weston
Scorer: Weston

Date: Saturday 18/01/1958
Result: **GLOUCESTER CITY 3 HASTINGS UNITED 1**
Competition: Southern League
Teamsheet: Teague, Kimberley, May, Docker, Smith, Carruthers, Dunbar, Johnson, Gallagher, Coldray, Weston
Scorers: Kimberley, Dunbar (2)

Date: Saturday 25/01/1958
Result: **GLOUCESTER CITY 2 BEDFORD TOWN 3**
Competition: Southern League
Teamsheet: Teague, Kimberley, May, Docker, Smith, Carruthers, Dunbar, Johnson, Gallagher, Coldray, Weston
Scorer: Coldray (2)

Date: Saturday 01/02/1958
Result: **KETTERING TOWN 2 GLOUCESTER CITY 2**
Competition: Southern League
Teamsheet: Teague, Kimberley, May, Docker, Smith, Carruthers, Dunbar, Johnson, Gallagher, Coldray, Weston
Scorer: Johnson (2)

Date: Saturday 08/02/1958
Result: **GLOUCESTER CITY 6 MERTHYR TYDFIL 1**
Competition: Southern League
Teamsheet: Teague, Kimberley, May, Docker, Smith, Carruthers, Dunbar, Johnson, Gallagher, Coldray, Weston
Scorers: Johnson (5), Weston

Date: Saturday 15/02/1958
Result: **GLOUCESTER CITY 5 LOVELLS ATHLETIC 2**
Competition: Southern League
Teamsheet: Teague, Kimberley, May, Docker, Smith, Carruthers, Dunbar, Johnson, Gallagher, Coldray, Weston
Scorers: Kimberley, Coldray (4)
Attendance: 1400

Date: Saturday 22/02/1958
Result: **YEOVIL TOWN 1 GLOUCESTER CITY 0**
Competition: Southern League
Teamsheet: Teague, Kimberley, May, Docker, Smith, Carruthers, Dunbar, Johnson, Gallagher, Coldray, Weston

Date: Saturday 01/03/1958
Result: **GLOUCESTER CITY 2 KIDDERMINSTER HARRIERS 1**
Competition: Southern League
Teamsheet: Teague, Kimberley, May, Docker, Smith, Carruthers, Dunbar, Johnson, Gallagher, Coldray, Weston
Scorers: Carruthers, Coldray

Date: Saturday 08/03/1958
Result: **TONBRIDGE 0 GLOUCESTER CITY 1**
Competition: Southern League
Teamsheet: Teague, Kimberley, May, Etheridge, Smith, Myers, Dunbar, Bell, Gallagher, Johnson, Knox
Scorer: Gallagher

Date: Saturday 15/03/1958
Result: **GLOUCESTER CITY 1 GRAVESEND & NORTHFLEET 0**
Competition: Southern League
Teamsheet: Teague, Kimberley, May, Etheridge, Smith, Myers, Dunbar, Johnson, Gallagher, Bell, Knox
Scorer: Knox
Attendance: 2000

Date: Saturday 22/03/1958
Result: **CHELMSFORD CITY 4 GLOUCESTER CITY 0**
Competition: Southern League
Teamsheet: Teague, Kimberley, May, Docker, Smith, Carruthers, Dunbar, Bell, Gallagher, Johnson, Knox
Attendance: 2151

Date: Wednesday 26/03/1958
Result: **GLOUCESTER CITY 0 CHELTENHAM TOWN 0**
Competition: Gloucestershire FA Northern Senior Professional Cup Semi-Final
Teamsheet: Teague, Kimberley, Volpe, Docker, Smith, Carruthers, Knox, Johnson, Gallagher, Coldray, Weston

Date: Saturday 29/03/1958
Result: **GLOUCESTER CITY 2 HEADINGTON UNITED 3**
Competition: Southern League
Teamsheet: Teague, Kimberley, May, Docker, Smith, Lloyd, Dunbar, Johnson, Gallagher, Carruthers, Knox
Scorers: Carruthers, Dunbar

Date: Friday 04/04/1958
Result: **GLOUCESTER CITY 1 GUILDFORD CITY 2**
Competition: Southern League
Teamsheet: Teague, Kimberley, May, Docker, Smith, Carruthers, Dunbar, Knox, McNiven, Gallagher, Box
Scorer: Dunbar

Date: Saturday 05/04/1958
Result: POOLE TOWN 2 GLOUCESTER CITY 1
Competition: Southern League
Teamsheet: Teague, Kimberley, May, Docker, Smith, Carruthers, Dunbar, Johnson, McNiven, Gallagher, Box
Scorer: McNiven

Date: Monday 07/04/1958
Result: GUILDFORD CITY 0 GLOUCESTER CITY 2
Competition: Southern League
Teamsheet: Teague, Dunkley, May, Lloyd, Smith, Carruthers, Dunbar, Knox, McNiven, Johnson, Box
Scorers: Knox, Box

Date: Saturday 12/04/1958
Result: LOVELLS ATHLETIC 4 GLOUCESTER CITY 1
Competition: Southern League
Teamsheet: Teague, Dunkley, May, Lloyd, Smith, Carruthers, Dunbar, Johnson, McNiven, Knox, Box
Scorer: Lloyd

Date: Saturday 19/04/1958
Result: HEREFORD UNITED 0 GLOUCESTER CITY 0
Competition: Southern League
Teamsheet: Teague, Kimberley, Volpe, Etheridge, Smith, Carruthers, Dunbar, Gallagher, Johnson, Coldray, Box

Date: Monday 21/04/1958
Result: CHELTENHAM TOWN 1 GLOUCESTER CITY 2
Competition: Gloucestershire FA Northern Senior Professional Cup Semi-Final Replay
Teamsheet: Teague, Volpe, May, Docker, Smith, Carruthers, Knox, Gallagher, McNiven, Coldray, Weston
Scorers: Coldray, Knox

Date: Thursday 24/04/1958
Result: GLOUCESTER CITY 4 CINDERFORD TOWN 0
Competition: Gloucestershire FA Northern Senior Professional Cup Final
Teamsheet: Teague, Kimberley, Volpe, Docker, Smith, Carruthers, Knox, Johnson, Gallagher, Coldray, Weston
Scorers: Carruthers, Coldray, Johnson, Weston

Date: Saturday 26/04/1958
Result: GLOUCESTER CITY 2 CHELTENHAM TOWN 2
Competition: Southern League
Teamsheet: Teague, Kimberley, May, Etheridge, Smith, Myers, Chilvers, Bell, Dunbar, McNiven, Box
Scorers: Dunbar, Bell

Date: Monday 28/04/1958
Result: GLOUCESTER CITY 0 HEREFORD UNITED 2
Competition: Southern League
Teamsheet: Teague, Kimberley, May, Docker, Smith, Carruthers, Knox, Bell, Gallagher, Coldray, Weston

Appearances – E Bell 8, AF Box 6, J Carruthers 43, ? Chilvers 1, RA Coldray 29, RL Coltman 21, A Docker 30, J Dunbar 26, G Dunkley 2, RF Etheridge 11, J Gallagher 41, MW Johnson 39, P Johnston 8, A Kimberley 30, J Knox 29, AC Lloyd 3, H May 31, D McNiven 8, D Meek 7, S Myers 11, AB Proudfoot 16, JDJ Rutherford 1, T Sloan 16, A Smith 48, WE Teague 27, KS Volpe 4, S Watson 2, J Weston 28.
Scorers – RA Coldray 16, MW Johnson 16, J Knox 9, J Weston 7, J Carruthers 6, J Dunbar 6, D McNiven 3, T Sloan 3, J Gallagher 2, P Johnston 2, A Kimberley 2, E Bell 1, AF Box 1, RF Etheridge 1, AC Lloyd 1, A Smith 1.

SOUTHERN LEAGUE

POS	CLUB	P	W	D	L	F	A	PTS
1	GRAVESEND & NORTHFLEET	42	27	5	10	109	71	59
2	BEDFORD TOWN	42	25	7	10	112	64	57
3	CHELMSFORD CITY	42	24	9	9	93	57	57
4	WEYMOUTH	42	25	5	12	90	61	55
5	WORCESTER CITY	42	23	7	12	95	59	53
6	CHELTENHAM TOWN	42	21	10	11	115	66	52
7	HEREFORD UNITED	42	21	6	15	79	56	48
8	KETTERING TOWN	42	18	9	15	99	76	45
9	HEADINGTON UNITED	42	18	7	17	90	83	43
10	POOLE TOWN	42	17	9	16	82	81	43
11	HASTINGS UNITED	42	13	15	14	78	77	41
12	**GLOUCESTER CITY**	**42**	**17**	**7**	**18**	**70**	**70**	**41**
13	YEOVIL TOWN	42	16	9	17	70	84	41
14	DARTFORD	42	14	9	19	66	92	37
15	LOVELLS ATHLETIC	42	15	6	21	60	83	36
16	BATH CITY	42	13	9	20	65	64	35
17	GUILDFORD CITY	42	12	10	20	58	92	34
18	TONBRIDGE	42	13	7	22	77	100	33
19	EXETER CITY RESERVES	42	12	8	22	60	94	32
20	BARRY TOWN	42	11	9	22	72	101	31
21	KIDDERMINSTER HARRIERS	42	10	10	22	60	101	30
22	MERTHYR TYDFIL	42	9	3	30	69	137	21
		924	374	176	374	1769	1769	924

SEASON 1958-1959
(Home Ground: The Ground, Cheltenham Road, Longlevens)

Date: Saturday 23/08/1958
Result: **GLOUCESTER CITY 3 NUNEATON BOROUGH 1**
Competition: Southern League North Western Zone
Teamsheet: Teague, Kimberley, Cook, Gallagher, Smith, Carruthers, Callaghan, Morris, Coldray, Collins, Milne
Scorers: -----, -----, -----

Date: Saturday 30/08/1958
Result: **STONEHOUSE 2 GLOUCESTER CITY 2**
Competition: Gloucestershire FA Northern Senior Professional Cup Semi-Final
Teamsheet: Teague, Kimberley, Cook, Gallagher, Smith, Carruthers, Callaghan, Morris, Collins, Coldray, Milne
Scorers: Collins, Morris

Date: Thursday 04/09/1958
Result: **GLOUCESTER CITY 4 BURTON ALBION 0**
Competition: Southern League Cup 1st Round 1st Leg
Teamsheet: Teague, Kimberley, Cook, Gallagher, Smith, Carruthers, Callaghan, Morris, Collins, Coldray, Milne
Scorers: Coldray (3), Milne

Date: Saturday 06/09/1958
Result: **GLOUCESTER CITY 4 STONEHOUSE 1**
Competition: Gloucestershire FA Northern Senior Professional Cup Semi-Final Replay
Teamsheet: Teague, Kimberley, Cook, Gallagher, Smith, Carruthers, Callaghan, Morris, Collins, Coldray, Milne
Scorers: Morris (3), Collins

Date: Wednesday 10/09/1958
Result: **BURTON ALBION 0 GLOUCESTER CITY 1**
Competition: Southern League Cup 1st Round 2nd Leg
Teamsheet: Coltman, Kimberley, Cook, Gallagher, Smith, Carruthers, Callaghan, Collins, Morris, Coldray, Milne
Scorer: Coldray
Attendance: 2091

Date: Saturday 13/09/1958
Result: **KETTERING TOWN 2 GLOUCESTER CITY 2**
Competition: Southern League North Western Zone
Teamsheet: Coltman, Kimberley, Cook, Gallagher, Smith, Carruthers, Callaghan, Collins, Morris, Coldray, Milne
Scorers: Morris (2)

Date: Wednesday 17/09/1958
Result: **GLOUCESTER CITY 1 CHELTENHAM TOWN 2**
Competition: Southern League North Western Zone
Teamsheet: Coltman, Kimberley, Cook, Gallagher, Smith, Carruthers, Callaghan, Collins, Morris, Coldray, Milne
Scorer: Coldray

Date: Saturday 20/09/1958
Result: **GLOUCESTER CITY 3 CINDERFORD TOWN 2**
Competition: FA Cup 1st Qualifying Round
Teamsheet: Coltman, Kimberley, Cook, Gallagher, Smith, Carruthers, Callaghan, Collins, Morris, Coldray, Milne
Scorers: Collins, Milne, -----

Date: Wednesday 24/09/1958
Result: **CHELTENHAM TOWN 2 GLOUCESTER CITY 2**
Competition: Southern League North Western Zone
Teamsheet: Coltman, Kimberley, Cook, Gallagher, Smith, Carruthers, Callaghan, Collins, Morris, Coldray, Milne
Scorers: Morris, Coldray
Attendance: 2700

Date: Saturday 27/09/1958
Result: **RUGBY TOWN 1 GLOUCESTER CITY 3**
Competition: Southern League North Western Zone
Teamsheet: Coltman, Kimberley, Cook, Gallagher, Smith, Carruthers, Callaghan, Collins, Morris, Coldray, Milne
Scorers: Coldray, Collins, Milne

Date: Thursday 02/10/1958
Result: **GLOUCESTER CITY 3 WORCESTER CITY 2**
Competition: Southern League Inter-Zone Competition
Teamsheet: Coltman, Myers, Weston, Gallagher, Smith, Carruthers, Bell, Collins, Morris, Coldray, Milne
Scorers: Morris (2), Bell
Attendance: 2400

Date: Saturday 04/10/1958
Result: **LOVELLS ATHLETIC 2 GLOUCESTER CITY 3**
Competition: FA Cup 2nd Qualifying Round
Teamsheet: Coltman, Kimberley, Weston, Gallagher, Smith, Carruthers, Callaghan, Collins, Morris, Coldray, Milne
Scorers: Coldray, Morris (2)

Date: Wednesday 08/10/1958
Result: **GLOUCESTER CITY 2 WISBECH TOWN 0**
Competition: Southern League North Western Zone
Teamsheet: Coltman, Kimberley, Weston, Gallagher, Smith, Carruthers, Bell, Collins, Morris, Coldray, Milne
Scorers: Morris, Carruthers

Date: Saturday 11/10/1958
Result: **GLOUCESTER CITY 4 MERTHYR TYDFIL 1**
Competition: Southern League North Western Zone
Teamsheet: Coltman, Kimberley, Weston, Gallagher, Smith, Carruthers, Callaghan, Collins, Morris, Coldray, Milne
Scorers: Milne, Coldray (3)

Date: Wednesday 15/10/1958
Result: **YIEWSLEY 0 GLOUCESTER CITY 0**
Competition: Southern League Inter-Zone Competition
Teamsheet: Coltman, Myers, Cook, Etheridge, Volpe, Carruthers, Bell, Morris, Gallagher, Coldray, Milne

Date: Saturday 18/10/1958
Result: **MERTHYR TYDFIL 2 GLOUCESTER CITY 1**
Competition: FA Cup 3rd Qualifying Round
Teamsheet: Coltman, Kimberley, Myers, Gallagher, Smith, Carruthers, Callaghan, Collins, Morris, Coldray, Milne
Scorer: own goal

Date: Thursday 23/10/1958
Result: **GLOUCESTER CITY 2 YIEWSLEY 1**
Competition: Southern League Inter-Zone Competition
Teamsheet: Coltman, Kimberley, Myers, Gallagher, Volpe, Carruthers, Bell, McNiven, Cook, Coldray, Milne
Scorers: Milne, Bell

Date: Saturday 25/10/1958
Result: **GLOUCESTER CITY 2 HEADINGTON UNITED 1**
Competition: Southern League North Western Zone
Teamsheet: Coltman, Kimberley, Myers, Gallagher, Smith, Carruthers, Bell, Collins, Morris, Coldray, Milne
Scorers: Milne, Morris

Date: Saturday 01/11/1958
Result: **CHELTENHAM TOWN 3 GLOUCESTER CITY 2**
Competition: Southern League Inter-Zone Competition
Teamsheet: Coltman, Kimberley, Weston, Gallagher, Smith, Carruthers, Bell, Collins, Morris, Coldray, Milne
Scorers: Collins, Milne
Attendance: 2500

Date: Saturday 08/11/1958
Result: **GLOUCESTER CITY 2 CORBY TOWN 1**
Competition: Southern League North Western Zone
Teamsheet: Coltman, Myers, Weston, Gallagher, Smith, Carruthers, Collins, Morris, McNiven, Coldray, Milne
Scorer: McNiven (2)

Date: Wednesday 12/11/1958
Result: **DARTFORD 3 GLOUCESTER CITY 1**
Competition: Southern League Inter-Zone Competition
Teamsheet: Coltman, Volpe, Cook, Myers, Smith, Carruthers, Bell, Morris, Etheridge, Jones, Milne
Scorer: Milne

Date: Saturday 15/11/1958
Result: **KIDDERMINSTER HARRIERS 1 GLOUCESTER CITY 2**
Competition: Southern League North Western Zone
Teamsheet: Coltman, Kimberley, Weston, Gallagher, Smith, Carruthers, Callaghan, Morris, McNiven, Coldray, Milne
Scorers: Coldray, McNiven

Date: Wednesday 19/11/1958
Result: **RUGBY TOWN 3 GLOUCESTER CITY 0**
Competition: Southern League Cup 2nd Round
Teamsheet: Coltman, Kimberley, Cook, Myers, Volpe, Carruthers, Bell, Morris, Etheridge, Coldray, Milne

Date: Saturday 22/11/1958
Result: **KIDDERMINSTER HARRIERS 2 GLOUCESTER CITY 3**
Competition: Welsh FA Cup 3rd Round
Teamsheet: Coltman, Kimberley, Weston, Gallagher, Smith, Carruthers, Callaghan, Morris, McNiven, Coldray, Milne
Scorers: McNiven, Morris (2)

Date: Saturday 29/11/1958
Result: **BATH CITY 4 GLOUCESTER CITY 2**
Competition: Southern League North Western Zone
Teamsheet: Coltman, Kimberley, Weston, Gallagher, Smith, Carruthers, Callaghan, Morris, McNiven, Coldray, Milne
Scorers: Coldray, Callaghan
Attendance: 4000

Date: Saturday 06/12/1958
Result: **GLOUCESTER CITY 3 BARRY TOWN 2**
Competition: Southern League North Western Zone
Teamsheet: Coltman, Kimberley, Weston, Gallagher, Smith, Carruthers, Callaghan, Morris, McNiven, Coldray, Milne
Scorers: Milne, Coldray (2)

Date: Saturday 13/12/1958
Result: **MERTHYR TYDFIL 1 GLOUCESTER CITY 0**
Competition: Southern League North Western Zone
Teamsheet: Coltman, Kimberley, Weston, Gallagher, Smith, Carruthers, Callaghan, Morris, McNiven, Coldray, Milne

Date: Saturday 20/12/1958
Result: **NUNEATON BOROUGH 2 GLOUCESTER CITY 1**
Competition: Southern League North Western Zone
Teamsheet: Coltman, Kimberley, Weston, Gallagher, Smith, Carruthers, Callaghan, Morris, Etheridge, Coldray, Box
Scorer: Coldray

Date: Friday 26/12/1958
Result: **WORCESTER CITY 1 GLOUCESTER CITY 0**
Competition: Southern League North Western Zone
Teamsheet: Coltman, Kimberley, Weston, Gallagher, Smith, Carruthers, Callaghan, Morris, Etheridge, Coldray, McNiven
Attendance: 5051

Date: Saturday 27/12/1958
Result: **GLOUCESTER CITY 3 CAEREAU ATHLETIC 0**
Competition: Welsh FA Cup 4th Round
Teamsheet: Coltman, Lacey, Weston, Gallagher, Smith, Carruthers, Callaghan, Morris, Etheridge, Coldray, McNiven
Scorers: Carruthers, Morris (2, 1 pen)

Date: Saturday 17/01/1959
Result: **WISBECH TOWN 0 GLOUCESTER CITY 0**
Competition: Southern League North Western Zone
Teamsheet: Coltman, Kimberley, Weston, Gallagher, Smith, Carruthers, Callaghan, Morris, Etheridge, Coldray, McNiven

Date: Saturday 24/01/1959
Result: **GLOUCESTER CITY 1 CHELTENHAM TOWN 1**
Competition: Southern League Inter-Zone Competition
Teamsheet: Coltman, Kimberley, Weston, Gallagher, Smith, Carruthers, Callaghan, Morris, Etheridge, Coldray, McNiven
Scorer: Coldray

Date: Saturday 31/01/1959
Result: **GLOUCESTER CITY 1 KETTERING TOWN 2**
Competition: Southern League North Western Zone
Teamsheet: Coltman, Kimberley, Weston, Gallagher, Smith, Carruthers, McNiven, Etheridge, Morris, Coldray, Box
Scorer: Kimberley (pen)

Date: Thursday 05/02/1959
Result: **GLOUCESTER CITY 1 CARDIFF CITY 1**
Competition: Welsh FA Cup 5th Round
Teamsheet: Teague, Kimberley, Weston, Myers, Smith, Gallagher, Adlam, Morris, Etheridge, Coldray, Box
Scorer: Kimberley (pen)

Date: Saturday 07/02/1959
Result: **BOSTON UNITED 1 GLOUCESTER CITY 1**
Competition: Southern League North Western Zone
Teamsheet: Coltman, Kimberley, Weston, Myers, Smith, Carruthers, Etheridge, Morris, Callaghan, Coldray, Bell
Scorer: Morris
Attendance: 3951

Date: Monday 09/02/1959
Result: **WORCESTER CITY 6 GLOUCESTER CITY 3**
Competition: Southern League Inter-Zone Competition
Teamsheet: Coltman, Kimberley, Weston, Cook, Volpe, Carruthers, McNiven, Morris, Smith, Coldray, Box
Scorers: Morris (2), Coldray

Date: Wednesday 11/02/1959
Result: **CARDIFF CITY 3 GLOUCESTER CITY 0**
Competition: Welsh FA Cup 5th Round Replay
Teamsheet: Halls, Weston, Volpe, Kimberley, Smith, Carruthers, Callaghan, Morris, Gallagher, Coldray, McNiven
Attendance: 2500

Date: Saturday 14/02/1958
Result: **GLOUCESTER CITY 3 RUGBY TOWN 3**
Competition: Southern League North Western Zone
Teamsheet: Roberts, Volpe, Lacey, Kimberley, Smith, Carruthers, Adlam, Etheridge, Callaghan, Coldray, Weston
Scorers: Weston, Smith, Callaghan

Date: Saturday 21/02/1958
Result: **BURTON ALBION 0 GLOUCESTER CITY 1**
Competition: Southern League North Western Zone
Teamsheet: Roberts, Kimberley, Weston, Gallagher, Smith, Carruthers, Callaghan, Morris, Etheridge, Coldray, Milne
Scorer: Etheridge
Attendance: 805

Date: Saturday 28/02/1959
Result: **HEADINGTON UNITED 3 GLOUCESTER CITY 1**
Competition: Southern League North Western Zone
Teamsheet: Teague, Kimberley, Weston, Gallagher, Smith, Carruthers, Myers, Morris, Etheridge, Coldray, Milne
Scorer: Milne

Date: Saturday 07/03/1959
Result: **GLOUCESTER CITY 0 HEREFORD UNITED 6**
Competition: Southern League North Western Zone
Teamsheet: Wilkinson, Kimberley, Weston, Gallagher, Smith, Carruthers, Myers, Etheridge, Morris, Coldray, Milne

Date: Saturday 14/03/1959
Result: **CORBY TOWN 0 GLOUCESTER CITY 0**
Competition: Southern League North Western Zone
Teamsheet: Roberts, Kimberley, Weston, Callaghan, Smith, Myers, Preest, Coldray, Morris, Carruthers, Box

Date: Thursday 19/03/1959
Result: **GLOUCESTER CITY 1 WORCESTER CITY 2**
Competition: Southern League North Western Zone
Teamsheet: Roberts, Kimberley, Weston, Etheridge, Smith, Myers, Bell, Morris, Gallagher, Carruthers, Milne
Scorer: Gallagher

Date: Saturday 21/03/1959
Result: **GLOUCESTER CITY 1 KIDDERMINSTER HARRIERS 2**
Competition: Southern League North Western Zone
Teamsheet: Roberts, Kimberley, Weston, Etheridge, Smith, Myers, Bell, Morris, Gallagher, Carruthers, Milne
Scorer: Weston

Date: Tuesday 24/03/1959
Result: **GLOUCESTER CITY 1 DARTFORD 1**
Competition: Southern League Inter-Zone Competition
Teamsheet: Roberts, Kimberley, Myers, Gallagher, Smith, Carruthers, Preest, Etheridge, Coldray, Weston, Box
Scorer: Gallagher

[161]

Date: Friday 27/03/1959
Result: **GLOUCESTER CITY 1 LOVELLS ATHLETIC 0**
Competition: Southern League North Western Zone
Teamsheet: Coltman, Kimberley, Myers, Gallagher, Smith, Carruthers, Preest, Etheridge, Coldray, Weston, Box
Scorer: Coldray
Note: Author's prerogative. First match attended, aged 12

Date: Monday 30/03/1959
Result: **LOVELLS ATHLETIC 4 GLOUCESTER CITY 0**
Competition: Southern League North Western Zone
Teamsheet: Coltman, Kimberley, Myers, Gallagher, Smith, Carruthers, Preest, Morris, Coldray, Weston, Box

Date: Thursday 09/04/1959
Result: **GLOUCESTER CITY 6 BOSTON UNITED 2**
Competition: Southern League North Western Zone
Teamsheet: Coltman, Kimberley, Weston, Gallagher, Smith, Carruthers, Callaghan, Rutherford, Morris, Coldray, Milne
Scorers: Morris (3), Coldray (2), Milne

Date: Saturday 11/04/1959
Result: **BARRY TOWN 4 GLOUCESTER CITY 1**
Competition: Southern League North Western Zone
Teamsheet: Coltman, Kimberley, Weston, Gallagher, Smith, Carruthers, Callaghan, Rutherford, Morris, Coldray, Milne
Scorer: Carruthers

Date: Monday 13/04/1959
Result: **WELLINGTON TOWN 1 GLOUCESTER CITY 0**
Competition: Southern League North Western Zone
Teamsheet: Coltman, Kimberley, Weston, Gallagher, Smith, Carruthers, Preest, Callaghan, Morris, Coldray, Milne

Date: Saturday 18/04/1959
Result: **GLOUCESTER CITY 0 WELLINGTON TOWN 4**
Competition: Southern League North Western Zone
Teamsheet: Coltman, Kimberley, Weston, Gallagher, Smith, Carruthers, Preest, Callaghan, Morris, Coldray, Milne

Date: Monday 20/04/1959
Result: **GLOUCESTER CITY 2 BURTON ALBION 0**
Competition: Southern League North Western Zone
Teamsheet: Coltman, Myers, Weston, Gallagher, Smith, Carruthers, Preest, Morris, Callaghan, Coldray, Milne
Scorers: Morris (pen), Callaghan

Date: Saturday 25/04/1959
Result: **HEREFORD UNITED 5 GLOUCESTER CITY 1**
Competition: Southern League North Western Zone
Teamsheet: Coltman, Myers, Weston, Gallagher, Smith, Carruthers, Preest, Morris, Callaghan, Coldray, Milne
Scorer: Morris

Date: Wednesday 29/04/1959
Result: **CHELTENHAM TOWN 2 GLOUCESTER CITY 1**
Competition: Gloucestershire FA Northern Senior Professional Cup Final
Teamsheet: Coltman, Volpe, Weston, Myers, Smith, Gallagher, Dunbar, Morris, Preest, Coldray, Milne
Scorer: Milne

Date: Saturday 02/05/1959
Result: **GLOUCESTER CITY 0 BATH CITY 4**
Competition: Southern League North Western Zone
Teamsheet: Coltman, Myers, Volpe, Etheridge, Smith, Gallagher, Bell, Morris, Preest, Coldray, Milne

Appearances – B Adlam 2, E Bell 12, AF Box 8, R Callaghan 34, J Carruthers 52, RA Coldray 52, RD Collins 18, RL Coltman 41, CI Cook 15, J Dunbar 1, RF Etheridge 20, J Gallagher 49, TW Halls 1, DH Jones 1, A Kimberley 46, B Lacey 2, D McNiven 14, M Milne 40, MJG Morris 51, S Myers 22, R Preest 10, T Roberts 6, JDJ Rutherford 2, A Smith 52, WE Teague 6, KS Volpe 9, J Weston 38, K Wilkinson 1.
Scorers – MJG Morris 25, RA Coldray 21, M Milne 12, RD Collins 5, D McNiven 4, R Callaghan 3, J Carruthers 3, E Bell 2, J Gallagher 2, A Kimberley 2, J Weston 2, RF Etheridge 1, A Smith 1, own goal 1.

SOUTHERN LEAGUE – NORTH WESTERN ZONE

POS	CLUB	P	W	D	L	F	A	PTS
1	HEREFORD UNITED	34	22	5	7	80	37	49
2	KETTERING TOWN	34	20	7	7	83	63	47
3	BOSTON UNITED	34	18	8	8	73	47	44
4	CHELTENHAM TOWN	34	20	4	10	65	47	44
5	WORCESTER CITY	34	19	4	11	74	47	42
6	BATH CITY	34	17	5	12	89	62	39
7	WELLINGTON TOWN	34	15	9	10	74	58	39
8	NUNEATON BOROUGH	34	17	5	12	76	66	39
9	WISBECH TOWN	34	16	5	13	77	54	37
10	HEADINGTON UNITED	34	16	3	15	76	61	35
11	BARRY TOWN	34	15	5	14	64	67	35
12	MERTHYR TYDFIL	34	16	3	15	54	59	35
13	**GLOUCESTER CITY**	**34**	**12**	**6**	**16**	**50**	**65**	**30**
14	CORBY TOWN	34	10	8	16	59	79	28
15	LOVELLS ATHLETIC	34	10	3	21	51	70	23
16	RUGBY TOWN	34	7	6	21	45	93	20
17	KIDDERMINSTER HARRIERS	34	7	3	24	42	94	17
18	BURTON ALBION	34	3	3	28	41	104	9
		612	260	92	260	1173	1173	612

GLOUCESTER CITY 1959-1960
(Photograph courtesy of Phil Warren)

Back Row – Alan Kimberley, Dick Etheridge, Ron Coltman, Alan Smith, Mike Gerrish, Jimmy Weston, Fred Howell (Trainer)
Front Row – Willie Symington, Mal Morris, Ollie Norris (Player-Manager), Rob Coldray, Alex Bowman

PROGRAMME

POSTER

1958-1959

SPECIAL
SOCCER ATTRACTION !!
STAN MYERS/ROB COLDRAY BENEFIT
GLOUCESTER CITY
v.
SELECTED
FOOTBALL LEAGUE XI
at LONGLEVENS
Monday 14th March, 1960
Kick Off 7 p.m.

ADMISSION
Ground 2/-, Stands 3/6, Boys & O.A.P. 9d.
Tickets available at Usual Agencies

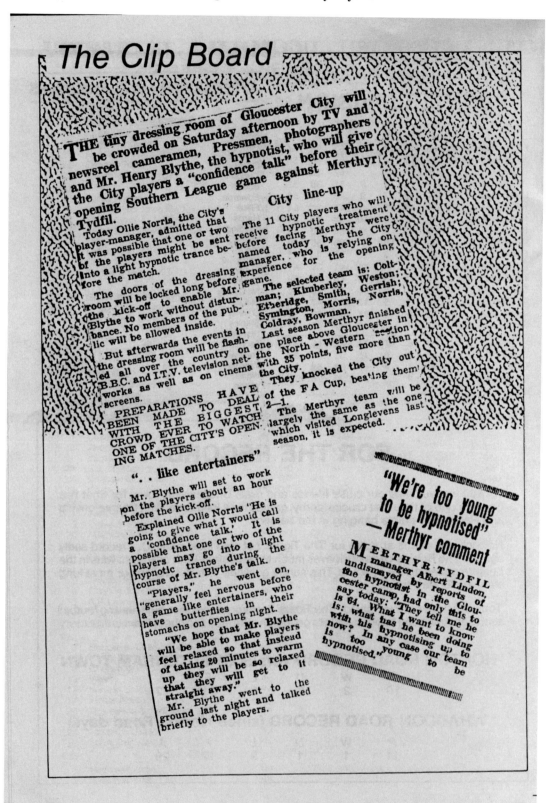

The Clip Board

THE tiny dressing room of Gloucester City will be crowded on Saturday afternoon by TV and newsreel cameramen, Pressmen, photographers and Mr. Henry Blythe, the hypnotist, who will give the City players a "confidence talk" before their opening Southern League game against Merthyr Tydfil.

Today Ollie Norris, the City's player-manager, admitted that it was possible that one or two of the players might be sent into a light hypnotic trance before the match.

The doors of the dressing room will be locked long before the kick-off to enable Mr. Blythe to work without disturbance. No members of the public will be allowed inside.

But afterwards the events in the dressing room will be flashed all over the country on B.B.C. and I.T.V. television networks as well as on cinema screens.

PREPARATIONS HAVE BEEN MADE TO DEAL WITH THE BIGGEST CROWD EVER TO WATCH ONE OF THE CITY'S OPENING MATCHES.

City line-up

The 11 City players who will receive hypnotic treatment before facing Merthyr were named today by the City manager, who is relying on experience for the opening game.

The selected team is: Coltman; Kimberley, Weston; Etheridge, Smith, Gerrish; Symington, Morris, Norris, Coldray, Bowman.

Last season Merthyr finished one place above Gloucester in the North - Western section with 35 points, five more than the City.

They knocked the City out of the FA Cup, beating them 2—1.

The Merthyr team will be largely the same as the one which visited Longlevens last season, it is expected.

". . like entertainers"

Mr. Blythe will set to work on the players about an hour before the kick-off.

Explained Ollie Norris "He is going to give what I would call a 'confidence talk.' It is possible that one or two of the players may go into a light hypnotic trance during the course of Mr. Blythe's talk.

"Players," he went on, "generally feel nervous before a game like entertainers, who have butterflies in their stomachs on opening night.

"We hope that Mr. Blythe will be able to make players feel relaxed so that instead of taking 20 minutes to warm up they will be so relaxed that they will get to it straight away."

Mr. Blythe went to the ground last night and talked briefly to the players.

"We're too young to be hypnotised" — Merthyr comment

MERTHYR TYDFIL manager Albert Lindon, undismayed by reports of the hypnotist in the Gloucester camp, had only this to say today: "They tell me he is 64. What I want to know is: what has he been doing with his hypnotising up to now? In any case our team is too young to be hypnotised."

[164]

Parade Magazine of 1 September 1962 used this photograph in an article entitled 'Hypnotism – A Power for Evil'.
(Courtesy of Dick Etheridge)

Gloucester City (amateur) F.C. players being hypnotised to victory. The experiment was abandoned after a few games.

From the end of the Second World War until 1958-1959 there had been insufficient clubs in the league to form more than one division. The number of clubs had in fact steadily increased from eleven in 1945-1946 to twenty-two in 1951-1952 and had remained constant at that figure until 1958-1959. Suddenly there was a great number of additional clubs wanting to join the league.

The teams were split into a South Eastern with seventeen clubs and a North Western Zone comprising eighteen clubs. This situation led many of the clubs to ask the Chairman to introduce a supplementary competition to augment the reduction in the number of league fixtures.

SOUTHERN LEAGUE – INTER-ZONE COMPETITION

POS	CLUB	P	W	D	L	F	A	PTS
1	DARTFORD	8	5	1	2	19	14	11
2	CHELTENHAM TOWN	8	3	3	2	17	16	9
3	WORCESTER CITY	8	3	2	3	17	15	8
4	**GLOUCESTER CITY**	**8**	**2**	**3**	**3**	**13**	**17**	**7**
5	YIEWSLEY	8	1	3	4	7	11	5
		40	14	12	14	73	73	40

A Special General Meeting was held at the Great Western Hotel at Paddington on Saturday, 9th August, 1958 and after some discussion the delegates overwhelmingly agreed to an Inter-Zone competition divided into seven geographical groups.

Early in March 1959, the Management Committee decided that, in order to prevent congestion of fixtures and as the competition had achieved its object of filling vacant Saturdays, the competition should end when all clubs had played eight games. A small trophy was awarded to the winners of each zone.

SEASON 1959-1960
(Home Ground: The Ground, Cheltenham Road, Longlevens)

Date: Saturday 22/08/1959
Result: **GLOUCESTER CITY 3 MERTHYR TYDFIL 1**
Competition: Southern League Division 1
Teamsheet: Coltman, Kimberley, Weston, Etheridge, Smith, Gerrish, Symington, Morris, Norris, Coldray, Bowman
Scorers: Coldray, Symington, Morris
Note: Gloucester City were hypnotised by local hypnotist, Henry Blythe

Date: Monday 24/08/1959
Result: **CAMBRIDGE UNITED 2 GLOUCESTER CITY 1**
Competition: Southern League Division 1
Teamsheet: Coltman, Kimberley, Weston, Etheridge, Smith, Gerrish, Symington, Morris, Norris, Coldray, Bowman
Scorer: Bowman
Attendance: 4000

Date: Saturday 29/08/1959
Result: **RUGBY TOWN 1 GLOUCESTER CITY 1**
Competition: Southern League Division 1
Teamsheet: Teague, Kimberley, Weston, Gallagher, Smith, Gerrish, Symington, Morris, Ireland, Coldray, Bowman
Scorer: Morris
Attendance: 2000

Date: Monday 31/08/1959
Result: **WORCESTER CITY 2 GLOUCESTER CITY 0**
Competition: Southern League Cup Qualifying Round 1st Leg
Teamsheet: Teague, Kimberley, Weston, Gallagher, Smith, Gerrish, Symington, Morris, Coldray, Ireland, Bowman
Attendance: 4358

Date: Saturday 05/09/1959
Result: **YIEWSLEY 4 GLOUCESTER CITY 1**
Competition: Southern League Division 1
Teamsheet: Teague, Kimberley, Weston, Gerrish, Dear, Smith, Symington, Gallagher, Etheridge, Coldray, Hickey
Scorer: Smith

Date: Wednesday 09/09/1959
Result: **GLOUCESTER CITY 2 WORCESTER CITY 2**
Competition: Southern League Cup Qualifying Round 2nd Leg
Teamsheet: Barton, Myers, Weston, Gallagher, Smith, Bell, Symington, Coldray, Horlick, Box, Bowman
Scorers: own goal, Coldray

Date: Saturday 12/09/1959
Result: **GLOUCESTER CITY 5 MARGATE 1**
Competition: Southern League Division 1
Teamsheet: Teague, Myers, Weston, Gallagher, Smith, Bell, Symington, Coldray, Norris, Box, Bowman
Scorers: Coldray (3), Norris (2)

Date: Saturday 19/09/1959
Result: **GLOUCESTER CITY 1 CHELTENHAM TOWN 3**
Competition: FA Cup 1st Qualifying Round
Teamsheet: Teague, Myers, Weston, Gallagher, Smith, Bell, Symington, Coldray, Norris, Box, Bowman
Scorer: Coldray
Note: Gloucester City were hypnotised by local hypnotist, Henry Blythe

Date: Wednesday 23/09/1959
Result: **FOLKESTONE TOWN 3 GLOUCESTER CITY 0**
Competition: Southern League Division 1
Teamsheet: Barton, Kimberley, Myers, Etheridge, Dear, Bell, Symington, Coldray, Norris, Box, Bowman

Date: Saturday 26/09/1959
Result: **GLOUCESTER CITY 4 SITTINGBOURNE 2**
Competition: Southern League Division 1
Teamsheet: Barton, Myers, Kimberley, Gallagher, Smith, Bell, Symington, Morris, Norris, Coldray, Bowman
Scorers: Coldray, Norris, Myers (pen), Morris

Date: Saturday 03/10/1959
Result: **GUILDFORD CITY 6 GLOUCESTER CITY 0**
Competition: Southern League Division 1
Teamsheet: Barton, Kimberley, Lacey, Gallagher, Smith, Bell, Symington, Morris, Norris, Coldray, Bowman

Date: Saturday 10/10/1959
Result: **GLOUCESTER CITY 2 BEXLEYHEATH & WELLING 1**
Competition: Southern League Division 1
Teamsheet: Barton, Myers, Kimberley, Norris, Volpe, Bell, Symington, Coldray, Morris, Ireland, Bowman
Scorers: Coldray, Symington

Date: Saturday 17/10/1959
Result: **ROMFORD 3 GLOUCESTER CITY 1**
Competition: Southern League Division 1
Teamsheet: Teague, Myers, Weston, Bell, Smith, Gerrish, Symington, Coldray, Norris, Morris, Bowman
Scorer: Morris

Date: Wednesday 21/10/1959
Result: **GLOUCESTER CITY 2 CAMBRIDGE UNITED 3**
Competition: Southern League Division 1
Teamsheet: Barton, Myers, Weston, Bell, Smith, Gerrish, Symington, Norris, Gallagher, Coldray, Bowman
Scorers: Symington, Smith

Date: Saturday 24/10/1959
Result: **GLOUCESTER CITY 1 EXETER CITY RESERVES 0**
Competition: Southern League Division 1
Teamsheet: Barton, Myers, Weston, Etheridge, Smith, Bell, Symington, Norris, Gallagher, Ireland, Bowman
Scorer: Ireland

Date: Saturday 31/10/1959
Result: **HINCKLEY ATHLETIC 3 GLOUCESTER CITY 1**
Competition: Southern League Division 1
Teamsheet: Barton, Myers, Weston, Etheridge, Smith, Bell, Adlam, Norris, Ireland, Symington, Bowman
Scorer: Ireland

Date: Saturday 07/11/1959
Result: **GLOUCESTER CITY 0 BURTON ALBION 0**
Competition: Southern League Division 1
Teamsheet: Barton, Kimberley, Weston, Myers, Smith, Bell, Adlam, Norris, Horlick, Coldray, Bowman

Date: Saturday 14/11/1959
Result: **STONEHOUSE 2 GLOUCESTER CITY 2**
Competition: Gloucestershire FA Northern Senior Professional Cup Semi-Final
Teamsheet: Barton, Kimberley, Weston, Myers, Smith, Bell, Symington, Norris, Horlick, Coldray, Bowman
Scorers: Smith, Myers

Date: Saturday 21/11/1959
Result: **GLOUCESTER CITY 3 DOVER 4**
Competition: Southern League Division 1
Teamsheet: Barton, Dear, Kimberley, Myers, Smith, Bell, Symington, Coldray, Norris, Weston, Bowman
Scorers: Kimberley (pen), Coldray (2)
Attendance: 1400

Date: Thursday 26/11/1959
Result: **GLOUCESTER CITY 2 STONEHOUSE 1**
Competition: Gloucestershire FA Northern Senior Professional Cup Semi-Final Replay
Teamsheet: Barton, Dear, Kimberley, Etheridge, Volpe, Bell, Symington, Coldray, Norris, Weston, Box
Scorers: Kimberley (pen), Box

Date: Saturday 28/11/1959
Result: **ASHFORD TOWN 2 GLOUCESTER CITY 1**
Competition: Southern League Division 1
Teamsheet: Barton, Dear, Weston, Etheridge, Smith, Bell, Symington, Coldray, Horlick, Box, Bowman
Scorer: Bowman

Date: Saturday 05/12/1959
Result: **GLOUCESTER CITY 2 RAMSGATE ATHLETIC 2**
Competition: Southern League Division 1
Teamsheet: Barton, Dear, Kimberley, Bell, Volpe, Smith, Symington, Myers, Horlick, Weston, Bowman
Scorers: Kimberley (pen), Myers

Date: Saturday 12/12/1959
Result: **CLACTON TOWN 2 GLOUCESTER CITY 0**
Competition: Southern League Division 1
Teamsheet: Teague, Dear, Kimberley, Bell, Volpe, Smith, Symington, Myers, Lauder, Etheridge, Box
Attendance: 808

Date: Saturday 19/12/1959
Result: **MERTHYR TYDFIL 0 GLOUCESTER CITY 0**
Competition: Southern League Division 1
Teamsheet: Teague, Myers, Volpe, Etheridge, Smith, Bell, Symington, Horlick, Lauder, Box, Bowman

Date: Saturday 26/12/1959
Result: **KIDDERMINSTER HARRIERS 0 GLOUCESTER CITY 1**
Competition: Southern League Division 1
Teamsheet: Teague, Kimberley, Volpe, Myers, Smith, Bell, Adlam, Myers, Norris, Weston, Bowman
Scorer: Norris
Attendance: 1200

Date: Monday 28/12/1959
Result: **GLOUCESTER CITY 4 KIDDERMINSTER HARRIERS 0**
Competition: Southern League Division 1
Teamsheet: Teague, Kimberley, Clark, Myers, Volpe, Bell, Horlick, Etheridge, Norris, Box, Bowman
Scorers: Norris (2), Etheridge (2)

Date: Saturday 02/01/1960
Result: **GLOUCESTER CITY 1 RUGBY TOWN 0**
Competition: Southern League Division 1
Teamsheet: Teague, Kimberley, Volpe, Myers, Smith, Bell, Adlam, Etheridge, Norris, Box, Bowman
Scorer: Norris

Date: Saturday 09/01/1960
Result: **CORBY TOWN 1 GLOUCESTER CITY 0**
Competition: Southern League Division 1
Teamsheet: Teague, Kimberley, Volpe, Myers, Smith, Bell, Symington, Etheridge, Norris, Lauder, Box

Date: Saturday 16/01/1960
Result: **GLOUCESTER CITY 1 YIEWSLEY 2**
Competition: Southern League Division 1
Teamsheet: Teague, Kimberley, Volpe, Myers, Smith, Bell, Symington, Etheridge, Horlick, Box, Hickey
Scorer: Box

Date: Saturday 23/01/1960
Result: **MARGATE 5 GLOUCESTER CITY 2**
Competition: Southern League Division 1
Teamsheet: Barton, Kimberley, Volpe, Myers, Smith, Bell, Symington, Etheridge, Horlick, Box, Bowman
Scorers: -----, -----
Attendance: 1720

Date: Saturday 30/01/1960
Result: **GLOUCESTER CITY 0 CORBY TOWN 0**
Competition: Southern League Division 1
Teamsheet: Teague, Tredgett, Clark, Myers, Smith, Bell, Hickey, Symington, Etheridge, Day, Bowman

Date: Saturday 06/02/1960
Result: **GLOUCESTER CITY 0 FOLKESTONE TOWN 2**
Competition: Southern League Division 1
Teamsheet: Teague, Tredgett, Clark, Myers, Smith, Bell, Symington, Day, Etheridge, Lauder, Hickey

Date: Saturday 20/02/1960
Result: **GLOUCESTER CITY 1 GUILDFORD CITY 1**
Competition: Southern League Division 1
Teamsheet: Teague, Clark, Dear, Etheridge, Smith, Myers, Symington, Lauder, Horlick, Bell, Hickey
Scorer: Horlick

Date: Saturday 27/02/1960
Result: **BEXLEYHEATH & WELLING 10 GLOUCESTER CITY 0**
Competition: Southern League Division 1
Teamsheet: Teague, Kimberley, Dear, Etheridge, Smith, Myers, Symington, Iddles, Horlick, Bell, Hickey

Date: Saturday 12/03/1960
Result: **EXETER CITY RESERVES 3 GLOUCESTER CITY 2**
Competition: Southern League Division 1
Teamsheet: Teague, Kimberley, Volpe, Myers, Smith, Bell, Adlam, Gallagher, Horlick, Kettleborough, Hickey
Scorer: Horlick (2)
Attendance: 1767

Date: Saturday 19/03/1960
Result: **GLOUCESTER CITY 1 HINCKLEY ATHLETIC 1**
Competition: Southern League Division 1
Teamsheet: Teague, Kimberley, Volpe, Myers, Smith, Bell, Adlam, Gallagher, Horlick, Kettleborough, Hickey
Scorer: Hickey

Date: Saturday 26/03/1960
Result: **BURTON ALBION 0 GLOUCESTER CITY 0**
Competition: Southern League Division 1
Teamsheet: Teague, Kimberley, Volpe, Myers, Smith, Bell, Adlam, Gallagher, Horlick, Lauder, Hickey
Attendance: 1000

Date: Saturday 02/04/1960
Result: **GLOUCESTER CITY 0 ROMFORD 1**
Competition: Southern League Division 1
Teamsheet: Teague, Kimberley, Volpe, Myers, Smith, Bell, Adlam, Gallagher, Horlick, Kettleborough, Hickey

Date: Saturday 09/04/1960
Result: **DOVER 2 GLOUCESTER CITY 3**
Competition: Southern League Division 1
Teamsheet: Teague, Clark, Lacey, Gallagher, Tredgett, Bell, Symington, Etheridge, Smith, Day, Hickey
Scorers: Symington (2), Smith
Attendance: 1207

Date: Friday 15/04/1960
Result: **TROWBRIDGE TOWN 3 GLOUCESTER CITY 2**
Competition: Southern League Division 1
Teamsheet: Teague, Clark, Lacey, Gallagher, Tredgett, Etheridge, Adlam, Symington, Smith, Day, Hickey
Scorers: Smith, Tredgett
Attendance: 1683

Date: Saturday 16/04/1960
Result: **GLOUCESTER CITY 2 ASHFORD TOWN 0**
Competition: Southern League Division 1
Teamsheet: Teague, Clark, Lacey, Gallagher, Tredgett, Etheridge, Adlam, Symington, Smith, Day, Hickey
Scorers: Smith, Gallagher (pen)

Date: Monday 18/04/1960
Result: **GLOUCESTER CITY 1 TROWBRIDGE TOWN 0**
Competition: Southern League Division 1
Teamsheet: Teague, Clark, Lacey, Gallagher, Tredgett, Etheridge, Adlam, Symington, Smith, Day, Hickey
Scorer: Hickey

Date: Wednesday 20/04/1960
Result: **GLOUCESTER CITY 1 TUNBRIDGE WELLS UNITED 0**
Competition: Southern League Division 1
Teamsheet: Teague, Clark, Lacey, Gallagher, Tredgett, Etheridge, Adlam, Symington, Smith, Day, Hickey
Scorer: Day

Date: Saturday 23/04/1960
Result: **RAMSGATE ATHLETIC 3 GLOUCESTER CITY 3**
Competition: Southern League Division 1
Teamsheet: Barton, Clark, Lacey, Myers, Smith, Etheridge, Adlam, Symington, Horlick, Day, Hickey
Scorers: Day, Horlick (2)

Date: Wednesday 27/04/1960
Result: **CHELTENHAM TOWN 1 GLOUCESTER CITY 0**
Competition: Gloucestershire FA Northern Senior Professional Cup Final
Teamsheet: Barton, Myers, Lacey, Gallagher, Clark, Bell, Adlam, Symington, Horlick, Day, Hickey

Date: Saturday 30/04/1960
Result: **GLOUCESTER CITY 3 CLACTON TOWN 1**
Competition: Southern League Division 1
Teamsheet: Barton, Clark, Lacey, Bell, Tredgett, Etheridge, Adlam, Symington, Smith, Day, Hickey
Scorers: Symington, Smith (2)

Date: Wednesday 04/05/1960
Result: **SITTINGBOURNE 3 GLOUCESTER CITY 0**
Competition: Southern League Division 1
Teamsheet: Barton, Myers, Lacey, Etheridge, Tredgett, Bell, Adlam, Symington, Smith, Day, Hickey

Date: ?
Result:**TUNBRIDGE WELLS UNITED 6 GLOUCESTER CITY 0**
Competition: Southern League Division 1
Teamsheet: -----, -----, -----, -----, -----, -----, -----, -----, -----, -----, -----

Appearances – B Adlam 16, P Barton 19, E Bell 37, A Bowman 26, AF Box 13, JD Clark 12, RA Coldray 19, RL Coltman 2, H Day 11, GA Dear 9, RF Etheridge 27, J Gallagher 20, MC Gerrish 7, W Hickey 19, G Horlick 17, ? Iddles 1, R Ireland 5, A Kettleborough 3, A Kimberley 26, B Lacey 10, ? Lauder 6, MJG Morris 8, S Myers 34, OP Norris 20, A Smith 42, AGW Symington 39, WE Teague 26, KF Tredgett 9, KS Volpe 15, J Weston 19.
Scorers – RA Coldray 10, A Smith 8, OP Norris 7, AGW Symington 6, G Horlick 5, MJG Morris 4, A Kimberley 3, S Myers 3, A Bowman 2, AF Box 2, H Day 2, RF Etheridge 2, W Hickey 2, R Ireland 2, J Gallagher 1, KF Tredgett 1, own goal 1.

SOUTHERN LEAGUE DIVISION 1

POS	CLUB	P	W	D	L	F	A	PTS
1	CLACTON TOWN	42	27	5	10	106	69	59
2	ROMFORD	42	21	11	10	65	40	53
3	FOLKESTONE TOWN	42	23	5	14	93	71	51
4	EXETER CITY RESERVES	42	23	3	16	85	63	49
5	GUILDFORD CITY	42	19	9	14	79	56	47
6	SITTINGBOURNE	42	20	7	15	66	56	47
7	MARGATE	42	20	6	16	88	77	46
8	TROWBRIDGE TOWN	42	18	9	15	89	78	45
9	CAMBRIDGE UNITED	42	18	9	15	71	72	45
10	YIEWSLEY	42	17	10	15	83	71	44
11	BEXLEYHEATH & WELLING	42	16	11	15	85	77	43
12	MERTHYR TYDFIL	42	16	10	16	63	65	42
13	RAMSGATE ATHLETIC	42	16	8	18	84	85	40
14	ASHFORD TOWN	42	14	12	16	61	70	40
15	TUNBRIDGE WELLS UNITED	42	17	5	20	77	73	39
16	HINCKLEY ATHLETIC	42	14	8	20	62	74	36
17	**GLOUCESTER CITY**	**42**	**13**	**9**	**20**	**56**	**84**	**35**
18	DOVER	42	14	6	22	59	85	34
19	KIDDERMINSTER HARRIERS	42	14	6	22	59	97	34
20	CORBY TOWN	42	15	3	24	75	91	33
21	BURTON ALBION	42	11	10	21	51	79	32
22	RUGBY TOWN	42	10	11	21	67	91	31
		924	376	173	375	1624	1624	925

SEASON 1960-1961
(Home Ground: The Ground, Cheltenham Road, Longlevens)

Date: Saturday 20/08/1960
Result: **GLOUCESTER CITY 3 TUNBRIDGE WELLS UNITED 0**
Competition: Southern League Division 1
Teamsheet: Barton, Weston, B Lacey, Myers, Greenaway, Bell, Adlam, Symington, Horlick, Box, Bowman
Scorers: Bell (pen), Adlam, Horlick

Date: Tuesday 23/08/1960
Result: **CORBY TOWN 3 GLOUCESTER CITY 0**
Competition: Southern League Division 1
Teamsheet: Barton, Weston, B Lacey, Myers, Greenaway, Bell, Adlam, Symington, Horlick, Box, Bowman

Date: Saturday 27/08/1960
Result: **RUGBY TOWN 3 GLOUCESTER CITY 0**
Competition: Southern League Division 1
Teamsheet: Barton, Meek, B Lacey, Elliott, Greenaway, Box, Adlam, Symington, Horlick, Weston, Bowman

Date: Wednesday 31/08/1960
Result: **GLOUCESTER CITY 1 MERTHYR TYDFIL 3**
Competition: Southern League Cup Qualifying Round 1st Leg
Teamsheet: Barton, Meek, B Lacey, Elliott, Greenaway, J Lacey, Bowman, Symington, Horlick, Weston, Box
Scorer: Weston

Date: Saturday 03/09/1960
Result: **GLOUCESTER CITY 1 CANTERBURY CITY 1**
Competition: Southern League Division 1
Teamsheet: Barton, Meek, B Lacey, Bell, Greenaway, Box, Adlam, Symington, Horlick, Weston, Bowman
Scorer: Symington

Date: Wednesday 07/09/1960
Result: **MERTHYR TYDFIL 6 GLOUCESTER CITY 1**
Competition: Southern League Cup Qualifying Round 2nd Leg
Teamsheet: Wood, Meek, Weston, Elliott, Greenaway, Bell, Adlam, Symington, Horlick, Cooper, Box
Scorer: Symington

Date: Saturday 10/09/1960
Result: **GLOUCESTER CITY 1 CHELTENHAM TOWN 4**
Competition: FA Cup 1st Qualifying Round
Teamsheet: Barton, Meek, B Lacey, Myers, Greenaway, Bell, Bowman, Symington, Horlick, Weston, Box
Scorer: Horlick

Date: Wednesday 14/09/1960
Result: **GLOUCESTER CITY 0 CORBY TOWN 0**
Competition: Southern League Division 1
Teamsheet: Barton, Meek, B Lacey, Elliott, Bell, Weston, Adlam, Horlick, Greenaway, Symington, Bowman

Date: Saturday 17/09/1960
Result: **RAMSGATE ATHLETIC 4 GLOUCESTER CITY 0**
Competition: Southern League Division 1
Teamsheet: Barton, Meek, B Lacey, Elliott, Greenaway, Bell, Adlam, Weston, Horlick, Bowman, Cooper
Attendance: 2100

Date: Wednesday 21/09/1960
Result: **GLOUCESTER CITY 1 TROWBRIDGE TOWN 1**
Competition: Southern League Division 1
Teamsheet: Barton, Meek, B Lacey, McLean, Bell, Weston, Adlam, Horlick, Dunleavy, Greenaway, Bowman
Scorer: own goal

Date: Saturday 24/09/1960
Result: **GLOUCESTER CITY 1 ASHFORD TOWN 2**
Competition: Southern League Division 1
Teamsheet: Barton, Meek, B Lacey, McLean, Bell, Weston, Adlam, Horlick, Dunleavy, Symington, Bowman
Scorer: Dunleavy

Date: Saturday 01/10/1960
Result: **NUNEATON BOROUGH 4 GLOUCESTER CITY 0**
Competition: Southern League Division 1
Teamsheet: Barton, Meek, B Lacey, McLean, Bell, Weston, Adlam, Cooper, Greenaway, Symington, Bowman

Date: Saturday 08/10/1960
Result: **GLOUCESTER CITY 2 STONEHOUSE 0**
Competition: Gloucestershire FA Northern Senior Professional Cup Semi-Final
Teamsheet: Barton, Meek, B Lacey, McLean, Bell, Weston, Adlam, England, Symington, Day, Bowman
Scorers: -----, -----

Date: Saturday 15/10/1960
Result: **GLOUCESTER CITY 0 MARGATE 3**
Competition: Southern League Division 1
Teamsheet: Barton, Meek, B Lacey, McLean, Bell, Weston, Adlam, Simkin, England, Day, Bowman
Attendance: 900

Date: Saturday 22/10/1960
Result: **YIEWSLEY 4 GLOUCESTER CITY 0**
Competition: Southern League Division 1
Teamsheet: Barton, Meek, B Lacey, Myers, Bell, Weston, Symington, Simkin, Horlick, Day, Bowman

Date: Saturday 29/10/1960
Result: **GLOUCESTER CITY 0 BURTON ALBION 3**
Competition: Southern League Division 1
Teamsheet: Barton, Meek, Weston, McLean, Bell, Myers, Symington, England, Dunleavy, Horlick, Bowman

Date: Saturday 05/11/1960
Result: **SITTINGBOURNE 3 GLOUCESTER CITY 2**
Competition: Southern League Division 1
Teamsheet: Barton, Myers, B Lacey, Elliott, Meek, Bell, Symington, England, Horlick, Weston, Bowman
Scorers: Bell, England

Date: Saturday 12/11/1960
Result: **GLOUCESTER CITY 2 MERTHYR TYDFIL 6**
Competition: Southern League Division 1
Teamsheet: Barton, Myers, B Lacey, Day, Meek, Bell, Symington, England, Horlick, Weston, Bowman
Scorer: Horlick (2)

Date: Saturday 19/11/1960
Result: **ASHFORD TOWN 5 GLOUCESTER CITY 1**
Competition: Southern League Division 1
Teamsheet: Barton, Meek, B Lacey, Myers, Bell, McLean, Adlam, Symington, Horlick, Day, Weston
Scorer: Day

Date: Saturday 03/12/1960
Result: **DOVER 1 GLOUCESTER CITY 2**
Competition: Southern League Division 1
Teamsheet: Barton, Weston, Dunn, Myers, Coltman, Bell, Adlam, England, Horlick, Symington, Box
Scorers: Bell, Horlick
Attendance: 540

Date: Saturday 10/12/1960
Result: **GLOUCESTER CITY 1 BARRY TOWN 0**
Competition: Southern League Division 1
Teamsheet: Barton, Weston, Dunn, Myers, Coltman, Bell, Adlam, England, Horlick, Symington, Box
Scorer: England

Date: Saturday 17/12/1960
Result: **TUNBRIDGE WELLS UNITED 4 GLOUCESTER CITY 0**
Competition: Southern League Division 1
Teamsheet: Barton, Weston, Dunn, Myers, Coltman, Bell, Adlam, England, Horlick, Symington, Box

Date: Saturday 24/12/1960
Result: **POOLE TOWN 5 GLOUCESTER CITY 0**
Competition: Southern League Division 1
Teamsheet: Barton, Weston, Dunn, Myers, Coltman, Bell, Symington, Adlam, Horlick, Cooper, Bowman

Date: Monday 26/12/1960
Result: **GLOUCESTER CITY 1 POOLE TOWN 0**
Competition: Southern League Division 1
Teamsheet: Barton, Myers, Weston, McLean, Coltman, Bell, Adlam, Symington, Horlick, Cooper, Bowman
Scorer: Horlick

Date: Saturday 07/01/1961
Result: **HINCKLEY ATHLETIC 2 GLOUCESTER CITY 1**
Competition: Southern League Division 1
Teamsheet: Barton, Weston, Dunn, Myers, Coltman, Day, Adlam, Symington, Horlick, Bell, Cooper
Scorer: Adlam

Date: Saturday 14/01/1961
Result: **CANTERBURY CITY 1 GLOUCESTER CITY 0**
Competition: Southern League Division 1
Teamsheet: Barton, Weston, Dunn, Myers, Coltman, Day, Adlam, Symington, Horlick, Bell, Cooper

Date: Saturday 21/01/1961
Result: **TROWBRIDGE TOWN 2 GLOUCESTER CITY 1**
Competition: Southern League Division 1
Teamsheet: Barton, Weston, Dunn, Myers, Coltman, Bell, Adlam, Day, Horlick, Symington, Friel
Scorer: Symington

Date: Saturday 28/01/1961
Result: **GLOUCESTER CITY 1 HINCKLEY ATHLETIC 1**
Competition: Southern League Division 1
Teamsheet: Barton, Weston, Myers, McLean, Coltman, Bell, Adlam, Day, Horlick, Symington, Friel
Scorer: Adlam

Date: Saturday 04/02/1961
Result: **GLOUCESTER CITY 0 RAMSGATE ATHLETIC 1**
Competition: Southern League Division 1
Teamsheet: Barton, Weston, Myers, McLean, Coltman, Bell, Adlam, Day, Horlick, Symington, Friel

Date: Saturday 11/02/1961
Result: **CAMBRIDGE UNITED 3 GLOUCESTER CITY 2**
Competition: Southern League Division 1
Teamsheet: Barton, Myers, Weston, McLean, Coltman, Bell, Adlam, England, Horlick, Symington, Box
Scorer: Adlam (2)
Attendance: 2875

Date: Saturday 18/02/1961
Result: **GLOUCESTER CITY 2 RUGBY TOWN 1**
Competition: Southern League Division 1
Teamsheet: Barton, Myers, Weston, McLean, Coltman, Bell, Adlam, Walker, Horlick, Symington, Box
Scorer: Symington (2)

Date: Saturday 25/02/1961
Result: **GLOUCESTER CITY 3 NUNEATON BOROUGH 0**
Competition: Southern League Division 1
Teamsheet: Barton, Weston, Dunn, McLean, Coltman, Bell, Adlam, Symington, Horlick, England, Box
Scorers: Adlam, Symington, Bell

Date: Saturday 04/03/1961
Result: **MARGATE 1 GLOUCESTER CITY 1**
Competition: Southern League Division 1
Teamsheet: Barton, Myers, B Lacey, McLean, Coltman, Bell, Adlam, Elliott, Horlick, England, Box
Scorer: England
Attendance: 1296

Date: Saturday 11/03/1961
Result: **GLOUCESTER CITY 0 YIEWSLEY 0**
Competition: Southern League Division 1
Teamsheet: Barton, Weston, B Lacey, McLean, Coltman, Bell, Adlam, Symington, Horlick, England, Box

Date: Thursday 16/03/1961
Result: **GLOUCESTER CITY 4 CAMBRIDGE UNITED 4**
Competition: Southern League Division 1
Teamsheet: Barton, Weston, B Lacey, McLean, Coltman, Bell, Adlam, Symington, Horlick, England, Box
Scorers: Symington, England, Adlam, Horlick

Date: Saturday 18/03/1961
Result: **MERTHYR TYDFIL 2 GLOUCESTER CITY 0**
Competition: Southern League Division 1
Teamsheet: Barton, Weston, B Lacey, McLean, Coltman, Bell, Adlam, Symington, Horlick, England, Box

Date: Saturday 25/03/1961
Result: **GLOUCESTER CITY 3 SITTINGBOURNE 1**
Competition: Southern League Division 1
Teamsheet: Barton, Weston, B Lacey, McLean, Coltman, Myers, Adlam, Symington, Horlick, Bell, Box
Scorers: Symington (2, 1 pen), Box

Date: Friday 31/03/1961
Result: **GLOUCESTER CITY 0 BEXLEYHEATH & WELLING 3**
Competition: Southern League Division 1
Teamsheet: Wood, Dunn, B Lacey, McLean, Coltman, Myers, Adlam, Symington, Horlick, Bell, Box

Date: Saturday 01/04/1961
Result: **BURTON ALBION 8 GLOUCESTER CITY 1**
Competition: Southern League Division 1
Teamsheet: Barton, B Lacey, Dunn, McLean, Coltman, Myers, Cooper, Symington, Horlick, Bell, Box
Scorer: Cooper

Date: Monday 10/04/1961
Result: **GLOUCESTER CITY 0 KETTERING TOWN 2**
Competition: Southern League Division 1
Teamsheet: Trigg, Weston, Dunn, Day, Coltman, Myers, Adlam, Elliott, Symington, Box, B Lacey

Date: Saturday 15/04/1961
Result: **KETTERING TOWN 6 GLOUCESTER CITY 1**
Competition: Southern League Division 1
Teamsheet: Barton, Dunn, B Lacey, Myers, Coltman, Bell, Adlam, Symington, Horlick, England, Box
Scorer: Adlam

Date: Tuesday 18/04/1961
Result: **BARRY TOWN 2 GLOUCESTER CITY 1**
Competition: Southern League Division 1
Teamsheet: Trigg, Goode, B Lacey, Elliott, Coltman, Meek, Adlam, Symington, Horlick, Box, Cooper
Scorer: Horlick

Date: Saturday 22/04/1961
Result: **GLOUCESTER CITY 3 DOVER 4**
Competition: Southern League Division 1
Teamsheet: Barton, Weston, Dunn, Elliott, Coltman, Bell, Adlam, Symington, Horlick, Box, B Lacey
Scorers: Horlick (2), Symington
Attendance: 600

Date: Monday 24/04/1961
Result: **BEXLEYHEATH & WELLING 7 GLOUCESTER CITY 1**
Competition: Southern League Division 1
Teamsheet: Trigg, Dunn, B Lacey, Elliott, Meek, Bell, Adlam, Symington, Horlick, Box, Cooper
Scorer: Box
Attendance: 1060

Date: Thursday 04/05/1961
Result: **GLOUCESTER CITY 1 CHELTENHAM TOWN 3**
Competition: Gloucestershire FA Northern Senior Professional Cup Final
Teamsheet: Barton, Weston, Dunn, Horlick, Coltman, Bell, Adlam, England, Reynolds, Symington, Box
Scorer: Symington

Appearances – B Adlam 38, P Barton 40, E Bell 41, A Bowman 19, AF Box 26, MJ Coltman 25, J Cooper 10, H Day 11, MD Dunleavy 3, R Dunn 15, H Elliott 11, M England 16, P Friel 3, ? Goode 1, G Greenaway 11, G Horlick 41, B Lacey 29, J Lacey 1, I McLean 20, D Meek 19, S Myers 26, D Reynolds 1, FG Simkin 2, AGW Symington 41, IM Trigg 3, ? Walker 1, J Weston 39, LB Wood 2.
Scorers – AGW Symington 11, G Horlick 10, B Adlam 8, E Bell 4, M England 4, AF Box 2, J Cooper 1, H Day 1, MD Dunleavy 1, J Weston 1, own goal 1.

PROGRAMME

1961-1962

SOUTHERN LEAGUE DIVISION 1

POS	CLUB	P	W	D	L	F	A	PTS
1	KETTERING TOWN	40	26	7	7	100	55	59
2	CAMBRIDGE UNITED	40	25	5	10	100	53	55
3	BEXLEYHEATH & WELLING	40	22	8	10	93	46	52
4	MERTHYR TYDFIL	40	23	6	11	88	65	52
5	SITTINGBOURNE	40	21	10	9	77	63	52
6	HINCKLEY ATHLETIC	40	17	13	10	73	59	47
7	RAMSGATE ATHLETIC	40	19	7	14	77	56	45
8	RUGBY TOWN	40	18	9	13	89	71	45
9	CORBY TOWN	40	16	10	14	82	73	42
10	POOLE TOWN	40	18	5	17	71	65	41
11	BARRY TOWN	40	16	9	15	65	74	41
12	YIEWSLEY	40	17	7	16	65	76	41
13	TROWBRIDGE TOWN	40	14	10	16	71	73	38
14	ASHFORD TOWN	40	14	8	18	61	67	36
15	MARGATE	40	11	12	17	62	75	34
16	DOVER	40	12	7	21	67	74	31
17	CANTERBURY CITY	40	10	10	20	52	75	30
18	NUNEATON BOROUGH	40	11	7	22	60	91	29
19	BURTON ALBION	40	12	4	24	64	85	28
20	TUNBRIDGE WELLS UNITED	40	8	5	27	56	115	21
21	**GLOUCESTER CITY**	**40**	**7**	**7**	**26**	**40**	**102**	**21**
		840	337	166	337	1513	1513	840

SEASON 1961-1962
(Home Ground: The Ground, Cheltenham Road, Longlevens)

Date: Saturday 19/08/1961
Result: **GLOUCESTER CITY 2 RAMSGATE ATHLETIC 1**
Competition: Southern League Division 1
Teamsheet: Barton, Weston, Dunn, Reeves, Hyde, Bell, Adlam, Sampson, Skull, Evans, Rothin
Scorers: -----, -----

Date: Saturday 26/08/1961
Result: **TROWBRIDGE TOWN 3 GLOUCESTER CITY 1**
Competition: Southern League Division 1
Teamsheet: Barton, Weston, Dunn, Reeves, Hyde, Bell, Adlam, Sampson, Skull, Evans, Keylock
Scorer: -----

Date: Thursday 31/08/1961
Result: **GLOUCESTER CITY 1 YEOVIL TOWN 2**
Competition: Southern League Cup Qualifying Round 1st Leg
Teamsheet: Barton, Weston, Dunn, Keylock, Hyde, Bell, Adlam, Skull, Horlick, Sampson, Evans
Scorer: Horlick

Date: Saturday 02/09/1961
Result: **GLOUCESTER CITY 3 HASTINGS UNITED 2**
Competition: Southern League Division 1
Teamsheet: Barton, Weston, Dunn, Keylock, Hyde, Bell, Adlam, Skull, Horlick, Sampson, Evans
Scorers: Skull, Sampson, Evans

Date: Wednesday 06/09/1961
Result: **YEOVIL TOWN 5 GLOUCESTER CITY 0**
Competition: Southern League Cup Qualifying Round 2nd Leg
Teamsheet: Barton, Reeves, Weston, Keylock, Hyde, Bell, Adlam, Sampson, Skull, Rothin, Evans

Date: Saturday 09/09/1961
Result: **GLOUCESTER CITY 5 STONEHOUSE 1**
Competition: FA Cup 1st Qualifying Round
Teamsheet: Barton, Weston, Dunn, Keylock, Hyde, Bell, Adlam, Skull, Horlick, Sampson, Evans
Scorers: Skull, Bell, Horlick (3)

Date: Saturday 16/09/1961
Result: **GLOUCESTER CITY 2 YIEWSLEY 3**
Competition: Southern League Division 1
Teamsheet: Barton, Reeves, Weston, Evans, Hyde, Bell, Adlam, Skull, Horlick, Sampson, Cooper
Scorers: Evans (pen), Hyde

Date: Saturday 23/09/1961
Result: **GLOUCESTER CITY 0 BARRY TOWN 0**
Competition: FA Cup 2nd Qualifying Round
Teamsheet: Barton, Weston, Dunn, Keylock, Hyde, Bell, Adlam, Skull, Horlick, Sampson, Evans

Date: Wednesday 27/09/1961
Result: **BARRY TOWN 2 GLOUCESTER CITY 1**
Competition: FA Cup 2nd Qualifying Round Replay
Teamsheet: Barton, Reeves, Weston, Evans, Hyde, Keylock, Adlam, Horlick, Skull, Bell, Day
Scorer: Horlick

[174]

Date: Saturday 30/09/1961
Result: **GLOUCESTER CITY 2 TUNBRIDGE WELLS UNITED 1**
Competition: Southern League Division 1
Teamsheet: Barton, Weston, Dunn, Evans, Hyde, Keylock, Adlam, Skull, Horlick, Bell, England
Scorers: England, Adlam

Date: Saturday 07/10/1961
Result: **GLOUCESTER CITY 0 SITTINGBOURNE 2**
Competition: Southern League Division 1
Teamsheet: Barton, Reeves, Dunn, Evans, Hyde, Keylock, Adlam, Skull, Horlick, England, Bell

Date: Wednesday 11/10/1961
Result: **BARRY TOWN 5 GLOUCESTER CITY 0**
Competition: Southern League Division 1
Teamsheet: Trigg, Reeves, Clark, Evans, Keylock, Bell, England, Skull, Horlick, Rothin, Cooper

Date: Saturday 14/10/1961
Result: **DOVER 1 GLOUCESTER CITY 1**
Competition: Southern League Division 1
Teamsheet: Barton, Reeves, Weston, Keylock, Hyde, Bell, Adlam, Skull, Horlick, Cooper, Clark
Scorer: Clark (pen)
Attendance: 1920

Date: Thursday 19/10/1961
Result: **GLOUCESTER CITY 8 STONEHOUSE 1**
Competition: Gloucestershire FA Northern Senior Professional Cup Semi-Final
Teamsheet: Barton, Clark, Weston, Keylock, Hyde, Bell, Adlam, Horlick, Skull, Day, Cooper
Scorers: Skull (4), Horlick (3), Cooper

Date: Saturday 21/10/1961
Result: **NUNEATON BOROUGH 4 GLOUCESTER CITY 1**
Competition: Southern League Division 1
Teamsheet: Barton, Clark, Weston, Keylock, Hyde, Bell, Adlam, Horlick, Skull, Day, England
Scorer: Horlick
Attendance: 1955

Date: Saturday 28/10/1961
Result: **CORBY TOWN 4 GLOUCESTER CITY 0**
Competition: Southern League Division 1
Teamsheet: Barton, Reeves, Dunn, Keylock, Hyde, Bell, Adlam, Horlick, Skull, Weston, Day

Date: Saturday 04/11/1961
Result: **GLOUCESTER CITY 3 HINCKLEY ATHLETIC 3**
Competition: Southern League Division 1
Teamsheet: Barton, Reeves, Dunn, Keylock, Hyde, Bell, Adlam, Evans, Horlick, Weston, England
Scorers: -----, -----, -----

Date: Saturday 11/11/1961
Result: **CANTERBURY CITY 4 GLOUCESTER CITY 0**
Competition: Southern League Division 1
Teamsheet: Barton, Reeves, Dunn, Keylock, Hyde, Bell, Adlam, Evans, Horlick, Weston, Clark

Date: Saturday 18/11/1961
Result: **GLOUCESTER CITY 1 RUGBY TOWN 2**
Competition: Southern League Division 1
Teamsheet: Barton, Reeves, Dunn, Keylock, Hyde, Bell, Adlam, Horlick, Skull, Weston, Killan
Scorer: Hyde (pen)

Date: Saturday 25/11/1961
Result: **BURTON ALBION 4 GLOUCESTER CITY 1**
Competition: Southern League Division 1
Teamsheet: Barton, Clark, Dunn, Keylock, Reeves, Bell, Adlam, Hyde, Horlick, Weston, Killan
Scorer: Weston
Attendance: 1020

Date: Saturday 02/12/1961
Result: **GLOUCESTER CITY 4 MARGATE 1**
Competition: Southern League Division 1
Teamsheet: Barton, Reeves, Dunn, Keylock, Hyde, Bell, Adlam, England, Skull, Weston, Killan
Scorers: Killan, Skull (3)
Attendance: 650

Date: Saturday 09/12/1961
Result: **SITTINGBOURNE 3 GLOUCESTER CITY 1**
Competition: Southern League Division 1
Teamsheet: Barton, Reeves, Dunn, Keylock, Hyde, Bell, Anderson, Weston, Skull, England, Cooper
Scorer: -----

Date: Saturday 16/12/1961
Result: **RAMSGATE ATHLETIC 1 GLOUCESTER CITY 0**
Competition: Southern League Division 1
Teamsheet: Barton, Reeves, Dunn, Keylock, Hyde, Bell, Anderson, Weston, Skull, Sampson, Neuman
Attendance: 922

Date: Saturday 23/12/1961
Result: **GLOUCESTER CITY 1 TROWBRIDGE TOWN 2**
Competition: Southern League Division 1
Teamsheet: Barton, Reeves, Dunn, Keylock, Hyde, Bell, Anderson, Weston, Skull, Sampson, England
Scorer: -----

Date: Tuesday 26/12/1961
Result: **POOLE TOWN 6 GLOUCESTER CITY 0**
Competition: Southern League Division 1
Teamsheet: Barton, Reeves, Goode, Keylock, Hyde, Bell, Cooper, Weston, Skull, Sampson, Cullunbine

Date: Saturday 13/01/1962
Result**: HASTINGS UNITED 3 GLOUCESTER CITY 2**
Competition: Southern League Division 1
Teamsheet: Barton, Reeves, Clark, Keylock, Hyde, Bell, Skull, Weston, Horlick, Cooper, Cherry
Scorers: Cooper, Weston
Attendance: 585

Date: Saturday 20/01/1962
Result: **GLOUCESTER CITY 2 NUNEATON BOROUGH 2**
Competition: Southern League Division 1
Teamsheet: Barton, Reeves, Dunn, Keylock, Hyde, Bell, Simcock, Weston, Skull, Anderson, Day
Scorer: Day (2)

Date: Saturday 27/01/1962
Result: **WISBECH TOWN 1 GLOUCESTER CITY 0**
Competition: Southern League Division 1
Teamsheet: Barton, Reeves, Dunn, Keylock, Hyde, Bell, Simcock, Weston, Skull, Gallagher, Day

Date: Saturday 03/02/1962
Result: **YIEWSLEY 3 GLOUCESTER CITY 2**
Competition: Southern League Division 1
Teamsheet: Barton, Bell, Dunn, Small, Hyde, Keylock, Skull, Horlick, Gallagher, Weston, Simcock
Scorers: Weston, Skull

Date: Saturday 10/02/1962
Result: **GLOUCESTER CITY 3 BARRY TOWN 1**
Competition: Southern League Division 1
Teamsheet: Wood, Bell, Dunn, Small, Hyde, Keylock, Skull, Horlick, Gallagher, Weston, Simcock
Scorers: Gallagher, Small, Weston

Date: Saturday 17/02/1962
Result: **TUNBRIDGE WELLS UNITED 3 GLOUCESTER CITY 2**
Competition: Southern League Division 1
Teamsheet: Wood, Reeves, Bell, Small, Hyde, Keylock, Blythe, Gallagher, Skull, Weston, Simcock
Scorers: Blythe, Weston

Date: Saturday 24/02/1962
Result: **ASHFORD TOWN 3 GLOUCESTER CITY 1**
Competition: Southern League Division 1
Teamsheet: Wood, Bell, Dunn, Small, Hyde, Keylock, Horlick, Weston, Skull, Gallagher, Blythe
Scorer: Small

Date: Saturday 03/03/1962
Result: **GLOUCESTER CITY 0 CORBY TOWN 4**
Competition: Southern League Division 1
Teamsheet: Barton, Bell, Dunn, Small, Keylock, Day, Horlick, Gallagher, Skull, Weston, Simcocks

Date: Saturday 10/03/1962
Result: **HINCKLEY ATHLETIC 7 GLOUCESTER CITY 2**
Competition: Southern League Division 1
Teamsheet: Barton, Reeves, Dunn, Small, Hyde, Bell, Hobbs, Keylock, Horlick, Gallagher, Blythe
Scorer: Horlick (2)

Date: Thursday 15/03/1962
Result: **GLOUCESTER CITY 1 WISBECH TOWN 1**
Competition: Southern League Division 1
Teamsheet: Barton, Bell, Weston, Small, Clark, Keylock, Blythe, Gallagher, Horlick, Anderson, Cooper
Scorer: Cooper

Date: Saturday 17/03/1962
Result: **GLOUCESTER CITY 1 CANTERBURY CITY 3**
Competition: Southern League Division 1
Teamsheet: Barton, Bell, Reeves, Hobbs, Hyde, Keylock, Skull, Sampson, Horlick, Anderson, Simcock
Scorer: Skull

Date: Saturday 24/03/1962
Result: **RUGBY TOWN 3 GLOUCESTER CITY 1**
Competition: Southern League Division 1
Teamsheet: Barton, Reeves, Weston, Bell, Hyde, Keylock, Cooper, Sampson, Skull, Gallagher, Simcock
Scorer: Simcock

Date: Saturday 31/03/1962
Result: **GLOUCESTER CITY 2 BURTON ALBION 0**
Competition: Southern League Division 1
Teamsheet: Barton, Reeves, Bell, Small, Hyde, Keylock, Day, Sampson, Horlick, Gallagher, Cooper
Scorers: Horlick, Sampson
Attendance: 400

Date: Wednesday 11/04/1962
Result: **GLOUCESTER CITY 0 POOLE TOWN 2**
Competition: Southern League Division 1
Teamsheet: Barton, Reeves, Bell, Small, Hyde, Keylock, Simcock, Sampson, Horlick, Gallagher, Cooper

Date: Saturday 14/04/1962
Result: **GLOUCESTER CITY 0 DOVER 1**
Competition: Southern League Division 1
Teamsheet: Barton, Reeves, Bell, Small, Hobbs, Keylock, Simcock, Sampson, Horlick, Gallagher, Cooper
Attendance: 300

Date: Friday 20/04/1962
Result: **GLOUCESTER CITY 3 DARTFORD 5**
Competition: Southern League Division 1
Teamsheet: Barton, Bell, Clark, Small, Hobbs, Keylock, Day, Sampson, Horlick, Gallagher, Cooper
Scorers: Horlick, Day, Small

Date: Monday 23/04/1962
Result: **DARTFORD 5 GLOUCESTER CITY 0**
Competition: Southern League Division 1
Teamsheet: Barton, Bell, Clark, Small, Keylock, Sampson, Simcock, Skull, Horlick, Cooper, Wood

Date: Thursday 26/04/1962
Result: **CHELTENHAM TOWN 3 GLOUCESTER CITY 0**
Competition: Gloucestershire FA Northern Senior Professional Cup Final
Teamsheet: Barton, Bell, Lacey, Small, Clark, Keylock, Hyde, Day, Horlick, Sampson, Cooper
Attendance: 1420

Date: Saturday 28/04/1962
Result: **GLOUCESTER CITY 1 ASHFORD TOWN 2**
Competition: Southern League Division 1
Teamsheet: Wood, Bell, Clark, Small, Hobbs, Keylock, Skull, Day, Horlick, Sampson, Cooper
Scorer: Day

Date: Saturday 05/05/1962
Result: **MARGATE 3 GLOUCESTER CITY 0**
Competition: Southern League Division 1
Teamsheet: Wood, Clark, Bell, Small, Hyde, Keylock, Skull, Day, Horlick, Sampson, Cooper
Attendance: 1547

Appearances – B Adlam, M Anderson 6, P Barton 39, E Bell 45, J Blythe 4, D Cherry 1, JD Clark 13, J Cooper 17, LO Cullunbine 1, H Day 12, R Dunn 24, M England 8, R Evans 14, J Gallagher 13, ? Goode 1, P Hobbs 5, G Horlick 33, J Hyde 38, B Keylock 43, P Killan 3, B Lacey 1, ? Neuman 1, R Reeves 28, AJ Rothin 3, RV Sampson 21, P Simcock 11, J Skull 35, S Small 15, IM Trigg 1, J Weston 33, LB Wood 6.
Scorers – G Horlick 13, J Skull 11, J Weston 5, H Day 4, J Cooper 3, S Small 3, R Evans 2, J Hyde 2, RV Sampson 2, B Adlam 1, E Bell 1, J Blythe 1, JD Clark 1, M England 1, J Gallagher 1, P Killan 1, P Simcock 1.

SOUTHERN LEAGUE DIVISION 1

POS	CLUB	P	W	D	L	F	A	PTS
1	WISBECH TOWN	38	21	11	6	76	42	53
2	POOLE TOWN	38	23	6	9	81	47	52
3	DARTFORD	38	21	8	9	89	50	50
4	RUGBY TOWN	38	20	9	9	82	49	49
5	MARGATE	38	20	6	12	74	55	46
6	CORBY TOWN	38	19	6	13	82	60	44
7	SITTINGBOURNE	38	16	12	10	69	51	44
8	DOVER	38	19	6	13	66	55	44
9	YIEWSLEY	38	18	6	14	64	51	42
10	BARRY TOWN	38	14	11	13	55	51	39
11	ASHFORD TOWN	38	14	11	13	66	70	39
12	HINCKLEY ATHLETIC	38	15	8	15	75	65	38
13	BURTON ALBION	38	16	5	17	70	79	37
14	NUNEATON BOROUGH	38	12	12	14	63	71	36
15	TUNBRIDGE WELLS UNITED	38	12	7	19	61	85	31
16	CANTERBURY CITY	38	11	8	19	60	82	30
17	RAMSGATE ATHLETIC	38	10	9	19	49	70	29
18	TROWBRIDGE TOWN	38	9	9	20	45	67	27
19	**GLOUCESTER CITY**	**38**	**6**	**4**	**28**	**46**	**104**	**16**
20	HASTINGS UNITED	38	5	4	29	46	115	14
		760	301	158	301	1319	1319	760

SEASON 1962-1963
(Home Ground: The Ground, Cheltenham Road, Longlevens)

Date: Saturday 18/08/1962
Result: **RAMSGATE ATHLETIC 3 GLOUCESTER CITY 1**
Competition: Southern League Division 1
Teamsheet: McCluskey, Palmer, Bell, Head, Hyde, Keylock, Day, Coldray, Horlick, Humphrey, Thomas
Scorer: Coldray

Date: Saturday 25/08/1962
Result: **GLOUCESTER CITY 1 FOLKESTONE TOWN 0**
Competition: Southern League Division 1
Teamsheet: McCluskey, Palmer, Bell, Head, Hyde, Keylock, Day, Coldray, Horlick, Humphrey, Thomas
Scorer: Horlick

Date: Monday 27/08/1962
Result: **BATH CITY 2 GLOUCESTER CITY 1**
Competition: Southern League Cup Qualifying Round 1st Leg
Teamsheet: McCluskey, Palmer, Bell, Head, Hyde, Keylock, Thomas, Coldray, Horlick, Humphrey, Quinlan
Scorer: Coldray
Attendance: 1958

SEASON BY SEASON

Date: Saturday 01/09/1962
Result: **CORBY TOWN 0 GLOUCESTER CITY 0**
Competition: Southern League Division 1
Teamsheet: McCluskey, Palmer, Bell, Head, Hyde, Keylock, Thomas, Coldray, Horlick, Humphrey, Quinlan

Date: Wednesday 05/09/1962
Result: **GLOUCESTER CITY 0 BATH CITY 3**
Competition: Southern League Cup Qualifying Round 2nd Leg
Teamsheet: McCluskey, Palmer, Bell, Head, Hyde, Keylock, Thomas, Coldray, Horlick, Humphrey, Quinlan
Attendance: 2000

Date: Saturday 08/09/1962
Result: **GLOUCESTER CITY 3 MERTHYR TYDFIL 2**
Competition: FA Cup 1st Qualifying Round
Teamsheet: McCluskey, Palmer, Bell, Head, Hyde, Keylock, Thomas, Coldray, Horlick, Humphrey, Quinlan
Scorers: Horlick (2), Bell (pen)
Attendance: 1500

Date: Saturday 15/09/1962
Result: **BURTON ALBION 4 GLOUCESTER CITY 1**
Competition: Southern League Division 1
Teamsheet (from): McCluskey, Palmer, Bell, Hyde, Keylock, Thomas, Coldray, Horlick, Humphrey, Quinlan, Day
Scorer: Horlick
Attendance: 1300

Date: Saturday 22/09/1962
Result: **GLOUCESTER CITY 2 BARRY TOWN 0**
Competition: FA Cup 2nd Qualifying Round
Teamsheet: McCluskey, Palmer, Bell, Cox, Hyde, Keylock, Thomas, Head, Horlick, Humphrey, Weston
Scorer: Weston (2)

Date: Saturday 29/09/1962
Result: **KING'S LYNN 0 GLOUCESTER CITY 2**
Competition: Southern League Division 1
Teamsheet: McCluskey, Palmer, Bell, Cox, Hyde, Keylock, Thomas, Head, Horlick, Humphrey, Weston
Scorers: Bell (pen), Head

Date: Saturday 06/10/1962
Result: **GLOUCESTER CITY 1 CHELTENHAM TOWN 2**
Competition: FA Cup 3rd Qualifying Round
Teamsheet: McCluskey, Palmer, Bell, Cox, Hyde, Keylock, Humphrey, Head, Horlick, Coldray, Weston
Scorer: Coldray
Attendance: 4600

Date: Saturday 13/10/1962
Result: **YIEWSLEY 5 GLOUCESTER CITY 2**
Competition: Southern League Division 1
Teamsheet: McCluskey, Palmer, Bell, Cox, Hyde, Keylock, Humphrey, Head, Horlick, Coldray, Weston
Scorers: Horlick, Humphrey

Date: Saturday 20/10/1962
Result: **GLOUCESTER CITY 0 CANTERBURY CITY 2**
Competition: Southern League Division 1
Teamsheet: McCluskey, Palmer, Bell, Head, Hyde, Keylock, Thomas, Coldray, Horlick, Humphrey, Weston

Date: Saturday 27/10/1962
Result: **TUNBRIDGE WELLS UNITED 2 GLOUCESTER CITY 3**
Competition: Southern League Division 1
Teamsheet: McCluskey, Palmer, Quinlan, Head, Hyde, Cox, Humphrey, Day, Horlick, Coldray, Cooper
Scorers: Horlick (2), Cooper

Date: Saturday 03/11/1962
Result: **GLOUCESTER CITY 2 NUNEATON BOROUGH 2**
Competition: Southern League Division 1
Teamsheet: McCluskey, Palmer, Quinlan, Head, Hyde, Cox, Humphrey, Day, Horlick, Coldray, Cooper
Scorers: Head, Horlick
Attendance: 1100

Date: Saturday 10/11/1962
Result: **ASHFORD TOWN 3 GLOUCESTER CITY 0**
Competition: Southern League Division 1
Teamsheet: McCluskey, Palmer, Quinlan, Head, Hyde, Cox, Humphrey, Day, Horlick, Coldray, Cooper

Date: Saturday 17/11/1962
Result: **GLOUCESTER CITY 1 TROWBRIDGE TOWN 0**
Competition: Southern League Division 1
Teamsheet: McCluskey, Palmer, Quinlan, Head, Hyde, Cox, Humphrey, Coldray, Horlick, Bell, Cooper
Scorer: Horlick

Date: Saturday 24/11/1962
Result: **DOVER 5 GLOUCESTER CITY 1**
Competition: Southern League Division 1
Teamsheet: McCluskey, Palmer, Quinlan, Head, Hyde, Bell, Humphrey, Coldray, Horlick, Day, Cooper
Scorer: Coldray
Attendance: 1263

Date: Saturday 01/12/1962
Result: **GLOUCESTER CITY 2 MARGATE 2**
Competition: Southern League Division 1
Teamsheet: McCluskey, Palmer, Quinlan, Head, Hyde, Cox, Thomas, Coldray, Horlick, Humphrey, Short
Scorers: Coldray, Hyde (pen)
Attendance: 800

Date: Saturday 08/12/1962
Result: **HASTINGS UNITED 3 GLOUCESTER CITY 0**
Competition: Southern League Division 1
Teamsheet: McCluskey, Palmer, Quinlan, Head, Hyde, Cox, Thomas, Humphrey, Horlick, Small, Short

Date: Saturday 15/12/1962
Result: **GLOUCESTER CITY 1 RAMSGATE ATHLETIC 2**
Competition: Southern League Division 1
Teamsheet: McCluskey, Palmer, Quinlan, Head, Hyde, Cox, Thomas, Coldray, Horlick, Humphrey, Short
Scorer: Horlick

Date: Saturday 22/12/1962
Result: **FOLKESTONE TOWN 5 GLOUCESTER CITY 0**
Competition: Southern League Division 1
Teamsheet: McCluskey, Palmer, Weston, Keylock, Hyde, Bell, Humphrey, Head, Horlick, Coldray, Short

Date: Saturday 02/03/1963
Result: **GLOUCESTER CITY 1 TUNBRIDGE WELLS UNITED 0**
Competition: Southern League Division 1
Teamsheet: McCluskey, Palmer, Bell, Head, Hyde, Cox, Humphrey, Coldray, Horlick, Day, Short
Scorer: Horlick

Date: Wednesday 06/03/1963
Result: **GLOUCESTER CITY 2 HASTINGS UNITED 1**
Competition: Southern League Division 1
Teamsheet: McCluskey, Quinlan, Weston, Head, Hyde, Cox, Short, Coldray, Horlick, Day, Bell
Scorer: Coldray (2)

Date: Saturday 09/03/1963
Result: **NUNEATON BOROUGH 4 GLOUCESTER CITY 0**
Competition: Southern League Division 1
Teamsheet: McCluskey, Quinlan, Bell, Head, Hyde, Cox, Humphrey, Coldray, Horlick, Day, Short

Date: Saturday 16/03/1963
Result: **GLOUCESTER CITY 0 CHELTENHAM TOWN 3**
Competition: Gloucestershire FA Northern Senior Professional Cup Final
Teamsheet: McCluskey, Palmer, Weston, Quinlan, Hyde, Keylock, Short, Horlick, Medcroft, Day, Bell
Attendance: 1500

Date: Saturday 23/03/1963
Result: **TROWBRIDGE TOWN 2 GLOUCESTER CITY 2**
Competition: Southern League Division 1
Teamsheet: McCluskey, Palmer, Weston, Quinlan, Hyde, Cox, Humphrey, Coldray, Horlick, Medcroft, Short
Scorers: Hyde (pen), Horlick

Date: Tuesday 26/03/1963
Result: **GLOUCESTER CITY 1 KING'S LYNN 1**
Competition: Southern League Division 1
Teamsheet: McCluskey, Quinlan, Weston, Keylock, Hyde, Cox, Humphrey, Coldray, Horlick, Medcroft, Short
Scorer: Horlick

Date: Thursday 28/03/1963
Result: **HINCKLEY ATHLETIC 3 GLOUCESTER CITY 0**
Competition: Southern League Division 1
Teamsheet: McCluskey, Quinlan, Palmer, Keylock, Hyde, Cox, Humphrey, Coldray, Horlick, Medcroft, Short

Date: Saturday 30/03/1963
Result: **GLOUCESTER CITY 1 YIEWSLEY 1**
Competition: Southern League Division 1
Teamsheet: McCluskey, Quinlan, Weston, Keylock, Hyde, Cox, Humphrey, Coldray, Horlick, Bell, Short
Scorer: Horlick

Date: Wednesday 03/04/1963
Result: **GLOUCESTER CITY 3 BARRY TOWN 0**
Competition: Southern League Division 1
Teamsheet: McCluskey, Quinlan, Weston, Keylock, Hyde, Cox, Humphrey, Coldray, Horlick, Bell, Short
Scorer: Horlick (3)

Date: Saturday 06/04/1963
Result: **MARGATE 5 GLOUCESTER CITY 1**
Competition: Southern League Division 1
Teamsheet: McCluskey, Quinlan, Weston, Keylock, Hyde, Cox, Humphrey, Coldray, Horlick, Bell, Short
Scorer: Horlick
Attendance: 1620

Date: Wednesday 10/04/1963
Result: **BARRY TOWN 3 GLOUCESTER CITY 0**
Competition: Southern League Division 1
Teamsheet: McCluskey, Quinlan, Weston, Keylock, Hyde, Cox, Thomas, Coldray, Horlick, Head, Bell

Date: Friday 12/04/1963
Result: **GLOUCESTER CITY 2 CHELTENHAM TOWN 2**
Competition: Southern League Division 1
Teamsheet: McCluskey, Quinlan, Palmer, Keylock, Hyde, Cox, Short, Humphrey, Horlick, Weston, Bell
Scorers: own goal, Weston
Attendance: 3000

Date: Saturday 13/04/1963
Result: **GLOUCESTER CITY 2 DOVER 2**
Competition: Southern League Division 1
Teamsheet: McCluskey, Quinlan, Palmer, Keylock, Hyde, Cox, Short, Humphrey, Horlick, Weston, Bell
Scorers: own goal, Short

Date: Monday 15/04/1963
Result: **CHELTENHAM TOWN 2 GLOUCESTER CITY 0**
Competition: Southern League Division 1
Teamsheet: McCluskey, Quinlan, Weston, Keylock, Hyde, Cox, Short, Coldray, Horlick, Head, Bell
Attendance: 2175

Date: Friday 19/04/1963
Result: **GLOUCESTER CITY 1 ASHFORD TOWN 4**
Competition: Southern League Division 1
Teamsheet: McCluskey, Quinlan, Palmer, Keylock, Hyde, Cox, Short, Humphrey, Horlick, Coldray, Bell
Scorer: Humphrey

Date: Saturday 20/04/1963
Result: **GLOUCESTER CITY 1 HINCKLEY ATHLETIC 2**
Competition: Southern League Division 1
Teamsheet: McCluskey, Quinlan, Palmer, Head, Hyde, Cox, Short, Humphrey, Horlick, Medcroft, Cooper
Scorer: Humphrey

Date: Monday 22/04/1963
Result: **TONBRIDGE 2 GLOUCESTER CITY 0**
Competition: Southern League Division 1
Teamsheet: McCluskey, Quinlan, Palmer, Coldray, Hyde, Keylock, Short, Medcroft, Horlick, Bell, Cooper

Date: Saturday 27/04/1963
Result: **GLOUCESTER CITY 3 BURTON ALBION 0**
Competition: Southern League Division 1
Teamsheet: McCluskey, Quinlan, Palmer, Coldray, Hyde, Keylock, Short, Humphrey, Horlick, Weston, Bell
Scorers: Weston, Short (2)
Attendance: 483

Date: Tuesday 30/04/1963
Result: **GLOUCESTER CITY 0 TONBRIDGE 2**
Competition: Southern League Division 1
Teamsheet: McCluskey, Quinlan, Palmer, Coldray, Hyde, Keylock, Short, Humphrey, Horlick, Weston, Bell
Attendance: 500

Date: Saturday 04/05/1963
Result: **GLOUCESTER CITY 0 CORBY TOWN 0**
Competition: Southern League Division 1
Teamsheet: McCluskey, Quinlan, Palmer, Coldray, Hyde, Keylock, Short, Humphrey, Horlick, Weston, Bell

Date: Saturday 11/05/1963
Result: **SITTINGBOURNE 2 GLOUCESTER CITY 2**
Competition: Southern League Division 1
Teamsheet: McCluskey, Quinlan, Palmer, Keylock, Hyde, Cox, Cooper, Coldray, Horlick, Humphrey, Bell
Scorers: Humphrey, Coldray

Date: Thursday 16/05/1963
Result: **CANTERBURY CITY 1 GLOUCESTER CITY 1**
Competition: Southern League Division 1
Teamsheet: McCluskey, Palmer, Bell, Keylock, Hyde, Cox, Cooper, Humphrey, Medcroft, Coldray, Rothin
Scorer: Coldray

Date: Saturday 18/05/1963
Result: **GLOUCESTER CITY 2 SITTINGBOURNE 1**
Competition: Southern League Division 1
Teamsheet: McCluskey, Quinlan, Palmer, Keylock, Hyde, Cox, Cooper, Medcroft, Horlick, Coldray, Rothin
Scorers: Medcroft, Palmer

Appearances – E Bell 33, RA Coldray 37, J Cooper 10, A Cox 29, H Day 11, DG Head 27, G Horlick 43, TR Humphrey 38, J Hyde 44, B Keylock 31, R McCluskey 44, PD Medcroft 8, G Palmer 36, M Quinlan 34, AJ Rothin 2, D Short 23, S Small 1, M Thomas 14, J Weston 20.
Scorers – G Horlick 18, RA Coldray 9, TR Humphrey 4, J Weston 4, D Short 3, E Bell 2, DG Head 2, J Hyde 2, J Cooper 1, PD Medcroft 1, G Palmer 1, own goals 2.

SEASON BY SEASON

SOUTHERN LEAGUE DIVISION 1

POS	CLUB	P	W	D	L	F	A	PTS
1	MARGATE	38	21	13	4	86	47	55
2	HINCKLEY ATHLETIC	38	22	9	7	66	38	53
3	HASTINGS UNITED	38	22	8	8	86	36	52
4	NUNEATON BOROUGH	38	21	10	7	82	40	52
5	TONBRIDGE	38	22	8	8	81	51	52
6	DOVER	38	22	7	9	78	56	51
7	CORBY TOWN	38	19	8	11	79	50	46
8	KING'S LYNN	38	19	7	12	76	66	45
9	CHELTENHAM TOWN	38	18	7	13	83	52	43
10	FOLKESTONE TOWN	38	15	10	13	79	57	40
11	CANTERBURY CITY	38	14	8	16	42	56	36
12	YIEWSLEY	38	11	10	17	63	71	32
13	RAMSGATE ATHLETIC	38	12	7	19	58	82	31
14	TROWBRIDGE TOWN	38	11	9	18	50	81	31
15	BURTON ALBION	38	10	10	18	48	76	30
16	**GLOUCESTER CITY**	**38**	**9**	**11**	**18**	**42**	**78**	**29**
17	SITTINGBOURNE	38	12	3	23	56	75	27
18	ASHFORD TOWN	38	9	6	23	48	76	24
19	BARRY TOWN	38	6	5	27	35	75	17
20	TUNBRIDGE WELLS UNITED	38	6	2	30	43	118	14
		760	301	158	301	1281	1281	760

SEASON 1963-1964

(Home Ground: The Ground, Cheltenham Road, Longlevens)

Date: Saturday 24/08/1963
Result: **GLOUCESTER CITY 3 KING'S LYNN 0**
Competition: Southern League Division 1
Teamsheet: McCluskey, Quinlan, Palmer, Coldray, Hyde, Casey, Humphrey, Wells, Horlick, Brown, Hawkins
Scorers: Humphrey, Wells, Brown

Date: Wednesday 28/08/1963
Result: **CLACTON TOWN 5 GLOUCESTER CITY 2**
Competition: Southern League Division 1
Teamsheet: McCluskey, McMillan, Palmer, Coldray, Hyde, Casey, Humphrey, Murney, Horlick, Brown, Hawkins
Scorers: Casey, Humphrey

Date: Saturday 31/08/1963
Result: **CANTERBURY CITY 1 GLOUCESTER CITY 0**
Competition: Southern League Division 1
Teamsheet: McCluskey, McMillan, Palmer, Coldray, Hyde, Casey, Humphrey, Wells, Horlick, Murney, Hawkins

Date: Tuesday 03/09/1963
Result: **WEYMOUTH 5 GLOUCESTER CITY 1**
Competition: Southern League Cup Qualifying Round 1st Leg
Teamsheet: McCluskey, McMillan, Palmer, Coldray, Hyde, Casey, Humphrey, Wells, Horlick, Murney, Hawkins
Scorer: Coldray
Attendance: 2416

Date: Saturday 07/09/1963
Result: **GLOUCESTER CITY 2 MERTHYR TYDFIL 2**
Competition: FA Cup 1st Qualifying Round
Teamsheet: McCluskey, Quinlan, Palmer, Coldray, Hyde, Cox, Humphrey, Wells, Horlick, Brown, Hawkins
Scorers: Quinlan, Hawkins
Attendance: 1400

Date: Wednesday 11/09/1963
Result: **MERTHYR TYDFIL 2 GLOUCESTER CITY 3**
Competition: FA Cup 1st Qualifying Round Replay
Teamsheet: McCluskey, Quinlan, Palmer, Coldray, Hyde, Casey, Humphrey, Wells, Horlick, Brown, Hawkins
Scorers: Wells, Coldray, Horlick

Date: Saturday 14/09/1963
Result: **TUNBRIDGE WELLS RANGERS 3 GLOUCESTER CITY 1**
Competition: Southern League Division 1
Teamsheet: McCluskey, Quinlan, Palmer, Coldray, Hyde, Cox, Humphrey, Wells, Horlick, Brown, Hawkins
Scorer: Humphrey

Date: Tuesday 17/09/1963
Result: **GLOUCESTER CITY 2 CLACTON TOWN 4**
Competition: Southern League Division 1
Teamsheet: Wood, Quinlan, Palmer, Coldray, Hyde, Casey, Humphrey, Williams, Emery, Brown, Hawkins
Scorer: Hawkins (2)

Date: Saturday 21/09/1963
Result: **GLOUCESTER CITY 1 CHELTENHAM TOWN 2**
Competition: FA Cup 2nd Qualifying Round
Teamsheet: McCluskey, Quinlan, Palmer, Coldray, Hyde, Casey, Humphrey, Williams, Emery, Brown, Hawkins
Scorer: Casey (pen)
Attendance: 5000

Date: Thursday 26/09/1963
Result: **GLOUCESTER CITY 1 CHELTENHAM TOWN 1**
Competition: Southern League Division 1
Teamsheet: McCluskey, Quinlan, Palmer, Coldray, Hyde, Durrant, Humphrey, Emery, Horlick, Wells, Hawkins
Scorer: own goal
Attendance: 2000

Date: Saturday 28/09/1963
Result: **DEAL TOWN 1 GLOUCESTER CITY 2**
Competition: Southern League Division 1
Teamsheet: McCluskey, Quinlan, Palmer, Coldray, Hyde, Durrant, Humphrey, Emery, Horlick, Wells, Hawkins
Scorer: Horlick (2)

Date: Tuesday 01/10/1963
Result: **GLOUCESTER CITY 3 WEYMOUTH 2**
Competition: Southern League Cup Qualifying Round 2nd Leg
Teamsheet: McCluskey, Quinlan, Palmer, Coldray, Hyde, Durrant, Humphrey, Williams, Horlick, Wells, Hawkins
Scorers: Durrant (pen), Horlick, Humphrey

Date: Thursday 03/10/1963
Result: **GLOUCESTER CITY 2 RAMSGATE ATHLETIC 1**
Competition: Southern League Division 1
Teamsheet: McCluskey, Quinlan, Palmer, Coldray, Hyde, Casey, Humphrey, Wells, Horlick, Williams, Hawkins
Scorer: Horlick (2)

Date: Saturday 05/10/1963
Result: **GLOUCESTER CITY 1 TUNBRIDGE WELLS RANGERS 4**
Competition: Southern League Division 1
Teamsheet: McCluskey, Quinlan, Palmer, Coldray, Durrant, Casey, Humphrey, Wells, Horlick, Williams, Hawkins
Scorer: Humphrey
Attendance: 1200

Date: Saturday 12/10/1963
Result: **GRAVESEND & NORTHFLEET 2 GLOUCESTER CITY 2**
Competition: Southern League Division 1
Teamsheet: McCluskey, Quinlan, Palmer, Coldray, Durrant, Casey, Humphrey, Wells, Horlick, Williams, Hawkins
Scorers: Casey (pen), Williams
Attendance: 959

Date: Saturday 19/10/1963
Result: **GLOUCESTER CITY 3 SITTINGBOURNE 0**
Competition: Southern League Division 1
Teamsheet: McCluskey, Quinlan, Palmer, Coldray, Cox, Casey, Humphrey, Wells, Horlick, Williams, Hawkins
Scorers: Horlick (2), Wells
Attendance: 1200

Date: Saturday 26/10/1963
Result: **POOLE TOWN 1 GLOUCESTER CITY 0**
Competition: Southern League Division 1
Teamsheet: McCluskey, Quinlan, Palmer, Coldray, Cox, Casey, Humphrey, Wells, Horlick, Williams, Hawkins

Date: Saturday 02/11/1963
Result: **GLOUCESTER CITY 1 TONBRIDGE 2**
Competition: Southern League Division 1
Teamsheet: McCluskey, Quinlan, Palmer, Coldray, Cox, Casey, Humphrey, Wells, Thomas, Williams, Hawkins
Scorer: -----
Attendance: 1400

Date: Saturday 09/11/1963
Result: **DOVER 1 GLOUCESTER CITY 3**
Competition: Southern League Division 1
Teamsheet: McCluskey, Quinlan, Palmer, Brown, Cox, Casey, Humphrey, Wells, Coldray, Williams, Hawkins
Scorers: Coldray, Hawkins, Wells
Attendance: 1445

Date: Saturday 16/11/1963
Result: **GLOUCESTER CITY 2 ASHFORD TOWN 0**
Competition: Southern League Division 1
Teamsheet: McCluskey, Quinlan, Palmer, Durrant, Cox, Casey, Humphrey, Wells, Coldray, Williams, Hawkins
Scorers: Casey, Coldray
Attendance: 1186

Date: Thursday 21/11/1963
Result: **GLOUCESTER CITY 4 CORBY TOWN 1**
Competition: Southern League Division 1
Teamsheet: McCluskey, Quinlan, Palmer, Durrant, Cox, Casey, Humphrey, Wells, Coldray, Williams, Hawkins
Scorers: Williams (2), Humphrey, Coldray
Attendance: 1586

Date: Saturday 23/11/1963
Result: **CRAWLEY TOWN 3 GLOUCESTER CITY 1**
Competition: Southern League Division 1
Teamsheet: McCluskey, Quinlan, Palmer, Durrant, Cox, Casey, Humphrey, Wells, Coldray, Williams, Hawkins
Scorer: Humphrey

Date: Saturday 30/11/1963
Result: **GLOUCESTER CITY 7 TROWBRIDGE TOWN 0**
Competition: Southern League Division 1
Teamsheet: McCluskey, Quinlan, Palmer, Coldray, Cox, Casey, Humphrey, Wells, Horlick, Williams, Hawkins
Scorers: Williams (2), Horlick (2), Wells, Hawkins, own goal

Date: Saturday 07/12/1963
Result: **YIEWSLEY 5 GLOUCESTER CITY 2**
Competition: Southern League Division 1
Teamsheet: McCluskey, Quinlan, Palmer, Coldray, Cox, Casey, Humphrey, Wells, Horlick, Williams, Hawkins
Scorers: Williams, Horlick

Date: Saturday 14/12/1963
Result: **KING'S LYNN 2 GLOUCESTER CITY 1**
Competition: Southern League Division 1
Teamsheet: McCluskey, Quinlan, Palmer, Coldray, Cox, Casey, Humphrey, Wells, Horlick, Williams, Hawkins
Scorer: Hawkins

Date: Saturday 21/12/1963
Result: **GLOUCESTER CITY 2 CANTERBURY CITY 2**
Competition: Southern League Division 1
Teamsheet: McCluskey, Quinlan, Palmer, Coldray, Cox, Casey, Humphrey, Wells, Horlick, Williams, Hawkins
Scorers: Williams, Hawkins

Date: Thursday 26/12/1963
Result: **GLOUCESTER CITY 7 BURTON ALBION 3**
Competition: Southern League Division 1
Teamsheet: McCluskey, Quinlan, Palmer, Coldray, Cox, Casey, Humphrey, Wells, Horlick, Williams, Hawkins
Scorers: Horlick (3), Williams (2), Wells (2)
Attendance: 1376

Date: Saturday 28/12/1963
Result: **BURTON ALBION 1 GLOUCESTER CITY 2**
Competition: Southern League Division 1
Teamsheet: McCluskey, Quinlan, Palmer, Coldray, Cox, Casey, Humphrey, Wells, Horlick, Williams, Hawkins
Scorer: Williams (2)
Attendance: 950

Date: Saturday 04/01/1964
Result: **GLOUCESTER CITY 4 BARRY TOWN 1**
Competition: Southern League Division 1
Teamsheet: McCluskey, Quinlan, Palmer, Coldray, Cox, Casey, Humphrey, Wells, Horlick, Williams, Hawkins
Scorers: Wells, Coldray, Humphrey, Williams

Date: Saturday 11/01/1964
Result: **RAMSGATE ATHLETIC 3 GLOUCESTER CITY 1**
Competition: Southern League Division 1
Teamsheet: McCluskey, Quinlan, Palmer, Coldray, Hyde, Casey, Humphrey, Wells, Horlick, Williams, Hawkins
Scorer: Horlick

Date: Saturday 18/01/1964
Result: **CHELTENHAM TOWN 4 GLOUCESTER CITY 1**
Competition: Gloucestershire FA Northern Senior Professional Cup Final
Teamsheet: McCluskey, Quinlan, Palmer, Coldray, Cox, Casey, Humphrey, Wells, Horlick, Williams, Hawkins
Scorer: Wells
Attendance: 1742

Date: Saturday 25/01/1964
Result: **BARRY TOWN 1 GLOUCESTER CITY 4**
Competition: Southern League Division 1
Teamsheet: McCluskey, Quinlan, Palmer, Coldray, Cox, Casey, Humphrey, Wells, Horlick, Williams, Hawkins
Scorers: Wells, Casey, Williams (2)

Date: Saturday 01/02/1964
Result: **FOLKESTONE TOWN 3 GLOUCESTER CITY 1**
Competition: Southern League Division 1
Teamsheet: McCluskey, Quinlan, Palmer, Coldray, Cox, Casey, Humphrey, Hyde, Horlick, Williams, Hawkins
Scorer: Horlick

Date: Saturday 08/02/1964
Result: **GLOUCESTER CITY 6 DEAL TOWN 1**
Competition: Southern League Division 1
Teamsheet: Pellant, Hyde, Palmer, Coldray, Cox, Casey, Humphrey, Thomas, Medcroft, Williams, Hawkins
Scorers: Thomas (2), Medcroft (2), Williams, Coldray

Date: Saturday 15/02/1964
Result: **CORBY TOWN 5 GLOUCESTER CITY 2**
Competition: Southern League Division 1
Teamsheet: Pellant, Quinlan, Palmer, Coldray, Cox, Casey, Humphrey, Thomas, Medcroft, Williams, Hawkins
Scorer: Williams (2)

Date: Saturday 22/02/1964
Result: **GLOUCESTER CITY 4 GRAVESEND & NORTHFLEET 1**
Competition: Southern League Division 1
Teamsheet: Pellant, Quinlan, Palmer, Coldray, Cox, Casey, Humphrey, Thomas, Horlick, Williams, Hawkins
Scorers: Thomas, Horlick, Coldray, Williams
Attendance: 1016

Date: Saturday 29/02/1964
Result: **SITTINGBOURNE 3 GLOUCESTER CITY 1**
Competition: Southern League Division 1
Teamsheet: Pellant, Quinlan, Palmer, Coldray, Cox, Casey, Wells, Thomas, Horlick, Williams, Hawkins
Scorer: Horlick

Date: Saturday 07/03/1964
Result: **GLOUCESTER CITY 1 POOLE TOWN 1**
Competition: Southern League Division 1
Teamsheet: McCluskey, Quinlan, Palmer, Coldray, Cox, Casey, Humphrey, Wells, Horlick, Williams, Hawkins
Scorer: Casey

[183]

Date: Saturday 14/03/1964
Result: **TONBRIDGE 6 GLOUCESTER CITY 2**
Competition: Southern League Division 1
Teamsheet: Pellant, Quinlan, Palmer, Coldray, Cox, Casey, Brown, Wells, Horlick, Humphrey, Hawkins
Scorers: Horlick, Humphrey

Date: Saturday 21/03/1964
Result: **GLOUCESTER CITY 4 DOVER 3**
Competition: Southern League Division 1
Teamsheet: Pellant, Quinlan, Palmer, Coldray, Cox, Casey, Humphrey, Wells, Horlick, Williams, Hawkins
Scorers: Williams (2), Wells (2)
Attendance: 1015

Date: Friday 27/03/1964
Result: **GLOUCESTER CITY 2 STEVENAGE TOWN 1**
Competition: Southern League Division 1
Teamsheet: Pellant, Quinlan, Palmer, Coldray, Cox, Durrant, Humphrey, Thomas, Horlick, Williams, Hawkins
Scorers: Horlick, Coldray

Date: Saturday 28/03/1964
Result: **CHELTENHAM TOWN 3 GLOUCESTER CITY 1**
Competition: Southern League Division 1
Teamsheet: Pellant, Quinlan, Palmer, Coldray, Hyde, Durrant, Humphrey, Wells, Horlick, Williams, Hawkins
Scorer: Wells
Attendance: 2283

Date: Monday 30/03/1964
Result: **STEVENAGE TOWN 5 GLOUCESTER CITY 0**
Competition: Southern League Division 1
Teamsheet: Pellant, Quinlan, Palmer, Coldray, Cox, Casey, Humphrey, Wells, Hyde, Williams, Hawkins

Date: Saturday 04/04/1964
Result: **GLOUCESTER CITY 0 CRAWLEY TOWN 1**
Competition: Southern League Division 1
Teamsheet: McCluskey, Quinlan, Palmer, Coldray, Hyde, Casey, Parrish, Wells, Horlick, Williams, Hawkins
Attendance: 875

Date: Saturday 11/04/1964
Result: **TROWBRIDGE TOWN 3 GLOUCESTER CITY 1**
Competition: Southern League Division 1
Teamsheet: McCluskey, Quinlan, Palmer, Cox, Hyde, Durrant, Thomas, Coldray, Wells, Williams, Hawkins
Scorer: Williams

Date: Thursday 16/04/1964
Result: **GLOUCESTER CITY 3 FOLKESTONE TOWN 0**
Competition: Southern League Division 1
Teamsheet: McCluskey, Quinlan, Palmer, Wixey, Cox, Durrant, Thomas, Coldray, Wells, Williams, Hawkins
Scorers: Wells, Coldray, Durrant

Date: Saturday 18/04/1964
Result: **GLOUCESTER CITY 0 YIEWSLEY 1**
Competition: Southern League Division 1
Teamsheet: McCluskey, Quinlan, Palmer, Wixey, Cox, Durrant, Thomas, Coldray, Wells, Williams, Hawkins

Date: Saturday 25/04/1964
Result: **ASHFORD TOWN 4 GLOUCESTER CITY 0**
Competition: Southern League Division 1
Teamsheet: Wood, Smith, Palmer, Durrant, Cox, Pratt, Medcroft, Thomas, Wells, Williams, Hawkins

Appearances – AE Brown 9, T Casey 37, RA Coldray 46, A Cox 32, A Durrant 14, J Emery 4, M Hawkins 48, G Horlick 34, TR Humphrey 42, J Hyde 20, R McCluskey 37, W McMillan 3, PD Medcroft 3, HP Murney 3, G Palmer 48, R Parrish 1, GA Pellant 9, D Pratt 1, M Quinlan 43, R Smith 1, RJ Thomas 10, B Wells 40, A Williams 38, R Wixey 2, LB Wood 2.
Scorers – A Williams 21, G Horlick 20, B Wells 14, RA Coldray 10, TR Humphrey 9, M Hawkins 7, T Casey 6, RJ Thomas 3, A Durrant 2, PD Medcroft 2, AE Brown 1, M Quinlan 1, own goals 2.

In April 1965 before the Sittingbourne game, Rob Coldray was presented with the Gloucester City Football Club's Player of the Year Award. It was presented by Miss Gloucester (Judith Wellsted). A total of 1,200 ballot forms were distributed and 350 people voted. This was the very first Player of the Year Award.

[184]

SOUTHERN LEAGUE DIVISION 1

POS	CLUB	P	W	D	L	F	A	PTS
1	FOLKESTONE TOWN	42	28	7	7	82	38	63
2	KING'S LYNN	42	28	5	9	94	44	61
3	CHELTENHAM TOWN	42	25	10	7	92	48	60
4	TONBRIDGE	42	24	11	7	98	54	59
5	CORBY TOWN	42	24	7	11	114	56	55
6	STEVENAGE TOWN	42	21	6	15	70	59	48
7	ASHFORD TOWN	42	19	9	14	73	57	47
8	BURTON ALBION	42	19	8	15	76	70	46
9	POOLE TOWN	42	17	11	14	75	61	45
10	DOVER	42	18	9	15	86	75	45
11	CANTERBURY CITY	42	16	12	14	66	66	44
12	CRAWLEY TOWN	42	20	2	20	81	71	42
13	TROWBRIDGE TOWN	42	16	9	17	70	78	41
14	CLACTON TOWN	42	19	1	22	76	88	39
15	**GLOUCESTER CITY**	**42**	**17**	**4**	**21**	**88**	**89**	**38**
16	YIEWSLEY	42	15	8	19	63	77	38
17	SITTINGBOURNE	42	15	8	19	52	70	38
18	RAMSGATE ATHLETIC	42	13	9	20	57	55	35
19	TUNBRIDGE WELLS RANGERS	42	10	8	24	47	89	28
20	GRAVESEND & NORTHFLEET	42	7	9	26	43	96	23
21	DEAL TOWN	42	5	7	30	48	106	17
22	BARRY TOWN	42	3	6	33	33	137	12
		924	379	166	379	1584	1584	924

SEASON 1964-1965
(Home Ground: Horton Road Stadium)

Date: Saturday 22/08/1964
Result: **HILLINGDON BOROUGH 1 GLOUCESTER CITY 0**
Competition: Southern League Division 1
Teamsheet: McCluskey, Ashall, Palmer, Prosser, Cox, Casey, Livingstone, Coldray, Wells, Williams, Durrant

Date: Thursday 27/08/1964
Result: **GLOUCESTER CITY 2 WIMBLEDON 2**
Competition: Southern League Division 1
Teamsheet: McCluskey, Ashall, Palmer, Prosser, Cox, Casey, Livingstone, Coldray, Wells, Jacques, Durrant
Scorers: Coldray, own goal
Attendance: 5000

Date: Saturday 29/08/1964
Result: **GLOUCESTER CITY 0 BURTON ALBION 1**
Competition: Southern League Division 1
Teamsheet: McCluskey, Ashall, Palmer, Prosser, Cox, Coldray, Livingstone, Jacques, Wells, Williams, Adlam
Attendance: 2563

Date: Tuesday 01/09/1964
Result: **POOLE TOWN 2 GLOUCESTER CITY 3**
Competition: Southern League Cup 1st Round 1st Leg
Teamsheet: McCluskey, Palmer, Foote, Prosser, Cox, Coldray, Adlam, Wells, Jacques, Williams, Durrant
Scorers: Wells, Jacques, Williams

Date: Saturday 05/09/1964
Result: **GLOUCESTER CITY 3 ABERGAVENNY THURSDAYS 1**
Competition: FA Cup 1st Qualifying Round
Teamsheet: McCluskey, Ashall, Palmer, Prosser, Cox, Coldray, Livingstone, Wells, Jacques, Williams, Adlam
Scorers: Jacques, Williams (2)

Date: Tuesday 08/09/1964
Result: **GLOUCESTER CITY 3 POOLE TOWN 1**
Competition: Southern League Cup 1st Round 2nd Leg
Teamsheet: McCluskey, Ashall, Palmer, Prosser, Cox, Durrant, Livingstone, Wells, Jacques, Williams, Hawkins
Scorers: Wells (2), Jacques

Date: Saturday 12/09/1964
Result: **POOLE TOWN 4 GLOUCESTER CITY 2**
Competition: Southern League Division 1
Teamsheet: McCluskey, Ashall, Palmer, Prosser, Cox, Durrant, Livingstone, Wells, Jacques, Williams, Hawkins
Scorers: Williams, own goal

Date: Tuesday 15/09/1964
Result: **WIMBLEDON 4 GLOUCESTER CITY 4**
Competition: Southern League Division 1
Teamsheet: McCluskey, Ashall, Palmer, Prosser, Cox, Casey, Livingstone, Wells, Jacques, Williams, Hawkins
Scorers: Prosser, Jacques, Williams, Hawkins

Date: Saturday 19/09/1964
Result: **GLOUCESTER CITY 0 LLANELLY 1**
Competition: FA Cup 2nd Qualifying Round
Teamsheet: McCluskey, Ashall, Palmer, Prosser, Cox, Casey, Livingstone, Wells, Jacques, Williams, Hawkins

Date: Saturday 26/09/1964
Result: **DOVER 5 GLOUCESTER CITY 1**
Competition: Southern League Division 1
Teamsheet: McCluskey, Ashall, Palmer, Prosser, Cox, Casey, Livingstone, Wells, Jacques, Williams, Hawkins
Scorer: Williams

Date: Monday 28/09/1964
Result: **SITTINGBOURNE 0 GLOUCESTER CITY 1**
Competition: Southern League Division 1
Teamsheet: McCluskey, Ashall, Palmer, Prosser, Cox, Casey, Livingstone, Coldray, Jacques, Durrant, Hawkins
Scorer: Hawkins

Date: Saturday 03/10/1964
Result: **GLOUCESTER CITY 1 RAMSGATE ATHLETIC 0**
Competition: Southern League Division 1
Teamsheet: McCluskey, Ashall, Palmer, Prosser, Cox, Casey, Livingstone, Coldray, Jacques, Durrant, Hawkins
Scorer: Jacques

Date: Wednesday 07/10/1964
Result: **WEYMOUTH 4 GLOUCESTER CITY 0**
Competition: Southern League Cup 2nd Round
Teamsheet: McCluskey, Ashall, Palmer, Prosser, Cox, Casey, Livingstone, Coldray, Jacques, Durrant, Hawkins
Attendance: 2819

Date: Saturday 10/10/1964
Result: **GLOUCESTER CITY 0 BARRY TOWN 0**
Competition: Southern League Division 1
Teamsheet: McCluskey, Ashall, Palmer, Prosser, Cox, Casey, Livingstone, Coldray, Jacques, Durrant, Hawkins

Date: Saturday 24/10/1964
Result: **GLOUCESTER CITY 2 TUNBRIDGE WELLS RANGERS 1**
Competition: Southern League Division 1
Teamsheet: Pellant, Ashall, Palmer, Coldray, Cox, Durrant, Livingstone, Wells, Jacques, Williams, Wise
Scorers: Livingstone, Wells

Date: Tuesday 27/10/1964
Result: **MERTHYR TYDFIL 1 GLOUCESTER CITY 1**
Competition: Southern League Division 1
Teamsheet: Pellant, Ashall, Palmer, Coldray, Cox, Casey, Livingstone, Wells, Jacques, Williams, Durrant
Scorer: Jacques

Date: Saturday 31/10/1964
Result: **KETTERING TOWN 0 GLOUCESTER CITY 0**
Competition: Southern League Division 1
Teamsheet: Pellant, Ashall, Palmer, Coldray, Cox, Casey, Livingstone, Williams, Jacques, Wells, Durrant

Date: Saturday 07/11/1964
Result: **GLOUCESTER CITY 1 HEREFORD UNITED 1**
Competition: Southern League Division 1
Teamsheet: Pellant, Ashall, Palmer, Coldray, Cox, Casey, Livingstone, Wells, Jacques, Durrant, Williams
Scorer: Williams

Date: Saturday 14/11/1964
Result: **GLOUCESTER CITY 3 POOLE TOWN 3**
Competition: Southern League Division 1
Teamsheet: Pellant, Ashall, Palmer, Coldray, Cox, Casey, Livingstone, Wells, Jacques, Durrant, Williams
Scorer: Williams (3)

Date: Saturday 21/11/1964
Result: **GLOUCESTER CITY 2 CANTERBURY CITY 1**
Competition: Southern League Division 1
Teamsheet: McCluskey, Ashall, Palmer, Coldray, Cox, Durrant, Livingstone, Williams, Jacques, Hawkins, Wise
Scorers: Jacques, Hawkins

Date: Saturday 28/11/1964
Result: **DEAL TOWN 3 GLOUCESTER CITY 2**
Competition: Southern League Division 1
Teamsheet: Pellant, Palmer, Foote, Coldray, Cox, Casey, Hawkins, Wise, Jacques, Durrant, Williams
Scorers: Wise, Jacques

Date: Saturday 05/12/1964
Result: **GLOUCESTER CITY 2 STEVENAGE TOWN 1**
Competition: Southern League Division 1
Teamsheet: Pellant, Ashall, Palmer, Coldray, Cox, Durrant, Livingstone, Wells, Jacques, Williams, Hawkins
Scorers: Livingstone, Williams

Date: Saturday 12/12/1964
Result: **GLOUCESTER CITY 2 HILLINGDON BOROUGH 1**
Competition: Southern League Division 1
Teamsheet: Pellant, Ashall, Palmer, Durrant, Cox, Casey, Livingstone, Coldray, Wells, Hargreaves, Hawkins
Scorers: Livingstone, own goal

Date: Saturday 19/12/1964
Result: **BURTON ALBION 2 GLOUCESTER CITY 1**
Competition: Southern League Division 1
Teamsheet: Pellant, Ashall, Palmer, Wixey, Cox, Casey, Livingstone, Wells, Jacques, Durrant, Hargreaves
Scorer: Jacques
Attendance: 1256

HORTON ROAD

THE DEVELOPMENT PLAN

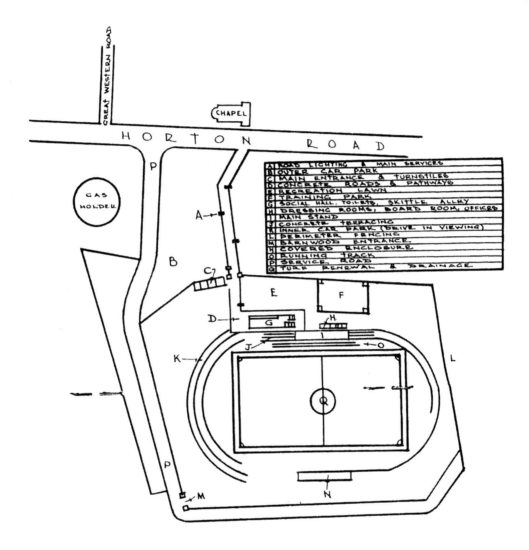

GREAT WESTERN ROAD

CHAPEL

H O R T O N   R O A D

GAS HOLDER

A	ROAD LIGHTING & MAIN SERVICES
B	OUTER CAR PARK
C	MAIN ENTRANCE & TURNSTILES
D	CONCRETE ROADS & PATHWAYS
E	RECREATION LAWN
F	TRAINING PARK
G	SOCIAL HALL, TOILETS, SKITTLE ALLEY
H	DRESSING ROOMS, BOARD ROOM, OFFICES
I	MAIN STAND
J	CONCRETE TERRACING
K	INNER CAR PARK (DRIVE IN VIEWING)
L	PERIMETER FENCING
M	BARNWOOD ENTRANCE
N	COVERED ENCLOSURE
O	RUNNING TRACK
P	SERVICE ROAD
Q	TURF RENEWAL & DRAINAGE

L A Y O U T   P L A N   ~   F I R S T   P H A S E

G L O U C E S T E R   S P O R T S   S T A D I U M

(Under the auspices of Gloucester City A.F.C. Ltd)

			£
COST OF BOWL to 1963			12,000
COST OF ITEMS A - G			24,000
		TOTAL	36,000
CASH AND LOANS			21,000
URGENTLY REQUIRED			15,000

10 August 1964 – The Mayor of Gloucester, Councillor W.J. Lewis, 'kicks off' the first training session of Gloucester City AFC at Horton Road Stadium, watched by directors of the club, player-manager Tom Casey and players.

Date: Saturday 26/12/1964
Result: **GLOUCESTER CITY 0 TROWBRIDGE TOWN 1**
Competition: Southern League Division 1
Teamsheet: Pellant, Ashall, Palmer, Wixey, Cox, Durrant, Livingstone, Williams, Wells, Hargreaves, Hawkins

Date: Monday 28/12/1964
Result: **TROWBRIDGE TOWN 2 GLOUCESTER CITY 3**
Competition: Southern League Division 1
Teamsheet: Pellant, Ashall, Palmer, Coldray, Cox, Casey, Livingstone, Wells, Jacques, Durrant, Williams
Scorers: Wells, Williams (2)

Date: Saturday 02/01/1965
Result: **GLOUCESTER CITY 4 CRAWLEY TOWN 0**
Competition: Southern League Division 1
Teamsheet: Pellant, Ashall, Palmer, Coldray, Cox, Casey, Livingstone, Wells, Jacques, Durrant, Williams
Scorers: Livingstone, Jacques (2), Williams

Date: Saturday 09/01/1965
Result: **CORBY TOWN 4 GLOUCESTER CITY 0**
Competition: Southern League Division 1
Teamsheet: Pellant, Ashall, Palmer, Wixey, Cox, Coldray, Livingstone, Edwards, Jacques, Durrant, Williams

Date: Saturday 23/01/1965
Result: **ASHFORD TOWN 0 GLOUCESTER CITY 1**
Competition: Southern League Division 1
Teamsheet: Pellant, Ashall, Palmer, Coldray, Cox, Casey, Livingstone, Edwards, Jacques, Durrant, Williams
Scorer: Williams

Date: Saturday 30/01/1965
Result: **GLOUCESTER CITY 2 CORBY TOWN 3**
Competition: Southern League Division 1
Teamsheet: Pellant, Ashall, Palmer, Coldray, Cox, Durrant, Livingstone, Edwards, Jacques, Williams, Hawkins
Scorer: Hawkins (2)

Date: Saturday 06/02/1965
Result: **GLOUCESTER CITY 1 DOVER 1**
Competition: Southern League Division 1
Teamsheet: Pellant, Ashall, Palmer, Coldray, Cox, Casey, Livingstone, Wells, Crichton, Durrant, Jacques
Scorer: Durrant

Date: Saturday 13/02/1965
Result: **RAMSGATE ATHLETIC 2 GLOUCESTER CITY 0**
Competition: Southern League Division 1
Teamsheet: Pellant, Ashall, Palmer, Wixey, Cox, Casey, Hawkins, Wells, Crichton, Durrant, Williams

Date: Saturday 20/02/1965
Result: **BARRY TOWN 2 GLOUCESTER CITY 0**
Competition: Southern League Division 1
Teamsheet: McCluskey, Ashall, Palmer, Coldray, Cox, Durrant, Livingstone, Crichton, Jacques, Williams, Edwards

Date: Saturday 27/02/1965
Result: **GLOUCESTER CITY 2 MERTHYR TYDFIL 1**
Competition: Southern League Division 1
Teamsheet: McCluskey, Ashall, Palmer, Wixey, Cox, Coldray, Livingstone, Wells, Medcroft, Williams, Edwards
Scorers: Wixey, Wells

Date: Saturday 06/03/1965
Result: **STEVENAGE TOWN 2 GLOUCESTER CITY 2**
Competition: Southern League Division 1
Teamsheet: McCluskey, Ashall, Palmer, Wixey, Cox, Coldray, Livingstone, Wells, Medcroft, Williams, Edwards
Scorers: Medcroft, Edwards

Date: Saturday 13/03/1965
Result: **GLOUCESTER CITY 1 KETTERING TOWN 0**
Competition: Southern League Division 1
Teamsheet: McCluskey, Ashall, Palmer, Wixey, Cox, Coldray, Livingstone, Wells, Medcroft, Williams, Edwards
Scorer: Wells

Date: Saturday 20/03/1965
Result: **HEREFORD UNITED 7 GLOUCESTER CITY 0**
Competition: Southern League Division 1
Teamsheet: McCluskey, Ashall, Palmer, Wixey, Cox, Coldray, Livingstone, Wells, Medcroft, Edwards, Williams

Date: Saturday 27/03/1965
Result: **GLOUCESTER CITY 5 GRAVESEND & NORTHFLEET 2**
Competition: Southern League Division 1
Teamsheet: McCluskey, Ashall, Palmer, Wixey, Cox, Coldray, Livingstone, Wells, Medcroft, Williams, Edwards
Scorers: Livingstone, Wells, Medcroft, Williams (2)

Date: Saturday 03/04/1965
Result: **CANTERBURY CITY 1 GLOUCESTER CITY 3**
Competition: Southern League Division 1
Teamsheet: McCluskey, Ashall, Palmer, Wixey, Cox, Coldray, Livingstone, Wells, Medcroft, Williams, Edwards
Scorers: Coldray, Wells, Edwards

Date: Wednesday 07/04/1965
Result: **CRAWLEY TOWN 0 GLOUCESTER CITY 2**
Competition: Southern League Division 1
Teamsheet: McCluskey, Ashall, Palmer, Wixey, Cox, Casey, Livingstone, Wells, Medcroft, Williams, Edwards
Scorers: Livingstone, Medcroft

SEASON BY SEASON

Date: Saturday 10/04/1965
Result: **GLOUCESTER CITY 1 DEAL TOWN 0**
Competition: Southern League Division 1
Teamsheet: McCluskey, Ashall, Palmer, Wixey, Cox, Coldray, Livingstone, Wells, Medcroft, Williams, Edwards
Scorer: Edwards

Date: Monday 12/04/1965
Result: **GLOUCESTER CITY 1 CHELTENHAM TOWN 5**
Competition: Gloucestershire FA Northern Senior Professional Cup Final
Teamsheet: McCluskey, Ashall, Palmer, Wixey, Cox, Coldray, Livingstone, Wells, Medcroft, Williams, Edwards
Scorer: Medcroft
Attendance: 1800

Date: Friday 16/04/1965
Result: **GLOUCESTER CITY 3 HINCKLEY ATHLETIC 2**
Competition: Southern League Division 1
Teamsheet: Pellant, Ashall, Palmer, Williams, Cox, Coldray, Livingstone, Wells, Medcroft, Crichton, Edwards
Scorers: Coldray, Medcroft, Crichton
Attendance: 2000

Date: Saturday 17/04/1965
Result: **TUNBRIDGE WELLS RANGERS 1 GLOUCESTER CITY 1**
Competition: Southern League Division 1
Teamsheet: Pellant, Ashall, Palmer, Coldray, Cox, Casey, Livingstone, Wells, Crichton, Edwards, Williams
Scorer: Crichton

Date: Monday 19/04/1965
Result: **HINCKLEY ATHLETIC 3 GLOUCESTER CITY 0**
Competition: Southern League Division 1
Teamsheet: McCluskey, Ashall, Palmer, Coldray, Cox, Durrant, Livingstone, Wells, Medcroft, Crichton, Edwards
Attendance: 150

Date: Saturday 24/04/1965
Result: **GLOUCESTER CITY 3 SITTINGBOURNE 0**
Competition: Southern League Division 1
Teamsheet: Pellant, Ashall, Palmer, Coldray, Cox, Durrant, Livingstone, Wells, Medcroft, Crichton, Edwards
Scorers: Coldray, Medcroft, own goal

Date: Tuesday 27/04/1965
Result: **GLOUCESTER CITY 5 ASHFORD TOWN 0**
Competition: Southern League Division 1
Teamsheet: Pellant, Ashall, Palmer, Coldray, Cox, Durrant, Livingstone, Wells, Medcroft, Crichton, Edwards
Scorers: Coldray, Durrant, Medcroft, Crichton (2)

Date: Saturday 01/05/1965
Result: **GRAVESEND & NORTHFLEET 0 GLOUCESTER CITY 2**
Competition: Southern League Division 1
Teamsheet: Pellant, Ashall, Palmer, Coldray, Cox, Durrant, Livingstone, Wells, Medcroft, Crichton, Edwards
Scorers: Coldray, Crichton
Attendance: 500

Appearances – B Adlam 3, J Ashall 46, T Casey 23, RA Coldray 39, A Cox 48, R Crichton 9, A Durrant 32, K Edwards 19, TE Foote 2, T Hargreaves 3, M Hawkins 16, A Jacques 29, I Livingstone 45, R McCluskey 26, G Medcroft 14, G Palmer 48, GA Pellant 22, I Prosser 14, B Wells 38, A Williams 36, C Wise 3, R Wixey 13.
Scorers – A Williams 17, A Jacques 10, B Wells 9, G Medcroft 8, RA Coldray 6, I Livingstone 6, R Crichton 5, M Hawkins 5, K Edwards 3, A Durrant 2, I Prosser 1, C Wise 1, R Wixey 1, own goals 4.

SOUTHERN LEAGUE DIVISION 1

POS	CLUB	P	W	D	L	F	A	PTS
1	HEREFORD UNITED	42	34	4	4	124	39	72
2	WIMBLEDON	42	24	13	5	108	52	61
3	POOLE TOWN	42	26	6	10	92	56	58
4	CORBY TOWN	42	24	7	11	88	55	55
5	STEVENAGE TOWN	42	19	13	10	83	43	51
6	HILLINGDON BOROUGH	42	21	7	14	105	63	49
7	CRAWLEY TOWN	42	22	5	15	83	52	49
8	MERTHYR TYDFIL	42	20	9	13	75	59	49
9	**GLOUCESTER CITY**	**42**	**19**	**10**	**13**	**68**	**65**	**48**
10	BURTON ALBION	42	20	7	15	83	75	47
11	CANTERBURY CITY	42	13	16	13	73	53	42
12	KETTERING TOWN	42	14	13	15	74	64	41
13	RAMSGATE ATHLETIC	42	16	8	18	51	59	40
14	DOVER	42	14	10	18	54	59	38
15	HINCKLEY ATHLETIC	42	12	9	21	55	81	33
16	TROWBRIDGE TOWN	42	14	5	23	68	104	33
17	ASHFORD TOWN	42	11	8	23	60	98	30
18	BARRY TOWN	42	11	7	24	47	103	29
19	DEAL TOWN	42	7	13	22	61	127	27
20	TUNBRIDGE WELLS RANGERS	42	10	6	26	51	107	26
21	GRAVESEND & NORTHFLEET	42	9	7	26	57	101	25
22	SITTINGBOURNE	42	8	5	29	58	103	21
		924	368	188	368	1618	1618	924

SEASON BY SEASON

SEASON 1965-1966
(Home Ground: Horton Road Stadium)

Date: Saturday 21/08/1965
Result: **GLOUCESTER CITY 4 GRAVESEND & NORTHFLEET 1**
Competition: Southern League Division 1
Teamsheet: McCluskey, Ashall, Palmer, Wixey, Cox, Coldray, Livingstone, B Wells, Grant, Williams, Hargreaves
Scorers: Livingstone, Grant (2), Hargreaves
Attendance: 1426

Date: Monday 23/08/1965
Result: **HILLINGDON BOROUGH 5 GLOUCESTER CITY 1**
Competition: Southern League Division 1
Teamsheet: McCluskey, Palmer, Ashall, Wixey, Cox, Coldray, Hargreaves, Crichton, Grant, B Wells, Livingstone
Scorer: Wixey

Date: Saturday 28/08/1965
Result: **BURTON ALBION 2 GLOUCESTER CITY 1**
Competition: Southern League Division 1
Teamsheet: McCluskey, Ashall, Palmer, Wixey, Northcott, Coldray, Livingstone, Williams, Medcroft, Grant, Hargreaves
Scorer: Hargreaves
Attendance: 1627

Date: Monday 30/08/1965
Result: **GLOUCESTER CITY 2 MERTHYR TYDFIL 1**
Competition: Southern League Cup 1st Round 1st Leg
Teamsheet: Pellant, Ashall, Palmer, Grant, Northcott, Coldray, Livingstone, B Wells, Medcroft, Williams, Hargreaves
Scorers: Livingstone, Medcroft

Date: Saturday 04/09/1965
Result: **GLOUCESTER CITY 1 LLANELLY 0**
Competition: FA Cup 1st Qualifying Round
Teamsheet: McCluskey, Ashall, Palmer, Cox, Northcott, Coldray, Livingstone, Grant, Crichton, Williams, Hargreaves
Scorer: Hargreaves

Date: Saturday 11/09/1965
Result: **MERTHYR TYDFIL 5 GLOUCESTER CITY 1**
Competition: Southern League Division 1
Teamsheet: McCluskey, Ashall, Palmer, Grant, Cox, Coldray, Livingstone, Crichton, D Wells, Williams, Hargreaves
Scorer: D Wells

Date: Wednesday 15/09/1965
Result: **GLOUCESTER CITY 0 HILLINGDON BOROUGH 2**
Competition: Southern League Division 1
Teamsheet: McCluskey, Ashall, Palmer, Coldray, Northcott, Cox, Livingstone, Crichton, Grant, Williams, Hargreaves

Date: Saturday 18/09/1965
Result: **LOVELLS ATHLETIC 1 GLOUCESTER CITY 2**
Competition: FA Cup 2nd Qualifying Round
Teamsheet: McCluskey, Ashall, Palmer, Wixey, Northcott, Coldray, Livingstone, Grant, Medcroft, B Wells, Crichton
Scorers: Medcroft, Crichton

Date: Wednesday 22/09/1965
Result: **GLOUCESTER CITY 1 CANTERBURY CITY 1**
Competition: Southern League Division 1
Teamsheet: McCluskey, Ashall, Palmer, Wixey, Northcott, Cox, Livingstone, Grant, Medcroft, Hargreaves, Crichton
Scorer: Crichton

Date: Saturday 25/09/1965
Result: **RAMSGATE ATHLETIC 0 GLOUCESTER CITY 1**
Competition: Southern League Division 1
Teamsheet: McCluskey, Ashall, Palmer, Wixey, Northcott, Grant, Livingstone, Medcroft, D Wells, Hargreaves, Crichton
Scorer: D Wells
Attendance: 560

Date: Monday 27/09/1965
Result: **CANTERBURY CITY 3 GLOUCESTER CITY 4**
Competition: Southern League Division 1
Teamsheet: McCluskey, Ashall, Palmer, Wixey, Northcott, Grant, Livingstone, Medcroft, D Wells, Hargreaves, Crichton
Scorers: Hargreaves, D Wells (2), Medcroft

Date: Saturday 02/10/1965
Result: **GLOUCESTER CITY 1 MERTHYR TYDFIL 1**
Competition: FA Cup 3rd Qualifying Round
Teamsheet: McCluskey, Ashall, Palmer, Coldray, Northcott, Grant, Livingstone, Medcroft, D Wells, Hargreaves, Crichton
Scorer: Livingstone
Attendance: 2384

Date: Wednesday 06/10/1965
Result: **MERTHYR TYDFIL 1 GLOUCESTER CITY 1**
Competition: FA Cup 3rd Qualifying Round Replay
Teamsheet: McCluskey, Ashall, Palmer, Wixey, Coldray, Grant, Livingstone, B Wells, D Wells, Hargreaves, Crichton
Scorer: D Wells
Attendance: 3400

Date: Saturday 09/10/1965
Result: **GLOUCESTER CITY 1 HASTINGS UNITED 3**
Competition: Southern League Division 1
Teamsheet: McCluskey, Ashall, Palmer, Wixey, Northcott, Grant, Livingstone, Williams, D Wells, B Wells, Crichton
Scorer: Grant
Attendance: 1320

[191]

Date: Monday 11/10/1965
Result: **MERTHYR TYDFIL 1 GLOUCESTER CITY 0**
Competition: FA Cup 3rd Qualifying Round 2nd Replay
Teamsheet: McCluskey, Ashall, Palmer, Coldray, Northcott, Wixey, Hargreaves, Livingstone, Grant, B Wells, Crichton
Attendance: 2500
Note: Played at Hereford

Date: Saturday 16/10/1965
Result: **TUNBRIDGE WELLS RANGERS 2 GLOUCESTER CITY 2**
Competition: Southern League Division 1
Teamsheet: McCluskey, Ashall, Palmer, Coldray, Northcott, Grant, Livingstone, Wixey, B Wells, Hargreaves, Crichton
Scorers: B Wells, Hargreaves

Date: Wednesday 20/10/1965
Result: **MERTHYR TYDFIL 2 GLOUCESTER CITY 0**
Competition: Southern League Cup 1st Round 2nd Leg
Teamsheet: McCluskey, Palmer, Wixey, Coldray, Grant, Livingstone, B Wells, D Wells, Medcroft, Hargreaves, Crichton

Date: Saturday 23/10/1965
Result: **GLOUCESTER CITY 1 BARNET 0**
Competition: Southern League Division 1
Teamsheet: McCluskey, Ashall, Palmer, Grant, Northcott, Coldray, Gay, Williams, D Wells, Hargreaves, Crichton
Scorer: D Wells

Date: Saturday 30/10/1965
Result: **CRAWLEY TOWN 3 GLOUCESTER CITY 4**
Competition: Southern League Division 1
Teamsheet: McCluskey, Ashall, Palmer, Coldray, Northcott, Grant, Gay, Hargreaves, D Wells, B Wells, Crichton
Scorers: Grant, Hargreaves, D Wells, B Wells

Date: Saturday 06/11/1965
Result: **GLOUCESTER CITY 0 BEXLEY UNITED 0**
Competition: Southern League Division 1
Teamsheet: McCluskey, Ashall, Palmer, Grant, Northcott, Coldray, Gay, Hargreaves, D Wells, B Wells, Crichton

Date: Saturday 13/11/1965
Result: **KETTERING TOWN 2 GLOUCESTER CITY 1**
Competition: Southern League Division 1
Teamsheet: McCluskey, Ashall, Palmer, Grant, Northcott, Coldray, Gay, B Wells, D Wells, McCool, Hargreaves
Scorer: Grant

Date: Saturday 20/11/1965
Result: **GLOUCESTER CITY 0 STEVENAGE TOWN 0**
Competition: Southern League Division 1
Teamsheet: McCluskey, Ashall, Palmer, Grant, Northcott, Coldray, Gay, Hargreaves, B Wells, McCool, Crichton

Date: Saturday 27/11/1965
Result: **DEAL TOWN 1 GLOUCESTER CITY 2**
Competition: Southern League Division 1
Teamsheet: McCluskey, Ashall, Palmer, Coldray, Northcott, Grant, Gay, B Wells, Medcroft, Hargreaves, McCool
Scorers: Medcroft, McCool

Date: Saturday 04/12/1965
Result: **GLOUCESTER CITY 0 WISBECH TOWN 2**
Competition: Southern League Division 1
Teamsheet: McCluskey, Ashall, Palmer, Wixey, Northcott, Grant, Gay, B Wells, Crichton, Hargreaves, McCool

Date: Saturday 11/12/1965
Result: **DUNSTABLE TOWN 3 GLOUCESTER CITY 1**
Competition: Southern League Division 1
Teamsheet: McCluskey, Ashall, Palmer, Wixey, Northcott, Coldray, Gay, McCool, Grant, Hargreaves, Wise
Scorer: McCool

Date: Saturday 18/12/1965
Result: **GLOUCESTER CITY 3 TUNBRIDGE WELLS RANGERS 0**
Competition: Southern League Division 1
Teamsheet: McCluskey, Ashall, Palmer, Wixey, Northcott, Coldray, Gay, Hargreaves, Grant, McCool, Wise
Scorers: Wixey, Northcott, Grant

Date: Saturday 01/01/1966
Result: **HASTINGS UNITED 6 GLOUCESTER CITY 2**
Competition: Southern League Division 1
Teamsheet: McCluskey, Ashall, Palmer, Wixey, Coldray, Grant, Gay, Hargreaves, B Wells, McCool, D Wells
Scorers: Grant, McCool

Date: Saturday 08/01/1966
Result: **GLOUCESTER CITY 1 CRAWLEY TOWN 3**
Competition: Southern League Division 1
Teamsheet: McCluskey, Ashall, Palmer, Wixey, Northcott, Coldray, B Wells, Grant, D Wells, McCool, Hargreaves
Scorer: B Wells

Date: Saturday 15/01/1966
Result: **BARNET 2 GLOUCESTER CITY 0**
Competition: Southern League Division 1
Teamsheet: McCluskey, Ashall, Palmer, Grant, Northcott, Coldray, Gay, Hargreaves, Crichton, McCool, Wise

Date: Saturday 22/01/1966
Result: **GLOUCESTER CITY 6 DOVER 1**
Competition: Southern League Division 1
Teamsheet: McCluskey, Ashall, Palmer, Grant, Northcott, Coldray, Gay, Hargreaves, Crichton, McCool, Wise
Scorers: Gay (3), Crichton, McCool, Wise

[192]

Date: Saturday 29/01/1966
Result: **GRAVESEND & NORTHFLEET 3 GLOUCESTER CITY 3**
Competition: Southern League Division 1
Teamsheet: McCluskey, Ashall, Palmer, Grant, Northcott, Coldray, Gay, Hargreaves, Crichton, McCool, Wise
Scorers: Grant, Crichton, Wise
Attendance: 759

Date: Saturday 12/02/1966
Result: **DOVER 5 GLOUCESTER CITY 1**
Competition: Southern League Division 1
Teamsheet: McCluskey, Ashall, Palmer, Grant, Northcott, Coldray, Gay, McCool, Crichton, Hargreaves, Wise
Scorer: Hargreaves
Attendance: 491

Date: Saturday 19/02/1966
Result: **BARRY TOWN 5 GLOUCESTER CITY 2**
Competition: Southern League Division 1
Teamsheet: McCluskey, Coldray, Palmer, Moulsdale, Northcott, Grant, Gay, Hargreaves, Crichton, McCool, Wise
Scorers: Grant, McCool

Date: Saturday 26/02/1966
Result: **GLOUCESTER CITY 1 MERTHYR TYDFIL 2**
Competition: Southern League Division 1
Teamsheet: McCluskey, Ashall, Palmer, Moulsdale, Coldray, Grant, Gay, Hargreaves, Crichton, McCool, Wise
Scorer: Wise

Date: Saturday 05/03/1966
Result: **ASHFORD TOWN 1 GLOUCESTER CITY 2**
Competition: Southern League Division 1
Teamsheet: Pellant, Ashall, Palmer, Moulsdale, Northcott, Coldray, Gay, Hargreaves, McCool, Grant, Wise
Scorers: McCool, Grant

Date: Monday 07/03/1966
Result: **BATH CITY 4 GLOUCESTER CITY 1**
Competition: Southern League Division 1
Teamsheet: Pellant, Ashall, Palmer, Moulsdale, Coldray, Grant, Gay, Collins, McCool, Crichton, Wise
Scorer: Collins

Date: Saturday 12/03/1966
Result: **HINCKLEY ATHLETIC 4 GLOUCESTER CITY 4**
Competition: Southern League Division 1
Teamsheet: Pellant, Ashall, Palmer, Moulsdale, Northcott, Grant, Gay, Collins, McCool, Hargreaves, Crichton
Scorers: Grant, McCool (3)

Date: Saturday 19/03/1966
Result: **GLOUCESTER CITY 0 RAMSGATE ATHLETIC 0**
Competition: Southern League Division 1
Teamsheet: McCluskey, Ashall, Palmer, Moulsdale, Northcott, Coldray, Gay, Hargreaves, McCool, Grant, Collins

Date: Thursday 24/03/1966
Result: **GLOUCESTER CITY 1 BATH CITY 1**
Competition: Southern League Division 1
Teamsheet: McCluskey, Ashall, Palmer, Moulsdale, Grant, Etheridge, Gay, Collins, D Wells, Coldray, Hargreaves
Scorer: Moulsdale

Date: Saturday 26/03/1966
Result: **SITTINGBOURNE 2 GLOUCESTER CITY 2**
Competition: Southern League Division 1
Teamsheet: McCluskey, Ashall, Palmer, Moulsdale, Northcott, Etheridge, Hargreaves, Grant, D Wells, Coldray, Collins
Scorer: D Wells (2)

Date: Thursday 31/03/1966
Result: **GLOUCESTER CITY 2 BURTON ALBION 5**
Competition: Southern League Division 1
Teamsheet: McCluskey, Ashall, Palmer, Moulsdale, Grant, Etheridge, Gay, Collins, D Wells, Coldray, McCool
Scorers: McCool, D Wells
Attendance: 573

Date: Saturday 02/04/1966
Result: **BEXLEY UNITED 3 GLOUCESTER CITY 1**
Competition: Southern League Division 1
Teamsheet: Pellant, Ashall, Palmer, Moulsdale, Etheridge, Wixey, Grant, Collins, D Wells, McCool, Wise
Scorer: Collins
Attendance: 831

Date: Friday 08/04/1966
Result: **TROWBRIDGE TOWN 0 GLOUCESTER CITY 1**
Competition: Southern League Division 1
Teamsheet: Pellant, Ashall, Palmer, Moulsdale, Northcott, Grant, Gay, Collins, D Wells, McCool, Wise
Scorer: Grant

Date: Saturday 09/04/1966
Result: **GLOUCESTER CITY 0 KETTERING TOWN 1**
Competition: Southern League Division 1
Teamsheet: Pellant, Ashall, Palmer, Moulsdale, Northcott, Wixey, Grant, Gay, D Wells, McCool, Wise

Date: Monday 11/04/1966
Result: **GLOUCESTER CITY 3 TROWBRIDGE TOWN 2**
Competition: Southern League Division 1
Teamsheet: Pellant, Ashall, Palmer, Moulsdale, Northcott, Grant, McCool, Gay, D Wells, Hargreaves, Wise
Scorers: D Wells (2), Hargreaves
Note: Rob Kujawa's first match attended, aged 11

[193]

Date: Saturday 16/04/1966
Result: **STEVENAGE TOWN 5 GLOUCESTER CITY 1**
Competition: Southern League Division 1
Teamsheet: Pellant, Ashall, Palmer, Moulsdale, Northcott, Coldray, Hargreaves, Gay, D Wells, McCool, McCluskey
Scorer: McCool (pen)

Date: Monday 18/04/1966
Result: **GLOUCESTER CITY 1 CINDERFORD TOWN 0**
Competition: Gloucestershire FA Northern Senior Professional Cup Semi-Final
Teamsheet: McCluskey, Ashall, Palmer, Moulsdale, Etheridge, Wixey, McCool, Gay, D Wells, Grant, Hargreaves
Scorer: D Wells

Date: Thursday 21/04/1966
Result: **GLOUCESTER CITY 2 HINCKLEY ATHLETIC 3**
Competition: Southern League Division 1
Teamsheet: McCluskey, Ashall, Palmer, Moulsdale, Etheridge, Wixey, McCool, Gay, D Wells, Grant, Hargreaves
Scorers: Wixey, Gay

Date: Saturday 23/04/1966
Result: **GLOUCESTER CITY 3 DEAL TOWN 0**
Competition: Southern League Division 1
Teamsheet: McCluskey, Ashall, Palmer, Moulsdale, Northcott, Wixey, McCool, Gay, D Wells, Grant, Hargreaves
Scorers: Gay, Grant (2)

Date: Monday 25/04/1966
Result: **GLOUCESTER CITY 1 BARRY TOWN 1**
Competition: Southern League Division 1
Teamsheet: McCluskey, Ashall, Palmer, Moulsdale, Grant, Wixey, McCool, Gay, D Wells, Hargreaves, Collins
Scorer: Ashall

Date: Thursday 28/04/1966
Result: **GLOUCESTER CITY 2 SITTINGBOURNE 2**
Competition: Southern League Division 1
Teamsheet: McCluskey, Ashall, Palmer, Moulsdale, Grant, Wixey, Collins, Gay, McCool, Hargreaves, Wise
Scorers: McCool, Wise

Date: Saturday 30/04/1966
Result: **WISBECH TOWN 2 GLOUCESTER CITY 2**
Competition: Southern League Division 1
Teamsheet: McCluskey, Ashall, Palmer, Moulsdale, Grant, Wixey, Hargreaves, Gay, D Wells, McCool, Wise
Scorers: Grant, Gay

Date: Monday 02/05/1966
Result: **GLOUCESTER CITY 2 DUNSTABLE TOWN 0**
Competition: Southern League Division 1
Teamsheet: McCluskey, Ashall, Palmer, Moulsdale, Grant, Wixey, Hargreaves, Gay, D Wells, McCool, Wise
Scorers: Gay, D Wells

Date: Thursday 05/05/1966
Result: **GLOUCESTER CITY 1 ASHFORD TOWN 0**
Competition: Southern League Division 1
Teamsheet: McCluskey, Ashall, Palmer, Moulsdale, Grant, Wixey, McCool, Gay, D Wells, Hargreaves, Wise
Scorer: Gay

Date: Saturday 07/05/1966
Result: **GLOUCESTER CITY 2 CHELTENHAM TOWN 0**
Competition: Gloucestershire FA Northern Senior Professional Cup Final
Teamsheet: McCluskey, Ashall, Palmer, Moulsdale, Northcott, Wixey, McCool, Gay, D Wells, Grant, Wise
Scorers: D Wells, Grant
Attendance: 2200

Appearances – J Ashall 53, RA Coldray 36, D Collins 10, A Cox 6, R Crichton 27, RF Etheridge 6, GAM Gay 36, R Grant 54, T Hargreaves 46, I Livingstone 17, R McCluskey 47, R McCool 32, G Medcroft 9, CB Moulsdale 23, GE Northcott 37, G Palmer 55, GA Pellant 9, B Wells 17, D Wells 29, A Williams 8, C Wise 19, R Wixey 28.
Scorers – R Grant 16, D Wells 15, R McCool 12, GAM Gay 8, T Hargreaves 8, R Crichton 4, G Medcroft 4, C Wise 4, I Livingstone 3, B Wells 3, R Wixey 3, D Collins 2, J Ashall 1, CB Moulsdale 1, GE Northcott 1.

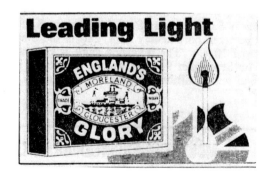

[194]

SOUTHERN LEAGUE DIVISION 1

POS	CLUB	P	W	D	L	F	A	PTS
1	BARNET	46	30	9	7	114	49	69
2	HILLINGDON BOROUGH	46	27	10	9	101	46	64
3	BURTON ALBION	46	28	8	10	121	60	64
4	BATH CITY	46	25	13	8	88	50	63
5	HASTINGS UNITED	46	25	10	11	104	59	60
6	WISBECH TOWN	46	25	9	12	98	54	59
7	CANTERBURY CITY	46	25	8	13	89	66	58
8	STEVENAGE TOWN	46	23	9	14	86	49	55
9	KETTERING TOWN	46	22	9	15	77	74	53
10	MERTHYR TYDFIL	46	22	6	18	95	68	50
11	DUNSTABLE TOWN	46	15	14	17	76	72	44
12	CRAWLEY TOWN	46	17	10	19	72	71	44
13	BEXLEY UNITED	46	20	4	22	65	71	44
14	TROWBRIDGE TOWN	46	16	11	19	79	81	43
15	DOVER	46	17	8	21	59	62	42
16	BARRY TOWN	46	16	10	20	72	94	42
17	GRAVESEND & NORTHFLEET	46	16	9	21	84	86	41
18	**GLOUCESTER CITY**	**46**	**14**	**12**	**20**	**75**	**98**	**40**
19	SITTINGBOURNE	46	11	12	23	77	121	34
20	RAMSGATE ATHLETIC	46	9	15	22	35	76	33
21	HINCKLEY ATHLETIC	46	10	12	24	58	93	32
22	TUNBRIDGE WELLS RANGERS	46	12	8	26	47	88	32
23	ASHFORD TOWN	46	9	10	27	44	92	28
24	DEAL TOWN	46	3	4	39	29	165	10
		1104	437	230	437	1845	1845	1104

SEASON 1966-1967
(Home Ground: Horton Road Stadium)

Date: Saturday 20/08/1966
Result: **HASTINGS UNITED 2 GLOUCESTER CITY 1**
Competition: Southern League Division 1
Teamsheet: Webb, Ashall, Pugsley, Ballinger, Northcott, Moulsdale, McCool, Grant, Bayliss, Gay, Wise
Substitute: Wells (for Gay)
Scorer: Bayliss

Date: Thursday 25/08/1966
Result: **GLOUCESTER CITY 3 BARRY TOWN 0**
Competition: Southern League Division 1
Teamsheet: Webb, Ashall, Wixey, Ballinger, Northcott, Moulsdale, McCool, Grant, Bayliss, Gay, Wise
Substitute: Wells (nps)
Scorers: McCool, Grant, Wise
Attendance: 1373

Date: Saturday 27/08/1966
Result: **GLOUCESTER CITY 0 MARGATE 1**
Competition: Southern League Division 1
Teamsheet: Webb, Ashall, Johnson, Ballinger, Northcott, Moulsdale, McCool, Bayliss, Grant, Gay, Wise
Substitute: Wells (nps)
Attendance: 1299

Date: Wednesday 31/08/1966
Result: **TROWBRIDGE TOWN 4 GLOUCESTER CITY 3**
Competition: Southern League Cup 1st Round 1st Leg
Teamsheet: Webb, Ashall, Johnson, Ballinger, Northcott, Moulsdale, McKellar, Hargreaves, Wells, Grant, Gay
Substitute: Wise (nps)
Scorers: Wells, Johnson, own goal
Attendance: 686

Date: Saturday 03/09/1966
Result: **GLOUCESTER CITY 4 ABERGAVENNY THURSDAYS 1**
Competition: FA Cup 1st Qualifying Round
Teamsheet: Webb, Ashall, Johnson, Moulsdale, Northcott, Ballinger, McCool, Gay, Grant, Wells, Hargreaves
Substitute: No sub
Scorers: Grant (3), McCool

Date: Thursday 08/09/1966
Result: **GLOUCESTER CITY 0 TROWBRIDGE TOWN 0**
Competition: Southern League Cup 1st Round 2nd Leg
Teamsheet: Webb, Ashall, Johnson, Ballinger, Northcott, Moulsdale, Gay, McCool, Grant, Wells, Hargreaves
Substitute: Wise (nps)
Attendance: 673

Date: Saturday 10/09/1966
Result: **GLOUCESTER CITY 2 RUGBY TOWN 0**
Competition: Southern League Division 1
Teamsheet: Webb, Ashall, Cottle, Moulsdale, Northcott, Ballinger, McIntosh, Hargreaves, Grant, Johnson, Wise
Substitute: Gay (nps)
Scorers: Grant, Johnson
Attendance: 893

[195]

Date: Monday 12/09/1966
Result: **BARRY TOWN 2 GLOUCESTER CITY 5**
Competition: Southern League Division 1
Teamsheet: Webb, Ashall, Cottle, Moulsdale, Northcott, Ballinger, Gay, Hargreaves, Grant, Johnson, Wise
Substitute: McCool (for Ballinger)
Scorers: Johnson (2), Grant (3)

Date: Saturday 17/09/1966
Result: **CINDERFORD TOWN 2 GLOUCESTER CITY 2**
Competition: FA Cup 2nd Qualifying Round
Teamsheet: Webb, Ashall, Cottle, Moulsdale, Northcott, Ballinger, Gay, Hargreaves, Grant, Johnson, Wise
Substitute: No sub
Scorers: Johnson, Grant
Attendance: 1200

Date: Thursday 22/09/1966
Result: **GLOUCESTER CITY 0 CINDERFORD TOWN 3**
Competition: FA Cup 2nd Qualifying Round Replay
Teamsheet: Webb, Ashall, Cottle, Moulsdale, Northcott, Ballinger, McCool, Hargreaves, Grant, Johnson, Wise
Substitute: No sub

Date: Saturday 24/09/1966
Result: **GLOUCESTER CITY 3 HINCKLEY ATHLETIC 0**
Competition: Southern League Division 1
Teamsheet: Webb, Pugsley, Cottle, Moulsdale, Northcott, Ballinger, McIntosh, Gay, Grant, Johnson, Wise
Substitute: McCool (nps)
Scorers: Johnson, own goal, Grant
Attendance: 803

Date: Thursday 29/09/1966
Result: **GLOUCESTER CITY 0 MERTHYR TYDFIL 1**
Competition: Southern League Division 1
Teamsheet: Webb, Pugsley, Cottle, Moulsdale, Northcott, Wixey, McIntosh, Tabor, Grant, Johnson, Gay
Substitute: Wise (nps)
Attendance: 902

Date: Saturday 01/10/1966
Result: **TUNBRIDGE WELLS RANGERS 0 GLOUCESTER CITY 1**
Competition: Southern League Division 1
Teamsheet: Webb, Pugsley, Cottle, Moulsdale, Grant, Wixey, Gay, Tabor, Johnson, McIntosh, Wise
Substitute: No sub
Scorer: Johnson

Date: Tuesday 04/10/1966
Result: **MERTHYR TYDFIL 4 GLOUCESTER CITY 1**
Competition: Southern League Division 1
Teamsheet: Webb, Pugsley, Cottle, Wixey, Grant, Moulsdale, Gay, Tabor, Johnson, McIntosh, Hargreaves
Substitute: McCool (nps)
Scorer: Hargreaves

Date: Saturday 08/10/1966
Result: **ASHFORD TOWN 3 GLOUCESTER CITY 1**
Competition: Southern League Division 1
Teamsheet: Webb, Pugsley, Cottle, Wixey, Northcott, Moulsdale, Hargreaves, Grant, Tabor, Johnson, Wise
Substitute: Gay (nps)
Scorer: Hargreaves

Date: Wednesday 19/10/1966
Result: **BEXLEY UNITED 2 GLOUCESTER CITY 0**
Competition: Southern League Division 1
Teamsheet: Webb, Pugsley, Cottle, Moulsdale, Northcott, Wixey, Hargreaves, Tabor, Johnson, Collins, Gay
Substitute: No sub

Date: Saturday 22/10/1966
Result: **GRAVESEND & NORTHFLEET 3 GLOUCESTER CITY 1**
Competition: Southern League Division 1
Teamsheet: Webb, Ashall, Cottle, Moulsdale, Northcott, Wixey, Gay, Tabor, Johnson, Collins, Hargreaves
Substitute: Pugsley (nps)
Scorer: Tabor
Attendance: 696

Date: Saturday 29/10/1966
Result: **GLOUCESTER CITY 2 KETTERING TOWN 1**
Competition: Southern League Division 1
Teamsheet: Webb, Ashall, Pugsley, Moulsdale, Northcott, Wixey, Gay, Grant, Johnson, Collins, Hargreaves
Substitute: Wise (nps)
Scorers: Gay, Johnson
Attendance: 678

Date: Wednesday 02/11/1966
Result: **DARTFORD 3 GLOUCESTER CITY 1**
Competition: Southern League Division 1
Teamsheet: Webb, Ashall, Cottle, Moulsdale, Northcott, Wixey, Gay, Grant, Johnson, Collins, Hargreaves
Substitute: Wise (nps)
Scorer: Johnson
Attendance: 600

Date: Saturday 05/11/1966
Result: **DUNSTABLE TOWN 2 GLOUCESTER CITY 1**
Competition: Southern League Division 1
Teamsheet: Webb, Ashall, Cottle, Moulsdale, Northcott, Wixey, Gay, Grant, Johnson, Collins, Hargreaves
Substitute: Williams (for Ashall)
Scorer: Johnson

Date: Saturday 12/11/1966
Result: **GLOUCESTER CITY 1 CANTERBURY CITY 0**
Competition: Southern League Division 1
Teamsheet: Webb, Wixey, Cottle, Moulsdale, Northcott, McCool, Gay, Grant, Johnson, Collins, Hargreaves
Substitute: McKellar (nps)
Scorer: Collins
Attendance: 710

Date: Saturday 26/11/1966
Result: **GLOUCESTER CITY 3 SITTINGBOURNE 0**
Competition: Southern League Division 1
Teamsheet: Webb, Wixey, Cottle, Moulsdale, Northcott, McCool, Gay, Grant, Johnson, Collins, Hargreaves
Substitute: Wise (nps)
Scorers: Collins, Johnson (2)
Attendance: 702

Date: Saturday 03/12/1966
Result: **TROWBRIDGE TOWN 1 GLOUCESTER CITY 1**
Competition: Southern League Division 1
Teamsheet: Webb, Wixey, Cottle, Moulsdale, Northcott, McCool, Gay, Grant, Johnson, Collins, Hargreaves
Substitute: Williams (nps)
Scorer: Gay

Date: Saturday 10/12/1966
Result: **GLOUCESTER CITY 6 BANBURY UNITED 3**
Competition: Southern League Division 1
Teamsheet: Webb, Wixey, Cottle, Moulsdale, Northcott, McCool, Gay, Grant, Johnson, Collins, Hargreaves
Substitute: Wise (nps)
Scorers: Collins (4), Johnson, Grant
Attendance: 806

Date: Saturday 17/12/1966
Result: **GLOUCESTER CITY 3 HASTINGS UNITED 2**
Competition: Southern League Division 1
Teamsheet: Webb, Wixey, Cottle, Moulsdale, Northcott, McCool, Gay, Grant, Johnson, Collins, Hargreaves
Substitute: Wise (nps)
Scorers: Johnson, Grant (2, 1 pen)
Attendance: 859

Date: Saturday 24/12/1966
Result: **TONBRIDGE 5 GLOUCESTER CITY 1**
Competition: Southern League Division 1
Teamsheet: Webb, Wixey, Cottle, Moulsdale, Northcott, McCool, Gay, Grant, Johnson, Collins, Hargreaves
Substitute: Williams (nps)
Scorer: Hargreaves

Date: Monday 26/12/1966
Result: **GLOUCESTER CITY 1 TONBRIDGE 4**
Competition: Southern League Division 1
Teamsheet: Webb, Wixey, Cottle, Moulsdale, Northcott, McCool, Gay, Grant, Johnson, Collins, Hargreaves
Substitute: Wise (nps)
Scorer: Collins
Attendance: 1010

Date: Saturday 31/12/1966
Result: **MARGATE 4 GLOUCESTER CITY 2**
Competition: Southern League Division 1
Teamsheet: Webb, Ashall, Cottle, Moulsdale, Grant, McCool, Gay, Collins, Johnson, Wise, Hargreaves
Substitute: Williams (nps)
Scorers: Johnson, Gay
Attendance: 1533

Date: Saturday 07/01/1967
Result: **GLOUCESTER CITY 0 WISBECH TOWN 2**
Competition: Southern League Division 1
Teamsheet: Webb, Ashall, Cottle, Grant, Northcott, McCool, Gay, Collins, Johnson, Wise, Hargreaves
Substitute: Moulsdale (nps)
Attendance: 509

Date: Saturday 14/01/1967
Result: **RUGBY TOWN 0 GLOUCESTER CITY 0**
Competition: Southern League Division 1
Teamsheet: Webb, Ashall, Cottle, Moulsdale, Northcott, McCool, Gay, Grant, Johnson, Collins, Wise
Substitute: Williams (nps)

Date: Saturday 21/01/1967
Result: **GLOUCESTER CITY 2 DARTFORD 2**
Competition: Southern League Division 1
Teamsheet: Webb, Ashall, Cottle, Moulsdale, Northcott, McCool, Gay, Grant, Johnson, Collins, Wise
Substitute: Hargreaves (nps)
Scorers: Gay, Ashall
Attendance: 523

Date: Saturday 28/01/1967
Result: **RAMSGATE ATHLETIC 5 GLOUCESTER CITY 1**
Competition: Southern League Division 1
Teamsheet: Webb, Ashall, Cottle, Moulsdale, Northcott, McCool, Gay, Grant, Johnson, Collins, Wise
Substitute: Hargreaves (nps)
Scorer: Gay
Attendance: 761

[197]

Date: Saturday 04/02/1967
Result: **HINCKLEY ATHLETIC 0 GLOUCESTER CITY 0**
Competition: Southern League Division 1
Teamsheet: Webb, Ashall, Cottle, Moulsdale, Northcott, McCool, Hargreaves, Collins, Grant, Johnson, Wise
Substitute: Williams (nps)

Date: Saturday 11/02/1967
Result: **GLOUCESTER CITY 0 TROWBRIDGE TOWN 1**
Competition: Southern League Division 1
Teamsheet: Webb, Ashall, Cottle, Moulsdale, Northcott, McCool, Hargreaves, Grant, Johnson, Collins, Wise
Substitute: Duke (nps)
Attendance: 612

Date: Wednesday 15/02/1967
Result: **WISBECH TOWN 2 GLOUCESTER CITY 0**
Competition: Southern League Division 1
Teamsheet: Webb, Ashall, Cottle, Moulsdale, Northcott, McCool, Gay, Hargreaves, Johnson, Collins, Wise
Substitute: Williams (nps)
Attendance: 301

Date: Saturday 18/02/1967
Result: **GLOUCESTER CITY 5 RAMSGATE ATHLETIC 0**
Competition: Southern League Division 1
Teamsheet: Webb, Ashall, Cottle, Moulsdale, Northcott, McCool, Gay, Grant, Johnson, Hargreaves, Wise
Substitute: Collins (nps)
Scorers: Wise, Gay (2), Johnson (2)
Attendance: 675

Date: Saturday 25/02/1967
Result: **GLOUCESTER CITY 2 ASHFORD TOWN 1**
Competition: Southern League Division 1
Teamsheet: Webb, Ashall, Cottle, Moulsdale, Northcott, McCool, Collins, Grant, Johnson, Hargreaves, Wise
Substitute: Wixey (nps)
Scorers: Grant, Collins
Attendance: 623

Date: Saturday 04/03/1967
Result: **STEVENAGE TOWN 6 GLOUCESTER CITY 0**
Competition: Southern League Division 1
Teamsheet: Webb, Ashall, Cottle, Moulsdale, Northcott, McCool, Barber, Grant, Johnson, Hargreaves, Wise
Substitute: Wixey (nps)

Date: Saturday 11/03/1967
Result: **GLOUCESTER CITY 0 DOVER 2**
Competition: Southern League Division 1
Teamsheet: Pellant, Ashall, Cottle, Moulsdale, Northcott, McCool, Gay, Grant, Johnson, Hargreaves, Wise
Substitute: Collins (nps)
Attendance: 633

Date: Saturday 18/03/1967
Result: **GLOUCESTER CITY 2 GRAVESEND & NORTHFLEET 0**
Competition: Southern League Division 1
Teamsheet: Pellant, Ashall, Cottle, Moulsdale, Northcott, McCool, Gay, Grant, Johnson, Hargreaves, Wise
Substitute: Collins (nps)
Scorers: Johnson, Grant
Attendance: 601

Date: Friday 24/03/1967
Result: **CRAWLEY TOWN 1 GLOUCESTER CITY 2**
Competition: Southern League Division 1
Teamsheet: Pellant, Wixey, Cottle, Moulsdale, Ashall, McCool, Gay, Grant, Howells, Collins, Wise
Substitute: Hargreaves (nps)
Scorers: Wise, own goal
Attendance: 1300

Date: Saturday 25/03/1967
Result: **KETTERING TOWN 1 GLOUCESTER CITY 2**
Competition: Southern League Division 1
Teamsheet: Pellant, Wixey, Cottle, Moulsdale, Ashall, McCool, Gay, Grant, Howells, Hargreaves, Wise
Substitute: Collins (nps)
Scorer: Gay (2)

Date: Monday 27/03/1967
Result: **GLOUCESTER CITY 2 CRAWLEY TOWN 2**
Competition: Southern League Division 1
Teamsheet: Pritchard, Wixey, Cottle, Moulsdale, Ashall, McCool, Gay, Grant, Johnson, Hargreaves, Wise
Substitute: Howells (nps)
Scorer: Grant (2)
Attendance: 1461

Date: Saturday 01/04/1967
Result: **GLOUCESTER CITY 1 DUNSTABLE TOWN 0**
Competition: Southern League Division 1
Teamsheet: Pritchard, Wixey, Johnson, Moulsdale, Ashall, McCool, Gay, Grant, Collins, Hargreaves, Wise
Substitute: Duke (nps)
Scorer: Wise
Attendance: 873

Date: Saturday 08/04/1967
Result: **CANTERBURY CITY 2 GLOUCESTER CITY 1**
Competition: Southern League Division 1
Teamsheet: Pritchard, Wixey, Cottle, Moulsdale, Ashall, McCool, Collins, Grant, Johnson, Hargreaves, Wise
Substitute: No sub
Scorer: Grant

Date: Saturday 15/04/1967
Result: **GLOUCESTER CITY 4 TUNBRIDGE WELLS RANGERS 0**
Competition: Southern League Division 1
Teamsheet: Pritchard, Wixey, Cottle, Ashall, Northcott, Moulsdale, Gay, Collins, Johnson, McCool, Wise
Substitute: Howells (nps)
Scorers: Wise (2), Wixey, Johnson
Attendance: 609

Date: Sunday 16/04/1967
Result: **GLOUCESTER CITY 1 CHELTENHAM TOWN 2**
Competition: Gloucestershire FA Northern Senior Professional Cup Final
Teamsheet: Webb, Ashall, Cottle, Moulsdale, Northcott, Wixey, Gay, Grant, Johnson, McCool, Wise
Substitute: No sub
Scorer: Grant
Attendance: 2650

Date: Thursday 20/04/1967
Result: **GLOUCESTER CITY 1 BEXLEY UNITED 0**
Competition: Southern League Division 1
Teamsheet: Webb, Wixey, Cottle, Moulsdale, Ashall, McCool, Gay, Grant, Johnson, Collins, Williams
Substitute: Howells (nps)
Scorer: Gay
Attendance: 457

Date: Saturday 22/04/1967
Result: **SITTINGBOURNE 3 GLOUCESTER CITY 3**
Competition: Southern League Division 1
Teamsheet: Webb, Wixey, Cottle, Moulsdale, Ashall, McCool, Williams, Gay, Johnson, Grant, Wise
Substitute: Collins (for Gay)
Scorers: Williams, Grant, Collins

Date: Thursday 27/04/1967
Result: **GLOUCESTER CITY 0 STEVENAGE TOWN 1**
Competition: Southern League Division 1
Teamsheet: Webb, Wixey, Cottle, Moulsdale, Ashall, McCool, Williams, Grant, Johnson, Collins, Wise
Substitute: Pendrick (nps)
Attendance: 611

Date: Saturday 06/05/1967
Result: **BANBURY UNITED 2 GLOUCESTER CITY 1**
Competition: Southern League Division 1
Teamsheet: Pritchard, Gapper, Cottle, Moulsdale, Ashall, Wixey, Williams, McCool, Johnson, Pendrick, Collins
Substitute: Gay (nps)
Scorer: McCool

Date: Saturday 13/05/1967
Result: **DOVER 7 GLOUCESTER CITY 0**
Competition: Southern League Division 1
Teamsheet: Pritchard, Gapper, Cottle, Wixey, Ashall, McCool, Williams, Duke, Johnson, Collins, Pendrick
Substitute: No sub
Attendance: 2063

Appearances – J Ashall 39, BP Ballinger 11, D Barber 1, C Bayliss 3, D Collins 29(1), T Cottle 44, DJ Duke 1, D Gapper 2, GAM Gay 41, R Grant 46, T Hargreaves 35, B Howells 2, H Johnson 48, R McCool 18(1), JM McIntosh 25, R McKellar 1, CB Moulsdale 50, GE Northcott 39, GA Pellant 4, S Pendrick 2, S Pritchard 6, D Pugsley 8, R Tabor 6, D Webb 42, D Wells 3(1), A Williams 5(1), C Wise 32, R Wixey 29.
Scorers: - R Grant 20, H Johnson 19, GAM Gay 10, D Collins 9, C Wise 5, T Hargreaves 3, R McCool 3, J Ashall 1, C Bayliss 1, R Tabor 1, D Wells 1, A Williams 1, R Wixey 1, own goals 3.

PROGRAMME

1968-1969

PROGRAMME

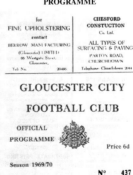

1969-1970

SOUTHERN LEAGUE DIVISION 1

POS	CLUB	P	W	D	L	F	A	PTS
1	DOVER	46	29	12	5	92	35	70
2	MARGATE	46	31	7	8	127	54	69
3	STEVENAGE TOWN	46	29	8	9	90	32	66
4	HASTINGS UNITED	46	25	16	5	89	45	66
5	KETTERING TOWN	46	27	9	10	105	62	63
6	CRAWLEY TOWN	46	26	8	12	81	48	60
7	RAMSGATE ATHLETIC	46	23	8	15	79	62	54
8	DARTFORD	46	19	15	12	92	67	53
9	TONBRIDGE	46	21	10	15	91	69	52
10	TROWBRIDGE TOWN	46	20	12	14	73	60	52
11	ASHFORD TOWN	46	18	8	20	74	68	44
12	MERTHYR TYDFIL	46	17	9	20	81	71	43
13	**GLOUCESTER CITY**	**46**	**18**	**6**	**22**	**69**	**83**	**42**
14	CANTERBURY CITY	46	17	8	21	57	75	42
15	WISBECH TOWN	46	16	9	21	87	93	41
16	BEXLEY UNITED	46	13	15	18	53	69	41
17	BANBURY UNITED	46	13	14	19	88	100	40
18	RUGBY TOWN	46	15	7	24	57	77	37
19	DUNSTABLE TOWN	46	14	6	26	55	87	34
20	BARRY TOWN	46	11	11	24	62	89	33
21	GRAVESEND & NORTHFLEET	46	11	9	26	63	106	31
22	HINCKLEY ATHLETIC	46	10	8	28	44	100	28
23	TUNBRIDGE WELLS RANGERS	46	4	15	27	31	96	23
24	SITTINGBOURNE	46	5	10	31	44	136	20
		1104	432	240	432	1784	1784	1104

SEASON 1967-1968
(Home Ground: Horton Road Stadium)

Date: Saturday 19/08/1967
Result: **BRENTWOOD TOWN 0 GLOUCESTER CITY 2**
Competition: Southern League Division 1
Teamsheet: Pellant, Wixey, Walker, Moulsdale, McDonald, McCool, Gay, Rice, Bell, Mortimer, Partridge
Substitute: Batty (nps)
Scorer: Bell (2)

Date: Tuesday 22/08/1967
Result: **RAMSGATE ATHLETIC 1 GLOUCESTER CITY 1**
Competition: Southern League Division 1
Teamsheet: Pellant, Wixey, Walker, Moulsdale, McDonald, McCool, Gay, Rice, Bell, Mortimer, Partridge
Substitute: Ashall (nps)
Scorer: McCool
Attendance: 1082

Date: Saturday 26/08/1967
Result: **GLOUCESTER CITY 0 KETTERING TOWN 1**
Competition: Southern League Division 1
Teamsheet: Pellant, Wixey, Walker, Moulsdale, McDonald, McCool, Gay, Rice, Bell, Mortimer, Partridge
Substitute: Ashall (nps)
Attendance: 1217

Date: Monday 28/08/1967
Result: **BATH CITY 8 GLOUCESTER CITY 1**
Competition: Southern League Cup 1st Round 1st Leg
Teamsheet: Pellant, Wixey, Ashall, Moulsdale, McDonald, McCool, Gay, Rice, Bell, Basey, Partridge
Substitute: Mortimer (nps)
Scorer: Basey
Attendance: 1300

Date: Saturday 02/09/1967
Result: **GRAVESEND & NORTHFLEET 1 GLOUCESTER CITY 3**
Competition: Southern League Division 1
Teamsheet: Pellant, McDonald, Walker, Moulsdale, Ashall, McCool, Gay, Rice, Bell, Mortimer, Partridge
Substitute: Basey (nps)
Scorers: Bell, Gay (2)
Attendance: 550

Date: Thursday 07/09/1967
Result: **GLOUCESTER CITY 2 BATH CITY 2**
Competition: Southern League Cup 1st Round 2nd Leg
Teamsheet: Pellant, McDonald, Walker, Moulsdale, Ashall, McCool, Gay, Rice, Bell, Basey, Mortimer
Substitute: McIntosh (nps)
Scorers: Mortimer, Basey
Attendance: 783

5 November 1966
Was there 'poaching' at the time?

Date: Saturday 09/09/1967
Result: **GLOUCESTER CITY 2 WISBECH TOWN 0**
Competition: Southern League Division 1
Teamsheet: Pellant, McDonald, Walker, Moulsdale, Ashall, McCool, Gay, Partridge, Bell, Basey, Mortimer
Substitute: Rice (nps)
Scorers: Bell, Partridge
Attendance: 1050

Date: Saturday 16/09/1967
Result: **LOVELLS ATHLETIC 0 GLOUCESTER CITY 4**
Competition: FA Cup 1st Qualifying Round
Teamsheet: Pellant, McDonald, Walker, Moulsdale, Ashall, McCool, Gay, Partridge, Bell, Basey, Mortimer
Substitute: Rice (nps)
Scorers: Basey (2), Bell (2)

Date: Saturday 23/09/1967
Result: **ASHFORD TOWN 3 GLOUCESTER CITY 0**
Competition: Southern League Division 1
Teamsheet: Pellant, McDonald, Walker, Moulsdale, Ashall, McCool, Gay, Rice, Bell, Basey, Mortimer
Substitute: Batty (nps)

Date: Saturday 30/09/1967
Result: **GLOUCESTER CITY 0 CHELTENHAM TOWN 1**
Competition: FA Cup 2nd Qualifying Round
Teamsheet: Pellant, McDonald, Walker, Wixey, Ashall, McCool, Gay, Rice, Bell, Basey, Mortimer
Substitute: Moulsdale (nps)
Attendance: 4753

Date: Saturday 07/10/1967
Result: **GLOUCESTER CITY 0 BEXLEY UNITED 0**
Competition: Southern League Division 1
Teamsheet: Pellant, McDonald, Walker, Wixey, Ashall, Moulsdale, Gay, Basey, Bell, McCool, Mortimer
Substitute: Rice (nps)
Attendance: 859

Date: Saturday 14/10/1967
Result: **CINDERFORD TOWN 1 GLOUCESTER CITY 0**
Competition: Gloucestershire FA Northern Senior Professional Cup Semi-Final
Teamsheet: Pellant, McDonald, Walker, Rice, Ashall, Moulsdale, Gay, Basey, Bell, McCool, Mortimer
Substitute: Wixey (nps)

Date: Saturday 21/10/1967
Result: **GLOUCESTER CITY 4 RUGBY TOWN 0**
Competition: Southern League Division 1
Teamsheet: Pellant, McDonald, Walker, Ashall, Rusher, McCool, Gay, Basey, Bell, Johnson, Partridge
Substitute: Moulsdale (nps)
Scorers: Bell (2), Johnson (2)
Attendance: 806

Date: Saturday 28/10/1967
Result: **DARTFORD 2 GLOUCESTER CITY 0**
Competition: Southern League Division 1
Teamsheet: Pellant, McDonald, Walker, Ashall, Rusher, McCool, Gay, Basey, Bell, Johnson, Partridge
Substitute: Wixey (nps)

Date: Saturday 11/11/1967
Result: **TONBRIDGE 0 GLOUCESTER CITY 1**
Competition: Southern League Division 1
Teamsheet: Pellant, Ashall, McDonald, Moulsdale, Rusher, McCool, Gay, Basey, Bell, Johnson, Partridge
Substitute: Wixey (nps)
Scorer: Partridge
Attendance: 1264

Date: Saturday 18/11/1967
Result: **GLOUCESTER CITY 1 BARRY TOWN 0**
Competition: Southern League Division 1
Teamsheet: Pellant, Ashall, McDonald, Moulsdale, Rusher, McCool, Gay, Basey, Bell, Rice, Partridge
Substitute: Mortimer (nps)
Scorer: Bell
Attendance: 1021

Date: Tuesday 21/11/1967
Result: **BANBURY UNITED 4 GLOUCESTER CITY 2**
Competition: Southern League Division 1
Teamsheet: Pellant, Ashall, McDonald, Mortimer, Moulsdale, McCool, Gay, Rice, Bell, Basey, Partridge
Substitute: No sub
Scorers: Gay, Partridge

Date: Saturday 25/11/1967
Result: **BEDFORD TOWN 1 GLOUCESTER CITY 1**
Competition: Southern League Division 1
Teamsheet: Jones, Ashall, McDonald, Moulsdale, Rusher, McCool, Gay, Wallace, Bell, Mortimer, Partridge
Substitute: Basey (for Mortimer)
Scorer: Mortimer

Date: Saturday 02/12/1967
Result: **GLOUCESTER CITY 2 FOLKESTONE TOWN 4**
Competition: Southern League Division 1
Teamsheet: Jones, Ashall, McDonald, Moulsdale, Rusher, Wallace, Gay, Basey, Bell, McCool, Partridge
Substitute: Rice (nps)
Scorers: Partridge, Bell
Attendance: 875

Date: Saturday 16/12/1967
Result: **GLOUCESTER CITY 2 BRENTWOOD TOWN 4**
Competition: Southern League Division 1
Teamsheet: Pellant, Ashall, Walker, Moulsdale, Rusher, McCool, Gay, Basey, Bell, Rice, Partridge
Substitute: Wallace (nps)
Scorers: Partridge, Rice
Attendance: 711

Date: Saturday 23/12/1967
Result: **KETTERING TOWN 2 GLOUCESTER CITY 1**
Competition: Southern League Division 1
Teamsheet: Jones, McDonald, Walker, Moulsdale, Ashall, Wixey, Gay, Rice, Batty, Basey, Partridge
Substitute: McCool (nps)
Scorer: Rice

Date: Tuesday 26/12/1967
Result: **CRAWLEY TOWN 1 GLOUCESTER CITY 1**
Competition: Southern League Division 1
Teamsheet: Jones, McDonald, Walker, Moulsdale, Ashall, Wixey, Gay, Rice, Batty, Basey, Partridge
Substitute: No sub
Scorer: Rice

Date: Saturday 30/12/1967
Result: **GLOUCESTER CITY 4 CRAWLEY TOWN 2**
Competition: Southern League Division 1
Teamsheet: Jones, McDonald, Walker, Moulsdale, Ashall, Wixey, Gay, Basey, Bell, Rice, Partridge
Substitute: McCool (nps)
Scorers: Gay (2), Basey, Partridge
Attendance: 548

Date: Saturday 06/01/1968
Result: **GLOUCESTER CITY 2 GRAVESEND & NORTHFLEET 0**
Competition: Southern League Division 1
Teamsheet: Jones, McDonald, Walker, Moulsdale, Ashall, Wixey, Gay, Rice, Bell, Basey, Partridge
Substitute: McCool (nps)
Scorers: Gay, Bell
Attendance: 479

Date: Saturday 13/01/1968
Result: **WISBECH TOWN 3 GLOUCESTER CITY 2**
Competition: Southern League Division 1
Teamsheet: Jones, McDonald, Walker, Moulsdale, Ashall, Wixey, Gay, Rice, Bell, Basey, Partridge
Substitute: McCool (for Walker)
Scorers: Basey, Partridge (pen)

Date: Saturday 20/01/1968
Result: **GLOUCESTER CITY 1 RAMSGATE ATHLETIC 1**
Competition: Southern League Division 1
Teamsheet: Jones, Wixey, McDonald, Moulsdale, Ashall, Rice, Gay, Mortimer, Bell, Basey, Partridge
Substitute: McCool (nps)
Scorer: Basey
Attendance: 510

Date: Saturday 27/01/1968
Result: **DUNSTABLE TOWN 1 GLOUCESTER CITY 1**
Competition: Southern League Division 1
Teamsheet: Jones, Wixey, McDonald, Moulsdale, Ashall, McCool, Gay, Rice, Bell, Mortimer, Partridge
Substitute: No sub
Scorer: Mortimer

Date: Saturday 03/02/1968
Result: **GLOUCESTER CITY 1 ASHFORD TOWN 2**
Competition: Southern League Division 1
Teamsheet: Jones, Ashall, McDonald, Moulsdale, Neville, Wixey, Gay, Partridge, Bell, Mortimer, Wardle
Substitute: McCool (nps)
Scorer: Wardle
Attendance: 763

Date: Saturday 10/02/1968
Result: **TROWBRIDGE TOWN 2 GLOUCESTER CITY 2**
Competition: Southern League Division 1
Teamsheet: Pellant, Wixey, McDonald, Moulsdale, Neville, McCool, Ashall, Gay, Bell, Mortimer, Walker
Substitute: Basey (nps)
Scorers: Walker, McCool

Date: Saturday 17/02/1968
Result: **GLOUCESTER CITY 1 DUNSTABLE TOWN 2**
Competition: Southern League Division 1
Teamsheet: Pellant, Wixey, McDonald, Moulsdale, Neville, McCool, Gay, Basey, Medcroft, Bell, Mortimer
Substitute: Ashall (nps)
Scorer: Gay

Date: Saturday 24/02/1968
Result: **BEXLEY UNITED 1 GLOUCESTER CITY 2**
Competition: Southern League Division 1
Teamsheet: Pellant, Wixey, McDonald, Moulsdale, Ashall, Neville, Gay, Basey, Medcroft, Mortimer, McCool
Substitute: Batty (nps)
Scorers: Basey, Medcroft
Attendance: 752

Date: Saturday 02/03/1968
Result: **GLOUCESTER CITY 0 BANBURY UNITED 1**
Competition: Southern League Division 1
Teamsheet: Pellant, Wixey, McDonald, Moulsdale, Ashall, Neville, Gay, Basey, Medcroft, Mortimer, McCool
Substitute: Batty (nps)
Attendance: 610

Date: Saturday 09/03/1968
Result: **GLOUCESTER CITY 2 CANTERBURY CITY 1**
Competition: Southern League Division 1
Teamsheet: Pellant, Wixey, McDonald, Moulsdale, Ashall, Neville, Gay, Basey, Medcroft, Mortimer, McCool
Substitute: Duke (nps)
Scorers: McCool, Gay
Attendance: 510

Date: Wednesday 13/03/1968
Result: **MERTHYR TYDFIL 4 GLOUCESTER CITY 1**
Competition: Southern League Division 1
Teamsheet: Jones, Gapper, McDonald, Moulsdale, Ashall, Neville, Gay, Nunez, Wixey, Mortimer, McCool
Substitute: Duke (nps)
Scorer: Neville

Date: Friday 15/03/1968
Result: **RUGBY TOWN 5 GLOUCESTER CITY 1**
Competition: Southern League Division 1
Teamsheet: Pellant, Wixey, McDonald, Moulsdale, Ashall, Neville, Gay, Basey, Medcroft, Mortimer, McCool
Substitute: Duke (for Gay)
Scorer: Mortimer
Attendance: 846

Date: Saturday 23/03/1968
Result: **GLOUCESTER CITY 0 DARTFORD 1**
Competition: Southern League Division 1
Teamsheet: Pellant, Wixey, McDonald, Moulsdale, Ashall, Neville, Medcroft, Rice, Basey, Mortimer, McCool
Substitute: Duke (nps)
Attendance: 463

Date: Saturday 30/03/1968
Result: **WORCESTER CITY 3 GLOUCESTER CITY 0**
Competition: Southern League Division 1
Teamsheet: Pellant, Wixey, McDonald, Moulsdale, Ashall, Neville, Rice, Basey, Stevens, Mortimer, McCool
Substitute: Medcroft (for Ashall)
Attendance: 1530

Date: Saturday 06/04/1968
Result: **GLOUCESTER CITY 5 TONBRIDGE 0**
Competition: Southern League Division 1
Teamsheet: Pellant, Wixey, McDonald, Moulsdale, Neville, McCool, Medcroft, Barker, Stevens, Basey, Mortimer
Substitute: Nunez (nps)
Scorers: Medcroft (2), Basey, Stevens, Barker
Attendance: 580

Date: Friday 12/04/1968
Result: **BATH CITY 1 GLOUCESTER CITY 0**
Competition: Southern League Division 1
Teamsheet: Pellant, Wixey, McDonald, Moulsdale, Neville, McCool, Medcroft, Basey, Stevens, Barker, Mortimer
Substitute: Batty (nps)
Attendance: 2844

Date: Saturday 13/04/1968
Result: **BARRY TOWN 2 GLOUCESTER CITY 1**
Competition: Southern League Division 1
Teamsheet: Pellant, Ashall, Walker, Moulsdale, Neville, McCool, Medcroft, Basey, Stevens, Barker, Mortimer
Substitute: McDonald (nps)
Scorer: Medcroft

Date: Monday 15/04/1968
Result: **GLOUCESTER CITY 2 BATH CITY 0**
Competition: Southern League Division 1
Teamsheet: Pellant, Gapper, McDonald, Moulsdale, Neville, McCool, Medcroft, Barker, Stevens, Basey, Mortimer
Substitute: Batty (for Medcroft)
Scorers: McCool, Mortimer
Attendance: 823

Date: Saturday 20/04/1968
Result: **GLOUCESTER CITY 0 BEDFORD TOWN 1**
Competition: Southern League Division 1
Teamsheet: Pellant, Gapper, McDonald, Moulsdale, Neville, McCool, Medcroft, Barker, Stevens, Basey, Mortimer
Substitute: Duke (nps)
Attendance: 815

Date: Thursday 25/04/1968
Result: **GLOUCESTER CITY 0 TROWBRIDGE TOWN 3**
Competition: Southern League Division 1
Teamsheet: Pellant, Gapper, Walker, Moulsdale, Neville, Rice, McKellar, Barker, Stevens, Basey, Mortimer
Substitute: Nunez (nps)
Attendance: 611

[205]

Date: Saturday 27/04/1968
Result: **FOLKESTONE TOWN 5 GLOUCESTER CITY 1**
Competition: Southern League Division 1
Teamsheet: Jones, Gapper, McDonald, Moulsdale, Neville, McCool, Rice, Barker, Stevens, Basey, Mortimer
Substitute: No sub
Scorer: own goal
Attendance: 720

Date: Saturday 04/05/1968
Result: **GLOUCESTER CITY 0 MERTHYR TYDFIL 1**
Competition: Southern League Division 1
Teamsheet: Jones, Gapper, McDonald, Ashall, Neville, McCool, Rice, Barker, Stevens, Basey, Mortimer
Substitute: Batty (nps)
Attendance: 536

Date: Thursday 09/05/1968
Result: **GLOUCESTER CITY 1 WORCESTER CITY 1**
Competition: Southern League Division 1
Teamsheet: Jones, Gapper, McDonald, Moulsdale, Neville, McCool, Rice, Barker, Stevens, Basey, Mortimer
Substitute: Ashall (nps)
Scorer: McCool
Attendance: 1193

Date: Saturday 11/05/1968
Result: **CANTERBURY CITY 1 GLOUCESTER CITY 1**
Competition: Southern League Division 1
Teamsheet: Jones, Gapper, McDonald, Moulsdale, Neville, McCool, Rice, Duke, Stevens, Basey, Mortimer
Substitute: Ashall (nps)
Scorer: Duke

Appearances – J Ashall 35(1), G Barker 9, PJ Basey 38(1), R Batty 2(1), E Bell 28, DJ Duke 1(1), D Gapper 8, GAM Gay 35, H Johnson 3, R Jones 15, R McCool 39, R McKellar 1, L McDonald 44, G Medcroft 11(1), KEW Mortimer 35, CB Moulsdale 43, J Neville 20, L Nunez 1, B Partridge 23, GA Pellant 32, S Rice 26, B Rusher 7, JM Stevens 11, D Walker 22, I Wallace 2, B Wardle 1, R Wixey 25.
Others selected but did not play: JM McIntosh.
Scorers – E Bell 11, PJ Basey 9, GAM Gay 8, B Partridge 7, R McCool 5, KEW Mortimer 5, G Medcroft 4, S Rice 3, H Johnson 2, G Barker 1, DJ Duke 1, J Neville 1, JM Stevens 1, D Walker 1, B Wardle 1, own goal 1.

SOUTHERN LEAGUE DIVISION 1

POS	CLUB	P	W	D	L	F	A	PTS
1	WORCESTER CITY	42	23	14	5	92	35	60
2	KETTERING TOWN	42	24	10	8	88	40	58
3	BEDFORD TOWN	42	24	7	11	101	40	55
4	RUGBY TOWN	42	20	15	7	72	44	55
5	DARTFORD	42	23	9	10	71	48	55
6	BATH CITY	42	21	12	9	78	51	54
7	BANBURY UNITED	42	22	9	11	79	59	53
8	RAMSGATE ATHLETIC	42	17	17	8	70	37	51
9	MERTHYR TYDFIL	42	18	13	11	80	66	49
10	TONBRIDGE	42	18	9	15	76	71	45
11	CANTERBURY CITY	42	16	11	15	66	63	43
12	ASHFORD TOWN	42	18	6	18	73	78	42
13	BRENTWOOD TOWN	42	16	9	17	63	73	41
14	BEXLEY UNITED	42	12	13	17	56	64	37
15	TROWBRIDGE TOWN	42	12	11	19	64	70	35
16	**GLOUCESTER CITY**	42	12	9	21	54	68	33
17	WISBECH TOWN	42	11	10	21	43	78	32
18	CRAWLEY TOWN	42	10	8	24	54	85	28
19	FOLKESTONE TOWN	42	10	7	25	49	80	27
20	DUNSTABLE TOWN	42	8	10	24	44	94	26
21	BARRY TOWN	42	7	12	23	36	81	26
22	GRAVESEND & NORTHFLEET	42	6	7	29	28	112	19
		924	348	228	348	1437	1437	924

SEASON 1968-1969

(Home Ground: Horton Road Stadium)

Date: Saturday 10/08/1968
Result: **GRAVESEND & NORTHFLEET 0 GLOUCESTER CITY 2**
Competition: Southern League Division 1
Teamsheet: Jones, Vale, Anderson, McIntosh, Neville, Page-Jones, Rice, Rodgerson, Stevens, Fraser, McCool
Substitute: Smith (nps)
Scorers: Stevens, Rodgerson
Attendance: 1031

Date: Thursday 15/08/1968
Result: **GLOUCESTER CITY 1 SALISBURY 2**
Competition: Southern League Division 1
Teamsheet: Jones, Vale, Anderson, McIntosh, Neville, Page-Jones, Rice, Rodgerson, Stevens, Ferns, McCool
Substitute: Fraser (nps)
Scorer: Rodgerson
Attendance: 2065

Date: Saturday 17/08/1968
Result: **GLOUCESTER CITY 5 TONBRIDGE 0**
Competition: Southern League Division 1
Teamsheet: Jones, Vale, Anderson, McIntosh, Neville, Page-Jones, Fraser, Rodgerson, Stevens, Ferns, McCool
Substitute: Rice (nps)
Scorers: Stevens, Rodgerson, Vale, Fraser (2, 1 pen)
Attendance: 1500

Date: Thursday 22/08/1968
Result: **GLOUCESTER CITY 1 TROWBRIDGE TOWN 2**
Competition: Southern League Cup 1st Round 1st Leg
Teamsheet: Jones, Vale, Anderson, McIntosh, Neville, Page-Jones, Fraser, Rodgerson, Stevens, Ferns, McCool
Substitute: Rice (nps)
Scorer: Ferns
Attendance: 1243

Date: Saturday 24/08/1968
Result: **CRAWLEY TOWN 0 GLOUCESTER CITY 2**
Competition: Southern League Division 1
Teamsheet: Jones, Vale, Page-Jones, McIntosh, Anderson, Ferns, Rice, Rodgerson, Stevens, Fraser, McCool
Substitute: Neville (nps)
Scorers: Fraser (pen), Stevens
Attendance: 911

Date: Tuesday 27/08/1968
Result: **TROWBRIDGE TOWN 1 GLOUCESTER CITY 2**
Competition: Southern League Cup 1st Round 2nd Leg
Teamsheet: Jones, Anderson, Page-Jones, McIntosh, Neville, Ferns, Rice, Rodgerson, Stevens, Fraser, McCool
Substitute: Smith (nps)
Scorers: McCool, Fraser
Attendance: 924

Date: Saturday 31/08/1968
Result: **GLOUCESTER CITY 3 CANTERBURY CITY 1**
Competition: Southern League Division 1
Teamsheet: Jones, Vale, Page-Jones, McIntosh, Anderson, Ferns, Rice, Rodgerson, Stevens, Fraser, McCool
Substitute: Smith (for Rodgerson)
Scorers: Stevens (2), Ferns
Attendance: 1883

Date: Monday 02/09/1968
Result: **SALISBURY 0 GLOUCESTER CITY 1**
Competition: Southern League Division 1
Teamsheet: Jones, Vale, Page-Jones, Anderson, Neville, McIntosh, Rice, Ferns, Stevens, Fraser, McCool
Substitute: Smith (nps)
Scorer: McCool
Attendance: 1288

Date: Wednesday 04/09/1968
Result: **TROWBRIDGE TOWN 2 GLOUCESTER CITY 0**
Competition: Southern League Cup 1st Round Replay
Teamsheet: Jones, Vale, Page-Jones, Anderson, Neville, McIntosh, Rice, Ferns, Stevens, Fraser, McCool
Substitute: Walker (nps)
Attendance: 974

Date: Saturday 07/09/1968
Result: **CORBY TOWN 1 GLOUCESTER CITY 1**
Competition: Southern League Division 1
Teamsheet: Jones, Vale, Page-Jones, McIntosh, Anderson, Ferns, Rice, Rodgerson, Stevens, Fraser, McCool
Substitute: Neville (for Rodgerson)
Scorer: McCool
Attendance: 1419

Date: Saturday 14/09/1968
Result: **GLOUCESTER CITY 1 DUNSTABLE TOWN 1**
Competition: Southern League Division 1
Teamsheet: Jones, Vale, Page-Jones, McIntosh, Anderson, Ferns, Gay, McCool, Stevens, Fraser, Rice
Substitute: Smith (for Rice)
Scorer: own goal
Attendance: 1020

Date: Sunday 15/09/1968
Result: **GLOUCESTER CITY 1 CINDERFORD TOWN 1**
Competition: Gloucestershire FA Northern Senior Professional Cup Semi-Final
Teamsheet: Jones, Vale, Page-Jones, Anderson, Neville, McIntosh, Gay, Ferns, Stevens, Fraser, McCool
Substitute: Smith (nps)
Scorer: Gay

Date: Saturday 21/09/1968
Result: **GLOUCESTER CITY 3 DEVIZES TOWN 1**
Competition: FA Cup 1st Qualifying Round
Teamsheet: Jones, Vale, Page-Jones, McIntosh, Anderson, Ferns, Gay, Rodgerson, Stevens, Fraser, McCool
Substitute: No sub
Scorers: McCool, Fraser (2)

Date: Sunday 29/09/1968
Result: **DARTFORD 1 GLOUCESTER CITY 2**
Competition: Southern League Division 1
Teamsheet: Jones, Vale, Page-Jones, McIntosh, Anderson, Ferns, Gay, Rodgerson, Stevens, Fraser, McCool
Substitute: Rice (nps)
Scorers: McCool, Fraser

Date: Saturday 05/10/1968
Result: **WELTON ROVERS 1 GLOUCESTER CITY 2**
Competition: FA Cup 2nd Qualifying Round
Teamsheet: Jones, Vale, Page-Jones, McIntosh, Anderson, Ferns, Gay, Rodgerson, Stevens, Fraser, McCool
Substitute: No sub
Scorers: Gay, Fraser
Attendance: 870

Date: Saturday 12/10/1968
Result: **BEXLEY UNITED 2 GLOUCESTER CITY 2**
Competition: Southern League Division 1
Teamsheet: Jones, Vale, Page-Jones, McIntosh, Anderson, Ferns, Rice, Rodgerson, Stevens, McQuarrie, Fraser
Substitute: Gay (nps)
Scorer: Stevens (2)
Attendance: 975

Date: Saturday 19/10/1968
Result: **POOLE TOWN 1 GLOUCESTER CITY 1**
Competition: FA Cup 3rd Qualifying Round
Teamsheet: Jones, Vale, Page-Jones, McIntosh, Anderson, Ferns, Rice, Rodgerson, Stevens, Fraser, McCool
Substitute: No sub
Scorer: Stevens
Attendance: 793

Date: Thursday 24/10/1968
Result: **GLOUCESTER CITY 1 POOLE TOWN 2**
Competition: FA Cup 3rd Qualifying Round Replay
Teamsheet: Jones, Vale, Page-Jones, McIntosh, Anderson, Ferns, Rice, Rodgerson, Stevens, Fraser, McCool
Substitute: Gay (nps)
Scorer: Fraser
Attendance: 1347

Date: Saturday 26/10/1968
Result: **FOLKESTONE 5 GLOUCESTER CITY 2**
Competition: Southern League Division 1
Teamsheet: Jones, Vale, Page-Jones, McIntosh, Anderson, Ferns, Rice, Rodgerson, Stevens, Fraser, McCool
Substitute: McQuarrie (nps)
Scorers: Page-Jones, Rodgerson
Attendance: 902

Date: Saturday 02/11/1968
Result: **GLOUCESTER CITY 3 TROWBRIDGE TOWN 3**
Competition: Southern League Division 1
Teamsheet: Jones, Vale, Page-Jones, McIntosh, Anderson, Ferns, Fraser, Rodgerson, Stevens, McQuarrie, McCool
Substitute: Rice (nps)
Scorers: Stevens, Fraser (pen), Ferns
Attendance: 825

Date: Saturday 09/11/1968
Result: **WISBECH TOWN 1 GLOUCESTER CITY 2**
Competition: Southern League Division 1
Teamsheet: Jones, Vale, Page-Jones, McIntosh, Anderson, Ferns, Fraser, Rodgerson, Stevens, McQuarrie, McCool
Substitute: Rice (nps)
Scorer: Ferns (2)
Attendance: 570

Date: Saturday 16/11/1968
Result: **GLOUCESTER CITY 2 CAMBRIDGE CITY 0**
Competition: Southern League Division 1
Teamsheet: Jones, Vale, Page-Jones, McIntosh, Anderson, Ferns, Fraser, Rodgerson, Stevens, McQuarrie, McCool
Substitute: Rice (nps)
Scorers: McCool, Ferns
Attendance: 836

Date: Saturday 23/11/1968
Result: **RAMSGATE ATHLETIC 3 GLOUCESTER CITY 2**
Competition: Southern League Division 1
Teamsheet: Jones, Vale, Page-Jones, McIntosh, Anderson, Ferns, Fraser, Rodgerson, Stevens, McQuarrie, McCool
Substitute: Rice (for McQuarrie)
Scorers: Rodgerson, Fraser (pen)
Attendance: 697

Date: Saturday 30/11/1968
Result: **GLOUCESTER CITY 1 DARTFORD 1**
Competition: Southern League Division 1
Teamsheet: Jones, Vale, Page-Jones, McIntosh, Anderson, Ferns, Fraser, Rodgerson, Stevens, McQuarrie, McCool
Substitute: Rice (for McQuarrie)
Scorer: Stevens
Attendance: 684

Date: Saturday 07/12/1968
Result: **CAMBRIDGE CITY 3 GLOUCESTER CITY 1**
Competition: Southern League Division 1
Teamsheet: Jones, Vale, Page-Jones, McIntosh, Anderson, Ferns, Fraser, Rodgerson, Stevens, McQuarrie, McCool
Substitute: Rice (for McQuarrie)
Scorer: Ferns
Attendance: 1808

Date: Sunday 08/12/1968
Result: **GLOUCESTER CITY 3 CINDERFORD TOWN 1**
Competition: Gloucestershire FA Northern Senior Professional Cup Semi-Final Replay
Teamsheet: Jones, Vale, Page-Jones, McIntosh, Anderson, Ferns, McQuarrie, Rodgerson, Stevens, Rice, McCool
Substitute: No sub
Scorers: McQuarrie (2), Stevens

Date: Thursday 26/12/1968
Result: **GLOUCESTER CITY 3 BATH CITY 0**
Competition: Southern League Division 1
Teamsheet: Jones, Vale, Page-Jones, McIntosh, Anderson, Ferns, Rice, Rodgerson, Stevens, McQuarrie, McCool
Substitute: Fraser (nps)
Scorers: McQuarrie, Stevens, Rice
Attendance: 2486

Date: Saturday 04/01/1969
Result: **GLOUCESTER CITY 5 FOLKESTONE 0**
Competition: Southern League Division 1
Teamsheet: Jones, Vale, Page-Jones, McIntosh, Anderson, Ferns, Rice, Rodgerson, Stevens, McQuarrie, McCool
Substitute: Fraser (for McQuarrie)
Scorers: Rodgerson, Rice, Stevens (2), Ferns
Attendance: 1523

Date: Saturday 11/01/1969
Result: **BANBURY UNITED 1 GLOUCESTER CITY 4**
Competition: Southern League Division 1
Teamsheet: Jones, Vale, Page-Jones, McIntosh, Anderson, Ferns, Rice, Rodgerson, Stevens, McQuarrie, McCool
Substitute: Fraser (nps)
Scorers: Ferns, Rice (2), Stevens
Attendance: 1047

Date: Saturday 25/01/1969
Result: **BRENTWOOD TOWN 3 GLOUCESTER CITY 1**
Competition: Southern League Division 1
Teamsheet: Jones, Vale, Page-Jones, McIntosh, Anderson, Ferns, Rice, Rodgerson, Stevens, McQuarrie, McCool
Substitute: Walker (nps)
Scorer: Stevens
Attendance: 1350

Date: Saturday 01/02/1969
Result: **GLOUCESTER CITY 2 GRAVESEND & NORTHFLEET 1**
Competition: Southern League Division 1
Teamsheet: Jones, Vale, Page-Jones, McIntosh, Anderson, Ferns, Rice, Rodgerson, Stevens, McQuarrie, McCool
Substitute: Fraser (nps)
Scorers: McQuarrie, Ferns
Attendance: 1234

Date: Monday 10/02/1969
Result: **BATH CITY 6 GLOUCESTER CITY 1**
Competition: Southern League Division 1
Teamsheet: Jones, Vale, Page-Jones, McIntosh, Anderson, Ferns, Gay, Rodgerson, Rice, McQuarrie, Fraser
Substitute: Walker (nps)
Scorer: Rice
Attendance: 2265

Date: Saturday 15/02/1969
Result: **GLOUCESTER CITY 3 CORBY TOWN 1**
Competition: Southern League Division 1
Teamsheet: Jones, Vale, Page-Jones, McIntosh, Anderson, Ferns, Rice, Rodgerson, Stevens, McQuarrie, McCool
Substitute: Fraser (for Rodgerson)
Scorers: Stevens, Fraser (pen), McQuarrie
Attendance: 1110

Date: Wednesday 26/02/1969
Result: **MERTHYR TYDFIL 3 GLOUCESTER CITY 1**
Competition: Southern League Division 1
Teamsheet: Jones, Vale, Walker, Page-Jones, Anderson, Ferns, Rice, Fraser, Stevens, McQuarrie, McCool
Substitute: McIntosh (for Fraser)
Scorer: Stevens

Date: Saturday 01/03/1969
Result: **GLOUCESTER CITY 2 BEXLEY UNITED 1**
Competition: Southern League Division 1
Teamsheet: Jones, Vale, Page-Jones, McIntosh, Anderson, Fraser, Rice, Rodgerson, Stevens, McQuarrie, Ferns
Substitute: Walker or McCool (nps)
Scorers: McQuarrie, Stevens
Attendance: 905

Date: Saturday 08/03/1969
Result: **HASTINGS UNITED 2 GLOUCESTER CITY 1**
Competition: Southern League Division 1
Teamsheet: Jones, Vale, Page-Jones, McIntosh, Anderson, Ferns, Rice, Rodgerson, Stevens, McQuarrie, Fraser
Substitute: Walker (nps)
Scorer: Stevens
Attendance: 1113

Date: Saturday 15/03/1969
Result: **GLOUCESTER CITY 5 BANBURY UNITED 1**
Competition: Southern League Division 1
Teamsheet: Jones, Vale, Page-Jones, McIntosh, McQuarrie, Ferns, Rice, Rodgerson, Stevens, Fraser, McCool
Substitute: Walker (nps)
Scorers: Rodgerson, Rice (2), Stevens, McCool
Attendance: 1210

[209]

Date: Saturday 22/03/1969
Result: **GLOUCESTER CITY 4 HASTINGS UNITED 0**
Competition: Southern League Division 1
Teamsheet: Jones, Vale, Page-Jones, McIntosh, McQuarrie, Ferns, Rice, Rodgerson, Stevens, Fraser, McCool
Substitute: Anderson (nps)
Scorers: Fraser (3), Stevens
Attendance: 1256

Date: Tuesday 25/03/1969
Result: **CANTERBURY CITY 2 GLOUCESTER CITY 4**
Competition: Southern League Division 1
Teamsheet: Jones, Vale, Page-Jones, McIntosh, McQuarrie, Ferns, Rice, Rodgerson, Stevens, Fraser, McCool
Substitute: Anderson (nps)
Scorers: McIntosh, Fraser (2), Stevens

Date: Saturday 29/03/1969
Result: **GLOUCESTER CITY 3 CRAWLEY TOWN 2**
Competition: Southern League Division 1
Teamsheet: Jones, Vale, Page-Jones, McIntosh, McQuarrie, Ferns, Rice, Rodgerson, Stevens, Fraser, McCool
Substitute: Anderson (nps)
Scorers: Ferns, Stevens (2)
Attendance: 1786

Date: Monday 31/03/1969
Result: **TONBRIDGE 0 GLOUCESTER CITY 3**
Competition: Southern League Division 1
Teamsheet: Jones, Vale, Page-Jones, McIntosh, McQuarrie, Ferns, Rice, Rodgerson, Stevens, Fraser, McCool
Substitute: Anderson (nps)
Scorers: McCool, Fraser (pen), Rice
Attendance: 220

Date: Friday 04/04/1969
Result: **BARRY TOWN 0 GLOUCESTER CITY 0**
Competition: Southern League Division 1
Teamsheet: Jones, Vale, McIntosh, Page-Jones, McQuarrie, Ferns, Rice, Rodgerson, Stevens, Fraser, McCool
Substitute: Anderson (nps)
Attendance: 616

Date: Saturday 05/04/1969
Result: **TROWBRIDGE TOWN 1 GLOUCESTER CITY 1**
Competition: Southern League Division 1
Teamsheet: Jones, Vale, Anderson, Page-Jones, McQuarrie, Ferns, Rice, McIntosh, Stevens, Fraser, McCool
Substitute: Rodgerson (nps)
Scorer: Stevens
Attendance: 1255

Date: Monday 07/04/1969
Result: **GLOUCESTER CITY 3 BARRY TOWN 0**
Competition: Southern League Division 1
Teamsheet: Jones, Vale, Page-Jones, McIntosh, McQuarrie, Ferns, Rice, Rodgerson, Stevens, Fraser, McCool
Substitute: Anderson (nps)
Scorers: Fraser, own goal, Stevens
Attendance: 2886

Date: Thursday 10/04/1969
Result: **DUNSTABLE TOWN 0 GLOUCESTER CITY 5**
Competition: Southern League Division 1
Teamsheet: Jones, Vale, Page-Jones, McIntosh, McQuarrie, Ferns, Anderson, Rodgerson, Stevens, Fraser, McCool
Substitute: Gay (for Rodgerson)
Scorers: Stevens (2), Fraser (2), own goal
Attendance: 220

Date: Saturday 12/04/1969
Result: **ASHFORD TOWN 2 GLOUCESTER CITY 2**
Competition: Southern League Division 1
Teamsheet: Jones, Vale, Page-Jones, McIntosh, McQuarrie, Ferns, Anderson, Rodgerson, Stevens, Fraser, McCool
Substitute: Rice (nps)
Scorer: Ferns (2)
Attendance: 554

Date: Thursday 17/04/1969
Result: **GLOUCESTER CITY 1 BRENTWOOD TOWN 1**
Competition: Southern League Division 1
Teamsheet: Jones, Vale, Page-Jones, McIntosh, McQuarrie, Ferns, Anderson, Rodgerson, Stevens, Fraser, McCool
Substitute: Rice (nps)
Scorer: Stevens
Attendance: 3687

Date: Saturday 19/04/1969
Result: **GLOUCESTER CITY 2 ASHFORD TOWN 0**
Competition: Southern League Division 1
Teamsheet: Jones, Vale, Anderson, McIntosh, McQuarrie, Ferns, Rice, Page-Jones, Stevens, Fraser, McCool
Substitute: Rodgerson (nps)
Scorers: Stevens, own goal
Attendance: 1810

Date: Thursday 24/04/1969
Result: **GLOUCESTER CITY 5 WISBECH TOWN 1**
Competition: Southern League Division 1
Teamsheet: Jones, Vale, Page-Jones, Anderson, McQuarrie, Ferns, Rice, Rodgerson, Stevens, Fraser, McCool
Substitute: Gay (nps)
Scorers: Fraser (2), Rice, Rodgerson, Stevens
Attendance: 2118

SEASON BY SEASON

Date: Thursday 01/05/1969
Result: **GLOUCESTER CITY 2 RAMSGATE ATHLETIC 0**
Competition: Southern League Division 1
Teamsheet: Jones, Vale, Page-Jones, Anderson, McQuarrie, Ferns, Rice, Rodgerson, Stevens, Fraser, McCool
Substitute: McIntosh (nps)
Scorers: Ferns, Fraser
Attendance: 2068

Date: Saturday 03/05/1969
Result: **GLOUCESTER CITY 4 MERTHYR TYDFIL 1**
Competition: Southern League Division 1
Teamsheet: Jones, Vale, Page-Jones, Anderson, McQuarrie, Ferns, Rice, Rodgerson, Stevens, Fraser, McCool
Substitute: McIntosh (nps)
Scorers: Fraser (pen), McQuarrie, Rodgerson, Stevens
Attendance: 1426

Date: Thursday 08/05/1969
Result: **GLOUCESTER CITY 2 CHELTENHAM TOWN 0**
Competition: Gloucestershire FA Northern Senior Professional Cup Final
Teamsheet: Jones, Vale, Page-Jones, Anderson, McQuarrie, Ferns, Rice, Rodgerson, Stevens, Fraser, McCool
Substitute: McIntosh (nps)
Scorers: Stevens, Rodgerson
Attendance: 3559

Appearances – R Anderson 45, W Ferns 51, I Fraser 44(3), GAM Gay 6(1), R Jones 52, R McCool 48, JG McIntosh 47(2), A McQuarrie 34, J Neville 8(1), N Page-Jones 52, S Rice 37(3), AR Rodgerson 45, P Smith 0(2), JM Stevens 51, ST Vale 51, D Walker 1.
Scorers – JM Stevens 34, I Fraser 25, W Ferns 14, AR Rodgerson 10, S Rice 9, R McCool 8, A McQuarrie 7, GAM Gay 2, I McIntosh 1, N Page-Jones 1, ST Vale 1, own goals 4.

SOUTHERN LEAGUE DIVISION 1

POS	CLUB	P	W	D	L	F	A	PTS
1	BRENTWOOD TOWN	42	26	12	4	94	37	64
2	BATH CITY	42	26	10	6	96	40	62
3	**GLOUCESTER CITY**	**42**	**25**	**9**	**8**	**100**	**53**	**59**
4	CRAWLEY TOWN	42	21	13	8	65	32	55
5	CORBY TOWN	42	22	6	14	81	65	50
6	DARTFORD	42	20	8	14	79	51	48
7	RAMSGATE ATHLETIC	42	19	9	14	72	57	47
8	SALISBURY	42	20	6	16	69	52	46
9	CAMBRIDGE CITY	42	18	10	14	73	63	46
10	TROWBRIDGE TOWN	42	15	14	13	70	60	44
11	BANBURY UNITED	42	16	12	14	67	72	44
12	FOLKESTONE	42	19	5	18	53	59	43
13	CANTERBURY CITY	42	17	7	18	67	63	41
14	ASHFORD TOWN	42	16	8	18	72	73	40
15	BEXLEY UNITED	42	15	9	18	64	75	39
16	HASTINGS UNITED	42	15	9	18	58	69	39
17	WISBECH TOWN	42	11	13	18	57	70	35
18	DUNSTABLE TOWN	42	14	6	22	73	99	34
19	MERTHYR TYDFIL	42	10	7	25	49	101	27
20	BARRY TOWN	42	8	10	24	39	78	26
21	GRAVESEND & NORTHFLEET	42	8	9	25	51	79	25
22	TONBRIDGE	42	2	6	34	36	137	10
		924	363	198	363	1485	1485	924

Gloucester City were the Southern League Merit Cup winners for scoring the most league goals in the Southern League.

SEASON 1969-1970
(Home Ground: Horton Road Stadium)

Date: Saturday 09/08/1969
Result: **CHELMSFORD CITY 3 GLOUCESTER CITY 1**
Competition: Southern League Premier Division
Teamsheet: Jones, Vale, Anderson, McIntosh, McQuarrie, Page-Jones, Rice, Rodgerson, Stevens, Fraser, Ferns
Substitute: Hurford (for Rice)
Scorer: Stevens
Attendance: 1938

Date: Thursday 14/08/1969
Result: **GLOUCESTER CITY 3 TELFORD UNITED 1**
Competition: Southern League Premier Division
Teamsheet: Jones, Vale, Anderson, McIntosh, McQuarrie, Page-Jones, Rice, Rodgerson, Stevens, Fraser, McCool
Substitute: Ferns (nps)
Scorers: Rice (2), McCool
Attendance: 2103

Date: Saturday 16/08/1969
Result: **GLOUCESTER CITY 1 CAMBRIDGE UNITED 2**
Competition: Southern League Premier Division
Teamsheet: Jones, Vale, Anderson, Ferns, McQuarrie, Page-Jones, Rice, Rodgerson, Fraser, McIntosh, McCool
Substitute: Hurford (for McIntosh)
Scorer: Fraser
Attendance: 2363

Date: Thursday 21/08/1969
Result: **GLOUCESTER CITY 3 MERTHYR TYDFIL 0**
Competition: Southern League Cup 1st Round 1st Leg
Teamsheet: Jones, Vale, Anderson, Ferns, McQuarrie, Page-Jones, Rice, Rodgerson, Stevens, Fraser, McCool
Substitute: McIntosh (nps)
Scorers: Rice (2), Ferns
Attendance: 1250

Date: Saturday 23/08/1969
Result: **BRENTWOOD TOWN 2 GLOUCESTER CITY 0**
Competition: Southern League Premier Division
Teamsheet: Jones, Vale, Anderson, McIntosh, McQuarrie, Page-Jones, Hurford, Ferns, Fraser, Rice, McCool
Substitute: Hall (nps)

Date: Wednesday 27/08/1969
Result: **MERTHYR TYDFIL 1 GLOUCESTER CITY 0**
Competition: Southern League Cup 1st Round 2nd Leg
Teamsheet: Jones, Vale, Anderson, McIntosh, McQuarrie, Page-Jones, Hall, Ferns, Fraser, Rice, McCool
Substitute: Hurford (nps)

Date: Saturday 30/08/1969
Result: **GLOUCESTER CITY 2 DOVER 3**
Competition: Southern League Premier Division
Teamsheet: Jones, Vale, Anderson, McIntosh, Page-Jones, Ferns, Rice, McQuarrie, Stevens, Fraser, McCool
Substitute: Hall (nps)
Scorers: Ferns, McCool
Attendance: 1871

Date: Monday 01/09/1969
Result: **TELFORD UNITED 3 GLOUCESTER CITY 3**
Competition: Southern League Premier Division
Teamsheet: Jones, Vale, Anderson, Ferns, McQuarrie, Page-Jones, Rice, Moulsdale, Stevens, Fraser, McCool
Substitute: Hall (for Moulsdale)
Scorers: Fraser, Stevens (2)
Attendance: 1721

Date: Saturday 06/09/1969
Result: **KETTERING TOWN 2 GLOUCESTER CITY 1**
Competition: Southern League Premier Division
Teamsheet: Jones, Vale, Anderson, AT Harris, McQuarrie, Page-Jones, McCool, Ferns, Stevens, Fraser, Shenton
Substitute: Rice (nps)
Scorer: Fraser

Date: Monday 08/09/1969
Result: **POOLE TOWN 1 GLOUCESTER CITY 1**
Competition: Southern League Premier Division
Teamsheet: Jones, Vale, Page-Jones, AT Harris, McQuarrie, Ferns, Hurford, McCool, Stevens, Fraser, Shenton
Substitute: Anderson (for Stevens)
Scorer: Fraser
Attendance: 501

Date: Saturday 13/09/1969
Result: **GLOUCESTER CITY 2 KING'S LYNN 0**
Competition: Southern League Premier Division
Teamsheet: Jones, Vale, Page-Jones, AT Harris, McQuarrie, Ferns, Hurford, Rodgerson, Fraser, McCool, Shenton
Substitute: Anderson (for AT Harris)
Scorers: Fraser, own goal
Attendance: 1211

Date: Saturday 20/09/1969
Result: **TON PENTRE 2 GLOUCESTER CITY 2**
Competition: FA Cup 1st Qualifying Round
Teamsheet: Jones, Vale, Page-Jones, Anderson, McQuarrie, Ferns, Hurford, Rodgerson, Fraser, Rice, McCool
Substitute: McIntosh (for Rice)
Scorers: Fraser, McQuarrie
Attendance: 1200

Date: Thursday 25/09/1969
Result: **GLOUCESTER CITY 0 TON PENTRE 1**
Competition: FA Cup 1st Qualifying Round Replay
Teamsheet: Jones, Vale, Page-Jones, Anderson, McQuarrie, McIntosh, Rice, Rodgerson, Fraser, Ferns, McCool
Substitute: AT Harris (nps)

Date: Saturday 27/09/1969
Result: **GLOUCESTER CITY 1 POOLE TOWN 1**
Competition: Southern League Premier Division
Teamsheet: Jones, Vale, Page-Jones, McIntosh, McQuarrie, Ferns, Hurford, Rodgerson, McCool, Fraser, Shenton
Substitute: Anderson (for Shenton)
Scorer: Ferns
Attendance: 1180

Date: Saturday 04/10/1969
Result: **DOVER 3 GLOUCESTER CITY 0**
Competition: Southern League Premier Division
Teamsheet: Jones, Vale, Page-Jones, Anderson, McQuarrie, Ferns, Hurford, Rodgerson, Amos, Rice, McCool
Substitute: McIntosh (nps)

Date: Saturday 11/10/1969
Result: **GLOUCESTER CITY 1 BARNET 1**
Competition: Southern League Premier Division
Teamsheet: Jones, Vale, Page-Jones, Anderson, McQuarrie, Ferns, Hurford, Rodgerson, Fraser, Rice, McCool
Substitute: Amos (nps)
Scorer: McCool
Attendance: 1156

Date: Wednesday 15/10/1969
Result: **GLOUCESTER CITY 3 WORCESTER CITY 0**
Competition: Southern League Cup 2nd Round
Teamsheet: Jones, Vale, Page-Jones, Anderson, McQuarrie, Ferns, Hurford, Rodgerson, Williams, Fraser, McCool
Substitute: Rice (nps)
Scorers: Hurford, Fraser (pen), own goal
Attendance: 1470

Date: Saturday 18/10/1969
Result: **GLOUCESTER CITY 1 WEYMOUTH 3**
Competition: Southern League Premier Division
Teamsheet: Jones, Vale, Page-Jones, Anderson, McQuarrie, Ferns, Rice, Rodgerson, M Harris, Fraser, McCool
Substitute: Stevens (for M Harris)
Scorer: McCool (nps)
Attendance: 1411

Date: Saturday 25/10/1969
Result: **ROMFORD 2 GLOUCESTER CITY 1**
Competition: Southern League Premier Division
Teamsheet: Jones, Vale, Page-Jones, Anderson, McQuarrie, Ferns, Hurford, Rodgerson, Stevens, Fraser, McCool
Substitute: McIntosh (for McCool)
Scorer: Fraser
Attendance: 1252

Date: Saturday 01/11/1969
Result: **GLOUCESTER CITY 2 WORCESTER CITY 1**
Competition: Southern League Premier Division
Teamsheet: Jones, Vale, Page-Jones, Anderson, McQuarrie, Ferns, Hurford, Rodgerson, Stevens, Williams, McCool
Substitute: Rice (nps)
Scorers: McQuarrie, Ferns
Attendance: 1673

Date: Saturday 08/11/1969
Result: **GLOUCESTER CITY 4 CHIPPENHAM TOWN 0**
Competition: FA Trophy 1st Qualifying Round
Teamsheet: Jones, Vale, Page-Jones, Anderson, McQuarrie, Ferns, Hurford, Fraser, Stevens, Williams, McCool
Substitute: McIntosh (for Williams)
Scorers: Williams (2), Stevens (2)
Attendance: 663

Date: Saturday 15/11/1969
Result: **GLOUCESTER CITY 3 ROMFORD 0**
Competition: Southern League Premier Division
Teamsheet: Jones, Vale, Page-Jones, Anderson, McQuarrie, Ferns, Reffold, Rodgerson, Stevens, Williams, McCool
Substitute: Fraser (for Reffold)
Scorers: Williams, Stevens, Fraser
Attendance: 1010

Date: Saturday 22/11/1969
Result: **TROWBRIDGE TOWN 0 GLOUCESTER CITY 0**
Competition: FA Trophy 2nd Qualifying Round
Teamsheet: Jones, Vale, Page-Jones, Anderson, McQuarrie, Ferns, Fraser, Rodgerson, Stevens, Williams, McCool
Substitute: Rice (for Williams)
Attendance: 911

Date: Monday 24/11/1969
Result: **CRAWLEY TOWN 2 GLOUCESTER CITY 2**
Competition: Southern League Premier Division
Teamsheet: Jones, Vale, Page-Jones, Anderson, McQuarrie, Ferns, McIntosh, Rodgerson, Stevens, Williams, McCool
Substitute: Fraser (for McIntosh)
Scorer: Stevens (2)

Date: Wednesday 26/11/1969
Result: **GLOUCESTER CITY 3 TROWBRIDGE TOWN 2**
Competition: FA Trophy 2nd Qualifying Round Replay
Teamsheet: Jones, Vale, Page-Jones, Anderson, McQuarrie, Ferns, Hurford, Rodgerson, Stevens, Williams, McCool
Substitute: Fraser (for Williams)
Scorers: Ferns (pen), Williams, Hurford
Attendance: 641
Note: Played at Whaddon Road, Cheltenham

Date: Saturday 06/12/1969
Result: **GLOUCESTER CITY 3 KETTERING TOWN 2**
Competition: Southern League Premier Division
Teamsheet: Jones, Vale, Page-Jones, Anderson, McQuarrie, Ferns, Hurford, Rodgerson, Stevens, Williams, McCool
Substitute: Fraser (nps)
Scorers: McCool, Vale, Rodgerson
Attendance: 1156

Date: Wednesday 10/12/1969
Result: **YEOVIL TOWN 0 GLOUCESTER CITY 1**
Competition: Southern League Cup 3rd Round
Teamsheet: Jones, Vale, Page-Jones, Anderson, McQuarrie, Ferns, Hurford, Rodgerson, Stevens, Williams, McCool
Substitute: Fraser (for Hurford)
Scorer: McCool
Attendance: 1661

Date: Saturday 13/12/1969
Result: **GLOUCESTER CITY 0 CHELTENHAM TOWN 1**
Competition: FA Trophy 3rd Qualifying Round
Teamsheet: Jones, Vale, Page-Jones, Anderson, McQuarrie, Ferns, Hurford, Rodgerson, Stevens, Williams, McCool
Substitute: Fraser (for Williams)
Attendance: 1517

Date: Saturday 20/12/1969
Result: **GLOUCESTER CITY 4 CRAWLEY TOWN 2**
Competition: Southern League Premier Division
Teamsheet: Jones, Vale, Page-Jones, Anderson, McQuarrie, Ferns, McIntosh, Rodgerson, Stevens, Fraser, McCool
Substitute: Williams (for McIntosh)
Scorers: Fraser (pen), Stevens (2), Rodgerson
Attendance: 673

Date: Saturday 27/12/1969
Result: **HEREFORD UNITED 4 GLOUCESTER CITY 2**
Competition: Southern League Premier Division
Teamsheet: Jones, Vale, Page-Jones, Anderson, McQuarrie, McCool, Fraser, Rodgerson, Stevens, Williams, Hurford
Substitute: McIntosh (for Williams)
Scorer: Rodgerson (2)

Date: Saturday 03/01/1970
Result: **WEYMOUTH 1 GLOUCESTER CITY 0**
Competition: Southern League Premier Division
Teamsheet: Jones, Vale, Page-Jones, Anderson, McQuarrie, Ferns, Fraser, Rodgerson, Stevens, Williams, McCool
Substitute: Rice (for Williams)
Attendance: 1229

Date: Saturday 17/01/1970
Result: **KING'S LYNN 6 GLOUCESTER CITY 1**
Competition: Southern League Premier Division
Teamsheet: Jones, Vale, Page-Jones, Anderson, McQuarrie, Ferns, Hurford, Rodgerson, Stevens, Fraser, McCool
Substitute: Williams (for Hurford)
Scorer: Stevens

Date: Wednesday 21/01/1970
Result: **GLOUCESTER CITY 2 BATH CITY 1**
Competition: Southern League Cup 4th Round
Teamsheet: Jones, Vale, Page-Jones, Anderson, McQuarrie, Ferns, Hurford, Rodgerson, Stevens, Williams, McCool
Substitute: McIntosh (for Hurford)
Scorers: Stevens, McCool
Attendance: 782

Date: Saturday 24/01/1970
Result: **WORCESTER CITY 1 GLOUCESTER CITY 2**
Competition: Southern League Premier Division
Teamsheet: Jones, Vale, Page-Jones, Anderson, McQuarrie, Ferns, Hurford, Rodgerson, Stevens, Williams, McCool
Substitute: McIntosh (nps)
Scorers: Ferns, Rodgerson
Attendance: 2290

Date: Wednesday 28/01/1970
Result: **YEOVIL TOWN 1 GLOUCESTER CITY 0**
Competition: Southern League Premier Division
Teamsheet: Jones, Vale, Page-Jones, Anderson, McQuarrie, Ferns, Hurford, Rodgerson, Williams, Stevens, McCool
Substitute: McIntosh (for Williams)
Attendance: 2160

Date: Saturday 31/01/1970
Result: **GLOUCESTER CITY 0 YEOVIL TOWN 3**
Competition: Southern League Premier Division
Teamsheet: Jones, Vale, Page-Jones, Anderson, McQuarrie, Ferns, Hurford, Rodgerson, Williams, Stevens, McCool
Substitute: McIntosh (for Ferns)
Attendance: 791

Date: Saturday 07/02/1970
Result: **WIMBLEDON 1 GLOUCESTER CITY 1**
Competition: Southern League Premier Division
Teamsheet: Jones, Vale, Page-Jones, Anderson, McQuarrie, McCool, Rice, Rodgerson, Stevens, Fraser, Hurford
Substitute: McIntosh (nps)
Scorer: own goal
Attendance: 1796

Date: Tuesday 10/02/1970
Result: **HILLINGDON BOROUGH 0 GLOUCESTER CITY 1**
Competition: Southern League Premier Division
Teamsheet: Jones, Vale, Page-Jones, Anderson, McQuarrie, McCool, Rice, Rodgerson, Stevens, Fraser, Ferns
Substitute: McIntosh (nps)
Scorer: Rice

[214]

Date: Saturday 28/02/1970
Result: **BARNET 0 GLOUCESTER CITY 0**
Competition: Southern League Premier Division
Teamsheet: Jones, Vale, Page-Jones, Anderson, McQuarrie, McCool, Rice, Rodgerson, Stevens, Fraser, Hurford
Substitute: McIntosh (for Rodgerson)
Attendance: 1290

Date: Monday 02/03/1970
Result: **MARGATE 2 GLOUCESTER CITY 0**
Competition: Southern League Premier Division
Teamsheet: Jones, Vale, Page-Jones, Anderson, McQuarrie, McIntosh, Rice, Williams, Stevens, Fraser, Hurford
Substitute: No sub
Attendance: 891

Date: Saturday 07/03/1970
Result: **BATH CITY 1 GLOUCESTER CITY 0**
Competition: Southern League Premier Division
Teamsheet: Jones, Vale, Page-Jones, Anderson, McQuarrie, McCool, Rice, Ferns, Stevens, Fraser, Hurford
Substitute: McIntosh (nps)

Date: Saturday 14/03/1970
Result: **GLOUCESTER CITY 2 MARGATE 0**
Competition: Southern League Premier Division
Teamsheet: Jones, Vale, Page-Jones, Anderson, McQuarrie, McCool, Rice, Ferns, Stevens, Fraser, Hurford
Substitute: McIntosh (nps)
Scorers: Fraser, own goal
Attendance: 716

Date: Thursday 19/03/1970
Result: **ROMFORD 2 GLOUCESTER CITY 2**
Competition: Southern League Cup Semi-Final
Teamsheet: Jones, Vale, Page-Jones, Anderson, McQuarrie, McCool, Rice, Ferns, Williams, Fraser, Hurford
Substitute: Stevens (for Rice)
Scorers: Williams, Stevens
Attendance: 1329

Date: Saturday 21/03/1970
Result: **NUNEATON BOROUGH 1 GLOUCESTER CITY 0**
Competition: Southern League Premier Division
Teamsheet: Jones, Vale, Page-Jones, Anderson, McQuarrie, McCool, Rice, Stevens, Williams, Ferns, Fraser
Substitute: McIntosh (for Rice)

Date: Thursday 25/03/1970
Result: **GLOUCESTER CITY 2 ROMFORD 4**
Competition: Southern League Cup Semi-Final Replay
Teamsheet: Jones, Vale, Page-Jones, Anderson, McQuarrie, McCool, Fraser, Ferns, Williams, Stevens, Hurford
Substitute: Moulsdale (for Williams)
Scorers: Fraser, Moulsdale
Attendance: 1058

Date: Friday 27/03/1970
Result: **BURTON ALBION 1 GLOUCESTER CITY 3**
Competition: Southern League Premier Division
Teamsheet: Jones, Vale, Page-Jones, Anderson, McQuarrie, McCool, Fraser, Stevens, Coldray, Ferns, Hurford
Substitute: Moulsdale (for Ferns)
Scorers: Stevens, Fraser, Coldray
Attendance: 545

Date: Saturday 28/03/1970
Result: **GLOUCESTER CITY 0 BRENTWOOD TOWN 4**
Competition: Southern League Premier Division
Teamsheet: Jones, Vale, Page-Jones, Anderson, McQuarrie, McCool, Fraser, Ferns, Coldray, Stevens, Hurford
Substitute: Rice (for Fraser)
Attendance: 1014

Date: Monday 30/03/1970
Result: **GLOUCESTER CITY 1 BURTON ALBION 1**
Competition: Southern League Premier Division
Teamsheet: Jones, Vale, Page-Jones, Anderson, McQuarrie, Ferns, Hurford, Coldray, Stevens, Fraser, McCool
Substitute: Rice (nps)
Scorer: Fraser
Attendance: 868

Date: Thursday 09/04/1970
Result: **GLOUCESTER CITY 1 CHELMSFORD CITY 3**
Competition: Southern League Premier Division
Teamsheet: Jones, Vale, Page-Jones, Anderson, McQuarrie, Ferns, Hurford, McCool, Stevens, Rodgerson, Fraser
Substitute: McIntosh (for Rodgerson)
Scorer: Rodgerson
Attendance: 486

Date: Monday 13/04/1970
Result: **CAMBRIDGE UNITED 3 GLOUCESTER CITY 0**
Competition: Southern League Premier Division
Teamsheet: Jones, Vale, Page-Jones, Anderson, McQuarrie, Ferns, Hurford, Rice, Stevens, Fraser, McCool
Substitute: McIntosh (nps)
Attendance: 3225

Date: Saturday 18/04/1970
Result: **GLOUCESTER CITY 0 BATH CITY 1**
Competition: Southern League Premier Division
Teamsheet: Jones, Vale, Page-Jones, Anderson, McQuarrie, McCool, Rice, Ferns, Stevens, Fraser, Hurford
Substitute: Coldray (for Rice)
Attendance: 846

Date: Monday 20/04/1970
Result: **GLOUCESTER CITY 0 CHELTENHAM TOWN 2**
Competition: Gloucestershire FA Northern Senior Professional Cup Final
Teamsheet: Jones, Vale, Page-Jones, McQuarrie, Biggart, Ferns, Hurford, Hutchison, Stevens, Anderson, McCool
Substitute: Fraser (for Hurford)
Attendance: 516

Date: Thursday 23/04/1970
Result: **GLOUCESTER CITY 3 WIMBLEDON 0**
Competition: Southern League Premier Division
Teamsheet: Jones, Vale, Page-Jones, Anderson, Biggart, Ferns, Hurford, Stevens, McQuarrie, McCool, Fraser
Substitute: Rodgerson (for Ferns)
Scorers: Ferns, McQuarrie, Stevens
Attendance: 488

Date: Monday 27/04/1970
Result: **GLOUCESTER CITY 1 NUNEATON BOROUGH 1**
Competition: Southern League Premier Division
Teamsheet: Jones, Vale, Page-Jones, Anderson, Biggart, Ferns, Hurford, McCool, McQuarrie, Stevens, Fraser
Substitute: Rodgerson (for Fraser)
Scorer: Hurford
Attendance: 876

Date: Thursday 30/04/1970
Result: **GLOUCESTER CITY 2 HEREFORD UNITED 0**
Competition: Southern League Premier Division
Teamsheet: Jones, Vale, Page-Jones, Anderson, Biggart, Ferns, Hurford, Fraser, McQuarrie, Stevens, McCool
Substitute: Coldray (nps)
Scorers: Ferns, Stevens
Attendance: 1215

Date: Saturday 02/05/1970
Result: **GLOUCESTER CITY 1 HILLINGDON BOROUGH 4**
Competition: Southern League Premier Division
Teamsheet: Jones, Vale, Page-Jones, Anderson, Biggart, Ferns, Hurford, Stevens, McQuarrie, Fraser, McCool
Substitute: Coldray (for Biggart)
Scorer: McCool
Attendance: 826

Appearances – PA Amos 1, R Anderson 53(3), SA Biggart 5, RA Coldray 3(2), W Ferns 51, I Fraser 43(6), R Hall 1(2), AT Harris 3(1), M Harris 1, DG Hurford 39(2), D Hutchison 1, R Jones 56, R McCool 54, JG McIntosh 11(11), A McQuarrie 56, MC Moulsdale 1(2), N Page-Jones 56, J Reffold 1, S Rice 23(3), AR Rodgerson 33(2), A Shenton 4, JM Stevens 44(2), ST Vale 56, M Williams 20(2).
Scorers – JM Stevens 16, I Fraser 14, W Ferns 8, R McCool 8, AR Rodgerson 6, S Rice 5, M Williams 5, DG Hurford 3, A McQuarrie 3, RA Coldray 1, MC Moulsdale 1, ST Vale 1, own goals 4.

SOUTHERN LEAGUE PREMIER DIVISION

POS	CLUB	P	W	D	L	F	A	PTS
1	CAMBRIDGE UNITED	42	26	6	10	84	50	58
2	YEOVIL TOWN	42	25	7	10	78	48	57
3	CHELMSFORD CITY	42	20	11	11	76	58	51
4	WEYMOUTH	42	18	14	10	59	37	50
5	WIMBLEDON	42	19	12	11	64	52	50
6	HILLINGDON BOROUGH	42	19	12	11	56	50	50
7	BARNET	42	16	15	11	71	54	47
8	TELFORD UNITED	42	18	10	14	61	62	46
9	BRENTWOOD TOWN	42	16	13	13	61	38	45
10	HEREFORD UNITED	42	18	9	15	74	65	45
11	BATH CITY	42	18	8	16	63	55	44
12	KING'S LYNN	42	16	11	15	72	68	43
13	MARGATE	42	17	8	17	70	64	42
14	DOVER	42	15	10	17	51	50	40
15	KETTERING TOWN	42	18	3	21	64	75	39
16	WORCESTER CITY	42	14	10	18	35	44	38
17	ROMFORD	42	13	11	18	50	62	37
18	POOLE TOWN	42	8	19	15	48	57	35
19	**GLOUCESTER CITY**	**42**	**12**	**9**	**21**	**53**	**73**	**33**
20	NUNEATON BOROUGH	42	11	10	21	52	74	32
21	CRAWLEY TOWN	42	6	15	21	53	101	27
22	BURTON ALBION	42	3	9	30	24	82	15
		924	346	232	346	1319	1319	924

SEASON 1970-1971
(Home Ground: Horton Road Stadium)

Date: Saturday 15/08/1970
Result: **DARTFORD 1 GLOUCESTER CITY 1**
Competition: Southern League Premier Division
Teamsheet: Jones, Vale, Peacock, Anderson, Biggart, Ferns, Hurford, Hudd, Williams, Wetson, McCool
Substitute: Rice (nps)
Scorer: Williams

Date: Monday 17/08/1970
Result: **WORCESTER CITY 0 GLOUCESTER CITY 0**
Competition: Southern League Premier Division
Teamsheet: Jones, Vale, Peacock, Anderson, Biggart, Ferns, Hurford, Hudd, Williams, Wetson, McCool
Substitute: Rice (nps)
Attendance: 1991

Date: Saturday 22/08/1970
Result: **GLOUCESTER CITY 0 KETTERING TOWN 0**
Competition: Southern League Premier Division
Teamsheet: Jones, Vale, Peacock, Anderson, Biggart, Ferns, Hurford, Hudd, Williams, Wetson, Holder
Substitute: Rice (for Holder)

Date: Wednesday 26/08/1970
Result: **HEREFORD UNITED 3 GLOUCESTER CITY 2**
Competition: Southern League Cup 1st Round 1st Leg
Teamsheet: Jones, Vale, Peacock, Anderson, Biggart, Ferns, Hurford, Hudd, Williams, Wetson, Rice
Substitute: McCool (nps)
Scorers: own goal, Williams
Attendance: 4477

Date: Saturday 29/08/1970
Result: **BEDFORD TOWN 1 GLOUCESTER CITY 0**
Competition: Southern League Premier Division
Teamsheet: Jones, Vale, Peacock, Anderson, Biggart, Ferns, Hurford, Hudd, Williams, Wetson, Rice
Substitute: McCool (for Rice)

Date: Thursday 03/09/1970
Result: **GLOUCESTER CITY 1 HEREFORD UNITED 1**
Competition: Southern League Cup 1st Round 2nd Leg
Teamsheet: Jones, Vale, Peacock, Anderson, Biggart, Ferns, Hurford, Holder, Williams, Wetson, Rice
Substitute: McCool (for Wetson)
Scorer: Rice
Attendance: 1923

Date: Saturday 05/09/1970
Result: **GLOUCESTER CITY 0 YEOVIL TOWN 3**
Competition: Southern League Premier Division
Teamsheet: Jones, Vale, Peacock, Anderson, Biggart, Ferns, Hurford, McCool, Williams, Wetson, Rice
Substitute: Holder (for Wetson)

Date: Thursday 10/09/1970
Result: **GLOUCESTER CITY 0 WORCESTER CITY 1**
Competition: Southern League Premier Division
Teamsheet: Jones, Vale, Peacock, Anderson, Biggart, Ferns, Hurford, Hudd, Williams, Wetson, McCool
Substitute: Rice (nps)
Attendance: 500

Date: Saturday 12/09/1970
Result: **HILLINGDON BOROUGH 4 GLOUCESTER CITY 0**
Competition: Southern League Premier Division
Teamsheet: Jones, Vale, Peacock, Hurford, Anderson, Ferns, Rice, Hudd, Holder, Wetson, McCool
Substitute: No sub
Attendance: 562

Date: Saturday 19/09/1970
Result: **CINDERFORD TOWN 3 GLOUCESTER CITY 2**
Competition: FA Cup 1st Qualifying Round
Teamsheet: Jones, Vale, Peacock, Hurford, Anderson, Ferns, Rice, Hudd, Williams, Wetson, McCool
Substitute: Holder (for Ferns)
Scorers: Williams, Hudd
Attendance: 717

Date: Saturday 26/09/1970
Result: **GLOUCESTER CITY 0 POOLE TOWN 4**
Competition: Southern League Premier Division
Teamsheet: Jones, Vale, Peacock, Holder, Anderson, Rice, Hurford, Hudd, Williams, Wetson, McCool
Substitute: Ferns (nps)
Attendance: 415

Date: Tuesday 29/09/1970
Result: **POOLE TOWN 2 GLOUCESTER CITY 1**
Competition: Southern League Premier Division
Teamsheet: Goodman, Vale, Peacock, Holder, Hall, Ferns, Hurford, Hudd, Williams, Rice, Wetson
Substitute: McCool (nps)
Scorer: Hudd

Date: Saturday 03/10/1970
Result: **GLOUCESTER CITY 0 HILLINGDON BOROUGH 2**
Competition: Southern League Premier Division
Teamsheet: Goodman, Vale, Holder, Anderson, Hall, Ferns, Hurford, Rice, Williams, Turner, Wetson
Substitute: Hudd (nps)

[217]

Date: Saturday 10/10/1970
Result: **GLOUCESTER CITY 2 CHELTENHAM TOWN 0**
Competition: Gloucestershire FA Northern Senior Professional Cup Final
Teamsheet: Goodman, Vale, Holder, Anderson, Hall, Hudd, Hurford, Rice, Williams, Turner, McCool
Substitute: Wetson (nps)
Scorer: McCool (2)
Attendance: 503

Date: Saturday 17/10/1970
Result: **GLOUCESTER CITY 3 BARNET 1**
Competition: Southern League Premier Division
Teamsheet: Goodman, Vale, Holder, Anderson, Hall, Hudd, Hurford, Rice, Williams, Turner, McCool
Substitute: Wetson (nps)
Scorers: Hudd, Turner, own goal
Attendance: 723

Date: Saturday 24/10/1970
Result: **KETTERING TOWN 1 GLOUCESTER CITY 1**
Competition: Southern League Premier Division
Teamsheet: Goodman, Vale, Holder, Anderson, Hall, Hudd, Hurford, Rice, Williams, Turner, Wetson
Substitute: Ferns (nps)
Scorer: Williams
Attendance: 889

Date: Saturday 31/10/1970
Result: **GLOUCESTER CITY 3 ABERGAVENNY THURSDAYS 1**
Competition: FA Trophy 1st Qualifying Round
Teamsheet: Goodman, Vale, Holder, Anderson, Biggart, Hudd, Hurford, Ferns, Williams, Turner, Rice
Substitute: Hall (nps)
Scorers: Vale, own goal, Williams
Attendance: 500

Date: Saturday 07/11/1970
Result: **GLOUCESTER CITY 1 DOVER 3**
Competition: Southern League Premier Division
Teamsheet: Goodman, Vale, Holder, Anderson, Biggart, Hudd, Hurford, Ferns, Williams, Rice, McCool
Substitute: Hall (for Williams)
Scorer: Ferns
Attendance: 510

Date: Saturday 14/11/1970
Result: **GLOUCESTER CITY 0 LOCKHEED LEAMINGTON 0**
Competition: FA Trophy 2nd Qualifying Round
Teamsheet: Goodman, Vale, Holder, Anderson, Biggart, Hudd, Hurford, Ferns, Turner, Rice, McCool
Substitute: Williams (nps)

Date: Tuesday 17/11/1970
Result: **LOCKHEED LEAMINGTON 1 GLOUCESTER CITY 2** (aet)
Competition: FA Trophy 2nd Qualifying Round Replay
Teamsheet: Goodman, Vale, Holder, Anderson, Biggart, Hudd, Ferns, Rice, Williams, Turner, Wetson
Substitute: Peacock (nps)
Scorer: Ferns (2)

Date: Saturday 21/11/1970
Result: **ROMFORD 4 GLOUCESTER CITY 1**
Competition: Southern League Premier Division
Teamsheet: Goodman, Vale, Holder, Anderson, Biggart, Hudd, Ferns, Rice, Williams, Turner, Wetson
Substitute: Jacobs (for Williams)
Scorer: Turner
Attendance: 1463

Date: Saturday 28/11/1970
Result: **GLOUCESTER CITY 0 MARGATE 0**
Competition: Southern League Premier Division
Teamsheet: Goodman, Vale, Holder, Anderson, Biggart, Hudd, Scarrott, Rice, Williams, Turner, Ferns
Substitute: Jacobs (nps)
Attendance: 563

Date: Saturday 05/12/1970
Result: **GLOUCESTER CITY 1 TON PENTRE 0**
Competition: FA Trophy 3rd Qualifying Round
Teamsheet: Goodman, Vale, Holder, Anderson, Biggart, Hudd, Hurford, Rice, Williams, Turner, Ferns
Substitute: Jacobs (nps)
Scorer: Williams
Attendance: 520

Date: Saturday 19/12/1970
Result: **GLOUCESTER CITY 3 KING'S LYNN 0**
Competition: Southern League Premier Division
Teamsheet: Goodman, Vale, Holder, Anderson, Biggart, Hudd, Scarrott, Rice, Round, Williams, Ferns
Substitute: Hurford (for Ferns)
Scorers: Williams, Hudd, Vale
Attendance: 606

Date: Saturday 26/12/1970
Result: **HEREFORD UNITED 1 GLOUCESTER CITY 0**
Competition: Southern League Premier Division
Teamsheet: Goodman, Vale, Holder, Anderson, Biggart, Hudd, Scarrott, Rice, Round, Williams, Ferns
Substitute: Hurford (nps)
Attendance: 4364

Date: Saturday 02/01/1971
Result: **GLOUCESTER CITY 3 ASHFORD TOWN 3**
Competition: Southern League Premier Division
Teamsheet: Goodman, Vale, Holder, Anderson, Biggart, Hudd, Scarrott, Rice, Round, Williams, Ferns
Substitute: Hurford (for Williams)
Scorers: Hudd, Round, Scarrott
Attendance: 750

Date: Saturday 09/01/1971
Result: **BATH CITY 2 GLOUCESTER CITY 2**
Competition: Southern League Premier Division
Teamsheet: Goodman, Vale, Holder, Anderson, Biggart, Hurford, Scarrott, Rice, Williams, Wetson, Jacobs
Substitute: Hudd (nps)
Scorers: Biggart, Vale
Attendance: 1113

Date: Saturday 16/01/1971
Result: **HEREFORD UNITED 3 GLOUCESTER CITY 1**
Competition: FA Trophy 1st Round
Teamsheet: Goodman, Vale, Holder, Anderson, Biggart, Hudd, Scarrott, Rice, Round, Hurford, Ferns
Substitute: Williams (for Holder)
Scorer: Hurford
Attendance: 3921

Date: Saturday 06/02/1971
Result: **NUNEATON BOROUGH 2 GLOUCESTER CITY 1**
Competition: Southern League Premier Division
Teamsheet: Jones, Vale, Hughes, Anderson, Biggart, Hudd, Hurford, Rice, Round, Shepherd, Ferns
Substitute: Wetson (for Hughes)
Scorer: Ferns

Date: Tuesday 09/02/1971
Result: **BARNET 4 GLOUCESTER CITY 1**
Competition: Southern League Premier Division
Teamsheet: Jones, Vale, Hughes, Anderson, Biggart, Hudd, Hurford, Rice, Round, Shepherd, Ferns
Substitute: Wetson (nps)
Scorer: Ferns
Attendance: 770

Date: Saturday 13/02/1971
Result: **GLOUCESTER CITY 0 CAMBRIDGE CITY 1**
Competition: Southern League Premier Division
Teamsheet: Jones, Vale, Hughes, Anderson, Biggart, Hudd, Scarrott, Rice, Round, Hurford, Ferns
Substitute: Shepherd (nps)
Attendance: 518

Date: Saturday 20/02/1971
Result: **GLOUCESTER CITY 0 CHELMSFORD CITY 2**
Competition: Southern League Premier Division
Teamsheet: Jones, Vale, Hughes, Anderson, Biggart, Hudd, Scarrott, Rice, Round, Shepherd, Ferns
Substitute: Hurford (for Round)

Date: Wednesday 24/02/1971
Result: **KING'S LYNN 0 GLOUCESTER CITY 0**
Competition: Southern League Premier Division
Teamsheet: Jones, Vale, Hughes, Anderson, Biggart, Hudd, Hurford, Rice, Shepherd, Ferns, Wetson
Substitute: Jacobs (nps)
Attendance: 1056

Date: Saturday 27/02/1971
Result: **GLOUCESTER CITY 0 DARTFORD 1**
Competition: Southern League Premier Division
Teamsheet: Jones, Vale, Hughes, Anderson, Biggart, Rice, Scarrott, Hurford, Andrews, Ferns, Wetson
Substitute: Shepherd (nps)
Attendance: 406

Date: Wednesday 03/03/1971
Result: **WEYMOUTH 3 GLOUCESTER CITY 1**
Competition: Southern League Premier Division
Teamsheet: Goodman, Vale, Hughes, Anderson, Biggart, Hudd, Rice, Round, Andrews, Shepherd, Ferns
Substitute: Hurford (nps)
Scorer: own goal
Attendance: 795

Date: Wednesday 10/03/1971
Result: **GLOUCESTER CITY 0 BATH CITY 0**
Competition: Southern League Premier Division
Teamsheet: Goodman, Vale, Hughes, Anderson, Biggart, Hudd, Rice, Round, Andrews, Shepherd, Ferns
Substitute: Hurford (nps)
Attendance: 310
Note: Played at Whaddon Road, Cheltenham

Date: Saturday 13/03/1971
Result: **GLOUCESTER CITY 2 NUNEATON BOROUGH 1**
Competition: Southern League Premier Division
Teamsheet: Goodman, Vale, Hughes, Anderson, Biggart, Hudd, Rice, Round, Andrews, Shepherd, Ferns
Substitute: Hurford (for Ferns)
Scorers: Shepherd (pen), Round
Attendance: 413

Date: Wednesday 17/03/1971
Result: **GLOUCESTER CITY 1 BEDFORD TOWN 0**
Competition: Southern League Premier Division
Teamsheet: Goodman, Vale, Hughes, Anderson, Biggart, Hudd, Rice, Round, Andrews, Shepherd, McCool
Substitute: Hurford (nps)
Scorer: Round
Attendance: 330

Date: Saturday 20/03/1971
Result: **MARGATE 0 GLOUCESTER CITY 1**
Competition: Southern League Premier Division
Teamsheet: Goodman, Vale, Hughes, Anderson, Biggart, Hudd, Rice, Round, Andrews, Shepherd, Ferns
Substitute: Hurford (nps)
Scorer: Andrews
Attendance: 673

Date: Monday 22/03/1971
Result: **CHELMSFORD CITY 1 GLOUCESTER CITY 0**
Competition: Southern League Premier Division
Teamsheet: Goodman, Vale, Ferns, Anderson, Biggart, Hudd, Rice, Shepherd, Round, Jacobs, Hurford
Substitute: No sub
Attendance: 1507

Date: Saturday 27/03/1971
Result: **GLOUCESTER CITY 1 WEYMOUTH 4**
Competition: Southern League Premier Division
Teamsheet: Jones, Vale, Ferns, Anderson, Biggart, Hudd, Rice, Round, Andrews, Shepherd, McCool
Substitute: Jacobs (for Hudd)
Scorer: McCool
Attendance: 555

Date: Saturday 03/04/1971
Result: **CAMBRIDGE CITY 5 GLOUCESTER CITY 0**
Competition: Southern League Premier Division
Teamsheet: Goodman, Vale, Layton, Anderson, Biggart, Hudd, Rice, Hurford, Andrews, Fraser, Ferns
Substitute: Holder (for Hudd)
Attendance: 1624

Date: Friday 09/04/1971
Result: **GLOUCESTER CITY 1 TELFORD UNITED 2**
Competition: Southern League Premier Division
Teamsheet: Goodman, Vale, Layton, Anderson, Biggart, Hughes, Rice, Ferns, Andrews, Fraser, McCool
Substitute: Hurford (nps)
Scorer: McCool
Attendance: 680

Date: Saturday 10/04/1971
Result: **YEOVIL TOWN 5 GLOUCESTER CITY 0**
Competition: Southern League Premier Division
Teamsheet: Goodman, Vale, Layton, Anderson, Biggart, Hughes, Hurford, Rice, Andrews, Fraser, Ferns
Substitute: Holder (nps)

Date: Monday 12/04/1971
Result: **TELFORD UNITED 2 GLOUCESTER CITY 0**
Competition: Southern League Premier Division
Teamsheet: Goodman, Vale, Holder, Anderson, Biggart, Rice, Scarrott, Hurford, Andrews, Fraser, Ferns
Substitute: Jacobs (nps)

Date: Saturday 17/04/1971
Result: **WIMBLEDON 3 GLOUCESTER CITY 2**
Competition: Southern League Premier Division
Teamsheet: Goodman, Vale, Layton, Anderson, Biggart, Rice, Hurford, Holder, Andrews, Fraser, Ferns
Substitute: Jacobs (for Andrews)
Scorers: Holder, Ferns

Date: Saturday 24/04/1971
Result: **GLOUCESTER CITY 2 WIMBLEDON 1**
Competition: Southern League Premier Division
Teamsheet: Goodman, Vale, Layton, Anderson, Biggart, Rice, Hurford, Holder, Andrews, Hudd, Ferns
Substitute: Fraser (nps)
Scorers: Andrews, Holder
Attendance: 327

Date: Wednesday 28/04/1971
Result: **GLOUCESTER CITY 0 ROMFORD 1**
Competition: Southern League Premier Division
Teamsheet: Goodman, Vale, Layton, Anderson, Biggart, Rice, Hurford, Hudd, Holder, Ferns, McCool
Substitute: Fraser (nps)
Attendance: 384

Date: Friday 30/04/1971
Result: **DOVER 5 GLOUCESTER CITY 1**
Competition: Southern League Premier Division
Teamsheet: Goodman, Vale, Layton, Anderson, Biggart, Rice, Hurford, Hudd, Andrews, Holder, Ferns
Substitute: Fraser (nps)
Scorer: Ferns
Attendance: 634

Date: Saturday 01/05/1971
Result: **ASHFORD TOWN 3 GLOUCESTER CITY 2**
Competition: Southern League Premier Division
Teamsheet: Goodman, Vale, Layton, Anderson, Biggart, Hudd, Hurford, Fraser, Andrews, Holder, Ferns
Substitute: Jacobs (nps)
Scorers: Fraser, Ferns
Attendance: 398

Date: Thursday 06/05/1971
Result: **GLOUCESTER CITY 2 HEREFORD UNITED 2**
Competition: Southern League Premier Division
Teamsheet: Goodman, Vale, Layton, Anderson, Biggart, Rice, Hurford, Hudd, Andrews, Ferns, McCool
Substitute: Fraser (nps)
Scorer: Vale (2)
Attendance: 1156

Appearances – R Anderson 50, G Andrews 16, SA Biggart 43, W Ferns 40, I Fraser 6, C Goodman 33, R Hall 5(1), CW Holder 32(3), DC Hudd 42, B Hughes 13, DG Hurford 37(4), C Jacobs 2(3), R Jones 18, JH Layton 9, R McCool 16(2), S Peacock 12, S Rice 46(1), SG Round 15, AR Scarrott 10, JA Shepherd 11, J Turner 10, ST Vale 51, RS Wetson 19(1), M Williams 25(1).
Scorers – W Ferns 8, M Williams 7, DC Hudd 5, ST Vale 5, R McCool 4, SG Round 3, G Andrews 2, CW Holder 2, J Turner 2, SA Biggart 1, I Fraser 1, DG Hurford 1, S Rice 1, AR Scarrott 1, JA Shepherd 1, own goals 4.

SOUTHERN LEAGUE PREMIER DIVISION

POS	CLUB	P	W	D	L	F	A	PTS
1	YEOVIL TOWN	42	25	7	10	66	31	57
2	CAMBRIDGE CITY	42	22	11	9	67	38	55
3	ROMFORD	42	23	9	10	63	42	55
4	HEREFORD UNITED	42	23	8	11	71	53	54
5	CHELMSFORD CITY	42	20	11	11	61	32	51
6	BARNET	42	18	14	10	69	49	50
7	BEDFORD TOWN	42	20	10	12	62	46	50
8	WIMBLEDON	42	20	8	14	72	54	48
9	WORCESTER CITY	42	20	8	14	61	46	48
10	WEYMOUTH	42	14	16	12	64	48	44
11	DARTFORD	42	15	12	15	53	51	42
12	DOVER	42	16	9	17	64	63	41
13	MARGATE	42	15	10	17	64	70	40
14	HILLINGDON BOROUGH	42	17	6	19	61	68	40
15	BATH CITY	42	13	12	17	48	68	38
16	NUNEATON BOROUGH	42	12	12	18	43	66	36
17	TELFORD UNITED	42	13	8	21	64	70	34
18	POOLE TOWN	42	14	6	22	57	75	34
19	KING'S LYNN	42	11	7	24	44	67	29
20	ASHFORD TOWN	42	8	13	21	52	86	29
21	KETTERING TOWN	42	8	11	23	48	84	27
22	**GLOUCESTER CITY**	**42**	**6**	**10**	**26**	**34**	**81**	**22**
		924	353	218	353	1288	1288	924

SEASON 1971-1972
(Home Ground: Horton Road Stadium)

Date: Tuesday 17/08/1971
Result: **ILKESTON TOWN 3 GLOUCESTER CITY 1**
Competition: Southern League Cup Group 4
Teamsheet: Miles, Winrow, Layton, Anderson, Biggart, Hudd, Meredith, Hargreaves, Blackburn, Andrews, Hughes
Substitute: Vale (nps)
Scorer: Andrews
Attendance: 779

Date: Saturday 21/08/1971
Result: **BURTON ALBION 3 GLOUCESTER CITY 0**
Competition: Southern League Cup Group 4
Teamsheet: Miles, Winrow, Layton, Anderson, Biggart, Ferns, Meredith, Hargreaves, Blackburn, Andrews, Hughes
Substitute: Vale (nps)
Attendance: 922

Date: Tuesday 24/08/1971
Result: **WELLINGBOROUGH TOWN 1 GLOUCESTER CITY 1**
Competition: Southern League Division 1 North
Teamsheet: Miles, Winrow, Layton, Anderson, Biggart, Ferns, Meredith, Hargreaves, Blackburn, Andrews, Hughes
Substitute: Vale (nps)
Scorer: Andrews
Attendance: 436

Date: Thursday 26/08/1971
Result: **GLOUCESTER CITY 1 STOURBRIDGE 2**
Competition: Southern League Cup Group 4
Teamsheet: Miles, Winrow, Layton, Anderson, Biggart, Ferns, Meredith, Hargreaves, Blackburn, Andrews, Hughes
Substitute: Vale (nps)
Scorer: Hughes
Attendance: 510

Date: Saturday 28/08/1971
Result: **GLOUCESTER CITY 2 CHELTENHAM TOWN 3**
Competition: Southern League Cup Group 4
Teamsheet: Miles, Winrow, Layton, Anderson, Biggart, Ferns, Meredith, Vale, Andrews, Hargreaves, Hughes
Substitute: Hudd (for Hargreaves)
Scorers: Meredith, Vale
Attendance: 717

Date: Saturday 04/09/1971
Result: **BARRY TOWN 1 GLOUCESTER CITY 2**
Competition: Southern League Cup Group 4
Teamsheet: Miles, Winrow, Layton, Anderson, Biggart, Ferns, Meredith, Hudd, Blackburn, Vale, Hughes
Substitute: Andrews (nps)
Scorers: Hughes, Vale

Date: Saturday 11/09/1971
Result: **GLOUCESTER CITY 0 BURTON ALBION 1**
Competition: Southern League Division 1 North
Teamsheet: Miles, Winrow, Layton, Anderson, Biggart, Ferns, Meredith, Vale, Blackburn, McCool, Hughes
Substitute: Hargreaves (for Blackburn)
Attendance: 502

Date: Saturday 18/09/1971
Result: **GLOUCESTER CITY 2 MERTHYR TYDFIL 3**
Competition: FA Cup 1st Qualifying Round
Teamsheet: Miles, Winrow, Layton, Anderson, Biggart, Ferns, Meredith, Vale, McCool, Hargreaves, Hughes
Substitute: Andrews (nps)
Scorers: Ferns, Hargreaves

Date: Saturday 25/09/1971
Result: **WEALDSTONE 2 GLOUCESTER CITY 1**
Competition: Southern League Division 1 North
Teamsheet: Miles, Winrow, Layton, Anderson, Biggart, Hargreaves, Meredith, Vale, McCool, Andrews, Hughes
Substitute: Hudd (for Layton)
Scorer: Vale
Attendance: 1021

Date: Thursday 30/09/1971
Result: **TON PENTRE 2 GLOUCESTER CITY 0**
Competition: FA Trophy 1st Qualifying Round
Teamsheet: Miles, Vale, Winrow, Anderson, Biggart, Ferns, Hargreaves, Hudd, Blackburn, Andrews, Hughes
Substitute: Meredith (nps)

Date: Saturday 02/10/1971
Result: **GLOUCESTER CITY 3 KING'S LYNN 0**
Competition: Southern League Division 1 North
Teamsheet: Miles, Vale, Winrow, Anderson, Biggart, Ferns, Hargreaves, Blackburn, McCool, Andrews, Hughes
Substitute: Meredith (nps)
Scorers: Blackburn (2), own goal
Attendance: 510

Date: Saturday 09/10/1971
Result: **BANBURY UNITED 1 GLOUCESTER CITY 0**
Competition: Southern League Division 1 North
Teamsheet: Miles, Vale, Winrow, Anderson, Biggart, Ferns, Hargreaves, Blackburn, McCool, Andrews, Hughes
Substitute: Meredith (nps)

Date: Saturday 16/10/1971
Result: **GLOUCESTER CITY 0 BANBURY UNITED 2**
Competition: Southern League Division 1 North
Teamsheet: Miles, Vale, Winrow, Anderson, Biggart, Ferns, Hargreaves, Blackburn, McCool, Andrews, Hughes
Substitute: Meredith (nps)
Attendance: 451

Date: Saturday 23/10/1971
Result: **GLOUCESTER CITY 3 BARRY TOWN 1**
Competition: Southern League Division 1 North
Teamsheet: Miles, Winrow, Vale, Anderson, Biggart, Ferns, Hughes, Hudd, Blackburn, Hargreaves, McCool
Substitute: Andrews (nps)
Scorers: McCool, Hargreaves, Blackburn
Attendance: 485

Date: Saturday 06/11/1971
Result: **GLOUCESTER CITY 4 STEVENAGE ATHLETIC 1**
Competition: Southern League Division 1 North
Teamsheet: Miles, Winrow, Timms, Anderson, Biggart, Ferns, Hurford, Vale, Blackburn, Hudd, McCool
Substitute: Hargreaves (nps)
Scorers: McCool (2), Ferns (pen), Hudd
Attendance: 410

Date: Saturday 13/11/1971
Result: **BURY TOWN 2 GLOUCESTER CITY 0**
Competition: Southern League Division 1 North
Teamsheet: Miles, Winrow, Timms, Anderson, Biggart, Ferns, Hurford, Vale, Blackburn, Hudd, McCool
Substitute: Hargreaves (for Anderson)

Date: Saturday 20/11/1971
Result: **GLOUCESTER CITY 3 ILKESTON TOWN 1**
Competition: Southern League Division 1 North
Teamsheet: Miles, Vale, Timms, Winrow, Biggart, Ferns, Hurford, Laycock, Blackburn, Hudd, McCool
Substitute: Hargreaves (for McCool)
Scorers: McCool, Hargreaves, Hurford
Attendance: 401

[222]

Date: Tuesday 23/11/1971
Result: **RUGBY TOWN 0 GLOUCESTER CITY 0**
Competition: Southern League Division 1 North
Teamsheet: Miles, Vale, Timms, Winrow, Biggart, Ferns, Hurford, Hudd, Blackburn, Laycock, Hargreaves
Substitute: Layton (nps)

Date: Saturday 27/11/1971
Result: **GLOUCESTER CITY 0 CORBY TOWN 1**
Competition: Southern League Division 1 North
Teamsheet: Miles, Vale, Timms, Winrow, Biggart, Ferns, Hurford, Laycock, Blackburn, Hudd, McCool
Substitute: Hargreaves (for Hudd)
Attendance: 510

Date: Wednesday 01/12/1971
Result: **KETTERING TOWN 4 GLOUCESTER CITY 4**
Competition: Southern League Division 1 North
Teamsheet: Miles, Vale, Layton, Winrow, Biggart, Ferns, Hurford, Laycock, Hargreaves, Hudd, McCool
Substitute: Blackburn (for Hurford)
Scorers: Vale (2), Ferns (pen), Blackburn
Attendance: 713

Date: Saturday 04/12/1971
Result: **GLOUCESTER CITY 4 WELLINGBOROUGH TOWN 1**
Competition: Southern League Division 1 North
Teamsheet: Miles, Vale, Timms, Winrow, Biggart, Ferns, Hurford, Laycock, Hargreaves, Baker, Hudd
Substitute: Blackburn (for Baker)
Scorers: Laycock, Hudd, Hurford, own goal
Attendance: 412

Date: Saturday 11/12/1971
Result: **LOCKHEED LEAMINGTON 2 GLOUCESTER CITY 1**
Competition: Southern League Division 1 North
Teamsheet: Miles, Vale, Timms, Winrow, Biggart, Ferns, Hurford, Layton, Hargreaves, Hudd, McCool
Substitute: Blackburn (nps)
Scorer: Hudd

Date: Saturday 18/12/1971
Result: **CORBY TOWN 4 GLOUCESTER CITY 1**
Competition: Southern League Division 1 North
Teamsheet: Miles, Vale, Timms, Winrow, Biggart, Layton, Hurford, Laycock, Hargreaves, Baker, McCool
Substitute: Hudd (nps)
Scorer: Vale

Date: Monday 27/12/1971
Result: **GLOUCESTER CITY 2 STOURBRIDGE 2**
Competition: Southern League Division 1 North
Teamsheet: Miles, Vale, Timms, Winrow, Anderson, Laycock, Hargreaves, Hudd, Blackburn, Baker, McCool
Substitute: Layton (nps)
Scorers: Hargreaves, Hudd
Attendance: 1052

Date: Saturday 01/01/1972
Result: **STOURBRIDGE 3 GLOUCESTER CITY 0**
Competition: Southern League Division 1 North
Teamsheet: Cameron, Vale, Timms, Winrow, Anderson, Ferns, Hargreaves, Hudd, Blackburn, Laycock, Hurford
Substitute: McCool (nps)

Date: Saturday 08/01/1972
Result: **GLOUCESTER CITY 1 WEALDSTONE 3**
Competition: Southern League Division 1 North
Teamsheet: Miles, Vale, Winrow, Laycock, Biggart, Ferns, Hargreaves, Hudd, Anderson, McCool, Hurford
Substitute: Blackburn (nps)
Scorer: McCool
Attendance: 410

Date: Saturday 22/01/1972
Result: **GLOUCESTER CITY 0 BLETCHLEY TOWN 1**
Competition: Southern League Division 1 North
Teamsheet: Miles, Vale, Timms, Winrow, Biggart, Laycock, Hurford, Hudd, Stevens, Hargreaves, McCool
Substitute: Baker (for Hurford)
Attendance: 410

Date: Saturday 29/01/1972
Result: **KING'S LYNN 1 GLOUCESTER CITY 0**
Competition: Southern League Division 1 North
Teamsheet: Miles, Vale, Timms, Winrow, Biggart, Ferns, Hurford, Blackburn, Stevens, Baker, Hargreaves
Substitute: Tandy (nps)

Date: Saturday 12/02/1972
Result: **BARRY TOWN 1 GLOUCESTER CITY 3**
Competition: Southern League Division 1 North
Teamsheet: Miles, Hurford, Laycock, Anderson, Biggart, Ferns, Vale, Blackburn, Stevens, Hargreaves, McCool
Substitute: Hudd (for Hargreaves)
Scorers: Blackburn, Hudd (2)

Date: Saturday 19/02/1972
Result: **GLOUCESTER CITY 1 DUNSTABLE TOWN 1**
Competition: Southern League Division 1 North
Teamsheet: Miles, Winrow, Hargreaves, Anderson, Biggart, Ferns, Vale, Blackburn, Stevens, Hudd, McCool
Substitute: Hurford (nps)
Scorer: Blackburn
Attendance: 345

Date: Saturday 26/02/1972
Result: **STEVENAGE ATHLETIC 1 GLOUCESTER CITY 1**
Competition: Southern League Division 1 North
Teamsheet: Miles, Winrow, Laycock, Anderson, Biggart, Ferns, Vale, Blackburn, Stevens, Hudd, Hargreaves
Substitute: Hurford (nps)
Scorer: Stevens

Date: Saturday 11/03/1972
Result: **ILKESTON TOWN 2 GLOUCESTER CITY 3**
Competition: Southern League Division 1 North
Teamsheet: Miles, Winrow, Laycock, Anderson, Biggart, Ferns, Vale, Blackburn, Stevens, Hudd, Hurford
Substitute: Hargreaves (nps)
Scorers: Hudd, Stevens, Hurford

Date: Saturday 18/03/1972
Result: **GLOUCESTER CITY 2 RUGBY TOWN 4**
Competition: Southern League Division 1 North
Teamsheet: Miles, Winrow, Laycock, Anderson, Biggart, Ferns, Vale, Blackburn, Stevens, Hudd, Hurford
Substitute: Hargreaves (for Hurford)
Scorers: Vale, Blackburn
Attendance: 411

Date: Saturday 25/03/1972
Result: **BURTON ALBION 0 GLOUCESTER CITY 0**
Competition: Southern League Division 1 North
Teamsheet: Miles, Vale, Laycock, Winrow, Biggart, Ferns, Hargreaves, Blackburn, Stevens, Hudd, McCool
Substitute: Anderson (for Ferns)
Attendance: 1008

Date: Saturday 01/04/1972
Result: **GLOUCESTER CITY 1 LOCKHEED LEAMINGTON 2**
Competition: Southern League Division 1 North
Teamsheet: Miles, Anderson, Laycock, Timms, Biggart, Ferns, Hargreaves, Blackburn, Stevens, Hudd, McCool
Substitute: Baker (nps)
Scorer: Blackburn
Attendance: 356

Date: Monday 03/04/1972
Result: **GLOUCESTER CITY 0 CHELTENHAM TOWN 4**
Competition: Southern League Division 1 North
Teamsheet: Miles, Anderson, Laycock, Timms, Biggart, Ferns, Hargreaves, Blackburn, Stevens, Hudd, McCool
Substitute: Baker (for Timms)
Attendance: 1220

Date: Tuesday 04/04/1972
Result: **CHELTENHAM TOWN 2 GLOUCESTER CITY 1**
Competition: Southern League Division 1 North
Teamsheet: Miles, Hargreaves, Timms, Anderson, Biggart, Ferns, Hudd, Blackburn, Stevens, Laycock, McCool
Substitute: Baker (nps)
Scorer: Ferns
Attendance: 1198

Date: Saturday 15/04/1972
Result: **BLETCHLEY TOWN 3 GLOUCESTER CITY 3**
Competition: Southern League Division 1 North
Teamsheet: Miles, Hargreaves, Timms, Anderson, Biggart, Ferns, Hudd, Blackburn, Stevens, Laycock, McCool
Substitute: Winrow (nps)
Scorers: McCool, Laycock, Stevens

Date: Sunday 16/04/1972
Result: **CHELTENHAM TOWN 4 GLOUCESTER CITY 1**
Competition: Gloucestershire FA Northern Senior Professional Cup Final
Teamsheet: Miles, Hargreaves, Layton, Anderson, Biggart, Ferns, Hudd, Blackburn, Stevens, Laycock, McCool
Substitute: Hall (nps)
Scorer: Ferns
Attendance: 850

Date: Saturday 22/04/1972
Result: **DUNSTABLE TOWN 2 GLOUCESTER CITY 0**
Competition: Southern League Division 1 North
Teamsheet: Miles, Hargreaves, Timms, Anderson, Biggart, Ferns, Hudd, Blackburn, Stevens, Laycock, McCool
Substitute: Hall (nps)

Date: Monday 24/04/1972
Result: **GLOUCESTER CITY 1 BURY TOWN 4**
Competition: Southern League Division 1 North
Teamsheet: Miles, Hall, Timms, Anderson, Biggart, Ferns, Hargreaves, Blackburn, Stevens, Laycock, McCool
Substitute: Winrow (nps)
Scorer: Ferns
Attendance: 121

Date: Saturday 29/04/1972
Result: **GLOUCESTER CITY 2 KETTERING TOWN 1**
Competition: Southern League Division 1 North
Teamsheet: Miles, Hall, Timms, Anderson, Biggart, Ferns, Hargreaves, Blackburn, Stevens, Laycock, McCool
Substitute: Winrow (nps)
Scorers: McCool, Hargreaves
Attendance: 150

Appearances – R Anderson 32(1), G Andrews 10, GA Baker 4(2), SA Biggart 40, KA Blackburn 33(2), A Cameron 1, W Ferns 37, R Hall 2, T Hargreaves 34(5), DC Hudd 27(3), A Hughes 14, DG Hurford 16, J Laycock 23, JH Layton 13, R McCool 28, M Meredith 9, JM Miles 41, JM Stevens 16, PN Timms 19, ST Vale 30, B Winrow 28.
Others selected but did not play: BI Tandy.
Scorers – KA Blackburn 8, DC Hudd 7, R McCool 7, ST Vale 7, W Ferns 6, T Hargreaves 5, DG Hurford 3, JM Stevens 3, G Andrews 2, A Hughes 2, J Laycock 2, M Meredith 1, own goals 2.

SOUTHERN LEAGUE DIVISION 1 NORTH

POS	CLUB	P	W	D	L	F	A	PTS
1	KETTERING TOWN	34	23	6	5	70	27	52
2	BURTON ALBION	34	18	13	3	58	27	49
3	CHELTENHAM TOWN	34	20	4	10	72	51	44
4	RUGBY TOWN	34	18	7	9	52	36	43
5	WELLINGBOROUGH TOWN	34	15	10	9	73	44	40
6	STOURBRIDGE	34	13	14	7	59	42	40
7	KING'S LYNN	34	14	11	9	62	45	39
8	CORBY TOWN	34	15	9	10	47	35	39
9	ILKESTON TOWN	34	14	11	9	44	38	39
10	BANBURY UNITED	34	14	5	15	54	46	33
11	BURY TOWN	34	14	5	15	47	44	33
12	WEALDSTONE	34	14	5	15	51	58	33
13	LOCKHEED LEAMINGTON	34	15	3	16	41	52	33
14	GLOUCESTER CITY	34	8	8	18	46	61	24
15	STEVENAGE ATHLETIC	34	8	8	18	41	69	24
16	BLETCHLEY TOWN	34	7	7	20	36	70	21
17	DUNSTABLE TOWN	34	5	7	22	29	75	17
18	BARRY TOWN	34	1	7	26	22	84	9
		612	236	140	236	904	904	612

SEASON 1972-1973
(Home Ground: Horton Road Stadium)

Date: Saturday 12/08/1972
Result: **GLOUCESTER CITY 1 BROMSGROVE ROVERS 3**
Competition: Southern League Division 1 North
Teamsheet: Miles, Hargreaves, Layton, McCool, Biggart, McQuarrie, Corr, Vale, Stevens, Bird, J Whitehouse
Substitute: Sayer (for Corr)
Scorer: Stevens
Attendance: 669

Date: Monday 14/08/1972
Result: **WORCESTER CITY 2 GLOUCESTER CITY 1**
Competition: Southern League Cup Preliminary Round
Teamsheet: Miles, Wixey, Hargreaves, Vale, Layton, McQuarrie, Corr, Bird, Stevens, J Whitehouse, McCool
Substitute: Foxwell (for Corr)
Scorer: J Whitehouse
Attendance: 1326

Date: Saturday 19/08/1972
Result: **ATHERSTONE TOWN 3 GLOUCESTER CITY 0**
Competition: Southern League Division 1 North
Teamsheet: Miles, Wixey, Hargreaves, Vale, Layton, McQuarrie, Corr, Bird, Stevens, J Whitehouse, McCool
Substitute: Biggart (nps)

Date: Saturday 26/08/1972
Result: **GLOUCESTER CITY 2 ENDERBY TOWN 0**
Competition: Southern League Division 1 North
Teamsheet: Miles, Wixey, Biggart, Vale, Layton, McQuarrie, Corr, Bird, Stevens, Hargreaves, J Whitehouse
Substitute: McCool (nps)
Scorers: Stevens, Corr
Attendance: 366

Date: Monday 28/08/1972
Result: **KING'S LYNN 2 GLOUCESTER CITY 0**
Competition: Southern League Division 1 North
Teamsheet: Miles, Wixey, Biggart, Vale, Layton, McQuarrie, Corr, Bird, Stevens, J Whitehouse, Hargreaves
Substitute: Foxwell (for Stevens)
Attendance: 533

Date: Thursday 07/09/1972
Result: **GLOUCESTER CITY 0 REDDITCH UNITED 1**
Competition: Southern League Division 1 North
Teamsheet: Miles, Wixey, Biggart, Vale, Layton, McQuarrie, Corr, Bird, Stevens, Hargreaves, J Whitehouse
Substitute: McCool (for Corr)
Attendance: 268

Date: Saturday 09/09/1972
Result: **GLOUCESTER CITY 0 GRANTHAM 1**
Competition: Southern League Division 1 North
Teamsheet: Miles, Wixey, Biggart, Vale, Layton, McQuarrie, Hargreaves, Bird, Stevens, Foxwell, J Whitehouse
Substitute: McCool (for Bird)
Attendance: 302

Date: Thursday 14/09/1972
Result: **GLOUCESTER CITY 1 CHELTENHAM TOWN 4**
Competition: Southern League Division 1 North
Teamsheet: Miles, Wixey, Biggart, Vale, Layton, McQuarrie, McCool, Foxwell, Stevens, Hargreaves, J Whitehouse
Substitute: Corr (for Vale)
Scorer: Foxwell
Attendance: 410

Date: Saturday 16/09/1972
Result: **GLOUCESTER CITY 2 TROWBRIDGE TOWN 2**
Competition: FA Cup 1st Qualifying Round
Teamsheet: Miles, Wixey, Biggart, Corr, Layton, McQuarrie, McCool, Foxwell, Stevens, Hargreaves, J Whitehouse
Substitute: Sayer (nps)
Scorers: J Whitehouse, McCool (pen)

Date: Wednesday 20/09/1972
Result: **TROWBRIDGE TOWN 2 GLOUCESTER CITY 0**
Competition: FA Cup 1st Qualifying Round Replay
Teamsheet: Miles, Wixey, Biggart, Corr, Layton, McQuarrie, McCool, Foxwell, Hargreaves, Vale, J Whitehouse
Substitute: Stevens (for Foxwell)
Attendance: 1005

Date: Saturday 23/09/1972
Result: **GLOUCESTER CITY 0 MERTHYR TYDFIL 0**
Competition: Southern League Division 1 North
Teamsheet: Miles, Wixey, Layton, McQuarrie, Biggart, Corr, McCool, Vale, Stevens, Hargreaves, J Whitehouse
Substitute: Foxwell (nps)
Attendance: 340

Date: Tuesday 26/09/1972
Result: **REDDITCH UNITED 0 GLOUCESTER CITY 1**
Competition: Southern League Division 1 North
Teamsheet: Miles, Wixey, Myatt, McQuarrie, Biggart, Layton, Hargreaves, Foxwell, J Whitehouse, Corr, McCool
Substitute: Stevens (nps)
Scorer: Corr
Attendance: 600

Date: Saturday 30/09/1972
Result: **TROWBRIDGE TOWN 2 GLOUCESTER CITY 0**
Competition: Southern League Division 1 North
Teamsheet: Miles, Wixey, Layton, McQuarrie, Biggart, Corr, Hargreaves, Stevens, J Whitehouse, McCool, Bird
Substitute: Vale (nps)
Attendance: 711

Date: Saturday 07/10/1972
Result: **CINDERFORD TOWN 0 GLOUCESTER CITY 2**
Competition: Gloucestershire FA Northern Senior Professional Cup Semi-Final
Teamsheet: Miles, Wixey, Myatt, McQuarrie, Biggart, Layton, McCool, Hargreaves, Stevens, J Whitehouse, Bird
Substitute: Vale (nps)
Scorers: McCool, Stevens
Attendance: 401

Date: Saturday 14/10/1972
Result: **GLOUCESTER CITY 2 LOCKHEED LEAMINGTON 1**
Competition: Southern League Division 1 North
Teamsheet: Miles, Wixey, Myatt, McQuarrie, Biggart, Layton, Corr, Vale, Stevens, Hargreaves, Bird
Substitute: J Whitehouse (nps)
Scorers: Corr, Hargreaves
Attendance: 341

Date: Monday 16/10/1972
Result: **BROMSGROVE ROVERS 3 GLOUCESTER CITY 0**
Competition: Southern League Division 1 North
Teamsheet: Miles, Vale, Myatt, McQuarrie, Layton, Wixey, Corr, Hargreaves, McCool, J Whitehouse, Bird
Substitute: Stevens (nps)
Attendance: 528

Date: Saturday 21/10/1972
Result: **TAMWORTH 1 GLOUCESTER CITY 3**
Competition: Southern League Division 1 North
Teamsheet: Miles, Wixey, Myatt, McQuarrie, Biggart, Vale, Corr, Hargreaves, J Whitehouse, Bird, Croft
Substitute: Stevens (nps)
Scorers: Corr, J Whitehouse, Bird
Attendance: 557

Date: Saturday 28/10/1972
Result: **GLOUCESTER CITY 2 STOURBRIDGE 0**
Competition: Southern League Division 1 North
Teamsheet: Miles, Wixey, Myatt, Vale, McQuarrie, Bird, Corr, Croft, Stevens, Hargreaves, J Whitehouse
Substitute: McCool (nps)
Scorers: Stevens, Croft
Attendance: 320

Date: Saturday 04/11/1972
Result: **ILKESTON TOWN 0 GLOUCESTER CITY 1**
Competition: Southern League Division 1 North
Teamsheet: Miles, Wixey, Vale, McQuarrie, Biggart, Bird, Corr, Croft, K Whitehouse, Hargreaves, J Whitehouse
Substitute: McCool (nps)
Scorer: Corr

Date: Saturday 18/11/1972
Result: **GLOUCESTER CITY 1 BEDWORTH UNITED 1**
Competition: Southern League Division 1 North
Teamsheet: Miles, Wixey, Myatt, McQuarrie, Biggart, Bird, Vale, Croft, J Whitehouse, Hargreaves, McCool
Substitute: K Whitehouse (nps)
Scorer: J Whitehouse
Attendance: 363

Date: Saturday 25/11/1972
Result: **RUGBY TOWN 2 GLOUCESTER CITY 1**
Competition: Southern League Division 1 North
Teamsheet: Miles, Wixey, Myatt, McQuarrie, Biggart, Vale, Corr, Croft, J Whitehouse, Hargreaves, Bird
Substitute: McCool (for J Whitehouse)
Scorer: J Whitehouse

Date: Saturday 02/12/1972
Result: **ENDERBY TOWN 1 GLOUCESTER CITY 3**
Competition: Southern League Division 1 North
Teamsheet: Miles, Wixey, Myatt, McQuarrie, Biggart, Ferns, Corr, Hargreaves, K Whitehouse, McCool, Bird
Substitute: Stevens (nps)
Scorers: McCool, Corr, Hargreaves

Date: Saturday 09/12/1972
Result: **STEVENAGE ATHLETIC 1 GLOUCESTER CITY 1**
Competition: Southern League Division 1 North
Teamsheet: Miles, Wixey, Myatt, McQuarrie, Biggart, Vale, Corr, Hargreaves, K Whitehouse, McCool, Bird
Substitute: Stevens (nps)
Scorer: K Whitehouse

Date: Saturday 16/12/1972
Result: **GLOUCESTER CITY 3 BANBURY UNITED 3**
Competition: Southern League Division 1 North
Teamsheet: Miles, Wixey, Myatt, McQuarrie, Biggart, Vale, Corr, McCool, K Whitehouse, Hargreaves, Bird
Substitute: Stevens (nps)
Scorers: Biggart, K Whitehouse, Hargreaves
Attendance: 326

Date: Wednesday 20/12/1972
Result: **MERTHYR TYDFIL 4 GLOUCESTER CITY 1**
Competition: Southern League Division 1 North
Teamsheet: Miles, Wixey, Myatt, McQuarrie, Biggart, Vale, Corr, Croft, K Whitehouse, Hargreaves, Bird
Substitute: Stevens (for Hargreaves)
Scorer: K Whitehouse

Date: Saturday 23/12/1972
Result: **GLOUCESTER CITY 2 BARRY TOWN 1**
Competition: Southern League Division 1 North
Teamsheet: Miles, Wixey, Myatt, McQuarrie, Biggart, Vale, Corr, McCool, K Whitehouse, Hargreaves, Bird
Substitute: Stevens (nps)
Scorers: Myatt (pen), Corr
Attendance: 256

Date: Tuesday 26/12/1972
Result: **CORBY TOWN 1 GLOUCESTER CITY 1**
Competition: Southern League Division 1 North
Teamsheet: Miles, Wixey, Vale, McQuarrie, Biggart, Bird, Corr, Stevens, K Whitehouse, Croft, McCool
Substitute: Hargreaves (nps)
Scorer: Stevens
Attendance: 269

Date: Saturday 13/01/1973
Result: **GLOUCESTER CITY 2 BURY TOWN 1**
Competition: Southern League Division 1 North
Teamsheet: Miles, Keen, Myatt, McQuarrie, Biggart, Wixey, Corr, Stevens, K Whitehouse, Hargreaves, Bird
Substitute: Vale (nps)
Scorers: Bird, Stevens
Attendance: 306

Date: Monday 15/01/1973
Result: **KIDDERMINSTER HARRIERS 1 GLOUCESTER CITY 2**
Competition: Southern League Division 1 North
Teamsheet: Miles, Keen, Myatt, McQuarrie, Biggart, Wixey, Corr, Croft, K Whitehouse, Hargreaves, Bird
Substitute: Vale (nps)
Scorers: Bird, K Whitehouse
Attendance: 700

Date: Saturday 20/01/1973
Result: **GLOUCESTER CITY 2 KIDDERMINSTER HARRIERS 0**
Competition: Southern League Division 1 North
Teamsheet: Miles, Keen, Vale, McQuarrie, Biggart, Wixey, Corr, Stevens, K Whitehouse, Hargreaves, Bird
Substitute: Myatt (nps)
Scorers: Stevens, Bird
Attendance: 310

Date: Saturday 27/01/1973
Result: **GRANTHAM 5 GLOUCESTER CITY 0**
Competition: Southern League Division 1 North
Teamsheet: Miles, Vale, Myatt, McQuarrie, Biggart, Wixey, McCool, Croft, Stevens, Hargreaves, Bird
Substitute: Corr (nps)
Attendance: 1180

[227]

Date: Saturday 03/02/1973
Result: **WELLINGBOROUGH TOWN 4 GLOUCESTER CITY 1**
Competition: Southern League Division 1 North
Teamsheet: Miles, Vale, Myatt, McQuarrie, Biggart, Wixey, McCool, Croft, K Whitehouse, Stevens, Bird
Substitute: Corr (nps)
Scorer: Croft

Date: Saturday 10/02/1973
Result: **GLOUCESTER CITY 2 KING'S LYNN 1**
Competition: Southern League Division 1 North
Teamsheet: Miles, Myatt, Hallam, McQuarrie, Biggart, Wixey, Corr, Hargreaves, Stevens, K Whitehouse, Bird
Substitute: Croft (for Corr)
Scorers: K Whitehouse, Biggart
Attendance: 310

Date: Saturday 17/02/1973
Result: **GLOUCESTER CITY 3 WELLINGBOROUGH TOWN 1**
Competition: Southern League Division 1 North
Teamsheet: Miles, Myatt, Hallam, McQuarrie, Biggart, Wixey, Croft, Stevens, K Whitehouse, Hargreaves, Bird
Substitute: Vale (nps)
Scorers: Croft, Hallam, Bird
Attendance: 356

Date: Saturday 24/02/1973
Result: **BURY TOWN 0 GLOUCESTER CITY 2**
Competition: Southern League Division 1 North
Teamsheet: Miles, Wixey, Myatt, Hallam, McQuarrie, Vale, Croft, Lobban, Stevens, Hargreaves, Bird
Substitute: McCool (nps)
Scorer: Bird (2)
Attendance: 262

Date: Saturday 03/03/1973
Result: **GLOUCESTER CITY 1 TAMWORTH 2**
Competition: Southern League Division 1 North
Teamsheet: Miles, Wixey, Myatt, Lobban, McQuarrie, Hallam, Corr, Croft, Stevens, Hargreaves, Bird
Substitute: Vale (nps)
Scorer: Stevens
Attendance: 515

Date: Saturday 10/03/1973
Result: **LOCKHEED LEAMINGTON 3 GLOUCESTER CITY 2**
Competition: Southern League Division 1 North
Teamsheet: Miles, Wixey, Myatt, Vale, McQuarrie, Hallam, Croft, Lobban, Stevens, Hargreaves, Bird
Substitute: K Whitehouse (for Vale)
Scorer: Bird (2)

Date: Saturday 17/03/1973
Result: **GLOUCESTER CITY 3 ILKESTON TOWN 0**
Competition: Southern League Division 1 North
Teamsheet: Miles, Myatt, Lobban, Wixey, Biggart, McQuarrie, Croft, Stevens, K Whitehouse, Hargreaves, Bird
Substitute: Vale (nps)
Scorer: Stevens (3)
Attendance: 383

Date: Wednesday 21/03/1973
Result: **CHELTENHAM TOWN 3 GLOUCESTER CITY 2**
Competition: Southern League Division 1 North
Teamsheet: Miles, Wixey, Lobban, McQuarrie, Biggart, Vale, Croft, Corr, Stevens, Hargreaves, Bird
Substitute: Hallam (nps)
Scorer: Bird (2, 1 pen)
Attendance: 1871

Date: Saturday 24/03/1973
Result: **STOURBRIDGE 5 GLOUCESTER CITY 1**
Competition: Southern League Division 1 North
Teamsheet: Miles, Wixey, Lobban, Hallam, McQuarrie, Myatt, Croft, Vale, Stevens, Hargreaves, Bird
Substitute: K Whitehouse (nps)
Scorer: Bird

Date: Saturday 31/03/1973
Result: **GLOUCESTER CITY 0 RUGBY TOWN 0**
Competition: Southern League Division 1 North
Teamsheet: Miles, Wixey, Myatt, Lobban, Biggart, Vale, Croft, Corr, Stevens, McCool, Lewis
Substitute: Hallam (nps)
Attendance: 316

Date: Saturday 07/04/1973
Result: **BANBURY UNITED 1 GLOUCESTER CITY 0**
Competition: Southern League Division 1 North
Teamsheet: Miles, Wixey, Hallam, McQuarrie, Biggart, Vale, Lewis, Lobban, Stevens, Hargreaves, Bird
Substitute: Croft (nps)

Date: Monday 09/04/1973
Result: **BARRY TOWN 2 GLOUCESTER CITY 0**
Competition: Southern League Division 1 North
Teamsheet: Miles, Wixey, Hallam, McQuarrie, Biggart, Vale, Lewis, Lobban, Stevens, Hargreaves, Bird
Substitute: Croft (for Lewis)
Attendance: 106

Date: Saturday 14/04/1973
Result: **GLOUCESTER CITY 1 STEVENAGE ATHLETIC 0**
Competition: Southern League Division 1 North
Teamsheet: Miles, Wixey, Hallam, McQuarrie, Biggart, Lobban, Croft, Stevens, K Whitehouse, Hargreaves, Bird
Substitute: Vale (for Lobban)
Scorer: Hargreaves
Attendance: 306

Date: Wednesday 18/04/1973
Result: **CHELTENHAM TOWN 3 GLOUCESTER CITY 2**
Competition: Gloucestershire FA Northern Senior Professional Cup Final
Teamsheet: Miles, Myatt, Hallam, McQuarrie, Biggart, McCool, Croft, Wixey, K Whitehouse, Hargreaves, Bird
Substitute: Vale (nps)
Scorers: Croft, Hargreaves
Attendance: 966

Date: Saturday 21/04/1973
Result: **BEDWORTH UNITED 0 GLOUCESTER CITY 0**
Competition: Southern League Division 1 North
Teamsheet: Miles, Wixey, Hallam, McQuarrie, Biggart, Lobban, Lewis, Vale, Stevens, Hargreaves, Bird
Substitute: McCool (nps)

Date: Monday 23/04/1973
Result: **GLOUCESTER CITY 3 CORBY TOWN 2**
Competition: Southern League Division 1 North
Teamsheet: Miles, Wixey, Myatt, Hallam, Biggart, Vale, Croft, Stevens, K Whitehouse, Hargreaves, McCool
Substitute: Corr (nps)
Scorers: K Whitehouse, McCool (2)
Attendance: 310

Date: Thursday 26/04/1973
Result: **GLOUCESTER CITY 2 ATHERSTONE TOWN 0**
Competition: Southern League Division 1 North
Teamsheet: Miles, Wixey, Hallam, Lobban, Biggart, Vale, Croft, McCool, Stevens, Hargreaves, Bird
Substitute: McQuarrie (nps)
Scorers: Croft, McCool
Attendance: 710

Appearances – SA Biggart 40, RP Bird 41, JJ Corr 30(1), M Croft 22(2), W Ferns 1, DP Foxwell 5(2), K Hallam 13, T Hargreaves 45, R Keen 3, JH Layton 16, M Lewis 4, B Lobban 12, R McCool 23(3), A McQuarrie 46, JM Miles 48, G Myatt 27, D Sayer 0(1), JM Stevens 34(2), ST Vale 35(1), J Whitehouse 19, K Whitehouse 17(1), R Wixey 47.
Scorers – RP Bird 12, JM Stevens 11, JJ Corr 7, R McCool 6, K Whitehouse 6, M Croft 5, T Hargreaves 5, J Whitehouse 5, SA Biggart 2, DP Foxwell 1, K Hallam 1, G Myatt 1.

SOUTHERN LEAGUE DIVISION 1 NORTH

POS	CLUB	P	W	D	L	F	A	PTS
1	GRANTHAM	42	29	8	5	113	41	66
2	ATHERSTONE TOWN	42	23	11	8	82	48	57
3	CHELTENHAM TOWN	42	24	8	10	87	47	56
4	RUGBY TOWN	42	20	10	12	60	47	50
5	KIDDERMINSTER HARRIERS	42	19	12	11	67	56	50
6	MERTHYR TYDFIL	42	17	12	13	51	40	46
7	CORBY TOWN	42	14	16	12	62	56	44
8	STOURBRIDGE	42	16	11	15	70	64	43
9	**GLOUCESTER CITY**	42	18	7	17	55	64	43
10	BROMSGROVE ROVERS	42	17	8	17	63	54	42
11	REDDITCH UNITED	42	18	6	18	58	59	42
12	BANBURY UNITED	42	18	5	19	60	53	41
13	WELLINGBOROUGH TOWN	42	17	7	18	58	71	41
14	KING'S LYNN	42	14	12	16	45	49	40
15	LOCKHEED LEAMINGTON	42	13	12	17	51	58	38
16	ENDERBY TOWN	42	12	14	16	50	61	38
17	STEVENAGE ATHLETIC	42	12	13	17	50	63	37
18	TAMWORTH	42	14	8	20	45	65	36
19	BURY TOWN	42	13	9	20	52	69	35
20	BARRY TOWN	42	11	10	21	42	71	32
21	ILKESTON TOWN	42	9	6	27	35	68	24
22	BEDWORTH UNITED	42	10	3	29	42	94	23
		924	358	208	358	1298	1298	924

SEASON 1973-1974
(Home Ground: Horton Road Stadium)

Date: Saturday 11/08/1973
Result: **BEDWORTH UNITED 4 GLOUCESTER CITY 2**
Competition: Southern League Division 1 North
Teamsheet: Miles, Wixey, Hallam, Lobban, Biggart, Bird, Croft, Gardner, Foxwell, Hargreaves, Lewis
Substitute: Vale (nps)
Scorers: Lewis, Gardner

Date: Thursday 16/08/1973
Result: **GLOUCESTER CITY 0 REDDITCH UNITED 1**
Competition: Southern League Division 1 North
Teamsheet: Stow, Wixey, Lewis, Lobban, Biggart, Vale, Croft, Gardner, Foxwell, Hargreaves, Bird
Substitute: J Whitehouse (nps)
Attendance: 310

[229]

Date: Saturday 18/08/1973
Result: **GLOUCESTER CITY 1 STOURBRIDGE 1**
Competition: Southern League Division 1 North
Teamsheet: Stow, Wilby, Lewis, Lobban, Biggart, Wixey, Gardner, McCool, Foxwell, Hargreaves, Bird
Substitute: Croft (for Foxwell)
Scorer: Foxwell
Attendance: 305

Date: Tuesday 21/08/1973
Result: **ANDOVER 3 GLOUCESTER CITY 3**
Competition: Southern League Cup 1st Round 1st Leg
Teamsheet: Stow, Searls, Lewis, Lobban, Biggart, Wixey, Gardner, McCool, Foxwell, Hargreaves, Bird
Substitute: Croft (nps)
Scorers: Foxwell, Bird, Gardner

Date: Saturday 25/08/1973
Result: **KING'S LYNN 3 GLOUCESTER CITY 1**
Competition: Southern League Division 1 North
Teamsheet: Stow, Searls, Lewis, Lobban, Biggart, Wixey, Croft, Gardner, Foxwell, McCool, Bird
Substitute: Hallam (nps)
Scorer: Croft
Attendance: 738

Date: Thursday 30/08/1973
Result: **GLOUCESTER CITY 0 ANDOVER 6**
Competition: Southern League Cup 1st Round 2nd Leg
Teamsheet: Stow, Wixey, Lewis, Lobban, Biggart, Bird, Croft, Gardner, K Whitehouse, Foxwell, McCool
Substitute: Hallam (nps)
Attendance: 240

Date: Saturday 01/09/1973
Result: **GLOUCESTER CITY 1 BEDWORTH UNITED 2**
Competition: Southern League Division 1 North
Teamsheet: Stow, Wixey, Lewis, Williams, Biggart, Lobban, Croft, Gardner, Foxwell, Ferns, Bird
Substitute: Hallam (for Wixey)
Scorer: Bird
Attendance: 200

Date: Thursday 06/09/1973
Result: **GLOUCESTER CITY 1 BANBURY UNITED 2**
Competition: Southern League Division 1 North
Teamsheet: Stow, Wilby, Lewis, Lobban, Biggart, Williams, Croft, Gardner, McCool, Foxwell, Bird
Substitute: Hallam (nps)
Scorer: Bird
Attendance: 250

Date: Saturday 08/09/1973
Result: **DUNSTABLE TOWN 0 GLOUCESTER CITY 2**
Competition: Southern League Division 1 North
Teamsheet: Stow, Wilby, Lewis, Lobban, Biggart, Williams, Croft, Gardner, McCool, Foxwell, Bird
Substitute: Ferns (for McCool)
Scorers: Bird (pen), Lewis

Date: Thursday 13/09/1973
Result: **GLOUCESTER CITY 3 MERTHYR TYDFIL 2**
Competition: Southern League Division 1 North
Teamsheet: Stow, Wixey, Lewis, Lobban, Biggart, Williams, Croft, Gardner, McCool, Foxwell, Bird
Substitute: Wilby (nps)
Scorers: Gardner, McCool, Williams
Attendance: 300

Date: Saturday 15/09/1973
Result: **STONEHOUSE 1 GLOUCESTER CITY 1**
Competition: FA Cup 1st Qualifying Round
Teamsheet: Stow, Wixey, Lewis, Lobban, Biggart, Williams, Croft, Gardner, McCool, Foxwell, Bird
Substitute: Wilby (nps)
Scorer: Croft

Date: Wednesday 19/09/1973
Result: **GLOUCESTER CITY 0 STONEHOUSE 1**
Competition: FA Cup 1st Qualifying Round Replay
Teamsheet: Stow, Wixey, Lewis, Lobban, Biggart, Williams, Croft, Gardner, McCool, Foxwell, Bird
Substitute: Hargreaves (for Croft)

Date: Saturday 22/09/1973
Result: **CINDERFORD TOWN 3 GLOUCESTER CITY 0**
Competition: FA Trophy Preliminary Round
Teamsheet: Stow, Vale, Lewis, Wixey, Biggart, Williams, Ferns, Gardner, J Whitehouse, Hargreaves, Bird
Substitute: Lobban (nps)
Attendance: 520

Date: Saturday 29/09/1973
Result: **GLOUCESTER CITY 3 KING'S LYNN 2**
Competition: Southern League Division 1 North
Teamsheet: Stow, Vale, Hallam, Wixey, Biggart, Williams, Hargreaves, Gardner, Ferns, Lewis, Bird
Substitute: J Whitehouse (nps)
Scorers: Ferns, Hargreaves, Gardner
Attendance: 186

16 May 1973

Did George Best want a job?

"There's a face I can't quite place — wonder what he wants?"

"WE SHOULD GET OUR HEADS TOGETHER, DICK.
LIKE—BANGING 'EM TOGETHER—**HARD!**"

Date: Saturday 06/10/1973
Result: **GLOUCESTER CITY 0 STEVENAGE ATHLETIC 1**
Competition: Southern League Division 1 North
Teamsheet: Stow, Wilby, Lewis, Wixey, Biggart, Williams, Lobban, Gardner, Ferns, Hargreaves, Bird
Substitute: J Whitehouse (for Ferns)
Attendance: 240

Date: Saturday 13/10/1973
Result: **WITNEY TOWN 3 GLOUCESTER CITY 0**
Competition: Southern League Division 1 North
Teamsheet: Stow, Vale, Lewis, Wixey, Biggart, Williams, Ferns, Gardner, J Whitehouse, Hargreaves, Bird
Substitute: Croft (nps)

Date: Saturday 20/10/1973
Result: **BURTON ALBION 3 GLOUCESTER CITY 1**
Competition: Southern League Division 1 North
Teamsheet: Stow, Vale, Lewis, Wixey, Biggart, Williams, Croft, Gardner, McCool, Hallam, Bird
Substitute: Hargreaves (for Bird)
Scorer: Wixey
Attendance: 881

Date: Saturday 27/10/1973
Result: **GLOUCESTER CITY 2 WELLINGBOROUGH TOWN 2**
Competition: Southern League Division 1 North
Teamsheet: Stow, Vale, Lewis, Wixey, Biggart, Williams, Hargreaves, Gardner, Ferns, Lobban, Bird
Substitute: McCool (nps)
Scorers: Gardner, own goal
Attendance: 225

Date: Wednesday 31/10/1973
Result: **ENDERBY TOWN 2 GLOUCESTER CITY 2**
Competition: Southern League Division 1 North
Teamsheet: Stow, Vale, Lewis, Wixey, Gough, Williams, Lobban, Gardner, Ferns, Hargreaves, Bird
Substitute: McCool (nps)
Scorer: Bird (2)

Date: Saturday 03/11/1973
Result: **STEVENAGE ATHLETIC 2 GLOUCESTER CITY 0**
Competition: Southern League Division 1 North
Teamsheet: Stow, Vale, Lewis, Wixey, Gough, Williams, Lobban, Gardner, G Davies, Ferns, Bird
Substitute: Hargreaves (nps)

Date: Friday 09/11/1973
Result: **MERTHYR TYDFIL 1 GLOUCESTER CITY 0**
Competition: Southern League Division 1 North
Teamsheet: Stow, Hallam, Lewis, Lobban, Gough, Williams, Hargreaves, Gardner, G Davies, McCool, Bird
Substitute: Biggart (nps)

Date: Saturday 17/11/1973
Result: **TAMWORTH 2 GLOUCESTER CITY 0**
Competition: Southern League Division 1 North
Teamsheet: Stow, Vale, Lewis, Wixey, Gough, Williams, Hargreaves, Gardner, G Davies, McCool, Bird
Substitute: Biggart (nps)
Attendance: 411

Date: Saturday 24/11/1973
Result: **GLOUCESTER CITY 1 AUTOMOTIVE PRODUCTS LEAMINGTON 3**
Competition: Southern League Division 1 North
Teamsheet: Stow, Vale, Hallam, Wixey, Gough, Williams, Ferns, Gardner, G Davies, Hargreaves, Lewis
Substitute: Biggart (nps)
Scorer: Vale
Attendance: 210

Date: Sunday 02/12/1973
Result: **CINDERFORD TOWN 0 GLOUCESTER CITY 1**
Competition: Gloucestershire FA Northern Senior Professional Cup Semi-Final
Teamsheet: Miles, Vale, Wixey, Hargreaves, Gough, Williams, McCool, Gardner, G Davies, Bird, Reid
Substitutes: Biggart (nps), Lewis (nps)
Scorer: Bird

Date: Saturday 08/12/1973
Result: **GLOUCESTER CITY 0 BURY TOWN 5**
Competition: Southern League Division 1 North
Teamsheet: Miles, Vale, Wixey, Hargreaves, Gough, Williams, McCool, J Davies, G Davies, Bird, Reid
Substitute: Lewis (for McCool)
Attendance: 166

Date: Saturday 15/12/1973
Result: **GLOUCESTER CITY 2 BARRY TOWN 0**
Competition: Southern League Division 1 North
Teamsheet: Miles, Vale, Lewis, Wixey, Biggart, Williams, Gardner, J Davies, G Davies, Bird, Reid
Substitute: Hargreaves (nps)
Scorers: G Davies, Bird
Attendance: 140

Date: Wednesday 26/12/1973
Result: **GLOUCESTER CITY 0 CHELTENHAM TOWN 1**
Competition: Southern League Division 1 North
Teamsheet: Miles, Vale, Lewis, Wixey, Biggart, Williams, Gardner, J Davies, G Davies, Bird, Reid
Substitute: Hargreaves (for Reed)
Attendance: 650

[233]

Date: Saturday 29/12/1973
Result: **GLOUCESTER CITY 2 DUNSTABLE TOWN 0**
Competition: Southern League Division 1 North
Teamsheet: Miles, Vale, Lewis, Wixey, Biggart, Williams, Gardner, J Davies, G Davies, Bird, Reid
Substitute: Hargreaves (for Lewis)
Scorers: G Davies, J Davies
Attendance: 200

Date: Saturday 05/01/1974
Result: **GLOUCESTER CITY 1 KIDDERMINSTER HARRIERS 1**
Competition: Southern League Division 1 North
Teamsheet: Stow, Vale, Wixey, Williams, Biggart, Hargreaves, Gardner, J Davies, G Davies, Bird, Reid
Substitute: McCool (nps)
Scorer: Bird
Attendance: 182

Date: Sunday 13/01/1974
Result: **AUTOMOTIVE PRODUCTS LEAMINGTON 3 GLOUCESTER CITY 1**
Competition: Southern League Division 1 North
Teamsheet: Stow, Vale, Lewis, Wixey, Biggart, Williams, Gardner, G Davies, J Davies, Bird, Hargreaves
Substitute: McCool (nps)
Scorer: Vale

Date: Saturday 19/01/1974
Result: **GLOUCESTER CITY 1 ENDERBY TOWN 3**
Competition: Southern League Division 1 North
Teamsheet: Miles, Vale, Wixey, Hargreaves, Gough, Williams, Lobban, G Davies, J Davies, Bird, McCool
Substitute: Biggart (for Wixey)
Scorers: G Davies
Attendance: 181

Date: Sunday 27/01/1974
Result: **KIDDERMINSTER HARRIERS 3 GLOUCESTER CITY 0**
Competition: Southern League Division 1 North
Teamsheet: Miles, Hargreaves, Hallam, Lobban, Gough, Biggart, Gardner, G Davies, J Davies, Bird, McCool
Substitute: Hudd (nps)

Date: Saturday 02/02/1974
Result: **REDDITCH UNITED 4 GLOUCESTER CITY 2**
Competition: Southern League Division 1 North
Teamsheet: Miles, Hargreaves, Hallam, Lobban, Gough, Biggart, Gardner, J Davies, G Davies, Bird, Lewis
Substitute: McCool (nps)
Scorers: J Davies, G Davies

Date: Saturday 16/02/1974
Result: **BARRY TOWN 2 GLOUCESTER CITY 3**
Competition: Southern League Division 1 North
Teamsheet: Miles, Vale, Hargreaves, Wixey, Gough, Biggart, Gardner, J Davies, G Davies, Lobban, Bird
Substitute: Hallam (nps)
Scorers: G Davies, Lobban, own goal

Date: Saturday 23/02/1974
Result: **STOURBRIDGE 3 GLOUCESTER CITY 0**
Competition: Southern League Division 1 North
Teamsheet: Miles, Vale, Hargreaves, Wixey, Gough, Biggart, Saunders, G Davies, Gardner, Lobban, Bird
Substitute: J Davies (nps)

Date: Saturday 09/03/1974
Result: **WELLINGBOROUGH TOWN 2 GLOUCESTER CITY 0**
Competition: Southern League Division 1 North
Teamsheet: Miles, Vale, Wixey, Lobban, Gough, Biggart, Saunders, J Davies, G Davies, Gardner, Bird
Substitute: Hargreaves (nps)
Attendance: 48

Date: Saturday 16/03/1974
Result: **GLOUCESTER CITY 1 CORBY TOWN 2**
Competition: Southern League Division 1 North
Teamsheet: Miles, Vale, Hargreaves, Lobban, Biggart, Wixey, Saunders, Gardner, G Davies, J Davies, Bird
Substitute: Gough (nps)
Scorer: Lobban
Attendance: 105

Date: Saturday 23/03/1974
Result: **BLETCHLEY TOWN 1 GLOUCESTER CITY 0**
Competition: Southern League Division 1 North
Teamsheet: Miles, Hargreaves, Lewis, Lobban, Biggart, Wixey, Saunders, Gardner, G Davies, Bird, McCool
Substitute: Gough (nps)

Date: Saturday 30/03/1974
Result: **GLOUCESTER CITY 1 BURTON ALBION 2**
Competition: Southern League Division 1 North
Teamsheet: Townsend, Vale, Lewis, Lobban, Biggart, Wixey, Saunders, Gardner, G Davies, Bird, McCool
Substitute: J Davies (nps)
Scorer: McCool
Attendance: 186

Date: Thursday 04/04/1974
Result: **GLOUCESTER CITY 3 BROMSGROVE ROVERS 1**
Competition: Southern League Division 1 North
Teamsheet: Townsend, Vale, Lewis, Lobban, Biggart, Wixey, J Davies, Gardner, G Davies, Bird, McCool
Substitute: Hargreaves (for J Davies)
Scorers: Gardner (2), G Davies
Attendance: 130

Date: Sunday 07/04/1974
Result: **GLOUCESTER CITY 1 CHELTENHAM TOWN 4**
Competition: Gloucestershire FA Northern Senior Professional Cup Final
Teamsheet: Miles, Vale, Lewis, Wixey, Biggart, Lobban, Hargreaves, Gardner, G Davies, Bird, McCool
Substitute: Gough (nps)
Scorer: Lobban
Attendance: 410

Date: Monday 08/04/1974
Result: **BROMSGROVE ROVERS 2 GLOUCESTER CITY 1**
Competition: Southern League Division 1 North
Teamsheet: Stow, Vale, Lewis, Lobban, Gough, Wixey, Hargreaves, Gardner, G Davies, Bird, McCool
Substitute: J Davies (for Bird)
Scorers: J Davies
Attendance: 266

Date: Saturday 13/04/1974
Result: **GLOUCESTER CITY 2 TAMWORTH 0**
Competition: Southern League Division 1 North
Teamsheet: Miles, Vale, Hargreaves, Lobban, Biggart, Wixey, Saunders, Gardner, G Davies, Bird, McCool
Substitute: J Davies (nps)
Scorer: G Davies (2)
Attendance: 150

Date: Monday 15/04/1974
Result: **CHELTENHAM TOWN 3 GLOUCESTER CITY 2**
Competition: Southern League Division 1 North
Teamsheet: Miles, Vale, Lewis, Lobban, Biggart, Wixey, J Davies, Gardner, G Davies, Bird, McCool
Substitute: Hargreaves (nps)
Scorers: Gardner, G Davies
Attendance: 1245

Date: Tuesday 16/04/1974
Result: **GLOUCESTER CITY 3 WITNEY TOWN 0**
Competition: Southern League Division 1 North
Teamsheet: Miles, Vale, Lewis, Biggart, Gough, Wixey, Lobban, Gardner, G Davies, J Davies, Bird
Substitute: Hargreaves (nps)
Scorers: G Davies (2), J Davies
Attendance: 210

Date: Saturday 20/04/1974
Result: **BURY TOWN 2 GLOUCESTER CITY 2**
Competition: Southern League Division 1 North
Teamsheet: Miles, Vale, Lewis, Biggart, Gough, Wixey, Lobban, Gardner, G Davies, J Davies, Bird
Substitute: Hargreaves (nps)
Scorers: Gardner, J Davies

Date: Thursday 25/04/1974
Result: **GLOUCESTER CITY 1 BLETCHLEY TOWN 1**
Competition: Southern League Division 1 North
Teamsheet: Miles, Vale, Lewis, Biggart, Gough, Wixey, Lobban, Gardner, G Davies, J Davies, Bird
Substitute: Hargreaves (nps)
Scorer: own goal
Attendance: 203

Date: Saturday 27/04/1974
Result: **BANBURY UNITED 4 GLOUCESTER CITY 2**
Competition: Southern League Division 1 North
Teamsheet: Miles, Vale, Lewis, Biggart, Gough, Wixey, Lobban, Gardner, G Davies, J Davies, Bird
Substitute: Hargreaves (for -----)
Scorers: Gardner, Gough

Date: Sunday 28/04/1974
Result: **CORBY TOWN 0 GLOUCESTER CITY 2**
Competition: Southern League Division 1 North
Teamsheet: Miles, Vale, Lewis, Lobban, Biggart, Wixey, Hargreaves, Gardner, G Davies, J Davies, Bird
Substitute: Gough (for -----)
Scorers: G Davies, J Davies

Appearances – SA Biggart 40(1), RP Bird 48, M Croft 11(1), G Davies 30, J Davies 19(1), W Ferns 9(1), DP Foxwell 12, CR Gardner 47, A Gough 18(1), K Hallam 7(1), T Hargreaves 28(6), M Lewis 39(1), B Lobban 36, R McCool 23, JM Miles 22, J Reid 6, J Saunders 6, A Searls 2, RT Stow 25, M Townsend 2, ST Vale 33, J Whitehouse 2(1), K Whitehouse 1, P Wilby 4, A Williams 25, R Wixey 44.
Others selected but did not play: DC Hudd.
Scorers – G Davies 12, CR Gardner 10, RP Bird 9, J Davies 6, B Lobban 3, M Croft 2, DP Foxwell 2, M Lewis 2, R McCool 2, ST Vale 2, W Ferns 1, A Gough 1, T Hargreaves 1, A Williams 1, R Wixey 1, own goals 3.

PROGRAMME	RECORD BREAKER	PROGRAMME	PROGRAMME

1973-1974	Doug Foxwell Most Seasons Played (jointly) - 12	1975-1976	1976-1977

SEASON BY SEASON

SOUTHERN LEAGUE DIVISION 1 NORTH

POS	CLUB	P	W	D	L	F	A	PTS
1	STOURBRIDGE	42	29	11	2	103	36	69
2	BURTON ALBION	42	27	9	6	88	32	63
3	CHELTENHAM TOWN	42	24	8	10	75	51	56
4	AUTOMOTIVE PRODUCTS LEAMINGTON	42	21	12	9	82	45	54
5	ENDERBY TOWN	42	19	14	9	60	36	52
6	WITNEY TOWN	42	20	10	12	69	55	50
7	STEVENAGE ATHLETIC	42	19	11	12	65	46	49
8	BANBURY UNITED	42	19	11	12	69	57	49
9	KING'S LYNN	42	19	10	13	65	50	48
10	KIDDERMINSTER HARRIERS	42	15	14	13	67	53	44
11	MERTHYR TYDFIL	42	16	12	14	70	61	44
12	REDDITCH UNITED	42	14	11	17	56	73	39
13	BROMSGROVE ROVERS	42	14	10	18	54	61	38
14	BEDWORTH UNITED	42	14	10	18	49	76	38
15	TAMWORTH	42	13	11	18	42	51	37
16	CORBY TOWN	42	12	11	19	40	58	35
17	BLETCHLEY TOWN	42	10	15	17	47	71	35
18	BARRY TOWN	42	10	8	24	54	85	28
19	BURY TOWN	42	10	6	26	57	84	26
20	**GLOUCESTER CITY**	**42**	**10**	**6**	**26**	**52**	**81**	**26**
21	WELLINGBOROUGH TOWN	42	7	9	26	42	87	23
22	DUNSTABLE TOWN	42	5	11	26	26	83	21
		924	347	230	347	1332	1332	924

SEASON 1974-1975
(Home Ground: Horton Road Stadium)

Date: Saturday 17/08/1974
Result: **GLOUCESTER CITY 1 STEVENAGE ATHLETIC 1**
Competition: Southern League Division 1 North
Teamsheet: Miles, Wixey, Lewis, Moughton, Gough, Hayden, Dangerfield, Gardner, J Davies, G Davies, Feighery
Substitute: Hargreaves (nps)
Scorer: Gough
Attendance: 284

Date: Wednesday 21/08/1974
Result: **GLOUCESTER CITY 1 BANBURY UNITED 2**
Competition: Southern League Division 1 North
Teamsheet: Miles, Wixey, Lewis, Moughton, Gough, Hayden, Dangerfield, Gardner, J Davies, G Davies, Feighery
Substitute: Hargreaves (nps)
Scorer: G Davies
Attendance: 290

Date: Saturday 24/08/1974
Result: **DUNSTABLE TOWN 4 GLOUCESTER CITY 1**
Competition: Southern League Division 1 North
Teamsheet: Miles, Wixey, Lewis, Moughton, Gough, Hayden, Dangerfield, Gardner, G Davies, J Davies, Feighery
Substitute: Hargreaves (nps)
Scorer: G Davies
Attendance: 211

Date: Tuesday 27/08/1974
Result: **REDDITCH UNITED 1 GLOUCESTER CITY 1**
Competition: Southern League Cup 1st Round 1st Leg
Teamsheet: Miles, Hargreaves, Lewis, Moughton, Gough, Hayden, Dangerfield, Gardner, J Davies, G Davies, Feighery
Substitute: Wixey (nps)
Scorer: G Davies

Date: Saturday 31/08/1974
Result: **GLOUCESTER CITY 3 KING'S LYNN 2**
Competition: Southern League Division 1 North
Teamsheet: Miles, Wixey, Hargreaves, Moughton, Gough, Hayden, Dangerfield, Gardner, J Davies, G Davies, Feighery
Substitute: Langley (nps)
Scorers: G Davies (2), J Davies
Attendance: 220

Date: Wednesday 04/09/1974
Result: **GLOUCESTER CITY 0 REDDITCH UNITED 0**
Competition: Southern League Cup 1st Round 2nd Leg
Teamsheet: Miles, Wixey, Hargreaves, Moughton, Gough, Hayden, Dangerfield, Gardner, J Davies, G Davies, Feighery
Substitute: Lewis (nps)
Attendance: 260

Date: Saturday 07/09/1974
Result: **MILTON KEYNES CITY 0 GLOUCESTER CITY 3**
Competition: Southern League Division 1 North
Teamsheet: Miles, Hargreaves, Lewis, Moughton, Gough, Wixey, Dangerfield, Gardner, J Davies, G Davies, Feighery
Substitute: Langley (nps)
Scorer: G Davies (3)

Date: Tuesday 10/09/1974
Result: **BANBURY UNITED 2 GLOUCESTER CITY 0**
Competition: Southern League Division 1 North
Teamsheet: Miles, Hargreaves, Lewis, Wixey, Moughton, Hayden, Dangerfield, Gardner, J Davies, G Davies, Feighery
Substitute: Langley (nps)

Date: Saturday 14/09/1974
Result: **GLOUCESTER CITY 3 MERTHYR TYDFIL 2**
Competition: FA Cup 1st Qualifying Round
Teamsheet: Miles, Wixey, Hargreaves, Moughton, Gough, Hayden, Dangerfield, Gardner, J Davies, G Davies, Feighery
Substitute: Lewis (nps)
Scorers: Feighery, J Davies, Hayden (pen)

Date: Monday 16/09/1974
Result: **KIDDERMINSTER HARRIERS 3 GLOUCESTER CITY 1**
Competition: Southern League Division 1 North
Teamsheet: Miles, Wixey, Hargreaves, Moughton, Gough, Hayden, Dangerfield, Gardner, J Davies, G Davies, Feighery
Substitute: Lewis (nps)
Scorer: Hayden
Attendance: 602

Date: Saturday 21/09/1974
Result: **TROWBRIDGE TOWN 4 GLOUCESTER CITY 1**
Competition: FA Trophy Preliminary Round
Teamsheet: Miles, Wixey, Hargreaves, Moughton, Gough, Hayden, Dangerfield, Gardner, J Davies, G Davies, Feighery
Substitute: Lewis (nps)
Scorer: G Davies

Date: Wednesday 25/09/1974
Result: **REDDITCH UNITED 0 GLOUCESTER CITY 2**
Competition: Southern League Cup 1st Round Replay
Teamsheet: Miles, Wixey, Hargreaves, Lewis, Moughton, Hayden, Dangerfield, Gardner, J Davies, G Davies, Feighery
Substitute: Gough (nps)
Scorers: Dangerfield, Gardner

Date: Saturday 28/09/1974
Result: **GLOUCESTER CITY 1 CORBY TOWN 3**
Competition: Southern League Division 1 North
Teamsheet: Miles, Hargreaves, Lewis, Wixey, Moughton, Hayden, Dangerfield, Gardner, J Davies, G Davies, Feighery
Substitute: Langley (nps)
Scorer: Feighery
Attendance: 275

Date: Monday 30/09/1974
Result: **BEDFORD TOWN 2 GLOUCESTER CITY 1**
Competition: Southern League Division 1 North
Teamsheet: Miles, Hargreaves, Lewis, Wixey, Moughton, Hayden, Dangerfield, Gardner, J Davies, G Davies, Feighery
Substitute: Langley (nps)
Scorer: J Davies

Date: Saturday 05/10/1974
Result: **CHELTENHAM TOWN 4 GLOUCESTER CITY 1**
Competition: FA Cup 2nd Qualifying Round
Teamsheet: Miles, Wixey, Hargreaves, Moughton, Gough, Hayden, Dangerfield, Gardner, J Davies, G Davies, Feighery
Substitute: Lewis (nps)
Scorer: J Davies
Attendance: 1309

Date: Saturday 12/10/1974
Result: **GLOUCESTER CITY 4 BARRY TOWN 1**
Competition: Southern League Division 1 North
Teamsheet: Miles, Wixey, Hargreaves, Moughton, Gough, Hayden, Dangerfield, Gardner, J Davies, G Davies, Feighery
Substitute: Lewis (nps)
Scorers: Hayden, Gardner, J Davies, G Davies
Attendance: 210

Date: Monday 14/10/1974
Result: **GLOUCESTER CITY 1 ATHERSTONE TOWN 0**
Competition: Southern League Cup 2nd Round
Teamsheet: Miles, Hargreaves, Lewis, Wixey, Moughton, Hayden, Dangerfield, Gardner, J Davies, McCool, Feighery
Substitute: G Davies (nps)
Scorer: Hayden
Attendance: 210
Note: Played at Whaddon Road, Cheltenham

Date: Saturday 19/10/1974
Result: **GLOUCESTER CITY 0 WITNEY TOWN 2**
Competition: Southern League Division 1 North
Teamsheet: Miles, Hargreaves, Lewis, Wixey, Moughton, Hayden, Dangerfield, Gardner, J Davies, McCool, Feighery
Substitute: G Davies (nps)
Attendance: 340

Date: Saturday 26/10/1974
Result: **ENDERBY TOWN 2 GLOUCESTER CITY 0**
Competition: Southern League Division 1 North
Teamsheet: Miles, Hargreaves, Lewis, Wixey, Moughton, Hayden, Dangerfield, Gardner, J Davies, McCool, Feighery
Substitute: G Davies (nps)

Date: Tuesday 29/10/1974
Result: **TAMWORTH 1 GLOUCESTER CITY 1**
Competition: Southern League Division 1 North
Teamsheet: Miles, Hargreaves, Lewis, Wixey, Moughton, Hayden, Dangerfield, Gardner, J Davies, McCool, Feighery
Substitute: G Davies (nps)
Scorer: J Davies
Attendance: 292

Date: Saturday 02/11/1974
Result: **GLOUCESTER CITY 1 MERTHYR TYDFIL 0**
Competition: Southern League Division 1 North
Teamsheet: Miles, Hargreaves, Lewis, Wixey, Moughton, Hayden, Dangerfield, Gardner, J Davies, G Davies, Feighery
Substitute: Gough (nps)
Scorer: Hargreaves
Attendance: 291

Date: Saturday 09/11/1974
Result: **WORCESTER CITY 1 GLOUCESTER CITY 1**
Competition: Southern League Division 1 North
Teamsheet: Miles, Hargreaves, Lewis, Wixey, Moughton, Hayden, Dangerfield, Gardner, J Davies, G Davies, Feighery
Substitute: Gough (nps)
Scorer: J Davies
Attendance: 698

Date: Saturday 16/11/1974
Result: **GLOUCESTER CITY 3 BROMSGROVE ROVERS 3**
Competition: Southern League Division 1 North
Teamsheet: Miles, Hargreaves, Lewis, Wixey, Gough, Hayden, Dangerfield, Gardner, J Davies, G Davies, Feighery
Substitute: Moughton (nps)
Scorers: J Davies, Gough, Dangerfield
Attendance: 280

Date: Saturday 23/11/1974
Result: **MARGATE 3 GLOUCESTER CITY 1**
Competition: Southern League Cup 3rd Round
Teamsheet: Miles, Hargreaves, Lewis, Wixey, Moughton, Hayden, Dangerfield, Gardner, J Davies, G Davies, Feighery
Substitute: Gough (nps)
Scorer: G Davies
Attendance: 490

Date: Saturday 30/11/1974
Result: **GLOUCESTER CITY 3 ENDERBY TOWN 2**
Competition: Southern League Division 1 North
Teamsheet: Miles, Hargreaves, Lewis, Wixey, Moughton, Hayden, Dangerfield, Gardner, J Davies, G Davies, Feighery
Substitute: Gough (nps)
Scorers: Dangerfield, Hayden, G Davies
Attendance: 210

Date: Saturday 14/12/1974
Result: **GLOUCESTER CITY 0 KIDDERMINSTER HARRIERS 2**
Competition: Southern League Division 1 North
Teamsheet: Miles, Hargreaves, Lewis, Wixey, Moughton, Hayden, Dangerfield, Gardner, J Davies, G Davies, Feighery
Substitute: Gough (nps)
Attendance: 275

Date: Thursday 26/12/1974
Result: **CHELTENHAM TOWN 3 GLOUCESTER CITY 1**
Competition: Southern League Division 1 North
Teamsheet: Miles, Wixey, Hayden, Turner, Moughton, Lewis, Dangerfield, Gardner, G Davies, J Davies, Feighery
Substitute: Gough (nps)
Scorer: G Davies
Attendance: 1548

Date: Saturday 28/12/1974
Result: **GLOUCESTER CITY 1 WORCESTER CITY 2**
Competition: Southern League Division 1 North
Teamsheet: Miles, Wixey, Lewis, Moughton, Gough, Hayden, Dangerfield, Gardner, G Davies, Turner, Feighery
Substitute: McCool (nps)
Scorer: Gardner
Attendance: 450

Date: Saturday 04/01/1975
Result: **BURY TOWN 0 GLOUCESTER CITY 2**
Competition: Southern League Division 1 North
Teamsheet: Stow, Hargreaves, Lewis, Moughton, Gough, Wixey, Dangerfield, Gardner, Feighery, G Davies, Hayden
Substitute: Parkes
Scorer: Feighery (2)

Date: Saturday 11/01/1975
Result: **GLOUCESTER CITY 0 AUTOMOTIVE PRODUCTS LEAMINGTON 3**
Competition: Southern League Division 1 North
Teamsheet: Stow, Hargreaves, Lewis, Moughton, Gough, Wixey, Dangerfield, Gardner, Feighery, G Davies, Hayden
Substitute: Parkes (nps)
Attendance: 270

Date: Saturday 18/01/1975
Result: **STEVENAGE ATHLETIC 1 GLOUCESTER CITY 0**
Competition: Southern League Division 1 North
Teamsheet: Miles, Hargreaves, Lewis, Moughton, Gough, Wixey, Dangerfield, Gardner, Feighery, G Davies, Hayden
Substitute: Parkes (nps)

[238]

Date: Saturday 08/02/1975
Result: **REDDITCH UNITED 4 GLOUCESTER CITY 0**
Competition: Southern League Division 1 North
Teamsheet: Miles, Hargreaves, Lewis, Moughton, Gough, Wixey, Dangerfield, Gardner, Feighery, G Davies, Hayden
Substitute: McCool (nps)

Date: Tuesday 11/02/1975
Result: **AUTOMOTIVE PRODUCTS LEAMINGTON 4 GLOUCESTER CITY 1**
Competition: Southern League Division 1 North
Teamsheet: Stow, Hargreaves, Lewis, Moughton, Gough, Wixey, Dangerfield, Gardner, G Davies, Turner, Feighery
Substitute: Langley (nps)
Scorer: G Davies

Date: Saturday 22/02/1975
Result: **BROMSGROVE ROVERS 0 GLOUCESTER CITY 0**
Competition: Southern League Division 1 North
Teamsheet: Stow, Hargreaves, Lewis, Moughton, Gough, Wixey, Dangerfield, Gardner, Feighery, G Davies, Hayden
Substitute: McCool (nps)

Date: Saturday 01/03/1975
Result: **GLOUCESTER CITY 2 REDDITCH UNITED 2**
Competition: Southern League Division 1 North
Teamsheet: Stow, Hargreaves, Lewis, Moughton, Gough, Wixey, Dangerfield, Gardner, Feighery, G Davies, Hayden
Substitute: McCool (nps)
Scorers: G Davies, Gardner
Attendance: 220

Date: Tuesday 04/03/1975
Result: **WELLINGBOROUGH TOWN 1 GLOUCESTER CITY 1**
Competition: Southern League Division 1 North
Teamsheet: Clark, Hargreaves, Lewis, Moughton, Gough, Wixey, Dangerfield, Langley, Feighery, G Davies, Hayden
Substitute: McCool (nps)
Scorer: G Davies
Attendance: 98

Date: Saturday 15/03/1975
Result: **MERTHYR TYDFIL 2 GLOUCESTER CITY 0**
Competition: Southern League Division 1 North
Teamsheet: Stow, Wixey, Lewis, Moughton, Gough, Hayden, Dangerfield, Gardner, Feighery, G Davies, Bitchenor
Substitute: Miles (nps)

Date: Saturday 22/03/1975
Result: **GLOUCESTER CITY 1 WELLINGBOROUGH TOWN 0**
Competition: Southern League Division 1 North
Teamsheet: Stow, Wixey, Hargreaves, Moughton, Gough, Hayden, Dangerfield, Gardner, Feighery, G Davies, Bitchenor
Substitute: Lewis (nps)
Scorer: Bitchenor
Attendance: 150

Date: Friday 28/03/1975
Result: **BARRY TOWN 0 GLOUCESTER CITY 1**
Competition: Southern League Division 1 North
Teamsheet: Stow, Wixey, Hargreaves, Moughton, Gough, Hayden, Dangerfield, Gardner, Feighery, G Davies, Bitchenor
Substitute: Lewis (for Feighery)
Scorer: Wixey

Date: Saturday 29/03/1975
Result: **GLOUCESTER CITY 1 BEDWORTH UNITED 1**
Competition: Southern League Division 1 North
Teamsheet: Stow, Hargreaves, Lewis, Moughton, Gough, Wixey, Dangerfield, Gardner, Bitchenor, G Davies, Hayden
Substitute: Millyard (nps)
Scorer: G Davies
Attendance: 214

Date: Monday 31/03/1975
Result: **GLOUCESTER CITY 3 CHELTENHAM TOWN 2**
Competition: Southern League Division 1 North
Teamsheet: Stow, Hargreaves, Lewis, Moughton, Gough, Wixey, Dangerfield, Gardner, Matchwick, Hayden, Foxwell
Substitute: G Davies (nps)
Scorers: Gardner, Wixey, Foxwell
Attendance: 1200

Date: Saturday 05/04/1975
Result: **WITNEY TOWN 1 GLOUCESTER CITY 0**
Competition: Southern League Division 1 North
Teamsheet: Stow, Hargreaves, Lewis, Moughton, Gough, Wixey, Dangerfield, Gardner, Eves, G Davies, Hayden
Substitute: Bitchenor (nps)

Date: Thursday 10/04/1975
Result: **GLOUCESTER CITY 5 BURY TOWN 2**
Competition: Southern League Division 1 North
Teamsheet: Stow, Hargreaves, Lewis, Moughton, Gough, Wixey, Dangerfield, Hayden, Gardner, Turner, Foxwell
Substitute: G Davies (nps)
Scorers: Foxwell (2), Dangerfield, Wixey, Gardner
Attendance: 150

Date: Saturday 12/04/1975
Result: **GLOUCESTER CITY 4 MILTON KEYNES CITY 3**
Competition: Southern League Division 1 North
Teamsheet: Stow, Hargreaves, Lewis, Moughton, Gough, Wixey, Dangerfield, Gardner, Bitchenor, Hayden, McCool
Substitute: Parkes (nps)
Scorers: McCool, Bitchenor, Gardner (2)
Attendance: 266

Date: Tuesday 15/04/1975
Result: **CORBY TOWN 1 GLOUCESTER CITY 2**
Competition: Southern League Division 1 North
Teamsheet: Stow, Hargreaves, Lewis, Moughton, Gough, Wixey, Dangerfield, Gardner, Eves, McCool, Hayden
Substitute: Bitchenor (for Hayden)
Scorers: McCool, Gough
Attendance: 130

Date: Saturday 19/04/1975
Result: **BEDWORTH UNITED 1 GLOUCESTER CITY 2**
Competition: Southern League Division 1 North
Teamsheet: Stow, Hargreaves, Lewis, Moughton, Gough, Wixey, Dangerfield, Gardner, Bitchenor, Eves, McCool
Substitute: G Davies (nps)
Scorers: Bitchenor, Gardner

Date: Tuesday 22/04/1975
Result: **GLOUCESTER CITY 0 TAMWORTH 1**
Competition: Southern League Division 1 North
Teamsheet: Stow, Hargreaves, Lewis, Moughton, Gough, Wixey, Dangerfield, Gardner, Bitchenor, Eves, McCool
Substitute: G Davies (nps)
Attendance: 378

Date: Wednesday 23/04/1975
Result: **KING'S LYNN 3 GLOUCESTER CITY 0**
Competition: Southern League Division 1 North
Teamsheet: Stow, Hargreaves, Hayden, Moughton, Gough, Lewis, G Davies, Eves, Bitchenor, Gardner, Wixey
Substitute: Tandy (nps)

Date: Sunday 27/04/1975
Result: **CHELTENHAM TOWN 0 GLOUCESTER CITY 2**
Competition: Gloucestershire FA Northern Senior Professional Cup Final
Teamsheet: Stow, Wixey, Hargreaves, Moughton, Gough, Hayden, Dangerfield, Gardner, Turner, Foxwell, Lewis
Substitute: McCool (nps)
Scorers: Turner, Dangerfield
Attendance: 521

Date: Tuesday 29/04/1975
Result: **GLOUCESTER CITY 2 BEDFORD TOWN 3**
Competition: Southern League Division 1 North
Teamsheet: Stow, Hargreaves, Lewis, Moughton, Gough, Wixey, Dangerfield, Eves, Gardner, Hayden, Bitchenor
Substitute: Matchwick (for Hayden)
Scorers: Gardner, Dangerfield
Attendance: 284

Date: Thursday 01/05/1975
Result: **GLOUCESTER CITY 1 DUNSTABLE TOWN 2**
Competition: Southern League Division 1 North
Teamsheet: Stow, Hargreaves, Lewis, Moughton, Gough, Wixey, Dangerfield, Eves, Gardner, McCool, Matchwick
Substitute: Turner (nps)
Scorer: Eves
Attendance: 290

Appearances – KD Bitchenor 9(1), M Clark 1, JR Dangerfield 50, G Davies 38, J Davies 27, JD Eves 7, E Feighery 39, DP Foxwell 3, CR Gardner 50, A Gough 37, T Hargreaves 45, M Hayden 46, M Langley 1, M Lewis 42(1), P Matchwick 2(1), R McCool 9, JM Miles 30, CE Moughton 50, RT Stow 20, J Turner 5, R Wixey 50.
Others selected but did not play: MR Millyard, D Parkes, BI Tandy.
Scorers – G Davies 17, CR Gardner 10, J Davies 8, JR Dangerfield 6, M Hayden 5, E Feighery 4, KD Bitchenor 3, DP Foxwell 3, A Gough 3, R Wixey 3, R McCool 2, JD Eves 1, T Hargreaves 1, J Turner 1.

SOUTHERN LEAGUE DIVISION 1 NORTH

POS	CLUB	P	W	D	L	F	A	PTS
1	BEDFORD TOWN	42	28	9	5	85	33	65
2	DUNSTABLE TOWN	42	25	8	9	105	61	58
3	AUTOMOTIVE PRODUCTS LEAMINGTON	42	25	7	10	68	48	57
4	REDDITCH UNITED	42	22	12	8	76	40	56
5	WORCESTER CITY	42	24	8	10	84	50	56
6	CHELTENHAM TOWN	42	21	9	12	72	53	51
7	TAMWORTH	42	21	8	13	74	53	50
8	KING'S LYNN	42	19	10	13	71	64	48
9	ENDERBY TOWN	42	17	12	13	61	48	46
10	BANBURY UNITED	42	18	10	14	52	51	46
11	STEVENAGE ATHLETIC	42	16	13	13	62	48	45
12	BROMSGROVE ROVERS	42	18	9	15	63	52	45
13	MERTHYR TYDFIL	42	11	15	16	53	64	37
14	WITNEY TOWN	42	16	4	22	57	76	36
15	CORBY TOWN	42	11	13	18	60	57	35
16	KIDDERMINSTER HARRIERS	42	12	11	19	50	66	35
17	**GLOUCESTER CITY**	**42**	**13**	**8**	**21**	**55**	**75**	**34**
18	WELLINGBOROUGH TOWN	42	9	13	20	42	61	31
19	BARRY TOWN	42	10	10	22	49	73	30
20	BEDWORTH UNITED	42	9	9	24	60	91	27
21	MILTON KEYNES CITY	42	7	5	30	48	100	19
22	BURY TOWN	42	5	7	30	36	119	17
		924	357	210	357	1383	1383	924

SEASON 1975-1976
(Home Ground: Horton Road Stadium)

Date: Saturday 16/08/1975
Result: **GLOUCESTER CITY 2 ENDERBY TOWN 1**
Competition: Southern League Division 1 North
Teamsheet: Stow, Wixey, Hayden, Moulsdale, Gough, Moughton, Eves, CR Gardner, Cooper, Feighery, Wise
Substitute: Wood (nps)
Scorer: Feighery (2)
Attendance: 270

Date: Wednesday 20/08/1975
Result: **BARRY TOWN 0 GLOUCESTER CITY 2**
Competition: Southern League Division 1 North
Teamsheet: Stow, Chapman, Birch, Moulsdale, Moughton, Gough, PW Gardner, CR Gardner, Feighery, Cooper, Wise
Substitute: E Jones (for PW Oardbner)
Scorers: Gough, PW Gardner

Date: Saturday 23/08/1975
Result: **GLOUCESTER CITY 0 BURY TOWN 3**
Competition: Southern League Division 1 North
Teamsheet: Stow, Chapman, Birch, Moulsdale, Gough, Moughton, PW Gardner, CR Gardner, Feighery, Cooper, Wise
Substitute: Etheridge (nps)

Date: Thursday 28/08/1975
Result: **GLOUCESTER CITY 0 DORCHESTER TOWN 2**
Competition: Southern League Cup 1st Round 1st Leg
Teamsheet: Stow, Chapman, Birch, Moulsdale, Gough, Moughton, Cooper, CR Gardner, Smith, Feighery, Wise
Substitute: Bitchenor (nps)
Attendance: 230

Date: Saturday 30/08/1975
Result: **GLOUCESTER CITY 1 CHELTENHAM TOWN 1**
Competition: Southern League Division 1 North
Teamsheet: Stow, Sperti, Birch, Moulsdale, Gough, Moughton, Cooper, Eves, CR Gardner, Feighery, Wise
Substitute: Bitchenor (nps)
Scorer: Feighery
Attendance: 620

Date: Tuesday 02/09/1975
Result: **DORCHESTER TOWN 2 GLOUCESTER CITY 1**
Competition: Southern League Cup 1st Round 2nd Leg
Teamsheet: Stow, Sperti, Birch, Moulsdale, Gough, Moughton, Cooper, M Jones, CR Gardner, Feighery, Foxwell
Substitute: Wood (nps)
Scorer: Cooper

Date: Saturday 06/09/1975
Result: **TAMWORTH 1 GLOUCESTER CITY 0**
Competition: Southern League Division 1 North
Teamsheet: Stow, Sperti, Birch, Cooper, Gough, Moughton, PW Gardner, CR Gardner, Feighery, M Jones, Wise
Substitute: Wood (nps)
Attendance: 303

Date: Tuesday 09/09/1975
Result: **GLOUCESTER CITY 1 STEVENAGE ATHLETIC 1**
Competition: Southern League Division 1 North
Teamsheet: Stow, Sperti, Birch, Wixey, Gough, Moughton, Cooper, CR Gardner, Wood, Feighery, Foxwell
Substitute: M Jones (nps)
Scorer: Foxwell
Attendance: 250

Date: Saturday 13/09/1975
Result: **BRIERLEY HILL ALLIANCE 2 GLOUCESTER CITY 1**
Competition: FA Cup 1st Qualifying Round
Teamsheet: Stow, Moughton, Birch, Cooper, Moulsdale, Gough, CR Gardner, Feighery, Wood, Wise, E Jones
Substitute: Etheridge (nps)
Scorer: E Jones

Date: Tuesday 16/09/1975
Result: **GLOUCESTER CITY 0 MILTON KEYNES CITY 1**
Competition: Southern League Division 1 North
Teamsheet: Stow, Moughton, Birch, PW Gardner, Gough, Moulsdale, Cooper, Fiocca, Wood, Feighery, Foxwell
Substitute: Wise (nps)
Attendance: 260

Date: Saturday 20/09/1975
Result: **GLOUCESTER CITY 1 EVERWARM 1**
Competition: FA Trophy Preliminary Round
Teamsheet: Stow, Moughton, Birch, Wixey, Gough, Moulsdale, Sperti, Cooper, Wood, CR Gardner, Fiocca
Substitute: Feighery (for Moughton)
Scorer: Cooper
Attendance: 300

Date: Tuesday 23/09/1975
Result: **EVERWARM 2 GLOUCESTER CITY 4** (aet)
Competition: FA Trophy Preliminary Round Replay
Teamsheet: Stow, Sperti, Birch, Wixey, Gough, Moulsdale, Cooper, Fiocca, CR Gardner, Feighery, Foxwell
Substitute: No sub
Scorers: Gough, Feighery (pen), Foxwell (2)

Date: Saturday 27//09/1975
Result: **BEDWORTH UNITED 1 GLOUCESTER CITY 1**
Competition: Southern League Division 1 North
Teamsheet: Stow, Sperti, Chapman, Moulsdale, Gough, Wixey, Cooper, CR Gardner, Wood, Feighery, Fiocca
Substitute: E Jones (nps)
Scorer: Gough

Date: Saturday 04/10/1975
Result: **GLOUCESTER CITY 2 CORBY TOWN 2**
Competition: Southern League Division 1 North
Teamsheet: Wright, Sperti, Birch, Moulsdale, Gough, Wixey, Cooper, CR Gardner, Feighery, Fiocca, Foxwell
Substitute: Chapman (for Wixey)
Scorers: Foxwell, Feighery
Attendance: 200

Date: Saturday 11/10/1975
Result: **TON PENTRE 2 GLOUCESTER CITY 0**
Competition: FA Trophy 1st Qualifying Round
Teamsheet: Stow, Moughton, Birch, Sperti, Moulsdale, Gough, Eves, Cooper, CR Gardner, Feighery, Foxwell
Substitute: Fiocca (for Moughton)
Attendance: 500

Date: Saturday 18/10/1975
Result: **GLOUCESTER CITY 2 KING'S LYNN 1**
Competition: Southern League Division 1 North
Teamsheet: Stow, Chapman, Birch, Sperti, Gough, Moulsdale, Eves, Feighery, Cooper, Fiocca, Foxwell
Substitute: Wood (nps)
Scorers: Cooper, Feighery
Attendance: 186

Date: Saturday 25/10/1975
Result: **GLOUCESTER CITY 2 BARNET 2**
Competition: Southern League Division 1 North
Teamsheet: Stow, Chapman, Birch, Sperti, Gough, Etheridge, Cooper, Fiocca, Wood, Feighery, Foxwell
Substitute: Boots (nps)
Scorers: Fiocca, Wood
Attendance: 290

Date: Tuesday 28/10/1975
Result: **AUTOMOTIVE PRODUCTS LEAMINGTON 2 GLOUCESTER CITY 1**
Competition: Southern League Division 1 North
Teamsheet: Stow, Chapman, Birch, Sperti, Gough, Anderson, Cooper, Fiocca, Wood, Feighery, Foxwell
Substitute: Boots (nps)
Scorer: own goal
Attendance: 288

Date: Saturday 01/11/1975
Result: **MERTHYR TYDFIL 4 GLOUCESTER CITY 2**
Competition: Southern League Division 1 North
Teamsheet: Stow, Birch, Chapman, Sperti, Gough, Cooper, PW Gardner, Fiocca, Wood, Feighery, Foxwell
Substitute: Etheridge (nps)
Scorers: Wood, Foxwell

Date: Saturday 08/11/1975
Result: **GLOUCESTER CITY 4 KIDDERMINSTER HARRIERS 3**
Competition: Southern League Division 1 North
Teamsheet: Stow, Chapman, Birch, Wixey, Gough, Cooper, Eves, Sperti, Wood, CR Gardner, Foxwell
Substitute: Fiocca (nps)
Scorers: Foxwell (2), CR Gardner, Sperti
Attendance: 240

Date: Saturday 15/11/1975
Result: **KING'S LYNN 3 GLOUCESTER CITY 2**
Competition: Southern League Division 1 North
Teamsheet: Stow, Chapman, Birch, Sperti, Gough, Wixey, Cooper, Eves, Wood, CR Gardner, Fiocca
Substitute: Etheridge (nps)
Scorers: own goal, CR Gardner

Date: Saturday 29/11/1975
Result: **WELLINGBOROUGH TOWN 2 GLOUCESTER CITY 3**
Competition: Southern League Division 1 North
Teamsheet: Stow, Chapman, Birch, Moulsdale, Gough, Cooper, Eves, CR Gardner, Wood, PW Gardner, Foxwell
Substitute: Wixey (nps)
Scorers: CR Gardner, Wood (2)

Date: Saturday 06/12/1975
Result: **GLOUCESTER CITY 1 REDDITCH UNITED 3**
Competition: Southern League Division 1 North
Teamsheet: Stow, Chapman, Birch, Moulsdale, Gough, Cooper, Eves, Wixey, Wood, CR Gardner, Foxwell
Substitute: PW Gardner (nps)
Scorer: Eves
Attendance: 400

Date: Saturday 13/12/1975
Result: **GLOUCESTER CITY 4 WORCESTER CITY 2**
Competition: Southern League Division 1 North
Teamsheet: Stow, Wixey, Birch, Moulsdale, Gough, Cooper, Eves, PW Gardner, Wood, CR Gardner, Foxwell
Substitute: Chapman (nps)
Scorers: Cooper, Wood, CR Gardner, Foxwell
Attendance: 500

Date: Saturday 20/12/1975
Result: **OSWESTRY TOWN 0 GLOUCESTER CITY 1**
Competition: Southern League Division 1 North
Teamsheet: Stow, Sperti, Birch, Wixey, Gough, Moulsdale, Cooper, Eves, CR Gardner, PW Gardner, Foxwell
Substitute: Wood (nps)
Scorer: Foxwell (pen)
Attendance: 800

Date: Friday 26/12/1975
Result: **GLOUCESTER CITY 1 BANBURY UNITED 0**
Competition: Southern League Division 1 North
Teamsheet: Stow, Wixey, Birch, Eves, Gough, Moulsdale, Cooper, CR Gardner, Wood, PW Gardner, Foxwell
Substitute: Etheridge (nps)
Scorer: CR Gardner
Attendance: 650

Date: Saturday 27/12/1975
Result: **MILTON KEYNES CITY 1 GLOUCESTER CITY 0**
Competition: Southern League Division 1 North
Teamsheet: Stow, Wixey, Birch, Eves, Gough, Moulsdale, Cooper, CR Gardner, Wood, PW Gardner, Foxwell
Substitute: Moughton (nps)

Date: Thursday 01/01/1976
Result: **BROMSGROVE ROVERS 2 GLOUCESTER CITY 0**
Competition: Southern League Division 1 North
Teamsheet: Wright, Wixey, Birch, Moughton, Gough, Moulsdale, Cooper, King, Wood, CR Gardner, Foxwell
Substitute: PW Gardner (for King)

Date: Saturday 03/01/1976
Result: **GLOUCESTER CITY 0 TAMWORTH 4**
Competition: Southern League Division 1 North
Teamsheet: Wright, Moughton, Birch, Cooper, Gough, Moulsdale, Eves, PW Gardner, Wood, CR Gardner, Foxwell
Substitute: Wixey (nps)
Attendance: 220

Date: Tuesday 13/01/1976
Result: **WITNEY TOWN 1 GLOUCESTER CITY 0**
Competition: Southern League Division 1 North
Teamsheet: Wright, Moughton, Birch, Cooper, Moulsdale, Wood, Gough, Eves, CR Gardner, PW Gardner, Foxwell
Substitute: G Jones (nps)
Attendance: 400

Date: Saturday 17/01/1976
Result: **GLOUCESTER CITY 3 BURY TOWN 1**
Competition: Southern League Division 1 North
Teamsheet: Stow, Boots, Birch, PW Gardner, Gough, Moulsdale, Eves, Cooper, Wood, CR Gardner, Foxwell
Substitute: G Jones (nps)
Scorers: Wood (2), Foxwell
Attendance: 200

Date: Saturday 24/01/1976
Result: **WORCESTER CITY 3 GLOUCESTER CITY 0**
Competition: Southern League Division 1 North
Teamsheet: Stow, Wixey, Birch, PW Gardner, Gough, Moulsdale, Eves, Cooper, Wood, CRGardner, Hancock
Substitute: Boots (nps)
Attendance: 741

Date: Tuesday 27/01/1976
Result: **BANBURY UNITED 3 GLOUCESTER CITY 0**
Competition: Southern League Division 1 North
Teamsheet: Stow, Wixey, Birch, PW Gardner, Gough, Moulsdale, Eves, Cooper, Wood, CR Gardner, E Jones
Substitute: Boots (nps)

Date: Saturday 07/02/1976
Result: **GLOUCESTER CITY 1 BEDWORTH UNITED 1**
Competition: Southern League Division 1 North
Teamsheet: Stow, Wixey, Birch, Eves, Gough, Moulsdale, Smith, CR Gardner, Coburn, PW Gardner, Cooper
Substitute: Wood (for Cooper)
Scorer: PW Gardner
Attendance: 195

Date: Saturday 14/02/1976
Result: **GLOUCESTER CITY 1 WITNEY TOWN 2**
Competition: Southern League Division 1 North
Teamsheet: Stow, Wixey, Birch, Moulsdale, Gough, Coburn, Cooper, Eves, Wood, CR Gardner, PW Gardner
Substitute: Smith (nps)
Scorer: Wood
Attendance: 255

Date: Saturday 21/02/1976
Result: **GLOUCESTER CITY 0 AUTOMOTIVE PRODUCTS LEAMINGTON 3**
Competition: Southern League Division 1 North
Teamsheet: Stow, Allen, Birch, Cooper, Gough, Moulsdale, Eves, CR Gardner, Wood, PW Gardner, Coburn
Substitute: Smith (nps)
Attendance: 197

Date: Saturday 28/02/1976
Result: **KIDDERMINSTER HARRIERS 4 GLOUCESTER CITY 1**
Competition: Southern League Division 1 North
Teamsheet: Stow, Allen, Wixey, Coburn, Gough, Moulsdale, Cooper, PW Gardner, Wood, CR Gardner, Eves
Substitute: Smith (nps)
Scorer: Wood
Attendance: 257

[243]

Date: Saturday 06/03/1976
Result: **GLOUCESTER CITY 1 MERTHYR TYDFIL 0**
Competition: Southern League Division 1 North
Teamsheet: Stow, Wixey, Allen, Moulsdale, Gough, Eves, Cooper, Wood, Smith, CR Gardner, PW Gardner
Substitute: Birch (nps)
Scorer: Smith
Attendance: 147

Date: Saturday 13/03/1976
Result: **BARNET 1 GLOUCESTER CITY 2**
Competition: Southern League Division 1 North
Teamsheet: Stow, Allen, Birch, Coburn, Gough, Moulsdale, Cooper, Eves, Wood, Smith, CR Gardner
Substitute: Etheridge (nps)
Scorer: Wood (2)

Date: Saturday 20/03/1976
Result: **GLOUCESTER CITY 3 WELLINGBOROUGH TOWN 1**
Competition: Southern League Division 1 North
Teamsheet: Stow, Allen, Birch, Eves, Gough, Moulsdale, Cooper, Coburn, Wood, Smith, CR Gardner
Substitute: PW Gardner (nps)
Scorers: Cooper (2, 1 pen), Smith
Attendance: 197

Date: Saturday 27/03/1976
Result: **REDDITCH UNITED 2 GLOUCESTER CITY 0**
Competition: Southern League Division 1 North
Teamsheet: Stow, Allen, Birch, Chapman, Gough, Moulsdale, Eves, CR Gardner, Wood, Smith, PW Gardner
Substitute: Cooper (for Chapman)

Date: Tuesday 30/03/1976
Result: **ENDERBY TOWN 1 GLOUCESTER CITY 2**
Competition: Southern League Division 1 North
Teamsheet: Stow, Allen, Birch, Chapman, Boots, Moulsdale, Cooper, Hancock, Wood, CR Gardner, PW Gardner
Substitute: Smith (nps)
Scorer: Wood (2)

Date: Saturday 03/04/1976
Result: **CHELTENHAM TOWN 5 GLOUCESTER CITY 0**
Competition: Southern League Division 1 North
Teamsheet: Stow, Allen, Birch, Chapman, Gough, Moulsdale, Cooper, Ewart, Wood, Smith, PW Gardner
Substitute: Hancock (for Smith)
Attendance: 655

Date: Saturday 10/04/1976
Result: **GLOUCESTER CITY 1 BROMSGROVE ROVERS 1**
Competition: Southern League Division 1 North
Teamsheet: Stow, Allen, Birch, PW Gardner, Gough, Moulsdale, Eves, Cooper, Wood, King, Hancock
Substitute: Chapman (nps)
Scorer: Wood
Attendance: 187

Date: Saturday 17/04/1976
Result: **STEVENAGE ATHLETIC 2 GLOUCESTER CITY 2**
Competition: Southern League Division 1 North
Teamsheet: Stow, Allen, Birch, PW Gardner, Gough, Moulsdale, Cooper, Chapman, Wood, CR Gardner, Hancock
Substitute: Smith (nps)
Scorers: PW Gardner, Wood

Date: Monday 19/04/1976
Result: **GLOUCESTER CITY 0 OSWESTRY TOWN 0**
Competition: Southern League Division 1 North
Teamsheet: Wright, Allen, Birch, P Gardner, Gough, Moulsdale, Boots, Cooper, Wood, CR Gardner, Hancock
Substitute: King (for Boots)
Attendance: 214

Date: Thursday 22/04/1976
Result: **GLOUCESTER CITY 0 BARRY TOWN 2**
Competition: Southern League Division 1 North
Teamsheet: Stow, Allen, Birch, PW Gardner, Gough, Moulsdale, Cooper, CR Gardner, Wood, Boots, Eves
Substitute: Smith (nps)
Attendance: 150

Date: Saturday 24/04/1976
Result: **GLOUCESTER CITY 0 CHELTENHAM TOWN 2**
Competition: Gloucestershire FA Northern Senior Professional Cup Final
Teamsheet: Stow, Allen, Birch, PW Gardner, Gough, Moulsdale, Cooper, CR Gardner, Wood, Smith, Boots
Substitutes: King (nps), Eves (nps)
Attendance: 370

Date: Tuesday 27/04/1976
Result: **CORBY TOWN 5 GLOUCESTER CITY 0**
Competition: Southern League Division 1 North
Teamsheet: Stow, Allen, Birch, PW Gardner, Gough, Moulsdale, Cooper, Smith, Wood, CR Gardner, Boots
Substitute: Hancock (nps)

Appearances – K Allen 14, R Anderson 1, A Birch 45, AP Boots 6, D Chapman 16(1), A Coburn 6, A Cooper 48(1), RJ Etheridge 1, JD Eves 27, D Ewart 1, E Feighery 18(1), P Fiocca 10(1), DP Foxwell 21, CR Gardner 44, PW Gardner 27(1), A Gough 48, M Hancock 5(1), M Hayden 1, E Jones 2, M Jones 2, JR King 2(1), CE Moughton 15, CB Moulsdale 42, D Smith 9, F Sperti 16, RT Stow 44, C Wise 7, R Wixey 20, K Wood 36(1), B Wright 5.
Others selected but did not play: KD Bitchenor, G Jones.
Scorers – K Wood 15, DP Foxwell 10, A Cooper 6, E Feighery 6, CR Gardner 5, PW Gardner 3, A Gough 3, D Smith 2, JD Eves 1, P Fiocca 1, E Jones 1, F Sperti 1, own goals 2.

SOUTHERN LEAGUE DIVISION 1 NORTH

POS	CLUB	P	W	D	L	F	A	PTS
1	REDDITCH UNITED	42	29	11	2	101	39	69
2	AUTOMOTIVE PRODUCTS LEAMINGTON	42	27	10	5	85	31	64
3	WITNEY TOWN	42	24	9	9	66	40	57
4	WORCESTER CITY	42	24	8	10	90	49	56
5	CHELTENHAM TOWN	42	20	10	12	87	55	50
6	BARRY TOWN	42	19	10	13	52	47	48
7	KING'S LYNN	42	17	14	11	52	48	48
8	TAMWORTH	42	18	11	13	65	43	47
9	BARNET	42	15	12	15	56	57	42
10	OSWESTRY TOWN	42	16	8	18	63	71	40
11	ENDERBY TOWN	42	16	6	20	48	51	38
12	BANBURY UNITED	42	15	8	19	58	67	38
13	MERTHYR TYDFIL	42	11	15	16	59	67	37
14	BROMSGROVE ROVERS	42	13	11	18	49	65	37
15	MILTON KEYNES CITY	42	15	6	21	51	63	36
16	BURY TOWN	42	12	11	19	52	72	35
17	**GLOUCESTER CITY**	**42**	**13**	**9**	**20**	**49**	**78**	**35**
18	KIDDERMINSTER HARRIERS	42	13	8	21	54	70	34
19	BEDWORTH UNITED	42	8	18	16	41	65	34
20	CORBY TOWN	42	11	10	21	50	65	32
21	WELLINGBOROUGH TOWN	42	9	11	22	42	68	29
22	STEVENAGE ATHLETIC	42	6	6	30	46	105	18
		924	351	222	351	1316	1316	924

SEASON 1976-1977
(Home Ground: Horton Road Stadium)

Date: Saturday 21/08/1976
Result: **MERTHYR TYDFIL 6 GLOUCESTER CITY 0**
Competition: Southern League Cup 1st Round 1st Leg
Teamsheet: Stow, Hargreaves, Mortimer, Gardner, Gough, Allen, Eves, Cooper, Evans, Wood, Foxwell
Substitute: Blackburn (nps)

Date: Tuesday 24/08/1976
Result: **GLOUCESTER CITY 2 MERTHYR TYDFIL 0**
Competition: Southern League Cup 1st Round 2nd Leg
Teamsheet: Stow, Hargreaves, Mortimer, Gardner, Gough, Allen, Cooper, Eves, Evans, Wood, Foxwell
Substitute: Blackburn (for Mortimer)
Scorers: Wood, Cooper (pen)
Attendance: 233

Date: Saturday 28/08/1976
Result: **GLOUCESTER CITY 1 WELLINGBOROUGH TOWN 0**
Competition: Southern League Division 1 North
Teamsheet: Stow, Allen, Hargreaves, Moulsdale, Gough, Eves, Cooper, Evans, Wood, Gardner, Foxwell
Substitute: Blackburn (for Cooper)
Scorer: Blackburn
Attendance: 142

Date: Monday 30/08/1976
Result: **WITNEY TOWN 2 GLOUCESTER CITY 1**
Competition: Southern League Division 1 North
Teamsheet: Stow, Allen, Carroll, Moulsdale, Gough, Eves, Gardner, Evans, Wood, Foxwell, Blackburn
Substitute: Smith (nps)
Scorer: Blackburn

Date: Saturday 04/09/1976
Result: **GLOUCESTER CITY 1 TROWBRIDGE TOWN 1**
Competition: FA Cup Preliminary Round
Teamsheet: Stow, Allen, Carroll, Moulsdale, Gough, Mortimer, Eves, Blackburn, Wood, Evans, Foxwell
Substitute: Hargreaves (nps)
Scorer: Wood

Date: Wednesday 08/09/1976
Result: **TROWBRIDGE TOWN 1 GLOUCESTER CITY 2**
Competition: FA Cup Preliminary Round Replay
Teamsheet: Stow, Allen, Moulsdale, Gough, Carroll, Hargreaves, Wood, Mortimer, Evans, Blackburn, Foxwell
Substitute: Gardner (nps)
Scorers: Evans, Foxwell

Date: Tuesday 14/09/1976
Result: **GLOUCESTER CITY 1 CORBY TOWN 1**
Competition: Southern League Division 1 North
Teamsheet: Stow, Allen, Carroll, Moulsdale, Gough, Hargreaves, Mortimer, Evans, Wood, Blackburn, Foxwell
Substitute: Gardner (for Mortimer)
Scorer: Blackburn
Attendance: 120

Date: Saturday 18/09/1976
Result: **MERTHYR TYDFIL 4 GLOUCESTER CITY 1**
Competition: FA Cup 1st Qualifying Round
Teamsheet: Stow, Allen, Smith, Moulsdale, Gough, Hargreaves, Gardner, Blackburn, Wood, Evans, Foxwell
Substitute: Eves (for Foxwell)
Scorer: Wood

Date: Saturday 25/09/1976
Result: **GLOUCESTER CITY 2 BRIERLEY HILL ALLIANCE 2**
Competition: FA Trophy 1st Qualifying Round
Teamsheet: Stow, Allen, Hargreaves, Carroll, Gough, Eves, Gardner, Blackburn, Wood, Evans, Foxwell
Substitute: Bitchenor (nps)
Scorers: Wood, Evans

Date: Tuesday 28/09/1976
Result: **BRIERLEY HILL ALLIANCE 1 GLOUCESTER CITY 3**
Competition: FA Trophy 1st Qualifying Round Replay
Teamsheet: Stow, Allen, Hargreaves, Medcroft, Gough, Gardner, Eves, Blackburn, Wood, Evans, Foxwell
Substitute: Smith (nps)
Scorers: Blackburn, Evans (2)

Date: Saturday 02/10/1976
Result: **GLOUCESTER CITY 2 KING'S LYNN 0**
Competition: Southern League Division 1 North
Teamsheet: Stow, Allen, Carroll, Hargreaves, Gough, Gardner, Eves, Blackburn, Wood, Evans, Foxwell
Substitute: Bitchenor (nps)
Scorer: Evans (2)
Attendance: 151

Date: Wednesday 06/10/1976
Result: **CHELTENHAM TOWN 2 GLOUCESTER CITY 0** (aet)
Competition: Gloucestershire FA Northern Senior Professional Cup Final
Teamsheet: Stow, Allen, Carroll, Gough, Hargreaves, Gardner, Eves, Evans, Wood, Blackburn, Foxwell
Substitute: Bitchenor (for Eves)
Attendance: 360

Date: Saturday 09/10/1976
Result: **OSWESTRY TOWN 0 GLOUCESTER CITY 1**
Competition: Southern League Division 1 North
Teamsheet: Stow, Allen, Carroll, Hargreaves, Gough, Gardner, Mortimer, Blackburn, Wood, Evans, Foxwell
Substitute: Eves (nps)
Scorer: Blackburn

Date: Saturday 16/10/1976
Result: **GLOUCESTER CITY 2 BANBURY UNITED 4**
Competition: Southern League Division 1 North
Teamsheet: Stow, Allen, Carroll, Hargreaves, Gough, Gardner, Mortimer, Blackburn, Wood, Evans, Foxwell
Substitute: Eves (nps)
Scorers: Evans, Foxwell
Attendance: 400

Date: Saturday 23/10/1976
Result: **BEDWORTH UNITED 0 GLOUCESTER CITY 2**
Competition: Southern League Division 1 North
Teamsheet: Stow, Allen, Carroll, Moulsdale, Gough, Jones, Mortimer, Blackburn, Wood, Evans, Hargreaves
Substitute: Foxwell (for -----)
Scorers: Blackburn, Evans

Date: Saturday 30/10/1976
Result: **FERNDALE ATHLETIC 3 GLOUCESTER CITY 1**
Competition: FA Trophy 2nd Qualifying Round
Teamsheet: Stow, Allen, Carroll, Moulsdale, Gough, Jones, Hargreaves, Blackburn, Wood, Evans, Foxwell
Substitute: Gardner (nps)
Scorer: Blackburn

Date: Saturday 06/11/1976
Result: **KIDDERMINSTER HARRIERS 4 GLOUCESTER CITY 1**
Competition: Southern League Division 1 North
Teamsheet: Stow, Allen, Carroll, Moulsdale, Gough, Jones, Hargreaves, Blackburn, Mortimer, Evans, Foxwell
Substitute: Gardner (nps)
Scorer: Blackburn
Attendance: 441

Date: Saturday 13/11/1976
Result: **BROMSGROVE ROVERS 5 GLOUCESTER CITY 1**
Competition: Southern League Division 1 North
Teamsheet: Stow, Allen, Carroll, Moulsdale, Gough, Gardner, Hargreaves, Blackburn, Jones, Evans, Foxwell
Substitute: Wood (nps)
Scorer: Foxwell (pen)

Date: Monday 15/11/1976
Result: **WORCESTER CITY 5 GLOUCESTER CITY 1**
Competition: Southern League Division 1 North
Teamsheet: Stow, Allen, Hargreaves, Moulsdale, Gough, Jones, Eves, Gardner, Wood, Evans, Foxwell
Substitute: Blackburn (for Hargreaves)
Scorer: Evans
Attendance: 1062

Date: Saturday 20/11/1976
Result: **GLOUCESTER CITY 5 DUNSTABLE TOWN 1**
Competition: Southern League Division 1 North
Teamsheet: Stow, Allen, Hargreaves, Moulsdale, Gough, Jones, Gardner, Eves, Wood, Evans, Foxwell
Substitute: Blackburn (nps)
Scorers: Foxwell (3), Wood, Evans
Attendance: 220

Date: Saturday 27/11/1976
Result: **ENDERBY TOWN 1 GLOUCESTER CITY 2**
Competition: Southern League Division 1 North
Teamsheet: Stow, Allen, Hargreaves, Moulsdale, Carroll, Gardner, Eves, Jones, Wood, Evans, Foxwell
Substitute: Blackburn (for Gardner)
Scorers: Jones, Foxwell

Date: Saturday 11/12/1976
Result: **TAMWORTH 8 GLOUCESTER CITY 2**
Competition: Southern League Division 1 North
Teamsheet: Stow, Allen, Hargreaves, Moulsdale, Carroll, Jones, Medcroft, Mortimer, Wood, Evans, Foxwell
Substitute: Blackburn (nps)
Scorers: Medcroft, Wood

Date: Monday 27/12/1976
Result: **BARRY TOWN 5 GLOUCESTER CITY 1**
Competition: Southern League Division 1 North
Teamsheet: Stow, Allen, Hargreaves, Moulsdale, Gough, Medcroft, Jones, Mortimer, Wood, Evans, Foxwell
Substitute: Blackburn (nps)
Scorer: Jones
Attendance: 300

Date: Saturday 08/01/1977
Result: **GLOUCESTER CITY 0 WORCESTER CITY 3**
Competition: Southern League Division 1 North
Teamsheet: Stow, Allen, Bitchenor, Moulsdale, Gough, Mortimer, Rowe, Gardner, Jones, Evans, Foxwell
Substitute: Wood (nps)
Attendance: 472

Date: Saturday 15/01/1977
Result: **GLOUCESTER CITY 5 MILTON KEYNES CITY 3**
Competition: Southern League Division 1 North
Teamsheet: Stow, Allen, Mortimer, Boots, Gough, Hargreaves, Pocock, Rowe, Jones, Evans, Foxwell
Substitute: Wood (for Allen)
Scorers: Evans, Jones (2), Foxwell, Wood
Attendance: 150

Date: Saturday 22/01/1977
Result: **GLOUCESTER CITY 3 BEDWORTH UNITED 1**
Competition: Southern League Division 1 North
Teamsheet: Stow, Allen, Mortimer, Boots, Gough, Hargreaves, Pocock, Rowe, Jones, Evans, Foxwell
Substitute: Wood (for Jones)
Scorers: Foxwell (2), Jones
Attendance: 165

Date: Tuesday 25/01/1977
Result: **BANBURY UNITED 4 GLOUCESTER CITY 2**
Competition: Southern League Division 1 North
Teamsheet: Stow, Allen, Mortimer, Boots, Gough, Hargreaves, Pocock, Rowe, Jones, Evans, Foxwell
Substitute: Wood (nps)
Scorer: Evans (2)

Date: Saturday 29/01/1977
Result: **DUNSTABLE TOWN 0 GLOUCESTER CITY 2**
Competition: Southern League Division 1 North
Teamsheet: Stow, Allen, Mortimer, Moulsdale, Gough, Gardner, Pocock, Boots, Wood, Evans, Foxwell
Substitute: Eves (nps)
Scorers: Foxwell, Evans

Date: Saturday 05/02/1977
Result: **WELLINGBOROUGH TOWN 2 GLOUCESTER CITY 3**
Competition: Southern League Division 1 North
Teamsheet: Stow, Allen, Mortimer, Moulsdale, Gough, Gardner, Pocock, Boots, Jones, Evans, Foxwell
Substitute: Wood (nps)
Scorer: Evans (3)

Date: Saturday 12/02/1977
Result: **GLOUCESTER CITY 1 WITNEY TOWN 1**
Competition: Southern League Division 1 North
Teamsheet: Wright, Allen, Mortimer, Moulsdale, Gough, Gardner, Pocock, Boots, Jones, Evans, Foxwell
Substitute: Wood (nps)
Scorer: Jones
Attendance: 292

Date: Saturday 19/02/1977
Result: **MERTHYR TYDFIL 4 GLOUCESTER CITY 1**
Competition: Southern League Division 1 North
Teamsheet: Wright, Allen, Mortimer, Moulsdale, Gough, Medcroft, Pocock, Wood, Jones, Gardner, Foxwell
Substitute: Smith (nps)
Scorer: Jones

Date: Saturday 05/03/1977
Result: **GLOUCESTER CITY 2 CAMBRIDGE CITY 4**
Competition: Southern League Division 1 North
Teamsheet: Wright, Allen, Mortimer, Moulsdale, Gough, Boots, Pocock, Gardner, Jones, Evans, Foxwell
Substitute: Wood (nps)
Scorers: Gough, Gardner
Attendance: 150

Date: Saturday 12/03/1977
Result: **KING'S LYNN 1 GLOUCESTER CITY 2**
Competition: Southern League Division 1 North
Teamsheet: Stow, Allen, Mortimer, Boots, Gough, Gardner, Eves, Moulsdale, Wood, Evans, Foxwell
Substitute: Pocock (nps)
Scorer: Evans (2)

Date: Saturday 19/03/1977
Result: **GLOUCESTER CITY 5 OSWESTRY TOWN 1**
Competition: Southern League Division 1 North
Teamsheet: Stow, Allen, Mortimer, Moulsdale, Gough, Gardner, Pocock, Eves, Wood, Evans, Foxwell
Substitute: Hancock (for Gardner)
Scorers: Gough, Wood, Evans (2), Foxwell
Attendance: 173

Date: Saturday 26/03/1977
Result: **STOURBRIDGE 1 GLOUCESTER CITY 1**
Competition: Southern League Division 1 North
Teamsheet: Stow, Allen, Mortimer, Moulsdale, Gough, Eves, Pocock, Gardner, Wood, Evans, Foxwell
Substitute: Medcroft (nps)
Scorer: Evans

Date: Tuesday 29/03/1977
Result: **CORBY TOWN 4 GLOUCESTER CITY 3**
Competition: Southern League Division 1 North
Teamsheet: Stow, Allen, Mortimer, Moulsdale, Gough, Gardner, Eves, Pocock, Wood, Evans, Foxwell
Substitute: Medcroft (nps)
Scorers: Evans (2), Eves

Date: Saturday 02/04/1977
Result: **GLOUCESTER CITY 1 KIDDERMINSTER HARRIERS 2**
Competition: Southern League Division 1 North
Teamsheet: Stow, Allen, Mortimer, Moulsdale, Gough, Pocock, Eves, Gardner, Jones, Evans, Foxwell
Substitute: Wood (for Evans)
Scorer: Foxwell (pen)
Attendance: 214

Date: Saturday 09/04/1977
Result: **CHELTENHAM TOWN 4 GLOUCESTER CITY 0**
Competition: Southern League Division 1 North
Teamsheet: Stow, Allen, Mortimer, Moulsdale, Boots, Pocock, Eves, Gardner, Jones, Medcroft, Foxwell
Substitute: Short (for -----)
Attendance: 1095

Date: Monday 11/04/1977
Result: **GLOUCESTER CITY 3 BARRY TOWN 0**
Competition: Southern League Division 1 North
Teamsheet: Stow, Allen, Mortimer, Moulsdale, Boots, Pocock, Eves, Gardner, Wood, Medcroft, Foxwell
Substitute: No sub
Scorer: Foxwell (3, 1 pen)
Attendance: 245

Date: Saturday 16/04/1977
Result: **MILTON KEYNES CITY 2 GLOUCESTER CITY 2**
Competition: Southern League Division 1 North
Teamsheet: Stow, Allen, Mortimer, Moulsdale, Boots, Pocock, Eves, Gardner, Wood, Medcroft, Foxwell
Substitute: Gough (nps)
Scorers: Moulsdale, Wood

Date: Saturday 23/04/1977
Result: **GLOUCESTER CITY 1 BROMSGROVE ROVERS 3**
Competition: Southern League Division 1 North
Teamsheet: Stow, Allen, Moulsdale, Boots, Gough, Pocock, Eves, gardner, Jones, Evans, Foxwell
Substitute: Wood (nps)
Scorer: Foxwell
Attendance: 282

Date: Tuesday 26/04/1977
Result: **GLOUCESTER CITY 1 STOURBRIDGE 0**
Competition: Southern League Division 1 North
Teamsheet: Stow, Allen, Moulsdale, Boots, Gough, Perry, Pocock, Gardner, Medcroft, Evans, Foxwell
Substitute: Wood (nps)
Scorer: Evans
Attendance: 168

Date: Saturday 30/04/1977
Result: **GLOUCESTER CITY 2 ENDERBY TOWN 1**
Competition: Southern League Division 1 North
Teamsheet: Stow, Allen, Smith, Moulsdale, Gough, Gardner, Pocock, Boots, Medcroft, Evans, Foxwell
Substitute: Wood (nps)
Scorers: Foxwell, Evans
Attendance: 165

Date: Tuesday 03/05/1977
Result: **GLOUCESTER CITY 3 MERTHYR TYDFIL 2**
Competition: Southern League Division 1 North
Teamsheet: Stow, Allen, Smith, Moulsdale, Gough, Gardner, Pocock, Boots, Medcroft, Evans, Foxwell
Substitute: Wood (for Medcroft)
Scorers: Foxwell, Gough, Evans
Attendance: 208

Date: Saturday 07/05/1977
Result: **GLOUCESTER CITY 3 TAMWORTH 0**
Competition: Southern League Division 1 North
Teamsheet: Stow, Allen, Smith, Moulsdale, Gough, Gardner, Pocock, Boots, Wood, Evans, Foxwell
Substitute: Mortimer (nps)
Scorers: Evans, Gough, Pocock
Attendance: 226

Date: Tuesday 10/05/1977
Result: **GLOUCESTER CITY 0 CHELTENHAM TOWN 2**
Competition: Southern League Division 1 North
Teamsheet: Stow, Allen, Smith, Moulsdale, Gough, Gardner, Pocock, Boots, Wood, Evans, Foxwell
Substitute: Mortimer (nps)
Attendance: 1010

Date: Saturday 14/05/1977
Result: **CAMBRIDGE CITY 0 GLOUCESTER CITY 1**
Competition: Southern League Division 1 North
Teamsheet: Stow, Allen, Mortimer, Moulsdale, Gough, Gardner, Pocock, Boots, Wood, Evans, Foxwell
Substitute: Medcroft (nps)
Scorer: Foxwell

Appearances – K Allen 47, KD Bitchenor 1(1), KA Blackburn 15(4), AP Boots 18, M Carroll 16, A Cooper 3, JA Evans 43, JD Eves 21(1), DP Foxwell 45(2), PW Gardner 36(1), A Gough 42, M Hancock 0(1), T Hargreaves 24, T Jones 20, G Medcroft 10, KEW Mortimer 29, CB Moulsdale 36, I Perry 1, B Pocock 22, M Rowe 4, R Short 0(1), LF Smith 5, RT Stow 44, K Wood 32(4), B Wright 3.
Scorers – JA Evans 28, DP Foxwell 20, K Wood 9, KA Blackburn 8, T Jones 7, A Gough 4, JD Eves 1, PW Gardner 1, G Medcroft 1, CB Moulsdale 1, B Pocock 1.

SOUTHERN LEAGUE DIVISION 1 NORTH

POS	CLUB	P	W	D	L	F	A	PTS
1	WORCESTER CITY	38	32	5	1	97	22	69
2	CHELTENHAM TOWN	38	23	8	7	85	35	54
3	WITNEY TOWN	38	21	8	9	48	31	50
4	BROMSGROVE ROVERS	38	20	8	10	61	37	48
5	BARRY TOWN	38	19	8	11	62	45	46
6	CAMBRIDGE CITY	38	17	10	11	68	43	44
7	STOURBRIDGE	38	17	9	12	48	35	43
8	KIDDERMINSTER HARRIERS	38	17	6	15	74	65	40
9	BANBURY UNITED	38	15	10	13	51	47	40
10	**GLOUCESTER CITY**	**38**	**18**	**4**	**16**	**70**	**81**	**40**
11	ENDERBY TOWN	38	15	9	14	50	44	39
12	KING'S LYNN	38	13	11	14	47	53	37
13	CORBY TOWN	38	11	13	14	56	64	35
14	TAMWORTH	38	11	13	14	49	58	35
15	MERTHYR TYDFIL	38	12	6	20	60	69	30
16	OSWESTRY TOWN	38	8	10	20	30	60	26
17	WELLINGBOROUGH TOWN	38	8	7	23	37	73	23
18	DUNSTABLE TOWN	38	7	7	24	38	84	21
19	BEDWORTH UNITED	38	5	10	23	28	68	20
20	MILTON KEYNES CITY	38	7	6	25	31	76	20
		760	296	168	296	1090	1090	760

SEASON 1977-1978
(Home Ground: Horton Road Stadium)

Date: Saturday 20/08/1977
Result: **CHELTENHAM TOWN 5 GLOUCESTER CITY 0**
Competition: Southern League Cup 1st Round 1st Leg
Teamsheet: Stow, Allen, Mortimer, Moulsdale, Boots, Eves, Pocock, Perry, Wood, Evans, Turner
Substitute: PW Gardner (nps)
Attendance: 706

Date: Tuesday 23/08/1977
Result: **GLOUCESTER CITY 0 CHELTENHAM TOWN 5**
Competition: Southern League Cup 1st Round 2nd Leg
Teamsheet: Stow, Allen, Mortimer, Moulsdale, Boots, Turner, Pocock, PW Gardner, Wood, Evans, Perry
Substitute: Eves (for Wood)
Attendance: 612

Date: Saturday 27/08/1977
Result: **GLOUCESTER CITY 2 STOURBRIDGE 4**
Competition: Southern League Division 1 North
Teamsheet: Stow, Allen, Mortimer, Boots, Adams, Turner, Eves, Evans, Wood, Perry, Foxwell
Substitute: Pocock (for Mortimer)
Scorers: Evans, Foxwell
Attendance: 250

Date: Monday 29/08/1977
Result: **ENDERBY TOWN 2 GLOUCESTER CITY 1**
Competition: Southern League Division 1 North
Teamsheet: Trevarthan, Allen, Medcroft, Moulsdale, Boots, Perry, Eves, Evans, Wood, Turner, Foxwell
Substitute: Pocock (nps)
Scorer: Foxwell

Date: Saturday 03/09/1977
Result: **BARRY TOWN 0 GLOUCESTER CITY 2**
Competition: Southern League Division 1 North
Teamsheet: Trevarthan, Allen, Smith, Adams, Boots, Perry, Eves, Turner, Wood, Evans, Foxwell
Substitute: Moulsdale (nps)
Scorers: Wood, Evans

Date: Tuesday 06/09/1977
Result: **GLOUCESTER CITY 1 BROMSGROVE ROVERS 1**
Competition: Southern League Division 1 North
Teamsheet: Trevarthan, Allen, Moulsdale, Adams, Boots, Perry, Eves, Turner, Wood, Evans, Foxwell
Substitute: Smith (nps)
Scorer: Evans
Attendance: 191

Date: Saturday 10/09/1977
Result: **FROME TOWN 2 GLOUCESTER CITY 3**
Competition: FA Trophy Preliminary Round
Teamsheet: Trevarthan, Allen, Boots, Adams, Moulsdale, Eves, Turner, Perry, Evans, Wood, Foxwell
Substitute: Mortimer (for Moulsdale)
Scorers: Turner, Foxwell, Evans

Date: Saturday 17/09/1977
Result: **DUDLEY TOWN 1 GLOUCESTER CITY 1**
Competition: FA Cup 1ˢᵗ Qualifying Round
Teamsheet: Trevarthan, Allen, Mortimer, Boots, Adams, Perry, Eves, Turner, Wood, Medcroft, Foxwell
Substitute: Evans (nps)
Scorer: Foxwell

Date: Tuesday 20/09/1977
Result: **GLOUCESTER CITY 1 DUDLEY TOWN 2**
Competition: FA Cup 1ˢᵗ Qualifying Round Replay
Teamsheet: Trevarthan, Allen, Mortimer, Bitchenor, Adams, Perry, Eves, Turner, Wood, Medcroft, Evans
Substitute: -----
Scorer: Wood

Date: Saturday 24/09/1977
Result: **GLOUCESTER CITY 2 CAMBRIDGE CITY 3**
Competition: Southern League Division 1 North
Teamsheet: Trevarthan, Allen, Mortimer, Adams, Turner, Perry, Eves, PW Gardner, Medcroft, Evans, Hayden
Substitute: Wood (nps)
Scorers: Evans (pen), Hayden
Attendance: 173

Date: Tuesday 27/09/1977
Result: **BRIDGEND TOWN 2 GLOUCESTER CITY 1**
Competition: Southern League Division 1 North
Teamsheet: Trevarthan, Allen, Mortimer, Adams, Turner, Perry, Medcroft, PW Gardner, Wood, Evans, Feighery
Substitute: Smith (nps)
Scorer: Evans

Date: Saturday 01/10/1977
Result: **KING'S LYNN 4 GLOUCESTER CITY 3**
Competition: Southern League Division 1 North
Teamsheet: Trevarthan, Allen, Mortimer, Moulsdale, Turner, Perry, Eves, PW Gardner, Medcroft, Evans, Hayden
Substitute: Wood (nps)
Scorers: Hayden (2), own goal
Attendance: 417

Date: Saturday 15/10/1977
Result: **GLOUCESTER CITY 2 PAULTON ROVERS 3**
Competition: FA Trophy 1ˢᵗ Qualifying Round
Teamsheet: Trevarthan, Allen, Mortimer, Boots, Turner, Perry, Eves, Moulsdale, Wood, Evans, Hayden
Substitute: PW Gardner (nps)
Scorers: Turner, Evans

Date: Saturday 22/10/1977
Result: **GLOUCESTER CITY 0 KING'S LYNN 2**
Competition: Southern League Division 1 North
Teamsheet: Trevarthan, Allen, Hayden, Boots, Turner, PW Gardner, Eves, Perry, Wood, Evans, Foxwell
Substitute: Moulsdale (nps)
Attendance: 163

Date: Saturday 29/10/1977
Result: **CORBY TOWN 0 GLOUCESTER CITY 2**
Competition: Southern League Division 1 North
Teamsheet: Trevarthan, Allen, Mortimer, Boots, Turner, Eves, PW Gardner, Perry, Hayden, Evans, Foxwell
Substitute: Moulsdale (nps)
Scorer: Evans (2)

Date: Saturday 12/11/1977
Result: **GLOUCESTER CITY 1 OSWESTRY TOWN 2**
Competition: Southern League Division 1 North
Teamsheet: Trevarthan, Allen, Moulsdale, Boots, Gough, Hayden, Eves, Callaway, Foxwell, Evans, Turner
Substitute: PW Gardner (nps)
Scorer: Turner
Attendance: 153

Date: Monday 14/11/1977
Result: **KIDDERMINSTER HARRIERS 1 GLOUCESTER CITY 2**
Competition: Southern League Division 1 North
Teamsheet: Trevarthan, Allen, Hayden, Boots, Gough, PW Gardner, Eves, Callaway, Foxwell, Evans, Turner
Substitute: Moulsdale (nps)
Scorer: Foxwell (2)
Attendance: 310

Date: Saturday 19/11/1977
Result: **GLOUCESTER CITY 0 WELLINGBOROUGH TOWN 2**
Competition: Southern League Division 1 North
Teamsheet: Trevarthan, Allen, Hayden, Boots, Gough, PW Gardner, Eves, Callaway, Foxwell, Evans, Turner
Substitute: Perry (for -----)
Attendance: 150

Date: Saturday 26/11/1977
Result: **BEDWORTH UNITED 2 GLOUCESTER CITY 2**
Competition: Southern League Division 1 North
Teamsheet: Trevarthan, Allen, Scarrott, Boots, Gough, Turner, Eves, Hayden, Callaway, Evans, Foxwell
Substitute: PW Gardner (nps)
Scorers: Callaway, Evans

Date: Saturday 03/12/1977
Result: **TAMWORTH 0 GLOUCESTER CITY 3**
Competition: Southern League Division 1 North
Teamsheet: Trevarthan, Allen, Scarrott, Boots, Gough, Turner, Boseley, CR Gardner, Callaway, Evans, Foxwell
Substitute: PW Gardner (nps)
Scorers: Turner, Callaway (2)
Attendance: 133

Date: Saturday 10/12/1977
Result: **BANBURY UNITED 3 GLOUCESTER CITY 2**
Competition: Southern League Division 1 North
Teamsheet: Trevarthan, Allen, Scarrott, Boots, Gough, Turner, Hayden, CR Gardner, Callaway, Evans, Foxwell
Substitute: PW Gardner (nps)
Scorers: Turner, CR Gardner

Date: Tuesday 13/12/1977
Result: **WITNEY TOWN 2 GLOUCESTER CITY 1**
Competition: Southern League Division 1 North
Teamsheet: Trevarthan, Allen, Scarrott, Boots, Gough, Turner, CR Gardner, Boseley, Callaway, Foxwell, Hayden
Substitute: Evans (nps)
Scorer: CR Gardner

Date: Saturday 17/12/1977
Result: **GLOUCESTER CITY 2 DUNSTABLE TOWN 1**
Competition: Southern League Division 1 North
Teamsheet: Trevarthan, Allen, Scarrott, Boots, Gough, Turner, CR Gardner, Boseley, Callaway, Evans, Foxwell
Substitute: Hayden (for -----)
Scorers: Turner, Foxwell
Attendance: 217

Date: Tuesday 27/12/1977
Result: **GLOUCESTER CITY 2 MILTON KEYNES CITY 0**
Competition: Southern League Division 1 North
Teamsheet: Trevarthan, Allen, Scarrott, Boots, Gough, Turner, CR Gardner, Callaway, Foxwell, Evans, Boseley
Substitute: Reid (nps)
Scorers: Gough, Turner
Attendance: 382

Date: Saturday 31/12/1977
Result: **GLOUCESTER CITY 3 CORBY TOWN 2**
Competition: Southern League Division 1 North
Teamsheet: Trevarthan, Allen, Scarrott, Boots, Gough, Turner, CR Gardner, Boseley, Callaway, Evans, Foxwell
Substitute: Reid (for Callaway)
Scorers: Turner (2), Evans
Attendance: 286

Date: Monday 02/01/1978
Result: **MERTHYR TYDFIL 7 GLOUCESTER CITY 1**
Competition: Southern League Division 1 North
Teamsheet: Trevarthan, Allen, Scarrott, Boots, Gough, Turner, CR Gardner, Boseley, Callaway, Evans, Foxwell
Substitute: Reid (for Callaway)
Scorer: Evans
Attendance: 300

Date: Saturday 07/01/1978
Result: **GLOUCESTER CITY 0 BURTON ALBION 1**
Competition: Southern League Division 1 North
Teamsheet: Trevarthan, Appleyard, Scarrott, Boots, Gough, Turner, CR Gardner, Boseley, Wood, Evans, Foxwell
Substitute: Hayden (nps)
Attendance: 239

Date: Saturday 14/01/1978
Result: **STOURBRIDGE 5 GLOUCESTER CITY 1**
Competition: Southern League Division 1 North
Teamsheet: Trevarthan, Appleyard, Scarrott, Boots, Gough, Turner, CR Gardner, Boseley, Callaway, Evans, Foxwell
Substitute: Hayden (for Callaway)
Scorer: Evans

Date: Saturday 28/01/1978
Result: **OSWESTRY TOWN 3 GLOUCESTER CITY 5**
Competition: Southern League Division 1 North
Teamsheet: Stow, Appleyard, Scarrott, Boots, Gough, Turner, Eves, CR Gardner, Foxwell, Evans, Boseley
Substitute: Allen (nps)
Scorers: Foxwell (3), Boseley, Evans

Date: Saturday 18/02/1978
Result: **CAMBRIDGE CITY 4 GLOUCESTER CITY 0**
Competition: Southern League Division 1 North
Teamsheet: Trevarthan, Appleyard, Scarrott, Mockridge, Gough, PW Gardner, Boseley, CR Gardner, Foxwell, Evans, Bell
Substitute: Eves (nps)

Date: Saturday 25/02/1978
Result: **BURTON ALBION 0 GLOUCESTER CITY 0**
Competition: Southern League Division 1 North
Teamsheet: Stow, Appleyard, Scarrott, Newman, Gough, Boseley, Moulsdale, Eves, Foxwell, Evans, Bell
Substitute: CR Gardner (nps)
Attendance: 417

Date: Saturday 04/03/1978
Result: **GLOUCESTER CITY 3 WITNEY TOWN 1**
Competition: Southern League Division 1 North
Teamsheet: Stow, Appleyard, Moulsdale, Eves, Gough, Callaway, Boseley, Newman, Foxwell, Evans, Bell
Substitute: CR Gardner (for Callaway)
Scorers: Foxwell (2), Callaway
Attendance: 236

Date: Saturday 11/03/1978
Result: **GLOUCESTER CITY 1 BRIDGEND TOWN 4**
Competition: Southern League Division 1 North
Teamsheet: Stow, Appleyard, Moulsdale, Newman, Gough, Turner, Boseley, Eves, Foxwell, Evans, Bell
Substitute: CR Gardner (nps)
Scorer: Turner
Attendance: 276

Date: Tuesday 14/03/1978
Result: **BROMSGROVE ROVERS 1 GLOUCESTER CITY 1**
Competition: Southern League Division 1 North
Teamsheet: Stow, Appleyard, Moulsdale, Scarrott, Mockridge, Turner, CR Gardner, Boseley, Foxwell, Evans, Bell
Substitute: Eves (nps)
Scorer: Foxwell

Date: Saturday 18/03/1978
Result: **GLOUCESTER CITY 2 BEDWORTH UNITED 2**
Competition: Southern League Division 1 North
Teamsheet: Stow, Appleyard, Scarrott, Moulsdale, Newman, Turner, Boseley, CR Gardner, Foxwell, Evans, Bell
Substitute: Eves (for -----)
Scorers: Foxwell, Eves
Attendance: 146

Date: Saturday 25/03/1978
Result: **MILTON KEYNES CITY 0 GLOUCESTER CITY 2**
Competition: Southern League Division 1 North
Teamsheet: Stow, Appleyard, Scarrott, Moulsdale, Gough, Turner, Eves, CR Gardner, Foxwell, Evans, Bell
Substitute: PW Gardner (nps)
Scorers: Gough, Evans

Date: Monday 27/03/1978
Result: **GLOUCESTER CITY 2 BARRY TOWN 2**
Competition: Southern League Division 1 North
Teamsheet: Trevarthan, Appleyard, Scarrott, Moulsdale, Gough, Turner, Woodruff, CR Gardner, Foxwell, Evans, Bell
Substitute: PW Gardner (nps)
Scorers: Evans, Foxwell (pen)
Attendance: 225

Date: Saturday 01/04/1978
Result: **GLOUCESTER CITY 3 KIDDERMINSTER HARRIERS 1**
Competition: Southern League Division 1 North
Teamsheet: Stow, Appleyard, Scarrott, Moulsdale, Gough, Turner, Eves, CR Gardner, Foxwell, Evans, Bell
Substitute: Boseley (nps)
Scorers: Turner, Foxwell (2)
Attendance: 212

Date: Saturday 08/04/1978
Result: **GLOUCESTER CITY 2 BANBURY UNITED 2**
Competition: Southern League Division 1 North
Teamsheet: Trevarthan, Boseley, Scarrott, Moulsdale, Gough, Turner, Eves, CR Gardner, Foxwell, Evans, Bell
Substitute: PW Gardner (nps)
Scorers: Foxwell, Evans
Attendance: 202

Date: Saturday 15/04/1978
Result: **DUNSTABLE TOWN 0 GLOUCESTER CITY 1**
Competition: Southern League Division 1 North
Teamsheet: Stow, Appleyard, Scarrott, Moulsdale, Turner, Boseley, Eves, CR Gardner, Foxwell, Evans, Bell
Substitute: PW Gardner (nps)
Scorer: Turner

Date: Tuesday 18/04/1978
Result: **GLOUCESTER CITY 4 ENDERBY TOWN 3**
Competition: Southern League Division 1 North
Teamsheet: Stow, Appleyard, Scarrott, Moulsdale, Boseley, Turner, Eves, CR Gardner, Foxwell, Evans, Bell
Substitute: PW Gardner (nps)
Scorers: Foxwell (3, 1 pen), Evans
Attendance: 150

Date: Saturday 22/04/1978
Result: **WELLINGBOROUGH TOWN 3 GLOUCESTER CITY 2**
Competition: Southern League Division 1 North
Teamsheet: Stow, Appleyard, Scarrott, Moulsdale, Gough, Turner, Eves, PW Gardner, Foxwell, Evans, Bell
Substitute: Wood (nps)
Scorers: Evans, Eves

Date: Tuesday 25/04/1978
Result: **GLOUCESTER CITY 4 MERTHYR TYDFIL 1**
Competition: Southern League Division 1 North
Teamsheet: Stow, Appleyard, Scarrott, Moulsdale, Turner, Bell, Eves, PW Gardner, Foxwell, Evans, Boseley
Substitute: Wood (nps)
Scorers: Evans, Foxwell, PW Gardner, Bell
Attendance: 169

Date: Tuesday 02/05/1978
Result: **GLOUCESTER CITY 2 TAMWORTH 2**
Competition: Southern League Division 1 North
Teamsheet: Stow, Appleyard, Scarrott, Moulsdale, Mockridge, Boseley, Woodruff, Turner, Foxwell, Evans, Bell
Substitute: Eves (nps)
Scorer: Mockridge (2)
Attendance: 179

Date: Thursday 04/05/1978
Result: **GLOUCESTER CITY 1 CHELTENHAM TOWN 2**
Competition: Gloucestershire FA Northern Senior Professional Cup Final
Teamsheet: Stow, Appleyard, Scarrott, Moulsdale, Mockridge, Boseley, Woodruff, Turner, Foxwell, Evans, Bell
Substitutes: Eves (nps), Dick (nps)
Scorer: Foxwell
Attendance: 500

Appearances – P Adams 8, K Allen 26, J Appleyard 18, G Bell 16, KD Bitchenor 1, AP Boots 25, SJ Boseley 21, CJ Callaway 13, JA Evans 43, JD Eves 28(2), E Feighery 1, DP Foxwell 38, CR Gardner 19(1), PW Gardner 11, A Gough 23, M Hayden 11(2), G Medcroft 6, GD Mockridge 4, KEW Mortimer 10(1), CB Moulsdale 23, B Newman 4, I Perry 15(1), B Pocock 2(1), J Reid 0(2), SW Scarrott 25, LF Smith 1, RT Stow 17, C Trevarthan 28, J Turner 42, K Wood 13, RW Woodruff 3.
Others selected but did not play: R Dick.
Scorers – DP Foxwell 23, JA Evans 20, J Turner 12, CJ Callaway 4, M Hayden 3, JD Eves 2, CR Gardner 2, A Gough 2, GD Mockridge 2, K Wood 2, G Bell 1, PW Gardner 1, SJ Boseley 1, own goal 1.

SOUTHERN LEAGUE DIVISION 1 NORTH

POS	CLUB	P	W	D	L	F	A	PTS
1	WITNEY TOWN	38	20	15	3	54	27	55
2	BRIDGEND TOWN	38	20	9	9	59	45	49
3	BURTON ALBION	38	17	11	10	48	32	45
4	ENDERBY TOWN	38	17	10	11	59	44	44
5	BROMSGROVE ROVERS	38	16	12	10	56	41	44
6	BANBURY UNITED	38	17	10	11	52	47	44
7	KIDDERMINSTER HARRIERS	38	16	11	11	58	41	43
8	MERTHYR TYDFIL	38	18	6	14	85	62	42
9	CAMBRIDGE CITY	38	14	12	12	56	45	40
10	BARRY TOWN	38	14	11	13	58	48	39
11	WELLINGBOROUGH TOWN	38	12	15	11	47	43	39
12	KING'S LYNN	38	12	13	13	55	55	37
13	**GLOUCESTER CITY**	**38**	**14**	**8**	**16**	**68**	**75**	**36**
14	CORBY TOWN	38	9	17	12	46	48	35
15	DUNSTABLE TOWN	38	11	13	14	49	59	35
16	STOURBRIDGE	38	8	15	15	52	53	31
17	TAMWORTH	38	10	11	17	37	48	31
18	BEDWORTH UNITED	38	8	14	16	36	58	30
19	MILTON KEYNES CITY	38	5	11	22	26	74	21
20	OSWESTRY TOWN	38	6	8	24	29	85	20
		760	264	232	264	1030	1030	760

SEASON 1978-1979

(Home Ground: Horton Road Stadium)

Date: Saturday 19/08/1978
Result: **GLOUCESTER CITY 2 CHELTENHAM TOWN 1**
Competition: Southern League Cup 1st Round 1st Leg
Teamsheet: Main, Scarrott, Perrott, Pepworth, GD Mockridge, Turner, Bell, Perry, Foxwell, Evans, Brake
Substitute: Eves (nps)
Scorers: Scarrott, Perry
Attendance: 612

Date: Wednesday 23/08/1978
Result: **CHELTENHAM TOWN 2 GLOUCESTER CITY 4**
Competition: Southern League Cup 1st Round 2nd Leg
Teamsheet: Main, Scarrott, Perrott, Pepworth, GD Mockridge, Turner, Bell, Perry, Foxwell, Evans, Brake
Substitute: Eves (nps)
Scorers: Evans, Foxwell (2), Brake
Attendance: 803

Date: Saturday 26/08/1978
Result: **BROMSGROVE ROVERS 2 GLOUCESTER CITY 3**
Competition: Southern League Division 1 North
Teamsheet: Main, Scarrott, Perrott, Pepworth, GD Mockridge, Turner, Bell, Perry, Foxwell, Evans, Gardner
Substitute: Eves (nps)
Scorers: Foxwell, GD Mockridge, Gardner

Date: Saturday 02/09/1978
Result: **FROME TOWN 0 GLOUCESTER CITY 3**
Competition: FA Cup Preliminary Round
Teamsheet: Main, Scarrott, Perrott, GD Mockridge, Pepworth, Perry, Bell, Brake, Foxwell, Evans, Turner
Substitute: Eves (for -----)
Scorer: Evans (3, 1 pen)

Date: Tuesday 05/09/1978
Result: **GLOUCESTER CITY 2 STOURBRIDGE 2**
Competition: Southern League Division 1 North
Teamsheet: Main, Eves, Scarrott, Pepworth, GD Mockridge, Turner, Bell, Perry, Foxwell, Evans, Brake
Substitute: Gardner (nps)
Scorers: Scarrott (pen), Brake
Attendance: 216

Date: Saturday 09/09/1978
Result: **TROWBRIDGE TOWN 2 GLOUCESTER CITY 2**
Competition: FA Trophy Preliminary Round
Teamsheet: Main, Eves, Scarrott, GD Mockridge, Pepworth, Perry, Turner, Brake, Bell, Evans, Foxwell
Substitute: Perrott (nps)
Scorers: GD Mockridge, Evans
Attendance: 340

Date: Tuesday 12/09/1978
Result: **GLOUCESTER CITY 1 TROWBRIDGE TOWN 2**
Competition: FA Trophy Preliminary Round Replay
Teamsheet: Main, Scarrott, Perrott, GD Mockridge, Pepworth, Perry, Bell, Brake, Turner, Evans, Foxwell
Substitute: Eves (nps)
Scorer: Foxwell

Date: Saturday 16/09/1978
Result: **MELKSHAM TOWN 1 GLOUCESTER CITY 0**
Competition: FA Cup 1st Qualifying Round
Teamsheet: Main, Perrott, Scarrott, Pepworth, GD Mockridge, Perry, Bell, Turner, Foxwell, Eves, Brake
Substitute: Gardner (for Eves)

Date: Saturday 23/09/1978
Result: **GLOUCESTER CITY 1 TAMWORTH 0**
Competition: Southern League Division 1 North
Teamsheet: Main, Gittings, Scarrott, GD Mockridge, Brinkworth, Turner, Bell, Brake, Pepworth, Evans, Foxwell
Substitute: Gardner (for Foxwell)
Scorer: GD Mockridge
Attendance: 250

Date: Monday 25/09/1978
Result: **BATH CITY 1 GLOUCESTER CITY 0**
Competition: Southern League Cup 2nd Round
Teamsheet: Main, Gittings, Scarrott, Pepworth, GD Mockridge, Turner, Bell, Brinkworth, Gardner, Brake, Perrott
Substitute: Eves (nps)

Date: Saturday 30/09/1978
Result: **ALVECHURCH 1 GLOUCESTER CITY 1**
Competition: Southern League Division 1 North
Teamsheet: Main, Gittings, Scarrott, Pepworth, GD Mockridge, Turner, Bell, Brinkworth, Gardner, Brake, Perrott
Substitute: Eves (nps)
Scorer: Pepworth

Date: Saturday 07/10/1978
Result: **ENDERBY TOWN 3 GLOUCESTER CITY 1**
Competition: Southern League Division 1 North
Teamsheet: Main, Gittings, Scarrott, Pepworth, GD Mockridge, Turner, Bell, Brinkworth, Foxwell, Evans, Perrott
Substitute: Brake (nps)
Scorer: Scarrott (pen)

Date: Saturday 14/10/1978
Result: **GRANTHAM 3 GLOUCESTER CITY 0**
Competition: Southern League Division 1 North
Teamsheet: Main, Gittings, Scarrott, Pepworth, GD Mockridge, Turner, Bell, Gardner, Foxwell, Evans, Brake
Substitute: Davies (for Gardner)
Attendance: 429

Date: Monday 16/10/1978
Result: **KIDDERMINSTER HARRIERS 1 GLOUCESTER CITY 3**
Competition: Southern League Division 1 North
Teamsheet: Main, Gittings, Scarrott, Pepworth, GD Mockridge, Turner, Bell, Perry, Foxwell, Evans, Brake
Substitute: Davies (nps)
Scorers: Foxwell (2), Evans

Date: Saturday 21/10/1978
Result: **GLOUCESTER CITY 0 ALVECHURCH 3**
Competition: Southern League Division 1 North
Teamsheet: Main, Gittings, Scarrott, Pepworth, GD Mockridge, Turner, Bell, Perry, Foxwell, Evans, Brake
Substitute: Davies (for Pepworth)
Attendance: 350

Date: Saturday 28/10/1978
Result: **CORBY TOWN 1 GLOUCESTER CITY 2**
Competition: Southern League Division 1 North
Teamsheet: Main, Gittings, Scarrott, Pepworth, GD Mockridge, Turner, Bell, Perry, Foxwell, Evans, Brake
Substitute: Davies (nps)
Scorers: Foxwell, Evans

Date: Saturday 04/11/1978
Result: **GLOUCESTER CITY 3 WELLINGBOROUGH TOWN 0**
Competition: Southern League Division 1 North
Teamsheet: Main, Scarrott, Gittings, Pepworth, Turner, Bell, Perry, Davies, Foxwell, Evans, Brake
Substitute: Gardner (nps)
Scorers: Foxwell, Turner, Evans
Attendance: 231

Date: Saturday 11/11/1978
Result: **CAMBRIDGE CITY 0 GLOUCESTER CITY 1**
Competition: Southern League Division 1 North
Teamsheet: Main, Gittings, Scarrott, Pepworth, Turner, Perrott, Perry, Bell, Evans, Foxwell, Brake
Substitute: Rice (for Foxwell)
Scorer: Evans

Date: Saturday 18/11/1978
Result: **BARRY TOWN 3 GLOUCESTER CITY 1**
Competition: Southern League Division 1 North
Teamsheet: Main, Gittings, GD Mockridge, Turner, Scarrott, Perry, Bell, Rice, Brake, Evans, Foxwell
Substitute: Perrott (nps)
Scorer: Brake

Date: Saturday 25/11/1978
Result: **GLOUCESTER CITY 4 OSWESTRY TOWN 3**
Competition: Southern League Division 1 North
Teamsheet: Main, Gittings, Scarrott, Pepworth, Turner, Paterson, Brake, Perry, Rice, Evans, Foxwell
Substitute: Perrott (nps)
Scorers: Turner, Paterson (2), Foxwell
Attendance: 320

Date: Saturday 02/12/1978
Result: **WELLINGBOROUGH TOWN 1 GLOUCESTER CITY 2**
Competition: Southern League Division 1 North
Teamsheet: Main, Gittings, Scarrott, Turner, Perry, Rice, Paterson, Pepworth, Foxwell, Evans, Brake
Substitute: GD Mockridge (nps)
Scorers: Scarrott (pen), Evans

Date: Saturday 09/12/1978
Result: **GLOUCESTER CITY 1 BEDWORTH UNITED 2**
Competition: Southern League Division 1 North
Teamsheet: Main, Scarrott, Gittings, Pepworth, Turner, Perry, Davies, Rice, Paterson, Evans, Foxwell
Substitute: GD Mockridge (nps)
Scorer: Davis
Attendance: 287

Date: Tuesday 26/12/1978
Result: **BANBURY UNITED 2 GLOUCESTER CITY 2**
Competition: Southern League Division 1 North
Teamsheet: Main, Bell, Scarrott, Turner, Pepworth, Perry, Rice, Paterson, Brake, Evans, Foxwell
Substitute: Davies (nps)
Scorers: Pepworth, Rice

Date: Saturday 30/12/1978
Result: **MERTHYR TYDFIL 3 GLOUCESTER CITY 2**
Competition: Southern League Division 1 North
Teamsheet: Main, Scarrott, Bell, Pepworth, Turner, Perry, Paterson, Brake, Evans, Rice, Foxwell
Substitute: Davies (nps)
Scorers: Paterson, Evans

Date: Saturday 03/02/1979
Result: **TAMWORTH 4 GLOUCESTER CITY 3**
Competition: Southern League Division 1 North
Teamsheet: Main, Davies, Bell, Pepworth, GD Mockridge, Turner, Brake, Paterson, Rice, Evans, Bruton
Substitute: Perry (nps)
Scorers: Brake, Turner, Bruton

Date: Saturday 24/02/1979
Result: **GLOUCESTER CITY 1 GRANTHAM 2**
Competition: Southern League Division 1 North
Teamsheet: Main, Davies, Bell, GD Mockridge, Mallender, Rice, Turner, Brake, Paterson, Bruton, Evans
Substitute: Hall (nps)
Scorer: Paterson
Attendance: 228

Date: Saturday 03/03/1979
Result: **BEDFORD TOWN 2 GLOUCESTER CITY 0**
Competition: Southern League Division 1 North
Teamsheet: Main, Davies, Bell, GD Mockridge, Mallender, Turner, Rice, Paterson, Bruton, Evans, Brake
Substitute: Hall (nps)

Date: Saturday 10/03/1979
Result: **GLOUCESTER CITY 4 CORBY TOWN 1**
Competition: Southern League Division 1 North
Teamsheet: Emmerson, Davies, Bell, GD Mockridge, Mallender, Turner, Paterson, Hall, Bruton, Evans, Brake
Substitute: Rice (for Mallender)
Scorers: Davies, GD Mockridge, Hall, Brake
Attendance: 201

Date: Monday 19/03/1979
Result: **STOURBRIDGE 3 GLOUCESTER CITY 4**
Competition: Southern League Division 1 North
Teamsheet: Emmerson, Davies, Bell, DC Mockridge, GD Mockridge, Turner, Brake, Paterson, Bruton, Evans, Griffin
Substitute: Hall (nps)
Scorers: DC Mockridge, Turner, Brake, Paterson

Date: Wednesday 21/03/1979
Result: **CHELTENHAM TOWN 3 GLOUCESTER CITY 4** (aet)
Competition: Gloucestershire FA Northern Senior Professional Cup Final
Teamsheet: Main, Davies, Brake, GD Mockridge, DC Mockridge, Turner, Hall, Paterson, Griffin, Evans, Bruton
Substitutes: Shatford (for Hall), Northover (for Griffin)
Scorers: Griffin, Bruton, Paterson, Davies
Attendance: 259

Date: Saturday 24/03/1979
Result: **GLOUCESTER CITY 0 CAMBRIDGE CITY 2**
Competition: Southern League Division 1 North
Teamsheet: Main, Bell, Davies, DC Mockridge, GD Mockridge, Turner, Watts, Paterson, Griffin, Evans, Bruton
Substitute: Shatford (for Griffin)
Attendance: 252

Date: Saturday 31/03/1979
Result: **OSWESTRY TOWN 1 GLOUCESTER CITY 0**
Competition: Southern League Division 1 North
Teamsheet: Lewis, Davies, Bell, DC Mockridge, GD Mockridge, Turner, Paterson, Eves, Bruton, Hall, Brake
Substitute: Wood (for -----)

Date: Tuesday 03/04/1979
Result: **GLOUCESTER CITY 1 BARRY TOWN 1**
Competition: Southern League Division 1 North
Teamsheet: Emmerson, Davies, Bell, DC Mockridge, Turner, Brake, Eves, Paterson, Bruton, Brinkworth, Griffin
Substitute: Northover (nps)
Scorer: Griffin
Attendance: 120

Date: Saturday 07/04/1979
Result: **GLOUCESTER CITY 3 KING'S LYNN 0**
Competition: Southern League Division 1 North
Teamsheet: Nicholls, Bell, Hall, DC Mockridge, GD Mockridge, Turner, Paterson, Eves, Griffin, Northover, Bruton
Substitute: Hill (nps)
Scorers: Griffin (2), Paterson
Attendance: 163

Date: Tuesday 10/04/1979
Result: **GLOUCESTER CITY 1 BROMSGROVE ROVERS 1**
Competition: Southern League Division 1 North
Teamsheet: Nicholls, Bell, Hall, DC Mockridge, GD Mockridge, Turner, Paterson, Eves, Bruton, Gardner, Griffin
Substitute: Brinkworth (nps)
Scorer: Paterson
Attendance: 123

Date: Saturday 14/04/1979
Result: **GLOUCESTER CITY 2 BANBURY UNITED 1**
Competition: Southern League Division 1 North
Teamsheet: Nicholls, Bell, Davies, DC Mockridge, GD Mockridge, Turner, Paterson, Griffin, Gardner, Hall, Bruton
Substitute: Hill (nps)
Scorers: Davies, Gardner
Attendance: 219

Date: Monday 16/04/1979
Result: **BURTON ALBION 1 GLOUCESTER CITY 1**
Competition: Southern League Division 1 North
Teamsheet: Nicholls, Hall, Davies, DC Mockridge, GD Mockridge, Turner, Paterson, Griffin, Gardner, Bruton, Brinkworth
Substitute: Hill (nps)
Scorer: Bruton

Date: Wednesday 18/04/1979
Result: **MILTON KEYNES CITY 0 GLOUCESTER CITY 7**
Competition: Southern League Division 1 North
Teamsheet: Nicholls, Davies, Rice, GD Mockridge, DC Mockridge, Turner, Paterson, Gardner, Bruton, Brinkworth, Griffin
Substitute: Hill (nps)
Scorers: GD Mockridge (2), Paterson (2), Gardner, Bruton, Griffin

Date: Saturday 21/04/1979
Result: **GLOUCESTER CITY 5 MERTHYR TYDFIL 0**
Competition: Southern League Division 1 North
Teamsheet: Nicholls, Hall, Davies, DC Mockridge, GD Mockridge, Turner, Paterson, Rice, Griffin, Gardner, Bruton
Substitute: Bell (for Griffin)
Scorers: Gardner, Griffin (3), Hall
Attendance: 410

Date: Tuesday 24/04/1979
Result: **GLOUCESTER CITY 1 BURTON ALBION 1**
Competition: Southern League Division 1 North
Teamsheet: Nicholls, Davies, Hall, DC Mockridge, GD Mockridge, Turner, Paterson, Rice, Griffin, Bruton, Gardner
Substitute: Bell (nps)
Scorer: Griffin
Attendance: 310

Date: Saturday 28/04/1979
Result: **BEDWORTH UNITED 0 GLOUCESTER CITY 2**
Competition: Southern League Division 1 North
Teamsheet: Nicholls, Davies, Bell, DC Mockridge, GD Mockridge, Turner, Paterson, Rice, Griffin, Gardner, Bruton
Substitute: Shatford (nps)
Scorers: Bruton, DC Mockridge

Date: Tuesday 01/05/1979
Result: **GLOUCESTER CITY 3 BEDFORD TOWN 1**
Competition: Southern League Division 1 North
Teamsheet: Nicholls, Davies, Bell, GD Mockridge, DC Mockridge, Turner, Brinkworth, Paterson, Griffin, Gardner, Bruton
Substitute: Shatford (nps)
Scorers: Griffin, Turner, Bruton
Attendance: 150

Date: Thursday 03/05/1979
Result: **GLOUCESTER CITY 2 KIDDERMINSTER HARRIERS 2**
Competition: Southern League Division 1 North
Teamsheet: Nicholls, Davies, Bell, DC Mockridge, GD Mockridge, Turner, Paterson, Brinkworth, Griffin, Gardner, Bruton
Substitute: Hall (nps)
Scorers: Griffin, GD Mockridge
Attendance: 268

Date: Saturday 05/05/1979
Result: **GLOUCESTER CITY 4 ENDERBY TOWN 1**
Competition: Southern League Division 1 North
Teamsheet: Nicholls, Davies, Rice, DC Mockridge, GD Mockridge, Turner, Brinkworth, Paterson, Bruton, Hall, Shatford
Substitute: Hill (nps)
Scorers: Paterson, Bruton, Hall, Shatford
Attendance: 267

Date: Monday 07/05/1979
Result: **KING'S LYNN 4 GLOUCESTER CITY 1**
Competition: Southern League Division 1 North
Teamsheet: Nicholls, Davies, Eves, DC Mockridge, GD Mockridge, Turner, Paterson, Gardner, Brinkworth, Bruton, Hall
Substitute: Hill (nps)
Scorer: Paterson
Attendance: 359

Date: Thursday 10/05/1979
Result: **GLOUCESTER CITY 2 MILTON KEYNES CITY 1**
Competition: Southern League Division 1 North
Teamsheet: Nicholls, Davies, Hall, DC Mockridge, GD Mockridge, Turner, Paterson, Brinkworth, Gardner, Evans, Bruton
Substitute: Hill (nps)
Scorers: own goal, Paterson
Attendance: 243

Appearances – G Bell 35, P Brake 29, RA Brinkworth 12, M Bruton 22, TG Davies 22(2), M Emmerson 3, JA Evans 29, JD Eves 8(1), DP Foxwell 22, CR Gardner 15(2), FH Gittings 15, KR Griffin 14, CT Hall 12, R Lewis 1, IR Main 29, K Mallender 3, DC Mockridge 18, GD Mockridge 38, LB Nicholls 13, S Northover 1(1), TJ Paterson 27, R Pepworth 23, R Perrott 10, B Perry 19, S Rice 14(2), SW Scarrott 24, CC Shatford 1(2), J Turner 46, A Watts 1, K Wood 0(1).
Others selected but did not play: R Hill.
Scorers – TJ Paterson 13, JA Evans 11, KR Griffin 11, DP Foxwell 9, M Bruton 7, GD Mockridge 7, P Brake 6, J Turner 5, TG Davies 4, CR Gardner 4, SW Scarrott 4, CT Hall 3, DC Mockridge 2, R Pepworth 2, B Perry 1, S Rice 1, CC Shatford 1, own goal 1.

SOUTHERN LEAGUE DIVISION 1 NORTH

POS	CLUB	P	W	D	L	F	A	PTS
1	GRANTHAM	38	21	10	7	70	45	52
2	MERTHYR TYDFIL	38	22	7	9	90	53	51
3	ALVECHURCH	38	20	10	8	70	42	50
4	BEDFORD TOWN	38	19	9	10	74	49	47
5	KING'S LYNN	38	17	11	10	57	46	45
6	OSWESTRY TOWN	38	18	8	12	63	43	44
7	**GLOUCESTER CITY**	**38**	**18**	**8**	**12**	**76**	**59**	**44**
8	BURTON ALBION	38	16	10	12	51	40	42
9	KIDDERMINSTER HARRIERS	38	13	14	11	70	60	40
10	BEDWORTH UNITED	38	13	14	11	41	34	40
11	TAMWORTH	38	15	8	15	47	45	38
12	STOURBRIDGE	38	15	7	16	64	61	37
13	BARRY TOWN	38	14	9	15	51	53	37
14	ENDERBY TOWN	38	14	8	16	46	55	36
15	BANBURY UNITED	38	10	13	15	42	58	33
16	WELLINGBOROUGH TOWN	38	13	6	19	50	71	32
17	CAMBRIDGE CITY	38	9	9	20	37	62	27
18	BROMSGROVE ROVERS	38	6	14	18	33	61	26
19	MILTON KEYNES CITY	38	7	9	22	37	87	23
20	CORBY TOWN	38	5	6	27	40	85	16
		760	285	190	285	1109	1109	760

SEASON 1979-1980
(Home Ground: Horton Road Stadium)

Date: Saturday 18/08/1979
Result: **MERTHYR TYDFIL 2 GLOUCESTER CITY 0**
Competition: Southern League Cup 1st Round 1st Leg
Teamsheet: Berry, Davies, Hall, DC Mockridge, GD Mockridge, Turner, Paterson, Rice, Griffin, Evans, Steel
Substitute: Gardner (nps)

Date: Tuesday 21/08/1979
Result: **GLOUCESTER CITY 1 MERTHYR TYDFIL 4**
Competition: Southern League Cup 1st Round 2nd Leg
Teamsheet: Berry, Davies, Hall, DC Mockridge, GD Mockridge, Turner, Paterson, Rice, Griffin, Gardner, Steel
Substitute: Evans (for Davies)
Scorer: Turner
Attendance: 450

Date: Saturday 25/08/1979
Result: **GLOUCESTER CITY 1 MILTON KEYNES CITY 2**
Competition: Southern League Midland Division
Teamsheet: Cole, Steel, Ferris, DC Mockridge, GD Mockridge, Turner, Rice, Paterson, Gardner, Evans, Griffin
Substitute: Watts (for Evans)
Scorer: Griffin
Attendance: 250

Date: Monday 27/08/1979
Result: **BROMSGROVE ROVERS 2 GLOUCESTER CITY 6**
Competition: Southern League Midland Division
Teamsheet: Cole, Steel, Ferris, DC Mockridge, GD Mockridge, Turner, Paterson, Rice, Sutton, Griffin, Davies
Substitute: Gardner (nps)
Scorers: Griffin (2), Turner, Paterson, Sutton (2)

Date: Saturday 01/09/1979
Result: **GLOUCESTER CITY 0 BRIDGEND TOWN 2**
Competition: FA Cup Preliminary Round
Teamsheet: Harris, Steel, Ferris, GD Mockridge, DC Mockridge, Turner, Rice, Paterson, Gardner, Griffin, Lewis
Substitute: Wood (nps)
Attendance: 314

Date: Saturday 08/09/1979
Result: **GLOUCESTER CITY 2 LLANELLI 2**
Competition: FA Trophy Preliminary Round
Teamsheet: Harris, Steel, Hall, GD Mockridge, DC Mockridge, Turner, Davies, Paterson, Sutton, Griffin, Rice
Substitute: Evans (nps)
Scorers: Paterson, GD Mockridge
Attendance: 169

Date: Tuesday 11/09/1979
Result: **GLOUCESTER CITY 7 LLANELLI 0**
Competition: FA Trophy Preliminary Round Replay
Teamsheet: Harris, Davies, Steel, GD Mockridge, DC Mockridge, Turner, Rice, Paterson, Sutton, Griffin, Evans
Substitute: Jones (nps)
Scorers: Turner, Paterson (2), Sutton (2), Griffin (2)
Attendance: 242

6 October 1979

(Photograph courtesy of Dick Etheridge)

Back row – Paul Crew-Smith, Keith Pitman, John Smith, Rob Coldray Front row – Peter Robins, Dick Etheridge, Geoff Hester

Sign here. Chairman Dick Etheridge (left) and Westbury Estates managing director Geoff Hester formally complete the takeover of Gloucester City Football Club. City directors John Smith and Rob Coldray look on.

SEASON BY SEASON

GLOUCESTER CITY 1979-1980

BACK ROW (left to right) : Bob Mursell (Manager), Roy Hillman (Coach), JohnEvans, Greg Steele, Gary Mockridge, Timmy Harris, Dave Mockridge, Neil Sutton, Bernard Tandy (Trainer).

FRONT ROW (left to right) : Selwyn Rice, Kevin Griffin, Colin Hall, Terry Paterson, John Turner, Timmy Davies.

PROGRAMME

1978-1979

PROGRAMME

1979-1980

Date: Saturday 15/09/1979
Result: **CAMBRIDGE CITY 3 GLOUCESTER CITY 2**
Competition: Southern League Midland Division
Teamsheet: Harris, Davies, GD Mockridge, DC Mockridge, Steel, Rice, Turner, Paterson, Hall, Griffin, Evans
Substitute: T Brinkworth (nps)
Scorers: Griffin, own goal

Date: Tuesday 18/09/1979
Result: **GLOUCESTER CITY 1 BARRY TOWN 0**
Competition: Southern League Midland Division
Teamsheet: Harris, Davies, Steel, GD Mockridge, DC Mockridge, Turner, Rice, Paterson, R Brinkworth, Griffin, Evans
Substitute: Hall (nps)
Scorer: Paterson
Attendance: 280

Date: Saturday 22/09/1979
Result: **GLOUCESTER CITY 1 ENDERBY TOWN 3**
Competition: Southern League Midland Division
Teamsheet: Harris, Davies, GD Mockridge, DC Mockridge, Steel, Turner, Paterson, Evans, R Brinkworth, Sutton, Griffin
Substitute: Hall (for Turner)
Scorer: Paterson
Attendance: 295

Date: Saturday 29/09/1979
Result: **WITNEY TOWN 2 GLOUCESTER CITY 2**
Competition: Southern League Midland Division
Teamsheet: Harris, Davies, GD Mockridge, DC Mockridge, Steel, Turner, Rice, Paterson, Sutton, Evans, R Brinkworth
Substitute: Griffin (for R Brinkworth)
Scorers: Turner, Evans

Date: Tuesday 02/10/1979
Result: **WELLINGBOROUGH TOWN 0 GLOUCESTER CITY 2**
Competition: Southern League Midland Division
Teamsheet: Harris, Davies, Steel, GD Mockridge, DC Mockridge, Turner, Rice, Paterson, Sutton, Evans, R Brinkworth
Substitute: Griffin (nps)
Scorer: Sutton (2)

Date: Saturday 06/10/1979
Result: **GLOUCESTER CITY 0 BANBURY UNITED 0**
Competition: Southern League Midland Division
Teamsheet: Harris, Hall, Davies, GD Mockridge, DC Mockridge, Turner, Paterson, Rice, Sutton, Evans, R Brinkworth
Substitute: Griffin (nps)
Attendance: 275

Date: Saturday 13/10/1979
Result: **GLOUCESTER CITY 2 REDDITCH UNITED 2**
Competition: FA Trophy 1st Qualifying Round
Teamsheet: Harris, Davies, Hall, GD Mockridge, DC Mockridge, Turner, Rice, Griffin, Sutton, Evans, R Brinkworth
Substitute: Steel (nps)
Scorers: Evans, Griffin
Attendance: 263

Date: Wednesday 17/10/1979
Result: **REDDITCH UNITED 4 GLOUCESTER CITY 3**
Competition: FA Trophy 1st Qualifying Round Replay
Teamsheet: Harris, Davies, Hall, GD Mockridge, DC Mockridge, Turner, Rice, Paterson, Sutton, Evans, R Brinkworth
Substitute: Steel (nps)
Scorer: GD Mockridge (3)
Attendance: 206

Date: Saturday 20/10/1979
Result: **GLOUCESTER CITY 0 TROWBRIDGE TOWN 2**
Competition: Southern League Midland Division
Teamsheet: Book, Davies, Hall, DC Mockridge, GD Mockridge, Paterson, Rice, Griffin, Sutton, Evans, R Brinkworth
Substitute: Steel (for R Brinkworth)
Attendance: 293

Date: Tuesday 23/10/1979
Result: **TROWBRIDGE TOWN 4 GLOUCESTER CITY 2**
Competition: Western Floodlight League
Teamsheet (from): Book, Davies, Hall, GD Mockridge, DC Mockridge, Turner, Rice, Paterson, Sutton, Evans, Burford, Griffin, R Brinkworth, Steel
Substitute: -----
Scorers: -----, -----

Date: Saturday 27/10/1979
Result: **BRIDGEND TOWN 1 GLOUCESTER CITY 1**
Competition: Southern League Midland Division
Teamsheet: Book, Steel, Hall, GD Mockridge, DC Mockridge, Turner, Paterson, Davies, Griffin, Evans, R Brinkworth
Substitute: Ferris (nps)
Scorer: Evans

Date: Saturday 03/11/1979
Result: **GLOUCESTER CITY 2 CAMBRIDGE CITY 2**
Competition: Southern League Midland Division
Teamsheet: Book, Davies, Steel, GD Mockridge, DC Mockridge, Turner, Kelly, Paterson, R Brinkworth, Evans, Griffin
Substitute: Rice (for -----)
Scorers: Turner, Paterson
Attendance: 236

Date: Saturday 10/11/1979
Result: **MINEHEAD 1 GLOUCESTER CITY 1**
Competition: Southern League Midland Division
Teamsheet: Book, Steel, Kelly, GD Mockridge, DC Mockridge, Turner, Paterson, Rice, Sutton, Evans, Davies
Substitute: R Brinkworth (nps)
Scorer: Evans

Date: Wednesday 14/11/1979
Result: **CHELTENHAM TOWN 2 GLOUCESTER CITY 1**
Competition: Southern League Midland Division
Teamsheet: Book, Steel, Kelly, GD Mockridge, DC Mockridge, Turner, Paterson, Davies, Sutton, Evans, Rice
Substitute: Risdale (nps)
Scorer: Paterson
Attendance: 335

Date: Saturday 17/11/1979
Result: **GLOUCESTER CITY 2 CORBY TOWN 1**
Competition: Southern League Midland Division
Teamsheet: Book, Kelly, Davies, GD Mockridge, DC Mockridge, Turner, Paterson, Rice, Sutton, Evans, Risdale
Substitute: Griffin (for Risdale)
Scorers: Turner, Griffin
Attendance: 209

Date: Saturday 24/11/1979
Result: **KING'S LYNN 0 GLOUCESTER CITY 0**
Competition: Southern League Midland Division
Teamsheet: Book, Davies, Kelly, GD Mockridge, DC Mockridge, Turner, Paterson, Griffin, Sutton, Evans, R Brinkworth
Substitute: Rice (nps)
Attendance: 213

Date: Tuesday 27/11/1979
Result: **GLOUCESTER CITY 5 KIDDERMINSTER HARRIERS 2**
Competition: Southern League Midland Division
Teamsheet: Book, Davies, Kelly, GD Mockridge, DC Mockridge, Turner, Rice, Paterson, Sutton, Evans, Risdale
Substitute: Boseley (nps)
Scorers: Evans (4), GD Mockridge
Attendance: 311

Date: November/December 1979
Result: **TAUNTON TOWN 1 GLOUCESTER CITY 1**
Competition: Western Floodlight League
Teamsheet: -----, -----, -----, GD Mockridge (?), DC Mockridge (?), -----, Harris, Risdale (?), -----, -----, Burford
Substitute: No sub
Scorer: Harris

Date: Tuesday 04/12/1979
Result: **GLOUCESTER CITY 0 STOURBRIDGE 3**
Competition: Southern League Midland Division
Teamsheet: Book, Davies, Kelly, GD Mockridge, DC Mockridge, Turner, Paterson, R Brinkworth, Sutton, Evans, Risdale
Substitute: Boseley (nps)
Attendance: 265

Date: Saturday 08/12/1979
Result: **BARRY TOWN 1 GLOUCESTER CITY 0**
Competition: Southern League Midland Division
Teamsheet: Book, Steel, Kelly, GD Mockridge, DC Mockridge, Boseley, Rice, Paterson, Risdale, Evans, Griffin
Substitute: R Brinkworth (nps)

Date: Wednesday 17/12/1979
Result: **GLOUCESTER CITY 2 MINEHEAD 3**
Competition: Western Floodlight League
Teamsheet: Book, Davies, Kelly, GD Mockridge, DC Mockridge, Turner, R Brinkworth, Paterson, Sutton, Evans, Griffin
Substitutes: Risdale (nps), Rice (nps)
Scorers: -----, -----

Date: Saturday 22/12/1979
Result: **TAUNTON TOWN 0 GLOUCESTER CITY 3**
Competition: Southern League Midland Division
Teamsheet: Book, Davies, Steel, GD Mockridge, DC Mockridge, Turner, Boseley, Paterson, Griffin, Evans, Risdale
Substitute: R Brinkworth (nps)
Scorers: Evans (2), Paterson

Date: Wednesday 26/12/1979
Result: **GLOUCESTER CITY 0 BEDWORTH UNITED 0**
Competition: Southern League Midland Division
Teamsheet: Book, Davies, Steel, GD Mockridge, DC Mockridge, Turner, Boseley, Paterson, Callaway, Evans, Burford
Substitute: R Brinkworth (nps)
Attendance: 242

Date: Tuesday 01/01/1980
Result: **MERTHYR TYDFIL 0 GLOUCESTER CITY 0**
Competition: Southern League Midland Division
Teamsheet: Book, Davies, Steel, GD Mockridge, DC Mockridge, Turner, Boseley, Paterson, Callaway, Evans, Risdale
Substitute: R Brinkworth (nps)

Date: Saturday 05/01/1980
Result: **GLOUCESTER CITY 2 WELLINGBOROUGH TOWN 3**
Competition: Southern League Midland Division
Teamsheet: Book, Davies, Steel, GD Mockridge, DC Mockridge, Turner, Boseley, Paterson, Risdale, Callaway, Griffin
Substitute: Evans (nps)
Scorers: Risdale, Davies
Attendance: 206

[262]

SEASON BY SEASON

Date: Saturday 12/01/1980
Result: **GLOUCESTER CITY 1 BROMSGROVE ROVERS 3**
Competition: Southern League Midland Division
Teamsheet: Book, Davies, Kelly, GD Mockridge, DC Mockridge, Turner, R Brinkworth, Paterson, Evans, Callaway, Griffin
Substitute: Burford (for Griffin)
Scorer: Paterson
Attendance: 203

Date: Saturday 26/01/1980
Result: **ALVECHURCH 1 GLOUCESTER CITY 1**
Competition: Southern League Midland Division
Teamsheet: Book, Steel, Hall, GD Mockridge, DC Mockridge, Turner, Paterson, Boseley, Callaway, Evans, Burford
Substitute: Griffin (for -----)
Scorer: Callaway

Date: Saturday 02/02/1980
Result: **GLOUCESTER CITY 3 BEDFORD TOWN 2**
Competition: Southern League Midland Division
Teamsheet: Book, Steel, Hall, DC Mockridge, GD Mockridge, Turner, Boseley, Paterson, Callaway, Evans, Burford
Substitute: Griffin (nps)
Scorers: Paterson (2), Turner
Attendance: 181

Date: Saturday 09/02/1980
Result: **ENDERBY TOWN 4 GLOUCESTER CITY 1**
Competition: Southern League Midland Division
Teamsheet: Book, Hall, Steel, GD Mockridge, DC Mockridge, Turner, Paterson, Boseley, Callaway, Evans, Burford
Substitute: Griffin (for -----)
Scorer: Callaway

Date: Tuesday 12/02/1980
Result: **BANBURY UNITED 3 GLOUCESTER CITY 5**
Competition: Southern League Midland Division
Teamsheet: Book, Hall, Steel, GD Mockridge, DC Mockridge, Turner, Boseley, Paterson, Callaway, Evans, Burford
Substitute: Griffin (nps)
Scorers: DC Mockridge (2), Boseley, Turner (pen), Evans

Date: Saturday 16/02/1980
Result: **GLOUCESTER CITY 1 WITNEY TOWN 1**
Competition: Southern League Midland Division
Teamsheet: Book, Hall, Steel, GD Mockridge, DC Mockridge, Turner, Paterson, Boseley, Callaway, Evans, Burford
Substitute: Griffin (nps)
Scorer: Callaway
Attendance: 222

Date: Saturday 23/02/1980
Result: **GLOUCESTER CITY 1 CHELTENHAM TOWN 3**
Competition: Southern League Midland Division
Teamsheet: Book, Steel, Hall, GD Mockridge, DC Mockridge, Turner, Stephens, Boseley, Paterson, Evans, Griffin
Substitute: Burford (nps)
Scorer: Paterson
Attendance: 485

Date: Tuesday 26/02/1980
Result: **GLOUCESTER CITY 1 BATH CITY 4**
Competition: Western Floodlight League
Teamsheet: Book, Steel, Davies, GD Mockridge, DC Mockridge, Turner, Boseley, Paterson, Griffin, Evans, Burford
Substitutes: Harris (for Book), Jones (nps)
Scorer: Paterson

Date: Saturday 01/03/1980
Result: **TROWBRIDGE TOWN 1 GLOUCESTER CITY 0**
Competition: Southern League Midland Division
Teamsheet: Book, Davies, Hall, GD Mockridge, DC Mockridge, Turner, Stephens, Paterson, Callaway, Evans, Burford
Substitute: Griffin (nps)

Date: Saturday 08/03/1980
Result: **GLOUCESTER CITY 1 BRIDGEND TOWN 2**
Competition: Southern League Midland Division
Teamsheet: Book, Davies, Tanner, Stroud, GD Mockridge, Turner, Paterson, Stephens, Callaway, Evans, Burford
Substitute: DC Mockridge (nps)
Scorer: Paterson
Attendance: 214

Date: Saturday 22/03/1980
Result: **GLOUCESTER CITY 0 MINEHEAD 2**
Competition: Southern League Midland Division
Teamsheet: Book, Davies, Tanner, Stroud, DC Mockridge, Turner, Stephens, Paterson, GD Mockridge, Evans, Griffin
Substitute: Boseley (nps)
Attendance: 205

Date: Tuesday 25/03/1980
Result: **GLOUCESTER CITY 3 CHELTENHAM TOWN 2** (aet)
Competition: Gloucestershire FA Northern Senior Professional Cup Final
Teamsheet: Harris, Davies, Tanner, GD Mockridge, Turner, Boseley, Paterson, Callaway, Evans, Stephens, Burford
Substitute: Stroud (nps)
Scorers: Boseley, Turner, own goal

Date: Saturday 29/03/1980
Result: **STOURBRIDGE 4 GLOUCESTER CITY 1**
Competition: Southern League Midland Division
Teamsheet: Book, Hall, Tanner, GD Mockridge, Stroud, Turner, Paterson, Boseley, Callaway, Evans, Stephens
Substitute: Burford (for Boseley)
Scorer: Paterson

Date: Thursday 03/04/1980
Result: **GLOUCESTER CITY 1 TAUNTON TOWN 0**
Competition: Southern League Midland Division
Teamsheet: Book, Davies, Tanner, DC Mockridge, GD Mockridge, Turner, Boseley, Paterson, Callaway, Evans, Burford
Substitute: Stroud (nps)
Scorer: Evans
Attendance: 187

Date: Saturday 05/04/1980
Result: **BEDWORTH UNITED 1 GLOUCESTER CITY 1**
Competition: Southern League Midland Division
Teamsheet: Book, GD Mockridge, Tanner, Stroud, DC Mockridge, Turner, Paterson, Boseley, Callaway, Evans, Burford
Substitute: Griffin (nps)
Scorer: GD Mockridge

Date: Monday 07/04/1980
Result: **GLOUCESTER CITY 1 MERTHYR TYDFIL 1**
Competition: Southern League Midland Division
Teamsheet: Book, Davies, Tanner, GD Mockridge, Boseley, Turner, Stroud, Paterson, Callaway, Evans, Burford
Substitute: Griffin (nps)
Scorer: GD Mockridge
Attendance: 294

Date: Monday 14/04/1980
Result: **BEDFORD TOWN 3 GLOUCESTER CITY 0**
Competition: Southern League Midland Division
Teamsheet: Book, Davies, Tanner, G Mockridge, Ferris, Turner, Boseley, Paterson, Griffin, Evans, Burford
Substitute: Hall (nps)

Date: Saturday 19/04/1980
Result: **GLOUCESTER CITY 3 KING'S LYNN 1**
Competition: Southern League Midland Division
Teamsheet: Harris, Davies, Tanner, GD Mockridge, D Mockridge, Hall, Boseley, Paterson, Griffin, Evans, Burford
Substitute: Ferris (nps)
Scorers: Griffin (2), Burford
Attendance: 189

Date: Tuesday 22/04/1980
Result: **CORBY TOWN 1 GLOUCESTER CITY 0**
Competition: Southern League Midland Division
Teamsheet: Book, Davies, Tanner, GD Mockridge, DC Mockridge, Ferris, Boseley, Paterson, Griffin, Evans, Jones
Substitute: Hall (nps)

Date: Thursday 24/04/1980
Result: **KIDDERMINSTER HARRIERS 1 GLOUCESTER CITY 1**
Competition: Southern League Midland Division
Teamsheet: Book, Davies, Tanner, GD Mockridge, DC Mockridge, Turner, Boseley, Paterson, Griffin, Evans, Jones
Substitute: Callaway (nps)
Scorer: own goal
Attendance: 387

Date: Thursday 01/05/1980
Result: **MILTON KEYNES CITY 3 GLOUCESTER CITY 0**
Competition: Southern League Midland Division
Teamsheet: Ferris, Davies, Hall, GD Mockridge, DC Mockridge, Turner, Boseley, Paterson, Griffin, Evans, Jones
Substitute: Harris (nps)

Date: Saturday 03/05/1980
Result: **GLOUCESTER CITY 1 ALVECHURCH 1**
Competition: Southern League Midland Division
Teamsheet: Harris, Davies, Tanner, GD Mockridge, DC Mockridge, Turner, Boseley, Paterson, Callaway, Evans, Burford
Substitute: Hall (nps)
Scorer: Paterson
Attendance: 190

Appearances – NM Berry 2, KA Book 34, SJ Boseley 23, RA Brinkworth 15, MT Burford 17(3), CJ Callaway 16, P Cole 2, TG Davies 42, JA Evans 48(1), A Ferris 6, CR Gardner 3, KR Griffin 30(4), CT Hall 20(1), T Harris 15(1), J Jones 3, J Kelly 10, K Lewis 1, DC Mockridge 49, GD Mockridge 54, TJ Paterson 52, S Rice 21(1), S Risdale 8, GR Steel 29(1), KJ Stephens 6, V Stroud 5, NF Sutton 18, K Tanner 12, J Turner 49, A Watts 0(1).
Others selected but did not play: TG Brinkworth, K Wood.
Scorers – TJ Paterson 17, JA Evans 12, KR Griffin 10, J Turner 9, GD Mockridge 7, NF Sutton 6, CJ Callaway 3, SJ Boseley 2, DC Mockridge 2, MT Burford 1, TG Davies 1, T Harris 1, S Risdale 1, own goals 3.

SOUTHERN LEAGUE MIDLAND DIVISION

POS	CLUB	P	W	D	L	F	A	PTS
1	BRIDGEND TOWN	42	28	6	8	85	39	62
2	MINEHEAD	42	22	15	5	70	42	59
3	BEDFORD TOWN	42	20	12	10	71	42	52
4	KIDDERMINSTER HARRIERS	42	23	6	13	81	59	52
5	MERTHYR TYDFIL	42	20	11	11	70	47	51
6	ENDERBY TOWN	42	21	8	13	62	50	50
7	STOURBRIDGE	42	19	11	12	67	49	49
8	ALVECHURCH	42	17	14	11	78	60	48
9	TROWBRIDGE TOWN	42	19	9	14	62	61	47
10	BROMSGROVE ROVERS	42	18	10	14	67	56	46
11	BARRY TOWN	42	15	12	15	64	58	42
12	KING'S LYNN	42	15	11	16	48	55	41
13	BANBURY UNITED	42	13	14	15	56	56	40
14	TAUNTON TOWN	42	16	8	18	55	62	40
15	WITNEY TOWN	42	10	19	13	43	45	39
16	BEDWORTH UNITED	42	12	15	15	40	42	39
17	MILTON KEYNES CITY	42	15	7	20	46	59	37
18	**GLOUCESTER CITY**	**42**	**10**	**14**	**18**	**55**	**68**	**32***
19	CHELTENHAM TOWN	42	13	5	24	49	70	31
20	WELLINGBOROUGH TOWN	42	9	7	26	54	106	25
21	CAMBRIDGE CITY	42	6	9	27	30	73	21
22	CORBY TOWN	42	5	9	28	40	94	19
		924	346	232	346	1293	1293	922

* Two points deducted for playing ineligible player.

WESTERN FLOODLIGHT LEAGUE

POS	CLUB	P	W	D	L	F	A	PTS
1	BATH CITY	4	4	0	0	9	3	8
2	TROWBRIDGE TOWN	2	1	0	1	5	4	2
3	MINEHEAD	2	1	0	1	4	4	2
4	TAUNTON TOWN	2	0	1	1	1	2	1
5	**GLOUCESTER CITY**	**4**	**0**	**1**	**3**	**6**	**12**	**1**
		14	6	2	6	25	25	14

Incomplete. Only Gloucester City and Bath City results known.

SEASON 1980-1981
(Home Ground: Horton Road Stadium)

Date: Saturday 16/08/1980
Result: **GLOUCESTER CITY 0 BEDFORD TOWN 1**
Competition: Southern League Midland Division
Teamsheet: Miles, J Davies, Dangerfield, Mockridge, Dixon, Turner, Paterson, Stephens, Bruton, Evans, Lewis
Substitute: Bouston (nps)
Attendance: 361

Date: Tuesday 19/08/1980
Result: **GLOUCESTER CITY 5 TAUNTON TOWN 1**
Competition: Southern League Cup 1st Round 1st Leg
Teamsheet: Miles, J Davies, Dangerfield, Mockridge, Dixon, Turner, Stephens, Paterson, Bruton, Evans, Lewis
Substitute: Bouston (for J Davies)
Scorers: Lewis (3), Bruton, Paterson
Attendance: 288

Date: Saturday 23/08/1980
Result: **WITNEY TOWN 0 GLOUCESTER CITY 4**
Competition: Southern League Midland Division
Teamsheet: Miles, J Davies, Dangerfield, Mockridge, Dixon, Turner, Stephens, Paterson, Bruton, Evans, Lewis
Substitute: Bouston (for -----)
Scorers: Lewis (2, 1 pen), Bruton, Paterson

Date: Wednesday 27/08/1980
Result: **TAUNTON TOWN 2 GLOUCESTER CITY 0**
Competition: Southern League Cup 1st Round 2nd Leg
Teamsheet: Miles, J Davies, Dangerfield, Bouston, Mockridge, Turner, Paterson, Boseley, Bruton, Evans, Lewis
Substitute: Williams (nps)

Date: Saturday 30/08/1980
Result: **BRIDGEND TOWN 4 GLOUCESTER CITY 0**
Competition: Southern League Midland Division
Teamsheet: Miles, J Davies, Dangerfield, Mockridge, Dixon, Turner, Burford, Paterson, Bruton, Evans, Lewis
Substitute: Bouston (nps)

Date: Tuesday 02/09/1980
Result: **GLOUCESTER CITY 3 MILTON KEYNES CITY 2**
Competition: Southern League Midland Division
Teamsheet: Miles, J Davies, Dangerfield, Mockridge, Dixon, Turner, Paterson, Stephens, Bruton, Evans, Lewis
Substitute: Bouston (for Dixon)
Scorers: Turner, Lewis, Evans
Attendance: 303

Date: Saturday 06/09/1980
Result: **GLOUCESTER CITY 1 REDDITCH UNITED 2**
Competition: Southern League Midland Division
Teamsheet: Miles, J Davies, Bouston, Mockridge, Layton, Dangerfield, Stephens, Paterson, Bruton, Evans, Lewis
Substitute: Turner (nps)
Scorer: Paterson
Attendance: 320

Date: Saturday 13/09/1980
Result: **GLOUCESTER CITY 1 DORCHESTER TOWN 0**
Competition: FA Cup 1st Qualifying Round
Teamsheet: Miles, Bouston, J Davies, Mockridge, Layton, Dangerfield, Stephens, Paterson, Bruton, Evans, Lewis
Substitute: Turner (for Mockridge)
Scorer: Paterson
Attendance: 531

Date: Saturday 20/09/1980
Result: **BROMSGROVE ROVERS 2 GLOUCESTER CITY 2**
Competition: Southern League Midland Division
Teamsheet: Miles, J Davies, Bouston, Mockridge, Layton, Dangerfield, Stephens, Paterson, Bruton, Evans, Lewis
Substitute: Turner (nps)
Scorers: Lewis, Bruton

Date: Saturday 27/09/1980
Result: **GLOUCESTER CITY 2 BEDWORTH UNITED 0**
Competition: Southern League Midland Division
Teamsheet: Miles, J Davies, Bouston, Mockridge, Layton, Dangerfield, Stephens, Paterson, Bruton, Evans, Lewis
Substitute: Turner (nps)
Scorers: Paterson, Bruton
Attendance: 294

Date: Tuesday 30/09/1980
Result: **ENDERBY TOWN 2 GLOUCESTER CITY 1**
Competition: Southern League Midland Division
Teamsheet: Miles, J Davies, Bouston, Mockridge, Layton, Dangerfield, Turner, Paterson, Bruton, Evans, Lewis
Substitute: TG Davies (nps)
Scorer: Paterson

Date: Saturday 04/10/1980
Result: **GLOUCESTER CITY 0 TROWBRIDGE TOWN 1**
Competition: FA Cup 2nd Qualifying Round
Teamsheet: Miles, Bouston, J Davies, Mockridge, Layton, Dangerfield, TG Davies, Paterson, Bruton, Evans, Lewis
Substitute: Stephens (for -----)
Attendance: 637

Date: Monday 06/10/1980
Result: **BATH CITY 3 GLOUCESTER CITY 0**
Competition: Western Floodlight League
Teamsheet: Dawes, Bouston, Mockridge, Dixon, Board, Dangerfield, Boseley, TG Davies, Jones, J Davies, Turner
Substitutes: Stephens (nps), Oldfield (nps)

Date: Saturday 11/10/1980
Result: **GLOUCESTER CITY 3 GLASTONBURY 1**
Competition: FA Trophy 1st Qualifying Round
Teamsheet: Miles, Bouston, J Davies, Mockridge, Layton, Dangerfield, Stephens, Paterson, Bruton, Evans, Lewis
Substitute: TG Davies (nps)
Scorers: Bruton (2), Lewis
Attendance: 250

Date: Wednesday 22/10/1980
Result: **MILTON KEYNES CITY 0 GLOUCESTER CITY 3**
Competition: Southern League Midland Division
Teamsheet: Miles, Bouston, Dangerfield, Mockridge, Layton, Preece, Stephens, Paterson, Lewis, Evans, Burford
Substitute: Dixon (nps)
Scorers: Evans (2), Paterson
Attendance: 329

Date: Saturday 25/10/1980
Result: **GLOUCESTER CITY 3 MINEHEAD 1**
Competition: Southern League Midland Division
Teamsheet: Miles, Bouston, Dangerfield, Mockridge, Layton, Preece, Stephens, Paterson, Lewis, Evans, Burford
Substitute: Dixon (nps)
Scorers: Lewis (2, 1 pen), Stephens
Attendance: 520

Date: Saturday 01/11/1980
Result: **ALVECHURCH 3 GLOUCESTER CITY 2**
Competition: Southern League Midland Division
Teamsheet: Miles, Bouston, Dangerfield, Mockridge, Layton, Preece, Stephens, Paterson, Lewis, Evans, Burford
Substitute: Dixon (nps)
Scorers: Preece, Lewis

Date: Saturday 08/11/1980
Result: **GLOUCESTER CITY 1 BRIDGWATER TOWN 0**
Competition: FA Trophy 2nd Qualifying Round
Teamsheet: Miles, Bouston, Dangerfield, Mockridge, Layton, Preece, Stephens, Paterson, Lewis, Evans, Burford
Substitute: Dixon (nps)
Scorer: Lewis
Attendance: 485

Date: Tuesday 11/11/1980
Result: **GLOUCESTER CITY 1 EXETER CITY 1**
Competition: Western Floodlight League
Teamsheet: Miles, Bouston, Taylor, Dixon, Layton, Preece, Stephens, Northam, Lewis, Evans, Burford
Substitutes: Mockridge (for Dixon), Paterson (for Northam)
Scorer: Mockridge

Date: Saturday 15/11/1980
Result: **BANBURY UNITED 1 GLOUCESTER CITY 1**
Competition: Southern League Midland Division
Teamsheet: Miles, Bouston, Taylor, Mockridge, Layton, Preece, Stephens, Paterson, Lewis, Evans, Burford
Substitute: Dangerfield (nps)
Scorer: Burford

Date: Tuesday 18/11/1980
Result: **GLOUCESTER CITY 4 DORCHESTER TOWN 3**
Competition: Southern League Cup 3rd Round
Teamsheet: Miles, Taylor, Bouston, Mockridge, Layton, Preece, Stephens, Paterson, Lewis, Evans, Burford
Substitute: Dangerfield (nps)
Scorers: Stephens, Burford (2), own goal
Attendance: 424

Date: Saturday 22/11/1980
Result: **GLOUCESTER CITY 2 ENDERBY TOWN 4**
Competition: Southern League Midland Division
Teamsheet: Dawes, Bouston, Taylor, Mockridge, Layton, Preece, Stephens, Paterson, Lewis, Evans, Burford
Substitute: Dangerfield (nps)
Scorers: Evans, Burford
Attendance: 409

Date: Tuesday 25/11/1980
Result: **GLOUCESTER CITY 1 TAUNTON TOWN 0**
Competition: Southern League Midland Division
Teamsheet: Miles, Bouston, Dangerfield, Mockridge, Layton, Preece, Stephens, Paterson, Lewis, Evans, Burford
Substitute: Taylor (nps)
Scorer: Stephens
Attendance: 416

Date: Saturday 29/11/1980
Result: **GRANTHAM 1 GLOUCESTER CITY 3**
Competition: FA Trophy 3rd Qualifying Round
Teamsheet: Miles, Bouston, J Davies, Mockridge, Layton, Preece, Dangerfield, Paterson, Lewis, Evans, Burford
Substitutes: Taylor (nps), Dixon (nps)
Scorer: Lewis (3, 1 pen)
Attendance: 334

Date: Tuesday 02/12/1980
Result: **GLOUCESTER CITY 1 STOURBRIDGE 0**
Competition: Southern League Midland Division
Teamsheet: Miles, Bouston, Taylor, Mockridge, Layton, Preece, Stephens, Paterson, Lewis, Feighery, Burford
Substitute: Dixon (nps)
Scorer: Paterson
Attendance: 438

Date: Saturday 06/12/1980
Result: **GLOUCESTER CITY 6 WELLINGBOROUGH TOWN 2**
Competition: Southern League Midland Division
Teamsheet: Miles, Bouston, Parsons, Mockridge, Layton, Preece, Stephens, Paterson, Lewis, Evans, Burford
Substitute: Taylor (nps)
Scorers: Preece (2), Burford, Evans, Lewis, Paterson
Attendance: 410

Date: Tuesday 09/12/1980
Result: **TROWBRIDGE TOWN 4 GLOUCESTER CITY 0**
Competition: Southern League Midland Division
Teamsheet: Dangerfield, Bouston, Parsons, Mockridge, Layton, Preece, Stephens, Paterson, Lewis, Evans, Burford
Substitute: Taylor (nps)

Date: Saturday 13/12/1980
Result: **CAMBRIDGE CITY 1 GLOUCESTER CITY 3**
Competition: Southern League Midland Division
Teamsheet: Dawes, Bouston, Parsons, Mockridge, Layton, Preece, Stephens, Paterson, Lewis, Evans, Burford
Substitute: Taylor (nps)
Scorers: Stephens, Evans, Burford

Date: Wednesday 17/12/1980
Result: **MINEHEAD 3 GLOUCESTER CITY 2**
Competition: Western Floodlight League
Teamsheet: Dawes, Taylor, Mockridge, Dixon, Prictor, Adams, Bruno, Northam, Feighery, Parsons, Evans
Substitute: Burford (nps)
Scorers: -----, -----

Date: Friday 26/12/1980
Result: **CHELTENHAM TOWN 0 GLOUCESTER CITY 0**
Competition: Southern League Midland Division
Teamsheet: Miles, Bouston, Parsons, Mockridge, Layton, Preece, Stephens, Paterson, Lewis, Evans, J Davies
Substitute: Taylor (nps)
Attendance: 1165

[267]

Date: Thursday 01/01/1981
Result: **GLOUCESTER CITY 1 BARRY TOWN 3**
Competition: Southern League Midland Division
Teamsheet: Miles, Bouston, Taylor, Parsons, Layton, Preece, Stephens, Paterson, Lewis, Evans, J Davies
Substitute: Feighery (nps)
Scorer: Stephens
Attendance: 672

Date: Saturday 03/01/1981
Result: **KIDDERMINSTER HARRIERS 3 GLOUCESTER CITY 1**
Competition: Southern League Midland Division
Teamsheet: Miles, Bouston, J Davies, Parsons, Layton, Preece, Stephens, Paterson, Lewis, Evans, Feighery
Substitute: Taylor (nps)
Scorer: Lewis
Attendance: 412

Date: Saturday 10/01/1981
Result: **LEYTONSTONE & ILFORD 7 GLOUCESTER CITY 0**
Competition: FA Trophy 1st Round
Teamsheet: Miles, Bouston, Taylor, Mockridge, Layton, Preece, Stephens, Paterson, Lewis, Evans, J Davies
Substitute: Feighery (nps)

Date: Saturday 17/01/1981
Result: **MERTHYR TYDFIL 2 GLOUCESTER CITY 3**
Competition: Southern League Midland Division
Teamsheet: Miles, Bouston, Parsons, Mockridge, Layton, Preece, Prue, Paterson, Lewis, Evans, Burford
Substitute: Stephens (nps)
Scorers: Paterson, Lewis, Burford

Date: Tuesday 20/01/1981
Result: **GLOUCESTER CITY 2 ALVECHURCH 1**
Competition: Southern League Cup 4th Round
Teamsheet: Miles, Bouston, Parsons, Mockridge, Layton, Preece, Prue, Paterson, Lewis, Evans, Burford
Substitute: J Davies (nps)
Scorers:Lewis, Paterson
Attendance: 550

Date: Saturday 24/01/1981
Result: **GLOUCESTER CITY 1 WITNEY TOWN 1**
Competition: Southern League Midland Division
Teamsheet: Miles, Bouston, Norman, Mockridge, Layton, Preece, Prue, Paterson, Lewis, Evans, Burford
Substitute: Hams (nps)
Scorer: Lewis
Attendance: 468

Date: Saturday 31/01/1981
Result: **GLOUCESTER CITY 2 TROWBRIDGE TOWN 1**
Competition: Southern League Midland Division
Teamsheet: Miles, Bouston, Parsons, Mockridge, Layton, Preece, Evans, Paterson, Lewis, Prue, Burford
Substitute: Norman (for Layton)
Scorers: Lewis, Prue
Attendance: 392

Date: Saturday 07/02/1981
Result: **REDDITCH UNITED 1 GLOUCESTER CITY 3**
Competition: Southern League Midland Division
Teamsheet: Miles, Bouston, Norman, Mockridge, Hams, Preece, Prue, Paterson, Lewis, Evans, Burford
Substitute: J Davies (nps)
Scorers: Lewis (2, 1 pen), Paterson

Date: Tuesday 10/02/1981
Result: **GLOUCESTER CITY 1 BEDFORD TOWN 3**
Competition: Southern League Cup Semi-Final 1st Leg
Teamsheet: Miles, Bouston, Parsons, Mockridge, Hams, Preece, Paterson, Prue, Lewis, Evans, Burford
Substitute: Norman (nps)
Scorer: Lewis
Attendance: 827

Date: Saturday 14/02/1981
Result: **GLOUCESTER CITY 3 BRIDGEND TOWN 2**
Competition: Southern League Midland Division
Teamsheet: Miles, Norman, Bouston, Mockridge, Hams, Evans, Preece, Paterson, Lewis, Prue, Burford
Substitute: J Davies (nps)
Scorers: Preece, Paterson, Lewis
Attendance: 329

Date: Tuesday 17/02/1981
Result: **GLOUCESTER CITY 1 TROWBRIDGE TOWN 2**
Competition: Western Floodlight League
Teamsheet: Dawes, Newman, Norman, Lewis, Hams, Adams, Stephens, J Davies, Paterson, Prue, Meecham
Substitute: Field (nps)
Scorer: Lewis

Date: Saturday 21/02/1981
Result: **BEDWORTH UNITED 0 GLOUCESTER CITY 0**
Competition: Southern League Midland Division
Teamsheet: Miles, Bouston, Norman, Mockridge, Parsons, Preece, Paterson, Evans, Lewis, Prue, Burford
Substitute: Hams (nps)

Date: Monday 23/02/1981
Result: **BEDFORD TOWN 0 GLOUCESTER CITY 1**
Competition: Southern League Cup Semi-Finals 2nd Leg
Teamsheet: Miles, Bouston, Parsons, Mockridge, Norman, Preece, Evans, Paterson, Lewis, Prue, Stephens
Substitute: J Davies (nps)
Scorer: Paterson

Date: Saturday 28/02/1981
Result: **GLOUCESTER CITY 1 BROMSGROVE ROVERS 0**
Competition: Southern League Midland Division
Teamsheet: Miles, Bouston, Parsons, Mockridge, Norman, Preece, Evans, Paterson, Lewis, Prue, Burford
Substitute: J Davies (nps)
Scorer: Evans
Attendance: 347

Date: Saturday 14/03/1981
Result: **TAUNTON TOWN 2 GLOUCESTER CITY 0**
Competition: Southern League Midland Division
Teamsheet: Miles, Bouston, Parsons, Mockridge, Norman, Prue, Evans, Paterson, Lewis, Preece, Burford
Substitute: Stephens (nps)

Date: Tuesday 17/03/1981
Result: **GLOUCESTER CITY 5 BANBURY UNITED 4**
Competition: Southern League Midland Division
Teamsheet: Miles, Bouston, Parsons, Mockridge, Norman, Prue, Evans, Paterson, Lewis, Swankie, Burford
Substitute: Preece (nps)
Scorers: Lewis (2, 1 pen), own goals (2), Paterson
Attendance: 297

Date: Tuesday 24/03/1981
Result: **CORBY TOWN 1 GLOUCESTER CITY 4**
Competition: Southern League Midland Division
Teamsheet: Dawes, Bouston, Norman, Mockridge, Hams, Preece, Evans, Paterson, Lewis, Prue, Burford
Substitute: Stephens (nps)
Scorers: Paterson (2), Hams, Burford

Date: Saturday 28/03/1981
Result: **MINEHEAD 0 GLOUCESTER CITY 2**
Competition: Southern League Midland Division
Teamsheet: Dawes, Bouston, Norman, Mockridge, Hams, Preece, Evans, Stephens, Lewis, Prue, Burford
Substitute: J Davies (nps)
Scorers: Preece, Lewis

Date: Saturday 04/04/1981
Result: **GLOUCESTER CITY 6 CORBY TOWN 2**
Competition: Southern League Midland Division
Teamsheet: Dawes, Norman, Bouston, Mockridge, Parsons, Preece, Evans, Paterson, Lewis, Doyle, Burford
Substitute: Prue (nps)
Scorers: Doyle (3), Burford, Lewis (pen), Paterson
Attendance: 350

Date: Wednesday 08/04/1981
Result: **CHELTENHAM TOWN 3 GLOUCESTER CITY 2**
Competition: Gloucestershire FA Northern Senior Professional Cup Final
Teamsheet: Dawes, Norman, Bouston, Mockridge, Hams, Preece, Evans, Paterson, Lewis, Prue, J Davies
Substitute: Parsons (nps), Doyle (nps)
Scorers: Prue, Lewis
Attendance: 431

Date: Thursday 09/04/1981
Result: **GLOUCESTER CITY 1 ALVECHURCH 2**
Competition: Southern League Midland Division
Teamsheet: Dawes, Bouston, Norman, Mockridge, Parsons, Preece, Evans, Paterson, Lewis, Doyle, Burford
Substitute: Prue (for Norman)
Scorer: Mockridge
Attendance: 585

Date: Saturday 11/04/1981
Result: **STOURBRIDGE 3 GLOUCESTER CITY 3**
Competition: Southern League Midland Division
Teamsheet: Dawes, Hams, Norman, Mockridge, Parsons, Preece, Evans, Paterson, Lewis, Doyle, Burford
Substitute: Prue (nps)
Scorers: Doyle (2), Paterson

Date: Tuesday 14/04/1981
Result: **GLOUCESTER CITY 1 KIDDERMINSTER HARRIERS 2**
Competition: Southern League Midland Division
Teamsheet: Dawes, Norman, Hams, Mockridge, Parsons, Preece, Evans, Paterson, Lewis, Prue, Doyle
Substitute: Bouston (nps)
Scorer: Evans
Attendance: 498

Date: Thursday 16/04/1981
Result: **GLOUCESTER CITY 0 MERTHYR TYDFIL 1**
Competition: Southern League Midland Division
Teamsheet: Dawes, Bouston, Norman, Mockridge, Parsons, Preece, Hams, Paterson, Lewis, Prue, Burford
Substitute: Evans (for -----)
Attendance: 375

Date: Saturday 18/04/1981
Result: **BARRY TOWN 5 GLOUCESTER CITY 2**
Competition: Southern League Midland Division
Teamsheet: Dawes, Bouston, Dangerfield, Parsons, Mockridge, Adams, Evans, Paterson, Lewis, Prue, Burford
Substitute: Leach (nps)
Scorer: Prue (2)

Date: Monday 20/04/1981
Result: **GLOUCESTER CITY 3 CHELTENHAM TOWN 4**
Competition: Southern League Midland Division
Teamsheet: Dawes, Bouston, Parsons, Mockridge, Norman, Evans, Dangerfield, Paterson, Lewis, Doyle, Feighery
Substitute: Adams (nps)
Scorers: Lewis (2), Paterson
Attendance: 845

Date: Saturday 25/04/1981
Result: **WELLINGBOROUGH TOWN 2 GLOUCESTER CITY 1**
Competition: Southern League Midland Division
Teamsheet: Dawes, Bouston, Leach, Mockridge, Parsons, Prue, Paterson, Evans, Lewis, Adams, Burford
Substitute: Norman (nps)
Scorer: Lewis

Date: Monday 27/04/1981
Result: **BEDFORD TOWN 3 GLOUCESTER CITY 2**
Competition: Southern League Midland Division
Teamsheet: Dawes, Bouston, Norman, Parsons, Adams, Prue, Evans, Paterson, Lewis, Doyle, Burford
Substitute: Mockridge (nps)
Scorers: Prue, Paterson

Date: Saturday 02/05/1981
Result: **GLOUCESTER CITY 2 CAMBRIDGE CITY 0**
Competition: Southern League Midland Division
Teamsheet: Cornwell, Bouston, Norman, Adams, Parsons, Evans, Prue, Paterson, Lewis, Mockridge, Burford
Substitute: Feighery (nps)
Scorers: Lewis, Burford
Attendance: 269

Appearances – P Adams 6, JP Board 1, SJ Boseley 2, BJ Bouston 50(3), D Bruno 1, M Bruton 13, MT Burford 37, NT Cornwell 1, DA Dangerfield 23, J Davies 20, TG Davies 3, S Dawes 17, D Dixon 8, IP Doyle 6, JA Evans 55(1), E Feighery 4, P Field 1, WK Hams 10, J Jones 1, JH Layton 29, W Leach 1, DD Lewis 58, A Meecham 1, JM Miles 40, GD Mockridge 54(1), ? Newman 1, K Norman 20(1), T Northam 2, LW Parsons 26, TJ Paterson 55(1), BJ Preece 38, ? Prictor 1, KJ Prue 22(1), KJ Stephens 29(1), IR Swankie 1, J Taylor 8, J Turner 7(1).
Others selected but did not play: N Oldfield, C Williams.
Scorers – DD Lewis 35, TJ Paterson 21, MT Burford 10, JA Evans 8, M Bruton 6, IP Doyle 5, BJ Preece 5, KJ Prue 5, KJ Stephens 5, GD Mockridge 2, WK Hams 1, J Turner 1, own goals 3.

SOUTHERN LEAGUE MIDLAND DIVISION

POS	CLUB	P	W	D	L	F	A	PTS
1	ALVECHURCH	42	26	9	7	76	40	61
2	BEDFORD TOWN	42	25	11	6	63	32	61
3	TROWBRIDGE TOWN	42	24	9	9	69	39	57
4	KIDDERMINSTER HARRIERS	42	23	9	10	67	41	55
5	BARRY TOWN	42	21	9	12	60	40	51
6	STOURBRIDGE	42	17	16	9	75	49	50
7	ENDERBY TOWN	42	21	8	13	71	47	50
8	CHELTENHAM TOWN	42	18	12	12	70	59	48
9	BROMSGROVE ROVERS	42	19	9	14	65	50	47
10	CORBY TOWN	42	19	7	16	69	58	45
11	BRIDGEND TOWN	42	19	7	16	74	64	45
12	MINEHEAD	42	19	7	16	54	60	45
13	**GLOUCESTER CITY**	**42**	**19**	**6**	**17**	**82**	**72**	**44**
14	MERTHYR TYDFIL	42	15	12	15	60	50	42
15	BEDWORTH UNITED	42	14	12	16	49	46	40
16	BANBURY UNITED	42	11	11	20	51	65	33
17	TAUNTON TOWN	42	10	9	23	48	68	29
18	CAMBRIDGE CITY	42	8	12	22	46	87	28
19	WITNEY TOWN	42	9	9	24	44	65	27
20	WELLINGBOROUGH TOWN	42	10	7	25	43	91	27
21	REDDITCH UNITED	42	11	4	27	54	92	26
22	MILTON KEYNES CITY	42	3	7	32	28	103	13
		924	361	202	361	1318	1318	924

WESTERN FLOODLIGHT LEAGUE

POS	CLUB	P	W	D	L	F	A	PTS
1	TROWBRIDGE TOWN	2	2	0	0	4	1	4
2	BATH CITY	4	2	0	2	6	4	4
3	MINEHEAD	2	2	0	0	4	2	4
4	EXETER CITY	2	0	1	1	2	4	1
5	**GLOUCESTER CITY**	**4**	**0**	**1**	**3**	**4**	**9**	**1**
		14	6	2	6	20	20	14

Incomplete. Only Gloucester City and Bath City results known.

1980-1981
Dave Lewis receiving the Match Ball Trophy from the Mayor of Gloucester, Councillor Miss Freda Wilton, as a momento of the occasion when he scored his 300th goal in Southern League Football before the match against his previous club Cheltenham Town.
Left to Right: J.M. Purves, Chairman Cheltenham Town, Dave Lewis, Bobby Campbell Manager Gloucester City, The Mayor of Gloucester, Alan Grundy Manager Cheltenham Town and Geoff Hester Chairman Gloucester City

1981
A visit from Terry Wogan. Note he is wearing the City club tie.
With him in the forefront are on the left Westbury Estates Director and Vice President Member, Richard Fraser and to the right Club Director Brian Howe

(Home Ground: Horton Road Stadium)

Date: Tuesday 11/08/1981
Result: **GLOUCESTER CITY 6 CHELTENHAM TOWN 2**
Competition: Gloucestershire FA Northern Senior Professional Cup Final
Teamsheet: Miles, Ryan, Parsons, Mockridge, Blockley, Evans, Brown, Paterson, Lewis, Doyle, Burford
Substitute: Cornwell (nps)
Scorers: Burford, Lewis (3, 2 pens), Doyle, Paterson
Attendance: 608

Date: Saturday 15/08/1981
Result: **ENDERBY TOWN 5 GLOUCESTER CITY 1**
Competition: Southern League Midland Division
Teamsheet: Miles, Ryan, Parsons, Mockridge, Blockley, Paterson, Brown, Doyle, Lewis, Evans, Burford
Substitute: CR Gardner (nps)
Scorer: Paterson

Date: Tuesday 18/08/1981
Result: **GLOUCESTER CITY 0 MERTHYR TYDFIL 0**
Competition: Southern League Cup 1st Round 1st Leg
Teamsheet: Cornwell, Ryan, Parsons, Mockridge, Blockley, Brown, Bruton, Paterson, Lewis, Doyle, Burford
Substitute: Evans (nps)
Attendance: 489

Date: Saturday 22/08/1981
Result: **GLOUCESTER CITY 2 WELLINGBOROUGH TOWN 2**
Competition: Southern League Midland Division
Teamsheet: Cornwell, Ryan, Parsons, Mockridge, Blockley, Bruton, Brown, Paterson, Lewis, Doyle, Burford
Substitute: Evans (for Lewis)
Scorers: Bruton, Paterson
Attendance: 361

Date: Tuesday 25/08/1981
Result: **GLOUCESTER CITY 0 ALVECHURCH 1**
Competition: Southern League Midland Division
Teamsheet: Cornwell, Ryan, Parsons, Mockridge, Blockley, Brown, Bruton, Paterson, CR Gardner, Doyle, Evans
Substitute: Burford (for CR Gardner)
Attendance: 425

Date: Saturday 29/08/1981
Result: **TAUNTON TOWN 1 GLOUCESTER CITY 3**
Competition: Southern League Midland Division
Teamsheet: Cornwell, Ryan, Parsons, Bruton, Blockley, Adams, Brown, Paterson, Lewis, Doyle, Burford
Substitute: Mockridge (nps)
Scorers: Bruton, Paterson, Doyle

Date: Monday 31/08/1981
Result: **MERTHYR TYDFIL 1 GLOUCESTER CITY 1**
Competition: Southern League Cup 1st Round 2nd Leg
Teamsheet: Cornwell, Ryan, Parsons, Mockridge, Blockley, Brown, Bruton, Paterson, Lewis, Doyle, Burford
Substitute: Evans (nps)
Scorer: Mockridge

Date: Saturday 05/09/1981
Result: **CLANDOWN 1 GLOUCESTER CITY 3**
Competition: FA Cup Preliminary Round
Teamsheet: Cornwell, Ryan, Parsons, Mockridge, Blockley, Bruton, Brown, Paterson, Lewis, Doyle, Burford
Substitute: Evans (nps)
Scorers: Blockley, Doyle, Lewis
Attendance: 246

Date: Tuesday 08/09/1981
Result: **BRIDGEND TOWN 0 GLOUCESTER CITY 0**
Competition: Southern League Midland Division
Teamsheet: Cornwell, Ryan, Parsons, Mockridge, Blockley, Brown, Bruton, Paterson, Evans, Doyle, Burford
Substitute: Lewis (nps)

Date: Saturday 12/09/1981
Result: **BEDWORTH UNITED 0 GLOUCESTER CITY 1**
Competition: Southern League Midland Division
Teamsheet: Cornwell, Ryan, Parsons, Mockridge, Blockley, Bruton, Brown, Paterson, Evans, Doyle, Burford
Substitute: Lewis (nps)
Scorer: Doyle

Date: Tuesday 15/09/1981
Result: **GLOUCESTER CITY 2 BARRY TOWN 2**
Competition: Southern League Midland Division
Teamsheet: Cornwell, Ryan, Parsons, Mockridge, Blockley, Bruton, Brown, Paterson, Evans, Doyle, Burford
Substitute: Lewis (for Mockridge)
Scorer: Lewis (2)
Attendance: 390

Date: Saturday 19/09/1981
Result: **GLOUCESTER CITY 2 FOREST GREEN ROVERS 1**
Competition: FA Cup 1st Qualifying Round
Teamsheet: Cornwell, Ryan, Parsons, Bruton, Blockley, Brown, Mockridge, Paterson, Evans, Doyle, Lewis
Substitute: Burford (nps)
Scorers: Lewis, Evans
Attendance: 700

Date: Saturday 26/09/1981
Result: **GLOUCESTER CITY 2 CORBY TOWN 0**
Competition: Southern League Midland Division
Teamsheet: Cornwell, Ryan, Mockridge, Blockley, Bruton, Brown, CR Gardner, Paterson, Lewis, Doyle, Evans
Substitute: Burford (nps)
Scorers: Lewis, Paterson
Attendance: 352

Date: Monday 28/09/1981
Result: **MERTHYR TYDFIL 0 GLOUCESTER CITY 0** (6-5 pens)
Competition: Southern League Cup 1st Round Replay
Teamsheet: Cornwell, CR Gardner, Parsons, Mockridge, Blockley, Brown, Bruton, Paterson, Lewis, Evans, Doyle
Substitute: Burford (for -----)

Date: Saturday 03/10/1981
Result**: GLOUCESTER CITY 2 DEVIZES TOWN 4**
Competition: FA Cup 2nd Qualifying Round
Teamsheet: Cornwell, Brown, Mockridge, Bruton, Blockley, CR Gardner, Lewis, Paterson, Evans, Doyle, Burford
Substitute: Adams (for Burford)
Scorer: Doyle (2)
Attendance: 389

Date: Saturday 10/10/1981
Result: **NUNEATON BOROUGH 3 GLOUCESTER CITY 0**
Competition: Southern League Midland Division
Teamsheet: Cornwell, Ryan, Mockridge, Adams, Bruton, Evans, Brown, Paterson, Lewis, Doyle, Burford
Substitute: Feighery (for Ryan)

Date: Friday 16/10/1981
Result: **GLOUCESTER CITY 3 BANBURY UNITED 0**
Competition: Southern League Midland Division
Teamsheet: Cornwell, Brown, Mockridge, Bruton, Adams, Leach, CR Gardner, Paterson, Lewis, Doyle, Burford
Substitute: Feighery (nps)
Scorers: Lewis (2), CR Gardner
Attendance: 328

Date: Tuesday 20/10/1981
Result: **GLOUCESTER CITY 2 MERTHYR TYDFIL 0**
Competition: Southern League Midland Division
Teamsheet: Cornwell, Evans, Mockridge, Bruton, Adams, Brown, CR Gardner, Paterson, Lewis, Doyle, Burford
Substitute: Feighery (nps)
Scorers: Bruton, Lewis
Attendance: 392

Date: Saturday 24/10/1981
Result: **GLOUCESTER CITY 2 SALISBURY 1**
Competition: FA Trophy 1st Qualifying Round
Teamsheet: Cornwell, Ryan, Mockridge, Adams, Bruton, Brown, CR Gardner, Paterson, Evans, Doyle, Burford
Substitute: Feighery (for Doyle)
Scorers: Evans, Feighery
Attendance: 324

Date: Saturday 07/11/1981
Result: **GLOUCESTER CITY 3 CAMBRIDGE CITY 0**
Competition: Southern League Midland Division
Teamsheet: Cornwell, Ryan, Mockridge, Parsons, Bruton, Brown, Evans, Paterson, Lewis, Doyle, Burford
Substitute: CR Gardner (nps)
Scorers: Bruton, Burford, Lewis
Attendance: 329

Date: Tuesday 10/11/1981
Result: **GLOUCESTER CITY 2 SALISBURY 0**
Competition: Southern League Cup 3rd Round
Teamsheet: Cornwell, Ryan, Parsons, Mockridge, Bruton, Brown, Evans, Paterson, Lewis, Doyle, Burford
Substitute: CR Gardner (nps)
Scorers: Brown, Ryan
Attendance: 343

Date: Saturday 14/11/1981
Result: **MILTON KEYNES CITY 1 GLOUCESTER CITY 1**
Competition: Southern League Midland Division
Teamsheet: Cornwell, Ryan, Mockridge, Parsons, Bruton, Brown, Evans, Paterson, Lewis, Doyle, C Gardner
Substitute: Feighery (nps)
Scorer: Doyle

Date: Saturday 21/11/1981
Result: **GLOUCESTER CITY 2 WITNEY TOWN 0**
Competition: Southern League Midland Division
Teamsheet: Cornwell, Ryan, Mockridge, Parsons, Bruton, Brown, Paterson, Wheeler, Lewis, Doyle, Foxwell
Substitute: Evans (nps)
Scorers: Doyle, Paterson
Attendance: 335

Date: Tuesday 24/11/1981
Result: **GLOUCESTER CITY 1 STOURBRIDGE 1**
Competition: Southern League Midland Division
Teamsheet: Cornwell, Ryan, Mockridge, Parsons, Bruton, Brown, Paterson, Wheeler, Lewis, Doyle, Foxwell
Substitute: Evans (nps)
Scorer: Doyle
Attendance: 421

Date: Saturday 28/11/1981
Result: **GLOUCESTER CITY 4 MAESTEG PARK 0**
Competition: FA Trophy 2nd Qualifying Round
Teamsheet: Cornwell, Ryan, Mockridge, Parsons, Bruton, Brown, Lewis, Paterson, Evans, Doyle, Burford
Substitute: CR Gardner (nps)
Scorers: own goal, Lewis, Burford, Doyle
Attendance: 309

Date: Saturday 05/12/1981
Result: **MINEHEAD 0 GLOUCESTER CITY 2**
Competition: Southern League Midland Division
Teamsheet: Cornwell, Ryan, Mockridge, Parsons, Bruton, Brown, Wheeler, Paterson, Lewis, Doyle, Burford
Substitute: Foxwell (for Burford)
Scorers: Doyle, Bruton

Date: Tuesday 22/12/1981
Result: **BRIDGEND TOWN 0 GLOUCESTER CITY 3**
Competition: FA Trophy 3rd Qualifying Round
Teamsheet: Cornwell, Ryan, Mockridge, Bruton, Parsons, Brown, Paterson, Wheeler, Lewis, Foxwell, Burford
Substitute: Evans (nps)
Scorers: Paterson, Burford, Foxwell
Attendance: 44

Date: Monday 28/12/1981
Result: **GLOUCESTER CITY 2 CHELTENHAM TOWN 1**
Competition: Southern League Midland Division
Teamsheet: Cornwell, Ryan, Mockridge, Parsons, Bruton, Brown, Wheeler, Paterson, Lewis, Doyle, Burford
Substitute: Evans (nps)
Scorers: Wheeler, Paterson
Attendance: 1063

Date: Wednesday 20/01/1982
Result: **WEALDSTONE 3 GLOUCESTER CITY 1**
Competition: FA Trophy 1st Round
Teamsheet: Cornwell, Ryan, Mockridge, Bruton, Parsons, Brown, Evans, Paterson, Doyle, Wheeler, Burford
Substitute: Foxwell (for Burford)
Scorer: Wheeler
Attendance: 470

Date: Saturday 23/01/1982
Result: **GLOUCESTER CITY 2 MINEHEAD 0**
Competition: Southern League Midland Division
Teamsheet: Cornwell, Ryan, Mockridge, Parsons, Bruton, Wheeler, Brown, Paterson, Lewis, Doyle, Foxwell
Substitute: CR Gardner (for Mockridge)
Scorer: Lewis (2, 1 pen)
Attendance: 313

Date: Tuesday 26/01/1982
Result: **GLOUCESTER CITY 1 WITNEY TOWN 1**
Competition: Southern League Cup 4th Round
Teamsheet: Cornwell, Ryan, Mockridge, Parsons, Adams, Brown, Wheeler, Paterson, Lewis, Foxwell, Burford
Substitute: CR Gardner (nps)
Scorer: Lewis
Attendance: 373

Date: Saturday 30/01/1982
Result: **CAMBRIDGE CITY 0 GLOUCESTER CITY 1**
Competition: Southern League Midland Division
Teamsheet: Cornwell, Ryan, Mockridge, Parsons, Adams, Brown, Wheeler, Paterson, Lewis, Foxwell, Burford
Substitute: Evans (nps)
Scorer: Paterson

Date: Tuesday 02/02/1982
Result: **WITNEY TOWN 0 GLOUCESTER CITY 2**
Competition: Southern League Cup 4th Round Replay
Teamsheet: Cornwell, Ryan, Mockridge, Parsons, Adams, Brown, Wheeler, Paterson, Lewis, Foxwell, Burford
Substitute: Evans (nps)
Scorers: Adams, Lewis

Date: Saturday 06/02/1982
Result: **GLOUCESTER CITY 2 TAUNTON TOWN 4**
Competition: Southern League Midland Division
Teamsheet: Cornwell, Ryan, Mockridge, Parsons, Adams, Brown, Wheeler, Paterson, Lewis, Foxwell, Burford
Substitute: Prince (for -----)
Scorers: Lewis (pen), Foxwell
Attendance: 250

Date: Tuesday 09/02/1982
Result: **MINEHEAD 3 GLOUCESTER CITY 2**
Competition: Western Floodlight League
Teamsheet: Tilling, NH Gardner, Leach, Gannon, Medcroft, Brown, Evans, Locke, Westlake, Gayle, CR Gardner
Substitutes: M Williams (nps), H Williams (nps), Browning (nps)
Scorers: CR Gardner, Westlake

Date: Wednesday 10/02/1982
Result: **WELLINGBOROUGH TOWN 2 GLOUCESTER CITY 0**
Competition: Southern League Midland Division
Teamsheet: Cornwell, Brown, Mockridge, Parsons, Adams, Wheeler, Paterson, Foxwell, Lewis, Doyle, Burford
Substitute: Ryan (for Burford)

Date: Saturday 13/02/1982
Result: **CORBY TOWN 2 GLOUCESTER CITY 1**
Competition: Southern League Midland Division
Teamsheet: Cornwell, Evans, Mockridge, Parsons, Bruton, Wheeler, Brown, Paterson, Lewis, Foxwell, CR Gardner
Substitute: Adams (for Lewis)
Scorer: Foxwell

Date: Tuesday 16/02/1982
Result: **GLOUCESTER CITY 0 AYLESBURY UNITED 0**
Competition: Southern League Cup Semi-Final 1st Leg
Teamsheet: Cornwell, Brown, Mockridge, Bruton, Parsons, Adams, Paterson, CR Gardner, Lewis, Foxwell, Burford
Substitute: Wheeler (nps)
Attendance: 628

Date: Saturday 20/02/1982
Result: **GLOUCESTER CITY 0 BEDWORTH UNITED 0**
Competition: Southern League Midland Division
Teamsheet: Cornwell, Adams, Mockridge, Parsons, Bruton, Brown, CR Gardner, Paterson, Foxwell, Doyle, Burford
Substitute: Wheeler (nps)
Attendance: 317

Date: Wednesday 24/02/1982
Result: **AYLESBURY UNITED 0 GLOUCESTER CITY 1**
Competition: Southern League Cup Semi-Final 2nd Leg
Teamsheet: Cornwell, Adams, Mockridge, Parsons, Bruton, Brown, CR Gardner, Foxwell, Lewis, Doyle, Burford
Substitute: Paterson (nps)
Scorer: Doyle

Date: Saturday 27/02/1982
Result: **GLOUCESTER CITY 0 NUNEATON BOROUGH 2**
Competition: Southern League Midland Division
Teamsheet: Cornwell, Adams, Mockridge, Parsons, Bruton, Brown, CR Gardner, Foxwell, Lewis, Day, Burford
Substitute: Wheeler (nps)
Attendance: 472

Date: Tuesday 02/03/1982
Result: **GLOUCESTER CITY 3 ENDERBY TOWN 3**
Competition: Southern League Midland Division
Teamsheet: Cornwell, Adams, Mockridge, Parsons, Bruton, Brown, Paterson, Wheeler, Lewis, Doyle, Evans
Substitute: Burford (nps)
Scorers: Paterson, Lewis (2)
Attendance: 289

Date: Saturday 06/03/1982
Result: **BANBURY UNITED 0 GLOUCESTER CITY 4**
Competition: Southern League Midland Division
Teamsheet: Cornwell, Adams, Mockridge, Parsons, Bruton, Brown, Paterson, Evans, Lewis, Wheeler, Burford
Substitute: CR Gardner (nps)
Scorers: Wheeler (2), Burford, Paterson

Date: Saturday 13/03/1982
Result: **MERTHYR TYDFIL 1 GLOUCESTER CITY 3**
Competition: Southern League Midland Division
Teamsheet: Cornwell, Adams, Mockridge, Parsons, Bruton, Brown, Paterson, Evans, Lewis, Wheeler, Burford
Substitute: CR Gardner (nps)
Scorers: Wheeler (2), Lewis

Date: Wednesday 17/03/1982
Result: **ALVECHURCH 3 GLOUCESTER CITY 0**
Competition: Southern League Midland Division
Teamsheet: Cornwell, Adams, Mockridge, Parsons, Bruton, Brown, Paterson, Evans, Lewis, Wheeler, Burford
Substitute: CR Gardner (nps)

Date: Saturday 20/03/1982
Result: **GLOUCESTER CITY 2 BEDFORD TOWN 1**
Competition: Southern League Midland Division
Teamsheet: Cornwell, Brown, Mockridge, Parsons, Bruton, CR Gardner, Paterson, Evans, Lewis, Wheeler, Foxwell
Substitute: Doyle (for -----)
Scorer: Lewis (2, 1 pen)
Attendance: 279

Date: Monday 22/03/1982
Result: **KIDDERMINSTER HARRIERS 1 GLOUCESTER CITY 0**
Competition: Southern League Midland Division
Teamsheet: Cornwell, Adams, Mockridge, Parsons, Layton, Brown, Griffiths, Evans, Lewis, Wheeler, Burford
Substitute: CR Gardner (for Parsons)
Attendance: 569

Date: Saturday 27/03/1982
Result: **STOURBRIDGE 2 GLOUCESTER CITY 0**
Competition: Southern League Midland Division
Teamsheet: Cornwell, Brown, Mockridge, Parsons, Bruton, Wheeler, Griffiths, Evans, Lewis, Doyle, Burford
Substitute: Paterson (for Mockridge)

Date: Tuesday 30/03/1982
Result: **BROMSGROVE ROVERS 1 GLOUCESTER CITY 1**
Competition: Southern League Midland Division
Teamsheet: Cornwell, Brown, Parsons, Bruton, Layton, Evans, Griffiths, Paterson, Doyle, Wheeler, Burford
Substitute: Lewis (nps)
Scorer: Burford (pen)

Date: Thursday 01/04/1982
Result: **GLOUCESTER CITY 6 BRIDGEND TOWN 0**
Competition: Southern League Midland Division
Teamsheet: Cornwell, Brown, Parsons, Layton, Bruton, Griffiths, Paterson, Evans, Doyle, Wheeler, Burford
Substitute: Lewis (nps)
Scorers: Burford (pen), Bruton, Paterson, Wheeler, Evans (2)
Attendance: 272

Date: Saturday 03/04/1982
Result: **GLOUCESTER CITY 3 MILTON KEYNES CITY 2**
Competition: Southern League Midland Division
Teamsheet: Cornwell, Brown, Parsons, Layton, Bruton, Griffiths, Paterson, Evans, Doyle, Wheeler, Burford
Substitute: Lewis (for Doyle)
Scorers: Burford, Paterson, Lewis
Attendance: 348

Date: Monday 05/04/1982
Result: **GLOUCESTER CITY 0 WEALDSTONE 1**
Competition: Southern League Cup Final 1st Leg
Teamsheet: Cornwell, Brown, Parsons, Bruton, Layton, Griffiths, Paterson, Evans, Doyle, Wheeler, Burford
Substitute: Lewis (nps)
Attendance: 2300

Date: Friday 09/04/1982
Result: **BARRY TOWN 3 GLOUCESTER CITY 0**
Competition: Southern League Midland Division
Teamsheet: Cornwell, Brown, Parsons, Bruton, Layton, Griffiths, Paterson, Evans, Doyle, Wheeler, Burford
Substitute: Lewis (nps)

Date: Saturday 10/04/1982
Result: **GLOUCESTER CITY 1 BROMSGROVE ROVERS 0**
Competition: Southern League Midland Division
Teamsheet: Cornwell, Brown, Mockridge, Bruton, Layton, Evans, Griffiths, Paterson, Doyle, Lewis, Foxwell
Substitute: CR Gardner (nps)
Scorer: Evans
Attendance: 302

Date: Monday 12/04/1982
Result: **CHELTENHAM TOWN 1 GLOUCESTER CITY 3**
Competition: Southern League Midland Division
Teamsheet: Cornwell, Brown, Mockridge, Bruton, Layton, Griffiths, Paterson, Evans, Lewis, Doyle, Foxwell
Substitute: Wheeler (for -----)
Scorers: Layton, Lewis (pen), Evans
Attendance: 800

Date: Wednesday 14/04/1982
Result: **WEALDSTONE 1 GLOUCESTER CITY 0**
Competition: Southern League Cup Final 2nd Leg
Teamsheet: Cornwell, Brown, Mockridge, Bruton, Layton, Griffiths, Paterson, Evans, Doyle, Wheeler, Burford
Substitute: Lewis (nps)

Date: Saturday 17/04/1982
Result: **WITNEY TOWN 1 GLOUCESTER CITY 2**
Competition: Southern League Midland Division
Teamsheet: Cornwell, Griffiths, Mockridge, Bruton, Layton, Brown, Evans, Paterson, Doyle, Wheeler, Burford
Substitute: Lewis (nps)
Scorers: Wheeler, Bruton

Date: Wednesday 21/04/1982
Result: **BEDFORD TOWN 0 GLOUCESTER CITY 0**
Competition: Southern League Midland Division
Teamsheet: Cornwell, Griffiths, Mockridge, Bruton, Layton, Brown, Evans, Paterson, Doyle, Wheeler, Burford
Substitute: Lewis (nps)

Date: Saturday 24/04/1982
Result: **GLOUCESTER CITY 1 KIDDERMINSTER HARRIERS 0**
Competition: Southern League Midland Division
Teamsheet: Cornwell, Griffiths, Mockridge, Bruton, Layton, Evans, Brown, Paterson, Doyle, Wheeler, Burford
Substitute: Lewis (for Burford)
Scorer: Doyle
Attendance: 370

Date: Tuesday 27/04/1982
Result: **GLOUCESTER CITY 1 REDDITCH UNITED 0**
Competition: Southern League Midland Division
Teamsheet: Cornwell, Griffiths, Paterson, Mockridge, Bruton, CR Gardner, Brown, Lewis, Doyle, Wheeler, Foxwell
Substitute: Evans (nps)
Scorer: Bruton
Attendance: 250

Date: Saturday 01/05/1982
Result: **REDDITCH UNITED 2 GLOUCESTER CITY 1**
Competition: Southern League Midland Division
Teamsheet: Cornwell, Griffiths, Mockridge, Bruton, Layton, Brown, Evans, Paterson, Doyle, Wheeler, Burford
Substitute: Lewis (nps)
Scorer: Burford

Appearances – P Adams 19(2), JP Blockley 15, R Brown 61, DE Bruton 48, MT Burford 46(2), NT Cornwell 58, GG Day 1, IP Doyle 47(1), JA Evans 39(1), E Feighery 0(2), DP Foxwell 18(2), A Gannon 1, CR Gardner 16(2), NH Gardner 1, ? Gayle 1, AR Griffiths 15, JH Layton 13, W Leach 2, DD Lewis 43(3), P Locke 1, G Medcroft 1, JM Miles 2, GD Mockridge 55, LW Parsons 46, TJ Paterson 56(1), FA Prince 0(1), NR Ryan 30(1), ? Tilling 1, M Westlake 1, M Wheeler 31(1).
Others selected but did not play: G Browning, H, Williams, M Williams.
Scorers – DD Lewis 26, TJ Paterson 14, IP Doyle 13, MT Burford 10, DE Bruton 9, M Wheeler 8, JA Evans 6, DP Foxwell 3, R Brown 2, CR Gardner 2, P Adams 1, JP Blockley 1, E Feighery 1, JH Layton 1, GD Mockridge 1, NR Ryan 1, M Westlake 1, own goal 1.

SOUTHERN LEAGUE MIDLAND DIVISION

POS	CLUB	P	W	D	L	F	A	PTS
1	NUNEATON BOROUGH	42	27	11	4	88	32	65
2	ALVECHURCH	42	26	10	6	79	34	62
3	KIDDERMINSTER HARRIERS	42	22	12	8	71	40	56
4	STOURBRIDGE	42	21	10	11	69	47	52
5	**GLOUCESTER CITY**	**42**	**21**	**9**	**12**	**64**	**48**	**51**
6	BEDWORTH UNITED	42	20	10	12	59	40	50
7	ENDERBY TOWN	42	20	10	12	79	66	50
8	WITNEY TOWN	42	19	8	15	71	49	46
9	BARRY TOWN	42	16	14	12	59	46	46
10	CORBY TOWN	42	19	8	15	70	59	46
11	MERTHYR TYDFIL	42	16	12	14	63	54	44
12	WELLINGBOROUGH TOWN	42	15	12	15	50	45	42
13	BRIDGEND TOWN	42	13	13	16	50	62	39
14	BROMSGROVE ROVERS	42	15	8	19	57	63	38
15	BEDFORD TOWN	42	12	13	17	45	54	37
16	CHELTENHAM TOWN	42	11	14	17	65	68	36
17	TAUNTON TOWN	42	12	8	22	46	76	32
18	BANBURY UNITED	42	11	8	23	63	91	30
19	MINEHEAD	42	12	6	24	38	69	30
20	CAMBRIDGE CITY	42	10	8	24	39	80	28
21	MILTON KEYNES CITY	42	6	11	25	34	70	23
22	REDDITCH UNITED	42	8	5	29	37	103	21
		924	352	220	352	1296	1296	924

WESTERN FLOODLIGHT LEAGUE

POS	CLUB	P	W	D	L	F	A	PTS
1	MINEHEAD	1	1	0	0	3	2	2
2	**GLOUCESTER CITY**	1	0	0	1	2	3	0
3	FROME TOWN							
		2	1	0	1	5	5	2

Incomplete. Not all fixtures completed. Indications are that Gloucester City v Frome Town cancelled.

SEASON 1982-1983
(Home Ground: Horton Road Stadium)

Date: Saturday 21/08/1982
Result: **GLOUCESTER CITY 1 STOURBRIDGE 0**
Competition: Southern League Premier Division
Teamsheet: Cornwell, Griffiths, Davies, Layton, DE Bruton, Evans, Williams, Hopkins, Cunningham, DJ Jones, Stirland
Substitute: Burford (nps)
Scorer: Stirland
Attendance: 466

Date: Tuesday 24/08/1982
Result: **GLOUCESTER CITY 1 FOREST GREEN ROVERS 2**
Competition: Southern League Cup 1st Round 1st Leg
Teamsheet: Cornwell, Griffiths, Davies, DE Bruton, Layton, Williams, Hopkins, Evans, DJ Jones, Cunningham, Stirland
Substitute: Burford (for -----)
Scorer: DJ Jones
Attendance: 818

Date: Saturday 28/08/1982
Result: **GLOUCESTER CITY 3 GRAVESEND & NORTHFLEET 4**
Competition: Southern League Premier Division
Teamsheet: Cornwell, Griffiths, Davies, DE Bruton, Layton, Williams, Hopkins, DJ Jones, Cunningham, Stirland, Burford
Substitute: Evans (nps)
Scorers: Stirland (2), Burford
Attendance: 420

Date: Saturday 04/09/1982
Result: **HASTINGS UNITED 2 GLOUCESTER CITY 1**
Competition: Southern League Premier Division
Teamsheet: Cornwell, Griffiths, Davies, DE Bruton, Layton, Williams, Hopkins, Cunningham, DJ Jones, Stirland, Burford
Substitute: Preece (nps)
Scorer: Stirland

Date: Tuesday 07/09/1982
Result: **FOREST GREEN ROVERS 3 GLOUCESTER CITY 2**
Competition: Southern League Cup 1st Round 2nd Leg
Teamsheet: Cornwell, Griffiths, Ledbury, DE Bruton, Layton, Williams, Hopkins, Cunningham, DJ Jones, Stirland, Burford
Substitute: Preece (nps)
Scorers: Burford, Cunningham
Attendance: 1000

[278]

Date: Saturday 11/09/1982
Result: **GLOUCESTER CITY 1 CORBY TOWN 1**
Competition: Southern League Premier Division
Teamsheet: GA Jones, Griffiths, Davies, DE Bruton, Layton, Williams, Hopkins, Cunningham, DJ Jones, Stirland, Burford
Substitute: Preece (nps)
Scorer: Stirland
Attendance: 323

Date: Saturday 18/09/1982
Result: **GLOUCESTER CITY 1 LLANELLI 0**
Competition: FA Cup 1st Qualifying Round
Teamsheet: GA Jones, Ledbury, Davies, Layton, DE Bruton, Williams, Preece, DJ Jones, Stirland, Cunningham, Evans
Substitute: Hopkins (nps)
Scorer: Williams
Attendance: 300

Date: Saturday 25/09/1982
Result: **GLOUCESTER CITY 2 WATERLOOVILLE 2**
Competition: Southern League Premier Division
Teamsheet: Cornwell, Griffiths, Davies, DE Bruton, Layton, Williams, Hopkins, Overson, DJ Jones, Stirland, Cunningham
Substitute: Burford (for Overson)
Scorers: Cunningham, Williams
Attendance: 325

Date: Saturday 02/10/1982
Result: **CHELTENHAM TOWN 5 GLOUCESTER CITY 1**
Competition: FA Cup 2nd Qualifying Round
Teamsheet: Gwinnett, Ledbury, Burford, Griffiths, DE Bruton, DJ Jones, Williams, Overson, Cunningham, Stirland, Evans
Substitute: Davies (nps)
Scorer: Williams
Attendance: 1070

Date: Saturday 09/10/1982
Result: **POOLE TOWN 3 GLOUCESTER CITY 3**
Competition: Southern League Premier Division
Teamsheet: GA Jones, Griffiths, Davies, DE Bruton, Ledbury, Williams, Cunningham, Overson, DJ Jones, Stirland, Lowe
Substitute: Burford (for Cunningham)
Scorers: DJ Jones (2), Cunningham (pen)

Date: Tuesday 12/10/1982
Result: **WEALDSTONE 3 GLOUCESTER CITY 1**
Competition: Championship Match
Teamsheet: GA Jones, Griffiths, Davies, DE Bruton, Lowe, Overson, Hopkins, Williams, DJ Jones, Stirland, Cunningham
Substitute: Layton (for DE Bruton)
Scorer: own goal
Note: Cup for winners of last seasons League and Cup in the Southern League

Date: Saturday 16/10/1982
Result: **WELLING UNITED 4 GLOUCESTER CITY 1**
Competition: Southern League Premier Division
Teamsheet: GA Jones, Griffiths, Davies, Layton, Lowe, Ledbury, Hopkins, Cunningham, DJ Jones, Stirland, Burford
Substitute: Preece (nps)
Scorer: DJ Jones

Date: Tuesday 19/10/1982
Result: **GLOUCESTER CITY 2 FOREST GREEN ROVERS 5**
Competition: Western Floodlight League
Teamsheet: Gwinnett, Ledbury, Tanner, Layton, DE Bruton, Williams, Lowe, DJ Jones, Cunningham, M Bruton, Burford
Substitutes: Davies (nps), Griffiths (nps), Hopkins (nps)
Scorers: M Bruton, DJ Jones

Date: Tuesday 26/10/1982
Result: **GLOUCESTER CITY 3 TAUNTON TOWN 0**
Competition: Western Floodlight League
Teamsheet: GA Jones, Griffiths, Ross, Tanner, DE Bruton, Aitken, Porter, DJ Jones, M Bruton, Burford, Cunningham
Substitutes: Williams (nps), Ledbury (nps), Lowe (nps)
Scorers: Porter, DE Bruton, Burford

Date: Saturday 30/10/1982
Result: **GLOUCESTER CITY 3 FAREHAM TOWN 4**
Competition: Southern League Premier Division
Teamsheet: GA Jones, Griffiths, Tanner, Lowe, DE Bruton, Ross, McNeill, Porter, DJ Jones, M Bruton, Burford
Substitute: Ledbury (nps)
Scorers: DJ Jones, Lowe, Porter
Attendance: 371

Date: Tuesday 02/11/1982
Result: **FOREST GREEN ROVERS 4 GLOUCESTER CITY 1**
Competition: Western Floodlight League
Teamsheet: GA Jones, Griffiths, Tanner, Ross, DE Bruton, Aitken, McNeill, Porter, DJ Jones, M Bruton, Burford
Substitutes: Lowe (nps), Thomas (nps), Ledbury (nps)
Scorer: DJ Jones

Date: Saturday 06/11/1982
Result: **DARTFORD 1 GLOUCESTER CITY 0**
Competition: Southern League Premier Division
Teamsheet: GA Jones, Griffiths, Tanner, Layton, DE Bruton, Lowe, Overson, McNeill, DJ Jones, M Bruton, Porter
Substitute: Ross (for Porter)

Date: Saturday 13/11/1982
Result: **GLOUCESTER CITY 2 ALVECHURCH 2**
Competition: Southern League Premier Division
Teamsheet: Cornwell, Ross, Tanner, DE Bruton, Layton, Lowe, McNeill, Porter, DJ Jones, M Bruton, Cunningham
Substitute: Williams (nps)
Scorers: McNeil, M Bruton
Attendance: 353

Date: Saturday 20/11/1982
Result: **GLOUCESTER CITY 0 ENDERBY TOWN 2**
Competition: Southern League Premier Division
Teamsheet: Harris, Griffiths, McNeill, DE Bruton, Layton, Walker, Lowe, Spencer, M Bruton, DJ Jones, Burford
Substitute: Ross (nps)
Attendance: 284

Date: Saturday 27/11/1982
Result: **GOSPORT BOROUGH 0 GLOUCESTER CITY 5**
Competition: Southern League Premier Division
Teamsheet: Harris, Gillies, McNeill, Layton, DE Bruton, Walker, Spencer, DJ Jones, Porter, M Bruton, Burford
Substitute: Tanner (nps)
Scorers: Walker (2), Spencer, Porter (2)

Date: Saturday 04/12/1982
Result: **GLOUCESTER CITY 0 WELLING UNITED 2**
Competition: Southern League Premier Division
Teamsheet: Cornwell, Gillies, McNeill, Layton, DE Bruton, Walker, Spencer, DJ Jones, Porter, M Bruton, Burford
Substitute: Tanner (nps)
Attendance: 280

Date: Tuesday 07/12/1982
Result: **STOURBRIDGE 2 GLOUCESTER CITY 2**
Competition: Southern League Premier Division
Teamsheet: Cornwell, Griffiths, McNeill, Gillies, Layton, DE Bruton, Porter, Walker, Gough, M Bruton, Burford
Substitute: Tanner (nps)
Scorers: M Bruton, Porter

Date: Saturday 11/12/1982
Result: **BEDWORTH UNITED 1 GLOUCESTER CITY 0**
Competition: Southern League Premier Division
Teamsheet: Cornwell, Spencer, McNeill, M Bruton, Layton, Gillies, Walker, Porter, Gough, DE Bruton, Foxwell
Substitute: Griffiths (for Spencer)

Date: Saturday 18/12/1982
Result: **GLOUCESTER CITY 4 MINEHEAD 1**
Competition: FA Trophy 3rd Qualifying Round
Teamsheet: Cornwell, Gillies, McNeill, Layton, DE Bruton, Walker, Spencer, Porter, M Bruton, DJ Jones, Burford
Substitutes: Griffiths, Tanner
Scorers: M Bruton, DE Bruton (pen), DJ Jones, Spencer

Date: Monday 27/12/1982
Result: **GLOUCESTER CITY 2 WITNEY TOWN 2**
Competition: Southern League Premier Division
Teamsheet: Cornwell, Gillies, McNeill, DE Bruton, Layton, Walker, Tanner, Porter, DJ Jones, Butt, Burford
Substitute: M Bruton (for McNeill)
Scorers: DE Bruton, M Bruton
Attendance: 473

Date: Saturday 01/01/1983
Result: **WITNEY TOWN 1 GLOUCESTER CITY 0**
Competition: Southern League Premier Division
Teamsheet: Cornwell, Williams, Tanner, DE Bruton, Layton, Spencer, Walker, Porter, DJ Jones, Butt, Foxwell
Substitute: M Bruton (nps)

Date: Monday 03/01/1983
Result: **KIDDERMINSTER HARRIERS 3 GLOUCESTER CITY 1**
Competition: Southern League Premier Division
Teamsheet: Cornwell, Williams, Davies, Layton, Harding, Tanner, Porter, Walker, Butt, M Bruton, Foxwell
Substitute: Burford (for Porter)
Scorer: M Bruton
Attendance: 630

Date: Saturday 08/01/1983
Result: **GLOUCESTER CITY 3 ADDLESTONE & WEYBRIDGE TOWN 3**
Competition: Southern League Premier Division
Teamsheet: Harris, McNeill, Davies, Layton, Harding, Williams, Walker, Tanner, Foxwell, M Bruton, Butt
Substitute: Gough (nps)
Scorers: Butt, M Bruton (2)
Attendance: 350

Date: Saturday 15/01/1983
Result: **DORCHESTER TOWN 3 GLOUCESTER CITY 2**
Competition: FA Trophy 1st Round
Teamsheet: Harris, McNeill, Tanner, DE Bruton, Harding, Williams, Walker, Porter, M Bruton, Gough, Burford
Substitutes: Butt (nps), Foxwell (nps)
Scorers: Harding, Gough

Date: Tuesday 18/01/1983
Result: **TAUNTON TOWN 1 GLOUCESTER CITY 3**
Competition: Western Floodlight League
Teamsheet: Watson, Williams, Wookey, Harding, Tanner, Curtis, Walker, Porter, M Bruton, Butt, Gough
Substitutes: Burford (for -----), Foxwell (for -----)
Scorers: Gough, Butt, Foxwell

GLOUCESTER CITY 1982-1983

GLOUCESTER CITY A.F.C.

Back Row Left to Right N. Cornwell. B. Tandy (Trainer). P. Hunt. S. Butt. D. Bruton. I. Watson. S. Harding. M. Bruton
J. Garwood. C. Porter. D. Gillies.

Front Row Left to Right B. Curtiss. S. Walker. G. Sweeney. B. Mirsell (Joint M.D.). M. Burford. K. Tanner. T. Peters (Coach)
(Missing from the squad J. Gough)   CUP   North Senior Cup.

PROGRAMME

1982-1983

[281]

GLOUCESTER CITY A.F.C. 1984/85

Back Row Left to Right: Mirek Kalewski, Mario Waite, Steve Harding, Neil Hards, Wayne Stokes, Dennis McCoy, Keith Tanner.
Front Row Left to Right: Kim Casey, Kevin Trusswell, Barry Vassallo, Chris O'Reilly, Melvyn Langford.

PROGRAMME

SEASON 1983–84

GLOUCESTER CITY A.F.C.

SOUTHERN PREMIER LEAGUE

WESTBURY HOMES LTD
CITY'S MAJOR SPONSORS

1983-1984

PROGRAMME

The T-Ender

Official Match Magazine

The Worcestershire Senior Cup Final 20p

Gloucester City
v
Worcester City

1983-1984

PROGRAMME

HORTON ROAD REVIEW

Official Matchday Magazine of Gloucester City A.F.C. No.1 10p

FRIENDLY
v TORQUAY UNITED
Tuesday, 7th August, 1984
Kickoff 7.30 p.m.

1984-1985

[282]

Date: Saturday 22/01/1983
Result: **GLOUCESTER CITY 3 POOLE TOWN 1**
Competition: Southern League Premier Division
Teamsheet: Watson, Gillies, Tanner, DE Bruton, Harding, Curtis, Walker, Porter, Gough, M Bruton, Butt
Substitute: Burford (for Gough)
Scorers: M Bruton (2), own goal
Attendance: 343

Date: Saturday 29/01/1983
Result: **WATERLOOVILLE 1 GLOUCESTER CITY 2**
Competition: Southern League Premier Division
Teamsheet: Watson, Gillies, Tanner, Harding, Sweeney, Garwood, Walker, Porter, Gough, M Bruton, Burford
Substitute: Butt (nps)
Scorers: M Bruton, Gough

Date: Saturday 05/02/1983
Result: **CHELMSFORD CITY 3 GLOUCESTER CITY 1**
Competition: Southern League Premier Division
Teamsheet: Watson, Gillies, Tanner, Harding, Garwood, DE Bruton, Porter, Curtis, Gough, Butt, Foxwell
Substitute: Burford (nps)
Scorer: DE Bruton (pen)

Date: Saturday 19/02/1983
Result: **GLOUCESTER CITY 2 CHELMSFORD CITY 2**
Competition: Southern League Premier Division
Teamsheet: Watson, Gillies, Tanner, DE Bruton, Harding, Walker, Sweeney, Gough, M Bruton, Curtis, Burford
Substitute: Porter (nps)
Scorers: M Bruton, Burford
Attendance: 383

Date: Tuesday 01/03/1983
Result: **CORBY TOWN 1 GLOUCESTER CITY 2**
Competition: Southern League Premier Division
Teamsheet: Watson, Curtis, Tanner, DE Bruton, Harding, Walker, Sweeney, Gillies, Gough, Butt, Burford
Substitute: Porter (nps)
Scorers: Butt, Gough

Date: Saturday 05/03/1983
Result: **GLOUCESTER CITY 1 DARTFORD 0**
Competition: Southern League Premier Division
Teamsheet: Watson, Gillies, Tanner, DE Bruton, Harding, Walker, Curtis, Gough, M Bruton, Sweeney, Burford
Substitute: Butt (nps)
Scorer: DE Bruton (pen)
Attendance: 380

Date: Saturday 12/03/1983
Result: **ALVECHURCH 1 GLOUCESTER CITY 1**
Competition: Southern League Premier Division
Teamsheet: Watson, Curtis, Tanner, DE Bruton, Harding, Sweeney, Walker, Gillies, Gough, M Bruton, Burford
Substitute: Porter (nps)
Scorer: Sweeney

Date: Monday 14/03/1983
Result: **GLOUCESTER CITY 3 CHELTENHAM TOWN 1** (aet)
Competition: Gloucestershire FA Northern Senior Professional Cup Final
Teamsheet: Watson, Curtis, Tanner, DE Bruton, Harding, Gillies, Sweeney, Walker, M Bruton, Gough, Burford
Substitute: Butt (for -----), Porter (nps), Williams (nps), Davies (nps), Cornwell (nps)
Scorers: M Bruton, Burford, Butt
Attendance: 700

Date: Saturday 19/03/1983
Result: **ADDLESTONE & WEYBRIDGE TOWN 1 GLOUCESTER CITY 2**
Competition: Southern League Premier Division
Teamsheet: Watson, Curtis, Tanner, DE Bruton, Harding, Walker, Gillies, Sweeney, M Bruton, Butt, Burford
Substitute: Porter (nps)
Scorers: Burford, own goal

Date: Saturday 26/03/1983
Result: **GLOUCESTER CITY 3 DORCHESTER TOWN 1**
Competition: Southern League Premier Division
Teamsheet: Watson, Garwood, Tanner, Harding, DE Bruton, Curtis, Walker, Porter, Gillies, M Bruton, Burford
Substitute: Butt (nps)
Scorers: DE Bruton, M Bruton (2)
Attendance: 385

Date: Tuesday 29/03/1983
Result: **GLOUCESTER CITY 4 HASTINGS UNITED 0**
Competition: Southern League Premier Division
Teamsheet: Watson, Garwood, Tanner, DE Bruton, Harding, Sweeney, Walker, Gillies, M Bruton, Gough, Burford
Substitute: Curtis (nps)
Scorers: Burford (2), M Bruton, Gillies
Attendance: 366

Date: Saturday 02/04/1983
Result: **AUTOMOTIVE PRODUCTS LEAMINGTON 2 GLOUCESTER CITY 2**
Competition: Southern League Premier Division
Teamsheet: Watson, Garwood, Tanner, DE Bruton, Harding, Hunt, Walker, Sweeney, Gough, M Bruton, Burford
Substitute: Butt (nps)
Scorers: Harding, M Bruton
Attendance: 591

Date: Monday 04/04/1983
Result: **GLOUCESTER CITY 2 AUTOMOTIVE PRODUCTS LEAMINGTON 1**
Competition: Southern League Premier Division
Teamsheet: Watson, Garwood, Tanner, Curtis, Harding, Hunt, Walker, Sweeney, Gough, M Bruton, Burford
Substitute: Butt (nps)
Scorer: M Bruton (2)
Attendance: 651

Date: Saturday 09/04/1983
Result: **GRAVESEND & NORTHFLEET 0 GLOUCESTER CITY 2**
Competition: Southern League Premier Division
Teamsheet: Watson, Garwood, Tanner, DE Bruton, Harding, Hunt, Walker, Sweeney, Gough, M Bruton, Burford
Substitute: Curtis (nps)
Scorers: M Bruton, Walker

Date: Monday 11/04/1983
Result: **FAREHAM TOWN 0 GLOUCESTER CITY 0**
Competition: Southern League Premier Division
Teamsheet: Watson, Garwood, Tanner, DE Bruton, Harding, Curtis, Walker, Sweeney, Gough, M Bruton, Burford
Substitute: Butt (nps)

Date: Saturday 16/04/1983
Result: **GLOUCESTER CITY 1 GOSPORT BOROUGH 0**
Competition: Southern League Premier Division
Teamsheet: Watson, Garwood, Tanner, DE Bruton, Harding, Hunt, Walker, Sweeney, Gough, M Bruton, Burford
Substitute: Curtis (nps)
Scorer: Gough
Attendance: 610

Date: Tuesday 19/04/1983
Result: **DORCHESTER TOWN 1 GLOUCESTER CITY 1**
Competition: Southern League Premier Division
Teamsheet: Watson, Garwood, Tanner, DE Bruton, Harding, Hunt, Walker, Sweeney, Gough, Butt, Burford
Substitute: Curtis (nps)
Scorer: Butt

Date: Friday 22/04/1983
Result: **ENDERBY TOWN 0 GLOUCESTER CITY 1**
Competition: Southern League Premier Division
Teamsheet: Watson, Garwood, Tanner, DE Bruton, Harding, Hunt, Walker, Sweeney, Butt, M Bruton, Burford
Substitute: Curtis (nps)
Scorer: Butt

Date: Tuesday 26/04/1983
Result: **GLOUCESTER CITY 0 BEDWORTH UNITED 1**
Competition: Southern League Premier Division
Teamsheet: Watson, Garwood, Tanner, DE Bruton, Harding, Hunt, Walker, Sweeney, Butt, M Bruton, Burford
Substitute: Curtis (nps)
Attendance: 400

Date: Monday 02/05/1983
Result: **GLOUCESTER CITY 1 KIDDERMINSTER HARRIERS 2**
Competition: Southern League Premier Division
Teamsheet: Watson, Garwood, Tanner, DE Bruton, Harding, Curtis, Walker, Sweeney, Gough, Gillies, Burford
Substitute: Butt (nps)
Scorer: DE Bruton (pen)
Attendance: 664

Appearances – P Aitken 2, DE Bruton 45, M Bruton 32(1), MT Burford 35(6), S Butt 12(1), NT Cornwell 14, D Cunningham 16, B Curtis 13, K Davies 13, JA Evans 4, DP Foxwell 5(1), J Garwood 13, DG Gillies 18, J Gough 20, AR Griffiths 18(1), ML Gwinnett 2, SJ Harding 24, T Harris 4, W Hopkins 10, P Hunt 7, DJ Jones 25, GAJones 9, JH Layton 22(1), PJ Ledbury 6, GW Lowe 8, B McNeill 13, RJ Overson 5, CJ Porter 19, BJ Preece 1, D Ross 4(1), D Spencer 6, G Stirland 13, G Sweeney 17, K Tanner 32, S Walker 31, I Watson 21, M Williams 18, D Wookey 1.
Others selected but did not play: RJ Thomas.
Scorers – M Bruton 20, DJ Jones 8, DE Bruton 7, MT Burford 7, S Butt 6, J Gough 5, CJ Porter 5, G Stirland 5, S Walker 3, M Williams 3, D Cunningham 2, S Harding 2, D Spencer 2, DP Foxwell 1, DG Gillies 1, GW Lowe 1, B McNeill 1, G Sweeney 1, own goals 3.

TIGERS SUPPORTERS CLUB
(Gloucester City)

Player of the Year

My Choice

_____

Supporter of the Year

My Choice

_____

O & I (INSTANT PRINT) Northgate, Gloucester

SEASON BY SEASON

SOUTHERN LEAGUE PREMIER DIVISION

POS	CLUB	P	W	D	L	F	A	PTS
1	AUTOMOTIVE PRODUCTS LEAMINGTON	38	25	4	9	78	50	79
2	KIDDERMINSTER HARRIERS	38	23	7	8	69	40	76
3	WELLING UNITED	38	21	6	11	63	40	69
4	CHELMSFORD CITY	38	16	11	11	57	40	59
5	BEDWORTH UNITED	38	16	11	11	47	39	59
6	DARTFORD	38	16	8	14	48	38	56
7	GOSPORT BOROUGH	38	14	13	11	47	43	55
8	FAREHAM TOWN	38	16	7	15	73	82	55
9	DORCHESTER TOWN	38	14	12	12	52	50	54
10	GRAVESEND & NORTHFLEET	38	14	12	12	49	50	54
11	**GLOUCESTER CITY**	**38**	**13**	**12**	**13**	**61**	**57**	**51**
12	WITNEY TOWN	38	12	13	13	60	48	47*
13	ALVECHURCH	38	13	8	17	60	66	47
14	STOURBRIDGE	38	12	11	15	48	54	47
15	CORBY TOWN	38	12	11	15	58	67	47
16	HASTINGS UNITED	38	11	11	16	48	61	44
17	ENDERBY TOWN	38	11	9	18	44	62	42
18	WATERLOOVILLE	38	10	9	19	62	83	39
19	POOLE TOWN	38	9	9	20	57	73	36
20	ADDLESTONE & WEYBRIDGE TOWN	38	5	10	23	24	62	25
		760	283	194	283	1105	1105	1041

* Two points deducted for ineligible player.
  3 points for a win introduced.

WESTERN FLOODLIGHT LEAGUE

POS	CLUB	P	W	D	L	F	A	PTS
1	FROME TOWN	4	2	2	0	6	3	8
2	FOREST GREEN ROVERS	4	2	1	1	11	6	7
3	**GLOUCESTER CITY**	**4**	**2**	**0**	**2**	**9**	**10**	**6**
4	TAUNTON TOWN	4	0	1	3	2	9	1
		16	6	4	6	28	28	22

Not all fixtures completed. Indications are that Gloucester City v Frome Town and Frome Town v Gloucester City were cancelled.

SEASON 1983-1984
(Home Ground: Horton Road Stadium)

Date: Saturday 20/08/1983
Result: **GLOUCESTER CITY 4 STOURBRIDGE 0**
Competition: Southern League Premier Division
Teamsheet: Hards, Gillies, Tanner, DE Bruton, Davies, Hunt, Walker, Sweeney, M Bruton, Gwyther, Burford
Substitute: Curtis (nps)
Scorers: Burford (2), DE Bruton (pen), M Bruton
Attendance: 466

Date: Tuesday 23/08/1983
Result: **GLOUCESTER CITY 3 FOREST GREEN ROVERS 2**
Competition: Southern League Cup 1st Round 1st Leg
Teamsheet: Hards, Garwood, Tanner, DE Bruton, Harding, Gillies, Walker, Sweeney, M Bruton, Gwyther, Burford
Substitute: Curtis (nps)
Scorers: DE Bruton, M Bruton (2)
Attendance: 925

Date: Saturday 27/08/1983
Result: **HASTINGS UNITED 1 GLOUCESTER CITY 1**
Competition: Southern League Premier Division
Teamsheet: Hards, Gillies, Tanner, DE Bruton, Garwood, Hunt, Walker, Sweeney, M Bruton, Gwyther, Burford
Substitute: Waite (nps)
Scorer: DE Bruton

Date: Tuesday 30/08/1983
Result: **FOREST GREEN ROVERS 1 GLOUCESTER CITY 1**
Competition: Southern League Cup 1st Round 2nd Leg
Teamsheet: Hards, Gillies, Tanner, DE Bruton, Garwood, Hunt, Walker, Sweeney, M Bruton, Gwyther, Burford
Substitute: Waite (nps)
Scorer: M Bruton

Date: Saturday 03/09/1983
Result: **GLOUCESTER CITY 2 CHELMSFORD CITY 0**
Competition: Southern League Premier Division
Teamsheet: Hards, Gillies, Tanner, DE Bruton, Garwood, Waite, Walker, Sweeney, M Bruton, Gwyther, Burford
Substitute: Curtis (nps)
Scorers: Burford, DE Bruton
Attendance: 418

Date: Saturday 10/09/1983
Result: **CORBY TOWN 0 GLOUCESTER CITY 0**
Competition: Southern League Premier Division
Teamsheet: Hards, Gillies, Tanner, Davies, Garwood, Waite, Walker, Sweeney, M Bruton, Gwyther, Burford
Substitute: Curtis (for Walker)

Date: Saturday 17/09/1983
Result: **HAVERFORDWEST COUNTY 1 GLOUCESTER CITY 2**
Competition: FA Cup 1st Qualifying Round
Teamsheet: Hards, Gillies, Tanner, Garwood, Davies, Waite, Curtis, Sweeney, M Bruton, Gwyther, Burford
Substitute: Harding (nps)
Scorer: Burford (2)

Date: Saturday 24/09/1983
Result: **GLOUCESTER CITY 1 WELLING UNITED 1**
Competition: Southern League Premier Division
Teamsheet: Hards, Gillies, Tanner, DE Bruton, Harding, Waite, Davies, Sweeney, M Bruton, Gwyther, Burford
Substitute: Hunt (nps)
Scorer: Waite
Attendance: 520

Date: Tuesday 27/09/1983
Result: **GLOUCESTER CITY 1 MERTHYR TYDFIL 0**
Competition: Southern League Cup 2nd Round
Teamsheet: Hards, Gillies, Tanner, DE Bruton, Harding, Waite, Hunt, Sweeney, M Bruton, Gwyther, Burford
Substitute: Garwood (for DE Bruton)
Scorer: M Bruton
Attendance: 525

Date: Saturday 01/10/1983
Result: **WELTON ROVERS 1 GLOUCESTER CITY 4**
Competition: FA Cup 2nd Qualifying Round
Teamsheet: Hards, Gillies, Tanner, Harding, DE Bruton, Davies, Waite, Sweeney, M Bruton, Gwyther, Burford
Substitute: Hunt (nps)
Scorers: DE Bruton (2), Burford, Gwyther

Date: Saturday 08/10/1983
Result: **GLOUCESTER CITY 2 AUTOMOTIVE PRODUCTS LEAMINGTON 1**
Competition: Southern League Premier Division
Teamsheet: Hards, Gillies, Tanner, DE Bruton, Harding, Waite, Walker, Sweeney, M Bruton, Gwyther, Hunt
Substitute: Davies (for Gillies)
Scorers: Waite, Gwyther
Attendance: 589

Date: Tuesday 18/10/1983
Result: **MERTHYR TYDFIL 3 GLOUCESTER CITY 2**
Competition: FA Cup 3rd Qualifying Round
Teamsheet: Hards, Gillies, Tanner, Harding, DE Bruton, Walker, Sweeney, Waite, M Bruton, Gwyther, Hunt
Substitute: Burford (nps)
Scorers: Walker, Waite
Attendance: 3000

Date: Saturday 29/10/1983
Result: **GOSPORT BOROUGH 1 GLOUCESTER CITY 1**
Competition: Southern League Premier Division
Teamsheet: Hards, Davies, Tanner, DE Bruton, Harding, Walker, Waite, Sweeney, M Bruton, Gwyther, Burford
Substitute: Hunt (nps)
Scorer: M Bruton

Date: Tuesday 01/11/1983
Result: **GLOUCESTER CITY 2 BROMSGROVE ROVERS 1** (aet)
Competition: Worcestershire FA Senior Challenge Cup Quarter-Final
Teamsheet: Cook, DE Bruton, Davies, Harding, Tanner, Walker, Sweeney, Waite, M Bruton, Gwyther, Burford
Substitute: Jeff Hughes (for M Bruton),
Scorers: Gwyther, Jeff Hughes

Date: Saturday 05/11/1983
Result: **GLOUCESTER CITY 1 ALVECHURCH 2**
Competition: Southern League Premier Division
Teamsheet: Cook, Davies, Hunt, DE Bruton, Harding, Walker, Waite, Sweeney, M Bruton, Gwyther, Burford
Substitute: Sillett (nps)
Scorer: M Bruton
Attendance: 450

Date: Tuesday 08/11/1983
Result: **GLOUCESTER CITY 0 WITNEY TOWN 0**
Competition: Southern League Cup 3rd Round
Teamsheet: Cook, Garwood, Merrick, DE Bruton, Harding, Waite, Hunt, Sweeney, Callaway, Gwyther, Burford
Substitute: Sillett (nps)
Attendance: 425

Date: Saturday 12/11/1983
Result: **FISHER ATHLETIC 2 GLOUCESTER CITY 0**
Competition: Southern League Premier Division
Teamsheet: Cook, Sweeney, Merrick, DE Bruton, Harding, Walker, Hunt, Waite, Sillett, Gwyther, Burford
Substitute: Jeff Hughes (nps)

Date: Saturday 19/11/1983
Result: **GLOUCESTER CITY 1 KING'S LYNN 2**
Competition: Southern League Premier Division
Teamsheet: Hards, Sillett, Merrick, DE Bruton, Harding, Walker, Hunt, Sweeney, M Bruton, Gwyther, Garland
Substitute: Burford (for Sillett)
Scorer: Garland
Attendance: 403

Date: Tuesday 22/11/1983
Result: **BEDWORTH UNITED 0 GLOUCESTER CITY 0**
Competition: Southern League Premier Division
Teamsheet: Hards, Hunt, Merrick, DE Bruton, Harding, Walker, Sillett, Sweeney, M Bruton, Gwyther, Burford
Substitute: Waite (nps)

Date: Wednesday 30/11/1983
Result: **FOLKESTONE TOWN 1 GLOUCESTER CITY 3**
Competition: Southern League Premier Division
Teamsheet: Hards, McCoy, Hunt, DE Bruton, Harding, Walker, Waite, Sweeney, M Bruton, Gwyther, Sillett
Substitute: Leitch (for Gwyther)
Scorers: M Bruton (2), Walker

Date: Saturday 03/12/1983
Result: **GLOUCESTER CITY 1 DARTFORD 1**
Competition: Southern League Premier Division
Teamsheet: Hards, John, Merrick, DE Bruton, Harding, Walker, Sillett, Sweeney, M Bruton, Waite, Burford
Substitute: Tanner (nps)
Scorer: Burford
Attendance: 460

Date: Tuesday 06/12/1983
Result: **WITNEY TOWN 0 GLOUCESTER CITY 3**
Competition: Southern League Cup 3rd Round Replay
Teamsheet: Hards, McCoy, Merrick, DE Bruton, Harding, Walker, John, Tanner, M Bruton, Waite, Burford
Substitute: Sillett (nps)
Scorers: Tanner (2), M Bruton

Date: Saturday 10/12/1983
Result: **GLOUCESTER CITY 3 DORCHESTER TOWN 3**
Competition: Southern League Premier Division
Teamsheet: Hards, McCoy, Merrick, DE Bruton, Harding, Walker, John, Tanner, M Bruton, Waite, Burford
Substitute: Gwyther (for Walker)
Scorers: Waite, Burford, McCoy
Attendance: 338

Date: Saturday 17/12/1983
Result: **SALISBURY 2 GLOUCESTER CITY 2**
Competition: FA Trophy 3rd Qualifying Round
Teamsheet: Hards, McCoy, Merrick, DE Bruton, Harding, John, Tanner, Sweeney, M Bruton, Waite, Burford
Substitute: Hunt (nps)
Scorer: M Bruton (2, 1 pen)

Date: Friday 23/12/1983
Result: **GLOUCESTER CITY 3 SALISBURY 3**
Competition: FA Trophy 3rd Qualifying Round Replay
Teamsheet: Hards, Sweeney, Tanner, DE Bruton, Harding, John, Walker, Hunt, M Bruton, Gwyther, Waite
Substitute: Burford (nps)
Scorers: M Bruton (pen), Gwyther (2)
Attendance: 390

Date: Monday 26/12/1983
Result: **CHELTENHAM TOWN 4 GLOUCESTER CITY 1**
Competition: Southern League Premier Division
Teamsheet: Hards, McCoy, Tanner, Walker, Garwood, Hunt, Waite, Sweeney, M Bruton, Gwyther, John
Substitute: Burford (nps)
Scorer: Waite
Attendance: 1127

Date: Wednesday 28/12/1983
Result: **GLOUCESTER CITY 2 SALISBURY 0**
Competition: FA Trophy 3rd Qualifying Round 2nd Replay
Teamsheet: Hards, McCoy, Hunt, Davies, Harding, Tanner, Walker, John, M Bruton, Gwyther, Waite
Substitute: Burford (nps)
Scorers: Gwyther, Waite
Attendance: 537

Date: Saturday 31/12/1983
Result: **GLOUCESTER CITY 0 WITNEY TOWN 4**
Competition: Southern League Premier Division
Teamsheet: Hards, McCoy, Hunt, Harding, Davies, Walker, Tanner, John, M Bruton, Gwyther, Waite
Substitute: Burford (nps)
Attendance: 320

Date: Monday 02/01/1984
Result: **FAREHAM TOWN 2 GLOUCESTER CITY 0**
Competition: Southern League Premier Division
Teamsheet: Cook, McCoy, Hunt, Sweeney, Davies, DE Bruton, John, Tanner, M Bruton, Gwyther, Burford
Substitute: Sillett (nps)

Date: Saturday 07/01/1984
Result: **ALVECHURCH 0 GLOUCESTER CITY 0**
Competition: Southern League Premier Division
Teamsheet: TA Hughes, McCoy, Hunt, DE Bruton, Harding, Walker, Sweeney, Mills, M Bruton, Gwyther, Burford
Substitute: Waite (nps)

Date: Tuesday 10/01/1984
Result: **AUTOMOTIVE PRODUCTS LEAMINGTON 4 GLOUCESTER CITY 1**
Competition: Southern League Cup 4th Round
Teamsheet: TA Hughes, McCoy, Hunt, DE Bruton, Harding, Waite, Sweeney, Mills, M Bruton, Gwyther, Burford
Substitute: John (nps)
Scorer: Burford

Date: Tuesday 17/01/1984
Result: **GLOUCESTER CITY 3 FISHER ATHLETIC 3**
Competition: FA Trophy 1st Round
Teamsheet: Hards, McCoy, Tanner, DE Bruton, Harding, Walker, Waite, Sweeney, M Bruton, Gwyther, Burford
Substitute: John (for Burford)
Scorer: M Bruton (3, 2 pens)
Attendance: 347

Date: Saturday 21/01/1984
Result: **GLOUCESTER CITY 1 SUTTON COLDFIELD TOWN 1**
Competition: Southern League Premier Division
Teamsheet: Hards, John, Tanner, DE Bruton, Harding, Waite, Walker, Sweeney, M Bruton, Gwyther, Jasper Hughes
Substitute: Taylor (nps)
Scorer: Sweeney
Attendance: 337

Date: Thursday 26/01/1984
Result: **FISHER ATHLETIC 2 GLOUCESTER CITY 1**
Competition: FA Trophy 1st Round Replay
Teamsheet: Hards, McCoy (?), John (?), Davies, Harding, Walker, Waite, Sweeney, M Bruton, Gwyther, Jasper Hughes (?)
Substitute: ----- (for Waite)
Scorers: Gwyther

Date: Saturday 28/01/1984
Result: **AUTOMOTIVE PRODUCTS LEAMINGTON 4 GLOUCESTER CITY 1**
Competition: Southern League Premier Division
Teamsheet: Hards, McCoy, John, Harding, O'Reilly, Walker, Garland, Sweeney, DE Bruton, Gwyther, Hunt
Substitute: Mockridge (nps)
Scorer: Gwyther
Attendance: 414

Date: Saturday 04/02/1984
Result: **GLOUCESTER CITY 1 GRAVESEND & NORTHFLEET 0**
Competition: Southern League Premier Division
Teamsheet: Hards, McCoy, Hunt, Harding, DE Bruton, Waite, Walker, Sweeney, M Bruton, Gwyther, Vassallo
Substitute: O'Reilly (nps)
Scorer: Walker
Attendance: 301

Date: Tuesday 07/02/1984
Result: **GLOUCESTER CITY 2 WILLENHALL TOWN 1**
Competition: Worcestershire FA Senior Challenge Cup Semi-Final
Teamsheet: Hards, McCoy, Hunt, DE Bruton, Harding, Walker, Waite, Sweeney, M Bruton, Gwyther, Vassallo
Substitute: O'Reilly (nps)
Scorers: DE Bruton, Waite

Date: Saturday 11/02/1984
Result: **WELLING UNITED 1 GLOUCESTER CITY 3**
Competition: Southern League Premier Division
Teamsheet: Hards, McCoy, Hunt, DE Bruton, Harding, O'Reilly, Walker, Sweeney, Waite, Gwyther, Vassallo
Substitute: John (nps)
Scorers: Gwyther, Waite, O'Reilly

Date: Saturday 18/02/1984
Result: **GLOUCESTER CITY 1 CORBY TOWN 1**
Competition: Southern League Premier Division
Teamsheet: Hards, John, Hunt, Harding, DE Bruton, O'Reilly, Sweeney, Walker, Tanner, M Bruton, Waite
Substitute: Lloyd (nps)
Scorer: M Bruton
Attendance: 335

Date: Monday 27/02/1984
Result: **CHELMSFORD CITY 2 GLOUCESTER CITY 1**
Competition: Southern League Premier Division
Teamsheet: Hards, McCoy, Hunt, DE Bruton, Gwyther, Mulraney, Walker, Sweeney, M Bruton, Waite, Vassallo
Substitute: O'Reilly (nps)
Scorer: M Bruton (pen)

Date: Saturday 03/03/1984
Result: **GLOUCESTER CITY 2 HASTINGS UNITED 2**
Competition: Southern League Premier Division
Teamsheet: Hards, McCoy, John, Harding, DE Bruton, Walker, Vassallo, O'Reilly, Waite, M Bruton, Gwyther
Substitute: Hunt (for O'Reilly)
Scorers: Harding, M Bruton
Attendance: 298

Date: Wednesday 07/03/1984
Result: **SUTTON COLDFIELD TOWN 1 GLOUCESTER CITY 1**
Competition: Southern League Premier Division
Teamsheet: Hards, McCoy, John, DE Bruton, Harding, Hunt, Walker, Sweeney, Gwyther, Waite, Vassallo
Substitute: Callaway (nps)
Scorers: DE Bruton

Date: Saturday 10/03/1984
Result: **DARTFORD 0 GLOUCESTER CITY 2**
Competition: Southern League Premier Division
Teamsheet: Hards, McCoy, Hunt, Harding, DE Bruton, Walker, Vassallo, Sweeney, Waite, Gwyther, M Bruton
Substitute: John (nps)
Scorers: M Bruton (2)

Date: Saturday 17/03/1984
Result: **GLOUCESTER CITY 0 FOLKESTONE TOWN 0**
Competition: Southern League Premier Division
Teamsheet: Hards, McCoy, John, Harding, Thompson, Walker, Vassallo, Sweeney, Waite, Gwyther, M Bruton
Substitute: Tanner (nps)
Attendance: 280

Date: Saturday 24/03/1984
Result: **KING'S LYNN 1 GLOUCESTER CITY 2**
Competition: Southern League Premier Division
Teamsheet: Hards, John, O'Reilly, DE Bruton, Harding, Walker, Vassallo, Sweeney, Waite, Gwyther, M Bruton
Substitute: Burford (for -----)
Scorers: Waite, Harding
Attendance: 254

Date: Tuesday 27/03/1984
Result: **GLOUCESTER CITY 1 WORCESTER CITY 1**
Competition: Worcestershire FA Senior Challnege Cup Final 1st Leg
Teamsheet: Hards, McCoy, DE Bruton, Hunt, Harding, Sweeney, Walker, Vassallo, M Bruton, Gwyther, Burford
Substitute: O'Reilly (nps)
Scorer: Gwyther

Date: Saturday 31/03/1984
Result: **GLOUCESTER CITY 2 FISHER ATHLETIC 1**
Competition: Southern League Premier Division
Teamsheet: Hards, McCoy, Hunt, DE Bruton, Harding, Walker, Vassallo, Sweeney, Waite, Gwyther, Burford
Substitute: Dangerfield (nps)
Scorers: Walker, Waite
Attendance: 267

Date: Tuesday 03/04/1984
Result: **GLOUCESTER CITY 3 GOSPORT BOROUGH 0**
Competition: Southern League Premier Division
Teamsheet: Hards, McCoy, Hunt, DE Bruton, Harding, Dangerfield, Vassallo, Sweeney, Waite, Gwyther, Burford
Substitute: M Bruton (nps)
Scorers: Vassallo, Harding, Burford
Attendance: 293

Date: Saturday 07/04/1984
Result: **WITNEY TOWN 1 GLOUCESTER CITY 0**
Competition: Southern League Premier Division
Teamsheet: Hards, McCoy, Hunt, DE Bruton, Harding, Walker, Vassallo, Sweeney, Waite, Thompson, Burford
Substitute: Dangerfield (nps)

Date: Wednesday 11/04/1984
Result: **GRAVESEND & NORTHFLEET 3 GLOUCESTER CITY 1**
Competition: Southern League Premier Division
Teamsheet: Hards, McCoy, John, Thompson, Harding, Hunt, Walker, Sweeney, Waite, Gwyther, Burford
Substitute: O'Reilly (nps)
Scorer: Waite

Date: Saturday 14/04/1984
Result: **DORCHESTER TOWN 1 GLOUCESTER CITY 3**
Competition: Southern League Premier Division
Teamsheet: Hards, McCoy, John, Dangerfield, Harding, Vassallo, Burford, Sweeney, Hunt, Gwyther, Leitch
Substitute: O'Reilly (nps)
Scorers: Gwyther (2), Harding

Date: Saturday 21/04/1984
Result: **GLOUCESTER CITY 5 BEDWORTH UNITED 2**
Competition: Southern League Premier Division
Teamsheet: Hards, McCoy, Dangerfield, DE Bruton, Harding, Hunt, Sweeney, Vassallo, Gwyther, Leitch, M Bruton
Substitute: Waite (nps)
Scorers: M Bruton (4, 1 pen), own goal
Attendance: 317

Date: Monday 23/04/1984
Result: **GLOUCESTER CITY 0 CHELTENHAM TOWN 0**
Competition: Southern League Premier Division
Teamsheet: Hards, McCoy, Dangerfield, DE Bruton, Harding, Vassallo, Leitch, Sweeney, Waite, Gwyther, M Bruton
Substitute: Hunt (nps)
Attendance: 1030

Date: Saturday 28/04/1984
Result: **STOURBRIDGE 1 GLOUCESTER CITY 2**
Competition: Southern League Premier Division
Teamsheet: Hards, McCoy, Dangerfield, DE Bruton, Harding, Vassallo, Waite, Sweeney, Leitch, Gwyther, M Bruton
Substitute: Hunt (nps)
Scorers: M Bruton, Harding

Date: Monday 30/04/1984
Result: **FOREST GREEN ROVERS 0 GLOUCESTER CITY 4**
Competition: Gloucestershire FA Northern Senior Professional Cup Final
Teamsheet: Hards, McCoy, Dangerfield, DE Bruton, Harding, Hunt, Waite, Sweeney, Leitch, Gwyther, M Bruton
Substitutes: Burford (nps), John (nps)
Scorers: Waite (2), Sweeney, Gwyther
Attendance: 1000

Date: Wednesday 02/05/1984
Result: **WORCESTER CITY 3 GLOUCESTER CITY 1**
Competition: Worcestershire FA Senior Challenge Cup Final 2nd Leg
Teamsheet: Hards, McCoy, Hunt, DE Bruton, Harding, Walker, Vassallo, Sweeney, Waite, Gwyther, M Bruton
Substitute: Burford (nps)
Scorer: M Bruton (pen)

Date: Saturday 05/05/1984
Result: **GLOUCESTER CITY 3 FAREHAM TOWN 3**
Competition: Southern League Premier Division
Teamsheet: Hards, McCoy, Dangerfield, John, Harding, Vassallo, Hunt, Sweeney, Waite, Gwyther, M Bruton
Substitute: Burford (nps)
Scorers: Sweeney, Harding, Waite
Attendance: 304

Appearances – DE Bruton 48, M Bruton 47, MT Burford 29(2), CJ Callaway 1, G Cook 4, B Curtis 1(1), DA Dangerfield 7, G Davies 12(1), CS Garland 2, J Garwood 9(1), DG Gillies 12, DJA Gwyther 50(1), SJ Harding 48, NA Hards 50, Jasper Hughes 2, Jeff Hughes 0(1), TA Hughes 2, P Hunt 38(1), I John 20(1), AB Leitch 5(1), D McCoy 33, G Merrick 8, T Mills 2, MG Mulraney 1, C O'Reilly 5, N Sillett 4, G Sweeney 51, K Tanner 25, M Thompson 3, BE Vassallo 18, M Waite 44, S Walker 41.
Others selected but did not play: J Lloyd, GD Mockridge, C Taylor.
Scorers – M Bruton 27, M Waite 14, DJA Gwyther 12, MT Burford 10, DE Bruton 8, SJ Harding 6, G Sweeney 3, S Walker 3, K Tanner 2, CS Garland 1, Jeff Hughes 1, D McCoy 1, C O'Reilly 1, B Vassallo 1, own goal 1.

SOUTHERN LEAGUE PREMIER DIVISION

POS	CLUB	P	W	D	L	F	A	PTS
1	DARTFORD	38	23	9	6	67	32	78
2	FISHER ATHLETIC	38	22	9	7	80	42	75
3	CHELMSFORD CITY	38	19	9	10	67	45	66
4	GRAVESEND & NORTHFLEET	38	18	9	11	50	38	63
5	WITNEY TOWN	38	18	6	14	75	50	60
6	KING'S LYNN	38	18	6	14	42	45	60
7	FOLKESTONE TOWN	38	16	9	13	60	56	57
8	CHELTENHAM TOWN	38	16	7	15	63	56	55
9	**GLOUCESTER CITY**	38	13	15	10	55	50	54
10	HASTINGS UNITED	38	15	9	14	55	57	54
11	BEDWORTH UNITED	38	15	9	14	51	55	54
12	WELLING UNITED	38	15	7	16	61	61	52
13	AUTOMOTIVE PRODUCTS LEAMINGTON	38	14	9	15	73	83	51
14	CORBY TOWN	38	12	14	12	55	54	50
15	FAREHAM TOWN	38	13	11	14	65	70	50
16	ALVECHURCH	38	12	12	14	56	63	48
17	SUTTON COLDFIELD TOWN	38	10	14	14	49	53	44
18	GOSPORT BOROUGH	38	6	15	17	31	64	33
19	DORCHESTER TOWN	38	4	8	26	40	69	20
20	STOURBRIDGE	38	4	7	27	30	82	19
		760	283	194	283	1125	1125	1043

SEASON 1984-1985
(Home Ground: Horton Road Stadium)

Date: Saturday 18/08/1984
Result: **BEDWORTH UNITED 0 GLOUCESTER CITY 2**
Competition: Southern League Premier Division
Teamsheet: Hards, O'Reilly, Tanner, Elliott, Harding, Burford, Vassallo, Waite, Kalewski, Casey, Truswell
Substitute: Langford (for Burford)
Scorers: Casey, Kalewski
Attendance: 240

Date: Tuesday 21/08/1984
Result: **GLOUCESTER CITY 4 REDDITCH UNITED 1**
Competition: Southern League Cup Group 14
Teamsheet: Hards, O'Reilly, Tanner, Stokes, Harding, Waite, Truswell, Casey, Kalewski, Vassallo, Langford
Substitute: McCoy (nps)
Scorers: Truswell, Casey (2), Langford
Attendance: 353

Date: Saturday 25/08/1984
Result: **GLOUCESTER CITY 4 CRAWLEY TOWN 2**
Competition: Southern League Premier Division
Teamsheet: Hards, O'Reilly, Tanner, Stokes, Harding, Waite, Truswell, Casey, Kalewski, Vassallo, Langford
Substitute: McCoy (nps)
Scorers: Casey, Langford (2), Kalewski
Attendance: 398

Date: Monday 27/08/1984
Result: **GLOUCESTER CITY 6 TROWBRIDGE TOWN 1**
Competition: Southern League Premier Division
Teamsheet: Hards, O'Reilly, Tanner, Harris, Harding, Waite, Truswell, Casey, Kalewski, Vassallo, Langford
Substitute: Burford (nps)
Scorers: Langford, Casey (3), Kalewski, Waite
Attendance: 562

Date: Saturday 01/09/1984
Result: **FISHER ATHLETIC 2 GLOUCESTER CITY 1**
Competition: Southern League Premier Division
Teamsheet: Hards, O'Reilly, Tanner, Harris, Harding, Waite, Truswell, Casey, Kalewski, Vassallo, Langford
Substitute: Burford (for Truswell)
Scorer: Waite
Attendance: 280

Date: Wednesday 05/09/1984
Result: **CHELTENHAM TOWN 4 GLOUCESTER CITY 0**
Competition: Southern League Cup Group 14
Teamsheet: Hards, O'Reilly, Tanner, Harris, Harding, Burford, Truswell, Waite, Kalewski, Casey, Langford
Substitute: Stokes (for Truswell)
Attendance: 903

Date: Saturday 08/09/1984
Result: **KING'S LYNN 2 GLOUCESTER CITY 2**
Competition: Southern League Premier Division
Teamsheet: Hards, Harris, Tanner, Stokes, Elliott, Truswell, Waite, Casey, Kalewski, Vassallo, Langford
Substitute: Burford (nps)
Scorers: Harris, Kalewski
Attendance: 450

Date: Tuesday 11/09/1984
Result: **BROMSGROVE ROVERS 1 GLOUCESTER CITY 1**
Competition: Southern League Cup Group 14
Teamsheet: Hards, O'Reilly, Tanner, Harris, Elliott, Waite, Truswell, Casey, Kalewski, Vassallo, Langford
Substitute: Burford (nps)
Scorer: Casey
Attendance: 485

Date: Saturday 15/09/1984
Result: **LLANELLI 2 GLOUCESTER CITY 5**
Competition: FA Cup 1st Qualifying Round
Teamsheet: Hards, O'Reilly, Tanner, Stokes, Elliott, Harris, Truswell, Casey, Kalewski, Vassallo, Waite
Substitute: Langford (for Waite)
Scorers: Casey (4), Harris
Attendance: 203

Date: Tuesday 18/09/1984
Result: **GLOUCESTER CITY 1 HALESOWEN TOWN 2**
Competition: Worcestershire FA Senior Challenge Cup 1st Round
Teamsheet: Hards, McCoy, O'Reilly, Stokes, Harding, Harris, Truswell, Casey, Kalewski, Vassallo, Langford
Substitutes: Waite (for -----), Tanner (for -----)
Scorer: Casey (pen)
Attendance: 336

Date: Saturday 22/09/1984
Result: **GLOUCESTER CITY 3 CORBY TOWN 2**
Competition: Southern League Premier Division
Teamsheet: Hards, O'Reilly, Tanner, Stokes, Harding, Harris, Economou, Casey, Kalewski, Vassallo, Langford
Substitute: Truswell (for Economou)
Scorer: Casey (3)
Attendance: 437

Date: Tuesday 25/09/1984
Result: **REDDITCH UNITED 1 GLOUCESTER CITY 1**
Competition: Southern League Cup Group 14
Teamsheet: Hards, O'Reilly, Tanner, Stokes, Harding, Harris, Truswell, Casey, Kalewski, Vassallo, Langford
Substitute: Waite (for Harris)
Scorer: Casey
Attendance: 293

Date: Saturday 06/10/1984
Result: **GLOUCESTER CITY 0 GRAVESEND & NORTHFLEET 1**
Competition: Southern League Premier Division
Teamsheet: Hards, Tanner, O'Reilly, Stokes, Harding, Harris, Economou, Casey, Kalewski, Vassallo, Langford
Substitute: Truswell (for Tanner)
Attendance: 504

Date: Tuesday 09/10/1984
Result: **GLOUCESTER CITY 1 CHELTENHAM TOWN 0**
Competition: Southern League Cup Group 14
Teamsheet: Hards, Tanner, O'Reilly, Stokes, Harding, Waite, Truswell, Casey, Kalewski, Vassallo, Economou
Substitute: Langford (for Waite)
Scorer: Waite
Attendance: 824

Date: Saturday 13/10/1984
Result: **GLOUCESTER CITY 1 BARRY TOWN 3**
Competition: FA Cup 3rd Qualifying Round
Teamsheet: Hards, Tanner, O'Reilly, Stokes, Harding, Truswell, Waite, Casey, Kalewski, Vassallo, Harris
Substitute: Langford (for Harris)
Scorer: Casey
Attendance: 626

Date: Tuesday 16/10/1984
Result: **GLOUCESTER CITY 1 BROMSGROVE ROVERS 2**
Competition: Southern League Cup Group 14
Teamsheet: Hards, O'Reilly, Andrews, Harris, Stokes, Waite, Truswell, Casey, Kalewski, Vassallo, Langford
Substitute: Elliott (for Casey)
Scorer: Casey
Attendance: 347

Date: Saturday 20/10/1984
Result: **WELLING UNITED 2 GLOUCESTER CITY 0**
Competition: Southern League Premier Division
Teamsheet: Hards, McCoy, Andrews, Stokes, Harris, Waite, Truswell, O'Reilly, Kalewski, Vassallo, Langford
Substitute: Elliott (for McCoy)
Attendance: 228

Date: Tuesday 30/10/1984
Result: **GLOUCESTER CITY 0 AUTOMOTIVE PRODUCTS LEAMINGTON 0**
Competition: Southern League Premier Division
Teamsheet: Hards, Andrews, McCoy, Stokes, Harris, Duggan, Waite, Casey, Kalewski, Vassallo, Shipley
Substitute: Langford (nps)
Attendance: 381

Date: Saturday 03/11/1984
Result: **FOLKESTONE TOWN 5 GLOUCESTER CITY 0**
Competition: Southern League Premier Division
Teamsheet: Hards, McCoy, Andrews, Stokes, Harris, Duggan, Truswell, Shipley, Kalewski, Vassallo, Langford
Substitute: Waite (nps)
Attendance: 662

Date: Saturday 10/11/1984
Result: **HASTINGS UNITED 3 GLOUCESTER CITY 2**
Competition: Southern League Premier Division
Teamsheet: Hards, McCoy, Harris, Stokes, Elliott, Duggan, Truswell, Shipley, Kalewski, Vassallo, Langford
Substitute: O'Reilly (for Harris)
Scorers: Langford, Kalewski
Attendance: 371

Date: Tuesday 13/11/1984
Result: **WITNEY TOWN 5 GLOUCESTER CITY 1**
Competition: Southern League Premier Division
Teamsheet: Hards, McCoy, Andrews, Stokes, Elliott, Duggan, Drinkwater, Shipley, Kalewski, Vassallo, Langford
Substitute: Waite (for Duggan)
Scorer: Langford
Attendance: 212

Date: Saturday 17/11/1984
Result: **GLOUCESTER CITY 1 SHEPSHED CHARTERHOUSE 2**
Competition: Southern League Premier Division
Teamsheet: Hards, Tanner, McCoy, Stokes, Elliott, Truswell, Waite, Casey, Kalewski, Vassallo, Langford
Substitute: Duggan (for McCoy)
Scorer: Kalewski
Attendance: 361

Date: Saturday 24/11/1984
Result: **WILLENHALL TOWN 1 GLOUCESTER CITY 0**
Competition: Southern League Premier Division
Teamsheet: Hards, O'Reilly, Tanner, Stokes, Harris, Waite, Truswell, Casey, Kalewski, Vassallo, Langford
Substitute: Shipley (nps)
Attendance: 224

Date: Saturday 01/12/1984
Result: **GLOUCESTER CITY 2 CHELMSFORD CITY 1**
Competition: Southern League Premier Division
Teamsheet: Hards, O'Reilly, Tanner, Stokes, Harris, Truswell, Waite, Casey, Langford, Vassallo, Shipley
Substitute: Andrews (for Casey)
Scorers: Casey, Waite
Attendance: 378

Date: Saturday 08/12/1984
Result: **ALVECHURCH 3 GLOUCESTER CITY 2**
Competition: Southern League Premier Division
Teamsheet: Hards, O'Reilly, Tanner, Stokes, Harris, Truswell, Waite, Casey, Kalewski, Vassallo, Langford
Substitute: Shipley (nps)
Scorers: Langford, Casey
Attendance: 321

Date: Saturday 15/12/1984
Result: **GLOUCESTER CITY 2 YEOVIL TOWN 0**
Competition: FA Trophy 3rd Qualifying Round
Teamsheet: Hards, Duggan, Tanner, Stokes, Harris, Truswell, Waite, Casey, Kalewski, Vassallo, Langford
Substitute: Shipley (nps)
Scorers: Waite, Langford
Attendance: 520

Date: Saturday 22/12/1984
Result: **GLOUCESTER CITY 2 ROAD SEA SOUTHAMPTON 1**
Competition: Southern League Premier Division
Teamsheet: Hards, Duggan, Tanner, Stokes, Harris, Truswell, Shipley, Casey, Waite, Vassallo, Langford
Substitute: O'Reilly (nps)
Scorers: Waite, Langford
Attendance: 306

Date: Wednesday 26/12/1984
Result: **CHELTENHAM TOWN 4 GLOUCESTER CITY 0**
Competition: Southern League Premier Division
Teamsheet: Hards, Duggan, Tanner, Stokes, Harris, Truswell, Shipley, Casey, Waite, Vassallo, Langford
Substitute: McCoy (for Duggan)
Attendance: 1150

Date: Saturday 29/12/1984
Result: **GLOUCESTER CITY 2 KING'S LYNN 3**
Competition: Southern League Premier Division
Teamsheet: Hards, Shipley, Tanner, Stokes, Elliott, Truswell, Waite, Casey, Kalewski, Vassallo, Langford
Substitute: McCoy (nps)
Scorer: Casey (2)
Attendance: 328

Date: Tuesday 01/01/1985
Result: **GLOUCESTER CITY 0 FAREHAM TOWN 5**
Competition: Southern League Premier Division
Teamsheet: Hards, Shipley, Tanner, Stokes, Elliott, Truswell, Waite, Casey, Kalewski, Vassallo, Langford
Substitute: McCoy (nps)
Attendance: 357

Date: Saturday 05/01/1985
Result: **CRAWLEY TOWN 3 GLOUCESTER CITY 1**
Competition: Southern League Premier Division
Teamsheet: Hards, Shipley, Tanner, Harris, Kalewski, Truswell, O'Reilly, Casey, Waite, Vassallo, Langford
Substitute: Elliott (nps)
Scorer: Langford
Attendance: 361

Date: Thursday 24/01/1985
Result: **GLOUCESTER CITY 0 MAIDSTONE UNITED 2**
Competition: FA Trophy 1st Round
Teamsheet: Hards, Duggan, Tanner, Stokes, Harris, Truswell, Waite, Casey, Kalewski, Vassallo, Langford
Substitute: Shipley (nps)
Attendance: 384

Date: Saturday 23/02/1985
Result: **GLOUCESTER CITY 1 ALVECHURCH 1**
Competition: Southern League Premier Division
Teamsheet: Hards, Harris, Edwards, Stokes, Lander, Duggan, Truswell, Wilton, Kalewski, Casey, Langford
Substitute: Vassallo (for Duggan)
Scorer: Casey
Attendance: 330

Date: Saturday 02/03/1985
Result: **TROWBRIDGE TOWN 0 GLOUCESTER CITY 3**
Competition: Southern League Premier Division
Teamsheet: Hards, Harris, Edwards, Stokes, Lander, Truswell, Shipley, Casey, Kalewski, Vassallo, Wilton
Substitute: Iddon (nps)
Scorers: Casey (2), Kalewski
Attendance: 305

Date: Saturday 09/03/1985
Result: **CHELMSFORD CITY 1 GLOUCESTER CITY 0**
Competition: Southern League Premier Division
Teamsheet: Hards, Harris, Edwards, Stokes, Lander, Shipley, Truswell, Casey, Kalewski, Vassallo, Wilton
Substitute: Iddon (for Harris)
Attendance: 767

Date: Tuesday 19/03/1985
Result: **AUTOMOTIVE PRODUCTS LEAMINGTON 1 GLOUCESTER CITY 0**
Competition: Southern League Premier Division
Teamsheet: Hards, Shipley, Tanner, Stokes, Lander, Truswell, Langford, Casey, Kalewski, Vassallo, Wilton
Substitute: Iddon (nps)

Date: Saturday 23/03/1985
Result: **ROAD SEA SOUTHAMPTON 2 GLOUCESTER CITY 0**
Competition: Southern League Premier Division
Teamsheet: Hards, Shipley, Edwards, Stokes, Lander, Langford, Truswell, Casey, Kalewski, Vassallo, Wilton
Substitute: McCoy (nps)

Date: Saturday 30/03/1985
Result: **GLOUCESTER CITY 1 FOLKESTONE TOWN 3**
Competition: Southern League Premier Division
Teamsheet: Hards, Truswell, Edwards, Stokes, Lander, Tanner, Macauley, Casey, Kalewski, Vassallo, Langford
Substitute: Iddon (nps)
Scorer: Casey
Attendance: 280

Date: Wednesday 03/04/1985
Result: **SHEPSHED CHARTERHOUSE 2 GLOUCESTER CITY 2**
Competition: Southern League Premier Division
Teamsheet: Hards, McCoy, Tanner, Stokes, Lander, Macauley, Duggan, Casey, Truswell, Vassallo, Wilton
Substitute: Langford (for Duggan)
Scorers: Truswell, Casey

Date: Saturday 06/04/1985
Result: **CORBY TOWN 2 GLOUCESTER CITY 0**
Competition: Southern League Premier Division
Teamsheet: Hards, McCoy, Edwards, Stokes, Lander, Macauley, Langford, Casey, Truswell, Vassallo, Wilton
Substitute: Kalewski (for Truswell)

Date: Saturday 13/04/1985
Result: **GLOUCESTER CITY 1 WITNEY TOWN 0**
Competition: Southern League Premier Division
Teamsheet: Hards, Harris, Edwards, Stokes, Lander, Macauley, Langford, Casey, Kalewski, Vassallo, Wilton
Substitute: Shipley (nps)
Scorer: Casey
Attendance: 268

Date: Sunday 14/04/1985
Result: **GLOUCESTER CITY 1 WELLING UNITED 1**
Competition: Southern League Premier Division
Teamsheet: Hards, Shipley, Edwards, Stokes, Lander, Truswell, Langford, Casey, Kalewski, Vassallo, Wilton
Substitute: McCoy (for Edwards)
Scorer: Casey
Attendance: 379

Date: Wednesday 17/04/1985
Result: **GLOUCESTER CITY 0 FISHER ATHLETIC 4**
Competition: Southern League Premier Division
Teamsheet: Hards, Shipley, Tanner, Stokes, Lander, Macauley, Langford, Casey, Kalewski, Vassallo, Truswell
Substitute: Wilton (for Langford)
Attendance: 308

Date: Saturday 20/04/1985
Result: **GRAVESEND & NORTHFLEET 2 GLOUCESTER CITY 1**
Competition: Southern League Premier Division
Teamsheet: Hards, Shipley, Edwards, Stokes, Lander, Macauley, Harris, Casey, Kalewski, Vassallo, Wilton
Substitute: Truswell (for -----)
Scorer: Truswell

Date: Monday 22/04/1985
Result: **FAREHAM TOWN 1 GLOUCESTER CITY 1**
Competition: Southern League Premier Division
Teamsheet: Hards, Shipley, Edwards, Stokes, Lander, Macauley, Langford, Casey, Truswell, Vassallo, Wilton
Substitute: Kalewski (for -----)
Scorer: Wilton

Date: Thursday 25/04/1985
Result: **GLOUCESTER CITY 4 HASTINGS UNITED 0**
Competition: Southern League Premier Division
Teamsheet: Hards, Shipley, Edwards, Stokes, Lander, Macauley, Langford, Casey, Kalewski, Harris, Truswell
Substitute: Wilton (nps)
Scorers: Harris, Casey (3)
Attendance: 248

Date: Monday 29/04/1985
Result: **GLOUCESTER CITY 2 FOREST GREEN ROVERS 3** (aet)
Competition: Gloucestershire FA Northern Senior Professional Cup Final
Teamsheet: Hards, McCoy, Edwards, Stokes, Elliott, Macauley, Langford, Iddon, Powell, Vassallo, Wilton
Substitutes: Shipley (nps), Casey (for -----)
Scorer: Casey (2)
Attendance: 324

Date: Tuesday 30/04/1985
Result: **GLOUCESTER CITY 2 CHELTENHAM TOWN 3**
Competition: Southern League Premier Division
Teamsheet: Hards, Shipley, Edwards, Stokes, Lander, Macauley, Harris, Casey, Kalewski, Vassallo, Iddon
Substitute: Truswell (nps)
Scorers: Macauley, Harris
Attendance: 1220

Date: Saturday 04/05/1985
Result: **GLOUCESTER CITY 1 BEDWORTH UNITED 0**
Competition: Southern League Premier Division
Teamsheet: Hards, Truswell, Edwards, Stokes, Elliott, Macauley, Harris, Casey, Kalewski, Iddon, Wilton
Substitute: Langford (nps)
Scorer: Casey
Attendance: 269

Date: Monday 06/05/1985
Result: **GLOUCESTER CITY 0 WILLENHALL TOWN 3**
Competition: Southern League Premier Division
Teamsheet: Hards, Truswell, Edwards, Stokes, Lander, Macauley, Harris, Casey, Kalewski, Iddon, Wilton
Substitute: Langford (for Edwards)
Attendance: 379

Appearances – R Andrews 5(1), MT Burford 3(1), KT Casey 45(1), D Drinkwater 1, D Duggan 10(1), J Economou 3, M Edwards 15, R Elliott 11(2), SJ Harding 12, NA Hards 50, GW Harris 33, D Iddon 4(1), MR Kalewski 43(2), MT Lander 16, MJ Langford 38(6), R Macauley 12, D McCoy 10(2), C O'Reilly 21(1), C Powell 1, P Shipley 20, WD Stokes 44(1), K Tanner 27(1), K Truswell 42(3), BE Vassallo 45(1), M Waite 25(3), RB Wilton 14(1).
Scorers – KT Casey 36, MJ Langford 10, MR Kalewski 7, M Waite 6, G Harris 4, K Truswell 3, R Macauley 1, RB Wilton 1.

SEASON BY SEASON

SOUTHERN LEAGUE PREMIER DIVISION

POS	CLUB	P	W	D	L	F	A	PTS
1	CHELTENHAM TOWN	38	24	5	9	83	41	77
2	KING'S LYNN	38	23	6	9	73	48	75
3	CRAWLEY TOWN	38	22	8	8	76	52	74
4	WILLENHALL TOWN	38	20	8	10	57	38	68
5	ROAD SEA SOUTHAMPTON	38	21	4	13	76	52	67
6	WELLING UNITED	38	18	11	9	55	38	65
7	FOLKESTONE TOWN	38	19	6	13	70	54	63
8	FISHER ATHLETIC	38	19	5	14	67	57	62
9	CHELMSFORD CITY	38	17	10	11	52	50	61
10	SHEPSHED CHARTERHOUSE	38	18	5	15	67	50	59
11	CORBY TOWN	38	15	6	17	56	54	51
12	BEDWORTH UNITED	38	14	8	16	48	52	50
13	GRAVESEND & NORTHFLEET	38	12	12	14	46	46	48
14	FAREHAM TOWN	38	13	8	17	52	55	47
15	ALVECHURCH	38	11	7	20	53	59	40
16	HASTINGS UNITED	38	11	7	20	46	71	40
17	WITNEY TOWN	38	9	12	17	51	58	39
18	**GLOUCESTER CITY**	**38**	**10**	**6**	**22**	**49**	**74**	**36**
19	TROWBRIDGE TOWN	38	10	5	23	45	83	35
20	AUTOMOTIVE PRODUCTS LEAMINGTON	38	2	5	31	22	112	11
		760	308	144	308	1144	1144	1068

SEASON 1985-1986
(Home Ground: Horton Road Stadium)

Date: Saturday 24/08/1985
Result: **GLOUCESTER CITY 1 STOURBRIDGE 1**
Competition: Southern League Midland Division
Teamsheet: S Smith, Norman, Edwards, Scarrott, Lander, Richardson, Spittle, Vassallo, Truswell, Macauley, Paterson
Substitute: Burford (for Spittle)
Scorer: Paterson
Attendance: 309

Date: Monday 26/08/1985
Result: **GLOUCESTER CITY 0 BILSTON TOWN 3**
Competition: Southern League Midland Division
Teamsheet: S Smith, Norman, Edwards, Scarrott, Lander, Vassallo, Spittle, Wilton, Truswell, Macauley, Paterson
Substitute: Burford (for Wilton)
Attendance: 354

Date: Saturday 31/08/1985
Result: **RUSHDEN TOWN 1 GLOUCESTER CITY 2**
Competition: Southern League Midland Division
Teamsheet: S Smith, Norman, Scarrott, Goodwin, Lander, Macauley, Spittle, Vassallo, Truswell, Paterson, Wilton
Substitute: Tanner (nps)
Scorers: Spittle, Paterson

Date: Tuesday 03/09/1985
Result: **FOREST GREEN ROVERS 4 GLOUCESTER CITY 2**
Competition: Southern League Cup Group 16
Teamsheet: S Smith, Norman, Scarrott, Goodwin, Lander, Macauley, Spittle, Vassallo, Truswell, Paterson, Wilton
Substitute: Tanner (for Macauley)
Scorer: Truswell (2)

Date: Saturday 07/09/1985
Result: **GLOUCESTER CITY 0 TON PENTRE 0**
Competition: FA Cup 1st Qualifying Round
Teamsheet: S Smith, Norman, Scarrott, Goodwin, Lander, Macauley, Spittle, Vassallo, Truswell, Paterson, Wilton
Substitute: Richardson (for Wilton)
Attendance: 246

Date: Wednesday 11/09/1985
Result: **TON PENTRE 3 GLOUCESTER CITY 3** (aet)
Competition: FA Cup 1st Qualifying Round Replay
Teamsheet: S Smith, Norman, Scarrott, Goodwin, Lander, Macauley, Spittle, Vassallo, Truswell, Paterson, Burford
Substitute: Wilton (for Burford)
Scorer: Spittle (3)
Attendance: 326

Date: Saturday 14/09/1985
Result: **GRANTHAM 1 GLOUCESTER CITY 1**
Competition: Southern League Midland Division
Teamsheet: S Smith, Norman, Scarrott, Goodwin, Lander, Macauley, Spittle, Vassallo, Truswell, Paterson, Wilton
Substitute: Edwards (nps)
Scorer: Truswell
Attendance: 286

[295]

Date: Monday 16/09/1985
Result: **TON PENTRE 2 GLOUCESTER CITY 1**
Competition: FA Cup 1st Qualifying Round 2nd Replay
Teamsheet: S Smith, Richardson, Scarrott, Goodwin, Lander, Macauley, Burford, Vassallo, Truswell, Paterson, Wilton
Substitute: Norman (nps)
Scorer: own goal
Attendance: 460

Date: Saturday 21/09/1985
Result: **GLOUCESTER CITY 0 VALLEY SPORTS RUGBY 0**
Competition: Southern League Midland Division
Teamsheet: S Smith, Goodwin, Edwards, Scarrott, Lander, Goff, Spittle, Vassallo, Truswell, Macauley, Burford
Substitute: Paterson (for Spittle)
Attendance: 313

Date: Tuesday 24/09/1985
Result: **GLOUCESTER CITY 2 WORCESTER CITY 1**
Competition: Southern League Cup Group 16
Teamsheet: S Smith, Goff, Scarrott, Goodwin, Edwards, Paterson, Spittle, Macauley, Truswell, Wilton, Burford
Substitute: Richardson (nps)
Scorers: Burford, Goff
Attendance: 300

Date: Saturday 28/09/1985
Result: **GLOUCESTER CITY 1 SUTTON COLDFIELD TOWN 1**
Competition: Southern League Midland Division
Teamsheet: S Smith, Edwards, Scarrott, Goodwin, Lander, Macauley, Simpson, Goff, Truswell, Paterson, Burford
Substitute: Vassallo (for Truswell)
Scorer: Scarrott (pen)
Attendance: 285

Date: Tuesday 01/10/1985
Result: **MERTHYR TYDFIL 0 GLOUCESTER CITY 1**
Competition: Southern League Cup Group 16
Teamsheet: S Smith, Goodwin, Edwards, Scarrott, Lander, Macauley, Simpson, Goff, Wright, Paterson, Burford
Substitute: Vassallo (nps)
Scorer: Edwards

Date: Saturday 05/10/1985
Result: **GLOUCESTER CITY 2 LEAMINGTON 3**
Competition: Southern League Midland Division
Teamsheet: S Smith, Goodwin, Edwards, Scarrott, Lander, Goff, Simpson, Macauley, Wright, Paterson, Spittle
Substitute: Vassallo (for -----)
Scorers: Goff, Vassallo
Attendance: 285

Date: Tuesday 08/10/1985
Result: **GLOUCESTER CITY 1 MERTHYR TYDFIL 1**
Competition: Southern League Cup Group 16
Teamsheet: S Smith, Goodwin, Edwards, Scarrott, Lander, Goff, Spittle, Vassallo, Wright, Macauley, Truswell
Substitute: Paterson (nps)
Scorer: Truswell
Attendance: 223

Date: Saturday 12/10/1985
Result: **MOOR GREEN 1 GLOUCESTER CITY 5**
Competition: Southern League Midland Division
Teamsheet: S Smith, Goodwin, Edwards, Scarrott, Lander, Macauley, Simpson, Goff, Wright, Vassallo, Truswell
Substitute: Paterson (for -----)
Scorers: Truswell, Wright (2), Truswell, Macauley, Paterson

Date: Tuesday 15/10/1985
Result: **GLOUCESTER CITY 0 FOREST GREEN ROVERS 3**
Competition: Southern League Cup Group 16
Teamsheet: S Smith, Goodwin, Edwards, Scarrott, Lander, Macauley, Simpson, Goff, Wright, Vassallo, Truswell
Substitute: Paterson (for Simpson)
Attendance: 370

Date: Saturday 19/10/1985
Result: **GLOUCESTER CITY 5 BANBURY UNITED 1**
Competition: Southern League Midland Division
Teamsheet: S Smith, Norman, Scarrott, Goodwin, Lander, Macauley, Simpson, Goff, Wright, Vassallo, Truswell
Substitute: Paterson (nps)
Scorers: Wright (2), Truswell (2), own goal
Attendance: 263

Date: Monday 21/10/1985
Result: **WORCESTER CITY 2 GLOUCESTER CITY 0**
Competition: Southern League Cup Group 16
Teamsheet: S Smith, Norman, Scarrott, Goodwin, Lander, Macauley, Goff, Paterson, Wright, Vassallo, Truswell
Substitute: Simpson (for Truswell)
Attendance: 948

Date: Saturday 26/10/1985
Result: **LEICESTER UNITED 1 GLOUCESTER CITY 2**
Competition: Southern League Midland Division
Teamsheet: S Smith, Norman, Scarrott, Goodwin, Lander, Macauley, Simpson, Goff, Wright, Vassallo, S Bell
Substitute: Paterson (for -----)
Scorers: Vassallo, Wright

Date: Tuesday 29/10/1985
Result: **GLOUCESTER CITY 4 MOOR GREEN 1**
Competition: Southern League Midland Division
Teamsheet: S Smith, Norman, Scarrott, Goodwin, Lander, Macauley, Simpson, Goff, Wright, Vassallo, Paterson
Substitute: Bayliss (nps)
Scorers: Wright (2), own goal, Norman
Attendance: 348

Date: Saturday 02/11/1985
Result: **GLOUCESTER CITY 1 BRIDGNORTH TOWN 2**
Competition: Southern League Midland Division
Teamsheet: S Smith, Norman, Scarrott, Goodwin, Lander, Macauley, Simpson, Goff, Wright, Vassallo, Paterson
Substitute: Bayliss (nps)
Scorer: Simpson
Attendance: 318

Date: Monday 11/11/1985
Result: **CHELTENHAM TOWN 7 GLOUCESTER CITY 1**
Competition: Gloucestershire FA Northern Senior Professional Cup Semi-Final
Teamsheet: S Smith, Norman, Scarrott, Goodwin, Lander, Macauley, Simpson, Goff, Wright, Vassallo, Bayliss
Substitute: Edwards (for Bayliss)
Scorer: Vassallo
Attendance: 753

Date: Saturday 16/11/1985
Result: **GLOUCESTER CITY 1 WELLINGBOROUGH TOWN 1**
Competition: Southern League Midland Division
Teamsheet: S Smith, Norman, Scarrott, Goodwin, Lander, Macauley, Simpson, Goff, Wright, Vassallo, Granger
Substitute: Edwards (Scarrott)
Scorer: Wright
Attendance: 265

Date: Tuesday 19/11/1985
Result: **LEAMINGTON 2 GLOUCESTER CITY 1**
Competition: Southern League Midland Division
Teamsheet: S Smith, Norman, Scarrott, Goodwin, Lander, Macauley, Simpson, Goff, Wright, Vassallo, Paterson
Substitute: Edwards (nps)
Scorer: Wright
Attendance: 134

Date: Saturday 23/11/1985
Result: **OLDBURY UNITED 0 GLOUCESTER CITY 1**
Competition: Southern League Midland Division
Teamsheet: S Smith, Norman, Scarrott, Goodwin, Lander, Macauley, Simpson, Goff, Wright, Vassallo, Paterson
Substitute: Truswell (nps)
Scorer: Simpson

Date: Saturday 30/11/1985
Result: **GLOUCESTER CITY 0 WORCESTER CITY 4**
Competition: FA Trophy 3rd Qualifying Round
Teamsheet: S Smith, Norman, Scarrott, Goodwin, Lander, Macauley, Truswell, Goff, Wright, Vassallo, Paterson
Substitute: Edwards (nps)
Attendance: 486

Date: Tuesday 03/12/1985
Result: **BROMSGROVE ROVERS 3 GLOUCESTER CITY 0**
Competition: Southern League Midland Division
Teamsheet: Martyn, Norman, Scarrott, Goodwin, Lander, Macauley, Simpson, Goff, Wright, Vassallo, Truswell
Substitute: Paterson (for Vassallo)

Date: Saturday 07/12/1985
Result: **SUTTON COLDFIELD TOWN 1 GLOUCESTER CITY 1**
Competition: Southern League Midland Division
Teamsheet: Martyn, Norman, Edwards, Goodwin, Lander, Macauley, Vassallo, Scarrott, Wright, Truswell, Goff
Substitute: Paterson (nps)
Scorer: Wright
Attendance: 200

Date: Saturday 14/12/1985
Result: **GLOUCESTER CITY 1 HEDNESFORD TOWN 0**
Competition: Southern League Midland Division
Teamsheet: Martyn, Norman, Edwards, Goodwin, Lander, Macauley, Goff, Scarrott, Simpson, Truswell, Vassallo
Substitute: Paterson (nps)
Scorer: Truswell
Attendance: 277

Date: Thursday 26/12/1985
Result: **GLOUCESTER CITY 0 FOREST GREEN ROVERS 1**
Competition: Southern League Midland Division
Teamsheet: Martyn, Goodwin, Edwards, Scarrott, Lander, Slattery, Vassallo, Goff, Wright, Macauley, Truswell
Substitute: Simpson (for Slattery)
Attendance: 472

Date: Saturday 28/12/1985
Result: **VALLEY SPORTS RUGBY 0 GLOUCESTER CITY 1**
Competition: Southern League Midland Division
Teamsheet: Martyn, Norman, Edwards, Goodwin, Lander, Macauley, Vassallo, Slattery, Wright, Truswell, N Bell
Substitute: Simpson (nps)
Scorer: Truswell

Date: Saturday 11/01/1986
Result: **BRIDGNORTH TOWN 3 GLOUCESTER CITY 3**
Competition: Southern League Midland Division
Teamsheet: Martyn, Norman, Edwards, Goodwin, Lander, Macauley, Vassallo, Slattery, Wright, Truswell, N Bell
Substitute: Scarrott (nps)
Scorers: Truswell (2), Vassallo

Date: Saturday 18/01/1986
Result: **GLOUCESTER CITY 1 COVENTRY SPORTING 1**
Competition: Southern League Midland Division
Teamsheet: Martyn, Norman, Edwards, Goodwin, Lander, Macauley, Scarrott, Slattery, Wright, Truswell, Goff
Substitute: Simpson (for Macauley)
Scorer: Goff
Attendance: 265

Date: Saturday 25/01/1986
Result: **GLOUCESTER CITY 4 RUSHDEN TOWN 0**
Competition: Southern League Midland Division
Teamsheet: Martyn, Norman, Scarrott, Goodwin, Lander, Macauley, Simpson, Goff, Wright, Truswell, Vassallo
Substitute: Slattery (for Vassallo)
Scorers: Simpson, Wright, Truswell (2)
Attendance: 242

Date: Saturday 01/02/1986
Result: **BILSTON TOWN 3 GLOUCESTER CITY 0**
Competition: Southern League Midland Division
Teamsheet: Martyn, Norman, Scarrott, Goodwin, Lander, Macauley, Truswell, Goff, Wright, N Bell, Simpson
Substitute: Edwards (nps)

Date: Saturday 22/02/1986
Result: **GLOUCESTER CITY 2 BROMSGROVE ROVERS 2**
Competition: Southern League Midland Division
Teamsheet: Martyn, Norman, Scarrott, Goodwin, Lander, Macauley, Truswell, Goff, Wright, N Bell, Simpson
Substitute: Slattery (nps)
Scorers: Scarrott (pen), N Bell
Attendance: 332

Date: Saturday 01/03/1986
Result: **GLOUCESTER CITY 0 MILE OAK ROVERS 0**
Competition: Southern League Midland Division
Teamsheet: Martyn, Norman, Scarrott, Goodwin, Lander, Macauley, Truswell, Goff, Wright, N Bell, Simpson
Substitute: Slattery (for N Bell)
Attendance: 197

Date: Tuesday 04/03/1986
Result: **GLOUCESTER CITY 2 REDDITCH UNITED 2**
Competition: Southern League Midland Division
Teamsheet: Martyn, Norman, Edwards, Goodwin, Lander, Macauley, Scarrott, Goff, Wright, Truswell, Simpson
Substitute: Slattery (for Simpson)
Scorer: Truswell (2)
Attendance: 212

Date: Saturday 08/03/1986
Result: **WELLINGBOROUGH TOWN 2 GLOUCESTER CITY 3**
Competition: Southern League Midland Division
Teamsheet: Martyn, Norman, Edwards, Goodwin, Lander, Macauley, Scarrott, Goff, Wright, Truswell, Slattery
Substitute: Waite (for Macauley)
Scorers: Scarrott (pen), Truswell, Edwards

Date: Sunday 09/03/1986
Result: **GLOUCESTER CITY 0 GRANTHAM 2**
Competition: Southern League Midland Division
Teamsheet: Martyn, Norman, Edwards, Goodwin, Lander, Macauley, Scarrott, Goff, Wright, Truswell, Slattery
Substitute: Waite (for Slattery)
Attendance: 235

Date: Saturday 15/03/1986
Result: **GLOUCESTER CITY 1 LEICESTER UNITED 3**
Competition: Southern League Midland Division
Teamsheet: Martyn, Norman, Scarrott, Goodwin, Lander, Macauley, N Smith, Goff, Truswell, Johnson, Waite
Substitute: Wright (for Waite)
Scorer: N Smith
Attendance: 234

Date: Saturday 22/03/1986
Result: **STOURBRIDGE 1 GLOUCESTER CITY 2**
Competition: Southern League Midland Division
Teamsheet: Harris, Norman, Scarrott, Goodwin, Lander, Macauley, N Smith, Goff, Wright, Johnson, Waite
Substitute: Truswell (for Macauley)
Scorers: Johnson, Lander

Date: Saturday 29/03/1986
Result: **GLOUCESTER CITY 2 MERTHYR TYDFIL 2**
Competition: Southern League Midland Division
Teamsheet: Martyn, Norman, Scarrott, Goodwin, Lander, Simpson, Goff, N Smith, Wright, Johnson, Waite
Substitute: Truswell (nps)
Scorers: Scarrott, Wright
Attendance: 269

5 April 1986

(Photograph courtesy of Simon Drake)

Players, officials and supporters say goodbye to soccer at Horton Road as the following season City moved to the new £350,000 stadium in Hempsted. The players pictured are, back row, from the left, Steve Johnson, Rob Simpson, Gary Goodwin, Steve Scarrott (player-manager), Bernie Wright, Mario Waite, Martin Lander. Front row, Tim Harris (assistant manager), Nigel Smith, Kenny Norman, Neil Goff, Stewart Martyn and Kevin Truswell. City beat Oldbury United 1-0.

PROGRAMME

1986-1987

MEADOW PARK
will be officially opened by
MR. BILLY WRIGHT, CBE
We extend to him a warm welcome
and our sincere thanks

1987 Streets named after former players on the old Horton Road Stadium site
(Courtesy of Stan Myers)

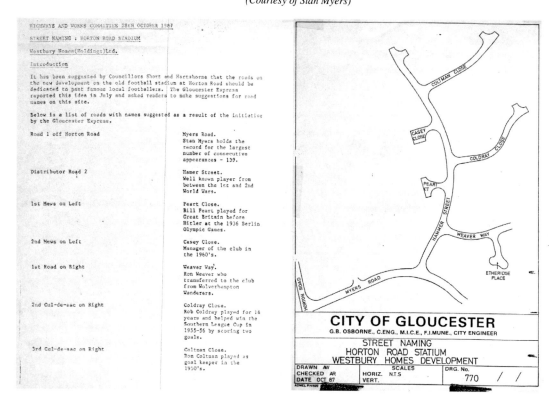

HIGHWAYS AND WORKS COMMITTEE 28th OCTOBER 1987

STREET NAMING : HORTON ROAD STADIUM

Westbury Homes(Holdings)Ltd.

Introduction

It has been suggested by Councillors Short and Hartshorne that the roads on the new development on the old football stadium at Horton Road should be dedicated to past famous local footballers. The Gloucester Express reported this idea in July and asked readers to make suggestions for road names on this site.

Below is a list of roads with names suggested as a result of the initiative by the Gloucester Express.

Road 1 off Horton Road	Myers Road. Stan Myers holds the record for the largest number of consecutive appearances - 139.
Distributor Road 2	Hamer Street. Well known player from between the 1st and 2nd World Wars.
1st Mews on Left	Peart Close. Bill Peart played for Great Britain before Hitler at the 1936 Berlin Olympic Games.
2nd Mews on Left	Casey Close. Manager of the club in the 1960's.
1st Road on Right	Weaver Way. Ron Weaver who transferred to the club from Wolverhampton Wanderers.
2nd Cul-de-sac on Right	Coldray Close. Rob Coldray played for 16 years and helped win the Southern League Cup in 1955-56 by scoring two goals.
3rd Cul-de-sac on Right	Coltman Close. Ron Coltman played as goal keeper in the 1950's.

CITY OF GLOUCESTER
G.B. OSBORNE, C.ENG., M.I.C.E., F.I.MUNE., CITY ENGINEER

STREET NAMING
HORTON ROAD STADIUM
WESTBURY HOMES DEVELOPMENT

DRAWN AW	SCALES	DRG. No.
CHECKED AR	HORIZ. N.T.S	770 / /
DATE OCT 87	VERT.	

Ron Coltman visits the Close named after him in 2006

Close encounter of the football kind

■ **TOUCHED:** Ron Coltman finally visits the street that bears his name. Left: Ron in action for Gloucester City against Cheltenham.

COLTMAN CLOSE

Date: Monday 31/03/1986
Result: **FOREST GREEN ROVERS 2 GLOUCESTER CITY 4**
Competition: Southern League Midland Division
Teamsheet: Martyn, Norman, Scarrott, Goodwin, Lander, Simpson, N Smith, Goff, Wright, Johnson, Waite
Substitute: Truswell (nps)
Scorers: Waite (3), Johnson

Date: Saturday 05/04/1986
Result: **GLOUCESTER CITY 1 OLDBURY UNITED 0**
Competition: Southern League Midland Division
Teamsheet: Martyn, Norman, Scarrott, Goodwin, Lander, Simpson, N Smith, Goff, Wright, Johnson, Waite
Substitute: Truswell (for Waite)
Scorer: Johnson
Attendance: 318

Date: Monday 07/04/1986
Result: **HEDNESFORD TOWN 3 GLOUCESTER CITY 2**
Competition: Southern League Midland Division
Teamsheet: Martyn, Goodwin, Edwards, Scarrott, Lander, Simpson, N Smith, Goff, Wright, Johnson, Truswell
Substitute: Macauley (for -----)
Scorers: Wright, N Smith
Attendance: 202

Date: Saturday 12/04/1986
Result: **COVENTRY SPORTING 3 GLOUCESTER CITY 0**
Competition: Southern League Midland Division
Teamsheet: Harris, Norman, Scarrott, Goodwin, Lander, Simpson, N Smith, Goff, Wright, Johnson, Waite
Substitute: Truswell (nps)

Date: Monday 14/04/1986
Result: **MILE OAK ROVERS 0 GLOUCESTER CITY 1**
Competition: Southern League Midland Division
Teamsheet: Harris, Norman, Edwards, Goodwin, Lander, Macauley, N Smith, Goff, Wright, Johnson, Truswell
Substitute: Simpson (nps)
Scorer: Truswell

Date: Tuesday 22/04/1986
Result: **MERTHYR TYDFIL 3 GLOUCESTER CITY 1**
Competition: Southern League Midland Division
Teamsheet: Harris, Norman, Scarrott, Goodwin, Lander, Edwards, N Smith, Goff, Wright, Johnson, Truswell
Substitute: Simpson (nps)
Scorer: N Smith

Date: Saturday 26/04/1986
Result: **BANBURY UNITED 0 GLOUCESTER CITY 2**
Competition: Southern League Midland Division
Teamsheet: Martyn, Norman, Scarrott, Goodwin, Lander, N Smith, Truswell, Goff, Wright, Johnson, Simpson
Substitute: Macauley (nps)
Scorers: Johnson, Lander

Date: Saturday 03/05/1986
Result: **REDDITCH UNITED 1 GLOUCESTER CITY 0**
Competition: Southern League Midland Division
Teamsheet: Martyn, Norman, Edwards, Goodwin, Scarrott, Macauley, N Smith, Goff, Wright, Johnson, Truswell
Substitute: Vassallo (nps)

Appearances – KA Bayliss 1, N Bell 5, S Bell 1, MT Burford 6(2), M Edwards 23(2), N Goff 41, G Goodwin 49, K Granger 1, T Harris 4, S Johnson 11, MT Lander 49, R Macauley 44(1), S Martyn 21, K Norman 40, TJ Paterson 18(5), P Richardson 2(1), SW Scarrott 48, RM Simpson 26(3), S Slattery 6(3), N Smith 11, S Smith 26, PD Spittle 11, K Tanner 0(1), K Truswell 37(2), BE Vassallo 29(2), M Waite 6(2), RB Wilton 7(1), BP Wright 38(1).
Scorers – K Truswell 17, BP Wright 13, S Johnson 4, SW Scarrott 4, PD Spittle 4, BE Vassallo 4, N Goff 3, TJ Paterson 3, RM Simpson 3, N Smith 3, M Waite 3, M Edwards 2, MT Lander 2, N Bell 1, MT Burford 1, R Macauley 1, K Norman 1, own goals 3.

PROGRAMME

PROGRAMME

1986-1987

1987-1988

SEASON BY SEASON

SOUTHERN LEAGUE MIDLAND DIVISION

POS	CLUB	P	W	D	L	F	A	PTS
1	BROMSGROVE ROVERS	40	29	5	6	95	44	92
2	REDDITCH UNITED	40	23	6	11	70	42	75
3	MERTHYR TYDFIL	40	21	10	9	60	40	73
4	VALLEY SPORTS RUGBY	40	17	14	9	41	31	65
5	STOURBRIDGE	40	15	14	11	62	39	59
6	RUSHDEN TOWN	40	17	7	16	69	74	58
7	BILSTON TOWN	40	15	12	13	60	48	57
8	BRIDGNORTH TOWN	40	13	18	9	56	45	57
9	**GLOUCESTER CITY**	**40**	**15**	**12**	**13**	**61**	**57**	**57**
10	GRANTHAM	40	16	7	17	46	59	55
11	WELLINGBOROUGH TOWN	40	15	9	16	56	56	54
12	SUTTON COLDFIELD TOWN	40	13	14	13	60	45	53
13	HEDNESFORD TOWN	40	14	9	17	67	70	51
14	FOREST GREEN ROVERS	40	14	9	17	52	56	51
15	MILE OAK ROVERS	40	14	8	18	56	73	50
16	LEICESTER UNITED	40	13	10	17	41	48	49
17	BANBURY UNITED	40	13	8	19	38	55	47
18	COVENTRY SPORTING	40	10	15	15	42	48	45
19	MOOR GREEN	40	12	6	22	63	91	42
20	LEAMINGTON	40	10	6	24	40	77	36
21	OLDBURY UNITED	40	8	7	25	50	87	31
		840	317	206	317	1185	1185	1157

SEASON 1986-1987
(Home Ground: City Stadium, Meadow Park, Hempsted)

Date: Saturday 16/08/1986
Result: **SUTTON COLDFIELD TOWN 1 GLOUCESTER CITY 1**
Competition: Southern League Midland Division
Teamsheet: Teasdale, Moore, Edwards, Bryant, Lander, Scarrott, Murphy, Vassallo, Westerberg, Johnson, Baddock
Substitute: Truswell (nps)
Scorer: Johnson

Date: Tuesday 19/08/1986
Result: **FOREST GREEN ROVERS 0 GLOUCESTER CITY 0**
Competition: Southern League Cup Group 2
Teamsheet: Teasdale, Moore, Scarrott, Bryant, Lander, Vassallo, Truswell, Murphy, Westerberg, Johnson, Baddock
Substitute: Davies (nps)

Date: Saturday 23/08/1986
Result: **GLOUCESTER CITY 3 HEDNESFORD TOWN 1**
Competition: Southern League Midland Division
Teamsheet: Teasdale, Goodwin, Scarrott, Bryant, Lander, Truswell, Murphy, Vassallo, Westerberg, Johnson, Baddock
Substitute: Payne (for Vassallo)
Scorers: Westerberg, Baddock, Johnson
Attendance: 461

Date: Monday 25/08/1986
Result: **GLOUCESTER CITY 4 HALESOWEN TOWN 1**
Competition: Southern League Midland Division
Teamsheet: Teasdale, Goodwin, Scarrott, Bryant, Lander, Truswell, Murphy, Payne, Westerberg, Johnson, Baddock
Substitute: Edwards (nps)
Scorers: Westerberg, Baddock (2), Murphy
Attendance: 549

Date: Saturday 30/08/1986
Result: **SALTASH UNITED 0 GLOUCESTER CITY 0**
Competition: FA Cup Preliminary Round
Teamsheet: Teasdale, Goodwin, Scarrott, Bryant, Lander, Truswell, Murphy, Payne, Westerberg, Johnson, Baddock
Substitutes: Edwards (nps), Harris (nps)

Date: Tuesday 02/09/1986
Result: **GLOUCESTER CITY 0 SALTASH UNITED 2**
Competition: FA Cup Preliminary Round Replay
Teamsheet: Teasdale, Goodwin, Scarrott, Bryant, Lander, Truswell, Murphy, Payne, Westerberg, Johnson, Baddock
Substitutes: Edwards (nps), Harris (nps)
Attendance: 419

Date: Saturday 06/09/1986
Result: **GLOUCESTER CITY 2 BUCKINGHAM TOWN 0**
Competition: Southern League Midland Division
Teamsheet: Teasdale, Goodwin, Scarrott, Bryant, Lander, Hughes, Murphy, Payne, Westerberg, Johnson, Baddock
Substitute: Truswell (for Westerberg)
Scorers: Baddock, Johnson
Attendance: 352

Date: Saturday 13/09/1986
Result: **VALLEY SPORTS RUGBY 1 GLOUCESTER CITY 0**
Competition: Southern League Midland Division
Teamsheet: Teasdale, Goodwin, Edwards, Bryant, Lander, Hughes, Murphy, Payne, Westerberg, Johnson, Baddock
Substitute: Truswell (for Hughes)

Date: Saturday 20/09/1986
Result: **GLOUCESTER CITY 2 LEAMINGTON 1**
Competition: Southern League Midland Division
Teamsheet: Teasdale, Moore, Goodwin, Bryant, Lander, Edwards, Murphy, Payne, Truswell, Johnson, Baddock
Substitute: Westerberg (for Moore)
Scorers: Baddock, Murphy
Attendance: 388

Date: Tuesday 23/09/1986
Result: **GLOUCESTER CITY 1 MERTHYR TYDFIL 1**
Competition: Southern League Cup Group 2
Teamsheet: Teasdale, Moore, Goodwin, Bryant, Lander, Edwards, Murphy, Payne, Truswell, Johnson, Baddock
Substitute: Westerberg (for Baddock)
Scorer: Truswell
Attendance: 365

Date: Saturday 27/09/1986
Result: **MOOR GREEN 0 GLOUCESTER CITY 4**
Competition: Southern League Midland Division
Teamsheet: Teasdale, Goodwin, Scarrott, Bryant, Lander, Edwards, Murphy, Payne, Baddock, Johnson, Truswell
Substitute: Westerberg (nps)
Scorers: Johnson (2), Truswell, Payne

Date: Saturday 04/10/1986
Result: **TROWBRIDGE TOWN 4 GLOUCESTER CITY 0**
Competition: FA Trophy 1st Qualifying Round
Teamsheet: Teasdale, Goodwin, Scarrott, Bryant, Lander, Edwards, Murphy, Payne, Baddock, Johnson, Truswell
Substitute: Goff (for Teasdale)
Attendance: 422

Date: Saturday 11/10/1986
Result: **GLOUCESTER CITY 6 RUSHDEN TOWN 3**
Competition: Southern League Midland Division
Teamsheet: Martyn, Goodwin, Scarrott, Bryant, Lander, Edwards, Murphy, Payne, Baddock, Johnson, Truswell
Substitute: Goff (nps)
Scorers: Truswell (2), Johnson (2), Baddock, Murphy
Attendance: 341

Date: Tuesday 14/10/1986
Result: **GLOUCESTER CITY 2 WITNEY TOWN 1**
Competition: Southern League Cup Group 2
Teamsheet: Martyn, Goodwin, Edwards, Bryant, Lander, Goff, Murphy, Payne, Westerberg, Johnson, Baddock
Substitute: Scarrott (for Payne)
Scorer: Goodwin (2)
Attendance: 361

Date: Saturday 18/10/1986
Result: **WELLINGBOROUGH TOWN 2 GLOUCESTER CITY 1**
Competition: Southern League Midland Division
Teamsheet: Martyn, Norman, Scarrott, Goodwin, Bryant, Foxwell, Murphy, Goff, Westerberg, Johnson, Baddock
Substitute: Hughes (nps)
Scorer: Goff

Date: Tuesday 21/10/1986
Result: **GLOUCESTER CITY 2 FOREST GREEN ROVERS 1**
Competition: Southern League Cup Group 2
Teamsheet: Martyn, Norman, Scarrott, Goodwin, Bryant, Edwards, Murphy, Goff, Westerberg, Johnson, Baddock
Substitute: Moore (nps)
Scorers: Westerberg, Baddock
Attendance: 423

Date: Saturday 25/10/1986
Result: **GLOUCESTER CITY 7 WELLINGBOROUGH TOWN 0**
Competition: Southern League Midland Division
Teamsheet: Martyn, Goodwin, Edwards, Bryant, Lander, Foxwell, Murphy, Goff, Westerberg, Johnson, Baddock
Substitute: Scarrott (nps)
Scorers: Westerberg, Johnson (4), Foxwell, Baddock
Attendance: 379

Date: Tuesday 28/10/1986
Result: **WITNEY TOWN 1 GLOUCESTER CITY 1**
Competition: Southern League Cup Group 2
Teamsheet: Martyn, Goodwin, Scarrott, Bryant, Lander, Edwards, Murphy, Goff, Westerberg, Johnson, Baddock
Substitute: Norman (nps)
Scorer: Baddock
Attendance: 102

Date: Monday 10/11/1986
Result: **CHELTENHAM TOWN 3 GLOUCESTER CITY 4** (aet)
Competition: Gloucestershire FA Northern Senior Professional Cup Semi-Final
Teamsheet: Martyn, Norman, Scarrott, Goodwin, Lander, Foxwell, Murphy, Goff, Westerberg, Johnson, Baddock
Substitutes: Moore (for Goodwin), Truswell (for Westerberg)
Scorers: Foxwell, Baddock (2), Murphy
Attendance: 1007

Date: Saturday 15/11/1986
Result: **GRANTHAM 2 GLOUCESTER CITY 5**
Competition: Southern League Midland Division
Teamsheet: Martyn, Norman, Scarrott, Moore, Lander, Foxwell, Murphy, Goff, Westerberg, Johnson, Baddock
Substitute: Truswell (for Baddock)
Scorers: Westerberg (4), Baddock
Attendance: 323

[303]

Date: Saturday 22/11/1986
Result: **BILSTON TOWN 1 GLOUCESTER CITY 2**
Competition: Southern League Midland Division
Teamsheet: Martyn, Norman, Scarrott, Bryant, Lander, Foxwell, Murphy, Goff, Westerberg, Johnson, Baddock
Substitute: Truswell (for Baddock)
Scorer: Baddock (2)

Date: Tuesday 25/11/1986
Result: **BANBURY UNITED 0 GLOUCESTER CITY 3**
Competition: Southern League Midland Division
Teamsheet: Martyn, Norman, Edwards, Lander, Bryant, Goff, Murphy, Foxwell, Johnson, Westerberg, Truswell
Substitute: Scarrott (for Bryant)
Scorers: Johnson (2), Goff

Date: Saturday 29/11/1986
Result: **GLOUCESTER CITY 2 BRIDGNORTH TOWN 2**
Competition: Southern League Midland Division
Teamsheet: Martyn, Norman, Edwards, Bryant, Lander, Foxwell, Murphy, Goff, Westerberg, Johnson, Truswell
Substitute: Scarrott (for Edwards)
Scorer: Truswell (2)
Attendance: 413

Date: Saturday 06/12/1986
Result: **GLOUCESTER CITY 1 GRANTHAM 5**
Competition: Southern League Midland Division
Teamsheet: Martyn, Norman, Edwards, Lander, Bryant, Foxwell, Murphy, Goff, Westerberg, Truswell, Baddock
Substitute: Scarrott (for Truswell)
Scorer: Westerberg
Attendance: 348

Date: Saturday 13/12/1986
Result: **STOURBRIDGE 1 GLOUCESTER CITY 0**
Competition: Southern League Midland Division
Teamsheet: Martyn, Goodwin, Scarrott, Bryant, Lander, Foxwell, Murphy, Goff, Westerberg, Baddock, Payne
Substitute: Norman (for Scarrott)

Date: Tuesday 16/12/1986
Result: **MERTHYR TYDFIL 5 GLOUCESTER CITY 2**
Competition: Southern League Cup Group 2
Teamsheet: Martyn, Goodwin, Edwards, Bryant, Lander, Norman, Murphy, Payne, Westerberg, Johnson, Baddock
Substitute: Young (nps)
Scorers: Goodwin, Westerberg

Date: Saturday 20/12/1986
Result: **GLOUCESTER CITY 0 VALLEY SPORTS RUGBY 1**
Competition: Southern League Midland Division
Teamsheet: Martyn, Norman, Edwards, Moore, Lander, Neale, Foxwell, Goff, Westerberg, Johnson, Baddock
Substitute: Payne (for Edwards)
Attendance: 311

Date: Friday 26/12/1986
Result: **FOREST GREEN ROVERS 2 GLOUCESTER CITY 0**
Competition: Southern League Midland Division
Teamsheet: Martyn, Norman, Lander, Moore, Neale, Goff, Emery, Foxwell, Johnson, Wiffle, Baddock
Substitute: Payne (for Goff)
Attendance: 800

Date: Saturday 27/12/1986
Result: **BRIDGNORTH TOWN 2 GLOUCESTER CITY 3**
Competition: Southern League Midland Division
Teamsheet: Martyn, Norman, Neale, Bryant, Lander, Foxwell, Emery, Murphy, Baddock, Johnson, Payne
Substitute: Goodwin (nps)
Scorers: Baddock (2), Lander

Date: Thursday 01/01/1987
Result: **GLOUCESTER CITY 4 MERTHYR TYDFIL 1**
Competition: Southern League Midland Division
Teamsheet: Teasdale, Norman, Scarrott, Bryant, Lander, Emery, Neale, Foxwell, Baddock, Johnson, Hyde
Substitute: Payne (nps)
Scorers: Hyde, Baddock (2), Johnson
Attendance: 652

Date: Saturday 03/01/1987
Result: **RUSHDEN TOWN 1 GLOUCESTER CITY 2**
Competition: Southern League Midland Division
Teamsheet: Martyn, Norman, Scarrott, Bryant, Lander, Emery, Neale, Foxwell, Baddock, Johnson, Hyde
Substitute: Payne (nps)
Scorers: Baddock, Foxwell

Date: Saturday 10/01/1987
Result: **GLOUCESTER CITY 1 MOOR GREEN 4**
Competition: Southern League Midland Division
Teamsheet: Martyn, Norman, Scarrott, Bryant, Lander, Foxwell, Emery, Neale, Baddock, Johnson, Hyde
Substitute: Payne (for Scarrott)
Scorer: Foxwell
Attendance: 462

Date: Saturday 24/01/1987
Result: **GLOUCESTER CITY 6 BANBURY UNITED 1**
Competition: Southern League Midland Division
Teamsheet: Martyn, Norman, Neale, Bryant, Lander, Foxwell, Emery, Payne, Baddock, Johnson, Hyde
Substitute: Goff (nps)
Scorers: Johnson, Baddock (2), Hyde (3)
Attendance: 355

Date: Tuesday 27/01/1987
Result: **GLOUCESTER CITY 1 DORCHESTER TOWN 1**
Competition: Southern League Cup 2nd Round
Teamsheet: Martyn, Norman, Edwards, Bryant, Lander, Payne, Emery, Goff, Baddock, Johnson, Beacock
Substitute: Scarrott (nps)
Scorer: Norman
Attendance: 272

Date: Saturday 31/01/1987
Result: **GLOUCESTER CITY 0 STOURBRIDGE 1**
Competition: Southern League Midland Division
Teamsheet: Martyn, Norman, Neale, Bryant, Lander, Foxwell, Emery, Payne, Baddock, Johnson, Hyde
Substitute: Goff (for Johnson)
Attendance: 402

Date: Saturday 07/02/1987
Result: **BUCKINGHAM TOWN 1 GLOUCESTER CITY 1**
Competition: Southern League Midland Division
Teamsheet: Martyn, Norman, Neale, Bryant, Lander, Foxwell, Emery, Payne, Baddock, Johnson, Hyde
Substitute: Beacock (nps)
Scorer: Hyde

Date: Tuesday 10/02/1987
Result: **DORCHESTER TOWN 1 GLOUCESTER CITY 0**
Competition: Southern League Cup 2nd Round Replay
Teamsheet: Martyn, Norman, Scarrott, Bryant, Lander, Payne, Emery, Goff, Baddock, Johnson, Beacock
Substitute: Edwards (nps)

Date: Saturday 14/02/1987
Result: **GLOUCESTER CITY 3 MILE OAK ROVERS 2**
Competition: Southern League Midland Division
Teamsheet: Martyn, Norman, Edwards, Bryant, Lander, Payne, Emery, Goff, Baddock, Johnson, Hyde
Substitute: Beacock (nps)
Scorers: Johnson, Baddock (2)
Attendance: 332

Date: Saturday 28/02/1987
Result: **LEICESTER UNITED 3 GLOUCESTER CITY 2**
Competition: Southern League Midland Division
Teamsheet: Martyn, Norman, Scarrott, Green, Lander, Payne, Emery, Goff, Baddock, Johnson, Hyde
Substitute: Foxwell (nps)
Scorers: Baddock, Johnson

Date: Saturday 14/03/1987
Result: **COVENTRY SPORTING 1 GLOUCESTER CITY 2**
Competition: Southern League Midland Division
Teamsheet: Bowles, Norman, Scarrott, Green, Lander, Collicutt, Goff, Payne, Foxwell, Johnson, Baddock
Substitute: Hyde (nps)
Scorers: Foxwell, Goff

Date: Saturday 21/03/1987
Result: **MILE OAK ROVERS 1 GLOUCESTER CITY 2**
Competition: Southern League Midland Division
Teamsheet: Bowles, Norman, Scarrott, Collicutt, Green, Goff, Foxwell, Payne, Baddock, Johnson, Hyde
Substitute: Wiffill (nps)
Scorers: Foxwell, Hyde

Date: Saturday 28/03/1987
Result: **GLOUCESTER CITY 2 LEICESTER UNITED 2**
Competition: Southern League Midland Division
Teamsheet: Bowles, Norman, Scarrott, Green, Collicutt, Goff, Foxwell, Payne, Baddock, Johnson, Hyde
Substitute: Wiffill (for Hyde)
Scorer: Baddock (2)
Attendance: 360

Date: Tuesday 07/04/1987
Result: **GLOUCESTER CITY 2 COVENTRY SPORTING 1**
Competition: Southern League Midland Division
Teamsheet: Bowles, Norman, Scarrott, Collicutt, Green, Goff, Foxwell, Payne, Baddock, Johnson, Wiffill
Substitute: Hyde (nps)
Scorers: Payne, Baddock
Attendance: 325

Date: Saturday 11/04/1987
Result: **LEAMINGTON 0 GLOUCESTER CITY 1**
Competition: Southern League Midland Division
Teamsheet: Teasdale, Norman, Scarrott, Collicutt, Green, Foxwell, Lander, Payne, Baddock, Johnson, Wiffill
Substitute: Hyde (for Payne)
Scorer: Hyde

[305]

Date: Tuesday 14/04/1987
Result: **GLOUCESTER CITY 1 BILSTON TOWN 2**
Competition: Southern League Midland Division
Teamsheet: Teasdale, Norman, Scarrott, Collicutt, Green, Payne, Lander, Foxwell, Baddock, Johnson, Wiffill
Substitute: Hyde (for Wiffill)
Scorer: Johnson
Attendance: 376

Date: Saturday 18/04/1987
Result: **MERTHYR TYDFIL 4 GLOUCESTER CITY 0**
Competition: Southern League Midland Division
Teamsheet: Teasdale, Norman, Scarrott, Collicutt, Green, Goff, Foxwell, Payne, Baddock, Johnson, Hyde
Substitute: Wiffill (nps)

Date: Monday 20/04/1987
Result: **GLOUCESTER CITY 0 FOREST GREEN ROVERS 1**
Competition: Southern League Midland Division
Teamsheet: Teasdale, Collicutt, Scarrott, Lander, Green, Goff, Foxwell, Payne, Wiffill, Hyde, Baddock
Substitute: Johnson (for Teasdale)
Attendance: 552

Date: Saturday 25/04/1987
Result: **GLOUCESTER CITY 2 SUTTON COLDFIELD TOWN 2**
Competition: Southern League Midland Division
Teamsheet: Bowles, Norman, Edwards, Collicutt, Green, Goff, Foxwell, Payne, Wiffill, Hyde, Baddock
Substitute: Lander (for Payne)
Scorers: Green, Hyde
Attendance: 211

Date: Monday 27/04/1987
Result: **GLOUCESTER CITY 2 FOREST GREEN ROVERS 3**
Competition: Gloucestershire FA Northern Senior Professional Cup Final
Teamsheet: Bowles, Norman, Edwards, Lander, Green, Goff, Foxwell, Payne, Wiffill, Hyde, Baddock
Substitute: Scarrott (nps)
Scorers: Baddock, Foxwell
Attendance: 362

Date: Wednesday 29/04/1987
Result: **HALESOWEN TOWN 2 GLOUCESTER CITY 0**
Competition: Southern League Midland Division
Teamsheet: Bowles, Norman, Edwards, Collicutt, Green, Scarrott, Lander, Goff, Baddock, Johnson, Hyde
Substitute: Foxwell (nps)

Date: Saturday 02/05/1987
Result: **HEDNESFORD TOWN 3 GLOUCESTER CITY 0**
Competition: Southern League Midland Division
Teamsheet: Bowles, Norman, Edwards, Collicutt, Green, Goff, Lander, Payne, Baddock, Scarrott, Hyde
Substitute: Wiffill (nps)

Appearances – SW Baddock 49, GC Beacock 2, R Bowles 8, RJ Bryant 34, P Collicutt 11, M Edwards 22, SR Emery 12, DP Foxwell 28, N Goff 28(2), G Goodwin 19, N Green 13, MC Hughes 2, C Hyde 16(2), S Johnson 45(1), MT Lander 44(1), S Martyn 26, G Moore 7(1), R Murphy 27, PA Neale 9, K Norman 33(1), MI Payne 32(4), SW Scarrott 32(4), M Teasdale 17, K Truswell 13(5), BE Vassallo 3, SA Westerberg 22(2), DP Wiffill 7(1).
Others selected but did not play: TG Davies, T Harris, N Young.
Scorers – SW Baddock 28, S Johnson 18, SA Westerberg 10, C Hyde 8, DP Foxwell 7, K Truswell 6, R Murphy 4, N Goff 3, G Goodwin 3, MI Payne 2, N Green 1, MT Lander 1, K Norman 1.

SOUTHERN LEAGUE MIDLAND DIVISION

POS	CLUB	P	W	D	L	F	A	PTS
1	VALLEY SPORTS RUGBY	38	25	5	8	81	43	80
2	LEICESTER UNITED	38	26	1	11	89	49	79
3	MERTHYR TYDFIL	38	23	6	9	95	54	75
4	MOOR GREEN	38	22	6	10	73	55	72
5	HALESOWEN TOWN	38	19	12	7	72	50	69
6	HEDNESFORD TOWN	38	21	5	12	84	56	68
7	**GLOUCESTER CITY**	**38**	**19**	**5**	**14**	**77**	**59**	**62**
8	COVENTRY SPORTING	38	17	8	13	55	54	59
9	FOREST GREEN ROVERS	38	16	9	13	65	53	57
10	STOURBRIDGE	38	16	7	15	56	56	55
11	GRANTHAM	38	15	9	14	74	54	54
12	BANBURY UNITED	38	14	7	17	55	65	49
13	BUCKINGHAM TOWN	38	13	9	16	55	59	48
14	BRIDGNORTH TOWN	38	12	9	17	59	63	45
15	WELLINGBOROUGH TOWN	38	13	6	19	55	76	45
16	MILE OAK ROVERS	38	11	10	17	50	63	43
17	SUTTON COLDFIELD TOWN	38	8	10	20	56	78	34
18	BILSTON TOWN	38	8	7	23	37	76	31
19	LEAMINGTON	38	4	13	21	37	80	25
20	RUSHDEN TOWN	38	1	10	27	42	124	13
		760	303	154	303	1267	1267	1063

SEASON 1987-1988
(Home Ground: City Stadium, Meadow Park, Hempsted)

Date: Saturday 22/08/1987
Result: **PAGET RANGERS 1 GLOUCESTER CITY 6**
Competition: Southern League Midland Division
Teamsheet: Teasdale, Steele, M Rogers, Delve, Green, Collicutt, Foxwell, PP Rogers, Baddock, Johnson, Harris
Substitute: Norman (for Delve)
Scorers: Baddock (2), Johnson (3), Harris

Date: Tuesday 25/08/1987
Result: **GLOUCESTER CITY 8 STOURBRIDGE 1**
Competition: Southern League Cup Group 13
Teamsheet: Teasdale, Steele, M Rogers, Delve, Green, Collicutt, Foxwell, PP Rogers, Baddock, Johnson, Harris
Substitute: Norman (for Delve)
Scorers: PP Rogers (2), Baddock (3, 1 pen), Foxwell (2), Green
Attendance: 413

Date: Saturday 29/08/1987
Result: **GLOUCESTER CITY 7 WESTBURY UNITED 0**
Competition: FA Cup Preliminary Round
Teamsheet: Teasdale, Steele, M Rogers, Delve, Green, Collicutt, Foxwell, PP Rogers, Baddock, Johnson, Harris
Substitutes: Norman (for PP Rogers), Lander (nps)
Scorers: Delve, Harris, Foxwell, Baddock (2), Johnson (2)
Attendance: 489

Date: Monday 31/08/1987
Result: **GLOUCESTER CITY 2 HALESOWEN TOWN 2**
Competition: Southern League Midland Division
Teamsheet: Teasdale, Steele, M Rogers, Delve, Green, Collicutt, Foxwell, PP Rogers, Baddock, Johnson, Harris
Substitute: Norman (nps)
Scorers: Baddock, Johnson
Attendance: 962

Date: Saturday 05/09/1987
Result: **WELLINGBOROUGH TOWN 4 GLOUCESTER CITY 0**
Competition: Southern League Midland Division
Teamsheet: Teasdale, Steele, M Rogers, Delve, Green, Collicutt, Foxwell, PP Rogers, Baddock, Johnson, Harris
Substitute: Lander (for Delve)

Date: Tuesday 08/09/1987
Result: **GLOUCESTER CITY 1 SUTTON COLDFIELD TOWN 0**
Competition: Southern League Midland Division
Teamsheet: Teasdale, Steele, M Rogers, Delve, Green, Collicutt, Foxwell, PP Rogers, Baddock, Lander, Harris
Substitute: Norman (for Delve)
Scorer: Green
Attendance: 437

Date: Saturday 12/09/1987
Result: **GLOUCESTER CITY 1 TON PENTRE 2**
Competition: FA Cup 1st Qualifying Round
Teamsheet: Teasdale, Steele, M Rogers, Delve, Green, Collicutt, Foxwell, PP Rogers, Baddock, Lander, Harris
Substitutes: Norman (for PP Rogers), Hyde (for Delve)
Scorer: own goal
Attendance: 470

Date: Saturday 19/09/1987
Result: **ATHERSTONE UNITED 2 GLOUCESTER CITY 3**
Competition: Southern League Midland Division
Teamsheet: Teasdale, Steele, M Rogers, Delve, Lander, Collicutt, Foxwell, PP Rogers, Baddock, Hyde, Harris
Substitute: Goff (for Hyde)
Scorers: Baddock (pen), PP Rogers (2)

Date: Tuesday 22/09/1987
Result: **GLOUCESTER CITY 2 DUDLEY TOWN 3**
Competition: Southern League Cup Group 13
Teamsheet: Martyn, Steele, M Rogers, Norman, Green, Lander, Goff, PP Rogers, Hyde, Harris, Johnson
Substitute: Baddock (for Lander)
Scorers: Johnson, Hyde
Attendance: 366

Date: Saturday 26/09/1987
Result: **GLOUCESTER CITY 1 BRIDGNORTH TOWN 2**
Competition: Southern League Midland Division
Teamsheet: Teasdale, Steele, M Rogers, Delve, Norman, Collicutt, Goff, PP Rogers, Baddock, Johnson, Harris
Substitute: Hyde (for Goff)
Scorer: Johnson
Attendance: 371

Date: Tuesday 29/09/1987
Result: **GLOUCESTER CITY 6 ALVECHURCH 2**
Competition: Southern League Cup Group 13
Teamsheet: Martyn, Steele, M Rogers, Delve, Davies, Collicutt, Foxwell, Hyde, Baddock, Johnson, Harris
Substitute: Norman (nps)
Scorers: Harris, Johnson (2), Foxwell (2), Hyde
Attendance: 306

Date: Saturday 03/10/1987
Result: **GLOUCESTER CITY 3 ANDOVER 0**
Competition: FA Trophy 1st Qualifying Round
Teamsheet: Martyn, Steele, M Rogers, Delve, Lander, Collicutt, Foxwell, Hyde, Baddock, Johnson, Harris
Substitutes: PP Rogers (nps), Norman (nps)
Scorers: Johnson (2), Hyde
Attendance: 362

Date: Saturday 10/10/1987
Result: **MILE OAK ROVERS 2 GLOUCESTER CITY 0**
Competition: Southern League Midland Division
Teamsheet: Teasdale, Steele, M Rogers, Delve, Lander, Collicutt, Foxwell, PP Rogers, Baddock, McKenzie, Harris
Substitute: Davies (nps)

Date: Thursday 15/10/1987
Result: **STOURBRIDGE 3 GLOUCESTER CITY 1**
Competition: Southern League Cup Group 13
Teamsheet: Teasdale, Green, M Rogers, Delve, Lander, Collicutt, Foxwell, PP Rogers, Baddock, Beacham, Harris
Substitute: Goff (nps)
Scorer: Collicutt

Date: Saturday 17/10/1987
Result: **GLOUCESTER CITY 2 GRANTHAM TOWN 2**
Competition: Southern League Midland Division
Teamsheet: Teasdale, Steele, Davies, Lander, Green, McKenzie, Foxwell, PP Rogers, Baddock, Johnson, Harris
Substitute: Collicutt (nps)
Scorers: Baddock, own goal
Attendance: 340

Date: Monday 19/10/1987
Result: **DUDLEY TOWN 0 GLOUCESTER CITY 4**
Competition: Southern League Cup Group 13
Teamsheet: Webb, Lander, Davies, Delve, Green, Collicutt, Foxwell, Hyde, Baddock, Johnson, Harris
Substitute: Young (nps)
Scorers: Harris, Baddock, Johnson (2)

Date: Saturday 24/10/1987
Result: **BUCKINGHAM TOWN 1 GLOUCESTER CITY 1**
Competition: Southern League Midland Division
Teamsheet: Martyn, Steele, Davies, McKenzie, Green, Lander, Hyde, PP Rogers, Baddock, Johnson, Harris
Substitute: Foxwell (nps)
Scorer: Hyde

Date: Tuesday 27/10/1987
Result: **ALVECHURCH 0 GLOUCESTER CITY 4**
Competition: Southern League Cup Group 13
Teamsheet: Martyn, Lander, Davies, Steele, Green, Collicutt, Foxwell, Hyde, Baddock, Johnson, Harris
Substitute: Young (nps)
Scorers: Green, Hyde, Johnson, Baddock (pen)

Date: Wednesday 04/11/1987
Result: **MELKSHAM TOWN 0 GLOUCESTER CITY 2**
Competition: FA Trophy 2nd Qualifying Round
Teamsheet: Martyn, Lander, Davies, Steele, Green, Collicutt, Foxwell, Hyde, Baddock, Johnson, Harris
Substitutes: McKenzie (for Davies), Young (nps)
Scorers: Harris, Foxwell

Date: Saturday 07/11/1987
Result: **KING'S LYNN 0 GLOUCESTER CITY 1**
Competition: Southern League Midland Division
Teamsheet: Webb, Lander, McKenzie, Steele, Green, Collicutt, Foxwell, Hyde, Baddock, Johnson, Harris
Substitute: Young (nps)
Scorer: Baddock
Attendance: 380

Date: Saturday 14/11/1987
Result: **GLOUCESTER CITY 5 COVENTRY SPORTING 0**
Competition: Southern League Midland Division
Teamsheet: Martyn, Lander, McKenzie, Steele, Green, Collicutt, Foxwell, Hyde, Baddock, Johnson, Harris
Substitute: Scarrott (for McKenzie)
Scorers: Hyde (3), Johnson (2)
Attendance: 360

Date: Tuesday 17/11/1987
Result: **GLOUCESTER CITY 1 BILSTON TOWN 1**
Competition: Southern League Midland Division
Teamsheet: Martyn, Lander, Scarrott, Steele, Green, Collicutt, Foxwell, Hyde, Malpas, Johnson, Harris
Substitute: Young (nps)
Scorer: Foxwell
Attendance: 428

Date: Saturday 21/11/1987
Result: **GLOUCESTER CITY 4 FOREST GREEN ROVERS 0**
Competition: FA Trophy 3rd Qualifying Round
Teamsheet: Martyn, Lander, McKenzie, Steele, Green, Collicutt, Foxwell, Hyde, Baddock, Johnson, Harris
Substitutes: Young (nps), Beacham (nps)
Scorers: Green, Johnson, Steele, Hyde
Attendance: 628

Date: Saturday 28/11/1987
Result: **GLOUCESTER CITY 2 PAGET RANGERS 2**
Competition: Southern League Midland Division
Teamsheet: Martyn, Lander, McKenzie, Steele, Malpas, Collicutt, Foxwell, Hyde, Baddock, Johnson, Harris
Substitute: Talboys (for Baddock)
Scorers: Steele, Hyde
Attendance: 425

Date: Saturday 05/12/1987
Result: **MOOR GREEN 1 GLOUCESTER CITY 3**
Competition: Southern League Midland Division
Teamsheet: Martyn, Lander, Collicutt, Steele, Green, Malpas, Foxwell, Hyde, Baddock, Talboys, Harris
Substitute: Johnson (for Hyde)
Scorers: Steele, Baddock (pen), Talboys

Date: Saturday 12/12/1987
Result: **GLOUCESTER CITY 5 WELLINGBOROUGH TOWN 1**
Competition: Southern League Midland Division
Teamsheet: Martyn, Lander, Collicutt, Steele, Green, Malpas, Foxwell, Hyde, Baddock, Talboys, Harris
Substitute: Johnson (for Foxwell)
Scorers: Hyde (4), Harris
Attendance: 425

Date: Tuesday 15/12/1987
Result: **CHELTENHAM TOWN 2 GLOUCESTER CITY 1**
Competition: Gloucestershire FA Northern Senior Professional Cup Semi-Final
Teamsheet: Martyn, McKenzie, Scarrott, Steele, Green, Malpas, Williams, Hyde, Truswell, Talboys, Harris
Substitutes: Lander (for McKenzie), Johnson (nps), Baddock (for Truswell), Collicutt (nps), Foxwell (for -----)
Scorer: Hyde
Attendance: 668

Date: Saturday 19/12/1987
Result: **GLOUCESTER CITY 1 YEOVIL TOWN 3**
Competition: FA Trophy 1st Round
Teamsheet: Martyn, Lander, Collicutt, Steele, Green, Malpas, Foxwell, Hyde, Baddock, Johnson, Harris
Substitutes: Truswell (for Hyde), Young (nps)
Scorer: Johnson
Attendance: 747

Date: Saturday 26/12/1987
Result: **GLOUCESTER CITY 0 FOREST GREEN ROVERS 0**
Competition: Southern League Midland Division
Teamsheet: Martyn, Lander, Scarrott, Steele, Collicutt, Malpas, Foxwell, Hyde, Baddock, Talboys, Harris
Substitute: Johnson (for Baddock)
Attendance: 732

Date: Monday 28/12/1987
Result: **TROWBRIDGE TOWN 5 GLOUCESTER CITY 2**
Competition: Southern League Midland Division
Teamsheet: Martyn, Lander, Scarrott, Steele, Collicutt, Malpas, Foxwell, Hyde, Baddock, Talboys, Harris
Substitute: Johnson (for Scarrott)
Scorers: Lander, Baddock (pen)

Date: Friday 01/01/1988
Result: **MERTHYR TYDFIL 3 GLOUCESTER CITY 1**
Competition: Southern League Midland Division
Teamsheet: Martyn, McKenzie, Scarrott, Steele, Malpas, Collicutt, Williams, Johnson, Talboys, Bray, Harris
Substitute: Baddock (for Bray)
Scorer: Malpas

Date: Saturday 02/01/1988
Result: **GLOUCESTER CITY 1 BANBURY UNITED 0**
Competition: Southern League Midland Division
Teamsheet: Martyn, Collicutt, Scarrott, Steele, Malpas, Bray, Foxwell, Johnson, Talboys, Williams, Harris
Substitute: Truswell (nps)
Scorer: Williams
Attendance: 455

Date: Saturday 09/01/1988
Result: **GLOUCESTER CITY 5 DUDLEY TOWN 1**
Competition: Southern League Midland Division
Teamsheet: Stevens, Steele, Scarrott, Malpas, Lander, Foxwell, Bray, Hyde, Talboys, Williams, Harris
Substitute: Johnson (for Hyde)
Scorers: Bray (2), Foxwell (2), Johnson
Attendance: 441

Date: Tuesday 12/01/1988
Result: **GLOUCESTER CITY 2 FOREST GREEN ROVERS 1**
Competition: Southern League Cup 2nd Round
Teamsheet: Stevens, Patterson, Hedges, Steele, Lander, Foxwell, Norman, McCreadie, Johnson, Baddock, Truswell
Substitute: Young (for Patterson)
Scorers: Truswell, Johnson
Attendance: 418

Date: Saturday 23/01/1988
Result: **GLOUCESTER CITY 5 HEDNESFORD TOWN 0**
Competition: Southern League Midland Division
Teamsheet: Stevens, Lander, Scarrott, Steele, Green, Malpas, Foxwell, Talboys, Morrison, Johnson, Williams
Substitute: Truswell (for Foxwell)
Scorers: Johnson (3), Morrison, Steele
Attendance: 466

Date: Tuesday 26/01/1988
Result: **GLOUCESTER CITY 2 RUSHDEN TOWN 1**
Competition: Southern League Midland Division
Teamsheet: Stevens, Lander, Scarrott, Steele, Green, Malpas, Foxwell, Talboys, Morrison, Johnson, Williams
Substitute: Bray (for Morrison)
Scorers: Johnson, Steele
Attendance: 507

Date: Saturday 06/02/1988
Result: **GLOUCESTER CITY 2 BUCKINGHAM TOWN 2**
Competition: Southern League Midland Division
Teamsheet: Stevens, Lander, Scarrott, Steele, Green, Malpas, Foxwell, Talboys, Morrison, Johnson, Williams
Substitute: Bray (for Williams)
Scorers: Talboys, Steele
Attendance: 484

Date: Wednesday 10/02/1987
Result: **GLOUCESTER CITY 3 SHEPSHED CHARTERHOUSE 0**
Competition: Southern League Cup 3rd Round
Teamsheet: Martyn, Lander, Truswell, Steele, Green, Hendry, Foxwell, Baddock, Tyler, Johnson, Harris
Substitute: Hyde (for Harris)
Scorers: Johnson, Harris (2)
Attendance: 310

Date: Saturday 13/02/1988
Result: **GRANTHAM TOWN 1 GLOUCESTER CITY 1**
Competition: Southern League Midland Division
Teamsheet: Stevens, Bray, Scarrott, Steele, Green, Malpas, Foxwell, Talboys, Morrison, Johnson, Hendry
Substitute: Harris (for Morrison)
Scorer: Talboys (pen)
Attendance: 357

Date: Saturday 20/02/1988
Result: **GLOUCESTER CITY 1 MOOR GREEN 3**
Competition: Southern League Midland Division
Teamsheet: Martyn, Bray, Scarrott, Steele, Green, Malpas, Foxwell, Hendry, Talboys, Johnson, Harris
Substitute: Morrison (for Scarrott)
Scorer: Talboys
Attendance: 495

Date: Tuesday 23/02/1988
Result: **COVENTRY SPORTING 0 GLOUCESTER CITY 0**
Competition: Southern League Midland Division
Teamsheet: Stevens, Lander, McKenzie, Steele, Green, Malpas, Foxwell, Bray, Talboys, Johnson, Harris
Substitute: Trusswell (for -----)

Date: Saturday 27/02/1988
Result: **SUTTON COLDFIELD TOWN 3 GLOUCESTER CITY 1**
Competition: Southern League Midland Division
Teamsheet: Stevens, Lander, Williams, Steele, Green, Malpas, Foxwell, Hyde, Talboys, Johnson, Harris
Substitute: Morrison (for Malpas)
Scorer: Green

Date: Saturday 05/03/1988
Result: **HEDNESFORD TOWN 2 GLOUCESTER CITY 2**
Competition: Southern League Midland Division
Teamsheet: Martyn, McKenzie, Williams, Steele, Green, Lander, Foxwell, Talboys, Tyler, Johnson, Morrison
Substitute: Harris (nps)
Scorers: Talboys (pen), Tyler
Attendance: 230

Date: Tuesday 08/03/1988
Result: **STOURBRIDGE 2 GLOUCESTER CITY 4**
Competition: Southern League Midland Division
Teamsheet: Martyn, McKenzie, Hendry, Lander, Green, Williams, Foxwell, Talboys, Tyler, Morrison, Harris
Substitute: Johnson (nps)
Scorers: Harris, Tyler, Foxwell, McKenzie

Date: Thursday 10/03/1987
Result: **ATHERSTONE UNITED 1 GLOUCESTER CITY 2**
Competition: Southern League Cup Quarter-Final
Teamsheet: Martyn, Truswell, Wilmott, Steele, Green, Lander, Foxwell, Hyde, Tyler, Johnson, Harris
Substitute: Hendry (nps)
Scorer: Hyde (2)
Attendance: 396

Date: Saturday 12/03/1988
Result: **GLOUCESTER CITY 4 ATHERSTONE UNITED 1**
Competition: Southern League Midland Division
Teamsheet: Martyn, Truswell, Hendry, Steele, Green, Williams, Foxwell, Hyde, Tyler, Talboys, Harris
Substitute: Johnson (nps)
Scorers: Hendry, Hyde (2), Tyler
Attendance: 387

Date: Thursday 17/03/1988
Result: **BILSTON TOWN 1 GLOUCESTER CITY 2**
Competition: Southern League Midland Division
Teamsheet: Martyn, Truswell, Wilmott, Lander, Green, Williams, Foxwell, Hyde, Tyler, Talboys, Harris
Substitute: Johnson (nps)
Scorers: Talboys, Hyde

Date: Saturday 19/03/1988
Result: **GLOUCESTER CITY 5 STOURBRIDGE 0**
Competition: Southern League Midland Division
Teamsheet: Martyn, Lander, Hendry, Steele, Green, Williams, Foxwell, Morrison, Tyler, Harris, Talboys
Substitute: Johnson (for Harris)
Scorers: Tyler, Morrison, Steele, Foxwell (2)
Attendance: 383

Date: Saturday 26/03/1988
Result: **BANBURY UNITED 1 GLOUCESTER CITY 1**
Competition: Southern League Midland Division
Teamsheet: Martyn, Bray, Hendry, Steele, Green, Lander, Foxwell, Williams, Tyler, Morrison, Harris
Substitute: Hyde (for Williams)
Scorer: Tyler
Attendance: 246

Date: Tuesday 29/03/1987
Result: **GLOUCESTER CITY 1 BROMSGROVE ROVERS 3**
Competition: Southern League Cup Semi-Final 1st Leg
Teamsheet: Martyn, Truswell, Hendry, Steele, Green, Lander, Foxwell, Hyde, Wilmott, Johnson, Harris
Substitute: Young (for Lander)
Scorer: Hyde
Attendance: 806

Date: Saturday 02/04/1988
Result: **GLOUCESTER CITY 0 MERTHYR TYDFIL 3**
Competition: Southern League Midland Division
Teamsheet: Martyn, Truswell, Hendry, Steele, Green, Bray, Foxwell, Talboys, Morrison, Hyde, Harris
Substitute: Johnson (nps)
Attendance: 1003

Date: Monday 04/04/1988
Result: **FOREST GREEN ROVERS 1 GLOUCESTER CITY 1**
Competition: Southern League Midland Division
Teamsheet: Martyn, Bray, Hendry, Steele, Green, Lander, Foxwell, Hyde, Tyler, Talboys, Harris
Substitute: Johnson (for Tyler)
Scorer: Talboys
Attendance: 485

Date: Thursday 07/04/1987
Result: **BROMSGROVE ROVERS 1 GLOUCESTER CITY 2**
Competition: Southern League Cup Semi-Final 2nd Leg
Teamsheet: Martyn, Truswell, Hendry, Steele, Green, Lander, Foxwell, Hyde, Tyler, Johnson, Harris
Substitute: Wilmott (nps)
Scorers: Tyler, Hyde

Date: Saturday 09/04/1988
Result: **GLOUCESTER CITY 3 MILE OAK ROVERS 1**
Competition: Southern League Midland Division
Teamsheet: Martyn, Bray, Wilmott, Steele, Green, Lander, Foxwell, Hyde, Tyler, Talboys, Harris
Substitute: Johnson (nps)
Scorers: Talboys, Green, Hyde
Attendance: 295

Date: Tuesday 12/04/1988
Result: **HALESOWEN TOWN 3 GLOUCESTER CITY 3**
Competition: Southern League Midland Division
Teamsheet: Martyn, Lander, Wilmott, Steele, Green, Malpas, Williams, Hyde, Tyler, Talboys, Harris
Substitute: Morrison (nps)
Scorers: Williams, Tyler, Malpas

Date: Saturday 16/04/1988
Result: **RUSHDEN TOWN 2 GLOUCESTER CITY 0**
Competition: Southern League Midland Division
Teamsheet: Stevens, Lander, Hendry, Steele, Green, Malpas, Williams, Morrison, Tyler, Talboys, Harris
Substitute: Johnson (for Harris)

Date: Tuesday 19/04/1988
Result: **BRIDGNORTH TOWN 3 GLOUCESTER CITY 2**
Competition: Southern League Midland Division
Teamsheet: Martyn, Lander, Scarrott, Steele, Green, Malpas, Foxwell, Williams, Tyler, Talboys, Harris
Substitute: Bray (nps)
Scorers: Tyler, Talboys

Date: Saturday 23/04/1988
Result: **GLOUCESTER CITY 3 KING'S LYNN 1**
Competition: Southern League Midland Division
Teamsheet: Martyn, Williams, Hendry, Steele, Green, Malpas, Foxwell, Morrison, Tyler, Talboys, Johnson
Substitute: Hyde (for Morrison)
Scorers: Talboys, Hyde (2)
Attendance: 305

Date: Monday 25/04/1988
Result: **DUDLEY TOWN 0 GLOUCESTER CITY 0**
Competition: Southern League Midland Division
Teamsheet: Martyn, Bray, Scarrott, Steele, Green, Malpas, Foxwell, Hyde, Tyler, Johnson, Williams
Substitute: Harris (for -----)

Date: Monday 02/05/1988
Result: **GLOUCESTER CITY 2 TROWBRIDGE TOWN 1**
Competition: Southern League Midland Division
Teamsheet: Martyn, Bray, Wilmott, Steele, Green, Lander, Foxwell, Hyde, Tyler, Talboys, Harris
Substitute: Williams (nps)
Scorer: Hyde (2)
Attendance: 359

Appearances – SW Baddock 29(3), A Beacham 1, M Bray 12(2), P Collicutt 28, IC Davies 6, JF Delve 14, DP Foxwell 53(1), N Goff 2(1), N Green 48, AG Harris 52(2), IA Hedges 1, I Hendry 13, C Hyde 32(4), S Johnson 37(8), MT Lander 44(2), M Malpas 23, S Martyn 37, M McCreadie 1, SL McKenzie 12(1), L Morrison 11(2), K Norman 3(4), N Patterson 1, M Rogers 14, PP Rogers 14, SW Scarrott 14(1), HV Steele 56, M Stevens 9, SJ Talboys 28(1), M Teasdale 12, K Truswell 9(3), S Tyler 17, R Webb 2, M Williams 19, IM Willmott 6, N Young 0(2).
Scorers – C Hyde 27, S Johnson 27, SW Baddock 15, DP Foxwell 13, SJ Talboys 11, AG Harris 8, S Tyler 8, HV Steele 7, N Green 6, PP Rogers 4, M Bray 2, M Malpas 2, L Morrison 2, M Williams 2, P Collicutt 1, JF Delve 1, I Hendry 1, MT Lander 1, SL McKenzie 1, K Truswell 1, own goal 1.

SOUTHERN LEAGUE MIDLAND DIVISION

POS	CLUB	P	W	D	L	F	A	PTS
1	MERTHYR TYDFIL	42	30	4	8	102	40	94
2	MOOR GREEN	42	26	8	8	91	49	86
3	GRANTHAM TOWN	42	27	4	11	97	53	85
4	ATHERSTONE UNITED	42	22	10	10	93	56	76
5	SUTTON COLDFIELD TOWN	42	22	6	14	71	47	72
6	HALESOWEN TOWN	42	18	15	9	75	59	69
7	**GLOUCESTER CITY**	**42**	**18**	**14**	**10**	**86**	**62**	**68**
8	DUDLEY TOWN	42	20	5	17	64	55	65
9	FOREST GREEN ROVERS	42	14	16	12	67	54	58
10	BANBURY UNITED	42	17	7	18	48	46	58
11	BRIDGNORTH TOWN	42	16	7	19	59	75	55
12	BUCKINGHAM TOWN	42	15	9	18	74	75	54
13	KING'S LYNN	42	16	6	20	53	63	54
14	WELLINGBOROUGH TOWN	42	14	10	18	67	70	52
15	RUSHDEN TOWN	42	14	9	19	69	85	51
16	TROWBRIDGE TOWN	42	14	3	25	53	82	45
17	BILSTON TOWN	42	12	8	22	52	87	44
18	HEDNESFORD TOWN	42	11	10	21	50	81	43
19	MILE OAK ROVERS	42	9	14	19	43	65	41
20	COVENTRY SPORTING	42	11	8	23	46	83	41
21	STOURBRIDGE	42	10	10	22	46	79	40
22	PAGET RANGERS	42	10	9	23	49	89	39
		924	366	192	366	1455	1455	1290

SEASON 1988-1989

(Home Ground: City Stadium, Meadow Park, Hempsted)

Date: Saturday 20/08/1988
Result: **GLOUCESTER CITY 2 ASHTREE HIGHFIELD 0**
Competition: Southern League Midland Division
Teamsheet: Shaw, Hedges, Williams, Lander, Malpas, Green, Talboys, Hughes, Penny, Morrison, Noble
Substitutes: Johnson (nps), Harris (nps)
Scorers: Penny, Morrison
Attendance: 625

Date: Wednesday 24/08/1988
Result: **SUTTON COLDFIELD TOWN 1 GLOUCESTER CITY 3**
Competition: Southern League Midland Division
Teamsheet: Shaw, Hedges, Williams, Lander, Malpas, Green, Talboys, Hughes, Penny, Morrison, Noble
Substitutes: Johnson (nps), Foxwell (nps)
Scorers: Penny (2), Morrison
Attendance: 419

Date: Saturday 27/08/1988
Result: **GLOUCESTER CITY 3 ATHERSTONE UNITED 1**
Competition: Southern League Midland Division
Teamsheet: Shaw, Hedges, Williams, Lander, Malpas, Green, Talboys, Hughes, Penny, Morrison, Noble
Substitutes: Johnson (nps), Foxwell (for Hughes)
Scorers: Penny (2), Malpas
Attendance: 629

Date: Monday 29/08/1988
Result: **BANBURY UNITED 1 GLOUCESTER CITY 1**
Competition: Southern League Midland Division
Teamsheet: Shaw, Hedges, Williams, Lander, Malpas, Green, Talboys, Hughes, Penny, Morrison, Noble
Substitutes: Johnson (for Penny), Andrews (nps)
Scorer: Williams
Attendance: 249

Date: Tuesday 06/09/1988
Result: **WILLENHALL TOWN 2 GLOUCESTER CITY 1**
Competition: Southern League Midland Division
Teamsheet: Shaw, Hedges, Bray, Lander, Malpas, Green, Talboys, Hughes, Morrison, Johnson, Noble
Substitutes: Hyde (for Johnson), Andrews (for Hedges)
Scorer: Hughes (pen)
Attendance: 198

Date: Saturday 10/09/1988
Result: **GLOUCESTER CITY 1 KING'S LYNN 0**
Competition: Southern League Midland Division
Teamsheet: Shaw, Lander, Williams, Foxwell, Malpas, Green, Talboys, Hughes, Morrison, Hyde, Noble
Substitutes: Harris (for Talboys), Andrews (for Malpas)
Scorer: Andrews
Attendance: 507

Date: Saturday 17/09/1988
Result: **MELKSHAM TOWN 0 GLOUCESTER CITY 5**
Competition: FA Cup 1st Qualifying Round
Teamsheet: Shaw, Lander, Williams, Foxwell, Malpas, Green, Talboys, Hughes, Morrison, Hyde, Noble
Substitutes: Penny (for Talboys), Andrews (for Morrison)
Scorers: Malpas (2), Morrison, Talboys, Williams
Attendance: 175

Date: Saturday 24/09/1988
Result: **FOREST GREEN ROVERS 1 GLOUCESTER CITY 2**
Competition: FA Trophy 1st Qualifying Round
Teamsheet: Shaw, Steel, Williams, Lander, Malpas, Green, Talboys, Hughes, Morrison, Penny, Noble
Substitutes: Hyde (nps), Harris (nps)
Scorers: Morrison, Noble
Attendance: 384

Date: Saturday 01/10/1988
Result: **GLOUCESTER CITY 3 CHELTENHAM TOWN 0**
Competition: FA Cup 2nd Qualifying Round
Teamsheet: Shaw, Steel, Williams, Lander, Malpas, Green, Talboys, Hughes, Penny, Morrison, Noble
Substitutes: Hedges (nps), Johnson (nps)
Scorers: Malpas (pen), Noble, Morrison
Attendance: 1730

Date: Saturday 08/10/1988
Result: **COVENTRY SPORTING 0 GLOUCESTER CITY 2**
Competition: Southern League Midland Division
Teamsheet: Shaw, Steel, Williams, Lander, Malpas, Green, Talboys, Hughes, Penny, Morrison, Noble
Substitutes: Johnson (nps), Hedges (nps)
Scorer: Penny (2)
Attendance: 120

Date: Tuesday 11/10/1988
Result: **GLOUCESTER CITY 0 BRIDGNORTH TOWN 0**
Competition: Southern League Cup 1st Round 1st Leg
Teamsheet: Webb, Hedges, Williams, Lander, Malpas, Steel, Johnson, Hughes, Andrews, Hyde, Noble
Substitutes: Harris (for Johnson), Penny (for Andrews)
Attendance: 316

Date: Saturday 15/10/1988
Result: **GLOUCESTER CITY 0 MERTHYR TYDFIL 1**
Competition: FA Cup 3rd Qualifying Round
Teamsheet: Shaw, Steel, Williams, Lander, Malpas, Green, Talboys, Hughes, Penny, Morrison, Noble
Substitutes: Harris (for Penny), Hedges (nps)
Attendance: 1429

Date: Tuesday 18/10/1988
Result: **BRIDGNORTH TOWN 0 GLOUCESTER CITY 3**
Competition: Southern League Cup 1st Round 2nd Leg
Teamsheet: Shaw, Hedges, Williams, Lander, Malpas, Steel, Chandler, Hughes, Penny, Morrison, Noble
Substitutes: Talboys (nps), Hyde (nps)
Scorers: Chandler, Morrison, Penny
Attendance: 135

Date: Saturday 22/10/1988
Result: **GLOUCESTER CITY 3 FROME TOWN 2**
Competition: FA Trophy 2nd Qualifying Round
Teamsheet: Shaw, Steel, Williams, Lander, Malpas, Green, Talboys, Hughes, Penny, Morrison, Noble
Substitutes: Hedges (nps), Hyde (for Penny)
Scorers: Lander, Green (2)
Attendance: 524

Date: Saturday 29/10/1988
Result: **HEDNESFORD TOWN 2 GLOUCESTER CITY 1**
Competition: Southern League Midland Division
Teamsheet: Shaw, Chandler, Williams, Lander, Malpas, Green, Talboys, Hughes, Penny, Morrison, Noble
Substitutes: Hyde (for Penny), Hedges (nps)
Scorer: Talboys
Attendance: 298

Date: Tuesday 01/11/1988
Result: **GOSPORT BOROUGH 4 GLOUCESTER CITY 0**
Competition: Southern League Cup 2nd Round 1st Leg
Teamsheet: Shaw, Hedges, Williams, Lander, Malpas, Green, Chandler, Foxwell, Hyde, Morrison, Noble
Substitutes: Talboys (nps), Penny (for Hyde)
Attendance: 180

Date: Saturday 05/11/1988
Result: **GLOUCESTER CITY 3 WELLINGBOROUGH TOWN 1**
Competition: Southern League Midland Division
Teamsheet: O'Hagan, Hedges, Williams, Lander, Foxwell, Green, Talboys, Chandler, Penny, Morrison, Noble
Substitutes: Andrews (nps), Bray (nps)
Scorers: Morrison, Penny, Talboys
Attendance: 388

Date: Tuesday 08/11/1988
Result: **GLOUCESTER CITY 2 FOREST GREEN ROVERS 3**
Competition: Gloucestershire FA Northern Senior Professional Cup Semi-Final
Teamsheet: O'Hagan, Hedges, Williams, Lander, Green, Bray, Talboys, Hughes, Penny, Chandler, Noble
Substitutes: Morrison (for Bray), Hyde (nps), Tandy (nps), Foxwell (for Chandler), Andrews (nps)
Scorer: Penny (2)
Attendance: 486

Date: Saturday 12/11/1988
Result: **GRANTHAM TOWN 1 GLOUCESTER CITY 1**
Competition: Southern League Midland Division
Teamsheet: Shaw, Steel, Williams, Lander, Malpas, Green, Chandler, Hughes, Penny, Morrison, Noble
Substitutes: Talboys (nps), Hedges (nps)
Scorer: Penny
Attendance: 441

Date: Tuesday 15/11/1988
Result: **GLOUCESTER CITY 6 GOSPORT BOROUGH 1** (aet)
Competition: Southern League Cup 2nd Round 2nd Leg
Teamsheet: Shaw, Steel, Williams, Lander, Malpas, Green, Chandler, Hughes, Penny, Morrison, Noble
Substitutes: Talboys (for Williams), Hedges (for Penny)
Scorers: Penny (2), Morrison, Malpas, Talboys (2)
Attendance: 273

Date: Saturday 19/11/1988
Result: **GLOUCESTER CITY 8 MILE OAK ROVERS 0**
Competition: Southern League Midland Division
Teamsheet: Shaw, Steel, Williams, Lander, Malpas, Green, Chandler, Hughes, Penny, Morrison, Noble
Substitutes: Talboys (nps), Hedges (nps)
Scorers: Morrison (4), Penny (2), Chandler (2)
Attendance: 426

Date: Tuesday 22/11/1988
Result: **GLOUCESTER CITY 1 TAMWORTH 1**
Competition: Southern League Midland Division
Teamsheet: Shaw, Steel, Williams, Lander, Hedges, Green, Chandler, Hughes, Penny, Morrison, Noble
Substitutes: Talboys (for Penny), Bray (for Hedges)
Scorer: Green
Attendance: 990

Date: Saturday 26/11/1988
Result: **GLOUCESTER CITY 1 DUDLEY TOWN 1**
Competition: Southern League Midland Division
Teamsheet: Shaw, Steel, Williams, Lander, Hedges, Green, Chandler, Hughes, Talboys, Morrison, Noble
Substitutes: Andrews (nps), Harris (for Talboys)
Scorer: Hughes
Attendance: 497

Date: Sunday 27/11/1988
Result: **SPALDING UNITED 1 GLOUCESTER CITY 4**
Competition: Southern League Midland Division
Teamsheet: Shaw, Steel, Williams, Lander, Hedges, Harris, Chandler, Hughes, Andrews, Morrison, Noble
Substitutes: Bray (nps), Godfrey (nps)
Scorers: Andrews (2), Lander, Chandler
Attendance: 239

Date: Tuesday 29/11/1988
Result: **GLOUCESTER CITY 2 BILSTON TOWN 1**
Competition: Southern League Midland Division
Teamsheet: Shaw, Steel, Williams, Andrews, Hedges, Harris, Chandler, Hughes, Penny, Morrison, Noble
Substitutes: Talboys (for -----), Bray (for Talboys)
Scorers: Hughes, own goal
Attendance: 507

Date: Saturday 03/12/1988
Result: **DORCHESTER TOWN 1 GLOUCESTER CITY 1**
Competition: FA Trophy 3rd Qualifying Round
Teamsheet: Shaw, Steel, Williams, Lander, Hedges, Harris, Chandler, Hughes, Andrews, Morrison, Noble
Substitutes: Talboys (for Andrews), Malpas (nps)
Scorer: Noble
Attendance: 301

Date: Tuesday 06/12/1988
Result: **GLOUCESTER CITY 1 DORCHESTER TOWN 3**
Competition: FA Trophy 3rd Qualifying Round Replay
Teamsheet: Shaw, Steel, Williams, Lander, Hedges, Harris, Chandler, Hughes, Talboys, Morrison, Noble
Substitutes: Andrews (for Hedges), Malpas (nps)
Scorer: Talboys
Attendance: 687

Date: Saturday 10/12/1988
Result: **ASHTREE HIGHFIELD 0 GLOUCESTER CITY 0**
Competition: Southern League Midland Division
Teamsheet: Shaw, Steel, Hedges, Lander, Malpas, Green, Chandler, Hughes, Townsend, Morrison, Noble
Substitutes: Harris (nps), Andrews (nps)
Attendance: 113

Date: Wednesday 14/12/1988
Result: **SALISBURY 0 GLOUCESTER CITY 2**
Competition: Southern League Cup 3rd Round 1st Leg
Teamsheet: Shaw, Harris, Hedges, Lander, Malpas, Green, Talboys, Hughes, Morrison, Townsend, Noble
Substitutes: Steel (nps), Chandler (nps)
Scorer: Townsend (2)
Attendance: 220

Date: Saturday 17/12/1988
Result: **GLOUCESTER CITY 4 BANBURY UNITED 1**
Competition: Southern League Midland Division
Teamsheet: Shaw, Steel, Hedges, Lander, Malpas, Green, Chandler, Hughes, Townsend, Morrison, Noble
Substitutes: Penny (nps), Talboys (nps)
Scorers: Green (2), Townsend (2)
Attendance: 524

Date: Tuesday 20/12/1988
Result: **GLOUCESTER CITY 3 SALISBURY 2**
Competition: Southern League Cup 3rd Round 2nd Leg
Teamsheet: Shaw, Steel, Williams, Lander, Malpas, Green, Talboys, Hughes, Penny, Townsend, Noble
Substitutes: Morrison (for Talboys), Hedges (nps)
Scorer: Townsend (3)
Attendance: 470

Date: Monday 26/12/1988
Result: **FOREST GREEN ROVERS 0 GLOUCESTER CITY 2**
Competition: Southern League Midland Division
Teamsheet: Shaw, Steel, Williams, Lander, Malpas, Green, Chandler, Hughes, Penny, Townsend, Noble
Substitutes: Hedges (nps), Harris (nps)
Scorer: Townsend (2)
Attendance: 772

Date: Saturday 31/12/1988
Result: **NUNEATON BOROUGH 1 GLOUCESTER CITY 2**
Competition: Southern League Midland Division
Teamsheet: Shaw, Steel, Williams, Lander, Malpas, Green, Chandler, Hughes, Penny, Townsend, Noble
Substitutes: Hedges (nps), Talboys (nps)
Scorers: Penny, Townsend
Attendance: 648

Date: Monday 02/01/1989
Result: **GLOUCESTER CITY 2 STOURBRIDGE 1**
Competition: Southern League Midland Division
Teamsheet: Shaw, Steel, Williams, Lander, Malpas, Green, Chandler, Hughes, Penny, Townsend, Noble
Substitutes: Hedges (nps), Morrison (nps)
Scorers: Penny, Townsend
Attendance: 1011

Date: Saturday 07/01/1989
Result: **GLOUCESTER CITY 2 RUSHDEN TOWN 1**
Competition: Southern League Midland Division
Teamsheet: Shaw, Steel, Williams, Lander, Malpas, Green, Chandler, Hughes, Penny, Townsend, Noble
Substitutes: Morrison (for Townsend), Talboys (nps)
Scorers: Green, Hughes
Attendance: 1021

Date: Saturday 14/01/1989
Result: **BILSTON TOWN 0 GLOUCESTER CITY 3**
Competition: Southern League Midland Division
Teamsheet: Shaw, Steel, Williams, Lander, Malpas, Green, Chandler, Hughes, Penny, Townsend, Noble
Substitutes: Morrison (for Malpas), Talboys (for Penny)
Scorers: Penny, Townsend, Noble
Attendance: 250

Date: Saturday 21/01/1989
Result: **GLOUCESTER CITY 1 WILLENHALL TOWN 1**
Competition: Southern League Midland Division
Teamsheet: Shaw, Steel, Williams, Lander, Talboys, Green, Chandler, Hughes, Penny, Morrison, Noble
Substitutes: Payne (for Noble), Hedges (nps)
Scorer: Talboys
Attendance: 828

Date: Saturday 28/01/1989
Result: **BRIDGNORTH TOWN 2 GLOUCESTER CITY 4**
Competition: Southern League Midland Division
Teamsheet: Shaw, Steel, Williams, Lander, Talboys, Green, Chandler, Hughes, Penny, Townsend, Noble
Substitutes: Payne (nps), Morrison (nps)
Scorers: Noble, Penny, Townsend (2)
Attendance: 380

Date: Tuesday 31/01/1989
Result: **BALDOCK TOWN 0 GLOUCESTER CITY 1**
Competition: Southern League Cup Quarter-Final 1st Leg
Teamsheet: Webb, Steel, Williams, Hedges, Payne, Green, Chandler, Hughes, Morrison, Townsend, Talboys
Substitutes: Harris (for Payne), Penny (nps)
Scorer: Townsend
Attendance: 368

Date: Saturday 04/02/1989
Result: **WELLINGBOROUGH TOWN 1 GLOUCESTER CITY 2**
Competition: Southern League Midland Division
Teamsheet: Shaw, Steel, Williams, Lander, Talboys, Green, Chandler, Hughes, Penny, Townsend, Noble
Substitutes: Morrison (for Talboys), Hedges (for Chandler)
Scorer: Townsend (2)
Attendance: 160

Date: Tuesday 07/02/1989
Result: **GLOUCESTER CITY 1 BALDOCK TOWN 1**
Competition: Southern League Cup Quarter-Final 2nd Leg
Teamsheet: Shaw, Steel, Williams, Lander, Hedges, Green, Morrison, Hughes, Penny, Townsend, Noble
Substitutes: Payne (nps), Harris (for Noble)
Scorer: Townsend
Attendance: 769

Date: Saturday 11/02/1989
Result: **GLOUCESTER CITY 2 HEDNESFORD TOWN 1**
Competition: Southern League Midland Division
Teamsheet: Shaw, Steel, Williams, Hedges, Morrison, Green, Chandler, Hughes, Penny, Townsend, Noble
Substitutes: Harris (nps), Payne (nps)
Scorers: Noble, Hughes
Attendance: 712

Date: Saturday 18/02/1989
Result: **GLOUCESTER CITY 7 COVENTRY SPORTING 0**
Competition: Southern League Midland Division
Teamsheet: Shaw, Steel, Williams, Lander, Hedges, Green, Talboys, Hughes, Penny, Townsend, Noble
Substitutes: Morrison (nps), Payne (nps)
Scorers: own goal, Talboys, Penny (3), Williams, Noble
Attendance: 508

Date: Tuesday 21/02/1989
Result: **HALESOWEN TOWN 0 GLOUCESTER CITY 0**
Competition: Southern League Midland Division
Teamsheet: Shaw, Steel, Williams, Lander, Hedges, Green, Talboys, Hughes, Penny, Townsend, Noble
Substitutes: Morrison (for Penny), Harris (nps)
Attendance: 1580

Date: Saturday 25/02/1989
Result: **MILE OAK ROVERS 0 GLOUCESTER CITY 2**
Competition: Southern League Midland Division
Teamsheet: Shaw, Steel, Williams, Lander, Fullbrook, Green, Talboys, Hughes, Penny, Townsend, Noble
Substitutes: Morrison (nps), Payne (nps)
Scorer: Townsend (2)
Attendance: 450

Date: Tuesday 07/03/1989
Result: **GLOUCESTER CITY 2 BURTON ALBION 1**
Competition: Southern League Cup Semi-Final 1st Leg
Teamsheet: Shaw, Steel, Williams, Lander, Fullbrook, Green, Chandler, Hughes, Penny, Townsend, Noble
Substitutes: Talboys (for Chandler), Morrison (for Penny)
Scorers: Townsend, Noble (pen)
Attendance: 1032

Date: Saturday 11/03/1989
Result: **GLOUCESTER CITY 4 BRIDGNORTH TOWN 1**
Competition: Southern League Midland Division
Teamsheet: Shaw, Steel, Williams, Lander, Fullbrook, Green, Hughes, Chandler, Penny, Townsend, Noble
Substitutes: Morrison (for Penny), Talboys (for Steel)
Scorers: own goal, Townsend (2), Talboys
Attendance: 724

Date: Tuesday 14/03/1989
Result: **BURTON ALBION 3 GLOUCESTER CITY 1** (aet)
Competition: Southern League Cup Semi-Final 2nd Leg
Teamsheet: Shaw, Steel, Williams, Lander, Fullbrook, Green, Chandler, Hughes, Penny, Townsend, Talboys
Substitutes: Noble (for Penny), Morrison (for Talboys)
Scorer: Steel
Attendance: 1001

Date: Saturday 18/03/1989
Result: **GLOUCESTER CITY 1 NUNEATON BOROUGH 2**
Competition: Southern League Midland Division
Teamsheet: Shaw, Hedges, Williams, Lander, Fullbrook, Green, Chandler, Hughes, Penny, Townsend, Noble
Substitutes: Morrison (for Penny), Talboys (for Chandler)
Scorer: Lander
Attendance: 600

Date: Wednesday 22/03/1989
Result: **GLOUCESTER CITY 1 SUTTON COLDFIELD TOWN 3**
Competition: Southern League Midland Division
Teamsheet: Shaw, Steel, Williams, Lander, Fullbrook, Green, Chandler, Hughes, Morrison, Townsend, Noble
Substitutes: Talboys (nps), Harris (for Fullbrook)
Scorer: Green
Attendance: 661

Date: Saturday 25/03/1989
Result: **STOURBRIDGE 1 GLOUCESTER CITY 2**
Competition: Southern League Midland Division
Teamsheet: Shaw, Steel, Williams, Lander, Fullbrook, Green, Chandler, Hughes, Penny, Townsend, Noble
Substitutes: Morrison (for Townsend), Talboys (nps)
Scorers: Chandler, Townsend
Attendance: 313

Date: Monday 27/03/1989
Result: **GLOUCESTER CITY 7 FOREST GREEN ROVERS 1**
Competition: Southern League Midland Division
Teamsheet: Shaw, Steel, Williams, Lander, Fullbrook, Green, Chandler, Hughes, Penny, Townsend, Noble
Substitutes: Morrison (nps), Payne (nps)
Scorers: Penny (2), Townsend (2), Hughes, Chandler, Noble
Attendance: 1216

Date: Saturday 01/04/1989
Result: **ATHERSTONE UNITED 1 GLOUCESTER CITY 1**
Competition: Southern League Midland Division
Teamsheet: Shaw, Steel, Williams, Lander, Talboys, Green, Chandler, Hughes, Penny, Townsend, Noble
Substitutes: Morrison (nps), Hedges (for Lander)
Scorer: Townsend
Attendance: 822

Date: Saturday 08/04/1989
Result: **RUSHDEN TOWN 2 GLOUCESTER CITY 3**
Competition: Southern League Midland Division
Teamsheet: Shaw, Steel, Williams, Lander, Bradder, Green, Chandler, Hughes, Penny, Morrison, Noble
Substitutes: Payne (for Morrison), Talboys (nps)
Scorers: Penny, Noble, Morrison
Attendance: 294

Date: Tuesday 11/04/1989
Result: **TAMWORTH 1 GLOUCESTER CITY 2**
Competition: Southern League Midland Division
Teamsheet: Shaw, Steel, Williams, Lander, Bradder, Green, Chandler, Hughes, Penny, Townsend, Noble
Substitutes: Morrison (nps), Talboys (nps)
Scorers: Chandler, Townsend
Attendance: 1806

Date: Saturday 15/04/1989
Result: **GLOUCESTER CITY 0 SPALDING UNITED 1**
Competition: Southern League Midland Division
Teamsheet: Shaw, Steel, Williams, Lander, Bradder, Green, Chandler, Hughes, Penny, Townsend, Noble
Substitutes: Payne (nps), Morrison (for Penny)
Attendance: 793

Date: Saturday 22/04/1989
Result: **DUDLEY TOWN 0 GLOUCESTER CITY 2**
Competition: Southern League Midland Division
Teamsheet: Shaw, Steel, Williams, Lander, Bradder, Green, Chandler, Hughes, Penny, Townsend, Noble
Substitutes: Morrison (nps), Payne (nps)
Scorers: Noble, Penny
Attendance: 437

Date: Saturday 29/04/1989
Result: **GLOUCESTER CITY 1 HALESOWEN TOWN 2**
Competition: Southern League Midland Division
Teamsheet: Shaw, Steel, Williams, Lander, Bradder, Green, Chandler, Hughes, Penny, Townsend, Noble
Substitutes: Payne (nps), Morrison (for Chandler)
Scorer: Townsend
Attendance: 1709

Date: Monday 01/05/1989
Result: **GLOUCESTER CITY 2 GRANTHAM TOWN 0**
Competition: Southern League Midland Division
Teamsheet: Shaw, Steel, Williams, Fullbrook, Bradder, Green, Talboys, Hughes, Penny, Townsend, Noble
Substitutes: Payne (nps), Morrison (for Penny)
Scorers: Townsend, Morrison
Attendance: 1194

Date: Saturday 06/05/1989
Result: **KING'S LYNN 0 GLOUCESTER CITY 2**
Competition: Southern League Midland Division
Teamsheet: Shaw, Steel, Williams, Fullbrook, Bradder, Green, Chandler, Hughes, Payne, Townsend, Noble
Substitutes: Penny (for Chandler), Talboys (for Noble)
Scorers: Townsend, Penny
Attendance: 266

Appearances – M Andrews 4(4), GV Bradder 7, M Bray 2(2), RD Chandler 40, DP Foxwell 4(2), G Fullbrook 10, N Green 54, AG Harris 5(7), IA Hedges 25(3), BD Hughes 58, C Hyde 4(3), S Johnson 2(1), MT Lander 55, M Malpas 28, L Morrison 34(14), WI Noble 58(1), P O'Hagan 2, D Payne 2(2), S Penny 45(4), J Shaw 56, GR Steel 47, SJ Talboys 29(9), CG Townsend 31, R Webb 2, M Williams 56.
Others selected but did not play: BC Godfrey, DM Tandy.
Scorers – CG Townsend 31, S Penny 28, L Morrison 14, WI Noble 11, SJ Talboys 9, RD Chandler 7, N Green 7, BD Hughes 6, M Malpas 5, M Andrews 3, MT Lander 3, M Williams 3, GR Steel 1 own goals 3.

SEASON BY SEASON

SOUTHERN LEAGUE MIDLAND DIVISION

POS	CLUB	P	W	D	L	F	A	PTS
1	**GLOUCESTER CITY**	**42**	**28**	**8**	**6**	**95**	**37**	**92**
2	TAMWORTH	42	26	9	7	85	45	87
3	ATHERSTONE UNITED	42	25	10	7	84	38	85
4	HALESOWEN TOWN	42	25	10	7	85	42	85
5	GRANTHAM TOWN	42	23	11	8	66	37	80
6	NUNEATON BOROUGH	42	19	9	14	71	58	66
7	RUSHDEN TOWN	42	19	8	15	71	50	65
8	SPALDING UNITED	42	17	13	12	72	64	64
9	DUDLEY TOWN	42	16	13	13	73	62	61
10	SUTTON COLDFIELD TOWN	42	18	7	17	56	56	61
11	WILLENHALL TOWN	42	16	12	14	65	71	60
12	FOREST GREEN ROVERS	42	12	16	14	64	67	52
13	HEDNESFORD TOWN	42	12	16	14	49	56	52
14	BILSTON TOWN	42	15	7	20	63	71	52
15	ASHTREE HIGHFIELD	42	12	15	15	57	62	51
16	BANBURY UNITED	42	10	14	18	53	74	44
17	BRIDGNORTH TOWN	42	12	7	23	59	77	43
18	STOURBRIDGE	42	11	10	21	37	65	43
19	KING'S LYNN	42	7	13	22	31	67	34
20	COVENTRY SPORTING	42	6	13	23	39	91	31
21	WELLINGBOROUGH TOWN	42	5	15	22	39	72	30
22	MILE OAK ROVERS	42	5	10	27	46	98	25
		924	339	246	339	1360	1360	1263

SEASON 1989-1990
(Home Ground: City Stadium, Meadow Park, Hempsted)

Date: Saturday 19/08/1989
Result: **GRAVESEND & NORTHFLEET 1 GLOUCESTER CITY 1**
Competition: Southern League Premier Division
Teamsheet: Webb, Fullbrook, M Williams, Bradder, Webster, Steel, Chandler, Hughes, Morrison, Townsend, Noble
Substitutes: Talboys (for Webster), Payne (for Noble)
Scorer: Hughes
Attendance: 626

Date: Tuesday 22/08/1989
Result: **GLOUCESTER CITY 1 WEYMOUTH 1**
Competition: Southern League Premier Division
Teamsheet: Webb, Fullbrook, M Williams, Bradder, Steel, Green, Chandler, Hughes, Penny, Townsend, Noble
Substitutes: Talboys (for Chandler), Payne (for Penny)
Scorer: Townsend
Attendance: 914

Date: Saturday 26/08/1989
Result: **GLOUCESTER CITY 3 CAMBRIDGE CITY 2**
Competition: Southern League Premier Division
Teamsheet: Hopps, Lander, M Williams, Bradder, Green, Webster, Chandler, Hughes, Morrison, Townsend, Noble
Substitutes: Talboys (for Webster), Payne (for Noble)
Scorers: Townsend (2), Bradder
Attendance: 790

Date: Monday 28/08/1989
Result: **GOSPORT BOROUGH 2 GLOUCESTER CITY 3**
Competition: Southern League Premier Division
Teamsheet: Hopps, Hedges, M Williams, Bradder, Green, Steel, Chandler, Hughes, Morrison, Townsend, Noble
Substitutes: Talboys (for Hedges), Payne (for Townsend)
Scorers: Townsend (2), Noble (pen)
Attendance: 306

Date: Saturday 02/09/1989
Result: **GLOUCESTER CITY 2 VALLEY SPORTS RUGBY 3**
Competition: Southern League Premier Division
Teamsheet: Webb, Hedges, M Williams, Bradder, Green, Steel, Chandler, Hughes, Morrison, Townsend, Noble
Substitutes: Talboys (for Noble), Payne (for Townsend)
Scorers: M Williams, Noble (pen)
Attendance: 900

Date: Tuesday 05/09/1989
Result: **WATERLOOVILLE 2 GLOUCESTER CITY 4**
Competition: Southern League Premier Division
Teamsheet: Shaw, Lander, M Williams, Bradder, Green, Webster, Chandler, Hughes, Morrison, Townsend, Payne
Substitutes: Noble (for Payne), Talboys (nps)
Scorers: Townsend (3, 1 pen), Payne
Attendance: 250

Date: Saturday 09/09/1989
Result: **CORBY TOWN 1 GLOUCESTER CITY 4**
Competition: Southern League Premier Division
Teamsheet: Shaw, Lander, M Williams, Bradder, Green, Webster, Chandler, Hughes, Morrison, Townsend, Payne
Substitutes: Talboys (for Chandler), Noble (for Morrison)
Scorers: Hughes, Townsend, Bradder, Payne
Attendance: 240

GLOUCESTER CITY 1988-1989
SOUTHERN LEAGUE MIDLAND DIVISION CHAMPIONS

Gloucester City won the Midland Division title: — Back row (l-r): Brian Godfrey (Manager), Bernard Tandy (Trainer), Nigel Green, Gary Fulbrook, Lance Morrison, Martin Lander, Gary Bradder, John Shaw, Steve Talboys, Ian Hedges, Greg Steel, Dennis Savery. — Front row: Dave Payne, Ricky Chandler, Shaun Penny, Brian Hughes, Wayne Noble, Chris Townsend, Martyn Williams, Adrian Harris.

(Photograph courtesy of Steve Turk)
The Board and Brian Hughes with the cup

[319]

Date: Tuesday 12/09/1989
Result: **GLOUCESTER CITY 3 ATHERSTONE UNITED 1**
Competition: Southern League Premier Division
Teamsheet: Hopps, Fullbrook, M Williams, Bradder, Green, Steel, Talboys, Hughes, Morrison, Townsend, Payne
Substitutes: Noble (for Payne), Lander (for Bradder)
Scorers: Morrison, Payne (2, 1 pen)
Attendance: 1116

Date: Wednesday 20/09/1989
Result: **GLOUCESTER CITY 4 MANGOTSFIELD UNITED 0**
Competition: FA Cup 1st Qualifying Round
Teamsheet: Hopps, Fullbrook, M Williams, Bradder, Green, Steel, Talboys, Hughes, Morrison, Townsend, Payne
Substitutes: Noble (for Payne), Chandler (for Talboys)
Scorers: Morrison (2), Hughes (2)
Attendance: 867

Date: Saturday 23/09/1989
Result: **GLOUCESTER CITY 4 DORCHESTER TOWN 0**
Competition: FA Trophy 1st Qualifying Round
Teamsheet: Hopps, Fullbrook, M Williams, Chandler, Green, Steel, Talboys, Hughes, Morrison, Townsend, Payne
Substitutes: Noble (for Talboys), Bradder (nps)
Scorers: Townsend (2), Talboys, Morrison
Attendance: 582

Date: Saturday 30/09/1989
Result: **BARRY TOWN 2 GLOUCESTER CITY 2**
Competition: FA Cup 2nd Qualifying Round
Teamsheet: Hopps, Fullbrook, M Williams, Chandler, Green, Steel, Talboys, Hughes, Morrison, Townsend, Payne
Substitutes: Noble (for Payne), Bradder (for Chandler)
Scorers: Chandler, Townsend
Attendance: 594

Date: Tuesday 03/10/1989
Result: **GLOUCESTER CITY 2 BARRY TOWN 0**
Competition: FA Cup 2nd Qualifying Round Replay
Teamsheet: Hopps, Hedges, M Williams, Chandler, Green, Steel, Noble, Hughes, Morrison, Townsend, Payne
Substitutes: Talboys (for Payne), Lander (for Hedges)
Scorers: Morrison, M Williams
Attendance: 972

Date: Saturday 07/10/1989
Result: **CHELMSFORD CITY 3 GLOUCESTER CITY 1**
Competition: Southern League Premier Division
Teamsheet: Hopps, Hedges, M Williams, Chandler, Lander, Steel, Talboys, Hughes, Morrison, Noble, Payne
Substitutes: Bradder (for Chandler), Fullbrook (nps)
Scorer: Talboys
Attendance: 930

Date: Tuesday 10/10/1989
Result: **BATH CITY 2 GLOUCESTER CITY 1**
Competition: Clubcall Cup 1st Round
Teamsheet: Shaw, Fullbrook, M Williams, Bradder, Lander, Steel, Talboys, Hughes, Morrison, Payne, Noble
Substitutes: Hedges (nps), Andrews (for Fulbrook)
Scorer: Payne
Attendance: 543

Date: Saturday 14/10/1989
Result: **GLOUCESTER CITY 4 WORCESTER CITY 2**
Competition: FA Cup 3rd Qualifying Round
Teamsheet: Shaw, Hedges, M Williams, Lander, Green, Steel, Talboys, Hughes, Morrison, Payne, Noble
Substitutes: Hyde (nps), Fullbrook (nps)
Scorers: Hughes, Morrison, Payne (2)
Attendance: 1213

Date: Monday 16/10/1989
Result: **HEDNESFORD TOWN 0 GLOUCESTER CITY 4**
Competition: Southern League Cup 1st Round 1st Leg
Teamsheet: Shaw, Hedges, M Williams, Lander, Green, Steel, Hyde, Hughes, Morrison, Payne, Noble
Substitutes: Talboys (for Noble), Fullbrook (for Lander)
Scorers: Noble, Hyde, Payne, Talboys
Attendance: 375

Date: Saturday 21/10/1989
Result: **GLOUCESTER CITY 2 BARRY TOWN 1**
Competition: FA Trophy 2nd Qualifying Round
Teamsheet: Shaw, Hedges, M Williams, Lander, Green, Steel, Talboys, Hughes, Morrison, Payne, Noble
Substitutes: Hyde (for Payne), Fullbrook (nps)
Scorer: Talboys (2)
Attendance: 659

Date: Saturday 28/10/1989
Result: **FOLKESTONE TOWN 0 GLOUCESTER CITY 1**
Competition: FA Cup 4th Qualifying Round
Teamsheet: Shaw, Hedges, M Williams, Lander, Green, Steel, Talboys, Hughes, Morrison, Payne, Noble
Substitutes: Townsend (for Morrison), Hyde (nps)
Scorer: Payne
Attendance: 974

Date: Tuesday 31/10/1989
Result: **GLOUCESTER CITY 2 HEDNESFORD TOWN 2**
Competition: Southern League Cup 1st Round 2nd Leg
Teamsheet: Shaw, Fullbrook, M Williams, Chandler, Green, Steel, Payne, Hughes, Hyde, Townsend, Noble
Substitutes: Andrews (for Chandler), Morrison (for Andrews)
Scorers: Green, Hyde
Attendance: 518

Date: Saturday 04/11/1989
Result: **WORCESTER CITY 2 GLOUCESTER CITY 0**
Competition: Southern League Premier Division
Teamsheet: Shaw, Hedges, M Williams, Lander, Green, Steel, Talboys, Hughes, Morrison, Townsend, Payne
Substitutes: Noble (for Payne), Hyde (for Morrison)
Attendance: 1115

Date: Tuesday 07/11/1989
Result: **GLOUCESTER CITY 3 CHELTENHAM TOWN 3** (5-6 pens)
Competition: Gloucestershire FA Northern Senior Professional Cup Semi-Final
Teamsheet: Hopps, Hedges, M Williams, Lander, Green, Steel, Talboys, Hughes, Morrison, Townsend, Noble
Substitutes: Fullbrook (for Lander), Hyde (for Townsend), Andrews (nps), Shaw (nps)
Scorers: Talboys (2), Townsend
Attendance: 968

Date: Saturday 11/11/1989
Result: **GLOUCESTER CITY 2 WEALDSTONE 2**
Competition: Southern League Premier Division
Teamsheet: Hopps, Hedges, M Williams, Lander, Fullbrook, Steel, Talboys, Hughes, Morrison, Payne, Noble
Substitutes: Chandler (nps), Hyde (for Morrison)
Scorers: Steel, Payne
Attendance: 620

Date: Saturday 18/11/1989
Result: **GLOUCESTER CITY 1 DORCHESTER TOWN 0**
Competition: FA Cup 1st Round
Teamsheet: Shaw, Hedges, M Williams, Lander, Green, Steel, Talboys, Hughes, Morrison, Payne, Noble
Substitutes: Hyde (nps), Chandler (nps)
Scorer: Talboys
Attendance: 1754

Date: Tuesday 21/11/1989
Result: **DORCHESTER TOWN 0 GLOUCESTER CITY 1**
Competition: Southern League Cup 2nd Round 1st Leg
Teamsheet: Mogg, Fulbrook, M Williams, Lander, Webster, Steel, Talboys, Hughes, Hyde, Payne, Noble
Substitutes: Morrison (for Payne), Hedges (for Lander)
Scorer: Talboys
Attendance: 316

Date: Saturday 25/11/1989
Result: **GLOUCESTER CITY 3 GRAVESEND & NORTHFLEET 0**
Competition: Southern League Premier Division
Teamsheet: Mogg, Hedges, M Williams, Lander, Webster, Steel, Talboys, Hughes, Morrison, Payne, Noble
Substitutes: Hyde (nps), Chandler (nps)
Scorers: Talboys, Hughes, Morrison
Attendance: 644

Date: Tuesday 28/11/1989
Result: **GLOUCESTER CITY 3 DORCHESTER TOWN 0**
Competition: Southern League Cup 2nd Round 2nd Leg
Teamsheet: Mogg, Fullbrook, M Williams, Chandler, Green, Steel, Talboys, Hughes, Morrison, Hyde, Noble
Substitutes: Payne (for Morrison), Hedges (nps)
Scorers: Noble, Hyde (2)
Attendance: 471

Date: Saturday 02/12/1989
Result: **GLOUCESTER CITY 0 WORCESTER CITY 1**
Competition: FA Trophy 3rd Qualifying Round
Teamsheet: Mogg, Hedges, M Williams, Lander, Green, Steel, Talboys, Hughes, Morrison, Payne, Noble
Substitutes: Hyde (for Noble), Chandler (for Steel)
Attendance: 799

Date: Tuesday 05/12/1989
Result: **GLOUCESTER CITY 0 WATERLOOVILLE 1**
Competition: Southern League Premier Division
Teamsheet: Mogg, Fullbrook, M Williams, Lander, Green, Steel, Chandler, Hughes, Morrison, Payne, Noble
Substitutes: Talboys (for Hughes), Hyde (for Noble)
Attendance: 468

Date: Saturday 09/12/1989
Result: **CARDIFF CITY 2 GLOUCESTER CITY 2**
Competition: FA Cup 2nd Round
Teamsheet: Shaw, Hedges, M Williams, Lander, Green, Steel, Talboys, Payne, Morrison, Townsend, Noble
Substitutes: Chandler (for Lander), Hyde (nps)
Scorers: Talboys, Townsend
Attendance: 4531

Date: Tuesday 12/12/1989
Result: **GLOUCESTER CITY 0 CARDIFF CITY 1**
Competition: FA Cup 2nd Round Replay
Teamsheet: Shaw, Hedges, M Williams, Payne, Green, Steel, Talboys, Hughes, Morrison, Townsend, Noble
Substitutes: Hyde (for Noble), Lander (for Hughes)
Attendance: 3877

Date: Saturday 16/12/1989
Result: **MOOR GREEN 4 GLOUCESTER CITY 1**
Competition: Southern League Premier Division
Teamsheet: Mogg, Hedges, M Williams, Lander, Green, Steel, Talboys, Payne, Morrison, Townsend, Noble
Substitutes: Hyde (for Morrison), Chandler (for Townsend)
Scorer: Morrison
Attendance: 314

Date: Thursday 21/12/1989
Result: **MOOR GREEN 2 GLOUCESTER CITY 2**
Competition: Southern League Cup 3rd Round 1st Leg
Teamsheet: Mogg, Fullbrook, M Williams, Lander, Green, Steel, Talboys, Webster, Morrison, Payne, Noble
Substitutes: Hedges (nps), Chandler (nps)
Scorers: Noble, Talboys
Attendance: 161

Date: Tuesday 26/12/1989
Result: **GLOUCESTER CITY 0 BATH CITY 0**
Competition: Southern League Premier Division
Teamsheet: Mogg, Hedges, M Williams, Payne, Green, Steel, Talboys, Hughes, Morrison, Thompson, Noble
Substitutes: Lander (nps), Fullbrook (nps)
Attendance: 1223

Date: Saturday 30/12/1989
Result: **GLOUCESTER CITY 0 BURTON ALBION 0**
Competition: Southern League Premier Division
Teamsheet: Mogg, Hedges, M Williams, Payne, Green, Steel, Talboys, Hughes, Morrison, Thompson, Noble
Substitutes: Fullbrook (nps), Lander (nps)
Attendance: 828

Date: Monday 01/01/1990
Result: **DORCHESTER TOWN 3 GLOUCESTER CITY 2**
Competition: Southern League Premier Division
Teamsheet: Mogg, Fullbrook, M Williams, Payne, Green, Steel, Talboys, Hughes, Morrison, Townsend, Noble
Substitutes: Thompson (for Morrison), Lander (nps)
Scorers: Talboys, Townsend
Attendance: 404

Date: Saturday 06/01/1990
Result: **CRAWLEY TOWN 2 GLOUCESTER CITY 3**
Competition: Southern League Premier Division
Teamsheet: Mogg, Fullbrook, M Williams, Lander, Green, Steel, Talboys, Hughes, Morrison, Payne, Noble
Substitutes: Thompson (nps), Hedges (nps)
Scorers: Payne, Morrison, Talboys
Attendance: 363

Date: Tuesday 09/01/1990
Result: **GLOUCESTER CITY 4 MOOR GREEN 3** (aet)
Competition: Southern League Cup 3rd Round 2nd Leg
Teamsheet: Mogg, Fullbrook, M Williams, Lander, Green, Steel, Talboys, Hughes, Morrison, Payne, Noble
Substitutes: Thompson (for Payne), Chandler (for Steel)
Scorers: Noble, Hughes, Talboys (2)
Attendance: 548

Date: Saturday 13/01/1990
Result: **GLOUCESTER CITY 1 CRAWLEY TOWN 1**
Competition: Southern League Premier Division
Teamsheet: Mogg, Fullbrook, M Williams, Lander, Green, Bryant, Talboys, Hughes, Morrison, Payne, Noble
Substitutes: Chandler (for Talboys), Hedges (for Fulbrook)
Scorer: Noble
Attendance: 694

Date: Saturday 20/01/1990
Result: **GLOUCESTER CITY 0 DARTFORD 4**
Competition: Southern League Premier Division
Teamsheet: Mogg, Hedges, M Williams, Lander, Green, Bryant, Talboys, Hughes, Morrison, Payne, Noble
Substitutes: Chandler (for Bryant), Thompson (nps)
Attendance: 948

Date: Saturday 27/01/1990
Result: **DOVER ATHLETIC 1 GLOUCESTER CITY 0**
Competition: Southern League Premier Division
Teamsheet: Mogg, Fullbrook, M Williams, Lander, Green, Chandler, Talboys, Hughes, Morrison, Withey, Noble
Substitutes: Payne (for Morrison), Hedges (nps)
Attendance: 1268

Date: Saturday 10/02/1990
Result: **WEALDSTONE 2 GLOUCESTER CITY 3**
Competition: Southern League Premier Division
Teamsheet: Mogg, Steel, M Williams, Lander, Green, Bryant, Talboys, Hughes, Withey, Townsend, Noble
Substitutes: Morrison (for Townsend), Chandler (for Steel)
Scorers: Green, Withey (2)
Attendance: 497

Date: Tuesday 13/02/1990
Result: **ATHERSTONE UNITED 2 GLOUCESTER CITY 1**
Competition: Southern League Premier Division
Teamsheet: Mogg, Chandler, M Williams, Lander, Green, Bryant, Talboys, Hughes, Withey, Townsend, Noble
Substitutes: Morrison (for Townsend), Payne (nps)
Scorer: Townsend
Attendance: 373

[323]

Date: Thursday 22/02/1990
Result: **GLOUCESTER CITY 2 REDDITCH UNITED 0**
Competition: Southern League Cup 4th Round 1st Leg
Teamsheet: Mogg, Chandler, Payne, Lander, Green, Bryant, Talboys, Hughes, Withey, Morrison, Noble
Substitutes: Browning (for Payne), Hedges (for Bryant)
Scorers: Talboys (pen), Morrison
Attendance: 495

Date: Saturday 24/02/1990
Result: **BROMSGROVE ROVERS 0 GLOUCESTER CITY 2**
Competition: Southern League Premier Division
Teamsheet: Mogg, Chandler, Payne, Lander, Green, Hedges, Talboys, Hughes, Withey, Morrison, Noble
Substitutes: Browning (for Payne), Townsend (for Noble)
Scorers: Withey, Noble
Attendance: 665

Date: Tuesday 27/02/1990
Result: **ALVECHURCH 2 GLOUCESTER CITY 2**
Competition: Southern League Premier Division
Teamsheet: Mogg, Chandler, Payne, Bryant, Green, Hedges, Talboys, Hughes, Withey, Townsend, Noble
Substitutes: Browning (for Townsend), Lander (nps)
Scorers: Green, Talboys
Attendance: 217

Date: Thursday 01/03/1990
Result: **REDDITCH UNITED 3 GLOUCESTER CITY 0**
Competition: Southern League Cup 4th Round 2nd Leg
Teamsheet: Mogg, Hedges, Noble, Lander, Green, Hughes, Talboys, Payne, Withey, Fulbrook, Townsend
Substitutes: Steel (nps), Shaw (nps)
Attendance: 237

Date: Saturday 03/03/1990
Result: **CAMBRIDGE CITY 0 GLOUCESTER CITY 2**
Competition: Southern League Premier Division
Teamsheet: Mogg, Chandler, Fullbrook, Lander, Green, Bryant, Talboys, Hughes, Withey, Townsend, Noble
Substitutes: Steel (nps), Browning (for Townsend)
Scorers: Talboys, Withey
Attendance: 287

Date: Tuesday 06/03/1990
Result: **GLOUCESTER CITY 2 MOOR GREEN 3**
Competition: Southern League Premier Division
Teamsheet: Mogg, Chandler, Fullbrook, Browning, Green, Steel, Talboys, Hughes, Withey, Townsend, Noble
Substitutes: Hedges (nps), M Williams (nps)
Scorers: Browning, Talboys
Attendance: 503

Date: Saturday 10/03/1990
Result: **GLOUCESTER CITY 0 DOVER ATHLETIC 1**
Competition: Southern League Premier Division
Teamsheet: Mogg, Chandler, Hedges, Lander, Payne, Browning, Talboys, Hughes, Withey, Townsend, Noble
Substitutes: Fullbrook (nps), M Williams (nps)
Attendance: 663

Date: Tuesday 13/03/1990
Result: **GLOUCESTER CITY 9 GOSPORT BOROUGH 0**
Competition: Southern League Premier Division
Teamsheet: Mogg, M Williams, Chandler, Lander, Payne, Hedges, Talboys, Hughes, Withey, Townsend, Noble
Substitutes: Browning (for Lander), Morrison (for Talboys)
Scorers: Payne, Withey (2), Townsend (5, 2 pens), Browning
Attendance: 514

Date: Saturday 17/03/1990
Result: **VALLEY SPORTS RUGBY 3 GLOUCESTER CITY 0**
Competition: Southern League Premier Division
Teamsheet: Mogg, Chandler, Morrison, Lander, Payne, Hedges, Talboys, Hughes, Withey, Townsend, Noble
Substitutes: Browning (for Townsend), M Williams (for Payne)
Attendance: 528

Date: Wednesday 21/03/1990
Result: **WEYMOUTH 1 GLOUCESTER CITY 1**
Competition: Southern League Premier Division
Teamsheet: Mogg, Chandler, M Williams, Lander, Steel, Hedges, Talboys, Hughes, Withey, Townsend, Noble
Substitutes: Payne (nps), Morrison (for Townsend)
Scorer: Withey
Attendance: 369

Date: Saturday 24/03/1990
Result: **GLOUCESTER CITY 3 CHELMSFORD CITY 1**
Competition: Southern League Premier Division
Teamsheet: Mogg, Chandler, M Williams, Lander, Steel, Hedges, Talboys, Hughes, Withey, Townsend, Noble
Substitutes: Payne (for Steel), Morrison (for Noble)
Scorer: Townsend (3)
Attendance: 542

Date: Tuesday 27/03/1990
Result: **GLOUCESTER CITY 5 ASHFORD TOWN 2**
Competition: Southern League Premier Division
Teamsheet: Mogg, Chandler, M Williams, Lander, Steel, Hedges, Talboys, Hughes, Withey, Townsend, Noble
Substitutes: Morrison (for Talboys), Fullbrook (for M Williams)
Scorers: Chandler (3), M Williams, Withey
Attendance: 487

Date: Saturday 31/03/1990
Result: **GLOUCESTER CITY 5 ALVECHURCH 2**
Competition: Southern League Premier Division
Teamsheet: Mogg, Chandler, M Williams, Morrison, Steel, Hedges, Talboys, Hughes, Withey, Townsend, Noble
Substitutes: Green (for Chandler), Fullbrook (for Townsend)
Scorers: Morrison (2), Hughes, Withey, Noble
Attendance: 534

Date: Tuesday 03/04/1990
Result: **GLOUCESTER CITY 3 CORBY TOWN 2**
Competition: Southern League Premier Division
Teamsheet: Mogg, Hedges, M Williams, Morrison, Green, Steel, Talboys, Hughes, Withey, Townsend, Noble
Substitutes: Fullbrook (nps), P Williams (nps)
Scorers: Morrison, Townsend (2 pens)
Attendance: 529

Date: Saturday 07/04/1990
Result: **BURTON ALBION 0 GLOUCESTER CITY 0**
Competition: Southern League Premier Division
Teamsheet: Mogg, Hedges, M Williams, Fullbrook, Green, Steel, Talboys, Hughes, Morrison, Townsend, Noble
Substitutes: Shaw (nps), Godfrey (nps)
Attendance: 698

Date: Saturday 14/04/1990
Result: **GLOUCESTER CITY 0 DORCHESTER TOWN 0**
Competition: Southern League Premier Division
Teamsheet: Mogg, Hedges, M Williams, Steel, Lander, Chandler, Talboys, Hughes, Withey, Morrison, Noble
Substitutes: Townsend (nps), Fullbrook (nps)
Attendance: 542

Date: Monday 16/04/1990
Result: **BATH CITY 2 GLOUCESTER CITY 0**
Competition: Southern League Premier Division
Teamsheet: Mogg, Hedges, M Williams, Chandler, Green, Steel, Talboys, Hughes, Withey, Townsend, Noble
Substitutes: Morrison (for Townsend), Lander (for Chandler)
Attendance: 1166

Date: Saturday 21/04/1990
Result: **DARTFORD 6 GLOUCESTER CITY 2**
Competition: Southern League Premier Division
Teamsheet: Mogg, Hedges, M Williams, Chandler, Green, Lander, Talboys, Hughes, Withey, Townsend, Noble
Substitutes: Morrison (for Withey), Fulbrook (for Hedges)
Scorers: M Williams, Chandler
Attendance: 653

Date: Tuesday 24/04/1990
Result: **ASHFORD TOWN 1 GLOUCESTER CITY 2**
Competition: Southern League Premier Division
Teamsheet: Mogg, Steel, M Williams, Lander, Green, Chandler, Talboys, Hughes, Morrison, Day, Noble
Substitutes: Hedges (for Chandler), Fullbrook (nps)
Scorers: Steel, Talboys
Attendance: 361

Date: Saturday 28/04/1990
Result: **GLOUCESTER CITY 3 WORCESTER CITY 1**
Competition: Southern League Premier Division
Teamsheet: Mogg, Steel, M Williams, Hancocks, Green, Lander, Talboys, Hughes, Chandler, Morrison, Noble
Substitutes: Hedges (nps), Townsend (nps)
Scorers: Talboys (2), own goal
Attendance: 516

Date: Saturday 05/05/1990
Result: **GLOUCESTER CITY 1 BROMSGROVE ROVERS 1**
Competition: Southern League Premier Division
Teamsheet: Mogg, Steel, Fullbrook, Lander, Hancocks, Hedges, Talboys, Hughes, Morrison, Chandler, Noble
Substitutes: Townsend (for Steel), M Williams (for Chandler)
Scorer: Talboys
Attendance: 426

Appearances – T Andrews 0(2), GV Bradder 10(2), MT Browning 2(6), M Bryant 7, RD Chandler 34(8), I Day 1, G Fullbrook 23(5), N Green 48(1), GM Hancocks 2, IA Hedges 36(4), T Hopps 10, BD Hughes 60, C Hyde 4(8), MT Lander 42(4), DJ Mogg 38, L Morrison 47(10), WI Noble 56(7), D Payne 39(8), S Penny 1, J Shaw 12, GRSteel 47, SJ Talboys 52(9), RJ Thompson 2(2), CG Townsend 36(3), R Webb 3, L Webster 7, M Williams 54(3), GA Withey 20.
Others selected but did not play: BC Godfrey, P Williams.
Scorers – CG Townsend 26, SJ Talboys 24, L Morrison 13, D Payne 12, WI Noble 9, GA Withey 9, BD Hughes 8, RD Chandler 5, C Hyde 4, M Williams 4, N Green 3, GV Bradder 2, MT Browning 2, GR Steel 2, own goal 1.

RECORD BREAKER	RECORD BREAKER

Ian Hedges
Record Transfer Received - £25,000

Wayne Noble
Most Appearances In One Season In All Matches - 63

SOUTHERN LEAGUE PREMIER DIVISION

POS	CLUB	P	W	D	L	F	A	PTS
1	DOVER ATHLETIC	42	32	6	4	87	27	102
2	BATH CITY	42	30	8	4	81	28	98
3	DARTFORD	42	26	9	7	80	35	87
4	BURTON ALBION	42	20	12	10	64	40	72
5	VALLEY SPORTS RUGBY	42	19	12	11	51	35	69
6	ATHERSTONE UNITED	42	19	10	13	60	52	67
7	GRAVESEND & NORTHFLEET	42	18	12	12	44	50	66
8	CAMBRIDGE CITY	42	17	11	14	76	56	62
9	**GLOUCESTER CITY**	**42**	**17**	**11**	**14**	**80**	**68**	**62**
10	BROMSGROVE ROVERS	42	17	10	15	56	48	61
11	MOOR GREEN	42	18	7	17	62	59	61
12	WEALDSTONE	42	16	9	17	55	54	57
13	DORCHESTER TOWN	42	16	7	19	52	67	55
14	WORCESTER CITY	42	15	10	17	62	63	54*
15	CRAWLEY TOWN	42	13	12	17	53	57	51
16	WATERLOOVILLE	42	13	10	19	63	81	49
17	WEYMOUTH	42	11	13	18	50	70	46
18	CHELMSFORD CITY	42	11	10	21	52	72	43
19	ASHFORD TOWN	42	10	7	25	43	75	37
20	CORBY TOWN	42	10	6	26	57	77	36
21	ALVECHURCH	42	7	5	30	46	95	26
22	GOSPORT BOROUGH	42	6	5	31	28	93	23
		924	361	202	361	1302	1302	1284

* One point deducted.

SEASON 1990-1991
(Home Ground: City Stadium, Meadow Park, Hempsted)

Date: Saturday 18/08/1990
Result: **GLOUCESTER CITY 3 RUSHDEN TOWN 2**
Competition: Southern League Premier Division
Teamsheet: Mogg, Abbley, Bater, Chandler, Hancocks, Hedges, Talboys, Hughes, Withey, Meacham, Noble
Substitutes: Williams (nps), Webb (nps)
Scorers: Talboys (2), Withey
Attendance: 719

Date: Wednesday 22/08/1990
Result: **WEYMOUTH 1 GLOUCESTER CITY 1**
Competition: Southern League Premier Division
Teamsheet: Mogg, Abbley, Baverstock, Webb, Hancocks, Hedges, Talboys, Hughes, Withey, Meacham, Noble
Substitutes: Jenkins (nps), Steel (nps)
Scorer: Withey
Attendance: 838

Date: Saturday 25/08/1990
Result: **VALLEY SPORTS RUGBY 0 GLOUCESTER CITY 1**
Competition: Southern League Premier Division
Teamsheet: Mogg, Abbley, Baverstock, Lander, Hancocks, Hedges, Talboys, Hughes, Withey, Meacham, Noble
Substitutes: Webb (nps), Chandler (for Lander)
Scorer: Withey
Attendance: 509

Date: Monday 27/08/1990
Result: **GLOUCESTER CITY 1 FARNBOROUGH TOWN 1**
Competition: Southern League Premier Division
Teamsheet: Mogg, Abbley, Baverstock, Bater, Hancocks, Hedges, Talboys, Hughes, Withey, Chandler, Noble
Substitutes: Meacham (nps), Webb (nps)
Scorer: Withey
Attendance: 825

Date: Saturday 01/09/1990
Result: **CHELMSFORD CITY 0 GLOUCESTER CITY 2**
Competition: Southern League Premier Division
Teamsheet: Mogg, Abbley, Baverstock, Chandler, Hancocks, Hedges, Talboys, Hughes, Withey, Meacham, Noble
Substitutes: Williams (nps), Webb (nps)
Scorers: own goal, Withey
Attendance: 747

Date: Tuesday 04/09/1990
Result: **GLOUCESTER CITY 3 BROMSGROVE ROVERS 1**
Competition: Southern League Premier Division
Teamsheet: Mogg, Abbley, Baverstock, Chandler, Hancocks, Hedges, Talboys, Hughes, Withey, Meacham, Noble
Substitutes: Williams (nps), Webb (for Abbley)
Scorers: Talboys (2), Webb
Attendance: 786

Date: Saturday 08/09/1990
Result: **GLOUCESTER CITY 1 CAMBRIDGE CITY 1**
Competition: Southern League Premier Division
Teamsheet: Mogg, Webb, Baverstock, Chandler, Hancocks, Hedges, Talboys, Hughes, Brown, Meacham, Noble
Substitutes: Lander (for Hughes), Williams (for Brown)
Scorer: Webb
Attendance: 1011

Date: Tuesday 11/09/1990
Result: **WEALDSTONE 2 GLOUCESTER CITY 1**
Competition: Southern League Premier Division
Teamsheet: Mogg, Webb, Baverstock, Chandler, Hancocks, Hedges, Talboys, Lander, Brown, Williams, Noble
Substitutes: Steel (for Williams), Craig (nps)
Scorer: Williams
Attendance: 545

Date: Saturday 22/09/1990
Result: **GLOUCESTER CITY 2 TON PENTRE 2**
Competition: FA Trophy 1st Qualifying Round
Teamsheet: Mogg, Abbley, Baverstock, Webb, Hancocks, Hedges, Talboys, Hughes, Steel, Meacham, Noble
Substitutes: Lander (nps), Morrison (for Abbley)
Scorers: Hancocks, Morrison
Attendance: 551

Date: Wednesday 26/09/1990
Result: **TON PENTRE 0 GLOUCESTER CITY 2**
Competition: FA Trophy 1st Qualifying Round Replay
Teamsheet: Mogg, Hughes, Baverstock, Chandler, Hancocks, Hedges, Talboys, Lander, Morrison, Meacham, Noble
Substitutes: Webb (nps), Williams (nps)
Scorers: Talboys, Morrison
Attendance: 381

Date: Saturday 29/09/1990
Result: **GLOUCESTER CITY 2 DARTFORD 0**
Competition: Southern League Premier Division
Teamsheet: Mogg, Webb, Baverstock, Chandler, Hancocks, Hedges, Talboys, Hughes, Morrison, Meacham, Noble
Substitutes: Williams (nps), Lander (nps)
Scorers: Chandler, Morrison
Attendance: 662

Date: Saturday 06/10/1990
Result: **DOVER ATHLETIC 3 GLOUCESTER CITY 0**
Competition: Southern League Premier Division
Teamsheet: Mogg, Lander, Craig, Chandler, Hancocks, Hedges, Talboys, Hughes, Morrison, Meacham, Noble
Substitutes: Webb (for Chandler), Jenkins (for Noble)
Attendance: 1306

Date: Monday 08/10/1990
Result: **WORCESTER CITY 4 GLOUCESTER CITY 0**
Competition: Premier Inter League Cup 1st Round
Teamsheet: Mogg, Lander, Craig, Chandler, Hancocks, Hedges, Talboys, Hughes, Morrison, Meacham, Noble
Substitutes: Webb (for Talboys), Jenkins (for Morrison)
Attendance: 1491

Date: Saturday 13/10/1990
Result: **GLOUCESTER CITY 4 POOLE TOWN 0**
Competition: Southern League Premier Division
Teamsheet: Mogg, Lander, Craig, Chandler, Williams, Hedges, Webb, Hughes, Morrison, Meacham, Noble
Substitutes: Jenkins (for Williams), Tucker (for Meacham)
Scorers: Noble (2, 1 pen), Morrison (2)
Attendance: 684

Date: Tuesday 16/10/1990
Result: **WITNEY TOWN 2 GLOUCESTER CITY 1**
Competition: Southern League Cup 1st Round 1st Leg
Teamsheet: Roberts, Webb, Baverstock, Chandler, Craig, Hedges, Knight, Hughes, Morrison, Meacham, Noble
Substitutes: Jenkins (for Craig), Tucker (nps)
Scorer: Noble
Attendance: 335

Date: Saturday 20/10/1990
Result: **GLOUCESTER CITY 3 LLANELLI 0**
Competition: FA Trophy 2nd Qualifying Round
Teamsheet: Mogg, Jenkins, Baverstock, Chandler, Hancocks, Hedges, Webb, Hughes, Morrison, Meacham, Noble
Substitutes: Williams (nps), Lander (for Hancocks)
Scorers: Hancocks, Morrison, Webb
Attendance: 638

Date: Saturday 27/10/1990
Result: **FARNBOROUGH TOWN 4 GLOUCESTER CITY 1**
Competition: FA Cup 4th Qualifying Round
Teamsheet: Mogg, Lander, Baverstock, Chandler, Hancocks, Hedges, Knight, Hughes, Withey, Morrison, Noble
Substitutes: Meacham (for Noble), Webb (for Lander)
Scorer: Meacham
Attendance: 838

Date: Tuesday 30/10/1990
Result: **GLOUCESTER CITY 1 WITNEY TOWN 2**
Competition: Southern League Cup 1st Round 2nd Leg
Teamsheet: Brain, Webb, Baverstock, Chandler, Hancocks, Hedges, Knight, Hughes, Withey, Morrison, Noble
Substitutes: Meacham (for Withey), Jenkins (nps)
Scorer: Morrison
Attendance: 485

Date: Saturday 03/11/1990
Result: **MOOR GREEN 3 GLOUCESTER CITY 2**
Competition: Southern League Premier Division
Teamsheet: Roberts, Webb, Baverstock, Chandler, Meacham, Hendy, Knight, Hughes, Withey, Browning, Williams
Substitutes: Noble (nps), Steel (for Hendy)
Scorers: Webb, Withey
Attendance: 504

Date: Saturday 10/11/1990
Result: **GLOUCESTER CITY 3 BASHLEY 0**
Competition: Southern League Premier Division
Teamsheet: Bond, Webb, Baverstock, Chandler, Hancocks, Meacham, Knight, Hughes, Morrison, Browning, Noble
Substitutes: Williams (for Hughes), Jenkins (for Knight)
Scorers: Browning (2), Noble
Attendance: 641

Date: Saturday 17/11/1990
Result: **GLOUCESTER CITY 1 DORCHESTER TOWN 1**
Competition: Southern League Premier Division
Teamsheet: Bond, Webb, Steel, Madge, Hancocks, Meacham, Knight, Jenkins, Eaton, Browning, Noble
Substitutes: Morrison (for Knight), Lander (for Jenkins)
Scorer: Browning
Attendance: 640

Date: Monday 26/11/1990
Result: **GLOUCESTER CITY 3 YATE TOWN 2**
Competition: Gloucestershire FA Northern Senior Professional Cup Semi-Final
Teamsheet: Mogg, Madge, Meacham, Webb, Hancocks, Sherwood, Morrison, Dawkins, Eaton, Browning, Noble
Substitutes: Malpas (nps), Jenkins (nps), Lander (nps), Steel (nps), Roberts (nps)
Scorers: Webb (2), Morrison
Attendance: 328

Date: Saturday 01/12/1990
Result: **WEYMOUTH 1 GLOUCESTER CITY 1**
Competition: FA Trophy 3rd Qualifying Round
Teamsheet: Bond, Madge, Meacham, Webb, Hancocks, Sherwood, Morrison, Dawkins, Eaton, Browning, Noble
Substitutes: Withey (for Eaton), Jenkins (nps)
Scorer: Meacham
Attendance: 684

Date: Tuesday 04/12/1990
Result: **GLOUCESTER CITY 3 WEYMOUTH 0**
Competition: FA Trophy 3rd Qualifying Round Replay
Teamsheet: Mogg, Madge, Baverstock, Webb, Hancocks, Sherwood, Eaton, Dawkins, Morrison, Browning, Meacham
Substitutes: Withey (nps), Noble (nps)
Scorers: Eaton, Browning (pen), Meacham
Attendance: 682

Date: Saturday 15/12/1990
Result: **WATERLOOVILLE 2 GLOUCESTER CITY 2**
Competition: Southern League Premier Division
Teamsheet: Mogg, Slattery, Baverstock, Chandler, Malpas, Sherwood, Webb, Dawkins, Eaton, Browning, Meacham
Substitutes: Withey (for Eaton), Talboys (for Slattery)
Scorer: Chandler (2)
Attendance: 305

Date: Saturday 22/12/1990
Result: **GLOUCESTER CITY 5 CRAWLEY TOWN 0**
Competition: Southern League Premier Division
Teamsheet: Mogg, Noble, Baverstock, Chandler, Malpas, Sherwood, Webb, Dawkins, Eaton, Browning, Meacham
Substitutes: Withey (nps), Knight (nps)
Scorers: Browning (3), Eaton, Chandler
Attendance: 644

Date: Wednesday 26/12/1990
Result: **WORCESTER CITY 1 GLOUCESTER CITY 1**
Competition: Southern League Premier Division
Teamsheet: Mogg, Meacham, Baverstock, Chandler, Hancocks, Sherwood, Webb, Dawkins, Eaton, Browning, Noble
Substitutes: Knight (for Eaton), Hendy (nps)
Scorer: Browning
Attendance: 1515

Date: Saturday 29/12/1990
Result: **DORCHESTER TOWN 1 GLOUCESTER CITY 0**
Competition: Southern League Premier Division
Teamsheet: Mogg, Meacham, Baverstock, Chandler, Hancocks, Sherwood, Webb, Dawkins, Eaton, Meacham, Noble
Substitutes: Malpas (for Dawkins), Withey (for Eaton)
Attendance: 710

Date: Tuesday 01/01/1991
Result: **GLOUCESTER CITY 2 HALESOWEN TOWN 1**
Competition: Southern League Premier Division
Teamsheet: Mogg, Knight, Baverstock, Chandler, Hancocks, Sherwood, Webb, Dawkins, Withey, Eaton, Meacham
Substitutes: Noble (nps), Hendy (nps)
Scorers: Knight (pen), Hancocks
Attendance: 1131

4 February 1990
A sign of things to come!
(Photograph courtesy of Tony Gaze)

PROGRAMME

PROGRAMME

PROGRAMME

1989-1990

1990-1991

1991-1992

Gloucester City tour of Georgia July 1991
City's only venture abroad

v Napereuli Tevali 26 July 1991

v Mesxti Achalziche 28 July 1991

Some of the tour party in Tbilisi for the match v Shevardeni Tbilisi 30 July 1991

The tour party included Brian Godfrey (manager), Steve Millard (assistant manager), Steve Abbley, Ray Baverstock, Len Bond, Ricky Chandler, Derek Dawkins, Jason Eaton, Steve Fergusson, Jon Freegard, Brendan Hackett, Geoff Hancocks, Brian Hughes, Mark Madge, Mike Malpas, Jeff Meacham, Wayne Noble, Sean Penny, Jeff Sherwood, Lee Rogers, Chris Smith, Steve Talboys and Dave Webb

Date: Saturday 12/01/1991
Result: **GLOUCESTER CITY 1 YEOVIL TOWN 0**
Competition: FA Trophy 1st Round
Teamsheet: Mogg, Meacham, Baverstock, Chandler, Hancocks, Sherwood, Noble, Dawkins, Withey, Eaton, Knight
Substitutes: Talboys (for Noble), Hendy (nps)
Scorer: Eaton
Attendance: 1368

Date: Saturday 19/01/1991
Result: **GLOUCESTER CITY 2 BURTON ALBION 1**
Competition: Southern League Premier Division
Teamsheet: Mogg, Meacham, Baverstock, Chandler, Hancocks, Sherwood, Talboys, Dawkins, Withey, Eaton, Knight
Substitutes: Noble (for Talboys), Malpass (for Sherwood)
Scorer: Eaton (2)
Attendance: 644

Date: Tuesday 22/01/1991
Result: **GLOUCESTER CITY 3 MOOR GREEN 2**
Competition: Southern League Premier Division
Teamsheet: Mogg, Meacham, Baverstock, Chandler, Hancocks, Malpas, Talboys, Dawkins, Withey, Eaton, Knight
Substitutes: Noble (for Dawkins), Webb (nps)
Scorers: Talboys, Withey, Eaton
Attendance: 512

Date: Saturday 26/01/1991
Result: **POOLE TOWN 1 GLOUCESTER CITY 2**
Competition: Southern League Premier Division
Teamsheet: Mogg, Meacham, Baverstock, Chandler, Hancocks, Malpas, Talboys, Sherwood, Withey, Eaton, Noble
Substitutes: Freegard (for Withey), Webb (for Baverstock)
Scorers: Withey, Eaton
Attendance: 541

Date: Sunday 17/02/1991
Result: **CAMBRIDGE CITY 1 GLOUCESTER CITY 2**
Competition: Southern League Premier Division
Teamsheet: Mogg, Sherwood, Meacham, Chandler, Hancocks, Malpas, Talboys, Baverstock, Withey, Eaton, Noble
Substitutes: Freegard (for Withey), Webb (for Malpas)
Scorers: Meacham, Eaton
Attendance: 509

Date: Tuesday 19/02/1991
Result: **MERTHYR TYDFIL 1 GLOUCESTER CITY 3**
Competition: FA Trophy 2nd Round
Teamsheet: Mogg, Sherwood, Meacham, Chandler, Kemp, Dawkins, Talboys, Baverstock, Withey, Eaton, Noble
Substitutes: Freegard (for Talboys), Webb (nps)
Scorers: Withey, Freegard (2)
Attendance: 752

Date: Saturday 23/02/1991
Result: **WITTON ALBION 3 GLOUCESTER CITY 0**
Competition: FA Trophy 3rd Round
Teamsheet: Mogg, Sherwood, Meacham, Chandler, Hancocks, Malpas, Talboys, Baverstock, Withey, Eaton, Noble
Substitutes: Smith (for Withey), Webb (for Hancocks)
Attendance: 1162

Date: Tuesday 26/02/1991
Result: **GLOUCESTER CITY 2 WEALDSTONE 1**
Competition: Southern League Premier Division
Teamsheet: Mogg, Sherwood, Meacham, Chandler, Hancocks, Dawkins, Talboys, Baverstock, Freegard, Eaton, Noble
Substitutes: Smith (for Hancocks), Webb (for Smith)
Scorers: Freegard, Eaton
Attendance: 706

Date: Saturday 02/03/1991
Result: **RUSHDEN TOWN 1 GLOUCESTER CITY 1**
Competition: Southern League Premier Division
Teamsheet: Mogg, Sherwood, Meacham, Chandler, Hancocks, Dawkins, Talboys, Baverstock, Freegard, Eaton, Noble
Substitutes: Penny (nps), Webb (for Noble)
Scorer: Meacham (pen)
Attendance: 360

Date: Wednesday 06/03/1991
Result: **ATHERSTONE UNITED 2 GLOUCESTER CITY 2**
Competition: Southern League Premier Division
Teamsheet: Mogg, Sherwood, Meacham, Webb, Kemp, Dawkins, Talboys, Baverstock, Freegard, Eaton, Noble
Substitutes: Penny (for Baverstock), Tregale (nps)
Scorer: Talboys (2)
Attendance: 223

Date: Saturday 09/03/1991
Result: **GLOUCESTER CITY 3 CHELMSFORD CITY 2**
Competition: Southern League Premier Division
Teamsheet: Mogg, Sherwood, Meacham, Chandler, Kemp, Madge, Talboys, Webb, Freegard, Eaton, Noble
Substitutes: Penny (nps), Baverstock (nps)
Scorers: Noble, Freegard, Talboys
Attendance: 695

Date: Tuesday 12/03/1991
Result: **GLOUCESTER CITY 1 WEYMOUTH 1**
Competition: Southern League Premier Division
Teamsheet: Mogg, Sherwood, Meacham, Chandler, Kemp, Madge, Talboys, Webb, Freegard, Eaton, Noble
Substitutes: Penny (nps), Baverstock (for Webb)
Scorer: Noble
Attendance: 672

Date: Saturday 16/03/1991
Result: **DARTFORD 2 GLOUCESTER CITY 1**
Competition: Southern League Premier Division
Teamsheet: Mogg, Sherwood, Meacham, Chandler, Kemp, Madge, Talboys, Baverstock, Freegard, Eaton, Noble
Substitutes: Penny (for Baverstock), Webb (nps)
Scorer: Meacham
Attendance: 502

Date: Tuesday 19/03/1991
Result: **BURTON ALBION 1 GLOUCESTER CITY 2**
Competition: Southern League Premier Division
Teamsheet: Mogg, Dawkins, Meacham, Webb, Kemp, Sherwood, Talboys, Madge, Freegard, Eaton, Penny
Substitutes: Noble (nps), Chandler (nps)
Scorer: Freegard (2)
Attendance: 428

Date: Saturday 23/03/1991
Result: **GLOUCESTER CITY 2 ATHERSTONE UNITED 2**
Competition: Southern League Premier Division
Teamsheet: Mogg, Dawkins, Meacham, Webb, Hancocks, Sherwood, Talboys, Smith, Freegard, Eaton, Penny
Substitutes: Noble (for Smith), Chandler (for Penny)
Scorers: Freegard, Talboys
Attendance: 602

Date: Tuesday 26/03/1991
Result: **CRAWLEY TOWN 3 GLOUCESTER CITY 3**
Competition: Southern League Premier Division
Teamsheet: Bond, Dawkins, Meacham, Smith, Baverstock, Sherwood, Talboys, Hughes, Freegard, Eaton, Noble
Substitutes: Penny (for Baverstock), Chandler (for Hughes)
Scorers: Eaton, Penny (2)
Attendance: 472

Date: Saturday 30/03/1991
Result: **GLOUCESTER CITY 3 WORCESTER CITY 1**
Competition: Southern League Premier Division
Teamsheet: Bond, Rogers, Meacham, Chandler, Kemp, Sherwood, Talboys, Dawkins, Freegard, Eaton, Noble
Substitutes: Penny (nps), Webb (for Dawkins)
Scorers: Eaton, Talboys (2)
Attendance: 873

Date: Monday 01/04/1991
Result: **HALESOWEN TOWN 0 GLOUCESTER CITY 0**
Competition: Southern League Premier Division
Teamsheet: Bond, Rogers, Meacham, Chandler, Kemp, Sherwood, Talboys, Fergusson, Freegard, Eaton, Hackett
Substitutes: Penny (for Freegard), Noble (nps)
Attendance: 1334

Date: Saturday 06/04/1991
Result: **GRAVESEND & NORTHFLEET 0 GLOUCESTER CITY 4**
Competition: Southern League Premier Division
Teamsheet: Bond, Rogers, Meacham, Chandler, Kemp, Sherwood, Talboys, Fergusson, Noble, Eaton, Hackett
Substitutes: Penny (for Rogers), Freegard (nps)
Scorers: Eaton (2), Hackett, Penny
Attendance: 377

Date: Tuesday 09/04/1991
Result: **CHELTENHAM TOWN 1 GLOUCESTER CITY 2**
Competition: Gloucestershire FA Northern Senior Professional Cup Final
Teamsheet: Mogg, Rogers, Madge, Webb, Hendy, Dawkins, Fergusson, Hughes, Freegard, Penny, Hackett
Substitutes: Chandler (for Freegard), Sherwood (nps), Talboys (nps), Eaton (nps), Noble (nps)
Scorer: Hackett (2)
Attendance: 705

Date: Saturday 13/04/1991
Result: **GLOUCESTER CITY 4 DOVER ATHLETIC 1**
Competition: Southern League Premier Division
Teamsheet: Bond, Rogers, Meacham, Chandler, Kemp, Sherwood, Talboys, Fergusson, Noble, Eaton, Hackett
Substitutes: Freegard (nps), Penny (nps)
Scorers: Noble, Hackett, Fergusson, Talboys
Attendance: 1887

Date: Tuesday 16/04/1991
Result: **FARNBOROUGH TOWN 1 GLOUCESTER CITY 1**
Competition: Southern League Premier Division
Teamsheet: Bond, Rogers, Meacham, Chandler, Kemp, Sherwood, Talboys, Fergusson, Noble, Eaton, Hackett
Substitutes: Freegard (for Noble), Penny (nps)
Scorer: Eaton
Attendance: 1202

Date: Saturday 20/04/1991
Result: **BASHLEY 0 GLOUCESTER CITY 1**
Competition: Southern League Premier Division
Teamsheet: Bond, Rogers, Meacham, Chandler, Kemp, Sherwood, Talboys, Fergusson, Noble, Eaton, Hackett
Substitutes: Freegard (nps), Hughes (nps)
Scorer: Meacham
Attendance: 451

Date: Tuesday 23/04/1991
Result: **GLOUCESTER CITY 6 GRAVESEND & NORTHFLEET 3**
Competition: Southern League Premier Division
Teamsheet: Mogg, Rogers, Meacham, Chandler, Kemp, Sherwood, Talboys, Fergusson, Noble, Eaton, Hackett
Substitutes: Freegard (nps), Penny (nps)
Scorers: Fergusson, Talboys, Eaton (2), Meacham, Hackett
Attendance: 1417

Date: Saturday 27/04/1991
Result: **GLOUCESTER CITY 3 WATERLOOVILLE 1**
Competition: Southern League Premier Division
Teamsheet: Mogg, Rogers, Meacham, Chandler, Kemp, Sherwood, Talboys, Fergusson, Noble, Eaton, Hackett
Substitutes: Freegard (nps), Hughes (for Kemp)
Scorers: Fergusson, Hughes, Eaton
Attendance: 1579

Date: Tuesday 30/04/1991
Result: **GLOUCESTER CITY 2 VALLEY SPORTS RUGBY 2**
Competition: Southern League Premier Division
Teamsheet: Mogg, Rogers, Meacham, Chandler, Hughes, Sherwood, Talboys, Fergusson, Noble, Eaton, Hackett
Substitutes: Freegard (for Talboys), Dawkins (for Hughes)
Scorers: Meacham, Eaton
Attendance: 2550

Date: Saturday 04/05/1991
Result: **BROMSGROVE ROVERS 0 GLOUCESTER CITY 1**
Competition: Southern League Premier Division
Teamsheet: Mogg, Rogers, Meacham, Chandler, Dawkins, Sherwood, Talboys, Fergusson, Noble, Eaton, Hackett
Substitutes: Freegard (for Sherwood), Penny (for Eaton)
Scorer: Freegard
Attendance: 1782

Appearances – SG Abbley 7, PT Bater 2, R Baverstock 34(1), LA Bond 10, M Brain 1, R Brown 2, MT Browning 10, RD Chandler 44(4), D Craig 4, DA Dawkins 21(1), JC Eaton 35, SJ Fergusson 10, JP Freegard 12(6), BJ Hackett 10, GM Hancocks 33, IA Hedges 18, N Hendy 2, BD Hughes 22(1), P Jenkins 2(5), GJ Kemp 14, K Knight 10(1), M Lander 7(3), M Madge 9, M Malpas 6(2), J Meacham 51(2), DJ Mogg 43, L Morrison 13(2), WI Noble 46(3), S Penny 3(6), P Roberts 2, LM Rogers 11, J Sherwood 33, NJ Slatter 1, CJ Smith 2(2), GR Steel 2(2), SJ Talboys 38(2), S Tucker 0(1), DA Webb 26(10), M Williams 3(2), GA Withey 17(3).
Others selected but did not play: S Tregale.
Scorers – JC Eaton 18, SJ Talboys 14, J Meacham 9, GA Withey 9, MT Browning 8, JP Freegard 8, L Morrison 8, WI Noble 7, DA Webb 6, BJ Hackett 5, RD Chandler 4, SJ Fergusson 3, GM Hancocks 3, S Penny 3, BD Hughes 1, K Knight 1, M Williams 1.

SOUTHERN LEAGUE PREMIER DIVISION

POS	CLUB	P	W	D	L	F	A	PTS
1	FARNBOROUGH TOWN	42	26	7	9	79	43	85
2	**GLOUCESTER CITY**	**42**	**23**	**14**	**5**	**86**	**49**	**83**
3	CAMBRIDGE CITY	42	21	14	7	63	43	77
4	DOVER ATHLETIC	42	21	11	10	56	37	74
5	BROMSGROVE ROVERS	42	20	11	11	68	49	71
6	WORCESTER CITY	42	18	12	12	55	42	66
7	BURTON ALBION	42	15	15	12	59	48	60
8	HALESOWEN TOWN	42	17	9	16	73	67	60
9	VALLEY SPORTS RUGBY	42	16	11	15	56	46	59
10	BASHLEY	42	15	12	15	56	52	57
11	DORCHESTER TOWN	42	15	12	15	47	54	57
12	WEALDSTONE	42	16	8	18	57	58	56
13	DARTFORD	42	15	9	18	61	64	54
14	RUSHDEN TOWN	42	14	11	17	64	66	53
15	ATHERSTONE UNITED	42	14	10	18	55	58	52
16	MOOR GREEN	42	15	6	21	64	75	51
17	POOLE TOWN	42	12	13	17	56	69	49
18	CHELMSFORD CITY	42	11	15	16	57	68	48
19	CRAWLEY TOWN	42	12	12	18	45	67	48
20	WATERLOOVILLE	42	11	13	18	51	70	46
21	GRAVESEND & NORTHFLEET	42	9	7	26	46	91	34
22	WEYMOUTH	42	4	12	26	50	88	24
		924	340	244	340	1304	1304	1264

SEASON 1991-1992
(Home Ground: City Stadium, Meadow Park, Hempsted)

Date: Saturday 17/08/1991
Result: **GLOUCESTER CITY 3 WEALDSTONE 2**
Competition: Southern League Premier Division
Teamsheet: Mogg, Sherwood, Meacham, Smith, Hancocks, Rogers, Talboys, Hughes, Freegard, Eaton, Hackett
Substitutes: Chandler (nps), Madge (nps)
Scorers: Eaton (2), Talboys
Attendance: 779

Date: Wednesday 21/08/1991
Result: **BASHLEY 2 GLOUCESTER CITY 1**
Competition: Southern League Premier Division
Teamsheet: Mogg, Sherwood, Meacham, Smith, Hancocks, Rogers, Talboys, Hughes, Freegard, Eaton, Hackett
Substitutes: Chandler (nps), Penny (nps)
Scorer: Freegard
Attendance: 496

Date: Saturday 24/08/1991
Result: **GRAVESEND & NORTHFLEET 1 GLOUCESTER CITY 0**
Competition: Southern League Premier Division
Teamsheet: Mogg, Sherwood, Meacham, Smith, Hancocks, Rogers, Talboys, Madge, Freegard, Eaton, Hackett
Substitutes: Penny (for Freegard), Chandler (for Smith)
Attendance: 430

Date: Monday 26/08/1991
Result: **GLOUCESTER CITY 5 POOLE TOWN 1**
Competition: Southern League Premier Division
Teamsheet: Mogg, Sherwood, Meacham, Chandler, Hancocks, Rogers, Talboys, Madge, Freegard, Eaton, Hackett
Substitutes: Noble (for Hancocks), Smith (for Rogers)
Scorers: Eaton (2), Hackett, Talboys, own goal
Attendance: 749

Date: Saturday 31/08/1991
Result: **GLOUCESTER CITY 3 CORBY TOWN 2**
Competition: Southern League Premier Division
Teamsheet: Mogg, Sherwood, Meacham, Chandler, Noble, Rogers, Talboys, Madge, Freegard, Eaton, Hackett
Substitutes: Penny (for Freegard), Hughes (nps)
Scorers: Freegard, Noble, Eaton
Attendance: 743

Date: Tuesday 03/09/1991
Result: **BROMSGROVE ROVERS 0 GLOUCESTER CITY 2**
Competition: Southern League Premier Division
Teamsheet: Mogg, Madge, Noble, Chandler, Sherwood, Rogers, Talboys, Hughes, Freegard, Eaton, Hackett
Substitutes: Penny (for Eaton), Kemp (nps)
Scorers: Talboys, Eaton
Attendance: 550

Date: Saturday 07/09/1991
Result: **GLOUCESTER CITY 2 FISHER ATHLETIC 0**
Competition: Southern League Premier Division
Teamsheet: Mogg, Madge, Noble, Chandler, Sherwood, Rogers, Talboys, Hughes, Freegard, Eaton, Hackett
Substitutes: Penny (for Hughes), Meacham (for Freegard)
Scorers: Meacham, Hackett
Attendance: 810

Date: Monday 09/09/1991
Result: **WORCESTER CITY 0 GLOUCESTER CITY 3**
Competition: Southern League Premier Division
Teamsheet: Bond, Madge, Meacham, Chandler, Sherwood, Rogers, Talboys, Noble, Freegard, Eaton, Hackett
Substitutes: Fergusson (for Freegard), Penny (for Eaton)
Scorers: Talboys (2), Eaton
Attendance: 1103

Date: Saturday 14/09/1991
Result: **GLOUCESTER CITY 4 SHORTWOOD UNITED 1**
Competition: FA Cup 1st Qualifying Round
Teamsheet: Mogg, Madge, Meacham, Penny, Sherwood, Rogers, Talboys, Noble, Freegard, Eaton, Hackett
Substitutes: Fergusson (for Meacham), Hughes (nps)
Scorers: Penny, Meacham, Noble, own goal
Attendance: 744

Date: Saturday 21/09/1991
Result: **CAMBRIDGE CITY 4 GLOUCESTER CITY 2**
Competition: Southern League Premier Division
Teamsheet: Mogg, Madge, Meacham, Chandler, Sherwood, Rogers, Talboys, Noble, Freegard, Eaton, Hackett
Substitutes: Penny (for Noble), Hughes (for Madge)
Scorers: Meacham, Freegard
Attendance: 390

Date: Saturday 28/09/1991
Result: **WORCESTER CITY 2 GLOUCESTER CITY 1**
Competition: FA Cup 2nd Qualifying Round
Teamsheet: Mogg, Rogers, Meacham, Chandler, Kemp, Sherwood, Talboys, Noble, Freegard, Eaton, Hackett
Substitutes: Fergusson (for Chandler), Penny (nps)
Scorer: Eaton
Attendance: 904

Date: Saturday 05/10/1991
Result: **GLOUCESTER CITY 3 CHELMSFORD CITY 1**
Competition: Southern League Premier Division
Teamsheet: Mogg, Kemp, Meacham, Noble, Hancocks, Sherwood, Talboys, Hughes, Fergusson, Eaton, Hackett
Substitutes: Penny (for Meacham), Madge (for Hughes)
Scorers: Eaton, Kemp, Hackett
Attendance: 650

Date: Tuesday 08/10/1991
Result: **TROWBRIDGE TOWN 1 GLOUCESTER CITY 0**
Competition: Southern League Cup 1st Round 1st Leg
Teamsheet: Mogg, Kemp, Meacham, Noble, Hancocks, Sherwood, Talboys, Hughes, Fergusson, Eaton, Hackett
Substitutes: Penny (nps), Madge (for Eaton)
Attendance: 478

[334]

Date: Saturday 12/10/1991
Result: **GLOUCESTER CITY 2 WATERLOOVILLE 1**
Competition: Southern League Premier Division
Teamsheet: Mogg, Madge, Meacham, Noble, Hancocks, Sherwood, Talboys, Hughes, Fergusson, Eaton, Hackett
Substitutes: Chandler (nps), Penny (nps)
Scorers: Talboys, Eaton
Attendance: 574

Date: Saturday 19/10/1991
Result: **GLOUCESTER CITY 0 DOVER ATHLETIC 4**
Competition: Southern League Premier Division
Teamsheet: Mogg, Rogers, Meacham, Noble, Hancocks, Sherwood, Talboys, Hughes, Fergusson, Eaton, Hackett
Substitutes: Penny (for Hughes), Chandler (for Meacham)
Attendance: 662

Date: Saturday 26/10/1991
Result: **DARTFORD 2 GLOUCESTER CITY 0**
Competition: Southern League Premier Division
Teamsheet: Mogg, Penny, Noble, Chandler, Kemp, Sherwood, Talboys, Hughes, Fergusson, Eaton, Hackett
Substitutes: Madge (for Talboys), Rogers (nps)
Attendance: 412

Date: Tuesday 29/10/1991
Result: **GLOUCESTER CITY 2 TROWBRIDGE TOWN 0**
Competition: Southern League Cup 1st Round 2nd Leg
Teamsheet: Bond, Kemp, Noble, Chandler, Hancocks, Sherwood, Penny, Hughes, Fergusson, Eaton, Madge
Substitutes: Hackett (nps), Rogers (nps)
Scorers: Eaton, own goal
Attendance: 465

Date: Saturday 02/11/1991
Result: **GLOUCESTER CITY 2 BURTON ALBION 2**
Competition: Southern League Premier Division
Teamsheet: Mogg, Rogers, Noble, Chandler, Kemp, Sherwood, Penny, Hughes, Fergusson, Eaton, Madge
Substitutes: Talboys (for Penny), Hackett (for Rogers)
Scorers: Noble, Eaton
Attendance: 337

Date: Tuesday 05/11/1991
Result: **GLOUCESTER CITY 2 STROUD 1**
Competition: Gloucestershire FA Northern Senior Professional Cup Semi-Final
Teamsheet: Bond, Madge, Sherwoood, Chandler, Kemp, Rogers, Talboys, Hackett, Noble, Eaton, Fergusson
Substitutes: Dean (for Rogers), Tucker (for Eaton)
Scorers: Eaton, Fergusson
Attendance: 391

Date: Saturday 09/11/1991
Result: **CHELMSFORD CITY 0 GLOUCESTER CITY 0**
Competition: Southern League Premier Division
Teamsheet: Mogg, Underhill, Sherwood, Kemp, Hancocks, Chandler, Talboys, Rogers, Townsend, Eaton, Noble
Substitutes: Madge (for Hancocks), Penny (nps)
Attendance: 567

Date: Tuesday 12/11/1991
Result: **GLOUCESTER CITY 3 BASHLEY 1**
Competition: Southern League Premier Division
Teamsheet: Mogg, Underhill, Meacham, Sherwood, Kemp, Penny, Noble, Rogers, Chandler, Eaton, Townsend
Substitutes: Madge (for Kemp), Tucker (nps)
Scorers: Noble, Townsend, own goal
Attendance: 458

Date: Saturday 16/11/1991
Result: **WEALDSTONE 3 GLOUCESTER CITY 2**
Competition: Southern League Premier Division
Teamsheet: Mogg, Underhill, Noble, Bywater, Kemp, Penny, Talboys, Rogers, Meacham, Eaton, Townsend
Substitutes: Madge (nps), Dean (nps)
Scorers: Talboys, Townsend
Attendance: 489

Date: Wednesday 20/11/1991
Result: **POOLE TOWN 2 GLOUCESTER CITY 1**
Competition: Southern League Premier Division
Teamsheet: Mogg, Underhill, Sherwood, Bywater, Kemp, Rogers, Talboys, Smith, Townsend, Eaton, Noble
Substitutes: Penny (for Noble), Tucker (for Underhill)
Scorer: Eaton
Attendance: 153

Date: Saturday 23/11/1991
Result: **GLOUCESTER CITY 0 GRAVESEND & NORTHFLEET 1**
Competition: Southern League Premier Division
Teamsheet: Mogg, Underhill, Noble, Sherwood, Kemp, Bywater, Talboys, Rogers, Townsend, Eaton, Smith
Substitutes: Penny (nps), Congrave (for Townsend)
Attendance: 553

Date: Monday 25/11/1991
Result: **BARRY TOWN 1 GLOUCESTER CITY 1**
Competition: Southern League Cup 2nd Round 1st Leg
Teamsheet: Mogg, Underhill, Noble, Bywater, Kemp, Rogers, Talboys, Townsend, Congrave, Eaton, Sherwood
Substitutes: Penny (nps), Madge (for Congrave)
Scorer: Eaton
Attendance: 239

Date: Saturday 07/12/1991
Result: **WATERLOOVILLE 1 GLOUCESTER CITY 0**
Competition: Southern League Premier Division
Teamsheet: Mogg, Underhill, Meacham, Bywater, Kemp, Sherwood, Talboys, Rogers, Musker, Eaton, Noble
Substitutes: Townsend (for Underhill), Penny (nps)
Attendance: 250

Date: Tuesday 17/12/1991
Result: **GLOUCESTER CITY 2 BARRY TOWN 0**
Competition: Southern League Cup 2nd Round 2nd Leg
Teamsheet: Mogg, Sherwood, Meacham, Kemp, Bywater, Crook, Talboys, Morgan, Penny, Eaton, Noble
Substitutes: Underhill (for Morgan), Tucker (nps)
Scorers: Talboys, Meacham
Attendance: 349

Date: Saturday 21/12/1991
Result: **ATHERSTONE UNITED 0 GLOUCESTER CITY 3**
Competition: Southern League Premier Division
Teamsheet: Mogg, Sherwood, Meacham, Kemp, Bywater, Crook, Talboys, Morgan, Penny, Eaton, Noble
Substitutes: Underhill (nps), Blackman (for Penny)
Scorers: Bywater (2), Penny
Attendance: 230

Date: Thursday 26/12/1991
Result: **GLOUCESTER CITY 1 HALESOWEN TOWN 1**
Competition: Southern League Premier Division
Teamsheet: Mogg, Sherwood, Meacham, Kemp, Bywater, Crook, Talboys, Morgan, Penny, Eaton, Noble
Substitutes: Musker (for Morgan), Blackman (for Noble)
Scorer: Penny
Attendance: 796

Date: Saturday 28/12/1991
Result: **GLOUCESTER CITY 0 CAMBRIDGE CITY 0**
Competition: Southern League Premier Division
Teamsheet: Mogg, Sherwood, Meacham, Kemp, Bywater, Crook, Talboys, Musker, Penny, Eaton, Noble
Substitutes: Morgan (nps), Blackman (for Penny)
Attendance: 649

Date: Wednesday 01/01/1992
Result: **DORCHESTER TOWN 4 GLOUCESTER CITY 2**
Competition: Southern League Premier Division
Teamsheet: Mogg, Crook, Meacham, Bywater, Kemp, Sherwood, Talboys, Blackman, Musker, Eaton, Noble
Substitutes: Townsend (for Blackman), Morgan (for Musker)
Scorers: Kemp, Townsend
Attendance: 1049

Date: Saturday 04/01/1992
Result: **MOOR GREEN 5 GLOUCESTER CITY 1**
Competition: Southern League Premier Division
Teamsheet: Mogg, Sherwood, Meacham, Underhill, Bywater, Crook, Chandler, Musker, Blackman, Eaton, Townsend
Substitutes: Morgan (for Crook), Rogers (for Underhill)
Scorer: Townsend
Attendance: 453

Date: Saturday 11/01/1992
Result: **GLOUCESTER CITY 1 HARROW BOROUGH 2**
Competition: FA Trophy 1st Round
Teamsheet: Mogg, Sherwood, Bywater, Rogers, Meacham, Chandler, Noble, Morgan, Crook, Townsend, Musker
Substitutes: Underhill (nps), Blackman (for Crook)
Scorer: Townsend
Attendance: 492

Date: Saturday 18/01/1992
Result: **GLOUCESTER CITY 2 TROWBRIDGE TOWN 2**
Competition: Southern League Premier Division
Teamsheet: Mogg, Underhill, Noble, Bywater, Morgan, Hazel, Chandler, Taylor, Evans, Townsend, Crook
Substitutes: Penny (for Townsend), Musker (nps)
Scorers: Morgan, own goal
Attendance: 549

Date: Saturday 25/01/1992
Result: **CRAWLEY TOWN 5 GLOUCESTER CITY 2**
Competition: Southern League Premier Division
Teamsheet: Jones, Taylor, Tripp, Bywater, Crook, Hazel, Chandler, Noble, Morgan, Townsend, Penny
Substitutes: Musker (for Townsend), Underhill (for Crook)
Scorers: Hazel, Penny
Attendance: 517

Date: Wednesday 05/02/1992
Result: **SALISBURY 1 GLOUCESTER CITY 2**
Competition: Southern League Cup 3rd Round 1st Leg
Teamsheet: Mogg, Kemp, Underhill, Hancocks, Bywater, Crouch, Morgan, Hughes, Penny, Townsend, Noble
Substitutes: Chandler (nps), Rogers (nps)
Scorers: Penny, Townsend
Attendance: 190

Date: Saturday 08/02/1992
Result: **GLOUCESTER CITY 1 MOOR GREEN 1**
Competition: Southern League Premier Division
Teamsheet: Mogg, Kemp, Underhill, Hancocks, Bywater, Crouch, Morgan, Hughes, Penny, Townsend, Noble
Substitutes: Sherwood (for Hancocks), Chandler (for Noble)
Scorer: Penny
Attendance: 585

Date: Tuesday 11/02/1992
Result: **GLOUCESTER CITY 0 SALISBURY 2**
Competition: Southern League Cup 3rd Round 2nd Leg
Teamsheet: Mogg, Kemp, Underhill, Hancocks, Bywater, Crouch, Morgan, Hughes, Penny, Townsend, Noble
Substitutes: Chandler (for Hancocks), Eaton (for Townsend)
Attendance: 382

Date: Saturday 15/02/1992
Result: **DOVER ATHLETIC 4 GLOUCESTER CITY 0**
Competition: Southern League Premier Division
Teamsheet: Mogg, Kemp, Sherwood, Rogers, Bywater, Crouch, Chandler, Hughes, Eaton, Townsend, Noble
Substitutes: Hancocks (for Townsend), Underhill (for Crouch)
Attendance: 930

Date: Tuesday 18/02/1992
Result: **GLOUCESTER CITY 2 WORCESTER CITY 0**
Competition: Southern League Premier Division
Teamsheet: Mogg, Kemp, Morgan, Hancocks, Bywater, Crouch, Chandler, Hughes, Penny, Townsend, Noble
Substitutes: Underhill (nps), Dean (nps)
Scorers: Townsend, Chandler
Attendance: 483

Date: Saturday 22/02/1992
Result: **CORBY TOWN 2 GLOUCESTER CITY 2**
Competition: Southern League Premier Division
Teamsheet: Mogg, Kemp, Morgan, Hancocks, Bywater, Crouch, Chandler, Hughes, Penny, Townsend, Noble
Substitutes: Underhill (nps), Eaton (nps)
Scorer: Townsend (2)
Attendance: 246

Date: Wednesday 04/03/1992
Result: **VALLEY SPORTS RUGBY 2 GLOUCESTER CITY 1**
Competition: Southern League Premier Division
Teamsheet: Mogg, Underhill, Jenkins, Kemp, Bywater, Crouch, Penny, Morgan, Eaton, Townsend, Noble
Substitutes: Clutterbuck (for Noble), Chandler (for Eaton)
Scorer: Clutterbuck
Attendance: 355

Date: Saturday 07/03/1992
Result: **GLOUCESTER CITY 0 DARTFORD 0**
Competition: Southern League Premier Division
Teamsheet: Mogg, Underhill, Jenkins, Kemp, Bywater, Hancocks, Penny, Crouch, Morgan, Townsend, Noble
Substitutes: Underhill (nps), Clutterbuck (for Townsend)
Attendance: 420

Date: Saturday 14/03/1992
Result: **FISHER ATHLETIC 3 GLOUCESTER CITY 0**
Competition: Southern League Premier Division
Teamsheet: Mogg, Morgan, Criddle, Kemp, Bywater, Crouch, Chandler, Hughes, Eaton, Penny, Noble
Substitutes: Townsend (for Crouch), Hancocks (nps)
Attendance: 174

Date: Saturday 21/03/1992
Result: **GLOUCESTER CITY 1 VALLEY SPORTS RUGBY 2**
Competition: Southern League Premier Division
Teamsheet: Mogg, Morgan, Criddle, Kemp, Bywater, Underhill, Chandler, Hughes, Eaton, Penny, Noble
Substitutes: Crouch (for Chandler), Hancocks (nps)
Scorer: Hughes
Attendance: 543

Date: Tuesday 24/03/1992
Result: **GLOUCESTER CITY 4 CRAWLEY TOWN 1**
Competition: Southern League Premier Division
Teamsheet: Mogg, Morgan, Criddle, Kemp, Bywater, Crouch, Underhill, Hughes, Eaton, Penny, Noble
Substitutes: Townsend (nps), Chandler (nps)
Scorers: Eaton (2), Penny, Morgan
Attendance: 328

Date: Saturday 28/03/1992
Result: **BURTON ALBION 4 GLOUCESTER CITY 3**
Competition: Southern League Premier Division
Teamsheet: Mogg, Underhill, Criddle, Bayliss, Bywater, Crouch, Morgan, Hughes, Penny, Eaton, Noble
Substitutes: Chandler (for Criddle), Griffiths (nps)
Scorers: Criddle, Penny, Noble (pen)
Attendance: 685

Date: Saturday 04/04/1992
Result: **TROWBRIDGE TOWN 1 GLOUCESTER CITY 1**
Competition: Southern League Premier Division
Teamsheet: Mogg, Penny, Criddle, Hancocks, Bywater, Crouch, Morgan, Hughes, Bayliss, Eaton, Noble
Substitutes: Underhill (nps), Chandler (nps)
Scorer: Eaton
Attendance: 443

Date: Tuesday 07/04/1992
Result: **CHELTENHAM TOWN 4 GLOUCESTER CITY 2**
Competition: Gloucestershire FA Northern Senior Professional Cup Final
Teamsheet: Mogg, Underhill, Belfitt, Bywater, Hancocks, Morgan, Chandler, Hughes, Penny, Eaton, Noble
Substitutes: Beacham (for Morgan), Griffiths (nps)
Scorer: Penny (2)
Attendance: 458

Date: Saturday 11/04/1992
Result: **GLOUCESTER CITY 2 ATHERSTONE UNITED 0**
Competition: Southern League Premier Division
Teamsheet: Mogg, Kemp, Criddle, Bywater, Hancocks, Crouch, Morgan, Hughes, Bayliss, Eaton, Chandler
Substitutes: Penny (nps), Underhill (nps)
Scorers: Bayliss, Bywater
Attendance: 411

Date: Saturday 18/04/1992
Result: **GLOUCESTER CITY 2 DORCHESTER TOWN 1**
Competition: Southern League Premier Division
Teamsheet: Mogg, Kemp, Criddle, Bywater, Hancocks, Crouch, Penny, Hughes, Bayliss, Eaton, Chandler
Substitutes: Noble (for Crouch), Underhill (nps)
Scorers: Penny, Eaton
Attendance: 353

Date: Monday 20/04/1992
Result: **HALESOWEN TOWN 0 GLOUCESTER CITY 2**
Competition: Southern League Premier Division
Teamsheet: Mogg, Kemp, Criddle, Bywater, Hancocks, Crouch, Penny, Hughes, Bayliss, Eaton, Chandler
Substitutes: Underhill (nps), Morgan (nps)
Scorer: Bayliss (2)
Attendance: 660

Date: Saturday 02/05/1992
Result: **GLOUCESTER CITY 1 BROMSGROVE ROVERS 2**
Competition: Southern League Premier Division
Teamsheet: Mogg, Kemp, Criddle, Bywater, Hancocks, Crouch, Chandler, Hughes, Bayliss, Eaton, Penny
Substitutes: Noble (for Criddle), Underhill (nps)
Scorer: Noble
Attendance: 875

Appearances – KA Bayliss 6, A Beacham 0(1), SR Belfitt 1, BG Blackman 2(4), LA Bond 3, PR Bywater 32, RD Chandler 27(6), R Clutterbuck 0(1), RJ Congrave 1(1), R Criddle 9, A Crook 9, SP Crouch 16(1), P Dean 0(1), JC Eaton 44(1), R Evans 1, SJ Fergusson 8(3), JP Freegard 11, BJ Hackett 17(1), GM Hancocks 22(1), I Hazell 2, BD Hughes 27(1), P Jenkins 2, M Jones 1, GJ Kemp 34, M Madge 12(6), J Meacham 23(1), DJ Mogg 49, JP Morgan 20(2), R Musker 5(2), WI Noble 44(3), S Penny 27(10), LM Rogers 23(1), J Sherwood 33(1), CJ Smith 5(1), SJ Talboys 28(1), GK Taylor 2, CG Townsend 18(3), N Tripp 1, S Tucker 0(2), P Underhill 18(3).
Others selected but did not play: K Griffiths.
Scorers – JC Eaton 19, S Penny 11, CG Townsend 9, SJ Talboys 8, WI Noble 6, J Meacham 4, KA Bayliss 3, PR Bywater 3, JP Freegard 3, BJ Hackett 3, GJ Kemp 2, JP Morgan 2, RD Chandler 1, R Clutterbuck 1, R Criddle 1, SJ Fergusson 1, I Hazel 1, BD Hughes 1, own goals 5.

SOUTHERN LEAGUE PREMIER DIVISION

POS	CLUB	P	W	D	L	F	A	PTS
1	BROMSGROVE ROVERS	42	27	9	6	78	34	90
2	DOVER ATHLETIC	42	23	15	4	66	30	84
3	VALLEY SPORTS RUGBY	42	23	11	8	70	44	80
4	BASHLEY	42	22	8	12	70	44	74
5	CAMBRIDGE CITY	42	18	14	10	71	53	68
6	DARTFORD	42	17	15	10	62	45	66
7	TROWBRIDGE TOWN	42	17	10	15	69	51	61
8	HALESOWEN TOWN	42	15	15	12	61	49	60
9	MOOR GREEN	42	15	11	16	61	59	56
10	BURTON ALBION	42	15	10	17	59	61	55
11	DORCHESTER TOWN	42	14	13	15	66	73	55
12	**GLOUCESTER CITY**	**42**	**15**	**9**	**18**	**67**	**70**	**54**
13	ATHERSTONE UNITED	42	15	8	19	54	66	53
14	CORBY TOWN	42	13	12	17	66	81	51
15	WATERLOOVILLE	42	13	11	18	43	56	50
16	WORCESTER CITY	42	12	13	17	56	59	49
17	CRAWLEY TOWN	42	12	12	18	62	67	48
18	CHELMSFORD CITY	42	12	12	18	49	56	48
19	WEALDSTONE	42	13	7	22	52	69	46
20	POOLE TOWN	42	10	13	19	46	77	43
21	FISHER ATHLETIC	42	9	11	22	53	89	38
22	GRAVESEND & NORTHFLEET	42	8	9	25	39	87	33
		924	338	248	338	1320	1320	1262

SEASON 1992-1993
(Home Ground: City Stadium, Meadow Park, Hempsted)

Date: Saturday 22/08/1992
Result: **GLOUCESTER CITY 2 CAMBRIDGE CITY 3**
Competition: Southern League Premier Division
Teamsheet: Knott, Crouch, Fishlock, Buckland, Bywater, Jenkins, Callinan, Hughes, Bayliss, Eaton, Noble
Substitutes: Darlaston (nps), Dixon (nps)
Scorer: Bayliss (2)
Attendance: 485

Date: Wednesday 26/08/1992
Result: **SOLIHULL BOROUGH 1 GLOUCESTER CITY 3**
Competition: Southern League Premier Division
Teamsheet: Knott, Crouch, Fishlock, Buckland, Bywater, Jenkins, Callinan, Hughes, Bayliss, Eaton, Noble
Substitutes: Darlaston (nps), Dixon (nps)
Scorers: Bayliss (2), Callinan
Attendance: 251

Date: Saturday 29/08/1992
Result: **CHELMSFORD CITY 3 GLOUCESTER CITY 1**
Competition: Southern League Premier Division
Teamsheet: Knott, Crouch, Fishlock, Buckland, Bywater, Jenkins, Callinan, Hughes, Bayliss, Eaton, Noble
Substitutes: Darlaston (nps), Dixon (for Hughes)
Scorer: Eaton
Attendance: 736

Date: Monday 31/08/1992
Result: **GLOUCESTER CITY 1 HEDNESFORD TOWN 3**
Competition: Southern League Premier Division
Teamsheet: Knott, Crouch, Fishlock, Buckland, Bywater, Jenkins, Callinan, GJ Kemp, Bayliss, Eaton, Noble
Substitutes: Darlaston (for Callinan), Dixon (for Bayliss)
Scorer: Noble
Attendance: 551

Date: Saturday 05/09/1992
Result: **HASTINGS TOWN 0 GLOUCESTER CITY 1**
Competition: Southern League Premier Division
Teamsheet: Oakes, Crouch, Criddle, Buckland, Bywater, Jenkins, Callinan, GJ Kemp, Bayliss, Eaton, Noble
Substitutes: Dixon (nps), Fishlock (for Noble)
Scorer: Callinan
Attendance: 487

Date: Tuesday 08/09/1992
Result: **GLOUCESTER CITY 1 WEYMOUTH 1**
Competition: Southern League Premier Division
Teamsheet: Oakes, Crouch, Criddle, Buckland, Bywater, Jenkins, Callinan, GJ Kemp, Bayliss, Eaton, Dixon
Substitutes: Fishlock (for Crouch), Darlaston (for Bayliss)
Scorer: Buckland
Attendance: 557

Date: Saturday 12/09/1992
Result: **GLOUCESTER CITY 2 WESTON-SUPER-MARE 3**
Competition: FA Cup 1st Qualifying Round
Teamsheet: Barrett, Fishlock, Criddle, Buckland, Bywater, Jenkins, Callinan, GJ Kemp, Bayliss, Eaton, Noble
Substitutes: Dixon (for Fishlock), Darlaston (for Jenkins)
Scorers: Callinan, Eaton
Attendance: 509

Date: Saturday 19/09/1992
Result: **GLOUCESTER CITY 4 ATHERSTONE UNITED 0**
Competition: Southern League Premier Division
Teamsheet: Oakes, Fishlock, Criddle, Buckland, Bywater, GJ Kemp, Callinan, Hughes, Bayliss, Eaton, Noble
Substitutes: Darlaston (nps), Dixon (nps)
Scorer: Bayliss (4)
Attendance: 427

Date: Saturday 26/09/1992
Result: **BURTON ALBION 0 GLOUCESTER CITY 3**
Competition: Southern League Premier Division
Teamsheet: Oakes, Fishlock, Criddle, Buckland, Bywater, GJ Kemp, Callinan, Hughes, Bayliss, Eaton, Noble
Substitutes: Darlaston (for Noble), Dixon (for Bayliss)
Scorer: Eaton (3)
Attendance: 495

Date: Tuesday 29/09/1992
Result: **MOOR GREEN 1 GLOUCESTER CITY 0**
Competition: Southern League Cup 1st Round 1st Leg
Teamsheet: Oakes, Fishlock, Criddle, Buckland, Bywater, GJ Kemp, Callinan, Hughes, Bayliss, Eaton, Noble
Substitutes: Dixon (for Noble), Crouch (for Callinan)
Attendance: 169

Date: Tuesday 06/10/1992
Result: **CHELTENHAM TOWN 1 GLOUCESTER CITY 2**
Competition: Gloucestershire FA Northern Senior Professional Cup Quarter-Final
Teamsheet: Oakes, Jones, Criddle, Buckland, Bywater, GJ Kemp, Hodges, Hughes, Dixon, Eaton, Banks
Substitutes: Crouch (nps), Fishlock (nps)
Scorers: Hodges, Eaton
Attendance: 402

Date: Saturday 10/10/1992
Result: **CRAWLEY TOWN 2 GLOUCESTER CITY 1**
Competition: Southern League Premier Division
Teamsheet: Oakes, Crouch, Criddle, Buckland, Bywater, GJ Kemp, Hodges, Hughes, Bayliss, Eaton, Noble
Substitutes: Dixon (for Bayliss), Fishlock (nps)
Scorer: Hodges
Attendance: 705

Date: Saturday 17/10/1992
Result: **GLOUCESTER CITY 4 WORCESTER CITY 0**
Competition: Southern League Premier Division
Teamsheet: Oakes, Crouch, Criddle, Buckland, Bywater, GJ Kemp, Hodges, Hughes, Bayliss, Eaton, Banks
Substitutes: Fishlock (nps), Penny (nps)
Scorers: Crouch, Banks (2), own goal
Attendance: 598

Date: Tuesday 20/10/1992
Result: **GLOUCESTER CITY 3 MOOR GREEN 0**
Competition: Southern League Cup 1st Round 2nd Leg
Teamsheet: Oakes, Crouch, Criddle, Buckland, Bywater, GJ Kemp, Hodges, Hughes, Bayliss, Dixon, Banks
Substitutes: Fishlock (nps), Penny (nps)
Scorers: Crouch, Bayliss (2)
Attendance: 224

Date: Saturday 24/10/1992
Result: **DORCHESTER TOWN 1 GLOUCESTER CITY 1**
Competition: Southern League Premier Division
Teamsheet: Oakes, Crouch, Criddle, Buckland, Bywater, GJ Kemp, Hodges, Hughes, Bayliss, Dixon, Banks
Substitutes: Penny (for Dixon), Fishlock (for Hodges)
Scorer: Criddle
Attendance: 378

Date: Tuesday 27/10/1992
Result: **GLOUCESTER CITY 1 SOLIHULL BOROUGH 1**
Competition: Southern League Premier Division
Teamsheet: Oakes, Crouch, Criddle, Buckland, Bywater, GJ Kemp, Hodges, Hughes, Bayliss, Dixon, Banks
Substitutes: Penny (for Banks), Noble (for Dixon)
Scorer: Dixon
Attendance: 408

Date: Saturday 31/10/1992
Result: **GLOUCESTER CITY 1 VALLEY SPORTS RUGBY 0**
Competition: Southern League Premier Division
Teamsheet: Oakes, Crouch, Noble, Buckland, Bywater, GJ Kemp, Hodges, Hughes, Bayliss, Dixon, Banks
Substitutes: Penny (for Dixon), Fishlock (nps)
Scorer: Bayliss
Attendance: 487

Date: Tuesday 03/11/1992
Result: **GLOUCESTER CITY 2 AFC NEWPORT 1**
Competition: Gloucestershire FA Northern Senior Professional Cup Semi-Final
Teamsheet: Oakes, Crouch, Noble, Buckland, Bywater, GJ Kemp, Hodges, Hughes, Bayliss, Penny, Fishlock
Substitutes: Dixon (for Penny), Jones (for Buckland)
Scorers: Fishlock, own goal
Attendance: 386

Date: Saturday 07/11/1992
Result: **WATERLOOVILLE 1 GLOUCESTER CITY 1**
Competition: Southern League Premier Division
Teamsheet: Oakes, Crouch, Criddle, Buckland, Bywater, GJ Kemp, Hodges, Hughes, Bayliss, Noble, Banks
Substitutes: Fishlock (for Criddle), Dixon (for Noble)
Scorer: Hodges
Attendance: 323

Date: Wednesday 11/11/1992
Result: **AFC NEWPORT 1 GLOUCESTER CITY 1**
Competition: Southern League Cup 2nd Round
Teamsheet: Oakes, Crouch, Fishlock, Buckland, Bywater, GJ Kemp, Jenkins, Hughes, Bayliss, Dixon, Noble
Substitutes: Hodges (for Jenkins), Banks (for Dixon)
Scorer: Bayliss
Attendance: 354

Date: Saturday 14/11/1992
Result: **GLOUCESTER CITY 1 DOVER ATHLETIC 1**
Competition: Southern League Premier Division
Teamsheet: Oakes, Crouch, Criddle, Buckland, Bywater, GJ Kemp, Hodges, Hughes, Bayliss, Jones, Noble
Substitutes: Fishlock (for Crouch), Banks (nps)
Scorer: Criddle
Attendance: 568

Date: Tuesday 24/11/1992
Result: **GLOUCESTER CITY 3 AFC NEWPORT 2**
Competition: Southern League Cup 2nd Round Replay
Teamsheet: Oakes, Crouch, Criddle, Buckland, Bywater, GJ Kemp, Callinan, Hughes, Bayliss, Penny, Noble
Substitutes: Fishlock (nps), Banks (for Crouch)
Scorers: Buckland, Hughes, Banks
Attendance: 301

Date: Saturday 28/11/1992
Result: **WEYMOUTH 1 GLOUCESTER CITY 5**
Competition: Southern League Premier Division
Teamsheet: Oakes, Crouch, Criddle, Buckland, Bywater, GJ Kemp, Callinan, Hughes, Bayliss, Penny, Noble
Substitutes: Hodges (for Crouch), Banks (nps)
Scorers: Bayliss (3), Noble, own goal
Attendance: 690

Date: Saturday 05/12/1992
Result: **BASHLEY 0 GLOUCESTER CITY 3**
Competition: Southern League Premier Division
Teamsheet: Utteridge, Crouch, Criddle, Buckland, Bywater, GJ Kemp, Callinan, Hughes, Bayliss, Penny, Noble
Substitutes: Hodges (nps), Banks (nps)
Scorers: Buckland, Bayliss (2)
Attendance: 241

Date: Tuesday 15/12/1992
Result: **GLOUCESTER CITY 2 HALESOWEN TOWN 2**
Competition: Southern League Cup 3rd Round
Teamsheet: Utteridge, Banks, Criddle, Buckland, Bywater, GJ Kemp, Hodges, Hughes, Bayliss, Penny, Noble
Substitutes: Cook (for Noble), Fishlock (for Criddle)
Scorers: Buckland, own goal
Attendance: 297

Date: Saturday 19/12/1992
Result: **ATHERSTONE UNITED 2 GLOUCESTER CITY 1**
Competition: Southern League Premier Division
Teamsheet: Utteridge, Crouch, Banks, Buckland, Bywater, GJ Kemp, Callinan, Hughes, Bayliss, Penny, Cook
Substitutes: Hodges (for Crouch), Fishlock (nps)
Scorer: Penny
Attendance: 321

Date: Monday 28/12/1992
Result: **CHELTENHAM TOWN 4 GLOUCESTER CITY 0**
Competition: Southern League Premier Division
Teamsheet: R Kemp, Crouch, Criddle, Buckland, Bywater, GJ Kemp, Callinan, Hughes, Bayliss, Cook, Noble
Substitutes: Penny (for Noble), Hodges (for Crouch)
Attendance: 2200

Date: Tuesday 05/01/1993
Result: **GLOUCESTER CITY 1 DORCHESTER TOWN 0**
Competition: Southern League Premier Division
Teamsheet: R Kemp, Hodges, Banks, Buckland, Bywater, GJ Kemp, Callinan, Hughes, Bayliss, Penny, Noble
Substitutes: Crouch (nps), Fishlock (nps)
Scorer: Callinan
Attendance: 359

Date: Saturday 09/01/1993
Result: **GLOUCESTER CITY 1 BURTON ALBION 3**
Competition: Southern League Premier Division
Teamsheet: Utteridge, Hodges, Banks, Buckland, Bywater, GJ Kemp, Callinan, Hughes, Bayliss, Penny, Noble
Substitutes: Crouch (nps), Fishlock (for Banks)
Scorer: Bywater
Attendance: 486

Date: Tuesday 12/01/1993
Result: **HALESOWEN TOWN 2 GLOUCESTER CITY 1**
Competition: Southern League Cup 3rd Round Replay
Teamsheet: Utteridge, Hodges, Fishlock, Buckland, Bywater, GJ Kemp, Callinan, Hughes, Bayliss, Penny, Noble
Substitutes: Banks (nps), Crouch (for Fishlock)
Scorer: own goal
Attendance: 361

Date: Saturday 16/01/1993
Result: **GLOUCESTER CITY 0 CORBY TOWN 1**
Competition: Southern League Premier Division
Teamsheet: Utteridge, Hodges, Fishlock, Buckland, Bywater, GJ Kemp, Callinan, Hughes, Bayliss, Penny, Crouch
Substitutes: Banks (nps), Jones (nps)
Attendance: 380

Date: Saturday 23/01/1993
Result: **CAMBRIDGE CITY 6 GLOUCESTER CITY 3**
Competition: Southern League Premier Division
Teamsheet: Utteridge, Hodges, Fishlock, Buckland, Bywater, GJ Kemp, Callinan, Hughes, Bayliss, Penny, Noble
Substitutes: Crouch (nps), Banks (for Fishlock)
Scorers: Fishlock, Noble (2)
Attendance: 351

Date: Saturday 30/01/1993
Result: **GLOUCESTER CITY 3 RUNCORN 3**
Competition: FA Trophy 2nd Round
Teamsheet: Utteridge, Hodges, Fishlock, Buckland, Bywater, GJ Kemp, Callinan, Hughes, Bayliss, Penny, Noble
Substitutes: Crouch (for Hodges), Banks (for Noble)
Scorers: Bayliss, Hughes, Buckland
Attendance: 577

Date: Tuesday 02/02/1993
Result: **RUNCORN 2 GLOUCESTER CITY 2**
Competition: FA Trophy 2nd Round Replay
Teamsheet: Bowles, Hodges, Criddle, Buckland, Bywater, GJ Kemp, Callinan, Hughes, Bayliss, Penny, Crouch
Substitutes: Fishlock (for Hughes), Banks (for Hodges)
Scorers: Bayliss, Buckland
Attendance: 600

Date: Saturday 06/02/1993
Result: **GLOUCESTER CITY 3 HALESOWEN TOWN 1**
Competition: Southern League Premier Division
Teamsheet: Utteridge, Hodges, Fishlock, Buckland, Bywater, GJ Kemp, Callinan, Jones, Bayliss, Penny, Crouch
Substitutes: Banks (for Callinan), Noble (nps)
Scorers: GJ Kemp, Bayliss (2)
Attendance: 469

Date: Monday 08/02/1993
Result: **GLOUCESTER CITY 0 RUNCORN 0**
Competition: FA Trophy 2nd Round 2nd Replay
Teamsheet: Bowles, Hodges, Fishlock, Buckland, Bywater, GJ Kemp, Callinan, Noble, Bayliss, Penny, Crouch
Substitutes: Darlaston (for Bayliss), Jones (nps)
Attendance: 771

[341]

Date: Thursday 11/02/1993
Result: **RUNCORN 4 GLOUCESTER CITY 1**
Competition: FA Trophy 2nd Round 3rd Replay
Teamsheet: Bowles, Hodges, Fishlock, Buckland, Bywater, GJ Kemp, Callinan, Crouch, Bayliss, Penny, Noble
Substitutes: Darlaston (for Hodges), Banks (for Noble)
Scorer: Crouch
Attendance: 701

Date: Saturday 13/02/1993
Result: **WORCESTER CITY 2 GLOUCESTER CITY 0**
Competition: Southern League Premier Division
Teamsheet: Utteridge, Abbley, Fishlock, Buckland, Bywater, Baverstock, Callinan, Noble, Bayliss, Penny, Crouch
Substitutes: Darlaston (for Crouch), Hodges (for Abbley)
Attendance: 771

Date: Saturday 20/02/1993
Result: **GLOUCESTER CITY 1 CRAWLEY TOWN 1**
Competition: Southern League Premier Division
Teamsheet: Utteridge, Abbley, Fishlock, Buckland, Bywater, Baverstock, Callinan, Hodges, Bayliss, Penny, Noble
Substitutes: Johnson (nps), Jones (nps)
Scorer: Noble
Attendance: 378

Date: Tuesday 23/02/1993
Result: **GLOUCESTER CITY 2 TROWBRIDGE TOWN 4**
Competition: Southern League Premier Division
Teamsheet: Utteridge, Jones, Fishlock, Buckland, Bywater, Hancocks, Callinan, Hodges, Bayliss, Meacham, Noble
Substitutes: Jenkins (nps), Johnson (for Hodges)
Scorers: Buckland, Bywater
Attendance: 472

Date: Saturday 27/02/1993
Result: **DOVER ATHLETIC 2 GLOUCESTER CITY 0**
Competition: Southern League Premier Division
Teamsheet: Crompton, Abbley, Criddle, Buckland, Bywater, Fishlock, Callinan, Crouch, Jones, Penny, Noble
Substitutes: Cook (for Criddle), Johnson (for Jones)
Attendance: 1540

Date: Saturday 06/03/1993
Result: **GLOUCESTER CITY 1 BASHLEY 1**
Competition: Southern League Premier Division
Teamsheet: Crompton, Abbley, Crouch, Buckland, Bywater, GJ Kemp, Callinan, Hughes, Bayliss, Cook, Noble
Substitutes: Penny (nps), Criddle (for Hughes)
Scorer: Bywater
Attendance: 385

Date: Saturday 13/03/1993
Result: **VALLEY SPORTS RUGBY 0 GLOUCESTER CITY 1**
Competition: Southern League Premier Division
Teamsheet: Crompton, Abbley, Crouch, Buckland, Bywater, GJ Kemp, Callinan, Hughes, Bayliss, Cook, Noble
Substitutes: Criddle (for Crouch), Penny (for Cook)
Scorer: Abbley
Attendance: 358

Date: Tuesday 16/03/1993
Result: **GLOUCESTER CITY 2 MOOR GREEN 2**
Competition: Southern League Premier Division
Teamsheet: Crompton, Abbley, Baverstock, Buckland, Bywater, GJ Kemp, Callinan, Hughes, Bayliss, Cook, Noble
Substitutes: Criddle (for Bywater), Penny (for Hughes)
Scorers: Callinan, Bayliss
Attendance: 330

Date: Saturday 20/03/1993
Result: **GLOUCESTER CITY 1 WATERLOOVILLE 1**
Competition: Southern League Premier Division
Teamsheet: Crompton, Abbley, Baverstock, Buckland, Criddle, GJ Kemp, Callinan, Hughes, Bayliss, Cook, Noble
Substitutes: Crouch (nps), Penny (for Hughes)
Scorer: Bayliss
Attendance: 352

Date: Monday 22/03/1993
Result: **HEDNESFORD TOWN 1 GLOUCESTER CITY 2**
Competition: Southern League Premier Division
Teamsheet: Crompton, Penny, Criddle, Buckland, Baverstock, G Kemp, Callinan, Hughes, Bayliss, Cook, Noble
Substitutes: Crouch (nps), Fishlock (nps)
Scorers: GJ Kemp, Penny
Attendance: 522

Date: Saturday 27/03/1993
Result: **CORBY TOWN 1 GLOUCESTER CITY 1**
Competition: Southern League Premier Division
Teamsheet: Crompton, Baverstock, Noble, Buckland, Bywater, GJ Kemp, Callinan, Hughes, Bayliss, Cook, Penny
Substitutes: Crouch (for Callinan), Abbley (for Hughes)
Scorer: Cook
Attendance: 321

Date: Saturday 03/04/1993
Result: **HALESOWEN TOWN 2 GLOUCESTER CITY 2**
Competition: Southern League Premier Division
Teamsheet: Crompton, Abbley, Baverstock, Criddle, Penny, GJ Kemp, Callinan, Hughes, Bayliss, Cook, Noble
Substitutes: Crouch (nps), Fishlock (for Penny)
Scorers: Bayliss, Penny
Attendance: 558

Date: Wednesday 07/04/1993
Result: **YATE TOWN 2 GLOUCESTER CITY 3**
Competition: Gloucestershire FA Northern Senior Professional Cup Final
Teamsheet: Crompton, Abbley, Noble, Crouch, Criddle, GJ Kemp, Callinan, Hughes, Bayliss, Cook, Penny
Substitutes: Fishlock (nps), Banks (nps)
Scorers: Callinan, Bayliss, Criddle
Attendance: 266

Date: Saturday 10/04/1993
Result: **TROWBRIDGE TOWN 1 GLOUCESTER CITY 2**
Competition: Southern League Premier Division
Teamsheet: Crompton, Abbley, Baverstock, Penny, Criddle, GJ Kemp, Callinan, Hughes, Bayliss, Cook, Noble
Substitutes: Crouch (for Penny), Fishlock (for Baverstock)
Scorers: Cook, Baverstock
Attendance: 363

Date: Monday 12/04/1993
Result: **GLOUCESTER CITY 1 CHELTENHAM TOWN 5**
Competition: Southern League Premier Division
Teamsheet: Bowles, Abbley, Baverstock, Criddle, Bywater, GJ Kemp, Callinan, Penny, Bayliss, Cook, Noble
Substitutes: Fishlock (for Abbley), Crouch (nps)
Scorer: Penny
Attendance: 1072

Date: Saturday 17/04/1993
Result: **GLOUCESTER CITY 1 CHELMSFORD CITY 2**
Competition: Southern League Premier Division
Teamsheet: Crompton, Baverstock, Criddle, Penny, Bywater, GJ Kemp, Callinan, Hughes, Fishlock, Cook, Noble
Substitutes: Crouch (nps), Buckland (nps)
Scorer: Criddle
Attendance: 379

Date: Saturday 24/04/1993
Result: **MOOR GREEN 6 GLOUCESTER CITY 0**
Competition: Southern League Premier Division
Teamsheet: Crompton, Baverstock, Fishlock, Buckland, Bywater, GJ Kemp, Callinan, Hughes, Penny, Cook, Crouch
Substitutes: Johnstone (for Callinan), Jones (for Baverstock)
Attendance: 276

Date: Saturday 01/05/1993
Result: **GLOUCESTER CITY 6 HASTINGS TOWN 2**
Competition: Southern League Premier Division
Teamsheet: Crompton, Jones, Fishlock, Buckland, Bywater, Crouch, Callinan, Hughes, Penny, Cook, Noble
Substitutes: Johnstone (nps), Criddle (nps)
Scorers: Penny (3), Cook, Crouch, Bywater
Attendance: 387

Appearances – SG Abbley 11(1), T Banks 11(7), M Barrett 1, R Baverstock 11, KA Bayliss 49, R Bowles 4, MC Buckland 49, PR Bywater 49, TJ Callinan 42, A Cook 15(2), R Criddle 28(3), SG Crompton 13, SP Crouch 33(5), S Darlaston 0(7), L Dixon 7(8), JC Eaton 13, ME Fishlock 24(11), GM Hancocks 1, DT Hodges 23(5), BD Hughes 42, P Jenkins 8, M Johnson 0(2), K Johnstone 0(1), P Jones 6(2), GJ Kemp 46, R Kemp 2, A Knott 4, J Meacham 1, WI Noble 43(1), MC Oakes 18, S Penny 28(7), M Utteridge 12.
Scorers – KA Bayliss 25, S Penny 7, MC Buckland 6, TJ Callinan 6, JC Eaton 6, WI Noble 6, PR Bywater 4, SP Crouch 4, R Criddle 4, Banks 3, A Cook 3, ME Fishlock 3, D Hodges 3, BD Hughes 2, GJ Kemp 2, SG Abbley 1, R Baverstock 1, L Dixon 1, own goals 4.

SOUTHERN LEAGUE PREMIER DIVISION

POS	CLUB	P	W	D	L	F	A	PTS
1	DOVER ATHLETIC	40	25	11	4	65	23	86
2	CHELTENHAM TOWN	40	21	10	9	76	40	73
3	CORBY TOWN	40	20	12	8	68	43	72
4	HEDNESFORD TOWN	40	21	7	12	72	52	70
5	TROWBRIDGE TOWN	40	18	8	14	70	66	62
6	CRAWLEY TOWN	40	16	12	12	68	59	60
7	SOLIHULL BOROUGH	40	17	9	14	68	59	60
8	BURTON ALBION	40	16	11	13	53	50	59
9	BASHLEY	40	18	8	14	60	60	59*
10	HALESOWEN TOWN	40	15	11	14	67	54	56
11	WATERLOOVILLE	40	15	9	16	59	62	54
12	CHELMSFORD CITY	40	15	9	16	59	69	54
13	**GLOUCESTER CITY**	**40**	**14**	**11**	**15**	**66**	**68**	**53**
14	CAMBRIDGE CITY	40	14	10	16	62	73	52
15	ATHERSTONE UNITED	40	13	14	13	56	60	50*
16	HASTINGS TOWN	40	13	11	16	50	55	50
17	WORCESTER CITY	40	12	9	19	45	62	45
18	DORCHESTER TOWN	40	12	6	22	52	74	42
19	MOOR GREEN	40	10	6	24	58	79	36
20	VALLEY SPORTS RUGBY	40	10	6	24	40	63	36
21	WEYMOUTH	40	5	10	25	39	82	23**
22	DARTFORD							
		840	320	200	320	1253	1253	1152

*Three points deducted. **Two points deducted.
Dartford withdrew in September after the Maidstone United collapse deprived them of their Watling Street ground and they were refused permission to ground share with Welling United. All scores were expunged from the records.

[343]

SEASON BY SEASON

SEASON 1993-1994
(Home Ground: City Stadium, Meadow Park, Hempsted)

Date: Saturday 21/08/1993
Result: **CORBY TOWN 2 GLOUCESTER CITY 1**
Competition: Southern League Premier Division
Teamsheet: Crompton, Bloomfield, Fishlock, Buckland, GJ Kemp, Criddle, Callinan, BD Hughes, Bayliss, Cook, Crouch
Substitutes: Boyland (for Crouch), Johnson (nps)
Scorer: Buckland
Attendance: 358

Date: Tuesday 24/08/1993
Result: **GLOUCESTER CITY 4 BURTON ALBION 2**
Competition: Southern League Premier Division
Teamsheet: Crompton, Bloomfield, Fishlock, Buckland, GJ Kemp, Criddle, Callinan, BD Hughes, Bayliss, Cook, Crouch
Substitutes: Boyland (for Fishlock), Johnson (nps)
Scorers: Cook (2), Bayliss (2)
Attendance: 569

Date: Saturday 28/08/1993
Result: **GLOUCESTER CITY 3 SOLIHULL BOROUGH 1**
Competition: Southern League Premier Division
Teamsheet: Crompton, Bloomfield, Fishlock, Buckland, GJ Kemp, Criddle, Callinan, BD Hughes, Bayliss, Cook, Crouch
Substitutes: Boyland (for Crouch), Johnson (nps)
Scorers: Cook, Bayliss (2)
Attendance: 570

Date: Monday 30/08/1993
Result: **CRAWLEY TOWN 0 GLOUCESTER CITY 0**
Competition: Southern League Premier Division
Teamsheet: Crompton, Bloomfield, Fishlock, Buckland, GJ Kemp, Criddle, Callinan, BD Hughes, Bayliss, Cook, Crouch
Substitutes: Boyland (for Callinan), Johnson (nps)
Attendance: 785

Date: Saturday 04/09/1993
Result: **GLOUCESTER CITY 1 GRESLEY ROVERS 1**
Competition: Southern League Premier Division
Teamsheet: Crompton, Bloomfield, Fishlock, Buckland, GJ Kemp, Criddle, Callinan, BD Hughes, Bayliss, Cook, Crouch
Substitutes: Boyland (for BD Hughes), Johnson (for Fishlock)
Scorer: Cook
Attendance: 566

Date: Tuesday 07/09/1993
Result: **HALESOWEN TOWN 1 GLOUCESTER CITY 0**
Competition: Southern League Premier Division
Teamsheet: Crompton, Bloomfield, Fishlock, Buckland, GJ Kemp, Criddle, Callinan, Boyland, Bayliss, Cook, Crouch
Substitutes: Johnson (nps), Jones (nps)
Attendance: 728

Date: Saturday 11/09/1993
Result: **GLOUCESTER CITY 1 CLEVEDON TOWN 2**
Competition: FA Cup 1st Qualifying Round
Teamsheet: Crompton, Bloomfield, Criddle, Buckland, Bywater, GJ Kemp, Callinan, BD Hughes, Bayliss, Cook, Olner
Substitutes: Boyland (for BD Hughes), Fishlock (for Callinan)
Scorer: Callinan
Attendance: 436

Date: Sunday 19/09/1993
Result: **GLOUCESTER CITY 2 WATERLOOVILLE 1**
Competition: Southern League Premier Division
Teamsheet: Crompton, Bloomfield, Fishlock, Buckland, Bywater, GJ Kemp, Callinan, BD Hughes, Bayliss, Cook, Olner
Substitutes: Crouch (nps), Boyland (nps)
Scorers: Olner, Bayliss
Attendance: 475

Date: Saturday 25/09/1993
Result: **HEDNESFORD TOWN 1 GLOUCESTER CITY 1**
Competition: Southern League Premier Division
Teamsheet: Crompton, Bloomfield, Criddle, Buckland, Bywater, GJ Kemp, Callinan, Smith, Bayliss, Cook, Olner
Substitutes: Boyland (nps), Johnson (for GJ Kemp)
Scorer: Bayliss
Attendance: 402

Date: Tuesday 28/09/1993
Result: **WITNEY TOWN 1 GLOUCESTER CITY 2**
Competition: Southern League Cup 1st Round 1st Leg
Teamsheet: Crompton, Bloomfield, Fishlock, Buckland, Bywater, Criddle, Crouch, BD Hughes, Boyland, Cook, Olner
Substitutes: Bayliss (for Cook), Callinan (for Bloomfield)
Scorers: Boyland, Fishlock
Attendance: 286

Date: Saturday 02/10/1993
Result: **CHELMSFORD CITY 2 GLOUCESTER CITY 1**
Competition: Southern League Premier Division
Teamsheet: Crompton, Bloomfield, Criddle, Buckland, Bywater, Fletcher, Callinan, Smith, Bayliss, Cook, Olner
Substitutes: Boyland (for Fletcher), BD Hughes (nps)
Scorer: Callinan
Attendance: 525

Date: Saturday 09/10/1993
Result: **GLOUCESTER CITY 2 MOOR GREEN 1**
Competition: Southern League Premier Division
Teamsheet: Crompton, Bloomfield, Criddle, Buckland, Bywater, GJ Kemp, Callinan, Smith, Bayliss, Cook, Olner
Substitutes: Boyland (for Bloomfield), Fishlock (for Criddle)
Scorers: Bayliss, Buckland
Attendance: 435

Date: Saturday 16/10/1993
Result: **GLOUCESTER CITY 2 HASTINGS TOWN 1**
Competition: Southern League Premier Division
Teamsheet: Crompton, Bloomfield, Fishlock, Buckland, Bywater, GJ Kemp, Callinan, Smith, Bayliss, Cook, Olner
Substitutes: Boyland (for Smith), Crouch (nps)
Scorers: Bloomfield, Boyland
Attendance: 457

Date: Tuesday 19/10/1993
Result: **GLOUCESTER CITY 1 WITNEY TOWN 1**
Competition: Southern League Cup 1st Round 2nd Leg
Teamsheet: Crompton, Crouch, Criddle, Buckland, Bywater, GJ Kemp, Callinan, BD Hughes, Bayliss, Boyland, Olner
Substitutes: Cook (for Boyland), Bloomfield (nps)
Scorer: Callinan
Attendance: 132

Date: Saturday 23/10/1993
Result: **SITTINGBOURNE 0 GLOUCESTER CITY 0**
Competition: Southern League Premier Division
Teamsheet: Crompton, Bloomfield, Fishlock, Buckland, Bywater, GJ Kemp, Callinan, Crouch, Bayliss, Cook, Olner
Substitutes: Boyland (nps), BD Hughes (nps)
Attendance: 963

Date: Tuesday 26/10/1993
Result: **BURTON ALBION 4 GLOUCESTER CITY 1**
Competition: Southern League Premier Division
Teamsheet: Crompton, Crouch, Fishlock, Buckland, Bywater, GJ Kemp, Callinan, BD Hughes, Boyland, Cook, Olner
Substitutes: Bayliss (for Callinan), Bloomfield (for Fishlock)
Scorer: Cook
Attendance: 526

Date: Saturday 30/10/1993
Result: **GLOUCESTER CITY 1 DORCHESTER TOWN 0**
Competition: Southern League Premier Division
Teamsheet: Crompton, Bloomfield, Fishlock, Buckland, Bywater, GJ Kemp, Callinan, Crouch, Bayliss, Cook, Olner
Substitutes: BD Hughes (nps), Smith (nps)
Scorer: Bloomfield
Attendance: 405

Date: Tuesday 02/11/1993
Result: **CHELTENHAM TOWN 0 GLOUCESTER CITY 1**
Competition: Gloucestershire FA Northern Senior Professional Cup Quarter-Final
Teamsheet: Crompton, Bloomfield, Fishlock, Buckland, Bywater, GJ Kemp, Callinan, Crouch, Bayliss, Cook, Olner
Substitutes: BD Hughes (nps), Smith (nps), Boyland (nps)
Scorer: Buckland
Attendance: 449

Date: Saturday 06/11/1993
Result: **CAMBRIDGE CITY 2 GLOUCESTER CITY 0**
Competition: Southern League Premier Division
Teamsheet: Crompton, Bloomfield, Fishlock, Buckland, Bywater, GJ Kemp, Callinan, Crouch, Bayliss, Cook, Olner
Substitutes: Boyland (for Callinan), BD Hughes (nps)
Attendance: 447

Date: Saturday 13/11/1993
Result: **TROWBRIDGE TOWN 2 GLOUCESTER CITY 0**
Competition: Southern League Premier Division
Teamsheet: Crompton, Bloomfield, Fishlock, Buckland, Bywater, GJ Kemp, Callinan, Crouch, Boyland, Cook, Olner
Substitutes: BD Hughes (nps), Smith (for Bloomfield)
Attendance: 390

Date: Tuesday 16/11/1993
Result: **GLOUCESTER CITY 3 CRAWLEY TOWN 0**
Competition: Southern League Premier Division
Teamsheet: Crompton, Crouch, Fishlock, Buckland, Bywater, GJ Kemp, Callinan, BD Hughes, Bayliss, Cook, Boyland
Substitutes: Bloomfield (nps), Smith (nps)
Scorers: Buckland, Bayliss, Cook
Attendance: 430

Date: Saturday 20/11/1993
Result: **FARNBOROUGH TOWN 1 GLOUCESTER CITY 0**
Competition: Southern League Premier Division
Teamsheet: Crompton, Crouch, Fishlock, Buckland, Bywater, GJ Kemp, Callinan, BD Hughes, Bayliss, Cook, Boyland
Substitutes: Bloomfield (for BD Hughes), Smith (for Boyland)
Attendance: 426

Date: Saturday 27/11/1993
Result: **DULWICH HAMLET 2 GLOUCESTER CITY 1**
Competition: FA Trophy 3rd Qualifying Round
Teamsheet: Crompton, Crouch, Fishlock, Buckland, Bywater, GJ Kemp, Callinan, BD Hughes, Bayliss, Cook, Boyland
Substitutes: Bloomfield (for BD Hughes), Smith (for Boyland)
Scorer: Bayliss
Attendance: 313

Date: Saturday 11/12/1993
Result: **GLOUCESTER CITY 2 CORBY TOWN 4**
Competition: Southern League Premier Division
Teamsheet: Crompton, Crouch, Fishlock, Buckland, Bywater, GJ Kemp, Callinan, BD Hughes, Bayliss, Cook, Boyland
Substitutes: Bloomfield (for Callinan), Johnstone (nps)
Scorers: Bywater, Boyland
Attendance: 389

Date: Tuesday 14/12/1993
Result: **GLOUCESTER CITY 0 SITTINGBOURNE 1**
Competition: Southern League Premier Division
Teamsheet: Crompton, Crouch, Fishlock, Buckland, Bywater, GJ Kemp, Callinan, BD Hughes, Bayliss, Cook, Boyland
Substitutes: Bloomfield (for Boyland), Smith (nps)
Attendance: 352

Date: Monday 27/12/1993
Result: **WORCESTER CITY 2 GLOUCESTER CITY 0**
Competition: Southern League Premier Division
Teamsheet: Crompton, Crouch, Fishlock, Buckland, Bywater, GJ Kemp, Callinan, BD Hughes, Bayliss, Cook, Boyland
Substitutes: Johnstone (for Boyland), Williams (nps)
Attendance: 1198

Date: Saturday 01/01/1994
Result: **GLOUCESTER CITY 1 CHELTENHAM TOWN 3**
Competition: Southern League Premier Division
Teamsheet: Crompton, Crouch, Fishlock, Buckland, Bywater, GJ Kemp, Callinan, BD Hughes, Bayliss, Criddle, Boyland
Substitutes: Cook (for Crouch), Johnstone (for Criddle)
Scorer: Cook
Attendance: 1239

Date: Monday 03/01/1994
Result: **BASHLEY 4 GLOUCESTER CITY 5**
Competition: Southern League Premier Division
Teamsheet: Crompton, Saunders, Criddle, Buckland, Bywater, GJ Kemp, Callinan, Tilley, Bayliss, Cook, BD Hughes
Substitutes: Boyland (for Criddle), N Hughes (for GJ Kemp)
Scorers: Callinan, Bayliss (2), N Hughes, Tilley
Attendance: 465

Date: Saturday 08/01/1994
Result: **GLOUCESTER CITY 3 ATHERSTONE UNITED 0**
Competition: Southern League Premier Division
Teamsheet: Crompton, Saunders, Criddle, Buckland, Bywater, Blackler, Callinan, Tilley, Bayliss, Cook, BD Hughes
Substitutes: Boyland (nps), N Hughes (nps)
Scorers: Bayliss, Cook, Tilley
Attendance: 577

Date: Monday 10/01/1994
Result: **EVESHAM UNITED 1 GLOUCESTER CITY 3**
Competition: Southern League Cup 2nd Round
Teamsheet: Crompton, Saunders, Criddle, Buckland, Crouch, Fishlock, Callinan, Tilley, Bayliss, Cook, BD Hughes
Substitutes: Boyland (nps), Johnstone (nps)
Scorers: Bayliss (2), Cook
Attendance: 140

Date: Saturday 15/01/1994
Result: **GLOUCESTER CITY 2 CHELMSFORD CITY 5**
Competition: Southern League Premier Division
Teamsheet: Crompton, Saunders, Criddle, Buckland, Bywater, Blackler, Callinan, Tilley, Bayliss, Cook, Lee
Substitutes: Birkby (for Callinan), Crouch (nps)
Scorers: Cook (pen), Lee
Attendance: 538

Date: Wednesday 19/01/1994
Result: **HEDNESFORD TOWN 0 GLOUCESTER CITY 1**
Competition: Southern League Cup 3rd Round
Teamsheet: Crompton, Saunders, Fishlock, Buckland, Bywater, Blackler, Birkby, BD Hughes, Bayliss, Cook, Crouch
Substitutes: Boyland (for Bayliss), Tilley (nps)
Scorer: Boyland
Attendance: 267

Date: Tuesday 25/01/1994
Result: **GLOUCESTER CITY 0 BURTON ALBION 1**
Competition: Southern League Cup 4th Round
Teamsheet: Crompton, Saunders, Fishlock, Buckland, Bywater, Blackler, Birkby, BD Hughes, Bayliss, Cook, Crouch
Substitutes: Boyland (for Birkby), Webb (for BD Hughes)
Attendance: 314

Date: Saturday 29/01/1994
Result: **WATERLOOVILLE 1 GLOUCESTER CITY 1**
Competition: Southern League Premier Division
Teamsheet: Crompton, Saunders, Criddle, Buckland, Bywater, Blackler, Callinan, Webb, Bayliss, Cook, Crouch
Substitutes: Birkby (for Crouch), Fishlock (for Criddle)
Scorer: Buckland
Attendance: 210

Date: Saturday 05/02/1994
Result: **GLOUCESTER CITY 2 HEDNESFORD TOWN 0**
Competition: Southern League Premier Division
Teamsheet: Crompton, Saunders, Vassell, Buckland, Bywater, Webb, Callinan, BD Hughes, Bayliss, Cook, Gordon
Substitutes: Bloomfield (nps), Blackler (for Cook)
Scorers: Buckland, Bayliss
Attendance: 396

Date: Tuesday 08/02/1994
Result: **HALESOWEN TOWN 0 GLOUCESTER CITY 0**
Competition: Southern League Premier Division
Teamsheet: Crompton, Saunders, Vassell, Buckland, Bywater, Blackler, Callinan, BD Hughes, Bayliss, Cook, Gordon
Substitutes: Fishlock (nps), Bloomfield (for BD Hughes)
Attendance: 459

Date: Saturday 12/02/1994
Result: **HASTINGS TOWN 1 GLOUCESTER CITY 0**
Competition: Southern League Premier Division
Teamsheet: Crompton, Saunders, Vassell, Buckland, Bywater, Webb, Callinan, Bloomfield, Bayliss, Cook, Willetts
Substitutes: Blackler (nps), Johnstone (nps)
Attendance: 333

Date: Saturday 19/02/1994
Result: **GLOUCESTER CITY 0 TROWBRIDGE TOWN 1**
Competition: Southern League Premier Division
Teamsheet: Crompton, Saunders, Cook, Buckland, Bywater, Webb, Callinan, BD Hughes, Bayliss, Hunt, Willetts
Substitutes: Bloomfield (nps), Vassell (for BD Hughes)
Attendance: 510

Date: Tuesday 01/03/1994
Result: **DORCHESTER TOWN 1 GLOUCESTER CITY 2**
Competition: Southern League Premier Division
Teamsheet: R Kemp, Saunders, Vassell, Buckland, Bywater, GJ Kemp, Hunt, Webb, Bayliss, Cook, Willetts
Substitutes: Callinan (for G Kemp), Bloomfield (nps)
Scorers: Webb, Bayliss
Attendance: 450

Date: Saturday 05/03/1994
Result: **MOOR GREEN 3 GLOUCESTER CITY 0**
Competition: Southern League Premier Division
Teamsheet: R Kemp, Saunders, Willetts, Buckland, Bywater, GJ Kemp, Callinan, Webb, Hunt, Cook, Bloomfield
Substitutes: Carty (for Hunt), Fishlock (for Cook)
Attendance: 253

Date: Saturday 12/03/1994
Result: **GLOUCESTER CITY 0 FARNBOROUGH TOWN 1**
Competition: Southern League Premier Division
Teamsheet: Crompton, Saunders, Willetts, Buckland, Bywater, GJ Kemp, Callinan, Webb, Bayliss, Carty, Hunt
Substitutes: Bloomfield (nps), Porter (for Hunt)
Attendance: 486

Date: Tuesday 15/03/1994
Result: **FOREST GREEN ROVERS 2 GLOUCESTER CITY 3** (aet)
Competition: Gloucestershire FA Northern Senior Professional Cup Semi-Final
Teamsheet: Crompton, Saunders, Porter, Buckland, Bywater, GJ Kemp, Callinan, Webb, Bayliss, Carty, Hunt
Substitutes: Bloomfield (for Hunt), Johnstone (nps)
Scorers: Bywater, Callinan, Porter
Attendance: 281

Date: Tuesday 22/03/1994
Result: **NUNEATON BOROUGH 1 GLOUCESTER CITY 3**
Competition: Southern League Premier Division
Teamsheet: Crompton, Saunders, Willetts, Buckland, Bywater, GJ Kemp, Callinan, Webb, Bayliss, Porter, Fishlock
Substitutes: Crouch (nps), Bloomfield (nps)
Scorers: Webb, Bayliss, Bywater
Attendance: 813

Date: Saturday 26/03/1994
Result: **SOLIHULL BOROUGH 2 GLOUCESTER CITY 4**
Competition: Southern League Premier Division
Teamsheet: Crompton, Saunders, Willetts, Buckland, Bywater, GJ Kemp, Crouch, Webb, Bayliss, Porter, Fishlock
Substitutes: Johnstone (nps), BD Hughes (nps)
Scorers: Bayliss (2), Porter, Fishlock
Attendance: 246

Date: Saturday 02/04/1994
Result: **GLOUCESTER CITY 1 WORCESTER CITY 2**
Competition: Southern League Premier Division
Teamsheet: Crompton, Saunders, Willetts, Crouch, Bywater, GJ Kemp, Callinan, Webb, Bayliss, Porter, Fishlock
Substitutes: Buckland (for Callinan), Iddles (for Crouch)
Scorer: Bayliss
Attendance: 624

Date: Monday 04/04/1994
Result: **CHELTENHAM TOWN 0 GLOUCESTER CITY 1**
Competition: Southern League Premier Division
Teamsheet: Crompton, Saunders, Willetts, Crouch, Bywater, GJ Kemp, Callinan, Webb, Bayliss, Porter, Fishlock
Substitutes: Buckland (nps), Iddles (For Porter)
Scorer: Bayliss
Attendance: 1806

Date: Saturday 09/04/1994
Result: **GLOUCESTER CITY 1 BASHLEY 0**
Competition: Southern League Premier Division
Teamsheet: Crompton, Saunders, Willetts, Crouch, Bywater, GJ Kemp, Callinan, Webb, Iddles, Cook, Fishlock
Substitutes: Buckland (for Iddles), Bloomfield (for Crouch)
Scorer: Cook
Attendance: 472

Date: Tuesday 12/04/1994
Result: **AFC NEWPORT 1 GLOUCESTER CITY 0**
Competition: Gloucestershire FA Northern Senior Professional Cup Final
Teamsheet: Crompton, Saunders, Fishlock, Buckland, Bywater, GJ Kemp, Callinan, Webb, Iddles, Cook, Bloomfield
Substitutes: Crouch (nps), Johnstone (for Bloomfield)
Attendance: 410

Date: Saturday 16/04/1994
Result: **ATHERSTONE UNITED 2 GLOUCESTER CITY 1**
Competition: Southern League Premier Division
Teamsheet: Crompton, Saunders, Willetts, Buckland, Bywater, GJ Kemp, Callinan, Crouch, Iddles, Cook, Fishlock
Substitutes: Bloomfield (nps), Webb (nps)
Scorer: Fishlock
Attendance: 277

Date: Saturday 23/04/1994
Result: **GLOUCESTER CITY 2 CAMBRIDGE CITY 1**
Competition: Southern League Premier Division
Teamsheet: Crompton, Saunders, Willetts, Buckland, Bywater, GJ Kemp, Callinan, Crouch, Webb, Cook, Fishlock
Substitutes: Bloomfield (for Willetts), Perris (nps)
Scorers: Cook, Buckland
Attendance: 455

Date: Saturday 30/04/1994
Result: **GRESLEY ROVERS 2 GLOUCESTER CITY 0**
Competition: Southern League Premier Division
Teamsheet: Crompton, Saunders, Willetts, Buckland, Bywater, GJ Kemp, Callinan, Crouch, Johnstone, Webb, Fishlock
Substitutes: Bloomfield (nps), Cook (for Johnstone)
Attendance: 574

Date: Saturday 07/05/1994
Result: **GLOUCESTER CITY 2 NUNEATON BOROUGH 1**
Competition: Southern League Premier Division
Teamsheet: Crompton, Saunders, Willetts, Buckland, Bywater, GJ Kemp, Callinan, Webb, Porter, Cook, Fishlock
Substitutes: Crouch (for Willetts), Johnstone (for Porter)
Scorers: Callinan, Cook
Attendance: 728

Appearances – KA Bayliss 42(2), D Birkby 2(2), MJ Blackler 6(1), P Bloomfield 21(9), M Boyland 12(13), MC Buckland 49(2), PR Bywater 45, TJ Callinan 47(2), PE Carty 2(1), A Cook 43(3), R Criddle 18, SG Crompton 50, SP Crouch 32(1), ME Fishlock 35(4), M Fletcher 1, CK Gordon 2, BD Hughes 25, N Hughes 0(1), P Hunt 5, D Iddles 3(2), M Johnson 0(2), K Johnstone 1(4), GJ Kemp 40, R Kemp 2, J Lee 1, PA Olner 14, D Porter 6(1), MA Saunders 25, G Smith 4(3), DJ Tilley 4(2), RA Vassell 4(1), DA Webb 17(1), KJ Willetts 14.
Others selected but did not play: P Jones, MJ Perris, M Williams.
Scorers – KA Bayliss 21, A Cook 13, MC Buckland 7, TJ Callinan 6, M Boyland 4, PR Bywater 3, ME Fishlock 3, P Bloomfield 2, D Porter 2, DJ Tilley 2, DA Webb 2, N Hughes 1, J Lee 1, PA Olner 1.

SOUTHERN LEAGUE PREMIER DIVISION

POS	CLUB	P	W	D	L	F	A	PTS
1	FARNBOROUGH TOWN	42	25	7	10	74	44	82
2	CHELTENHAM TOWN	42	21	12	9	67	38	75
3	HALESOWEN TOWN	42	21	11	10	69	46	74
4	ATHERSTONE UNITED	42	22	7	13	57	43	73
5	CRAWLEY TOWN	42	21	10	11	56	42	73
6	CHELMSFORD CITY	42	21	7	14	74	59	70
7	TROWBRIDGE TOWN	42	16	17	9	52	41	65
8	SITTINGBOURNE	42	17	13	12	65	48	64
9	CORBY TOWN	42	17	8	17	52	56	59
10	**GLOUCESTER CITY**	**42**	**17**	**6**	**19**	**55**	**60**	**57**
11	BURTON ALBION	42	15	11	16	57	49	56
12	HASTINGS TOWN	42	16	7	19	51	60	55
13	HEDNESFORD TOWN	42	15	9	18	67	66	54
14	GRESLEY ROVERS	42	14	11	17	61	72	53
15	WORCESTER CITY	42	14	9	19	61	70	51
16	SOLIHULL BOROUGH	42	13	11	18	52	57	50
17	CAMBRIDGE CITY	42	13	11	18	50	60	50
18	DORCHESTER TOWN	42	12	11	19	38	51	47
19	MOOR GREEN	42	11	10	21	49	66	43
20	WATERLOOVILLE	42	11	10	21	47	69	43
21	BASHLEY	42	11	10	21	47	80	43
22	NUNEATON BOROUGH	42	11	8	23	42	66	41
		924	354	216	354	1243	1243	1278

SEASON 1994-1995
(Home Ground: City Stadium, Meadow Park, Hempsted)

Date: Saturday 20/08/1994
Result: **GLOUCESTER CITY 3 VALLEY SPORTS RUGBY 0**
Competition: Southern League Premier Division
Teamsheet: Coles, Bird, Lester, Crowley, Kilgour, Shearer, Knight, Mitchell, Hallam, Bayliss, Harris
Substitutes: Kemp (nps), Boden (for Bayliss)
Scorers: Hallam, Bayliss (2)
Attendance: 802

Date: Tuesday 23/08/1994
Result: **CRAWLEY TOWN 0 GLOUCESTER CITY 1**
Competition: Southern League Premier Division
Teamsheet: Coles, Bird, Willetts, Crowley, Kilgour, Lester, Knight, Shearer, Hallam, Mitchell, Boden
Substitutes: Kemp (nps), Harris (for Boden)
Scorer: Shearer
Attendance: 734

Date: Saturday 27/08/1994
Result: **SUDBURY TOWN 0 GLOUCESTER CITY 1**
Competition: Southern League Premier Division
Teamsheet: Coles, Bird, Willetts, Kemp, Kilgour, Lester, Knight, Shearer, Hallam, Mitchell, Harris
Substitutes: Boden (nps), Bayliss (nps)
Scorer: Knight
Attendance: 513

Date: Monday 29/08/1994
Result: **GLOUCESTER CITY 3 GRAVESEND & NORTHFLEET 3**
Competition: Southern League Premier Division
Teamsheet: Coles, Bird, Willetts, Kemp, Kilgour, Lester, Knight, Shearer, Hallam, Mitchell, Bayliss
Substitutes: Harris (nps), Boden (nps)
Scorers: Hallam, Bayliss, Mitchell
Attendance: 906

Date: Saturday 03/09/1994
Result: **GLOUCESTER CITY 2 CHELMSFORD CITY 0**
Competition: Southern League Premier Division
Teamsheet: Coles, Bird, Willetts, Lester, Kilgour, Mitchell, Knight, Shearer, Hallam, Bayliss, Harris
Substitutes: Boden (nps), Callinan (nps)
Scorers: Hallam, Bayliss
Attendance: 733

Date: Tuesday 06/09/1994
Result: **HALESOWEN TOWN 1 GLOUCESTER CITY 1**
Competition: Southern League Premier Division
Teamsheet: Coles, Bird, Willetts, Lester, Kilgour, Mitchell, Knight, Shearer, Hallam, Bayliss, Harris
Substitutes: Boden (for Bayliss), Callinan (nps)
Scorer: Knight
Attendance: 674

Date: Saturday 10/09/1994
Result: **GLOUCESTER CITY 3 EXMOUTH TOWN 0**
Competition: FA Cup 1st Qualifying Round
Teamsheet: Coles, Bird, Willetts, Lester, Kilgour, Mitchell, Knight, Shearer, Hallam, Bayliss, Harris
Substitutes: Kemp (nps), Boden (for Bayliss)
Scorers: Mitchell, Knight (2, 1 pen)
Attendance: 557

Date: Saturday 17/09/1994
Result: **GLOUCESTER CITY 1 WEYMOUTH 0**
Competition: FA Trophy 1st Qualifying Round
Teamsheet: Coles, Bird, Willetts, Lester, Kilgour, Mitchell, Knight, Shearer, Hallam, Bayliss, Harris
Substitutes: Kemp (for Lester), Boden (for Bayliss)
Scorer: Kilgour
Attendance: 558

Date: Saturday 24/09/1994
Result: **GLOUCESTER CITY 7 MERTHYR TYDFIL 1**
Competition: FA Cup 2nd Qualifying Round
Teamsheet: Coles, Bird, Willetts, Kemp, Kilgour, Shearer, Knight, Mitchell, Hallam, Boden, Harris
Substitutes: Bayliss (for Knight), Hughes (for Hallam)
Scorers: Hallam (2), Mitchell (3), Kilgour, Knight
Attendance: 746

Date: Tuesday 27/09/1994
Result: **CLEVEDON TOWN 0 GLOUCESTER CITY 1**
Competition: Southern League Cup 1st Round 1st Leg
Teamsheet: Coles, Willetts, Lester, Kemp, Kilgour, Shearer, Hughes, Mitchell, Hallam, Boden, Harris
Substitutes: Bayliss (nps), Callinan (nps)
Scorer: Mitchell
Attendance: 285

Date: Saturday 01/10/1994
Result: **GLOUCESTER CITY 1 BURTON ALBION 0**
Competition: Southern League Premier Division
Teamsheet: Coles, Bird, Willetts, Kemp, Kilgour, Shearer, Knight, Mitchell, Hallam, Boden, Harris
Substitutes: Bayliss (nps), Lester (nps)
Scorer: Mitchell
Attendance: 704

Date: Tuesday 04/10/1994
Result: **AFC NEWPORT 1 GLOUCESTER CITY 1** (4-3 pens)
Competition: Gloucestershire FA Northern Senior Professional Cup Semi-Final
Teamsheet: Coles, Bird, Jackson, Kemp, Crowley, Lester, Knight, Callinan, Bayliss, Boden, Peacey
Substitutes: Harris (for Peacey), Hughes (for Callinan)
Scorer: Bayliss
Attendance: 313

Date: Saturday 08/10/1994
Result: **GLOUCESTER CITY 2 CINDERFORD TOWN 0**
Competition: FA Cup 3rd Qualifying Round
Teamsheet: Coles, Bird, Willetts, Kemp, Kilgour, Shearer, Knight, Mitchell, Hallam, Boden, Harris
Substitutes: Bayliss (nps), Lester (for Harris)
Scorers: Hallam, Mitchell
Attendance: 1022

Date: Saturday 15/10/1994
Result: **GLOUCESTER CITY 3 FAREHAM TOWN 0**
Competition: FA Trophy 2nd Qualifying Round
Teamsheet: Coles, Bird, Lester, Kemp, Kilgour, Crowley, Knight, Mitchell, Boden, Shearer, Willetts
Substitutes: Bayliss (for Boden), Harris (for Shearer)
Scorers: Lester, Knight (pen), Kilgour
Attendance: 531

Date: Tuesday 18/10/1994
Result: **GLOUCESTER CITY 2 CLEVEDON TOWN 1**
Competition: Southern League Cup 1st Round 2nd Leg
Teamsheet: Coles, Jackson, Howell, Bird, Crowley, Lester, Knight, Shearer, Boden, Bayliss, Harris
Substitutes: Peacey (for Harris), Hughes (nps)
Scorer: Bayliss (2)
Attendance: 238

Date: Saturday 22/10/1994
Result: **GLOUCESTER CITY 1 WORTHING 1**
Competition: FA Cup 4th Qualifying Round
Teamsheet: Coles, Bird, Howell, Lester, Crowley, Mitchell, Knight, Boden, Hallam, Bayliss, Harris
Substitutes: Peacey (for Mitchell), Hughes (nps)
Scorer: Crowley
Attendance: 1013

Date: Tuesday 25/10/1994
Result: **WORTHING 2 GLOUCESTER CITY 1**
Competition: FA Cup 4th Qualifying Round Replay
Teamsheet: Coles, Bird, Howell, Lester, Kilgour, Crowley, Knight, Boden, Hallam, Mitchell, Harris
Substitutes: Jackson (for Bird), Bayliss (for Kilgour)
Scorer: Hallam
Attendance: 1187

Date: Saturday 29/10/1994
Result: **RUSHDEN & DIAMONDS 1 GLOUCESTER CITY 2**
Competition: Southern League Premier Division
Teamsheet: Coles, Bird, Howell, Crowley, Kilgour, Lester, Knight, Mitchell, Hallam, Bayliss, Harris
Substitutes: Boden (for Bayliss), Hughes (nps)
Scorers: Howell, Mitchell
Attendance: 1553

Date: Saturday 05/11/1994
Result: **GLOUCESTER CITY 1 WORCESTER CITY 2**
Competition: Southern League Premier Division
Teamsheet: Coles, Bird, Lester, Crowley, Kilgour, Adebowale, Knight, Mitchell, Hallam, Shearer, Harris
Substitutes: Bayliss (for Mitchell), Howell (for Knight)
Scorer: Crowley
Attendance: 1127

Date: Monday 07/11/1994
Result: **WORCESTER CITY 2 GLOUCESTER CITY 1**
Competition: Southern League Cup 2nd Round
Teamsheet: Coles, Bird, Howell, Crowley, Kilgour, Lester, Adebowale, Shearer, Hallam, Bayliss, Harris
Substitutes: Boden (for Howell), Mitchell (for Kilgour)
Scorer: Bird
Attendance: 654

Date: Saturday 12/11/1994
Result: **CORBY TOWN 0 GLOUCESTER CITY 6**
Competition: Southern League Premier Division
Teamsheet: Coles, Bird, Lester, Kemp, Kilgour, Adebowale, Knight, Mitchell, Hallam, Shearer, Harris
Substitutes: Bayliss (for Mitchell), Willetts (for Bird)
Scorers: Hallam (3), Knight, Mitchell, Harris
Attendance: 238

Date: Tuesday 15/11/1994
Result: **GRAVESEND & NORTHFLEET 1 GLOUCESTER CITY 0**
Competition: Southern League Premier Division
Teamsheet: Coles, Bird, Lester, Kemp, Kilgour, Shearer, Knight, Mitchell, Hallam, Adebowale, Bayliss
Substitutes: Harris (for Mitchell), Willetts (for Kilgour)
Attendance: 606

Date: Saturday 19/11/1994
Result: **GLOUCESTER CITY 0 SITTINGBOURNE 0**
Competition: Southern League Premier Division
Teamsheet: Coles, Bird, Howell, Kemp, Kilgour, Lester, Knight, Shearer, Hallam, Adebowale, Harris
Substitutes: Bayliss (for Shearer), Mitchell (nps)
Attendance: 701

Date: Saturday 26/11/1994
Result: **GLOUCESTER CITY 0 CHELMSFORD CITY 2**
Competition: FA Trophy 3rd Qualifying Round
Teamsheet: Coles, Bird, Lester, Crowley, Kilgour, Kemp, Knight, Mitchell, Hallam, Shearer, Harris
Substitutes: Howell (nps), Willetts (for Kilgour)
Attendance: 576

Date: Saturday 03/12/1994
Result: **GRESLEY ROVERS 3 GLOUCESTER CITY 2**
Competition: Southern League Premier Division
Teamsheet: Coles, Bird, Lester, Kemp, Kilgour, Crowley, Mitchell, Adebowale, Hallam, Portway, Bayliss
Substitutes: Harris (for Bayliss), Willetts (for Kemp)
Scorers: Portway, Bird
Attendance: 649

Date: Tuesday 06/12/1994
Result: **GLOUCESTER CITY 4 CRAWLEY TOWN 1**
Competition: Southern League Premier Division
Teamsheet: Coles, Bird, Lester, Crowley, Kilgour, Kemp, Knight, Adebowale, Hallam, Portway, Mitchell
Substitutes: Bayliss (for Crowley), Willetts (for Lester)
Scorers: Adebowale, Kilgour, Mitchell, Portway
Attendance: 443

Date: Saturday 10/12/1994
Result: **GLOUCESTER CITY 4 ATHERSTONE UNITED 0**
Competition: Southern League Premier Division
Teamsheet: Coles, Bird, Willetts, Kemp, Crowley, Shearer, Knight, Adebowale, Hallam, Portway, Mitchell
Substitutes: Bayliss (for Portway), Harris (for Shearer)
Scorers: Adebowale, Mitchell (2), Hallam
Attendance: 573

Date: Saturday 17/12/1994
Result: **HEDNESFORD TOWN 1 GLOUCESTER CITY 3**
Competition: Southern League Premier Division
Teamsheet: Coles, Bird, Willetts, Crowley, Kilgour, Kemp, Knight, Adebowale, Hallam, Shearer, Mitchell
Substitutes: Harris (nps), Lester (nps)
Scorers: Kilgour, Adebowale (2)
Attendance: 995

Date: Tuesday 20/12/1994
Result: **GLOUCESTER CITY 3 GRESLEY ROVERS 3**
Competition: Southern League Premier Division
Teamsheet: Coles, Bird, Willetts, Kemp, Crowley, Lester, Knight, Shearer, Hallam, Adebowale, Mitchell
Substitutes: Harris (for Shearer), Bayliss (for Lester)
Scorers: Adebowale (2), Mitchell
Attendance: 803

Date: Monday 26/12/1994
Result: **GLOUCESTER CITY 1 CHELTENHAM TOWN 2**
Competition: Southern League Premier Division
Teamsheet: Coles, Bird, Willetts, Kemp, Kilgour, Crowley, Knight, Shearer, Hallam, Adebowale, Mitchell
Substitutes: Harris (for Shearer), Portway (for Kemp)
Scorer: Crowley
Attendance: 3018

Date: Saturday 31/12/1994
Result: **GLOUCESTER CITY 2 LEEK TOWN 0**
Competition: Southern League Premier Division
Teamsheet: Coles, Bird, Willetts, Kemp, Kilgour, Adebowale, Knight, Shearer, Hallam, Portway, Mitchell
Substitutes: Harris (nps), Lester (for Mitchell)
Scorers: Kilgour, Mitchell
Attendance: 832

Date: Monday 02/01/1995
Result: **DORCHESTER TOWN 4 GLOUCESTER CITY 2**
Competition: Southern League Premier Division
Teamsheet: Coles, Bird, Willetts, Kemp, Kilgour, Adebowale, Knight, Shearer, Hallam, Portway, Lester
Substitutes: Harris (for Lester), Crowley
Scorers: Willetts, Portway
Attendance: 1118

Date: Saturday 07/01/1995
Result: **SITTINGBOURNE 2 GLOUCESTER CITY 1**
Competition: Southern League Premier Division
Teamsheet: Coles, Jackson, Howell, Bird, Kilgour, Crowley, Knight, Adebowale, Hallam, Portway, Harris
Substitutes: Hughes (for Knight), Mitchell (for Crowley)
Scorer: Portway
Attendance: 569

Date: Saturday 14/01/1995
Result: **GLOUCESTER CITY 3 SUDBURY TOWN 0**
Competition: Southern League Premier Division
Teamsheet: Coles, Jackson, Willetts, Bird, Kemp, Shearer, Knight, Adebowale, Hallam, Portway, Mitchell
Substitutes: Harris (for Shearer), Lester (nps)
Scorers: Hallam (2), Portway
Attendance: 672

Date: Saturday 28/01/1995
Result: **BURTON ALBION 0 GLOUCESTER CITY 1**
Competition: Southern League Premier Division
Teamsheet: Coles, Jackson, Willetts, Lester, Bird, Adebowale, Knight, Dobbins, Hallam, Portway, Harris
Substitutes: McCluskey (nps), Hughes (nps)
Scorer: Knight (pen)
Attendance: 744

Date: Wednesday 01/02/1995
Result: **SOLIHULL BOROUGH 1 GLOUCESTER CITY 2**
Competition: Southern League Premier Division
Teamsheet: Coles, Jackson, Willetts, Lester, Bird, Adebowale, Knight, Dobbins, Hallam, Portway, Harris
Substitutes: McCluskey (nps), Hughes (nps)
Scorer: Portway (2)
Attendance: 214

Date: Saturday 04/02/1995
Result: **WORCESTER CITY 0 GLOUCESTER CITY 1**
Competition: Southern League Premier Division
Teamsheet: Coles, Jackson, Willetts, Cann, Kemp, Adebowale, Knight, Dobbins, Hallam, Portway, Bird
Substitutes: Lester (for Dobbins), Harris (nps)
Scorer: Portway
Attendance: 1036

Date: Tuesday 07/02/1995
Result: **GLOUCESTER CITY 5 CAMBRIDGE CITY 1**
Competition: Southern League Premier Division
Teamsheet: Coles, Jackson, Willetts, Cann, Kemp, Lester, Knight, Adebowale, Hallam, Portway, Bird
Substitutes: Kilgour (nps), Hughes (nps)
Scorers: Kemp, Adebowale, Hallam, Portway (2)
Attendance: 603

Date: Saturday 11/02/1995
Result: **GLOUCESTER CITY 1 HASTINGS TOWN 0**
Competition: Southern League Premier Division
Teamsheet: Coles, Jackson, Willetts, Cann, Kemp, Bird, Knight, Dobbins, Adebowale, Portway, Ullathorne
Substitutes: Lester (for Dobbins), Kilgour (for Jackson)
Scorer: Bird
Attendance: 742

Date: Saturday 18/02/1995
Result: **TROWBRIDGE TOWN 1 GLOUCESTER CITY 2**
Competition: Southern League Premier Division
Teamsheet: Coles, Cann, Willetts, Kemp, Kilgour, Lester, Knight, Bird, Adebowale, Portway, Ullathorne
Substitutes: Harris (nps), Jackson (nps)
Scorer: Knight (2, 1 pen)
Attendance: 606

Date: Saturday 04/03/1995
Result: **GLOUCESTER CITY 2 CORBY TOWN 2**
Competition: Southern League Premier Division
Teamsheet: Coles, Bird, Willetts, Cann, Kemp, Lester, Knight, Adebowale, Hallam, Portway, Ullathorne
Substitutes: Harris (nps), Mitchell (nps)
Scorers: Kemp, Portway
Attendance: 823

Date: Monday 06/03/1995
Result: **CHELMSFORD CITY 0 GLOUCESTER CITY 2**
Competition: Southern League Premier Division
Teamsheet: Coles, Jackson, Willetts, Kemp, Kilgour, Lester, Bird, Mitchell, Hallam, Portway, Ullathorne
Substitutes: Harris (nps), Cann (nps)
Scorers: Ullathorne, Hallam
Attendance: 536

Date: Saturday 11/03/1995
Result: **HASTINGS TOWN 2 GLOUCESTER CITY 1**
Competition: Southern League Premier Division
Teamsheet: Coles, Jackson, Willetts, Kemp, Kilgour, Adebowale, Bird, Lester, Hallam, Portway, Ullathorne
Substitutes: Mitchell (for Jackson), Knight (for Willetts)
Scorer: own goal
Attendance: 501

Date: Saturday 18/03/1995
Result: **GLOUCESTER CITY 1 RUSHDEN & DIAMONDS 0**
Competition: Southern League Premier Division
Teamsheet: Coles, Bird, Lester, Kemp, Kilgour, Dobbins, Knight, Adebowale, Hallam, Portway, Ullathorne
Substitutes: Willetts (nps), Mitchell (for Portway)
Scorer: Knight
Attendance: 614

Date: Tuesday 21/03/1995
Result: **GLOUCESTER CITY 1 HALESOWEN TOWN 2**
Competition: Southern League Premier Division
Teamsheet: Coles, Bird, Lester, Kemp, Kilgour, Mitchell, Knight, Adebowale, Hallam, Harris, Ullathorne
Substitutes: Dobbins (for Mitchell), Cann (nps)
Scorer: Ullathorne
Attendance: 817

Date: Saturday 25/03/1995
Result: **CAMBRIDGE CITY 0 GLOUCESTER CITY 1**
Competition: Southern League Premier Division
Teamsheet: Coles, Bird, Reeves, Kemp, Cann, Lester, Knight, Adebowale, Hallam, Dobbins, Ullathorne
Substitutes: Willetts (nps), Harris (nps)
Scorer: Hallam
Attendance: 468

Date: Wednesday 29/03/1995
Result: **VALLEY SPORTS RUGBY 3 GLOUCESTER CITY 3**
Competition: Southern League Premier Division
Teamsheet: Coles, Bird, Reeves, Kemp, Cann, Dobbins, Knight, Adebowale, Hallam, Holmes, Ullathorne
Substitutes: Willetts (nps), Lester (nps)
Scorers: Knight, Adebowale, Hallam
Attendance: 414

Date: Saturday 01/04/1995
Result: **GLOUCESTER CITY 2 TROWBRIDGE TOWN 0**
Competition: Southern League Premier Division
Teamsheet: Coles, Bird, Reeves, Kemp, Cann, Lester, Knight, Adebowale, Hallam, Holmes, Ullathorne
Substitutes: Harris (pen), Mitchell (nps)
Scorers: Hallam, Holmes
Attendance: 855

Date: Saturday 08/04/1995
Result: **LEEK TOWN 3 GLOUCESTER CITY 1**
Competition: Southern League Premier Division
Teamsheet: Coles, Willetts, Reeves, Cann, Kemp, Lester, Bird, Adebowale, Hallam, Holmes, Ullathorne
Substitutes: Mitchell (for Lester), Knight (for Ullathorne)
Scorer: Holmes
Attendance: 340

Date: Saturday 15/04/1995
Result: **GLOUCESTER CITY 0 DORCHESTER TOWN 3**
Competition: Southern League Premier Division
Teamsheet: Coles, Bird, Reeves, Kemp, Cann, Willetts, Knight, Adebowale, Hallam, Holmes, Ullathorne
Substitutes: Lester (nps), Kilgour (nps)
Attendance: 732

Date: Monday 17/04/1995
Result: **CHELTENHAM TOWN 1 GLOUCESTER CITY 1**
Competition: Southern League Premier Division
Teamsheet: Coles, Cann, Reeves, Kemp, Kilgour, Lester, Knight, Adebowale, Hallam, Holmes, Bird
Substitutes: Willetts (nps), Ullathorne (nps)
Scorer: Holmes
Attendance: 2691

Date: Saturday 22/04/1995
Result: **GLOUCESTER CITY 2 HEDNESFORD TOWN 2**
Competition: Southern League Premier Division
Teamsheet: Coles, Cann, Lester, Kemp, Kilgour, Bird, Knight, Adebowale, Hallam, Holmes, Ullathorne
Substitutes: Harris (for Kilgour), Willetts (nps)
Scorers: Hallam, Ullathorne
Attendance: 1123

Date: Saturday 29/04/1995
Result: **ATHERSTONE UNITED 1 GLOUCESTER CITY 0**
Competition: Southern League Premier Division
Teamsheet: Coles, Cann, Lester, Kemp, Kilgour, Bird, Knight, Adebowale, Hallam, Holmes, Ullathorne
Substitutes: Portway (for Kilgour), Harris (nps)
Attendance: 405

Date: Saturday 06/05/1995
Result: **GLOUCESTER CITY 1 SOLIHULL BOROUGH 2**
Competition: Southern League Premier Division
Teamsheet: Coles, Bird, Willetts, Kemp, Kilgour, Lester, Knight, Adebowale, Hallam, Holmes, Ullathorne
Substitutes: Cann (nps), Portway (nps)
Scorer: Hallam
Attendance: 802

Appearances – AA Adebowale 34, KA Bayliss 13(9), AM Bird 53, R Boden 10(6), TJ Callinan 1, DJ Cann 13, DA Coles 54, RS Crowley 18, LW Dobbins 7(1), MJHallam 49, AG Harris 23(11), DJ Holmes 8, I Howell 7(1), BD Hughes 1(3), T Jackson 11(1), GJ Kemp 39(1), M Kilgour 37(1), K Knight 48(2), S Lester 41(4), D Mitchell 30(5), C Peacey 1(2), SL Portway 17(3), N Reeves 6, M Shearer 27, S Ullathorne 15, KJ Willetts 31(5).
Others selected but did not play: DM McCluskey.
Scorers – MJ Hallam 19, D Mitchell 15, K Knight 12, SL Portway 11, AA Adebowale 8, KA Bayliss 7, M Kilgour 6, AM Bird 3, RS Crowley 3, D Holmes 3, S Ullathorne 3, GJ Kemp 2, AG Harris 1, I Howell 1, S Lester 1, M Shearer 1, KJ Willetts 1, own goal 1.

PROGRAMME

PROGRAMME

PROGRAMME

1993-1994

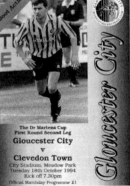

1994-1995

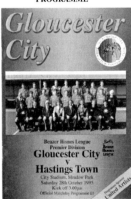

1995-1996

SOUTHERN LEAGUE PREMIER DIVISION

POS	CLUB	P	W	D	L	F	A	PTS
1	HEDNESFORD TOWN	42	28	9	5	99	49	93
2	CHELTENHAM TOWN	42	25	11	6	87	39	86
3	BURTON ALBION	42	20	15	7	55	39	75
4	**GLOUCESTER CITY**	**42**	**22**	**8**	**12**	**76**	**48**	**74**
5	RUSHDEN & DIAMONDS	42	19	11	12	99	65	68
6	DORCHESTER TOWN	42	19	10	13	84	61	67
7	LEEK TOWN	42	19	10	13	72	60	67
8	GRESLEY ROVERS	42	17	12	13	70	63	63
9	CAMBRIDGE CITY	42	18	8	16	60	55	62
10	WORCESTER CITY	42	14	15	13	46	34	57
11	CRAWLEY TOWN	42	15	10	17	64	71	55
12	HASTINGS TOWN	42	13	14	15	55	57	53
13	HALESOWEN TOWN	42	14	10	18	81	80	52
14	GRAVESEND & NORTHFLEET	42	13	13	16	38	55	52
15	CHELMSFORD CITY	42	14	6	22	56	60	48
16	ATHERSTONE UNITED	42	12	12	18	51	67	48
17	VALLEY SPORTS RUGBY	42	11	14	17	49	61	47
18	SUDBURY TOWN	42	12	10	20	50	77	46
19	SOLIHULL BOROUGH	42	10	15	17	39	65	45
20	SITTINGBOURNE	42	11	10	21	51	73	43
21	TROWBRIDGE TOWN	42	9	13	20	43	69	40
22	CORBY TOWN	42	4	10	28	36	113	21*
		924	339	246	339	1361	1361	1262

* One point deducted for fielding ineligible player.

SEASON 1995-1996
(Home Ground: City Stadium, Meadow Park, Hempsted)

Date: Saturday 19/08/1995
Result: **GLOUCESTER CITY 5 CHELMSFORD CITY 0**
Competition: Southern League Premier Division
Teamsheet: Coles, Dobbins, Reeves, Bird, Kemp, Rouse, Knight, Adebowale, Hallam, Holmes, Warner
Substitutes: Kilgour (nps), Lester (nps), Webb (nps)
Scorers: Rouse, Knight, Adebowale, Hallam, Holmes
Attendance: 764

Date: Wednesday 23/08/1995
Result: **AFC NEWPORT 1 GLOUCESTER CITY 0**
Competition: Southern League Premier Division
Teamsheet: Coles, Dobbins, Reeves, Bird, Kemp, Rouse, Knight, Adebowale, Hallam, Holmes, Warner
Substitutes: Kilgour (nps), Lester (nps), Webb (for Warner)
Attendance: 1524

Date: Saturday 26/08/1995
Result: **CAMBRIDGE CITY 0 GLOUCESTER CITY 4**
Competition: Southern League Premier Division
Teamsheet: Coles, Dobbins, Reeves, Bird, Kemp, Rouse, Knight, Adebowale, Hallam, Holmes, Portway
Substitutes: Webb (nps), Lester (for Reeves), Warner (for Portway)
Scorers: Adebowale, Hallam, Holmes, Portway
Attendance: 342

Date: Monday 28/08/1995
Result: **GLOUCESTER CITY 2 SALISBURY CITY 0**
Competition: Southern League Premier Division
Teamsheet: Coles, Dobbins, Lester, Bird, Kemp, Rouse, Knight, Adebowale, Hallam, Holmes, Portway
Substitutes: Kilgour (nps), Warner (for Hallam), Webb (nps)
Scorers: Kemp, Portway
Attendance: 1576

Date: Saturday 02/09/1995
Result: **GLOUCESTER CITY 3 GRAVESEND & NORTHFLEET 1**
Competition: Southern League Premier Division
Teamsheet: Coles, Dobbins, Lester, Bird, Kemp, Rouse, Knight, Adebowale, Holmes, Webb, Portway
Substitutes: Kilgour (nps), Warner (nps), Adams (for Portway)
Scorers: Knight, Holmes (2)
Attendance: 851

Date: Tuesday 05/09/1995
Result: **HALESOWEN TOWN 2 GLOUCESTER CITY 1**
Competition: Southern League Premier Division
Teamsheet: Coles, Dobbins, Lester, Bird, Kemp, Rouse, Knight, Adebowale, Holmes, Webb, Portway
Substitutes: Kilgour (nps), Warner (for Webb), Adams (for Portway)
Scorer: Knight
Attendance: 678

Date: Saturday 09/09/1995
Result: **GLOUCESTER CITY 8 BRISTOL MANOR FARM 0**
Competition: FA Cup 1st Qualifying Round
Teamsheet: Coles, Dobbins, Lester, Bird, Kemp, Rouse, Knight, Adebowale, Holmes, Webb, Portway
Substitutes: Kilgour (for Dobbins), Warner (for Holmes), Adams (for Lester)
Scorers: Rouse, Knight (pen), Adebowale, Webb, Portway (2), Warner, Adams
Attendance: 514

Date: Saturday 16/09/1995
Result: **GLOUCESTER CITY 2 BURTON ALBION 1**
Competition: Southern League Premier Division
Teamsheet: Coles, Bird, Rouse, Kemp, Freeman, Webb, Knight, Adebowale, Hallam, Holmes, Portway
Substitutes: Dobbins (nps), Lester (nps), Adams (for Portway)
Scorers: Adebowale, Holmes
Attendance: 867

Date: Tuesday 19/09/1995
Result: **GLOUCESTER CITY 1 AFC NEWPORT 1**
Competition: Southern League Premier Division
Teamsheet: Coles, Bird, Dobbins, Kemp, Freeman, Rouse, Knight, Adebowale, Hallam, Holmes, Portway
Substitutes: Webb (nps), Lester (nps), Adams (for Portway)
Scorer: Knight (pen)
Attendance: 1412

Date: Saturday 23/09/1995
Result: **GLOUCESTER CITY 0 CINDERFORD TOWN 1**
Competition: FA Cup 2nd Qualifying Round
Teamsheet: Coles, Dobbins, Reeves, Bird, Kemp, Rouse, Knight, Webb, Hallam, Holmes, Portway
Substitutes: Adams (for Reeves), Lester (for Webb), Cornwall (nps)
Attendance: 921

Date: Saturday 30/09/1995
Result: **SUDBURY TOWN 0 GLOUCESTER CITY 2**
Competition: Southern League Premier Division
Teamsheet: Coles, Dobbins, Reeves, Bird, Kemp, Rouse, Knight, Webb, Hallam, Holmes, Portway
Substitutes: Freeman (nps), Lester (for Adams), Adams (for Portway)
Scorers: Holmes, Knight
Attendance: 421

Date: Tuesday 03/10/1995
Result: **FOREST GREEN ROVERS 1 GLOUCESTER CITY 2**
Competition: Gloucestershire FA Northern Senior Professional Cup Quarter-Final
Teamsheet: Coles, Bird, Reeves, Kemp, Freeman, Rouse, Knight, Adebowale, Holmes, Phillips, Dobbins
Substitutes: Lester (nps), Adams (nps), Hallam (for Knight)
Scorers: Adebowale, Holmes
Attendance: 215

Date: Saturday 07/10/1995
Result: **CRAWLEY TOWN 0 GLOUCESTER CITY 0**
Competition: Southern League Premier Division
Teamsheet: Coles, Bird, Reeves, Kemp, Freeman, Rouse, Dobbins, Adebowale, Holmes, Webb, Portway
Substitutes: Hallam (nps), Adams (nps), Phillips (nps)
Attendance: 855

Date: Tuesday 10/10/1995
Result: **WITNEY TOWN 1 GLOUCESTER CITY 0**
Competition: Southern League Cup 1st Round 1st Leg
Teamsheet: Coles, Lester, Reeves, Kemp, Freeman, Phillips, Webb, Adebowale, Portway, Holmes, Dobbins
Substitutes: Hallam (for Portway), Adams (for Phillips), Medcroft (nps)
Attendance: 177

Date: Saturday 14/10/1995
Result: **GLOUCESTER CITY 2 WORCESTER CITY 1**
Competition: Southern League Premier Division
Teamsheet: Hamblin, Bird, Reeves, Kemp, Freeman, Rouse, Knight, Adebowale, Hallam, Holmes, Dobbins
Substitutes: Webb (nps), Phillips (nps), Adams (nps)
Scorers: Adebowale, Hallam
Attendance: 1285

Date: Tuesday 17/10/1995
Result: **GLOUCESTER CITY 3 WITNEY TOWN 0**
Competition: Southern League Cup 1st Round 2nd Leg
Teamsheet: Hamblin, Bird, Reeves, Kemp, Freeman, Rouse, Knight, Adams, Hallam, Holmes, Dobbins
Substitutes: Webb (for Dobbins), Phillips (for Knight), Wollen (nps)
Scorers: Holmes, Hallam (2)
Attendance: 276

Date: Saturday 21/10/1995
Result: **CHELMSFORD CITY 1 GLOUCESTER CITY 1**
Competition: Southern League Premier Division
Teamsheet: Hamblin, Bird, Reeves, Kemp, Freeman, Rouse, Webb, Adebowale, Hallam, Holmes, Milsom
Substitutes: Lester (nps), Phillips (nps), Adams (nps)
Scorer: Milsom
Attendance: 804

Date: Wednesday 25/10/1995
Result: **SALISBURY CITY 3 GLOUCESTER CITY 3**
Competition: Southern League Premier Division
Teamsheet: Hamblin, Bird, Reeves, Freeman, Kemp, Rouse, Webb, Phillips, Hallam, Milsom, Lester
Substitutes: Wollen (for Freeman), Adams (nps), Medcroft (nps)
Scorers: Milsom (2), Phillips
Attendance: 583

Date: Saturday 28/10/1995
Result: **GLOUCESTER CITY 0 HASTINGS TOWN 2**
Competition: Southern League Premier Division
Teamsheet: Hamblin, Wollen, Reeves, Bird, Kemp, Rouse, Lester, Webb, Hallam, Milsom, Phillips
Substitutes: Adams (for Wollen), Cornwall (for Rouse)
Attendance: 712

Date: Saturday 04/11/1995
Result: **ILKESTON TOWN 1 GLOUCESTER CITY 2**
Competition: Southern League Premier Division
Teamsheet: Hamblin, Dobbins, Reeves, Bird, Kemp, Rouse, Webb, Lester, Hallam, Milsom, Phillips
Substitutes: Freeman (nps), Holmes (for Webb), Adams (nps)
Scorers: Kemp, Phillips
Attendance: 751

Date: Saturday 11/11/1995
Result: **STAFFORD RANGERS 3 GLOUCESTER CITY 4**
Competition: Southern League Premier Division
Teamsheet: Hamblin, Bird, Reeves, Freeman, Kemp, Rouse, Dobbins, Webb, Milsom, Holmes, Phillips
Substitutes: Lester (nps), Wollen (nps), Medcroft (nps)
Scorers: Webb, Holmes, Phillips, Milsom
Attendance: 543

Date: Tuesday 14/11/1995
Result: **GLOUCESTER CITY 0 HALESOWEN TOWN 2**
Competition: Southern League Premier Division
Teamsheet: Coles, Bird, Reeves, Freeman, Kemp, Rouse, Dobbins, Webb, Milsom, Holmes, Phillips
Substitutes: Knight (for Rouse), Lester (nps), Hamblin (nps)
Attendance: 578

Date: Saturday 18/11/1995
Result: **GLOUCESTER CITY 3 BALDOCK TOWN 1**
Competition: Southern League Premier Division
Teamsheet: Coles, Wollen, Reeves, Bird, Freeman, Rouse, Knight, Webb, Milsom, Holmes, Adebowale
Substitutes: Lester (nps), Phillips (nps), Cornwall (nps)
Scorers: Holmes, Milsom (2)
Attendance: 584

Date: Saturday 25/11/1995
Result: **GLOUCESTER CITY 5 ALDERSHOT TOWN 1**
Competition: FA Trophy 3rd Qualifying Round
Teamsheet: Coles, Dobbins, Reeves, Bird, Freeman, Rouse, Hallam, Webb, Milsom, Holmes, Adebowale
Substitutes: Lester (for Dobbins), Knight (nps), Wollen (nps)
Scorers: Adebowale, Holmes (2), Webb, Milsom
Attendance: 1041

Date: Saturday 02/12/1995
Result: **WORCESTER CITY 1 GLOUCESTER CITY 3**
Competition: Southern League Premier Division
Teamsheet: Coles, Dobbins, Reeves, Bird, Freeman, Rouse, Hallam, Webb, Milsom, Holmes, Adebowale
Substitutes: Knight (nps), Lester (nps), Wollen (nps)
Scorers: Webb, Hallam, own goal
Attendance: 1109

Date: Tuesday 05/12/1995
Result: **CHELTENHAM TOWN 4 GLOUCESTER CITY 0**
Competition: Southern League Cup 2nd Round
Teamsheet: Coles, Dobbins, Reeves, Bird, Freeman, Rouse, Hallam, Webb, Milsom, Holmes, Adebowale
Substitutes: Knight (for Adebowale), Lester (nps), Kemp (for Dobbins)
Attendance: 551

Date: Saturday 09/12/1995
Result: **GLOUCESTER CITY 3 CAMBRIDGE CITY 1**
Competition: Southern League Premier Division
Teamsheet: Coles, Bird, Rouse, Kemp, Freeman, Phillips, Knight, Webb, Milsom, Holmes, Adebowale
Substitutes: Hallam (nps), Lester (for Knight), Hughes (nps)
Scorers: Phillips (2), Knight (pen)
Attendance: 666

Date: Tuesday 12/12/1995
Result: **RUSHDEN & DIAMONDS 3 GLOUCESTER CITY 2**
Competition: Southern League Premier Division
Teamsheet: Coles, Bird, Reeves, Kemp, Freeman, Rouse, Knight, Webb, Milsom, Holmes, Adebowale
Substitutes: Hallam (for Rouse), Lester (for Freeman), Hamblin (nps)
Scorers: Milsom, Adebowale
Attendance: 1666

Date: Saturday 23/12/1995
Result: **GLOUCESTER CITY 1 ATHERSTONE UNITED 2**
Competition: Southern League Premier Division
Teamsheet: Coles, Bird, Reeves, Kemp, Freeman, Rouse, Knight, Webb, Milsom, Holmes, Adebowale
Substitutes: Hallam (for Rouse), Lester (nps), Webber (nps)
Scorer: Knight
Attendance: 615

Date: Saturday 06/01/1996
Result: **VALLEY SPORTS RUGBY 1 GLOUCESTER CITY 2**
Competition: Southern League Premier Division
Teamsheet: Coles, Lester, Reeves, Kemp, Bird, Rouse, Phillips, Webb, Hallam, Holmes, Adebowale
Substitutes: Knight (nps), Freeman (for Webb), Webber (nps)
Scorers: Rouse, Hallam
Attendance: 446

Date: Saturday 13/01/1996
Result: **GLOUCESTER CITY 3 MERTHYR TYDFIL 1**
Competition: Southern League Premier Division
Teamsheet: Coles, Bird, Lester, Kemp, Adebowale, Rouse, Knight, Webb, Hallam, Holmes, Phillips
Substitutes: Freeman (nps), Reeves (nps), Webber (nps)
Scorers: Webb, Hallam (2)
Attendance: 781

Date: Saturday 20/01/1996
Result: **GLOUCESTER CITY 5 STAINES TOWN 0**
Competition: FA Trophy 1st Round
Teamsheet: Coles, Bird, Lester, Kemp, Freeman, Reeves, Knight, Webb, Hallam, Holmes, Phillips
Substitutes: Milsom (nps), Portway (for Phillips), Hughes (for Kemp)
Scorers: Knight, Phillips, Hallam (2), Portway
Attendance: 748

Date: Saturday 03/02/1996
Result: **GLOUCESTER CITY 1 CRAWLEY TOWN 1**
Competition: Southern League Premier Division
Teamsheet: Coles, Webb, Reeves, Bird, Lester, Rouse, Knight, Adebowale, Hallam, Holmes, Milsom
Substitutes: Phillips (for Knight), Hughes (nps), Dobbins (nps)
Scorer: Hallam
Attendance: 606

Date: Thursday 15/02/1996
Result: **SUDBURY TOWN 3 GLOUCESTER CITY 1**
Competition: FA Trophy 2nd Round
Teamsheet: Coles, Webb, Reeves, Bird, Lester, Rouse, Knight, Adebowale, Hallam, Holmes, Milsom
Substitutes: Phillips (nps), Hughes (nps), Dobbins (for Reeves)
Scorer: Hallam
Attendance: 262

Date: Tuesday 20/02/1996
Result: **GLOUCESTER CITY 3 CINDERFORD TOWN 2**
Competition: Gloucestershire FA Northern Senior Professional Cup Semi-Final
Teamsheet: Cook, Dobbins, Reeves, Bird, Lester, Rouse, Phillips, Adebowale, Hallam, Holmes, Webb
Substitutes: Milsom (nps), Medcroft (for Reeves), Webber (nps)
Scorers: Adebowale, Hallam, own goal
Attendance: 246

Date: Saturday 24/02/1996
Result: **BURTON ALBION 1 GLOUCESTER CITY 0**
Competition: Southern League Premier Division
Teamsheet: Coles, Webb, Lester, Bird, Kemp, Rouse, Medcroft, Adebowale, Hallam, Holmes, Milsom
Substitutes: Cornwall (nps), Webber (nps), Cook (nps)
Attendance: 672

Date: Tuesday 27/02/1996
Result: **CHELTENHAM TOWN 0 GLOUCESTER CITY 0**
Competition: Southern League Premier Division
Teamsheet: Coles, Charity, Lester, Bird, Kemp, Rouse, Webb, Adebowale, Hallam, Holmes, Milsom
Substitutes: Medcroft (nps), Webber (nps), Cook (nps)
Attendance: 1010

Date: Saturday 02/03/1996
Result: **GLOUCESTER CITY 1 VALLEY SPORTS RUGBY 1**
Competition: Southern League Premier Division
Teamsheet: Coles, Bird, Lester, Cooper, Kemp, Rouse, Tucker, Adebowale, Hallam, Holmes, Milsom
Substitutes: Webb (for Hallam), Charity (nps), Cook (nps)
Scorer: Holmes
Attendance: 509

Date: Saturday 09/03/1996
Result: **MERTHYR TYDFIL 1 GLOUCESTER CITY 0**
Competition: Southern League Premier Division
Teamsheet: Coles, Tucker, Lester, Bird, Kemp, Rouse, Webb, Adebowale, Hallam, Holmes, Milsom
Substitutes: Charity (for Tucker), Hughes (nps), Knight (nps)
Attendance: 456

Date: Tuesday 12/03/1996
Result: **GLOUCESTER CITY 3 STAFFORD RANGERS 2**
Competition: Southern League Premier Division
Teamsheet: Coles, Tucker, Lester, Bird, Kemp, Rouse, Webb, Adebowale, Hallam, Cooper, Milsom
Substitutes: Charity (for Hallam), Webber (for Tucker), Medcroft (nps)
Scorers: Webb (pen), Adebowale, Milsom
Attendance: 435

Date: Saturday 16/03/1996
Result: **GLOUCESTER CITY 1 SUDBURY TOWN 0**
Competition: Southern League Premier Division
Teamsheet: Coles, Tucker, Reeves, Bird, Kemp, Rouse, Webb, Adebowale, Milsom, Cooper, Charity
Substitutes: Webber (nps), Cornwall (nps), Rosenior (for Charity)
Scorer: Webb
Attendance: 509

Date: Tuesday 19/03/1996
Result: **GRESLEY ROVERS 1 GLOUCESTER CITY 0**
Competition: Southern League Premier Division
Teamsheet: Coles, Tucker, Reeves, Bird, Kemp, Rouse, Webb, Adebowale, Milsom, Cooper, Charity
Substitutes: Howell (for Charity), Webber (for Reeves), Rosenior (for Adebowale)
Attendance: 511

Date: Saturday 23/03/1996
Result: **ATHERSTONE UNITED 2 GLOUCESTER CITY 1**
Competition: Southern League Premier Division
Teamsheet: Coles, Holloway, Howell, Thorne, Kemp, Rouse, Webb, Mardenborough, Milsom, Cooper, Tucker
Substitutes: Webber (for Tucker), Charity (for Howell), Reeves (nps)
Scorer: Milsom
Attendance: 284

[357]

Date: Tuesday 26/03/1996
Result: **GRAVESEND & NORTHFLEET 0 GLOUCESTER CITY 0**
Competition: Southern League Premier Division
Teamsheet: Coles, Holloway, Johnson, Thorne, Webber, Tucker, Webb, Cooper, Milsom, Mardenborough, Vernon
Substitutes: Howell (for Tucker), Cornwall (nps), Adebowale (for Vernon)
Attendance: 383

Date: Saturday 30/03/1996
Result: **GLOUCESTER CITY 1 GRESLEY ROVERS 2**
Competition: Southern League Premier Division
Teamsheet: Coles, Holloway, Johnson, Thorne, Barnard, Rouse, Webb, Adebowale, Milsom, Cooper, Mardenborough
Substitutes: Vernon (for Cooper), Howell (for Barnard), Webber (nps)
Scorer: Holloway
Attendance: 613

Date: Tuesday 02/04/1996
Result: **CHELTENHAM TOWN 0 GLOUCESTER CITY 0** (3-1 pens)
Competition: Gloucestershire FA Northern Senior Professional Cup Final
Teamsheet: Coles, Holloway, Johnson, Thorne, Kemp, Rouse, Webb, Adebowale, Milsom, Black, Mardenborough
Substitutes: Tucker (for Rouse), Barnard (for Milsom), Vernon (for Mardenborough)
Attendance: 432

Date: Saturday 06/04/1996
Result: **DORCHESTER TOWN 0 GLOUCESTER CITY 1**
Competition: Southern League Premier Division
Teamsheet: Coles, Holloway, Johnson, Thorne, Kemp, Vernon, Webb, Adebowale, Milsom, Black, Mardenborough
Substitutes: Howell (For Vernon), Cooper (for Milsom), Cook (nps)
Scorer: Black
Attendance: 770

Date: Monday 08/04/1996
Result: **GLOUCESTER CITY 0 CHELTENHAM TOWN 3**
Competition: Southern League Premier Division
Teamsheet: Coles, Holloway, Johnson, Thorne, Kemp, Rouse, Webb, Adebowale, Black, Cooper, Mardenborough
Substitutes: Vernon (for Rouse), Milsom (for Cooper), Howell (for Holloway)
Attendance: 1523

Date: Saturday 13/04/1996
Result: **BALDOCK TOWN 0 GLOUCESTER CITY 1**
Competition: Southern League Premier Division
Teamsheet: Coles, Tucker, Johnson, Thorne, Kemp, Rouse, Webb, Adebowale, Rosenior, Black, Barnard
Substitutes: Milsom (for Rosenior), Howell (nps), Mardenborough (nps)
Scorer: Black
Attendance: 261

Date: Saturday 20/04/1996
Result: **GLOUCESTER CITY 2 RUSHDEN & DIAMONDS 1**
Competition: Southern League Premier Division
Teamsheet: Coles, Tucker, Johnson, Thorne, Kemp, Holloway, Webb, Adebowale, Milsom, Mardenborough, Howell
Substitutes: Barnard (nps), Vernon (nps), Rouse (for Howell)
Scorers: Mardenborough, Milsom
Attendance: 1226

Date: Saturday 27/04/1996
Result: **GLOUCESTER CITY 3 ILKESTON TOWN 1**
Competition: Southern League Premier Division
Teamsheet: Coles, Tucker, Johnson, Thorne, Kemp, Holloway, Webb, Adebowale, Black, Mardenborough, Howell
Substitutes: Cooper (for Adebowale), Rouse (nps), Vernon (nps)
Scorers: Kemp, Howell, Holloway
Attendance: 607

Date: Tuesday 30/04/1996
Result: **GLOUCESTER CITY 1 DORCHESTER TOWN 0**
Competition: Southern League Premier Division
Teamsheet: Coles, Tucker, Johnson, Thorne, Cooper, Holloway, Webb, Milsom, Black, Mardenborough, Howell
Substitutes: Webber (nps), Rouse (for Mardenborough), Vernon (nps)
Scorer: Black
Attendance: 523

Date: Saturday 04/05/1996
Result: **HASTINGS TOWN 2 GLOUCESTER CITY 0**
Competition: Southern League Premier Division
Teamsheet: Coles, Tucker, Johnson, Thorne, Cooper, Holloway, Webb, Milsom, Black, Mardenborough, Howell
Substitutes: Webber (for Cooper), Rouse (for Howell), Vernon (nps)
Attendance: 504

Appearances – M Adams 1(9), AA Adebowale 40(1), S Barnard 2(1), AM Bird 41, SA Black 7, SN Charity 3(3), DA Coles 45, S Cook 1, S Cooper 10(2), GR Cornwall 0(1), LW Dobbins 22, MW Freeman 19(1), MJ Hallam 28(4), CP Hamblin 7, JS Holloway 10, DJ Holmes 36(1), I Howell 5(5), BD Hughes 0(1), DD Johnson 11, GJ Kemp 42(1), M Kilgour 0(1), K Knight 22(2), S Lester 19(6), SA Mardenborough 10, S Medcroft 1(1), PJ Milsom 30(2), MS Phillips 12(3), SL Portway 11(1), N Reeves 29, LD Rosenior 1(2), S Rouse 45(3), GR Thorne 11, A Tucker 12(1), D Vernon 2(3), A Warner 2(4), DA Webb 44(3), A Webber 1(4), A Wollen 2(1).
Scorers – MJ Hallam 14, DJ Holmes 13, PJ Milsom 11, AA Adebowale 10, K Knight 8, DA Webb 7, MS Phillips 6, SL Portway 4, SA Black 3, GJ Kemp 3, S Rouse 3, JS Holloway 2, M Adams 1, I Howell 1, SA Mardenborough 1, A Warner 1, own goals 3.

SOUTHERN LEAGUE PREMIER DIVISION

POS	CLUB	P	W	D	L	F	A	PTS
1	RUSHDEN & DIAMONDS	42	29	7	6	99	41	94
2	HALESOWEN TOWN	42	27	11	4	70	36	92
3	CHELTENHAM TOWN	42	21	11	10	76	57	74
4	**GLOUCESTER CITY**	**42**	**21**	**8**	**13**	**65**	**47**	**71**
5	GRESLEY ROVERS	42	20	10	12	70	58	70
6	WORCESTER CITY	42	19	12	11	61	43	69
7	MERTHYR TYDFIL	42	19	6	17	67	59	63
8	HASTINGS TOWN	42	16	13	13	68	56	61
9	CRAWLEY TOWN	42	15	13	14	57	56	58
10	SUDBURY TOWN	42	15	10	17	69	71	55
11	GRAVESEND & NORTHFLEET	42	15	10	17	60	62	55
12	CHELMSFORD CITY	42	13	16	13	46	53	55
13	DORCHESTER TOWN	42	15	8	19	62	57	53
14	AFC NEWPORT	42	13	13	16	53	59	52
15	SALISBURY CITY	42	14	10	18	57	69	52
16	BURTON ALBION	42	13	12	17	55	56	51
17	ATHERSTONE UNITED	42	12	12	18	58	75	48
18	BALDOCK TOWN	42	11	14	17	51	56	47
19	CAMBRIDGE CITY	42	12	10	20	56	68	46
20	ILKESTON TOWN	42	11	10	21	53	87	43
21	STAFFORD RANGERS	42	11	4	27	58	90	37
22	VALLEY SPORTS RUGBY	42	5	10	27	37	92	25
		924	347	230	347	1348	1348	1271

SEASON 1996-1997

(Home Ground: City Stadium, Meadow Park, Hempsted)

Date: Saturday 17/08/1996
Result: **ASHFORD TOWN 0 GLOUCESTER CITY 3**
Competition: Southern League Premier Division
Teamsheet: Coles, Tucker, Johnson, Thorne, Kemp, Fergusson, Mardenborough, Webb, Mings, Watkins, Cooper
Substitutes: Howell (for Webb), Milsom (for Mings), Wright (for Mardenborough)
Scorers: Webb (2), Mings
Attendance: 648

Date: Tuesday 20/08/1996
Result: **GLOUCESTER CITY 6 MERTHYR TYDFIL 3**
Competition: Southern League Premier Division
Teamsheet: Coles, Tucker, Johnson, Thorne, Kemp, Fergusson, Mardenborough, Webb, Mings, Watkins, Cooper
Substitutes: Howell (for Webb), Milsom (for Mings), Wright (for Mardenborough)
Scorers: Webb (3), Watkins (3)
Attendance: 875

Date: Saturday 24/08/1996
Result: **CAMBRIDGE CITY 0 GLOUCESTER CITY 1**
Competition: Southern League Premier Division
Teamsheet: Coles, Tucker, Johnson, Thorne, Kemp, Fergusson, Mardenborough, Webb, Mings, Watkins, Cooper
Substitutes: Howell (for Webb), Milsom (for Mings), Wright (nps)
Scorer: Cooper
Attendance: 337

Date: Monday 26/08/1996
Result: **GLOUCESTER CITY 0 HALESOWEN TOWN 3**
Competition: Southern League Premier Division
Teamsheet: Coles, Tucker, Johnson, Thorne, Kemp, Fergusson, Mardenborough, Webb, Mings, Watkins, Cooper
Substitutes: Holloway (for Tucker), Holmes (for Mardenborough), Wright (for Mings)
Attendance: 1152

Date: Saturday 31/08/1996
Result: **GLOUCESTER CITY 1 KING'S LYNN 0**
Competition: Southern League Premier Division
Teamsheet: Coles, Tucker, Johnson, Thorne, Kemp, Fergusson, Mardenborough, Webb, Mings, Watkins, Cooper
Substitutes: Howell (for Webb), Holmes (for Watkins), Holloway (for Mardenborough)
Scorer: Mings
Attendance: 752

Date: Wednesday 04/09/1996
Result: **AFC NEWPORT 0 GLOUCESTER CITY 4**
Competition: Southern League Premier Division
Teamsheet: Coles, Holloway, Johnson, Thorne, Kemp, Fergusson, Holmes, Webb, Mings, Watkins, Cooper
Substitutes: Howell (for Cooper), Knight (for Watkins), Rouse (for Webb)
Scorers: Holmes, Watkins, Mings (2)
Attendance: 952

Date: Saturday 07/09/1996
Result: **GLOUCESTER CITY 3 BALDOCK TOWN 1**
Competition: Southern League Premier Division
Teamsheet: Coles, Holloway, Johnson, Thorne, Kemp, Fergusson, Holmes, Webb, Mings, Watkins, Howell
Substitutes: McGrath (for Johnson), Knight (for Mings), Rouse (for Howell)
Scorers: Holmes (2), Mings
Attendance: 718

Date: Saturday 14/09/1996
Result: **BASINGSTOKE TOWN 0 GLOUCESTER CITY 3**
Competition: FA Cup 1st Qualifying Round
Teamsheet: Coles, Holloway, Johnson, Thorne, Kemp, Fergusson, Holmes, Webb, Mings, Watkins, Howell
Substitutes: McGrath (for Webb), Cooper (for Howell), Rouse (for Thorne)
Scorers: Watkins, Webb, Mings
Attendance: 422

Date: Saturday 21/09/1996
Result: **GLOUCESTER CITY 3 CHELMSFORD CITY 1**
Competition: Southern League Premier Division
Teamsheet: Coles, Holloway, Johnson, Thorne, Kemp, Fergusson, Holmes, Webb, Mings, Watkins, Howell
Substitutes: Cooper (for Howell), Rouse (nps), McGrath (for Webb)
Scorers: Mings, Watkins (2)
Attendance: 816

Date: Tuesday 24/09/1996
Result: **MERTHYR TYDFIL 1 GLOUCESTER CITY 0**
Competition: Southern League Premier Division
Teamsheet: Coles, Holloway, Johnson, Thorne, Kemp, Fergusson, Holmes, Cooper, Mings, Watkins, Howell
Substitutes: McGrath (for Cooper), Knight (for Mings), Tucker (nps)
Attendance: 680

Date: Saturday 28/09/1996
Result: **GLOUCESTER CITY 1 THATCHAM TOWN 3**
Competition: FA Cup 2nd Qualifying Round
Teamsheet: Coles, Holloway, Johnson, Thorne, Kemp, Fergusson, Knight, Cooper, Holmes, Watkins, Howell
Substitutes: McGrath (for Howell), Milsom (for Holmes), Tucker (for Knight)
Scorer: Kemp
Attendance: 701

Date: Saturday 05/10/1996
Result: **SITTINGBOURNE 1 GLOUCESTER CITY 1**
Competition: Southern League Premier Division
Teamsheet: Coles, Holloway, McGrath, Thorne, Kemp, Yates, Holmes, Tucker, Milsom, Watkins, Johnson
Substitutes: Howell (nps), Cooper (for Holmes), Rosenior (for Milsom)
Scorer: Holmes
Attendance: 579

Date: Tuesday 08/10/1996
Result: **GLOUCESTER CITY 5 CINDERFORD TOWN 0**
Competition: Southern League Cup 1st Round 1st Leg
Teamsheet: Coles, Holloway, McGrath, Thorne, Kemp, Yates, Holmes, Tucker, Milsom, Watkins, Johnson
Substitutes: Rosenior (for Watkins), Howell (for Johnson), Cooper (for Kemp)
Scorers: Johnson, Kemp, Watkins (2), Rosenior
Attendance: 411

Date: Saturday 12/10/1996
Result: **GLOUCESTER CITY 1 NUNEATON BOROUGH 0**
Competition: Southern League Premier Division
Teamsheet: Coles, Yates, McGrath, Thorne, Kemp, Burns, Kirkup, Tucker, Holmes, Watkins, Johnson
Substitutes: Webb (for McGrath), Milsom (for Holmes), Cooper (for Tucker)
Scorer: Webb
Attendance: 1055

Date: Tuesday 15/10/1996
Result: **HALESOWEN TOWN 5 GLOUCESTER CITY 4**
Competition: Southern League Premier Division
Teamsheet: Coles, Yates, Holloway, Thorne, Kemp, Burns, Kirkup, Webb, Milsom, Watkins, Holmes
Substitutes: Mings (for Yates), Howell (nps), Tucker (nps)
Scorers: Holmes, Watkins (3)
Attendance: 903

Date: Saturday 19/10/1996
Result: **HASTINGS TOWN 0 GLOUCESTER CITY 2**
Competition: Southern League Premier Division
Teamsheet: Coles, Yates, Johnson, Thorne, Kemp, Burns, Kirkup, Webb, Milsom, Watkins, Holmes
Substitutes: McGrath (for Kemp), Tucker (for Holmes), Mings (for Milsom)
Scorers: Milsom, Watkins
Attendance: 418

Date: Saturday 26/10/1996
Result: **GLOUCESTER CITY 1 GRESLEY ROVERS 2**
Competition: Southern League Premier Division
Teamsheet: Coles, Fergusson, Johnson, Thorne, Kemp, Burns, Kirkup, Webb, Mings, Watkins, Holmes
Substitutes: Milsom (for Mings), Tucker (for Kirkup), Holloway (for Holmes)
Scorer: Mings
Attendance: 1552

Date: Tuesday 29/10/1996
Result: **CINDERFORD TOWN 2 GLOUCESTER CITY 1**
Competition: Southern League Cup 1st Round 2nd Leg
Teamsheet: Coles, Holloway, Howell, Thorne, O'Riordan, Fergusson, Holmes, Tucker, Mings, Milsom, Cooper
Substitutes: Kemp (for O'Riordan), Webb (for Holloway), Burns (for Tucker)
Scorer: Tucker
Attendance: 192

Date: Saturday 02/11/1996
Result: **BURTON ALBION 3 GLOUCESTER CITY 1**
Competition: Southern League Premier Division
Teamsheet: Coles, Fergusson, Johnson, Thorne, Kemp, Burns, Kirkup, Webb, Mings, Watkins, Holmes
Substitutes: Milsom (for Mings), Tucker (for Kirkup), McGrath (for Burns)
Scorer: Watkins (pen)
Attendance: 862

Date: Monday 04/11/1996
Result: **GLOUCESTER CITY 3 FOREST GREEN ROVERS 0**
Competition: Gloucestershire FA Northern Senior Professional Cup Semi-Final
Teamsheet: Coles, Holloway, McGrath, Thorne, Kemp, Burns, Kirkup, Cooper, Milsom, Watkins, Johnson
Substitutes: Webb (For Kirkup), Mings (nps), Tucker (nps)
Scorers: Watkins (2), own goal
Attendance: 265

Date: Saturday 09/11/1996
Result: **GLOUCESTER CITY 2 CRAWLEY TOWN 1**
Competition: Southern League Premier Division
Teamsheet: Mildenhall, Holloway, McGrath, Thorne, Kemp, Burns, Kirkup, Cooper, Milsom, Watkins, Johnson
Substitutes: Webb (for Burns), Fergusson (for Milsom), Tucker (nps)
Scorers: Fergusson, own goal
Attendance: 838

Date: Saturday 16/11/1996
Result: **SALISBURY CITY 0 GLOUCESTER CITY 4**
Competition: Southern League Premier Division
Teamsheet: Mildenhall, Holloway, McGrath, Thorne, Kemp, Burns, Kirkup, Webb, Milsom, Watkins, Cooper
Substitutes: Adcock (for Kirkup), Mings (nps), Fergusson (for Cooper)
Scorers: Milsom, Watkins (3)
Attendance: 489

Date: Saturday 23/11/1996
Result: **KING'S LYNN 2 GLOUCESTER CITY 1**
Competition: Southern League Premier Division
Teamsheet: Mildenhall, Holloway, McGrath, Thorne, Kemp, Burns, Kirkup, Webb, Milsom, Watkins, Cooper
Substitutes: Adcock (for Kirkup), Tucker (nps), Fergusson (for Milsom)
Scorer: Adcock
Attendance: 786

Date: Tuesday 26/11/1996
Result: **GLOUCESTER CITY 2 AFC NEWPORT 1**
Competition: Southern League Premier Division
Teamsheet: Mildenhall, Holloway, McGrath, Thorne, Kemp, Burns, Adcock, Webb, Fergusson, Watkins, Cooper
Substitutes: Kirkup (for Adcock), Mings (for Watkins), Tucker (for Webb)
Scorers: Fergusson, Adcock
Attendance: 816

Date: Saturday 30/11/1996
Result: **GLOUCESTER CITY 3 KINGSTONIAN 1**
Competition: FA Trophy 3rd Qualifying Round
Teamsheet: Rosenior, Holloway, McGrath, Thorne, Kemp, Burns, Johnson, Webb, Fergusson, Watkins, Cooper
Substitutes: Milsom (nps), Mings (for Fergusson), Tucker (for Webb)
Scorers: Webb, Watkins (2)
Attendance: 752

Date: Saturday 07/12/1996
Result: **GLOUCESTER CITY 2 BURTON ALBION 4**
Competition: Southern League Premier Division
Teamsheet: Mildenhall, Tucker, McGrath, Thorne, Kemp, Burns, Johnson, Webb, Fergusson, Watkins, Cooper
Substitutes: Mings (for Tucker), Kirkup (for McGrath), Adebowale (for Johnson)
Scorers: Kemp, Watkins
Attendance: 861

Date: Tuesday 10/12/1996
Result: **CHELTENHAM TOWN 1 GLOUCESTER CITY 0**
Competition: Southern League Cup 2nd Round
Teamsheet: Mildenhall, Tucker, Johnson, Thorne, Kemp, Burns, Mings, Webb, Fergusson, Watkins, Cooper
Substitutes: Adebowale (for Webb), Milsom (for Fergusson), Howell (for Tucker)
Attendance: 590

Date: Saturday 14/12/1996
Result: **GLOUCESTER CITY 1 SITTINGBOURNE 1**
Competition: Southern League Premier Division
Teamsheet: Mildenhall, Holloway, McGrath, Thorne, Kemp, Burns, Mings, Webb, Fergusson, Kirkup, Cooper
Substitutes: Johnson (for McGrath), Milsom (for Mings), Adebowale (for Cooper)
Scorer: Holloway
Attendance: 710

Date: Saturday 21/12/1996
Result: **NUNEATON BOROUGH 2 GLOUCESTER CITY 0**
Competition: Southern League Premier Division
Teamsheet: Mildenhall, Holloway, Howell, Johnson, Kemp, Burns, Kirkup, Webb, Fergusson, Adebowale, Cooper
Substitutes: Steadman (nps), O'Riordan (nps), Rosenior (for Kirkup)
Attendance: 824

Date: Thursday 26/12/1996
Result: **GLOUCESTER CITY 2 CHELTENHAM TOWN 1**
Competition: Southern League Premier Division
Teamsheet: Phillips, Holloway, Johnson, Fergusson, Kemp, Burns, Kirkup, Cooper, Milsom, Watkins, Howell
Substitutes: Tucker (nps), Webb (nps), McGrath (For Johnson)
Scorer: Watkins (2)
Attendance: 2145

[361]

Date: Saturday 18/01/1997
Result: **YEADING 0 GLOUCESTER CITY 3**
Competition: FA Trophy 1st Round
Teamsheet: Coles, Holloway, Johnson, Fergusson, Kemp, Burns, Tucker, Cooper, Milsom, Watkins, McGrath
Substitutes: Mings (for Watkins), Webb (for Mings), Thorne (for Tucker)
Scorers: Kemp, Burns, own goal
Attendance: 245

Date: Saturday 25/01/1997
Result: **GLOUCESTER CITY 2 CAMBRIDGE CITY 0**
Competition: Southern League Premier Division
Teamsheet: Coles, Holloway, Johnson, Fergusson, Kemp, Burns, Kirkup, Cooper, Mings, Watkins, McGrath
Substitutes: Webb (nps), Holmes (for Watkins), Thorne (for Kirkup)
Scorers: Fergusson, McGrath
Attendance: 606

Date: Tuesday 28/01/1997
Result: **ATHERSTONE UNITED 0 GLOUCESTER CITY 0**
Competition: Southern League Premier Division
Teamsheet: Coles, Holloway, Johnson, Fergusson, Kemp, Burns, Thorne, Cooper, Mings, Watkins, McGrath
Substitutes: Webb (for Mings), Kirkup (nps), Holmes (for Watkins)
Attendance: 315

Date: Saturday 01/02/1997
Result: **SUDBURY TOWN 2 GLOUCESTER CITY 1**
Competition: Southern League Premier Division
Teamsheet: Coles, Thorne, Johnson, Fergusson, Kemp, Burns, Kirkup, Cooper, Holmes, Watkins, McGrath
Substitutes: Webb (for Kirkup), Adcock (for Cooper), Tucker (for Kemp)
Scorer: Kemp
Attendance: 351

Date: Saturday 08/02/1997
Result: **GLOUCESTER CITY 3 HALIFAX TOWN 0**
Competition: FA Trophy 2nd Round
Teamsheet: Coles, Thorne, Johnson, Fergusson, Kemp, Burns, Kirkup, Cooper, Holmes, Watkins, McGrath
Substitutes: Webb (for Holmes), Tucker (for Burns), Rosenior (nps)
Scorers: Watkins (2), Holmes
Attendance: 1181

Date: Saturday 15/02/1997
Result: **GLOUCESTER CITY 2 HASTINGS TOWN 0**
Competition: Southern League Premier Division
Teamsheet: Coles, Holloway, Johnson, Thorne, Kemp, Burns, Kirkup, Cooper, Holmes, Watkins, McGrath
Substitutes: Webb (for McGrath), Tucker (for Kirkup), Mings (for Watkins)
Scorers: Watkins, Tucker
Attendance: 612

Date: Monday 17/02/1997
Result: **WORCESTER CITY 0 GLOUCESTER CITY 0**
Competition: Southern League Premier Division
Teamsheet: Coles, Holloway, Johnson, Thorne, Kemp, Burns, Tucker, Cooper, Holmes, Watkins, McGrath
Substitutes: Kirkup (nps), Webb (for Tucker), Mings (nps)
Attendance: 770

Date: Saturday 22/02/1997
Result: **GRAVESEND & NORTHFLEET 2 GLOUCESTER CITY 3**
Competition: Southern League Premier Division
Teamsheet: Coles, Holloway, Fergusson, Thorne, Kemp, Burns, Tucker, Cooper, Holmes, Watkins, McGrath
Substitutes: Webb (for McGrath), Kirkup (nps), Mings (nps)
Scorers: Fergusson, Kemp, Burns
Attendance: 696

Date: Saturday 01/03/1997
Result: **GLOUCESTER CITY 3 RUNCORN 1**
Competition: FA Trophy 3rd Round
Teamsheet: Coles, Holloway, Fergusson, Thorne, Kemp, Burns, Kirkup, Cooper, Holmes, Watkins, Webb
Substitutes: Tucker (nps), Adcock (nps), Rosenior (for Watkins)
Scorers: Burns, Kemp, own goal
Attendance: 1129

Date: Saturday 08/03/1997
Result: **GLOUCESTER CITY 3 SUDBURY TOWN 3**
Competition: Southern League Premier Division
Teamsheet: Coles, Holloway, Johnson, Thorne, Kemp, Burns, Fergusson, Cooper, Holmes, Watkins, Webb
Substitutes: Tucker (nps), Adcock (for Holloway), McGrath (nps)
Scorers: Watkins, Burns, Johnson
Attendance: 732

Date: Monday 10/03/1997
Result: **CHELMSFORD CITY 1 GLOUCESTER CITY 3**
Competition: Southern League Premier Division
Teamsheet: Coles, Holloway, Johnson, Thorne, Kemp, Burns, Adcock, Cooper, Holmes, Watkins, Webb
Substitutes: Tucker (for Adcock), McGrath (for Webb), Mings (for Watkins)
Scorers: Webb, Holmes, Tucker
Attendance: 550

Date: Saturday 15/03/1997
Result: **CRAWLEY TOWN 1 GLOUCESTER CITY 1**
Competition: Southern League Premier Division
Teamsheet: Coles, Holloway, Johnson, Thorne, Kemp, Burns, Tucker, Webb, Holmes, Mings, Fergusson
Substitutes: McGrath (for Johnson), Kirkup (nps), Rosenior (for Tucker)
Scorer: Mings
Attendance: 534

[362]

Date: Tuesday 18/03/1997
Result: **GLOUCESTER CITY 6 ASHFORD TOWN 1**
Competition: Southern League Premier Division
Teamsheet: Coles, Holloway, McGrath, Thorne, Kemp, Burns, Fergusson, Cooper, Holmes, Mings, Webb
Substitutes: Tucker (for Cooper), Kirkup (for Holloway), Rosenior (for Holmes)
Scorers: Webb (2), Mings (2), Holmes, own goal
Attendance: 556

Date: Saturday 22/03/1997
Result: **BISHOP AUCKLAND 0 GLOUCESTER CITY 0**
Competition: FA Trophy Quarter-Final
Teamsheet: Coles, Holloway, Johnson, Thorne, Kemp, Burns, Fergusson, Webb, Holmes, Watkins, Cooper
Substitutes: McGrath (nps), Mings (for Holmes), Tucker (nps)
Attendance: 832

Date: Tuesday 25/03/1997
Result: **GLOUCESTER CITY 4 BISHOP AUCKLAND 3**
Competition: FA Trophy Quarter-Final Replay
Teamsheet: Coles, Holloway, Johnson, Thorne, Kemp, Burns, Fergusson, Webb, Holmes, Watkins, Cooper
Substitutes: McGrath (nps), Mings (nps), Kirkup (nps)
Scorers: Holmes (2), Watkins (2)
Attendance: 1829

Date: Saturday 29/03/1997
Result: **GLOUCESTER CITY 1 WORCESTER CITY 1**
Competition: Southern League Premier Division
Teamsheet: Coles, Holloway, McGrath, Thorne, Kemp, Burns, Fergusson, Webb, Holmes, Watkins, Cooper
Substitutes: Tucker (nps), Mings (for Holloway), Kirkup (nps)
Scorer: Watkins
Attendance: 1082

Date: Monday 31/03/1997
Result: **CHELTENHAM TOWN 1 GLOUCESTER CITY 1**
Competition: Southern League Premier Division
Teamsheet: Coles, Holloway, McGrath, Thorne, Kemp, Burns, Fergusson, Webb, Holmes, Mings, Cooper
Substitutes: Kirkup (nps), Watkins (for Holmes), Tucker (nps)
Scorer: Webb
Attendance: 3005

Date: Saturday 05/04/1997
Result: **DAGENHAM & REDBRIDGE 0 GLOUCESTER CITY 0**
Competition: FA Trophy Semi-Final 1st Leg
Teamsheet: Coles, Holloway, McGrath, Thorne, Kemp, Burns, Fergusson, Webb, Holmes, Watkins, Cooper
Substitutes: Kirkup (nps), Mings (for Holmes), Tucker (nps)
Attendance: 2077

Date: Saturday 12/04/1997
Result: **GLOUCESTER CITY 2 DAGENHAM & REDBRIDGE 2** (aet)
Competition: FA Trophy Semi-Final 2nd Leg
Teamsheet: Coles, Holloway, Johnson, Thorne, Kemp, Burns, Fergusson, Webb, Holmes, Watkins, Cooper
Substitutes: Kirkup (for Holloway), Mings (for Holmes), McGrath (for Johnson)
Scorers: Watkins, Mings
Attendance: 4000

Date: Wednesday 16/04/1997
Result: **DAGENHAM & REDBRIDGE 2 GLOUCESTER CITY 1**
Competition: FA Trophy Semi-Final Replay
Teamsheet: Coles, Mings, Johnson, Thorne, Kemp, Burns, Fergusson, Webb, Holmes, Watkins, Cooper
Substitutes: Milsom (for Mings), Tucker (for Webb), McGrath (nps)
Scorer: Holmes
Attendance: 2053
Note: Played at Slough

Date: Saturday 19/04/1997
Result: **GLOUCESTER CITY 3 GRAVESEND & NORTHFLEET 1**
Competition: Southern League Premier Division
Teamsheet: Coles, Mings, Johnson, Thorne, Kemp, Burns, Fergusson, Webb, Holmes, Watkins, Cooper
Substitutes: Milsom (for Holmes), Tucker (for Webb), McGrath (for Burns)
Scorers: Watkins, Mings (2)
Attendance: 804

Date: Tuesday 22/04/1997
Result: **DORCHESTER TOWN 2 GLOUCESTER CITY 2**
Competition: Southern League Premier Division
Teamsheet: Coles, Holloway, Johnson, Thorne, Kemp, Burns, McGrath, Mings, Holmes, Watkins, Cooper
Substitutes: O'Riordan (for McGrath), Tucker (for Holmes), Milsom (for Mings)
Scorers: Watkins, Burns
Attendance: 472

Date: Thursday 24/04/1997
Result: **GLOUCESTER CITY 0 ATHERSTONE UNITED 0**
Competition: Southern League Premier Division
Teamsheet: Coles, Holloway, McGrath, Thorne, Kemp, Burns, Tucker, Webb, Milsom, Watkins, Cooper
Substitutes: Holmes (for Watkins), Mings (for Milsom), Howell (for Thorne)
Attendance: 927

Date: Saturday 26/04/1997
Result: **GRESLEY ROVERS 3 GLOUCESTER CITY 1**
Competition: Southern League Premier Division
Teamsheet: Coles, Holloway, Johnson, Fergusson, Kemp, Burns, Mings, Webb, Holmes, Watkins, Cooper
Substitutes: McGrath (nps), Howell (for Webb), Milsom (for Holmes)
Scorer: Watkins
Attendance: 1376

[363]

Date: Tuesday 29/04/1997
Result: **GLOUCESTER CITY 3 DORCHESTER TOWN 1**
Competition: Southern League Premier Division
Teamsheet: Coles, Holloway, Johnson, Fergusson, Kemp, Burns, Tucker, Webb, Mings, Watkins, Cooper
Substitutes: Holmes (for Mings), Kirkup (for Holloway), McGrath (nps)
Scorers: Kemp, Webb, Kirkup
Attendance: 1022

Date: Thursday 01/05/1997
Result: **BALDOCK TOWN 2 GLOUCESTER CITY 3**
Competition: Southern League Premier Division
Teamsheet: Coles, Holloway, Johnson, Fergusson, Kemp, Burns, Tucker, Webb, Milsom, Holmes, Cooper
Substitutes: Mings (for Milsom), Kirkup (for Holloway), Adcock (for Holmes)
Scorers: Fergusson, Webb, Adcock
Attendance: 301

Date: Saturday 03/05/1997
Result: **GLOUCESTER CITY 1 SALISBURY CITY 3**
Competition: Southern League Premier Division
Teamsheet: Coles, Tucker, Johnson, Fergusson, Kemp, Burns, Kirkup, Webb, Mings, Watkins, Cooper
Substitutes: Holmes (for Mings), Holloway (for Kirkup), Adcock (for Tucker)
Scorer: own goal
Attendance: 1863

Date: Tuesday 06/05/1997
Result: **CHELTENHAM TOWN 2 GLOUCESTER CITY 1**
Competition: Gloucestershire FA Northern Senior Professional Cup Final
Teamsheet: Coles, Holloway, McGrath, Fergusson, Kemp, Burns, Tucker, Webb, Holmes, Watkins, Cooper
Substitutes: Kirkup (for Tucker), Steadman (for Webb), Howell (for McGrath)
Scorer: Holmes
Attendance: 520

Appearances – PM Adcock 2(6), AA Adebowale 1(3), C Burns 44(1), DA Coles 48, S Cooper 47(5), SJ Fergusson 44(3), JS Holloway 42(4), DJ Holmes 36(7), I Howell 8(10), DD Johnson 48(1), GJ Kemp 53(1), A Kirkup 18(7), K Knight 1(3), SA Mardenborough 5, J McGrath 26(12), SJ Mildenhall 8, PJ Milsom 13(13), AL Mings 24(14), DJ O'Riordan 1(1), SJ Phillips 1, LD Rosenior 1(6), S Rouse 0(3), WCM Steadman 0(1), GR Thorne 49(2), A Tucker 20(14), DA Watkins 51(1), DA Webb 40(11), H Wright 0(3), L Yates 5.
Scorers – DA Watkins 35, AL Mings 14, DA Webb 14, DJ Holmes 13, GJ Kemp 7, C Burns 5, SJ Fergusson 5, PM Adcock 3, DD Johnson 2, PJ Milsom 2, A Tucker 2, S Cooper 1, JS Holloway 1, A Kirkup 1, J McGrath 1, LD Rosenior 1, own goals 6.

SOUTHERN LEAGUE PREMIER DIVISION

POS	CLUB	P	W	D	L	F	A	PTS
1	GRESLEY ROVERS	42	25	10	7	75	40	85
2	CHELTENHAM TOWN	42	21	11	10	76	44	74
3	**GLOUCESTER CITY**	**42**	**21**	**10**	**11**	**81**	**56**	**73**
4	HALESOWEN TOWN	42	21	10	11	77	54	73
5	KING'S LYNN	42	20	8	14	65	61	68
6	BURTON ALBION	42	18	12	12	70	53	66
7	NUNEATON BOROUGH	42	19	9	14	61	52	66
8	SITTINGBOURNE	42	19	7	16	76	65	64
9	MERTHYR TYDFIL	42	17	9	16	69	61	60
10	WORCESTER CITY	42	15	14	13	52	50	59
11	ATHERSTONE UNITED	42	15	13	14	46	47	58
12	SALISBURY CITY	42	15	13	14	57	66	58
13	SUDBURY TOWN	42	16	7	19	72	72	55
14	GRAVESEND & NORTHFLEET	42	16	7	19	63	73	55
15	DORCHESTER TOWN	42	14	9	19	62	66	51
16	HASTINGS TOWN	42	12	15	15	49	60	51
17	CRAWLEY TOWN	42	13	8	21	49	67	47
18	CAMBRIDGE CITY	42	11	13	18	57	65	46
19	ASHFORD TOWN	42	9	18	15	53	79	45
20	BALDOCK TOWN	42	11	8	23	52	90	41
21	AFC NEWPORT	42	9	13	20	40	60	40
22	CHELMSFORD CITY	42	6	14	22	49	70	32
		924	343	238	343	1351	1351	1267

SEASON 1997-1998
(Home Ground: City Stadium, Meadow Park, Hempsted)

Date: Saturday 16/08/1997
Result: **GLOUCESTER CITY 1 HASTINGS TOWN 1**
Competition: Southern League Premier Division
Teamsheet: Coles, Tucker, Elsey, Thorne, Kemp, Fergusson, Webb, Burns, Mings, Milsom, Preedy
Substitutes: Hoskins (for Milsom), Steadman (nps), Adcock (for Preedy)
Scorer: Webb
Attendance: 711

Date: Saturday 23/08/1997
Result: **CRAWLEY TOWN 3 GLOUCESTER CITY 1**
Competition: Southern League Premier Division
Teamsheet: Coles, Tucker, Elsey, Thorne, Kemp, Fergusson, Webb, Burns, Mings, Adcock, Hoskins
Substitutes: Preedy (nps), Steadman (nps), Milsom (for Hoskins)
Scorer: Mings
Attendance: 1178

[364]

1997
Keith Gardner's 'Vision of the Future'

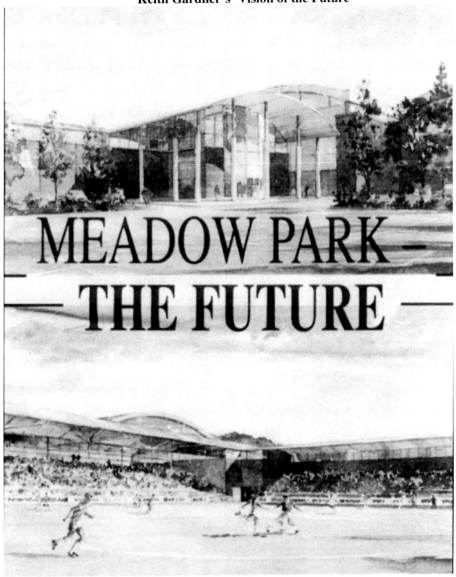

RECORD BREAKER

Steve Fergusson
Record Transfer Fee Paid (jointly) - £25,000

RECORD BREAKER

Gary Kemp
Most Appearances In Cup Matches – 84

RECORD BREAKER

David Holmes
Record Transfer Fee Paid (jointly) - £25,000

'Day of Destiny!'
3 May 1997 v Salisbury City
A City win and a Cheltenham Town loss would have been sufficient to promote City.
Unfortunately, City lost 1-3 and the rest is history.
Author's son, Simon Clark, mascot on the right next to Chris Burns

PROGRAMME   PROGRAMME   PROGRAMME

1996-1997   1997-1998   1998-1999

Date: Monday 25/08/1997
Result: **GLOUCESTER CITY 1 MERTHYR TYDFIL 0**
Competition: Southern League Premier Division
Teamsheet: Coles, Holloway, Elsey, Thorne, Kemp, Fergusson, Webb, Burns, Mings, Adcock, Cooper
Substitutes: Hoskins (nps), Tucker (nps), Rosenior (nps)
Scorer: Adcock
Attendance: 823

Date: Saturday 30/08/1997
Result: **GLOUCESTER CITY 0 ROTHWELL TOWN 1**
Competition: Southern League Premier Division
Teamsheet: Coles, Holloway, Elsey, Thorne, Kemp, Fergusson, Webb, Burns, Mings, Adcock, Cooper
Substitutes: Hoskins (for Adcock), Tucker (for Cooper), Preedy (for Elsey)
Attendance: 582

Date: Monday 01/09/1997
Result: **WESTON-SUPER-MARE 0 GLOUCESTER CITY 2**
Competition: Southern League Cup Preliminary Round 1st Leg
Teamsheet: Mokler, Holloway, Elsey, Thorne, Johnson, Fergusson, Webb, Burns, Mings, Adcock, Cooper
Substitutes: Hoskins (for Adcock), Tucker (for Webb), Rosenior (for Mings)
Scorers: Mings, Hoskins
Attendance: 220

Date: Friday 05/09/1997
Result: **TAMWORTH 1 GLOUCESTER CITY 3**
Competition: Southern League Premier Division
Teamsheet: Mokler, Holloway, Elsey, Thorne, Kemp, Fergusson, Webb, Burns, Mings, Adcock, Cooper
Substitutes: Hoskins (for Adcock), Tucker (for Cooper), Johnson (for Elsey)
Scorers: Mings, Adcock, Hoskins
Attendance: 730

Date: Tuesday 09/09/1997
Result: **GLOUCESTER CITY 1 WESTON-SUPER-MARE 0**
Competition: Southern League Cup Preliminary Round 2md Leg
Teamsheet: Mokler, Holloway, Johnson, Thorne, Kemp, Fergusson, Webb, Burns, Mings, Hoskins, Cooper
Substitutes: Rosenior (for Hoskins), Tucker (for Cooper), Preedy (for Johnson)
Scorer: Webb
Attendance: 306

Date: Saturday 13/09/1997
Result: **GLOUCESTER CITY 3 MANGOTSFIELD UNITED 0**
Competition: FA Cup 1st Qualifying Round
Teamsheet: Mokler, Holloway, Johnson, Thorne, Kemp, Fergusson, Tucker, Burns, Mings, Hoskins, Cooper
Substitutes: Rosenior (for Mings), Steadman (for Fergusson), Preedy (for Johnson)
Scorers: Burns (2), Hoskins
Attendance: 532

Date: Tuesday 16/09/1997
Result: **HALESOWEN TOWN 0 GLOUCESTER CITY 1**
Competition: Southern League Premier Division
Teamsheet: Mokler, Holloway, Elsey, Thorne, Kemp, Johnson, Tucker, Burns, Fergusson, Adcock, Cooper
Substitutes: Hoskins (nps), Rosenior (for Adcock), Steadman (nps)
Scorer: Fergusson
Attendance: 681

Date: Saturday 20/09/1997
Result: **GLOUCESTER CITY 1 SAINT LEONARDS STAMCROFT 1**
Competition: Southern League Premier Division
Teamsheet: Mokler, Holloway, Elsey, Thorne, Kemp, Johnson, Tucker, Burns, Fergusson, Adcock, Cooper
Substitutes: Hoskins (nps), Rosenior (for Tucker), Mings (for Adcock)
Scorer: Fergusson
Attendance: 612

Date: Tuesday 23/09/1997
Result: **BATH CITY 1 GLOUCESTER CITY 0**
Competition: Southern League Premier Division
Teamsheet: Mokler, Holloway, Elsey, Thorne, Kemp, Fergusson, Tucker, Burns, Mings, Adcock, Cooper
Substitutes: Hoskins (for Adcock), Rosenior (for Tucker), Preedy (nps)
Attendance: 704

Date: Saturday 27/09/1997
Result: **GLOUCESTER CITY 2 NEWPORT (Isle of Wight) 1**
Competition: FA Cup 2nd Qualifying Round
Teamsheet: Mokler, Holloway, Elsey, Thorne, Kemp, Johnson, Tucker, Burns, Fergusson, Mings, Cooper
Substitutes: Adcock (for Tucker), Steadman (for Holloway), Preedy (for Elsey)
Scorers: Burns, Fergusson
Attendance: 582

Date: Tuesday 30/09/1997
Result: **CINDERFORD TOWN 0 GLOUCESTER CITY 3**
Competition: Southern League Cup 1st Round 1st Leg
Teamsheet: Mokler, Tucker, Preedy, Thorne, Steadman, Rosenior, Adcock, Burns, Hoskins, Cooper, Colwell
Substitutes: Johnson (for Steadman), Kemp (nps), Fergusson (for Rosenior)
Scorers: Preedy, Rosenior, Adcock (pen)
Attendance: 260

Date: Saturday 04/10/1997
Result: **KING'S LYNN 0 GLOUCESTER CITY 3**
Competition: Southern League Premier Division
Teamsheet: Mokler, Holloway, Adcock, Thorne, Kemp, Johnson, Tucker, Burns, Fergusson, Cadette, Cooper
Substitutes: Mings (for Cadette), Hoskins (for Adcock), Rosenior (for Fergusson)
Scorers: Thorne, Burns, Fergusson
Attendance: 608

Date: Saturday 11/10/1997
Result: **GLOUCESTER CITY 2 WATERLOOVILLE 0**
Competition: FA Cup 3rd Qualifying Round
Teamsheet: Mokler, Holloway, Elsey, Thorne, Kemp, Johnson, Tucker, Burns, Fergusson, Cadette, Cooper
Substitutes: Mings (for Cadette), Webb (for Tucker), Steadman (for Holloway)
Scorers: Elsey, Fergusson
Attendance: 558

Date: Tuesday 14/10/1997
Result: **MERTHYR TYDFIL 1 GLOUCESTER CITY 0**
Competition: Southern League Premier Division
Teamsheet: Mokler, Holloway, Elsey, Thorne, Kemp, Steadman, Webb, Burns, Fergusson, Mings, Cooper
Substitutes: Cadette (for Fergusson), Tucker (for Steadman), Adcock (for Cooper)
Attendance: 635

Date: Saturday 18/10/1997
Result: **GLOUCESTER CITY 1 DORCHESTER TOWN 2**
Competition: Southern League Premier Division
Teamsheet: Coles, Holloway, Elsey, Thorne, Kemp, Johnson, Webb, Burns, Fergusson, Mings, Cooper
Substitutes: Tucker (for Webb), Rosenior (for Johnson), Adcock (for Elsey)
Scorer: Fergusson
Attendance: 648

Date: Saturday 25/10/1997
Result: **GLOUCESTER CITY 1 WISBECH TOWN 1**
Competition: FA Cup 4th Qualifying Round
Teamsheet: Coles, Holloway, Johnson, Thorne, Kemp, Steadman, Adcock, Burns, Fergusson, Mings, Cooper
Substitutes: Elsey (for Adcock), Webb (for Thorne), Rosenior (for Mings)
Scorer: Holloway
Attendance: 912

Date: Wednesday 29/10/1997
Result: **WISBECH TOWN 3 GLOUCESTER CITY 2**
Competition: FA Cup 4th Qualifying Round Replay
Teamsheet: Coles, Holloway, Johnson, Thorne, Kemp, Steadman, Tucker, Burns, Fergusson, Mings, Adcock
Substitutes: Hoskins (for Tucker), Howell (nps), Rosenior (for Steadman)
Scorers: Fergusson (pen), Mings
Attendance: 1094

Date: Saturday 01/11/1997
Result: **ROTHWELL TOWN 1 GLOUCESTER CITY 1**
Competition: Southern League Premier Division
Teamsheet: Coles, Holloway, Johnson, Thorne, Kemp, Hoskins, Tucker, Burns, Fergusson, Adcock, Hobbs
Substitutes: Steadman (for Hoskins), Rosenior (for Adcock), Elsey (for Hobbs)
Scorer: Hoskins
Attendance: 252

Date: Tuesday 04/11/1997
Result: **CINDERFORD TOWN 0 GLOUCESTER CITY 1**
Competition: Gloucestershire FA Northern Senior Professional Cup Quarter-Final
Teamsheet: Lambert, Holloway, Johnson, Thorne, Kemp, Rosenior, Tucker, Burns, Fergusson, Mings, Adcock
Substitutes: Steadman (for Kemp), Elsey (for Mings), Hobbs (for Johnson)
Scorer: Holloway
Attendance: 139

Date: Saturday 08/11/1997
Result: **GLOUCESTER CITY 1 HALESOWEN TOWN 0**
Competition: Southern League Premier Division
Teamsheet: Lambert, Holloway, Hobbs, Thorne, Johnson, Rosenior, Tucker, Burns, Fergusson, Mings, Hoskins
Substitutes: Kemp (nps), Elsey (nps), Smith (nps)
Scorer: Fergusson (pen)
Attendance: 718

Date: Monday 10/11/1997
Result: **GLOUCESTER CITY 2 CINDERFORD TOWN 0**
Competition: Southern League Cup 1st Round 2nd Leg
Teamsheet: Newman, Holloway, Hobbs, Thorne, Johnson, Evans, Tucker, Burns, Fergusson, Hoskins, Smith
Substitutes: Howell (nps), Steadman (nps), Elsey (for Hoskins)
Scorers: Burns, Smith
Attendance: 187

Date: Saturday 15/11/1997
Result: **HASTINGS TOWN 1 GLOUCESTER CITY 1**
Competition: Southern League Premier Division
Teamsheet: Lambert, Holloway, Hobbs, Thorne, Kemp, Johnson, Tucker, Burns, Fergusson, Mings, Hoskins
Substitutes: Evans (for Hobbs), Smith (for Hoskins), Adcock (for Tucker)
Scorer: Mings
Attendance: 436

Date: Tuesday 18/11/1997
Result: **GLOUCESTER CITY 4 BROMSGROVE ROVERS 2**
Competition: Southern League Premier Division
Teamsheet: Lambert, Holloway, Johnson, Thorne, Hobbs, Rosenior, Tucker, Burns, Fergusson, Mings, Hoskins
Substitutes: Adcock (for Hoskins), Evans (for Rosenior), Smith (for Mings)
Scorers: Tucker, Mings, Adcock (2)
Attendance: 518

Date: Saturday 22/11/1997
Result: **SITTINGBOURNE 2 GLOUCESTER CITY 0**
Competition: Southern League Premier Division
Teamsheet: Mokler, Holloway, Hobbs, Thorne, Kemp, Johnson, Tucker, Burns, Fergusson, Adcock, Hoskins
Substitutes: Evans (nps), Smith (for Hoskins), Cooper (for Hobbs)
Attendance: 467

[368]

Date: Tuesday 25/11/1997
Result: **FOREST GREEN ROVERS 2 GLOUCESTER CITY 1**
Competition: Gloucestershire FA Northern Senior Professional Cup Semi-Final
Teamsheet: Lambert, Holloway, Elsey, Thorne, Kemp, Evans, Tucker, Burns, Fergusson, Smith, Hoskins
Substitutes: Steadman (for Evans), Rosenior (for Elsey), Johnson (for Smith)
Scorer: Kemp
Attendance: 439

Date: Thursday 27/11/1997
Result: **GLOUCESTER CITY 2 AFC NEWPORT 2**
Competition: Southern League Cup 2nd Round
Teamsheet: Lambert, Holloway, Johnson, Thorne, Kemp, Steadman, Cooper, Burns, Fergusson, Adcock, Hoskins
Substitutes: Smith (for Steadman), Evans (for Adcock), Hobbs (for Hoskins)
Scorers: Holloway, Thorne
Attendance: 283

Date: Tuesday 02/12/1997
Result: **GLOUCESTER CITY 1 SALISBURY CITY 1**
Competition: Southern League Premier Division
Teamsheet: Lambert, Holloway, Elsey, Thorne, Kemp, Steadman, Evans, Burns, Fergusson, Rosenior, Cooper
Substitutes: Smith (for Rosenior), Hobbs (nps), Colwell (nps)
Scorer: Smith
Attendance: 328

Date: Saturday 06/12/1997
Result: **SAINT LEONARDS STAMCROFT 0 GLOUCESTER CITY 0**
Competition: Southern League Premier Division
Teamsheet: Lambert, Holloway, Johnson, Thorne, Kemp, Elsey, Tucker, Burns, Fergusson, Smith, Cooper
Substitutes: Webb (nps), Evans (for Smith), Hobbs (nps)
Attendance: 351

Date: Saturday 13/12/1997
Result: **WORCESTER CITY 2 GLOUCESTER CITY 1**
Competition: Southern League Premier Division
Teamsheet: Lambert, Evans, Elsey, Thorne, Harriott, Fergusson, Tucker, Burns, Mings, Adcock, Cooper
Substitutes: Smith (for Adcock), Hobbs (nps), Webb (for Evans)
Scorer: Burns
Attendance: 1010

Date: Tuesday 16/12/1997
Result: **NUNEATON BOROUGH 3 GLOUCESTER CITY 1**
Competition: Southern League Premier Division
Teamsheet: Lambert, Evans, Elsey, Thorne, Steadman, Fergusson, Tucker, Burns, Adcock, Mings, Cooper
Substitutes: Hobbs (nps), Webb (nps), Hughes (nps)
Scorer: Mings
Attendance: 526

Date: Saturday 20/12/1997
Result: **GLOUCESTER CITY 0 CRAWLEY TOWN 0**
Competition: Southern League Premier Division
Teamsheet: Sumpter, Adcock, Elsey, Thorne, Steadman, Fergusson, Tucker, Burns, Mainwaring, Mings, Cooper
Substitutes: Webb (for Tucker), Evans (nps), Hobbs (nps)
Attendance: 556

Date: Friday 26/12/1997
Result: **FOREST GREEN ROVERS 1 GLOUCESTER CITY 1**
Competition: Southern League Premier Division
Teamsheet: Mokler, Holloway, Elsey, Thorne, Tucker, Fergusson, Webb, Burns, Mainwaring, Mings, Cooper
Substitutes: Adcock (for Tucker), Steadman (for Holloway), Evans (nps)
Scorer: Mainwaring
Attendance: 1333

Date: Saturday 27/12/1997
Result: **GLOUCESTER CITY 1 GRESLEY ROVERS 0**
Competition: Southern League Premier Division
Teamsheet: Mokler, Evans, Elsey, Thorne, Steadman, Fergusson, Tucker, Burns, Adcock, Webb, Cooper
Substitutes: Smith (nps), Hobbs (nps), Nichols (nps)
Scorer: Tucker
Attendance: 606

Date: Thursday 01/01/1998
Result: **GLOUCESTER CITY 4 BATH CITY 0**
Competition: Southern League Premier Division
Teamsheet: Mokler, Holloway, Elsey, Thorne, Steadman, Webb, Tucker, Burns, Mainwaring, Mings, Cooper
Substitutes: Nichols (for Mings), Evans (for Holloway), Adcock (nps)
Scorers: Burns, Mainwaring (2), Mings
Attendance: 978

Date: Saturday 03/01/1998
Result: **DORCHESTER TOWN 3 GLOUCESTER CITY 0**
Competition: Southern League Premier Division
Teamsheet: Mokler, Holloway, Elsey, Thorne, Steadman, Webb, Tucker, Burns, Mainwaring, Mings, Cooper
Substitutes: Nichols (nps), Evans (for Mings), Adcock (for Steadman)
Attendance: 830

Date: Saturday 10/01/1998
Result: **BASINGSTOKE TOWN 0 GLOUCESTER CITY 1**
Competition: FA Trophy 1st Round
Teamsheet: Mokler, Holloway, Elsey, Thorne, Tucker, Fergusson, Webb, Burns, Adcock, Mings, Cooper
Substitutes: Evans (nps), Steadman (for Holloway), Smith (nps)
Scorer: Mings
Attendance: 713

Date: Wednesday 14/01/1998
Result: **AFC NEWPORT 1 GLOUCESTER CITY 2**
Competition: Southern League Cup 2nd Round Replay
Teamsheet: Mokler, Holloway, Elsey, Thorne, Kemp, Tucker, Evans, Burns, Mainwaring, Adcock, Cooper
Substitutes: Webb (for Elsey), Smith (nps), Mings (for Evans)
Scorers: Mainwaring, Adcock
Attendance: 302

Date: Saturday 17/01/1998
Result: **CAMBRIDGE CITY 1 GLOUCESTER CITY 1**
Competition: Southern League Premier Division
Teamsheet: Mokler, Tucker, Temple, Thorne, Kemp, Webb, Smith, Burns, Mainwaring, Mings, Cooper
Substitutes: Evans (for Temple), Colwell (for Webb), Sumpter (for Evans)
Scorer: Smith
Attendance: 284

Date: Tuesday 20/01/1998
Result: **GLOUCESTER CITY 1 TAMWORTH 0**
Competition: Southern League Premier Division
Teamsheet: Mokler, Holloway, Steadman, Thorne, Kemp, Smith, Tucker, Burns, Mainwaring, Mings, Cooper
Substitutes: Colwell (for Smith), Nichols (for Mainwaring), Temple (nps)
Scorer: Mings
Attendance: 519

Date: Saturday 24/01/1998
Result: **GLOUCESTER CITY 1 ATHERSTONE UNITED 2**
Competition: Southern League Premier Division
Teamsheet: Mokler, Holloway, Steadman, Thorne, Kemp, Elsey, Nichols, Burns, Mainwaring, Fergusson, Cooper
Substitutes: Smith (for Nichols), Webb (for Smith), Colwell (for Elsey)
Scorer: Fergusson
Attendance: 660

Date: Tuesday 27/01/1998
Result: **BEDWORTH UNITED 0 GLOUCESTER CITY 3**
Competition: Southern League Cup 3rd Round
Teamsheet: Sumpter, Holloway, Steadman, Thorne, Kemp, Fergusson, Elsey, Burns, Mainwaring, Adcock, Cooper
Substitutes: Nichols (for Adcock), Smith (for Mainwaring), Hughes (nps)
Scorers: Holloway (pen), Fergusson, Mainwaring
Attendance: 82

Date: Saturday 31/01/1998
Result: **GLOUCESTER CITY 1 BURTON ALBION 1**
Competition: FA Trophy 2nd Round
Teamsheet: Mokler, Holloway, Elsey, Thorne, Kemp, Fergusson, Tucker, Burns, Adcock, Mings, Cooper
Substitutes: Smith (nps), Colwell (nps), Powell (nps)
Scorer: Kemp
Attendance: 963

Date: Tuesday 03/02/1998
Result: **BURTON ALBION 2 GLOUCESTER CITY 2** (5-6 pens)
Competition: FA Trophy 2nd Round Replay
Teamsheet: Mokler, Holloway, Elsey, Thorne, Kemp, Fergusson, Tucker, Burns, Adcock, Nichols, Cooper
Substitutes: Smith (for Nichols), Colwell (for Tucker), Hughes (nps)
Scorers: Fergusson, Burns
Attendance: 701

Date: Saturday 07/02/1998
Result: **GLOUCESTER CITY 1 FOREST GREEN ROVERS 4**
Competition: Southern League Premier Division
Teamsheet: Mokler, Holloway, Elsey, Thorne, Kemp, Fergusson, Tucker, Burns, Mainwaring, Adcock, Steadman
Substitutes: Colwell (nps), Nichols (nps), Smith (for Tucker)
Scorer: Tucker
Attendance: 1095

Date: Tuesday 10/02/1998
Result: **GLOUCESTER CITY 2 REDDITCH UNITED 2**
Competition: Southern League Cup Quarter-Final
Teamsheet: Mokler, Holloway, Elsey, Thorne, Kemp, Fergusson, Steadman, Burns, Mainwaring, Adcock, Keeling
Substitutes: Powell (nps), Nichols (for Thorne), Smith (for Nichols)
Scorers: Burns, Mainwaring
Attendance: 302

Date: Saturday 14/02/1998
Result: **GRESLEY ROVERS 2 GLOUCESTER CITY 3**
Competition: Southern League Premier Division
Teamsheet: Mokler, Holloway, Elsey, Thorne, Kemp, Fergusson, Adcock, Loss, Mainwaring, Keeling, Cooper
Substitutes: Evans (nps), Colwell (nps), Powell (nps)
Scorers: Fergusson (pen), Mainwaring, Keeling
Attendance: 566

Date: Tuesday 17/02/1998
Result: **GLOUCESTER CITY 2 ASHFORD TOWN 3**
Competition: Southern League Premier Division
Teamsheet: Mokler, Holloway, Elsey, Thorne, Kemp, Fergusson, Adcock, Loss, Mainwaring, Keeling, Cooper
Substitutes: Evans (nps), Colwell (nps), Powell (nps)
Scorers: Fergusson (pen), Mainwaring
Attendance: 375

Date: Saturday 21/02/1998
Result: **STEVENAGE BOROUGH 1 GLOUCESTER CITY 1**
Competition: FA Trophy 3rd Round
Teamsheet: Mokler, Holloway, Powell, Thorne, Kemp, Fergusson, Webb, Burns, Mings, Keeling, Steadman
Substitutes: Nichols (nps), Colwell (nps), Elsey (nps)
Scorer: Fergusson (pen)
Attendance: 2835

Date: Tuesday 24/02/1998
Result: **GLOUCESTER CITY 1 STEVENAGE BOROUGH 2**
Competition: FA Trophy 3rd Round Replay
Teamsheet: Mokler, Holloway, Powell, Thorne, Kemp, Fergusson, Webb, Burns, Mings, Keeling, Steadman
Substitutes: Nichols (for Steadman), Cooper (for Powell), Elsey (nps)
Scorer: Webb
Attendance: 1540

Date: Saturday 28/02/1998
Result: **GLOUCESTER CITY 2 SITTINGBOURNE 1**
Competition: Southern League Premier Division
Teamsheet: Mokler, Holloway, Cooper, Thorne, Kemp, Fergusson, Keeling, Burns, Mainwaring, Mings, Webb
Substitutes: Steadman (nps), Tucker (for Webb), Adcock (nps)
Scorers: Thorne, Keeling
Attendance: 555

Date: Monday 02/03/1998
Result: **REDDITCH UNITED 4 GLOUCESTER CITY 1**
Competition: Southern League Cup Quarter-Final Replay
Teamsheet: Mokler, Holloway, Cooper, Thorne, Kemp, Fergusson, Keeling, Burns, Mainwaring, Mings, Tucker
Substitutes: Steadman (for Burns), Adcock (for Tucker), Smith (nps)
Scorer: Keeling
Attendance: 170

Date: Saturday 07/03/1998
Result: **BURTON ALBION 2 GLOUCESTER CITY 1**
Competition: Southern League Premier Division
Teamsheet: Mokler, Holloway, Huggins, Adcock, Kemp, Fergusson, Tucker, Burns, Mainwaring, Mings, Webb
Substitutes: Powell (for Tucker), Colwell (nps), Cooper (for Webb)
Scorer: Mainwaring
Attendance: 731

Date: Saturday 14/03/1998
Result: **GLOUCESTER CITY 1 NUNEATON BOROUGH 0**
Competition: Southern League Premier Division
Teamsheet: Mokler, Holloway, Huggins, Cooper, Kemp, Fergusson, Keeling, Webb, Mainwaring, Adcock, Tucker
Substitutes: Steadman (for Huggins), Powell (for Keeling), Nichols (nps)
Scorer: Mainwaring
Attendance: 649

Date: Saturday 21/03/1998
Result: **ASHFORD TOWN 0 GLOUCESTER CITY 1**
Competition: Southern League Premier Division
Teamsheet: Mokler, Holloway, Huggins, Thorne, Kemp, Fergusson, Webb, Cooper, Mainwaring, Adcock, Tucker
Substitutes: Elsey (for Adcock), Nichols (nps), Colwell (for Kemp)
Scorer: Mainwaring
Attendance: 318

Date: Saturday 28/03/1998
Result: **ATHERSTONE UNITED 2 GLOUCESTER CITY 2**
Competition: Southern League Premier Division
Teamsheet: Mokler, Tucker, Huggins, Thorne, Rowntree, Adcock, Webb, Burns, Mainwaring, Mings, Cooper
Substitutes: Colwell (nps), Powell (for Adcock), Elsey (nps)
Scorers: Mainwaring, Mings
Attendance: 317

Date: Saturday 04/04/1998
Result: **GLOUCESTER CITY 4 BURTON ALBION 2**
Competition: Southern League Premier Division
Teamsheet: Mokler, Steadman, Huggins, Thorne, Rowntree, Keeling, Webb, Burns, Mainwaring, Mings, Tucker
Substitutes: Cooper (for Huggins), Powell (nps), Elsey (nps)
Scorers: Webb, Mainwaring (3)
Attendance: 562

Date: Saturday 11/04/1998
Result: **GLOUCESTER CITY 0 WORCESTER CITY 0**
Competition: Southern League Premier Division
Teamsheet: Mokler, Steadman, Rowntree, Thorne, Fergusson, Keeling, Webb, Burns, Mainwaring, Huggins, Tucker
Substitutes: Cooper (for Steadman), Holloway (for Huggins), Colwell (for Mokler)
Attendance: 758

Date: Monday 13/04/1998
Result: **SALISBURY CITY 2 GLOUCESTER CITY 3**
Competition: Southern League Premier Division
Teamsheet: Sumpter, Holloway, Cooper, Thorne, Rowntree, Fergusson, Tucker, Burns, Mainwaring, Mings, Keeling
Substitutes: Powell (for Fergusson), Nichols (nps), Steadman (for Keeling)
Scorers: Tucker, Mainwaring, Mings
Attendance: 434

Date: Saturday 18/04/1998
Result: **KING'S LYNN 1 GLOUCESTER CITY 2**
Competition: Southern League Premier Division
Teamsheet: Sumpter, Holloway, Rowntree, Thorne, Powell, Keeling, Cooper, Burns, Mainwaring, Mings, Tucker
Substitutes: Webb (for Mainwaring), Fergusson (for Rowntree), Steadman (for Powell)
Scorers: Burns, Mainwaring
Attendance: 483

Date: Saturday 25/04/1998
Result: **GLOUCESTER CITY 3 CAMBRIDGE CITY 5**
Competition: Southern League Premier Division
Teamsheet: Sumpter, Holloway, Rowntree, Webb, Fergusson, Keeling, Cooper, Burns, Mainwaring, Mings, Tucker
Substitutes: Powell (for Cooper), Elsey (for Rowntree), Colwell (nps)
Scorers: Fergusson (2 pens), Mings
Attendance: 678

Date: Saturday 02/05/1998
Result: **BROMSGROVE ROVERS 3 GLOUCESTER CITY 1**
Competition: Southern League Premier Division
Teamsheet: Mokler, Holloway, Rowntree, Powell, Fergusson, Keeling, Webb, Burns, Mainwaring, Mings, Tucker
Substitutes: Elsey (nps), Cooper (nps), Colwell (nps)
Scorer: Mainwaring
Attendance: 1061

Appearances – PM Adcock 33(9), C Burns 59, R Cadette 2(1), DA Coles 8, R Colwell 1(6), S Cooper 44(5), DJ Elsey 33(6), M Evans 7(7), SJ Fergusson 55(2), M Harriott 1, DJ Hobbs 6(2), JS Holloway 52(1), AR Hoskins 12(7), D Huggins 6, DD Johnson 20(3), D Keeling 14, GJ Kemp 42, B Lambert 10, C Loss 2, AJ Mainwaring 25, PJ Milsom 1(1), AL Mings 39(4), S Mokler 39, R Newman 1, D Nichols 2(5), S Powell 4(5), P Preedy 2(4), LD Rosenior 5(13), ME Rowntree 7, D Smith 5(11), WCM Steadman 20(12), M Sumpter 5(1), C Temple 1, GR Thorne 59, A Tucker 46(7), DA Webb 26(7).
Others selected but did not play: I Howell, BD Hughes.
Scorers –AJ Mainwaring 18, SJ Fergusson 13, AL Mings 13, C Burns 10, PM Adcock 6, JS Holloway 4, AR Hoskins 4, GJ Kemp 4, A Tucker 4, DA Webb 4, D Keeling 3, D Smith 3, GR Thorne 3, P Preedy 1, LD Rosenior 1.

SOUTHERN LEAGUE PREMIER DIVISION

POS	CLUB	P	W	D	L	F	A	PTS
1	FOREST GREEN ROVERS	42	27	8	7	93	55	89
2	MERTHYR TYDFIL	42	24	12	6	80	42	84
3	BURTON ALBION	42	21	8	13	64	43	71
4	DORCHESTER TOWN	42	19	13	10	63	38	70
5	HALESOWEN TOWN	42	18	15	9	70	38	69
6	BATH CITY	42	19	12	11	72	51	69
7	WORCESTER CITY	42	19	12	11	54	44	69
8	KING'S LYNN	42	18	11	13	64	65	65
9	ATHERSTONE UNITED	42	17	12	13	55	49	63
10	CRAWLEY TOWN	42	17	8	17	63	60	59
11	**GLOUCESTER CITY**	**42**	**16**	**11**	**15**	**57**	**57**	**59**
12	NUNEATON BOROUGH	42	17	6	19	68	61	57
13	CAMBRIDGE CITY	42	16	8	18	62	70	56
14	HASTINGS TOWN	42	14	12	16	67	70	54
15	TAMWORTH	42	14	11	17	68	65	53
16	ROTHWELL TOWN	42	11	16	15	55	73	49
17	GRESLEY ROVERS	42	14	6	22	59	77	48
18	SALISBURY CITY	42	12	12	18	53	72	48
19	BROMSGROVE ROVERS	42	13	6	23	67	85	45
20	SITTINGBOURNE	42	12	8	22	47	66	44
21	ASHFORD TOWN	42	8	5	29	34	85	29
22	SAINT LEONARDS STAMCROFT	42	5	10	27	48	97	25
		924	351	222	351	1363	1363	1275

SEASON 1998-1999
(Home Ground: City Stadium, Meadow Park, Hempsted)

Date: Saturday 22/08/1998
Result: **CAMBRIDGE CITY 1 GLOUCESTER CITY 1**
Competition: Southern League Premier Division
Teamsheet: Mokler, Holloway, Steadman, Wyatt, Kemp, Fergusson, Webb, Burns, Mainwaring, Mings, Hemmings
Substitutes: Tucker (nps), Hoskins (nps), Rutter (nps)
Scorer: Mainwaring
Attendance: 359

Date: Tuesday 25/08/1998
Result: **GLOUCESTER CITY 4 DORCHESTER TOWN 1**
Competition: Southern League Premier Division
Teamsheet: Mokler, Holloway, Steadman, Wyatt, Kemp, Fergusson, Webb, Burns, Mainwaring, Mings, Hemmings
Substitutes: Rutter (for Mainwaring), Tucker (for Wyatt), GR Thorne (nps)
Scorers: Wyatt, Burns, Mings, Hemmings
Attendance: 606

Date: Saturday 29/08/1998
Result: **GLOUCESTER CITY 1 ILKESTON TOWN 1**
Competition: Southern League Premier Division
Teamsheet: Mokler, Holloway, Steadman, Wyatt, Kemp, Fergusson, Webb, Burns, Mainwaring, Mings, Hemmings
Substitutes: Rutter (for Webb), Tucker (for Wyatt), GR Thorne (for Steadman)
Scorer: Fergusson (pen)
Attendance: 703

Date: Monday 31/08/1998
Result: **BATH CITY 1 GLOUCESTER CITY 2**
Competition: Southern League Premier Division
Teamsheet: Mokler, Holloway, GR Thorne, Wyatt, Kemp, Fergusson, Webb, Burns, Keeling, Mings, Hemmings
Substitutes: Molloy (nps), Mainwaring (nps), Hoskins (nps)
Scorers: Wyatt, Fergusson (pen)
Attendance: 1029

Date: Saturday 05/09/1998
Result: **KING'S LYNN 2 GLOUCESTER CITY 0**
Competition: Southern League Premier Division
Teamsheet: Mokler, Holloway, GR Thorne, Wyatt, Kemp, Fergusson, Webb, Burns, Keeling, Mings, Hemmings
Substitutes: Molloy (nps), Mainwaring (for Keeling), Hoskins (for Mings)
Attendance: 561

Date: Tuesday 08/09/1998
Result: **GLOUCESTER CITY 0 WEYMOUTH 0**
Competition: Southern League Premier Division
Teamsheet: Mokler, Holloway, GR Thorne, Wyatt, Kemp, Tucker, Webb, Burns, Mainwaring, Mings, Hemmings
Substitutes: Molloy (nps), WP Thorne (for Webb), Keeling (for Hemmings)
Attendance: 516

Date: Satrurday 12/09/1998
Result: **GLOUCESTER CITY 1 NUNEATON BOROUGH 0**
Competition: Southern League Premier Division
Teamsheet: Mokler, Holloway, GR Thorne, Wyatt, Kemp, Fergusson, Webb, Burns, Rutter, Mings, Tucker
Substitutes: Keeling (for Rutter), Steadman (for Wyatt), Cairns (nps)
Scorer: Tucker
Attendance: 1010

Date: Saturday 19/09/1998
Result: **HASTINGS TOWN 0 GLOUCESTER CITY 0**
Competition: Southern League Premier Division
Teamsheet: Mokler, Holloway, GR Thorne, Wyatt, Kemp, Fergusson, Webb, Burns, Keeling, Hemmings, Tucker
Substitutes: Steadman (nps), Bennett (for Wyatt), Cairns (nps)
Attendance: 620

Date: Tuesday 22/09/1998
Result: **GLOUCESTER CITY 2 BATH CITY 1**
Competition: Southern League Premier Division
Teamsheet: Mokler, Holloway, GR Thorne, Tucker, Kemp, Fergusson, Webb, Burns, Keeling, Mings, Hemmings
Substitutes: Hoskins (nps), Wyatt (nps), Steadman (nps)
Scorers: Holloway, Fergusson (pen)
Attendance: 704

Date: Saturday 26/09/1998
Result: **BURTON ALBION 5 GLOUCESTER CITY 3**
Competition: Southern League Premier Division
Teamsheet: Mokler, Holloway, GR Thorne, Tucker, Kemp, Fergusson, Webb, Burns, Keeling, Mings, Hemmings
Substitutes: Steadman (nps), Hoskins (for Webb), Wyatt (for Hemmings)
Scorers: Keeling, Mings (2)
Attendance: 742

Date: Tuesday 29/09/1998
Result: **BROMSGROVE ROVERS 0 GLOUCESTER CITY 1**
Competition: Southern League Premier Division
Teamsheet: Mokler, Holloway, GR Thorne, Tucker, Kemp, Fergusson, Callinan, Burns, Keeling, Mings, Hemmings
Substitutes: Molloy (nps), Webb (for Callinan), Hoskins (for Hemmings)
Scorer: Kemp
Attendance: 634

Date: Saturday 03/10/1998
Result: **GLOUCESTER CITY 2 PAULTON ROVERS 1**
Competition: FA Cup 2nd Qualifying Round
Teamsheet: Mokler, Holloway, GR Thorne, Tucker, Kemp, Fergusson, Webb, Burns, Keeling, Mings, Hemmings
Substitutes: Steadman (nps), Bennett (for Hoskins), Hoskins (for Mings)
Scorers: Keeling, Bennett
Attendance: 507

Date: Tuesday 06/10/1998
Result: **CIRENCESTER TOWN 1 GLOUCESTER CITY 3** (aet)
Competition: Gloucestershire FA Northern Senior Professional Cup Quarter-Final
Teamsheet: Lambert, Holloway, Steadman, GR Thorne, Kemp, Wyatt, Webb, Tucker, Rutter, Mings, Callinan
Substitutes: Bennett (for Rutter), WP Thorne (for Kemp), Hoskins (nps)
Scorers: GR Thorne, Webb (2)
Attendance: 140

Date: Saturday 10/10/1998
Result: **GLOUCESTER CITY 0 ATHERSTONE UNITED 0**
Competition: Southern League Premier Division
Teamsheet: Mokler, Holloway, GR Thorne, Wyatt, Bennett, Fergusson, Webb, Burns, Callinan, Mings, Hemmings
Substitutes: Tucker (for Callinan), Hoskins (for Bennett), Steadman (nps)
Attendance: 563

Date: Saturday 17/10/1998
Result: **GLOUCESTER CITY 10 SUDBURY TOWN 0**
Competition: FA Cup 3rd Qualifying Round
Teamsheet: Mokler, Holloway, GR Thorne, Callinan, Kemp, Fergusson, Webb, Burns, Bennett, Mings, Hemmings
Substitutes: Tucker (for Webb), Hoskins (for Hemmings), Steadman (for Kemp)
Scorers: Bennett, Burns (2), Hemmings, Mings (3), Callinan, Kemp, Hoskins
Attendance: 621

[373]

Date: Saturday 24/10/1998
Result: **CHERTSEY TOWN 0 GLOUCESTER CITY 5**
Competition: FA Trophy 1st Round
Teamsheet: Mokler, Holloway, GR Thorne, Callinan, Kemp, Fergusson, Webb, Burns, Bennett, Mings, Hemmings
Substitutes: Keeling (for Hemmings), Wyatt (for Holloway), Tucker (for Burns)
Scorers: Hemmings (3), Mings (2)
Attendance: 246

Date: Saturday 31/10/1998
Result: **KIDDERMINSTER HARRIERS 2 GLOUCESTER CITY 1**
Competition: FA Cup 4th Qualifying Round
Teamsheet: Mokler, Holloway, GR Thorne, Callinan, Kemp, Fergusson, Webb, Burns, Bennett, Mings, Hemmings
Substitutes: Tucker (for Callinan), Steadman (nps), Keeling (for Bennett)
Scorer: Webb
Attendance: 1690

Date: Saturday 07/11/1998
Result: **GLOUCESTER CITY 0 TAMWORTH 1**
Competition: Southern League Premier Division
Teamsheet: Mokler, Holloway, GR Thorne, Callinan, Kemp, Fergusson, Webb, Burns, Bennett, Tucker, Hemmings
Substitutes: Wyatt (for Tucker), Steadman (nps), WP Thorne (nps)
Attendance: 702

Date: Tuesday 10/11/1998
Result: **GLOUCESTER CITY 1 CIRENCESTER TOWN 0**
Competition: Southern League Cup 1st Round 1st Leg
Teamsheet: Mokler, Holloway, GR Thorne, Callinan, Kemp, Fergusson, Webb, Burns, Tucker, Mings, Hemmings
Substitutes: Wyatt (for Mings), Bennett (for Hemmings), Steadman (nps)
Scorer: own goal
Attendance: 188

Date: Saturday 14/11/1998
Result: **CRAWLEY TOWN 2 GLOUCESTER CITY 1**
Competition: Southern League Premier Division
Teamsheet: Mokler, Holloway, GR Thorne, Callinan, Kemp, Fergusson, Wyatt, Burns, Steadman, Tucker, Hemmings
Substitutes: Bennett (for Callinan), WP Thorne (nps), Rutter (for Fergusson)
Scorer: Hemmings
Attendance: 911

Date: Saturday 21/11/1998
Result: **GLOUCESTER CITY 1 KINGSTONIAN 2**
Competition: FA Trophy 2nd Round
Teamsheet: Mokler, Holloway, GR Thorne, Callinan, Kemp, Fergusson, Wyatt, Burns, Mainwaring, Tucker, Hemmings
Substitutes: Bennett (nps), Mings (nps), Steadman (nps)
Scorer: Tucker
Attendance: 652

Date: Tuesday 24/11/1998
Result: **CIRENCESTER TOWN 1 GLOUCESTER CITY 3**
Competition: Southern League Cup 1st Round 2nd Leg
Teamsheet: Mokler, Holloway, GR Thorne, Tucker, Kemp, Steadman, Wyatt, Burns, Rutter, Mings, Hemmings
Substitutes: Callinan (nps), Hoskins (for Rutter), Bennett (for Hemmings)
Scorers: Kemp, Wyatt, Hoskins
Attendance: 125

Date: Saturday 28/11/1998
Result: **GRESLEY ROVERS 2 GLOUCESTER CITY 3**
Competition: Southern League Premier Division
Teamsheet: Lambert, Holloway, GR Thorne, Callinan, Kemp, Steadman, Wyatt, Burns, Mainwaring, Tucker, Hemmings
Substitutes: Fergusson (for Burns), Mings (for Mainwaring), Hoskins (nps)
Scorers: Burns, Hemmings, Mings
Attendance: 512

Date: Saturday 05/12/1998
Result: **GLOUCESTER CITY 4 BROMSGROVE ROVERS 3**
Competition: Southern League Premier Division
Teamsheet: Mokler, Fergusson, GR Thorne, Callinan, Kemp, Steadman, Wyatt, Webb, Mings, Tucker, Hemmings
Substitutes: Hoskins (nps), Rutter (nps), WP Thorne (nps)
Scorers: Wyatt (2), Hemmings, own goal
Attendance: 463

Date: Monday 07/12/1998
Result: **WEYMOUTH 5 GLOUCESTER CITY 3**
Competition: Southern League Premier Division
Teamsheet: Mokler, Holloway, GR Thorne, Callinan, Kemp, Fergusson, Wyatt, Burns, Mings, Tucker, Hemmings
Substitutes: Steadman (nps), Rutter (for Tucker), Hoskins (for Holloway)
Scorers: Kemp, Wyatt, Burns
Attendance: 505

Date: Saturday 12/12/1998
Result: **GLOUCESTER CITY 3 CAMBRIDGE CITY 1**
Competition: Southern League Premier Division
Teamsheet: Mokler, Holloway, GR Thorne, WP Thorne, Kemp, Webb, Wyatt, Burns, Mings, Tucker, Hemmings
Substitutes: Fergusson (nps), Callinan (nps), Hoskins (for Mings)
Scorers: Kemp (2), Mings
Attendance: 536

Date: Wednesday 16/12/1998
Result: **STOURBRIDGE 2 GLOUCESTER CITY 0**
Competition: Southern League Cup 2nd Round
Teamsheet: Mountain, Steadman, WP Thorne, Callinan, Fergusson, GR Thorne, Wyatt, Burns, Hoskins, Tucker, Hemmings
Substitutes: Bennett (for Steadman), Rutter (nps), Webb (nps)
Attendance: 111

Date: Saturday 19/12/1998
Result: **BOSTON UNITED 1 GLOUCESTER CITY 0**
Competition: Southern League Premier Division
Teamsheet: Mokler, Holloway, WP Thorne, Callinan, Kemp, Niblett, Wyatt, Burns, Mings, Tucker, Hemmings
Substitutes: GR Thorne (nps), Fergusson (nps), Hoskins (nps)
Attendance: 907

Date: Monday 28/12/1998
Result: **WORCESTER CITY 2 GLOUCESTER CITY 2**
Competition: Southern League Premier Division
Teamsheet: Mokler, Holloway, WP Thorne, Webb, GR Thorne, Niblett, Wyatt, Burns, Mings, Tucker, Hemmings
Substitutes: Mainwaring (for Tucker), Callinan (for Webb), Fergusson (nps)
Scorers: Holloway (pen), Mainwaring
Attendance: 1045

Date: Friday 01/01/1999
Result: **SALISBURY CITY 1 GLOUCESTER CITY 1**
Competition: Southern League Premier Division
Teamsheet: Mokler, Holloway, WP Thorne, GR Thorne, Kemp, Niblett, Tucker, Burns, Mainwaring, Mings, Hemmings
Substitutes: Callinan (for Tucker), Wyatt (for Mings), Fergusson (nps)
Scorer: Mainwaring
Attendance: 667

Date: Saturday 02/01/1999
Result: **GLOUCESTER CITY 2 ROTHWELL TOWN 1**
Competition: Southern League Premier Division
Teamsheet: Mokler, GR Thorne, WP Thorne, Callinan, Kemp, Niblett, Wyatt, Fergusson, Mainwaring, Tucker, Hemmings
Substitutes: Holloway (for WP Thorne), Mings (for GR Thorne), Bennett (nps)
Scorer: Mings (2)
Attendance: 442

Date: Saturday 09/01/1999
Result: **ATHERSTONE UNITED 1 GLOUCESTER CITY 2**
Competition: Southern League Premier Division
Teamsheet: Mokler, GR Thorne, WP Thorne, Callinan, Kemp, Niblett, Wyatt, Burns, Mainwaring, Tucker, Hemmings
Substitutes: Holloway (for Niblett), Mings (for Mainwaring), Fergusson (for Wyatt)
Scorer: Mainwaring (2)
Attendance: 278

Date: Saturday 16/01/1999
Result: **GLOUCESTER CITY 0 GRANTHAM TOWN 1**
Competition: Southern League Premier Division
Teamsheet: Mokler, Holloway, WP Thorne, Webb, Kemp, GR Thorne, Wyatt, Burns, Mainwaring, Tucker, Hemmings
Substitutes: Fergusson (for Webb), Bennett (nps), Hoskins (for Tucker)
Attendance: 593

Date: Saturday 23/01/1999
Result: **GLOUCESTER CITY 2 BOSTON UNITED 2**
Competition: Southern League Premier Division
Teamsheet: Mokler, Holloway, WP Thorne, Callinan, Kemp, GR Thorne, Wyatt, Burns, Mainwaring, Tucker, Hemmings
Substitutes: Mings (for Callinan), Fergusson (for Callinan), Hoskins (for WP Thorne)
Scorer: Mings (2)
Attendance: 510

Date: Tuesday 26/01/1999
Result: **MERTHYR TYDFIL 0 GLOUCESTER CITY 1**
Competition: Southern League Premier Division
Teamsheet: Mountain, Holloway, WP Thorne, Callinan, Kemp, GR Thorne, Tucker, Burns, Mainwaring, Mings, Hemmings
Substitutes: Fergusson (nps), Hoskins (nps), Bennett (nps)
Scorer: Kemp
Attendance: 343

Date: Saturday 30/01/1999
Result: **HALESOWEN TOWN 0 GLOUCESTER CITY 1**
Competition: Southern League Premier Division
Teamsheet: Mountain, Holloway, WP Thorne, Callinan, Kemp, GR Thorne, Tucker, Burns, Mainwaring, Mings, Hemmings
Substitutes: Fergusson (for Mainwaring), Hoskins (nps), Bennett (nps)
Scorer: Holloway (pen)
Attendance: 743

Date: Saturday 06/02/1999
Result: **GLOUCESTER CITY 0 GRESLEY ROVERS 0**
Competition: Southern League Premier Division
Teamsheet: Mountain, Holloway, WP Thorne, Callinan, Kemp, GR Thorne, Tucker, Burns, Mainwaring, Mings, Hemmings
Substitutes: Wyatt (for Tucker), Fergusson (for -----), Hoskins (for Mainwaring)
Attendance: 531

Date: Saturday 13/02/1999
Result: **GRANTHAM TOWN 0 GLOUCESTER CITY 1**
Competition: Southern League Premier Division
Teamsheet: Mountain, Holloway, WP Thorne, Callinan, Niblett, GR Thorne, Wyatt, Burns, Tucker, Mings, Hemmings
Substitutes: Fergusson (nps), Mainwaring (nps), Webb (for WP Thorne)
Scorer: own goal
Attendance: 522

Date: Tuesday 16/02/1999
Result: **FOREST GREEN ROVERS 2 GLOUCESTER CITY 4** (aet)
Competition: Gloucestershire FA Northern Senior Professional Cup Semi-Final
Teamsheet: Mountain, Holloway, Fergusson, Callinan, Kemp, Niblett, Webb, Burns, Mainwaring, Mings, Tucker
Substitutes: Jenkins (for Callinan), Smith (for Mings), Hoskins (nps)
Scorers: Holloway (2 pens), Mainwaring, Mings
Attendance: 501

Date: Saturday 20/02/1999
Result: GLOUCESTER CITY 2 CRAWLEY TOWN 0
Competition: Southern League Premier Division
Teamsheet: Mountain, Holloway, Fergusson, Callinan, Niblett, GR Thorne, Webb, Burns, Mainwaring, Tucker, Hemmings
Substitutes: Mings (for Hemmings), Smith (nps), Jenkins (nps)
Scorers: Mainwaring, Tucker
Attendance: 584

Date: Saturday 27/02/1999
Result: GLOUCESTER CITY 2 KING'S LYNN 1
Competition: Southern League Premier Division
Teamsheet: Mountain, Holloway, Fergusson, Callinan, Kemp, Niblett, Webb, GR Thorne, Mainwaring, Mings, Tucker
Substitutes: Hemmings (for Callinan), Smith (for Tucker), Hickey (nps)
Scorers: Kemp, Mings
Attendance: 610

Date: Saturday 06/03/1999
Result: ROTHWELL TOWN 0 GLOUCESTER CITY 1
Competition: Southern League Premier Division
Teamsheet: Mountain, Holloway, WP Thorne, Callinan, Kemp, Niblett, Webb, GR Thorne, Mainwaring, Mings, Tucker
Substitutes: Hemmings (for Tucker), Smith (for Mainwaring), Jenkins (nps)
Scorer: Holloway (pen)
Attendance: 239

Date: Tuesday 09/03/1999
Result: GLOUCESTER CITY 2 MERTHYR TYDFIL 1
Competition: Southern League Premier Division
Teamsheet: Mountain, Holloway, WP Thorne, GR Thorne, Kemp, Niblett, Webb, Burns, Tucker, Mings, Hemmings
Substitutes: Mainwaring (for Mings), Smith (for Tucker), Callinan (nps)
Scorers: Burns, Mings
Attendance: 576

Date: Saturday 13/03/1999
Result: TAMWORTH 1 GLOUCESTER CITY 1
Competition: Southern League Premier Division
Teamsheet: Mountain, Holloway, WP Thorne, GR Thorne, Kemp, Niblett, Webb, Burns, Callinan, Mings, Hemmings
Substitutes: Mainwaring (for Callinan), Fergusson (nps), Tucker (nps)
Scorer: GR Thorne
Attendance: 512

Date: Saturday 20/03/1999
Result: GLOUCESTER CITY 0 BURTON ALBION 1
Competition: Southern League Premier Division
Teamsheet: Mountain, Holloway, WP Thorne, GR Thorne, Kemp, Niblett, Webb, Burns, Smith, Mings, Hemmings
Substitutes: Mainwaring (for Smith), Fergusson (for Hemmings), Callinan (nps)
Attendance: 617

Date: Saturday 27/03/1999
Result: GLOUCESTER CITY 2 HASTINGS TOWN 3
Competition: Southern League Premier Division
Teamsheet: Mountain, Holloway, WP Thorne, GR Thorne, Kemp, Niblett, Jenkins, Burns, Fergusson, Smith, Webb
Substitutes: Mainwaring (for Webb), Griffiths (nps), Hickey (nps)
Scorers: Holloway, Burns
Attendance: 394

Date: Saturday 03/04/1999
Result: DORCHESTER TOWN 0 GLOUCESTER CITY 0
Competition: Southern League Premier Division
Teamsheet: Mountain, Holloway, GR Thorne, Webb, Kemp, Niblett, Wyatt, Burns, Mainwaring, Fergusson, Hemmings
Substitutes: Mings (nps), Rutter (nps), Jenkins (nps)
Attendance: 668

Date: Monday 05/04/1999
Result: GLOUCESTER CITY 0 WORCESTER CITY 2
Competition: Southern League Premier Division
Teamsheet: Mountain, Holloway, WP Thorne, GR Thorne, Kemp, Niblett, Wyatt, Burns, Fergusson, Rutter, Hemmings
Substitutes: Mainwaring (for Rutter), Mings (for WP Thorne), Webb (nps)
Attendance: 654

Date: Saturday 10/04/1999
Result: NUNEATON BOROUGH 2 GLOUCESTER CITY 0
Competition: Southern League Premier Division
Teamsheet: Mountain, Hickey, Fergusson, Webb, Kemp, Niblett, Rutter, Callinan, Mainwaring, Mings, Hemmings
Substitutes: Tucker (nps), Jenkins (nps), Griffiths (nps)
Attendance: 1538

Date: Saturday 17/04/1999
Result: GLOUCESTER CITY 2 HALESOWEN TOWN 0
Competition: Southern League Premier Division
Teamsheet: Mountain, Holloway, Fergusson, Callinan, Kemp, Niblett, Wyatt, Burns, Mainwaring, Webb, Hemmings
Substitutes: Tucker (for Callinan), Rutter (for Wyatt), Hickey (nps)
Scorers: Wyatt, Hemmings
Attendance: 535

Date: Saturday 24/04/1999
Result: ILKESTON TOWN 4 GLOUCESTER CITY 3
Competition: Southern League Premier Division
Teamsheet: Mountain, Holloway, Callinan, Fergusson, Kemp, Niblett, Wyatt, Burns, Mainwaring, Webb, Hemmings
Substitutes: Tucker (nps), Rutter (nps), Hickey (nps)
Scorers: Callinan (2), Mainwaring
Attendance: 639

[376]

Date: Saturday 01/05/1999
Result: **GLOUCESTER CITY 1 SALISBURY CITY 2**
Competition: Southern League Premier Division
Teamsheet: Mountain, Holloway, Fergusson, GR Thorne, Kemp, Niblett, Wyatt, Burns, Mainwaring, Webb, Hemmings
Substitutes: Tucker (nps), Rutter (for Mainwaring), Callinan (nps)
Scorer: Hemmings
Attendance: 448

Date: Tuesday 04/05/1999
Result: **GLOUCESTER CITY 0 CHELTENHAM TOWN 3**
Competition: Gloucestershire FA Northern Senior Professional Cup Final
Teamsheet: Mountain, Holloway, Fergusson, GR Thorne, Callinan, Niblett, Wyatt, Burns, Mainwaring, Mings, Hemmings
Substitutes: Webb (for Wyatt), Kemp (nps), Rutter (nps)
Attendance: 904

Appearances – SJ Bennett 6(6), C Burns 46, TJ Callinan 31(1), SJ Fergusson 34(7), T Hemmings 46(2), SMH Hickey 1, JS Holloway 47(2), AR Hoskins 1(12), S Jenkins 1(1), D Keeling 7(4), GJ Kemp 46, B Lambert 2, A Mainwaring 23(7), AL Mings 35(6), S Mokler 30, P Molloy 0(1), PD Mountain 20, N Niblett 20, T Rutter 5(6), JS Smith 2(4), WCM Steadman 9(2), GR Thorne 44(2), WP Thorne 18(2), A Tucker 33(7), DA Webb 35(4), M Wyatt 30(6).
Others selected but did not play: K Cairns, N Griffiths.
Scorers – AL Mings 17, T Hemmings 10, GJ Kemp 8, A Mainwaring 8, C Burns 7, JS Holloway 7, M Wyatt 7, TJ Callinan 3, SJ Fergusson 3, A Tucker 3, DA Webb 3, SJ Bennett 2, AR Hoskins 2, D Keeling 2, GR Thorne 2, own goals 3.

1998-1999 – SOUTHERN LEAGUE – PREMIER DIVISION

POS	CLUB	P	W	D	L	F	A	PTS
1	NUNEATON BOROUGH	42	27	9	6	91	33	90
2	BOSTON UNITED	42	17	16	9	69	51	67
3	ILKESTON TOWN	42	18	13	11	72	59	67
4	BATH CITY	42	18	11	13	70	44	65
5	HASTINGS TOWN	42	18	11	13	57	49	65
6	**GLOUCESTER CITY**	**42**	**18**	**11**	**13**	**57**	**52**	**65**
7	WORCESTER CITY	42	18	9	15	58	54	63
8	HALESOWEN TOWN	42	17	11	14	72	60	62
9	TAMWORTH	42	19	5	18	62	67	62
10	KING'S LYNN	42	17	10	15	53	46	61
11	CRAWLEY TOWN	42	17	10	15	57	58	61
12	SALISBURY CITY	42	16	12	14	56	61	60
13	BURTON ALBION	42	17	7	18	58	52	58
14	WEYMOUTH	42	14	14	14	56	55	56
15	MERTHYR TYDFIL	42	15	8	19	52	62	53
16	ATHERSTONE UNITED	42	12	14	16	47	52	50
17	GRANTHAM TOWN	42	14	8	20	51	58	50
18	DORCHESTER TOWN	42	11	15	16	49	63	48
19	ROTHWELL TOWN	42	13	9	20	47	67	48
20	CAMBRIDGE CITY	42	11	12	19	47	68	45
21	GRESLEY ROVERS	42	12	8	22	49	73	44
22	BROMSGROVE ROVERS	42	8	7	27	38	84	30*
		924	347	230	347	1268	1268	1270

* One point deducted.

SEASON 1999-2000
(Home Ground: City Stadium, Meadow Park, Hempsted)

Date: Saturday 14/08/1999
Result: **GLOUCESTER CITY 2 GRANTHAM TOWN 0**
Competition: Southern League Premier Division
Teamsheet: Gannaway, GR Thorne, WP Thorne, Wigg, Kemp, Niblett, Wyatt, Chenoweth, Keeling, Smith, Hackett
Substitutes: Cox (for Keeling), Tucker (for Chenoweth), Rose (for Wigg)
Scorers: Niblett, Smith
Attendance: 639

Date: Tuesday 17/08/1999
Result: **BURTON ALBION 3 GLOUCESTER CITY 0**
Competition: Southern League Premier Division
Teamsheet: Gannaway, GR Thorne, WP Thorne, Wigg, Kemp, Niblett, Wyatt, Chenoweth, Keeling, Smith, Hackett
Substitutes: Cox (for Hackett), Tucker (for Chenoweth), Rose (for Wyatt)
Attendance: 948

Date: Saturday 21/08/1999
Result: **MARGATE 3 GLOUCESTER CITY 0**
Competition: Southern League Premier Division
Teamsheet: Gannaway, Coupe, WP Thorne, GR Thorne, Kemp, Niblett, Wyatt, Wigg, Keeling, Smith, Hackett
Substitutes: Cox (for Hackett), Chenoweth (for Wigg), Rose (for Wyatt)
Attendance: 504

Date: Tuesday 24/08/1999
Result: **GLOUCESTER CITY 0 TAMWORTH 0**
Competition: Southern League Premier Division
Teamsheet: Hervin, Coupe, Chenoweth, GR Thorne, Kemp, Niblett, Wyatt, Tucker, Cox, Smith, Rose
Substitutes: Keeling (for Wyatt), Callinan (nps), WP Thorne (nps)
Attendance: 509

Date: Saturday 28/08/1999
Result: **GLOUCESTER CITY 1 CAMBRIDGE CITY 0**
Competition: Southern League Premier Division
Teamsheet: Hervin, Coupe, Chenoweth, GR Thorne, Kemp, Niblett, Wyatt, Tucker, Cox, Smith, Rose
Substitutes: Keeling (for Rose), Callinan (for Tucker), WP Thorne (for Chenoweth)
Scorer: Callinan
Attendance: 446

Date: Monday 30/08/1999
Result: **ATHERSTONE UNITED 1 GLOUCESTER CITY 0**
Competition: Southern League Premier Division
Teamsheet: Hervin, Coupe, Chenoweth, GR Thorne, Kemp, Niblett, Wyatt, Tucker, Callinan, Smith, WP Thorne
Substitutes: Keeling (for Wyatt), Cox (for Tucker), Hackett (for WP Thorne)
Attendance: 363

Date: Saturday 04/09/1999
Result: **GLOUCESTER CITY 0 DORCHESTER TOWN 0**
Competition: Southern League Premier Division
Teamsheet: Hervin, Coupe, Chenoweth, GR Thorne, Kemp, Niblett, Wyatt, Callinan, Cox, Smith, Hackett
Substitutes: Rose (for Chenoweth), Tucker (for Callinan), WP Thorne (for -----)
Attendance: 340

Date: Tuesday 07/09/1999
Result: **CLEVEDON TOWN 3 GLOUCESTER CITY 0**
Competition: Southern League Premier Division
Teamsheet: Hervin, Coupe, WP Thorne, GR Thorne, Kemp, Tucker, Callinan, Chenoweth, Cox, Smith, Rose
Substitutes: Hickey (for Tucker), Wyatt (nps), Hackett (nps)
Attendance: 481

Date: Saturday 11/09/1999
Result: **HAVANT & WATERLOOVILLE 1 GLOUCESTER CITY 1**
Competition: Southern League Premier Division
Teamsheet: Gannaway, Tucker, WP Thorne, GR Thorne, Kemp, Chenoweth, Wyatt, Rose, Callinan, Smith, Hackett
Substitutes: Jennings (nps), Fergusson (for WP Thorne), Cairns (nps)
Scorer: Smith (pen)
Attendance: 497

Date: Saturday 18/09/1999
Result: **WEYMOUTH 0 GLOUCESTER CITY 0**
Competition: FA Cup 2nd Qualifying Round
Teamsheet: Gannaway, Tucker, WP Thorne, GR Thorne, Niblett, Chenoweth, Wyatt, Rose, Callinan, Smith, Hackett
Substitutes: Jennings (nps), Fergusson (for Smith), Cairns (nps)
Attendance: 643

Date: Tuesday 21/09/1999
Result: **GLOUCESTER CITY 2 WEYMOUTH 1**
Competition: FA Cup 2nd Qualifying Round Replay
Teamsheet: Gannway, Tucker, WP Thorne, GR Thorne, Niblett, Chenoweth, Wyatt, Rose, Callinan, Smith, Hackett
Substitutes: Jennings (nps), Fergusson (for Smith), Cairns (nps)
Scorers: Smith (pen), Fergusson
Attendance: 491

Date: Saturday 25/09/1999
Result: **GLOUCESTER CITY 1 ILKESTON TOWN 0**
Competition: Southern League Premier Division
Teamsheet: Gannaway, Tucker, WP Thorne, GR Thorne, Niblett, Chenoweth, Wyatt, Rose, Callinan, Smith, Jennings
Substitutes: Fergusson (for Jennings), Hickey (for Rose), Cairns (nps)
Scorer: Chenoweth
Attendance: 558

Date: Saturday 02/10/1999
Result: **GLOUCESTER CITY 2 MERTHYR TYDFIL 3**
Competition: FA Cup 3rd Qualifying Round
Teamsheet: Gannway, Tucker, WP Thorne, GR Thorne, Fergusson, Chenoweth, Wyatt, Rose, Callinan, Smith, Jennings
Substitutes: Cox (for Jennings), Cairns (nps), Temple (nps)
Scorers: Wyatt, Smith
Attendance: 749

Date: Saturday 09/10/1999
Result: **GLOUCESTER CITY 4 CHESHAM UNITED 2**
Competition: FA Trophy 1st Round
Teamsheet: Gannway, Tucker, WP Thorne, GR Thorne, Fergusson, Chenoweth, Wyatt, Rose, Cox, Smith, Callinan
Substitutes: Jennings (for Wyatt), Devlin (nps), Cairns (for Chenoweth)
Scorers: Cox (2), Smith, Chenoweth
Attendance: 513

Date: Wednesday 13/10/1999
Result: **FOREST GREEN ROVERS 5 GLOUCESTER CITY 0**
Competition: Gloucestershire FA Northern Senior Professional Cup Quarter-Final
Teamsheet: Gannaway, Tucker, WP Thorne, GR Thorne, Fergusson, Cairns, Wyatt, Callinan, Cox, Smith, Rose
Substitutes: Temple (for Rose), Hickey (nps), Newton (nps)
Attendance: 365

Date: Saturday 16/10/1999
Result: **GLOUCESTER CITY 1 WEYMOUTH 1**
Competition: Southern League Premier Division
Teamsheet: Gannaway, Tucker, WP Thorne, GR Thorne, Fergusson, Chenoweth, Wyatt, Rose, Cox, Smith, Callinan
Substitutes: Cairns (for Fergusson), Devlin (for WP Thorne), Temple (nps)
Scorer: GR Thorne
Attendance: 454

Date: Saturday 23/10/1999
Result: **MERTHYR TYDFIL 5 GLOUCESTER CITY 0**
Competition: Southern League Premier Division
Teamsheet: Gannaway, Tucker, Temple, WP Thorne, Fergusson, Callinan, Wyatt, Rose, Cox, Smith, Cairns
Substitutes: Devlin (nps), Hickey (for Fergusson), Griffiths (nps)
Attendance: 528

Date: Tuesday 26/10/1999
Result: **GLOUCESTER CITY 2 BURTON ALBION 1**
Competition: Southern League Premier Division
Teamsheet: Gannaway, Tucker, WP Thorne, GR Thorne, Niblett, Chenoweth, Wyatt, Rose, Cox, Smith, Griffiths
Substitutes: Temple (nps), Cairns (nps), Fergusson (nps)
Scorer: Cox (2)
Attendance: 408

Date: Saturday 30/10/1999
Result: **GLOUCESTER CITY 2 BOSTON UNITED 2**
Competition: Southern League Premier Division
Teamsheet: Gannaway, Tucker, WP Thorne, GR Thorne, Fergusson, Chenoweth, Wyatt, Rose, Cox, Smith, Griffiths
Substitutes: Temple (nps), Cairns (nps), Hickey (nps)
Scorers: Cox, Smith
Attendance: 702

Date: Saturday 06/11/1999
Result: **BATH CITY 5 GLOUCESTER CITY 1**
Competition: Southern League Premier Division
Teamsheet: Gannaway, Tucker, WP Thorne, GR Thorne, Fergusson, Callinan, Wyatt, Rose, Cox, Smith, Griffiths
Substitutes: Temple (nps), Cairns (nps), Hickey (nps)
Scorer: Rose
Attendance: 926

Date: Saturday 13/11/1999
Result: **GLOUCESTER CITY 1 NEWPORT COUNTY 1**
Competition: Southern League Premier Division
Teamsheet: Gannaway, Tucker, WP Thorne, GR Thorne, Niblett, Callinan, Wyatt, Rose, Cox, Smith, Griffiths
Substitutes: Fergusson (for Griffiths), Cairns (for Niblett), Temple (nps)
Scorer: Rose
Attendance: 889

Date: Tuesday 16/11/1999
Result: **GLOUCESTER CITY 4 YATE TOWN 1**
Competition: Southern League Cup 1st Round
Teamsheet: Gannway, Tucker, Devlin, Hickey, Fergusson, Callinan, Temple, Rose, Cairns, Smith, Griffiths
Substitutes: Cox (for Fergusson), Futcher (for Griffiths), WP Thorne (for Tucker)
Scorers: Smith (3, 1 pen), Cairns
Attendance: 140

Date: Saturday 20/11/1999
Result: **GRANTHAM TOWN 1 GLOUCESTER CITY 1**
Competition: Southern League Premier Division
Teamsheet: Gannaway, Tucker, Devlin, GR Thorne, Fergusson, Cairns, Wyatt, Rose, Cox, Smith, Griffiths
Substitutes: Hickey (nps), Temple (nps), Futcher (nps)
Scorer: Cox
Attendance: 306

Date: Saturday 27/11/1999
Result: **WELLING UNITED 2 GLOUCESTER CITY 1**
Competition: FA Trophy 2nd Round
Teamsheet: Gannaway, Tucker, WP Thorne, GR Thorne, Fergusson, Chenoweth, Wyatt, Rose, Cox, Cairns, Griffiths
Substitutes: Smith (for Chenoweth), Temple (nps), Hickey (nps)
Scorer: Smith
Attendance: 423

Date: Saturday 04/12/1999
Result: **GLOUCESTER CITY 3 ROTHWELL TOWN 1**
Competition: Southern League Premier Division
Teamsheet: Gannaway, Tucker, WP Thorne, GR Thorne, Fergusson, Cairns, Wyatt, Rose, Cox, Smith, Griffiths
Substitutes: Casey (for Griffiths), Devlin (nps), Hickey (nps)
Scorers: Rose, Smith, Cox
Attendance: 395

Date: Tuesday 07/12/1999
Result: **GLOUCESTER CITY 3 SOLIHULL BOROUGH 1**
Competition: Southern League Cup 2nd Round
Teamsheet: Gannaway, Tucker, Devlin, GR Thorne, Hickey, Cairns, Wyatt, Callinan, Cox, Smith, Casey
Substitutes: Temple (for Callinan), Griffiths (for Casey), Futcher (for Cox)
Scorers: Smith (2), Callinan
Attendance: 250

Date: Saturday 18/12/1999
Result: **GLOUCESTER CITY 2 CRAWLEY TOWN 2**
Competition: Southern League Premier Division
Teamsheet: Gannaway, Abbott, WP Thorne, Callinan, Fergusson, Casey, Wyatt, Rose, Cairns, Smith, Griffiths
Substitutes: Hickey (for Griffiths), Devlin (nps), Newton (nps)
Scorers: Fergusson, Rose
Attendance: 416

Date: Monday 27/12/1999
Result: **WORCESTER CITY 4 GLOUCESTER CITY 0**
Competition: Southern League Premier Division
Teamsheet: Gannaway, Tucker, WP Thorne, Hughes, Fergusson, Casey, Wyatt, Rose, Callinan, Smith, Cairns
Substitutes: Hickey (for Hughes), Devlin (for -----), Newton (for Smith)
Attendance: 1609

[379]

Date: Monday 03/01/2000
Result: **GLOUCESTER CITY 2 HALESOWEN TOWN 2**
Competition: Southern League Premier Division
Teamsheet: Gannaway, Tucker, WP Thorne, GR Thorne, Abbott, Casey, Wyatt, Rose, Chenoweth, Smith, Callinan
Substitutes: Cairns (for Casey), Wigg (for Chenoweth), Devlin (nps)
Scorers: GR Thorne, Callinan
Attendance: 562

Date: Saturday 08/01/2000
Result: **GLOUCESTER CITY 1 CLEVEDON TOWN 5**
Competition: Southern League Premier Division
Teamsheet: Gannaway, Tucker, WP Thorne, GR Thorne, Abbott, Chenoweth, Wyatt, Rose, Cox, Wigg, Callinan
Substitutes: Smith (for Abbott), Casey (for Chenoweth), Cairns (for Callinan)
Scorer: Smith
Attendance: 452

Date: Saturday 15/01/2000
Result: **CAMBRIDGE CITY 2 GLOUCESTER CITY 1**
Competition: Southern League Premier Division
Teamsheet: Gannaway, Tucker, WP Thorne, GR Thorne, Abbott, Callinan, Casey, Rose, Cox, Smith, Wigg
Substitutes: Wyatt (for Casey), Devlin (nps), Cairns (nps)
Scorer: Smith
Attendance: 418

Date: Tuesday 18/01/2000
Result: **GLOUCESTER CITY 1 MERTHYR TYDFIL 0**
Competition: Southern League Premier Division
Teamsheet: Gannaway, Tucker, WP Thorne, Callinan, Abbott, Casey, Wyatt, Rose, Cox, Smith, Wigg
Substitutes: Cairns (for Wigg), Chenoweth (nps), Niblett (for Rose)
Scorer: Smith
Attendance: 404

Date: Saturday 22/01/2000
Result: **WEYMOUTH 4 GLOUCESTER CITY 1**
Competition: Southern League Premier Division
Teamsheet: Gannaway, Tucker, WP Thorne, GR Thorne, Abbott, Niblett, Wyatt, Chenoweth, Cox, Smith, Wigg
Substitutes: Casey (for WP Thorne), Cairns (nps), Callinan (for Chenoweth)
Scorer: Cox
Attendance: 649

Date: Tuesday 25/01/2000
Result: **BATH CITY 3 GLOUCESTER CITY 0**
Competition: Southern League Cup 3rd Round
Teamsheet: Gannaway, Tucker, WP Thorne, GR Thorne, Abbott, Chenoweth, Casey, Griffiths, Cox, Callinan, Cairns
Substitutes: Wigg (for Chenoweth), Smith (for Callinan), Devlin (for Cairns)
Attendance: 434

Date: Saturday 29/01/2000
Result: **DORCHESTER TOWN 1 GLOUCESTER CITY 2**
Competition: Southern League Premier Division
Teamsheet: King, Tucker, WP Thorne, GR Thorne, Niblett, Abbott, Wyatt, Rose, Cox, Smith, Wigg
Substitutes: Casey (nps), Griffiths (nps), Devlin (nps)
Scorers: WP Thorne, Abbott
Attendance: 574

Date: Wednesday 02/02/2000
Result: **NEWPORT COUNTY 2 GLOUCESTER CITY 1**
Competition: Southern League Premier Division
Teamsheet: King, Tucker, WP Thorne, GR Thorne, Niblett, Abbott, Wyatt, Rose, Cox, Smith, Wigg
Substitutes: Casey (nps), Griffiths (for Wyatt), Devlin (nps)
Scorer: Smith
Attendance: 577

Date: Saturday 05/02/2000
Result: **GLOUCESTER CITY 1 ATHERSTONE UNITED 1**
Competition: Southern League Premier Division
Teamsheet: King, Tucker, WP Thorne, GR Thorne, Niblett, Abbott, Wyatt, Rose, Cox, Smith, Wigg
Substitutes: Casey (for Wigg), Griffiths (for Rose), Devlin (nps)
Scorer: Smith
Attendance: 435

Date: Saturday 12/02/2000
Result: **KING'S LYNN 2 GLOUCESTER CITY 0**
Competition: Southern League Premier Division
Teamsheet: King, Tucker, Chenoweth, GR Thorne, Niblett, Callinan, Wyatt, Rose, Cox, Casey, Griffiths
Substitutes: Smith (nps), Wigg (nps), Cairns (nps)
Attendance: 565

Date: Saturday 19/02/2000
Result: **GLOUCESTER CITY 1 BATH CITY 1**
Competition: Southern League Premier Division
Teamsheet: King, Abbott, WP Thorne, GR Thorne, Callinan, Chenoweth, Wyatt, Rose, Casey, Smith, Griffiths
Substitutes: Cox (for Casey), Wigg (for Callinan), Devlin (nps)
Scorer: Smith
Attendance: 689

Date: Saturday 26/02/2000
Result: **SALISBURY CITY 2 GLOUCESTER CITY 0**
Competition: Southern League Premier Division
Teamsheet: King, Abbott, WP Thorne, GR Thorne, Callinan, Chenoweth, Wyatt, Rose, Casey, Smith, Griffiths
Substitutes: Cox (for Casey), Wigg (nps), Devlin (nps)
Attendance: 536

SEASON BY SEASON

Date: Saturday 04/03/2000
Result: **GLOUCESTER CITY 0 KING'S LYNN 1**
Competition: Southern League Premier Division
Teamsheet: King, Griffiths, Devlin, Abbott, Niblett, Wigg, Wyatt, Cox, Bayliss, Callinan, Casey
Substitutes: Cairns (for Callinan), Smith (for Casey), Hickey (nps)
Attendance: 429

Date: Tuesday 07/03/2000
Result: **TAMWORTH 1 GLOUCESTER CITY 1**
Competition: Southern League Premier Division
Teamsheet: King, Griffiths, WP Thorne, Abbott, Niblett, Callinan, Wigg, Cox, Bayliss, Casey, Wyatt
Substitutes: Cairns (for Cox), Smith (nps), Hickey (nps)
Scorer: Cox
Attendance: 493

Date: Saturday 11/03/2000
Result: **ILKESTON TOWN 1 GLOUCESTER CITY 0**
Competition: Southern League Premier Division
Teamsheet: King, Devlin, WP Thorne, Abbott, Niblett, Wyatt, Jenkins, Casey, Smith, Bayliss, Wigg
Substitutes: Gordon (for Smith), Cairns (for Devlin), Hickey (nps)
Attendance: 505

Date: Saturday 25/03/2000
Result: **GLOUCESTER CITY 1 HAVANT & WATERLOOVILLE 1**
Competition: Southern League Premier Division
Teamsheet: Gannaway, Griffiths, Steadman, Abbott, Niblett, Wigg, Wyatt, Smart, Bayliss, Gordon, Cook
Substitutes: Hunt (nps), Casey (for Wigg), Callinan (for Gordon)
Scorer: Cook
Attendance: 426

Date: Saturday 01/04/2000
Result: **CRAWLEY TOWN 2 GLOUCESTER CITY 1**
Competition: Southern League Premier Division
Teamsheet: Gannaway, Steadman, Hunt, Abbott, Niblett, Cook, Wyatt, Griffiths, Bayliss, Smart, Casey
Substitutes: Wigg (nps), Gordon (for Casey), Callinan (nps)
Scorer: Cook
Attendance: 713

Date: Saturday 08/04/2000
Result: **BOSTON UNITED 6 GLOUCESTER CITY 1**
Competition: Southern League Premier Division
Teamsheet: Gannaway, Steadman, Hunt, Abbott, Niblett, Wigg, Wyatt, Casey, Bayliss, Smart, Griffiths
Substitutes: Callinan (nps), Gordon (for Smart), Cairns (for Casey)
Scorer: Wyatt
Attendance: 2063

Date: Saturday 15/04/2000
Result: **GLOUCESTER CITY 3 SALISBURY CITY 3**
Competition: Southern League Premier Division
Teamsheet: Gannaway, Griffiths, Hunt, Abbott, Niblett, Cook, Wyatt, Talboys, Bayliss, Smart, WP Thorne
Substitutes: Tucker (for Smart), Gordon (for Griffiths), Casey (for Talboys)
Scorers: Niblett, Bayliss (2)
Attendance: 408

Date: Saturday 22/04/2000
Result: **HALESOWEN TOWN 4 GLOUCESTER CITY 2**
Competition: Southern League Premier Division
Teamsheet: Gannaway, Griffiths, Hunt, Steadman, Niblett, Cook, Wyatt, Callinan, Bayliss, Gordon, W Thorne
Substitutes: Wigg (for Callinan), Jenkins (for Griffiths), Devlin (for Gordon)
Scorers: Bayliss, Devlin
Attendance: 452

Date: Monday 24/04/2000
Result: **GLOUCESTER CITY 2 WORCESTER CITY 1**
Competition: Southern League Premier Division
Teamsheet: Gannaway, Griffiths, Hunt, Steadman, Niblett, Cook, Wyatt, Callinan, Bayliss, Smart, WP Thorne
Substitutes: Casey (for Steadman), Gordon (nps), Devlin (nps)
Scorers: Wyatt, Bayliss
Attendance: 560

Date: Saturday 29/04/2000
Result: **GLOUCESTER CITY 0 MARGATE 4**
Competition: Southern League Premier Division
Teamsheet: Gannaway, Griffiths, Hunt, Steadman, Niblett, Cook, Wyatt, Callinan, Bayliss, Smart, WP Thorne
Substitutes: Casey (for Steadman), Gordon (for Smart), Devlin (nps)
Attendance: 326

Date: Saturday 06/05/2000
Result: **ROTHWELL TOWN 2 GLOUCESTER CITY 0**
Competition: Southern League Premier Division
Teamsheet: King, Griffiths, Hunt, Steadman, Niblett, Cook, Wyatt, Jenkins, Bayliss, Callinan, WP Thorne
Substitutes: Casey (for Callinan), Gordon (for WP Thorne), Hickey (for Jenkins)
Attendance: 191

Appearances – M Abbott 19, KA Bayliss 11, K Cairns 10(10), TJ Callinan 32(3), RM Casey 15(8), P Chenoweth 24, RP Cook 7, MW Coupe 6, JD Cox 27(8), M Devlin 5(4), SJ Fergusson 13, SJ Futcher 0(2), RL Gannaway 36, D Gordon 2(6), N Griffiths 23(3), BJ Hackett 7(1), MP Hervin 5, SMH Hickey 2(6), BD Hughes 1, D Hunt 7, S Jenkins 2(1), P Jennings 2(1), D Keeling 3(3), GJ Kemp 9, TE King 10, JJ Newton 0(1), N Niblett 28(1), ML Rose 32(4), G Smart 6, JH Smith 37(4), WCM Steadman 7, SJ Talboys 1, M Temple 2(2), GR Thorne 35, WP Thorne 40(3), A Tucker 32(4), N Wigg 15(4), M Wyatt 47(1).
Scorers – JH Smith 19, JD Cox 9, KA Bayliss 4, ML Rose 4, TJ Callinan 3, M Wyatt 3, P Chenoweth 2, RP Cook 2, SJ Fergusson 2, GR Thorne 2, N Niblett 2, M Abbott 1, K Cairns 1, M Devlin 1, WP Thorne 1.

SOUTHERN LEAGUE – PREMIER DIVISION

POS	CLUB	P	W	D	L	F	A	PTS
1	BOSTON UNITED	42	27	11	4	102	39	92
2	BURTON ALBION	42	23	9	10	73	43	78
3	MARGATE	42	23	8	11	64	43	77
4	BATH CITY	42	19	15	8	70	49	72
5	KINGSTONIAN	42	19	14	9	59	43	71
6	TAMWORTH	42	20	10	12	80	51	70
7	NEWPORT COUNTY	42	16	18	8	67	50	66
8	CLEVEDON TOWN	42	18	9	15	52	52	63
9	ILKESTON TOWN	42	16	12	14	77	69	60
10	WEYMOUTH	42	14	16	12	60	51	58
11	HALESOWEN TOWN	42	14	14	14	52	54	56
12	CRAWLEY TOWN	42	15	8	19	68	82	53
13	HAVANT & WATERLOOVILLE	42	13	13	16	63	68	52
14	CAMBRIDGE CITY	42	14	10	18	52	66	52
15	WORCESTER CITY	42	13	11	18	60	66	50
16	SALISBURY CITY	42	14	8	20	70	84	50
17	MERTHYR TYDFIL	42	13	9	20	51	63	48
18	DORCHESTER TOWN	42	10	17	15	56	65	47
19	GRANTHAM TOWN	42	14	5	23	63	76	47
20	**GLOUCESTER CITY**	**42**	**8**	**14**	**20**	**40**	**82**	**38**
21	ROTHWELL TOWN	42	5	14	23	48	85	29
22	ATHERSTONE UNITED	42	5	13	24	30	76	28
		924	333	258	333	1357	1357	1257

SEASON 2000-2001
(Home Ground: City Stadium, Meadow Park, Hempsted)

Date: Saturday 19/08/2000
Result: **GLOUCESTER CITY 2 GRESLEY ROVERS 2**
Competition: Southern League Western Division
Teamsheet: Gannaway, Johnstone, Dicks, Hunt, Moore, Thorne, Meadows, Chenoweth, Rawlins, Griffiths, Cox
Substitutes: Tucker (for Meadows), Abbott (for Moore), Cairns (for Johnstone)
Scorers: Cox, Rawlins (pen)
Attendance: 367

Date: Tuesday 22/08/2000
Result: **RACING CLUB WARWICK 1 GLOUCESTER CITY 5**
Competition: Southern League Western Division
Teamsheet: Gannaway, Johnstone, Dicks, Hunt, Moore, Thorne, Tucker, Chenoweth, Rawlins, Griffiths, Cox
Substitutes: Bayliss (for Cox), Abbott (for Chenoweth), Meadows (for Tucker)
Scorers: Bayliss (2), Rawlins (2), Chenoweth
Attendance: 137

Date: Saturday 26/08/2000
Result: **BLAKENHALL 3 GLOUCESTER CITY 3**
Competition: Southern League Western Division
Teamsheet: Gannaway, Johnstone, Dicks, Hunt, Abbott, Thorne, Tucker, Chenoweth, Rawlins, Griffiths, Cox
Substitutes: Bayliss (for Cox), Meadows (for Johnstone), Steadman (for Gannaway)
Scorers: Hunt, Bayliss, Steadman
Attendance: 137

Date: Monday 28/08/2000
Result: **GLOUCESTER CITY 2 SOLIHULL BOROUGH 2**
Competition: Southern League Western Division
Teamsheet: Hines, Jenkins, Dicks, Hunt, Moore, Thorne, Tucker, Chenoweth, Rawlins, Bayliss, Cairns
Substitutes: Cox (for Jenkins), Steadman (for Rawlins), Abbott (nps)
Scorers: Bayliss, Cox
Attendance: 385

Date: Saturday 02/09/2000
Result: **ODD DOWN 0 GLOUCESTER CITY 2**
Competition: FA Cup Preliminary Round
Teamsheet: Hines, Johnstone, Dicks, Hunt, Moore, Thorne, Tucker, Chenoweth, Rawlins, Bayliss, Cairns
Substitutes: Cox (for Rawlins), Marshall (for Johnstone), Abbott (for Chenoweth)
Scorers: Tucker, Johnstone
Attendance: 108

Date: Saturday 09/09/2000
Result: **BEDWORTH UNITED 1 GLOUCESTER CITY 2**
Competition: Southern League Western Division
Teamsheet: Hines, Johnstone, Dicks, Hunt, Moore, Thorne, Tucker, Chenoweth, Rawlins, Bayliss, Cairns
Substitutes: Cox (for Rawlins), Steadman (for Chenoweth), Meadows (for Cairns)
Scorers: Johnstone, Cox
Attendance: 201

Date: Saturday 16/09/2000
Result: **GLOUCESTER CITY 2 EVESHAM UNITED 1**
Competition: FA Cup 1st Qualifying Round
Teamsheet: Hines, Johnstone, Dicks, Hunt, Moore, Thorne, Tucker, Chenoweth, Rawlins, Bayliss, Marshall
Substitutes: Cox (for Marshall), Gannaway (nps), Steadman (for Hunt)
Scorers: Bayliss, Tucker
Attendance: 403

Date: Saturday 23/09/2000
Result: **GLOUCESTER CITY 3 SUTTON COLDFIELD TOWN 3**
Competition: Southern League Western Division
Teamsheet: Hines, Johnstone, Dicks, Hunt, Moore, Thorne, Tucker, Chenoweth, Cox, Bayliss, Marshall
Substitutes: Rawlins (for Chenoweth), Steadman (for Marshall), Meadows (for Johnstone)
Scorers: Johnstone, Rawlins, Cox
Attendance: 323

Date: Tuesday 26/09/2000
Result: **MANGOTSFIELD UNITED 2 GLOUCESTER CITY 1**
Competition: Southern League Western Division
Teamsheet: Hines, Johnstone, Dicks, Hunt, Steadman, Thorne, Tucker, Meadows, Cox, Rawlins, Griffiths
Substitutes: Chenoweth (for Meadows), Bayliss (for Johnstone), Abbott (nps)
Scorer: Griffiths
Attendance: 386

Date: Saturday 30/09/2000
Result**:** **GLOUCESTER CITY 1 CHIPPENHAM TOWN 1**
Competition: FA Cup 2nd Qualifying Round
Teamsheet: Hines, Tucker, Dicks, Hunt, Moore, Thorne, Meadows, Griffiths, Cox, Rawlins, Bayliss
Substitutes: Cairns (for Meadows), Callinan (for Griffiths), Marshall (for Bayliss)
Scorer: Rawlins (pen)
Attendance: 565

Date: Wednesday 04/10/2000
Result: **CHIPPENHAM TOWN 3 GLOUCESTER CITY 5**
Competition: FA Cup 2nd Qualifying Round Replay
Teamsheet: Hines, Griffiths, Dicks, Hunt, Moore, Thorne, Tucker, Meadows, Cox, Rawlins, Marshall
Substitutes: Cairns (for Meadows), Johnstone (nps), Steadman (for Hunt)
Scorers: Meadows, Marshall, Rawlins, Griffiths, Cox
Attendance: 785

Date: Saturday 07/10/2000
Result: **HINCKLEY UNITED 1 GLOUCESTER CITY 1**
Competition: Southern League Western Division
Teamsheet: Gannaway, Griffiths, Dicks, Moore, Steadman, Thorne, Tucker, Cairns, Cox, Bayliss, Marshall
Substitutes: Johnstone (for Griffiths), Abbott (for Cairns), Callinan (nps)
Scorer: Cox
Attendance: 227

Date: Tuesday 10/10/2000
Result: **GLOUCESTER CITY 0 RACING CLUB WARWICK 1**
Competition: Southern League Western Division
Teamsheet: Gannaway, Marshall, Dicks, Johnstone, Abbott, Steadman, Moore, Thorne, Cox, Bayliss, Cairns
Substitutes: Meadows (for Marshall), Rawlins (for Moore), Tucker (for Thorne)
Attendance: 228

Date: Saturday 14/10/2000
Result: **TIVERTON TOWN 1 GLOUCESTER CITY 3**
Competition: FA Cup 3rd Qualifying Round
Teamsheet: Gannaway, Johnstone, Dicks, Moore, Abbott, Steadman, Tucker, Thorne, Rawlins, Bayliss, Marshall
Substitutes: Cox (for Rawlins), Hines (nps), Jenkins (nps)
Scorers: Bayliss (2, 1 pen), Rawlins
Attendance: 876

Date: Friday 20/10/2000
Result: **SUTTON COLDFIELD TOWN 1 GLOUCESTER CITY 2**
Competition: Southern League Western Division
Teamsheet: Gannaway, Tucker, Dicks, Moore, Abbott, Steadman, Thorne, Cox, Rawlins, Bayliss, Marshall
Substitutes: Jenkins (for Marshall), Cairns (for Cox), Callinan (for Bayliss)
Scorers: Rawlins, Cox
Attendance: 350

Date: Tuesday 24/10/2000
Result: **SOLIHULL BOROUGH 2 GLOUCESTER CITY 2**
Competition: Southern League Western Division
Teamsheet: Gannaway, Johnstone, Dicks, Moore, Abbott, Steadman, Tucker, Thorne, Cox, Rawlins, Marshall
Substitutes: Bayliss (for Tucker), Jenkins (for Thorne), Callinan (nps)
Scorers: Rawlins, Marshall
Attendance: 385

Date: Tuesday 31/10/2000
Result: **HAVANT & WATERLOOVILLE 1 GLOUCESTER CITY 1**
Competition: FA Cup 4th Qualifying Round
Teamsheet: Gannaway, Johnstone, Dicks, Moore, Abbott, Callinan, Steadman, Tucker, Cox, Rawlins, Marshall
Substitutes: Meadows (for Rawlins), Jenkins (for Callinan), Chenoweth (for Marshall)
Scorer: Moore
Attendance: 785

Date: Saturday 04/11/2000
Result: **CAMBRIDGE CITY 1 GLOUCESTER CITY 0**
Competition: FA Trophy 1st Round
Teamsheet: Gannaway, Johnstone, Dicks, Moore, Abbott, Steadman, Jenkins, Tucker, Cox, Rawlins, Marshall
Substitutes: Meadows (nps), Thorne (nps), Chenoweth (nps)
Attendance: 257

Date: Monday 06/11/2000
Result: **GLOUCESTER CITY 2 HAVANT & WATERLOOVILLE 3**
Competition: FA Cup 4th Qualifying Round Replay
Teamsheet: Gannaway, Johnstone, Dicks, Moore, Abbott, Steadman, Tucker, Jenkins, Cox, Rawlins, Marshall
Substitutes: Meadows (for Johnstone), Thorne (nps), Chenoweth (for Jenkins)
Scorers: Cox, Johnstone (pen)
Attendance: 321

Date: Saturday 11/11/2000
Result: **GRESLEY ROVERS 1 GLOUCESTER CITY 3**
Competition: Southern League Western Division
Teamsheet: Hines, Steadman, Dicks, Hunt, Moore, Callinan, Tucker, Chenoweth, Cox, Rawlins, Marshall
Substitutes: Thorne (for Marshall), Jenkins (for Callinan), Johnstone (for Chenoweth)
Scorers: Rawlins (2), Cox
Attendance: 342

Date: Tuesday 14/11/2000
Result: **GLOUCESTER CITY 2 CLEVEDON TOWN 1**
Competition: Southern League Cup 1st Round
Teamsheet: Hines, Steadman, Hunt, Abbott, Moore, Callinan, Jenkins, Chenoweth, Cox, Johnstone, Thorne
Substitutes: Dicks (for Thorne), Tucker (for Callinan), Rawlins (nps)
Scorer: Chenoweth (2)
Attendance: 141

Date: Saturday 18/11/2000
Result: **GLOUCESTER CITY 2 BEDWORTH UNITED 2**
Competition: Southern League Western Division
Teamsheet: Gannaway, Steadman, Dicks, Abbott, Moore, Callinan, Tucker, Chenoweth, Cox, Rawlins, Hunt
Substitutes: Jenkins (for Hunt), Bayliss (for Callinan), Hines (nps)
Scorers: Bayliss, Moore
Attendance: 291

Date: Tuesday 21/11/2000
Result: **GLOUCESTER CITY 0 MANGOTSFIELD UNITED 4**
Competition: Southern League Western Division
Teamsheet: Gannaway, Abbott, Dicks, Hunt, Moore, Steadman, Tucker, Chenoweth, Cox, Rawlins, Bayliss
Substitutes: Johnstone (for Rawlins), Jenkins (for Chenoweth), Callinan (nps)
Attendance: 220

Date: Saturday 25/11/2000
Result: **EVESHAM UNITED 3 GLOUCESTER CITY 2**
Competition: Southern League Western Division
Teamsheet: Gannaway, Griffiths, Dicks, Hunt, Moore, Johnstone, Tucker, Chenoweth, Cox, Bayliss, Callinan
Substitutes: Rawlins (for Bayliss), Jenkins (for Callinan), Abbott (nps)
Scorers: Chenoweth, Cox
Attendance: 131

Date: Saturday 02/12/2000
Result: **GLOUCESTER CITY 2 RUGBY UNITED 1**
Competition: Southern League Western Division
Teamsheet: Hines, Griffiths, Dicks, Hunt, Moore, Callinan, Johnstone, Jenkins, Cox, Bayliss, Chenoweth
Substitutes: Rawlins (for Bayliss), Steadman (for Jenkins), Abbott (nps)
Scorer: Rawlins (2)
Attendance: 256

Date: Saturday 09/12/2000
Result: **PAGET RANGERS 3 GLOUCESTER CITY 0**
Competition: Southern League Western Division
Teamsheet: Hines, Griffiths, Dicks, Hunt, Moore, Callinan, Johnstone, Jenkins, Cox, Rawlins, Chenoweth
Substitutes: Steadman (for Callinan), Abbott (for Johnstone), Tucker (for Chenoweth)
Attendance: 152

Date: Tuesday 26/12/2000
Result: **WESTON-SUPER-MARE 2 GLOUCESTER CITY 2**
Competition: Southern League Western Division
Teamsheet: Hines, Griffiths, Dicks, Moore, Steadman, Callinan, Tucker, Johnstone, Bayliss, Cox, Marshall
Substitutes: Jenkins (nps), Parnell (nps), Gannaway (nps)
Scorers: Marshall, Cox
Attendance: 175

Date: Tuesday 09/01/2001
Result: **BRISTOL CITY RESERVES 2 GLOUCESTER CITY 0**
Competition: Gloucestershire FA Northern Senior Professional Cup Quarter-Final
Teamsheet: Hines, Griffiths, Dicks, Parnell, Hunt, Callinan, Tucker, Chenoweth, Cox, Bayliss, Johnstone
Substitutes: Moore (for Bayliss), Thorne (for Chenoweth), Gannaway (nps)
Attendance: 236

Date: Saturday 13/01/2001
Result: **CINDERFORD TOWN 2 GLOUCESTER CITY 3**
Competition: Southern League Western Division
Teamsheet: Gannaway, Griffiths, Dicks, Hunt, Parnell, Callinan, Tucker, Steadman, Cox, Bayliss, Marshall
Substitutes: Thorne (for Callinan), Johnstone (for Cox), Jenkins (nps)
Scorers: Bayliss (2), Griffiths
Attendance: 247

Date: Saturday 27/01/2001
Result: **REDDITCH UNITED 2 GLOUCESTER CITY 1**
Competition: Southern League Western Division
Teamsheet: Hines, Griffiths, Dicks, Abbott, Parnell, Tucker, Jenkins, Chenoweth, Bayliss, Cox, Marshall
Substitutes: Davis (for Jenkins), Gannaway (nps), Callinan (for Davis)
Scorer: Chenoweth
Attendance: 272

Date: Saturday 03/02/2001
Result: **GLOUCESTER CITY 4 SHEPSHED DYNAMO 2**
Competition: Southern League Western Division
Teamsheet: Hines, Griffiths, Dicks, Hunt, Parnell, Tucker, Jenkins, Chenoweth, Bayliss, Cox, Marshall
Substitutes: Abbott (for Jenkins), Davis (for Chenoweth), Callinan (nps)
Scorers: Parnell, Cox, Griffiths, Davis
Attendance: 263

Date: Thursday 08/02/2001
Result: **MANGOTSFIELD UNITED 1 GLOUCESTER CITY 0**
Competition: Southern League Cup 2nd Round
Teamsheet: Hines, Griffiths, Dicks, Hunt, Steadman, Abbott, Davis, Chenoweth, Cox, Bayliss, Smith
Substitutes: Jenkins (nps), Marshall (nps), Callinan (for Smith)

Date: Saturday 10/02/2001
Result: **GLOUCESTER CITY 1 EVESHAM UNITED 3**
Competition: Southern League Western Division
Teamsheet: Hines, Griffiths, Dicks, Hunt, Steadman, Tucker, Abbott, Chenoweth, Bayliss, Cox, Marshall
Substitutes: Callinan (nps), Davis (for Marshall), Smith (for Griffiths)
Scorer: Cox
Attendance: 287

Date: Saturday 17/02/2001
Result: **BILSTON TOWN 3 GLOUCESTER CITY 0**
Competition: Southern League Western Division
Teamsheet: Hines, Griffiths, Dicks, Hunt, Steadman, Tucker, Abbott, Chenoweth, Bayliss, Cox, Marshall
Substitutes: Jenkins (for Griffiths), Smith (for Marshall), Callinan (nps)
Attendance: 258

Date: Saturday 24/02/2001
Result: **GLOUCESTER CITY 2 CINDERFORD TOWN 2**
Competition: Southern League Western Division
Teamsheet: Hines, Tucker, Dicks, Hunt, Parnell, Abbott, Jenkins, Chenoweth, Cox, Bayliss, Marshall
Substitutes: Griffiths (for Jenkins), Davis (nps), Callinan (for Marshall)
Scorers: Jenkins, Bayliss
Attendance: 382

Date: Saturday 03/03/2001
Result: **ATHERSTONE UNITED 2 GLOUCESTER CITY 3**
Competition: Southern League Western Division
Teamsheet: Hines, Abbott, Dicks, Hunt, Parnell, Jenkins, Griffiths, Bayliss, Cox, Chenoweth, Marshall
Substitutes: Steadman (nps), Davis (for Bayliss), Smith (for Cox)
Scorer: Cox (3)
Attendance: 220

Date: Saturday 10/03/2001
Result: **GLOUCESTER CITY 4 PAGET RANGERS 1**
Competition: Southern League Western Division
Teamsheet: Hines, Abbott, Dicks, Hunt, Parnell, Jenkins, Tucker, Bayliss, Cox, Chenoweth, Marshall
Substitutes: Steadman (for Abbott), Davis (for Marshall), Griffiths (for Jenkins)
Scorers: Chenoweth (2), Bayliss (2, 1 pen)
Attendance: 280

Date: Tuesday 13/03/2001
Result: **GLOUCESTER CITY 2 TIVERTON TOWN 3**
Competition: Southern League Western Division
Teamsheet: Hines, Abbott, Dicks, Hunt, Parnell, Jenkins, Tucker, Bayliss, Cox, Chenoweth, Marshall
Substitutes: Steadman (for Jenkins), Davis (for Dicks), Griffiths (for Marshall)
Scorers: Jenkins, Bayliss
Attendance: 289

Date: Tuesday 20/03/2001
Result: **GLOUCESTER CITY 1 BLAKENHALL 3**
Competition: Southern League Western Division
Teamsheet: Hines, Tucker, Dicks, Hunt, Parnell, Abbott, Jenkins, Bayliss, Cox, Chenoweth, Marshall
Substitutes: Steadman (for Dicks), Griffiths (nps), Smith (for Jenkins)
Scorer: Cox
Attendance: 119

Date: Saturday 24/03/2001
Result: **ROCESTER 4 GLOUCESTER CITY 3**
Competition: Southern League Western Division
Teamsheet: Hines, Griffiths, Dicks, Steadman, Parnell, Abbott, Jenkins, Tucker, Cox, Callinan, Marshall
Substitutes: Medcroft (for Marshall), Smith (for Callinan), Bayliss (nps)
Scorer: Marshall (3, 1 pen)
Attendance: 86

Date: Tuesday 27/03/2001
Result: **GLOUCESTER CITY 0 HINCKLEY UNITED 2**
Competition: Southern League Western Division
Teamsheet: Hines, Griffiths, Steadman, Callinan, Parnell, Tucker, Jenkins, Marshall, Cox, Johnstone, Abbott
Substitutes: Medcroft (for Callinan), Smith (for Jenkins), Rea (for Abbott)
Attendance: 220

Date: Saturday 31/03/2001
Result: **GLOUCESTER CITY 0 ROCESTER 1**
Competition: Southern League Western Division
Teamsheet: Hines, Steadman, Griffiths, Abbott, Parnell, Marshall, Tucker, Jenkins, Cox, Bayliss, Johnstone
Substitutes: Medcroft (for Jenkins), Smith (for Steadman), Rea (nps)
Attendance: 210

Date: Tuesday 03/04/2001
Result: **GLOUCESTER CITY 3 ATHERSTONE UNITED 4**
Competition: Southern League Western Division
Teamsheet: Hines, Griffiths, Marshall, Tucker, Parnell, Callinan, Abbott, Jenkins, Cox, Johnstone, Bayliss
Substitutes: Steadman (nps), Medcroft (for Jenkins), Smith (for Griffiths)
Scorer: Bayliss (3, 1 pen)
Attendance: 149

[385]

Date: Saturday 07/04/2001
Result: **RUGBY UNITED 3 GLOUCESTER CITY 2**
Competition: Southern League Western Division
Teamsheet: Hines, Steadman, Marshall, Tucker, Parnell, Callinan, Abbott, Medcroft, Cox, Smith, Bayliss
Substitutes: Griffiths (for Abbott), Rea (nps) Tovey (nps)
Scorers: Cox, Callinan
Attendance: 231

Date: Saturday 14/04/2001
Result: **TIVERTON TOWN 2 GLOUCESTER CITY 0**
Competition: Southern League Western Division
Teamsheet: Hines, Marshall, Medcroft, Tucker, Parnell, Callinan, Abbott, Smith, Cox, Bayliss, Griffiths
Substitutes: Steadman (for Marshall), Jenkins (for Callinan), Rea (for Tucker)
Attendance: 828

Date: Monday 16/04/2001
Result: **GLOUCESTER CITY 2 WESTON-SUPER-MARE 0**
Competition: Southern League Western Division
Teamsheet: Hines, Griffiths, Steadman, Tucker, Abbott, Callinan, Jenkins, Bayliss, Cox, Smith, Marshall
Substitutes: Medcroft (nps), Tovey (nps), Rea (nps)
Scorers: Cox, Bayliss
Attendance: 220

Date: Wednesday 18/04/2001
Result: **GLOUCESTER CITY 0 REDDITCH UNITED 0**
Competition: Southern League Western Division
Teamsheet: Hines, Griffiths, Steadman, Parnell, Abbott, Callinan, Jenkins, Bayliss, Cox, Smith, Marshall
Substitutes: Medcroft (for Callinan), Rea (for Marshall), Tovey (nps)
Attendance: 120

Date: Saturday 21/04/2001
Result: **BROMSGROVE ROVERS 0 GLOUCESTER CITY 1**
Competition: Southern League Western Division
Teamsheet: Hines, Steadman, Marshall, Tucker, Parnell, Abbott, Callinan, Bayliss, Cox, Jenkins, Smith
Substitutes: Medcroft (for Smith), Rea (nps), Webb (for Medcroft)
Scorer: Callinan
Attendance: 441

Date: Tuesday 24/04/2001
Result: **GLOUCESTER CITY 1 BILSTON TOWN 3**
Competition: Southern League Western Division
Teamsheet: Hines, Steadman, Rea, Tucker, Parnell, Abbott, Callinan, Medcroft, Cox, Bayliss, Marshall
Substitutes: Smith (for Marshall), Jenkins (for Callinan), Webb (for Rea)
Scorer: Abbott
Attendance: 172

Date: Saturday 28/04/2001
Result: **GLOUCESTER CITY 5 CIRENCESTER TOWN 0**
Competition: Southern League Western Division
Teamsheet: Hines, Abbott, Steadman, Callinan, Parnell, Webb, Jenkins, Medcroft, Cox, Bayliss, Marshall
Substitutes: Smith (for Medcroft), Davis (nps), Rea (nps)
Scorers: Jenkins, Cox, Medcroft, Bayliss, Smith
Attendance: 291

Date: Tuesday 01/05/2001
Result: **GLOUCESTER CITY 2 BROMSGROVE ROVERS 2**
Competition: Southern League Western Division
Teamsheet: Hines, Abbott, Steadman, Callinan, Parnell, Webb, Jenkins, Medcroft, Cox, Bayliss, Marshall
Substitutes: Smith (for Webb), Devlin (for Jenkins), Rea (for Callinan)
Scorer: Cox (2)
Attendance: 211

Date: Thursday 03/05/2001
Result: **CIRENCESTER TOWN 4 GLOUCESTER CITY 2**
Competition: Southern League Western Division
Teamsheet: Hines, Callinan, Steadman, Tucker, Parnell, Medcroft, Jenkins, Abbott, Cox, Bayliss, Marshall
Substitutes: Smith (for Steadman), Johnson (nps), Rea (for Marshall)
Scorers: Abbott, own goal
Attendance: 127

Date: Saturday 05/05/2001
Result: **SHEPSHED DYNAMO 3 GLOUCESTER CITY 0**
Competition: Southern League Western Division
Teamsheet: Hines, Abbott, Marshall, Tucker, Parnell, Callinan, Griffiths, Jenkins, Cox, Bayliss, Medcroft
Substitutes: Steadman (nps), Smith (for Bayliss), Rea (nps)
Attendance: 135

Appearances – M Abbott 34(6), KA Bayliss 38(5), K Cairns 5(4), TJ Callinan 23(5), P Chenoweth 26(3), JD Cox 48(5), B Davis 1(6), M Devlin 0(1), GE Dicks 39(1), RL Gannaway 15, N Griffiths 27(4), A Hines 38, D Hunt 29, S Jenkins 24(9), K Johnstone 23(3), GP Marshall 38(1), J Meadows 4(7), S Medcroft 7(6), R Moore 25(1), MK Parnell 22, MB Rawlins 20(5), GJ Rea 1(5), LF Smith 6(12), WCM Steadman 29(10), WP Thorne 16(3), A Tucker 43(4), TA Webb 2(2).
Others selected but did not play: M Johnson, L Tovey.
Scorers – JD Cox 22, KA Bayliss 19, MB Rawlins 13, P Chenoweth 6, GP Marshall 6, N Griffiths 4, K Johnstone 4, S Jenkins 3, M Abbott 2, TJ Callinan 2, R Moore 2, A Tucker 2, B Davis 1, D Hunt 1, J Meadows 1, S Medcroft 1, M Parnell 1, LF Smith 1, WCM Steadman 1, own goal 1.

SOUTHERN LEAGUE – WESTERN DIVISION

SOUTHERN LEAGUE – WESTERN DIVISION

POS	CLUB	P	W	D	L	F	A	PTS
1	HINCKLEY UNITED	42	30	8	4	102	38	98
2	TIVERTON TOWN	42	28	7	7	97	36	91
3	BILSTON TOWN	42	27	9	6	88	48	90
4	EVESHAM UNITED	42	27	5	10	86	46	86
5	MANGOTSFIELD UNITED	42	25	9	8	91	44	84
6	SOLIHULL BOROUGH	42	22	12	8	73	43	78
7	REDDITCH UNITED	42	17	13	12	76	69	64
8	WESTON-SUPER-MARE	42	17	10	15	68	58	61
9	ATHERSTONE UNITED	42	16	11	15	64	58	59
10	ROCESTER	42	18	5	19	57	77	59
11	CIRENCESTER TOWN	42	14	15	13	65	74	57
12	RUGBY UNITED	42	13	10	19	51	68	49
13	**GLOUCESTER CITY**	**42**	**12**	**11**	**19**	**76**	**86**	**47**
14	BLAKENALL	42	13	10	19	54	64	46*
15	SHEPSHED DYNAMO	42	12	9	21	56	73	45
16	BEDWORTH UNITED	42	12	9	21	38	60	45
17	RACING CLUB WARWICK	42	13	6	23	46	77	45
18	GRESLEY ROVERS	42	11	8	23	46	65	41
19	CINDERFORD TOWN	42	11	8	23	56	84	41
20	SUTTON COLDFIELD TOWN	42	7	14	21	45	66	35
21	PAGET RANGERS	42	9	4	29	38	93	31
22	BROMSGROVE ROVERS	42	7	9	26	47	92	30
		924	361	202	361	1420	1420	1282

* Three points deducted for an ineligible player.

SEASON 2001-2002
(Home Ground: City Stadium, Meadow Park, Hempsted)

Date: Saturday 18/08/2001
Result: **GLOUCESTER CITY 2 REDDITCH UNITED 1**
Competition: Southern League Western Division
Teamsheet: Morris, Dunton, C Temple, Griffiths, Sreadman, Rea, Burns, Jenkins, Marshall, Hoskins, Wilkinson
Substitutes: LF Smith (for Marshall), Webb (nps), Allen (nps)
Scorers: Jenkins, Griffiths
Attendance: 272

Date: Saturday 25/08/2001
Result: **GRESLEY ROVERS 2 GLOUCESTER CITY 0**
Competition: Southern League Western Division
Teamsheet: A Cook, Dunton, C Temple, Griffiths, Steadman, Randall, Burns, Jenkins, Allen, Hoskins, Wilkinson
Substitutes: LF Smith (for Randall), JS Smith (for C Temple), Rea (for Allen)
Attendance: 362

Date: Monday 27/08/2001
Result: **GLOUCESTER CITY 1 CLEVEDON TOWN 1**
Competition: Southern League Western Division
Teamsheet: A Cook, Dunton, C Temple, Griffiths, Steadman, Webb, Burns, Jenkins, Marshall, Hoskins, Wilkinson
Substitutes: LF Smith (nps), Rea (nps), Allen (nps)
Scorer: Jenkins
Attendance: 377

Date: Saturday 01/09/2001
Result: **CIRENCESTER TOWN 2 GLOUCESTER CITY 1**
Competition: FA Cup Preliminary Round
Teamsheet: A Cook, Dunton, C Temple, Griffiths, Steadman, LF Smith, Burns, Jenkins, Marshall, Hoskins, Wilkinson
Substitutes: Allen (for Marshall), JS Smith (for LF Smith), Tovey (nps)
Scorer: Marshall
Attendance: 207

Date: Saturday 08/09/2001
Result: **GLOUCESTER CITY 1 SHEPSHED DYNAMO 5**
Competition: Southern League Western Division
Teamsheet: Morris, Dunton, Rea, Griffiths, Steadman, LF Smith, Burns, Jenkins, Allen, Hoskins, C Temple
Substitutes: Delves (for Rea), Tovey (for Burns), JS Smith (for Allen)
Scorer: Hoskins
Attendance: 271

Date: Tuesday 11/09/2001
Result: **CIRENCESTER TOWN 1 GLOUCESTER CITY 1**
Competition: Southern League Western Division
Teamsheet: Taylor, Dunton, C Temple, Griffiths, Steadman, Delves, Wilkinson, Jenkins, Prince, Hoskins, LF Smith
Substitutes: Rea (nps), JS Smith (for Delves), Tovey (nps)
Scorer: LF Smith
Attendance: 167

Date: Tuesday 18/09/2001
Result: **WESTON-SUPER-MARE 0 GLOUCESTER CITY 1**
Competition: Southern League Western Division
Teamsheet: Taylor, Dunton, Marshall, Griffiths, Steadman, Delves, Jenkins, Wilkinson, LF Smith, Hoskins, Prince
Substitutes: JS Smith (nps), C Temple (nps), Tovey (nps)
Scorer: Hoskins
Attendance: 290

Date: Saturday 22/09/2001
Result: **GLOUCESTER CITY 1 BEDWORTH UNITED 7**
Competition: Southern League Western Division
Teamsheet: Taylor, Dunton, Marshall, Griffiths, Steadman, Delves, Hardcastle, Jenkins, LF Smith, Hoskins, Wilkinson
Substitutes: Rea (nps), Burns (for Delves), C Temple (for Wilkinson)
Scorer: Wilkinson
Attendance: 270

Date: Tuesday 25/09/2001
Result: **CINDERFORD TOWN 2 GLOUCESTER CITY 1**
Competition: Southern League Western Division
Teamsheet: Taylor, Dunton, C Temple, Griffiths, Steadman, Delves, Hardcastle, Jenkins, Marshall, Hoskins, Wilkinson
Substitutes: LF Smith (for Hardcastle), JS Smith (for Jenkins), Burns (for Delves)
Scorer: own goal
Attendance: 276

Date: Saturday 29/09/2001
Result: **GLOUCESTER CITY 2 ROCESTER 2**
Competition: Southern League Western Division
Teamsheet: Taylor, Dunton, C Temple, Griffiths, Steadman, Wilkinson, Burns, Jenkins, LF Smith, Hoskins, Marshall
Substitutes: Rea (nps), Webb (for LF Smith), Hardcastle (for Wilkinson)
Scorers: Marshall, Dunton
Attendance: 199

Date: Friday 05/10/2001
Result: **EVESHAM UNITED 3 GLOUCESTER CITY 0**
Competition: Southern League Western Division
Teamsheet: Taylor, Dunton, Rea, Griffiths, Steadman, Wilkinson, Burns, Jenkins, Marshall, Hoskins, C Temple
Substitutes: Hardcastle (for Marshall), Allen (nps), Delves (nps)
Attendance: 171

Date: Tuesday 09/10/2001
Result: **GLOUCESTER CITY 0 WESTON-SUPER-MARE 2**
Competition: Southern League Western Division
Teamsheet: Taylor, Dunton, C Temple, Griffiths, McCluskey, Steadman, Wilkinson, Marshall, Prince, Hoskins, Jenkins
Substitutes: Hardcastle (nps), Allen (for Hoskins), LF Smith (for Hoskins)
Attendance: 221

Date: Saturday 13/10/2001
Result: **SWINDON SUPERMARINE 1 GLOUCESTER CITY 2**
Competition: Southern League Western Division
Teamsheet: Taylor, Dunton, C Temple, Griffiths, Hardcastle, McCluskey, Marshall, Jenkins, Prince, LF Smith, Wilkinson
Substitutes: Allen (for Hardcastle), Rea (nps), Webb (for Jenkins)
Scorers: McCluskey, Marshall
Attendance: 201

Date: Saturday 20/10/2001
Result: **GLOUCESTER CITY 3 RACING CLUB WARWICK 2**
Competition: Southern League Western Division
Teamsheet: Taylor, Dunton, C Temple, Griffiths, Hardcastle, McCluskey, Burns, Jenkins, Marshall, Prince, Wilkinson
Substitutes: Allen (nps), LF Smith (for Marshall), Webb (for Hardcastle)
Scorers: Burns (2), Dunton (pen)
Attendance: 253

Date: Wednesday 24/10/2001
Result: **BRISTOL ROVERS RESERVES 3 GLOUCESTER CITY 0**
Competition: Gloucestershire FA Northern Senior Professional Cup 1st Round
Teamsheet: Taylor, Dunton, C Temple, Rea, Hardcastle, McCluskey, Burns, Jenkins, Prince, LF Smith, Webb
Substitutes: Marshall (nps), Allen (nps), M Temple (nps)
Attendance: 114

Date: Saturday 27/10/2001
Result: **SHEPSHED DYNAMO 0 GLOUCESTER CITY 2**
Competition: Southern League Western Division
Teamsheet: Taylor, Dunton, C Temple, Griffiths, McCluskey, Webb, Burns, Jenkins, Prince, Hoskins, Marshall
Substitutes: Steadman (nps), LF Smith (nps), Wilkinson (for Burns)
Scorer: Marshall (2)
Attendance: 198

Date: Saturday 03/11/2001
Result: **CAMBRIDGE CITY 4 GLOUCESTER CITY 1**
Competition: FA Trophy 1st Round
Teamsheet: Bennett, Dunton, C Temple, Griffiths, McCluskey, Webb, Burns, Jenkins, Prince, Hoskins, Marshall
Substitutes: Steadman (nps), Wilkinson (for Burns), LF Smith (for C Temple)
Scorer: Burns
Attendance: 289

Date: Saturday 10/11/2001
Result: **BILSTON TOWN 5 GLOUCESTER CITY 1**
Competition: Southern League Western Division
Teamsheet: Bennett, Steadman, C Temple, Griffiths, M Cook, McCluskey, Burns, Marshall, Wilkinson, Prince, Hoskins
Substitutes: LF Smith (for M Cook), Dunton (for Hoskins), Delves (nps)
Scorer: Burns
Attendance: 174

Date: Tuesday 13/11/2001
Result: **CINDERFORD TOWN 3 GLOUCESTER CITY 0**
Competition: Southern League Cup 1st Round
Teamsheet: Bennett, Dunton, C Temple, Griffiths, Steadman, McCluskey, LF Smith, Marshall, Prince, Hoskins, Wilkinson
Substitutes: Allen (nps), Delves (nps), M Cook (nps)
Attendance: 162

Date: Saturday 17/11/2001
Result: **GLOUCESTER CITY 0 EVESHAM UNITED 2**
Competition: Southern League Western Division
Teamsheet: Bennett, Dunton, Marshall, Webb, Steadman, McCluskey, Burns, M Cook, LF Smith, C Temple, Wilkinson
Substitutes: M Temple (nps), Delves (for Marshall), JS Smith (for C Temple)
Attendance: 285

Date: Tuesday 20/11/2001
Result: **GLOUCESTER CITY 1 MANGOTSFIELD UNITED 2**
Competition: Southern League Western Division
Teamsheet: Bath, Dunton, Marshall, Griffiths, Steadman, McCluskey, Webb, Wilkinson, LF Smith, Hoskins, Prince
Substitutes: M Cook (for McCluskey), C Temple (for LF Smith), Delves (nps)
Scorer: Griffiths
Attendance: 220

Date: Saturday 24/11/2001
Result: **SUTTON COLDFIELD TOWN 0 GLOUCESTER CITY 1**
Competition: Southern League Western Division
Teamsheet: Bath, Webb, Steadman, Griffiths, Wilkinson, McCluskey, Burns, Prince, Bayliss, Hoskins, Marshall
Substitutes: M Cook (nps), Dunton (nps), LF Smith (nps)
Scorer: Wilkinson
Attendance: 157

Date: Tuesday 27/11/2001
Result: **GLOUCESTER CITY 4 CINDERFORD TOWN 2**
Competition: Southern League Western Division
Teamsheet: Bath, Webb, Steadman, Griffiths, Wilkinson, McCluskey, Burns, Prince, Bayliss, Hoskins, Marshall
Substitutes: Dunton (nps), M Cook (nps), LF Smith (for Hoskins)
Scorers: Burns, Bayliss, Hoskins (2)
Attendance: 234

Date: Saturday 22/12/2001
Result: **GLOUCESTER CITY 2 GRESLEY ROVERS 0**
Competition: Southern League Western Division
Teamsheet: Bath, Webb, Prince, Griffiths, McCluskey, Steadman, Burns, Jenkins, Bayliss, Hoskins, Wilkinson
Substitutes: M Cook (nps), LF Smith (for Webb), Delves (nps)
Scorer: Bayliss (2, 1 pen)
Attendance: 281

Date: Wednesday 26/12/2001
Result: **CLEVEDON TOWN 1 GLOUCESTER CITY 3**
Competition: Southern League Western Division
Teamsheet: Bath, Marshall, Prince, Griffiths, McCluskey, Steadman, Burns, Jenkins, Bayliss, Hoskins, Wilkinson
Substitutes: M Cook (nps), LF Smith (nps), Webb (nps)
Scorers: Bayliss (2, 1 pen), Prince
Attendance: 368

Date: Saturday 29/12/2001
Result: **RACING CLUB WARWICK 0 GLOUCESTER CITY 0**
Competition: Southern League Western Division
Teamsheet: Bath, Marshall, Prince, Griffiths, McCluskey, Steadman, Burns, Jenkins, Bayliss, Hoskins, Wilkinson
Substitutes: M Cook (nps), LF Smith (for Hoskins), Webb (for Marshall)
Attendance: 130

Date: Saturday 05/01/2002
Result: **GLOUCESTER CITY 1 SUTTON COLDFIELD TOWN 1**
Competition: Southern League Western Division
Teamsheet: Bath, Marshall, Prince, Griffiths, McCluskey, Steadman, Burns, Jenkins, Bayliss, Hoskins, Wilkinson
Substitutes: M Cook (for Jenkins), LF Smith (for Prince), Webb (for Marshall)
Scorer: Prince
Attendance: 284

Date: Saturday 12/01/2002
Result: **REDDITCH UNITED 0 GLOUCESTER CITY 0**
Competition: Southern League Western Division
Teamsheet: Bath, Marshall, Prince, M Cook, Steadman, McCluskey, Burns, Jenkins, Bayliss, Hoskins, Wilkinson
Substitutes: LF Smith (for Hoskins), Webb (nps), Howard (for Marshall)
Attendance: 234

Date: Tuesday 15/01/2002
Result: **GLOUCESTER CITY 1 SWINDON SUPERMARINE 0**
Competition: Southern League Western Division
Teamsheet: Bath, M Cook, Prince, Steadman, McCluskey, Jenkins, Burns, Wilkinson, Bayliss, Hoskins, Griffiths
Substitutes: LF Smith (for Hoskins), Webb (for Wilkinson), Howard (nps)
Scorer: Griffiths
Attendance: 292

Date: Saturday 19/01/2002
Result: **GLOUCESTER CITY 0 HALESOWEN TOWN 2**
Competition: Southern League Western Division
Teamsheet: Bath, Steadman, Marshall, Griffiths, McCluskey, Prince, Burns, Jenkins, Bayliss, LF Smith, M Cook
Substitutes: Webb (for M Cook), Howard (for Prince), Archer (nps)
Attendance: 476

Date: Tuesday 29/01/2002
Result: **GLOUCESTER CITY 1 CHIPPENHAM TOWN 1**
Competition: Southern League Western Division
Teamsheet: Bath, Steadman, Marshall, Griffiths, McCluskey, Prince, Burns, Jenkins, Bayliss, LF Smith, M Cook
Substitutes: Webb (nps), Hampson (nps), Archer (nps)
Scorer: Bayliss
Attendance: 307

[389]

Date: Saturday 09/02/2002
Result: **GLOUCESTER CITY 1 SOLIHULL BOROUGH 1**
Competition: Southern League Western Division
Teamsheet: Bath, Steadman, Marshall, Griffiths, McCluskey, Prince, Burns, Jenkins, Bayliss, LF Smith, Wilkinson
Substitutes: M Cook (for McCluskey), Howard (for Jenkins), Stockley (for Marshall)
Scorer: Bayliss
Attendance: 239

Date: Saturday 16/02/2002
Result: **GLOUCESTER CITY 5 BILSTON TOWN 1**
Competition: Southern League Western Division
Teamsheet: Bath, LF Smith, Howard, Griffiths, McCluskey, Wilkinson, Burns, Jenkins, Bayliss, Hoskins, Prince
Substitutes: Steadman (for Howard), M Cook (for McCluskey), Stockley (for Bayliss)
Scorers: Hoskins (4), Burns (pen)
Attendance: 257

Date: Saturday 02/03/2002
Result: **BEDWORTH UNITED 4 GLOUCESTER CITY 1**
Competition: Southern League Western Division
Teamsheet: Bath, Marshall, Howard, Griffiths, McCluskey, Wilkinson, Burns, Jenkins, Bayliss, Hoskins, Prince
Substitutes: M Cook (for Wilkinson), Webb (for Howard), Stockley (for Hoskins)
Scorer: McCluskey
Attendance: 168

Date: Saturday 09/03/2002
Result: **GLOUCESTER CITY 2 STOURPORT SWIFTS 0**
Competition: Southern League Western Division
Teamsheet: Bath, Webb, Marshall, Griffiths, McCluskey, Wilkinson, Burns, Jenkins, Bayliss, Hoskins, Prince
Substitutes: Stockley (for Marshall), LF Smith (for Bayliss), Howard (for Jenkins)
Scorer: McCluskey, LF Smith
Attendance: 239

Date: Tuesday 12/03/2002
Result: **MANGOTSFIELD UNITED 1 GLOUCESTER CITY 1**
Competition: Southern League Western Division
Teamsheet: Bath, Hampson, Steadman, Griffiths, McCluskey, Wilkinson, Burns, Webb, LF Smith, Hoskins, Prince
Substitutes: Marshall (nps), Stockley (nps), M Cook (nps)
Scorer: McCluskey
Attendance: 220

Date: Saturday 16/03/2002
Result: **SOLIHULL BOROUGH 4 GLOUCESTER CITY 0**
Competition: Southern League Western Division
Teamsheet: Bath, Hampson, Steadman, Griffiths, McCluskey, Wilkinson, Burns, Webb, LF Smith, Hoskins, Prince
Substitutes: Jenkins (for Webb), Stockley (for McCluskey), Howard (for Steadman)
Attendance: 244

Date: Saturday 23/03/2002
Result: **STOURPORT SWIFTS 2 GLOUCESTER CITY 1**
Competition: Southern League Western Division
Teamsheet: Bath, Marshall, Steadman, Griffiths, McCluskey, M Cook, Burns, Jenkins, Prince, Hoskins, Wilkinson
Substitutes: Howard (for Steadman), Webb (for Wilkinson), LF Smith (for Burns)
Scorer: Prince
Attendance: 148

Date: Saturday 30/03/2002
Result: **GLOUCESTER CITY 0 CIRENCESTER TOWN 1**
Competition: Southern League Western Division
Teamsheet: Bath, Webb, Marshall, Griffiths, M Cook, Steadman, Burns, Jenkins, Prince, Hoskins, Thompson
Substitutes: Wilkinson (for Webb), LF Smith (for Thompson), Howard (for Marshall)
Attendance: 299

Date: Monday 01/04/2002
Result: **CHIPPENHAM TOWN 1 GLOUCESTER CITY 0**
Competition: Southern League Western Division
Teamsheet: Bath, Thompson, Hampson, Griffiths, Wilkinson, McCluskey, Burns, Jenkins, Bayliss, Hoskins, Prince
Substitutes: LF Smith (for Bayliss), Howard (for Hampson), Stockley (nps)
Attendance: 842

Date: Saturday 13/04/2002
Result: **HALESOWEN TOWN 0 GLOUCESTER CITY 0**
Competition: Southern League Western Division
Teamsheet: Bath, Steadman, Marshall, Griffiths, Wilkinson, McCluskey, Burns, Jenkins, Thompson, Hoskins, Prince
Substitutes: LF Smith (for Thompson), Webb (for Marshall), Howard (nps)
Attendance: 777

Date: Monday 15/04/2002
Result: **ATHERSTONE UNITED 1 GLOUCESTER CITY 0**
Competition: Southern League Western Division
Teamsheet: Bath, Webb, Howard, Griffiths, Marshall, McCluskey, Burns, LF Smith, Thompson, Hoskins, Prince
Substitutes: Steadman (nps), Wilkinson (nps), Stockley (nps)
Attendance: 250

Date: Saturday 20/04/2002
Result: **GLOUCESTER CITY 4 ATHERSTONE UNITED 1**
Competition: Southern League Western Division
Teamsheet: Bath, Webb, Marshall, Griffiths, Thompson, Steadman, Burns, Jenkins, Prince, Hoskins, Wilkinson
Substitutes: McCluskey (for Thompson), LF Smith (for Webb), Howard (for Wilkinson)
Scorers: Jenkins, Hoskins (2), Griffiths
Attendance: 293

Date: Saturday 27/04/2002
Result: **ROCESTER 0 GLOUCESTER CITY 1**
Competition: Southern League Western Division
Teamsheet: Bath, Webb, Howard, Griffiths, Steadman, McCluskey, Prince, Thompson, LF Smith, Hoskins, Wilkinson
Substitutes: Burns (nps), Stockley (for -----), Marshall (for -----)
Scorer: Stockley

Appearances – LP Allen 2(3), MR Bath 24, KA Bayliss 15, AD Bennett 4, C Burns 35(2), A Cook 3, MJ Cook 8(6), NJP Delves 4(2), DP Dunton 20(1), N Griffiths 41, C Hampson 3, MJ Hardcastle 5(2), AR Hoskins 37, KL Howard 4(9), S Jenkins 34(1), GP Marshall 33, DM McCluskey 31(1), S Morris 2, L Prince 34, L Randall 1, GJ Rea 4(1), JS Smith 0(6), LF Smith 19(19), WCM Steadman 34(1), N Stockley 0(6), MA Taylor 11, C Temple 18(2), CD Thompson 6, L Tovey 0(1), TA Webb 16(10), D Wilkinson 35(3).
Others selected but did not play: R Archer, M Temple.
Scorers – AR Hoskins 10, KA Bayliss 7, C Burns 6, GP Marshall 5, N Griffiths 4, DM McCluskey 4, S Jenkins 3, L Prince 3, DP Dunton 2, LF Smith 2, D Wilkinson 2, N Stockley 1, own goal 1.

SOUTHERN LEAGUE – WESTERN DIVISION

POS	CLUB	P	W	D	L	F	A	PTS
1	HALESOWEN TOWN	40	27	9	4	85	24	90
2	CHIPPENHAM TOWN	40	26	9	5	81	28	87
3	WESTON-SUPER-MARE	40	22	10	8	70	38	76
4	SOLIHULL BOROUGH	40	20	11	9	75	42	71
5	GRESLEY ROVERS	40	19	9	12	59	50	66
6	SUTTON COLDFIELD TOWN	40	17	11	12	53	46	62
7	MANGOTSFIELD UNITED	40	17	10	13	74	54	61
8	STOURPORT SWIFTS	40	18	6	16	59	59	60
9	ATHERSTONE UNITED	40	16	8	16	61	59	56
10	CLEVEDON TOWN	40	15	11	14	57	58	56
11	BEDWORTH UNITED	40	16	7	17	59	63	55
12	EVESHAM UNITED	42	16	7	17	54	70	55
13	CIRENCESTER TOWN	40	17	3	20	64	69	54
14	**GLOUCESTER CITY**	**40**	**14**	**10**	**16**	**48**	**63**	**52**
15	CINDERFORD TOWN	40	14	9	17	54	67	51
16	SHEPSHED DYNAMO	40	10	10	20	64	84	40
17	BILSTON TOWN	40	11	7	22	50	72	40
18	REDDITCH UNITED	40	11	6	23	47	77	39
19	SWINDON SUPERMARINE	40	11	4	25	52	76	37
20	RACING CLUB WARWICK	40	8	11	21	38	63	35
21	ROCESTER	40	5	12	23	33	75	27
22	BLOXWICH UNITED							
		840	330	180	327	1237	1237	1170

Bloxwich United withdrew. All scores were expunged from records.

SEASON 2002-2003
(Home Ground: City Stadium, Meadow Park, Hempsted)

Date: Saturday 17/08/2002
Result: **GLOUCESTER CITY 1 ATHERSTONE UNITED 2**
Competition: Southern League Western Division
Teamsheet: Taylor, Webb, Burby, Griffiths, Steadman, Wilkinson, Burns, Jenkins, Bayliss, Mustoe, Thompson
Substitutes: Smith (for Webb), Howard (nps), Marshall (for Burby)
Scorer: Burns
Attendance: 324

Date: Wednesday 21/08/2002
Result: **TAUNTON TOWN 0 GLOUCESTER CITY 2**
Competition: Southern League Western Division
Teamsheet: Taylor, Thompson, Marshall, Griffiths, Steadman, Wilkinson, Burns, Jenkins, Bayliss, Mustoe, Smith
Substitutes: Burby (for Marshall), Hampson (nps), Howard (for Smith)
Scorer: Smith (2)
Attendance: 478

Date: Saturday 24/08/2002
Result: **CINDERFORD TOWN 4 GLOUCESTER CITY 0**
Competition: Southern League Western Division
Teamsheet: Taylor, Thompson, Burby, Griffiths, Steadman, Marshall, Burns, Jenkins, Bayliss, Mustoe, Smith
Substitutes: Howard (for Burby), Harris (nps), Webb (nps)
Attendance: 247

Date: Monday 26/08/2002
Result: **GLOUCESTER CITY 2 MERTHYR TYDFIL 2**
Competition: Southern League Western Division
Teamsheet: Bath, Thompson, Marshall, Griffiths, Hampson, Harris, Burns, Jenkins, Bayliss, Mustoe, Smith
Substitutes: Howard (nps), Webb (nps), Wilkinson (for Jenkins)
Scorers: Griffiths, Wilkinson
Attendance: 422

Date: Saturday 31/08/2002
Result: **MINEHEAD TOWN 0 GLOUCESTER CITY 2**
Competition: FA Cup Preliminary Round
Teamsheet: Bath, Thompson, Marshall, Hampson, Webb, Wilkinson, Burns, Harris, Bayliss, Mustoe, Smith
Substitutes: Howard (for Bayliss), Steadman (for Wilkinson), Taylor (nps)
Scorers: Thompson, Howard
Attendance: 144

Date: Saturday 07/09/2002
Result: **GLOUCESTER CITY 2 REDDITCH UNITED 5**
Competition: Southern League Western Division
Teamsheet: Bath, Steadman, Hampson, Griffiths, Webb, Thompson, Burns, Cox, Bayliss, Mustoe, Harris
Substitutes: Smith (for Bayliss), Marshall (nps), Jenkins (for Steadman)
Scorers: Griffiths, Thompson
Attendance: 260

Date: Tuesday 10/09/2002
Result: **WESTON-SUPER-MARE 3 GLOUCESTER CITY 2**
Competition: Southern League Western Division
Teamsheet: Bath, Thompson, Smith, Mustoe, Hampson, Steadman, Burns, Cox, Jenkins, Hoskins, Harris
Substitutes: Webb (for Harris), Bayliss (nps), Taylor (nps)
Scorers: Cox, Burns (pen)
Attendance: 240

Date: Saturday 14/09/2002
Result: **GLOUCESTER CITY 3 BASHLEY 0**
Competition: FA Cup 1st Qualifying Round
Teamsheet: Bath, Thompson, Harris, Griffiths, Steadman, Mustoe, Burns, Cox, Bayliss, Hoskins, Jenkins
Substitutes: Hampson (for Jenkins), Webb (for Hoskins), Smith (for Bayliss)
Scorers: Cox, Harris, Thompson
Attendance: 305

Date: Saturday 21/09/2002
Result: **GLOUCESTER CITY 3 RACING CLUB WARWICK 1**
Competition: Southern League Western Division
Teamsheet: Bath, Thompson, Jenkins, Griffiths, Webb, Steadman, Burns, Smith, Mustoe, Hoskins, Harris
Substitutes: Marshall (nps), Wilkinson (nps), Cook (nps)
Scorers: Hoskins (2), Griffiths
Attendance: 233

Date: Tuesday 24/09/2002
Result: **GLOUCESTER CITY 2 SWINDON SUPERMARINE 1**
Competition: Southern League Western Division
Teamsheet: Bath, Thompson, Jenkins, Griffiths, Webb, Steadman, Burns, Smith, Mustoe, Hoskins, Harris
Substitutes: Marshall (for Hoskins), Wilkinson (for Webb), Temple (for Harris)
Scorers: Hoskins, Burns (pen)
Attendance: 203

Date: Saturday 28/09/2002
Result: **GLOUCESTER CITY 1 NEWPORT COUNTY 1**
Competition: FA Cup 2nd Qualifying Round
Teamsheet: Bath, Thompson, Harris, Griffiths, Steadman, Jenkins, Burns, Cox, Mustoe, Hoskins, Wilkinson
Substitutes: Smith (for Wilkinson), Marshall (nps), Webb (for Thompson)
Scorer: Hoskins
Attendance: 774

Date: Monday 30/09/2002
Result: **NEWPORT COUNTY 4 GLOUCESTER CITY 0**
Competition: FA Cup 2nd Qualifying Round Replay
Teamsheet: Bath, Webb, Harris, Griffiths, Steadman, Jenkins, Burns, Cox, Mustoe, Hoskins, Wilkinson
Substitutes: Smith (for Wilkinson), Marshall (for Harris), Bayliss (nps)
Attendance: 619

Date: Saturday 05/10/2002
Result: **ATHERSTONE UNITED 0 GLOUCESTER CITY 1**
Competition: FA Trophy Preliminary Round
Teamsheet: Bath, Smith, Jenkins, Griffiths, Steadman, Wilkinson, Burns, Cox, Mustoe, Hoskins, Harris
Substitutes: Marshall (nps), Webb (for Wilkinson), Bayliss (for Hoskins)
Scorer: Hoskins
Attendance: 170

Date: Saturday 12/10/2002
Result: **GLOUCESTER CITY 4 SOLIHULL BOROUGH 2**
Competition: Southern League Western Division
Teamsheet: Bath, Smith, Harris, Griffiths, Steadman, Mustoe, Jenkins, Cox, Bayliss, Hoskins, Wilkinson
Substitutes: Webb (for Bayliss), Temple (for Hoskins), Cook (nps)
Scorer: Cox (4)
Attendance: 250

Date: Tuesday 15/10/2002
Result: **MANGOTSFIELD UNITED 2 GLOUCESTER CITY 0**
Competition: Southern League Cup Preliminary Round
Teamsheet: Bath, Webb, Temple, Griffiths, Steadman, Chipps, Mustoe, Jenkins, Smith, Hoskins, Wilkinson
Substitutes: Marshall (for Wilkinson), Harris (nps), Delves (nps)
Attendance: 97

Date: Saturday 19/10/2002
Result: **SUTTON COLDFIELD TOWN 0 GLOUCESTER CITY 1**
Competition: Southern League Western Division
Teamsheet: Bath, Webb, Thompson, Griffiths, Steadman, Wilkinson, Burns, Harris, Mustoe, Hoskins, Jenkins
Substitutes: Bayliss (nps), Temple (nps), Smith (nps)
Scorer: Burns (pen)
Attendance: 124

Date: Tuesday 22/10/2002
Result: **CIRENCESTER TOWN 0 GLOUCESTER CITY 3**
Competition: Southern League Western Division
Teamsheet: Bath, Webb, Thompson, Griffiths, Steadman, Wilkinson, Burns, Harris, Mustoe, Hoskins, Jenkins
Substitutes: Marshall (for Thompson), Smith (for Harris), Temple (for Hoskins)
Scorers: Thompson, Wilkinson, Burns
Attendance: 196

[392]

Date: Saturday 26/10/2002
Result: **GLOUCESTER CITY 0 RUGBY UNITED 0**
Competition: Southern League Western Division
Teamsheet: Bath, Smith, Temple, Griffiths, Steadman, Wilkinson, Burns, Thompson, Mustoe, Webb, Harris
Substitutes: Marshall (for Temple), Hoskins (nps), Bayliss (nps)
Attendance: 329

Date: Saturday 02/11/2002
Result: **BANBURY UNITED 1 GLOUCESTER CITY 1**
Competition: FA Trophy 1st Round
Teamsheet: Bath, Thompson, Harris, Griffiths, Steadman, Jenkins, Burns, Smith, Bayliss, Mustoe, Wilkinson
Substitutes: Webb (for Thompson), Marshall (nps), Temple (for Jenkins)
Scorer: Bayliss
Attendance: 478

Date: Tuesday 05/11/2002
Result: **GLOUCESTER CITY 2 BANBURY UNITED 1**
Competition: FA Trophy 1st Round Replay
Teamsheet: Bath, Steadman, Jenkins, Griffiths, Thompson, Mustoe, Burns, Wilkinson, Harris, Smith, Bayliss
Substitutes: Hoskins (for Smith), Webb (for Burns), Temple (nps)
Scorers: Wilkinson, Hoskins
Attendance: 326

Date: Saturday 09/11/2002
Result: **GRESLEY ROVERS 1 GLOUCESTER CITY 1**
Competition: Southern League Western Division
Teamsheet: Bath, Thompson, Harris, Griffiths, Steadman, Jenkins, Burns, Mustoe, Bayliss, Hoskins, Wilkinson
Substitutes: Webb (nps), Smith (nps), Marshall (nps)
Scorer: Hoskins
Attendance: 362

Date: Tuesday 12/11/2002
Result: **GLOUCESTER CITY 3 SUTTON COLDFIELD TOWN 1**
Competition: Southern League Western Division
Teamsheet: Bath, Thompson, Harris, Griffiths, Steadman, Jenkins, Burns, Webb, Bayliss, Hoskins, Wilkinson
Substitutes: Marshall (for Burns), Smith (for Bayliss), Temple (nps)
Scorers: Wilkinson, Thompson, Steadman
Attendance: 204

Date: Saturday 16/11/2002
Result: **REDDITCH UNITED 1 GLOUCESTER CITY 0**
Competition: Southern League Western Division
Teamsheet: Bath, Thompson, Harris. Griffiths, Steadman, Jenkins, Burns, Mustoe, Smith, Hoskins, Wilkinson
Substitutes: Marshall (nps), Cox (for Smith), Webb (for Thompson)
Attendance: 175

Date: Monday 18/11/2002
Result: **GLOUCESTER CITY 1 BRISTOL CITY RESERVES 2**
Competition: Gloucestershire FA Northern Senior Professional Cup 1st Round
Teamsheet: Bath, Thompson, Harris, Griffiths, Steadman, Webb, Burns, Mustoe, Cox, Hoskins, Wilkinson
Substitutes: Marshall (for Thompson), Chipps (for Steadman), Smith (for Hoskins)
Scorer: Hoskins
Attendance: 136

Date: Tuesday 26/11/2002
Result: **GLOUCESTER CITY 4 TAUNTON TOWN 2**
Competition: Southern League Western Division
Teamsheet: Bath, Thompson, Harris, Griffiths, Steadman, Jenkins, Burns, Cox, Mustoe, Smith, Wilkinson
Substitutes: Webb (for Thompson), Chipps (for Steadman), Marshall (for Mustoe)
Scorers: Smith, Cox, Griffiths, Wilkinson
Attendance: 165

Date: Saturday 30/11/2002
Result: **GLOUCESTER CITY 0 MERTHYR TYDFIL 0**
Competition: FA Trophy 2nd Round
Teamsheet: Bath, Thompson, Harris, Griffiths, Steadman, Jenkins, Burns, Cox, Mustoe, Hoskins, Wilkinson
Substitutes: Webb (for Thompson), Smith (for Burns), Marshall (nps)
Attendance: 417

Date: Tuesday 03/12/2002
Result: **MERTHYR TYDFIL 0 GLOUCESTER CITY 1**
Competition: FA Trophy 2nd Round Replay
Teamsheet: Bath, Thompson, Harris, Griffiths, Steadman, Jenkins, Burns, Cox, Mustoe, Hoskins, Wilkinson
Substitutes: Webb (for Thompson), Smith (for Burns), Marshall (nps)
Scorer: Cox
Attendance: 340

Date: Saturday 07/12/2002
Result: **GLOUCESTER CITY 0 ROCESTER 0**
Competition: Southern League Western Division
Teamsheet: Bath, Smith, Harris, Griffiths, Steadman, Thompson, Burns, Cox, Mustoe, Hoskins, Wilkinson
Substitutes: Webb (for Harris), Marshall (for Thompson), Chipps (nps)
Attendance: 271

Date: Saturday 14/12/2002
Result: **GLOUCESTER CITY 3 SHEPSHED DYNAMO 1**
Competition: Southern League Western Division
Teamsheet: Bath, Smith, Marshall, Griffiths, Steadman, Harris, Burns, Cox, Mustoe, Hoskins, Wilkinson
Substitutes: Thompson (for Marshall), Webb (for Harris), Howard (nps)
Scorers: own goal, Hoskins, Cox
Attendance: 288

[393]

Date: Saturday 21/12/2002
Result: **STOURPORT SWIFTS 0 GLOUCESTER CITY 1**
Competition: Southern League Western Division
Teamsheet: Bath, Smith, Harris, Griffiths, Steadman, Chipps, Burns, Cox, Mustoe, Hoskins, Wilkinson
Substitutes: Jenkins (nps), Bayliss (nps), Howard (nps)
Scorer: Burns
Attendance: 132

Date: Thursday 26/12/2002
Result: **MERTHYR TYDFIL 3 GLOUCESTER CITY 2**
Competition: Southern League Western Division
Teamsheet: Bath, Smith, Harris, Griffiths, Steadman, Chipps, Jenkins, Cox, Mustoe, Hoskins, Wilkinson
Substitutes: Thompson (for Wilkinson), Webb (for Smith), Bayliss (for Chipps)
Scorer: Hoskins (2)
Attendance: 570

Date: Wednesday 01/01/2003
Result: **GLOUCESTER CITY 4 MANGOTSFIELD UNITED 3**
Competition: Southern League Western Division
Teamsheet: Bath, Thompson, Harris, Griffiths, Steadman, Jenkins, Burns, Cox, Mustoe, Hoskins, Wilkinson
Substitutes: Smith (for Harris), Webb (for Wilkinson), Bayliss (for Jenkins)
Scorers: Thompson (2), Wilkinson, Harris
Attendance: 283

Date: Saturday 04/01/2003
Result: **CLEVEDON TOWN 1 GLOUCESTER CITY 1**
Competition: Southern League Western Division
Teamsheet: Bath, Thompson, Harris, Griffiths, Steadman, Jenkins, Burns, Cox, Mustoe, Hoskins, Wilkinson
Substitutes: Smith (for Wilkinson), Webb (for Steadman), Bayliss (for Hoskins)
Scorer: Bayliss
Attendance: 233

Date: Tuesday 14/01/2003
Result: **GLOUCESTER CITY 3 LEWES 2**
Competition: FA Trophy 3rd Round
Teamsheet: Bath, Thompson, Harris, Griffiths, Chipps, Jenkins, Burns, Cox, Mustoe, Hoskins, Wilkinson
Substitutes: Smith (for Thompson), Webb (for Harris), Bayliss (for Hoskins)
Scorers: Griffiths, Smith, Cox
Attendance: 338

Date: Saturday 18/01/2003
Result: **GLOUCESTER CITY 1 GRESLEY ROVERS 0**
Competition: Southern League Western Division
Teamsheet: Bath, Smith, Harris, Griffiths, Chipps, Thompson, Marshall, Cox, Bayliss, Webb, Wilkinson
Substitutes: Stradling (nps), Radcliffe (for Harris), Hoskins (nps)
Scorer: Bayliss
Attendance: 302

Date: Saturday 25/01/2003
Result: **BROMSGROVE ROVERS 2 GLOUCESTER CITY 4**
Competition: Southern League Western Division
Teamsheet: Bath, Smith, Harris, Griffiths, Chipps, Thompson, Jenkins, Cox, Bayliss, Webb, Wilkinson
Substitutes: Hoskins (for Bayliss), Radcliffe (for Smith), Howard (nps)
Scorers: Smith (2), Wilkinson, Thompson
Attendance: 713

Date: Tuesday 28/01/2003
Result: **RACING CLUB WARWICK 1 GLOUCESTER CITY 6**
Competition: Southern League Western Division
Teamsheet: Bath, Smith, Harris, Griffiths, Chipps, Thompson, Jenkins, Cox, Webb, Hoskins, Wilkinson
Substitutes: Marshall (for Thompson), Radcliffe (for Harris), Howard (for Hoskins)
Scorers: Smith, Hoskins (2), Thompson, Cox, Griffiths
Attendance: 150

Date: Saturday 01/02/2003
Result: **GLOUCESTER CITY 0 WOKING 0**
Competition: FA Trophy 4th Round
Teamsheet: Bath, Smith, Harris, Griffiths, Chipps, Thompson, Burns, Cox, Webb, Hoskins, Wilkinson
Substitutes: Jenkins (nps), Bayliss (for Wilkinson), Radcliffe (nps)
Attendance: 1087

Date: Tuesday 04/02/2003
Result: **WOKING 0 GLOUCESTER CITY 2**
Competition: FA Trophy 4th Round Replay
Teamsheet: Bath, Smith, Harris, Griffiths, Chipps, Thompson, Burns, Cox, Webb, Hoskins, Wilkinson
Substitutes: Jenkins (for Smith), Bayliss (for Hoskins), Radcliffe (nps)
Scorers: Webb, Harris
Attendance: 1007

Date: Saturday 08/02/2003
Result: **SWINDON SUPERMARINE 1 GLOUCESTER CITY 2**
Competition: Southern League Western Division
Teamsheet: Bath, Radcliffe, Harris, Griffiths, Chipps, Thompson, Burns, Cox, Webb, Hoskins, Jenkins
Substitutes: Marshall (nps), Bayliss (for Radcliffe), Steadman (nps)
Scorers: Thompson, Cox
Attendance: 226

Date: Saturday 15/02/2003
Result: **GLOUCESTER CITY 4 BEDWORTH UNITED 1**
Competition: Southern League Western Division
Teamsheet: Bath, Smith, Harris, Griffiths, Chipps, Thompson, Burns, Cox, Webb, Jenkins, Wilkinson
Substitutes: Radcliffe (for Smith), Marshall (for Wilkinson), Bayliss (nps)
Scorers: Burns (pen), Smith, Jenkins, Cox
Attendance: 345

Date: Saturday 22/02/2003
Result: **GLOUCESTER CITY 1 SOUTHPORT 1**
Competition: FA Trophy 5th Round
Teamsheet: Bath, Smith, Harris, Griffiths, Chipps, Thompson, Burns, Cox, Webb, Jenkins, Wilkinson
Substitutes: Radcliffe (nps), Marshall (nps), Bayliss (for Smith)
Scorer: Cox
Attendance: 1237

Date: Tuesday 25/02/2003
Result: **SOUTHPORT 1 GLOUCESTER CITY 3**
Competition: FA Trophy 5th Round Replay
Teamsheet: Bath, Smith, Jenkins, Griffiths, Chipps, Thompson, Burns, Cox, Webb, Hoskins, Wilkinson
Substitutes: Radcliffe (for Jenkins), Marshall (nps), Steadman (nps)
Scorers: Cox (2), Webb
Attendance: 835

Date: Saturday 01/03/2003
Result: **GLOUCESTER CITY 0 WESTON-SUPER-MARE 2**
Competition: Southern League Western Division
Teamsheet: Bath, Smith, Harris, Griffiths, Chipps, Jenkins, Burns, Cox, Webb, Hoskins, Wilkinson
Substitutes: Radcliffe (for Smith), Marshall (nps), Bayliss (for Wilkinson)
Attendance: 583

Date: Tuesday 04/03/2003
Result: **BEDWORTH UNITED 2 GLOUCESTER CITY 2**
Competition: Southern League Western Division
Teamsheet: Bath, Steadman, Harris, Griffiths, Chipps, Jenkins, Burns, Cox, Webb, Hoskins, Wilkinson
Substitutes: Radcliffe (for Jenkins), Marshall (for Steadman), Barratt (nps)
Scorers: Hoskins, Burns
Attendance: 143

Date: Tuesday 11/03/2003
Result: **RUGBY UNITED 1 GLOUCESTER CITY 0**
Competition: Southern League Western Division
Teamsheet: Bath, Smith, Harris, Griffiths, Chipps, Jenkins, Steadman, Cox, Webb, Hoskins, Wilkinson
Substitutes: Radcliffe (for Hoskins), Bayliss (for Wilkinson), Marshall (for Harris)
Attendance: 271

Date: Saturday 15/03/2003
Result: **AYLESBURY UNITED 2 GLOUCESTER CITY 1**
Competition: FA Trophy Quarter-Final
Teamsheet: Bath, Thompson, Harris, Griffiths, Steadman, Bayliss, Burns, Cox, Webb, Hoskins, Wilkinson
Substitutes: Smith (for Wilkinson), Marshall (nps), Chipps (nps)
Scorer: Burns (pen)
Attendance: 1435

Date: Tuesday 18/03/2003
Result: **GLOUCESTER CITY 6 EVESHAM UNITED 1**
Competition: Southern League Western Division
Teamsheet: Bath, Smith, Harris, Griffiths, Chipps, Thompson, Steadman, Cox, Webb, Hoskins, Wilkinson
Substitutes: Marshall (for Harris), Howard (for Steadman), Radcliffe (for Webb)
Scorers: Cox, Hoskins (4, 1 pen), Griffiths
Attendance: 257

Date: Saturday 22/03/2003
Result: **GLOUCESTER CITY 1 STOURPORT SWIFTS 2**
Competition: Southern League Western Division
Teamsheet: Bath, Smith, Harris, Griffiths, Chipps, Thompson, Steadman, Cox, Webb, Hoskins, Wilkinson
Substitutes: Marshall (for Wilkinson), Howard (for Griffiths), Burns (for Thompson)
Scorer: Hoskins (pen)
Attendance: 309

Date: Monday 24/03/2003
Result: **ATHERSTONE UNITED 1 GLOUCESTER CITY 1**
Competition: Southern League Western Division
Teamsheet: Bath, Smith, Harris, Marshall, Chipps, Thompson, Steadman, Cox, Webb, Hoskins, Wilkinson
Substitutes: Burns (for Wilkinson), Howard (nps), Cook (nps)
Scorer: Harris
Attendance: 164

Date: Saturday 29/03/2003
Result: **GLOUCESTER CITY 1 BROMSGROVE ROVERS 0**
Competition: Southern League Western Division
Teamsheet: Bath, Smith, Jenkins, Griffiths, Chipps, Thompson, Burns, Cox, Bayliss, Hoskins, Webb
Substitutes: Marshall (for Bayliss), Howard (nps), Barratt (nps)
Scorer: Cox
Attendance: 355

Date: Monday 31/03/2003
Result: **SOLIHULL BOROUGH 2 GLOUCESTER CITY 1**
Competition: Southern League Western Division
Teamsheet: Bath, Smith, Marshall, Griffiths, Chipps, Thompson, Burns, Cox, Jenkins, Hoskins, Webb
Substitutes: Harris (for Marshall), Bayliss (for Hoskins), Steadman (nps)
Scorer: Cox
Attendance: 153

[395]

SEASON BY SEASON

Date: Saturday 05/04/2003
Result: **EVESHAM UNITED 0 GLOUCESTER CITY 1**
Competition: Southern League Western Division
Teamsheet: Bath, Smith, Harris, Griffiths, Chipps, Thompson, Jenkins, Cox, Bayliss, Webb, Wilkinson
Substitutes: Marshall (nps), Howard (nps), Steadman (nps)
Scorer: Cox
Attendance: 203

Date: Tuesday 08/04/2003
Result: **GLOUCESTER CITY 4 CINDERFORD TOWN 0**
Competition: Southern League Western Division
Teamsheet: Bath, Smith, Harris, Griffiths, Chipps, Thompson, Steadman, Cox, Bayliss, Webb, Wilkinson
Substitutes: Radcliffe (for Smith), Howard (for Harris), Hoskins (for Bayliss)
Scorers: Wilkinson, Bayliss, Harris, Cox
Attendance: 215

Date: Saturday 12/04/2003
Result: **SHEPSHED DYNAMO 1 GLOUCESTER CITY 0**
Competition: Southern League Western Division
Teamsheet: Bath, Smith, Harris, Griffiths, Chipps, Thompson, Steadman, Cox, Bayliss, Webb, Wilkinson
Substitutes: Howard (nps), Hoskins (for Bayliss), Radcliffe (nps)
Attendance: 141

Date: Saturday 19/04/2003
Result: **GLOUCESTER CITY 1 CLEVEDON TOWN 1**
Competition: Southern League Western Division
Teamsheet: Bath, Jenkins, Harris, Griffiths, Chipps, Thompson, Burns, Cox, Bayliss, Webb, Wilkinson
Substitutes: Hoskins (for Webb), Howard (nps), Smith (for Wilkinson)
Scorer: Burns (pen)
Attendance: 268

Date: Monday 21/04/2003
Result: **MANGOTSFIELD UNITED 1 GLOUCESTER CITY 4**
Competition: Southern League Western Division
Teamsheet: Bath, Smith, Harris, Griffiths, Chipps, Thompson, Steadman, Cox, Webb, Hoskins, Wilkinson
Substitutes: Bayliss (nps), Burns (nps), Jenkins (nps)
Scorers: Webb, Smith, Hoskins (2)
Attendance: 271

Date: Saturday 26/04/2003
Result: **ROCESTER 2 GLOUCESTER CITY 2**
Competition: Southern League Western Division
Teamsheet: Bath, Smith, Harris, Griffiths, Chipps, Thompson, Howard, Cox, Webb, Hoskins, Wilkinson
Substitutes: Jenkins (for Smith), Steadman (for Howard), Marshall (for Wilkinson)
Scorers: Cox, Webb
Attendance: 108

Date: Saturday 03/05/2003
Result: **GLOUCESTER CITY 5 CIRENCESTER TOWN 4**
Competition: Southern League Western Division
Teamsheet: Bath, Smith, Jenkins, Griffiths, Chipps, Thompson, Steadman, Cox, Webb, Hoskins, Wilkinson
Substitutes: Bayliss (for Hoskins), Howard (for Thompson), Burns (nps)
Scorers: Cox (3), Smith, Webb
Attendance: 388

Appearances – MR Bath 56, KA Bayliss 20(13), L Burby 2(1), C Burns 44(2), S Chipps 28(2), JD Cox 43(1), N Griffiths 55, C Hampson 5(2), AG Harris 51(1), AR Hoskins 43(5), KL Howard 1(11), S Jenkins 41(3), GP Marshall 8(19), NJ Mustoe 33, T Radcliffe 1(11), LF Smith 40(15), WCM Steadman 41(3), AJ Stradling 0(1), MA Taylor 3, C Temple 2(4), CD Thompson 49(2), TA Webb 37(18), D Wilkinson 49(2).
Others selected but did not play: E Barratt, A Cook, NJP Delves.
Scorers – JD Cox 22, AR Hoskins 21, C Burns 10, LF Smith 10, CD Thompson 10, D Wilkinson 8, N Griffiths 7, AG Harris 5, TA Webb 5, KA Bayliss 4, KL Howard 1, S Jenkins 1, WCM Steadman 1, own goal 1.

PROGRAMME   **PROGRAMME**   **PROGRAMME**

1999-2000

2001-2002

2002-2003

[396]

SOUTHERN LEAGUE – WESTERN DIVISION

POS	CLUB	P	W	D	L	F	A	PTS
1	MERTHYR TYDFIL	42	28	8	6	78	32	92
2	WESTON-SUPER-MARE	42	26	7	9	77	42	85
3	BROMSGROVE ROVERS	42	23	7	12	73	41	76
4	SOLIHULL BOROUGH	42	21	13	8	77	48	76
5	**GLOUCESTER CITY**	**42**	**22**	**9**	**11**	**87**	**58**	**75**
6	MANGOTSFIELD UNITED	42	21	10	11	106	53	73
7	REDDITCH UNITED	42	22	6	14	76	42	72
8	RUGBY UNITED	42	20	9	13	58	43	69
9	GRESLEY ROVERS	42	19	10	13	63	54	67
10	TAUNTON TOWN	42	20	7	15	76	78	67
11	SUTTON COLDFIELD TOWN	42	18	10	14	63	53	64
12	EVESHAM UNITED	42	19	6	17	76	72	63
13	CLEVEDON TOWN	42	14	13	15	54	60	55
14	CIRENCESTER TOWN	42	15	7	20	62	82	52
15	CINDERFORD TOWN	42	13	12	17	50	67	51
16	SHEPSHED DYNAMO	42	12	6	24	48	76	42
17	STOURPORT SWIFTS	42	10	11	21	48	66	41
18	BEDWORTH UNITED	42	11	7	24	46	74	40
19	SWINDON SUPERMARINE	42	11	5	26	52	85	38
20	ATHERSTONE UNITED	42	9	10	23	45	78	37
21	ROCESTER	42	9	10	23	34	74	37
22	RACING CLUB WARWICK	42	3	9	30	33	104	18
		924	366	192	366	1382	1382	1290

SEASON 2003-2004
(Home Ground: City Stadium, Meadow Park, Hempsted)

Date: Saturday 16/08/2003
Result: **RUGBY UNITED 1 GLOUCESTER CITY 0**
Competition: Southern League Western Division
Teamsheet: Bath, Smith, Knight, Griffiths, Jeffries, CD Thompson, Burns, Cox, Webb, Hoskins, Wilkinson
Substitutes: Tomkins (nps), Bayliss (nps), Steadman (for Smith), Howard (nps), Hemming (for Knight)
Attendance: 274

Date: Tuesday 19/08/2003
Result: **GLOUCESTER CITY 4 TEAM BATH 3**
Competition: Southern League Western Division
Teamsheet: Bath, Smith, Knight, Griffiths, Jeffries, CD Thompson, Burns, Cox, Webb, Hoskins, Wilkinson
Substitutes: Tomkins (nps), Steadman (for Burns), Howard (nps), Hemming (for Knight), Mustoe (for Webb)
Scorers: Hoskins, Cox (2), Hemming
Attendance: 383

Date: Saturday 23/08/2003
Result: GLOUCESTER CITY 4 ATHERSTONE UNITED 1
Competition: Southern League Western Division
Teamsheet: Bath, Smith, Knight, Griffiths, Jeffries, CD Thompson, Steadman, Cox, Webb, Hoskins, Wilkinson
Substitutes: Mustoe (for Webb), Tomkins (nps), Harris (for Smith), Hemming (for Knight), Howard (nps)
Scorers: Griffiths, Jeffries, own goal, Hemming
Attendance: 355
Note: Originally League game. Atherstone United withdrew after 5 games.

Date: Monday 25/08/2003
Result: **MANGOTSFIELD UNITED 3 GLOUCESTER CITY 2**
Competition: Southern League Western Division
Teamsheet: Bath, Smith, Hemming, Griffiths, Jeffries, CD Thompson, Mustoe, Cox, Webb, Hoskins, Wilkinson
Substitutes: Harris (for Hemming), Knight (nps), Burns (for Hoskins), Howard (for Wilkinson), Bayliss (nps)
Scorer: Hoskins (2, 1 pen)
Attendance: 267

Date: Saturday 30/08/2003
Result: **BRISTOL MANOR FARM 0 GLOUCESTER CITY 5**
Competition: FA Cup Preliminary Round
Teamsheet: Bath, Smith, Harris, Griffiths, Jeffries, CD Thompson, Mustoe, Cox, Webb, Hoskins, Wilkinson
Substitutes: Steadman (for Griffiths), Knight (for Wilkinson), Burns (nps), Hemming (for Harris), Bayliss (nps)
Scorers: Hoskins (4, 1 pen), Smith
Attendance: 151

Date: Satuday 06/09/2003
Result: **GLOUCESTER CITY 2 SOLIHULL BOROUGH 2**
Competition: Southern League Western Division
Teamsheet: Bath, Smith, Harris, Griffiths, Mustoe, CD Thompson, Burns, Cox, Webb, Hoskins, Wilkinson
Substitutes: Knight (for Smith), Jenkins (nps), Tomkins (nps), Hemming (for Harris), Bayliss (nps)
Scorer: Hoskins (2, 1 pen)
Attendance: 369

Date: Saturday 13/09/2003
Result: **GLOUCESTER CITY 0 TEAM BATH 0**
Competition: FA Cup 1st Qualifying Round
Teamsheet: Bath, Smith, Hemming, Griffiths, Mustoe, CD Thompson, Burns, Cox, Webb, Hoskins, Wilkinson
Substitutes: Harris (for Smith), Knight (for Wilkinson), Jenkins (for Mustoe), Bayliss (nps)
Attendance: 377

Date: Saturday 20/09/2003
Result: **BEDWORTH UNITED 1 GLOUCESTER CITY 2**
Competition: Southern League Western Division
Teamsheet: Bath, Webb, Harris, Griffiths, Knight, CD Thompson, Burns, Mustoe, Smith, Hoskins, Wilkinson
Substitutes: Cox (for Smith), Jenkins, (for Knight), Hemming (nps), Bayliss (nps), Howard (nps)
Scorers: Hoskins, Griffiths
Attendance: 162

Date: Monday 22/09/2003
Result: **TEAM BATH 0 GLOUCESTER CITY 2**
Competition: FA Cup 1st Qualifying Round Replay
Teamsheet: Bath, Smith, Jenkins, Griffiths, Jeffries, CD Thompson, Burns, Cox, Knight, Hoskins, Mustoe
Substitutes: Webb (for Burns), Wilkinson (for Knight), Hemming (for CD Thompson), Harris (nps), Tomkins (nps)
Scorer: Cox (2)
Attendance: 202

Date: Saturday 27/09/2003
Result: **GLOUCESTER CITY 2 MERTHYR TYDFIL 0**
Competition: FA Cup 2nd Qualifying Round
Teamsheet: Bath, Smith, Jenkins, Griffiths, Jeffries, CD Thompson, Burns, Cox, Knight, Hoskins, Mustoe
Substitutes: Wilkinson (for Burns), Harris (for Cox), Webb (for Knight), Hemming (nps), Jones (nps)
Scorer: Jeffries (2)
Attendance: 476

Date: Saturday 04/10/2003
Result: **GLOUCESTER CITY 2 EVESHAM UNITED 0**
Competition: FATrophy Preliminary Round
Teamsheet: Barratt, Webb, Harris, Griffiths, Jeffries, Mustoe, Jenkins, Cox, Knight, Hoskins, Wilkinson
Substitutes: Smith (for Hoskins), CD Thompson (for Knight), Jones (for Harris), Hemming (nps), Burns (nps)
Scorers: Hoskins, Smith
Attendance: 380

Date: Tuesday 07/10/2003
Result: **GLOUCESTER CITY 4 MANGOTSFIELD UNITED 2** (aet)
Competition: Gloucestershire FA Northern Senior Professional Cup 1st Round
Teamsheet: Barratt, Harris, Hemming, Griffiths, Bayliss, Howard, Jenkins, CD Thompson, Jones, Smith, Wilkinson
Substitutes: Mustoe (for Bayliss), Knight (for Jones), Cox (for Hemming), Bath (nps), Burns (nps)
Scorers: Smith, Cox, Jones, Wilkinson
Attendance: 110

Date: Saturday 11/10/2004
Result: **GLOUCESTER CITY 4 CHIPPENHAM TOWN 3**
Competition: FA Cup 3rd Qualifying Round
Teamsheet: Bath, Smith, Jenkins, Griffiths, Jeffries, CD Thompson, Burns, Cox, Knight, Hoskins, Mustoe
Substitutes: Wilkinson (for Jeffries), Harris (for Burns), Webb (for Knight), Hemming (nps), Jones (nps)
Scorers: Cox (2), Smith, Hoskins
Attendance: 611

Date: Tuesday 14/10/2003
Result: **GLOUCESTER CITY 2 HALESOWEN TOWN 2**
Competition: Southern League Western Division
Teamsheet: Bath, Smith, Jenkins, Griffiths, Jeffries, CD Thompson, Webb, Cox, Knight, Hoskins, Mustoe
Substitutes: Wilkinson (for Jenkins), Burns (for Knight), Harris (for CD Thompson), Hemming (nps), Jones (nps)
Scorers: Smith, Cox
Attendance: 368

Date: Saturday 18/10/2003
Result: **GLOUCESTER CITY 3 EVESHAM UNITED 1**
Competition: Southern League Western Division
Teamsheet: Bath, Smith, Webb, Griffiths, Wilkinson, CD Thompson, Burns, Cox, Knight, Hoskins, Mustoe
Substitutes: Harris (for Smith), Hemming (for CD Thompson), Bayliss (nps)
Scorers: Cox, Hoskins, Knight
Attendance: 316

Date: Saturday 25/10/2003
Result: **BISHOP'S STORTFORD 2 GLOUCESTER CITY 0**
Competition: FA Cup 4th Qualifying Round
Teamsheet: Bath, Smith, CD Thompson, Griffiths, Jeffries, Mustoe, Burns, Cox, Knight, Hoskins, Webb
Substitutes: Wilkinson (nps), Harris (nps), Howard (nps), Hemming (nps)
Attendance: 768

Date: Tuesday 28/10/2003
Result: **GLOUCESTER CITY 1 SOLIHULL BOROUGH 4**
Competition: Southern League Cup 1st Round
Teamsheet: Bath, Hemming, Howard, Griffiths, CD Thompson, Wilkinson, Burns, Webb, Knight, Smith, Harris
Substitutes: Mustoe (for Burns), Hoskins (nps), Cox (for Smith), Bayliss (for Harris), Jeffries (nps)
Scorer: Cox
Attendance: 112

Date: Saturday 01/11/2003
Result: **ROTHWELL TOWN 1 GLOUCESTER CITY 1**
Competition: FA Trophy 1st Round
Teamsheet: Bath, Smith, Webb, Griffiths, Jeffries, CD Thompson, Mustoe, Cox, Knight, Hoskins, Wilkinson
Substitutes: Howard (nps), Bayliss (nps), Burns (nps), Hemming (for Webb)
Scorer: Hoskins
Attendance: 137

Date: Tuesday 04/11/2003
Result: **GLOUCESTER CITY 4 ROTHWELL TOWN 1** (aet)
Competition: FA Trophy 1st Round Replay
Teamsheet: Bath, Smith, Webb, Griffiths, Jeffries, CD Thompson, Mustoe, Cox, Knight, Hoskins, Wilkinson
Substitutes: Howard (for Smith), Bayliss (nps), Burns (nps)
Scorers: Wilkinson, Hoskins (2, 1 pen), Cox
Attendance: 250

Date: Saturday 08/11/2003
Result: **CLEVEDON TOWN 0 GLOUCESTER CITY 2**
Competition: Southern League Western Division
Teamsheet: Bath, Smith, Hemming, Griffiths, Jeffries, CD Thomson, Burns, Cox, Knight, Bayliss, Mustoe
Substitutes: Wilkinson (for Mustoe), Webb (for Knight), Avery (nps), Harris (nps), Jenkins (for Bayliss)
Scorers: Wilkinson, Bayliss
Attendance: 224

Date: Saturday 15/11/2003
Result: **SUTTON COLDFIELD TOWN 0 GLOUCESTER CITY 1**
Competition: Southern League Western Division
Teamsheet: Bath, Smith, Hemming, Griffiths, Jeffries, CD Thompson, Burns, Cox, Webb, Hoskins, Wilkinson
Substitutes: Knight (nps), Harris (for Cox), Jenkins (for Burns), Bayliss (nps), Avery (nps)
Scorer: Cox
Attendance: 171

Date: Saturday 22/11/2003
Result: **GLOUCESTER CITY 2 BEDWORTH UNITED 1**
Competition: Southern League Western Division
Teamsheet: Bath, Smith, Harris, Griffiths, Jeffries, CD Thompson, Mustoe, Cox, Knight, Hoskins, Wilkinson
Substitutes: Webb (for Knight), Burns (nps), Avery (nps), Hemming (for Harris), Bayliss (nps)
Scorer: Wilkinson (2)
Attendance: 304

Date: Tuesday 25/11/2003
Result: **GLOUCESTER CITY 3 GRESLEY ROVERS 3**
Competition: Southern League Western Division
Teamsheet: Bath, Smith, Hemming, Griffiths, Jeffries, CD Thompson, Burns, Cox, Webb, Hoskins, Mustoe
Substitutes: Wilkinson (nps), Avery (for Jeffries), Knight (nps)
Scorer: Hoskins (3)
Attendance: 253

Date: Saturday 29/11/2003
Result: **BATH CITY 2 GLOUCESTER CITY 1**
Competition: FA Trophy 2nd Round
Teamsheet: Bath, Smith, Webb, Griffiths, Jeffries, CD Thompson, Mustoe, Cox, Knight, Hoskins, Wilkinson
Substitutes: Burns (for Wilkinson), Barratt (nps), Avery (nps), Bayliss (for Smith), Hemming (for Knight)
Scorer: Wilkinson
Attendance: 608

Date: Saturday 06/12/2003
Result: **ILKESTON TOWN 0 GLOUCESTER CITY 3**
Competition: Southern League Western Division
Teamsheet: Bath, Smith, Hemming, Griffiths, Jeffries, CD Thompson, Mustoe, Cox, Webb, Hoskins, Wilkinson
Substitutes: Knight (nps), Avery (nps), Burns (nps)
Scorers: Smith, Wilkinson, Cox
Attendance: 364

Date: Tuesday 09/12/2003
Result: **GLOUCESTER CITY 5 SHEPSHED DYNAMO 2**
Competition: Southern League Western Division
Teamsheet: Bath, Smith, Webb, Griffiths, Avery, CD Thompson, Mustoe, Cox, Knight, Hoskins, Wilkinson
Substitutes: Hemming (for Wilkinson), Howard (for CD Thompson), Burns (nps)
Scorers: Wilkinson, Hoskins (3), Knight
Attendance: 222

Date: Saturday 13/12/2003
Result: **GLOUCESTER CITY 0 RUGBY UNITED 1**
Competition: Southern League Western Division
Teamsheet: Bath, Smith, Webb, Griffiths, Burns, CD Thompson, Mustoe, Cox, Knight, Hoskins, Wilkinson
Substitutes: Avery (nps), Palmer (for Burns), Howard (nps), Hemming (for Knight), Bayliss (nps)
Attendance: 379

Date: Tuesday 16/12/2003
Result: **STOURPORT SWIFTS 1 GLOUCESTER CITY 2**
Competition: Southern League Western Division
Teamsheet: Bath, Smith, Hemming, Griffiths, Burns, CD Thompson, Mustoe, Cox, Webb, Hoskins, Wilkinson
Substitutes: Knight (for Webb), Avery (nps), Palmer (for Smith)
Scorer: Cox (2)
Attendance: 103

Date: Friday 26/12/2003
Result: **GLOUCESTER CITY 2 MANGOTSFIELD UNITED 2**
Competition: Southern League Western Division
Teamsheet: Bath, Smith, Webb, Griffiths, Jeffries, Burns, Mustoe, Cox, Knight, Hoskins, Wilkinson
Substitutes: Palmer (for Smith), Davis (for Knight), MP Thompson (for Wilkinson), Hemming (nps), Avery (nps)
Scorers: Wilkinson, Smith
Attendance: 439

[399]

Date: Thursday 01/01/2004
Result: **CINDERFORD TOWN 0 GLOUCESTER CITY 2**
Competition: Southern League Western Division
Teamsheet: Bath, Smith, Hemming, Griffiths, Jeffries, CD Thompson, Mustoe, Cox, Webb, Hoskins, Wilkinson
Substitutes: Davis (for Smith), MP Thompson (for Jeffries), Knight (nps), Harris (for Hemming), Burns (nps)
Scorers: Hoskins, Cox
Attendance: 487

Date: Saturday 03/01/2004
Result: **GLOUCESTER CITY 3 SWINDON SUPERMARINE 1**
Competition: Southern League Western Division
Teamsheet: Bath, Smith, Hemming, Griffiths, Jeffries, CD Thompson, Mustoe, Cox, Webb, Hoskins, Knight
Substitutes: Davis (for Cox), MP Thompson (nps), Wilkinson (nps), Avery (for Griffiths), Bayliss (for Hoskins)
Scorers: Hoskins, Webb, Cox
Attendance: 385

Date: Wednesday 07/01/2004
Result: **TAUNTON TOWN 5 GLOUCESTER CITY 0**
Competition: Southern League Western Division
Teamsheet: Bath, Smith, Hemming, Griffiths, Jeffries, CD Thompson, Mustoe, Cox, Webb, Hoskins, Wilkinson
Substitutes: Knight (nps), Bayliss (for Hoskins), Harris (for Hemming), Jenkins (for Wilkinson)
Attendance: 166

Date: Saturday 10/01/2004
Result: **GLOUCESTER CITY 1 YATE TOWN 2**
Competition: Southern League Western Division
Teamsheet: Bath, CD Thompson, Harris, Griffiths, Jeffries, Burns, Mustoe, Cox, Knight, Smith, Jenkins
Substitutes: Wilkinson (for Burns), Webb (for CD Thompson), Davis (for Harris), Hemming (nps), MP Thompson (nps)
Scorer: Wilkinson
Attendance: 356

Date: Monday 12/01/2004
Result: **SOLIHULL BOROUGH 0 GLOUCESTER CITY 0**
Competition: Southern League Western Division
Teamsheet: Bath, Smith, Harris, Griffiths, Jeffries, CD Thompson, Mustoe, Cox, Webb, Hoskins, Wilkinson
Substitutes: Knight (nps), Davis (nps), MP Thompson (nps), Jenkins (for Smith)
Attendance: 146

Date: Tuesday 20/01/2004
Result: **GRESLEY ROVERS 1 GLOUCESTER CITY 2**
Competition: Southern League Western Division
Teamsheet: Bath, Smith, Harris, Griffiths, MP Thompson, CD Thompson, Mustoe, Cox, Knight, Hoskins, Wilkinson
Substitutes: Davis (for Knight), Burns (nps), Bayliss (nps), Hemming (for Harris)
Scorers: Hoskins, MP Thompson
Attendance: 326

Date: Saturday 24/01/2004
Result: **YATE TOWN 2 GLOUCESTER CITY 1**
Competition: Southern League Western Division
Teamsheet: Bath, Knight, Harris, Griffiths, MP Thompson, CD Thompson, Mustoe, Cox, Mings, Hoskins, Wilkinson
Substitutes: Jeffries (for Wilkinson), Bayliss (for Mings), Davis (nps), Hemming (for Harris)
Scorer: Hoskins
Attendance: 292

Date: Tuesday 03/02/2004
Result: **GLOUCESTER CITY 1 BROMSGROVE ROVERS 0**
Competition: Southern League Western Division
Teamsheet: Bath, Webb, Harris, Griffiths, Jeffries, Burns, Mustoe, Cox, Mings, Hoskins, Knight
Substitutes: Hemming (for Harris), Davis (for Knight), CD Thompson (nps), Bayliss (nps), MP Thompson (nps)
Scorer: Hoskins
Attendance: 258

Date: Saturday 07/02/2004
Result: **GLOUCESTER CITY 3 TAUNTON TOWN 1**
Competition: Southern League Western Division
Teamsheet: Bath, Webb, Harris, Griffiths, Jeffries, Burns, Mustoe, Cox, Mings, Hoskins, Knight
Substitutes: Wilkinson (for Knight), MP Thompson (nps), Davis (for Hoskins), Hemming (nps), Howarth (for Burns)
Scorers: Griffiths, Mustoe, Hoskins
Attendance: 364

Date: Saturday 14/02/2004
Result: **HALESOWEN TOWN 0 GLOUCESTER CITY 0**
Competition: Southern League Western Division
Teamsheet: Bath, Webb, Harris, Howarth, Jeffries, Burns, Mustoe, Cox, Mings, Hoskins, Wilkinson
Substitutes: Smith (for Mings), MP Thompson (for Webb), Bayliss (nps), Hemming (for -----)
Attendance: 427

Date: Saturday 21/02/2004
Result: **CIRENCESTER TOWN 2 GLOUCESTER CITY 1**
Competition: Southern League Western Division
Teamsheet: Bath, Smith, Harris, Howarth, Jeffries, Burns, CD Thompson, Cox, Mings, Knight, Wilkinson
Substitutes: Davis (nps), MP Thompson (for Knight), Bayliss (nps), Hemming (for Smith)
Scorer: Mings
Attendance: 422

Date: Monday 23/02/2004
Result: **BRISTOL CITY RESERVES 6 GLOUCESTER CITY 1**
Competition: Gloucestershire FA Northern Senior Professional Cup Semi-Final
Teamsheet: Bath, Smith, Hemming, Griffiths, Jeffries, Howarth, CD Thompson, Cox, Bayliss, MP Thompson, Wilkinson
Substitutes: Hyde (for Wilkinson), Moody (for Bath), Burns (nps), Knight (nps), Harris (nps)
Scorer: Cox
Attendance: 176

Date: Saturday 28/02/2004
Result: **GLOUCESTER CITY 1 STOURPORT SWIFTS 0**
Competition: Southern League Western Division
Teamsheet: Bath, CD Thompson, Hemming, Griffiths, Jeffries, Burns, Mustoe, Cox, Howarth, Hoskins, Wilkinson
Substitutes: Knight (for Wilkinson), Bayliss (nps), Halliday (for Jeffries), Morrison (nps)
Scorer: Hoskins (pen)
Attendance: 336

Date: Saturday 06/03/2004
Result: **GLOUCESTER CITY 1 REDDITCH UNITED 1**
Competition: Southern League Western Division
Teamsheet: Bath, Smith, CD Thompson, Griffiths, Howarth, Burns, Mustoe, Cox, Webb, Hoskins, Wilkinson
Substitutes: Knight (for Wilkinson), Harris (for CD Thompson), Bayliss (nps), Hemming (nps)
Scorer: Hoskins (pen)
Attendance: 459

Date: Saturday 13/03/2004
Result: **SHEPSHED DYNAMO 0 GLOUCESTER CITY 6**
Competition: Southern League Western Division
Teamsheet: Bath, Smith, Knight, Griffiths, CD Thompson, Burns, Mustoe, Cox, Webb, Hoskins, Wilkinson
Substitutes: Harris (for Knight), Bayliss (for Hoskins), Hemming (for Cox)
Scorers: Cox (2), Hoskins, Wilkinson, Webb, Hemming
Attendance: 157

Date: Tuesday 16/03/2004
Result: **BROMSGROVE ROVERS 0 GLOUCESTER CITY 1**
Competition: Southern League Western Division
Teamsheet: Bath, Smith, Harris, Griffiths, CD Thompson, Burns, Mustoe, Cox, Webb, Hoskins, Wilkinson
Substitutes: Avery (nps), Hemming (for Harris), Bayliss (nps)
Scorer: Hoskins
Attendance: 414

Date: Saturday 27/03/2004
Result: **GLOUCESTER CITY 2 CIRENCESTER TOWN 0**
Competition: Southern League Western Division
Teamsheet: Bath, Smith, Harris, Griffiths, Howarth, Burns, Mustoe, Cox, Webb, Hoskins, CD Thompson
Substitutes: Knight (for Smith), Wilkinson (nps), Bayliss (nps), Hemming (for Cox), Jeffries (nps)
Scorers: Cox, CD Thompson
Attendance: 475

Date: Saturday 03/04/2004
Result: **TEAM BATH 1 GLOUCESTER CITY 3**
Competition: Southern League Western Division
Teamsheet: Bath, Smith, Harris, Griffiths, Howarth, Burns, Mustoe, Cox, Wilkinson, Hoskins, CD Thompson
Substitutes: Bayliss (nps), Jeffries (nps), Knight (for Smith), Hemming (for Cox)
Scorers: Wilkinson, Hoskins (2, 1 pen)
Attendance: 152

Date: Tuesday 06/04/2004
Result: **GLOUCESTER CITY 3 CLEVEDON TOWN 1**
Competition: Southern League Western Division
Teamsheet: Bath, Smith, Harris, Griffiths, Jeffries, Burns, Mustoe, Cox, Wilkinson, Hoskins, CD Thompson
Substitutes: Knight (for Wilkinson), Bayliss (nps), Webb (nps), Hemming (for Smith)
Scorers: Smith, Wilkinson, Hemming
Attendance: 291

Date: Saturday 10/04/2004
Result: **SWINDON SUPERMARINE 0 GLOUCESTER CITY 2**
Competition: Southern League Western Division
Teamsheet: Bath, Smith, Harris, Howarth, Jeffries, Burns, Mustoe, Cox, Wilkinson, Hoskins, CD Thompson
Substitutes: Knight (for CD Thompson), Bayliss (nps), Webb (for Wilkinson), Hemming (for Smith)
Scorer: Jeffries (2)
Attendance: 189

Date: Monday 12/04/2004
Result: **GLOUCESTER CITY 4 CINDERFORD TOWN 0**
Competition: Southern League Western Division
Teamsheet: Bath, Smith, Hemming, Howarth, Jeffries, CD Thompson, Mustoe, Cox, Webb, Hoskins, Knight
Substitutes: Griffiths (for Webb), Harris (for Smith), Bayliss (for Hoskins), Burns (nps)
Scorers: Hoskins, Griffiths, Cox (2)
Attendance: 572

Date: Saturday 17/04/2004
Result: **GLOUCESTER CITY 2 SUTTON COLDFIELD TOWN 1**
Competition: Southern League Western Division
Teamsheet: Bath, Smith, Harris, Griffiths, Jeffries, Burns, Howarth, Cox, Webb, Hoskins, CD Thompson
Substitutes: Knight (for Smith), Wilkinson (for Webb), Bayliss (nps), Hemming (nps)
Scorers: Hoskins, Cox
Attendance: 453

Date: Tuesday 20/04/2004
Result: **EVESHAM UNITED 4 GLOUCESTER CITY 2**
Competition: Southern League Western Division
Teamsheet: Bath, Smith, Harris, Griffiths, Jeffries, Burns, Howarth, Cox, Knight, Hoskins, CD Thompson
Substitutes: Wilkinson (for Knight), Hemming (for Harris), Bayliss (for Griffiths)
Scorers: Jeffries, Hoskins
Attendance: 279

Date: Saturday 24/04/2004
Result: **REDDITCH UNITED 0 GLOUCESTER CITY 1**
Competition: Southern League Western Division
Teamsheet: Bath, CD Thompson, Harris, Griffiths, Jeffries, Burns, Mustoe, Howarth, Smith, Hoskins, Wilkinson
Substitutes: Hemming (for Harris), Knight (for Mustoe), Bayliss (nps)
Scorer: Burns
Attendance: 1088

Date: Saturday 01/05/2004
Result: **GLOUCESTER CITY 0 ILKESTON TOWN 1**
Competition: Southern League Western Division
Teamsheet: Bath, CD Thompson, Hemming, Griffiths, Jeffries, Burns, Mustoe, Howarth, Smith, Hoskins, Wilkinson
Substitutes: Knight (for Hemming), Webb (for Wilkinson), Bayliss (for Smith)
Attendance: 902

Appearances – DJ Avery 1(2), E Barratt 2, MR Bath 52, KA Bayliss 3(9), C Burns 34(3), JD Cox 49(3), LM Davis 0(7), N Griffiths 50(1), LF Halliday 0(1), AG Harris 23(12), A Hemming 16(25), AR Hoskins 48, KL Howard 2(3), A Howarth 13, C Hyde 0(1), L Jeffries 38(1), S Jenkins 7(6), C Jones 1(1), K Knight 30(14), AL Mings 5, AT Moody 0(1), NJ Mustoe 44(4), KA Palmer 0(3), LF Smith 48(2), WCM Steadman 1(3), CD Thompson 49(2), MP Thompson 3(3), TA Webb 36(8), D Wilkinson 39(9).
Others selected but did not play: GT Morrison, LP Tomkins.
Scorers – AR Hoskins 37, JD Cox 24, D Wilkinson 13, LF Smith 8, L Jeffries 6, N Griffiths 4, A Hemming 4, K Knight 2, TA Webb 2, KA Bayliss 1, C Burns 1, C Jones 1, AL Mings 1, NJ Mustoe 1, CD Thompson 1, MP Thompson 1, own goal 1.

SOUTHERN LEAGUE – WESTERN DIVISION

POS	CLUB	P	W	D	L	F	A	PTS
1	REDDITCH UNITED	40	25	9	6	75	30	84
2	**GLOUCESTER CITY**	**40**	**24**	**7**	**9**	**77**	**46**	**79**
3	CIRENCESTER TOWN	40	24	4	12	73	40	76
4	HALESOWEN TOWN	40	20	13	7	64	40	73
5	RUGBY UNITED	40	21	8	11	57	40	71
6	TEAM BATH	40	21	6	13	62	41	69
7	SOLIHULL BOROUGH	40	19	9	12	50	31	66
8	SUTTON COLDFIELD TOWN	40	16	15	9	52	38	63
9	BROMSGROVE ROVERS	40	16	11	13	60	48	59
10	ILKESTON TOWN	40	16	10	14	58	59	58
11	CLEVEDON TOWN	40	16	5	19	55	59	53
12	GRESLEY ROVERS	40	15	7	18	52	60	52
13	MANGOTSFIELD UNITED	40	14	8	18	70	70	50
14	EVESHAM UNITED	40	15	5	20	56	57	50
15	TAUNTON TOWN	40	14	8	18	50	55	50
16	YATE TOWN	40	11	9	20	51	79	42
17	SWINDON SUPERMARINE	40	10	9	21	41	69	39
18	STOURPORT SWIFTS	40	9	11	20	43	62	38
19	BEDWORTH UNITED	40	8	12	20	39	61	36
20	CINDERFORD TOWN	40	7	9	24	50	94	30
21	SHEPSHED DYNAMO	40	5	13	22	31	87	28
22	ATHERSTONE UNITED							
		840	326	188	326	1166	1166	1166

Atherstone United withdrew after 5 games. All scores were expunged from records.

SEASON 2004-2005
(Home Ground: City Stadium, Meadow Park, Hempsted)

Date: Saturday 14/08/2004
Result: **BEDFORD TOWN 0 GLOUCESTER CITY 0**
Competition: Southern League Premier Division
Teamsheet: Bath, Smith, CD Thompson, Griffiths, MP Thompson, Burns, Mustoe, Webb, Aubrey, Davis, Wilkinson
Substitutes: Knight (for Burns), Harris (nps), Bayliss (for CD Thompson), Wood (nps), Palmer (nps)
Attendance: 515

Date: Tuesday 17/08/2004
Result: **GLOUCESTER CITY 2 TEAM BATH 1**
Competition: Southern League Premier Division
Teamsheet: Bath, Smith, Knight, Griffiths, MP Thompson, CD Thompson, Mustoe, Webb, Aubrey, Davis, Wilkinson
Substitutes: Cox (for Aubrey), Harris (for Webb), Bayliss (for Davis), Wood (nps), Palmer (nps)
Scorers: Knight (pen), Wilkinson
Attendance: 353

Date: Saturday 21/08/2004
Result: **GLOUCESTER CITY 3 DUNSTABLE TOWN 1**
Competition: Southern League Premier Division
Teamsheet: Bath, Smith, Knight, Griffiths, MP Thompson, CD Thompson, Mustoe, Webb, Aubrey, Davis, Wilkinson
Substitutes: Cox (for Davis), Harris (for Wilkinson), Palmer (nps), Wood (nps), Bayliss (for Aubrey)
Scorers: Wilkinson, Webb, MP Thompson
Attendance: 341

Date: Tuesday 24/08/2004
Result: **CHESHAM UNITED 3 GLOUCESTER CITY 2**
Competition: Southern League Premier Division
Teamsheet: Bath, Smith, Knight, Griffiths, MP Thompson, CD Thompson, Mustoe, Webb, Aubrey, Davis, Wilkinson
Substitutes: Cox (for Davis), Hoskins (for Aubrey), Harris (for Griffiths), Bayliss (nps)
Scorers: Davis, Cox
Attendance: 250

Date: Saturday 28/08/2004
Result: **GLOUCESTER CITY 1 HISTON 2**
Competition: Southern League Premier Division
Teamsheet: Bath, Davis, Webb, Griffiths, MP Thompson, CD Thompson, Mustoe, Cox, Aubrey, Hoskins, Wilkinson
Substitutes: Smith (for Davis), Wood (for Wilkinson), Styles (for Hoskins), Avery (nps), Bayliss (nps)
Scorer: Wilkinson
Attendance: 315

Date: Monday 30/08/2004
Result: **CHIPPENHAM TOWN 3 GLOUCESTER CITY 2**
Competition: Southern League Premier Division
Teamsheet: Bath, Smith, Avery, Griffiths, MP Thompson, CD Thompson, Mustoe, Cox, Aubrey, Webb, Wilkinson
Substitutes: Davis (for Avery), Wood (for Wilkinson), Styles (for Cox), Bayliss (nps)
Scorers: Cox (pen), Webb
Attendance: 651

Date: Saturday 04/09/2004
Result: **GLOUCESTER CITY 2 HEMEL HEMPSTEAD TOWN 3**
Competition: Southern League Premier Division
Teamsheet: Bath, CD Thompson, Avery, Griffiths, MP Thompson, Webb, Mustoe, Cox, Aubrey, Smith, Harris
Substitutes: Wood (nps), Styles (for Wilkinson), Davis (for MP Thompson), Bayliss (for Aubrey), Burns (nps)
Scorer: Smith (2)
Attendance: 354

Date: Tuesday 07/09/2004
Result: **BATH CITY 1 GLOUCESTER CITY 1**
Competition: Southern League Premier Division
Teamsheet: Bath, Smith, Harris, Griffiths, Aubrey, CD Thompson, Mustoe, Cox, Bayliss, Davis, Webb
Substitutes: Styles (for Smith), Hoskins (for Bayliss), Wilkinson (nps), Knight (nps)
Scorer: Cox
Attendance: 583

Date: Saturday 11/09/2004
Result: **STAMFORD 0 GLOUCESTR CITY 0**
Competition: Southern League Premier Division
Teamsheet: Bath, Smith, Styles, Griffiths, Aubrey, CD Thompson, Mustoe, Cox, Bayliss, Davis, Webb
Substitutes: Burns (for Griffiths), Knight (for Davis), Harris (nps)
Attendance: 262

Date: Saturday 18/09/2004
Result: **STREET 3 GLOUCESTER CITY 2**
Competition: FA Cup 1st Qualifying Round
Teamsheet: Bath, Smith, Styles, MP Thompson, CD Thompson, Burns, Mustoe, Cox, Bayliss, Webb, Knight
Substitutes: Avery (nps), Davis (for Styles), Griffiths (for Burns), Wilkinson (nps), Harris (nps)
Scorers: Cox, Bayliss
Attendance: 235

Date: Tuesday 21/09/2004
Result: **GLOUCESTER CITY 0 CHELTENHAM TOWN RESERVES 2** (aet)
Competition: Gloucestershire FA Northern Senior Professional Cup 1st Round
Teamsheet: Bath, Knight, Avery, Griffiths, MP Thompson, CD Thompson, Mustoe, Cox, Burns, Webb, Smith
Substitutes: Rimmer (for Knight), Forrester (for Burns), Reid (for Mustoe), Bayliss (nps)
Attendance: 364

Date: Saturday 25/09/2004
Result: **GLOUCESTER CITY 0 SOLIHULL BOROUGH 1**
Competition: Southern League Premier Division
Teamsheet: Bath, CD Thompson, MP Thompson, Griffiths, Tomkins, Webb, Mustoe, Cox, Bayliss, Burns, Smith
Substitutes: Davis (for Cox), Knight (for MP Thompson), Avery (nps), Reid (nps), Hoskins (nps)
Attendance: 288

Date: Saturday 09/10/2004
Result: **GRANTHAM TOWN 0 GLOUCESTER CITY 0**
Competition: Southern League Premier Division
Teamsheet: Bath, Smith, MP Thompson, Griffiths, Tomkins, CD Thompson, Mustoe, Burns, Webb, Hoskins, Knight
Substitutes: Wilkinson (for Knight), Harris (for MP Thompson), Cox (for Hoskins)
Attendance: 303

Date: Saturday 16/10/2004
Result: **GLOUCESTER CITY 0 STAMFORD 0**
Competition: Southern League Premier Division
Teamsheet: Bath, CD Thompson, MP Thompson, Griffiths, Tomkins, Burns, Mustoe, Webb, Smith, Hoskins, Wilkinson
Substitutes: Knight (for Tomkins), Davis (for Wilkinson), Harris (for MP Thompson), Reid (nps)
Attendance: 327

Date: Saturday 23/10/2004
Result: **DUNSTABLE TOWN 0 GLOUCESTER CITY 2**
Competition: Southern League Premier Division
Teamsheet: Bath, Smith, Knight, Griffiths, Tomkins, CD Thompson, Mustoe, Webb, DS Addis, Davis, Wilkinson
Substitutes: MP Thompson (for Knight), Harris (nps), Reid (for D Addis), Rimmer (nps), Cox (for Davis)
Scorers: Davis, Mustoe (pen)
Attendance: 95

Date: Saturday 30/10/2004
Result: **GLOUCESTER CITY 4 BANBURY UNITED 1**
Competition: Southern League Premier Division
Teamsheet: Bath, Smith, MP Thompson, Griffiths, Tomkins, CD Thompson, Mustoe, Webb, DS Addis, Davis, Wilkinson
Substitutes: Cox (for Davis), Rimmer (for Smith), Reid (for Mustoe), Knight (nps), Harris (nps)
Scorers: Wilkinson, Davis, Tomkins (2)
Attendance: 415

[403]

Date: Tuesday 02/11/2004
Result: **GLOUCESTER CITY 1 TIVERTON TOWN 1**
Competition: Southern League Premier Division
Teamsheet: Bath, Smith, MP Thompson, Griffiths, Tomkins, CD Thompson, Mustoe, Webb, DS Addis, Davis, Wilkinson
Substitutes: Cox (for Davis), Rimmer (nps), Reid (nps), Knight (nps), Harris (nps)
Scorer: Wilkinson
Attendance: 347

Date: Saturday 06/11/2004
Result: **GLOUCESTER CITY 0 KING'S LYNN 2**
Competition: FA Trophy 1st Round
Teamsheet: Bath, Smith, MP Thompson, Griffiths, Tomkins, CD Thompson, Mustoe, Webb, DS Addis, Davis, Wilkinson
Substitutes: Cox (for Davis), Knight (for Mustoe), Harris (nps), Burns (for MP Thompson)
Attendance: 383

Date: Saturday 13/11/2004
Result: **MERTHYR TYDFIL 2 GLOUCESTER CITY 2**
Competition: Southern League Premier Division
Teamsheet: Bath, Smith, CD Thompson, Griffiths, Tomkins, Burns, Mustoe, Cox, DS Addis, Webb, Wilkinson
Substitutes: Knight (nps), Harris (nps), MP Thompson (nps), Davis (nps)
Scorers: Griffiths, Wilkinson
Attendance: 346

Date: Wednesday 17/11/2004
Result: **TIVERTON TOWN 5 GLOUCESTER CITY 3**
Competition: Southern League Premier Division
Teamsheet: Bath, Smith, CD Thompson, Griffiths, Tomkins, Davis, Mustoe, Cox, DS Addis, Webb, Wilkinson
Substitutes: Knight (for Wilkinson), Harris (nps), MP Thompson (nps), Eaton (nps), Burns (nps)
Scorers: Davis, Wilkinson (2)
Attendance: 340

Date: Saturday 20/11/2004
Result: **GLOUCESTER CITY 3 CHESHAM UNITED 2**
Competition: Southern League Premier Division
Teamsheet: Bath, Smith, Knight, Griffiths, CD Thompson, Burns, Mustoe, Webb, Eaton, DS Addis, Wilkinson
Substitutes: Cox (for Eaton), MP Thompson (nps), Noakes (for Webb), Harris (nps)
Scorers: Mustoe, DS Addis, Noakes
Attendance: 289

Date: Saturday 04/12/2004
Result: **GLOUCESTER CITY 2 BEDFORD TOWN 2**
Competition: Southern League Premier Division
Teamsheet: Bath, Smith, Knight, Griffiths, CD Thompson, Burns, Mustoe, Webb, Eaton, DS Addis, Wilkinson
Substitutes: Cox (for Knight), Tomkins (nps), Davis (for Eaton), Reid (nps), Harris (nps)
Scorers: Knight, Eaton
Attendance: 407

Date: Saturday 11/12/2004
Result: **TEAM BATH 1 GLOUCESTER CITY 1**
Competition: Southern League Premier Division
Teamsheet: Bath, Smith, Knight, Griffiths, Tomkins, CD Thompson, Mustoe, Cox, Eaton, Webb, Wilkinson
Substitutes: DS Addis (for Eaton), Davis (for Cox), MP Thompson (for Knight), Burns (nps), Harris (nps)
Scorer: Smith
Attendance: 151

Date: Saturday 18/12/2004
Result: **HITCHIN TOWN 1 GLOUCESTER CITY 1**
Competition: Southern League Premier Division
Teamsheet: Bath, Smith, Davis, Griffiths, Burns, CD Thompson, Mustoe, Cox, DS Addis, Webb, Wilkinson
Substitutes: MP Thompson (for Davis), Knight (nps), Harris (nps), Tomkins (nps)
Scorer: Davis
Attendance: 252

Date: Monday 27/12/2004
Result: **GLOUCESTER CITY 3 HALESOWEN TOWN 3**
Competition: Southern League Premier Division
Teamsheet: Bath, Smith, Davis, Griffiths, CD Thompson, Burns, Mustoe, Cox, DS Addis, Webb, Wilkinson
Substitutes: Knight (nps), MP Thompson (for Davis), Reid (nps)
Scorers: Davis, Wilkinson, Cox
Attendance: 742

Date: Saturday 01/01/2005
Result: **CIRENCESTER TOWN 1 GLOUCESTER CITY 0**
Competition: Southern League Premier Division
Teamsheet: Bath, Smith, Knight, Griffiths, CD Thompson, MP Thompson, Mustoe, Cox, DS Addis, Webb, Wilkinson
Substitutes: Davis (for Smith), Rimmer (for Wilkinson), Reid (for Knight), Harris (nps)
Attendance: 476

Date: Monday 03/01/2005
Result: **GLOUCESTER CITY 3 MERTHYR TYDFIL 3**
Competition: Southern League Premier Division
Teamsheet: Bath, Smith, MP Thompson, Griffiths, Burns, CD Thompson, Mustoe, Cox, DS Addis, Webb, Wilkinson
Substitutes: Knight (nps), Davis (for Cox), Reid (for Burns), Rimmer (nps)
Scorers: Cox (2), Burns
Attendance: 521

Date: Saturday 08/01/2005
Result: **GLOUCESTER CITY 6 RUGBY UNITED 1**
Competition: Southern League Premier Division
Teamsheet: Bath, Smith, MP Thompson, Griffiths, Burns, CD Thompson, Mustoe, Cox, DS Addis, Webb, Wilkinson
Substitutes: Reid (for Cox), Rimmer (for Smith), Knight (for MP Thompson), Bennett (nps)
Scorers: Wilkinson, own goal, DS Addis (2), Knight, Rimmer
Attendance: 357

Date: Saturday 15/01/2005
Result: **HEMEL HEMPSTEAD TOWN 2 GLOUCESTER CITY 2**
Competition: Southern League Premier Division
Teamsheet: Bath, Smith, MP Thompson, Griffiths, Burns, CD Thompson, Mustoe, Cox, DS Addis, Webb, Wilkinson
Substitutes: Knight (for MP Thompson), Reid (for Wilkinson), Rimmer (nps), Tomkins (nps)
Scorers: Cox, DS Addis
Attendance: 199

Date: Tuesday 18/01/2005
Result: **GLOUCESTER CITY 0 PAULTON ROVERS 1**
Competition: Southern League Cup 1st Round
Teamsheet: Bennett, Smith, Knight, Griffiths, Tomkins, Avery, CD Thompson, Cox, DS Addis, Webb, Reid
Substitutes: Noakes (for Smith), Varnham (for Cox), Wilkinson (nps), MP Thompson (nps), Evans (for Bennett)
Attendance: 148

Date: Saturday 22/01/2005
Result: **GLOUCESTER CITY 0 AYLESBURY UNITED 3**
Competition: Southern League Premier Division
Teamsheet: Bath, Smith, MP Thompson, Griffiths, Burns, CD Thompson, Knight, Cox, DS Addis, Webb, Wilkinson
Substitutes: Reid (for Knight), Noakes (for MP Thompson), Tomkins (for Burns)
Attendance: 411

Date: Saturday 29/01/2005
Result: **SOLIHULL BOROUGH 3 GLOUCESTER CITY 3**
Competition: Southern League Premier Division
Teamsheet: Bath, Smith, Noakes, Griffiths, Burns, CD Thompson, Mustoe, Cox, DS Addis, Webb, Wilkinson
Substitutes: MP Thompson (for Noakes), Reid (nps), Knight (nps), Tomkins (nps)
Scorers: Cox, Wilkinson, DS Addis
Attendance: 245

Date: Saturday 12/02/2005
Result: **AYLESBURY UNITED 2 GLOUCESTER CITY 0**
Competition: Southern League Premier Division
Teamsheet: Bath, Smith, Tomkins, Griffiths, Burns, CD Thompson, Mustoe, Cox, DS Addis, Webb, Wilkinson
Substitutes: MP Thompson (for Tomkins), Reid (for Wilkinson), Knight (nps), Harris (for Burns)
Attendance: 369

Date: Tuesday 15/02/2005
Result: **GLOUCESTER CITY 2 HEDNESFORD TOWN 0**
Competition: Southern League Premier Division
Teamsheet: Bath, Knight, M Thompson, Griffiths, Tomkins, CD Thompson, Mustoe, Smith, DS Addis, Webb, Wilkinson
Substitutes: Cox (for Knight), Harris (for MP Thompson), Reid (nps), Bennett (nps)
Scorer: Smith (2)
Attendance: 344

Date: Saturday 19/02/2005
Result: **GLOUCESTER CITY 2 BATH CITY 1**
Competition: Southern League Premier Division
Teamsheet: Bath, Smith, MP Thompson, Griffiths, Tomkins, CD Thompson, Mustoe, Cox, DS Addis, Webb, Wilkinson
Substitutes: Reid (nps), Harris (for DS Addis), Knight (nps)
Scorer: Cox (2)
Attendance: 502

Date: Saturday 26/02/2005
Result: **KING'S LYNN 1 GLOUCESTER CITY 0**
Competition: Southern League Premier Division
Teamsheet: Bath, Smith, Knight, MP Thompson, Tomkins, CD Thompson, Mustoe, Cox, DS Addis, Webb, Wilkinson
Substitutes: Burns (nps), Harris (for Knight), Reid (for Wilkinson)
Attendance: 776

Date: Saturday 05/03/2005
Result: **GLOUCESTER CITY 1 GRANTHAM TOWN 1**
Competition: Southern League Premier Division
Teamsheet: Bath, Smith, MP Thompson, Griffiths, Tomkins, CD Thompson, Burns, Cox, DS Addis, Webb, Wilkinson
Substitutes: CD Addis (nps), Reid (nps), Harris (for Cox)
Scorer: DS Addis
Attendance: 381

Date: Saturday 12/03/2005
Result: **HISTON 0 GLOUCESTER CITY 1**
Competition: Southern League Premier Division
Teamsheet: Bath, Smith, MP Thompson, Griffiths, CD Thompson, Burns, Mustoe, Harris, DS Addis, Webb, Wilkinson
Substitutes: Knight (nps), Reid (for Harris), Varnham (nps)
Scorer: Smith
Attendance: 718

Date: Saturday 19/03/2005
Result: **GLOUCESTER CITY 0 CHIPPENHAM TOWN 3**
Competition: Southern League Premier Division
Teamsheet: Bath, Smith, Harris, Griffiths, MP Thompson, Burns, Mustoe, CD Thompson, DS Addis, Webb, Wilkinson
Substitutes: Tomkins (nps), Reid (nps), Varnham (for Harris), Knight (nps)
Attendance: 501

Date: Saturday 26/03/2005
Result: **HALESOWEN TOWN 0 GLOUCESTER CITY 2**
Competition: Southern League Premier Division
Teamsheet: Bath, CD Thompson, MP Thompson, Griffiths, Tomkins, Burns, Mustoe, Smith, DS Addis, Webb, Wilkinson
Substitutes: Harris (for MP Thompson), Knight (for Webb), Reid (nps), Varnham (for Griffiths)
Scorers: Smith, DS Addis
Attendance: 412

Date: Monday 28/03/2005
Result: **GLOUCESTER CITY 0 CIRENCESTER TOWN 0**
Competition: Southern League Premier Division
Teamsheet: Bath, Smith, CD Thompson, Griffiths, Tomkins, Burns, Mustoe, Harris, DS Addis, Knight, Wilkinson
Substitutes: MP Thompson (for Griffiths), Webb (nps), Reid (nps), Varnham (for Wilkinson), Bennett (nps)
Attendance: 523

Date: Saturday 02/04/2005
Result: **GLOUCESTER CITY 3 HITCHIN TOWN 1**
Competition: Southern League Premier Division
Teamsheet: Bath, Webb, Harris, CD Thompson, MP Thompson, Burns, Mustoe, Smith, DS Addis, Knight, Wilkinson
Substitutes: Reid (for Burns), Varnham (for Harris), Griffiths (nps)
Scorers: Burns, Smith, Knight
Attendance: 319

Date: Saturday 09/04/2005
Result: **RUGBY UNITED 2 GLOUCESTER CITY 0**
Competition: Southern League Premier Division
Teamsheet: Bath, Smith, Harris, CD Thompson, Tomkins, MP Thompson, Mustoe, Varnham, DS Addis, Webb, Wilkinson
Substitutes: Knight (nps), Bennett (nps), Burns (for Varnham), Reid (nps), Griffiths (nps)
Attendance: 289

Date: Saturday 16/04/2005
Result: **HEDNESFORD TOWN 4 GLOUCESTER CITY 1**
Competition: Southern League Premier Division
Teamsheet: Bath, Smith, Reid, Griffiths, MP Thompson, Burns, CD Thompson, Varnham, DS Addis, Webb, Wilkinson
Substitutes: Knight (for Reid), Cox (for DS Addis), Harris (nps), Varnham (for Wilkinson), Bennett (nps)
Scorer: Wilkinson
Attendance: 704

Date: Saturday 23/04/2005
Result: **GLOUCESTER CITY 2 KING'S LYNN 0**
Competition: Southern League Premier Division
Teamsheet: Bath, Smith, Avery, Griffiths, MP Thompson, Burns, CD Thompson, Cox, DS Addis, Webb, Wilkinson
Substitutes: Reid (nps), Varnham (for DS Addis), Knight (for Griffiths), Harris (nps)
Scorer: Griffiths (2)
Attendance: 424

Date: Saturday 30/04/2005
Result: **BANBURY UNITED 0 GLOUCESTER CITY 0**
Competition: Southern League Premier Division
Teamsheet: Bath, CD Thompson, Avery, Griffiths, MP Thompson, Burns, Webb, Cox, Varnham, Reid, Wilkinson
Substitutes: Harris (for M Thompson), Smith (for Reid), DS Addis (for Varnham), Knight (nps)
Attendance: 718

Appearances – DS Addis 30(2), MD Aubrey 9, DJ Avery 6, MR Bath 45, KA Bayliss 4(4), AD Bennett 1, C Burns 26(3), JD Cox 26(12), LM Davis 14(9), JC Eaton 3, D Evans 0(1), D Forrester 0(1), N Griffiths 42(1), AG Harris 7(12), AR Hoskins 3(2), K Knight 17(11), NJ Mustoe 40, MI Noakes 1(3), J Reid 3(12), E Rimmer 0(4), LF Smith 44(2), KSS Styles 2(4), CD Thompson 46, MP Thompson 32(7), LP Tomkins 19(1), A Varnham 3(6), TA Webb 45, D Wilkinson 38(1), B Wood 0(2).
Others selected but did not play: CD Addis, KA Palmer.
Scorers – JD Cox 12, D Wilkinson 11, LF Smith 8, DS Addis 7, LM Davis 6, K Knight 4, N Griffiths 3, C Burns 2, NJ Mustoe 2, LP Tomkins 2, TA Webb 2, KA Bayliss 1, JC Eaton 1, M Noakes 1, E Rimmer 1, MP Thompson 1, own goal 1.

SOUTHERN LEAGUE – PREMIER DIVISION

POS	CLUB	P	W	D	L	F	A	PTS
1	HISTON	42	24	6	12	93	57	78
2	CHIPPENHAM TOWN	42	22	9	11	81	55	75
3	MERTHYR TYDFIL	42	19	14	9	62	47	71
4	HEDNESFORD TOWN	42	20	10	12	68	40	70
5	BEDFORD TOWN	42	19	12	11	70	52	69
6	BATH CITY	42	19	12	11	57	43	69
7	CIRENCESTER TOWN	42	19	11	12	63	52	68
8	TIVERTON TOWN	42	18	13	11	70	55	67
9	HALESOWEN TOWN	42	19	9	14	64	52	66
10	AYLESBURY UNITED	42	20	3	19	67	66	63
11	KING'S LYNN	42	19	4	19	78	69	61
12	CHESHAM UNITED	42	18	5	19	84	82	59
13	GRANTHAM TOWN	42	17	7	18	57	55	58
14	TEAM BATH	42	14	12	16	54	68	54
15	**GLOUCESTER CITY**	**42**	**12**	**17**	**13**	**63**	**61**	**53**
16	RUGBY UNITED	42	13	12	17	48	60	51
17	BANBURY UNITED	42	13	9	20	56	69	48
18	HITCHIN TOWN	42	13	9	20	55	77	48
19	HEMEL HEMPSTEAD TOWN	42	11	10	21	60	88	42*
20	DUNSTABLE TOWN	42	11	6	25	56	98	39
21	STAMFORD	42	6	18	18	40	60	36
22	SOLIHULL BOROUGH	42	10	4	28	45	85	34
		924	356	212	356	1391	1391	1279

* One point deducted for fielding an ineligible player.

SEASON 2005-2006
(Home Ground: City Stadium, Meadow Park, Hempsted)

Date: Saturday 13/08/2005
Result: **GLOUCESTER CITY 1 KING'S LYNN 2**
Competition: Southern League Premier Division
Teamsheet: Bath, CD Thompson, Mansell, Griffiths, Tomkins, MP Thompson, Mustoe, Webb, Addis, Kear, Davis
Substitutes: Lewis (for Addis), Harris (for Kear), Rimmer (nps), Reid (for Tomkins), Randall (nps)
Scorer: Bath
Attendance: 372

Date: Tuesday 16/08/2005
Result: **CHIPPENHAM TOWN 3 GLOUCESTER CITY 0**
Competition: Southern League Premier Division
Teamsheet: Bath, Griffiths, MP Thompson, CD Thompson, Reid, Webb, Mustoe, Davis, Mansell, Addis, Kear
Substitutes: Rimmer (for Reid), Lewis (for Davis), Harris (for Kear), Randall (nps)
Attendance: 605

Date: Saturday 20/08/2005
Result: **CHESHUNT 1 GLOUCESTER CITY 1**
Competition: Southern League Premier Division
Teamsheet: Bath, Griffiths, MP Thompson, CD Thompson, Reid, Webb, Mustoe, Knight, Mansell, Addis, Davis
Substitutes: Randall (for Reid), Harris (for MP Thompson), Wilkinson (nps)
Scorer: Davis
Attendance: 110

Date: Tuesday 23/08/2005
Result: **GLOUCESTER CITY 1 MERTHYR TYDFIL 1**
Competition: Southern League Premier Division
Teamsheet: Bath, CD Thompson, Harris, Griffiths, Mansell, Burns, Mustoe, Webb, Addis, Davis, Knight
Substitutes: Lewis (for Knight), Randall (nps), Wilkinson (nps)
Scorer: Davis
Attendance: 355

Date: Saturday 27/08/2005
Result: **TIVERTON TOWN 1 GLOUCESTER CITY 0**
Competition: Southern League Premier Division
Teamsheet: Bath, Harris, Mansell, CD Thompson, Lewis, Burns, Mustoe, Webb, Addis, Davis, Knight
Substitutes: Kear (for Knight), Randall (for Lewis), Wilkinson (nps), Cook (nps)
Attendance: 471

Date: Monday 29/08/2005
Result: **GLOUCESTER CITY 1 MANGOTSFIELD UNITED 3**
Competition: Southern League Premier Division
Teamsheet: Bath, Harris, Mansell, CD Thompson, Lewis, Burns, Mustoe, Webb, Addis, Davis, Knight
Substitutes: Kear (for Knight), Randall (nps), Wilkinson (nps), Cook (nps)
Scorer: Mustoe (pen)
Attendance: 425

Date: Saturday 03/09/2005
Result: **GLOUCESTER CITY 5 RUGBY TOWN 2**
Competition: Southern League Premier Division
Teamsheet: Bath, Kear, Harris, CD Thompson, Mansell, Burns, Mustoe, Webb, Addis, Davis, Knight
Substitutes: Lewis (for Knight), Reid (for Kear), Rimmer (for Harris), Randall (nps), Cook (nps)
Scorers: Webb, Harris, Mustoe (pen), Davis, CD Thompson
Attendance: 223

Date: Saturday 10/09/2005
Result: **GLOUCESTER CITY 0 CHRISTCHURCH 0**
Competition: FA Cup 1st Qualifying Round
Teamsheet: Bath, Kear, Harris, CD Thompson, Mansell, Burns, Mustoe, Webb, Addis, Davis, Knight
Substitutes: Lewis (for Kear), Reid (for Knight), Griffiths (for Harris), Randall (nps), Cook (nps)
Attendance: 280

Date: Tuesday 13/09/2005
Result: **CHRISTCHURCH 3 GLOUCESTER CITY 0**
Competition: FA Cup 1st Qualifying Round Replay
Teamsheet: Bath, Kear, Harris, Griffiths, Mansell, Burns, Mustoe, Webb, Addis, Davis, CD Thompson
Substitutes: Lewis (for Kear), Reid (for Burns), Knight (nps), Randall (for Addis), Wilkinson (nps)
Attendance: 106

Date: Saturday 17/09/2005
Result: **TEAM BATH 1 GLOUCESTER CITY 0**
Competition: Southern League Premier Division
Teamsheet: Bath, Reid, Mansell, Griffiths, CD Thompson, Burns, Mustoe, Webb, Addis, Davis, Knight
Substitutes: Harris (for Reid), Lewis (for Knight), Kear (nps), Randall (nps), Rimmer (nps)
Attendance: 114

Date: Tuesday 27/09/2005
Result: **GLOUCESTER CITY 0 CIRENCESTER TOWN 1**
Competition: Southern League Premier Division
Teamsheet: Bath, Reid, Mansell, Griffiths, CD Thompson, Burns, Mustoe, Webb, Addis, Kear, Davis
Substitutes: Lewis (for Reid), Knight (nps), Harris (for Griffiths), Randall (nps), Wilkinson (for Kear)
Attendance: 329

Date: Saturday 01/10/2005
Result: **BEDFORD TOWN 5 GLOUCESTER CITY 3**
Competition: Southern League Premier Division
Teamsheet: Evans, Reid, Harris, Griffiths, Mansell, Burns, Mustoe, Webb, Addis, Kear, Davis
Substitutes: Knight (nps), Wilkinson (for Reid), Randall (nps), Rimmer (for Harris), Tomkins (nps)
Scorers: Webb, Addis, Kear
Attendance: 472

Date: Saturday 08/10/2005
Result: **GLOUCESTER CITY 4 NORTHWOOD 1**
Competition: Southern League Premier Division
Teamsheet: Bath, Reid, Mansell, Griffiths, CD Thompson, Burns, Mustoe, Webb, Addis, Kear, Davis
Substitutes: Knight (for Mustoe), Wilkinson (for Davis), Randall (for Addis), Harris (nps), Evans (nps)
Scorers: Reid, Davis, Kear, Wilkinson
Attendance: 264

Date: Tuesday 11/10/2005
Result: **EVESHAM UNITED 0 GLOUCESTER CITY 0**
Competition: Southern League Premier Division
Teamsheet: Bath, Reid, Mansell, Griffiths, Tomkins, Wilkinson, Mustoe, Webb, Addis, Kear, Davis
Substitutes: Knight (for Mustoe), Harris (nps), Randall (for Addis), Varnham (for Kear)
Attendance: 219

Date: Saturday 15/10/2005
Result: **CIRENCESTER TOWN 2 GLOUCESTER CITY 0**
Competition: FA Trophy 1st Qualifying Round
Teamsheet: Bath, CD Thompson, Mansell, Griffiths, Tomkins, Wilkinson, Mustoe, Webb, Addis, Kear, Davis
Substitutes: MP Thompson (nps), Varnham (for Kear), Harris (for Mansell), Reid (for CD Thompson), Randall (nps)
Attendance: 322

Date: Tuesday 25/10/2005
Result: **MANGOTSFIELD UNITED 5 GLOUCESTER CITY 4**
Competition: Southern League Premier Division
Teamsheet: Bath, Reid, Harris, Griffiths, MP Thompson, Tomkins, Mustoe, Webb, Corbett, Davis, Wilkinson
Substitutes: Knight (nps), Varnham (for Davis), Mansell (nps), Randall (nps), Burns (for Reid)
Scorers: Corbett (2), Reid, Wilkinson
Attendance: 332

Date: Saturday 29/10/2005
Result: **BATH CITY 0 GLOUCESTER CITY 0**
Competition: Southern League Premier Division
Teamsheet: Bath, Reid, Harris, Griffiths, Tomkins, Burns, Mustoe, Webb, Addis, Corbett, Wilkinson
Substitutes: Knight (nps), MP Thompson (for Reid), Varnham (nps), Davis (for Corbett), Mansell (for Harris)
Attendance: 583

Date: Saturday 05/11/2005
Result: **GLOUCESTER CITY 1 BANBURY UNITED 1**
Competition: Southern League Premier Division
Teamsheet: Bath, MP Thompson, Harris, Griffiths, Tomkins, Burns, Mustoe, Webb, Addis, Corbett, Wilkinson
Substitutes: Knight (nps), Mansell (for Harris), Davis (for Wilkinson), Reid (nps), Varnham (nps)
Scorer: Webb
Attendance: 341

Date: Saturday 12/11/2005
Result: **KING'S LYNN 4 GLOUCESTER CITY 0**
Competition: Southern League Premier Division
Teamsheet: Bath, MP Thompson, Mansell, Griffiths, Tomkins, Burns, Mustoe, Webb, Addis, Corbett, Wilkinson
Substitutes: CD Thompson (for Mansell), Harris (for Burns), Knight (nps), Randall (nps), Davis (for MP Thompson)
Attendance: 690

Date: Saturday 19/11/2005
Result: **CIRENCESTER TOWN 0 GLOUCESTER CITY 1**
Competition: Southern League Premier Division
Teamsheet: Bath, CD Thompson, MP Thompson, Griffiths, Tomkins, Davis, Mustoe, Webb, Addis, Corbett, Wilkinson
Substitutes: Rimmer (nps), Mansell (for Corbett), Randall (nps), Knight (nps), Harris (nps)
Scorer: Mustoe (pen)
Attendance: 230

Date: Saturday 26/11/2005
Result: **GLOUCESTER CITY 3 CHESHUNT 2**
Competition: Southern League Premier Division
Teamsheet: Bath, CD Thompson, MP Thompson, Griffiths, Tomkins, Davis, Mustoe, Webb, Addis, Corbett, Wilkinson
Substitutes: Rimmer (nps), Mansell (for MP Thompson), Randall (nps), Knight (for Corbett), Harris (nps)
Scorers: Addis, Corbett, Mustoe (pen)
Attendance: 234

Date: Saturday 03/12/2005
Result: **GLOUCESTER CITY 1 AYLESBURY UNITED 1**
Competition: Southern League Premier Division
Teamsheet: Bath, CD Thompson, Sykes, Griffiths, Tomkins, Davis, Mustoe, Webb, Addis, Corbett, Wilkinson
Substitutes: Mansell (for Sykes), MP Thompson (for Corbett), Pritchett (nps), Rimmer (nps), Randall (nps)
Scorer: Wilkinson
Attendance: 299

Date: Tuesday 06/12/2005
Result: **GLOUCESTER CITY 0 CHIPPENHAM TOWN 1**
Competition: Southern League Premier Division
Teamsheet: Bath, CD Thompson, Mansell, Griffiths, Tomkins, Sykes, Mustoe, Webb, Addis, Davis, Wilkinson
Substitutes: Corbett (for Davis), MP Thompson (for Sykes), Pritchett (nps), Rimmer (nps), Randall (for Mansell)
Attendance: 261

Date: Saturday 10/12/2005
Result: **RUGBY TOWN 0 GLOUCESTER CITY 1**
Competition: Southern League Premier Division
Teamsheet: Bath, CD Thompson, MP Thompson, Harris, Tomkins, Sykes, Mustoe, Webb, Addis, Corbett, Wilkinson
Substitutes: Davis (for Sykes), Randall (for Corbett), Knight (nps), Reid (for Mustoe), Rimmer (nps)
Scorer: Corbett
Attendance: 214

GLOUCESTER CITY 2004-2005
(Photograph courtesy of Neil Phelps)

Back Row (l to r) – Kenny Blackburn (Coach), Jamie Reid, Dan Avery, Chris Burns, Chris Thompson, Andy Hoskins, Matt Bath, Marvin Thompson, Dave Wilkinson, Lyndon Tompkins, Ade Tandy (Physio)
Front Row (l to r) – Jimmy Cox, Keith Knight, Tom Webb, Neil Griffiths, Neil Mustoe, Lee Smith, Adie Harris, Lee Davis

APRIL 2006 RE-UNION OF MEMBERS OF THE
1956 SOUTHERN LEAGUE CUP WINNING SIDE
(Photograph courtesy of Stan Myers)

Phil Warren (Supporters' Trust Chairman), George Beattie, Stan Myers, Rob Coldray, Archie Proudfoot, Frank Tredgett, Ken Turner (Chairman).
Peeking behind the pillar is the author

(Photograph courtesy of Daphne Tandy)
Bernard Tandy
Bernard Tandy completed 37 years service as Trainer/Physio up to his death in 1996.
His son Adrian took over as physio thus completing 50 years unbroken service

(Photograph courtesy of Neil Phelps)
Adrian Tandy

(Photograph courtesy of Neil Phelps)
Dr. Bob Byrne
In 2008 Dr. Bob Byrne completed 20
years service as Club Doctor

[410]

Date: Tuesday 13/12/2005
Result: **GLOUCESTER CITY 2 CIRENCESTER TOWN 4**
Competition: Southern League Cup 3rd Round
Teamsheet: Bath, Reid, Mansell, Griffiths, Pritchett, Rimmer, Burns, Webb, Wilkinson, Randall, Harris
Substitutes: Corbett (for Burns), Addis (nps), Knight (nps), CD Thompson (nps), Tomkins (nps)
Scorers: Reid, Randall
Attendance: 71
Note: Played at Supermarine Road, Swindon

Date: Saturday 17/12/2005
Result: **CHESHAM UNITED 0 GLOUCESTER CITY 2**
Competition: Southern League Premier Division
Teamsheet: Bath, Reid, MP Thompson, CD Thompson, Tomkins, Sykes, Harris, Webb, Addis, Corbett, Wilkinson
Substitutes: Knight (nps), Burns (nps), Randall (for Addis), Griffiths (for Reid), Mansell (for Harris)
Scorers: Corbett (2, 1 pen)
Attendance: 223

Date: Tuesday 27/12/2005
Result: **HALESOWEN TOWN 1 GLOUCESTER CITY 0**
Competition: Southern League Premier Division
Teamsheet: Bath, CD Thompson, MP Thompson, Griffiths, Tomkins, Sykes, Harris, Webb, Addis, Corbett, Wilkinson
Substitutes: Reid (for Tomkins), Burns (nps), Randall (nps), Davis (for Harris), Mansell (for MP Thompson)
Attendance: 468

Date: Saturday 31/12/2005
Result: **YATE TOWN 3 GLOUCESTER CITY 1**
Competition: Southern League Premier Division
Teamsheet: Bath, MP Thompson, Mansell, Griffiths, Tomkins, CD Thompson, Harris, Webb, Addis, Corbett, Wilkinson
Substitutes: Reid (for MP Thompson), Burns (nps), Knight (nps), Randall (for Corbett)
Scorer: Corbett
Attendance: 340

Date: Monday 02/01/2006
Result: **GLOUCESTER CITY 1 SALISBURY CITY 2**
Competition: Southern League Premier Division
Teamsheet: Bath, Griffiths, CD Thompson, Tomkins, Harris, Knight, Burns, Webb, Sykes, Wilkinson, Addis
Substitutes: Mansell (for Sykes), MP Thompson (for Harris), Corbett (for Burns), Reid (nps)
Scorer: Wilkinson
Attendance: 551

Date: Saturday 07/01/2006
Result: **GLOUCESTER CITY 4 TIVERTON TOWN 5**
Competition: Southern League Premier Division
Teamsheet: Bath, MP Thompson, Mansell, Griffiths, Tomkins, CD Thompson, Harris, Webb, Addis, Corbett, Wilkinson
Substitutes: Randall (nps), Reid (nps), Rimmer (nps), Mustoe (nps)
Scorers: Corbett (pen), Mansell, Wilkinson, own goal
Attendance: 392

Date: Saturday 14/01/2006
Result: **GRANTHAM TOWN 2 GLOUCESTER CITY 1**
Competition: Southern League Premier Division
Teamsheet: Bath, MP Thompson, Mansell, Griffiths, Tomkins, Mustoe, CD Thompson, Webb, Addis, Corbett, Harris
Substitutes: Davis (for Mustoe), Noakes (nps), Randall (for MP Thompson), Rimmer (for Addis)
Scorer: Harris
Attendance: 366

Date: Saturday 21/01/2006
Result: **GLOUCESTER CITY 0 BATH CITY 2**
Competition: Southern League Premier Division
Teamsheet: Bath, Miller, Mansell, Preece, Ferro, Mustoe, CD Thompson, Webb, Bevan, Whittington, Wilkinson
Substitutes: Rimmer (nps), Noakes (nps), Addis (for Miller), Randall (nps), Tomkins (nps)
Attendance: 521

Date: Saturday 04/02/2006
Result: **GLOUCESTER CITY 1 EVESHAM UNITED 1**
Competition: Southern League Premier Division
Teamsheet: Bath, Miller, Mansell, Preece, Ferro, Mustoe, CD Thompson, Webb, Bevan, Whittington, Wilkinson
Substitutes: Randall (nps), Harris (for Mansell), Corbett (for Miller), Reid (nps), Addis (for Whittington)
Scorer: Corbett
Attendance: 340

Date: Saturday 11/02/2006
Result: **MERTHYR TYDFIL 2 GLOUCESTER CITY 2**
Competition: Southern League Premier Division
Teamsheet: Bath, Miller, Stonehouse, Preece, Ferro, Corbett, CD Thompson, Webb, Bevan, Whittington, Wilkinson
Substitutes: Harris (for Whittington), Addis (for Corbett), Randall (nps), Rimmer (nps), Mansell (nps)
Scorers: Miller, Whittington
Attendance: 411

Date: Saturday 18/02/2006
Result: **GLOUCESTER CITY 4 GRANTHAM TOWN 1**
Competition: Southern League Premier Division
Teamsheet: Bath, Miller, Stonehouse, Preece, Tomkins, Addis, CD Thompson, Webb, Bevan, Whittington, Wilkinson
Substitutes: Harris (for Addis), Rimmer (nps), Reid (nps), Randall (for Stonehouse), Ferro (nps)
Scorers: Bevan (pen), Whittington (2), Wilkinson
Attendance: 339

Date: Saturday 25/02/2006
Result: **HITCHIN TOWN 2 GLOUCESTER CITY 2**
Competition: Southern League Premier Division
Teamsheet: Bath, Miller, Stonehouse, Preece, Tomkins, Holland, CD Thompson, Webb, Bevan, Whittington, Wilkinson
Substitutes: Harris (nps), Mansell (nps), Rimmer (nps), Randall (nps), Corbett (for Bevan)
Scorers: Miller, Whittington
Attendance: 338

Date: Tuesday 28/02/2006
Result: **GLOUCESTER CITY 1 BRISTOL ROVERS RESERVES 2**
Competition: Gloucestershire FA Northern Senior Professional Cup Quarter-Final
Teamsheet: Bath, Miller, Harris, Preece, Tomkins, Randall, CD Thompson, Webb, Bevan, Varnham, Wilkinson
Substitutes: Reid (nps), Mansell (for Randall), Avery (nps), Corbett (nps), Rimmer (nps)
Scorer: Preece
Attendance: 139

Date: Saturday 04/03/2006
Result: **NORTHWOOD 0 GLOUCESTER CITY 1**
Competition: Southern League Premier Division
Teamsheet: Bath, Miller, Stonehouse, Preece, Holland, Harris, CD Thompson, Webb, Bevan, Whittington, Wilkinson
Substitutes: Reid (nps), Corbett (for Bevan), Addis (for Whittington), Randall (nps), Mansell (nps)
Scorer: Whittington
Attendance: 182

Date: Saturday 11/03/2006
Result: **GLOUCESTER CITY 3 TEAM BATH 0**
Competition: Southern League Premier Division
Teamsheet: Bath, Miller, Stonehouse, Preece, Holland, Harris, CD Thompson, Webb, Bevan, Whittington, Wilkinson
Substitutes: Addis (for Bevan), Corbett (for Wilkinson), Mansell (nps), Randall (for Wilkinson), Tomkins (nps)
Scorers: Webb, Bevan, Corbett
Attendance: 347

Date: Tuesday 21/03/2006
Result: **GLOUCESTER CITY 2 YATE TOWN 0**
Competition: Southern League Premier Division
Teamsheet: Bath, Miller, Stonehouse, Preece, Holland, Harris, CD Thompson, Webb, Bevan, Whittington, Wilkinson
Substitutes: Addis (for Bevan), Corbett (for Whittington), Reid (nps), Randall (nps), Tomkins (nps)
Scorer: Whittington (2)
Attendance: 366

Date: Saturday 25/03/2006
Result: **AYLESBURY UNITED 0 GLOUCESTER CITY 1**
Competition: Southern League Premier Division
Teamsheet: Bath, Miller, Stonehouse, Preece, Holland, Harris, CD Thompson, Webb, Bevan, Addis, Wilkinson
Substitutes: Reid (nps), Corbett (for Harris), Tomkins (nps), Randall (nps), Varnham (nps)
Scorer: Wilkinson
Attendance: 267

Date: Saturday 01/04/2006
Result: **GLOUCESTER CITY 0 BEDFORD TOWN 0**
Competition: Southern League Premier Division
Teamsheet: Bath, Miller, Harris, Preece, Holland, Corbett, CD Thompson, Webb, Bevan, Addis, Wilkinson
Substitutes: Reid (nps), Noakes (for Harris), Eckhardt (for CD Thompson), Randall (nps), Varnham (for Bevan)
Attendance: 384

Date: Saturday 08/04/2006
Result: **GLOUCESTER CITY 3 CHESHAM UNITED 1**
Competition: Southern League Premier Division
Teamsheet: Bath, Miller, McKeever, Preece, Holland, Eckhardt, Corbett, Webb, Bevan, Addis, Wilkinson
Substitutes: Reid (for Bevan), Noakes (for Corbett), Tomkins (for Preece), Randall (nps), Varnham (nps)
Scorers: Holland, McKeever, Corbett
Attendance: 338

Date: Saturday 15/04/2006
Result: **SALISBURY CITY 2 GLOUCESTER CITY 0**
Competition: Southern League Premier Division
Teamsheet: Bath, Miller, McKeever, Tomkins, Holland, Eckhardt, Corbett, Webb, Bevan, Addis, Wilkinson
Substitutes: Reid (for Bevan), Harris (nps), Preece (for Corbett), Randall (nps), Varnham (for Eckhardt)
Attendance: 1609

Date: Monday 17/04/2006
Result: **GLOUCESTER CITY 1 HALESOWEN TOWN 0**
Competition: Southern League Premier Division
Teamsheet: Bath, Miller, McKeever, Preece, Tomkins, Eckhardt, Noakes, Webb, Corbett, Addis, Wilkinson
Substitutes: Reid (nps), Bevan (for Corbett), Pritchett (nps), Randall (for McKeever), Varnham (nps)
Scorer: Bevan
Attendance: 471

Date: Saturday 22/04/2006
Result: **GLOUCESTER CITY 1 HITCHIN TOWN 0**
Competition: Southern League Premier Division
Teamsheet: Bath, Miller, McKeever, Preece, Tomkins, Holland, Pritchard, Webb, Bevan, Addis, Wilkinson
Substitutes: Reid (for Holland), Corbett (for Wilkinson), Eckhardt (for Bevan), Randall (nps), Harris (nps)
Scorer: Corbett
Attendance: 391

Date: Saturday 29/04/2006
Result: **BANBURY UNITED 1 GLOUCESTER CITY 0**
Competition: Southern League Premier Division
Teamsheet: Bath, Reid, McKeever, Preece, Tomkins, Eckhardt, Addis, Webb, Bevan, Corbett, Pritchard
Substitutes: Wilkinson (for Eckhardt), Randall (for Corbett), Harris (for Pritchard), Varnham (nps), Rimmer (nps)
Attendance: 426

SEASON BY SEASON

Appearances – DS Addis 37(6), MR Bath 46, JK Bevan 15(1), C Burns 15(1), LJ Corbett 19(10), LM Davis 20(6), JE Eckhardt 4(2), D Evans 1, J Ferro 3, N Griffiths 25(2), AG Harris 24(12), CJ Holland 9, R Kear 10(2), K Knight 8(3), LW Lewis 2(8), RJ Mansell 23(9), MA McKeever 5, J Miller 15, NJ Mustoe 27, MI Noakes 1(2), M Preece 15(1), J Pritchard 2, MA Pritchett 1, L Randall 2(14), J Reid 12(11), E Rimmer 1(4), P Stonehouse 7, A Sykes 6, CD Thompson 35(1), MP Thompson 14(4), LP Tomkins 25(1), A Varnham 1(4), TA Webb 47, MJ Whittington 8, D Wilkinson 32(4).

Others selected but did not play: SD Avery, A Cook.

Scorers – LJ Corbett 12, MJ Whittington 7, D Wilkinson 7, LM Davis 4, NJ Mustoe 4, TA Webb 4, DS Addis 3, JK Bevan 3, J Reid 3, AG Harris 2, R Kear 2, J Miller 2, MR Bath 1, CJ Holland 1, RJ Mansell 1, MA McKeever 1, M Preece 1, L Randall 1, CD Thompson 1, own goal 1.

SOUTHERN LEAGUE – PREMIER DIVISION

POS	CLUB	P	W	D	L	F	A	PTS
1	SALISBURY CITY	42	30	5	7	83	27	95
2	BATH CITY	42	25	8	9	66	33	83
3	KING'S LYNN	42	25	7	10	73	41	82
4	CHIPPENHAM TOWN	42	22	11	9	69	45	77
5	BEDFORD TOWN	42	22	10	10	69	53	76
6	YATE TOWN	42	21	5	16	78	74	68
7	BANBURY UNITED	42	17	11	14	66	61	62
8	HALESOWEN TOWN	42	15	15	12	54	45	60
9	MERTHYR TYDFIL	42	17	9	16	62	58	60
10	MANGOTSFIELD UNITED	42	15	13	14	67	67	58
11	GRANTHAM TOWN	42	15	11	16	49	49	56
12	TIVERTON TOWN	42	14	10	18	69	65	52
13	**GLOUCESTER CITY**	**42**	**14**	**10**	**18**	**57**	**60**	**52**
14	HITCHIN TOWN	42	13	12	17	59	76	51
15	RUGBY TOWN	42	13	11	18	58	66	50
16	CHESHUNT	42	13	9	20	57	70	48
17	TEAM BATH	42	14	6	22	55	68	48
18	CIRENCESTER TOWN	42	14	4	24	49	68	46
19	NORTHWOOD	42	12	6	24	53	88	42
20	EVESHAM UNITED	42	9	14	19	46	58	41
21	AYLESBURY UNITED	42	9	12	21	43	69	39
22	CHESHAM UNITED	42	9	9	24	43	84	36
		924	358	208	358	1325	1325	1282

SEASON 2006-2007
(Home Ground: City Stadium, Meadow Park, Hempsted)

Date: Saturday 19/08/2006
Result: **GLOUCESTER CITY 2 MAIDENHEAD UNITED 1**
Competition: Southern League Premier Division
Teamsheet: Bath, Miller, Wilson, Thompson, Hamblin, Tomkins, Fowler, Webb, Welsh, Corbett, Sykes
Substitutes: Reid (for Miller), Randall (nps), Tustain (for Corbett), Mustoe (nps), Bevan (for Sykes)
Scorers: Wilson, Reid
Attendance: 406

Date: Tuesday 22/08/2006
Result: **RUGBY TOWN 2 GLOUCESTER CITY 1**
Competition: Southern League Premier Division
Teamsheet: Bath, Miller, Wilson, Thompson, Hamblin, Tomkins, Fowler, Webb, Welsh, Corbett, Reid
Substitutes: Sykes (for Reid), Randall (nps), Tustain (nps), Mustoe (nps), Bevan (nps)
Scorer: Sykes
Attendance: 231

Date: Saturday 26/08/2006
Result: **CHESHUNT 0 GLOUCESTER CITY 3**
Competition: Southern League Premier Division
Teamsheet: Bath, Miller, Reid, Thompson, Hamblin, Tomkins, Fowler, Webb, Welsh, Corbett, Sykes
Substitutes: Harris (for Sykes), Randall (for Reid), Tustain (nps), Mustoe (for Fowler), Bevan (nps)
Scorers: Welsh (2), Corbett
Attendance: 161

Date: Monday 28/08/2006
Result: **GLOUCESTER CITY 1 HALESOWEN TOWN 3**
Competition: Southern League Premier Division
Teamsheet: Bath, Miller, Reid, Thompson, Hamblin, Tomkins, Fowler, Webb, Welsh, Corbett, Sykes
Substitutes: Harris (nps), Randall (nps), Tustain (for Corbett), Mustoe (for Fowler), Bevan (for Miller)
Scorer: Tomkins
Attendance: 488

Date: Saturday 02/09/2006
Result: **GLOUCESTER CITY 1 HITCHIN TOWN 1**
Competition: Southern League Premier Division
Teamsheet: Bath, Miller, Reid, Thompson, Hamblin, Tomkins, Fowler, Webb, Welsh, Bevan, Sykes
Substitutes: Harris (for Hamblin), Randall (nps), Tustain (for Welsh), Corbett (nps), Mehew (nps)
Scorer: Tustain
Attendance: 320

Date: Tuesday 05/09/2006
Result: **YATE TOWN 2 GLOUCESTER CITY 2**
Competition: Southern League Premier Division
Teamsheet: Bath, Miller, Reid, Thompson, Tomkins, Harris, Fowler, Webb, Welsh, Bevan, Sykes
Substitutes: Robison (nps), Randall (nps), Tustain (for Sykes), Corbett (for Tustain), Mustoe (for Reid)
Scorers: Sykes, Bevan
Attendance: 381

Date: Saturday 09/09/2006
Result: **STAMFORD 3 GLOUCESTER CITY 2**
Competition: Southern League Premier Division
Teamsheet: Bath, Miller, Reid, Thompson, Hamblin, Tomkins, Fowler, Webb, Tustain, Bevan, Sykes
Substitutes: Harris (for Sykes), Randall (nps), Wilson (for Tustain), Mustoe (nps), Mehew (nps)
Scorers: Reid, Tomkins
Attendance: 244

Date: Saturday 16/09/2006
Result: **GLOUCESTER CITY 0 LISKEARD ATHLETIC 0**
Competition: FA Cup 1st Qualifying Round
Teamsheet: Bath, Miller, Reid, Thompson, Hamblin, Tomkins, Mustoe, Webb, Bevan, Whittington, Sykes
Substitutes: Harris (nps), Tustain (for Bevan), Wilson (for Miller), Noakes (for Sykes), Robison (nps),
Attendance: 344

Date: Tuesday 19/09/2006
Result: **LISKEARD ATHLETIC 0 GLOUCESTER CITY 3**
Competition: FA Cup 1st Qualifying Round Replay
Teamsheet: Bath, Miller, Reid, Thompson, Mustoe, Tomkins, Wilson, Webb, Bevan, Whittington, Sykes
Substitutes: Noakes (for Wilson), Randall (for Webb), Tustain (for Whittington), Mehew (nps)
Scorers: Webb, Bevan, Noakes
Attendance: 200

Date: Saturday 23/09/2006
Result: **GLOUCESTER CITY 3 NORTHWOOD 3**
Competition: Southern League Premier Division
Teamsheet: Bath, Miller, Reid, Mustoe, Thompson, Tomkins, Wilson, Webb, Bevan, Whittington, Sykes
Substitutes: Noakes (for Wilson), Randall (for Webb), Tustain (for Whittington), Hamblin (nps), Mehew (nps)
Scorers: Whittington, Tomkins, Noakes
Attendance: 303

Date: Saturday 30/09/2006
Result: **EASTLEIGH 3 GLOUCESTER CITY 2**
Competition: FA Cup 2nd Qualifying Round
Teamsheet: Bath, Thompson, Wilson, Mustoe, Hamblin, Tomkins, Fowler, Webb, Bevan, Whittington, Sykes
Substitutes: Miller (nps), Noakes (nps), Tustain (for Bevan), Randall (nps), Reid (for Fowler)
Scorers: Bevan (pen), Wilson
Attendance: 418

Date: Tuesday 03/10/2006
Result: **GLOUCESTER CITY 1 CHIPPENHAM TOWN 0**
Competition: Southern League Premier Division
Teamsheet: Giles, Thompson, Wilson, Mustoe, Hamblin, Tomkins, Fowler, Webb, Bevan, Whittington, Sykes
Substitutes: Miller (nps), Noakes (nps), Tustain (for Bevan), Reid (for Whittington), Bath (nps)
Scorer: Bevan
Attendance: 395

Date: Saturday 07/10/2006
Result: **BANBURY UNITED 1 GLOUCESTER CITY 2**
Competition: Southern League Premier Division
Teamsheet: Giles, Thompson, Wilson, Mustoe, Hamblin, Tomkins, Fowler, Webb, Bevan, Whittington, Sykes
Substitutes: Reid (for Whittington), Noakes (nps), Tustain (for Wilson), Randall (nps), Bath (nps)
Scorers: Whittington, Bevan (pen)
Attendance: 440

Date: Saturday 14/10/2006
Result: **GLOUCESTER CITY 2 TEAM BATH 2**
Competition: Southern League Premier Division
Teamsheet: Giles, Thompson, Wilson, Mustoe, Hamblin, Tomkins, Fowler, Webb, Bevan, Whittington, Sykes
Substitutes: Reid (for Thompson), Noakes (nps), Tustain (for Whittington), Randall (nps), Bath (nps)
Scorers: Whittington, Fowler
Attendance: 400

Date: Saturday 21/10/2006
Result: **TIVERTON TOWN 2 GLOUCESTER CITY 2**
Competition: FA Trophy 1st Qualifying Round
Teamsheet: Bath, Miller, Wilson, Mustoe, Hamblin, Welsh, Fowler, Reid, Bevan, Tustain, Sykes
Substitutes: Ashford (nps), Noakes (for Bevan), Harris (nps), Randall (for Tustain), Thompson (nps)
Scorers: Welsh, Noakes
Attendance: 479

Date: Tuesday 24/10/2006
Result: **GLOUCESTER CITY 2 TIVERTON TOWN 2** (aet, 4-2 pens)
Competition: FA Trophy 1st Qualifying Round Replay
Teamsheet: Bath, Miller, Wilson, Mustoe, Hamblin, Robison, Fowler, Wilkinson, Welsh, Tustain, Noakes
Substitutes: Johnson (nps), Thompson (nps), Reid (for Wilkinson), Mehew (for Welsh), Randall (nps)
Scorers: Welsh (2)
Attendance: 367

Date: Saturday 28/10/2006
Result: **GLOUCESTER CITY 1 STAMFORD 1**
Competition: Southern League Premier Division
Teamsheet: Bath, Miller, Wilson, Mustoe, Hamblin, Thompson, Fowler, Reid, Wood, Tustain, Noakes
Substitutes: Harris (nps), Sykes (for Miller), Wilkinson (for Fowler), Randall (nps), Mehew (nps)
Scorer: Wilkinson
Attendance: 344

Date: Wednesday 01/11/2006
Result: **BISHOP'S CLEEVE 3 GLOUCESTER CITY 1**
Competition: Gloucestershire FA Northern Senior Professional Cup 1st Round
Teamsheet: Bath, Miller, Noakes, Randall, Hamblin, Tomkins, Sykes, Webb, Reid, Tustain, Wilkinson
Substitutes: Thompson (for Hamblin), Wilson (for Wilkinson), Mustoe (for Randall), Fowler (nps)
Scorer: Wilkinson
Attendance: 100

Date: Saturday 04/11/2006
Result: **GLOUCESTER CITY 1 MARGATE 0**
Competition: FA Trophy 2nd Qualifying Round
Teamsheet: Bath, Thompson, Wilson, Mustoe, Hamblin, Tomkins, Fowler, Webb, Williams, Whittington, Sykes
Substitutes: Ashford (nps), Miller (for Webb), Wilkinson (for Wilson), Tustain (for Williams), Randall (nps)
Scorers: Whittington (pen)
Attendance: 428

Date: Saturday 11/11/2006
Result: **HEMEL HEMPSTEAD TOWN 3 GLOUCESTER CITY 3**
Competition: Southern League Premier Division
Teamsheet: Bath, Thompson, Noakes, Mustoe, Hamblin, Tomkins, Fowler, Webb, Wood, Whittington, Sykes
Substitutes: Miller (for Tomkins), Wilkinson (nps), Tustain (for Whittington), Welsh (for Sykes), Randall (nps)
Scorers: Fowler, Tomkins, Sykes
Attendance: 245

Date: Tuesday 14/11/2006
Result: **GLOUCESTER CITY 1 MANGOTSFIELD UNITED 2**
Competition: Southern League Premier Division
Teamsheet: Bath, Thompson, Noakes, Mustoe, Hamblin, Welsh, Fowler, Webb, Wood, Whittington, Wilson
Substitutes: Miller (for Wood), Wilkinson (nps), Tustain (for Whittington), Reid (nps), Harris (nps)
Scorer: Whittington
Attendance: 388

Date: Tuesday 28/11/2006
Result: **GLOUCESTER CITY 2 EASTBOURNE BOROUGH 5**
Competition: FA Trophy 3rd Qualifying Round
Teamsheet: Bath, Reid, Wilson, Mustoe, Thompson, Welsh, Fowler, Webb, Tustain, Whittington, Noakes
Substitutes: Harris (nps), Sykes (for Tustain), Miller (for Reid), Wilkinson (for Wilson), Ashford (nps)
Scorers: Whittington, Wilson
Attendance: 277

Date: Saturday 02/12/2006
Result: **GLOUCESTER CITY 1 BANBURY UNITED 4**
Competition: Southern League Premier Division
Teamsheet: Bath, Thompson, Wilson, Mustoe, Hamblin, Wilkinson, Fowler, Reid, Welsh, Whittington, Sykes
Substitutes: Harris (nps), Webb (for Reid), Tustain (nps), Ashford (nps), Mehew (nps)
Scorer: Wilson
Attendance: 363

Date: Saturday 09/12/2006
Result: **GLOUCESTER CITY 0 CHESHUNT 2**
Competition: Southern League Premier Division
Teamsheet: Bath, Thompson, Wilson, Mustoe, Barnes, Khan, Fowler, Reid, Welsh, Cox, Wilkinson
Substitutes: Harris (nps), Webb (for Wilkinson), Tustain (nps), Sykes (nps), Noakes (nps)
Attendance: 278

Date: Tuesday 12/12/2006
Result: **KING'S LYNN 0 GLOUCESTER CITY 1**
Competition: Southern League Premier Division
Teamsheet: Bath, Thompson, Noakes, Mustoe, Hamblin, Barnes, Sykes, Webb, Welsh, Reid, Wilkinson
Substitutes: Harris (nps), Khan (nps), Fowler (for Wilkinson), Wilson (for Sykes), Cox (for Welsh)
Scorer: Wilson
Attendance: 693

Date: Saturday 16/12/2006
Result: **HITCHIN TOWN 2 GLOUCESTER CITY 2**
Competition: Southern League Premier Division
Teamsheet: Bath, Thompson, Noakes, Mustoe, Khan, Barnes, Sykes, Webb, Welsh, Reid, Wilkinson
Substitutes: Harris (nps), Tustain (nps), Fowler (for Khan), Wilson (for Sykes), Cox (for Welsh)
Scorer: Sykes (2)
Attendance: 394

Date: Saturday 23/12/2006
Result: **CORBY TOWN 2 GLOUCESTER CITY 3**
Competition: Southern League Premier Division
Teamsheet: Bath, Thompson, Noakes, Mustoe, Hamblin, Cox, Sykes, Webb, Welsh, Reid, Wilkinson
Substitutes: Harris (nps), Wilson (for Wilkinson), Tustain (nps), Fowler (for Cox), Mehew (nps)
Scorers: Sykes, Welsh, Reid
Attendance: 151

Date: Tuesday 26/12/2006
Result: **GLOUCESTER CITY 3 MERTHYR TYDFIL 3**
Competition: Southern League Premier Division
Teamsheet: Bath, Thompson, Noakes, Mustoe, Hamblin, Barnes, Sykes, Webb, Welsh, Reid, Fowler
Substitutes: Harris (nps), Wilson (for Welsh), Tustain (nps), Wilkinson (for Fowler), Cox (for Sykes)
Scorers: Reid, Fowler, Webb
Attendance: 531

[415]

Date: Monday 01/01/2007
Result: **CLEVEDON TOWN 2 GLOUCESTER CITY 2**
Competition: Southern League Premier Division
Teamsheet: Bath, Thompson, Noakes, Mustoe, Cox, Barnes, Sykes, Webb, Welsh, Wilson, Fowler
Substitutes: Harris (for Cox), Wilkinson (for Thompson), Tustain (for Noakes)
Scorers: Welsh, Tustain
Attendance: 303

Date: Saturday 13/01/2007
Result: **GLOUCESTER CITY 3 HEMEL HEMPSTEAD TOWN 4**
Competition: Southern League Premier Division
Teamsheet: Bath, Thompson, Wilson, Mustoe, Hamblin, Cox, Sykes, Webb, Welsh, Reid, Wilkinson
Substitutes: Harris (nps), Noakes (nps), Tustain (for Wilkinson), Fowler (for Reid), Mehew (nps)
Scorers: Wilkinson, Cox, Sykes
Attendance: 337

Date: Tuesday 16/01/2007
Result: **GLOUCESTER CITY 2 DIDCOT TOWN 3** (aet)
Competition: Southern League Cup 3rd Round
Teamsheet: Matthews, Thompson, Noakes, Fowler, Ashford, Tomkins, Cox, Webb, Tustain, Wilson, Wilkinson
Substitutes: Harris (for Wilson), Welsh (for Tustain), Hamblin (for Tomkins), Bath (nps), Mehew (nps)
Scorers: Ashford, Fowler (pen)
Attendance: 126

Date: Saturday 20/01/2007
Result: **GLOUCESTER CITY 0 BATH CITY 4**
Competition: Southern League Premier Division
Teamsheet: Bath, Thompson, Noakes, Mustoe, Welsh, Tomkins, Fowler, Webb, Cox, Stonehouse, Wilkinson
Substitutes: Harris (nps), Wilson (for Wilkinson), Tustain (for Welsh), Hamblin (for Noakes), Mehew (nps)
Attendance: 568

Date: Saturday 27/01/2007
Result: **NORTHWOOD 0 GLOUCESTER CITY 2**
Competition: Southern League Premier Division
Teamsheet: Bath, Hodnett, Noakes, Mustoe, Welsh, Tomkins, Sykes, Reid, Cox, Stonehouse, Wilkinson
Substitutes: Harris (nps), Ashford (nps), Tustain (nps), Hamblin (nps), Mehew (nps)
Scorers: Welsh, Sykes
Attendance: 120

Date: Tuesday 30/01/2007
Result: **GLOUCESTER CITY 0 YATE TOWN 3**
Competition: Southern League Premier Division
Teamsheet: Bath, Thompson, Noakes, Mustoe, Welsh, Tomkins, Sykes, Reid, Cox, Stonehouse, Wilkinson
Substitutes: Harris (for Reid), Ashford (nps), Tustain (for Wilkinson), Wilson (for Sykes), Hamblin (nps)
Attendance: 299

Date: Saturday 03/02/2007
Result: **GLOUCESTER CITY 0 KING'S LYNN 2**
Competition: Southern League Premier Division
Teamsheet: Johnston, Reid, Stonehouse, Mustoe, Thompson, Tomkins, Sykes, Webb, Cox, Welsh, Wilkinson
Substitutes: Harris (for Sykes), Wilson (for Wilkinson), Tustain (for Cox), Noakes (nps), Matthews (nps)
Attendance: 284

Date: Saturday 10/02/2007
Result: **MANGOTSFIELD UNITED 3 GLOUCESTER CITY 4**
Competition: Southern League Premier Division
Teamsheet: Johnston, Hodnett, Noakes, Mustoe, Hamblin, Tomkins, Sykes, Webb, Reid, Welsh, Stonehouse
Substitutes: Harris (nps), Griffin (for Noakes), Allard (nps), Cox (nps), Mehew (nps)
Scorers: Welsh (2), Reid, Sykes
Attendance: 282

Date: Saturday 17/02/2007
Result: **GLOUCESTER CITY 1 TIVERTON TOWN 0**
Competition: Southern League Premier Division
Teamsheet: Johnston, Thompson, Stonehouse, Mustoe, Hamblin, Tomkins, Sykes, Webb, Reid, Welsh, Griffin
Substitutes: Harris (nps), Allard (for Hamblin), Wilkinson (for Griffin), Mehew (nps), Morse (nps)
Scorer: Welsh
Attendance: 327

Date: Tuesday 20/02/2007
Result: **GLOUCESTER CITY 2 CORBY TOWN 0**
Competition: Southern League Premier Division
Teamsheet: Johnston, Thompson, Stonehouse, Mustoe, Hamblin, Tomkins, Harris, Webb, Reid, Welsh, Griffin
Substitutes: Shaxton (for Griffin), Allard (nps), Wilkinson (for Harris), Tustain (nps), Cox (nps)
Scorers: Welsh, Webb
Attendance: 255

Date: Monday 26/02/2007
Result: **TEAM BATH 2 GLOUCESTER CITY 1**
Competition: Southern League Premier Division
Teamsheet: Johnston, Thompson, Buttery, Mustoe, Hamblin, Tomkins, Sykes, Webb, Reid, Welsh, Griffin
Substitutes: Shaxton (nps), Allard (nps), Wilkinson (for Webb), Cox (for Griffin), Morse (nps)
Scorer: Sykes
Attendance: 245

Date: Saturday 03/03/2007
Result: **GLOUCESTER CITY 0 CIRENCESTER TOWN 0**
Competition: Southern League Premier Division
Teamsheet: Johnston, Thompson, Buttery, Mustoe, Hamblin, Tomkins, Sykes, Webb, Reid, Welsh, Griffin
Substitutes: Shaxton (for Griffin), Allard (for Hamblin), Cox (nps), Wilkinson (for Welsh), Morse (nps)
Attendance: 408

Date: Saturday 10/03/2007
Result: **BATH CITY 2 GLOUCESTER CITY 2**
Competition: Southern League Premier Division
Teamsheet: Johnston, Thompson, Buttery, Allard, Hamblin, Tomkins, Sykes, Webb, Reid, Griffin, Wilkinson
Substitutes: Shaxton (for Allard), Cox (nps), Tustain (nps), Ellis (nps), Morse (nps)
Scorers: Sykes, Griffin
Attendance: 917

Date: Tuesday 20/03/2007
Result: **WEALDSTONE 0 GLOUCESTER CITY 1**
Competition: Southern League Premier Division
Teamsheet: Johnston, Thompson, Hodnett, Mustoe, Hamblin, Tomkins, Sykes, Webb, Reid, Cox, Wilkinson
Substitutes: Harris (nps), Ellis (nps), Allard (nps), Mehew (nps), Morse (nps)
Scorer: Cox
Attendance: 192

Date: Saturday 24/03/2007
Result: **CHIPPENHAM TOWN 1 GLOUCESTER CITY 0**
Competition: Southern League Premier Division
Teamsheet: Johnston, Thompson, Hodnett, Mustoe, Hamblin, Tomkins, Sykes, Webb, Reid, Griffin, Wilkinson
Substitutes: Allard (for Reid), Cox (for Hamblin), Richards (for Wilkinson), Shaxton (nps), Morse (nps)
Attendance: 482

Date: Saturday 31/03/2007
Result: **HALESOWEN TOWN 1 GLOUCESTER CITY 1**
Competition: Southern League Premier Division
Teamsheet: Johnston, Thompson, Allard, Mustoe, Reid, Tomkins, Sykes, Richards, Cox, Griffin, Wilkinson
Substitutes: Harris (nps), Shaxton (for Griffin), Ellis (nps), Webb (for Cox), Morse (nps)
Scorer: Richards
Attendance: 421

Date: Tuesday 03/04/2007
Result: **MERTHYR TYDFIL 1 GLOUCESTER CITY 1**
Competition: Southern League Premier Division
Teamsheet: Johnston, Thompson, Allard, Mustoe, Hodnett, Tomkins, Sykes, Richards, Shaxton, Griffin, Wilkinson
Substitutes: Harris (for Griffin), Cox (for Allard), Buttery (nps), Ellis (for Sykes), Morse (nps)
Scorer: Richards
Attendance: 325

Date: Saturday 07/04/2007
Result: **GLOUCESTER CITY 3 RUGBY TOWN 2**
Competition: Southern League Premier Division
Teamsheet: Johnston, Thompson, Buttery, Mustoe, Hamblin, Tomkins, Sykes, Richards, Cox, Shaxton, Wilkinson
Substitutes: Harris (for Sykes), Webb (for Wilkinson), Ellis (nps), Griffin (nps), Welsh (for Cox)
Scorers: Sykes, own goal, Shaxton
Attendance: 373

Date: Monday 09/04/2007
Result: **CIRENCESTER TOWN 1 GLOUCESTER CITY 3**
Competition: Southern League Premier Division
Teamsheet: Johnston, Allard, Buttery, Mustoe, Hamblin, Tomkins, Sykes, Richards, Cox, Griffin, Webb
Substitutes: Thompson (for Richards), Wilkinson (nps), Shaxton (for Cox), Welsh (for Griffin), Reid (nps)
Scorers: Griffin, Hamblin, Cox
Attendance: 356

Date: Saturday 14/04/2007
Result: **GLOUCESTER CITY 0 WEALDSTONE 2**
Competition: Southern League Premier Division
Teamsheet: Johnston, Allard, Buttery, Mustoe, Hamblin, Thompson, Reid, Richards, Cox, Griffin, Webb
Substitutes: Harris (nps), Shaxton (for Mustoe), Wilkinson (for Buttery), Welsh (for Griffin), Morse (nps)
Attendance: 392

Date: Tuesday 17/04/2007
Result: **MAIDENHEAD UNITED 1 GLOUCESTER CITY 0**
Competition: Southern League Premier Division
Teamsheet: Johnston, Reid, Buttery, Mustoe, Hamblin, Thompson, Sykes, Richards, Welsh, Shaxton, Webb
Substitutes: Allard (for Shaxton), Griffin (for Welsh), Wilkinson (nps), Cox (for Sykes), Morse (nps)
Attendance: 218

Date: Saturday 21/04/2007
Result: **TIVERTON TOWN 1 GLOUCESTER CITY 3**
Competition: Southern League Premier Division
Teamsheet: Johnston, Reid, Buttery, Thompson, Hamblin, Richards, Mustoe, Cox, Welsh, Griffin, Sykes
Substitutes: Webb (for Griffin), Shaxton (for Cox), Wilkinson (for Hamblin), Allard (nps), Morse (nps)
Scorers: Cox (2), Reid
Attendance: 388

Date: Saturday 28/04/2007
Result: **GLOUCESTER CITY 3 CLEVEDON TOWN 1**
Competition: Southern League Premier Division
Teamsheet: Johnston, Reid, Buttery, Thompson, Hamblin, Richards, Mustoe, Webb, Cox, Welsh, Sykes
Substitutes: Wilkinson (for Richards), Shaxton (for Cox), Griffin (for Hamblin), Allard (nps), Morse (nps)
Scorers: Sykes (2), Welsh
Attendance: 460

Appearances – AG Allard 5(4), B Ashford 1, OJP Barnes 5, MR Bath 30, JK Bevan 11(2), L Buttery 9, LJ Corbett 4(1), JD Cox 16(7), S Ellis 0(1), MD Fowler 24(4), JD Giles 3, S Griffin 11(3), TR Hamblin 37(2), AG Harris 2(9), DW Hodnett 5, RS Johnston 17, S Khan 2, LD Matthews 1, DS Mehew 0(1), J Miller 14(4), NJ Mustoe 41(4), MI Noakes 16(3), L Randall 1(4), J Reid 36(5), M Richards 8(1), D Robison 1, MJ Shaxton 3(8), P Stonehouse 7, AB Sykes 41(3), CD Thompson 45(2), LP Tomkins 34, JO Tustain 7(19), TA Webb 40(5), J Welsh 30(5), MJ Whittington 12, D Wilkinson 19(12), J Williams 1, AL Wilson 19(10), T Wood 3.
Others selected but did not play: J Morse.
Scorers – AB Sykes 14, J Welsh 13, JD Cox 6, MJ Whittington 6, JK Bevan 5, J Reid 5, AA Wilson 5, MD Fowler 4, LP Tomkins 4, MI Noakes 3, TA Webb 3, D Wilkinson 3, S Griffin 2, M Richards 2, JO Tustain 2, B Ashford 1, LJ Corbett 1, TR Hamblin 1, MJ Shaxton 1, own goal 1.

SEASON BY SEASON

SOUTHERN LEAGUE – PREMIER DIVISION

POS	CLUB	P	W	D	L	F	A	PTS
1	BATH CITY	42	27	10	5	84	29	91
2	TEAM BATH	42	23	9	10	66	42	78
3	KING'S LYNN	42	22	10	10	69	40	76
4	MAIDENHEAD UNITED	42	20	10	12	58	36	70
5	HEMEL HEMPSTEAD TOWN	42	19	12	11	79	60	69
6	HALESOWEN TOWN	42	18	13	11	66	53	67
7	CHIPPENHAM TOWN	42	19	9	14	61	56	66
8	STAMFORD	42	16	11	15	65	62	59
9	MANGOTSFIELD UNITED	42	13	19	10	44	45	58
10	**GLOUCESTER CITY**	**42**	**15**	**13**	**14**	**67**	**70**	**58**
11	HITCHIN TOWN	42	16	9	17	55	68	57
12	MERTHYR TYDFIL	42	14	14	14	47	46	56
13	BANBURY UNITED	42	15	10	17	60	64	55
14	YATE TOWN	42	14	12	16	59	71	54
15	TIVERTON TOWN	42	14	8	20	56	67	50
16	CHESHUNT	42	14	7	21	56	71	49
17	RUGBY TOWN	42	15	4	23	58	79	49
18	CLEVEDON TOWN	42	12	12	18	60	61	48
19	WEALDSTONE	42	13	9	20	69	82	48
20	CORBY TOWN	42	10	9	23	52	69	39
21	CIRENCESTER TOWN	42	9	12	21	46	76	39
22	NORTHWOOD	42	8	10	24	44	74	34
		924	346	232	346	1321	1321	1270

SEASON 2007-2008
(Home Ground: The New Lawn, Forest Green, Nailsworth – groundshare with Forest Green Rovers)

Date: Saturday 18/08/2007
Result: **CHESHUNT 0 GLOUCESTER CITY 3**
Competition: Southern League Premier Division
Teamsheet: Sawyer, Reid, Buttery, Mustoe, Hamblin, Tomkins, Rose, Richards, Pitcher, Sykes, Webb
Substitutes: Whittington (nps), Thompson (nps), Griffin (for Sykes), Allard (nps), Welsh (for Pitcher)
Scorers: Rose, Sykes (pen), Richards
Attendance: 241

Date: Tuesday 21/08/2007
Result: **SWINDON SUPERMARINE 4 GLOUCESTER CITY 1**
Competition: Southern League Premier Division
Teamsheet: Sawyer, Reid, Buttery, Mustoe, Hamblin, Tomkins, Rose, Richards, Pitcher, Sykes, Webb
Substitutes: Whittington (for Pitcher), Thompson (nps), Griffin (for Webb), Allard (nps), Welsh (for Buttery)
Scorer: Sykes
Attendance: 267

Date: Saturday 25/08/2007
Result: **BASHLEY 0 GLOUCESTER CITY 0**
Competition: Southern League Premier Division
Teamsheet: Sawyer, Allard, Buttery, Mustoe, Hamblin, Thompson, Rose, Webb, Pitcher, Whittington, Sykes
Substitutes: Griffin (for Pitcher), Tomkins (for Thompson), Richards (for Sykes), Wilkinson (nps), Welsh (nps)
Attendance: 280

Date: Tuesday 28/08/2007
Result: **GLOUCESTER CITY 1 HALESOWEN TOWN 1**
Competition: Southern League Premier Division
Teamsheet: Sawyer, Allard, Buttery, Mustoe, Tomkins, Thompson, Rose, Richards, Griffin, Whittington, Webb
Substitutes: Sykes (for -----), Hamblin (for Thompson), Wilkinson (for Rose), Taylor (nps), Welsh (nps)
Scorer: Webb
Attendance: 388

Date: Saturday 01/09/2007
Result: **GLOUCESTER CITY 2 RUGBY TOWN 3**
Competition: Southern League Premier Division
Teamsheet: Sawyer, Allard, Welsh, Mustoe, Richards, Thompson, Wilkinson, Webb, Griffin, Whittington, Sykes
Substitutes: Reid (for Allard), Ellis (for Wilkinson), Price (for Whittington), Harris (nps), Taylor (nps)
Scorers: Sykes, Griffin
Attendance: 314

Date: Tuesday 04/09/2007
Result: **BROMSGROVE ROVERS 1 GLOUCESTER CITY 4**
Competition: Southern League Premier Division
Teamsheet: Sawyer, Reid, Price, Mustoe, Richards, Thompson, Ellis, Webb, Griffin, Welsh, Sykes
Substitutes: Whittington (nps), Wilkinson (for Sykes), Taylor (nps), Allard (for Reid), Pitcher (for Griffin)
Scorers: Welsh, Ellis, Sykes (pen), Pitcher
Attendance: 548

Date: Saturday 08/09/2007
Result: **GLOUCESTER CITY 1 BRACKLEY TOWN 3**
Competition: Southern League Premier Division
Teamsheet: Sawyer, Reid, Price, Mustoe, Richards, Thompson, Ellis, Webb, Griffin, Welsh, Sykes
Substitutes: Whittington (for Griffin), Smith (for Ellis), Taylor (for Sykes), Allard (nps), Wilkinson (nps)
Scorer: Griffin
Attendance: 306

[418]

Meadow Park 23 July 2007
(Photographs courtesy of Neil Phelps)

2007
Supporters Simon Clark, Paul Clark, Joe Green and Marcus Chew collecting for Flood Fund
(Photograph courtesy of Neil Phelps)

Premonition forty years earlier!

Date: Saturday 15/09/2007
Result: **YATE TOWN 1 GLOUCESTER CITY 5**
Competition: FA Cup 1st Qualifying Round
Teamsheet: Sawyer, Reid, Price, Mustoe, Richards, Thompson, Smith, Webb, Pitcher, Welsh, Sykes
Substitutes: Whittington (nps), Allard (for Webb), Griffin (for Welsh), Tomkins (for Sykes), Harris (nps)
Scorer: Pitcher (5)
Attendance: 309

Date: Saturday 22/09/2007
Result: **KING'S LYNN 2 GLOUCESTER CITY 1**
Competition: Southern League Premier Division
Teamsheet: Sawyer, Reid, Price, Mustoe, Tomkins, Thompson, Smith, Webb, Pitcher, Griffin, Sykes
Substitutes: Whittington (for Price), Allard (for Griffin), Taylor (for Sykes), Hamblin (nps), Bevan (nps)
Scorer: Sykes (pen)
Attendance: 1198

Date: Sunday 30/09/2007
Result: **GLOUCESTER CITY 0 SHORTWOOD UNITED 2**
Competition: FA Cup 2nd Qualifying Round
Teamsheet: Sawyer, Reid, Price, Mustoe, Tomkins, Thompson, Smith, Webb, Pitcher, Welsh, Richards
Substitutes: Whittington (for Webb), Allard (nps), Rose (for Reid), Sykes (for Smith), Bevan (nps)
Attendance: 706

Date: Tuesday 02/10/2007
Result: **GLOUCESTER CITY 0 MANGOTSFIELD UNITED 1**
Competition: Southern League Premier Division
Teamsheet: Sawyer, Thompson, Allard, Mustoe, Tomkins, Richards, Smith, Rose, Pitcher, Griffin, Sykes
Substitutes: Whittington (for Pitcher), Ellis (for Rose), Price (for Sykes), Taylor (nps), Reid (nps)
Attendance: 259

Date: Saturday 06/10/2007
Result: **GLOUCESTER CITY 0 HEMEL HEMPSTEAD TOWN 0**
Competition: Southern League Premier Division
Teamsheet: Sawyer, Thompson, Allard, Mustoe, Tomkins, Richards, Smith, Rose, Pitcher, Price, Sykes
Substitutes: Whittington (nps), Webb (for Sykes), Reid (for Smith), Bevan (for Pitcher), Harris (nps)
Attendance: 242

Date: Saturday 13/10/2007
Result: **BEDFORD TOWN 2 GLOUCESTER CITY 0**
Competition: Southern League Premier Division
Teamsheet: Sawyer, Thompson, Allard, Mustoe, Tomkins, Richards, Smith, Rose, Pitcher, Price, Sykes
Substitutes: Whittington (for Pitcher), Reid (for Sykes), Ellis (nps), Bevan (nps), Morford (for Price)
Attendance: 294

Date: Saturday 20/10/2007
Result: **STOURBRIDGE 1 GLOUCESTER CITY 1**
Competition: FA Trophy 1st Qualifying Round
Teamsheet: Sawyer, Reid, Allard, Mustoe, Hamblin, Richards, Rose, Webb, Whittington, Morford, Smith
Substitutes: Harris (nps), Sykes (for Webb), Bevan (for Morford), Pitcher (for Whittington), Tomkins (nps)
Scorer: Sykes (pen)
Attendance: 176

Date: Wednesday 24/10/2007
Result: **GLOUCESTER CITY 2 STOURBRIDGE 0**
Competition: FA Trophy 1st Qualifying Round Replay
Teamsheet: Sawyer, Reid, Allard, Mustoe, Hamblin, Welsh, Rose, Webb, Pitcher, Whittington, Smith
Substitutes: Harris (nps), Morford (nps), Bevan (for Whittington), Sykes (for Pitcher), Noakes (nps)
Scorers: Pitcher, Whittington
Attendance: 180

Date: Saturday 27/10/2007
Result: **GLOUCESTER CITY 0 BANBURY UNITED 0**
Competition: Southern League Premier Division
Teamsheet: Sawyer, Reid, Noakes, Mustoe, Thomas, Ellis, Rose, Webb, Pitcher, Whittington, Smith
Substitutes: Harris (nps), Allard (for Noakes), Morford (for Pitcher), Bevan (nps), Sykes (for Whittington)
Attendance: 303

Date: Saturday 03/11/2007
Result: **GLOUCESTER CITY 3 HILLINGDON BOROUGH 3**
Competition: FA Trophy 2nd Qualifying Round
Teamsheet: Sawyer, Reid, Noakes, Mustoe, Thomas, Tomkins, Rose, Webb, Morford, Whittington, Smith
Substitutes: Allard (for Tomkins), Ellis (nps), Bevan (for Whittington), Sykes (for Noakes), Harris (nps)
Scorers: Morford, Thomas, Bevan
Attendance: 246

Date: Tuesday 06/11/2007
Result: **HILLINGDON BOROUGH 0 GLOUCESTER CITY 1**
Competition: FA Trophy 2nd Qualifying Round Replay
Teamsheet: Sawyer, Reid, Allard, Mustoe, Thomas, Sykes, Rose, Webb, Morford, Bevan, Smith
Substitutes: Harris (for Webb), Ellis (for Allard), Pitcher (for Bevan), Whittington (nps), Seddon (nps)
Scorer: Pitcher
Attendance: 96

Date: Saturday 10/11/2007
Result: **CLEVEDON TOWN 1 GLOUCESTER CITY 1**
Competition: Southern League Premier Division
Teamsheet: Seddon, Courtney, Noakes, Mustoe, Thomas, Sykes, Rose, Webb, Morford, Bevan, Smith
Substitutes: Harris (nps), Ellis (for Webb), Whittington (nps), Richards (for Bevan), Allard (for Noakes)
Scorer: Thomas
Attendance: 353

Date: Saturday 17/11/2007
Result: **HITCHIN TOWN 1 GLOUCESTER CITY 2**
Competition: Southern League Premier Division
Teamsheet: Sawyer, Reid, Noakes, Mustoe, Thomas, Sykes, Rose, Richards, Morford, Whittington, Smith
Substitutes: Harris (nps), Allard (nps), Pitcher (nps), Bevan (for Whittington), Mehew (nps)
Scorers: Morford, Whittington
Attendance: 267

Date: Tuesday 20/11/2007
Result: **EVESHAM UNITED 2 GLOUCESTER CITY 4**
Competition: Southern League Cup 2nd Round
Teamsheet: Seddon, Reid, Noakes, Mustoe, Thomas, Sykes, Rose, Sysum, Bevan, KA Palmer, Allard
Substitutes: Harris (for Noakes), Sawyer (nps), Smith (nps), Richards (for Reid), Whittington (for Bevan)
Scorers: Allard, Rose, Reid, Thomas
Attendance: 54

Date: Saturday 24/11/2007
Result: **GLOUCESTER CITY 1 UXBRIDGE 0**
Competition: FA Trophy 3rd Qualifying Round
Teamsheet: Sawyer, Reid, Noakes, Mustoe, Thomas, Sykes, Rose, Richards, Morford, Whittington, Smith
Substitutes: Harris (nps), Allard (for Sykes), Pitcher (for Whittington), Bevan (nps), Webb (for Reid)
Scorer: Allard
Attendance: 255

Date: Monday 26/11/2007
Result: **SUTTON COLDFIELD TOWN 3 GLOUCESTER CITY 1**
Competition: Southern League Cup 3rd Round
Teamsheet: Seddon, Allard, Mustoe, Hilder, Sysum, Sykes, Tomkins, KA Palmer, Bevan, Webb, Richards
Substitutes: Harris (nps), Rose (for Sysum), Reid (nps), Smith (for Sykes), Thomas (for Bevan)
Scorer: Richards
Attendance: 72

Date: Thursday 29/11/2007
Result: **GLOUCESTER CITY 0 CIRENCESTER TOWN 0**
Competition: Southern League Premier Division
Teamsheet: Sawyer, Reid, Noakes, Mustoe, Thomas, Webb, Rose, Richards, Pitcher, Sykes, Smith
Substitutes: Harris (nps), Whittington (nps), Allard (for Reid), Morford (for Webb), Bevan (for Pitcher)
Attendance: 244

Date: Tuesday 04/12/2007
Result: **GLOUCESTER CITY 5 BROMSGROVE ROVERS 0**
Competition: Southern League Premier Division
Teamsheet: Sawyer, Reid, Noakes, Mustoe, Thomas, Ashford, Rose, Sykes, Pitcher, Morford, Smith
Substitutes: Harris (nps), Bevan (for Morford), Webb (for Sykes), Morgan (for Pitcher), Allard (nps)
Scorers: own goal, Morford, Reid (2), Bevan (pen)
Attendance: 245

Date: Wednesday 12/12/2007
Result: **BISHOP'S CLEEVE 2 GLOUCESTER CITY 2** (aet, 7-8 pens)
Competition: Gloucestershire FA Northern Senior Professional Cup Quarter-Finals
Teamsheet: Seddon, Reid, Bailey, Mustoe, Tomkins, KA Palmer, Rose, Webb, Bevan, Whittington, Smith
Substitutes: Harris (for Mustoe), Sykes (for Bailey), Pitcher (for Tomkins), Mehew (nps)
Scorers: Bevan, Pitcher
Attendance: 72

Date: Saturday 15/12/2007
Result: **GLOUCESTER CITY 0 BRAINTREE TOWN 2**
Competition: FA Trophy 1st Round
Teamsheet: Sawyer, Allard, Noakes, Mustoe, Richards, Reid, Webb, Sykes, Pitcher, Morford, Smith
Substitutes: Harris (nps), Mehew (nps), Whittington (for Pitcher), Courtney (for Sykes), Seddon (nps)
Attendance: 269

Date: Saturday 22/12/2007
Result: **GLOUCESTER CITY 2 CORBY TOWN 1**
Competition: Southern League Premier Division
Teamsheet: Sawyer, Reid, Walsh, Mustoe, Thomas, Richards, Sykes, Webb, Pitcher, Morford, Smith
Substitutes: Harris (nps), Bevan (nps), Allard (for Pitcher), Sysum (for Morford), Seddon (nps)
Scorers: Pitcher, Smith
Attendance: 212

Date: Wednesday 26/12/2007
Result: **MERTHYR TYDFIL 1 GLOUCESTER CITY 3**
Competition: Southern League Premier Division
Teamsheet: Sawyer, Reid, Walsh, Mustoe, Thomas, Richards, Sykes, Webb, Pitcher, Morgan, Smith
Substitutes: Bevan (for Smith), Harris (nps), Allard (for Morgan), Sysum (for Reid), Mehew (nps)
Scorers: Pitcher, Morgan, Webb
Attendance: 458

Date: Tuesday 01/01/2008
Result: **GLOUCESTER CITY 3 CHIPPENHAM TOWN 0**
Competition: Southern League Premier Division
Teamsheet: Sawyer, Reid, Walsh, Mustoe, Thomas, Richards, Sykes, Webb, Pitcher, Morford, Smith
Substitutes: Morgan (for Pitcher), Bevan (nps), Allard (for Sykes), Sysum (nps), Rose (for Reid)
Scorers: Richards, Morford, Walsh
Attendance: 587

Date: Saturday 05/01/2008
Result: **TIVERTON TOWN 0 GLOUCESTER CITY 0**
Competition: Southern League Premier Division
Teamsheet: Sawyer, Reid, Walsh, Rose, Thomas, Richards, Sykes, Webb, Pitcher, Morford, Smith
Substitutes: Harris (nps), Bevan (for Morford), Allard (for Sykes), Sysum (nps), Morgan (for Pitcher)
Attendance: 385

Date: Saturday 12/01/2008
Result: **CORBY TOWN 2 GLOUCESTER CITY 5**
Competition: Southern League Premier Division
Teamsheet: Sawyer, Reid, Walsh, Mustoe, Thomas, Rose, Sykes, Webb, Pitcher, Morford, Smith
Substitutes: Harris (nps), Allard (for Sykes), Sysum (nps), Mehew (nps), Bevan (for Reid)
Scorers: Morford (2), Walsh, Bevan, Pitcher
Attendance: 248

Date: Saturday 26/01/2008
Result: **BRACKLEY TOWN 1 GLOUCESTER CITY 3**
Competition: Southern League Premier Division
Teamsheet: Sawyer, Reid, Allard, Rose, Thomas, Richards, Sykes, Webb, Pitcher, Morford, Smith
Substitutes: Harris (nps), Wixey (nps), Cant (for Thomas), Taylor (for Pitcher), Bevan (nps)
Scorers: Reid, Sykes, Smith
Attendance: 230

Date: Tuesday 29/01/2008
Result: **GLOUCESTER CITY 2 YATE TOWN 3**
Competition: Southern League Premier Division
Teamsheet: Sawyer, Reid, Allard, Mustoe, Thomas, Richards, Rose, Webb, Pitcher, Morford, Smith
Substitutes: Harris (nps), Bevan (for Reid), Mehew (nps), Badham (for Morford), Seddon (nps)
Scorers: Allard, Webb
Attendance: 265

Date: Saturday 02/02/2008
Result: **GLOUCESTER CITY 2 HITCHIN TOWN 0**
Competition: Southern League Premier Division
Teamsheet: Sawyer, Reid, Allard, Mustoe, Thomas, Richards, Rose, Webb, Pitcher, Morford, Smith
Substitutes: Harris (for Reid), Sysum (nps), Taylor (for Smith), Bevan (for Morford), Mehew (nps)
Scorers: Pitcher, Smith (pen)
Attendance: 301

Date: Saturday 09/02/2008
Result: **MANGOTSFIELD UNITED 0 GLOUCESTER CITY 2**
Competition: Southern League Premier Division
Teamsheet: Sawyer, Reid, Allard, Mustoe, Thomas, Richards, Rose, Webb, Pitcher, Morford, Smith
Substitutes: Harris (nps), Sykes (for Reid), Taylor (for Morford), Bevan (for Pitcher), Sysum (nps)
Scorers: Pitcher, Bevan
Attendance: 259

Date: Wednesday 13/02/2008
Result: **GLOUCESTER CITY 1 BEDFORD TOWN 2**
Competition: Southern League Premier Division
Teamsheet: Sawyer, Reid, Allard, Mustoe, Thomas, Richards, Rose, Webb, Pitcher, Morford, Smith
Substitutes: Harris (for Allard), Sysum (nps), Taylor (nps), Bevan (for Morford), Sykes (for Reid)
Scorer: Pitcher
Attendance: 260

Date: Saturday 16/02/2008
Result: **HEMEL HEMPSTEAD TOWN 1 GLOUCESTER CITY 1**
Competition: Southern League Premier Division
Teamsheet: Sawyer, Reid, Allard, Mustoe, Thomas, Richards, Rose, Webb, Pitcher, Sykes, Smith
Substitutes: Harris (nps), Sysum (nps), Taylor (nps), Bevan (for Allard), Morford (for Sykes)
Scorer: Sykes
Attendance: 206

Date: Wednesday 20/02/2008
Result: **GLOUCESTER CITY 2 TEAM BATH 1**
Competition: Southern League Premier Division
Teamsheet: Sawyer, Reid, Ashford, Mustoe, Thomas, Sykes, Rose, Webb, Pitcher, Bevan, Smith
Substitutes: Harris (nps), Sysum (nps), Taylor (for Smith), Thomson (nps), Richards (for Bevan),
Scorers: Sykes (pen), Rose
Attendance: 234

Date: Saturday 23/02/2008
Result: **YATE TOWN 1 GLOUCESTER CITY 1**
Competition: Southern League Premier Division
Teamsheet: Sawyer, Reid, Sykes, Mustoe, Thomas, Richards, Rose, Webb, Pitcher, Bevan, Smith
Substitutes: Harris (for Reid), Allard (for Sykes), Sysum (nps), Morford (for Bevan), Taylor (nps)
Scorer: Sykes (pen)
Attendance: 290

Date: Tuesday 26/02/2008
Result: **RUGBY TOWN 0 GLOUCESTER CITY 5**
Competition: Southern League Premier Division
Teamsheet: Sawyer, Reid, Sykes, Mustoe, Thomas, Sysum, Rose, Webb, Pitcher, MJ Palmer, Smith
Substitutes: Harris (for Sykes), Wixey (for Rose), Taylor (for Pitcher), Mehew (nps), Richards (nps)
Scorers: Thomas, Sykes (pen), MJ Palmer (3)
Attendance: 166

Date: Tuesday 04/03/2008
Result: **GLOUCESTER CITY 4 TIVERTON TOWN 1**
Competition: Southern League Premier Division
Teamsheet: Sawyer, Reid, Sykes, Mustoe, Thomas, Richards, Rose, Webb, Pitcher, MJ Palmer, Smith
Substitutes: Taylor (nps), Sysum (nps), Morford (for MJ Palmer), Allard (for Rose), Bevan (for Pitcher)
Scorers: Pitcher (2), MJ Palmer, Sykes
Attendance: 247

[423]

Date: Saturday 08/03/2008
Result: **GLOUCESTER CITY 0 BASHLEY 2**
Competition: Southern League Premier Division
Teamsheet: Sawyer, Reid, Sykes, Mustoe, Thomas, Richards, Rose, Webb, Pitcher, MJ Palmer, Smith
Substitutes: Harris (nps), Taylor (nps), Allard (for Webb), Morford (for Sykes), Bevan (for MJ Palmer)
Attendance: 321

Date: Tuesday 11/03/2008
Result: **HALESOWEN TOWN 2 GLOUCESTER CITY 1**
Competition: Southern League Premier Division
Teamsheet: Sawyer, Reid, Walsh, Mustoe, Thomas, Sysum, Rose, Webb, Pitcher, Sykes, Smith
Substitutes: Harris (nps), MJ Palmer (for Sysum), Bevan (for Smith), Taylor (nps), Wixey (nps)
Scorer: Sykes (pen)
Attendance: 450

Date: Saturday 15/03/2008
Result: **BANBURY UNITED 1 GLOUCESTER CITY 1**
Competition: Southern League Premier Division
Teamsheet: Sawyer, Reid, Sykes, Mustoe, Thomas, Richards, Rose, Webb, Pitcher, MJ Palmer, Smith
Substitutes: Harris (nps), Sysum (nps), Allard (for Webb), Morford (for MJ Palmer), Bevan (for Smith)
Scorer: Reid
Attendance: 298

Date: Monday 24/03/2008
Result: **CHIPPENHAM TOWN 4 GLOUCESTER CITY 1**
Competition: Southern League Premier Division
Teamsheet: Sawyer, Reid, Sykes, Mustoe, Thomas, Richards, Rose, Walsh, Pitcher, Morford, Smith
Substitutes: Taylor (nps), Sysum (nps), Allard (for Reid), Webb (for Sykes), Bevan (for Morford)
Scorer: Morford
Attendance: 685

Date: Thursday 27/03/2008
Result: **GLOUCESTER CITY 5 SWINDON SUPERMARINE 0**
Competition: Southern League Premier Division
Teamsheet: Sawyer, Allard, Walsh, Mustoe, Sysum, Richards, Sykes, Webb, Pitcher, Morford, Smith
Substitutes: Taylor (nps), Reid (for Sykes), MJ Palmer (for Pitcher), Rose (nps), Bevan (for Morford)
Scorers: Sykes (2), Pitcher, MJ Palmer, Reid
Attendance: 233

Date: Tuesday 01/04/2008
Result: **GLOUCESTER CITY 3 MERTHYR TYDFIL 1**
Competition: Southern League Premier Division
Teamsheet: Sawyer, Reid, Sykes, Mustoe, Sysum, Richards, Rose, Allard, Pitcher, Morford, Smith
Substitutes: Harris (nps), Webb (for Reid), Taylor (for Morford), Bevan (for Smith), Seddon (nps)
Scorers: Morford, own goal, Smith
Attendance: 250

Date: Saturday 05/04/2008
Result: **GLOUCESTER CITY 2 CLEVEDON TOWN 1**
Competition: Southern League Premier Division
Teamsheet: Sawyer, Walsh, Sykes, Mustoe, Allard, Richards, Rose, Webb, Pitcher, Morford, Smith
Substitutes: Harris (for Sykes), Sysum (for Walsh), Taylor (nps), Bevan (for Morford), Seddon (nps)
Scorer: Pitcher (2)
Attendance: 276

Date: Saturday 12/04/2008
Result: **TEAM BATH 4 GLOUCESTER CITY 2**
Competition: Southern League Premier Division
Teamsheet: Sawyer, Walsh, Sykes, Mustoe, Sysum, Richards, Rose, Webb, Pitcher, Morford, Smith
Substitutes: Harris (nps), Reid (for Sykes), Allard (for Sysum), Bevan (for Walsh), Seddon (nps)
Scorers: Smith (2)
Attendance: 225

Date: Tuesday 15/04/2008
Result: **GLOUCESTER CITY 4 CHESHUNT 0**
Competition: Southern League Premier Division
Teamsheet: Sawyer, Walsh, Sykes, Mustoe, Sysum, Richards, Rose, Allard, Pitcher, Morford, Smith
Substitutes: Harris (nps), Webb (for Richards), Reid (nps), Preece (for Sykes), Bevan (for Walsh)
Scorers: Sykes, Pitcher, Morford (2)
Attendance: 190

Date: Saturday 19/04/2008
Result: **GLOUCESTER CITY 1 KING'S LYNN 1**
Competition: Southern League Premier Division
Teamsheet: Sawyer, Walsh, Sykes, Mustoe, Reid, Richards, Rose, Webb, Pitcher, Morford, Smith
Substitutes: Harris (nps), Sysum (nps), Thomas (for Reid), Allard (nps), Bevan (for Webb)
Scorer: Sykes
Attendance: 660

Date: Saturday 26/04/2008
Result: **CIRENCESTER TOWN 1 GLOUCESTER CITY 4**
Competition: Southern League Premier Division
Teamsheet: Sawyer, Walsh, Sykes, Mustoe, Thomas, Richards, Rose, Webb, Pitcher, Morford, Smith
Substitutes: Taylor (nps), Reid (for Walsh), Allard (for Sykes), Sysum (nps), Bevan (for Pitcher)
Scorers: Pitcher, Morford (2), Bevan
Attendance: 340

Appearances – AG Allard 22(20), B Ashford 2, SDR Badham 0(1), S Bailey 1, JK Bevan 7(27), L Buttery 4, JJ Cant 0(1), RE Courtney 1(1), S Ellis 3(4), S Griffin 6(4), TR Hamblin 5(1), AG Harris 0(8), DG Hilder 1, WG Morford 25(8), DJ Morgan 1(3), NJ Mustoe 51, MI Noakes 9, KA Palmer 3, MJ Palmer 4(2), J Pitcher 40(5), CJ Preece 0(1), JM Price 7(2), J Reid 40(6), M Richards 39(4), ML Rose 41(3), KJ Sawyer 49, EJ Seddon 4, LF Smith 44(2), AB Sykes 42(9), MJ Sysum 8(3), JR Taylor 0(8), AJ Thomas 29(2), CD Thompson 11, LP Tomkins 11(2), MD Walsh 13, TA Webb 43(6), J Welsh 6(2), MJ Whittington 10(8), D Wilkinson 1(2), DJ Wixey 0(1).
Others selected but did not play: DS Mehew, AJ Thomson.
Scorers – J Pitcher 22, AB Sykes 17, WG Morford 12, JK Bevan 6, J Reid 6, LF Smith 6, MJ Palmer 5, AJ Thomas 4, AG Allard 3, M Richards 3, ML Rose 3, TA Webb 3, S Griffin 2, MD Walsh 2, MJ Whittington 2, S Ellis 1, DJ Morgan 1, J Welsh 1, own goals 2.

SOUTHERN LEAGUE – PREMIER DIVISION

POS	CLUB	P	W	D	L	F	A	PTS
1	KING'S LYNN	42	24	13	5	91	36	85
2	TEAM BATH	42	25	8	9	71	41	83
3	HALESOWEN TOWN	42	22	13	7	80	46	79
4	CHIPPENHAM TOWN	42	20	13	9	73	44	73
5	BASHLEY	42	19	12	11	60	46	69
6	**GLOUCESTER CITY**	**42**	**19**	**11**	**12**	**81**	**50**	**68**
7	HEMEL HEMPSTEAD TOWN	42	19	11	12	67	50	68
8	BRACKLEY TOWN	42	16	12	14	57	53	60
9	BANBURY UNITED	42	14	16	12	55	57	58
10	YATE TOWN	42	16	10	16	71	76	58
11	CLEVEDON TOWN	42	13	18	11	49	46	57
12	SWINDON SUPERMARINE	42	14	12	16	51	67	54
13	MERTHYR TYDFIL	42	13	14	15	65	70	53
14	MANGOTSFIELD UNITED	42	12	16	14	38	42	52
15	RUGBY TOWN	42	13	12	17	55	66	51
16	CORBY TOWN	42	14	8	20	60	67	50
17	TIVERTON TOWN	42	13	11	18	45	60	50
18	HITCHIN TOWN	42	12	11	19	46	61	47
19	BEDFORD TOWN	42	12	9	21	54	73	45
20	BROMSGROVE ROVERS	42	10	12	20	46	67	42
21	CIRENCESTER TOWN	42	8	8	26	44	80	32
22	CHESHUNT	42	5	8	29	42	103	23
		924	333	258	333	1301	1301	1257

SEASON 2008-2009
(Home Ground: Corinium Stadium, Cirencester – groundshare with Cirencester Town)

Date: Saturday 16/08/2008
Result: **GLOUCESTER CITY 4 STOURBRIDGE 0**
Competition: Southern League Premier Division
Teamsheet: Sawyer, Upcott, Marshall, Mustoe, Thomas, Rose, Smith, Webb, Pitcher, Symons, Ballinger
Substitutes: MJ Palmer (for Pitcher), Hamblin (nps), Allard (for Webb), Walsh (for Upcott), Ellis (nps)
Scorers: Symons (2), Ballinger, Marshall
Attendance: 245

Date: Tuesday 19/08/2008
Result: **TIVERTON TOWN 2 GLOUCESTER CITY 2**
Competition: Southern League Premier Division
Teamsheet: Sawyer, Walsh, Marshall, Mustoe, Thomas, Rose, Smith, Webb, MJ Palmer, Symons, Allard
Substitutes: Pitcher (for MJ Palmer), Hamblin (nps), Ballinger (for Allard), Sysum (nps), J Harris (nps)
Scorer: Mustoe (2 pens)
Attendance: 446

Date: Saturday 23/08/2008
Result: **EVESHAM UNITED 2 GLOUCESTER CITY 2**
Competition: Southern League Premier Division
Teamsheet: Sawyer, Walsh, Marshall, Mustoe, Thomas, Rose, Smith, Webb, Pitcher, Symons, Ballinger
Substitutes: MJ Palmer (for Pitcher), Hamblin (nps), Reid (for Ballinger), Sysum (nps), J Harris (nps)
Scorers: Ballinger, Symons
Attendance: 207

Date: Monday 25/08/2008
Result: **GLOUCESTER CITY 2 OXFORD CITY 2**
Competition: Southern League Premier Division
Teamsheet: Sawyer, J Harris, Marshall, Mustoe, Hamblin, Rose, Smith, Webb, Pitcher, Symons, Ballinger
Substitutes: MJ Palmer (nps), Thomas (for Hamblin), Sykes (for J Harris), Sysum (nps), Walsh (nps)
Scorers: J Harris, Symons
Attendance: 302

Date: Saturday 30/08/2008
Result: **YATE TOWN 0 GLOUCESTER CITY 2**
Competition: Southern League Premier Division
Teamsheet: Sawyer, J Harris, Marshall, Mustoe, Hamblin, Rose, Smith, Webb, Pitcher, Symons, Ballinger
Substitutes: Upcott (nps), Thomas (nps), Sykes (nps), Sysum (nps), Ellis (for Pitcher)
Scorers: Pitcher, Ballinger
Attendance: 403

Date: Tuesday 02/09/2008
Result: **GLOUCESTER CITY 3 BASHLEY 0**
Competition: Southern League Premier Division
Teamsheet: Sawyer, J Harris, Marshall, Mustoe, Hamblin, Rose, Smith, Webb, Pitcher, Symons, Ballinger
Substitutes: Upcott (nps), Thomas (nps), Sykes (nps), Sysum (for Ballinger), Ellis (nps)
Scorers: Ballinger, Symons (2)
Attendance: 236

Date: Saturday 06/09/2008
Result: **FARNBOROUGH 2 GLOUCESTER CITY 1**
Competition: Southern League Premier Division
Teamsheet: Sawyer, J Harris, Marshall, Mustoe, Hamblin, Rose, Smith, Webb, Pitcher, Symons, Ballinger
Substitutes: Upcott (nps), Thomas (for J Harris), Sykes (for Ballinger), Sysum (nps), Ellis (for Webb)
Scorer: Sykes (pen)
Attendance: 700

Date: Saturday 13/09/2008
Result: **CHALFONT SAINT PETER 5 GLOUCESTER CITY 3**
Competition: FA Cup 1st Qualifying Round
Teamsheet: Sawyer, Upcott, Marshall, Mustoe, Thomas, Rose, Smith, Webb, Pitcher, Symons, Ballinger
Substitutes: J Harris (for Ballinger), Hamblin (nps), Sykes (for Upcott), Sysum (for Marshall), AG Harris (nps)
Scorers: Pitcher, Sysum, Sykes (pen)
Attendance: 145

Date: Saturday 20/09/2008
Result: **GLOUCESTER CITY 0 BEDFORD TOWN 1**
Competition: Southern League Premier Division
Teamsheet: Sawyer, J Harris, Sysum, Mustoe, Hamblin, Rose, Smith, Webb, Pitcher, Ballinger, Sykes
Substitutes: Thomas (for Smith), Upcott (for Sykes), Marshall (for Mustoe), AG Harris (nps), Twyman (nps)
Attendance: 270

Date: Saturday 04/10/2008
Result: **GLOUCESTER CITY 2 CHIPPENHAM TOWN 0**
Competition: Southern League Premier Division
Teamsheet: Sawyer, Sysum, Marshall, Thomas, Hamblin, Rose, Smith, Webb, Pitcher, Sykes, J Harris
Substitutes: Ballinger (for Sykes), Upcott (nps), AG Harris (nps), Twyman (nps), James (nps)
Scorers: Pitcher, own goal
Attendance: 380

Date: Tuesday 07/10/2008
Result: **BANBURY UNITED 1 GLOUCESTER CITY 5**
Competition: Southern League Premier Division
Teamsheet: Sawyer, Sysum, Marshall, Thomas, Hamblin, Rose, Smith, Webb, Pitcher, Sykes, J Harris
Substitutes: Ballinger (for Mustoe), Morford (for Pitcher), AG Harris (nps), Mustoe (for Thomas), Mehew (nps)
Scorers: Webb, Sykes (pen), Pitcher, Smith, Hamblin
Attendance: 235

Date: Saturday 18/10/2008
Result: **BROMSGROVE ROVERS 1 GLOUCESTER CITY 4**
Competition: FA Trophy 1st Qualifying Round
Teamsheet: Sawyer, Sysum, Marshall, Richards, Hamblin, Rose, Smith, Webb, Pitcher, Sykes, J Harris
Substitutes: Morford (for Pitcher), Ballinger (for J Harris), Twyman (for Sysum), AG Harris (nps), Nash (nps)
Scorers: Sykes (2, 1 pen), Morford (2)
Attendance: 362

Date: Saturday 25/10/2008
Result: **GLOUCESTER CITY 1 HALESOWEN TOWN 2**
Competition: Southern League Premier Division
Teamsheet: Sawyer, Sysum, Marshall, Richards, Hamblin, Rose, Smith, Webb, Pitcher, Ballinger, J Harris
Substitutes: Morford (for Ballinger), Thomas (For Sysum), AG Harris (nps), Twyman (nps), James (nps)
Scorer: Smith (pen)
Attendance: 366

Date: Tuesday 28/10/2008
Result: **EVESHAM UNITED 0 GLOUCESTER CITY 3**
Competition: Southern League Cup 1st Round
Teamsheet: Sawyer, Sysum, Marshall, Twyman, Thomas, Rose, Smith, Webb, Nash, Morford, J Harris
Substitutes: James (for J Harris), Ward (for Sysum), Pitcher (for Twyman), AG Harris (nps), Richards (nps)
Scorers: Nash (2), Morford
Attendance: 37

Date: Saturday 01/11/2008
Result: **EAST THURROCK UNITED 4 GLOUCESTER CITY 2**
Competition: FA Trophy 2nd Qualifying Round
Teamsheet: Sawyer, Ballinger, Marshall, Thomas, Hamblin, Rose, Smith, Webb, Pitcher, Morford, J Harris
Substitutes: Sykes (for Ballinger), Sysum (for Webb), A Harris (nps), Nash (nps), Richards (for Marshall)
Scorers: J Harris, Sykes
Attendance: 134

Date: Saturday 08/11/2008
Result: **MERTHYR TYDFIL 2 GLOUCESTER CITY 1**
Competition: Southern League Premier Division
Teamsheet: Sawyer, Sykes, Richards, Mustoe, Hamblin, Rose, Smith, Webb, Pitcher, Morford, J Harris
Substitutes: Ballinger (for Pitcher), Thomas (nps), AG Harris (nps), Marshall (for J Harris), Sysum (for Webb)
Scorer: Sykes (pen)
Attendance: 328

Date: Tuesday 11/11/2008
Result: **GLOUCESTER CITY 5 MANGOTSFIELD UNITED 2**
Competition: Southern League Premier Division
Teamsheet: Sawyer, Sykes, Marshall, Mustoe, Richards, Rose, Smith, Webb, Pitcher, Morford, J Harris
Substitutes: Ballinger (for Morford), Hamblin (for J Harris), AG Harris (nps), James (for Mustoe), Sysum (nps)
Scorers: Sykes (3, 1 pen), Morford, Webb
Attendance: 201

Date: Saturday 15/11/2008
Result: **GLOUCESTER CITY 1 CORBY TOWN 3**
Competition: Southern League Premier Division
Teamsheet: Sawyer, Sykes, Marshall, Richards, Hamblin, Sysum, Smith, Webb, Pitcher, Morford, Ballinger
Substitutes: James (for Webb), Ward (for Sysum), AG Harris (nps), Mehew (nps), Twyman (for Ballinger)
Scorer: Sykes
Attendance: 291

Date: Saturday 22/11/2008
Result: **RUGBY TOWN 1 GLOUCESTER CITY 3**
Competition: Southern League Premier Division
Teamsheet: Sawyer, Sykes, Richards, Mustoe, Thomas, Rose, Smith, Webb, Pitcher, Morford, Marshall
Substitutes: Ballinger (for Morford), AG Harris (nps), J Harris (nps), Sysum (nps)
Scorers: Smith, Sykes (pen), Pitcher
Attendance: 193

Date: Tuesday 25/11/2008
Result: **GLOUCESTER CITY 3 ABINGDON UNITED 0**
Competition: Southern League Cup 2nd Round
Teamsheet: Sawyer, Sykes, J Harris, Mustoe, Sysum, Rose, Smith, Fathers, Keveren, Ballinger, Marshall
Substitutes: Morford (for Keveren), Richards (for Sykes), AG Harris (nps), Webb (nps), Thomas (for Mustoe)
Scorers: own goal, Ballinger, J Harris
Attendance: 74

Date: Saturday 29/11/2008
Result: **CLEVEDON TOWN 1 GLOUCESTER CITY 4**
Competition: Southern League Premier Division
Teamsheet: Sawyer, Sykes, Richards, Mustoe, Thomas, Rose, Smith, Webb, Pitcher, Morford, Marshall
Substitutes: Ballinger (for Webb), Sysum (nps), Keveren (nps), Fathers (for Fathers), J Harris (for Marshall)
Scorers: Marshall, Webb, Smith (pen), Pitcher
Attendance: 193

Date: Saturday 06/12/2008
Result: **GLOUCESTER CITY 0 BRACKLEY TOWN 1**
Competition: Southern League Premier Division
Teamsheet: Sawyer, Sykes, Richards, Mustoe, Thomas, Rose, Smith, Webb, Ballinger, Morford, Marshall
Substitutes: Pitcher (for Ballinger), Fathers (for Webb), AG Harris (nps), J Harris (for Marshall), Mehew (nps)
Attendance: 225

Date: Tuesday 16/12/2008
Result: **MANGOTSFIELD UNITED 1 GLOUCESTER CITY 3**
Competition: Gloucestershire FA Northern Senior Professional Cup Quarter-Finals
Teamsheet: Sawyer, Ballinger, Richards, Mustoe, Marshall, Rose, Smith, Webb, Pitcher, Morford, J Harris
Substitutes: Sykes (for Morford), Ward (for J Harris), AG Harris (nps), Mehew (for Smith), Hamblin (nps)
Scorers: Smith, Richards, Sykes
Attendance: 68

Date: Saturday 20/12/2008
Result: **HITCHIN TOWN 1 GLOUCESTER CITY 1**
Competition: Southern League Premier Division
Teamsheet: Sawyer, Sykes, Richards, Mustoe, Thomas, Rose, Smith, Fathers, Pitcher, Morford, J Harris
Substitutes: Webb (for Fathers), Hamblin (for Richards), AG Harris (nps), Mehew (nps)
Scorer: Thomas
Attendance: 288

Date: Saturday 27/12/2008
Result: **OXFORD CITY 1 GLOUCESTER CITY 1**
Competition: Southern League Premier Division
Teamsheet: Sawyer, Sykes, Richards, Mustoe, Hamblin, Rose, Smith, Webb, Pitcher, Ballinger, J Harris
Substitutes: Morford (for Ballinger), Thomas (nps), Mehew (nps), Fathers (for Webb), Marshall (for Sykes)
Scorer: Smith
Attendance: 265

Date: Thursday 01/01/2009
Result: **GLOUCESTER CITY 3 SWINDON SUPERMARINE 1**
Competition: Southern League Premier Division
Teamsheet: Sawyer, Sykes, Richards, Mustoe, Hamblin, Rose, Smith, Webb, Pitcher, Morford, J Harris
Substitutes: Ballinger (nps), Thomas (nps), Mehew (nps), AG Harris (nps), Marshall (nps)
Scorers: Sykes (2), Pitcher
Attendance: 382

Date: Tuesday 13/01/2009
Result: **GLOUCESTER CITY 3 YATE TOWN 0**
Competition: Southern League Cup 3rd Round
Teamsheet: Sawyer, Ballinger, Richards, Marshall, J Harris, JW Palmer, Smith, Webb, Arnold, Morford, James
Substitutes: Pitcher (for Morford), Sykes (nps), Keveren (for Arnold), Hamblin (nps), Twyman (for James)
Scorers: Smith, Keveren, Pitcher
Attendance: 130

Date: Saturday 17/01/2009
Result: **BASHLEY 1 GLOUCESTER CITY 1**
Competition: Southern League Premier Division
Teamsheet: Sawyer, Sykes, Richards, Mustoe, Hamblin, JW Palmer, Smith, Webb, Pitcher, Morford, J Harris
Substitutes: Marshall (for Sykes), Arnold (for Pitcher), James (nps), AG Harris (nps), Mehew (nps)
Scorer: Smith
Attendance: 300

Date: Tuesday 20/01/2009
Result: **GLOUCESTER CITY 2 HEMEL HEMPSTEAD TOWN 1**
Competition: Southern League Premier Division
Teamsheet: Sawyer, Sykes, Richards, Mustoe, Hamblin, JW Palmer, Smith, Webb, Pitcher, Morford, J Harris
Substitutes: Marshall (for Hamblin), Arnold (nps), Ballinger (for Sykes), AG Harris (nps), Mehew (nps)
Scorer: Sykes (2, 1 pen)
Attendance: 160

Date: Saturday 24/01/2009
Result: **GLOUCESTER CITY 2 TIVERTON TOWN 1**
Competition: Southern League Premier Division
Teamsheet: Sawyer, Sykes, Richards, Mustoe, Hamblin, JW Palmer, Smith, Webb, Pitcher, Morford, Ballinger
Substitutes: Marshall (nps), Rose (for Sykes), J Harris (for Ballinger), AG Harris (nps), James (nps)
Scorers: Pitcher, Sykes (pen)
Attendance: 285

Date: Tuesday 27/01/2009
Result: **GLOUCESTER CITY 1 BANBURY UNITED 1**
Competition: Southern League Premier Division
Teamsheet: Sawyer, Sykes, Richards, Mustoe, Marshall, JW Palmer, Smith, Webb, Pitcher, Morford, Ballinger
Substitutes: Keveren (for Morford), Rose (for Sykes), J Harris (for Ballinger), Twyman (nps), James (nps)
Scorer: Pitcher
Attendance: 215

Date: Saturday 31/01/2009
Result: **CHIPPENHAM TOWN 2 GLOUCESTER CITY 2**
Competition: Southern League Premier Division
Teamsheet: Sawyer, Sykes, Marshall, Mustoe, Hamblin, Rose, Smith, Webb, Pitcher, Morford, J Harris
Substitutes: AG Harris (nps), Mehew (nps), Keveren (for Morford), Twyman (nps), James (nps)
Scorers: Pitcher, Keveren
Attendance: 468

Date: Saturday 14/02/2009
Result: **HALESOWEN TOWN 1 GLOUCESTER CITY 2**
Competition: Southern League Premier Division
Teamsheet: Sawyer, Sykes, Marshall, Mustoe, Hamblin, Rose, Ballinger, Webb, Pitcher, Morford, Richards
Substitutes: Keveren (for Morford), J Harris (for Sykes), AG Harris (nps), Twyman (nps), James (nps)
Scorer: Sykes (2, 1 pen)
Attendance: 434

Date: Tuesday 17/02/2009
Result: **BRIDGWATER TOWN 2 GLOUCESTER CITY 1**
Competition: Southern League Cup 4th Round
Teamsheet: Jones, James, J Harris, Ballinger, Hamblin, Rose, Smith, Webb, Pitcher, Keveren, Marshall
Substitutes: Mustoe (nps), Morford (for Keveren), AG Harris (nps), Mehew (nps), Richards (for James)
Scorer: Smith (pen)
Attendance: 297

Date: Saturday 21/02/2009
Result: **GLOUCESTER CITY 0 FARNBOROUGH 0**
Competition: Southern League Premier Division
Teamsheet: Sawyer, Sykes, Richards, Mustoe, Hamblin, J Harris, Smith, Webb, Pitcher, Morford, Marshall
Substitutes: Keveren (nps), James (nps), Twyman (nps), Ward (nps), Fey (nps)
Attendance: 431

Date: Saturday 28/02/2009
Result: **BEDFORD TOWN 1 GLOUCESTER CITY 1**
Competition: Southern League Premier Division
Teamsheet: Sawyer, Sykes, Marshall, Mustoe, Richards, Rose, Smith, Webb, Pitcher, Symons, J Harris
Substitutes: Morford (for J Harris), Ballinger (for Smith), Mehew (nps), AG Harris (nps)
Scorer: Sykes
Attendance: 379

Date: Saturday 07/03/2009
Result: **GLOUCESTER CITY 1 MERTHYR TYDFIL 1**
Competition: Southern League Premier Division
Teamsheet: Sawyer, Sykes, Marshall, Mustoe, Hamblin, Rose, Smith, Ballinger, Pitcher, Symons, J Harris
Substitutes: Morford (for Pitcher), James (nps), Mehew (nps), AG Harris (nps)
Scorer: Pitcher
Attendance: 315

Date: Tuesday 10/03/2009
Result: **MANGOTSFIELD UNITED 0 GLOUCESTER CITY 1**
Competition: Southern League Premier Division
Teamsheet: Sawyer, Sykes, Richards, Mustoe, Hamblin, Rose, Ballinger, Webb, Morford, Symons, J Harris
Substitutes: Pitcher (nps), James (nps), Sysum (for Morford), Smith (for Ballinger), Marshall (for J Harris)
Scorer: Morford
Attendance: 185

Date: Saturday 14/03/2009
Result: **CORBY TOWN 1 GLOUCESTER CITY 2**
Competition: Southern League Premier Division
Teamsheet: Sawyer, Sykes, Marshall, Mustoe, Richards, Rose, Ballinger, Webb, Sysum, Symons, J Harris
Substitutes: Morford (nps), Smith (for Ballinger), Mehew (nps), Hamblin (nps), Pitcher (nps)
Scorers: Symons, Sykes
Attendance: 265

Date: Tuesday 17/03/2009
Result: **GLOUCESTER CITY 2 EVESHAM UNITED 0**
Competition: Southern League Premier Division
Teamsheet: Sawyer, Sykes, Marshall, Mustoe, Sysum, Smith, Ballinger, Webb, Morford, Symons, J Harris
Substitutes: Pitcher (nps), James (nps), Mehew (nps), Hamblin (nps), AG Harris (nps)
Scorer: Smith (2)
Attendance: 210

Date: Saturday 21/03/2009
Result: **GLOUCESTER CITY 2 CAMBRIDGE CITY 1**
Competition: Southern League Premier Division
Teamsheet: Sawyer, Sykes, Marshall, Mustoe, Richards, Rose, Ballinger, Webb, Sysum, Symons, J Harris
Substitutes: Smith (for Ballinger), Morford (for Sysum), Grubb (for J Harris), Hamblin (nps), Pitcher (nps)
Scorers: Richards, Morford
Attendance: 275

Date: Wednesday 25/03/2009
Result: **GLOUCESTER CITY 3 RUGBY TOWN 0**
Competition: Southern League Premier Division
Teamsheet: Sawyer, Sykes, Marshall, Mustoe, Richards, Rose, Smith, Webb, Morford, Symons, Grubb
Substitutes: Pitcher (for Symons), Ballinger (nps), J Harris (for Grubb), Sysum (for Sykes), AG Harris (nps)
Scorers: Sykes (pen), Morford, Smith
Attendance: 267

Date: Saturday 28/03/2009
Result: **BRACKLEY TOWN 2 GLOUCESTER CITY 3**
Competition: Southern League Premier Division
Teamsheet: Sawyer, Ballinger, Sysum, Mustoe, Richards, Rose, Smith, Webb, Morford, Symons, J Harris
Substitutes: Pitcher (for Symons), Sykes (nps), Grubb (for J Harris), Marshall (for Ballinger), AG Harris (nps)
Scorers: Symons, Morford, Smith
Attendance: 307

Date: Monday 30/03/2009
Result: **CAMBRIDGE CITY 2 GLOUCESTER CITY 1**
Competition: Southern League Premier Division
Teamsheet: Sawyer, Sykes, Marshall, Mustoe, Richards, Rose, Smith, Webb, Pitcher, Symons, Grubb
Substitutes: Morford (for Grubb), Ballinger (for Pitcher), J Harris (nps), Sysum (nps), AG Harris (nps)
Scorer: Sykes
Attendance: 301

Date: Saturday 04/04/2009
Result: **GLOUCESTER CITY 0 CLEVEDON TOWN 1**
Competition: Southern League Premier Division
Teamsheet: Sawyer, Sykes, Marshall, Mustoe, Richards, Rose, Smith, Webb, Pitcher, Morford, Grubb
Substitutes: Ballinger (for Sykes), J Harris (for Grubb), Sysum (for Webb), Symons (nps), AG Harris (nps)
Attendance: 300

Date: Tuesday 07/04/2009
Result: **STOURBRIDGE 1 GLOUCESTER CITY 1**
Competition: Southern League Premier Division
Teamsheet: Sawyer, Sykes, Marshall, Mustoe, Richards, Rose, Ballinger, Webb, Sysum, Symons, J Harris
Substitutes: Grubb (for J Harris), Morford (for Sysum), Smith (for Ballinger), Pitcher (nps), AG Harris (nps)
Scorer: Webb
Attendance: 236

Date: Saturday 11/04/2009
Result: **GLOUCESTER CITY 4 YATE TOWN 0**
Competition: Southern League Premier Division
Teamsheet: Sawyer, Sykes, Marshall, Mustoe, Richards, Rose, Smith, Webb, Morford, Symons, J Harris
Substitutes: Pitcher (nps), Ballinger (for J Harris), Grubb (for Sykes), Sysum (for Mustoe), AG Harris (nps)
Scorers: Symons (2), J Harris, Grubb
Attendance: 303

Date: Monday 13/04/2009
Result: **SWINDON SUPERMARINE 0 GLOUCESTER CITY 1**
Competition: Southern League Premier Division
Teamsheet: Sawyer, Ballinger, Marshall, Mustoe, Richards, Rose, Smith, Webb, Morford, Symons, Grubb
Substitutes: Pitcher (for Symons), Sykes (nps), J Harris (nps), Sysum (for Grubb), AG Harris (nps)
Scorer: Ballinger
Attendance: 301

Date: Wednesday 15/04/2009
Result: **GLOUCESTER CITY 2 YATE TOWN 2** (aet, 3-2 pens)
Competition: Gloucestershire FA Northern Senior Professional Cup Semi-Finals
Teamsheet: Delve, Sykes, Marshall, Sysum, Richards, Ballinger, James, J Harris, Pitcher, Nash, Grubb
Substitutes: Mehew (nps), AG Harris (nps), Webb (for Nash), Morford (for Richards), Smith (for James)
Scorers: Sysum, Sykes
Attendance: 82

Date: Saturday 18/04/2009
Result: **GLOUCESTER CITY 4 HITCHIN TOWN 1**
Competition: Southern League Premier Division
Teamsheet: Sawyer, Sykes, Marshall, Mustoe, Richards, Rose, Smith, Webb, Morford, Symons, Ballinger
Substitutes: Pitcher (for Symons), J Harris (for Rose), Grubb (nps), Sysum (for Marshall), AG Harris (nps)
Scorers: Symons, Smith, Sykes (2)
Attendance: 295

Date: Saturday 25/04/2009
Result: **HEMEL HEMPSTEAD TOWN 2 GLOUCESTER CITY 1**
Competition: Southern League Premier Division
Teamsheet: Sawyer, Grubb, Marshall, Sysum, Richards, Rose, Smith, J Harris, Morford, Pitcher, Ballinger
Substitutes: Mustoe (for Rose), Symons (for Morford), Webb (for Richards), Sykes (nps), AG Harris (nps)
Scorer: Pitcher
Attendance: 684

Date: Tuesday 28/04/2009
Result: **GLOUCESTER CITY 3 CAMBRIDGE CITY 1**
Competition: Southern League Premier Division Play-Off Semi-Finals
Teamsheet: Sawyer, Sykes, Marshall, Mustoe, Richards, Rose, Smith, Webb, Morford, Symons, J Harris
Substitutes: Ballinger (for Smith), Pitcher (nps), Grubb (nps), Sysum (for Sykes), Delve (nps)
Scorers: J Harris, Smith, Symons
Attendance: 745

Date: Saturday 02/05/2009
Result: **FARNBOROUGH 0 GLOUCESTER CITY 1**
Competition: Southern League Premier Division Play-Off Final
Teamsheet: Sawyer, Sykes, Marshall, Mustoe, Richards, Rose, Smith, Webb, Morford, Symons, J Harris
Substitutes: Ballinger (for Webb), Pitcher (for Sykes), Grubb (nps), Sysum (nps), Delve (nps)
Scorer: Rose
Attendance: 1715

Date: Wednesday 06/05/2009
Result: **BRISTOL CITY RESERVES 5 GLOUCESTER CITY 1**
Competition: Gloucestershire FA Northern Senior Professional Cup Final
Teamsheet: Sawyer, Sykes, Sysum, Mustoe, Richards, Rose, Smith, Ballinger, Morford, Pitcher, J Harris
Substitutes: Grubb (for Pitcher), James (for Smith), Nash (for Morford), AG Harris (nps), Mehew (nps)
Scorer: Ballinger
Attendance: 702

Appearances – AG Allard 1(1), JD Arnold 1(1), LR Ballinger 32(15), AK Delve 1, S Ellis 0(2), LO Fathers 2(3), DL Grubb 6(5), TR Hamblin 23(2), J Harris 37(9), BA James 3(4), SC Jones 1, AM Keveren 2(4), LA Marshall 43(7), DS Mehew 0(1), WG Morford 31(12), NJ Mustoe 43(2), KP Nash 2(1), JW Palmer 5, MJ Palmer 1(2), J Pitcher 37(9), J Reid 0(1), M Richards 36(3), ML Rose 45(2), KJ Sawyer 52, LF Smith 48(5), AB Sykes 37(5), MA Symons 23(1), MJ Sysum 16(11), AJ Thomas 12(5), JT Twyman 1(3), JM Upcott 2(1), MD Walsh 2, NS Ward 0(3), TA Webb 48(3).
Others selected but did not play: RL Fey, AG Harris.
Scorers – AB Sykes 27, LF Smith 15, J Pitcher 13, MA Symons 12, WG Morford 8, LR Ballinger 7, J Harris 5, TA Webb 4, AM Keveren 2, LA Marshall 2, NJ Mustoe 2, KP Nash 2, M Richards 2, MJ Sysum 2, DL Grubb 1, TR Hamblin 1, ML Rose 1, AJ Thomas 1, own goals 2.

SOUTHERN LEAGUE – PREMIER DIVISION

POS	CLUB	P	W	D	L	F	A	PTS
1	CORBY TOWN	42	25	9	8	85	38	84
2	FARNBOROUGH	42	23	14	5	67	36	83
3	**GLOUCESTER CITY**	**42**	**21**	**12**	**9**	**80**	**45**	**75**
4	CAMBRIDGE CITY	42	21	10	11	62	40	73
5	HEMEL HEMPSTEAD TOWN	42	21	7	14	71	48	70
6	OXFORD CITY	42	19	10	13	76	55	67
7	MERTHYR TYDFIL	42	19	10	13	66	55	67
8	CHIPPENHAM TOWN	42	20	8	14	64	51	65*
9	EVESHAM UNITED	42	16	13	13	48	39	61
10	HALESOWEN TOWN	42	19	6	17	65	73	60*
11	BRACKLEY TOWN	42	15	12	15	69	62	57
12	TIVERTON TOWN	42	16	9	17	51	50	57
13	SWINDON SUPERMARINE	42	15	12	15	59	61	57
14	BASHLEY	42	15	12	15	52	58	57
15	BEDFORD TOWN	42	14	8	20	44	55	50
16	STOURBRIDGE	42	13	11	18	62	78	50
17	RUGBY TOWN	42	11	10	21	63	71	43
18	CLEVEDON TOWN	42	11	10	21	51	80	43
19	BANBURY UNITED	42	11	8	23	43	83	41
20	HITCHIN TOWN	42	10	10	22	57	79	40
21	YATE TOWN	42	9	9	24	54	91	36
22	MANGOTSFIELD UNITED	42	10	6	26	39	80	36
		924	354	216	354	1328	1328	1272

* Three points deducted for fielding an ineligible player

PROMOTED TO THE FOOTBALL CONFERENCE NORTH
2009-2010

Alfreton Town, Blyth Spartans, Corby Town, Droylsden, Eastwood Town, Farsley Celtic, Fleetwood Town, Gainsborough Trinity, Gloucester City, Harrogate Town, Hinckley United, Hyde United, Ilkeston Town, Northwich Victoria, Redditch United, Solihull Moors, Southport, Stafford Rangers, Stalybridge Celtic, AFC Telford United, Vauxhall Motors, Workington.

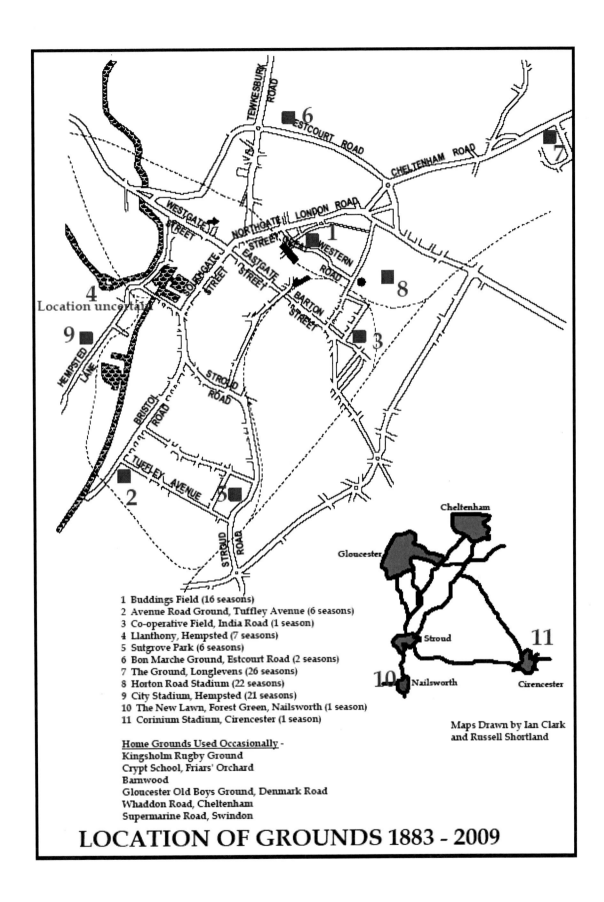

1 Buddings Field (16 seasons)
2 Avenue Road Ground, Tuffley Avenue (6 seasons)
3 Co-operative Field, India Road (1 season)
4 Llanthony, Hempsted (7 seasons)
5 Sutgrove Park (6 seasons)
6 Bon Marche Ground, Estcourt Road (2 seasons)
7 The Ground, Longlevens (26 seasons)
8 Horton Road Stadium (22 seasons)
9 City Stadium, Hempsted (21 seasons)
10 The New Lawn, Forest Green, Nailsworth (1 season)
11 Corinium Stadium, Cirencester (1 season)

Home Grounds Used Occasionally -
Kingsholm Rugby Ground
Crypt School, Friars' Orchard
Barnwood
Gloucester Old Boys Ground, Denmark Road
Whaddon Road, Cheltenham
Supermarine Road, Swindon

Maps Drawn by Ian Clark
and Russell Shortland

LOCATION OF GROUNDS 1883 - 2009

Jeff Eckhardt
Oldest Player on Debut – 40 years 176 days

Adie Harris
Most Playing Substitute Appearances – 74
Most Non Playing Substitute - 133
Oldest Goalscorer – 41 years 315 days
Oldest Player – 44 years 31 days

Callum Preece
Youngest Player – 15 years 30 days

Alex Sykes
Most Successful Penalty Taker - 19

GLOUCESTER CITY 2008-2009
(Photograph courtesy of Neil Phelps)

Back Row : Ken Blackburn (Youth Coach), Matt Sysum, Jack Pitcher, Jack Harris, Sam Ellis, Tom Hamblin, Kev Sawyer, Ollie Hall, Ash Thomas, Mike Symons, Alex Allard, Matt Rose, Lee Marshall, Lee Randall (Kit Manager)
Middle Row : Doug Foxwell (Chief Scout), Kevin Allard (Exec), Mike Dunstan (Exec), Phil Warren (Chairman Supporters Trust), Adie Tandy (Physio), Dave Mehew (Manager), David Phillips (Chairman), Tim Harris (General Manager), Adrian Harris (Assistant Manager), Nigel Hughes (Exec), Dave Hatton (Youth Secretary), John Davis (Exec), Stewart Martyn (Goalkeeping Coach)
Front Row : Dr Bob Byrne (Club Doctor), Jack Twyman, Lee Smith, Tom Webb, Luke Ballinger, Neil Mustoe (Captain), Alex Sykes, James Upcott, Karl Nash, Jamie Reid, Shaun Wetson (Secretary)

PROGRAMME   **PROGRAMME**   **PROGRAMME**   **PROGRAMME**

2005-2006   **2006-2007**   **2007-2008**   **2008-2009**

At last after 70 years.....
(Photographs courtesy of Neil Phelps)

The moment of realisation

Shaun Wetson, Kevin Allard and a happy Chairman, Dave Phillips

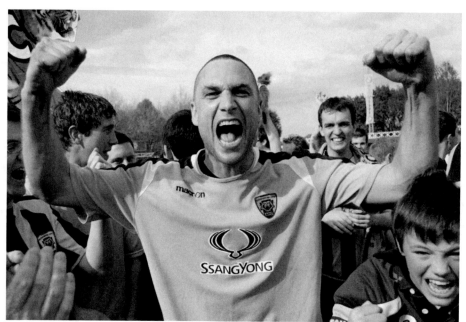

The unlikely match winner, Matt Rose

Dave Mehew with a
joyous fan!

Parmjit Dhanda M.P. and Matt Clift (Clifty)

FRIENDLIES

No doubt an incomplete list of friendlies. Pre World War One they were called Challenge Matches and probably had more significance than they do today due to the infrequency of competitive games.

Date	Opponent	H/A	Score	Scorers	Notes
1883/1884	Cheltenham	?	N/K		
1884/1885	Eastville Rovers	?	N/K		
02/01/1886	Eastville Rovers	A	0-1		
05/10/1889	Clifton Association	A	0-6		Dr.W.G.Grace refereed game
19/10/1889	Hereford Town	A	1-8	Taynton	
02/11/1889	Clifton Association	H	3-5	Henderson, Poole (pen), Wade	
16/11/1889	Swindon Town	A	0-10		
30/11/1889	Tewkesbury	A	1-9	Wade	
14/12/1889	Worcester Rovers	A	1-7	?	
21/12/1889	Nelson Villa	H	11-2	?	
26/12/1889	Cheltenham	H	7-0	?	
28/12/1889	Clifton Association	H	3-2	FB Fielding, Powell (2)	
25/01/1890	Hereford Town	H	2-3	?	
01/02/1890	Swindon Town	H	3-2	Wade, Hockin, Poole	
01/03/1890	Gloucester County Schools	H	1-4	?	
15/03/1890	Worcester Rovers	H	2-2	Poole (2)	
22/03/1890	Cardiff	A	1-1	Ely	
29/03/1890	Ledbury	A	1-4	?	
1889/1890	Cirencester	H	N/K		
1889/1890	Cirencester	A	N/K		
1889/1890	Tewkesbury	H	N/K		
1889/1890	Warmley	H	N/K		
1889/1890	Warmley	A	N/K		
04/10/1890	Gloucester Colts XIII	H	4-3	Henderson (3), FB Fielding	
11/10/1890	Evesham	A	9-0	Perkins (2), Henderson (2), FB Fielding (2), Wade (2), Macfarlane	
18/10/1890	Clifton Association	H	4-2	Henderson (2), Wade, King	
25/10/1890	Dean Close School	H	7-1	Henderson (6), King	
01/11/1890	Worcester Rovers	A	2-5	Matthews, Higginson	
08/11/1890	Tewkesbury	H	7-0	Henderson (4), Higginson, FB Fielding, ?	
15/11/1890	Cardiff	H	6-3	Higginson, Poole (3), wade, Henderson	
22/11/1890	Gloucester County Schools	H	4-5	FB Fielding (2), Poole (2)	
29/11/1890	Hereford	A	3-4	Henderson (2), Wade	
06/12/1890	Saint George (Bristol)	A	2-5	Walter Sessions (2)	
13/12/1890	Gloucester County Schools	A	2-4	?	
24/01/1891	Gloucester County Schools	A	5-4	Wade, Clemenson (2), Ely, FB Fielding	
31/01/1891	Gloucester County Schools	H	3-1	?	
07/02/1891	Nelson Villa	H	6-1	Henderson (3), Walter Sessions, FB Fielding, Clemenson	
14/02/1891	Worcester Rovers	H	7-2	Henderson (5), FB Fielding (2)	
21/02/1891	Dean Close School	A	0-2		
28/02/1891	Hereford	H	0-4		
07/03/1891	Cirencester	H	4-1	?	
14/03/1891	Nelson Villa	H	4-0	?	
21/03/1891	Saint George (Bristol)	H	3-2	Palmer (2), Matthews	
26/09/1891	Crypt Grammar School	A	1-2	?	
17/10/1891	United Schools of Gloucester	H	7-2	Bolland (3), Bagley, Wright, ?	
07/11/1891	Cirencester	A	1-1	Walter Sessions	
14/11/1891	Ledbury	H	4-0	Henderson (4)	
28/11/1891	Swindon Y.M.F.A.	H	2-4	?	
05/12/1891	Hereford	H	3-4	Poole, ?	Played at Crypt School Ground, Friars' Orchard
19/12/1891	Saint George (Bristol)	A	1-0	Stebbing	5000
28/12/1891	Wilfred Session's Holiday Team	H	4-3	?	
16/01/1892	Worcester Rovers	A	N/K		
23/01/1892	Dean Close School	A	N/K		
06/02/1892	Stroud Casuals	A	3-3	Harvey (2), Sherwood	
27/02/1892	Ledbury	A	N/K		
05/03/1892	Swindon Town	A	0-6		
19/03/1892	Saint George (Bristol)	A	1-3	?	
08/10/1892	Dean Close School	A	1-3	?	
15/10/1892	Swindon Saint Mark's	H	4-1	?	
22/10/1892	Cirencester	A	4-1	FB Fielding (2), Matthews (2)	
29/10/1892	Tewkesbury	H	5-0	Sherwood, FB Fielding, own goal, Crofts, ?	
05/11/1892	Ross	H	Won	?	
12/11/1892	Clifton	A	3-3	Robins, Gardner, FB Fielding	
19/11/1892	Winchcombe	A	5-0	Gardner, FB Fielding, Robins, PW Stout, Scott	
26/11/1892	Evesham	H	6-1	FB Fielding (3), Somerville, Sherwood, Robins, PW Stout	
10/12/1892	Ross	H	12-0	FB Fielding (5), Robins (3), Sherwood (3), Gardner	
17/12/1892	Saint George (Bristol)	H	3-0	FB Fielding (2), Gardner	
24/12/1892	Stroud Casuals	H	13-1	Walter Sessions, Robins (2), FB Fielding (3), Powell (2), McLinton (5)	
14/01/1893	Saint George (Bristol)	A	1-1	PW Stout	
04/02/1893	Dean Close School	H	1-2	?	
11/02/1893	Ledbury	H	1-2		
18/02/1893	Ross	A	8-0	FB Fielding (4), Robins (3), Jones	
04/03/1893	Evesham	A	3-2	Robins, Matthews, ?	
11/03/1893	Cirencester	H	7-0	?	
25/03/1893	Clifton	H	12-0	Sherwood (4), FB Fielding (3), Robins (3), Matthews, Jones	
07/10/1893	Swindon Town Athletic	H	3-1	PW Stout (2), FB Fielding	
21/10/1893	Cirencester	H	8-1	Sherwood (2), PW Stout (2), Robins, FB Fielding, AF Fielding, ?	
25/11/1893	Cirencester	H	5-0	?	

[435]

FRIENDLIES

09/12/1893	Dean Close School	A	1-2	?	
26/12/1893	Evesham Wanderers	A	4-3	?	
03/02/1894	Dean Close School	H	13-2	Sherwood (4), FB Fielding (4), AF Fielding (2), Scott, FM Stout, Cragg	
29/09/1894	Dean Close School	H	5-1	PW Stout, AF Fielding, Sherwood (2), ?	
13/10/1894	Dean Close School	A	1-2	Sherwood	
26/12/1894	Bristol South End	A	3-3	FB Fielding, PW Stout, Sherwood	1200
21/09/1895	Cheltenham	H	3-1	AF Fielding, Clutterbuck, Sherwood	
26/12/1895	Bristol South End	A	1-4	James	500
27/12/1895	Bedminster	A	2-1	FB Fielding, Sherwood	850
28/12/1895	Cheltenham	A	5-0	FB Fielding, Sherwood, Sewell, Scott, AF Fielding	
1895/1896	Bristol South End Wednesday	?	5-2	Wright (2), FB Fielding (2), AF Fielding	
10/10/1896	Tewkesbury Abbey	H	0-2		
17/10/1896	Ross Town	A	1-4	Stephens	
24/10/1896	Stroud	A	1-2	?	
31/10/1896	Wotton-Under-Edge	H	2-1	Sabin, Harris	
07/11/1896	Chalford	H	1-1	Arkell	
14/11/1896	Dean Close School	H	2-1	Arkell (2)	
21/11/1896	Wycliffe College	A	N/K		
05/12/1896	Cheltenham	H	2-0	Roberts, James	
12/12/1896	Price Walkers	H	0-1		
16/01/1897	Cheltenham	A	0-2		
06/02/1897	Price Walkers	H	1-2	Roberts	
13/02/1897	Cirencester	H	0-2		
20/02/1897	Dean Close School	A	N/K		
27/02/1897	Ross Town	H	1-2	Craggs	
27/03/1897	Wycliffe Collge	H	N/K		
09/10/1897	Wotton-Under-Edge	A	0-0		
16/10/1897	Bridstow	A	N/K		
23/10/1897	Gordon Wanderers	H	N/K		
06/11/1897	Stroud	H	3-2	Lane (2), Porter	
11/12/1897	Dean Close School	A	5-0	Arkell (3), Lane or Saunders, AF Fielding	
18/12/1897	Cheltenham	A	3-1	?	
08/01/1898	Stroud	A	7-2	Arkell (2), Porter, AF Fielding (2), Saunders, ?	
19/02/1898	Dean Close School	H	4-0	Beard (2), Saunders, own goal	
12/03/1898	Cirencester Royal Agricultural College	H	4-0	Oakey (2), Collins, Lane	
19/03/1898	Gordon Wanderers	A	3-0	Collins, own goal, ?	
01/10/1898	Dean Close School	A	2-0	AF Fielding, ?	
26/11/1898	Wycliffe College	H	4-0	?	
25/03/1899	Brimscombe	A	4-1	Long (2), AF Fielding, Rust	
30/09/1899	Dean Close School	A	2-1	Stock, Porter	
04/11/1899	Saint Michael's	H	0-1		
22/09/1900	Berkeley	A	9-1	?	
06/10/1900	Tewkesbury Abbey	A	2-3	?	
13/10/1900	Cheltenham Town	A	3-2	Wakefield, FT Rust, ?	
20/09/1902	Stonehouse	A	2-1	Rust (2)	
04/10/1902	Brimscombe	H	5-1	Parker, Eddowes, ?	
11/10/1902	Tewkesbury Abbey	A	1-2	Rust	
18/10/1902	Worcester Nondescripts	A	7-3	Romans (3), Parker (2), AF Fielding, Arkell	
25/10/1902	Wycliffe College	A	4-1	?	
08/11/1902	Tewkesbury Abbey	H	3-0	AF Fielding, Parker, Rust	
29/11/1902	Cirencester Town	A	4-1	?	
24/01/1903	Worcester Nondescripts	H	2-0	?	
31/01/1903	Cirencester Town	H	5-0	?	
14/02/1903	Brimscombe	A	2-2	Rust, ?	
19/09/1903	Cheltenham Town	A	0-2		
03/10/1903	Ross Town	A	7-2	FT Rust (5), AF Fielding, Parker	
31/10/1903	Dursley	A	4-1	Eddowes, FT Rust (3)	
09/01/1904	Brimscombe	A	7-1	?	
29/09/1906	Saint Paul's United	A	1-2	W Smith	
13/10/1906	Saint Paul's Training College	A	1-0	Baldwin	
20/10/1906	Swindon Amateurs	H	5-2	Haddon (2), Squier (3)	
27/10/1906	Chepstow Saint Mary's	A	1-2	?	
10/11/1906	Dursley	H	8-1	Squier (4), Haddon (2), Crouch (2)	
22/12/1906	Swindon Town Reserves	A	0-2		
12/01/1907	Brimscombe	H	2-1	Wilfred Nicholls (2)	
26/01/1907	Swindon Town Reserves	H	4-5	Squier, H Smith (2), Haddon	
16/03/1907	Swindon Amateurs	A	3-1	?	
30/03/1907	Brimscombe	A	1-1	Boughton	
13/04/1907	Rest of Cheltenham & District League	A	2-1	AJ Carter, Kent	
21/09/1907	Swindon Town Reserves	A	0-3		3000
05/10/1907	Saint Paul's Training College	A	3-2	Squier, Turner, Lucas	
19/10/1907	Swindon Town Reserves	H	0-1		
07/12/1907	Bristol City Reserves	A	2-3	Turner, Squier	
14/12/1907	Dursley	A	6-1	own goal, Squier (2), Lucas, Smith (2)	
28/12/1907	Bristol City Reserves	H	1-5	Harris	
18/01/1908	Cheltenham Town	H	1-0	Turner	
04/04/1908	Cheltenham Training College	H	1-4	Davy	
20/04/1908	Rest of North Gloucestershire League	N	3-3	Carter, Harris, Kent	Played at Sharpness
11/09/1908	Swindon Town Reserves	A	1-7	Squier	
18/09/1908	Brimscombe	A	3-3	Squier, Watts (2)	
25/09/1908	Colwall	H	3-2	Squier (3)	

FRIENDLIES

Date	Opponent		Score	Scorers	
10/10/1908	Stroud	A	2-2	Carter, Watts	
17/10/1908	Colwall	A	0-5		
31/10/1908	Saint Paul's Training College	H	4-5	W Smith, Watts (2,1 pen), Parsons	
26/12/1908	Tewkesbury Town	A	2-0	Harris (2)	
09/01/1909	Swindon Town Reserves	H	2-3	Jarman, Carter	
27/03/1909	Saint Paul's Training College	A	N/K		
10/04/1909	Tewkesbury Town	A	2-2	Watts (pen), Davy	
17/04/1909	Rest of North Gloucestershire League	N	2-3	Lucas, Carter	Played at Sharpness
17/03/1910	Swindon Town Reserves	A	1-4	Jarman	
02/04/1910	Swindon Town Reserves	H	2-3	Kent, Jarman	
20/09/1913	Leckhampton	A	N/K		
27/09/1913	Hartpury	A	N/K		
11/10/1913	Wycliffe College	A	2-10	?	
25/10/1913	Marling School	A	N/K		
22/11/1913	Saint Catharine's	?	2-0	Danks (2)	
17/01/1914	Leckhampton	H	2-2	Danks, Mills	
31/01/1914	Saint George's United	A	2-2	?	
14/02/1914	Wycliffe College	H	N/K		
28/02/1914	Ryecroft	A	0-2		
27/09/1919	Paper Mills	A	N/K		
04/10/1919	Hartpury	H	N/K		
11/10/1919	Churchdown	H	1-0	Probyn	
18/10/1919	Saint Catharine's	A	N/K		
25/10/1919	Westgate	H	1-4	Allen	
01/11/1919	Newnham	H	3-3	PH Crabtree, HR Crabtree, Horne	
08/11/1919	Cheltenham Y.M.C.A.	A	N/K		
15/11/1919	Atlas 'B'	H	4-0	Allen (2), Mills, Blandford	
22/11/1919	Sissons	H	4-1	PH Crabtree (2), Horne, Probyn	
06/12/1919	Hartpury	A	0-0		
13/12/1919	Technical Schools	H	7-1	Horne (3), Blandford (2), Mills, Bayliss	
20/12/1919	Atlas 'B'	H	N/K		
03/01/1920	Hartpury	H	4-0	PH Crabtree (2), Allen (2)	
10/01/1920	Saint Catherine's	H	N/K		
17/01/1920	Frampton	H	3-0	HR Crabtree (2), Allen	
24/01/1920	Churchdown	A	N/K		
07/02/1920	Paper Mills	H	1-0	PH Crabtree	
21/02/1920	Baptist Free Church	A	N/K		
20/03/1920	Longford & Twigworth	A	1-1	Jones	
27/03/1920	Newnham	A	1-2	Price	
06/11/1920	Cheltenham Town	H	N/K		
11/12/1920	Churcham	H	N/K		
18/12/1920	Longford & Twigworth	H	2-3	?	
01/01/1921	Staverton	H	5-1	Ford (2), Woodger, Beard, own goal	
08/01/1921	Newent	H	3-3	Woodger (2), Beard	
22/01/1921	Saint Catharine's	A	1-3	?	
29/01/1921	Powell Lane's	A	0-2		
19/03/1921	Wycliffe College	A	N/K		
10/09/1921	Longford & Twigworth	A	0-2		
01/10/1921	Cinderford Steam Mills	H	1-1	Hill	
08/10/1921	Wycliffe College	H	1-2	Goddard	
15/10/1921	G.W.R. (Great Western Railway?)	H	3-0	Hill, Woodger, Goddard	
29/10/1921	Newent	A	2-0	Tomlinson, Jarman	
17/12/1921	Upton Saint Leonards	A	1-1	Hall	
14/01/1922	Saint Peter (Cheltenham)	A	3-2	Clarke (2), Tomlinson	
28/01/1922	Newent	H	2-2	Surman, own goal	
04/02/1922	Wycliffe College	A	1-2	Bassett	
11/02/1922	Cinderford Steam Mills	A	Lost		
11/03/1922	Gloucester City Albion	?	Drew		
18/03/1922	Cheltenham Town II	H	5-0	Surman (2), Beddis, Woodger, Clarke	
15/04/1922	Upton Saint Leonards	H	2-1	Norcott, Ford	
22/04/1922	Cheltenham Saint Mary	A	5-1	Surman (2), Tomlinson, Jarman, Norcott	
09/09/1922	Longford & Twigworth	H	4-0	Surman (2), Norcott, Beddis	
14/09/1922	Gloucester YMCA Thursday Team	H	2-0	Surman, Hollingworth	
30/09/1922	Newent	A	1-0	Surman	
14/10/1922	Newent	H	4-2	Surman, Tomlinson (pen), Doel, Malpass	
08/12/1923	Brimscombe	A	2-1	Collins (2)	
29/08/1925	Hereford	?	5-3	Ringrose (2), Edwards, Tucker, Bailey	
24/10/1925	West Bromwich Albion Reserves	H	1-11	Alder	2000
14/11/1925	Saint Paul's Training College	H	2-2	Murdin, Alder	
28/12/1925	Cheltenham Town	H	12-2	Edwards (5), Perks (3), Burton, Tucker, Malpass, Hamer	
13/02/1926	Swindon Victoria	H	4-1	Edwards (2), Ringrose, Perks	400
29/04/1926	Bristol City Reserves	H	1-3	Edwards	2000
01/05/1926	Lovells Athletic	H	N/K		
06/09/1926	Cardiff City Reserves	H	1-2	Aubrey	
16/09/1926	Birmingham Reserves	H	4-8	Ringrose (2), Perks, Marler	
18/09/1926	Ross Town	A	4-1	?	
25/09/1926	Cardiff Corinthians	H	2-3	Perks (2)	
02/10/1926	Usk Town	A	5-2	Edwards (3), Marler (2)	
16/10/1926	Bristol City Reserves	H	0-5		
23/10/1926	West Bromwich Albion Reserves	H	1-5	Ringrose	
30/10/1926	Swindon Corinthians	A	Drew		
06/11/1926	Swindon Corinthians	H	2-2	Edwards, Collins	
13/11/1926	Saint Paul's Training College	A	2-4	Edwards, Burton	
20/11/1926	Sharpness	A	0-7		
27/11/1926	Sneyd Park	H	1-8	Edwards	

[437]

FRIENDLIES

04/12/1926	Saltley College	A	5-1	Perks (4), Gibson		
18/12/1926	Hereford United Reserves	H	7-3	Perks (5), Ringrose, Marler		
28/12/1926	Monmouth County	H	1-1	?		
15/01/1927	Cardiff University	H	3-1	DL Kibble, Ringrose, Marler		
19/02/1927	Caerleon College	H	6-2	Marler (2), Ringrose, Edwards (2), own goal		
05/03/1927	Usk Town	H	10-4	Collins (2), Tucker (2), Aubrey (2), May (3), Roche		
24/03/1927	Caerleon College	A	4-3	Perks (pen), Aubrey, Burton (2)		
13/04/1927	Pope's Hill	?	N/K			
19/04/1927	Lovells Athletic	H	0-2			
28/04/1927	Cheltenham Town	H	1-1	Stevens		
30/04/1927	Bristol Rovers	H	N/K			
01/09/1927	Cinderford Town	?	4-0	Mace (2), Marler, HF Kibble		
03/09/1927	Cardiff City Reserves	?	1-1	?	1000	
29/10/1927	Rodborough Old Boys	?	4-2	?		
19/11/1927	Saint Paul's College	H	3-5	DL Kibble, Monks, Williams		
03/12/1927	Cardiff University	H	2-1	Monks, S Alder		
27/12/1927	Ledbury Town	?	N/K			
28/01/1928	Tewkesbury Town	?	0-0			
28/04/1928	Tottenham Hotspur Reserves	H	3-3	Ringrose, Marler, Brain		
03/05/1028	Pick of the North Gloucestershire Thursday League	H	2-2	?		
08/09/1928	Ledbury Town	H	N/K			
22/09/1928	Chalford	A	3-4	?		
29/09/1928	Monmouth Training College	H	5-0	Marler (2), ?		
13/10/1928	Monmouth Training College	A	1-3	PK Alder		
26/12/1928	Pontypool	?	5-1	?		
29/03/1929	Ely United	H	2-2	Tingle, Marler		
01/04/1929	Llanelly Blwch Stars	H	4-2	Marler (2), Tingle, Ringrose		
20/04/1929	Cardiff City Reserves	H	4-5	?		
07/09/1929	West Bromwich Albion Reserves	H	0-8			
28/09/1929	Monmouth Training College	H	2-1	?		
19/10/1929	Cardiff Corinthians	H	3-3	AFT Murdock (2), Applin		
26/12/1929	District XI	H	3-1	?		
29/03/1930	Cardiff Corinthians	A	2-3	S Alder, Harrison		
18/04/1930	Ely United	H	2-0	Dee, Manders		
21/04/1930	Bristol Tramways	H	4-2	?		
05/05/1930	Cardiff Amateurs	H	3-1	?		
04/10/1930	Saint Paul's Training College	A	1-4	?		
11/10/1930	Cardiff Corinthians	H	2-2	?		
15/11/1930	Monmouth Training College	H	6-1	Taylor (4), Blackhouse, Causon		
26/12/1930	Weston-Super-Mare	H	2-0	?		
03/04/1931	Old Wulfrunians	H	3-0	AFT Murdock, Causon, Dee		
06/04/1931	Cardiff Fairoak	H	9-3	Finch, Taylor, Causon, ?		
18/04/1931	Lovells Athletic	H	3-3	Causon (2), Finch		
25/04/1931	Cardiff Amateurs	H	N/K			
30/04/1931	Brimscombe	H	N/K			Benefit for HF Maynall (reserve player)
02/05/1931	Weston-Super-Mare	A	N/K			
26/09/1931	Pope's Hill	A	2-2	?		
25/03/1932	Old Wulfrunians	H	5-1	?		
28/03/1932	Cardiff Fairoak	H	6-2	Dee (2), Causon (3), Applin		
26/12/1932	Purton Town	H	N/K			
27/12/1932	Gloucester City Albion	H	N/K			
14/04/1933	Stourbridge Old Edwardians	H	4-0	?		
17/04/1933	Wolverhampton Amateurs	H	2-4	?		
30/04/1934	Rest of League	H	2-0	Causon (2)		
02/10/1934	Brockworth Aerodrome	H	4-2	C Jones (3), Drew		
22/04/1935	Ledbury Town	H	2-4	Hartshorne (2)		
07/09/1935	Weston-Super-Mare	H	1-0	?		First game at Longlevens
09/05/1936	Cheltenham Town	H	7-0	Harris (2), Shelley (2), Edwards, Drew, Cox		
26/12/1936	Cardiff City 'A'	H	4-1	?		
08/05/1937	Swindon Town	A	1-0	Drew		Swindon Victoria Hospital Cup
02/09/1937	Swindon Victoria	H	4-3	Moore, Edwards (2), Stoles		
04/09/1937	Cardiff City 'A'	H	5-0	McNeil, Weaver (2), Gwatkin, Stoles	1000	
23/10/1937	Bristol University	H	2-3	Weaver (2)		
25/12/1937	Hereford United	H	2-2	Gwatkin, Drew		
05/05/1938	Bristol City XI	H	3-2	Gwatkin (2), Leach	1300	
22/10/1938	Bristol University	H	4-0	Riley, Taylor, Weaver (2)		
25/02/1939	Cheltenham Town	A	1-2	Gwatkin	700-800	
30/09/1939	Cheltenham Town	H	8-1	Edwards, ?		
07/10/1939	Lovells Athletic	H	N/K			
18/11/1939	Cardiff Corinthians	H	2-1	Beale, Gwatkin		
02/12/1939	Birmingham	H	4-5	Beale (4)		
09/12/1939	Bristol Aero	H	5-2	Beale (2,1 pen), Parris (2), Glaister		
13/01/1940	Ledbury Town	H	N/K			
10/02/1940	Bristol University	H	11-0	Farrelly (4), Roy Davis, Parks, J Landells, Gwatkin, Parris (2), own goal		
02/03/1940	R.H.A. (Royal Horse Artillery?)	H	3-0	Parris (2,1 pen), Farrelly		
28/09/1940	Naval XI	H	2-4	Poxton (2)		
05/10/1940	Naval XI	H	3-10	Edwards (2), K Griffiths		
12/10/1940	Royal Air Force XI	H	2-8	Stoles, Wilson		
19/10/1940	Newent	H	5-3	K Griffiths (3), Wilkins, D Kibble		
26/10/1940	Royal Air Force XI	H	1-1	Reeves		
02/11/1940	Royal Air Force XI	H	3-2	Hanson, Bevan, Wayman		

FRIENDLIES

Date	Opponent		Score	Scorers	Att.	Notes
09/11/1940	Royal Air Force Observer Training School XI	H	2-2	Wilkins (2)		
16/11/1940	Sunningend	H	5-2	Bevan (2), Stoles, Parris, Johns		
23/11/1940	Royal Air Force XI	H	2-3	McDonough (pen), Roy Davis		
30/11/1940	Royal Air Force Observer Training School XI	H	2-3	Roy Davis, Parris		
07/12/1940	Royal Air Force XI	H	1-2	Parris		
14/12/1940	Gloucestershire Regiment XI	H	3-6	?		
21/12/1940	Ledbury Town	H	1-5	Stoles		
04/01/1941	Gloucester Police	H	8-1	Stoles (2), McDonough (2), Hanson, Parris (3)		
18/01/1941	Army XI	H	N/K			
25/01/1941	Combined University of Bristol/Royal Naval College	H	5-0	Reeves, Wilkins (2), McDonough, Hanson		
01/02/1941	Gloucester Aero	H	5-2	Stoles, Wilkins (2), Parris, Hanson		
08/02/1941	Sunningend	H	4-4	Hanson (3), K Griffiths		
15/02/1941	Brimscombe Wanderers	H	7-4	Parris, Wilkins, K Griffiths (3), McDonough (pen), Waite		
22/02/1941	Saint Paul's Training College	H	3-2	K Griffiths (2), Hanson		
01/03/1941	Royal Air Force XI	H	1-7	K Griffiths		
08/03/1941	Royal Air Force XI	H	10-0	K Griffiths (4), Wilkins (2), Roy Davis (pen), Parris (3)		
15/03/1941	Departmental XI	H	1-2	McDonough (pen)		
22/03/1941	Royal Air Force XI	H	2-7	Reeves, Parris		
29/03/1941	Royal Air Force XI	H	3-3	Reeves, K Griffiths, Redwood		
05/04/1941	Army XI	H	0-0			
19/04/1941	Royal Air Force Observer Navigation School	H	6-3	Redwood (3), Traynor, Parris (2)		
26/04/1941	Army XI	H	1-3	K Griffiths		
03/05/1941	Army XI	H	6-1	K Griffiths, Wilkins, Reeves, Stoles, Parris (2)		
10/05/1941	Army XI	H	4-3	Reeves (2), Parris (2)		
17/05/1941	Royal Air Force XI	H	5-1	Reeves, Roy Davis (2), Parris (2)		
24/05/1941	Army Transport XI	H	1-7	Parris		
31/05/1941	Army XI	H	N/K			
30/08/1941	Naval XI	H	2-2	Parris, Gwatkin		
06/09/1941	Naval XI	H	3-6	Cassidy, K Griffiths, Anderson		
27/12/1941	Army XI	H	6-1	Wilkins (2), Carter (2), K Griffiths, Wilkins		
14/04/1942	Royal Army Service Corps Ashchurch	H	N/K			Played during an alert
18/04/1942	Kemble	H	3-1	Parris (3,1 pen)		
25/04/1942	South Cerney	H	N/K			
02/05/1942	Naval XI	H	4-4	Parris (2), Jenkins, Wilkins		
17/10/1942	N.F.S. (National Fire Service?)	H	16-0	Parris (6,1 pen), Burnett (4,1 pen), Ball, Anderson (pen), Webb (3), Stoles		
21/11/1942	Army Ordnance XI	H	5-3	Burnett (4), Reeves		
26/12/1942	Rotol AFC	H	6-1	Burnett (4), Webb, Stoles		
23/01/1943	Gloucester Aircraft Company	H	8-0	Reeves (4), Webb (2), Stoles, Wilkins		
20/02/1943	Royal Air Force XI	H	4-1	Wilkins, Stoles, Morris (2)		
10/04/1943	Royal Air Force XI	H	2-1	Stevenson (pen), Levey		
18/09/1946	Royal Air Force Records	H	N/K			
19/10/1946	Cardiff City Reserves	H	3-1	Cole, Dean, Sweeting		
17/05/1947	Combined Country XI	A	3-2	?		Gorsley's player benefit
10/04/1948	Tottenham Hotspur XI	H	2-2	Griffiths, Cowley	1500	
12/02/1949	Weston-Super-Mare	A	4-4	Boyd (2), ?		
18/03/1950	Charlton Athletic	H	0-3		2100	
30/08/1950	Forest Green Rovers	A	4-4	?	500	Official opening of FGR new changing room
10/03/1951	Coventry City XI	H	3-2	Robertson, Canavan (pen), Jenkins	1000	
20/08/1951	Cowley's XI	H	4-7	Nicholls (3), Canavan (pen)	1000	Eddie Cowley's Benefit
22/12/1951	Stonehouse	A	3-1	Grubb (pen), Wright, Barnfield		
19/01/1952	Cheltenham Town	A	1-4	Wright		
05/04/1952	Chelsea Reserves	H	2-0	Canavan (2,1 pen)		
29/04/1952	Cardiff City XI	H	1-1	Colenutt	1300	Gus Stow's Benefit
27/09/1952	Stonehouse Reserves	H	0-3			
08/10/1952	Southern Command	H	3-1	Price (2), Pullen	5000	First game under floodlights
14/10/1952	Swindon Town	H	0-2		5500	
27/10/1952	Tottenham Hotspur	H	2-1	Myers, Price	10500	
05/11/1952	Crystal Palace	H	2-2	Pullen, Price	4000	
11/11/1952	Torquay United	H	1-2	Wright	3000	
17/11/1952	Brentford	H	0-3		7000	
26/01/1953	Leyton Orient	H	1-4	Haines	1650	
31/01/1953	Street	A	2-2	Etheridge, ?		
02/02/1953	Queen's Park Rangers	H	2-2	Haines, Friel	1527	
07/02/1953	Reading Reserves	H	5-1	Haines (2), Etheridge, Myers, own goal		
09/02/1953	Cheltenham Town	H	5-1	Haines (2), Friel (2), Etheridge	643	Part of Ron Coltman deal
16/02/1953	East Fife	H	0-6		6000	
09/03/1953	Watford	H	2-3	Canavan, ?	1400	
11/03/1953	Cheltenham Town	A	3-3	Pullen, Price (2)		Part of Ron Coltman deal
16/03/1953	Gloucestershire Constabulary	H	5-0	Etheridge (4), Townsend	685	
23/03/1953	Poole Town	N	5-3	Pullen (2), Myers (2), Haines		Played at Plymouth
27/10/1953	Brentford	H	1-3	Etheridge	3500	
02/11/1953	East Fife	H	2-4	Own goal, Ross (pen)		
03/02/1954	Arsenal Reserves	H	2-2	Millar, Rutherford		
22/02/1954	ESV Austria-Innsbruck (Austria)	H	3-1	Tredgett (pen), Rutherford, Etheridge	3700	
22/03/1954	RAF Innsworth	H	3-2	Perkins (2), Barnfield		
22/11/1954	Portsmouth	H	2-4	RJ Etheridge (2)	5000	
10/01/1955	Ex-Gloucester City	H	2-2	Lawrence, J Rutherford		Stan Myer's Benefit
14/03/1955	All Star XI	H	4-2	Friel, Myers, Coldray, RJ Etheridge		Frank Tredgett's Benefit
22/03/1955	Newport County	H	1-1	Myers		

FRIENDLIES

Date	Opponent	H/A	Score	Scorers	Att.	Notes
19/11/1955	Tottenham Hotspur Reserves	H	0-4			
04/01/1956	RAF Home Command	H	3-2	T Rutherford, Friel, Dunbar		
16/04/1956	Portsmouth	H	1-2	JDJ Rutherford	6000	
15/10/1956	Bristol City	H	1-1	Rutherford		
26/01/1957	Leicester City Reserves	H	4-5	Dunbar, Coldray, Rutherford, Myers		
25/02/1958	Manager All Star XI	H	0-3			Ron Coltman, Phil Friel & Archie Proudfoot Benefit
11/11/1958	RAF Home Command	H	N/K			
07/12/1958	Salisbury	H	0-3			
10/03/1959	Barrow	H	3-0	Weston, McNiven, Gallagher		
14/03/1960	Football League XI	H	3-4	Horlick, Coldray, Etheridge	1300	Stan Myers & Rob Coldray Benefit
05/04/1961	RAF Technical Training Command	H	2-2	Reynolds, Hamilton		
14/08/1962	Swindon Town	A	2-2	Humphrey, Day		
26/09/1962	Ex-Claret Association	H	4-0	own goal, Bell (pen), Horlick, Weston	1000	
12/08/1964	Cheltenham Town	A	0-5			Public Trial Match
07/08/1965	Cinderford Town	H	4-2	Grant (2), D Wells, Crichton		
14/08/1965	Evesham United	H	1-1	B Wells		
18/08/1965	Cheltenham Town	A	1-1	Crichton		
11/08/1966	Weston-Super-Mare	A	2-5	Grant, D Wells		
07/08/1967	Trowbridge Town	A	1-4	Archibald		
14/08/1967	Kidderminster Harriers	A	0-5			
29/07/1968	Abergavenny Thursdays	A	1-1	Fraser		
04/08/1968	Minsterworth	A	5-1	Stevens, Fraser (2), McCool, Boyle		
05/08/1968	Coventry City XI	H	1-1	McCool	1800	
07/08/1968	Kidderminster Harriers	H	2-2	Ferns, McInnes		
24/07/1969	Sharpness	A	3-1	Stevens (2), Fraser		
28/07/1969	Cheltenham Town	A	2-4	Fraser (2)		
02/08/1969	Gloucester Y.M.C.A.	A	6-1	McIntosh, Anderson (2), Rodgerson, Fraser, Stevens		
05/08/1969	Abergavenny Thursdays	A	2-0	Stevens, Fraser		
02/08/1970	Forest Green Rovers	A	4-3	Hurford, McCool (2), Rice		
04/08/1970	Frampton United	A	6-1	Hudd (2), Williams (4)	200	
06/08/1970	Huntley	A	10-0	Holder (3,1 pen), Hudd (2), McCool (2), Rice, own goals (2)		
11/08/1970	Sharpness	A	2-0	McCool, Ferns		
12/08/1970	Cheltenham Town	A	2-2	Williams, Ferns		
07/08/1971	Birmingham City XI	H	2-1	Biggart, Meredith		
09/08/1971	Shrewsbury Town	H	1-3	Blackburn	471	
11/08/1971	Frampton United	A	5-0	Coburn (2), Ferns, Hargreaves, Meredith		
31/07/1972	Newport County	H	3-3	Stevens (2), J Whitehouse (pen)	519	
03/08/1972	Hereford United Reserves	H	4-0	Stevens (2), Biggart, J Whitehouse	585	
05/08/1972	Kington Town	A	3-2	Vale, J Whitehouse (2)		
07/08/1972	Frampton United	A	9-2	J Whitehouse (3), McCool (2,1 pen), Stevens (2), Vale (2)		
02/05/1973	Hereford United	H	1-1	Croft		Bobby McCool's Testimonial (abandoned 71 mins)
07/08/1973	Longlevens Star	H	3-0	Foxwell (2), Hargreaves		
06/08/1974	Forest Green Rovers	A	1-4	own goal		
08/08/1974	Ferndale Athletic	H	0-1			
13/08/1974	Sharpness	A	0-1			
08/05/1975	Wolverhampton Wanderers	H	2-7	?	6500	Combined City/Robins XI. Martin Millyard Memorial
07/08/1975	Viney Hill	A	3-0	Wood, C Gardner, Cooper		
1976/1977	Malvern Town	A	N/K			
16/08/1977	Cirencester Town	A	2-1	Evans, Pocock		
14/02/1978	Thornbury Town	?	10-1	?		
08/05/1978	Newport County	H	6-1	Turner (2), Foxwell (3), Evans		Charity Match
14/05/1978	Shortwood United	A	7-5	Wood (3), Turner (2), Scarrott (2)		Benefit Match
1977/1978	Frampton United	A	0-4			
1977/1978	Moreton Town	A	1-1	?		
29/07/1978	Cwmbran Town	H	3-2	Brake (2), Wood		
01/08/1978	Hereford United	H	3-1	Evans (2), Turner	250	
08/08/1978	Southampton XI	H	2-0	Foxwell, Evans		John Bishop Testimonial
12/08/1978	Cardiff City XI	H	3-0	Foxwell, Evans, Brake		
14/08/1978	Swindon Town XI	H	3-1	Foxwell (2), Evans		
01/08/1979	Forest Green Rovers	A	3-2	Turner, Griffin, Paterson		
04/08/1979	Newport County	H	0-5		500	
06/08/1979	Bridgewater Town	A	Drew			
08/08/1979	Sharpness	A	2-0	R Brinkworth, Gardner		James Mills Benefit
11/08/1979	Weymouth	H	3-2	Paterson, Gardner, Griffin	378	
15/08/1979	Newport Corinthians	H	3-0	D Mockridge, Hall, Turner		
07/1980	West Harptree	A	3-2	Lewis, Paterson, Mockridge		
24/07/1980	Yeovil Town	A	1-4	Lewis (pen)		
25/07/1980	Poole Town	A	0-3			
02/08/1980	Hereford United	H	1-2	Burford		
05/08/1980	Bristol Rovers	H	0-3			
07/1981	Yeovil Town	H	N/K			
04/08/1981	Bath City	H	0-1			
08/08/1981	Reading	H	0-4		353	
02/11/1981	Bristol Rovers XI	H	2-1	Stenhouse (2)		
02/01/1982	Barry Town	A	2-1	?		Originally League Game
08/03/1982	Birmingham City	H	P			John Evans Testimonial
24/03/1982	Cardiff City XI	H	2-1	Doyle, Chivers		
07/1982	Dales United	A	2-1	DJ Jones (2)		
31/07/1982	Caerleon	A	N/K			
07/08/1982	Hereford United	H	2-4	Waddle, DE Bruton		
10/08/1982	Westfield	H	3-0	DJ Jones, Williams, Lowe		
14/08/1982	Wolverhampton Wanderers XI	H	2-0	DJ Jones, Cunningham		

FRIENDLIES

23/10/1982	Bristol Saint George	A	6-1	Burford (2), Griffiths (2), DJ Jones, M Bruton		Behind closed doors
21/12/1982	Almondsbury Greenway	A	5-1	Butt (3), DE Bruton (pen), DJ Jones		
04/08/1983	West Bromwich Albion	H	0-1		1500	
10/08/1983	Cwmbran Town	A	4-4	M Bruton (3), DE Bruton		
13/08/1983	Exeter City	H	0-3			
18/08/1983	Aston Villa XI	H	N/K			
06/09/1983	Longlevens	H	2-0	Leitch, Burford (pen)	200	
13/09/1983	Radstock Town	H	2-1	Burford, M Bruton		
20/09/1983	Shortwood United	H	2-1	Gwyther, Burford		
25/10/1983	Newent Town	H	4-0	DE Bruton (2,1 pen), Gwyther, M Bruton		
15/11/1983	Gloucester Sunday League XI	H	2-1	M Bruton, Walker		
13/03/1984	Clevedon Town	A	N/K			
04/08/1984	Cinderford Town	A	2-2	Harding, Vassallo	117	
07/08/1984	Torquay United	H	0-2		252	
11/08/1984	Moreton Town	A	2-1	Trusswell, Casey	112	
14/08/1984	Aston Villa XI	H	1-4	Casey	457	
06/02/1985	Malvern Town	A	2-0	Langford, Duggan		
13/08/1985	Yate Town	A	3-0	Truswell, Vassallo, own goal		
15/08/1985	Shortwood United	H	1-3	Truswell		
20/08/1985	Thornbury Town	A	3-0	?		
05/11/1985	Cinderford Town	H	4-4	?		
09/11/1985	Loughborough Colleges	H	0-0			
29/07/1986	Wotton Rovers	A	2-1	Baddock (pen), Trusswell		
02/08/1986	Malvern Town	A	1-1	Vassallo		
06/08/1986	Alvechurch	A	1-0	Johnson		
09/08/1986	Leicester City	H	1-6	Johnson	1760	Official opening of Meadow Park
12/08/1986	Cardiff City	H	0-1			
05/11/1986	Oxford United	H	0-3			
08/11/1986	Highgate United	A	3-0	Baddock (2), Westerberg		
07/01/1987	Walsall Reserves	H	2-0	?		
01/1987	Sharpness	H	1-1	own goal		
21/07/1987	Arsenal	H	0-6		3952	Barrie Vassallo's Benefit
25/07/1987	Fairford Town	A	4-0	Foxwell, Johnson (2), own goal		
28/07/1987	Hereford United	H	0-2		461	
30/07/1987	West Bromwich Albion	H	1-2	Baddock	451	
01/08/1987	Hungerford Town	A	0-2			
06/08/1987	Swindon Town	H	1-2	Baddock	638	
08/08/1987	Malvern Town	A	2-2	Beacham (2)		
12/08/1987	Ellwood	A	2-3	Foxwell, Beacham		
15/08/1987	Thornbury Town	A	18-1	Green (4), Baddock (4), Johnson (7), Harris (3)		
18/08/1987	Wotton Rovers	H	5-1	Baddock, Johnson (4)		
30/07/1988	Tuffley Rovers	A	4-1	Talboys, Penny, Johnson (2)		
01/08/1988	Kidderminster Harriers	H	2-0	Green, Foxwell	331	
03/08/1988	Cardiff City	H	2-0	Hyde, Noble	506	
06/08/1988	Westbury United	A	5-2	Talboys (2), Hughes, Morrison, Andrews		
09/08/1988	Hereford United	H	0-0		342	
11/08/1988	Norwich City	H	1-3	own goal	724	
13/08/1988	Coventry City	H	0-2		1313	
25/07/1989	Worrall Hill	A	8-2	Townsend (4), Noble, Talboys, Bradder, Morrison		
26/07/1989	Burnley	H	3-1	Bradder, Talboys (2)	588	
29/07/1989	Coventry City	H	2-4	Bradder, Noble	1359	
01/08/1989	Fairford Town	A	0-0			
03/08/1989	Northampton Town	H	3-4	Townsend, Morrison (2)	659	
05/08/1989	Clevedon Town	A	4-0	Hedges, Williams, Penny, Talboys		
08/08/1989	Old Georgians	H	7-2	Chandler, Morrison (2), Noble (2), Penny, Talboys		
15/08/1989	Paulton Rovers	A	6-1	Bradder, Chandler, Townsend, Talboys (2), Tyler		
05/10/1989	Stroud	A	6-2	Noble, Talboys, Hyde (2), Williams, Harris	611	Doug Foxwell's Testimonial
26/07/1990	Barnet	H	3-2	Withey, Noble, Lander	408	
31/07/1990	AFC Newport	H	3-3	Abbley, Withey, Meacham	524	
02/08/1990	Cinderford Town	A	4-3	Withey, Brown, Meacham, Talboys		
04/08/1990	Millwall	H	2-0	Talboys (pen), Chandler	550	
07/08/1990	Newcastle United	H	0-2		1367	
09/08/1990	Bristol Rovers	H	0-4		733	
15/08/1990	Oxford United	H	2-2	Withey, Hancocks	521	
01/11/1990	Dinamo Minsk (Belarus)	H	1-4	Browning (pen)	851	
20/11/1990	Bristol City	H	2-4	Meacham, Browning	311	
22/07/1991	Queen's Park Rangers	H	0-1		1756	
26/07/1991	Napereuli Telavi (Georgia)	A	2-1	Meacham (pen), Freegard	2500	
28/07/1991	Mesxti (Georgia)	A	2-0	Fergusson, Noble	3000	
30/07/1991	Shevardeni Tbilisi (Georgia)	A	2-2	Meacham (pen), Fergusson (pen)	1000	
02/08/1991	Bristol Rovers	H	2-4	Talboys, Meacham (pen)	570	
05/08/1991	Bristol City	H	1-5	Freegard	614	
07/08/1991	Gornik Zabrze (Poland)	H	0-3		471	
10/08/1991	Torquay United	H	1-5	Meacham (pen)	392	
13/08/1991	Aston Villa	H	1-2	Hughes	1379	
17/09/1991	Almondsbury Picksons	H	5-2	Penny, Hackett, Eaton (2), Meacham (pen)	100	
03/12/1991	Bristol Rovers	H	1-1	Eaton	187	
25/02/1992	Cinderford Town	H	3-1	Hughes, Hancocks, own goal	89	
29/02/1992	Stroud	H	0-0		180	
25/07/1992	Moreton Town	A	3-1	Bayliss, Eaton, own goal		
28/07/1992	Bristol City	H	2-5	Eaton, Noble (pen)	500	
30/07/1992	Bristol Rovers	H	1-5	Boyland	380	
01/08/1992	Ellwood	A	4-1	Ackland, Bayliss, Jones, Dixon		
04/08/1992	Cinderford Town	A	2-1	Darlaston, Callinan	148	
08/08/1992	AFC Newport	H	3-0	Noble (pen), Ciany, Darlaston	345	
10/08/1992	Clevedon Town	A	3-2	Bywater, Eaton (2)	212	

FRIENDLIES

12/08/1992	Bishop's Cleeve	A	2-1	Bayliss, Ciany	
16/08/1992	Kettering Town	H	1-4	Eaton	212
17/11/1992	Moreton Town	A	2-3	Jenkins, Callinan	
24/07/1993	Bristol Rovers	H	1-3	Bayliss	
27/07/1993	Cinderford Town	A	0-0		
07/08/1993	Worrall Hill	A	7-2	Cook (3), Bayliss (3), Johnson	
03/08/1993	Pershore Town	A	3-1	Cook, Bayliss, Baverstock	
07/08/1993	Birmingham City	H	2-2	Callinan, Cook	325
14/08/1993	Ellwood	A	8-3	Cook (4), Bayliss (3), Callinan	
01/02/1994	Abingdon Town	A	N/K		
16/07/1994	Brockworth	A	4-0	Kilgour, Cook, Boden, Harris	
20/07/1994	Cirencester Town	A	6-0	Bird, Cook (2), Boden, Hallam, Callinan	
22/07/1994	Smiths Athletic	A	3-0	Webb, Knight, own goal	
24/07/1994	Swindon Town	H	1-3	Knight	1600
26/07/1994	Forest Green Rovers	A	4-2	Mitchell, Cook, Bayliss (2)	
28/07/1994	Fairford Town	A	3-0	Webb, Bayliss, Mitchell	
30/07/1994	Cinderford Town	A	0-2		300
02/08/1994	Mangotsfield United	A	2-1	Bayliss, Webb	
09/08/1994	Aston Villa	H	1-4	Mitchell	2012	Kevin Willett's Testimonial
11/08/1994	Bishop's Cleeve	A	4-0	Hallam (2), Crowley, Boden	
16/08/1994	Everton	H	1-1	Bayliss	2505
20/07/1995	Hereford United	H	1-1	Warner	
22/07/1995	Yeovil Town	H	0-0		
24/07/1995	Bristol Rovers	H	1-4	Knight	
29/07/1995	Cirencester Town	A	4-0	Warner, Holmes, Knight, Hallam	
01/08/1995	Shrewsbury Town	H	1-1	?	
03/08/1995	Bishop's Cleeve	A	8-1	Hallam, Warner (2), Adams (2), Mitchell, Holmes, Kilgour	
05/08/1995	Cambridge United	H	3-0	Portway, Adebowale, Hallam	
07/08/1995	Real Oviedo (Spain)	H	0-4		
08/08/1995	Tuffley Rovers	A	6-1	Hallam (2), Knight, Holmes, Warner, Rouse	
12/08/1995	Saint Marks	H	4-0	Holmes, Knight, Adebowale, Hallam	
20/07/1996	Cirencester Town	A	3-1	Holmes, Mardenborough, Watkins (pen)	
25/07/1996	Birmingham City	H	2-3	Watkins, Holmes	1144
27/07/1996	Kidderminster Harriers	H	2-3	Holmes (pen), Watkins	
31/07/1996	Tottenham Hotspur	H	3-1	Thorne, Holmes, Holloway	2712
03/08/1996	Wimbledon	H	1-1	Wright	1000
05/08/1996	Yeovil Town	A	0-0		
19/07/1997	Evesham United	A	1-1	Mings	
22/07/1997	Tuffley Rovers	H	3-1	Fergusson, Mings, Preedy	
24/07/1997	Bristol City XI	H	4-1	Webb, Hoskins (2), Preedy	269
26/07/1997	Barnstaple Town	A	2-2	Mings, Fergusson	
29/07/1997	Hereford United	H	1-4	Milsom	
02/08/1997	Harrow Hill	A	3-0	Cooper, Milsom, Hoskins	
06/08/1997	Chelsea XI	H	2-2	Webb, own goal	1258
09/08/1997	Hednesford Town	H	0-7		270
18/08/1997	Derby County	H	1-5	Burns	1011
05/05/1998	Cheltenham Town	H	N/K		
18/07/1998	Wolverhampton Wanderers	H	3-0	Keeling, Burns, Mings	575
21/07/1998	North Leigh	A	0-1		100
25/07/1998	Bristol Manor Farm	A	1-1	Hemmings	
01/08/1998	Coventry City	H	3-3	Rutter, Keeling, Cairns	614
03/08/1998	Swindon Town	H	0-1		513
08/08/1998	Bristol City Under 21s	H	0-6		212
15/08/1998	Evesham United	A	2-0	Mainwaring (2)	
13/07/1999	Harrow Hill	A	4-1	Barclay, Wyatt, Smith (2)	
14/07/1999	Worrall Hill	A	6-0	Cox (3), GJ Cook, Vittles, ?	
17/07/1999	Kidderminster Harriers	H	3-5	Wyatt, ?	441
20/07/1999	Bristol Rovers	H	0-1		400
23/07/1999	Northampton Town	H	3-1	Niblett, Cox, Chenoweth	
27/07/1999	Hardwicke	A	3-2	Roberts, Fergusson, Cox	
28/07/1999	Highworth Town	A	1-0	Smith	
01/08/1999	Witney Town	A	5-0	Barclay, Tucker, Wyatt, GJ Cook, Cox	
04/08/1999	Broadwell Amateurs	A	4-2	Cairns, Callinan, ?	
07/08/1999	Bristol City Under 21s	H	3-1	Smith, G Thorne, Hackett	
18/07/2000	Brockworth	A	3-0	Cox (3)	
21/07/2000	Manchester United Under 21s	H	4-1	Cox, Rawlins (2), Marshall	435
22/07/2000	Lydney Town	A	5-3	Johnstone, Freeman (2), Cairns, Casey	Combined City/United side
25/07/2000	Tuffley Rovers	H	2-1	Rawlins (2)	
29/07/2000	Clevedon Town	A	0-1		
02/08/2000	Broadwell Amateurs	A	3-2	Bayliss (2), Cox	
05/08/2000	Minehead Town	A	5-1	Rawling (3), Johnstone, Casey	
12/08/2000	Hereford United	H	1-1	Griffiths	
15/08/2000	Gloucester United	H	6-0	Bayliss, Callinan, Griffiths, Cairns (2), Roberts	
21/07/2001	Ellwood	A	2-1	Hoskins, Burns	
25/07/2001	Longford	A	4-1	JS Smith, Randall, Wilkinson, Jenkins	
28/07/2001	Port Talbot Town	A	N/K		
31/07/2001	Bishop's Cleeve	A	2-0	LF Smith, JS Smith	
02/08/2001	Yate Town	H	1-3	Dunton (pen)	
04/08/2001	Frome Town	A	1-1	Hoskins	
08/08/2001	Viney Saint Swithins	A	N/K		
15/07/2002	Army XI	H	2-1	Steadman, Stockley (pen)	
20/07/2002	Brockworth Albion	A	5-0	Hoskins (4), Hampson	
23/07/2002	Harrow Hill	A	2-4	Jenkins, Hoskins	
25/07/2002	Longhope	A	4-0	Howard, Burby, Johnson, Hampson	
27/07/2002	Yeovil Town	H	0-3		

FRIENDLIES

30/07/2002	Bilston Town	A	1-2	Griffiths		
03/08/2002	Bristol City	H	0-1			
09/08/2002	Garden Village	A	1-0	Thompson		
10/08/2002	Port Talbot Town	A	0-2			
13/08/2002	Tuffley Rovers	H	2-1	Mustoe (pen), Jenkins		
12/07/2003	Hardwicke	A	3-1	Griffiths, Wilkinson, Hoskins		
19/07/2003	Brockworth	A	7-0	Hoskins, Smith, Griffiths, Burns, Hemming, Walder (2)		
20/07/2003	Forest Green Rovers	H	2-2	Jeffries, Cox		
22/07/2003	Ellwood	A	4-0	Steadman, Howard, Hoskins, Burby		
26/07/2003	Bath City	H	3-1	Hoskins (2), Jenkins		
01/08/2003	Garden Village	A	3-0	Smith (2), Knight		
02/08/2003	Caldicot Town	A	3-0	Cox (2), Hoskins (pen)		
05/08/2003	Bishop's Cleeve	A	2-0	Hemming, Steadman		
09/08/2003	Weymouth	H	1-2	Hoskins (pen)		
12/08/2003	Chalford	A	4-1	Steadman, Wilkinson, Hoskins, Griffiths		
15/07/2004	Pegasus Juniors	A	2-1	Smith, Rirregah		
17/07/2004	Kidderminster Harriers	H	2-1	Davis, Avery	250	
20/07/2004	Ledbury Town	A	6-0	CD Thompson, Hoskins (2), Stiles, Palmer, Smith		
24/07/2004	West Bromwich Albion	H	1-4	MP Thompson		
27/07/2004	Rochdale	H	1-4	Stiles		
31/07/2004	Newent Town	A	4-0	Stiles, Wilkinson, Knight, CD Thompson		
04/08/2004	Aston Villa	H	0-3			Brian Godfrey's Testimonial
07/08/2004	Garden Village	A	6-0	Griffiths (2), Stiles (2), Smith, Webb		
09/02/2005	Wincanton Athletic	H	N/K			Tsunami Appeal Match
12/07/2005	Cheltenham Civil Service	A	9-0	Davis (2), Kear (3), Lewis (3), Reid		
19/07/2005	Rochdale	H	0-4			
21/07/2005	King's Stanley	A	7-0	Varnham (3), Lewis, Griffiths, Davis, Addis		
23/07/2005	Bristol Manor Farm	A	2-0	Tomkins, Lewis		
26/07/2005	Highworth Town	A	2-0	Lewis (2)		
30/07/2005	Brockworth	A	5-0	CD Thompson, Burns (3), Davis		
03/08/2005	Shortwood United	A	3-0	Addis, Kear (2)		
06/08/2005	Wellington	A	5-1	own goal, Webb, Mustoe, Reid, Randall		
22/10/2005	Cinderford Town	A	4-0	Wilkinson, Corbett, Kear (2)		
24/01/2006	Pegasus Juniors	H	4-0	Randall, Wilkinson, Bevan (2)		
30/01/2006	Forest Green Rovers	H	0-0			
15/02/2006	Abingdon United	H	3-2	Bevan, Randall, Stonehouse		
13/07/2006	Kidderminster Harriers	H	1-5	Corbett	245	
15/07/2006	Rochdale	H	1-2	Welsh	168	
22/07/2006	Slimbridge	A	0-1		172	
25/07/2006	Worcester City	H	0-0		197	
27/07/2006	Bristol City	H	1-3	Hamblin	241	
29/07/2006	Dawlish Town	A	0-1		61	
02/08/2006	Almondsbury Town	A	0-1			
05/08/2006	Newport County	H	1-4	Corbett	307	
11/08/2006	Staunton & Corse	A	14-0	Tomkins, Corbett (3), Wilson, Welsh (2), Harris, Tustain (3), Bevan (3)		
18/10/2006	Royal Air Force XI	H	3-0	Wilkinson, Welsh, Bevan		
11/07/2007	Ledbury Town	A	3-0	Taylor, Hamblin, Pitcher		
17/07/2007	Salisbury City	H	2-2	Taylor, Griffin	242	Last game at Meadow Park
19/07/2007	Cheltenham Saracens	A	3-1	Griffin (2), Bevan	76	
25/07/2007	Frome Town	A	2-2	Richards, Pitcher	103	
27/07/2007	Bath City	A	0-2		295	
04/08/2007	Forest Green Rovers	A	3-3	Pitcher, Sykes, Whittington	464	
07/08/2007	Shortwood United	A	2-0	Whittington, Taylor		
13/08/2007	Quedgeley Wanderers	A	9-0	Welsh (4), Wilkinson, Sykes, Richards, Webb, Rose		
14/07/2008	Cinderford Town	A	1-1	Sykes	150	Dave Wilkinson Benefit
19/07/2008	Pegasus Juniors	A	3-2	Ballinger (2), Sykes	77	
21/07/2008	Witney United	H	5-2	Sykes (pen), Smith, Symons, Bevan, Upcott	120	
26/07/2008	Malvern Town	A	0-0		130	
29/07/2008	Weston-Super-Mare	H	1-1	Ballinger	150	
01/08/2008	Bishop's Cleeve	H	1-2	Symons	70	
08/08/2008	Neath Athletic	A	1-1	Smith	200	
11/08/2008	Longlevens	A	5-0	Allard, Upcott (2), Reid, Nash	100	
22/09/2008	Tuffley Rovers	A	3-0	Sykes (2,1 pen), Ballinger (pen)	100	
14/07/2009	Ledbury Town	A	1-1	Sykes	150	
21/07/2009	Almondsbury Town	A	4-2	Symons, Pitcher (2), J Harris	70	
25/07/2009	Chasetown	H	2-3	Smith, Pitcher	177	
28/07/2009	Paulton Rovers	A	0-0		100	
30/07/2009	Bath City	H	1-2	Pitcher	142	
01/08/2009	Merthyr Tydfil	H	4-1	Morford, Smith, Ballinger, Jones	200	
03/08/2009	Gala Wilton	A	2-0	James, Robinson (pen)	200	

FRIENDLIES

Frank Tredgett's Benefit 14 March 1955 v All Star XI
(Photograph courtesy of Rob Coldray)
Back row – Maurice Tadman (Plymouth Argyle), Phil Gunter (Portsmouth), Eric Kerfoot (Leeds United), Ron Coltman, Arthur Rowley (Leicester City);
Middle Row – Ft/Sgt Kidd (Linesman), D Stephens (Linesman), BM Griffiths (Referee), Johnny Porteous (Plymouth Argyle), Ted Platt (Portsmouth), Len Allchurch
(Swansea Town), Phil Friel, Michael Lawrence, Rob Coldray, Ron Jackson (Leicester City), Bob Swankie, Jimmy Buist, Joey Martin;
Front row – Ivor Allchurch (Swansea Town), Bob Etheridge, Jack Froggatt (Leicester City), Harry Ferrier, John Charles (Leeds United), Frank Tredgett, Stan Myers,
Jimmy McLaughlin, Jim Clark

Frank Tredgett

[444]

All teams Gloucester City have played competitively.Teams are in their original names when playing Gloucester City. Cup games figures include all cup competitions. Expunged league results are also included. The years above the first column indicate the first and last time a Gloucester team played these opponents in a competitive game. Note some totals do not add up due to scores missing.

ABERDARE

1938	P	W	D	L	F	A		W	D	L	F	A
CUP	1	1	0	0	4	0		0	0	0	0	0
TOTAL	1	1	0	0	4	0		0	0	0	0	0

Formed 1892. Merged with Aberaman Athletic in 1926 to become Aberdare Athletic. In 1927, the merged club renamed themselves Aberdare & Aberaman Athletic until 1928 when reformed as Aberaman Athletic. Aberdare & Aberaman Athletic were reformed in 1945 but split with Aberaman and became Aberdare Athletic yet again in 1947.

ABERGAVENNY THURSDAYS

1964-1970	P	W	D	L	F	A		W	D	L	F	A
CUP	3	3	0	0	10	3		0	0	0	0	0
TOTAL	3	3	0	0	10	3		0	0	0	0	0

Formed 1927.

ABINGDON UNITED

2008	P	W	D	L	F	A		W	D	L	F	A
CUP	1	1	0	0	3	0		0	0	0	0	0
TOTAL	1	1	0	0	3	0		0	0	0	0	0

Formed 1946.

ADDLESTONE & WEYBRIDGE TOWN

1983	P	W	D	L	F	A		W	D	L	F	A
LEAGUE	2	0	1	0	3	3		1	0	0	2	1
TOTAL	2	0	1	0	3	3		1	0	0	2	1

Founded as Addlestone in 1885. Changed name to Addlestone & Weybridge Town in 1980. However, it ceased to exist in 1985.

ALDERSHOT TOWN

1995	P	W	D	L	F	A		W	D	L	F	A
CUP	1	1	0	0	5	1		0	0	0	0	0
TOTAL	1	1	0	0	5	1		0	0	0	0	0

Present club formed 1992 following the folding of Aldershot who had been in existence since 1926.

ALVECHURCH

1978-1990	P	W	D	L	F	A		W	D	L	F	A
LEAGUE	16	1	3	4	11	14		0	5	3	9	14
CUP	3	2	0	0	8	3		1	0	0	4	0
TOTAL	19	3	3	4	19	17		1	5	3	13	14

Formed 1929, the club closed in 1993 to be resurrected by supporters in 1994.

ANDOVER

1973-1987	P	W	D	L	F	A		W	D	L	F	A
CUP	3	1	0	1	3	6		0	1	0	3	3
TOTAL	3	1	0	1	3	6		0	1	0	3	3

Formed 1883.

ARMY 'E'

1942-1943	P	W	D	L	F	A		W	D	L	F	A
LEAGUE	2	2	0	0	19	2		0	0	0	0	0
TOTAL	2	2	0	0	19	2		0	0	0	0	0

Played in Gloucester. During World War II, all Services teams played under a nom-de-plume.

ARMY 'F'

1942	P	W	D	L	F	A		W	D	L	F	A
LEAGUE	2	2	0	0	11	2		0	0	0	0	0
TOTAL	2	2	0	0	11	2		0	0	0	0	0

Played in Gloucester. During World War II, all Services teams played under a nom-de-plume.

ARMY 'G'

1941-1942	P	W	D	L	F	A		W	D	L	F	A
LEAGUE	2	2	0	0	28	2		0	0	0	0	0
TOTAL	2	2	0	0	28	2		0	0	0	0	0

Played in Gloucester. During World War II, all Services teams played under a nom-de-plume.

ARMY 'J'

1941-1942	P	W	D	L	F	A		W	D	L	F	A
LEAGUE	2	1	0	1	2	3		0	0	0	0	0
TOTAL	2	1	0	1	2	3		0	0	0	0	0

Played in Gloucester. During World War II, all Services teams played under a nom-de-plume.

ARMY 'K'

1941-1942	P	W	D	L	F	A		W	D	L	F	A
LEAGUE	2	1	0	1	14	2		0	0	0	0	0
TOTAL	2	1	0	1	14	2		0	0	0	0	0

Played in Gloucester. During World War II, all Services teams played under a nom-de-plume.

[445]

ARMY 'L'

1941-1942	P	W	D	L	F	A		W	D	L	F	A
LEAGUE	2	0	1	1	4	5		0	0	0	0	0
TOTAL	**2**	**0**	**1**	**1**	**4**	**5**		**0**	**0**	**0**	**0**	**0**

Played in Gloucester. During World War II, all Services teams played under a nom-de-plume.

ARMY 'M'

1942	P	W	D	L	F	A		W	D	L	F	A
LEAGUE	2	2	0	0	13	2		0	0	0	0	0
TOTAL	**2**	**2**	**0**	**0**	**13**	**2**		**0**	**0**	**0**	**0**	**0**

Played in Gloucester. During World War II, all Services teams played under a nom-de-plume.

ASHFORD TOWN (Kent)

1959-1998	P	W	D	L	F	A		W	D	L	F	A
LEAGUE	28	8	1	5	34	20		5	1	8	17	30
TOTAL	**28**	**8**	**1**	**5**	**34**	**20**		**5**	**1**	**8**	**17**	**30**

Formed 1880 as Ashford United. United collapsed in 1906 to be reformed as South Eastern & Chatham Railway which collapsed in 1927. The current Ashford Town was founded in 1930. Not to be confused with the other Ashford Town which plays in Middlesex.

ASHTON-UNDER-HILL

1921	P	W	D	L	F	A		W	D	L	F	A
CUP	1	0	0	0	0	0		0	0	1	1	3
TOTAL	**1**	**0**	**0**	**0**	**0**	**0**		**0**	**0**	**1**	**1**	**3**

Ashton-Under-Hill is a village in Worcestershire.

ASHTREE HIGHFIELD

1988	P	W	D	L	F	A		W	D	L	F	A
LEAGUE	2	1	0	0	2	0		0	1	0	0	0
TOTAL	**2**	**1**	**0**	**0**	**2**	**0**		**0**	**1**	**0**	**0**	**0**

Formerly known as Smethwick Highfield. Changed name to Ashtree Highfield in 1986 and further changed their name to Sandwell Borough in 1989 which folded in 2001.

ASTON VILLA 'A'

1935-1939	P	W	D	L	F	A		W	D	L	F	A
LEAGUE	8	1	1	2	8	10		0	0	4	5	17
TOTAL	**8**	**1**	**1**	**2**	**8**	**10**		**0**	**0**	**4**	**5**	**17**

Aston Villa formed in 1874. This would probably be their third team.

ATHERSTONE TOWN

1935-1974	P	W	D	L	F	A		W	D	L	F	A
LEAGUE	10	5	0	0	19	2		1	0	4	5	10
CUP	1	1	0	0	1	0		0	0	0	0	0
TOTAL	**11**	**6**	**0**	**0**	**20**	**2**		**1**	**0**	**4**	**5**	**10**

Formed in 1888 and folded in 1978. New club bearing their name established 2004.

ATHERSTONE UNITED

1987-2003	P	W	D	L	F	A		W	D	L	F	A
LEAGUE	33	9	4	4	40	18		4	5	7	21	22
CUP	2	0	0	0	0	0		2	0	0	3	1
TOTAL	**35**	**9**	**4**	**4**	**40**	**18**		**6**	**5**	**7**	**24**	**23**

Formed in 1979 after the collapse of Atherstone Town. Club resigned 2003.

AUTOMOTIVE PRODUCTS LEAMINGTON

1973-1985	P	W	D	L	F	A		W	D	L	F	A
LEAGUE	12	2	1	3	5	11		0	1	5	6	16
CUP	1	0	0	0	0	0		0	0	1	1	4
TOTAL	**13**	**2**	**1**	**3**	**5**	**11**		**0**	**1**	**6**	**7**	**20**

Formerly Lockheed Leamington who were formed in 1945 and changed name to Automotive Products Leamington in 1973. Became Leamington in 1985.

AYLESBURY UNITED

1982-2006	P	W	D	L	F	A		W	D	L	F	A
LEAGUE	4	0	1	1	1	4		1	0	1	1	2
CUP	3	0	1	0	0	0		1	0	1	2	2
TOTAL	**7**	**0**	**2**	**1**	**1**	**4**		**2**	**0**	**2**	**3**	**4**

Formed 1897 as a merger between Night School FC, the Printing Works and Aylesbury Town.

BALDOCK TOWN

1989-1997	P	W	D	L	F	A		W	D	L	F	A
LEAGUE	4	2	0	0	6	2		2	0	0	4	2
CUP	2	0	1	0	1	1		1	0	0	1	0
TOTAL	**6**	**2**	**1**	**0**	**7**	**3**		**3**	**0**	**0**	**5**	**2**

Formed 1889.

BANBURY SPENCER

1936-1939	P	W	D	L	F	A		W	D	L	F	A
LEAGUE	9	1	1	2	12	15		0	0	5	6	17
TOTAL	**9**	**1**	**1**	**2**	**12**	**15**		**0**	**0**	**5**	**6**	**17**

Formed 1932 and changed their name to Banbury United in 1965.

BANBURY UNITED

1966-2009	P	W	D	L	F	A		W	D	L	F	A
LEAGUE	46	11	6	6	54	35		7	6	10	40	37
CUP	2	1	0	0	2	1		0	1	0	1	1
TOTAL	**48**	**12**	**6**	**6**	**56**	**36**		**7**	**7**	**10**	**41**	**38**

Formerly Banbury Spencer.

BARNET

1965-1976	P	W	D	L	F	A		W	D	L	F	A
LEAGUE	8	2	2	0	7	4		1	1	2	3	7
TOTAL	**8**	**2**	**2**	**0**	**7**	**4**		**1**	**1**	**2**	**3**	**7**

Formed 1888 out of Woodville FC and New Barnet FC until 1901 when it ceased to exist. Reformed 1912 following a merger between Barnet Avenue FC and Alston Works FC.

BARNSTAPLE TOWN

1948	P	W	D	L	F	A		W	D	L	F	A
CUP	1	1	0	0	5	2		0	0	0	0	0
TOTAL	**1**	**1**	**0**	**0**	**5**	**2**		**0**	**0**	**0**	**0**	**0**

Formed 1904 as Pilton Yeo Vale changing their name shortly thereafter.

BARRY

1938-1940	P	W	D	L	F	A		W	D	L	F	A
LEAGUE	2	1	0	0	3	2		0	0	1	2	6
CUP	2	0	0	1	1	2		1	0	0	3	2
TOTAL	**4**	**1**	**0**	**1**	**4**	**4**		**1**	**0**	**1**	**5**	**8**

Formed 1912 changing name to Barry Town 1945.

BARRY TOWN

1946-1991	P	W	D	L	F	A		W	D	L	F	A
LEAGUE	66	23	7	3	74	34		11	3	19	44	80
CUP	19	7	1	1	18	8		3	3	4	19	18
TOTAL	**85**	**30**	**8**	**4**	**92**	**42**		**14**	**6**	**23**	**63**	**98**

Formerly Barry.

BASHLEY

1990-2009	P	W	D	L	F	A		W	D	L	F	A
LEAGUE	12	4	1	1	11	4		3	2	1	11	7
CUP	1	1	0	0	3	0		0	0	0	0	0
TOTAL	**13**	**5**	**1**	**1**	**14**	**4**		**3**	**2**	**1**	**11**	**7**

Formed in 1947.

BASINGSTOKE TOWN

1996-1998	P	W	D	L	F	A		W	D	L	F	A
CUP	2	0	0	0	0	0		2	0	0	4	0
TOTAL	**2**	**0**	**0**	**0**	**0**	**0**		**2**	**0**	**0**	**4**	**0**

Formed in 1896 by the amalgamation of Basingstoke Albion and Aldsworth United.

BATH CITY

1939-2007	P	W	D	L	F	A		W	D	L	F	A
LEAGUE	54	14	5	8	42	37		5	6	16	25	56
CUP	12	2	1	1	7	8		1	0	7	9	23
TOTAL	**66**	**16**	**6**	**9**	**49**	**45**		**6**	**6**	**23**	**34**	**79**

Formed in 1889.

BATH CITY RESERVES

1932-1935	P	W	D	L	F	A		W	D	L	F	A
LEAGUE	8	2	1	1	9	5		0	0	4	4	16
TOTAL	**8**	**2**	**1**	**1**	**9**	**5**		**0**	**0**	**4**	**4**	**16**

BEDFORD TOWN

1946-2009	P	W	D	L	F	A		W	D	L	F	A
LEAGUE	46	11	5	7	42	30		2	8	13	29	42
CUP	2	0	0	1	1	3		1	0	0	1	0
TOTAL	**48**	**11**	**5**	**8**	**43**	**33**		**3**	**8**	**13**	**30**	**42**

Formed 1908.

BEDMINSTER

1893-1895	P	W	D	L	F	A		W	D	L	F	A
LEAGUE	5	2	0	0	8	2		1	1	1	7	6
CUP	1	1	0	0	5	0		0	0	0	0	0
TOTAL	**6**	**3**	**0**	**0**	**13**	**2**		**1**	**1**	**1**	**7**	**6**

Formed as Southville in 1887 were merged with Bedminster Cricket Club in 1889 as Bedminster. They merged with Bristol City in 1900.

BEDWORTH UNITED

1972-2003	P	W	D	L	F	A		W	D	L	F	A
LEAGUE	34	6	7	4	27	24		7	7	3	22	18
CUP	1	0	0	0	0	0		1	0	0	3	0
TOTAL	**35**	**6**	**7**	**4**	**27**	**24**		**8**	**7**	**3**	**25**	**18**

Formed in 1895 as Bedworth Town until disbanded in 1901. a second Bedworth Town was formed 1905 and played until the early 1920s. A third Bedworth Town was formed in 1925 and changed their name to Bedworth United in 1968.

RECORD AGAINST OPPONENTS

BERKELEY TOWN

1921-1924	P	W	D	L	F	A		W	D	L	F	A
LEAGUE	4	2	0	0	8	3		0	0	2	5	10
TOTAL	**4**	**2**	**0**	**0**	**8**	**3**		**0**	**0**	**2**	**5**	**10**

Formed 1898.

BEXLEY UNITED

1965-1969	P	W	D	L	F	A		W	D	L	F	A
LEAGUE	8	2	2	0	3	1		1	1	2	5	8
TOTAL	**8**	**2**	**2**	**0**	**3**	**1**		**1**	**1**	**2**	**5**	**8**

The name Bexley United was adopted in 1963. The club wound up in 1976.

BEXLEYHEATH & WELLING

1959-1961	P	W	D	L	F	A		W	D	L	F	A
LEAGUE	4	1	0	1	2	4		0	0	2	1	17
TOTAL	**4**	**1**	**0**	**1**	**2**	**4**		**0**	**0**	**2**	**1**	**17**

Formed 1917 as Bexleyheath Labour until 1921 when Bexleyheath Town took over their fixtures. Changed name to Bexleyheath & Welling in 1931 until they changed their name to Bexley United in 1963.

BIDEFORD

1949	P	W	D	L	F	A		W	D	L	F	A
CUP	2	1	0	0	3	1		0	1	0	1	1
TOTAL	**2**	**1**	**0**	**0**	**3**	**1**		**0**	**1**	**0**	**1**	**1**

Formed in 1946 as Bideford Town and subsequently dropped 'Town'.

BILSTON TOWN

1985-2002	P	W	D	L	F	A		W	D	L	F	A
LEAGUE	12	2	1	3	10	11		3	0	3	8	13
TOTAL	**12**	**2**	**1**	**3**	**10**	**11**		**3**	**0**	**3**	**8**	**13**

Formed in 1895 as Bilston United after amalgamation of Bilston Wanderers and Bilston Rovers and became bankrupt in 1927 reforming as Bilston FC. Changed their name to Bilston Borough in 1931. Reformed as Bilston again after World War II adding 'Town' in 1983.

BIRMINGHAM 'A'

1935-1939	P	W	D	L	F	A		W	D	L	F	A
LEAGUE	6	3	0	0	7	2		0	2	1	7	13
CUP	2	0	1	0	1	1		0	0	1	0	0
TOTAL	**8**	**3**	**1**	**0**	**8**	**3**		**0**	**2**	**2**	**7**	**13**

Formed in 1875 as Small Heath Alliance becoming Small Heath in 1888. They changed their name to Birmingham in 1905 adding 'City' in 1943. This would probably be their third team.

BIRMINGHAM TRAMS

1935-1939	P	W	D	L	F	A		W	D	L	F	A
LEAGUE	8	3	0	1	8	4		0	2	2	5	8
TOTAL	**8**	**3**	**0**	**1**	**8**	**4**		**0**	**2**	**2**	**5**	**8**

Full name was Birmingham Corporation Tramways.

BISHOP AUCKLAND

1997	P	W	D	L	F	A		W	D	L	F	A
CUP	2	1	0	0	4	3		0	1	0	0	0
TOTAL	**2**	**1**	**0**	**0**	**4**	**3**		**0**	**1**	**0**	**0**	**0**

Founded in 1886 as Auckland Town changing their name to Bishop Auckland in 1893.

BISHOP'S CLEEVE

2006-2007	P	W	D	L	F	A		W	D	L	F	A
CUP	2	0	0	0	0	0		0	0	2	3	5
TOTAL	**2**	**0**	**0**	**0**	**0**	**0**		**0**	**0**	**2**	**3**	**5**

Formed in 1905.

BISHOP'S STORTFORD

2003	P	W	D	L	F	A		W	D	L	F	A
CUP	1	0	0	0	0	0		0	0	1	0	2
TOTAL	**1**	**0**	**0**	**0**	**0**	**0**		**0**	**0**	**1**	**0**	**2**

Formed 1874.

BLAKENEY

1933-1935	P	W	D	L	F	A		W	D	L	F	A
LEAGUE	6	2	0	1	6	4		3	0	0	16	6
TOTAL	**6**	**2**	**0**	**1**	**6**	**4**		**3**	**0**	**0**	**16**	**6**

BLAKENHALL

2000-2001	P	W	D	L	F	A		W	D	L	F	A
LEAGUE	2	0	0	1	1	3		0	1	0	3	3
TOTAL	**2**	**0**	**0**	**1**	**1**	**3**		**0**	**1**	**0**	**3**	**3**

Formed 1946. Merged with Bloxwich Town to form Bloxwich United in 2001.

BLETCHLEY TOWN

1972-1974	P	W	D	L	F	A		W	D	L	F	A
LEAGUE	4	0	1	1	1	2		0	1	1	3	4
TOTAL	**4**	**0**	**1**	**1**	**1**	**2**		**0**	**1**	**1**	**3**	**4**

Formed in 1914 as Bletchley. Changed name to Milton Keynes City 1974 folding ten years later.

BOSTON UNITED

1958-2000	P	W	D	L	F	A		W	D	L	F	A
LEAGUE	6	1	2	0	10	6		0	1	2	2	8
TOTAL	6	1	2	0	10	6		0	1	2	2	8

Formed in 1933 out of an amalgamation of Boston Town and Boston Swifts.

BOURNEVILLE ATHLETIC

1935-1939	P	W	D	L	F	A		W	D	L	F	A
LEAGUE	8	4	0	0	16	4		2	2	0	11	4
TOTAL	8	4	0	0	16	4		2	2	0	11	4

Formed late 19th Century and was still in existence upto 1987.

BOURTON ROVERS

1902-1906	P	W	D	L	F	A		W	D	L	F	A
LEAGUE	5	1	1	0	3	2		2	1	0	8	1
CUP	2	0	1	0	1	1		1	0	0	1	0
TOTAL	7	1	2	0	4	3		3	1	0	9	1

Formed in 1894.

BRACKLEY TOWN

2007-2009	P	W	D	L	F	A		W	D	L	F	A
LEAGUE	4	0	0	2	1	4		2	0	0	6	3
TOTAL	4	0	0	2	1	4		2	0	0	6	3

Formed 1890.

BRAINTREE TOWN

2007	P	W	D	L	F	A		W	D	L	F	A
CUP	1	0	0	1	0	2		0	0	0	0	0
TOTAL	1	0	0	1	0	2		0	0	0	0	0

Formed in 1898 as Manor Works FC. In 1921 they changed their name to Crittall Athletic. In 1968 they changed their name once again to Braintree & Crittall Athletic when links with Crittall ended in 1981 when they became Braintree Town.

BREAM AMATEURS

1928-1935	P	W	D	L	F	A		W	D	L	F	A
LEAGUE	14	6	1	0	21	2		5	1	1	14	6
TOTAL	14	6	1	0	21	2		5	1	1	14	6

The club certainly existed pre-1907 and are still in existence today.

BRENTWOOD TOWN

1967-1970	P	W	D	L	F	A		W	D	L	F	A
LEAGUE	6	0	1	2	3	9		1	0	2	3	5
TOTAL	6	0	1	2	3	9		1	0	2	3	5

Formed in 1965 and folded 1970. The team currently named Brentwood Town were formed in 1954 as Manor Athletic. Following the demise of the 1970 team changed their name to Brentwood Athletic. In 2004 resorted back to Brentwood Town.

BRIDGEND TOWN

1977-1982	P	W	D	L	F	A		W	D	L	F	A
LEAGUE	8	2	0	2	11	8		0	2	2	2	7
CUP	2	0	0	1	0	2		1	0	0	3	0
TOTAL	10	2	0	3	11	10		1	2	2	5	7

Formed before the 1920s. Was reformed in 1954. Known as Everwarm for three years until 1976.

BRIDGNORTH TOWN

1985-1989	P	W	D	L	F	A		W	D	L	F	A
LEAGUE	8	1	1	2	8	7		2	1	1	12	10
CUP	2	0	1	0	0	0		1	0	0	3	0
TOTAL	10	1	2	2	8	7		3	1	1	15	10

Formed in 1938 and disbanded due to World War II. Re-formed in 1946 out of a club named Saint Leonard's Old Boys.

BRIDGWATER TOWN

1980-2009	P	W	D	L	F	A		W	D	L	F	A
CUP	2	1	0	0	1	0		0	0	1	1	2
TOTAL	2	1	0	0	1	0		0	0	1	1	2

Formed in 1898 and ceased in 1902. Re-established in 1903 as Bridgwater AFC and disbanded before World War I. Reformed in 1921 as Bridgwater Town.

BRIERLEY HILL ALLIANCE

1975-1976	P	W	D	L	F	A		W	D	L	F	A
CUP	3	0	1	0	2	2		1	0	1	4	3
TOTAL	3	0	1	0	2	2		1	0	1	4	3

Formed pre-1890 and folded in 1980.

BRIMSCOMBE

1899-1935	P	W	D	L	F	A		W	D	L	F	A
LEAGUE	31	7	2	6	35	23		8	2	5	37	41
CUP	1	0	0	0	0	0		0	0	1	1	7
TOTAL	32	7	2	6	35	23		8	2	6	38	48

Formed 1891. Became Brimscombe & Thrupp in the 1970s.

BRIMSCOMBE 'A'

1921-1922	P	W	D	L	F	A		W	D	L	F	A
LEAGUE	2	1	0	0	5	0		1	0	0	3	1
TOTAL	2	1	0	0	5	0		1	0	0	3	1

BRISTOL AMATEURS

1899	P	W	D	L	F	A		W	D	L	F	A
CUP	2	0	0	1	2	4		0	0	1	0	5
TOTAL	2	0	0	1	2	4		0	0	1	0	5

Formed pre-1898.

BRISTOL CITY

1950	P	W	D	L	F	A		W	D	L	F	A
CUP	1	0	0	0	0	0		0	0	1	0	4
TOTAL	1	0	0	0	0	0		0	0	1	0	4

Formed in 1897 when Bristol South End changed its name to Bristol City. In 1900 they merged with Bedminster.

BRISTOL CITY 'A'

1931-1935	P	W	D	L	F	A		W	D	L	F	A
LEAGUE	8	3	0	1	10	6		0	0	4	8	22
TOTAL	8	3	0	1	10	6		0	0	4	8	22

BRISTOL CITY RESERVES

1927-2009	P	W	D	L	F	A		W	D	L	F	A
LEAGUE	2	0	0	1	1	4		0	0	1	0	11
CUP	4	0	0	1	1	2		0	0	3	2	13
TOTAL	6	0	0	2	2	6		0	0	4	2	24

BRISTOL MANOR FARM

1995-2003	P	W	D	L	F	A		W	D	L	F	A
CUP	2	1	0	0	8	0		1	0	0	5	0
TOTAL	2	1	0	0	8	0		1	0	0	5	0

Formed in the late 1960s.

BRISTOL ROVERS 'A'

1934	P	W	D	L	F	A		W	D	L	F	A
LEAGUE	2	0	0	1	2	4		0	0	1	1	3
TOTAL	2	0	0	1	2	4		0	0	1	1	3

BRISTOL ROVERS RESERVES

1932-2006	P	W	D	L	F	A		W	D	L	F	A
LEAGUE	6	1	0	2	4	11		0	0	3	3	24
CUP	2	0	0	1	1	2		0	0	1	0	3
TOTAL	8	1	0	3	5	13		0	0	4	3	27

Founded in 1883 as Black Arabs changing their name to Eastville Rovers in 1884. The name changed briefly in 1897 to Bristol Eastville Rovers dropping 'Eastville' in 1898.

BRISTOL SAINT GEORGE

1929-1937	P	W	D	L	F	A		W	D	L	F	A
LEAGUE	8	1	1	2	15	5		1	0	3	8	17
CUP	3	3	0	0	15	6		0	0	0	0	0
TOTAL	11	4	1	2	30	11		1	0	3	8	17

Known as Saint George from at least 1892. Renamed Bristol Saint George in 1897.

BRISTOL SAINT PANCRAS

1933	P	W	D	L	F	A		W	D	L	F	A
CUP	1	1	0	0	5	4		0	0	0	0	0
TOTAL	1	1	0	0	5	4		0	0	0	0	0

Play in Knowle.

BRISTOL SAINT PHILIP'S

1929-1946	P	W	D	L	F	A		W	D	L	F	A
CUP	3	2	0	0	7	0		0	0	1	0	2
TOTAL	3	2	0	0	7	0		0	0	1	0	2

BROADWELL AMATEURS

1922-1934	P	W	D	L	F	A		W	D	L	F	A
LEAGUE	22	5	1	5	28	18		5	1	4	16	22
CUP	1	1	0	0	4	2		0	0	0	0	0
TOTAL	23	6	1	5	32	20		5	1	4	16	22

Formed 1905.

BROMSGROVE ROVERS

1935-2008	P	W	D	L	F	A		W	D	L	F	A
LEAGUE	48	13	7	4	56	33		12	5	7	43	38
CUP	6	1	0	2	4	6		2	1	0	7	3
TOTAL	54	14	7	6	60	39		14	6	7	50	41

Formed 1885.

RECORD AGAINST OPPONENTS

BUCKINGHAM TOWN

1986-1987	P	W	D	L	F	A		W	D	L	F	A
LEAGUE	4	1	1	0	4	2		0	2	0	2	2
TOTAL	4	1	1	0	4	2		0	2	0	2	2

Founded in 1883.

BURTON ALBION

1958-1999	P	W	D	L	F	A		W	D	L	F	A
LEAGUE	48	10	5	9	39	35		6	5	13	28	49
CUP	8	2	1	1	7	3		2	0	2	4	8
TOTAL	56	12	6	10	46	38		8	5	15	32	57

Formed in 1950.

BURY TOWN

1971-1976	P	W	D	L	F	A		W	D	L	F	A
LEAGUE	10	3	0	3	11	16		2	1	1	6	4
TOTAL	10	3	0	3	11	16		2	1	1	6	4

Formed in 1872 as Bury Saint Edmunds. Became Bury United in 1902 adopting the present title in 1906.

CADBURY'S ATHLETIC

1925-1928	P	W	D	L	F	A		W	D	L	F	A
LEAGUE	8	2	1	0	13	4		2	0	2	14	14
TOTAL	8	2	1	0	13	4		2	0	2	14	14

Played in Frampton.

CAERAU ATHLETIC

1958	P	W	D	L	F	A		W	D	L	F	A
CUP	1	1	0	0	3	0		0	0	0	0	0
TOTAL	1	1	0	0	3	0		0	0	0	0	0

Changed name to Caerau 1979. Changed yet again in 1996 to Caerau United.

CAM MILLS

1925-1935	P	W	D	L	F	A		W	D	L	F	A
LEAGUE	10	3	1	1	13	6		4	0	1	23	10
CUP	1	0	0	0	0	0		1	0	0	3	1
TOTAL	11	3	1	1	13	6		5	0	1	26	11

CAMBRIDGE CITY

1968-2009	P	W	D	L	F	A		W	D	L	F	A
LEAGUE	41	12	3	6	43	29		9	2	9	28	35
CUP	2	0	0	0	0	0		0	0	2	1	5
TOTAL	43	12	3	6	43	29		9	2	11	29	40

Formed in 1908 as Cambridge Town. The present name was adopted in 1952.

CAMBRIDGE UNITED

1959-1970	P	W	D	L	F	A		W	D	L	F	A
LEAGUE	6	0	1	2	7	9		0	0	3	3	8
TOTAL	6	0	1	2	7	9		0	0	3	3	8

Founded as Abbey United in 1919. Adopted Cambridge United in 1949.

CANTERBURY CITY

1960-1969	P	W	D	L	F	A		W	D	L	F	A
LEAGUE	18	4	3	2	13	12		3	2	4	14	16
TOTAL	18	4	3	2	13	12		3	2	4	14	16

Founded in 1947 as successor to Canterbury Waverley Club.

CARDIFF

1895	P	W	D	L	F	A		W	D	L	F	A
LEAGUE	1	0	0	1	0	2		0	0	0	0	0
TOTAL	1	0	0	1	0	2		0	0	0	0	0

There is no connection with the later Cardiff City FC.

CARDIFF CITY

1958-1989	P	W	D	L	F	A		W	D	L	F	A
CUP	4	0	1	1	1	2		0	1	1	2	5
TOTAL	4	0	1	1	1	2		0	1	1	2	5

Formed in 1899 as Riverside AFC. Became Cardiff City in 1907.

CAVENDISH HOUSE

1897-1898	P	W	D	L	F	A		W	D	L	F	A
LEAGUE	2	1	0	0	2	1		1	0	0	1	0
TOTAL	2	1	0	0	2	1		1	0	0	1	0

Played in Cheltenham. Presumably the team of the store of the same name.

CHALFONT SAINT PETER

2008	P	W	D	L	F	A		W	D	L	F	A
CUP	1	0	0	0	0	0		0	0	1	3	5
TOTAL	1	0	0	0	0	0		0	0	1	3	5

Formed 1926.

[451]

CHALFORD

1898-1935	P	W	D	L	F	A		W	D	L	F	A
LEAGUE	24	7	4	1	52	14		7	1	3	22	17
CUP	2	1	0	0	4	2		1	0	0	3	2
TOTAL	26	8	4	1	56	16		8	1	3	25	19

Formed 1891.

CHELMSFORD CITY

1946-1997	P	W	D	L	F	A		W	D	L	F	A
LEAGUE	50	17	4	4	62	35		4	4	17	32	63
CUP	2	1	0	1	1	2		0	0	0	0	0
TOTAL	52	18	4	5	63	37		4	4	17	32	63

Formed in 1922.

CHELTENHAM TOWN

1898-1999	P	W	D	L	F	A		W	D	L	F	A
LEAGUE	118	17	20	22	94	105		13	12	34	84	129
CUP	93	17	4	26	61	80		13	6	27	63	103
TOTAL	211	34	24	48	155	185		26	18	61	147	231

Founded in 1892.

CHELTENHAM TOWN RESERVES

1932-2004	P	W	D	L	F	A		W	D	L	F	A
LEAGUE	14	4	1	2	17	10		2	2	3	8	12
CUP	1	0	0	1	0	2		0	0	0	0	0
TOTAL	15	4	1	3	17	12		2	2	3	8	12

CHELTENHAM TRAINING COLLEGE

1900-1901	P	W	D	L	F	A		W	D	L	F	A
LEAGUE	2	1	0	0	1	0		0	0	1	1	3
TOTAL	2	1	0	0	1	0		0	0	1	1	3

CHEPSTOW TOWN

1927-1935	P	W	D	L	F	A		W	D	L	F	A
LEAGUE	16	6	1	1	24	11		2	2	4	15	19
CUP	2	0	0	1	0	2		1	0	0	5	0
TOTAL	18	6	1	2	24	13		3	2	4	20	19

Established in 1878.

CHERTSEY TOWN

1998	P	W	D	L	F	A		W	D	L	F	A
CUP	1	0	0	0	0	0		1	0	0	5	0
TOTAL	1	0	0	0	0	0		1	0	0	5	0

Established in 1890.

CHESHAM UNITED

1999-2006	P	W	D	L	F	A		W	D	L	F	A
LEAGUE	4	2	0	0	6	3		1	0	1	4	3
CUP	1	1	0	0	4	2		0	0	0	0	0
TOTAL	5	3	0	0	10	5		1	0	1	4	3

Founded in 1894 as Chesham FC. Renamed Chesham Town in 1899. In 1917 merged with Chesham Generals to form Chesham United.

CHESHUNT

2005-2008	P	W	D	L	F	A		W	D	L	F	A
LEAGUE	6	2	0	1	7	4		2	1	0	7	1
TOTAL	6	2	0	1	7	4		2	1	0	7	1

Formed c1880 and disbanded in 1931. The current club was reformed in 1946.

CHINGFORD TOWN

1949-1950	P	W	D	L	F	A		W	D	L	F	A
LEAGUE	5	3	0	0	16	4		0	1	1	6	7
TOTAL	5	3	0	0	16	4		0	1	1	6	7

Formed in 1947 and folded in 1951.

CHIPPENHAM TOWN

1969-2009	P	W	D	L	F	A		W	D	L	F	A
LEAGUE	12	3	1	2	7	5		0	1	5	5	14
CUP	4	2	1	0	9	4		1	0	0	5	3
TOTAL	16	5	2	2	16	9		1	1	5	10	17

Formed in 1873.

CHRISTCHURCH

2005	P	W	D	L	F	A		W	D	L	F	A
CUP	2	0	1	0	0	0		0	0	1	0	3
TOTAL	2	0	1	0	0	0		0	0	1	0	3

Founded in 1885.

CINDERFORD TOWN

1922-2004	P	W	D	L	F	A		W	D	L	F	A
LEAGUE	34	13	2	2	46	20		7	3	6	29	29
CUP	26	10	1	3	29	12		5	1	6	18	17
TOTAL	**60**	**23**	**3**	**5**	**75**	**32**		**12**	**4**	**12**	**47**	**46**

Formed in 1922.

CIRENCESTER TOWN

1904-2008	P	W	D	L	F	A		W	D	L	F	A
LEAGUE	18	4	3	2	16	7		5	1	3	21	10
CUP	8	2	0	0	4	0		3	0	3	13	11
TOTAL	**26**	**6**	**3**	**2**	**20**	**7**		**8**	**1**	**6**	**34**	**21**

Formed in 1889.

CLACTON TOWN

1959-1963	P	W	D	L	F	A		W	D	L	F	A
LEAGUE	4	1	0	1	5	5		0	0	2	2	7
TOTAL	**4**	**1**	**0**	**1**	**5**	**5**		**0**	**0**	**2**	**2**	**7**

Formed in 1892 as Clacton. Reformed c 1901 as Old Clactonians renaming to Clacton Town in 1905. Currently called FC Clacton.

CLANDOWN

1981	P	W	D	L	F	A		W	D	L	F	A
CUP	1	0	0	0	0	0		1	0	0	3	1
TOTAL	**1**	**0**	**0**	**0**	**0**	**0**		**1**	**0**	**0**	**3**	**1**

Formed pre-1920.

CLEVEDON

1893-1949	P	W	D	L	F	A		W	D	L	F	A
LEAGUE	6	3	0	0	15	2		1	0	1	7	5
CUP	6	3	1	0	17	5		1	0	1	4	6
TOTAL	**12**	**6**	**1**	**0**	**32**	**7**		**2**	**0**	**2**	**11**	**11**

Formed in 1880 as Clevedon. Changed name to Clevedon Town 1977.

CLEVEDON TOWN

1993-2009	P	W	D	L	F	A		W	D	L	F	A
LEAGUE	14	3	2	2	11	11		3	3	1	13	9
CUP	4	2	0	1	5	4		1	0	0	1	0
TOTAL	**18**	**5**	**2**	**2**	**16**	**15**		**4**	**3**	**1**	**14**	**9**

Formerly Clevedon.

CLIFTON

1893-1896	P	W	D	L	F	A		W	D	L	F	A
LEAGUE	6	2	0	1	7	5		1	0	2	11	12
CUP	2	1	0	0	8	0		1	0	0	6	1
TOTAL	**8**	**3**	**0**	**1**	**15**	**5**		**2**	**0**	**2**	**17**	**13**

Formed c1889 as Clifton Association. Dropped 'Association' in 1893. Resigned from league 1898.

CLIFTON ASSOCIATION RESERVES

1889	P	W	D	L	F	A		W	D	L	F	A
CUP	1	1	0	0	10	0		0	0	0	0	0
TOTAL	**1**	**1**	**0**	**0**	**10**	**0**		**0**	**0**	**0**	**0**	**0**

COLCHESTER UNITED

1946-1950	P	W	D	L	F	A		W	D	L	F	A
LEAGUE	8	1	0	3	11	12		1	1	2	5	17
TOTAL	**8**	**1**	**0**	**3**	**11**	**12**		**1**	**1**	**2**	**5**	**17**

Formed in 1937.

CORBY TOWN

1958-2009	P	W	D	L	F	A		W	D	L	F	A
LEAGUE	60	14	8	8	56	46		11	7	12	47	52
TOTAL	**60**	**14**	**8**	**8**	**56**	**46**		**11**	**7**	**12**	**47**	**52**

Founded 1948 out of Stewarts & Lloyds (Corby).

COVENTRY CITY 'A'

1938-1939	P	W	D	L	F	A		W	D	L	F	A
LEAGUE	4	1	0	1	1	1		1	1	0	2	1
TOTAL	**4**	**1**	**0**	**1**	**1**	**1**		**1**	**1**	**0**	**2**	**1**

Formed 1883 as Singers. Renamed Coventry City in 1898. This would probably be their third team.

COVENTRY SPORTING

1986-1989	P	W	D	L	F	A		W	D	L	F	A
LEAGUE	8	3	1	0	15	2		2	1	1	4	4
TOTAL	**8**	**3**	**1**	**0**	**15**	**2**		**2**	**1**	**1**	**4**	**4**

Formed as Coventry Amateurs in 1946 changing name to Coventry Sporting in 1974. Club folded 1989.

[453]

CRAWLEY TOWN

1963-2000	P	W	D	L	F	A		W	D	L	F	A
LEAGUE	38	11	6	2	47	22		6	6	7	29	33
TOTAL	38	11	6	2	47	22		6	6	7	29	33

Formed in 1896 as Crawley but folded in the 1920s. An amalgamation of Crawley Rangers and Crawley Athletic in 1938 but still as Crawley. Changed name to Crawley Town in 1958.

DAGENHAM & REDBRIDGE

1997	P	W	D	L	F	A		W	D	L	F	A
CUP	3	0	1	0	2	2		0	1	1	1	2
TOTAL	3	0	1	0	2	2		0	1	1	1	2

Formed in 1992 as a merger between Dagenham and Redbridge Forest.

DARLASTON

1935-1939	P	W	D	L	F	A		W	D	L	F	A
LEAGUE	8	2	1	1	9	8		0	1	3	1	14
TOTAL	8	2	1	1	9	8		0	1	3	1	14

Formed pre-1911. Changed name to Darlaston Town 1996.

DARTFORD

1946-1992	P	W	D	L	F	A		W	D	L	F	A
LEAGUE	46	9	8	6	36	30		3	2	18	27	61
TOTAL	46	9	8	6	36	30		3	2	18	27	61

Formed in 1888.

DEAL TOWN

1963-1966	P	W	D	L	F	A		W	D	L	F	A
LEAGUE	6	3	0	0	10	1		2	0	1	6	5
TOTAL	6	3	0	0	10	1		2	0	1	6	5

Founded in 1908 as Deal Cinque Ports FC changing name to Deal Town in 1920.

DEVIZES TOWN

1968-1981	P	W	D	L	F	A		W	D	L	F	A
CUP	2	1	0	1	5	5		0	0	0	0	0
TOTAL	2	1	0	1	5	5		0	0	0	0	0

Established in 1887.

DIDCOT TOWN

2007	P	W	D	L	F	A		W	D	L	F	A
CUP	1	0	0	1	2	3		0	0	0	0	0
TOTAL	1	0	0	1	2	3		0	0	0	0	0

Formed in 1907.

DORCHESTER TOWN

1975-2000	P	W	D	L	F	A		W	D	L	F	A
LEAGUE	26	7	4	2	20	13		4	4	5	18	22
CUP	13	5	1	2	15	9		1	1	3	5	7
TOTAL	39	12	5	4	35	22		5	5	8	23	29

Formed in 1880.

DOVER

1959-1971	P	W	D	L	F	A		W	D	L	F	A
LEAGUE	20	2	2	6	22	24		3	1	6	13	35
TOTAL	20	2	2	6	22	24		3	1	6	13	35

Formed 1891 disbanding 1910. Reformed as Dover United in 1920 winding up in 1933 and was reborn as Dover. Club wound up 1983.

DOVER ATHLETIC

1990-1993	P	W	D	L	F	A		W	D	L	F	A
LEAGUE	8	1	1	2	5	7		0	0	4	0	10
TOTAL	8	1	1	2	5	7		0	0	4	0	10

Club formed in 1983 after dissolution of Dover.

DUDLEY TOWN

1977-1989	P	W	D	L	F	A		W	D	L	F	A
LEAGUE	4	1	1	0	6	2		1	1	0	2	0
CUP	4	0	0	2	3	5		1	1	0	5	1
TOTAL	8	1	1	2	9	7		2	2	0	7	1

Formed in 1893.

DULWICH HAMLET

1993	P	W	D	L	F	A		W	D	L	F	A
CUP	1	0	0	0	0	0		0	0	1	1	2
TOTAL	1	0	0	0	0	0		0	0	1	1	2

Formed in 1893.

DUNSTABLE

1976-1978	P	W	D	L	F	A		W	D	L	F	A
LEAGUE	4	2	0	0	7	2		2	0	0	3	0
TOTAL	4	2	0	0	7	2		2	0	0	3	0

Formerly Dunstable Town changing name to Dunstable in 1975 disbanding 1994.

DUNSTABLE TOWN

1965-2004	P	W	D	L	F	A		W	D	L	F	A
LEAGUE	16	4	2	2	12	7		3	1	4	13	12
TOTAL	16	4	2	2	12	9		3	1	4	13	12

Formed 1895 as Dunstable Town lasted until 1914. Reformed 1950 changing name to Dunstable in 1975. Club reformed 1998.

DURSLEY

1909	P	W	D	L	F	A		W	D	L	F	A
LEAGUE	2	1	0	0	6	0		1	0	0	4	1
TOTAL	2	1	0	0	6	0		1	0	0	4	1

Formed 1893 as Dursley Saint James. Dropped 'Saint James' in 1898 and added 'Town' just after World War I.

DURSLEY ROVERS

1922-1926	P	W	D	L	F	A		W	D	L	F	A
LEAGUE	10	1	1	3	7	13		0	0	5	7	21
TOTAL	10	1	1	3	7	13		0	0	5	7	21

Formed 1919.

DURSLEY TOWN

1922-1932	P	W	D	L	F	A		W	D	L	F	A
LEAGUE	8	1	1	1	7	4		1	1	2	10	16
CUP	1	0	0	0	0	0		1	0	0	5	2
TOTAL	9	1	1	1	7	4		2	1	2	15	18

Formerly Dursley Saint James and Dursley. Became Dursley Town after World War I.

EAST THURROCK UNITED

2008	P	W	D	L	F	A		W	D	L	F	A
CUP	1	0	0	0	0	0		0	0	1	2	4
TOTAL	1	0	0	0	0	0		0	0	1	2	4

Formed 1969.

EASTBOURNE BOROUGH

2006	P	W	D	L	F	A		W	D	L	F	A
CUP	1	0	0	1	2	5		0	0	0	0	0
TOTAL	1	0	0	1	2	5		0	0	0	0	0

Formed 1964 as Langney Sports FC. Renamed Eastbourne Borough in 2001.

EASTINGTON

1930	P	W	D	L	F	A		W	D	L	F	A
CUP	2	1	0	0	5	1		0	1	0	2	2
TOTAL	2	1	0	0	5	1		0	1	0	2	2

Located near Northleach.

EASTLEIGH

2006	P	W	D	L	F	A		W	D	L	F	A
CUP	1	0	0	0	0	0		0	0	1	2	3
TOTAL	1	0	0	0	0	0		0	0	1	2	3

Formed 1946 as Swaythling Athletic dropping 'Athletic' to become just Swaythling in due course. Renamed Eastleigh in 1980.

EASTVILLE ROVERS

1893-1896	P	W	D	L	F	A		W	D	L	F	A
LEAGUE	6	1	0	2	6	5		2	0	1	9	9
CUP	1	0	0	1	0	1		0	0	0	0	0
TOTAL	7	1	0	3	6	6		2	0	1	9	9

Changed name to Bristol Rovers in 1898.

EBBW VALE

1951-1955	P	W	D	L	F	A		W	D	L	F	A
CUP	3	1	0	1	5	3		0	1	0	2	2
TOTAL	3	1	0	1	5	3		0	1	0	2	2

Formed pre-1903.

EBLEY

1898-1901	P	W	D	L	F	A		W	D	L	F	A
LEAGUE	8	4	0	0	17	4		3	1	0	9	1
TOTAL	8	4	0	0	17	4		3	1	0	9	1

ELLWOOD

1932-1935	P	W	D	L	F	A		W	D	L	F	A
LEAGUE	2	1	0	0	2	0		1	0	0	3	0
CUP	1	1	0	0	6	3		0	0	0	0	0
TOTAL	3	2	0	0	8	3		1	0	0	3	0

Established 1907.

ENDERBY TOWN

1972-1983	P	W	D	L	F	A		W	D	L	F	A
LEAGUE	22	6	1	4	24	23		4	1	6	15	23
TOTAL	22	6	1	4	24	23		4	1	6	15	23

Formed 1900. Changed name to Leicester United in 1981.

RECORD AGAINST OPPONENTS

EVERWARM

1975	P	W	D	L	F	A		W	D	L	F	A
CUP	2	0	1	0	1	1		1	0	0	4	2
TOTAL	**2**	**0**	**1**	**0**	**1**	**1**		**1**	**0**	**0**	**4**	**2**

Changed name to Everwarm temporarily for three years upto 1976 from Bridgend Town.

EVESHAM TOWN

1935-1938	P	W	D	L	F	A		W	D	L	F	A
LEAGUE	6	2	1	0	8	1		1	0	2	4	6
TOTAL	**6**	**2**	**1**	**0**	**8**	**1**		**1**	**0**	**2**	**4**	**6**

Formed pre-1922. Changed name to Evesham United (2) just after World War II.

EVESHAM UNITED (1)

1909-1910	P	W	D	L	F	A		W	D	L	F	A
LEAGUE	2	0	1	0	2	2		0	0	1	0	3
TOTAL	**2**	**0**	**1**	**0**	**2**	**2**		**0**	**0**	**1**	**0**	**3**

An Evesham United played in the Cheltenham & Distict League in 1909/10. Possibly no connection with the current club who were renamed from Evesham Town to Evesham United immediately after World War II.

EVESHAM UNITED (2)

1994-2009	P	W	D	L	F	A		W	D	L	F	A
LEAGUE	12	3	1	2	13	8		1	2	3	7	12
CUP	5	2	0	0	4	1		3	0	0	10	3
TOTAL	**17**	**4**	**1**	**2**	**17**	**9**		**4**	**2**	**3**	**17**	**15**

Formerly Evesham Town.

EXETER CITY

1980	P	W	D	L	F	A		W	D	L	F	A
LEAGUE	1	0	1	0	1	1		0	0	0	0	0
TOTAL	**1**	**0**	**1**	**0**	**1**	**1**		**0**	**0**	**0**	**0**	**0**

Formed 1904 as an amalgamation of Saint Sidwell's United and Exeter United.

EXETER CITY RESERVES

1947-1960	P	W	D	L	F	A		W	D	L	F	A
LEAGUE	26	7	4	2	26	13		2	3	8	18	35
CUP	1	1	0	0	4	1		0	0	0	0	0
TOTAL	**27**	**8**	**4**	**2**	**30**	**14**		**2**	**3**	**8**	**18**	**35**

EXMOUTH TOWN

1994	P	W	D	L	F	A		W	D	L	F	A
CUP	1	1	0	0	3	0		0	0	0	0	0
TOTAL	**1**	**1**	**0**	**0**	**3**	**0**		**0**	**0**	**0**	**0**	**0**

Formed 1933.

FAIRFORD TOWN

1926	P	W	D	L	F	A		W	D	L	F	A
CUP	1	1	0	0	13	0		0	0	0	0	0
TOTAL	**1**	**1**	**0**	**0**	**13**	**0**		**0**	**0**	**0**	**0**	**0**

Formed 1892.

FAREHAM TOWN

1982-1994	P	W	D	L	F	A		W	D	L	F	A
LEAGUE	6	0	1	2	6	12		0	2	1	1	3
CUP	1	1	0	0	3	0		0	0	0	0	0
TOTAL	**7**	**1**	**1**	**2**	**9**	**12**		**0**	**2**	**1**	**1**	**3**

Formed in 1946 by the amalgamation of three junior sides, each of which dated from the 19th Century.

FARNBOROUGH

2008-2009	P	W	D	L	F	A		W	D	L	F	A
LEAGUE	3	0	1	0	0	0		1	0	1	2	2
TOTAL	**3**	**0**	**1**	**0**	**0**	**0**		**1**	**0**	**1**	**2**	**2**

Reformed from Farnborough Town 2007.

FARNBOROUGH TOWN

1990-1994	P	W	D	L	F	A		W	D	L	F	A
LEAGUE	4	0	1	1	1	2		0	1	1	1	2
CUP	1	0	0	0	0	0		0	0	1	1	4
TOTAL	**5**	**0**	**1**	**1**	**1**	**2**		**0**	**1**	**2**	**2**	**6**

Formed 1967. Went into liquidation 2007 and reformed as Farnborough FC.

FERNDALE ATHLETIC

1976	P	W	D	L	F	A		W	D	L	F	A
CUP	1	0	0	0	0	0		0	0	1	1	3
TOTAL	**1**	**0**	**0**	**0**	**0**	**0**		**0**	**0**	**1**	**1**	**3**

Welsh club. A Ferndale club existed in 1922.

FISHER ATHLETIC

1983-1992	P	W	D	L	F	A		W	D	L	F	A
LEAGUE	6	2	0	1	4	5		0	0	3	1	7
CUP	2	0	1	0	3	3		0	0	1	1	2
TOTAL	**8**	**2**	**1**	**1**	**7**	**8**		**0**	**0**	**4**	**2**	**9**

Founded 1908 and named after the Catholic martyr Saint John Fisher. Changed name to Fisher Athletic London 1996.

FOLKESTONE

1968-1969	P	W	D	L	F	A		W	D	L	F	A
LEAGUE	2	1	0	0	5	0		0	0	1	2	5
TOTAL	**2**	**1**	**0**	**0**	**5**	**0**		**0**	**0**	**1**	**2**	**5**

Formerly Folkestone Town.

FOLKESTONE TOWN

1959-1989	P	W	D	L	F	A		W	D	L	F	A
LEAGUE	12	2	1	3	7	9		1	0	5	5	22
CUP	1	0	0	0	0	0		1	0	0	1	0
TOTAL	**13**	**2**	**1**	**3**	**7**	**9**		**2**	**0**	**5**	**6**	**22**

Formed 1884. Dropped 'Town' for one season 1968/69. Club folded 1990 but reformed same year as Folkestone and resigned after 17 games.

FOREST GREEN ROVERS

1899-1999	P	W	D	L	F	A		W	D	L	F	A
LEAGUE	34	6	5	7	43	26		6	2	8	35	35
CUP	23	6	0	5	23	19		6	2	4	26	22
TOTAL	**57**	**12**	**5**	**12**	**66**	**45**		**12**	**4**	**12**	**61**	**57**

Formed 1890 as Nailsworth & Forest Green. Became Forest Green Rovers in 1894. In 1989 changed name to Stroud (2) but changed back to Forest Green Rovers for the 1992-93 season.

FOREST GREEN ROVERS RESERVES

1921-1922	P	W	D	L	F	A		W	D	L	F	A
LEAGUE	2	0	0	1	1	5		0	0	1	0	3
TOTAL	**2**	**0**	**0**	**1**	**1**	**5**		**0**	**0**	**1**	**0**	**3**

FROME TOWN

1927-1988	P	W	D	L	F	A		W	D	L	F	A
LEAGUE	2	0	1	0	3	3		0	1	0	3	3
CUP	4	1	0	1	3	5		2	0	0	6	2
TOTAL	**6**	**1**	**1**	**1**	**6**	**8**		**2**	**1**	**0**	**9**	**5**

Formed 1904.

GILLINGHAM

1946-1949	P	W	D	L	F	A		W	D	L	F	A
LEAGUE	8	2	1	1	7	7		0	0	4	3	26
TOTAL	**8**	**2**	**1**	**1**	**7**	**7**		**0**	**0**	**4**	**3**	**26**

Formed 1893 as New Brompton. Renamed Gillingham in 1913.

GLASTONBURY

1948-1980	P	W	D	L	F	A		W	D	L	F	A
CUP	3	2	0	0	6	2		0	1	0	1	1
TOTAL	**3**	**2**	**0**	**0**	**6**	**2**		**0**	**1**	**0**	**1**	**1**

Founded in 1890 as Glastonbury Avalon Rovers. By 1901 they were just known as Glastonbury. Changed name to Glastonbury Town in 2003.

GLOUCESTER AERO

1941-1942	P	W	D	L	F	A		W	D	L	F	A
LEAGUE	2	2	0	0	5	1		0	0	0	0	0
TOTAL	**2**	**2**	**0**	**0**	**5**	**1**		**0**	**0**	**0**	**0**	**0**

GOSPORT BOROUGH

1982-1990	P	W	D	L	F	A		W	D	L	F	A
LEAGUE	6	3	0	0	13	0		2	1	0	9	3
CUP	2	1	0	0	6	1		0	0	1	0	4
TOTAL	**8**	**4**	**0**	**0**	**19**	**1**		**2**	**1**	**1**	**9**	**7**

Founded in 1944.

GRANTHAM

1972-1986	P	W	D	L	F	A		W	D	L	F	A
LEAGUE	8	0	0	4	2	10		1	1	2	6	11
CUP	1	0	0	0	0	0		1	0	0	3	1
TOTAL	**9**	**0**	**0**	**4**	**2**	**10**		**2**	**1**	**2**	**9**	**12**

Formed in 1874. Changed name to Grantham Town in 1987.

GRANTHAM TOWN

1987-2006	P	W	D	L	F	A		W	D	L	F	A
LEAGUE	12	3	2	1	11	5		1	4	1	5	5
TOTAL	**12**	**3**	**2**	**1**	**11**	**5**		**1**	**4**	**1**	**5**	**5**

Formerly Grantham.

GRAVESEND & NORTHFLEET

1946-1997	P	W	D	L	F	A		W	D	L	F	A
LEAGUE	54	18	3	6	67	38		10	10	7	40	31
TOTAL	54	18	3	6	67	38		10	10	7	40	31

Formed in 1946 with the merger of Gravesend United and Northfleet United. Now known as Ebbsfleet United from 2007.

GRESLEY ROVERS

1993-2004	P	W	D	L	F	A		W	D	L	F	A
LEAGUE	20	3	5	2	15	13		4	1	5	15	18
TOTAL	20	3	5	2	15	13		4	1	5	15	18

Formed 1882.

GUILDFORD CITY

1947-1960	P	W	D	L	F	A		W	D	L	F	A
LEAGUE	26	4	4	5	16	16		3	2	8	15	29
CUP	1	0	0	0	0	0		0	0	1	0	3
TOTAL	27	4	4	5	16	16		3	2	9	15	32

Formed as Guildford United in 1921. Became Guildford City in 1927 and folded in 1974. Emerged as Guildford & Dorking United but went into liquidation in 1976. Club is now known as AFC Guildford.

HALESOWEN TOWN

1935-2009	P	W	D	L	F	A		W	D	L	F	A
LEAGUE	48	8	8	7	39	34		8	9	8	38	32
CUP	3	0	1	1	3	4		0	0	1	1	2
TOTAL	51	8	9	8	42	38		8	9	9	39	34

Formed 1873.

HALIFAX TOWN

1997	P	W	D	L	F	A		W	D	L	F	A
CUP	1	1	0	0	3	0		0	0	0	0	0
TOTAL	1	1	0	0	3	0		0	0	0	0	0

Formed 1911.

HANHAM ATHLETIC

1928-1947	P	W	D	L	F	A		W	D	L	F	A
CUP	2	0	0	1	3	4		0	0	1	2	4
TOTAL	2	0	0	1	3	4		0	0	1	2	4

Formed 1896.

HARROW BOROUGH

1992	P	W	D	L	F	A		W	D	L	F	A
CUP	1	0	0	1	1	2		0	0	0	0	0
TOTAL	1	0	0	1	1	2		0	0	0	0	0

Founded 1933 as Roxonian. Changed name to Harrow Town in 1938. Changed name again to Harrow Borough in 1967.

HASTINGS TOWN

1992-1999	P	W	D	L	F	A		W	D	L	F	A
LEAGUE	14	4	1	2	14	9		2	2	3	5	6
TOTAL	14	4	1	2	14	9		2	2	3	5	6

Formed as Saint Leonards United in 1898. Became Hastings & Saint Leonards in 1906. Changed name to Hastings Town in 1980.

HASTINGS UNITED

1948-1985	P	W	D	L	F	A		W	D	L	F	A
LEAGUE	36	13	3	2	47	21		2	5	11	22	41
TOTAL	36	13	3	2	47	21		2	5	11	22	41

Formed in 1948 and wound up in 1985.

HAVANT & WATERLOOVILLE

1999-2000	P	W	D	L	F	A		W	D	L	F	A
LEAGUE	2	0	1	0	1	1		0	1	0	1	1
CUP	2	0	0	1	2	3		0	1	0	1	1
TOTAL	4	0	1	1	3	4		0	2	0	2	2

Formed 1998 as a merger between Havant Town and Waterlooville.

HAVERFORDWEST COUNTY

1983	P	W	D	L	F	A		W	D	L	F	A
CUP	1	0	0	0	0	0		1	0	0	2	1
TOTAL	1	0	0	0	0	0		1	0	0	2	1

Formed in 1899 as Haverfordwest and renamed Haverfordwest Town in 1901. In 1936 renamed Haverfordwest Athletic adopting the current name in 1956.

HEADINGTON UNITED

1949-1959	P	W	D	L	F	A		W	D	L	F	A
LEAGUE	20	6	2	2	16	13		2	0	8	6	25
CUP	2	1	0	0	2	1		0	1	0	0	0
TOTAL	22	7	2	2	18	14		2	1	8	6	25

Formed as Headington in 1896 adding 'United' in 1899. Changed name to Oxford United in 1960.

HEDNESFORD TOWN

1985-2005	P	W	D	L	F	A		W	D	L	F	A
LEAGUE	16	6	1	1	18	7		2	2	4	12	17
CUP	3	0	1	0	2	2		2	0	0	5	0
TOTAL	19	6	2	1	20	9		4	2	4	17	17

Formed 1880 by the amalgamation of West Hill and Hill Top.

HEMEL HEMPSTEAD TOWN

2004-2009	P	W	D	L	F	A		W	D	L	F	A
LEAGUE	8	1	1	2	7	8		0	3	1	7	8
TOTAL	8	1	1	2	7	8		0	3	1	7	8

Founded 1885 as Apsley. Changed name to Hemel Hempstead in 1952 adding 'Town' in 1955.

HEREFORD CITY

1909-1910	P	W	D	L	F	A		W	D	L	F	A
CUP	2	0	0	0	0	0		0	0	2	3	8
TOTAL	2	0	0	0	0	0		0	0	2	3	8

HEREFORD THISTLE

1894-1895?	P	W	D	L	F	A		W	D	L	F	A
LEAGUE	2	0	0	1	0	4		0	1	0	6	6
TOTAL	2	0	0	1	0	4		0	1	0	6	6

Formed pre-1894. They left the Birmingham League in 1899.

HEREFORD UNITED

1939-1971	P	W	D	L	F	A		W	D	L	F	A
LEAGUE	34	9	3	5	33	28		1	4	12	16	50
CUP	8	1	2	1	5	5		0	0	4	4	16
TOTAL	42	10	5	6	38	33		1	4	16	20	66

Formed in 1924 by the amalgamation of Saint Martins and RAOC.

HIGHBEECH

1934-1935?	P	W	D	L	F	A		W	D	L	F	A
LEAGUE	2	1	0	0	5	0		0	0	1	0	2
TOTAL	2	1	0	0	5	0		0	0	1	0	2

HILLINGDON BOROUGH

1964-2007	P	W	D	L	F	A		W	D	L	F	A
LEAGUE	8	1	0	3	3	9		1	0	3	2	10
CUP	2	0	1	0	3	3		1	0	0	1	0
TOTAL	10	1	1	3	6	12		2	0	3	3	10

Formed as Yiewsley in 1872. Folded 1987. Reformed 1990.

HINCKLEY ATHLETIC

1936-1967	P	W	D	L	F	A		W	D	L	F	A
LEAGUE	22	5	4	2	30	15		2	3	6	19	30
TOTAL	22	5	4	2	30	15		2	3	6	19	30

Formed in 1889. Merged with Hinckley Town to become United in 1997.

HINCKLEY UNITED

2000-2001	P	W	D	L	F	A		W	D	L	F	A
LEAGUE	2	0	0	1	0	2		0	1	0	1	1
TOTAL	2	0	0	1	0	2		0	1	0	1	1

Formerly Hinckley Athletic.

HISTON

2004-2005	P	W	D	L	F	A		W	D	L	F	A
LEAGUE	2	0	0	1	1	2		1	0	0	1	0
TOTAL	2	0	0	1	1	2		1	0	0	1	0

Formed in 1904 as Histon Institute. The 'Institute' was dropped by 1960.

HITCHIN TOWN

2004-2009	P	W	D	L	F	A		W	D	L	F	A
LEAGUE	10	4	1	0	11	3		1	4	0	8	7
TOTAL	10	4	1	0	11	3		1	4	0	8	7

Formed 1865 as Hitchin and wound up in 1911. Reformed as Hitchin Town in 1928.

ILKESTON TOWN

1971-2004	P	W	D	L	F	A		W	D	L	F	A
LEAGUE	12	4	1	1	11	4		4	0	2	12	8
CUP	1	0	0	0	0	0		0	0	1	1	3
TOTAL	13	4	1	1	11	4		4	0	3	13	11

Formed 1945 although a club known as Ilkeston played from 1894 until World War II.

KETTERING TOWN

1950-1972	P	W	D	L	F	A		W	D	L	F	A
LEAGUE	34	10	1	6	24	20		2	6	9	20	38
TOTAL	34	10	1	6	24	20		2	6	9	20	38

Founded 1872 as Kettering. Added 'Town' in 1924.

RECORD AGAINST OPPONENTS

KEYNSHAM TOWN

1929-1933	P	W	D	L	F	A		W	D	L	F	A
CUP	4	0	1	0	3	3		0	0	3	3	11
TOTAL	**4**	**0**	**1**	**0**	**3**	**3**		**0**	**0**	**3**	**3**	**11**

Formed 1895.

KIDDERMINSTER HARRIERS

1948-1998	P	W	D	L	F	A		W	D	L	F	A
LEAGUE	46	14	3	6	44	26		6	4	13	23	46
CUP	4	0	0	1	1	3		2	0	1	8	7
TOTAL	**50**	**14**	**3**	**7**	**45**	**29**		**8**	**4**	**14**	**31**	**53**

Formed 1886.

KING'S LYNN

1962-2008	P	W	D	L	F	A		W	D	L	F	A
LEAGUE	50	16	2	6	44	23		8	3	15	28	46
CUP	1	0	0	1	0	2		0	0	0	0	0
TOTAL	**51**	**16**	**2**	**7**	**44**	**25**		**8**	**3**	**15**	**28**	**46**

Founded 1879 as Lynn Town. Became King's Lynn in 1914.

KING'S STANLEY

1923	P	W	D	L	F	A		W	D	L	F	A
LEAGUE	2	0	1	0	0	0		1	0	0	3	1
TOTAL	**2**	**0**	**1**	**0**	**0**	**0**		**1**	**0**	**0**	**3**	**1**

Formed 1907.

KINGSTONIAN

1996-1998	P	W	D	L	F	A		W	D	L	F	A
CUP	2	1	0	1	4	3		0	0	0	0	0
TOTAL	**2**	**1**	**0**	**1**	**4**	**3**		**0**	**0**	**0**	**0**	**0**

Formed 1885.

KINGSWOOD

1922-1926	P	W	D	L	F	A		W	D	L	F	A
LEAGUE	10	2	2	1	14	10		0	1	4	7	14
CUP	2	0	0	0	0	0		0	0	2	1	4
TOTAL	**12**	**2**	**2**	**1**	**14**	**10**		**0**	**1**	**6**	**8**	**18**

Formed in the 1890s.

KINGSWOOD ROVERS

1903-1906	P	W	D	L	F	A		W	D	L	F	A
CUP	2	0	0	0	0	0		1	0	1	2	1
TOTAL	**2**	**0**	**0**	**0**	**0**	**0**		**1**	**0**	**1**	**2**	**1**

LEAMINGTON

1985-1987	P	W	D	L	F	A		W	D	L	F	A
LEAGUE	4	1	0	1	4	4		1	0	1	2	2
TOTAL	**4**	**1**	**0**	**1**	**4**	**4**		**1**	**0**	**1**	**2**	**2**

Formerly Automotive Products Leamington. Changed to Leamington in 1985.

LEAMINGTON TOWN

1936-1937	P	W	D	L	F	A		W	D	L	F	A
LEAGUE	4	1	0	1	4	3		1	1	0	4	3
TOTAL	**4**	**1**	**0**	**1**	**4**	**3**		**1**	**1**	**0**	**4**	**3**

Formed in 1891 folding 1937. Reformed as Lockheed Leamington in 1945.

LECKHAMPTON

1930	P	W	D	L	F	A		W	D	L	F	A
CUP	1	1	0	0	3	1		0	0	0	0	0
TOTAL	**1**	**1**	**0**	**0**	**3**	**1**		**0**	**0**	**0**	**0**	**0**

Formed pre-1913.

LEDBURY TOWN

1934-1935	P	W	D	L	F	A		W	D	L	F	A
LEAGUE	4	1	1	0	8	2		1	1	0	8	3
TOTAL	**4**	**1**	**1**	**0**	**8**	**2**		**1**	**1**	**0**	**8**	**3**

Formed 1893. Folded 1983 and reformed as Ledbury Town 84.

LEDBURY VICTORIA

1898-1900	P	W	D	L	F	A		W	D	L	F	A
LEAGUE	3	1	0	0	6	0		1	1	0	2	1
TOTAL	**3**	**1**	**0**	**0**	**6**	**0**		**1**	**1**	**0**	**2**	**1**

LEEK TOWN

1994-1995	P	W	D	L	F	A		W	D	L	F	A
LEAGUE	2	1	0	0	2	0		0	0	1	1	3
TOTAL	**2**	**1**	**0**	**0**	**2**	**0**		**0**	**0**	**1**	**1**	**3**

Formed in 1946 as Leek Lowe Hamil and adopted 'Town' in 1951.

LEICESTER UNITED

1985-1987	P	W	D	L	F	A		W	D	L	F	A
LEAGUE	4	0	1	1	3	5		1	0	1	4	4
TOTAL	4	0	1	1	3	5		1	0	1	4	4

Formerly Enderby Town. Club wound up 1996.

LEWES

2003	P	W	D	L	F	A		W	D	L	F	A
CUP	1	1	0	0	3	2		0	0	0	0	0
TOTAL	1	1	0	0	3	2		0	0	0	0	0

Formed 1885.

LEYTONSTONE & ILFORD

1981	P	W	D	L	F	A		W	D	L	F	A
CUP	1	0	0	0	0	0		0	0	1	0	7
TOTAL	1	0	0	0	0	0		0	0	1	0	7

Formed 1979 as a merger between Leytonstone and Ilford. Absorbed Walthamstowe Avenue in 1988 and changed name to Redbridge Forest in 1990. Subsequently merged with Dagenham in 1992 to become Dagenham & Redbridge.

LINDEN OLD BOYS

1908	P	W	D	L	F	A		W	D	L	F	A
LEAGUE	2	1	0	0	10	1		1	0	0	4	0
TOTAL	2	1	0	0	10	1		1	0	0	4	0

Played in Gloucester.

LISKEARD ATHLETIC

2006	P	W	D	L	F	A		W	D	L	F	A
CUP	2	0	1	0	0	0		1	0	0	3	0
TOTAL	2	0	1	0	0	0		1	0	0	3	0

Formed 1946.

LISTER'S WORKS

1928-1934	P	W	D	L	F	A		W	D	L	F	A
LEAGUE	11	4	0	1	18	4		2	1	3	15	19
CUP	3	0	0	0	0	0		2	0	1	14	9
TOTAL	14	4	0	1	18	4		4	1	4	29	28

Was the club side of the R.A. Lister Company in Dursley.

LLANELLI

1979-1990	P	W	D	L	F	A		W	D	L	F	A
CUP	5	3	1	0	13	2		1	0	0	5	2
TOTAL	5	3	1	0	13	2		1	0	0	5	2

Formerly Llanelly.

LLANELLY

1950-1965	P	W	D	L	F	A		W	D	L	F	A
LEAGUE	14	6	1	0	17	5		2	0	5	11	14
CUP	6	1	2	1	4	4		1	0	1	2	6
TOTAL	20	7	3	1	21	9		3	0	6	13	20

Formed in 1896. Now known as Llanelli.

LOCKHEED LEAMINGTON

1970-1973	P	W	D	L	F	A		W	D	L	F	A
LEAGUE	4	1	0	1	3	3		0	0	2	3	5
CUP	2	0	1	0	0	0		1	0	0	2	1
TOTAL	6	1	1	1	3	3		1	0	2	5	6

Reformed from the old Leamington Town in 1945 changing their name to Automotive Products Leamington in 1973.

LONGHOPE UNITED

1913-1914	P	W	D	L	F	A		W	D	L	F	A
LEAGUE	2	0	0	1	0	3		0	0	1	2	6
TOTAL	2	0	0	1	0	3		0	0	1	2	6

Formed pre-1913. There is a current club called Longhope.

LOVELLS ATHLETIC

1937-1967	P	W	D	L	F	A		W	D	L	F	A
LEAGUE	26	8	1	4	30	24		2	4	7	18	37
CUP	8	0	0	2	1	4		4	0	2	13	10
TOTAL	34	8	1	6	31	28		6	4	9	31	47

Formed 1918 and disbanded in 1969. Played in Newport.

MAESTEG PARK

1981	P	W	D	L	F	A		W	D	L	F	A
CUP	1	1	0	0	4	0		0	0	0	0	0
TOTAL	1	1	0	0	4	0		0	0	0	0	0

Formed 1945.

MAIDENHEAD UNITED

2006-2007	P	W	D	L	F	A		W	D	L	F	A
LEAGUE	2	1	0	0	2	1		0	0	1	0	1
TOTAL	2	1	0	0	2	1		0	0	1	0	1

Formed 1870 as Maidenhead. 'United' was added in 1920.

MAIDSTONE UNITED

1985	P	W	D	L	F	A		W	D	L	F	A
CUP	1	0	0	1	0	2		0	0	0	0	0
TOTAL	1	0	0	1	0	2		0	0	0	0	0

Formed in 1897. Went into liquidation in 1992. Reformed almost immediately as Maidstone Invicta and subsequently returned to Maidstone United circa 2000.

MANGOTSFIELD

1894-1896	P	W	D	L	F	A		W	D	L	F	A
LEAGUE	6	3	0	0	12	4		1	1	1	3	4
CUP	2	1	0	0	4	2		0	1	0	1	1
TOTAL	8	4	0	0	16	6		1	2	1	4	5

Formed 1888 disbanding 1898.

MANGOTSFIELD UNITED

1989-2009	P	W	D	L	F	A		W	D	L	F	A
LEAGUE	16	2	1	5	14	19		4	1	3	19	15
CUP	6	3	0	0	11	2		1	0	2	3	4
TOTAL	22	5	1	5	25	21		5	1	5	22	19

Founded 1951.

MANSFIELD TOWN

1948	P	W	D	L	F	A		W	D	L	F	A
CUP	1	0	0	0	0	0		0	0	1	0	4
TOTAL	1	0	0	0	0	0		0	0	1	0	4

Formed 1897 as Mansfield Wesleyans. The present name was adopted in 1910.

MARGATE

1959-2006	P	W	D	L	F	A		W	D	L	F	A
LEAGUE	16	3	2	3	13	12		1	1	6	7	23
CUP	2	1	0	0	1	0		0	0	1	1	3
TOTAL	18	4	2	3	14	12		1	1	7	8	26

Formed 1896. Between 1981 and 1989 known as Thanet United.

MARKET HARBOROUGH

1935	P	W	D	L	F	A		W	D	L	F	A
LEAGUE	1	1	0	0	7	1		0	0	0	0	0
TOTAL	1	1	0	0	7	1		0	0	0	0	0

Formed pre-1904. Disbanded 1935.

MELKSHAM TOWN

1978-1988	P	W	D	L	F	A		W	D	L	F	A
CUP	3	0	0	0	0	0		2	0	1	7	1
TOTAL	3	0	0	0	0	0		2	0	1	7	1

Formed 1876.

MERTHYR TYDFIL

1946-2009	P	W	D	L	F	A		W	D	L	F	A
LEAGUE	88	24	10	10	98	71		6	6	32	51	118
CUP	39	8	6	7	35	36		4	3	11	18	44
TOTAL	127	32	16	17	133	107		10	9	43	69	162

Formed 1945.

MIDLAND & SOUTH WESTERN JUNCTION RAILWAY

1903-1908	P	W	D	L	F	A		W	D	L	F	A
LEAGUE	6	2	0	1	7	4		2	1	0	11	3
TOTAL	6	2	0	1	7	4		2	1	0	11	3

Formed pre-1903. Railway company team that played in Cirencester. Absorbed as part of the Great Western Railway Company in 1923.

MILE OAK ROVERS

1986-1989	P	W	D	L	F	A		W	D	L	F	A
LEAGUE	8	3	1	0	14	3		3	0	1	5	3
TOTAL	8	3	1	0	14	3		3	0	1	5	3

Formed 1958.

MILLWALL

1946	P	W	D	L	F	A		W	D	L	F	A
LEAGUE	2	1	0	0	5	4		0	0	1	0	2
TOTAL	2	1	0	0	5	4		0	0	1	0	2

Formed 1885 as Millwall Rovers becoming Millwall Athletic in 1889. Known only as Millwall since 1899.

MILTON KEYNES CITY

1974-1982	P	W	D	L	F	A		W	D	L	F	A
LEAGUE	16	6	0	2	20	14		4	2	2	18	7
TOTAL	16	6	0	2	20	14		4	2	2	18	7

Formerly Bletchley Town. Club folded in 1985.

MINEHEAD

1979-1982	P	W	D	L	F	A		W	D	L	F	A
LEAGUE	9	2	0	2	7	6		2	1	2	9	7
CUP	1	1	0	0	4	1		0	0	0	0	0
TOTAL	10	3	0	2	11	7		2	1	2	9	7

Formed 1889. Changed name to Minehead Town in 1998.

MINEHEAD TOWN

2002	P	W	D	L	F	A		W	D	L	F	A
CUP	1	0	0	0	0	0		1	0	0	2	0
TOTAL	1	0	0	0	0	0		1	0	0	2	0

Formerly Minehead.

MINSTERWORTH

1913	P	W	D	L	F	A		W	D	L	F	A
LEAGUE	2	0	0	1	0	5		0	0	1	0	2
TOTAL	2	0	0	1	0	5		0	0	1	0	2

MITCHELDEAN

1913-1922	P	W	D	L	F	A		W	D	L	F	A
LEAGUE	5	1	1	0	9	2		0	1	1	1	3
TOTAL	5	1	1	0	9	2		0	1	1	1	3

Formed 1912.

MOOR GREEN

1985-1994	P	W	D	L	F	A		W	D	L	F	A
LEAGUE	16	3	2	3	16	17		3	0	5	16	23
CUP	4	2	0	0	7	3		0	1	1	2	3
TOTAL	20	5	2	3	23	20		3	1	6	18	26

Formed 1901. Merged with Solihull Borough in 2007 to become Solihull Moors.

MOUNT HILL ENTERPRISE

1934	P	W	D	L	F	A		W	D	L	F	A
CUP	1	0	0	0	0	0		1	0	0	4	3
TOTAL	1	0	0	0	0	0		1	0	0	4	3

NEWNHAM EXCELSIOR

1913-1914	P	W	D	L	F	A		W	D	L	F	A
LEAGUE	2	1	0	0	2	0		0	0	1	0	2
TOTAL	2	1	0	0	2	0		0	0	1	0	2

AFC NEWPORT

1992-1998	P	W	D	L	F	A		W	D	L	F	A
LEAGUE	4	1	1	0	3	2		1	0	1	4	1
CUP	7	2	1	0	7	5		1	1	2	4	4
TOTAL	11	3	2	0	10	7		2	1	3	8	5

Formed 1989 by the Newport County Supporters after the demise of that club. Changed name back to Newport County in 1999.

NEWPORT (Isle of Wight)

1997	P	W	D	L	F	A		W	D	L	F	A
CUP	1	1	0	0	2	1		0	0	0	0	0
TOTAL	1	1	0	0	2	1		0	0	0	0	0

Formed 1888.

NEWPORT COUNTY

1999-2002	P	W	D	L	F	A		W	D	L	F	A
LEAGUE	2	0	1	0	1	1		0	0	1	1	2
CUP	2	0	1	0	1	1		0	0	1	0	4
TOTAL	4	0	2	0	2	2		0	0	2	1	6

Original club founded 1912. Reformed by Supporters to become AFC Newport in 1989. Current club formed 1999.

NORTHWOOD

2005-2007	P	W	D	L	F	A		W	D	L	F	A
LEAGUE	4	1	1	0	7	4		2	0	0	3	0
TOTAL	4	1	1	0	7	4		2	0	0	3	0

Formed 1899.

NORWICH CITY

1949	P	W	D	L	F	A		W	D	L	F	A
CUP	1	0	0	1	2	3		0	0	0	0	0
TOTAL	1	0	0	1	2	3		0	0	0	0	0

Formed 1902.

NUNEATON BOROUGH

1938-1999	P	W	D	L	F	A		W	D	L	F	A
LEAGUE	26	8	3	2	22	14		4	0	9	18	27
TOTAL	**26**	**8**	**3**	**2**	**22**	**14**		**4**	**0**	**9**	**18**	**27**

Formed 1889 as Nuneaton Saint Nicholas. Changed name to Nuneaton Town in 1894 and disbanded in 1937. Nuneaton Borough took over a couple of days after disbandment.

ODD DOWN

2000	P	W	D	L	F	A		W	D	L	F	A
CUP	1	0	0	0	0	0		1	0	0	2	0
TOTAL	**1**	**0**	**0**	**0**	**0**	**0**		**1**	**0**	**0**	**2**	**0**

Founded 1901. Based in Bath.

OLD BOYS QUEEN ELIZABETH HOSPITAL

1889	P	W	D	L	F	A		W	D	L	F	A
CUP	1	1	0	0	8	1		0	0	0	0	0
TOTAL	**1**	**1**	**0**	**0**	**8**	**1**		**0**	**0**	**0**	**0**	**0**

Formed pre-1889. Played in Bristol.

OLDBURY UNITED

1985-1986	P	W	D	L	F	A		W	D	L	F	A
LEAGUE	2	1	0	0	1	0		1	0	0	1	0
TOTAL	**2**	**1**	**0**	**0**	**1**	**0**		**1**	**0**	**0**	**1**	**0**

Formed 1958.

OSWESTRY TOWN

1975-1979	P	W	D	L	F	A		W	D	L	F	A
LEAGUE	8	2	1	1	10	6		3	0	1	7	4
TOTAL	**8**	**2**	**1**	**1**	**10**	**6**		**3**	**0**	**1**	**7**	**4**

Formed as Oswestry United in 1860 and was one of the oldest football clubs in the world. Became Oswestry Town soon after folding in 1988. Reformed 1994 until they merged with Total Network Services Llansantffraid in 2003 subsequently changing the name to The New Saints in 2006.

OXFORD CITY

2008	P	W	D	L	F	A		W	D	L	F	A
LEAGUE	2	0	1	0	2	2		0	1	0	1	1
TOTAL	**2**	**0**	**1**	**0**	**2**	**2**		**0**	**1**	**0**	**1**	**1**

Formed 1882.

PAGET RANGERS

1987-2001	P	W	D	L	F	A		W	D	L	F	A
LEAGUE	4	1	1	0	6	3		1	0	1	6	4
TOTAL	**4**	**1**	**1**	**0**	**6**	**3**		**1**	**0**	**1**	**6**	**4**

Formed in 1938 and folded in 2002.

PAULTON ROVERS

1927-2005	P	W	D	L	F	A		W	D	L	F	A
LEAGUE	2	1	0	0	2	1		0	1	0	1	1
CUP	3	1	0	2	4	5		0	0	0	0	0
TOTAL	**5**	**2**	**0**	**2**	**6**	**6**		**0**	**1**	**0**	**1**	**1**

Formed 1881.

PIONEER CORPS

1943	P	W	D	L	F	A		W	D	L	F	A
CUP	1	1	0	0	6	4		0	0	0	0	0
TOTAL	**1**	**1**	**0**	**0**	**6**	**4**		**0**	**0**	**0**	**0**	**0**

Played in Gloucester.

POOLE TOWN

1957-1991	P	W	D	L	F	A		W	D	L	F	A
LEAGUE	20	5	3	2	25	13		1	2	7	11	27
CUP	4	1	0	1	4	3		1	1	0	4	3
TOTAL	**24**	**6**	**3**	**3**	**29**	**16**		**2**	**3**	**7**	**15**	**30**

Poole Town was formed 1890 with the merger of Poole Hornets and Poole Rovers.

POPE'S HILL

1931-1933	P	W	D	L	F	A		W	D	L	F	A
LEAGUE	4	2	0	0	6	1		2	0	0	7	3
CUP	1	1	0	0	3	0		0	0	0	0	0
TOTAL	**5**	**3**	**0**	**0**	**9**	**1**		**2**	**0**	**0**	**7**	**3**

Formed pre-1924.

PRICE WALKERS

1897-1898	P	W	D	L	F	A		W	D	L	F	A
LEAGUE	2	1	0	0	8	0		1	0	0	1	0
TOTAL	**2**	**1**	**0**	**0**	**8**	**0**		**1**	**0**	**0**	**1**	**0**

Company football team. Price Walkers & Co dealt with timber. Played in Gloucester.

[464]

RACING CLUB WARWICK

2000-2003	P	W	D	L	F	A		W	D	L	F	A
LEAGUE	6	2	0	1	6	4		2	1	0	11	2
TOTAL	6	2	0	1	6	4		2	1	0	11	2

Formed 1919 as Saltisford Rovers. Changed their name to Racing Club Warwick in 1970.

RADSTOCK TOWN

1927	P	W	D	L	F	A		W	D	L	F	A
LEAGUE	2	0	0	1	1	2		0	0	1	2	5
TOTAL	2	0	0	1	1	2		0	0	1	2	5

Formed 1895 as Radstock. Added 'Town' in 1903.

RAMSGATE ATHLETIC

1959-1969	P	W	D	L	F	A		W	D	L	F	A
LEAGUE	20	5	3	2	16	8		1	2	7	10	25
TOTAL	20	5	3	2	16	8		1	2	7	10	25

Formed 1886 as Ramsgate but folded in 1924. Ramsgate Glenville took over their ground but folded around World War II. A new club dubbed Ramsgate Athletic was formed in 1945. 'Athletic' was retained until 1972 going back to the original name of Ramsgate.

REDDITCH TOWN

1935-1939	P	W	D	L	F	A		W	D	L	F	A
LEAGUE	8	2	1	1	13	8		1	2	1	7	7
TOTAL	8	2	1	1	13	8		1	2	1	7	7

Formed 1891 changing name to Redditch post 1939. Renamed Redditch United in 1971.

REDDITCH UNITED

1972-2004	P	W	D	L	F	A		W	D	L	F	A
LEAGUE	22	2	4	5	12	18		3	1	7	9	17
CUP	11	2	3	0	10	5		1	2	3	8	13
TOTAL	33	4	7	5	22	23		4	3	10	17	30

Formerly Redditch Town.

ROAD SEA SOUTHAMPTON

1984-1985	P	W	D	L	F	A		W	D	L	F	A
LEAGUE	2	1	0	0	2	1		0	0	1	0	2
TOTAL	2	1	0	0	2	1		0	0	1	0	2

Formed 1973 folded 1987.

ROCESTER

2001-2003	P	W	D	L	F	A		W	D	L	F	A
LEAGUE	6	0	2	1	2	3		1	1	1	6	6
TOTAL	6	0	2	1	2	3		1	1	1	6	6

Formed 1876.

RODBOROUGH OLD BOYS

1930	P	W	D	L	F	A		W	D	L	F	A
CUP	1	1	0	0	8	1		0	0	0	0	0
TOTAL	1	1	0	0	8	1		0	0	0	0	0

ROMFORD

1959-1971	P	W	D	L	F	A		W	D	L	F	A
LEAGUE	6	1	0	2	3	2		0	0	3	3	9
CUP	2	0	0	1	2	4		0	1	0	2	2
TOTAL	8	1	0	3	5	6		0	1	3	5	11

Formed 1876.

ROSELEIGH

1900	P	W	D	L	F	A		W	D	L	F	A
LEAGUE	1	0	0	0	0	0		0	0	1	2	3
TOTAL	1	0	0	0	0	0		0	0	1	2	3

Played in Cheltenham.

ROSS KYRLE

1897-1900	P	W	D	L	F	A		W	D	L	F	A
LEAGUE	6	1	1	1	8	4		3	0	0	8	1
TOTAL	6	1	1	1	8	4		3	0	0	8	1

Formed pre-1897.

ROSS TOWN

1897-1903	P	W	D	L	F	A		W	D	L	F	A
LEAGUE	10	3	2	0	14	5		2	1	2	10	7
TOTAL	10	3	2	0	14	5		2	1	2	10	7

Formed pre-1897. There is a current club founded 1993.

ROTHWELL TOWN

1997-2003	P	W	D	L	F	A		W	D	L	F	A
LEAGUE	6	2	0	1	5	3		1	1	1	2	3
CUP	2	1	0	0	4	1		0	1	0	1	1
TOTAL	8	3	0	1	9	4		1	2	1	3	4

Formed 1894 as Rothwell Town Swifts dropping 'Swifts' soon after.

ROTOL AFC

1941-1943	P	W	D	L	F	A		W	D	L	F	A
LEAGUE	2	2	0	0	18	5		0	0	0	0	0
CUP	2	2	0	0	12	1		0	0	0	0	0
TOTAL	**4**	**4**	**0**	**0**	**30**	**6**		**0**	**0**	**0**	**0**	**0**

Company side played in Gloucester. The name is a contraction of 'ROlls-Royce' and 'BrisTOL'.

ROYAL AIR FORCE 'A'

1941-1943	P	W	D	L	F	A		W	D	L	F	A
LEAGUE	4	3	0	1	13	13		0	0	0	0	0
TOTAL	**4**	**3**	**0**	**1**	**13**	**13**		**0**	**0**	**0**	**0**	**0**

Played in Gloucester. During World War II, all Services teams played under a nom-de-plume.

ROYAL AIR FORCE 'B'

1941-1943	P	W	D	L	F	A		W	D	L	F	A
LEAGUE	4	4	0	0	27	6		0	0	0	0	0
CUP	2	0	0	1	1	3		0	0	0	0	0
TOTAL	**6**	**4**	**0**	**1**	**28**	**9**		**0**	**0**	**0**	**0**	**0**

Played in Gloucester. During World War II, all Services teams played under a nom-de-plume.

ROYAL AIR FORCE 'C'

1941-1943	P	W	D	L	F	A		W	D	L	F	A
LEAGUE	4	2	0	2	21	10		0	0	0	0	0
CUP	2	1	0	0	5	4		0	1	0	3	3
TOTAL	**6**	**3**	**0**	**2**	**26**	**14**		**0**	**1**	**0**	**3**	**3**

Played in Gloucester. During World War II, all Services teams played under a nom-de-plume.

ROYAL AIR FORCE 'D'

1941-1943	P	W	D	L	F	A		W	D	L	F	A
LEAGUE	4	3	0	0	19	5		0	0	0	0	0
CUP	1	1	0	0	13	1		0	0	0	0	0
TOTAL	**5**	**4**	**0**	**0**	**32**	**6**		**0**	**0**	**0**	**0**	**0**

Played in Gloucester. During World War II, all Services teams played under a nom-de-plume.

ROYAL AIR FORCE 'E'

1941-1942	P	W	D	L	F	A		W	D	L	F	A
LEAGUE	2	2	0	0	6	4		0	0	0	0	0
CUP	1	0	0	0	0	0		1	0	0	4	0
TOTAL	**3**	**2**	**0**	**0**	**6**	**4**		**1**	**0**	**0**	**4**	**0**

Played in Gloucester. During World War II, all Services teams played under a nom-de-plume.

ROYAL AIR FORCE 'F'

1941-1942	P	W	D	L	F	A		W	D	L	F	A
LEAGUE	2	1	1	0	12	3		0	0	0	0	0
CUP	1	0	0	1	5	6		0	0	0	0	0
TOTAL	**3**	**1**	**1**	**1**	**17**	**9**		**0**	**0**	**0**	**0**	**0**

Played in Gloucester. During World War II, all Services teams played under a nom-de-plume.

RUGBY TOWN (1)

1958-1973	P	W	D	L	F	A		W	D	L	F	A
LEAGUE	16	4	2	2	15	10		1	3	4	7	15
CUP	1	0	0	0	0	0		0	0	1	0	3
TOTAL	**17**	**4**	**2**	**2**	**15**	**10**		**1**	**3**	**5**	**7**	**18**

Formed pre-1919 folded 1934. A new club was formed 1945 folding yet again in 1973. Reformed 1993 folding again 1995 only to re-emerge briefly from 2000 to 2004. No connection to Rugby Town (2).

RUGBY TOWN (2)

2005-2009	P	W	D	L	F	A		W	D	L	F	A
LEAGUE	8	3	0	1	13	7		3	0	1	10	3
TOTAL	**8**	**3**	**0**	**1**	**13**	**7**		**3**	**0**	**1**	**10**	**3**

Formerly Rugby United.

RUGBY UNITED

2000-2005	P	W	D	L	F	A		W	D	L	F	A
LEAGUE	8	2	1	1	8	3		0	0	4	2	7
TOTAL	**8**	**2**	**1**	**1**	**8**	**3**		**0**	**0**	**4**	**2**	**7**

Changed name from Valley Sports Rugby to Rugby United in 2000 and subsequently renamed Rugby Town (2) in 2005.

RUNCORN

1993-1997	P	W	D	L	F	A		W	D	L	F	A
CUP	5	1	2	0	6	4		0	1	1	3	6
TOTAL	**5**	**1**	**2**	**0**	**6**	**4**		**0**	**1**	**1**	**3**	**6**

Formed 1918 as Highfield & Camden Tanneries Recreation Club changing to Runcorn in 1919. Changed name to Runcorn Halton in 2001.

RUSHDEN & DIAMONDS

1994-1996	P	W	D	L	F	A		W	D	L	F	A
LEAGUE	4	2	0	0	3	1		1	0	1	4	4
TOTAL	**4**	**2**	**0**	**0**	**3**	**1**		**1**	**0**	**1**	**4**	**4**

Formed in 1992 as a merger between Rushden Town and Irthlingborough Diamonds.

RUSHDEN TOWN

1985-1991	P	W	D	L	F	A		W	D	L	F	A
LEAGUE	10	5	0	0	17	7		3	1	1	8	7
TOTAL	10	5	0	0	17	7		3	1	1	8	7

Formed 1889 changing name to Rushden & Diamonds in 1992.

SAINT ANNE'S

1902	P	W	D	L	F	A		W	D	L	F	A
CUP	1	0	0	0	0	0		1	0	0	3	2
TOTAL	1	0	0	0	0	0		1	0	0	3	2

Played in Oldland, Bristol.

SAINT GEORGE

1892-1896	P	W	D	L	F	A		W	D	L	F	A
LEAGUE	6	1	0	2	4	4		1	0	2	4	8
CUP	2	0	0	1	3	4		0	0	1	3	4
TOTAL	8	1	0	3	7	8		1	0	3	7	12

Renamed Bristol Saint George in 1897.

SAINT JOHN'S

1946	P	W	D	L	F	A		W	D	L	F	A
CUP	1	0	0	0	0	0		1	0	0	5	0
TOTAL	1	0	0	0	0	0		1	0	0	5	0

Played in Weston-Super-Mare.

SAINT LEONARDS STAMCROFT

1997	P	W	D	L	F	A		W	D	L	F	A
LEAGUE	2	0	1	0	1	1		0	1	0	0	0
TOTAL	2	0	1	0	1	1		0	1	0	0	0

Formed 1971 as Stamco changing name to Saint Leonards Stamcroft in 1996. Renamed Saint Leonards in 1998.

SAINT MICHAEL'S

1904	P	W	D	L	F	A		W	D	L	F	A
LEAGUE	2	0	0	1	3	4		0	0	1	0	1
TOTAL	2	0	0	1	3	4		0	0	1	0	1

Played in Hempsted. Merged with Gloucester City 1906.

SAINT PAUL'S

1895-1896	P	W	D	L	F	A		W	D	L	F	A
LEAGUE	2	0	1	0	3	3		1	0	0	1	0
CUP	1	1	0	0	0	0		0	0	0	0	0
TOTAL	3	1	1	0	3	3		1	0	0	1	0

Played in Bristol.

SAINT PAUL'S UNITED

1906-1910	P	W	D	L	F	A		W	D	L	F	A
LEAGUE	10	4	0	1	16	3		3	1	1	12	9
TOTAL	10	4	0	1	16	3		3	1	1	12	9

Played in Cheltenham.

SAINT PHILIPS ATHLETIC

1927	P	W	D	L	F	A		W	D	L	F	A
CUP	1	0	0	1	1	2		0	0	0	0	0
TOTAL	1	0	0	1	1	2		0	0	0	0	0

Played in Bristol.

SAINT PHILIPS MARSH ADULT SCHOOL

1934	P	W	D	L	F	A		W	D	L	F	A
CUP	3	0	1	0	2	2		1	1	0	7	6
TOTAL	3	0	1	0	2	2		1	1	0	7	6

Formed 1892. Play in Bristol.

SALISBURY

1950-1992	P	W	D	L	F	A		W	D	L	F	A
LEAGUE	2	0	0	1	1	2		1	0	0	1	0
CUP	10	5	1	1	14	9		2	1	0	6	3
TOTAL	12	5	1	2	15	11		3	1	0	7	3

Formed 1947 as Salisbury. Changed name to Salisbury City in 1992.

SALISBURY CITY

1995-2006	P	W	D	L	F	A		W	D	L	F	A
LEAGUE	12	1	2	3	9	11		2	2	2	11	10
TOTAL	12	1	2	3	9	11		2	2	2	11	10

Formerly Salisbury.

SALTASH UNITED

1986	P	W	D	L	F	A		W	D	L	F	A
CUP	2	0	0	1	0	2		0	1	0	0	0
TOTAL	2	0	0	1	0	2		0	1	0	0	0

Formed 1946.

SHARPNESS

1907-1931	P	W	D	L	F	A		W	D	L	F	A
LEAGUE	26	6	3	3	35	24		3	1	8	25	38
CUP	3	0	0	0	0	0		0	0	3	5	14
TOTAL	29	6	3	3	35	24		3	1	11	30	52

Formed 1900.

SHARPNESS 'A'

1921-1922	P	W	D	L	F	A		W	D	L	F	A
LEAGUE	2	0	0	1	2	3		0	1	0	3	3
TOTAL	2	0	0	1	2	3		0	1	0	3	3

SHEPSHED CHARTERHOUSE

1984-1988	P	W	D	L	F	A		W	D	L	F	A
LEAGUE	2	0	0	1	1	2		0	1	0	2	2
CUP	1	1	0	0	3	0		0	0	0	0	0
TOTAL	3	1	0	1	4	2		0	1	0	2	2

Formed 1890 as Shepshed Albion. Changed name to Shepshed Charterhouse in 1975 reverting back briefly to Shepshed Albion 1992 to 1994. Changed name to Shepshed Dynamo in 1994.

SHEPSHED DYNAMO

2001-2004	P	W	D	L	F	A		W	D	L	F	A
LEAGUE	8	3	0	1	13	10		2	0	2	8	4
TOTAL	8	3	0	1	13	10		2	0	2	8	4

Formerly Shepshed Charterhouse.

SHIRLEY TOWN

1936-1938	P	W	D	L	F	A		W	D	L	F	A
LEAGUE	6	3	0	0	13	6		1	1	1	3	4
TOTAL	6	3	0	0	13	6		1	1	1	3	4

Changed name to West Shirley Athletic in 1974.

SHORTWOOD UNITED

1991-2007	P	W	D	L	F	A		W	D	L	F	A
CUP	2	1	0	1	4	3		0	0	0	0	0
TOTAL	2	1	0	1	4	3		0	0	0	0	0

Formed 1900.

SITTINGBOURNE

1959-1998	P	W	D	L	F	A		W	D	L	F	A
LEAGUE	24	7	3	2	23	11		1	5	6	14	24
TOTAL	24	7	3	2	23	11		1	5	6	14	24

Formed 1886.

SNEYD PARK

1927	P	W	D	L	F	A		W	D	L	F	A
CUP	1	1	0	0	4	2		0	0	0	0	0
TOTAL	1	1	0	0	4	2		0	0	0	0	0

Formed 1897.

SOLIHULL BOROUGH

1992-2005	P	W	D	L	F	A		W	D	L	F	A
LEAGUE	16	2	4	2	14	12		3	3	2	15	15
CUP	2	1	0	1	4	5		0	0	0	0	0
TOTAL	18	3	4	3	18	17		3	3	2	15	15

Formed in 1951 as Lincoln FC. Changed to Solihull Borough in 1969. Merged with Moor Green to become Solihull Moors in 2007.

SOLIHULL TOWN

1938-1939	P	W	D	L	F	A		W	D	L	F	A
LEAGUE	2	1	0	0	3	0		0	0	1	1	3
TOTAL	2	1	0	0	3	0		0	0	1	1	3

SOUTHPORT

2003	P	W	D	L	F	A		W	D	L	F	A
CUP	2	0	1	0	1	1		1	0	0	3	1
TOTAL	2	0	1	0	1	1		1	0	0	3	1

Formed 1881 as Southport Central. In 1918 changed name to Southport Vulcan becoming Southport in 1921.

SPALDING UNITED

1988-1989	P	W	D	L	F	A		W	D	L	F	A
LEAGUE	2	0	0	1	0	1		1	0	0	4	1
TOTAL	2	0	0	1	0	1		1	0	0	4	1

Formed 1921.

SPENCER MOULTON

1928	P	W	D	L	F	A		W	D	L	F	A
CUP	1	0	0	0	0	0		0	0	1	0	1
TOTAL	1	0	0	0	0	0		0	0	1	0	1

Played in Bradford-on-Avon.

STAFFORD RANGERS

1995-1996	P	W	D	L	F	A		W	D	L	F	A
LEAGUE	2	1	0	0	3	2		1	0	0	4	3
TOTAL	2	1	0	0	3	2		1	0	0	4	3

Formed 1876.

STAINES TOWN

1996	P	W	D	L	F	A		W	D	L	F	A
CUP	1	1	0	0	5	0		0	0	0	0	0
TOTAL	1	1	0	0	5	0		0	0	0	0	0

Formed 1892. Known as Staines and Staines Albany until it folded in 1935. Prior to World War II reformed as Staines Vale. Became Staines Town in 1953.

STAMFORD

2004-2006	P	W	D	L	F	A		W	D	L	F	A
LEAGUE	4	0	2	0	1	1		0	1	1	2	3
TOTAL	4	0	2	0	1	1		0	1	1	2	3

Formed 1894.

STAPLE HILL

1893-1900	P	W	D	L	F	A		W	D	L	F	A
LEAGUE	6	0	2	1	3	5		0	0	3	2	8
CUP	1	0	0	0	0	0		0	0	1	1	3
TOTAL	7	0	2	1	3	5		0	0	4	3	11

STEVENAGE ATHLETIC

1971-1976	P	W	D	L	F	A		W	D	L	F	A
LEAGUE	10	2	2	1	7	4		0	3	2	4	7
TOTAL	10	2	2	1	7	4		0	3	2	4	7

Formerly Stevenage Town.

STEVENAGE BOROUGH

1998	P	W	D	L	F	A		W	D	L	F	A
CUP	2	0	0	1	1	2		0	1	0	1	1
TOTAL	2	0	0	1	1	2		0	1	0	1	1

Formed 1976.

STEVENAGE TOWN

1964-1967	P	W	D	L	F	A		W	D	L	F	A
LEAGUE	8	2	1	1	4	3		0	1	3	3	18
TOTAL	8	2	1	1	4	3		0	1	3	3	18

Founded 1894. Merged with Stevenage Rangers in 1955 to become Stevenage reverting to Stevenage Town in 1959. Went into liquidation in 1968 when Stevenage Athletic was formed.

STONEHOUSE

1900-1973	P	W	D	L	F	A		W	D	L	F	A
LEAGUE	20	6	0	4	22	14		3	1	6	19	35
CUP	14	8	0	2	39	8		1	3	0	7	6
TOTAL	34	14	0	6	61	22		4	4	6	26	41

Formed pre-1900 became Stonehouse Town 2007.

STOURBRIDGE

1971-2009	P	W	D	L	F	A		W	D	L	F	A
LEAGUE	32	8	5	3	29	16		5	4	7	24	38
CUP	6	2	0	1	11	3		0	1	2	2	6
TOTAL	38	10	5	4	40	19		5	5	9	26	44

Formed 1876 as Stourbridge Standard. By the late 1880s just known as Stourbridge.

STOURPORT SWIFTS

2002-2004	P	W	D	L	F	A		W	D	L	F	A
LEAGUE	6	2	0	1	4	2		2	0	1	4	3
TOTAL	6	2	0	1	4	2		2	0	1	4	3

Formed 1882.

STREET

1948-2004	P	W	D	L	F	A		W	D	L	F	A
CUP	2	1	0	0	4	1		0	0	1	2	3
TOTAL	2	1	0	0	4	1		0	0	1	2	3

Formed 1880.

STROUD (1)

1907-1910	P	W	D	L	F	A		W	D	L	F	A
LEAGUE	6	2	1	0	14	2		1	1	1	12	5
CUP	1	0	0	0	0	0		1	0	0	5	2
TOTAL	7	2	1	0	14	2		2	1	1	17	7

Formed pre-1907. No connection to Stroud (2).

STROUD (2)

1991	P	W	D	L	F	A		W	D	L	F	A
CUP	1	1	0	0	2	1		0	0	0	0	0
TOTAL	1	1	0	0	2	1		0	0	0	0	0

Changed name from Forest Green Rovers 1989. Changed back to Forest Green Rovers from 1992-93 season.

[469]

SUDBURY TOWN

1994-1998	P	W	D	L	F	A		W	D	L	F	A
LEAGUE	6	2	1	0	7	3		2	0	1	4	2
CUP	2	1	0	0	10	0		0	0	1	1	3
TOTAL	8	3	1	0	17	3		2	0	1	5	5

Formed 1885 dissolved 1999. The same year Sudbury Town merged with Sudbury Wanderers to form AFC Sudbury.

SUNNINGEND

1927	P	W	D	L	F	A		W	D	L	F	A
CUP	1	1	0	0	6	0		0	0	0	0	0
TOTAL	1	1	0	0	6	0		0	0	0	0	0

Played in Cheltenham.

SUTTON COLDFIELD TOWN

1984-2007	P	W	D	L	F	A		W	D	L	F	A
LEAGUE	18	3	5	1	15	13		5	3	1	12	8
CUP	1	0	0	0	0	0		0	0	1	1	3
TOTAL	19	3	5	1	15	13		5	3	2	13	11

Founded 1879 as Sutton Coldfield. After World War II changed name to Sutton Town until 1964 when changed name to Sutton Coldfield Town.

SWINDON AMATEURS

1909	P	W	D	L	F	A		W	D	L	F	A
CUP	2	1	0	0	3	2		0	1	0	2	2
TOTAL	2	1	0	0	3	2		0	1	0	2	2

SWINDON SUPERMARINE

2001-2009	P	W	D	L	F	A		W	D	L	F	A
LEAGUE	10	5	0	0	14	3		4	0	1	8	6
TOTAL	10	5	0	0	14	3		4	0	1	8	6

Formed 1992 as a merger between Swindon Athletic and Supermarine.

SWINDON WANDERERS

1894-1896	P	W	D	L	F	A		W	D	L	F	A
LEAGUE	3	1	0	0	2	0		0	1	1	4	5
TOTAL	3	1	0	0	2	0		0	1	1	4	5

SYNWELL ROVERS

1922	P	W	D	L	F	A		W	D	L	F	A
LEAGUE	2	0	0	1	3	4		0	0	1	1	2
TOTAL	2	0	0	1	3	4		0	0	1	1	2

Formed 1890s as Synwell Star changing name to Synwell Rovers subsequently. In 1959 Synwell Rovers merged with Wotton-Under-Edge to form Wotton Rovers.

TAMWORTH

1935-2000	P	W	D	L	F	A		W	D	L	F	A
LEAGUE	31	5	4	7	17	22		5	4	6	25	40
TOTAL	31	5	4	7	17	22		5	4	6	25	40

Formed 1933.

TAUNTON TOWN

1979-2004	P	W	D	L	F	A		W	D	L	F	A
LEAGUE	13	5	0	1	14	7		4	1	2	12	10
CUP	2	1	0	0	5	1		0	0	1	0	2
TOTAL	15	6	0	1	19	8		4	1	3	12	12

Formed 1947 as Taunton. Added 'Town' in 1968.

TEAM BATH

2003-2008	P	W	D	L	F	A		W	D	L	F	A
LEAGUE	10	4	1	0	13	7		1	1	3	7	9
CUP	2	0	1	0	0	0		1	0	0	2	0
TOTAL	12	4	2	0	13	7		2	1	3	9	9

Formed 1999 and affiliated to the University of Bath.

TELFORD UNITED

1969-1971	P	W	D	L	F	A		W	D	L	F	A
LEAGUE	4	1	0	1	4	3		0	1	1	3	5
TOTAL	4	1	0	1	4	3		0	1	1	3	5

Formerly Wellington Town. Club folded 2004. A new club was formed through the Supporters Trust known as AFC Telford United.

TEWKESBURY ABBEY

1897-1903	P	W	D	L	F	A		W	D	L	F	A
LEAGUE	10	3	1	1	18	9		1	2	2	5	8
CUP	2	0	0	1	0	1		0	1	0	1	1
TOTAL	12	3	1	2	18	10		1	3	2	6	9

Formed pre-1897.

TEWKESBURY TOWN

1904-1935	P	W	D	L	F	A		W	D	L	F	A
LEAGUE	38	9	7	3	53	31		10	1	8	42	41
CUP	2	1	0	0	9	0		0	0	1	1	3
TOTAL	40	10	7	3	62	31		10	1	9	43	44

Formed pre-1904.

[470]

RECORD AGAINST OPPONENTS

THATCHAM TOWN

1996	P	W	D	L	F	A		W	D	L	F	A
CUP	1	0	0	1	1	3		0	0	0	0	0
TOTAL	**1**	**0**	**0**	**1**	**1**	**3**		**0**	**0**	**0**	**0**	**0**

Formed 1894 as Thatcham. Added 'Town' in 1974.

TIVERTON TOWN

2000-2009	P	W	D	L	F	A		W	D	L	F	A
LEAGUE	12	3	1	2	14	11		1	2	3	8	11
CUP	3	1	0	0	2	2		1	1	0	5	3
TOTAL	**15**	**4**	**1**	**2**	**16**	**13**		**2**	**3**	**3**	**13**	**14**

Founded 1913 as Tiverton Athletic. Changed to Tiverton Town in 1929.

TON PENTRE

1969-1990	P	W	D	L	F	A		W	D	L	F	A
CUP	11	1	2	2	4	5		1	2	3	8	11
TOTAL	**11**	**1**	**2**	**2**	**4**	**5**		**1**	**2**	**3**	**8**	**11**

Formed 1935.

TONBRIDGE

1949-1969	P	W	D	L	F	A		W	D	L	F	A
LEAGUE	30	7	4	3	33	15		4	2	10	20	38
TOTAL	**30**	**7**	**4**	**3**	**33**	**15**		**4**	**2**	**10**	**20**	**38**

Formed 1947 as Tonbridge and went into liquidation in 1976. Tonbridge Angels took over fixture list.

TORQUAY UNITED RESERVES

1947-1951	P	W	D	L	F	A		W	D	L	F	A
LEAGUE	8	1	2	1	5	4		0	1	3	3	11
CUP	2	0	0	1	1	2		0	0	1	1	4
TOTAL	**10**	**1**	**2**	**2**	**6**	**6**		**0**	**1**	**4**	**4**	**15**

Torquay United formed 1899.

TROWBRIDGE TOWN

1893-1995	P	W	D	L	F	A		W	D	L	F	A
LEAGUE	46	9	3	11	43	45		6	5	12	34	54
CUP	19	2	3	3	10	10		2	2	7	10	23
TOTAL	**65**	**11**	**6**	**14**	**53**	**55**		**8**	**7**	**19**	**44**	**77**

Formed 1880 and folded 1998 but reformed immediately.

TUFFLEY & WHADDON

1914	P	W	D	L	F	A		W	D	L	F	A
LEAGUE	2	0	0	1	1	5		0	0	1	0	4
TOTAL	**2**	**0**	**0**	**1**	**1**	**5**		**0**	**0**	**1**	**0**	**4**

TUNBRIDGE WELLS RANGERS

1963-1967	P	W	D	L	F	A		W	D	L	F	A
LEAGUE	8	3	0	1	10	5		1	2	1	5	6
TOTAL	**8**	**3**	**0**	**1**	**10**	**5**		**1**	**2**	**1**	**5**	**6**

Formerly Tunbridge Wells United. A Tunbridge Wells Rangers were formed in 1903 but were a separate side to United playing into the 1930s.

TUNBRIDGE WELLS UNITED

1960-1963	P	W	D	L	F	A		W	D	L	F	A
LEAGUE	8	4	0	0	7	1		1	0	3	5	15
TOTAL	**8**	**4**	**0**	**0**	**7**	**1**		**1**	**0**	**3**	**5**	**15**

Formed 1886 as Tunbridge Wells but closed down in 1914. Reformed after World War II changing name to Tunbridge Wells Rangers in 1963.

UXBRIDGE

2007	P	W	D	L	F	A		W	D	L	F	A
CUP	1	1	0	0	1	0		0	0	0	0	0
TOTAL	**1**	**1**	**0**	**0**	**1**	**0**		**0**	**0**	**0**	**0**	**0**

Formed 1871.

VALLEY SPORTS RUGBY

1985-1996	P	W	D	L	F	A		W	D	L	F	A
LEAGUE	16	2	3	3	10	9		4	1	3	9	10
TOTAL	**16**	**2**	**3**	**3**	**10**	**9**		**4**	**1**	**3**	**9**	**10**

Formed 1956 and changed name to Rugby United in 2000.

VINEY HILL

1927-1931	P	W	D	L	F	A		W	D	L	F	A
LEAGUE	9	2	1	1	8	7		1	1	3	8	17
TOTAL	**9**	**2**	**1**	**1**	**8**	**7**		**1**	**1**	**3**	**8**	**17**

WALSALL RESERVES

1935-1939	P	W	D	L	F	A		W	D	L	F	A
LEAGUE	8	1	0	3	5	7		1	0	3	6	10
TOTAL	**8**	**1**	**0**	**3**	**5**	**7**		**1**	**0**	**3**	**6**	**10**

Walsall formed 1888 as Walsall Town Swifts following a merger between Walsall Town and Walsall Swifts. Became Walsall in 1895.

WARMLEY

1893-1902	P	W	D	L	F	A		W	D	L	F	A
LEAGUE	6	1	0	2	4	9		0	0	3	1	11
CUP	2	0	0	0	0	0		1	0	1	4	5
TOTAL	**8**	**1**	**0**	**2**	**4**	**9**		**1**	**0**	**4**	**5**	**16**

Formed pre-1892 and folded 1899. Reformed pre-1902 but possibly folded again 1904.

WARMLEY AMATEURS

1906-1909	P	W	D	L	F	A		W	D	L	F	A
CUP	4	0	1	0	1	1		0	0	3	0	9
TOTAL	**4**	**0**	**1**	**0**	**1**	**1**		**0**	**0**	**3**	**0**	**9**

WARMLEY ATHLETIC

1910	P	W	D	L	F	A		W	D	L	F	A
CUP	1	1	0	0	2	0		0	0	0	0	0
TOTAL	**1**	**1**	**0**	**0**	**2**	**0**		**0**	**0**	**0**	**0**	**0**

WARMLEY RESERVES

1889	P	W	D	L	F	A		W	D	L	F	A
CUP	1	0	0	0	0	0		0	0	1	2	3
TOTAL	**1**	**0**	**0**	**0**	**0**	**0**		**0**	**0**	**1**	**2**	**3**

WATERLOOVILLE

1982-1997	P	W	D	L	F	A		W	D	L	F	A
LEAGUE	12	3	2	1	10	7		2	3	1	10	8
CUP	1	1	0	0	2	0		0	0	0	0	0
TOTAL	**13**	**3**	**2**	**1**	**12**	**7**		**2**	**3**	**1**	**10**	**8**

Formed 1905. Merged with Havant to form Havant & Waterlooville in 1998.

WEALDSTONE

1971-2007	P	W	D	L	F	A		W	D	L	F	A
LEAGUE	10	2	1	2	8	10		2	0	3	8	9
CUP	3	0	0	1	0	1		0	0	2	1	4
TOTAL	**13**	**2**	**1**	**3**	**8**	**11**		**2**	**0**	**5**	**9**	**13**

Formed 1899.

WELLING UNITED

1982-1999	P	W	D	L	F	A		W	D	L	F	A
LEAGUE	6	0	2	1	2	4		1	0	2	4	7
CUP	1	0	0	0	0	0		0	0	1	1	2
TOTAL	**7**	**0**	**2**	**1**	**2**	**4**		**1**	**0**	**3**	**5**	**9**

Formed 1963

WELLINGBOROUGH TOWN

1971-1989	P	W	D	L	F	A		W	D	L	F	A
LEAGUE	30	10	3	2	43	17		6	2	7	22	29
TOTAL	**30**	**10**	**3**	**2**	**43**	**17**		**6**	**2**	**7**	**22**	**29**

Formed 1867. In 1905 changed name to Wellingborough Redwell reverting back to 'Town' after World War I. Club folded 2002. A new club was formed 2004.

WELLINGTON TOWN

1959	P	W	D	L	F	A		W	D	L	F	A
LEAGUE	2	0	0	1	0	4		0	0	1	0	1
TOTAL	**2**	**0**	**0**	**1**	**0**	**4**		**0**	**0**	**1**	**0**	**1**

Formed 1872 as Wellington Parish Church Institute changing name to Wellington Town in 1879. Changed name again in 1969 to Telford United.

WELTON ROVERS

1926-1983	P	W	D	L	F	A		W	D	L	F	A
LEAGUE	4	0	0	2	2	6		0	0	1	2	7
CUP	2	0	0	0	0	0		2	0	0	6	2
TOTAL	**6**	**0**	**0**	**2**	**2**	**6**		**2**	**0**	**1**	**8**	**9**

Formed 1887.

WESLEY RANGERS

1932	P	W	D	L	F	A		W	D	L	F	A
CUP	1	0	0	0	0	0		0	0	1	0	3
TOTAL	**1**	**0**	**0**	**0**	**0**	**0**		**0**	**0**	**1**	**0**	**3**

WEST BROMWICH ALBION 'A'

1935-1938	P	W	D	L	F	A		W	D	L	F	A
LEAGUE	8	1	1	3	7	10		0	1	2	6	9
TOTAL	**8**	**1**	**1**	**3**	**7**	**10**		**0**	**1**	**2**	**6**	**9**

Formed 1878 as West Bromwich Strollers. Renamed West Bromwich Albion 1880. This would probably be their third team.

WESTBURY UNITED

1921-1987	P	W	D	L	F	A		W	D	L	F	A
CUP	2	2	0	0	7	0		0	0	0	0	0
TOTAL	**2**	**2**	**0**	**0**	**7**	**0**		**0**	**0**	**0**	**0**	**0**

Formed pre-1921.

WESTGATE

1913-1914	P	W	D	L	F	A		W	D	L	F	A
LEAGUE	2	1	0	0	4	0		0	0	1	1	2
TOTAL	2	1	0	0	4	0		0	0	1	1	2

Played in Gloucester.

WESTON-SUPER-MARE

1930-2003	P	W	D	L	F	A		W	D	L	F	A
LEAGUE	10	2	0	3	11	10		2	1	2	8	11
CUP	6	1	1	1	3	3		2	0	1	5	3
TOTAL	16	3	1	4	14	13		4	1	3	13	14

Formed 1887 and disbanded 1914. Reformed 1919 and disbanded 1939. Reformed again in 1948.

WEYMOUTH

1950-2000	P	W	D	L	F	A		W	D	L	F	A
LEAGUE	32	6	6	4	23	20		4	4	8	26	32
CUP	8	4	0	0	9	3		0	2	2	2	10
TOTAL	40	10	6	4	32	23		4	6	10	28	42

Formed 1890 but folded 1928. Reformed 1933 but folded yet again in 1939. Reformed again in 1947.

WICKWAR

1923-1924	P	W	D	L	F	A		W	D	L	F	A
LEAGUE	4	1	0	1	7	3		0	1	1	1	7
TOTAL	4	1	0	1	7	3		0	1	1	1	7

There has been a Wickwar club with varying names since the 1890s.

WILLENHALL TOWN

1984-1989	P	W	D	L	F	A		W	D	L	F	A
LEAGUE	4	0	1	1	1	4		0	0	2	1	3
CUP	1	1	0	0	2	1		0	0	0	0	0
TOTAL	5	1	1	1	3	5		0	0	2	1	3

Formed 1953.

WIMBLEDON

1964-1971	P	W	D	L	F	A		W	D	L	F	A
LEAGUE	6	2	1	0	7	3		0	2	1	7	8
TOTAL	6	2	1	0	7	3		0	2	1	7	8

Formed 1889 as Wimbledon Old Centrals changing name to Wimbledon in 1905. Wimbledon relocated to Milton Keynes calling themselves Milton Keynes Dons in 2002 effectively becoming another franchise. Dissident supporters of Wimbledon formed AFC Wimbledon in 2002.

WINCHCOMBE TOWN

1906-1910?	P	W	D	L	F	A		W	D	L	F	A
LEAGUE	4	2	0	0	9	2		0	2	0	2	2
TOTAL	4	2	0	0	9	2		0	2	0	2	2

WINCHCOMBE UNITED

1922	P	W	D	L	F	A		W	D	L	F	A
CUP	2	1	0	0	4	1		0	1	0	0	0
TOTAL	2	1	0	0	4	1		0	1	0	0	0

WISBECH TOWN

1958-1997	P	W	D	L	F	A		W	D	L	F	A
LEAGUE	12	3	1	2	10	6		1	2	3	6	9
CUP	2	0	1	0	1	1		0	0	1	2	3
TOTAL	14	3	2	2	11	7		1	2	4	8	12

Formed 1920.

WITNEY TOWN

1973-1995	P	W	D	L	F	A		W	D	L	F	A
LEAGUE	22	4	4	3	15	14		2	1	8	11	19
CUP	12	2	3	1	8	5		3	1	2	9	5
TOTAL	34	6	7	4	23	19		5	2	10	20	24

Formed in 1885 as Witney. Reformed as Witney Town in 1922 and folded in 2001. Witney United was formed the same year by a group of Witney Town supporters following its demise.

WITTON ALBION

1991	P	W	D	L	F	A		W	D	L	F	A
CUP	1	0	0	0	0	0		0	0	1	0	3
TOTAL	1	0	0	0	0	0		0	0	1	0	3

Formed 1887.

WOKING

2003	P	W	D	L	F	A		W	D	L	F	A
CUP	2	0	1	0	0	0		1	0	0	2	0
TOTAL	2	0	1	0	0	0		1	0	0	2	0

Formed 1889.

WOLVERHAMPTON WANDERERS 'A'

1935-1939	P	W	D	L	F	A		W	D	L	F	A
LEAGUE	8	2	1	1	11	5		1	2	1	8	7
TOTAL	8	2	1	1	11	5		1	2	1	8	7

Formed 1877 as Saint Luke's. Became Wolverhampton Wanderers in 1879. This would probably be their third team.

WOODCHESTER

1901-1935	P	W	D	L	F	A		W	D	L	F	A
LEAGUE	16	4	2	2	26	14		4	1	3	27	20
CUP	1	0	0	0	0	0		1	0	0	4	3
TOTAL	17	4	2	2	26	14		5	1	3	31	23

WOODCHESTER 'A'

1921	P	W	D	L	F	A		W	D	L	F	A
LEAGUE	2	1	0	0	5	2		0	0	1	1	4
TOTAL	2	1	0	0	5	2		0	0	1	1	4

WOODMANCOTE

1921	P	W	D	L	F	A		W	D	L	F	A
CUP	1	0	0	0	0	0		1	0	0	7	4
TOTAL	1	0	0	0	0	0		1	0	0	7	4

Woodmancote is a hamlet in the parish of Bishop's Cleeve.

WORCESTER CITY

1939-2000	P	W	D	L	F	A		W	D	L	F	A
LEAGUE	64	13	8	11	55	49		5	5	22	36	87
CUP	25	6	3	3	27	21		1	1	11	12	39
TOTAL	89	19	11	14	82	70		6	6	33	48	126

Formed 1902 following the liquidation of Berwick Rangers taking over their fixtures.

WORTHING

1994	P	W	D	L	F	A		W	D	L	F	A
CUP	2	0	1	0	1	1		0	0	1	1	2
TOTAL	2	0	1	0	1	1		0	0	1	1	2

Formed 1886 as Worthing Assocation changing to Worthing in 1899.

WOTTON-UNDER-EDGE

1898-1926	P	W	D	L	F	A		W	D	L	F	A
LEAGUE	11	5	0	1	21	8		1	0	4	12	13
TOTAL	11	5	0	1	21	8		1	0	4	12	13

Formed pre-1898. In 1959 Wotton-Under-Edge merged with Synwell Rovers to become Wotton Rovers.

YATE TOWN

1990-2009	P	W	D	L	F	A		W	D	L	F	A
LEAGUE	10	2	0	3	9	8		1	2	2	7	8
CUP	6	3	0	0	9	5		3	0	0	11	3
TOTAL	16	5	0	3	18	13		4	2	2	18	11

Formed 1906 as Yate Rovers changing their name to Yate YMCA in 1946. Became Yate Town in 1969.

YEADING

1997	P	W	D	L	F	A		W	D	L	F	A
CUP	1	0	0	0	0	0		1	0	0	3	0
TOTAL	1	0	0	0	0	0		1	0	0	3	0

Formed 1960 and dissolved 2007.

YEOVIL & PETTERS UNITED

1940	P	W	D	L	F	A		W	D	L	F	A
LEAGUE	2	0	0	1	0	1		1	0	0	3	2
TOTAL	2	0	0	1	0	1		1	0	0	3	2

Founded 1890 as Yeovil changed name to Yeovil Casuals in 1895. Became Yeovil Town in 1907 amalgamating with Petters United in 1915 to become Yeovil & Petters United. After World War II resorted back to Yeovil Town.

YEOVIL TOWN

1946-1991	P	W	D	L	F	A		W	D	L	F	A
LEAGUE	28	4	3	7	15	21		0	2	12	7	38
CUP	11	4	1	2	14	6		1	0	3	3	11
TOTAL	39	8	4	9	29	27		1	2	15	10	49

Formerly Yeovil & Petters United.

YIEWSLEY

1958-1964	P	W	D	L	F	A		W	D	L	F	A
LEAGUE	12	1	2	3	6	8		0	1	5	7	21
TOTAL	12	1	2	3	6	8		0	1	5	7	21

Changed name to Hillingdon Borough in 1983.

PLAYERS' RECORDS

GLOUCESTER/GLOUCESTER CITY/GLOUCESTER YMCA PLAYERS 1883-2009

(TOTAL = 1891 of which 1520 have been involved competitively)

For information: Pre World War II many records missing. From 1966/67 to1988/89 I was very much reliant on The Citizen match reports to find out if the designated substitutes actually played. On some occasions the substitution was not reported therefore the figure is included as a non playing substitute until verified. 1974/75 to 1983/84 were particularly bad seasons for non reporting of substitutions. Also on a few occasions I was only able to find a squad selection (usually 13 players) and all players in squad are included in the statistics. Therefore some players statistics may be distorted. This will take a lot of researching and even then may not be conclusive.

Controversially and contrary to FA instructions I have also included in the players records the league games against opponents who for varying reasons withdrew from the league during a season and subsequently had their records expunged. I take the view that as the players would have been in the mindset of playing these games competitively they should therefore count and not be reduced to just a friendly game which they patently were not. However, the FA do recognise the bookings from expunged games! These matches are indicated in *italics* in the Season by Season section.The players indicated with (?) in the same section are also counted as they are my educated guesses.

PLAYERS WHO PARTICIPATED IN THE FOLLOWING COMPETITIVE GAMES HAVE BEEN RECORDED

Gloucestershire FA Junior Challenge Cup	Bristol Charity League
Gloucestershire FA Senior Challenge Cup	FA Cup
Bristol & District League	Birmingham Combination
Western League	Birmingham Senior Cup
Gloucester & District League	Southern League
Mid Gloucestershire League	Southern League Cup
Cheltenham & District League	Worcestershire Senior FA Cup
North Gloucestershire League	Welsh FA Cup
Gloucestershire FA Intermediate Cup	Western Floodlight League
English Amateur Cup	Championship Game
North Gloucestershire Minor Cup	Clubcall Cup
Gloucestershire Northern Senior League	Premier Inter League Cup
Gloucestershire FA Northern Senior Amateur Challenge Cup	FA Trophy
Gloucestershire FA Northern Senior Professional Challenge Cup	

++ PLAYERS WHO PLAYED FOR GLOUCESTER CITY DURING WORLD WAR 2 ONLY HAVE BEEN RECORDED

Gloucester City Hurran Cup League	City Cup
Godsman Cup	

PLAYERS IN ITALICS HAVE NOT PLAYED IN A COMPETITIVE GAME FOR A GLOUCESTER TEAM (These are added as and when seen and are not complete)
Only seasons played indicated - sometimes in note section of players who participated competitively.

Players who had Football League experience at Levels 1-4 and in some cases Scottish League have their League record included. The year shown is the first year of the season played. Thus, 1997 indicates the season 1997-98, '1979-85' means that the player made his debut in 1979-80 and his last appearance in 1985-86, but does not necessarily mean that he played in every intervening season. Statistics upto 2008/09.

Club Record: This is playing record only. It is nigh on impossible to keep track of non-league players movements. Some may not be in the order of clubs played for. If anybody can add to this I would be grateful. If + at the end indicates Club Record may be incomplete or ongoing.
International Record: Have only counted Amateur and from Under 21 Level and up.
Birth/Death Dates: The places after Quarters (Qu) indicate the Registration District of Birth or Death. Qu1 = Jan-Mar, Qu2 = Apr-Jun, Qu3 = Jul-Sep, Qu4 = Oct-Dec; bef = before; aft = after; abt = about.

Key: app = Appearances; sub = Substitute; gls = Goals Scored; nps = Non Playing Substitute; ++ = Indicates played during WWII.
Favoured Positions: CD = Central Defender; CF = Centre Forward; CH = Centre Half; D = Defender; F = Forward; FB = Full back; GK = Goalkeeper; HB = Half Back; IF = Inside Forward; M = Midfield; Sub = Substitute; W = Winger; WH = Wing Half.

These players were killed in action or died of injuries sustained during WW1 and WW2. I would suggest there are more than the thirteen I have identified.

(Photograph courtesy of Stan Myers)
Gloucester Member of Parliament, Parmjit Dhanda with Stan Myers, April 2006

ABBLEY, Stephen George (Steve) (F)
b. 19/03/1957 Liverpool, Lancs.
1990/91 7 apps 0 gls
1992/93 11 apps 1 sub 1 gl
TOTAL 18 apps 1 sub 1 gl
Club Record: Parks FC, 1979-81 Swindon Town (23-0), Cheltenham Town, Witney Town, Cheltenham Town, Wycombe Wanderers, Trowbridge Town, Gloucester City, Cirencester Town.
Note: Played for Gloucester City 1991/92.

ABBOTT, F (IF) ++
1941/42 1 app 0 gls
TOTAL 1 app 0 gls

ABBOTT, Mark (CD/M)
b. Biggin Hill, London
1999/00 19 apps 1 gl
2000/01 34 apps 6 subs 2 gls (6 nps)
TOTAL 53 apps 6 subs 2 gls (6 nps)
Club Record: Croydon FC, Gloucester City, Carshalton Athletic, Sevenoaks Town, Westerham +.

ABBOTT, R.E (IF)
1922/23 1 app 0 gls
TOTAL 1 app 0 gls

ACKLAND, Nick (M)
1992/93
Club Record: Forest Green Rovers, Shortwood United, Gloucester City, Charfield AFC +.

ACTON, ? (WH)
1909/10 1 app 0 gls
TOTAL 1 app 0 gls

ADAMS, A.H (W)
1907/08

ADAMS, Mark (W)
b. 1971
1995/96 1 app 9 subs 1 gl (6 nps)
TOTAL 1 app 9 subs 1 gl (6 nps)
Club Record: Larkhall Athletic, Trowbridge Town, Gloucester City, Cheltenham Town +.

ADAMS, Paul (D)
b. 1956
1977/78 8 apps 0 gls
1980/81 6 apps 0 gls (1 nps)
1981/82 19 apps 2 subs 1 gl
TOTAL 33 apps 2 subs 1 gl (1 nps)
Club Record: Brockworth, Matson, Dowty Staverton, Gloucester City +.

ADCOCK, Paul Malcolm (F)
b. 02/05/1972 Ilminster, Somerset
1996/97 2 apps 6 subs 3 gls (1 nps)
1997/98 33 apps 9 subs 6 gls (2 nps)
TOTAL 35 apps 15 subs 9 gls (3 nps)
Club Record: 1990-92 Plymouth Argyle (21-2), Bath City, 1996 Torquay United (3-0), Bath City, Weymouth (loan), Gloucester City, Baldock Town, Saltash United, Tavistock, Bodmin Town +.

ADDIS, Christopher David (Chris) (D)
b. Qu3 1983 Coleford, Glos.
2004/05 0 apps 0 gls (1 nps)
TOTAL 0 apps 0 gls (1 nps)
Club Record: Gloucester United, Cinderford Town, Gloucester City, Ellwood +.
Note: Brother of Darryl Addis.

ADDIS, Darryl Stephen (F)
b. Qu3 1980 Coleford, Glos.
2004/05 30 apps 2 subs 7 gls
2005/06 37 apps 6 subs 3 gls (1 nps)
TOTAL 67 apps 8 subs 10 gls (1 nps)
Club Record: Cinderford Town, Westfields, Cinderford Town, Gloucester City, Cinderford Town, Ellwood, Westfields +.
Note: Brother of Chris Addis.

ADEBOWALE, Andrew Adecla (Andy) (M)
b. 25/02/1967 Hampstead, London
1994/95 34 apps 8 gls
1995/96 40 apps 1 sub 10 gls
1996/97 1app 3 subs 0 gls
TOTAL 75 apps 4 subs 18 gls
Club Record: Arsenal (0), Merthyr Tydfil, Gloucester City, Saint Albans City, Gravesend & Northfleet, Chesham United, Saint Albans City, Berkhamsted Town, Bishop's Stortford, Hertford Town, Balls Park, Chesham United .

ADLAM, Brian (W)
b. 1941
1958/59 2 apps 0 gls
1959/60 16 apps 0 gls
1960/61 38 apps 8 gls
1961/62 20 apps 1 gl
1964/65 3 apps 0 gls
TOTAL 79 apps 9 gls
Club Record: Gloucester City, Shrewsbury Town (0), Leeds United (trials) (0), Bristol Rovers (0), Norwich City (trials) (0), Cambridge United, Yeovil Town, Margate, Wilton Rovers, Gloucester City, Melbourne Croatia (Australia), Sydney Croatia (Australia).

AFTON, Dave (IF)
1983/84

AITKEN, Peter Gerald (WH)
b. 30/06/1954 Cardiff, Wales
1982/83 2 apps 0 gls
TOTAL 2 apps 0 gls
Club Record: 1972-79 Bristol Rovers (234-3), 1980-81 Bristol City (41-1), 1981 York City (18-2), Bulova (Hong Kong), 1982 AFC Bournemouth (1-0), Forest Green Rovers, Gloucester City, Bath City, Trowbridge Town.
International Record: Wales U23 (2).

ALDEN, E (IF)
1935/36 3 apps 1 gl
TOTAL 3 apps 1 gl
Club Record: Wells City, Gloucester City +.

ALDER, Percy Kenneth (CH/FB)
b. 02/09/1904 Gloucester d. Qu3 1984 Gloucester
1927/28 3 apps 0 gls
1928/29 22 apps 1 gl
1929/30 31 apps 2 gls
TOTAL 56 apps 3 gls
Club Record: The Army, Gloucester City +.
Note: Club Captain 1929-30. Played for Gloucester City 1930/31, 1940/41. Brother of Walter Alder and Samuel Alder.

ALDER, Samuel (Sammy) (CH/FB)
b. Qu2 1899 Gloucester d. ?
1925/26 29 apps 5 gls
1926/27 17 apps 1 gl
1927/28 19 apps 0 gls
1928/29 13 apps 3 gls
1929/30 8 apps 1 gl
TOTAL 86 apps 10 gls
Club Record: Gloucester Westgate, Gloucester City +.
Note: Club Captain 1925-26. Brother of Walter Alder and Percy Alder.

ALDER, Walter R (GK)
b. 1895 Gloucester d. ?
1930/31
Note: Brother of Samuel Alder and Percy Alder.

ALDRIDGE, Rob (D)
2004/05

ALDWINKLE, Neil (GK)
1969/70
Club Record: Gloucester City, Longlevens +.

ALLARD, Alexander Gregory (Alex) (M)
b. 14/09/1988 West Bromwich, West Midlands
2006/07 5 apps 4 subs 0 gls (7 nps)
2007/08 22 apps 20 subs 3 gls (7 nps)
2008/09 1 app 1 sub 0 gls
TOTAL 28 apps 25 subs 3 gls (14 nps)
Club Record: Cheltenham Town, Gloucester City, Forest Green Rovers (loan), Shortwood United +.

ALLEN, ? (FB)
1926/27

PLAYERS' RECORDS

ALLEN, E (GK)
1924/25 2 apps 0 gls
TOTAL 2 apps 0 gls

ALLEN, Ernest Edward (IF)
b. Qu3 1894 Gloucester d. ?
1913/14 7 apps 0 gls
1923/24 5 apps 0 gls
TOTAL 12 apps 0 gls
Note: Also played for Gloucester YMCA 1919/20.

ALLEN, F (HB)
1919/20

ALLEN, Keith (FB)
b. 30/04/1952 Cheltenham, Glos.
1975/76 14 apps 0 gls
1976/77 47 apps 0 gls
1977/78 26 apps 0 gls (1 nps)
TOTAL 87 apps 0 gls (1 nps)
Club Record: Swindon Town (0), Hereford United, Worcester City, Bromsgrove Rovers, Cheltenham Town, Gloucester City, Clevedon Town +.

ALLEN, Lee Paul (F)
b. 21/02/1979 Gloucester
2001/02 2 apps 3 subs 0 gls (6 nps)
TOTAL 2 apps 3 subs 0 gls (6 nps)
Club Record: Longlevens, Gloucester City, Gloucester United, Tuffley Rovers, Swindon Supermarine, Longlevens, Ledbury Town +.

AMOS, Peter A (Pete) (WH)
b. 05/11/1946 Kingswood, Glos.
1969/70 1 app 0 gls (1 nps)
TOTAL 1 app 0 gls (1 nps)
Club Record: Gloucester City, Cheltenham Town, Tiverton Town +.

ANDERSON, ? (IF) ++
1941/42 2 apps 1 gl
TOTAL 2 apps 1 gl

ANDERSON, Donald (Don) (HB/FB)
1933/34 27 apps 1 gl
1934/35 47 apps 4 gls
1935/36 8 apps 2 gls
1937/38 1 app 0 gls
1941/42 26 apps 1 gl
1942/43 21 apps 0 gls
TOTAL 130 apps 8 gls
Note: Played for Gloucester City 1939/40, 1940/41. Father of Michael Anderson.

ANDERSON, Michael (W)
b. 1945
1961/62 6 apps 0 gls
TOTAL 6 apps 0 gls
Club Record: Churchdown United, Gloucester City +.
Note: Son of Donald Anderson.

ANDERSON, Robert (Bob) (WH)
b. 1943 Scotland d. 14/05/1999
1968/69 45 apps 0 gls (6 nps)
1969/70 53 apps 3 subs 0 gls
1970/71 50 apps 0 gls
1971/72 32 apps 1 sub 0 gls
1975/76 1 app 0 gls
TOTAL 181 apps 4 subs 0 gls (6 nps)
Club Record: Berwick Rangers (0), Bedford Town, Gloucester City, Cape Town FC (South Africa), Wilton Rovers, Gloucester City (loan) +.
Note: Club Captain 1968-69, 1970-72. Club Player of the Season 1970/71.

ANDREWS, Glendon (Glen) (FB)
b. 11/02/1945 Dudley, Worcs.
1970/71 16 apps 2 gls
1971/72 10 apps 2 gls (3 nps)
TOTAL 26 apps 4 gls (3 nps)
Club Record: 1963 Manchester United (0), 1966 Wolverhampton Wanderers (0), 1967-68 Bradford Park Avenue (48-6), Chelmsford City, Worcester City, Gloucester City, Stourbridge, Cinderford Town +.

ANDREWS, Michael (Mike) (M)
b. 1963
1988/89 4 apps 4 subs 3 gls (5 nps)
TOTAL 4 apps 4 subs 3 gls (5 nps)
Club Record: Gloucester City, Redditch United +.

ANDREWS, Robert (Rob) (D)
b. 1965
1984/85 5 apps 1 sub 0 gls
TOTAL 5 apps 1 sub 0 gls
Club Record: Newport County (0), Pontllanfraith, Gloucester City +.

ANDREWS, Toby (Sub)
1989/90 0 apps 2 subs 0 gls (1 nps)
TOTAL 0 apps 2 subs 0 gls (1 nps)
Club Record: Gloucester City, Shortwood United +.

ANGROVE, E (W)
1935/36 3 apps 1 gl
TOTAL 3 apps 1 gl
Club Record: Cardiff City (0), Gloucester City +.

ANSON, Shayne David (M)
b. Qu2 1988 Gloucester
2006/07
Club Record: Gloucester City, Slimbridge, Hardwicke +.

APPERLEY, G (CF)
1928/29 18 apps 4 gls
TOTAL 18 apps 4 gls
Note: This could be George Applin. Citizen consistently printed Apperley for this season.

APPLEYARD, John (D)
1977/78 18 apps 0 gls
TOTAL 18 apps 0 gls
Club Record: Cheltenham Town, Gloucester City +.

APPLIN, George (IF)
b. 02/12/1904 Gloucester d. Qu1 1974 Gloucester
1929/30 29 apps 7 gls
1930/31 12 apps 1 gl
1931/32 33 apps 11 gls
1932/33 35 apps 5 gls
1933/34 26 apps 4 gls
1934/35 1 app 0 gls
TOTAL 136 apps 28 gls

ARCHER, Richard (D)
2001/02 0 apps 0 gls (2 nps)
TOTAL 0 apps 0 gls (2 nps)
Club Record: Gloucester City, Chipping Norton Town +.

ARCHIBALD, ? (IF)
1967/68

ARKELL, HENRY WITCOMB (IF/FB)
b. Qu3 1878, Gloucester d. ?
1897/98 4 apps 2 gls
1898/99 18 apps 3 gls
1899/00 19 apps 2 gls
1900/01 12 apps 0 gls
1902/03 12 apps 0 gls
1903/04 3 apps 0 gls
TOTAL 68 apps 7 gls
Note: Played for Gloucester 1896/97. Joint Club Secretary 1902-1903.

ARMIT, Peter Annand (W)
b. 1926 Edinburgh, Scotland
1953/54 17 apps 4 gls
TOTAL 17 apps 4 gls
Club Record: Saint Johnstone (0), Gloucester City +.

ARMSTRONG, William (Bill) (IF)
1955/56 7 apps 0 gls
TOTAL 7 apps 0 gls
Club Record: Third Lanark (0), Gloucester City +.

ARNOLD, George Robarts (FB)
b. Qu1 1883 Potton, Beds. d. ?
1899/00 3 apps 0 gls
1900/01 4 apps 0 gls
1903/04 2 apps 1 gl
TOTAL 9 apps 1 gl

ARNOLD, Joseph Daniel (Joe) (F)
b. 20/05/1988 Truro, Cornwall
2008/09 1 app 1 sub 0 gls (1 nps)
TOTAL 1 app 1 sub 0 gls (1 nps)
Club Record: Derby County (0), Swindon Town (0), Team Bath, Gloucester City (loan) +.

[477]

ARTUS, Colin Jack (W)
b. Qu2 1910 Stroud, Glos. d. ?
1930/31 7 apps 0 gls
TOTAL 7 apps 0 gls

ASH, Wally (FB)
1948/49 6 apps 0 gls
TOTAL 6 apps 0 gls
Club Record: Aston Villa (0), Gloucester City +.

ASHALL, James (Jimmy) (FB)
b. 13/12/1933 Normanton, Yorks.
1964/65 46 apps 0 gls
1965/66 53 apps 1 gl
1966/67 39 apps 1 gl
1967/68 35 apps 1 sub 0 gls (4 nps)
TOTAL 173 apps 1 sub 2 gls (4 nps)
Club Record: Hasland Old Boys, 1955-60 Leeds United (89-0), Weymouth, Gloucester City +.
Note: Club Captain 1966-67.

ASHER, Sydney James (Syd) (CF)
b. 24/12/1930 Portsmouth, Hants. d. Qu3 1994 Portsmouth, Hants.
1951/52 25 apps 12 gls
TOTAL 25 apps 12 gls
Club Record: 1948 Portsmouth (0), Gloucester City, Hastings United, 1956 Northampton Town (21-11), Bedford Town, Guildford City, Weymouth, Poole Town, Sittingbourne, Canterbury City, Chelmsford City, Trowbridge Town, Crawley Town.

ASHFORD, Ben (M)
b. 01/04/1989 Exeter, Devon
2006/07 1 app 1 gl (6 nps)
2007/08 2 apps 0 gls
TOTAL 3 apps 1 gl (6 nps)
Club Record: Gloucester City, Forest Green Rovers +.

ASHTON, Dave (M)
b. 1965
1983/84
Club Record: Cirencester Town, Fulham (trial) (0), Gloucester City +.

ATHERTON, F (HB)
1931/32 1 app 1 gl
1932/33 3 apps 0 gls
1933/34 1 app 0 gls
TOTAL 5 apps 1 gl

ATKINS, ? (GK)
1903/04

ATKINSON, ? (CF)
1946/47 4 apps 3 gls
TOTAL 4 apps 3 gls
Club Record: Bradford City, Gloucester City +.

AUBREY, Matthew Dennis (Matt) (F)
b. 04/09/1984 Hereford, Herefordshire
2004/05 9 apps 0 gls
TOTAL 9 apps 0 gls
Club Record: Bristol City (0), Westfields, Forest Green Rovers, Gloucester City (loan), Cinderford Town (loan), Redditch United, Rushall Olympic, Westfields, Pegasus Juniors, Malvern Town +.

AUBREY, R (IF)
1926/27 20 apps 2 gls
1927/28 9 apps 0 gls
TOTAL 29 apps 2 gls
Club Record: Old Plutonians, Gloucester City +.

AUCKLAND, Niel (D)
1984/85

AVERY, Daniel James (Dan) (D)
b. Qu1 1987 Cheltenham, Glos.
2003/04 1 apps 2 subs 0 gls (9 nps)
2004/05 6 apps 0 gls (3 nps)
TOTAL 7 apps 2 subs 0 gls (12 nps)
Club Record: Gloucester City, Gloucester United (loan), Chipping Norton Town, Bishop's Cleeve +.
Note: Brother of Sam Avery.

AVERY, Samuel David (Sam) (D)
b. Qu2 1989 Cheltenham, Glos.
2005/06 0 apps 0 gls (1 nps)
TOTAL 0 apps 0 gls (1 nps)
Club Record: Gloucester City, Chipping Norton Town, Bishop's Cleeve, Carterton, Bishop's Cleeve +.
Note: Brother of Dan Avery.

AXFORD, Thomas E (WH)
b. 1873 Monkton, Wilts. d. ?
1900/01 15 apps 0 gls
TOTAL 15 apps 0 gls

AYLAND, Albert Frederick Lot (Bert) (W)
b. 04/05/1906 Westbury-on-Severn, Glos. d. Qu4 1971 Gloucester
1925/26 2 apps 0 gls
1926/27 4 apps 0 gls
1928/29 1 app 0 gls
1929/30 21 apps 1 gl
1937/38 1 app 0 gls
TOTAL 29 app 1 gl
Club Record: Gloucester City, Pope's Hill, Gloucester City Albion +.
Note: Played for Gloucester City 1930/31, 1932/33, 1940/41.

BADDOCK, Stephen William (Steve) (F)
b. 10/09/1958 Kensington, London
1986/87 49 apps 28 gls
1987/88 29 apps 3 subs 15 gls
TOTAL 78 apps 3 subs 43 gls
Club Record: Bristol Portway, 1985 Bristol Rovers (17-3), Gloucester City, Wokingham Town +.
Note: Supporter's Player of the Season 1986/87.

BADHAM, Steven David R (Steve) (F)
b. 03/12/1978 Gloucester
2007/08 0 apps 1 sub 0 gls
TOTAL 0 apps 1 sub 0 gls
Club Record: Slimbridge, Gloucester City (loan) +.

BADHAM, William Land (W)
b. Qu3 1876 Kingstone, Herefordshire d. ?
1896/97

BAGLEY, R (IF)
1891/92

BAILEY, B (WH)
1931/32

BAILEY, F (CF)
1924/25 2 apps 0 gls
1925/26 2 apps 0 gls
TOTAL 4 apps 0 gls

BAILEY, Shaun (D)
b. 14/01/1989 Gloucester
2007/08 1 app 0 gls
TOTAL 1 app 0 gls
Club Record: Stonehouse Town, Gloucester City (loan) +.

BAILLIE, J (HB) ++
1941/42 23 apps 4 gls
TOTAL 23 apps 4 gls
Club Record: Dunfermline Athletic (0), Gloucester City +.

BAIN, C (HB)
1906/07 2 apps 0 gls
TOTAL 2 apps 0 gls

BAIRD, ? (HB)
1988/89

BAKER, Gerald A (Gerry) (CF)
b. 05/06/1953 Worcester, Worcs.
1971/72 4 apps 2 subs 0 gls (2 nps)
TOTAL 4 apps 2 subs 0 gls (2 nps)
Club Record: Gloucester City, Bromsgrove Rovers, Worcester City, Oldbury United +.

BAKER, J
1920s

PLAYERS' RECORDS

BAKKER, John (Johnny) (W)
b. 1919 Holland
1947/48 17 apps 2 gls
1948/49 13 apps 4 gls
1949/50 5 apps 1 gl
1950/51 7 apps 2 gls
TOTAL 42 apps 9 gls
Club Record: Oxford City, Gloucester City +.

BALDWIN, ? (CH)
1896/97

BALDWIN, Joseph Melville (IF)
b. Qu2 1887 Tibberton, Glos. d. ?
1906/07 13 apps 7 gls
TOTAL 13 apps 7 gls

BALL, Norman George (W) ++
b. 24/12/1923 Gloucester d. 11/1987 Torquay, Devon.
1942/43 4 apps 8 gls
TOTAL 4 apps 8 gls

BALLINGER, Brian Peter (WH)
b. 13/08/1943 Chippenham, Wilts.
1966/67 11 apps 0 gls
TOTAL 11 apps 0 gls
Club Record: Swindon Town (0), Chippenham United, Gloucester City,
Chippenham Town, Melksham Town.
Note: Grandfather of Luke Ballinger.

BALLINGER, Luke Richard (F)
b. 19/02/1987 Bath, Avon
2008/09 32 apps 15 subs 7 gls (2 nps)
TOTAL 32 apps 15 subs 7 gls (2 nps)
Club Record: Bristol City (0), Melksham Town, Bournemouth Sports AFC,
Mangotsfield United, Gloucester City +.
International Record: England Futsal (23+).
Note: Grandson of Brian Ballinger.

BAMPTON, G (HB)
1926/27 1 app 0 gls
TOTAL 1 app 0 gls

BANKS, H (FB)
1923/24 12 apps 0 gls
1924/25 5 apps 0 gls
1925/26 10 apps 0 gls
1926/27 13 apps 1 gl
TOTAL 40 apps 1 gl

BANKS, Timothy (Tim) (M)
b. 09/03/1964 Bristol
1992/93 11 apps 7 subs 3 gls (6 nps)
TOTAL 11 apps 7 subs 3 gls (6 nps)
Club Record: Old Georgians, Gloucester City, Forest Green Rovers +.

BARBER, David (Dave) (W)
b. 1943
1966/67 1 app 0 gls
TOTAL 1 app 0 gls
Club Record: Birmingham City (0), Kidderminster Harriers, Bromsgrove
Rovers, Worcester City, Gloucester City +.

BARCLAY, Dominic Alexander (F)
b. 05/09/1976 Bristol, Avon
1999/00
Club Record: 1995-97 Bristol City (12-0), 1998 Macclesfield Town (9-1),
Gloucester City, Kettering Town, Yate Town, Chippenham Town,
Salisbury City, Sutton United, Croydon, Saint Leonards, Croydon, Saint
Leonards, Erith & Belvedere, Slough Town, Lewes, Erith & Belvedere,
Whyteleafe +.

BARKER, Gerry (IF)
1967/68 9 apps 1 gl
TOTAL 9 apps 1 gl

BARNARD, H (FB)
1894/95 1 app 0 gls
TOTAL 1 app 0 gls
Note: Played for Gloucester 1889/90, 1890/91, 1892/93.

BARNARD, Leigh Kenneth (M)
b. 29/10/1958 Worsley, Salford, Lancs.
1991/92
Club Record: 1977-81 Portsmouth (79-8), Yeovil Town (loan), 1981
Peterborough United (loan) (4-0), 1982-89 Swindon Town (217-22), 1984
Exeter City (loan) (6-2), 1989-90 Cardiff City (63-9), Stroud, Gloucester
City (trial).

BARNARD, Simon (D)
b. 1975
1995/96 2 apps 1 sub 0 gls (1 nps)
TOTAL 2 apps 1 sub 0 gls (1 nps)
Club Record: Portsmouth (0), Worcester City, Gloucester City +.

BARNES, C (W)
1909/10 1 app 0 gls
TOTAL 1 app 0 gls
Note: Played for Gloucester 1906/07.

BARNES, H.L (GK)
1919/20

BARNES, Oliver James P (Ollie) (D)
b. Qu2 1987 Bristol, Avon
2006/07 5 apps 0 gls
TOTAL 5 apps 0 gls
Club Record: Bristol City (0), Bristol Rovers (0), Gloucester City (loan),
Salisbury City, Team Bath, Worcester City, Weymouth +.

BARNES, W.B (IF)
1933/34 3 apps 0 gls
TOTAL 3 apps 0 gls
Club Record: Camberley, Gloucester City +.

BARNETT, W.J (FB)
1934/35 2 apps 0 gls
TOTAL 2 apps 0 gls
Club Record: Lister's Works, Gloucester City +.

BARNFIELD, Bryan R (W)
b. Qu3 1931 Fairford, Glos.
1951/52 25 apps 8 gls
1952/53 44 apps 4 gls
1953/54 36 apps 4 gls
1954/55 15 apps 1 gl
TOTAL 120 apps 17 gls
Club Record: Gloucester City, Bath City +.

BARRATT, Eric (GK)
b. 1985
2002/03 0 apps 0 gls (10 nps)
2003/04 2 apps 0 gls (1 nps)
TOTAL 2 apps 0 gls (11 nps)
Club Record: Brighton & Hove Albion (0), Crawley Town, Tuffley Rovers,
Gloucester City (loan), Chippenham Town, Bishop's Cleeve +.

BARRETT, Archibald Manning (IF)
b. Qu1 1893 Gloucester d. 23/03/1916 Merville, France
1913/14 1 app 0 gls
TOTAL 1 app 0 gls
Note: Killed in action WW1.

BARRETT, Michael (Mike) (GK)
b. 20/10/1963 Exeter, Devon
1992/93 1 app 0 gls
TOTAL 1 app 0 gls
Club Record: Liskeard Athletic, 1994 Exeter City (4-0), Exmouth Town,
Cheltenham Town, Exmouth Town, Gloucester City, Crediton +.

BARROW, ? (W) ++
1939/40 1 app 0 gls
TOTAL 1 app 0 gls
Club Record: Leicester City (0), Gloucester City +.

BARRY, Nigel (F)
1979/80

BARTLETT, Frederick Leslie (Fred) (CH)
b. 05/03/1913 Reading, Berks. d. Qu3 1968 Henley-on-Thames, Oxon.
1946/47 3 apps 0 gls
1948/49 39 apps 0 gls
1949/50 27 apps 0 gls
TOTAL 69 apps 0 gls
Club Record: Club Francais (France), 1934-36 Queen's Park Rangers
(48-0), 1937-47 Clapton Orient (96-0), Gloucester City.

BARTON, Peter (Broncho) (GK)
b. 1942
1959/60 19 apps 0 gls
1960/61 40 apps 0 gls
1961/62 39 apps 0 gls
TOTAL 98 apps 0 gls
Club Record: Swindon Town (0), Gloucester City, Cheltenham Town +.

BASEY, Philip J (Phil) (W)
b. 27/08/1948 Cardiff, Wales
1967/68 38 apps 1 sub 9 gls (2 nps)
TOTAL 38 apps 1 sub 9 gls (2 nps)
Club Record: 1966 Brentford (2-0), Gloucester City, Crawley Town, Maidstone United, Hillingdon Borough, Tooting & Mitcham, Bromley.

BASFORD, Walter David (Jock) (D)
b. 03/12/1919 Basford, Notts. d. 03/1982 Mansfield, Notts.
1941/42 1 app 0 gls
1948/49 11 apps 0 gls
TOTAL 12 apps 0 gls
Club Record: Brush Sports, Wolverhampton Wanderers (0), Gainsborough Trinity, Portsmouth (0), Bournemouth & Boscombe Athletic (0), Bath City, Southampton (0), West Ham United (0), Birmingham (0), Grantham Town, Gloucester City, Margate, Sittingbourne, Holbeach United.

BASSETT, F.A (CF)
1921/22 1 app 1 gl
TOTAL 1 app 1 gl

BATER, Philip Thomas (Phil) (D)
b. 26/10/1955 Cardiff, Wales
1990/91 2 apps 0 gls
TOTAL 2 apps 0 gls
Club Record: Clifton Athletic, 1974-80 Bristol Rovers (212-2), 1981-82 Wrexham (73-1), 1983-85 Bristol Rovers (98-1), 1986 Brentford (19-2), 1987-88 Cardiff City (76-0), Gloucester City.
International Record: Wales U21 (2).

BATES, E (FB)
1891/92
1892/93

BATH, Matthew Ryan (Matt) (GK)
b. 12/06/1976 Stroud, Glos.
2001/02 24 apps 0 gls
2002/03 56 apps 0 gls
2003/04 52 apps 0 gls
2004/05 45 apps 0 gls
2005/06 46 apps 1 gl
2006/07 30 apps 0 gls (4 nps)
TOTAL 253 apps 1 gl (4 nps)
Club Record: Whitminster Town, Gloucester City, Cinderford Town, Cirencester Town +.
Note: Supporter's Player of the Season 2001/02.

BATH, W (W)
1927/28

BATHURST, Leonard Williams (IF)
b. Qu3 1882 Tewkesbury, Glos. d. ?
1909/10 3 apps 0 gls
TOTAL 3 apps 0 gls
Club Record: Tewkesbury Abbey, Gloucester City +.

BATSTONE, Victor Frank (CF) ++
b. 23/08/1916 Marlborough, Wilts. d. Qu1 1997 Gloucester
1941/42 7 apps 16 gls
TOTAL 7 apps 16 gls
Club Record: Gloucester Police, Gloucester City +.

BATTY, Roger (CF)
1967/68 2 apps 1 sub 0 gls (6 nps)
TOTAL 2 apps 1 sub 0 gls (6 nps)

BAVERSTOCK, Raymond (Ray) (D)
b. 03/12/1963 Southall, London
1990/91 34 apps 1 sub 0 gls (1 nps)
1992/93 11 apps 1 gl
TOTAL 45 apps 1 sub 1 gl (1 nps)
Club Record: 1982 Swindon Town (17-0), Cheltenham Town, Gloucester City, Worcester City, Moreton Town (loan), Worcester City, Bath City, Trowbridge Town, Forest Green Rovers, Cirencester Town.
Note: Played for Gloucester City 1993/94.

BAYLISS, Charles (CF)
b. 1945
1966/67 3 apps 1 gl
TOTAL 3 apps 1 gl
Club Record: Chippenham United, Horfield Old Boys, Gloucester City +.

BAYLISS, F (FB)
1923/24 3 apps 0 gls
1924/25 4 apps 1 gl
1925/26 15 apps 0 gls
1927/28 11 apps 1 gl
1932/33 2 apps 0 gls
TOTAL 35 apps 2 gls

BAYLISS, Karl Allan (F)
b. 24/02/1968 Gloucester
1985/86 1 app 0 gls (2 nps)
1991/92 6 apps 3 gls
1992/93 49 apps 25 gls
1993/94 42 apps 2 subs 21 gls
1994/95 13 apps 9 subs 7 gls (4 nps)
1999/00 11 apps 4 gls
2000/01 38 apps 5 subs 19 gls
2001/02 15 apps 7 gls
2002/03 20 apps 13 subs 4 gls
2003/04 3 apps 8 subs 1 gl (26 nps)
2004/05 4 apps 4 subs 1 gl (4 nps)
TOTAL 202 apps 41 subs 92 gls (36 nps)
Club Record: Cheltenham Town, Forest Green Rovers, Shortwood United, Sharpness, Salisbury City, Malvern Town, Tamworth, Stroud, Gloucester City, Cirencester Town (loan), Weston-Super-Mare (loan), Forest Green Rovers, Newport AFC, Gloucester City, Clevedon Town, Gloucester City, Stroud Ramblers +.

BAYLISS, T.W (FB)
1919/20
1920/21

BAZELEY, Stanley (Stan) (CF)
1948/49 24 apps 11 gls
1949/50 16 apps 6 gls
TOTAL 40 apps 17 gls
Club Record: Aston Villa (0), Gloucester City +.

BEACHAM, Andrew (Andy) (M)
1987/88 1 app 0 gls (1 nps)
1991/92 0 apps 1 sub 0 gls
TOTAL 1 app 1 sub 0 gls (1 nps)

BEACOCK, Gary Cedric (M)
b. 22/01/1960 Scunthorpe, Lincs.
1986/87 2 apps 0 gls (2 nps)
TOTAL 2 apps 0 gls (2 nps)
Club Record: 1977 Sheffield United (0), unknown Dutch club, 1980-82 Grimsby Town (17-0), 1983-85 Hereford United (27-4), Gloucester City, Dudley Town.

BEALE, W (CF) ++
1939/40 7 apps 3 gls
TOTAL 7 apps 3 gls
Club Record: Dursley Town, Gloucester City +.

BEALE, Walter (Paper) (IF)
b. Qu2 1890 Avening, Glos. d. ?
1927/28 1 app 0 gls
TOTAL 1 app 0 gls
Club Record: Forest Green Rovers, Avening, Forest Green Rovers, Gloucester City +.

BEARD, ? (WH) ++
1939/40

BEARD, C (HB)
1920/21

BEARD, G.J.A (IF)
1897/98

BEARD, L (GK)
1926/27

BEATTIE, Andrew (Andy) (M)
1981/82
Club Record: Merthyr Tydfil, Gloucester City (trial) +.
Note: Son of George Beattie.

PLAYERS' RECORDS

BEATTIE, George (IF)
b. 16/06/1925 Aberdeen, Scotland
1948/49 27 apps 8 gls
1949/50 48 apps 13 gls
1950/51 8 apps 9 gls
1955/56 32 apps 13 gls
TOTAL 115 apps 43 gls
Club Record: Rosslyn Rosemount, 1947 Southampton (1-0), Gloucester City, 1950-52 Newport County (113-23), 1953-54 Bradford Park Avenue (53-16), Tonbridge, Merthyr Town, Gloucester City, Dursley Town.
Note: Father of Andrew Beattie.

BEAVAN, A (FB)
1890/91

BEDDIS, Lemuel Archibald (HB/IF)
b. 03/10/1895 Stratford-Upon-Avon, Warks. d. Qu1 1971 Gloucester
1921/22 4 apps 2 gls
1922/23 7 apps 1 gl
1923/24 14 apps 4 gls
1924/25 6 apps 1 gl
1925/26 1 app 0 gls
TOTAL 32 apps 8 gls
Note: Also played for Gloucester YMCA 1920/21. Secretary-Manager 1919-31.

"BEDMAN", W (IF)
1894/95 1 app 0 gls
TOTAL 1 app 0 gls
Note: A pseudonym which cloaks the identity of this player!

BELFITT, Steven Richard (Steve) (D)
b. Qu2 1975 Gloucester
1991/92 1 app 0 gls
TOTAL 1 app 0 gls
Club Record: Gloucester City, Ellwood, Broadwell Amateurs +.

BELL, Eddie (IF)
b. 1941
1957/58 8 apps 1 gl
1958/59 12 apps 2 gls
1959/60 37 apps 0 gls
1960/61 41 apps 4 gls
1961/62 45 apps 1 gl
1962/63 33 apps 2 gls
1967/68 28 apps 11 gls
TOTAL 204 apps 21 gls
Club Record: Hardwicke, Gloucester City, Aston Villa (trial) (0), Dudley Town, Halesowen Town, Evesham United, Gloucester City +.

BELL, Gary (FB)
b. 04/04/1947 Stourbridge, Worcs.
1977/78 16 apps 1 gl
1978/79 35 apps 1 sub 0 gls (1 nps)
TOTAL 51 apps 1 sub 1 gl (1 nps)
Club Record: Halesowen Town, 1964 West Bromwich Albion (0), Lower Gormal Athletic, 1966-73 Cardiff City (223-10), 1973 Hereford United (loan) (8-0), 1974-77 Newport County (126-5), Gloucester City, Bridgend Town, Lydney Town.
Note: Club Captain 1978-79.

BELL, Nick (IF)
b. 1962
1985/86 5 apps 1 gl
TOTAL 5 apps 1 gl
Club Record: Shortwood United, Gloucester City +.

BELL, S (W)
1985/86 1 app 0 gls
TOTAL 1 app 0 gls

BELL, Steve (GK)
2007/08
Club Record: Hereford Lads Club, Gloucester City (trial) +.

BELLOWS, William (W)
b. 1874 Gloucester d. 29/03/1942 Gloucester
1896/97

BENBOW, Luke John (IF)
b. Qu2 1890 Gloucester d. ?
1909/10 1 app 0 gls
TOTAL 1 app 0 gls

BENFIELD, W. H (WH)
1891/92
1892/93
Note: Club Secretary 1890-1893.

BENNETT, Adam David (GK)
b. 28/08/1979 Bristol, Avon
2001/02 4 apps 0 gls
2004/05 1 app 0 gls (5 nps)
TOTAL 5 apps 0 gls (5 nps)
Club Record: Brockworth Albion, Gloucester City, Stroud Ramblers, Tuffley Rovers +.

BENNETT, Steven James (Steve) (M)
b. 29/03/1980 Cirencester, Glos.
1998/99 6 apps 6 subs 2 gls (5 nps)
TOTAL 6 apps 6 subs 2 gls (5 nps)
Club Record: Hungerford Town, Cirencester Town, Gloucester City, Swindon Supermarine +.

BENTON, Dave (D)
b. 1970
1999/00
Club Record: Burton Albion, Moor Green, Bilston Town, Stourbridge, Bromsgrove Rovers, Gloucester City (trial) +.

BERRY, J (CF)
1930/31 1 app 0 gls
TOTAL 1 app 0 gls

BERRY, Nigel M (GK)
b. 24/07/1954 Cheltenham, Glos.
1979/80 2 apps 0 gls
TOTAL 2 apps 0 gls
Club Record: Leckhampton, Cheltenham Town, Gloucester City, Cheltenham Town, Saint Marks CA +.

BEVAN, J (CF)
1933/34 1 app 1 gl
1941/42 3 apps 0 gls
1942/43 1 app 1 gl
TOTAL 5 apps 2 gls
Note: Played for Gloucester City 1940/41.

BEVAN, Jody Keith (F)
b. 21/10/1978 Gloucester
2005/06 15 apps 1 sub 3 gls
2006/07 11 apps 3 subs 5 gls (2 nps)
2007/08 7 apps 27 subs 6 gls (8 nps)
TOTAL 33 apps 31 subs 14 gls (10 nps)
Club Record: Gloucester City, Trowbridge Town, Cinderford Town, Weston-Super-Mare, Cirencester Town, Cinderford Town, Gloucester City, Almondsbury (loan), Cinderford Town, Cirencester Town +.
Note: Played for Gloucester City 2008/09.

BIBBY, Philip Robert (Phil) (F)
b. 23/01/1926 Ledbury, Herefordshire d. 03/1999 Derby, Derbys.
1950s
Club Record: Nottingham Forest (0), Margate, Gloucester City +.

BIGGART, Stewart A (CH)
b. Qu3 1951 Evesham, Worcs.
1969/70 5 apps 0 gls
1970/71 43 apps 1 gl
1971/72 40 apps 0 gls
1972/73 40 apps 2 gls (1 nps)
1973/74 40 apps 1 sub 0 gls (4 nps)
TOTAL 168 apps 1 sub 3 gls (5 nps)
Club Record: Pinvin United, Gloucester City, Worcester City, Moreton Town +.

BIRCH, Alan (D)
1975/76 45 apps 0 gls (1 nps)
TOTAL 45 apps 0 gls (1 nps)
Club Record: Frampton United, Gloucester City +.

BIRCH, Alfred (GK)
1932/33 33 apps 0 gls
1933/34 3 apps 0 gls
1934/35 1 app 0 gls
TOTAL 37 apps 0 gls
Club Record: Gloucester City, Maisemore +.

[481]

BIRCH, J (HB)
1938/39 1 app 0 gls
TOTAL 1 app 0 gls
Club Record: Gloucester City, Saint Paul's Training College +.
Note: Played for Gloucester City 1940/41.

BIRD, Alan Martin (D)
b. 06/05/1967 Chippenham, Wilts.
1994/95 53 apps 3 gls
1995/96 41 apps 0 gls
TOTAL 94 apps 3 gls
Club Record: Kington Langley, Chippenham Town, Trowbridge Town, Gloucester City , Worcester City, Witney Town, Weston-Super-Mare +.

BIRD, Ronald Philip (Ronnie) (W)
b. 27/12/1941 Erdington, Warks. d. Qu1 2005 Cardiff, Wales
1972/73 41 apps 12 gls
1973/74 48 apps 9 gls
TOTAL 89 apps 21 gls
Club Record: 1959 Birmingham City (0), 1961-65 Bradford PA (129-39), 1965 Bury (13-3), 1965-70 Cardiff City (108-25), 1971 Crewe Alexandra (20-0), Gloucester City, Barry Town.
Note: Club Captain 1973-74.

BIRKBY, Dean (M)
b. 03/03/1971 Pontefract, Yorks.
1993/94 2 apps 2 subs 0 gls
TOTAL 2 apps 2 subs 0 gls
Club Record: Yate Town, Clevedon Town, Gloucester City, Bath City, Yeovil Town, Forest Green Rovers (loan), Weymouth (loan), Forest Green Rovers, Clevedon Town, Paulton Rovers, Merthyr Tydfil (loan), Forest Green Rovers, Newport County (loan), Mangotsfield United (loan), Cinderford Town, Aberystwyth Town, Bath City, Weston-Super-Mare, unknown Australian club, Mangotsfield United +.

BIRKENSHAW, ? (GK)
1990/91

BIRT, J (W)
1932/33 32 apps 4 gls
1933/34 3 apps 0 gls
TOTAL 35 apps 4 gls

BISHOP, C (IF)
1929/30 1 app 0 gls
TOTAL 1 app 0 gls

BITCHENOR, Kevin D (CF)
b. Qu3 1958 Plymouth, Devon
1974/75 9 apps 1 sub 3 gls (1 nps)
1975/76 0 apps 0 gls (2 nps)
1976/77 1 app 1sub 0 gls (2 nps)
1977/78 1 app 0 gls
TOTAL 11 apps 2 subs 3 gls (5 nps)
Club Record: Churchdown Panthers, Gloucester City, Forest Green Rovers, Stonehouse +.

BLACK, Simon Anthony (F)
b. 09/11/1975 Marston Green, West Midlands
1995/96 7 apps 3 gls
TOTAL 7 apps 3 gls
Club Record: 1993 Birmingham City (2-0), Yeovil Town, Gloucester City (loan), 1996 Doncaster Rovers (0), Halesowen Town +.

BLACKBURN, Kenneth Alan (Ken) (CF)
b. 13/05/1951 Wembley, London
1971/72 33 apps 2 subs 8 gls (2 nps)
1976/77 15 apps 4 subs 8 gls (4 nps)
TOTAL 48 apps 6 subs 16 gls (6 nps)
Club Record: 1968 Brighton & Hove Albion (1-1), Gloucester City, Dover, Matson Athletic, Cinderford Town, Sharpness, Gloucester City, Stonehouse, Frampton United, Longlevens, Gloucester United.

BLACKHOUSE, J (IF)
1930/31 17 apps 10 gls
TOTAL 17 apps 10 gls

BLACKLER, Martin John (M)
b. 14/03/1963 Swindon, Wilts.
1993/94 6 apps 1 sub 0 gls (1 nps)
TOTAL 6 apps 1 sub 0 gls (1 nps)
Club Record: 1982 Swindon Town (9-0), Witney Town, Cheltenham Town, Trowbridge Town, Wycombe Wanderers, Wealdstone, Yeovil Town, Gloucester City, Salisbury City, Cirencester Town, Accrington Stanley, Stalybridge Celtic.

BLACKMAN, Barry George (F)
b. 15/09/1967 Southwark, London
1991/92 2 apps 4 subs 0 gls
TOTAL 2 apps 4 subs 0 gls
Club Record: Crystal Palace (0), Dulwich Hamlet, Gloucester City, Yeovil Town, Wealdstone, Tooting & Mitcham, Croydon, Edsbro (Sweden), Uppsala (Sweden), Hendon, Kingstonian, Saint Albans City, Sutton United, Croydon (loan) +.

BLACKMORE, ? (HB)
1920/21

BLAKE, John H (W)
b. 1873 Nailsworth, Glos. d. ?
1889/90
Club Record: Gloucester, Forest Green, Nailsworth, Stroud, Woodchester +.

BLAKE, W.T (GK)
1907/08 6 apps 0 gls
TOTAL 6 apps 0 gls
Club Record: Cheltenham Town, Gloucester City +.

BLAND, Archibald Evatt (IF)
b. Qu1 1886 Gloucester d. 23/07/1916 Somme, France
1906/07 2 apps 5 gls
1909/10 2 apps 1 gl
TOTAL 4 apps 6 gls
Club Record: Stroud, Gloucester +.
Note: Killed in action WW1.

BLANDFORD, Rev. A.J (IF)
1919/20

BLOCKLEY, Jeffrey Paul (Jeff) (CD)
b. 12/09/1949 Leicester, Leics.
1981/82 15 apps 1 gl
TOTAL 15 apps 1 gl
Club Record: 1968-72 Coventry City (146-6), 1972-74 Arsenal (52-1), 1974-77 Leicester City (76-2), 1977 Derby County (0) (loan), 1978-79 Notts County (59-5), Enderby Town, Gloucester City.
International Record: England (1), England U23 (10).
Note: Club Captain 1981.

BLOOMFIELD, Paul (D)
b. 1970
1993/94 21 apps 9 subs 2 gls (9 nps)
TOTAL 21 apps 9 subs 2 gls (9 nps)
Club Record: Saint Marks CA, Cheltenham Town, Worcester City (loan), Gloucester City, Forest Green Rovers, Weston-Super-Mare, Evesham United +.
Note: Played for Gloucester City 1994/95.

BLYTHE, James (Jimmy) (W)
1961/62 4 apps 1 gl
TOTAL 4 apps 1 gl
Club Record: Torquay United (0), Gloucester City +.
Note: Son of hypnotist Henry Blythe who hypnotised the Gloucester City team in 1959.

BOARD, Jeffrey Paul (Jeff) (CH)
b. 17/11/1962 Bristol d. Qu2 1981 Weston-Super-Mare, Somerset
1980/81 1 app 0 gls
TOTAL 1 app 0 gls

BODEN, Rich (F)
1994/95 10 apps 6 subs 0 gls (3 nps)
TOTAL 10 apps 6 subs 0 gls (3 nps)
Club Record: Trowbridge Town, Gloucester City, Trowbridge Town +.

BOGGIS, Brian (GK)
1971/72
Club Record: Wisbech Town, Gloucester City (trial) +.

BOLLAND, Rev. Arthur Middleton (W)
b. Qu4 1867 Kirkstall, Leeds, Yorks. d. ?
1890/91
1891/92

BOLTING, ? (CF) ++
1942/43 1 app 4 gls
TOTAL 1 app 4 gls

BOND, Leonard Allan (Len) (GK)
b. 12/02/1954 Ilminster, Somerset
1990/91 10 apps 0 gls
1991/92 3 apps 0 gls
TOTAL 13 apps 0 gls
Club Record: 1970-76 Bristol City (30-0), 1974 Exeter City (loan) (30-0), 1975 Torquay United (loan) (3-0), 1975 Scunthorpe United (loan) (8-0), 1975 Colchester United (loan) (3-0), 1977-79 Brentford (122-0), Saint Louis Stars (USA), 1980-83 Exeter City (138-0), Weymouth, Bath City, Yeovil Town, Gloucester City.

BONNOR, George Ricketts (FB)
b. Qu3 1868 Barnwood, Gloucester d. Qu4 1925 Williton, Somerset
1889/90 2 apps 0 gls
TOTAL 2 apps 0 gls

BOOK, Kim Alistair (GK)
b. 12/02/1946 Bath, Somerset
1979/80 34 apps 0 gls
TOTAL 34 apps 0 gls
Club Record: Frome Town, 1967-68 Bournemouth & Boscombe Athletic (2-0), 1969-71 Northampton Town (78-0), 1971 Mansfield Town (loan) (4-0), 1971-73 Doncaster Rovers (84-0), Trowbridge Town, Gloucester City, Yeovil Town, Bath City, Weston-Super-Mare.
Note: Father of Steven Book, brother of Tony Book ex-captain of Manchester City. Notably let in 6 George Best goals in FA Cup tie when at Northampton Town losing 2-8.

BOOK, Steven Kim (Steve) (GK)
b. 07/07/1969 Bournemouth, Hants.
1992/93
Club Record: 1987 Brighton & Hove Albion (0), Slough Town (loan), 1988 Lincoln City (0), Forest Green Rovers, 1999-03 Cheltenham Town (172-0), Gloucester City (loan), 2004 Swindon Town (2-0), Cirencester Town, 2005 Bristol Rovers (1-0), Mangotsfield United, 2007 Bristol Rovers (0), Tiverton Town +.
Note: Son of Kim Book.

BOONAVALLE, ? (IF)
1903/04 1 app 1 gl
TOTAL 1 app 1 gl
Note: Surname could be Boonaville.

BOONHAM, Gerald (George) (CF)
b. Qu4 1918 Atherstone, Warks.
1947/48 2 apps 1 gl
TOTAL 2 apps 1 gl
Club Record: Aston Villa (0), Gloucester City +.

BOOTS, Andrew P (Andy) (M)
b. Qu3 1957 Swindon, Wilts.
1975/76 6 apps 0 gls (4 nps)
1976/77 18 apps 0 gls
1977/78 25 apps 0 gls
TOTAL 49 apps 0 gls (4 nps)
Club Record: Marston United, Gloucester City, Matson Athletic +.

BOSELEY, Lesley Gordon (IF)
b. Qu3 1934 Westbury-on-Severn, Glos.
1950/51 5 apps 2 gls
1951/52 5 apps 2 gls
TOTAL 10 apps 4 gls
Club Record: Harrow Hill, Gloucester City, Tottenham Hotspur (0), Stonehouse +.
Note: Father of Steve Boseley.

BOSELEY, Stephen J (Steve) (W)
b. Qu4 1956 Gloucester
1977/78 21 apps 1 gl (1 nps)
1979/80 23 apps 2 gls (3 nps)
1980/81 2 apps 0 gls
TOTAL 46 apps 3 gls (4 nps)
Club Record: Derby County (0), Harrow Hill, Gloucester City, Forest Green Rovers +.
Note: Son of Gordon Boseley.

BOTTOMLEY, F (W)
1907/08 3 apps 0 gls
TOTAL 3 apps 0 gls

BOUGHTON, ? (D)
1985/86

BOUGHTON, Albert Victor (Bert) (WH)
b. Qu1 1885 Droitwich, Worcs. d. ?
1906/07 16 apps 1 gl
1907/08 16 apps 0 gls
1908/09 1 app 0 gls
TOTAL 33 apps 1 gl

BOURNE, Richard (M)
b. 1972
1994/95
Club Record: Bristol Rovers (0), Salisbury City, Gloucester City, Calne Town, Swindon Supermarine, Witney Town, Chippenham Town, Wantage Town +.

BOURTON, Harold Charles (Tiny) (GK)
b. 06/06/1902 Tewkesbury, Glos. d. Qu2 1986 Cheltenham, Glos.
1927/28 9 apps 0 gls
TOTAL 9 apps 0 gls
Club Record: Tewkesbury Town, Gloucester City +.

BOUSTON, Bryan John (FB)
b. 03/10/1960 Hereford, Herefordshire
1980/81 50 apps 3 subs 0 gls (3 nps)
TOTAL 50 apps 3 subs 0 gls (3 nps)
Club Record: 1977 Hereford United (6-0), Ledbury Town, Gloucester City +.

BOWKER, A (W)
1929/30 5 apps 0 gls
TOTAL 5 apps 0 gls
Club Record: Metropolitan Works (Birmingham), Gloucester City +.

BOWKLEY, Ken (Sub)
1954/55

BOWLES, John Charles (Jack) (GK) ++
b. 04/08/1914 Cheltenham, Glos. d. Qu1 1987 Shrewsbury, Shrops.
1939/40 1 app 0 gls
TOTAL 1 app 0 gls
Club Record: Cheltenham Town, 1936 Newport County (4-0), 1937 Accrington Stanley (12-0), 1938-52 Stockport County (277-0), Gloucester City, Winsford United.

BOWLES, Russell (GK)
1986/87 8 apps 0 gls
1992/93 4 apps 0 gls
TOTAL 12 apps 0 gls
Club Record: Cinderford Town, Gloucester City (loan), Harrow Hill, Cinderford Town, Newport AFC.

BOWLING, ? (FB)
1940/41
Club Record: Yorkshire Amateurs +.

BOWMAN, Alex (W)
b. 1940
1959/60 26 apps 2 gls
1960/61 19 apps 0 gls
TOTAL 45 apps 2 gls
Club Record: Leicester City (0), Gloucester City +.

BOX, Anthony F (Tony) (W)
b. Qu4 1939 Forest of Dean, Glos.
1957/58 6 apps 1 gl
1958/59 8 apps 0 gls
1959/60 13 apps 2 gls
1960/61 26 apps 2 gls
TOTAL 53 apps 5 gls
Club Record: Lydney Town, Newport County (0) (trials), Gloucester City +.

BOYD, John (Jackie) (CF)
b. 10/09/1926 Boston, Massachusetts, USA
1948/49 12 apps 7 gls
1949/50 43 apps 20 gls
1950/51 21 apps 8 gls
TOTAL 76 apps 35 gls
Club Record: Arthurlie, Gloucester City, 1950-51 Bristol City (31-6), Bath City, Weymouth.

BOYLAND, Mark (F)
b. 30/03/1958
1993/94 12 apps 13 subs 4 gls (6 nps)
TOTAL 12 apps 13 subs 4 gls (6 nps)
Club Record: Oxford City, Banbury United, Witney Town, Cheltenham Town, Wycombe Wanderers, Aylesbury United, Cheltenham Town, Valley Sports Rugby, Tamworth, Cheltenham Town, Worcester City, Gloucester City, Cirencester Town +.

BOYLE, James (Jim) (Sub)
1968/69

BRACE, G.B (GK)
1909/10 3 apps 0 gls
TOTAL 3 app 0 gls
Note: Played for Gloucester 1907/08, 1908/09.

BRADDER, Gary V (M)
b. 06/03/1961 Nuneaton, Warks.
1988/89 7 apps 0 gls
1989/90 10 apps 2 subs 2 gls (1 nps)
TOTAL 17 apps 2 subs 2 gls (1 nps)
Club Record: Bermuda FC, Bedworth United, Atherstone United, Gloucester City, Atherstone United, Valley Sports Rugby, Nuneaton Griff +.

BRADFORD, ? (GK)
1896/97

BRAIN, Mark (GK)
1990/91 1 app 0 gls
TOTAL 1 app 0 gls

BRAIN, W (CH)
1927/28 14 apps 0 gls
TOTAL 14 apps 0 gls

BRAKE, Philip (Phil) (M)
b. 1954
1978/79 29 apps 6 gls (1 nps)
TOTAL 29 apps 6 gls (1 nps)
Club Record: Minehead, Clevedon Town, Cinderford Town, Gloucester City +.

BRANIGAN, J (FB)
1932/33 1 app 0 gls
TOTAL 1 app 0 gls

BRAY, A.J.W (W)
1937/38 2 apps 0 gls
TOTAL 2 apps 0 gls

BRAY, Marcus (D)
b. 1967
1987/88 12 apps 2 subs 2 gls (1 nps)
1988/89 2 apps 2 subs 0 gls (2 nps)
TOTAL 14 apps 4 subs 2 gls (3 nps)
Club Record: Gloucester City, Cheltenham Town, Trowbridge Town, Marlborough Town +.

BRAZIER, J (IF)
1891/92

BRERETON, Rev. Henry Lloyd (FB)
b. 13/01/1864 South Molton, Devon d. Qu4 1917 Freebridge Lynn, Norfolk
1889/90 2 apps 0 gls
TOTAL 2 apps 0 gls
Note: Club Secretary 1889 -1890.

BRETHERTON, Charles Archibald (FB)
b. Qu3 1886 Gloucester d. ?
1913/14 8 apps 0 gls
1921/22 1 app 0 gls
TOTAL 9 apps 0 gls
Note: Club Captain 1913-1914. Also played for Gloucester YMCA 1919/20, 1920/21.

BRIDGES, S (FB)
1927/28 4 apps 0 gls
TOTAL 4 apps 0 gls

BRINKWORTH, Arthur (CH)
1931/32 30 apps 1 gl
1932/33 14 apps 0 gls
TOTAL 44 apps 1 gl

BRINKWORTH, Richard A (Dick) (M)
b. Qu1 1959 Swindon, Wilts.
1978/79 12 apps 0 gls (1 nps)
1979/80 15 apps 0 gls (5 nps)
TOTAL 27 apps 0 gls (6 nps)
Club Record: Swindon Town (0), Margate, Gloucester City, Cheltenham Town, Fairford Town.
Note: Brother of Trevor Brinkworth.

BRINKWORTH, Trevor (Sub)
b. Qu1 1958 Swindon, Wilts.
1979/80 0 apps 0 gls (1 nps)
TOTAL 0 apps 0 gls (1 nps)
Club Record: Dorchester Town, Gloucester City +.
Note: Brother of Richard Brinkworth.

BRINSFORD, Neil (GK)
1950/51 1 app 0 gls
TOTAL 1 app 0 gls
Club Record: Torquay United (0), Gloucester City +.

BROADBENT, S (HB)
1947/48 2 apps 0 gls
TOTAL 2 apps 0 gls

BROCK, John George Graham (GK)
b. 15/12/1915 Bromsgrove, Worcs. d. Qu1 1976 Chipping Sodbury, Glos.
1937/38 4 apps 0 gls
1938/39 7 apps 0 gls
TOTAL 11 apps 0 gls
Club Record: Bristol University, Forest Green Rovers, 1936 Swindon Town (5-0), Gloucester City +.

BROMAGE, Alfred (IF)
1937/38 1 app 0 gls
TOTAL 1 app 0 gls

BROOKES, ?
1980s

BROOMFIELD, ? (Sub)
1987/88

BROTHERTON, Les (FB)
1957/58
Club Record: Northampton Town (0), Newport County (0), Gloucester City +.

BROWN, A (W)
1919/20

BROWN, Albert Edward (Bert/Joe) (WH)
b. 04/03/1934 Bristol
1963/64 9 apps 1 gl
TOTAL 9 apps 1 gl
Club Record: Wolverhampton Wanderers (0), Bristol City (0), Exeter University, 1957 Crystal Palace (3-0), 1959 Queen's Park Rangers (0), Exeter City (0), Bath City, Gloucester City +.

BROWN, C.E (WH)
1909/10 1 app 0 gls
TOTAL 1 app 0 gls
Note: Played for Gloucester 1908/09.

BROWN, L (W)
1920/21

BROWN, Robert (Bobby) (IF)
b. 14/05/1949 Bristol
1981/82 61 apps 2 gls
TOTAL 61 apps 2 gls
Club Record: 1968-71 Bristol Rovers (35-4), 1969 Newport County (loan) (9-0), Weymouth, Yeovil Town, 1974 Hereford United (0), Weymouth, Minehead, Bath City, Gloucester City, Forest Green Rovers, Yate Town.

BROWN, Rod (F)
b. 1960
1990/91 2 apps 0 gls
TOTAL 2 apps 0 gls
Club Record: Dundee United (0), Brechin City (0), 1983 Montrose (1-0), 1984 Arbroath (21-6), Gloucester City, Forest Green Rovers, Bromsgrove Rovers.

BROWN, W.A (HB)
1897/98 3 apps 0 gls
TOTAL 3 apps 0 gls
Note: Played for Gloucester 1896/97.

BROWN, William Henry (Bill) (FB)
1946/47 27 apps 0 gls
1947/48 43 apps 0 gls
1948/49 41 apps 0 gls
1949/50 2 apps 0 gls
TOTAL 113 apps 0 gls
Club Record: Newport County (0), Gloucester City +.

BROWNING, Gary (Sub)
1981/82 0 apps 0 gls (1 nps)
TOTAL 0 apps 0 gls (1 nps)
Club Record: Bymacks, Gloucester City +.

BROWNING, Hubert Charles (GK)
b. 23/12/1903 Gloucester d. Qu1 1996 Gloucester
1925/26 30 apps 0 gls
1926/27 13 apps 0 gls
1928/29 5 apps 0 gls
1930/31 1 app 0 gls
TOTAL 49 apps 0 gls
Club Record: Gloucester City, Bristol Tramways +.
Note: Brother of William Browning.

BROWNING, Marcus Trevor (F)
b. 22/04/1971 Bristol
1989/90 2 apps 6 subs 2 gls
1990/91 10 apps 8 gls
TOTAL 12 apps 6 subs 10 gls
Club Record: 1989-96 Bristol Rovers (174-13), Weymouth (loan), Gloucester City (loan), 1992 Hereford United (loan) (7-5), 1996-98 Huddersfield Town (33-0), 1998 Gillingham (loan) (1-0), 1998-01 Gillingham (77-3), 2002-05 AFC Bournemouth (188-3), Weymouth +.
International Record: Wales (5).

BROWNING, William (FB)
b. Qu1 1902 Gloucester d. ?
1922/23 1 app 0 gls
TOTAL 1 app 0 gls
Note: Brother of Hubert Browning.

BRUNO, David (Dave) (F)
b. 1956 Bristol
1980/81 1 app 0 gls
TOTAL 1 app 0 gls
Club Record: Almondsbury Greenway, Gloucester City (trial) +.

BRUTON, David Edward (Dave) (D)
b. 31/10/1952 Uley, Glos.
1981/82 52 apps 9 gls
1982/83 45 apps 7 gls
1983/84 48 apps 8 gls
TOTAL 145 apps 24 gls
Club Record: 1971-72 Bristol City (17-0), 1973-78 Swansea City (193-19), 1976 Newport County (loan) (6-1), 1978-80 Newport County (82-9), Gloucester City, Forest Green Rovers.
Note: Club Captain 1981-82. Club Player of the Season 1982/83. Brother of Michael Bruton.

BRUTON, Michael (Mike) (F)
b. 06/05/1958 Uley, Glos.
1978/79 22 apps 7 gls
1980/81 13 apps 6 gls
1982/83 32 apps 1 sub 20 gls (1 nps)
1983/84 47 apps 27 gls (1 nps)
TOTAL 114 apps 1 sub 60 gls (2 nps)
Club Record: Sharpness, Gloucester City, 1979 Newport County (9-1), Oxford City, Gloucester City, Forest Green Rovers.
Note: Brother of David Bruton.

BRYAN, ? (IF) ++
1942/43
Club Record: West Ham United (0), Gloucester City +.

BRYANT, Matthew (Matt) (D)
b. 21/09/1970 Bristol
1989/90 7 apps 0 gls
TOTAL 7 apps 0 gls
Club Record: Gloucester City (loan), 1990-95 Bristol City (203-7), 1990 Walsall (loan) (13-0), 1996-99 Gillingham (103-0).

BRYANT, Richard John (D)
b. 20/06/1963 Bristol
1986/87 34 apps 0 gls
TOTAL 34 apps 0 gls
Club Record: Robinson's DRG, 1985 Bristol City (2-1), Gloucester City, Forest Green Rovers +.

BRYANT, W (W)
1946/47 5 apps 2 gls
TOTAL 5 apps 2 gls
Club Record: Bristol City (0), Gloucester City +.

BRYCELAND, Samuel (Sammy) (IF)
b. 1931 Greenock, Scotland
1956/57 43 apps 10 gls
TOTAL 43 apps 10 gls
Club Record: Greenock Morton (0), Gloucester City, Worcester City, Redditch United, Halesowen Town +.

BUCHANAN, ? (W) ++
1939/40

BUCHANAN, Wilfred Lawrence (GK)
b. Qu1 1874 Gloucester d. Qu1 1929 Gloucester
1890/91

BUCKLAND, Mark Christopher (D)
b. 18/08/1961 Cheltenham, Glos.
1992/93 49 apps 6 gls (1 nps)
1993/94 49 apps 2 subs 7 gls (1 nps)
TOTAL 98 apps 2 subs 13 gls (2 nps)
Club Record: Kidderminster Harriers, Cheltenham Town, 1979 Lincoln City (trial) (0), Automotive Products Leamington, 1983-84 Wolverhampton Wanderers (50-5), Cheltenham Town, Gloucester City, Moreton Town, Endsleigh, Crescent United, Gas Green.

BUCKLAND, William Albert (Bill) (HB)
b. Qu1 1900 Shipston-on-Stour, Warks. d. ?
1926/27
Club Record: Cheltenham Town, Cinderford Town, 1924 Bristol City (1-0), Gloucester City +.

BUIST, James Gibb (Jimmy) (W)
b. 19/06/1918 Falkirk, Scotland d. 1999 Inverness, Scotland
1949/50 57 apps 10 gls
1950/51 50 apps 7 gls
1951/52 29 apps 4 gls
1952/53 9 apps 1 gl
1953/54 1 app 0 gls
TOTAL 146 apps 22 gls
Club Record: King's Park, Dundee (0), Raith Rovers (0), Stirling Albion (0), 1946 New Brighton (21-6), 1948 Plymouth Argyle (1-0), Gloucester City, Hereford United.
Note: Club Manager Aug 1952- Apr 1954.

BURBY, Lee (M)
b. Qu3 1981 Gloucester
2002/03 2 apps 1 sub 0 gls
TOTAL 2 apps 1 sub 0 gls
Club Record: Cheltenham Town, Cinderford Town (loan), Gloucester City, Cinderford Town, Slimbridge +.

BURFORD, Michael T (Mike) (M)
b. 19/04/1960 Gloucester
1979/80 17 apps 3 subs 1 gl (1 nps)
1980/81 37 apps 10 gls (1 nps)
1981/82 46 apps 2 subs 10 gls (3 nps)
1982/83 35 apps 6 subs 7 gls (2 nps)
1983/84 29 apps 2 subs 10 gls (8 nps)
1984/85 3 apps 1 sub 0 gls (3 nps)
1985/86 6 apps 2 subs 1 gl
TOTAL 173 apps 16 subs 39 gls (18 nps)
Club Record: Hereford United, Gloucester City, Cheltenham Town, Sharpness, Brockworth +.

BURGESS, Ronald J (Ron) (GK)
b. Qu2 1919 Bristol
1946/47 26 apps 0 gls
1947/48 2 apps 0 gls
TOTAL 28 apps 0 gls
Club Record: Bristol Rovers (0), Gloucester City +.

BURLEY, D (CH)
1946/47 1 app 0 gls
TOTAL 1 app 0 gls

BURNETT, ? (CF) ++
1942/43 11 apps 14 gls
TOTAL 11 apps 14 gls
Club Record: Millwall (0), Cardiff City (0), Gloucester City +.
Note: Is this Stan Burnett from Saltash who was still associated with the club in 1950/51 in the reserves?

BURNS, Christopher (Chris) (D/M)
b. 09/11/1967 Manchester, Lancs.
1996/97 44 apps 1 sub 5 gls
1997/98 59 apps 10 gls
1998/99 46 apps 7 gls
2001/02 35 apps 2 subs 6 gls
2002/03 44 apps 2 subs 10 gls (3 nps)
2003/04 34 apps 3 subs 1 gl (12 nps)
2004/05 26 apps 3 subs 2 gls (4 nps)
2005/06 15 apps 1 sub 0 gls (3 nps)
TOTAL 303 apps 12 subs 41 gls (22 nps)
Club Record: Brockworth, Sharpness, Cheltenham Town, 1990-94 Portsmouth (90-10), 1993 Swansea City (loan) (4-0), 1994 AFC Bournemouth (14-1), 1994 Swansea City (5-0), 1994-98 Northampton Town (66-9), Gloucester City, Forest Green Rovers, Gloucester City, Cinderford Town, UD Horadada (Spain), Brockworth +.
Note: Club Captain 1999-2000. Club Manager Jun 2001 – Jan 2006. Father of Jake Burns.

BURNS, Jake Thomas J (F)
b. Qu4 1990 Gloucester
2005/06
Club Record: Brockworth, Gloucester City, Brockworth, Gala Wilton +.
Note: Son of Chris Burns.

BURNS, Mickey (Sub)
1970/71

BURT, ? (FB)
1894/95 1 app 0 gls
TOTAL 1 app 0 gls

BURTON, J. T (W)
1925/26 20 apps 5 gls
1926/27 17 apps 6 gls
TOTAL 37 apps 11 gls

BURTON, Paul Stewart (F)
b. 06/08/1973 Hereford, Herefordshire
1990s
Club Record: 1989-91 Hereford United (5-1), Westfields, Newport County, Redditch United, Evesham United, Kington Town, Westfields +.

BURY, James (Jimmy) (IF)
b. 1927
1950/51 39 apps 4 gls
TOTAL 39 apps 4 gls
Club Record: Blackburn Rovers (0), Torquay United (0), Gloucester City +.

BUTLER, A (HB)
1924/25 7 apps 2 gls
TOTAL 7 apps 2 gls

BUTLER, J (W)
1930/31 2 apps 0 gls
TOTAL 2 apps 0 gls

BUTLER, L (IF)
1908/09 1 app 0 gls
TOTAL 1 app 0 gls

BUTT, ? (FB) ++
1941/42

BUTT, Steve (F)
b. 1963
1982/83 12 apps 1 sub 6 gls (8 nps)
TOTAL 12 apps 1 sub 6 gls (8 nps)
Club Record: Bridgwater Town, Gloucester City +.

BUTTERY, Luke (D)
b. 12/02/1985 Wegberg, West Germany
2006/07 9 apps 0 gls (1 nps)
2007/08 4 apps 0 gls
TOTAL 13 apps 0 gls (1 nps)
Club Record: Cheltenham Town, Swindon Supermarine (loan), Chippenham Town (loan), Cinderford Town, Gloucester City, Forest Green Rovers +.

BYE, E (W)
1937/38 1 app 0 gls
TOTAL 1 app 0 gls

BYGRAVE, P (HB)
1913/14 1 app 0 gls
TOTAL 1 app 0 gls

BYWATER, Paul Richard (D)
b. 10/08/1971 Bridgnorth, Shrops.
1991/92 32 apps 3 gls
1992/93 49 apps 4 gls
1993/94 45 apps 3 gls
TOTAL 126 apps 10 gls
Club Record: Shrewsbury Town (0), Worcester City, Gloucester City , Bridgnorth Town, Stafford Rangers +.
Note: Supporter's Player of the Season 1992/93, 1993/94.

CADETTE, Richard Raymond (F)
b. 21/03/1965 Hammersmith, London
1997/98 2 apps 1 sub 0 gls
TOTAL 2 apps 1 sub 0 gls
Club Record: Wembley, 1984 Orient (21-4), 1985-86 Southend United (90-49), 1987 Sheffield United (28-7), 1988-91 Brentford (87-20), 1989 AFC Bournemouth (loan) (8-1), 1991-95 Falkirk (92-31), 1994-96 Millwall (24-5), 1997-98 Clydebank (4-1), Gloucester City, Shelbourne (Eire).

CAIRNS, Kwesi (D)
b. 05/08/1979 London
1998/99 0 apps 0 gls (2 nps)
1999/00 10 apps 10 subs 1 gl (11 nps)
2000/01 5 apps 4 subs 0 gls (2 nps)
TOTAL 15 apps 14 subs 1 gl (13 nps)
Club Record: Southampton (0), Stoke City (0), Gloucester City, Gloucester United (loan), Shortwood United, Slimbridge +.

CALE, ? (WH)
1937/38 1 app 0 gls
TOTAL 1 app 0 gls

CALLAGHAN, Robert (Bobby) (W)
b. 05/10/1931 Glasgow, Scotland d. Qu2 1991 Scunthorpe and Barton-Upon-Humber, Lincs.
1958/59 34 apps 3 gls
TOTAL 34 apps 3 gls
Club Record: Duntocher Hibernian, 1955 Scunthorpe United (19-6), 1956-57 Barrow (40-10), Gloucester City.

CALLAWAY, Colin J (IF)
b. Qu2 1947 Bristol
1977/78 13 apps 4 gls
1979/80 16 apps 3 gls (1 nps)
1983/84 1 app 0 gls (1 nps)
TOTAL 30 apps 7 gls (2 nps)
Club Record: Clevedon Town, Gloucester City, Taunton Town, Gloucester City +.

CALLINAN, Thomas Joseph (Tommy) (M)
b. 06/06/1966 Cheltenham, Glos.
1992/93 42 apps 6 gls
1993/94 47 apps 2 subs 6 gls
1994/95 1 app 0 gls (3 nps)
1998/99 31 apps 1 sub 3 gls (5 nps)
1999/00 32 apps 3 subs 3 gls (3 nps)
2000/01 23 apps 5 subs 2 gls (7 nps)
TOTAL 176 apps 11 subs 20 gls (18 nps)
Club Record: Saint Marks CA, Cheltenham Town, Bishop's Cleeve, Cheltenham Saracens, Cheltenham Town, Worcester City (trial), Cinderford Town, Gloucester City, Cinderford Town (loan), Cirencester Town (loan), Forest Green Rovers, Dorchester Town, Gloucester City, Clevedon Town, Cinderford Town, Swindon Supermarine, Cinderford Town, Slimbridge, Chippenham Town, Taunton Town, Malvern Town, Yate Town.
Note: Club Manager Feb 2000 – Jun 2001.

CAMERON, Alistair (GK)
b. 1955
1971/72 1 app 0 gls
TOTAL 1 app 0 gls
Club Record: Frampton United, Gloucester City +.

CAMPBELL, ? (W)
1946/47 1 app 0 gls
TOTAL 1 app 0 gls

CAMPBELL, Gary (Sub)
1993/94

CANAVAN, James (Jimmy) (WH)
b. 1924 Croy, Lanarkshire, Scotland
1950/51 42 apps 5 gls
1951/52 38 apps 6 gls
1952/53 32 apps 4 gls
TOTAL 112 apps 15 gls
Club Record: Croy Juveniles, 1946-48 East Fife (1-0), 1949 Saint Johnstone (6-0), Gloucester City, Stonehouse +.
Note: Club Captain 1950-52.

CANN, Darren John (D)
b. 17/06/1968 Torquay, Devon
1994/95 13 apps 0 gls (2 nps)
TOTAL 13 apps 0 gls (2 nps)
Club Record: 1986-87 Torquay United (13-0), Weymouth (loan), Barnstaple Town, Clevedon Town, Gloucester City, Elmore, Taunton Town, Bath City (loan), Minehead Town, Taunton Town, Dartmouth, Newton Abbott, Penzance.

CANNOCK, J (FB)
1934/35 1 app 0 gls
TOTAL 1 app 0 gls
Club Record: Cinderford Town, Gloucester City +.

CANT, John Joseph (D)
b. 06/11/1983 Bromley, Kent
2007/08 0 apps 1 sub 0 gls
TOTAL 0 apps 1 sub 0 gls
Club Record: Forest Green Rovers, Melksham Town (loan), Slimbridge, Shortwood United, Gloucester City (loan), Bishop's Cleeve +.

CAPENER, A.G (W)
1919/20

CARELY, F (WH)
1895/96 1 app 0 gls
TOTAL 1 app 0 gls

CARLETON, L.A (FB)
1909/10 12 apps 0 gls
TOTAL 12 apps 0 gls

CARMAN, ? (CH) ++
1941/42

CARPENTER, ? (CF)
1899/00 1 app 1 gl
TOTAL 1 app 1 gl

CARR, Lance Lanyon (IF) ++
b. 18/02/1910 Johannesburg, South Africa d. Qu2 1983 Greenwich, London
1939/40 1 app 0 gls
TOTAL 1 app 0 gls
Club Record: Johannesburg Calies (South Africa), Boksburg (South Africa), 1933-35 Liverpool (31-8), 1936 Newport County (25-5), South Liverpool, 1938-45 Newport County (39-9), Gloucester City, 1946 Bristol Rovers (42-8), Merthyr Tydfil.

CARROLL, Mick (D)
1976/77 15 apps 0 gls
TOTAL 15 apps 0 gls
Club Record: Forest Green Rovers, Cheltenham Town, Gloucester City, Shortwood United +.

CARRUTHERS, ? (WH) ++
1941/42 1 app 0 gls
TOTAL 1 app 0 gls
Club Record: Huddersfield Town (0), Gloucester City +.

CARRUTHERS, James (Jimmy) (IF)
b. 1934
1956/57 14 apps 2 gls
1957/58 43 apps 6 gls
1958/59 52 apps 3 gls
TOTAL 109 apps 11 gls
Club Record: Heart of Midlothian (0), Gloucester City +.

CARTER, Alfred J (Alf) (IF)
b. 1880 Gloucester d. ?
1906/07 4 apps 3 gls
1907/08 17 apps 10 gls
1908/09 6 apps 3 gls
1909/10 1 app 0 gls
TOTAL 28 apps 16 gls

CARTER, C (W)
1909/10 3 apps 0 gls
TOTAL 3 apps 0 gls
Note: Played for Gloucester City 1907/08.

CARTER, C (IF)
1928/29 8 apps 0 gls
TOTAL 8 apps 0 gls

CARTER, Charles G (WH)
b. 1890 Gloucester d. ?
1909/10 9 apps 3 gls
TOTAL 9 apps 3 gls

CARTER, H (CF) ++
1941/42
Club Record: Huddersfield Town (0), Gloucester City +.

CARTER, Lytton Haines (FB)
b. Qu4 1873 Gloucester d. ?
1894/95 1 app 0 gls
TOTAL 1 app 0 gls
Note: Played for Gloucester 1889/90.

CARTER, Oliver John Arthur (Olly) (IF)
b. Qu1 1885 Gloucester d. 13/01/1953 Winchester, Hants.
1906/07 1 app 0 gls
TOTAL 1 app 0 gls
Note: Club Secretary 1909-1910.

CARTY, Paul Eugene (M)
b. 22/10/1966 Birmingham, Warks.
1993/94 2 apps 1 sub 0 gls
TOTAL 2 apps 1 sub 0 gls
Club Record: Everton (0), Nuneaton Borough, Valley Sports Rugby, Bromsgrove Rovers, Gloucester City, Hednesford Town, Worcester City, Nuneaton Borough (loan), Bromsgrove Rovers +.

CASEY, Kim T (F)
b. 03/03/1961 Birmingham, Warks.
1984/85 45 apps 1 sub 36 gls
TOTAL 45 apps 1 sub 36 gls
Club Record: Sutton Coldfield Town, Automotive Products Leamington, Gloucester City, Kidderminster Harriers, Cheltenham Town, Wycombe Wanderers, Solihull Borough, Kidderminster Harriers, Solihull Motors, Moor Green, Rushall Olympic +.
Note: Club Player of the Season 1984/85.

CASEY, Matthew James (Matt) (M)
b. Qu4 1976 Stroud, Glos.
2000/01
Club Record: Gloucester City, Gloucester United, Slimbridge, King's Stanley +.
Note: Brother of Ross Casey.

CASEY, Ross Mark (M)
b. 07/08/1979 Stroud, Glos.
1999/00 15 apps 0 gls (3 nps)
TOTAL 15 apps 0 gls (3 nps)
Club Record: Cheltenham Town, Newport County, Inter Cardiff, Gloucester City, Yate Town, Bath City, Mangotsfield United, Paulton Rovers, Slimbridge, Shortwood United, Taverners (Nailsworth) +.
Note: Played for Gloucester City 2000/01. Brother of Matthew Casey.

CASEY, Thomas (Tommy) (WH)
b. 11/03/1930 Belfast, Northern Ireland d. 11/01/2009 Nailsea, Somerset
1963/64 37 apps 6 gls
1964/65 23 apps 0 gls
TOTAL 60 apps 6 gls
Club Record: Comber, Clara Park, Belfast YMCA, Bangor, 1949 Leeds United (4-0), 1950-51 Bournemouth & Boscombe Athletic (66-1), 1952-57 Newcastle United (116-8), 1958 Portsmouth (24-1), 1958-1962 Bristol City (122-9), Gloucester City, Inter Roma Toronto (Canada).
International Record: Northern Ireland (12).
Note: Club Manager Aug 1963 – May 1965.

CASSIDY, ? (CF) ++
1941/42 4 apps 0 gls
TOTAL 4 apps 0 gls

CASSWELL, T (GK)
1890/91

CASTLEDINE, Steve (?)

CAUSON, Walter John (Jerry) (CF)
b. 09/09/1911 Gloucester d. Qu4 1990 Gloucester
1930/31 27 apps 26 gls
1931/32 33 apps 33 gls
1932/33 34 apps 35 gls
1933/34 40 apps 47 gls
1934/35 39 apps 49 gls
1935/36 19 apps 4 gls
1936/37 2 apps 1 gl
TOTAL 194 apps 195 gls
Club Record: Saint James, Gloucester City, Bristol City (0), Bath City, Gloucester City +.
Note: First Gloucester player to score 100 competitive goals and all-time record scorer for the club.

CHADBORN, Arthur John (FB)
b. Qu3 1870 Gloucester d. ?
1889/90
Note: Brother of Charles Chadborn and William Chadborn.

CHADBORN, Charles Nugent (CF)
b. Qu4 1872 Gloucester d. 2/1949 Lewes, Sussex
1889/90
Note: Brother of Arthur Chadborn and William Chadborn.

CHADBORN, William Henry (Harry) (HB)
b. 12/1871 Gloucester d. Qu2 1955 Gloucester
1889/90 1 app 0 gls
TOTAL 1 app 0 gls
Note: Brother of Arthur Chadborn and Charles Chadborn.

CHADD, R.T (IF)
1932/33 9 apps 6 gls
TOTAL 9 apps 6 gls

CHAMBERS, T (W)
1935/36 3 apps 0 gls
TOTAL 3 apps 0 gls

CHANDLER, Richard David (Ricky) (M)
b. 26/09/1961 Bristol
1988/89 40 apps 7 gls (1 nps)
1989/90 34 apps 8 subs 5 gls (4 nps)
1990/91 44 apps 4 subs 4 gls (1 nps)
1991/92 27 apps 6 subs 1 gl (7 nps)
TOTAL 145 apps 18 subs 17 gls (13 nps)
Club Record: 1980-82 Bristol City (61-12), Bath City, Yeovil Town, Bath City, Gloucester City, Weston-Super-Mare.

CHAPMAN, Dave (D)
1975/76 16 apps 1 sub 0 gls (2 nps)
TOTAL 16 apps 1 sub 0 gls (2 nps)

CHARITY, Simon Nicholas (M)
b. 20/02/1975 Bath, Somerset
1995/96 3 apps 3 subs 0 gls (1 nps)
TOTAL 3 apps 3 subs 0 gls (1 nps)
Club Record: Gloucester City, Paulton Rovers, Mangotsfield United, Chippenham Town +.

CHENOWETH, Paul (M)
b. 05/02/1973 Bristol
1999/00 24 apps 2 gls (4 nps)
2000/01 26 apps 3 subs 6 gls (1 nps)
TOTAL 50 apps 3 subs 8 gls (5 nps)
Club Record: Bristol Rovers (0), Bath City, Cheltenham Town, Bath City, Worcester City, Gloucester City, Merthyr Tydfil, Gloucester City, Tiverton Town, Yate Town, Almondsbury Town +.

CHERRY, David (W)
1961/62 1 app 0 gls
TOTAL 1 app 0 gls

CHILVERS, ? (W)
1957/58 1 app 0 gls
TOTAL 1 app 0 gls

CHIPPETTE, L (W) ++
1940/41
Club Record: Walthamstow Avenue, Barking Town, West Ham United (0), Gloucester City +.

CHIPPS, Stephen (D)
b. 1980 Sydney, Australia
2002/03 28 apps 2 subs 0 gls (2 nps)
TOTAL 28 apps 2 subs 0 gls (2 nps)
Club Record: Macarthur Rams (Australia), Parametta Melita Eagles (Australia), Gloucester City, Hajduk Wanderers (Australia), Sydney Wanderers (Australia), Northern Tigers (Australia) +.

CHIVERS, John (Sub)
1981/82

CHURCHWARD, Alan John (GK)
b. 19/08/1968 Swindon, Wilts.
1992/93
Club Record: Swindon Town (0), Cheltenham Town, Bath City, Gloucester City, Cheltenham Town, Trowbridge Town, Cirencester Town, Clevedon Town, Highworth Town +.

CIANY, Gary (F)
b. U.S.A. ?
1992/93

CLARK, H (IF)
1953/54

CLARK, Harold (FB)
1947/48 7 apps 0 gls
TOTAL 7 apps 0 gls
Club Record: Bristol Rovers (0), Bristol City (0), Gloucester City +.

CLARK, James Donald (Jim) (FB)
b. 01/05/1923 Dornoch, Scotland d. 02/1994 Forest of Dean, Glos.
1952/53 1 app 0 gls
1953/54 35 apps 5 gls
1954/55 51 apps 5 gls
1955/56 50 apps 0 gls
1956/57 31 apps 0 gls
1959/60 12 apps 0 gls
1961/62 13 app 1 gl
TOTAL 193 apps 11 gls
Club Record: Keith Juniors, Glasgow Rangers (0), Brechin City (0), Aberdeen (0), 1948-52 Exeter City (95-5), 1952 Bradford City (loan) (6-0), Gloucester City, Kidderminster Harriers, Stonehouse, Gloucester City.
Note: Club Captain 1955-57.

CLARK, Michael (GK)
1974/75 1 app 0 gls
TOTAL 1 app 0 gls
Club Record: Viney Hill, Gloucester City +.

CLARK, T (HB)
1893/94 2 apps 0 gls
TOTAL 2 apps 0 gls

CLARKE, Roy (GK)
1946/47 9 apps 0 gls
TOTAL 9 apps 0 gls
Club Record: G.W.R., Gloucester City +.

CLARKE, V.P (IF/GK)
1921/22 3 apps 2 gls
1922/23 1 app 0 gls
TOTAL 4 apps 2 gls

CLARKE, W (FB)
1926/27 1 app 0 gls
TOTAL 1 app 0 gls

CLEMENSON, R (CF)
1890/91

CLOUGH, B (GK) ++
1940/41
Club Record: Charlton Athletic (0), Gloucester City +.

CLUTTERBUCK, A (W)
1922/23

CLUTTERBUCK, George Charles (IF)
b. Qu2 1875 Clifton, Bristol, GLS d. ?
1894/95 4 apps 0 gls
1895/96 11 apps 3 gls
TOTAL 15 apps 3 gls

CLUTTERBUCK, Ricky (Sub)
1991/92 0 apps 2 subs 1 gl
TOTAL 0 apps 2 subs 1 gl

COBURN, Andrew (Andy) (M)
1975/76 6 apps 0 gls
TOTAL 6 apps 0 gls
Club Record: Matson Athletic, Cinderford Town, Gloucester City +.

COCKS, ? (FB)
1920/21

COLDRAY, Robert Alexander (Rob) (CF/CH)
b. 14/01/1935 Gloucester
1954/55 22 apps 9 gls
1955/56 28 apps 9 gls
1956/57 35 apps 17 gls
1957/58 29 apps 16 gls
1958/59 52 apps 21 gls
1959/60 19 apps 10 gls
1962/63 37 apps 9 gls
1963/64 46 apps 10 gls
1964/65 39 apps 6 gls
1965/66 36 apps 0 gls
1969/70 3 apps 2 subs 1 gl (1 nps)
TOTAL 346 apps 2 subs 108 gls (1 nps)
Club Record: Longford, Gloucester City, Cheltenham Town, Gloucester City, Cinderford Town, Gloucester City, Stonehouse.
Note: Club Captain 1964-66. Club Player of the Season 1964/65. Club Manager May 1970 – Oct 1970.

COLE, Phil (GK)
1979/80 2 apps 0 gls
TOTAL 2 apps 0 gls

COLE, Wally (CF)
1946/47 5 apps 3 gls
TOTAL 5 apps 3 gls
Club Record: Pontypridd Town, Gloucester City, Cinderford Town +.

COLENUTT, John Michael W (Johnny) (FB)
b. 30/10/1924 Bristol d. Qu3 1986 Cheltenham, Glos.
1947/48 7 apps 0 gls
1948/49 42 apps 0 gls
1949/50 16 apps 0 gls
1950/51 3 apps 0 gls
1951/52 8 apps 0 gls
TOTAL 76 apps 0 gls
Club Record: Bristol Rovers (0), Gloucester City, Bath City, Chippenham Town +.

COLES, David Andrew (Dave) (GK)
b. 15/06/1964 Wandsworth, London
1994/95 54 apps 0 gls
1995/96 45 apps 0 gls
1996/97 48 apps 0 gls
1997/98 8 apps 0 gls
TOTAL 155 apps 0 gls
Club Record: 1982 Birmingham City (0), 1982 Mansfield Town (3-0), 1983-87 Aldershot (120-0), Newport County (loan) (14-0), HJK Helsinki (Finland), 1988 Crystal Palace (0), 1989-90 Aldershot (30-0), Yeovil Town, 1991 Fulham (0), Basingstoke Town, Gloucester City, Farnborough Town.

COLEY, V (WH)
1934/35 1 app 0 gls
TOTAL 1 app 0 gls

COLLEY, J (HB)
1921/22 1 app 0 gls
TOTAL 1 app 0 gls

COLLICUTT, Paul (D)
b. 14/01/1959 Shipston-on-Stour, Warks.
1986/87 11 apps 0 gls
1987/88 28 apps 1 gl (2 nps)
TOTAL 39 apps 1 gl (2 nps)
Club Record: Cheltenham Town, Swindon Town (0), Trowbridge Town, Cheltenham Town, Gloucester City, Newport AFC, Cinderford Town, Forest Green Rovers.
Note: Was Cheltenham Town's youngest ever player.

COLLINS, A (IF)
1897/98

COLLINS, A.F (IF)
1923/24 5 apps 4 gls
1925/26 1 app 0 gls
1926/27 18 apps 7 gls
1928/29 9 apps 2 gls
TOTAL 33 apps 13 gls

COLLINS, D (FB)
1926/27 3 apps 0 gls
TOTAL 3 apps 0 gls

COLLINS, David (Dave) (W)
b. 11/07/1945 Gloucester
1965/66 10 apps 2 gls
1966/67 29 apps 1 sub 9 gls (4 nps)
TOTAL 39 apps 1 sub 11 gls (4 nps)
Club Record: Longlevens, Cinderford Town, Gloucester City, Cinderford Town, Cheltenham Town, Merthyr Tydfil, Sharpness, Matson Athletic, Worrall Hill.

COLLINS, Ronald Dudley (Sammy) (IF)
b. 13/01/1923 Bristol d. Qu2 1998 North Somerset, Somerset
1958/59 18 apps 5 gls
TOTAL 18 apps 5 gls
Club Record: 1946-47 Bristol City (14-2), 1948-57 Torquay United (356-204), Gloucester City.

COLTMAN, Michael John (Mick) (CH)
b. 07/07/1932 Cheltenham, Glos. d. Qu1 2005 Kettering, Northants.
1960/61 25 apps 0 gls
TOTAL 25 apps 0 gls
Club Record: Gloucester City, Worcester City.
Note: Brother of Ron Coltman and cousin of Jeff Miles.

COLTMAN, Ronald Leslie (Ron) (GK)
b. 26/09/1930 Cheltenham, Glos.
1952/53 20 apps 0 gls
1953/54 32 apps 0 gls
1954/55 52 apps 0 gls
1955/56 55 apps 0 gls
1956/57 23 apps 0 gls
1957/58 21 apps 0 gls
1958/59 41 apps 0 gls
1959/60 2 apps 0 gls
TOTAL 246 apps 0 gls
Club Record: Cheltenham Town, Gloucester City, Worcester City, Cinderford Town.
Note: Brother of Mick Coltman and cousin of Jeff Miles. Awarded MBE in 2009 for voluntary service to the Sandford Parks Lido in Cheltenham.

COLWELL, Robbie (F)
1997/98 1 app 6 subs 0 gls (10 nps)
TOTAL 1 app 6 subs 0 gls (10 nps)
Club Record: Gloucester City, Ledbury Town, Slimbridge +.

COMER, W.C (IF)
1936/37 9 apps 0 gls
TOTAL 9 apps 0 gls
Club Record: Paulton Rovers, Gloucester City +.

CONGRAVE, Richard John (F)
b. 22/08/1972 Birmingham, Warks.
1991/92 1 app 1 sub 0 gls
TOTAL 1 app 1 sub 0 gls
Club Record: Gloucester City, Pershore Town, Kidderminster Harriers, Worcester City, Stourbridge +.

CONNOR, J (HB)
1936/37 16 apps 0 gls
1937/38 16 apps 0 gls
1938/39 2 apps 0 gls
TOTAL 34 apps 0 gls

COOK, ? (WH)
1949/50 1 app 0 gls
1952/53 4 apps 0 gls
TOTAL 5 apps 0 gls

COOK, Andrew (Andy) (GK)
b. 1965
2001/02 3 apps 0 gls
2002/03 0 apps 0 gls (4 nps)
2005/06 0 apps 0 gls (4 nps)
TOTAL 3 apps 0 gls (8 nps)
Club Record: Brockworth, Gloucester City, Brockworth, Gloucester City +.

COOK, Anthony (Tony) (F)
b. 26/07/1973 Bristol
1992/93 15 apps 2 subs 3 gls
1993/94 43 apps 3 subs 13 gls
TOTAL 58 apps 5 subs 16 gls
<u>Club Record:</u> Bristol City (0), Weymouth (loan), Weymouth, Gloucester City, KFC Izegem (Belgium), Weston-Super-Mare, Clevedon Town, Brislington +.
<u>Note:</u> Played for Gloucester City 1994/95.

COOK, C (FB)
1931/32 26 apps 0 gls
1932/33 2 apps 0 gls
TOTAL 28 apps 0 gls
<u>Note:</u> Played for Gloucester City 1928/29.

COOK, Charles Ivor (Charlie) (FB)
b. 28/01/1937 Cheltenham, Glos.
1954/55 1 app 0 gls
1955/56 21 apps 0 gls
1956/57 27 apps 3 gls
1958/59 15 apps 0 gls
TOTAL 64 apps 3 gls
<u>Club Record:</u> Gloucester City, 1956-57 Bristol City (2-0), Gloucester City +.

COOK, Garry John (M)
b. 31/03/1978 Northampton, Northants.
1999/00
<u>Club Record:</u> 1996 Hereford United (20-0), Gloucester City (trial), Saint Albans City, Aylesbury United, Buckingham Town (loan) +.

COOK, Gary (GK)
1983/84 4 apps 0 gls
TOTAL 4 apps 0 gls

COOK, H. J (CH)
1934/35 1 app 0 gls
TOTAL 1 app 0 gls
<u>Club Record:</u> Stroud, Gloucester City +.

COOK, Michael John (Mike) (M)
b. 18/10/1968 Stroud, Glos.
2001/02 8 apps 6 subs 0 gls (5 nps)
TOTAL 8 apps 6 subs 0 gls (5 nps)
<u>Club Record:</u> 1987 Coventry City (0), 1987 York City (loan) (6-1), 1989-90 Cambridge United (17-1), 1990 York City (loan) (6-0), Corby Town, Gloucester City, Cinderford Town.

COOK, Robert Paul (Rob) (M)
b. 28/03/1970 Nailsworth, Glos.
1999/00 7 apps 2 gls
TOTAL 7 apps 2 gls
<u>Club Record:</u> Shortwood United, Forest Green Rovers, Gloucester City (loan), Basingstoke Town, Forest Green Rovers, unknown Australian club? +.

COOK, S (W)
1908/09 2 apps 0 gls
1909/10 16 apps 6 gls
TOTAL 18 apps 6 gls

COOK, Shane (GK)
1995/96 1 app 0 gls (4 nps)
TOTAL 1 app 0 gls (4 nps)
<u>Club Record:</u> Swindon Town (0), Cheltenham Town, Gloucester City +.

COOKE, Arthur Bishop (GK)
b. Qu1 1869 Gloucester d. Qu4 1910 Fulham, London
1889/90 3 apps 0 gls
TOTAL 3 apps 0 gls

COOKSON, ? (WH) ++
1942/43

COOPER, Anthony (Tony) (W)
b. 1949 Gloucester
1975/76 48 apps 1 sub 6 gls
1976/77 3 apps 0 gls
TOTAL 51 apps 1 sub 6 gls
<u>Club Record:</u> Longlevens, Bristol City (0), Bishop's Cleeve, Cheltenham Town, Gloucester City, Ledbury Town +.
<u>Note:</u> Brother of James Cooper.

COOPER, James (Jimmy) (IF)
b. 1942
1960/61 10 apps 1 gl
1961/62 17 apps 3 gls
1962/63 10 apps 1 gl
TOTAL 37 apps 5 gls
<u>Note:</u> Brother of Anthony Cooper.

COOPER, R (?)

COOPER, Simon (M)
b. 18/03/1975
1995/96 10 apps 2 subs 0 gls
1996/97 47 apps 5 subs 1 gl
1997/98 44 apps 5 subs 0 gls (1 nps)
TOTAL 101 apps 12 subs 1 gl (1 nps)
<u>Club Record:</u> Cheltenham Town, Dorchester Town (loan), Gloucester City, Dorchester Town +.
<u>Note:</u> Supporter's Player of the Season 1996/97.

COOPER, W (FB)
1889/90

CORBETT, F (HB)
1913/14 1 app 0 gls
TOTAL 1 app 0 gls

CORBETT, Luke John (F)
b. 10/08/1984 Worcester, Worcs.
2005/06 19 apps 10 subs 12 gls (1 nps)
2006/07 4 apps 1 sub 1 gl (1 nps)
TOTAL 23 apps 11 subs 13 gls (2 nps)
<u>Club Record:</u> 2003 Cheltenham Town (1-0), Cirencester Town (loan), Hednesford Town (loan), Weston-Super-Mare (loan), Bath City (loan), Mangotsfield United, Gloucester City, Bishop's Cleeve, Leamington +.

CORLETT, Wilfred Albert (HB)
b. 02/10/1895 Gloucester d. Qu2 1985 Gloucester
1921/22 1 app 0 gls
1922/23 3 apps 0 gls
1923/24 7 apps 1 gl
TOTAL 11 apps 1 gl

CORNELIUS, ? (W) ++
1941/42 3 apps 4 gls
TOTAL 3 apps 4 gls
<u>Club Record:</u> Lanark, Peebles, Gloucester City +.

CORNWALL, Gary Richard (F)
b. Qu11978 Gloucester
1995/96 0 apps 1 sub 0 gls (5 nps)
TOTAL 0 apps 1 sub 0 gls (5 nps)
<u>Club Record:</u> Gloucester City, Bishop's Cleeve, Carterton Town +.
<u>Note:</u> Played for Gloucester City 1997/98.

CORNWELL, Nicholas T (Nicky) (GK)
b. Qu2 1961 Lydney, Glos.
1980/81 1 app 0 gls
1981/82 58 apps 0 gls (1 nps)
1982/83 14 apps 0 gls (1 nps)
TOTAL 73 apps 0 gls (2 nps)
<u>Club Record:</u> Mangotsfield United, Gloucester City +.

CORR, John Joseph (W)
b. 18/12/1946 Glasgow, Scotland
1972/73 30 apps 1 sub 7 gls (3 nps)
TOTAL 30 apps 1 sub 7 gls (3 nps)
<u>Club Record:</u> Possilpark Juniors, 1965 Arsenal (0), 1967-70 Exeter City (81-19), Cheltenham Town, Gloucester City, Worcester City.

CORRAL, ? (CH)
1970/71

COTTLE, Anthony (Tony) (FB)
1966/67 44 apps 0 gls
TOTAL 44 apps 0 gls
<u>Club Record:</u> Bristol City (0), Gloucester City, Yeovil Town +.
<u>Note:</u> Club Captain 1966-67.

COUPE, Matthew William (Matt) (D/M)
b. 07/10/1978 Saint Asaph, Denbighshire, Wales
1999/00 6 apps 0 gls
TOTAL 6 apps 0 gls
<u>Club Record:</u> Swindon Town (0), Forest Green Rovers, Gloucester City, Clevedon Town, Aberystwyth Town, Bath City, Forest Green Rovers, Chippenham Town, Bath City +.

COURTNEY, Russell Edward (D)
b. 11/10/1988 Stockport, Greater Manchester
2007/08 1 app 1 sub 0 gls
TOTAL 1 app 1 sub 0 gls
Club Record: Crewe Alexandra (0), Forest Green Rovers, Gloucester City, Cirencester Town, Forest Green Rovers, Shortwood United +.

COWLEY, A (GK)
1896/97

COWLEY, Edgar Manville (Ted/Eddie) (WH)
b. 12/09/1922 Blakenhall, Wolverhampton, Staffs.
1946/47 30 apps 1 gl
1947/48 42 apps 5 gls
1948/49 46 apps 0 gls
1949/50 45 apps 1 gl
1950/51 8 apps 0 gls
TOTAL 171 apps 7 gls
Club Record: Rotol AFC, Gloucester City, Cheltenham Town, Cinderford Town +.

COX, ? (F)
1906/07

COX, Anthony (Tony) (WH)
b. 1942 Hucclecote, Gloucester
1962/63 29 apps 0 gls
1963/64 32 apps 0 gls
1964/65 48 apps 0 gls
1965/66 6 apps 0 gls
TOTAL 115 apps 0 gls
Club Record: Bristol City (0), Gloucester City, Swindon Town (0), Gloucester City +.
Note: Son of Bob Cox.

COX, C (W)
1932/33 1 app 0 gls
TOTAL 1 app 0 gls

COX, James Darryl (Jimmy) (F)
b. 11/04/1980 Gloucester
1999/00 27 apps 8 subs 9 gls
2000/01 48 apps 5 subs 22 gls
2002/03 43 apps 1 sub 24 gls
2003/04 49 apps 3 subs 24 gls
2004/05 26 apps 12 subs 11 gls
2006/07 16 apps 7 subs 6 gls (4 nps)
TOTAL 209 apps 36 subs 96 gls (4 nps)
Club Record: Longlevens, 1998 Luton Town (8-0), Gloucester City, Bath City, Gloucester City, Weston-Super-Mare, Gloucester City, Bishop's Cleeve, Yate Town, Gloucester City, Cinderford Town, Tuffley Rovers +.
Note: Joint Supporter's Player of the Season 2000/01.

COX, Robert D (Bob) (FB)
b. 1909 d. ?
1935/36 37 apps 0 gls
1936/37 34 apps 1 gl
1937/38 18 apps 0 gls
1938/39 6 apps 0 gls
1946/47 2 app 0 gls
TOTAL 97 apps 1 gl
Club Record: The Army, Gloucester City +.
Note: Father of Tony Cox.

CRABTREE, Archibald Havelock (FB)
b. Qu2 1900 Gloucester d. ?
1919/20
Note: Brother of Harold Crabtree, Percy Crabtree and James Crabtree. I suspect F Crabtree is also a brother.

CRABTREE, F (CH)
b. abt. 1896 Rotherham, Yorks. d. ?
1919/20
Note: Suspect brother of Harold Crabtree, Percy Crabtree, Archibald Crabtree and James Crabtree.

CRABTREE, Harold Reginald (IF)
b. Qu4 1893 Rotherham, Yorks. d. ?
1919/20
Note: Brother of Percy Crabtree, Archibald Crabtree and James Crabtree. I suspect F Crabtree is also a brother.

CRABTREE, James William (W)
b. Qu1 1902 Rotherham, Yorks. d. ?
1919/20
Note: Brother of Harold Crabtree, Percy Crabtree and Archibald Crabtree. I suspect F Crabtree is also a brother.

CRABTREE, Percy Herbert (IF)
b. 1898 Rotherham, Yorks. d. ?
1919/20
1920/21
Note: Brother of Halord Crabtree, Archibald Crabtree and James Crabtree. I suspect F Crabtree is also a brother.

CRADDOCK, ? (W)
1920/21

CRAGG, Albert C (HB)
b. 1865 Saint Spauby, Lincs. d. ?
1892/93 3 apps 0 gls
1893/94 14 apps 0 gls
1894/95 19 apps 1 gl
1895/96 10 apps 0 gls
TOTAL 46 apps 1 gl
Note: Played for Gloucester 1896/97.

CRAIG, David (D)
b. 07/07/1961 Hamilton, Scotland
1990/91 4 apps 0 gls (1 nps)
TOTAL 4 apps 0 gls (1 nps)
Club Record: Weston-Super-Mare, Yeovil Town, Bath City, Cheltenham Town, Gloucester City +.

CRAWFORD, Maurice (FB)
1952/53 48 apps 0 gls
TOTAL 48 apps 0 gls
Club Record: 1949 Third Lanark (7-0), Arbroath (0), Gloucester City, Cheltenham Town +.

CRAWLEY, Frank R (WH)
b. 1883 Hull, Yorks. d. ?
1900/01 12 apps 1 gl
1902/03 10 apps 0 gls
1903/04 11 apps 1 gl
TOTAL 33 apps 2 gls
Note: Club Secretary 1903-1905.

CREBER, Leslie Charles Frederick (IF)
b. Qu3 1890 Stoke Damerel, Devon d. ?
1913/14

CREESE, Percival Harold (GK)
b. Qu4 1893 Cheltenham, Glos. d. ?
1926/27

CREESE, Percy Edward (W)
b. Qu2 1870 Tewkesbury, Glos. d. ?
1889/90

CRICHTON, James (Jimmy) (W)
b. 29/04/1932 Glasgow, Scotland
1955/56 33 apps 10 gls
TOTAL 33 apps 10 gls
Club Record: Ayr United (0), Third Lanark (0), Gloucester City, Toronto Scottish (Canada) +.

CRICHTON, Ronald (Ronnie) (IF)
b. 1941 Arbroath, Scotland
1964/65 9 apps 5 gls
1965/66 27 apps 4 gls
TOTAL 36 apps 9 gls
Club Record: Arbroath YM, 1960 Dundee (11-1), Heart of Midlothian (0), Cheltenham Town, Gloucester City +.

CRIDDLE, Richard (Rich) (D)
1991/92 9 apps 1 gl
1992/93 28 apps 3 subs 4 gls (1 nps)
1993/94 18 apps 0 gls
TOTAL 55 apps 3 subs 5 gls (1 nps)
Club Record: Cheltenham Town, Sharpness, Newent Town, Alvechurch, Cinderford Town, Stroud, Gloucester City +.

CRIPPS, Kenneth (Ken) (GK)
1948/49 2 apps 0 gls
TOTAL 2 apps 0 gls
Club Record: Leyton Orient (0), Gloucester City +.

CROFT, Mike (IF)
1972/73 22 apps 2 subs 5 gls (1 nps)
1973/74 11 apps 1 sub 2 gls (2 nps)
TOTAL 33 apps 3 subs 7 gls (3 nps)
Club Record: Worcester City, Gloucester City +.

CROFTS, J.M (W)
1892/93

CROMPTON, Steven Geoffrey (Steve) (GK)
b. 20/04/1968 Partington, Nr. Manchester, Lancs.
1992/93 13 apps 0 gls
1993/94 50 apps 0 gls
TOTAL 63 apps 0 gls
Club Record: 1986 Manchester City (0), 1987 Carlisle United (10-0),
1987-88 Stockport County (2-0), Wycombe Wanderers, Gloucester City,
Cirencester Town, Chesham United +.
Note: Played for Gloucester City 1994/95.

CROOK, Alex (M)
b. 1972 Devon
1991/92 9 apps 0 gls
TOTAL 9 apps 0 gls
Club Record: Torquay United (0), Gloucester City, Bideford +.

CROPPER, H.E (IF)
1913/14

CROSS, Des (GK/F)
b. 1926
1948/49 39 apps 0 gls
TOTAL 39 apps 0 gls
Club Record: Bristol Rovers (0), Gloucester City, Margate, Gloucester
City, Bridgewater Town.

CROUCH, Francis Edward Anson (W)
b. Qu4 1879 St Blazey, Cornwall d. ?
1906/07 2 apps 1 gl
TOTAL 2 apps 1 gl
Club Record: Plymouth Phoenix/Argyle, Loughborough Corinthians, Saint
Michael's, Gloucester City +.

CROUCH, Stephen Paul (Steve) (M)
b. 15/10/1969 Gloucester
1991/92 16 apps 1 sub 0 gls
1992/93 33 apps 5 subs 4 gls (9 nps)
1993/94 32 apps 1 sub 0 gls (5 nps)
TOTAL 81 apps 7 subs 4 gls (14 nps)
Club Record: Cheltenham Town, Stroud, Shepshed Albion, Gloucester
City, Weston-Super-Mare, Witney Town, Newport AFC, Cinderford Town
+.
Note: Played for Gloucester City 1994/95.

CROWLEY, Richard S (D)
b. 28/12/1959 Bristol
1994/95 18 apps 3 gls (1 nps)
TOTAL 18 apps 3 gls (1 nps)
Club Record: Bristol Rovers (0), Frome Town, Bath City, Forest Green
Rovers, Cheltenham Town, Bath City, Gloucester City, Bath City +.

CROWTHER, ? (IF)
1947/48 6 apps 0 gls
TOTAL 6 apps 0 gls
Club Record: Burnley (0), Royal Air Force, Gloucester City +.

CROWTHER, S.R (FB)
1919/20

CRUMP, Leonard Oliver (HB)
b. Qu3 1904 Gloucester d. ?
1923/24 1 app 0 gls
1924/25 2 apps 0 gls
TOTAL 3 app 0 gls

CULLUNBINE, Leslie O (W)
b. Qu1 1940 Newark, Notts.
1961/62 1 app 0 gls
TOTAL 1 app 0 gls
Club Record: Nottingham Forest (0), Swindon Town (0), Gloucester City
+.

CUNNAH, ? (W)
1946/47 1 app 0 gls
TOTAL 1 app 0 gls

CUNNINGHAM, David (Dave) (F)
b. 10/08/1953 Kirkcaldy, Scotland
1982/83 16 apps 2 gls
TOTAL 16 apps 2 gls
Club Record: Glenrothes, 1971-73 Brechin City (49-14), 1973-76 Southend
United (59-4), 1976 Hartlepool (loan) (12-1), 1977-78 Swindon Town
(23-3), 1978 Peterborough United (loan) (4-1), 1978 Aston Villa (0), 1979
Hereford United (30-2), Gloucester City, Trowbridge Town.

CURTIS, Brian (D)
b. 1964
1982/83 13 apps 0 gls (6 nps)
1983/84 1 app 1 sub 0 gls (3 nps)
TOTAL 14 apps 1 sub 0 gls (9 nps)
Club Record: Paulton Rovers, Gloucester City +.

DAINTY, George Edward (HB)
b. Qu3 1902 Gloucester d. ?
1923/24 2 apps 0 gls
1925/26 19 apps 0 gls
1926/27 15 app 0 gls
1928/29 5 apps 0 gls
1929/30 3 app 0 gls
1930/31 1 app 0 gls
TOTAL 45 apps 0 gls

DALL, ? (WH) ++
1939/40 1 app 0 gls
TOTAL 1 app 0 gls

DANGERFIELD, David Anthony (M)
b. 27/09/1951 Tetbury, Glos.
1980/81 23 apps 0 gls (3 nps)
1983/84 7 apps 0 gls (2 nps)
TOTAL 30 apps 0 gls (5 nps)
Club Record: 1968-72 Swindon Town (20-0), Charlton Athletic (0),
Cheltenham Town, Forest Green Rovers, Gloucester City, Shortwood
United +.
Note: Brother of John Dangerfield.

DANGERFIELD , John R (M)
b. Qu2 1950 Tetbury, Glos.
1974/75 50 apps 6 gls
TOTAL 50 apps 6 gls
Club Record: Forest Green Rovers, Cheltenham Town, Gloucester City,
Cinderford Town, Forest Green Rovers +.
Note: Brother of David Dangerfield.

DANIELLS, H (W)
1895/96 1 app 1 gl
TOTAL 1 app 1 gl
Club Record: Gloucester, Gloucester Post Office +.
Note: Played for Gloucester 1896/97.

DANKS, Ernest Reginald (W)
b. 20/11/1895 Old Hill, Staffs. d. 26/06/1921 Gloucester
1913/14 8 apps 1 gl
TOTAL 8 apps 1 gl
Note: Died of injuries sustained in WW1. Buried at St Philip and James,
Hucclecote.

DARKIN, ? (GK)
1892/93

DARLASTON, Simon (F)
1992/93 0 apps 7 subs 0 gls (4 nps)
TOTAL 0 apps 7 subs 0 gls (4 nps)
Club Record: Bristol City (0), Gloucester City, Forest Green Rovers,
Gloucester City +.

DAVIDSON, H (W)
1928/29 6 apps 1 gl
TOTAL 6 apps 1 gl

DAVIES, ? (GK)
1947/48 1 app 0 gls
TOTAL 1 app 0 gls

DAVIES, E (CH)
1930/31 1 app 0 gls
TOTAL 1 app 0 gls

DAVIES, G.P (WH)
1889/90
1890/91

PLAYERS' RECORDS

DAVIES, Glyn (IF)
1973/74 30 apps 12 gls
1974/75 38 apps 17 gls (8 nps)
TOTAL 68 apps 29 gls (8 nps)
Club Record: Stonehouse, Gloucester City +.

DAVIES, Grant (D)
b. 13/10/1959 Barrow, Lancs.
1983/84 12 apps 1 sub 0 gls
TOTAL 12 apps 1 sub 0 gls
Club Record: 1977 Preston North End (0), 1978-82 Newport County (150-1), 1982 Exeter City (7-0) (loan), Gloucester City, Yeovil Town, Risca United.

DAVIES, Ian Claude (FB)
b. 29/03/1957 Bristol
1987/88 6 apps 0 gls (1 nps)
TOTAL 6 apps 0 gls (1 nps)
Club Record: 1973-77 Norwich City (29-2), Detroit Express (USA), 1978 Norwich City (3-0), 1979-81 Newcastle United (75-3), 1982-83 Manchester City (7-0), 1982 Bury (loan) (14-0), 1983 (loan) Brentford (2-0), 1983 Cambridge United (loan) (5-0), 1984 Carlisle United (4-0), 1984 Exeter City (5-0), Bath City, Yeovil Town, Bury Town, Diss Town, 1985 Bristol Rovers (14-1), 1985 Swansea City (11-0), Gloucester City.
International Record: Wales U21 (1).

DAVIES, J.G (W/GK)
1919/20

DAVIES, John (CF)
b. 23/09/1951 Gloucester
1973/74 19 apps 1 sub 6 gls (3 nps)
1974/75 27 apps 8 gls
1980/81 20 apps 0 gls (6 nps)
TOTAL 66 apps 1 sub 14 gls (9 nps)
Club Record: Cinderford Town, Gloucester City, Cheltenham Town, Gloucester City +.

DAVIES, Kevin (D)
b. 1963
1982/83 13 apps 2 subs 0 gls (3 nps)
TOTAL 13 apps 0 gls (3 nps)
Club Record: Hereford United (0), Trowbridge Town, Gloucester City, Taunton Town (loan) +.

DAVIES, Timothy George (Tim) (D)
b. 09/07/1959 Kempley, Glos.
1978/79 22 apps 2 subs 4 gls (4 nps)
1979/80 42 apps 1 gl
1980/81 3 apps 0 gls (2 nps)
1986/87 0 app 0 gls (1 nps)
TOTAL 67 apps 2 subs 5 gls (7 nps)
Club Record: Hereford United (0), Newent Town, Ledbury Town, Gloucester City, Forest Green Rovers, Gloucester City +.

DAVIS, ? (WH)
1932/33

DAVIS, G (W)
1946/47

DAVIS, Lee Michael (F/M)
b. 07/11/1984 Cheltenham, Glos.
2003/04 0 apps 7 subs 0 gls (3 nps)
2004/05 14 apps 9 subs 6 gls (1 nps)
2005/06 20 apps 6 subs 4 gls
TOTAL 34 apps 22 subs 10 gls (4 nps)
Club Record: Cheltenham Town (0), Mangotsfield United (loan), Gloucester City (loan), Forest Green Rovers, Gloucester City, Cirencester Town , Bishop's Cleeve, Cinderford Town +.

DAVIS, Ray (GK)
1946/47 4 apps 0 gls
1947/48 1 app 0 gls
TOTAL 5 apps 0 gls

DAVIS, Ron (W)
1938/39 2 apps 0 gls
TOTAL 2 apps 0 gls
Club Record: Gloucester Co-op, Gloucester City +.

DAVIS, Roy (IF/GK)
b. 1918
1938/39 20 apps 1 gl
1939/40 8 apps 0 gls
1941/42 22 apps 3 gls
1942/43 12 apps 1 gl
1946/47 19 apps 8 gls
TOTAL 81 apps 13 gls
Club Record: Bristol Rovers (0), Royal Air Force, Gloucester City +.
Note: Club Captain 1940-41. Played for Gloucester City 1940/41.

DAVIS, Trevor (F)
b. abt. 1954
1972/73
Club Record: Gloucester YMCA, Gloucester City (trial) +.

DAVIS, William (Billy) (M)
2000/01 1 app 6 subs 1 gl (2 nps)
TOTAL 1 app 6 subs 1 gl (2 nps)

DAVOLL, Henry George Hooper (W/GK)
b. 1890 Gloucester d. 30/11/1918 Cairo, Egypt
1909/10 1 app 0 gls
1913/14 8 apps 1 gl
TOTAL 9 apps 1 gl
Club Record: Gloucester City, Gloucester YMCA +.
Note: Played in goal for YMCA 1913/14. Killed in action WW1.

DAVY, Ernest Francis (FB)
b. Qu2 1883 Wootton Bassett, Wilts. d. ?
1902/03 6 apps 0 gls
1903/04 11 apps 0 gls
1906/07 9 apps 0 gls
1907/08 17 apps 2 gls
TOTAL 43 apps 2 gls
Club Record: YMCA Pioneer Club, Gloucester City, Sir Thomas Rich's Old Boys, Gloucester City +.
Note: Club Captain 1906-08. Played for Gloucester City 1908/09.

DAWES, ? (IF)
1921/22 1 app 1 gl
TOTAL 1 app 1 gl

DAWES, Steve (GK)
b. Tredegar, Monmouth, Wales
1980/81 17 apps 0 gls
TOTAL 17 apps 0 gls
Club Record: Cardiff University, Merthyr Tydfil, Chepstow Town, Gloucester City +.

DAWKINS, Derek Anthony (The Dude) (M)
b. 29/11/1959 Edmonton, London
1990/91 21 apps 1 sub 0 gls
TOTAL 21 apps 1 sub 0 gls
Club Record: 1977 Leicester City (3-0), 1978-80 Mansfield Town (73-0), 1981-82 AFC Bournemouth (8-0), Weymouth, 1983-89 Torquay United (175-7), Newport County, Yeovil Town, Gloucester City +.
Note: Played for Gloucester City 1991/92.

DAY, Graham George (CD)
b. 22/11/1953 Bristol
1981/82 1 app 0 gls
TOTAL 1 app 0 gls
Club Record: Bristol Saint George, 1974-78 Bristol Rovers (130-1), Portland Timbers (USA), Forest Green Rovers, Gloucester City (trial) +.

DAY, Harold (Harry) (IF)
1959/60 11 apps 2 gls
1960/61 11 apps 1 gl
1961/62 12 apps 4 gls
1962/63 11 apps 0 gls
TOTAL 45 apps 7 gls

DAY, Ian (M)
1989/90 1 app 0 gls
TOTAL 1 app 0 gls

DAY, J (IF)
1926/27 5 apps 2 gls
TOTAL 5 apps 2 gls

DEAN, C (W)
1924/25 2 apps 0 gls
1928/29 2 apps 0 gls
TOTAL 4 app 0 gls

[493]

PLAYERS' RECORDS

DEAN, Cyril George (IR)
b. 27/07/1915 Bournemouth, Hants. d. Qu3 1997 Bournemouth, Hants.
1946/47 36 apps 19 gls
1947/48 25 apps 14 gls
TOTAL 61 apps 33 gls
Club Record: 1935 Aston Villa (0), 1936-37 Reading (16-3), Rouen (France), 1939 Southampton (0), Gloucester City, Cheltenham Town, Trowbridge Town, Dursley Town.
Note: Club Captain 1946-47. Club Manager 1946-1948.

DEAN, Paul (M)
1991/92 0 apps 1 sub 0 gls (2 nps)
TOTAL 0 apps 1 sub 0 gls (2 nps)

DEAR, Gerald Albert (Gerry) (CH)
b. 05/01/1937 Kensington, LND
1959/60 9 apps 0 gls
TOTAL 9 apps 0 gls
Club Record: 1956 Swindon Town (4-0), Gloucester City +.

DEE, F (IF)
1929/30 1 app 0 gls
1930/31 5 apps 1 gl
1931/32 3 apps 2 gls
1932/33 7 apps 4 gls
1933/34 10 apps 9 gls
1934/35 2 apps 0 gls
TOTAL 28 apps 16 gls

DEE, F.W (FB)
1906/07 2 apps 0 gls
TOTAL 2 apps 0 gls

DEE, W.H (FB)
1902/03 1 app 0 gls
TOTAL 1 app 0 gls

DELANEY, ? (CF) ++
1941/42 2 apps 0 gls
TOTAL 2 apps 0 gls

DELVE, Andrew Keith (Andy) (GK)
b. 08/09/1985 Newport, Wales
2008/09 1 app 0 gls (2 nps)
TOTAL 1 app 0 gls (2 nps)
Club Record: Newport County, Fields Park Pontllanfraith, Caldicot Town, Newport County, Carmarthen Town, Caerleon, Caldicot Town, Merthyr Tydfil, Gloucester City +.

DELVE, John Frederick (M)
b. 27/09/1953 Ealing, London
1987/88 14 apps 1 gl
TOTAL 14 apps 1 gl
Club Record: 1972-73 Queen's Park Rangers (15-0), 1974-77 Plymouth Argyle (132-6), 1977-82 Exeter City (215-20), 1983 Hereford United (36-3), Gloucester City, 1987 Exeter City (13-1), Taunton Town, Elmore.

DELVES, Nicholas James Philip (Nick) (D)
b. 13/11/1975 Cheltenham, Glos.
2001/02 4 apps 2 subs 0 gls (4 nps)
2002/03 0 apps 0 gls (1 nps)
TOTAL 4 apps 2 subs 0 gls (5 nps)
Club Record: Brockworth Albion, Gloucester City, Gloucester United +.

DENNION, Rory (M)
2008/09

DEVEREUX, G (CH)
1922/23 1 app 0 gls
TOTAL 1 app 0 gls

DEVLIN, Mike (Spike) (D)
1999/00 5 apps 4 subs 1 gl (13 nps)
2000/01 0 apps 1 sub 0 gls
TOTAL 5 apps 5 subs 1 gl (13 nps)

DICK, Ronald (Ron) (Sub)
1977/78 0 apps 0 gls (1 nps)
TOTAL 0 apps 0 gls (1 nps)
Club Record: Frome Town, Gloucester City +.

DICKS, Grantley Edward (M)
b. 17/10/1966 Bristol
2000/01 39 apps 1 sub 0 gls
TOTAL 39 apps 1 sub 0 gls
Club Record: Paulton Rovers, Bath City, Trowbridge Town, Forest Green Rovers, Newport AFC, Clevedon Town, Weston-Super-Mare, Gloucester City, Chippenham Town, Clevedon Town, Taunton Town, Brislington, Hallen +.
Note: Grantley Dicks is the brother of West Ham United legend Julian Dicks.

DIMMERY, Alan (GK)
1970/71
Club Record: Sharpness, Gloucester City (loan) +.

DIMMERY, V (GK)
1921/22

DIX, W (IF)
1923/24 14 apps 4 gls
1924/25 14 apps 5 gls
TOTAL 28 apps 9 gls

DIXON, ? (IF)
b. 1919
1938/39 2 apps 0 gls
TOTAL 2 apps 0 gls
Club Record: Partick Thistle (0), Gloucester City +.

DIXON, David (CD)
b. 1961 Hereford, Herefordshire
1980/81 8 apps 0 gls (6 nps)
TOTAL 8 apps 0 gls (6 nps)
Club Record: Hereford United (0), Gloucester City, Forest Green Rovers +.

DIXON, Liam (F)
1992/93 7 apps 8 subs 1 gl (4 nps)
TOTAL 7 apps 8 subs 1 gl (4 nps)
Club Record: Swindon Town (0), Nottingham Forest (0), Crewe Alexandra (0), Yeovil Town, Happy Valley (Hong Kong), Gloucester City, Moreton Town +.

DOBBINS, Lionel Wayne (FB)
b.30/08/1968 Bromsgrove, Worcs.
1994/95 7 apps 1 sub 0 gls
1995/96 22 apps 0 gls (3 nps)
TOTAL 29 apps 1 sub 0 gls (3 nps)
Club Record: Burlish Olympic, 1986-90 West Bromwich Albion (45-0), 1991 Torquay United (21-1), Yeovil Town, Gloucester City, Redditch United +

DOCKER, Arthur (WH)
b. 05/10/1932 Haddington, Scotland d. 11/1995 Gloucester
1955/56 40 apps 1 gl
1956/57 47 apps 4 gls
1957/58 30 apps 0 gls
TOTAL 117 apps 5 gls
Club Record: Heart of Midlothian (0), Gloucester City, Worcester City +.

DOEL, H.E (IF)
1922/23 4 apps 1 gl
1926/27 19 apps 1 gl
1927/28 15 apps 0 gls
1928/29 16 apps 0 gls
TOTAL 54 apps 2 gls

DONOVAN, J (W)
1946/47 2 apps 1 gl
TOTAL 2 apps 1 gl

DORRIAN, Ryan James (Dozzer) (M)
b. 31/01/1983 Panteg, Wales
2006/07
Club Record: Newport County, Clevedon Town, Merthyr Tydfil, Bath City, Merthyr Tydfil, Mangotsfield United, Gloucester City (trial), Cinderford Town, Merthyr Tydfil.

DOVEY, W.E (W)
1931/32 3 app 0 gls
TOTAL 3 app 0 gls
Note: Played for Gloucester City 1928/29.

[494]

PLAYERS' RECORDS

DOWLE, C (W)
1931/32 36 apps 6 gls
1932/33 1 app 0 gls
1933/34 29 apps 8 gls
TOTAL 66 apps 14 gls

DOWLER, Michael J (Mike) (GK)
b. 12/10/1957 Caldicot, Wales
1981/82
Club Record: Hereford United (0), 1975-80 Newport County (19-0), Gloucester City (trial), Wichita Wings (USA), Tacoma (USA), Sacramento Knights (USA) +.

DOYLE, Ian Patrick (F)
b. 27/02/1959 Torquay, Devon
1980/81 6 apps 5 gls (1 nps)
1981/82 47 apps 1 sub 13 gls
TOTAL 53 apps 1 sub 18 gls (1 nps)
Club Record: Barnstaple Town, 1979-80 Bristol City (3-0), Bideford Town, Gloucester City +.

DREW, Enos William (IF)
b. 21/01/1909 Westbury-on-Severn, Glos. d. Qu1 1985 Gloucester
1931/32 20 apps 15 gls
1932/33 34 apps 15 gls
1933/34 39 apps 11 gls
1934/35 46 apps 16 gls
1935/36 39 apps 7 gls
1936/37 35 apps 7 gls
1937/38 39 apps 8 gls
TOTAL 252 apps 79 gls
Club Record: Viney Hill, Blakeney, Gloucester City, Cheltenham Town +.
Note: Club Captain 1934-35.

DREWETT, O (FB)
1889/90

DRINKWATER, Douglas (Doug) (M)
b. 1965
1984/85 1 app 0 gls
TOTAL 1 app 0 gls
Club Record: Campden Town, Gloucester City +.

DUDBRIDGE, Leslie Francis (W)
b. Qu3 1890 Gloucester d. ?
1913/14 6 apps 0 gls
TOTAL 6 apps 0 gls
Club Record: Gloucester Amateurs, Gloucester YMCA +.

DUDFIELD, James (GK/HB)
1929/30 25 apps 0 gls
1930/31 27 apps 0 gls
1931/32 2 apps 0 gls
TOTAL 54 apps 0 gls
Club Record: Gloucester City, Cheltenham Town, Tewkesbury Town +.
Note: Father of Tim Dudfield.

DUDFIELD, Timothy J.B (Tim) (GK)
b. Qu1 1935 Newent, Glos.
1951/52
Note: Son of James Dudfield.

DUGGAN, Derek (M)
b. 1961
1984/85 10 apps 1 sub 0 gls
TOTAL 10 apps 1 sub 0 gls
Club Record: Birmingham City (0), Gloucester City, Worcester City, Corby Town, Kettering Town, Nuneaton Borough, Aylesbury United +.

DUKE, Dennis J (IF)
b. Qu3 1948 Cheltenham, Glos.
1966/67 1 app 0 gls (2 nps)
1967/68 1 app 1 sub 1 gl (4 nps)
TOTAL 2 apps 1 sub 1 gl (6 nps)
Club Record: Cinderford Town, Gloucester City +.

DUNBAR, John (Jackie) (W)
b. 06/10/1928 Scotland d. 05/2005 Gloucester
1955/56 52 apps 12 gls
1956/57 37 apps 15 gls
1957/58 26 apps 6 gls
1958/59 1 app 0 gls
TOTAL 116 apps 33 gls
Club Record: Kilbimie Ladeside, 1952-53 Aberdeen (4-0), Gloucester City, Stonehouse +.

DUNKLEY, Graham (FB)
1957/58 2 apps 0 gls
TOTAL 2 apps 0 gls

DUNLEAVY, Michael D (Mike) (CF)
b. Qu4 1938 Cardiff, Wales
1960/61 3 apps 1 gl
TOTAL 3 apps 1 gl
Club Record: Cardiff City (0), Cardiff Corinthians, Gloucester City +.

DUNN, Robert (Bob) (FB)
b. 1941
1960/61 15 apps 0 gls
1961/62 24 apps 0 gls
TOTAL 39 apps 0 gls
Club Record: The Army, Gloucester City +.

DUNTON, Dominic Pascal (D)
b. 12/08/1980 Barking/Dagenham, London
2001/02 20 apps 1 sub 2 gls (2 nps)
TOTAL 20 apps 1 sub 2 gls (2 nps)
Club Record: Norwich City (0), Peterborough United (0), Cirencester Town, Witney Town (loan), Swindon Supermarine, Gloucester City (loan), Marbella (Spain), Cirencester United, Devizes Town, Hungerford Town, Tytherington Rocks, Marbella (Spain) +.

DURHAM, Edward (Ted) (FB) ++
1939/40 1 app 0 gls
TOTAL 1 app 0 gls
Note: Played for Gloucester City 1940/41, 1941/42, 1946/47.

DURRANT, Alan (IF)
b. 1940 London
1963/64 14 apps 2 gls
1964/65 32 apps 2 gls
TOTAL 46 apps 4 gls
Club Record: West Ham United (0), Arsenal (0), Romford, Bristol Rovers (0), Gravesend & Northfleet, Bath City, Gloucester City +.

DURRETT, Charles (IF)
b. Qu4 1891 Gloucester d. ?
1909/10 1 app 2 gls
1913/14 2 apps 0 gls
TOTAL 3 apps 2 gls
Club Record: Gloucester City, Gloucester YMCA +.

DYER, ? (WH)
1937/38 2 apps 0 gls
TOTAL 2 apps 0 gls
Club Record: Wotton-under-Edge, Gloucester City +.

DYKE, J.G (FB)
1927/28 1 app 0 gls
TOTAL 1 app 0 gls

EAKERS, Gareth (GK)
1999/00
Club Record: Gloucester City, Hardwicke, Wotton Rovers, Longlevens, Longford +.

EAMER, A (GK/HB)
1922/23 12 apps 0 gls
1923/24 20 apps 0 gls
1924/25 8 apps 2 gls
1926/27 4 apps 1 gl
1930/31 2 apps 0 gls
TOTAL 46 apps 3 gls
Club Record: Gloucester Westgate, Gloucester YMCA +.

EARDLEY, G (CF)
1897/98

EASTER, G (FB)
1933/34 4 apps 0 gls
TOTAL 4 apps 0 gls

EATON, Jason Cord (F)
b. 29/01/1969 Bristol
1990/91 35 apps 18 gls (1 nps)
1991/92 44 apps 1 sub 19 gls (1 nps)
1992/93 13 apps 6 gls
2004/05 3 apps 1 sub 1 gl (1 nps)
TOTAL 95 apps 2 subs 44 gls (3 nps)
Club Record: Olveston, 1987 Bristol Rovers (2-0), Clevedon Town, Trowbridge Town, 1988-89 Bristol City (13-1), Trowbridge Town, 1990 Bristol City (0), Gloucester City, Cheltenham Town, Yeovil Town, Newport County, Forest Green Rovers, Merthyr Tydfil (loan), Basingstoke Town, Bath City, Merthyr Tydfil, Brislington (loan), Gloucester City (loan), Brislington, Mangotsfield United +.
Note: Club record equalling fee of £10,000 paid to Bristol City 1990/91.

ECKHARDT, Jeffrey Edward (Jeff) (D)
b. 07/10/1965 Sheffield, Yorks.
2005/06 4 apps 2 subs 0 gls
TOTAL 4 apps 2 subs 0 gls
Club Record: 1983-87 Sheffield United (74-2), 1987-93 Fulham (249-25), 1994-95 Stockport County (62-7), 1996-00 Cardiff City (140-14), Newport County, Merthyr Tydfil, Gloucester City, Risca United +.

ECONOMOU, Jonathan (Jon/Joe) (M)
b. 25/10/1961 Holloway, London
1984/85 3 apps 0 gls
TOTAL 3 apps 0 gls
Club Record: 1981-83 Bristol City (65-3), Cardiff City (loan) (0), Gloucester City, Yeovil Town, Forest Green Rovers, Weston-Super-Mare, Minehead +.

EDDOWES, Charles Frederic Beaumont (CH)
b. Qu1 1883 Loughborough, Leics. d. ?
1902/03 10 apps 0 gls
1903/04 11 apps 0 gls
TOTAL 21 apps 0 gls
Note: Played for Gloucester City 1907/08.

EDWARDS, David Samuel (Dai) (OL)
b. 11/09/1916 Bargoed, Wales d. Qu3 1990 Canterbury, Kent
1938/39 31 apps 8 gls
1946/47 8 apps 1 gl
TOTAL 39 apps 9 gls
Club Record: Deri, 1937 Newport County (2-0), Gloucester City, 1945 Ipswich Town (0), 1946 Swindon Town (3-1), Bath City.

EDWARDS, George (Archie) (W/GK)
b. 14/09/1897 Bristol d. 25/07/1948 Gloucester
1925/26 30 apps 24 gls
1926/27 19 apps 1 gl
1927/28 23 apps 4 gls
1928/29 24 apps 1 gl
1929/30 9 apps 0 gls
1938/39 4 apps 2 gls
1939/40 2 apps 0 gls
TOTAL 111 apps 32 gls
Club Record: Bristol Rovers (0), Gloucester City, Longford & Twigworth, Gloucester City, Sandhurst.
Note: Club Captain 1926-28. Played for Gloucester City 1940/41.

EDWARDS, Jamie (M)
b. 18/02/1983 Hereford, Herefordshire
2006/07
Club Record: Aston Villa (0), Bristol City (0), Cwmbran Town, Gloucester City (trial), Newtown AFC, Merthyr Tydfil +.

EDWARDS, Keith (W)
b. 1941 Hereford, Herefordshire
1964/65 19 apps 3 gls
TOTAL 19 apps 3 gls
Club Record: Birmingham City (0), Hereford United, Merthyr Tydfil, Gloucester City +.

EDWARDS, M (IF)
1935/36 1 app 2 gls
1936/37 18 apps 2 gls
1937/38 11 apps 4 gls
TOTAL 30 apps 8 gls

EDWARDS, Mark (D)
1984/85 15 apps 0 gls
1985/86 23 apps 2 subs 2 gls (4 nps)
1986/87 22 apps 0 gls (4 nps)
TOTAL 60 apps 2 subs 2 gls (8 nps)
Club Record: Blackburn Rovers (0), Royal Air Force, Lincoln United, Gloucester City +.

EGGLETON, Joe (D)
b. 1986
2004/05
Club Record: Gloucester United, Gloucester City, Bishop's Cleeve +.

ELDRIDGE, James Golby (FB)
b. Qu4 1887 Wardington, Oxon. d. ?
1909/10 5 apps 0 gls
TOTAL 5 apps 0 gls

ELLIOTT, Frank (HB)
1946/47 18 apps 1 gl
TOTAL 18 apps 1 gl
Club Record: Woking Town, Gloucester City +.

ELLIOTT, Harold (WH)
b. 1942
1960/61 11 apps 0 gls
TOTAL 11 apps 0 gls

ELLIOTT, Jack (W)
1950/51 5 apps 0 gls
TOTAL 5 apps 0 gls
Club Record: Millwall (0), Gloucester City, Headington United +.

ELLIOTT, Russell (D)
b. 1968
1984/85 11 apps 2 subs 0 gls (1 nps)
TOTAL 11 apps 2 subs 0 gls (1 nps)
Club Record: FC Lakeside, Cheltenham Town, Swindon Town (0), Gloucester City, Cheltenham Town.

ELLIS, Brinley R (Bryn) (LB/OL)
b. 12/03/1917 Pontypridd, Wales d. Qu1 1992 Pontypridd, Wales
1938/39 43 apps 2 gls
1939/40 10 apps 0 gls
TOTAL 53 apps 2 gls
Club Record: 1936-37 Newport County (2-0), Gloucester City.

ELLIS, Herbert Pearce (IF)
b. Qu1 1886 Upton-On-Severn, Worcs. d. 01/12/1917 Jerusalem, Palestine
1903/04
Note: Killed in action WW1. Awarded MC for gallantry.

ELLIS, Samuel (Sam) (M)
b. 10/01/1990 Gloucester
2006/07 0 apps 1 sub 0 gls (4 nps)
2007/08 3 apps 4 subs 1 gl (2 nps)
2008/09 0 apps 2 subs 0 gls (2 nps)
TOTAL 3 apps 7 subs 1 gl (8 nps)

ELSE, S.O (WH)
1902/03 1 app 0 gls
TOTAL 1 app 0 gls

ELSEY, David John (D)
b. 19/11/1975 Swindon, Wilts.
1997/98 33 apps 6 subs 0 gls (6 nps)
TOTAL 33 apps 6 subs 0 gls (6 nps)
Club Record: Swindon Town (0), Cheltenham Town, Gloucester City, Fairford Town (loan), Bath City, Mangotsfield United, Yate Town +.
Note: Played for Gloucester City 1995/96.

ELY, William Anthony S (HB)
b. 1869 Gloucester d. ?
1889/90 1 app 0 gls
TOTAL 1 app 0 gls
Note: Played for Gloucester 1890/91.

EMERY, James (Jim) (CF)
b. 02/03/1940 Lisburn, Northern Ireland
1963/64 4 apps 0 gls
TOTAL 4 apps 0 gls
Club Record: Distillery, 1959 Exeter City (0), 1960 Barrow (2-0), Portadown, Gloucester City, +.

EMERY, Stephen Roger (Steve) (M)
b. 07/02/1956 Ledbury, Herefordshire
1986/87 12 apps 0 gls
TOTAL 12 apps 0 gls
Club Record: 1973-79 Hereford United (204-10), 1979-81 Derby County (75-4), 1983 Newport County (0), 1983-84 Hereford United (75-2), 1985 Wrexham (9-0), Gloucester City, Westfields.

PLAYERS' RECORDS

EMMERSON, Michael (Mike) (GK)
b. Qu3 1963
1978/79 3 apps 0 gls
TOTAL 3 apps 0 gls
Club Record: Bristol City (0), Gloucester City (loan), Luton Town (0) +.
Note: Mike Emmerson was 15 years old when he made his debut and is possibly City's youngest ever goalkeeper. In a programme he is referred to as Kevin (!).

ENGLAND, Michael (Mike) (IF)
b. 1938
1960/61 16 apps 4 gls
1961/62 8 apps 1 gl
TOTAL 24 apps 5 gls
Club Record: Plymouth Argyle (0), Gloucester City +.

ETHERIDGE, R (W)
1919/20

ETHERIDGE, Richard Fredrick (Dick) (WH)
b. 07/07/1935 Gloucester
1954/55 1 app 0 gls
1956/57 14 apps 5 gls
1957/58 11 apps 1 gl
1958/59 20 apps 1 gl
1959/60 27 apps 2 gls
1965/66 6 apps 0 gls
TOTAL 79 apps 9 gls
Club Record: Longford, The Army, Gloucester City, Kidderminster Harriers, Cinderford Town, Bream Amateurs, Gloucester City.
Note: Caretaker Manager Mar 1967 – Jun 1967, Caretaker Manager Oct 1970 – Nov 1970, Club Manager Dec 1972 – Nov 1973, Caretaker Manager Sep 1980 – Oct 1980. Club Secretary 1969-71, 1972-74, Club Chairman 1975-80 and Club President 1987-2004. Brother of Robert Etheridge. Played for Gloucester City 1977/78.

ETHERIDGE, Robert James (Bob) (WH)
b. 25/03/1934 Gloucester d. 04/04/1988 Gloucester
1952/53 18 apps 2 gls
1953/54 36 apps 7 gls
1954/55 46 apps 17 gls
1955/56 44 apps 11 gls
1956/57 7 apps 5 gls
1975/76 1 app 0 gls (6 nps)
TOTAL 152 apps 42 gls (6 nps)
Club Record: Gloucester City, 1956-63 Bristol City (259-42), Cheltenham Town, Gloucester City.
Note: Club Manager Nov 1973 – May 1976, Caretaker Manager Mar 1985 – May 1985. Brother of Richard Etheridge. Played cricket for Gloucestershire CCC 1955-56.

EVANS, ? (IF)
1938/39 8 apps 2 gls
TOTAL 8 apps 2 gls

EVANS, Arthur (IF)
1950/51 2 apps 0 gls
TOTAL 2 apps 0 gls
Club Record: Newtown, Gloucester City, Bangor City +.
International Record: Wales Amateur.

EVANS, David (Dave) (GK)
b. 19/09/1987
2004/05 0 app 1 sub 0 gls
2005/06 1 app 0 gls (1 nps)
TOTAL 1 apps 1 sub 0 gls (1 nps)
Club Record: Gloucester City, Slimbridge, Hardwicke +.

EVANS, John Anthony (F)
b. 16/07/1952 Wellington, Shrops.
1976/77 43 apps 28 gls
1977/78 43 apps 20 gls (2 nps)
1978/79 29 apps 11 gls
1979/80 48 app 1 sub 12 gls (2 nps)
1980/81 55 apps 1 sub 8 gls
1981/82 39 apps 1 sub 6 gls (10 nps)
1982/83 4 apps 0 gls (1 nps)
TOTAL 261 apps 3 subs 85 gls (15 nps)
Club Record: Saint Paul's College, Cinderford Town, Forest Green Rovers, Gloucester City, Trowbridge Town, Cheltenham Town, Forest Green Rovers +.
Note: Club Player of the Season 1976/77.

EVANS, Mark (D)
1997/98 7 apps 7 subs 0 gls (6 nps)
TOTAL 7 apps 7 subs 0 gls (6 nps)
Club Record: Gloucester City, Merthyr Tydfil +.

EVANS, R (Sub)
1994/95

EVANS, Richard (F)
1991/92 1 app 0 gls
TOTAL 1 app 0 gls
Club Record: Weymouth, Bristol Rovers (0), Gloucester City +.

EVANS, Roy (W)
1961/62 14 apps 2 gls
TOTAL 14 apps 2 gls
Club Record: Canterbury City, Gloucester City +.

EVANS, T (IF)
1929/30 1 app 0 gls
TOTAL 1 app 0 gls

EVANS, W.S (W)
1934/35 1 app 0 gls
TOTAL 1 app 0 gls

EVES, John David (Geordie) (W)
b. 18/04/1946 Gateshead, County Durham d. 15/09/1981 Northallerton, Yorks.
1974/75 7 apps 1 gl
1975/76 27 apps 1 gl (1 nps)
1976/77 21 apps 1sub 1 gl (3 nps)
1977/78 28 apps 2 subs 2 gls (4 nps)
1978/79 8 apps 1 sub 0 gls (6 nps)
TOTAL 91 apps 4 subs 5 gls (14 nps)
Club Record: Weston-Super-Mare, Clanfield, Oxford City, RAF Innsworth, Gloucester City +.

EWART, David (F)
b. 1958
1975/76 1 app 0 gls
TOTAL 1 app 0 gls

FARMER, ? (GK)
1950/51 2 apps 0 gls
TOTAL 2 apps 0 gls

FARNALL, Thomas (Tot) (WH)
b. 1871 Gloucester d. ?
1900s
Club Record: Eastville Rovers, 1895-96 Small Heath (26-1), Watford, Bristol Eastville Rovers, Bradford City, 1899 Small Heath (19-1), Worcester City, 1903 Bradford City (25-1), Barrow, Gloucester.
Note: Some sources have Tot Farnall associated with Gloucester. Thus far have not found anything.

FARNELL, E (IF)
1930/31 1 app 0 gls
TOTAL 1 app 0 gls

FARNEN, Austin Leslie (Les) (CH)
b. 17/09/1919 St. Helens, Lancs. d. Qu1 1985 Harrow, London
1949/50 23 apps 0 gls
1950/51 2 apps 0 gls
TOTAL 25 apps 0 gls
Club Record: 1946-48 Watford (77-0), 1949 Bradford City (8-0), Gloucester City +.

FARRELL, Vincent (Vince) (W)
b. 11/09/1908 Preston, Lancs. d. 25/04/1987 Preston, Lancs.
1946/47 4 apps 1 gl
TOTAL 4 apps 1 gl
Club Record: Dick Kerr's XI, 1930-32 Preston North End (16-5), 1934-36 Clapton Orient (79-21), 1937 Exeter City (6-4), 1938 Clapton Orient (0), Gloucester City, Leyland Motors.

FARRELLY, ? (CF) ++
1939/40 13 apps 8 gls
TOTAL 13 apps 8 gls
Club Record: Brentford (0), Northampton Town (0), Gloucester City +.

FATHERS, Lewis Oliver (M)
b. 26/12/1990 Leamington, Warks.
2008/09 2 apps 3 subs 0 gls
TOTAL 2 apps 3 subs 0 gls
Club Record: Coventry City (0), Cheltenham Town, Gloucester City (loan)
+.

FAULKNER, J (D)
2001/02

FAWKES, S (CH)
1908/09

FEARIS, Edward Norman (CH)
b. Qu2 1904 Gloucester d. ?
1923/24 3 apps 0 gls
TOTAL 3 apps 0 gls

FEATHERSTONE, R (IF)
1934/35 3 apps 0 gls
TOTAL 3 apps 0 gls

FEIGHERY, Edward (Eddie) (IF)
b. Qu2 1953 Gloucester
1974/75 39 apps 4 gls
1975/76 18 apps 1 sub 6 gls
1977/78 1 app 0 gls
1980/81 4 apps 0 gls (3 nps)
1981/82 0 apps 2 subs 1 gl (3 nps)
TOTAL 62 apps 3 subs 11 gls (6 nps)
Club Record: Matson Athletic, Gloucester City, Cinderford Town, Ellwood
+.

FELLOWS, D (CH)
1930/31 1 app 0 gls
TOTAL 1 app 0 gls

FERGUSSON, Stephen J (Steve) (D)
b. 21/04/1961 Birmingham, Warks.
1990/91 10 apps 3 gls
1991/92 8 apps 3 subs 1 gl
1996/97 44 apps 3 subs 5 gls
1997/98 55 apps 2 subs 13 gls
1998/99 34 apps 7 subs 3 gls (6 nps)
1999/00 13 apps 3 subs 2 gls
TOTAL 164 apps 20 subs 27 gls (6 nps)
Club Record: Bromsgrove Rovers, Redditch United, Moor Green,
Alvechurch, Redditch United, Worcester City, Gloucester City, Telford
United, Worcester City, Gloucester City, Stratford Town, Feckenham.
Note: Club record fee of £25,000 paid to Worcester City 1990/91.

FERNS, Willie (IF)
b. 1941 Scotland
1968/69 51 apps 14 gls
1969/70 51 apps 8 gls (1 nps)
1970/71 40 apps 8 gls (2 nps)
1971/72 37 apps 5 gls
1972/73 1 app 0 gls
1973/74 9 apps 1 sub 1 gl
TOTAL 189 apps 1 sub 36 gls (3 nps)
Club Record: Third Lanark (0), Liverpool (0), 1961-62 Hamilton
Academicals (35-17), Cheltenham Town, Gloucester City, Stourbridge,
Gloucester City, Lydbrook Athletic.

FERRIER, Henry (Harry) (FB)
b. 20/05/1920 Ratho, Nr. Edinburgh, Scotland d. 16/10/2002 Earls Colne,
Colchester, Essex
1954/55 51 apps 2 gls
1955/56 18 apps 3 gls
TOTAL 69 apps 5 gls
Club Record: Ratho Amateurs, 1945 Barnsley (0), 1946-53 Portsmouth
(241-8), Gloucester City.
Note: Club Manager Apr 1954 - May 1959.

FERRIS, Andrew (Andy) (D)
b. 1963
1979/80 6 apps 0 gls (2 nps)
TOTAL 6 apps 0 gls (2 nps)
Club Record: Mangotsfield United, Gloucester City +.

FERRIS, Rod (GK)
1962/63
Club Record: Hereford United, Gloucester City (trial) +.

FERRO, Jorge (D)
b. 29/10/1972 Angola
2005/06 3 apps 0 gls (1 nps)
TOTAL 3 apps 0 gls (1 nps)
Club Record: Porto (Portugal), Benfica (Portugal), Forest Green Rovers,
Bridgwater Town, Gloucester City +.

FEY, Richard Lee (GK)
b. 26/01/1979 Bristol, Avon
2008/09 0 apps 0 gls (1 nps)
TOTAL 0 apps 0 gls (1 nps)
Club Record: Clevedon Town, Bitton, Bath City, Bristol Manor Farm,
Frome Town, Gloucester City (loan), Cadbury Heath +.

FIELD, Pat (Sub)
1980/81 0 apps 0 gls (1 nps)
TOTAL 0 apps 0 gls (1 nps)

FIELDING, Arthur Fitton (F)
b. Qu1 1877 Gloucester d. Qu3 1948 Gloucester
1893/94 4 apps 0 gls
1894/95 22 apps 6 gls
1895/96 18 apps 0 gls
1897/98 3 apps 3 gls
1898/99 16 apps 7 gls
1899/00 11 apps 5 gls
1900/01 10 apps 1 gl
1902/03 9 apps 0 gls
1903/04 9 apps 1 gl
TOTAL 102 apps 23 gls
Club Record: Gloucester, 1896 Bristol City (0), Gloucester City +.
Note: Club Captain 1897-1900. Played for Gloucester 1896/97. Brother of
Frank Fielding and Samuel Fielding. Grandson of founders of Fielding &
Platt.

FIELDING, Frank Berry (F)
b. Qu3 1872 Gloucester d. Qu1 1955 Gloucester
1889/90 3 apps 2 gls
1892/93 3 app 4 gls
1893/94 18 apps 9 gls
1894/95 22 apps 14 gls
1895/96 17 apps 11 gls
1897/98 4 apps 5 gls
1898/99 2 apps 2 gls
TOTAL 69 apps 47 gls
Club Record: Gloucester, 1896 Bristol City (0), Gloucester City +.
Note: Club Captain 1893-94. Played for Gloucester 1890/91, 1891/92.
Brother of Arthur Fielding and Samuel Fielding. Grandson of founders of
Fielding & Platt.

FIELDING, Samuel John (IF)
b. Qu4 1882 Gloucester d. Qu3 1960 Christchurch, Dorset
1902/03 1 app 0 gls
TOTAL 1 app 0 gls
Note: Brother of Frank Fielding and Arthur Fielding. Grandson of founders
of Fielding & Platt.

FIGGURES, Frederick William George (IF)
b. Qu2 1906 Bristol d. 02/12/1940 Bristol
1935/36 1 app 0 gls
TOTAL 1 app 0 gls
Club Record: Bristol City (0), Barrow (0), Gloucester City +.
Note: Killed during an air raid in WW2 whilst at 'Swan Hotel', Doveton
Street, Bedminster.

FINCH, R (HB)
1930/31 1 app 0 gls
1931/32 1 app 0 gls
TOTAL 2 apps 0 gls
Note: Played for Gloucester City 1932/33.

FINDLAY, Alexander (Alex) (RH/IR/IL)
b. 26/12/1902 Wishaw, Lanarkshire, Scotland d. 1985
1930s
Club Record: Musselburgh Rose, Musselburgh Bruntonians, Heart of
Midlothian (0), 1929-31 Bristol Rovers (37-9), 1932-34 Wrexham (22-4),
Cheltenham Town, Gloucester City.

FIOCCA, Paul (M)
b. 13/01/1955 Italy
1975/76 10 apps 1 sub 1 gl (1 nps)
TOTAL 10 apps 1 sub 1 gl (1 nps)
Club Record: 1973 Swindon Town (1-0), Bath City, Gloucester City +.

FISHER, ? (?)
1903/04

FISHLOCK, Murray Edward (FB)
b. 23/09/1973 Marlborough, Wilts.
1992/93 24 apps 11 subs 3 gls (10 nps)
1993/94 35 apps 4 subs 3 gls (1 nps)
TOTAL 59 apps 15 subs 6 gls (11 nps)
Club Record: Gloucester City, Trowbridge Town, 1994-96 Hereford United (71-4), Yeovil Town, Woking, Melksham Town (loan), Chippenham Town +.
Note: Played for Gloucester City 1994/95.

FITZSIMMONS, ? (CF) ++
1941/42 9 apps 14 gls
TOTAL 9 apps 14 gls
Club Record: Petershill, Gloucester City +.

FLETCHER, ? (CF)
1923/24 1 app 1 gl
TOTAL 1 app 1 gl

FLETCHER, F (WH)
1889/90
1890/91

FLETCHER, Michael (Mike) (D)
1993/94 1 app 0 gls
TOTAL 1 app 0 gls
Club Record: Tuffley Rovers, Gloucester City +.
Note: Played for Gloucester City 1990/91.

FLOOD, William (Bill) (W)
1954/55 8 apps 0 gls
TOTAL 8 apps 0 gls
Club Record: Bournemouth & Boscombe Athletic (0), Gloucester City +.

FLOWER, A (FB)
1896/97

FOOTE, Ernest (CH)
b. Qu1 1916 Ebbw Vale, Wales d. 18/08/1944 Normandy, France
1938/39 41 apps 0 gls
1939/40 17 apps 0 gls
1941/42 1 app 0 gls
1942/43 1 app 4 gls
TOTAL 60 apps 4 gls
Club Record: Ebbw Vale Town, Charlton, Cwm United, Bristol Rovers (0), 1937 Newport County (1-0), Gloucester City.
Note: Played for Gloucester City 1940/41. Father of Terry Foote. Killed in action WW2.

FOOTE, S. B (FB)
1929/30 1 app 0 gls
1931/32 2 apps 0 gls
1932/33 11 apps 0 gls
1933/34 5 apps 0 gls
1934/35 18 apps 0 gls
TOTAL 37 app 0 gls
Note: Played for Gloucester City 1930/31.

FOOTE, Terence Ernest (Terry) (FB)
b. 09/02/1941 Gloucester
1964/65 2 apps 0 gls
TOTAL 2 apps 0 gls
Club Record: Spa Rangers, Wilton Rovers, Gloucester City, Matson Athletic.
Note: Son of Ernest Foote.

FORD, H arry Gilbert (IF)
b. Qu2 1900 Gloucester d. ?
1920/21
Note: Brother of Leslie Ford.

FORD, Leslie Stanley (FB/HB)
b. Qu3 1898 Gloucester d. ?
1921/22 4 apps 1 gl
1923/24 10 apps 1 gl
1924/25 6 apps 0 gls
1925/26 4 apps 1 gl
1926/27 10 apps 0 gls
1927/28 3 apps 0 gls
1928/29 4 apps 1 gl
1929/30 1 app 0 gls
TOTAL 42 apps 4 gls
Note: Brother of Harry Ford. Also played for Gloucester YMCA 1920/21.

FORD, Trevor (CF)
b. 01/10/1923 Swansea, Wales d. 29/05/2003 Swansea, Wales
1955/56
Club Record: Tawe United, 1946 Swansea Town (16-9), 1946-50 Aston Villa (120-60), 1950-53 Sunderland (108-67), 1953-56 Cardiff City (96-42), PSV Eindhoven (Holland), 1960 Newport County (8-3), Romford.
International Record: Wales (38), Wales War-Time (1).
Note: Played for Gloucester City as a guest in a friendly against Portsmouth. In 1950 broke Britain's record transfer fee signing for Sunderland for £30,000.

FORD, W (CH)
1924/25 5 apps 0 gls
1926/27 1 app 0 gls
TOTAL 6 apps 0 gls

FORDHAM, Rob (WH)
b. 1937
1954/55 5 apps 0 gls
1955/56 2 apps 0 gls
TOTAL 7 apps 0 gls

FORDLAND, A.J (CF)
1919/20

FOREST, A (CF)
1892/93

FORRESTER, ? (CH) ++
1942/43

FORRESTER, Dan (M)
2004/05 0 apps 1 sub 0 gls
TOTAL 0 apps 1 sub 0 gls

FOWLER, G.W (IF)
1902/03 6 apps 0 gls
TOTAL 6 apps 0 gls

FOWLER, H.O (FB)
1893/94 2 apps 0 gls
TOTAL 2 apps 0 gls

FOWLER, Harry (CH)
1947/48 3 apps 0 gls
TOTAL 3 apps 0 gls
Club Record: Royal Air Force, Gloucester City +.

FOWLER, Michael David (Mike) (M)
b. 22/08/1981 Cardiff, Wales
2006/07 24 apps 4 subs 4 gls (1 nps)
TOTAL 24 apps 4 subs 4 gls (1 nps)
Club Record: Crystal Palace (0), Wrexham (loan) (0), Stevenage Borough (loan), Woking, Newport County, Welling United, Cwmbran Town, Merthyr Tydfil, Gloucester City, Salisbury City +.

FOWLER, R.C (FB)
1894/95 12 apps 0 gls
1895/96 5 apps 0 gls
TOTAL 17 apps 0 gls
Club Record: Lancing College, Gloucester +.

FOXWELL, Douglas Patrick (Doug) (M)
b. 06/10/1954 Stroud, Glos.
1972/73 5 apps 2 subs 1 gl (1 nps)
1973/74 12 apps 2 gls
1974/75 3 apps 3 gls
1975/76 21 apps 10 gls
1976/77 45 apps 2 subs 20 gls
1977/78 38 apps 23 gls
1978/79 22 apps 9 gls
1981/82 18 apps 2 subs 3 gls
1982/83 5 apps 1 sub 1 gl (1 nps)
1986/87 28 apps 7 gls (2 nps)
1987/88 53 apps 1 sub 13 gls (1 nps)
1988/89 4 apps 2 subs 0 gls (1 nps)
TOTAL 254 apps 10 subs 92 gls (6 nps)
Club Record: Arsenal (trial) (0), Swindon Town (trial) (0), Spa Rangers, Gloucester YMCA, Matson Athletic, Bristol Rovers (trial) (0), Burnley (trial) (0), Gloucester City, Cardiff City (trial) (0), Peterborough United (trial) (0), Kidderminster Harriers, Trowbridge Town, Gloucester City, Shortwood United, Stroud, Forest Green Rovers, Cinderford Town, Tuffley Rovers,.
Note: Club Player of the Season 1977/78.

FRANKLIN, J (W)
1895/96 2 apps 0 gls
TOTAL 2 apps 0 gls

FRASER, Ian (IF)
b. 1948 Glasgow, Scotland
1968/69 44 apps 3 subs 25 gls (3 nps)
1969/70 43 apps 6 subs 14 gls (1 nps)
1970/71 6 apps 1 gl (4 nps)
TOTAL 93 apps 9 subs 40 gls (8 nps)
Club Record: Hereford United, Gloucester City, Cheltenham Town +.

FREAM, John Russell (FB)
b. Qu2 1902 Gloucester d. ?
1919/20

FREEGARD, Jonathan P (Jon/Friggy) (F)
b. 17/03/1961 Bath, Somerset
1990/91 12 apps 6 subs 8 gls (5 nps)
1991/92 11 apps 3 gls
TOTAL 23 apps 6 subs 11 gls (5 nps)
Club Record: Trowbridge Town, Bath City, Chippenham Town, Bath City, Gloucester City, Trowbridge Town, Corsham Town +.

FREEMAN, Mark Wayne (D)
b. 27/01/1970 Walsall, Staffs.
1995/96 19 apps 1 sub 0 gls (3 nps)
TOTAL 19 apps 1 sub 0 gls (3 nps)
Club Record: Bilston Town, 1987 Wolverhampton Wanderers (0), Bilston Town, Willenhall Town, Hednesford Town, Gloucester City, 1999-00 Cheltenham Town (65-2), Boston United, Oldbury United.

FREETH, Andy (M)
1987/88

FRENCH, ? (HB)
1946/47

FREW, ? (W) ++
1941/42 1 app 0 gls
TOTAL 1 app 0 gls

FRIEL, Philip (Phil) (W)
b. 1927 Cumbernauld, Scotland d. 1985 Cumbernauld, Scotland
1952/53 9 apps 4 gls
1953/54 23 apps 14 gls
1954/55 50 apps 6 gls
1955/56 52 apps 19 gls
1956/57 37 apps 4 gls
1960/61 3 apps 0 gls
TOTAL 174 apps 47 gls
Club Record: Croy Juveniles, Third Lanark (0), Arbroath (0), Saint Johnstone (0), Gloucester City.
Note: Temporary Player-Coach Aug 1960 – Sep 1960.

FRITH, Arthur P (IF)
b. 1877 Gloucester d. ?
1894/95 1 app 0 gls
1895/96 10 apps 0 gls
1898/99 1 app 0 gls
TOTAL 12 apps 0 gls
Note: Played for Gloucester 1896/97.

FUDGE, Steve (?)
1980/81

FULLBROOK, Gary Lee (D)
b. 04/05/1966 Twerton, Bath, Somerset
1988/89 10 apps 0 gls
1989/90 23 apps 5 subs 0 gls (9 nps)
TOTAL 33 apps 5 subs 0 gls (9 nps)
Club Record: 1984 Swindon Town (1-0), Southampton (0), Bath City, 1987 Carlisle United (6-0), Bath City, Gloucester City, Weymouth.

FURBER, Archibald James (W)
b. 11/02/1900 Chard, Somerset d. Qu1 1988 Coventry, Warks.
1919/20

FUTCHER, Simon Jon (F)
07/10/1979 Swindon, Wilts.
1999/00 0 apps 2 subs 0 gls (1 nps)
TOTAL 0 apps 2 subs 0 gls (1 nps)
Club Record: Swindon Town (0), Chelsea (0), Swindon Supermarine, Forest Green Rovers, Chippenham Town (loan), Ilkeston Town (loan), Gloucester City, North Leigh +.

GAINSBORO, ? (FB) ++
1941/42 1 app 0 gls
TOTAL 1 app 0 gls

GALLAGHER, David (Dave) (D)
1972/73

GALLAGHER, John (Johnny) (WH)
b. 1931 Scotland
1957/58 41 apps 2 gls
1958/59 49 apps 2 gls
1959/60 20 apps 1 gl
1961/62 13 apps 1 gl
TOTAL 123 apps 6 gls
Club Record: Dumbarton (0), Gloucester City, Evesham United, Gloucester City +.
Note: Club Captain 1958-59.

GANNAWAY, Ryan Lee (GK)
b. 28/08/1973 Stroud, Glos.
1999/00 36 apps 0 gls
2000/01 15 apps 0 gls (6 nps)
TOTAL 51 apps 0 gls (6 nps)
Club Record: Forest Green Rovers, Shortwood United, Cheltenham Town, Witney Town (loan), Gloucester City, Endsleigh, Taverners FC +.

GANNON, Anthony (Tony) (M)
b. 1963
1981/82 1 app 0 gls
TOTAL 1 app 0 gls

GAPPER, Don (FB)
1966/67 2 apps 0 gls
1967/68 8 apps 0 gls
TOTAL 10 apps 0 gls
Club Record: Dursley Town, Gloucester City, unknown Australian club +.

GARDINER, Dave (CF)
b. 1934
1954/55 4 apps 1 gl
TOTAL 4 apps 1 gl
Club Record: Ruardean, Gloucester City +.

GARDNER, ? (FB) ++
1941/42 1 app 0 gls
TOTAL 1 app 0 gls
Club Record: The Army, Gloucester City +.

GARDNER, A (FB)
b. abt. 1871 d. ?
1889/90 2 apps 0 gls
TOTAL 2 apps 0 gls
Note: Played for Gloucester 1890/91.

GARDNER, A.G (IF)
1902/03

GARDNER, Christopher R (Chris/Digger) (IF)
b. 03/03/1954 Gloucester
1973/74 47 apps 10 gls
1974/75 50 apps 10 gls
1975/76 44 apps 5 gls
1977/78 19 apps 1 sub 2 gls (2 nps)
1978/79 15 apps 2 subs 4 gls (2 nps)
1979/80 3 apps 0 gls (2 nps)
1981/82 16 apps 2 subs 3 gls (9 nps)
TOTAL 194 apps 5 subs 34 gls (15 nps)
Club Record: Swindon Town (0), Frampton United, Gloucester City, Cheltenham Town, Gloucester City, Cheltenham Town, Gloucester City, Cinderford Town (loan), Cheltenham Town, Saint Marks CA +.
Note: Brother of Nick Gardner and Phil Gardner. Played for Gloucester City 1989/90.

GARDNER, Nicholas Henry (Nick) (D)
b. Qu1 1966 Gloucester
1981/82 1 app 0 gls
TOTAL 1 app 0 gls
Note: Brother of Chris Gardner and Phil Gardner.

GARDNER, Phillip W (Phil) (F)
b. 25/05/1957 Gloucester
1975/76 27 apps 1 sub 3 gls (2 nps)
1976/77 36 apps 1 sub 1 gl (3 nps)
1977/78 11 apps 1 gl (11 nps)
TOTAL 74 apps 2 subs 5 gls (16 nps)
Club Record: Gloucester YMCA, Minsterworth, Wilton Rovers, Gloucester City +.
Note: Brother of Chris Gardner and Nick Gardner.

PLAYERS' RECORDS

GARDNER, W.T (W)
1892/93 1 app 0 gls
1897/98 1 app 0 gls
TOTAL 2 apps 0 gls

GARLAND, Christopher Steven (Chris) (F)
b. 24/04/1949 Bristol
1983/84 2 apps 1 gl
TOTAL 2 apps 1 gl
Club Record: 1966-71 Bristol City (143-31), 1971-74 Chelsea (92-22), 1974-76 Leicester City (55-15), 1976-82 Bristol City (64-11), Gloucester City, Minehead.
International Record: England U23 (1).

GARWOOD, John (D)
b. Wales
1982/83 13 apps 0 gls
1983/84 9 apps 1 sub 0 gls
TOTAL 22 apps 1 sub 0 gls
Club Record: Spencer Works (Newport), Gloucester City +.

GAUGHAN, Patrick (Pat) (IF)
b. 1916 Eastwood, Lanark, Scotland
1938/39 1 app 0 gls
TOTAL 1 app 0 gls
Club Record: Glasgow Celtic (0), Gloucester City +.

GAY, Graham A.M (IF)
b. Qu2 1942 Gloucester
1965/66 35 apps 8 gls
1966/67 41 apps 10 gls (3 nps)
1967/68 35 apps 8 gls
1968/69 6 apps 1 sub 2 gls (3 nps)
TOTAL 117 apps 1 sub 28 gls (6 nps)
Club Record: Gloucester YMCA, Gloucester City, Cheltenham Town, Stonehouse +.

GAY, W (HB)
1919/20

GAYLE, ? (M)
b. 1963
1981/82 1 app 0 gls
TOTAL 1 app 0 gls

GAZE, ? (W)
1920/21

GENT, A (FB)
1926/27 1 app 0 gls
TOTAL 1 app 0 gls

GERRISH, Michael C (Mike) (WH)
b. Qu2 1935 Bristol
1959/60 7 apps 0 gls
TOTAL 7 apps 0 gls
Club Record: Bristol City (0), Gloucester City +.

GETGOOD, Brian (FB)
b. 1927
1949/50 1 app 0 gls
TOTAL 1 app 0 gls

GIBBS, Nick (F)
1979/80

GIBSON, A.J (IF)
1926/27 9 apps 0 gls
TOTAL 9 apps 0 gls

GIBSON, L (GK)
1926/27 23 apps 0 gls
1933/34 1 app 0 gls
TOTAL 24 apps 0 gls

GILES, Albert Edgar (CF)
b. 04/05/1924 Swansea, Wales
1947/48 36 apps 11 gls
1948/49 13 apps 1 gl
TOTAL 49 apps 12 gls
Club Record: 1946 Bristol Rovers (1-0), Gloucester City, Glastonbury +.

GILES, Jacob Douglas (GK)
b. 12/10/1985 Huddersfield, Yorks.
2006/07 3 apps 0 gls
TOTAL 3 apps 0 gls
Club Record: Huddersfield Town (0), Taunton Town, Team Bath, Newport County, Gloucester City, Bradford Park Avenue, Harrogate Town +.

GILL, ? (IF) ++
1941/42 1 app 0 gls
TOTAL 1 app 0 gls

GILLESPIE, Eric John (WH)
b. 1948 Glasgow, Scotland
1971/72
Club Record: Carmunnock Downcraig, Cambuslang Rangers, 1969 Burnley (0), 1970 Kilmarnock (2-0), 1971 Motherwell (11-0), Gloucester City (trial), 1972-73 Hamilton Academicals (21-3), Albion Rovers (28-2), Cumnock Juniors.

GILLIES, Donald George (Don/Donnie) (FB)
b. 20/06/1951 Glencoe, Scotland
1982/83 18 apps 1 gl
1983/84 12 apps 0 gls
TOTAL 30 apps 1 gl
Club Record: Inverness Clachnacuddin, 1971-72 Morton (47-23), 1972-79 Bristol City (200-26), 1980-81 Bristol Rovers (59-0), Paulton Rovers, Gloucester City, Trowbridge Town, Anorthosis (Cyprus), Trowbridge Town, Yeovil Town, Clutton, Bristol Manor Farm.
International Record: Scotland U23 (1).
Note: Club Captain 1983.

GITTINGS, Frederick Henry (Fred) (FB)
b. 04/05/1954 Newent, Glos.
1978/79 15 apps 0 gls
TOTAL 15 apps 0 gls
Club Record: Newent Town, Huntley, Dowty Rotol, Gloucester City +.

GLAISTER, George (W) ++
b. 18/05/1918 Bywell, Northumberland
1939/40 9 apps 4 gls
TOTAL 9 apps 4 gls
Club Record: North Shields, Gloucester City, 1946 Blackburn Rovers (8-1), 1946-49 Stockport County (92-21), 1950 Halifax Town (34-7), 1951 Accrington Stanley (24-1), Bangor City.

GODBY, W.H (WH)
1896/97
Note: Club Captain 1896-97.

GODDARD, N (W/HB)
1921/22 3 apps 1 gl
1922/23 1 app 0 gls
1927/28 17 apps 1 gl
TOTAL 21 apps 2 gls

GODFREY, Brian Cameron (F)
b. 01/05/1940 Flint, Wales
1988/89 0 apps 0 gls (1 nps)
1989/90 0 apps 0 gls (1 nps)
TOTAL 0 apps 0 gls (2 nps)
Club Record: Wrexham (0), Chester (0), Tranmere Rovers (0), Flint Alexandra, 1959 Everton (1-0), 1960-63 Scunthorpe United (87-24), 1963-67 Preston North End (127-52), 1967-70 Aston Villa (143-22), 1971-72 Bristol Rovers (81-16), 1973-75 Newport County (118-14), Portland Timbers (USA), Bath City, Clevedon Town, Gloucester City.
International Record: Wales (3), Wales U23 (1).
Note: Club Manager Jun 1987-Nov 1991, Feb 1992 – Mar 1994.

GOFF, Neil (M)
b. 1965 Wales
1985/86 41 apps 3 gls
1986/87 28 apps 2 subs 3 gls (2 nps)
1987/88 2 apps 1 sub 0 gls (1 nps)
TOTAL 71 apps 3 subs 6 gls (3 nps)
Club Record: Newport County (0), Pontllanfraith, Cheltenham Town, Gloucester City, Cwmbran Town +.

GOODALL, J (W)
1936/37 2 apps 0 gls
TOTAL 2 apps 0 gls

GOODBURN, ? (IF)
1937/38 3 apps 1 gl
TOTAL 3 apps 1 gl

PLAYERS' RECORDS

GOODE, ? (FB)
1960/61 1 app 0 gls
1961/62 1 app 0 gls
TOTAL 2 apps 0 gls

GOODMAN, A (CF)
1908/09

GOODMAN, A (WH)
1922/23 3 apps 0 gls
1928/29 2 apps 0 gls
TOTAL 5 apps 0 gls
Note: Played for Gloucester YMCA 1919/20.

GOODMAN, Chris (GK)
b. 1949
1970/71 33 apps 0 gls
TOTAL 33 apps 0 gls
Club Record: Manchester United (0), AFC Newbury, Gloucester City +.

GOODWIN, A.E (FB)
1894/95 5 apps 0 gls
1895/96 3 apps 0 gls
TOTAL 8 apps 0 gls

GOODWIN, Gary (D)
b. 1956
1985/86 49 apps 0 gls
1986/87 19 apps 3 gls (1 nps)
TOTAL 68 apps 3 gls (1 nps)
Club Record: Fairford Town, Witney Town, Oxford City, Banbury United, Gloucester City , Swindon Supermarine +.
Note: Joint Temporary Club Manager Mar 1994 – May 1994.

GOODWIN, Tony (F)
1993/94
Club Record: Gloucester City, Cinderford Town, Tuffley Rovers (loan) +.

GORDON, Colin Kenneth (F)
b. 17/01/1963 Stourbridge, Worcs.
1993/94 2 apps 0 gls
TOTAL 2 apps 0 gls
Club Record: Lye Town, Stourbridge, Worcester City, Oldbury United, 1984-85 Swindon Town (72-34), 1986 Wimbledon (3-0), 1986 Gillingham (loan) (4-2), 1987-88 Reading (24-9), 1987 Bristol City (loan) (8-4), 1988 Fulham (17-2), 1989-90 Birmingham City (26-3), 1990 Hereford United (loan) (6-0), 1990 Walsall (loan) (6-1), 1990 Bristol Rovers (loan) (4-0), 1991-92 Leicester City (24-5), Kidderminster Harriers, Gloucester City (loan), Stourbridge.

GORDON, Dominic (M)
1999/00 2 apps 6 subs 0 gls (1 nps)
TOTAL 2 apps 6 subs 0 gls (1 nps)

GOSLING, Paul (FB)
1970/71
Club Record: Forest Green Rovers, Gloucester City +.

GOTHING, F (WH)
1936/37 1 app 0 gls
TOTAL 1 app 0 gls

GOUGH, Alan (CH)
b. 1956
1973/74 18 apps 1 sub 1 gl (3 nps)
1974/75 37 apps 3 gls (7 nps)
1975/76 48 apps 3 gls
1976/77 42 apps 4 gls (1 nps)
1977/78 23 apps 2 gls
TOTAL 168 apps 1 sub 13 gls (11 nps)
Club Record: Swindon Town (0), Swansea City (0), Kidderminster Harriers (trials), Gloucester City, Cinderford Town +.
Note: Club Player of the Season 1975/76.

GOUGH, Jimmy (F)
b. 26/09/1956 Oban, Scotland
1982/83 20 apps 5 gls (1 nps)
TOTAL 20 apps 5 gls (1 nps)
Club Record: Corby Town, Avon Bradford, Trowbridge Town, Cheltenham Town, Gloucester City, Bath City, Bridgwater Town, Paulton Rovers +.

GOUGH, N (IF)
1928/29 3 apps 0 gls
TOTAL 3 apps 0 gls

GRACE, Arnold (CF)
b. Qu1 1924 Derby, Derbyshire
1946/47 16 apps 5 gls
1947/48 15 apps 1 gl
TOTAL 31 apps 6 gls
Club Record: Derby County (0), Gloucester City +.

GRANGER, Karl (W)
1985/86 1 app 0 gls
TOTAL 1 app 0 gls
Club Record: Almondsbury Greenway, Gloucester City +.

GRANT, Robert (Bobby) (IF)
b. 25/09/1940 Edinburgh, Scotland
1965/66 54 apps 16 gls
1966/67 46 apps 20 gls
TOTAL 100 app 36 gls
Club Record: Ormiston Primrose, 1959 Glasgow Rangers (1-0), 1960 Leyton Orient (0), Chelmsford City, Stirling Albion (0), 1961 Saint Johnstone (3-0), 1962 Carlisle United (2-1), Chelmsford City, Cheltenham Town, Gloucester City, Queen of the South (0).
Note: Club Player of the Season 1965/66. Club Manager Aug 1965 – May 1966.

GRANVILLE, Norman Trevor (IF)
b. 25/11/1919 Newport, Monmouth, Wales d. Qu4 1992 South Glamorgan, Wales
1949/50 19 apps 4 gls
TOTAL 19 apps 4 gls
Club Record: Raith Rovers, Cliftonville, 1946 Newport County (1-0), 1946-47 Exeter City (20-1), Gillingham, Gloucester City.

GREAVES, L (FB)
1890/91

GREEN, F.H (FB)
1891/92

GREEN, G (CH)
1919/20

GREEN, H (W)
1927/28 2 apps 0 gls
TOTAL 2 apps 0 gls

GREEN, H.D (CF)
1895/96 3 apps 2 gls
TOTAL 3 apps 2 gls

GREEN, Nigel (D)
1986/87 13 apps 1 gl
1987/88 48 apps 6 gls
1988/89 54 apps 7 gls
1989/90 48 apps 1 sub 3 gls
TOTAL 163 apps 1 sub 17 gls
Club Record: Oldbury United, Alvechurch, Gloucester City +.
Note: Supporter's Player of the Season 1988/89.

GREEN, R.N (FB)
1892/93 3 apps 0 gls
1893/94 7 apps 0 gls
TOTAL 10 apps 0 gls

GREEN, Scott (?)

GREENAWAY, Graham (CF)
1960/61 11 apps 0 gls
TOTAL 11 apps 0 gls
Club Record: Arsenal (0), Gloucester City +.

GREY, ? (HB)
1935/36 1 app 0 gls
TOTAL 1 app 0 gls

GRIBBLE, ? (WH)
1937/38 12 apps 0 gls
TOTAL 12 apps 0 gls
Club Record: The Army, Gloucester City +.

[502]

GRIFFIN, Kevin Russell (F)
b. 05/10/1953 Plymouth, Devon
1978/79 14 apps 11 gls
1979/80 30 apps 4 subs 10 gls (8 nps)
TOTAL 44 apps 4 subs 21 gls (8 nps)
Club Record: 1971-74 Bristol City (8-0), 1974 Mansfield Town (loan)
(4-2), 1975 Cambridge United (loan) (8-1), Bath City, Yeovil Town,
Trowbridge Town, Gloucester City +.

GRIFFIN, Scott (F)
b. 20/06/1979 Gloucester
2006/07 11 apps 3 subs 2 gls (1 nps)
2007/08 6 apps 4 subs 2 gls
TOTAL 17 apps 7 subs 4 gls (1 nps)
Club Record: Salisbury City, Newport County, Clevedon Town, Cinderford
Town, Cirencester Town, Gloucester City, Devizes Town, Cinderford
Town, Cirencester Town +.

GRIFFITHS, Andrew John (Andy) (Sub)
b. Qu1 1971 Gloucester
1989/90

GRIFFITHS, Ashley Russell (M)
b. 05/01/1961 Barry, Wales
1981/82 15 apps 0 gls
1982/83 18 apps 1 sub 0 gls (2 nps)
TOTAL 33 apps 1 sub 0 gls (2 nps)
Club Record: 1979-80 Bristol Rovers (7-0), 1981 Torquay United (0), 1981
Bristol City (0), Yeovil Town, Gloucester City, Barry Town.

GRIFFITHS, David E (CH)
b. 1872 Saint Dogmaels, Pembrokeshire, Wales d. ?
1900/01 3 apps 2 gls
1902/03 1 app 0 gls
TOTAL 4 apps 2 gls

GRIFFITHS, J (WH) ++
1941/42 5 apps 0 gls
TOTAL 5 apps 0 gls
Club Record: Gloucester City, Gloucester Aero +.
Note: Played for Gloucester City 1927/28, 1940/41.

GRIFFITHS, Ken (IF)
b. 1922
1938/39 5 apps 0 gls
1939/40 1 app 0 gls
1941/42 26 apps 24 gls
1942/43 1 app 2 gls
1946/47 3 apps 1 gl
1949/50 1 app 0 gls
TOTAL 37 apps 27 gls
Club Record: Notts County (0), Gloucester City, Tottenham Hotspur (0)
(trial) +.
Note: Played for Gloucester City 1940/41.

GRIFFITHS, Kevin (Sub)
1991/92 0 apps 0 gls (2 nps)
TOTAL 0 apps 0 gls (2 nps)
Note: Played for Gloucester City 1990/91.

GRIFFITHS, Neil (D/M)
b. 07/11/1981 Gloucester
1998/99 0 apps 0 gls (2 nps)
1999/00 23 apps 3 subs 0 gls (2 nps)
2000/01 27 apps 4 subs 4 gls
2001/02 41 apps 4 gls
2002/03 55 apps 7 gls
2003/04 50 apps 1 sub 4 gls
2004/05 42 apps 1 sub 3 gls (2 nps)
2005/06 25 apps 2 subs 0 gls
TOTAL 263 apps 11 subs 22 gls (6 nps)
Club Record: Longlevens, Gloucester City, Shortwood United (loan),
Cinderford Town, Cirencester Town +.
Note: Club Captain 2000-05. Was youngest Captain at 19.

GRIFFITHS, W (GK/CF/FB)
1932/33 1 app 0 gls
1933/34 3 apps 0 gls
1934/35 10 apps 2 gls
1935/36 1 app 0 gls
1936/37 1 app 0 gls
1941/42 2 apps 1 gl
TOTAL 18 apps 3 gls

GRIMLEY, Horace F (HB)
b. 1871 Handsworth, Staffordshire d. ?
1889/90 1 app 1 gl
TOTAL 1 app 1 gl

GRIMSHAW, Frederick William (GK)
b. Qu3 1872 Torquay, Devon d. Qu2 1913 York, Yorks.
1889/90

GRIST, N (W)
1929/30 1 app 0 gls
1930/31 1 app 0 gls
TOTAL 2 apps 0 gls

GRUBB, Alan Johnstone (W)
b. 05/02/1928 Leven, Scotland
1951/52 24 apps 6 gls
TOTAL 24 apps 6 gls
Club Record: Largo Villa, Leslie Hearts, 1950 East Fife (1-0), Gloucester
City, 1952 Tottenham Hotspur (2-0), 1953 Walsall (15-0), Worcester City.

GRUBB, Dean Leslie (M)
b. 04/10/1987 Weston-Super-Mare, Somerset
2008/09 6 apps 5 subs 1 gl (3 nps)
TOTAL 6 apps 5 subs 1 gl (3 nps)
Club Record: Bristol City (0), Weston-Super-Mare, Burnley (trial) (0),
Gloucester City, Weymouth, Tiverton Town (trial) +.
International Record: Wales U21 (1).

GRUNDY, W.J (W)
1934/35 10 apps 1 gl
TOTAL 10 apps 1 gl
Club Record: Gloucester City Albion, Gloucester City +.

GUNNELL, D (D)
1987/88

GUY, Bert (HB)
1898/99 2 apps 1 gl
TOTAL 2 apps 1 gl

GWATKIN, Ivor William (W)
b. 09/03/1919 Gloucester d. Qu11993 Cheltenham, Glos.
1935/36 1 app 0 gls
1936/37 12 apps 1 gl
1937/38 42 apps 6 gls
1938/39 42 apps 14 gls
1939/40 22 apps 7 gls
1947/48 14 apps 3 gls
TOTAL 133 apps 31 gls
Club Record: Aberavon, Gloucester Aircraft Club, Gloucester City +.
Note: Played for Gloucester City 1940/41, 1941/42.

GWINNETT, Melvyn Lawrence (Mel) (GK)
b. 14/05/1963 Worcester, Worcs.
1982/83 2 apps 0 gls
TOTAL 2 apps 0 gls
Club Record: West Bromwich Albion (0), Stourbridge, 1981 Peterborough
United (0), 1982 Hereford United (1-0), Gloucester City, Bralanda IF
(Sweden), 1984 Bradford City (0), 1985-88 Exeter City (46-0), Yeovil
Town, Weymouth.

GWYTHER, David Jeffrey Andrew (Dave) (IF)
b. 06/12/1948 Birmingham,Warks.
1983/84 50 apps 1 sub 12 gls
TOTAL 50 apps 1 sub 12 gls
Club Record: South Gower, 1965-72 Swansea Town (216-80), 1973-75
Halifax Town (104-26), 1975-79 Rotherham United (162-45), 1979-82
Newport County (105-28), 1981Crewe Alexandra (loan) (7-1), Gloucester
City, Port Talbot Athletic, 1984 Newport County (2-0), Briton Ferry,
Llanelli.
International Record: Wales U23 (2).

HACKETT, Brendan James (F)
b. 02/03/1966 Wolverhampton, Staffs.
1990/91 10 apps 5 gls
1991/92 17 apps 1 sub 3 gls (1 nps)
1999/00 7 apps 1 sub 0 gls (1 nps)
TOTAL 34 apps 2 subs 8 gls (2 nps)
Club Record: Dudley Town, Worcester City, Gloucester City, Telford
United, Bilston, Stourbridge, Stourport Swifts, Redditch United +.

HADDON, B (FB) ++
1940/41
Club Record: Blackburn Rovers (0), Gloucester City +.

HADDON, C.H (IF)
1906/07 13 apps 3 gls
1907/08 7 apps 1 gl
1908/09 1 app 0 gls

HAILE, F (CF)
1936/37 4 apps 1 gl
TOTAL 4 apps 1 gl
Club Record: Cheltenham Town, Gloucester City +.

HAINES, Albert (IF)
1934/35 17 apps 8 gls
TOTAL 17 apps 8 gls

HAINES, Mervyn John (W)
b. 02/05/1923 Llanwonno, Wales
1952/53 36 apps 4 gls
TOTAL 36 apps 4 gls
Club Record: Swansea Town (0), 1948 Bournemouth (0), Hereford United, Yeovil Town, 1950 Newport County (14-2), Gloucester City.

HALE, H.W (IF)
1907/08 2 apps 0 gls
TOTAL 2 apps 0 gls

HALL, Colin Thomas (M)
b. 02/02/1945 Wolverhampton, Staffs.
1978/79 12 apps 3 gls (4 nps)
1979/80 20 apps 1 sub 0 gls (4 nps)
TOTAL 32 apps 1 sub 3 gls (8 nps)
Club Record: 1967-69 Nottingham Forest (36-2), 1970-71 Bradford City (66-7), 1972 Bristol City (1-0), 1972 Hereford United (5-0) (loan), Bath City, Cheltenham Town, Ledbury Town, Gloucester City +.

HALL, Oliver John (Ollie) (GK)
b. 11/01/1992 Gloucester
2008/09
Club Record: Swindon Town (0), Gloucester City +.

HALL, Robert (CH)
b. Qu4 1950 Gloucester
1969/70 1 app 2 subs 0 gls (2 nps)
1970/71 5 apps 1 sub 0 gls (1 nps)
1971/72 2 apps 0 gls (2 nps)
TOTAL 8 apps 3 subs 0 gls (5 nps)
Club Record: Gloucester City, Cheltenham Town +.

HALL, Thomas George (HB)
b. Qu2 1890 Tetbury, Glos. d. ?
1921/22 5 apps 2 gls
TOTAL 5 apps 2 gls
Note: Played for Gloucester YMCA 1922/23.

HALLAM, Ken (HB)
b. 1951
1972/73 13 apps 1 gl (2 nps)
1973/74 7 apps 1 sub 0 gls (4 nps)
TOTAL 20 apps 1 sub 1 gl (6 nps)
Club Record: Worcester City, Bath City, Sheffield United (0), Stourbridge, Gloucester City, Forest Green Rovers +.

HALLAM, Mark John (F)
b. 29/08/1967 Leicester, Leics.
1994/95 49 apps 19 gls
1995/96 28 apps 4 subs 14 gls (2 nps)
TOTAL 77 apps 4 subs 33 gls (2 nps)
Club Record: Leicester United, Boston United, Ilkeston Town, Hednesford Town, Gloucester City, Hinckley Athletic, Worcester City, Forest Green Rovers, Tamworth +.
Note: Supporter's Player of the Season 1994/95.

HALLETT, Frank (GK)
b. 1878 Kingswood, Glos. d. ?
1899/00 21 apps 0 gls
TOTAL 21 apps 0 gls

HALLIDAY, Liam Francis (M)
b. 14/03/1986 Gloucester
2003/04 0 apps 1 sub 0 gls
TOTAL 0 apps 1 sub 0 gls
Club Record: Gloucester City, Tuffley Rovers, Gala Wilton, Ledbury Town +.

HALLS, Trevor W (GK)
b. Qu4 1929 Gloucester
1958/59 1 app 0 gls
TOTAL 1 app 0 gls
Note: Halls replaced Ron Coltman at the last moment v Cardiff City in Welsh FA Cup match. He was a Gloucester RFC player.

HAMBLIN, Christopher Paul (Chris/Wiggy) (GK)
b. 26/05/1977 Bristol, Avon
1995/96 7 apps 0 gls (2 nps)
TOTAL 7 apps 0 gls (2 nps)
Club Record: Swindon Town (0), Gloucester City, Evesham United, Trowbridge Town, Boston College Eagles (USA), Boston Bulldogs (USA) +.

HAMBLIN, Thomas Robert (Tom) (D)
b. 27/09/1986 Bristol, Avon
2006/07 37 apps 2 subs 1 gl (3 nps)
2007/08 5 apps 1 sub 0 gls (1 nps)
2008/09 23 apps 2 subs 1 gl (9 nps)
TOTAL 65 apps 5 subs 2 gls (13 nps)
Club Record: Mangotsfield United, Bristol Manor Farm, Gloucester City, Paulton Rovers (loan) +.

HAMER, Samuel Charles (Sam) (FB)
b. 06/06/1904 d. Qu2 1990 Gloucester
1923/24 15 apps 0 gls
1924/25 10 apps 0 gls
1925/26 31 apps 0 gls
1926/27 17 apps 0 gls
1927/28 18 apps 0 gls
1928/29 25 apps 0 gls
1929/30 2 apps 0 gls
1930/31 27 apps 0 gls
1931/32 23 apps 0 gls
1932/33 32 apps 1 gl
1933/34 34 apps 0 gls
1934/35 14 apps 0 gls
TOTAL 248 apps 1 gl
Club Record: Gloucester Wagon Works, Gloucester City +.
Note: Club Captain 1933-34. Played for Gloucester City 1940/41. Played more seasons than any other City player.

HAMILTON, ? (W)
1960/61

HAMMOND, J.C (IF)
1896/97

HAMPSON, Craig (D)
b. 11/07/1972 Newcastle-under-Lyme, Staffs.
2001/02 3 apps 0 gls (1 nps)
2002/03 5 apps 2 subs 0 gls
TOTAL 8 apps 2 subs 0 gls (1 nps)
Club Record: Gloucester City, Forest Green Rovers, Whitminster, King's Stanley, Stonehouse Freeway +.

HAMS, Wayne K (D)
b. 19/03/1961 Kensington, London
1980/81 10 apps 1 gl (2 nps)
TOTAL 10 apps 1 gl (2 nps)
Club Record: Brimscombe & Thrupp, Stonehouse, Forest Green Rovers, Cheltenham Town, Gloucester City, Tooting & Mitcham, Basingstoke Town, Cheltenham Town, Forest Green Rovers +.

HANCOCK, Mike (F)
b. 1959
1975/76 5 apps 1 sub 0 gls (1 nps)
1976/77 0 apps 1 sub 0 gls
TOTAL 5 apps 2 subs 0 gls (1 nps)
Club Record: Churchdown Youth, Gloucester City +.

HANCOCKS, Geoffrey M (Geoff/Basher) (D/M)
b. Qu3 1959 Warwick, Warks.
1989/90 2 apps 0 gls
1990/91 33 apps 3 gls
1991/92 22 apps 1 sub 0 gls (2 nps)
1992/93 1 app 0 gls
TOTAL 58 apps 1 sub 3 gls (2 nps)
Club Record: Cambridge City, Germania Teveren (West Germany), Gloucester City, Barry Town, Moreton Town +.

HANDLEY, J (IF) ++
1940/41

PLAYERS' RECORDS

HANSON, Adolf Jonathan (Alf) (W) ++
b. 27/02/1912 Bootle, Lancs. d. Qu4 1993 St Helens, Lancs.
1941/42 1 app 2 gls
TOTAL 1 app 2 gls
Club Record: 1930 Everton (0), 1932-37 Liverpool (166-50), 1938-39
Chelsea (40-8), Gloucester City, South Liverpool, Shelbourne United
(Eire), Ellesmere Port Town, Tranmere Rovers (0).
International Record: England War-Time (1).
Note: Played for Gloucester City 1940/41.

HARDCASTLE, Mark John (M)
b. 21/04/1984 Gloucester
2001/02 5 apps 2 subs 0 gls (1 nps)
TOTAL 5 apps 2 subs 0 gls (1 nps)
Club Record: Bristol Rovers (0), Gloucester City +.

HARDING, ? (IF)
1936/37 1 app 0 gls
TOTAL 1 app 0 gls

HARDING, ? (W)
1948/49 1 app 0 gls
TOTAL 1 app 0 gls

HARDING, Stephen John (Steve/Dolly) (D)
b. 23/07/1956 Bristol
1982/83 24 apps 2 gls
1983/84 48 apps 6 gls (1 nps)
1984/85 12 apps 0 gls
TOTAL 84 apps 8 gls (1 nps)
Club Record: 1975 Bristol City (2-0), 1975 Southend United (loan) (2-0),
1976 Grimsby Town (loan) (8-0), 1977-79 Bristol Rovers (38-1), 1979
Brentford (loan) (4-0), unknown USA club, Trowbridge Town, Cardiff City
(0), Gloucester City +.

HARDMAN, A (FB)
1923/24 4 apps 0 gls
TOTAL 4 apps 0 gls

HARDS, Neil Andrew (GK)
b. 28/01/1962 Portsmouth, Hants.
1983/84 50 apps 0 gls
1984/85 50 apps 0 gls
TOTAL 100 apps 0 gls
Club Record: Havant Town, 1979-82 Plymouth Argyle (6-0), Wimbledon
(loan) (0), Gloucester City, Cheltenham Town, Waterlooville, Havant
Town, Newport (IOW), Newport AFC.

HARE, W (FB)
1889/90

HARGREAVES, Terry (IF)
b. 1946
1964/65 3 apps 0 gls
1965/66 46 apps 8 gls
1966/67 35 apps 3 gls (3 nps)
1971/72 34 apps 5 subs 5 gls (2 nps)
1972/73 45 apps 5 gls (1 nps)
1973/74 28 apps 6 subs 1 gl (7 nps)
1974/75 45 apps 1 gl (3 nps)
1976/77 24 apps 0 gls (1 nps)
TOTAL 260 apps 11 subs 23 gls (17 nps)
Club Record: Gloucester City, Cinderford Town, Stonehouse, Ledbury
Town, Gloucester City, Sydney Croatia (Australia) +.

HARPER, Robert (Bobby) (W)
b. 06/06/1920 Glasgow, Scotland d. 1980
1951/52 3 apps 1 gl
TOTAL 3 apps 1 gl
Club Record: Partick Thistle (0), Ayr United (0), 1946 Huddersfield Town
(0), 1946-49 Newport County (114-12), 1950 Southend United (6-0),
Gloucester City, Linfield.

HARRIOTT, Marvin Lee (FB)
b. 20/04/1974 Dulwich, London
1997/98 1 game 0 gls
TOTAL 1 game 0 gls
Club Record: 1991 West Ham United (0), 1992 Oldham Athletic (0), 1993
Barnsley (0), 1993 Leyton Orient (loan) (8-0), 1993-94 Bristol City (36-0),
Fortuna Cologne (Germany), Enfield, Gloucester City, Gray's Athletic,
Stevenage Borough, Cambridge City, Cardiff City (0), Aylesbury United,
Scarborough, Chesham United, Enfield, Kingstonian +.

HARRIS, Adrian Gerald (Adie) (M)
b. 05/03/1964 Hereford, Herefordshire
1987/88 52 apps 2 subs 8 gls (1 nps)
1988/89 5 apps 7 subs 0 gls (5 nps)
1994/95 23 apps 11 subs 1 gl (11 nps)
2002/03 51 apps 1 sub 5 gls (3 nps)
2003/04 23 apps 12 subs 0 gls (5 nps)
2004/05 7 apps 12 subs 0 gls (16 nps)
2005/06 24 apps 12 subs 2 gls (6 nps)
2006/07 2 apps 9 subs 0 gls (19 nps)
2007/08 0 apps 8 subs 0 gls (30 nps)
2008/09 0 apps 0 gls (37 nps)
TOTAL 188 apps 74 subs 16 gls (133 nps)
Club Record: Dales United, Llandrindod Wells, Aberystwyth Town,
Gloucester City, Bath City, Trowbridge Town, Gloucester City, Cinderford
Town, Trowbridge Town, Cinderford Town, Gloucester City, Pegasus
Juniors (loan) +.
Note: There's only one Adie Harris! Played for Gloucester City 1989/90.
Supporter's Player of the Season 2002/03. Joint Temporary Club Manager
Jan 2006 (1 match).

HARRIS, Anthony Thomas (Tony) (D)
b. 20/12/1945 Berrington, Shrops.
1969/70 3 apps 1 sub 0 gls (1 nps)
TOTAL 3 apps 1 sub 0 gls (1 nps)
Club Record: 1963-66 Shrewsbury Town (55-4), 1968 Bradford PA (10-0),
Gloucester City (trial).

HARRIS, Bertram Griffiths (HB)
b. Qu2 1883 Gloucester d. ?
1906/07 2 apps 0 gls
TOTAL 2 apps 0 gls
Club Record: Gloucester City, Gloucester City Albions +.
Note: Played for Gloucester City 1907/08.

HARRIS, Geoffrey (IF)
1946/47 1 app 0 gls
TOTAL 1 app 0 gls
Club Record: Blakeney, Gloucester City +.

HARRIS, Gary Wayne (D)
b. 31/05/1959 Birmingham, Warks.
1984/85 33 apps 4 gls
TOTAL 33 apps 4 gls
Club Record: 1978-79 Cardiff City (4-0), Trowbridge Town, Gloucester
City +.

HARRIS, H (CF)
1895/96 7 apps 1 gl
TOTAL 7 apps 1 gl

HARRIS, Jack (D)
b. 07/06/1989 Bristol, Avon
2008/09 37 apps 9 subs 5 gls (5 nps)
TOTAL 37 apps 9 subs 5 gls (5 nps)
Club Record: Avonmouth, Hallen, Gloucester City +.

HARRIS, Mick (F)
1969/70 1 app 0 gls
TOTAL 1 app 0 gls
Club Record: Hereford United, 1967-69 Berwick Rangers (21-6), Merthyr
Tydfil, Gloucester City +.

HARRIS, Sidney Samuel (Sid) (FB)
b. Qu4 1877 Gloucester d. ?
1897/98 3 apps 0 gls
1898/99 14 apps 0 gls
TOTAL 17 apps 0 gls

HARRIS, Timothy (Tim) (GK)
b. 17/10/1959 Dymock, Glos.
1979/80 15 apps 1 sub 1 gl (1 nps)
1982/83 4 apps 0 gls
1985/86 4 apps 0 gls
1986/87 0 apps 0 gls (2 nps)
TOTAL 23 apps 1 sub 1 gl (3 nps)
Club Record: Ledbury Town, Shrewsbury Town (0), Newport County,
Gloucester City, Melksham Town (loan), Gloucester City, Cheltenham
Town, Banbury United, Redditch United, Cheltenham Town.
Note: Club Manager Jan 2006 – Jun 2008.

HARRIS, W.A (W)
1896/97

HARRIS, William A.H (Bill) (W)
b. 1913
1932/33 1 app 0 gls
1935/36 24 apps 10 gls
1936/37 5 apps 0 gls
TOTAL 30 app 10 gls
<u>Club Record:</u> Cardiff City (0), Gloucester City, Gloucester Post Office, Gloucester City +.

HARRISON, Paul (Sub)
1991/92

HARRISON, W. Richard (Dick) (W)
1929/30 16 apps 1 gl
1930/31 19 apps 3 gls
1933/34 7 apps 1 gl
TOTAL 42 apps 5 gls
<u>Note:</u> Club Captain 1930-31.

HART, James Patrick (IF) ++
b. 14/02/1914 Glasgow, Scotland d. Qu2 1997 Liverpool, Merseyside
1939/40 1 app 1 gl
TOTAL 1 app 1 gl
<u>Club Record:</u> Wishaw Juniors, 1935 Preston North End (0), 1937 Torquay United (5-1), Gloucester City, Hibernian (0) +.

HART, W.J (CF)
1899/00 6 apps 2 gls
1900/01 1 app 0 gls
TOTAL 7 apps 2 gls

HARTLAND, L
1890s

HARTSHORNE, C (IF)
1930/31 10 apps 1 gl
1931/32 30 apps 7 gls
1932/33 20 apps 6 gls
1933/34 39 apps 9 gls
1934/35 32 apps 7 gls
1936/37 11 apps 0 gls
1937/38 14 apps 4 gls
TOTAL 156 apps 34 gls
<u>Club Record:</u> Saint James, Gloucester City +.

HARVEY, Frederick (HB)
b. 1929
1949/50 5 apps 0 gls
TOTAL 5 apps 0 gls
<u>Club Record:</u> Southampton (0), Gloucester City +.

HARVEY, Rev. J.H (HB)
1892/93 3 apps 0 gls
1893/94 7 apps 0 gls
TOTAL 10 apps 0 gls
<u>Club Record:</u> Gloucester, Cheltenham Town +.
<u>Note:</u> Played for Gloucester 1891/92.

HASTINGS, ? (IF)
1920/21

HATCHER, Clifford Henry (Cliff) (GK)
b. 27/06/1925 Keynsham, Somerset d. Qu4 1978 Bath, Somerset
1949/50 36 apps 0 gls
TOTAL 36 apps 0 gls
<u>Club Record:</u> 1947-48 Reading (2-0), Gloucester City, Bath City +.

HAWKES, ? (GK)
1920/21

HAWKINS, David (Dave) (IF)
b. 1926 Gloucester
1946/47 13 apps 2 gls
TOTAL 13 apps 2 gls
<u>Club Record:</u> Royal Navy, Swindon Town (0), Gloucester City, Cinderford Town +.

HAWKINS, J (GK)
1902/03 1 app 0 gls
TOTAL 1 app 0 gls
<u>Note:</u> Played for Gloucester City 1903/04.

HAWKINS, Martin (W)
b. 1944 Bristol
1963/64 48 apps 7 gls
1964/65 16 apps 5 gls
TOTAL 64 apps 12 gls
<u>Club Record:</u> Bristol City (0), Gloucester City +.

HAYDEN, Micky (WH)
b. 1952
1974/75 46 apps 5 gls
1975/76 1 app 0 gls
1977/78 11 apps 2 subs 3 gls (1 nps)
TOTAL 58 apps 2 subs 8 gls (1 nps)
<u>Club Record:</u> Gloucester City, Cheltenham Town, Cinderford Town, Cheltenham Town, Gloucester City, Saint Marks CA +.
<u>Note:</u> Club Captain 1974-75.

HAYDON, Arthur Leonard (IF)
b. Qu3 1887 Romford, Essex d. ?
1907/08 1 app 0 gls
1909/10 1 app 1 gl
TOTAL 2 apps 1 gl

HAYDON, Trevor J (IF)
b. 17/03/1927 Bristol d. 09/11/2006 Bristol
1949/50 13 apps 5 gls
1950/51 30 apps 11 gls
TOTAL 43 apps 16 gls
<u>Club Record:</u> Bristol City (0), Norwich City (0), Gloucester City, Bath City +.

HAYES, George Edward (CF)
b. 10/10/1910 Hartley Wintney, Hants. d. Qu2 1993 Swindon, Wilts.
1933/34 2 apps 1 gl
TOTAL 2 apps 1 gl
<u>Club Record:</u> 1932 Swindon Town (5-1), Gloucester City, Cricklade Road Primitives +.

HAYNES, F (IF)
1909/10 1 app 1 gl
TOTAL 1 app 1 gl

HAZEL, Ian (M)
b. 01/12/1967 Merton, Surrey
1991/92 2 apps 1 gl
TOTAL 2 apps 1 gl
<u>Club Record:</u> 1987-88 Wimbledon (7-0), 1988 Bristol Rovers (loan) (3-0), 1989-90 Bristol Rovers (14-0), 1991 Maidstone United (8-0), Slough Town, Gloucester City +.

HEAD, David George (IF)
b. 11/08/1940 Midsomer Norton, Somerset
1962/63 27 apps 2 gls
TOTAL 27 apps 2 gls
<u>Club Record:</u> 1958 Swindon Town (0), 1959 Arsenal (0), 1960 Reading (12-0), 1961 Bristol Rovers (0), Trowbridge Town, Gloucester City +.
<u>Note:</u> Club Captain 1962-63. Son of Bert Head, ex-Swindon Town manager.

HEDGE, ? (IF)
1948/49 1 app 0 gls
TOTAL 1 app 0 gls

HEDGES, Ian Austin (D)
b. 05/02/1969 Bristol
1987/88 1 app 0 gls
1988/89 25 apps 3 subs 0 gls (12 nps)
1989/90 36 apps 4 subs 0 gls (7 nps)
1990/91 18 apps 0 gls
TOTAL 80 apps 7 subs 0 gls (19 nps)
<u>Club Record:</u> Bristol City (0), Newport County (0), Bristol Manor Farm, Gloucester City, AFC Bournemouth (0), Bath City (loan), Bath City, Forest Green Rovers, Merthyr Tydfil (loan), Paulton Rovers +.
<u>Note:</u> Club record fee of £25,000 received from AFC Bournemouth 1989/90.

HEMMING, Adam (M)
b. 18/07/1985 Gloucester
2003/04 16 apps 25 subs 4 gls (11 nps)
TOTAL 16 apps 25 subs 4 gls (11 nps)
<u>Club Record:</u> Longlevens, Gloucester City, Cirencester Town, Cinderford Town, Gala Wilton, Ledbury Town +.

HEMMINGS, Anthony George (Tony) (M)
b. 21/09/1967 Burton-on-Trent, Staffs.
1998/99 46 apps 2 subs 10 gls
TOTAL 46 apps 2 subs 10 gls
Club Record: Burton Albion, Rocester, Northwich Victoria, 1993-95 Wycombe Wanderers (49-12), Macclesfield Town, Hednesford Town, Gloucester City, Ilkeston Town, 1999 Chester City (19-2), 2000 Carlisle United (22-0), Altrincham, Ilkeston Town, Tamworth, Ilkeston Town, Alfreton Town, Grantham Town (loan), Gresley Rovers +.

HENDERSON, C.M (CF)
1889/90 2 apps 4 gls
TOTAL 2 apps 4 gls
Note: Played for Gloucester 1890/91, 1891/92.

HENDERSON, Vincent John D (IF)
b. 01/12/1908 Conway, Wales d. Qu4 1988 Cheltenham, Glos.
1934/35 42 apps 22 gls
1935/36 1 app 0 gls
TOTAL 43 apps 22 gls
Club Record: Sunningend, Gloucester City +.

HENDRY, Ian (D)
b. 19/10/1959 Glasgow, Scotland
1987/88 13 apps 1 gl (1 nps)
TOTAL 13 apps 1 gl (1 nps)
Club Record: Eastercraigs, 1977 Aston Villa (0), 1978-79 Hereford United (21-0), Gloucester City (loan), Cambridge United (loan) (0), 1980-82 Hibernian (2-0), Nuneaton Borough, Hereford United, Worcester City, Stafford Rangers +.

HENDY, Nicholas (Nick) (D)
b. 1972
1990/91 2 apps 0 gls (3 nps)
TOTAL 2 apps 0 gls (3 nps)
Club Record: Bristol Rovers (0), Bath City, Trowbridge Town, Gloucester City, Forest Green Rovers, Taunton Town, Forest Green Rovers +.

HERVIN, Mark Peter (GK)
b. 20/09/1972 Bristol
1999/00 5 apps 0 gls
TOTAL 5 apps 0 gls
Club Record: Yeovil Town, Forest Green Rovers (loan), Bristol Rovers (0), Mangotsfield United, Frome Town, Yeovil Town, Bath City, Gloucester City, Clevedon Town, Bath City, Cirencester Town (loan), Chippenham Town +.

HEYDEN, H (IF)
1922/23 1 app 1 gl
1924/25 5 apps 0 gls
TOTAL 6 apps 1 gl

HIBBITT, Kenneth (Ken) (M)
b. 03/01/1951 Bradford, Yorks.
1989/90
Club Record: 1967-68 Bradford Park Avenue (15-0), 1968-83 Wolverhampton Wanderers (466-89), Seattle Sounders (USA) (loan), 1984-85 Coventry City (47-4), 1986-88 Bristol Rovers (53-5).
International Record: England U23 (1)
Note: Played as a guest for Gloucester City in Doug Foxwell's Testimonial.

HICKEY, Steven Michael Henry (Steve) (D)
b. 18/10/1980 Gloucester
1998/99 1 app 0 gls (4 nps)
1999/00 2 apps 6 subs 0 gls (8 nps)
TOTAL 3 apps 6 subs 0 gls (12 nps)
Club Record: Gloucester City, Tuffley Rovers, Gala Wilton, Ledbury Town +.

HICKEY, William (Bill) (W)
1959/60 19 apps 2 gls
TOTAL 19 apps 2 gls

HICKMAN, Harold C (IF)
1929/30 20 apps 3 gls
1930/31 1 app 0 gls
1932/33 15 apps 3 gls
TOTAL 36 apps 6 gls
Club Record: Gloucester City, Pope's Hill, Gloucester City +.

HICKS, Walter H (FB)
1895/96 3 apps 0 gls
1897/98 3 apps 0 gls
1898/99 3 apps 0 gls
TOTAL 9 apps 0 gls
Note: Played for Gloucester 1896/97.

HIGGINSON, S (HB)
1889/90 2 apps 0 gls
TOTAL 2 apps 0 gls
Note: Played for Gloucester 1890/91.

HILDER, Daniel Gary (Dan) (D)
b. 11/09/1988 Cheltenham, Glos.
2007/08 1 app 0 gls
TOTAL 1 app 0 gls
Club Record: Cirencester Town, Gloucester City, Highworth Town +.

HILL, J (HB)
1906/07 1 app 0 gls
1907/08 3 apps 1 gl
1908/09 15 apps 1 gl
1909/10 15 apps 0 gls
TOTAL 34 apps 2 gls
Club Record: Exeter City, Gloucester City +.

HILL, Robert (Bob) (Sub)
1978/79 0 apps 0 gls (7 nps)
TOTAL 0 apps 0 gls (7 nps)

HILLMAN, Roy A (FB)
b. 08/04/1938 West Ham, London
1977/78
Club Record: Bristol City (0), Romford, Glastonbury +.

HILLS, H (FB)
1926/27

HINDLE, ? (W)
1957/58
Club Record: Oldham Athletic (0), Gloucester City +.

HINES, Alistair (GK)
b. 1981
2000/01 38 apps 0 gls (5 nps)
TOTAL 38 apps 0 gls (5 nps)
Club Record: Bristol Rovers (0), Forest Green Rovers, Gloucester City, Team Bath, Bristol Manor Farm +.

HOARE, A.S (GK)
1903/04 3 apps 0 gls
TOTAL 3 apps 0 gls
Club Record: Gloucester Thursday, Gloucester City +.

HOBBS, Darren James (D)
b. 18/01/1979 Bristol, Avon
1997/98 6 apps 2 subs 0 gls (6 nps)
TOTAL 6 apps 2 subs 0 gls (6 nps)
Club Record: Bristol City (0), Gloucester City, Yate Town, Clevedon Town, Paulton Rovers, Chippenham Town +.

HOBBS, Philip (CH)
b. 1945
1961/62 5 apps 0 gls
TOTAL 5 apps 0 gls
Club Record: Churchdown United, Gloucester City +.

HOCKIN, Henry Valentine (CF)
b. 14/02/1864 Lewisham, Kent d. 10/03/1945 Swansea, Wales
1889/90 1 app 1 gl
TOTAL 1 app 1 gl
Note: Played for Gloucester 1890/91.

HODGES, David Thomas (Dave) (M)
b. 17/01/1970 Ross-on-Wye, Herefordshire
1992/93 23 apps 5 subs 3 gls (1 nps)
TOTAL 23 apps 5 subs 3 gls (1 nps)
Club Record: 1986-90 Mansfield Town (75-7), 1990-91 Torquay United (16-0), 1992 Bolton Wanderers (0), 1992 Shrewsbury Town (1-0), Gloucester City, Kettering Town, Worcester City, Ross Town.

HODGES, K (W)
1923/24 1 app 0 gls
TOTAL 1 app 0 gls

HODNETT, Danny William (FB)
b. 19/11/1986 Worcester, Worcs.
2006/07 5 apps 0 gls
TOTAL 5 apps 0 gls
Club Record: Kidderminster Harriers, Stoke City (0), Solihull Borough, Worcester City (trial), Evesham United (loan), Gloucester City (loan), Evesham United +.

HOITT, A.C (HB)
1893/94 6 apps 0 gls
TOTAL 6 apps 0 gls

HOLDER, Colin Walter (CF)
b. 06/01/1944 Cheltenham, Glos.
1970/71 32 apps 3 subs 2 gls (1 nps)
TOTAL 32 apps 3 subs 2 gls (1 nps)
Club Record: 1960-61 Coventry City (9-4), Lockheed Leamington, Chelmsford City, Weymouth, Nuneaton Borough, Stourbridge, Deal, Margate, Cheltenham Town, Banbury United, Rugby Town, Gloucester City, Salisbury, Kidderminster Harriers, Burton Albion, Hednesford Town, Coleshill, Armitage.

HOLDER, Oliver (Ollie) (D)
b. 03/06/1989 Cirencester, Glos.
2007/08
Club Record: Cheltenham Saracens, Cirencester Town, Gloucester City +.

HOLLAND, Christopher James (Chris) (D)
b. 29/08/1980 Taunton, Somerset
2005/06 9 apps 1 gl
TOTAL 9 apps 1 gl
Club Record: AFC Bournemouth (0), 1999 Bristol City (0), Exeter City, Team Bath, Bath City, Weston-Super-Mare (loan), Gloucester City (loan) +.

HOLLAND, Con (IF)
1947/48 4 apps 1 gl
TOTAL 4 apps 1 gl
Club Record: Grimsby Town (0), Gloucester City +.

HOLLINGWORTH, George Philip (IF)
b. Qu3 1902 East Ashford, Kent d. ?
1922/23
Club Record: Gloucester City Albion, Gloucester YMCA, Cambridge University +.

HOLLOWAY, Jonathan Stuart (Jon) (D)
b. 11/02/1977 Swindon, Wilts.
1995/96 10 apps 2 gls
1996/97 42 apps 4 subs 1 gl
1997/98 52 apps 1 sub 4 gls
1998/99 47 apps 2 subs 7 gls
TOTAL 151 apps 7 subs 14 gls
Club Record: Swindon Town (0), Scarborough (0), Gloucester City, Bath City, Worcester City, Forest Green Rovers, Redditch United, Merthyr Tydfil, Bath City +.

HOLMAN, J (FB)
1929/30

HOLMES, David James (F)
b. 22/11/1972 Derby, Derbyshire.
1994/95 8 apps 3 gls
1995/96 36 apps 1 sub 13 gls
1996/97 36 apps 7 subs 13 gls
TOTAL 80 apps 8 subs 29 gls
Club Record: 1989-91 Scarborough (11-1), Gresley Rovers, Gloucester City, Hednesford Town (loan), Burton Albion, Ilkeston Town, Worcester City, Halesowen Town (loan), Alfreton Town, Ilkeston Town, Mickleover Sports, Gresley Rovers +.
Note: Club record equalling fee of £25,000 paid to Gresley Rovers 1994/95.

HOLTHAM, Dean Mark (D)
b. 30/09/1963 Pontypridd, Wales
1989/90
Club Record: 1981 Cardiff City (0), 1983 Swansea City (6-0), Weymouth, Yeovil Town, Bath City, Ebbw Vale, 1987 Newport County (6-0), Ebbw Vale, Bridgend Town.
Note: Played as a guest for Gloucester City in Doug Foxwell's Testimonial.

HOPEWELL, R (W)
1923/24 2 apps 0 gls
TOTAL 2 apps 0 gls

HOPKINS, ? (W)
1935/36 11 apps 5 gls
TOTAL 11 apps 5 gls

HOPKINS, Wynne (M)
b. 1956
1982/83 10 apps 0 gls (2 nps)
TOTAL 10 apps 0 gls (2 nps)
Club Record: Newport County (0), Gloucester City +.

HOPPS, Trevor (GK)
1989/90 10 apps 0 gls
TOTAL 10 apps 0 gls
Club Record: Rushden Town, Gloucester City +.

HORLICK, Gerald (Gerry) (F)
b. 20/09/1941 Wincanton, Somerset d. 07/07/2009 Hereford, Herefordshire
1959/60 17 apps 5 gls
1960/61 41 apps 10 gls
1961/62 33 apps 13 gls
1962/63 43 apps 18 gls
1963/64 34 apps 20 gls
TOTAL 168 apps 66 gls
Club Record: Bristol City (trial) (0), Gloucester City, Cheltenham Town.

HORNE, P (IF)
1913/14
1919/20

HORNSBY, R.H (GK)
1892/93

HORSFALL, Kevin (F)
1993/94
Club Record: Gloucester City, Ross Town +.

HOSKINS, Andrew Richard (Andy) (F)
b. 07/07/1972 Gloucester
1997/98 12 apps 7 subs 4 gls (3 nps)
1998/99 1 app 12 subs 2 gls (10 nps)
2001/02 37 apps 10 gls
2002/03 43 apps 5 subs 21 gls (2 nps)
2003/04 48 apps 37 gls (1 nps)
2004/05 3 apps 2 subs 0 gls (1 nps)
TOTAL 144 apps 26 subs 74 gls (17 nps)
Club Record: Brockworth, Tuffley Rovers, Forest Green Rovers, Cinderford Town, Gloucester City, Cinderford Town, Brockworth, Gloucester City, Cinderford Town, Shortwood United +.
Note: Supporter's Player of the Season 2003/04.

HOWARD, ? (GK)
1920/21

HOWARD, H (WH) ++
1940/41
Club Record: The Army, Gloucester City +.

HOWARD, Ken Leslie (Kenny) (D)
b. 27/10/1971 Gloucester
2001/02 4 apps 9 subs 0 gls (2nps)
2002/03 1 app 11 subs 1 gl (15 nps)
2003/04 2 apps 3 subs 0 gls (7 nps)
TOTAL 7 apps 23 subs 1 gl (24 nps)
Club Record: Brockworth Albion, Gloucester City +.

HOWARTH, Adam (D)
b. 06/09/1984 Newport, Isle of Wight
2003/04 13 apps 1 sub 0 gls
TOTAL 13 apps 1 sub 0 gls
Club Record: Eastleigh, Newport (IOW), Cheltenham Town, Bath City, Gloucester City, Cirencester Town, Newport (IOW), Western Massachusetts Pioneers (USA), New York Red Bulls (USA), Saint Mirren (trial), Milton Keynes Dons (trial), AC Kajaani (Finland) +.

HOWELL, Ian (D)
b. 24/08/1971
1994/95 7 apps 1 sub 1 gl (1 nps)
1995/96 5 apps 5 subs 1 gl (1 nps)
1996/97 8 apps 10 subs 0 gls (2 nps)
1997/98 0 apps 0 gls (2 nps)
TOTAL 20 apps 16 subs 2 gls (6 nps)
Club Record: Swindon Supermarine, , Trowbridge Town, Gloucester City, Cirencester Town (loan), Cheltenham Town, Newport (IOW) (loan), Bashley, Salisbury, Wokingham, Cinderford Town, Swindon Supermarine, Weston-Super-Mare, Swindon Supermarine +.
Note: Brother of Ryder Cup golfer, David Howell.

HOWELLS, Brian (CF)
1966/67 2 apps 0 gls (3 nps)
TOTAL 2 apps 0 gls (3 nps)

PLAYERS' RECORDS

HUDD, David Clive (Dave) (WH)
b. 09/07/1944 Bristol
1970/71 42 apps 5 gls (2 nps)
1971/72 27 apps 3 subs 7 gls (1 nps)
1973/74 0 apps 0 gls (1 nps)
TOTAL 69 apps 3 subs 12 gls (4 nps)
Club Record: Old Georgians, 1964 Bristol Rovers (5-1), Cheltenham Town, Worcester City, Gloucester City +.

HUDSON, D (D)
2001/02

HUGGINS, Dean S (D)
b. 21/11/1976 Cardiff, Wales
1997/98 6 apps 0 gls
TOTAL 6 apps 0 gls
Club Record: Bristol City (0), Barry Town, Carmarthen Town, Gloucester City +.
International Record: Wales U21 (1).

HUGHES, Anthony (Tony) (W)
b. 1953
1971/72 14 apps 2 gls
TOTAL 14 apps 2 gls
Club Record: Worcester City, Gloucester City, Stourbridge +.

HUGHES, Brian (FB)
b. 22/11/1937 Skewen, Glamorgan, Wales
1970/71 13 apps 0 gls
TOTAL 13 apps 0 gls
Club Record: 1958-66 Swansea Town (219-7), Merthyr Tydfil, 1968 Swansea Town (12-0), Gloucester City +.
International Record: Wales U23 (2).

HUGHES, Brian David (M)
b. 20/08/1962 Ludgershall, Nr.Andover, Hants.
1988/89 58 apps 6 gls
1989/90 60 apps 8 gls
1990/91 22 apps 1 sub 1 gl (1 nps)
1991/92 27 apps 1 sub 1 gl (2 nps)
1992/93 42 apps 2 gls
1993/94 25 apps 0 gls (7 nps)
1994/95 1 app 3 subs 0 gls (6 nps)
1995/96 0 app 1 sub 0 gls (4 nps)
1997/98 0 apps 0 gls (3 nps)
1999/00 1 app 0 gls
TOTAL 236 apps 6 subs 19 gls (23 nps)
Club Record: 1980-82 Swindon Town (70-5), 1983 Torquay United (38-6), Cheltenham Town, Gloucester City, Barry Town, Gloucester City, Witney Town, Gloucester City, Highworth Town.
Note: Club Captain 1988-95. Joint Temporary Club Manager Mar 1994 – May 1994, Club Manager Oct 1998 – Feb 2000.

HUGHES, Jasper (M)
1983/84 2 apps 0 gls
TOTAL 2 apps 0 gls

HUGHES, Jeff (Sub)
1983/84 0 apps 1 sub 1 gl (1 nps)
TOTAL 0 apps 1 sub 1 gl (1 nps)
Club Record: Newport County (0), Gloucester City +.

HUGHES, Mark Christopher (M)
b. 17/07/1967 Swindon, Wilts.
1986/87 2 apps 0 gls (1 nps)
TOTAL 2 apps 0 gls (1 nps)
Club Record: 1983 Swindon Town (1-0), Gloucester City +.

HUGHES, Nicky (Sub)
1993/94 0 apps 1 sub 1 gl (1 nps)
TOTAL 0 apps 1 sub 1 gl (1 nps)
Club Record: Gloucester City, Moreton Town +.

HUGHES, Thomas Alexander (Tommy) (GK)
b. 11/07/1947 Dalmuir, Scotland
1983/84 2 apps 0 gls
TOTAL 2 apps 0 gls
Club Record: Clydebank Juniors, 1966-69 Chelsea (11-0), 1971 Aston Villa (16-0), 1972 Brighton & Hove Albion (loan) (3-0), 1973-81 Hereford United (240-0), Gloucester City, Trowbridge Town.
International Record: Scotland U23 (2).

HUMPHREY, Thomas Robson (Tommy/Steptoe) (W)
b. 27/10/1937 Houghton-le-Spring, County Durham
1962/63 38 apps 4 gls
1963/64 42 apps 9 gls
TOTAL 80 apps 13 gls
Club Record: The Army, 1958-60 Aldershot (22-3), Poole Town, Gloucester City +.

HUMPHRIES, ? (HB)
1920/21

HUNT, Danny (M)
b. 29/11/1978
1999/00 7apps 0 gls (1 nps)
2000/01 29 apps 1 gl (1 nps)
TOTAL 36 apps 1 gl (2 nps)
Club Record: Swindon Town (0), Newport AFC, Clevedon Town, Gloucester City, Cinderford Town, Chippenham Town, Weston-Super-Mare +.
Note: Played for Gloucester City 1997/98.

HUNT, Douglas Arthur (Doug) (CF/IR)
b. 19/05/1914 Shipton Bellinger, Hants. d. Qu2 1989 Yeovil, Somerset
1948/49 47 apps 25 gls
1949/50 36 apps 17 gls
1950/51 10 apps 3 gls
1951/52 2 apps 0 gls
TOTAL 95 apps 45 gls
Club Record: Winchester City, 1931 Southampton (0), Northfleet, 1934-36 Tottenham Hotspur (17-6), 1936-37 Barnsley (36-18), 1937-39 Sheffield Wednesday (42-30), 1946-47 Leyton Orient (61-16), Gloucester City.
International Record: England War-Time (1).
Note: Club Captain 1948-49. Club Player-Manager Nov 1948-Jul 1952.

HUNT, Paul Craig (Oggie) (F)
b. 08/10/1970 Swindon, Wilts.
1993/94 5 apps 0 gls
TOTAL 5 apps 0 gls
Club Record: 1989-92 Swindon Town (11-0), Gloucester City, (loan), 1993 Charlton Athletic (0), 1993 Cardiff City (0), 1993 Bristol Rovers (0), Brann Bergen (Norway), Andover, Cirencester Town, Forest Green Rovers, Aberystwyth Town, Taunton Town, Clevedon Town, Swindon Supermarine, Highworth Town, Hungerford Town, Weston-Super-Mare, Mangotsfield United (loan), Cirencester Town, Fairford Town, Andover +.

HUNT, Paul Leslie (D)
b. 07/03/1959 Hereford, Herefordshire
1982/83 7 apps 0 gls
1983/84 38 apps 1 sub 0 gls (6 nps)
TOTAL 45 apps 1 sub 0 gls (6 nps)
Club Record: Coventry City (0), 1978-80 Hereford United (51-4), Trowbridge Town, Worcester City, Gloucester City +.

HUNT, Ralph Robert Arthur (CF)
b. 14/08/1933 Portsmouth, Hants. d. 1964
1950s
Club Record: Gloucester City, 1952-53 Portsmouth (5-0), 1953-54 Bournemouth (33-7), 1955-57 Norwich City (124-67), 1958 Derby County (24-10), 1959-60 Grimsby Town (53-39), 1961 Swindon Town (21-13), 1961 Port Vale (14-6), 1962-63 Newport County (83-38), 1964 Chesterfield (17-5).
Note: Any relation to Doug Hunt?

HURCUM, G (HB)
1932/33 8 apps 0 gls
TOTAL 8 apps 0 gls
Note: Played for Gloucester City 1928/29.

HURFORD, David George (W)
b. 17/01/1945 Chipping Sodbury, Glos.
1969/70 39 apps 2 subs 3 gls (1 nps)
1970/71 37 apps 4 subs 1 gl (6 nps)
1971/72 16 apps 3 gls (2 nps)
TOTAL 92 apps 6 subs 7 gls (9 nps)
Club Record: Old Sodbury, 1962-64 Bristol Rovers (6-0), Cheltenham Town, Gloucester City.

HUTCHINS, ? (IF)
1936/37 1 app 0 gls
TOTAL 1 app 0 gls

HUTCHISON, Douglas (Doug) (IF)
1969/70 1 app 0 gls
TOTAL 1 app 0 gls

HYDE, Christopher (Chris) (F)
b. 22/02/1963
1986/87 16 apps 2 subs 8 gls (2 nps)
1987/88 32 apps 4 subs 27 gls (1 nps)
1988/89 4 apps 3 subs 0 gls (3 nps)
1989/90 4 apps 8 subs 4 gls (5 nps)
TOTAL 56 apps 17 subs 39 gls (11 nps)
Club Record: Pegasus Juniors, Worcester City, Gloucester City, Cinderford Town, Abergavenny Thursdays, Stroud +.
Note: Father of Cory Hyde.

HYDE, Cory (F)
b. Qu4 1985 Hereford, Herefordshire
2003/04 0 apps 1 sub 0 gls
TOTAL 0 apps 1 sub 0 gls
Club Record: Gloucester City, Pegasus Juniors +.
Note: Son of Christopher Hyde.

HYDE, Joe (CH)
b. 1936 Cheltenham, Glos.
1961/62 38 apps 2 gls
1962/63 44 apps 2 gls
1963/64 20 apps 0 gls
TOTAL 102 apps 4 gls
Club Record: Cheltenham Town, Gloucester City, Evesham United.

IDDLES, ? (IF)
1959/60 1 app 0 gls
TOTAL 1 app 0 gls
Club Record: Cheltenham Town, Gloucester City +.

IDDLES, Danny (F)
1993/94 3 apps 2 subs 0 gls
TOTAL 3 apps 2 subs 0 gls
Club Record: Yate Town, Trowbridge Town, Cheltenham Town, Gloucester City, Forest Green Rovers, Sharpness, Shortwood United, Clevedon Town, Trowbridge Town (loan), Yate Town +

IDDON, Dave (F)
1984/85 4 apps 1 sub 0 gls (3 nps)
TOTAL 4 apps 1 sub 0 gls (3 nps)
Club Record: Royal Air Force, Gloucester City +.

INGLES, W (FB)
1909/10 23 apps 2 gls
TOTAL 23 apps 2 gls

IRELAND, Ron (IF)
b. 1935
1955/56 7 apps 1 gl
1959/60 5 apps 2 gls
TOTAL 12 apps 3 gls
Club Record: Cinderford Town, Stonehouse, Gloucester City +.

JACKSON, C (?)

JACKSON, R (CF)
1927/28 9 apps 4 gls
TOTAL 9 apps 4 gls

JACKSON, R.T (CF)
1932/33 1 app 2 gls
TOTAL 1 app 2 gls
Club Record: Gloucester City, Swindon Town (0) +.

JACKSON, Toby (D)
b. Bath, Somerset
1994/95 11 apps 1 sub 0 gls (1 nps)
TOTAL 11 apps 1 sub 0 gls (1 nps)
Club Record: Bath City, Trowbridge Town, Gloucester City, Clevedon Town, Witney Town, Forest Green Rovers, Salisbury City, Newport AFC +.

JACOBS, Clive (IF)
b. 1943
1970/71 2 apps 3 subs 0 gls (5 nps)
TOTAL 2 apps 3 subs 0 gls (5 nps)
Club Record: Bristol Rovers (0), Minehead, Gloucester City +.

JACQUES, Anthony (Tony/Hattie) (HB)
b. 10/10/1942 Oddington, Oxon.
1964/65 29 apps 10 gls
TOTAL 29 apps 10 gls
Club Record: 1962 Oxford United (7-0), Hereford United, Gloucester City, Banbury United, Nuneaton Borough, Kettering Town, Banbury United, Northampton Town (0).

JAMES, Allan (FB)
b. 1883 Goodrich, Herefordshire d. ?
1900/01 2 apps 0 gls
TOTAL 2 apps 0 gls

JAMES, Brett Anthony (F)
b. 10/09/1991 Gloucester
2008/09 3 apps 4 subs 0 gls (11 nps)
TOTAL 3 apps 4 subs 0 gls (11 nps)

JAMES, Edward T (IF)
b. 1876 Gloucester d. ?
1895/96 3 apps 0 gls
TOTAL 3 apps 0 gls
Note: Played for Gloucester 1896/97.

JAMES, H (IF/HB)
1921/22 2 apps 1 gl
1922/23 2 apps 0 gls
TOTAL 4 apps 1 gl

JAMES, Jimmy (GK)
1952/53 6 apps 0 gls
1953/54 4 apps 0 gls
TOTAL 10 apps 0 gls
Club Record: Uplands, Aston Villa (trial) (0), Gloucester City +.

JAMES, Lea (D/M)
b. 1970
1994/95
Club Record: Westbury United, Trowbridge Town, Gloucester City (trial), Bath City, Chippenham Town, Cinderford Town, Swindon Supermarine, Paulton Rovers, Odd Down +.

JARMAN, W (IF)
1921/22 8 apps 10 gls
1922/23 2 apps 0 gls
1923/24 1 app 0 gls
TOTAL 11 apps 10 gls

JARMAN, W.A (CF)
1908/09 12 apps 17 gls
1909/10 22 apps 12 gls
TOTAL 34 apps 29 gls

JARRETT, ? (IF) ++
1942/43 1 app 0 gls
TOTAL 1 app 0 gls

JEFFRIES, Lee (Jethro) (D)
b. 16/03/1973 Bristol
2003/04 38 apps 1 sub 6 gls (3 nps)
TOTAL 38 apps 1 sub 6 gls (3 nps)
Club Record: Yate Town, Clevedon Town, Gloucester City, Yate Town, Brislington +.

JENKINS, ? (IF) ++
1941/42 15 apps 19 gls
TOTAL 15 apps 19 gls
Club Record: The Army, Gloucester City +.

JENKINS, Jim (IF)
1954/55

JENKINS, Mansel (Taffy) (IF)
b. 26/11/1924 Pontypridd, Wales d. Qu3 1982 Gloucester
1948/49 38 apps 13 gls
1949/50 12 apps 3 gls
1950/51 39 apps 13 gls
1951/52 30 apps 7 gls
TOTAL 119 apps 36 gls
Club Record: Port Vale (0), Gloucester City, Bath City +.

JENKINS, Mark (GK)
2006/07

JENKINS, Paul (D)
1990/91 2 apps 5 subs 0 gls (4 nps)
1991/92 2 apps 0 gls
1992/93 8 apps 0 gls (1 nps)
TOTAL 12 apps 5 subs 0 gls (5 nps)
Club Record: Gloucester City, Malvern Town, Cinderford Town, Gloucester City +.

PLAYERS' RECORDS

JENKINS, Steve (M/D)
b. 23/01/1981 Gloucester
1998/99 1 app 1 sub 0 gls (4 nps)
1999/00 2 apps 1 sub 0 gls
2000/01 24 apps 9 subs 3 gls
2001/02 33 apps 1 sub 3 gls
2002/03 41 apps 3 subs 1 gl (3 nps)
2003/04 7 apps 6 subs 0 gls (1 nps)
TOTAL 108 apps 21 subs 7 gls (8 nps)
Club Record: Longlevens,Gloucester City, Cirencester Town, Gloucester City, Gloucester United (loan), Cinderford Town, Swindon Supermarine, Longlevens +.

JENNINGS, Paul (M)
1999/00 2 apps 1 sub 0 gls (3 nps)
TOTAL 2 apps 1 sub 0 gls (3 nps)

JENNINGS, Roy C (WH)
b. 1919
1946/47 38 apps 1 gl
1947/48 42 apps 1 gl
TOTAL 80 apps 2 gls
Club Record: Bristol City (0), Bristol Rovers (0), Gloucester City +.

JEPSON, Arthur (GK)
b. 12/07/1915 Selston, Notts. d. Qu3 1997 Mansfield, Notts.
1951/52 34 apps 0 gls
1952/53 12 apps 0 gls
TOTAL 46 apps 0 gls
Club Record: Newark Town, 1934 Mansfield Town (2-0), Grantham, 1938-45 Port Vale (39-0), 1946-47 Stoke City (28-0), 1948-49 Lincoln City (58-0), Gloucester City, Northwich Victoria, Hinckley United.
Note: Played cricket for Nottinghamshire CCC 1938-1959. Was Test Match Umpire 1960-1969.

JESSOP, A (CF)
1893/94 1 app 1 gl
TOTAL 1 app 1 gl

JESSOP, Gilbert Laird (CF)
b. 19/05/1874 Cheltenham, Glos. d. 11/05/1955 Fordington, Dorset
1895/96 2 apps 0 gls
TOTAL 2 apps 0 gls
Club Record: Gloucester, Cheltenham, Cambridge University, The Casuals +.
Note: Gilbert Jessop played cricket for Gloucestershire CCC 1894-1914 (Captain 1900-12), Cambridge University 1896-1899 and London County 1900-1903 and represented England 18 times between 1899 and 1912. He also played rugby for Gloucester RFC and Clifton RFC.

JEW, Percy (HB)
1896/97

JOHN, ? (Sub)
1988/89

JOHN, Iuen (D)
1983/84 20 apps 1 sub 0 gls (4 nps)
TOTAL 20 apps 1 sub 0 gls (4 nps)
Club Record: Merthyr Tydfil, Gloucester City, Forest Green Rovers +.

JOHNS, ? (W) ++
1940/41

JOHNSON, ? (W)
1937/38 1 app 0 gls
TOTAL 1 app 0 gls
Club Record: Hanham Athletic, Cadbury Heath, Gloucester City +.

JOHNSON, Albert E (HB)
b. 1871 Bristol d. ?
1889/90 1 app 0 gls
1891/92 1 app 0 gls
1893/94 1 app 0 gls
TOTAL 3 apps 0 gls
Note: Played for Gloucester 1890/91, 1892/93.

JOHNSON, David Donald (D)
b. 10/03/1967 Northampton, Northants.
1995/96 11 apps 0 gls
1996/97 48 apps 1 sub 2 gls
1997/98 20 apps 3 subs 0 gls
TOTAL 79 apps 4 subs 2 gls
Club Record: Irthlingborough Diamonds, 1989-91 Northampton Town (47-0), Kettering Town, Rushden & Diamonds, Gloucester City, Raunds Town +.

JOHNSON, E (WH) ++
1940/41

JOHNSON, Herbie (IF)
1966/67 48 apps 19 gls
1967/68 3 apps 2 gls
TOTAL 51 apps 21 gls
Club Record: Mangotsfield United, Gloucester City, Bath City, Cinderford Town +.

JOHNSON, Mark (Sub)
1992/93 0 apps 2 subs 0 gls (1 nps)
2000/01 0 apps 0 gls (1 nps)
TOTAL 0 apps 2 subs 0 gls (2 nps)
Note: Played for Gloucester City 2002/03.

JOHNSON, Michael (Sub)
1993/94 0 apps 2 subs 0 gls (5 nps)
TOTAL 0 apps 2 subs 0 gls (5 nps)

JOHNSON, Michael W (Mick) (W)
b. 04/10/1933 York, Yorks. d. 19/07/2004 Wollongong, New South Wales, Australia
1957/58 39 apps 16 gls
TOTAL 39 apps 16 gls
Club Record: 1951 Newcastle United (0), Blyth Spartans, 1956 Brighton & Hove Albion (2-0), Gloucester City, 1958-61 Fulham (23-6), 1962 Doncaster Rovers (15-2), 1962 Barrow (12-1), South Coast United (Australia), Metropolitan Adriatic (Australia), Sutherland (Australia).

JOHNSON, Steve (Jonno) (M)
b. 18/02/1961 Coventry, Warks.
1985/86 11 apps 4 gls
1986/87 45 apps 1 sub 18 gls
1987/88 37 apps 8 subs 27 gls (6 nps)
1988/89 2 apps 1 subs 0 gls (5 nps)
TOTAL 95 apps 10 subs 49 gls (11 nps)
Club Record: Stratford Town, Dulwich Hamlet, Hendon Town, Leamington, Gloucester City, Bilston Town, Grantham Town, Willenhall Town, Tamworth.

JOHNSTON, Peter (CF)
b. 1936
1957/58 8 apps 2 gls
TOTAL 8 apps 2 gls
Club Record: Newcastle United (0), Brighton & Hove Albion (0), Headington United, Millwall (0), Gloucester City +.

JOHNSTON, Raymond Steven (Ray) (GK)
b. 05/05/1981 Bristol, Avon
2006/07 17 apps 0 gls (1 nps)
TOTAL 17 apps 0 gls (1 nps)
Club Record: Bath City, 1998 Bristol Rovers (1-0), Southampton (loan) (0), Weston-Super-Mare, Frome Town, Bishop Sutton, Clevedon Town, Frome Town, Gloucester City, Tiverton Town +.

JOHNSTONE, Kacey (D)
b. 22/01/1976 Gloucester
1992/93 0 apps 1 sub 0 gls (1 nps)
1993/94 1 app 4 subs 0 gls (5 nps)
2000/01 23 apps 3 subs 4 gls (2 nps)
TOTAL 24 apps 8 subs 4 gls (8 nps)
Club Record: Gloucester City, Forest Green Rovers, Evesham United, Cinderford Town, Gloucester City, Bishop's Cleeve, Slimbridge, Tuffley Rovers, Bishop's Cleeve, Shortwood United, Almondsbury Town +.
Note: Played for Gloucester City 1994/95.

JONES, A (W)
1891/92

JONES, Rev. A (CF)
1922/23 2 apps 1 gl
1923/24 1 app 0 gls
TOTAL 3 apps 1 gl

JONES, C.A (WH)
1926/27

JONES, Christopher (Chris) (IF)
1933/34 4 apps 1 gl
1934/35 5 apps 1 gl
TOTAL 9 app 2 gls
Club Record: Sunningend, Gloucester City +.

PLAYERS' RECORDS

JONES, Christopher Philip (Chris) (D)
b. 07/11/1984 Cheltenham, Glos.
2004/05

JONES, Craig (F)
2003/04 1 app 1 sub 1 gl (3 nps)
TOTAL 1 app 1 sub 1 gl (3 nps)

JONES, Cyril (W)
b. 08/05/1922 Merthyr Tydfil, Wales d. 14/11/2008 Gloucester
1946/47 1 app 0 gls
1947/48 36 apps 9 gls
1948/49 28 apps 9 gls
TOTAL 65 app 18 gls
Club Record: Royal Air Force, Exeter City (0), Gloucester City, Hereford United, Bideford.

JONES, David (FB)
1968/69
Club Record: Hereford United, Gloucester City (trial) +.

JONES, David Henry (HB)
b. 04/08/1937 Tetbury, Glos.
1958/59 1 app 0 gls
TOTAL 1 app 0 gls
Club Record: 1954 Leeds United (0), Gloucester City, 1960-61 Crewe Alexandra (15-0) +.

JONES, David John (Dave) (F)
b. 16/09/1952 Ruabon, Wales
1982/83 25 apps 8 gls
TOTAL 25 apps 8 gls
Club Record: Ledbury Town, Oswestry Town, Telford United, 1978-79 Hereford United (47-11), Gloucester City, Cheltenham Town +.

JONES, David Owen (Dai) (FB) ++
b. 28/10/1910 Cardiff, Wales d. Qu2 1971 Leicester, Leics.
1942/43
Club Record: Ely United, Ebbw Vale, 1929 Charlton Athletic (0), 1930 Millwall (0), 1931-32 Clapton Orient (55-0), 1933-46 Leicester City (229-4), Gloucester City, 1947-48 Mansfield Town (74-0), Hinckley Athletic.
International Record: Wales (7).

JONES, E.J (CF)
1913/14 8 apps 1 gl
TOTAL 8 apps 1 gl

JONES, Eric (W)
1975/76 2 apps 1 sub 1 gl (1 nps)
TOTAL 2 apps 1 sub 1 g1 (1 nps)

JONES, Gary (Sub)
1975/76 0 apps 0 gls (2 nps)
TOTAL 0 apps 0 gls (2 nps)

JONES, Glyn Alan (GK)
b. 29/03/1959 Newport, Monmouth, Wales
1982/83 9 apps 0 gls
TOTAL 9 apps 0 gls
Club Record: 1977-79 Bristol Rovers (9-0), Shrewsbury Town (0), Gloucester City, Yeovil Town, Newport YMCA, Bath City, 1983 Newport County (3-0), Albion Rovers (Newport).

JONES, H.W (IF)
1892/93 1 app 0 gls
TOTAL 1 app 0 gls

JONES, Harold (Harry) (GK)
1931/32 35 apps 0 gls
1932/33 2 apps 0 gls
TOTAL 37 apps 0 gls

JONES, John (M)
b. 1963
1979/80 3 apps 0 gls (2 nps)
1980/81 1 app 0 gls
TOTAL 4 apps 0 gls (2 nps)

JONES, Mark (GK)
1991/92 1 app 0 gls
TOTAL 1 app 0 gls

JONES, Mike (IF)
1975/76 2 apps 0 gls (1 nps)
TOTAL 2 apps 0 gls (1 nps)

JONES, Phil (D)
b. 1974 Gloucester
1992/93 6 apps 2 subs 0 gls (3 nps)
1993/94 0 apps 0 gls (1 nps)
TOTAL 6 apps 2 subs 0 gls (4 nps)

JONES, R (FB)
1921/22 2 apps 1 gl
1922/23 5 apps 0 gls
TOTAL 7 apps 1 gl

JONES, Raymond (Ray) (GK)
b. 1949 Reading, Berks.
1967/68 15 apps 0 gls
1968/69 52 apps 0 gls
1969/70 56 apps 0 gls
1970/71 18 apps 0 gls
TOTAL 141 apps 0 gls
Club Record: Evesham United, Gloucester City, Cheltenham Town +.

JONES, Ronald (WH)
1950/51 4 apps 0 gls
TOTAL 4 apps 0 gls

JONES, Stuart Clive (GK)
b. 24/10/1977 Bristol, Avon
2008/09 1 app 0 gls
TOTAL 1 app 0 gls
Club Record: Weston-Super-Mare, 1997 Sheffield Wednesday (0), 1998 Crewe Alexandra (loan) (0), 1999-00 Torquay United (32-0), Gloucester City (loan), Hereford United, Chester City, Barry Town, Weston-Super-Mare, 2003 Brighton & Hove Albion (3-0), 2004 Doncaster Rovers (4-0), Weston-Super-Mare, Accrington Stanley, Gloucester City (loan) +.
Note: Played for Gloucester City 1990s.

JONES, T (W)
1926/27
Club Record: Highbeech, Gloucester City +.

JONES, Trevor (F)
b. 1948
1976/77 20 apps 7 gls
TOTAL 20 apps 7 gls
Club Record: Worcester City, Hereford United, Cheltenham Town, Cinderford Town, Malvern Town, Gloucester City +.

JONES, W (GK)
1903/04 2 apps 0 gls
TOTAL 2 apps 0 gls
Note: Played for Gloucester 1890/91, 1898/99.

JONES, W (Pepper) (W)
1933/34 43 apps 15 gls
1934/35 12 apps 4 gls
1935/36 16 apps 3 gls
1936/37 2 apps 0 gls
TOTAL 73 apps 22 gls
Club Record: Cinderford Town, Gloucester City, Cinderford Town +.

JORDAN, ? (FB) ++
1939/40 5 apps 0 gls
TOTAL 5 apps 0 gls
Club Record: Bristol University, Gloucester City +.

JORDAN, Roy Antony (W)
b. 17/04/1978 Plymouth, Devon
1999/00
Club Record: 1996 Hereford United (1-0), Newport County, Merthyr Tydfil, Worcester City, Gloucester City, Pegasus Juniors, Kington Town, Westfields +.

KALEWSKI, Miroslaw R (Mirek) (F)
b. 18/03/1956 Cirencester, Glos.
1984/85 43 apps 2 subs 7 gls
TOTAL 43 apps 2 subs 7 gls
Club Record: Worcester City, Ledbury Town, Bromsgrove Rovers, Gloucester City +.

KEAR, Richard (F)
b. 05/11/1983 Gloucester
2005/06 10 apps 3 subs 2 gls (1 nps)
TOTAL 10 apps 3 subs 2 gls (1 nps)
Club Record: Cheltenham Town, Weston-Super-Mare (loan), Chippenham Town (loan), Cirencester Town, Cinderford Town, Yate Town, Gloucester City, Cinderford Town, Swindon Supermarine, Almondsbury Town, Cinderford Town +.

KEELING, Darren (F)
1997/98 14 apps 3 gls
1998/99 7 apps 4 subs 2 gls
1999/00 3 apps 3 subs 0 gls
TOTAL 24 apps 7 subs 5 gls
Club Record: Bristol City (0), Exeter City (0), Weymouth, Gloucester City, Yeovil Town, Clevedon Town +.

KEEN, Roger (FB)
1972/73 3 apps 0 gls
TOTAL 3 apps 0 gls

KEEPING, Allan Sedgwick (FB)
b. Qu1 1886 Gloucester d. ?
1906/07 1 app 0 gls
TOTAL 1 app 0 gls

KELLY, Jerry (D)
1979/80 10 apps 0 gls
TOTAL 10 apps 0 gls
Club Record: Swindon Town (0), Gloucester City, Fairford Town +.

KEMP, Gary John (D)
b. 29/05/1969 Thornbury, Glos.
1990/91 14 apps 0 gls
1991/92 34 apps 2 gls (1 nps)
1992/93 46 apps 2 gls
1993/94 40 apps 0 gls
1994/95 39 apps 1 sub 2 gls (3 nps)
1995/96 42 apps 1 sub 3 gls
1996/97 53 apps 1 sub 7 gls
1997/98 42 apps 4 gls (2 nps)
1998/99 46 apps 8 gls
1999/00 9 apps 0 gls
TOTAL 365 apps 3 subs 28 gls (6 nps)
Club Record: Olveston, Almondsbury Picksons, Gloucester City, Cirencester Town (loan), Newport County, Bath City, Mangotsfield United, Brislington.
Note: Club Captain 1995-99. Supporter's Player of the Season 1995/96, 1998/99.

KEMP, Robbie (GK)
b. 08/10/1968
1992/93 2 apps 0 gls
1993/94 2 apps 0 gls
TOTAL 4 apps 0 gls
Club Record: Swindon Town (0), Moreton Town, Worcester City, Gloucester City, Salisbury City +.
Note: Played for Gloucester City 1994/95.

KENT, Albert Edward (IF)
b. Qu4 1882 Gloucester d. ?
1906/07 4 apps 2 gls
1907/08 17 apps 5 gls
1908/09 15 apps 3 gls
1909/10 21 apps 5 gls
TOTAL 57 apps 15 gls

KENT, Sydney Joseph Frederick (GK)
b. Qu3 1870 Southsea, Hants. d. ?
1893/94 16 apps 0 gls
TOTAL 16 apps 0 gls
Club Record: Weymouth, Gloucester +.

KERNICK, Dudley Henry John (IF) ++
b. 29/08/1921 Camelford, Cornwall
1942/43
Club Record: Tintagel, Gloucester City, 1946-47 Torquay United (38-7), 1948 Northampton Town (0), 1948 Birmingham City (0), Kettering Town, Brierley Hill Alliance, Nuneaton Borough, Evesham United..

KERSLAKE, A (IF)
1928/29 6 apps 0 gls
1930/31 2 apps 0 gls
TOTAL 8 apps 0 gls

KETTLEBOROUGH, Albert (IF)
b. 1940
1959/60 3 apps 0 gls
TOTAL 3 apps 0 gls
Club Record: Plymouth Argyle (0), Gloucester City +.

KEVEREN, Andrew Mark (Andy) (F)
b. 26/04/1978 Limavady, Northern Ireland
2008/09 2 apps 4 subs 2 gls (2 nps)
TOTAL 2 apps 4 subs 2 gls (2 nps)
Club Record: Tuffley Rovers, Harrow Hill, Witney Town, Bishop's Cleeve, Gairloch/Altbea United, Golspie Sutherland, Gloucester City, Harrow Hill (loan), Bishop's Cleeve +.

KEYLOCK, Brian (WH)
b. 1940
1961/62 43 apps 0 gls
1962/63 31 apps 0 gls
TOTAL 74 apps 0 gls
Club Record: Cheltenham Town, Gloucester City, Evesham United +.

KEYS, George Eric H (CH)
b. Qu3 1878 Gloucester d. ?
1899/00 20 apps 2 gls
1900/01 2 apps 0 gls
1903/04 2 apps 0 gls
TOTAL 24 apps 2 gls
Club Record: Gloucester Teachers, Gloucester City +.

KHAN, Shabir (D)
b. 10/11/1985 Worcester, Worcs.
2006/07 2 apps 0 gls (1 nps)
TOTAL 2 apps 0 gls (1 nps)
Club Record: Worcester City, Gloucester City (loan) +.

KIBBLE, Donald Leslie (IF)
b. Qu1 1906 Pontypridd, Glamorgan, Wales d. ?
1926/27 9 apps 1 gl
1927/28 19 apps 4 gls
TOTAL 28 apps 5 gls
Club Record: Pope's Hill, Gloucester City, Pope's Hill +.
Note: Brother of Herbert Kibble.

KIBBLE, Herbert Frederick (HB)
b. 03/02/1904 Westbury-on-Severn, Glos. d. Qu3 1984 Gloucester
1926/27 11 apps 1 gl
1927/28 12 apps 0 gls
1928/29 1 app 0 gls
TOTAL 24 apps 1 gl
Club Record: Pope's Hill, Gloucester City, Pope's Hill, Cinderford Town +.
Note: Brother of Donald Kibble.

KIBBLE, J (IF) ++
1940/41

KILGOUR, Michael (Mike/Killer) (D)
b. 1965
1994/95 37 apps 1 sub 6 gls (2 nps)
1995/96 0 apps 1 sub 0 gls (5 nps)
TOTAL 37 apps 2 subs 6 gls (7 nps)
Club Record: Trowbridge Town, Salisbury City, Stroud, Trowbridge Town, Bath City, Gloucester City, Dorchester Town, Newport AFC, Forest Green Rovers, Weston-Super-Mare, Mangotsfield United.

KILLAN, Patrick (Paddy) (W)
b. 1940 Belfast, Northern Ireland
1961/62 3 apps 1 gl
TOTAL 3 apps 1 gl
Club Record: RAF Innsworth, Gloucester City +.

KILMINSTER, E (CH)
b. 1917
1934/35 18 apps 1 gl
TOTAL 18 apps 1 gl

KIMBERLEY, Alan (FB)
b. Birmingham, Warks.
1957/58 30 apps 2 gls
1958/59 46 apps 2 gls
1959/60 26 apps 3 gls
TOTAL 102 apps 7 gls
Club Record: West Bromwich Albion (0), Gloucester City +.

KING, ? (WH) ++
1942/43 10 apps 0 gls
TOTAL 10 apps 0 gls
Club Record: Colchester United, Gloucester City +.

KING, A.S (W)
1889/90
1891/92

KING, Harold (GK)
b. 1927 d. ?
1948/49 11 apps 0 gls
1949/50 19 apps 0 gls
1950/51 47 apps 0 gls
1951/52 7 apps 0 gls
TOTAL 84 apps 0 gls
Club Record: Brimscombe, Leicester City (trial) (0), Gloucester City, Stonehouse +.

KING, J (W)
1890/91
1891/92

KING, John R (Johnny) (M)
b. 05/05/1958 Gloucester
1975/76 2 apps 1 sub 0 gls (1 nps)
TOTAL 2 apps 1 sub 0 gls (1 nps)
Club Record: Churchdown Panthers, Gloucester City, Cheltenham Town, Wilton Rovers, Frampton Athletic +.

KING, Thomas Edward (Tom) (GK)
b. 16/12/1980 Stroud, Glos.
1999/00 10 apps 0 gls
TOTAL 10 apps 0 gls
Club Record: Forest Green Rovers, Gloucester City, Shortwood United, Highworth Town, Swindon Supermarine, Cirencester Town +.

KIRBY, A.Thomas (Tom) (W)
b. 1916 d. 2007
1933/34 1 app 0 gls
1937/38 6 apps 1 gl
TOTAL 7 app 1 gl
Club Record: Gloucester City Albion, Gloucester City +.

KIRK, J (WH) ++
1940/41

KIRKUP, Andy (M)
1996/97 18 apps 7 subs 1 gl (8 nps)
TOTAL 18 apps 7 subs 1 gl (8 nps)
Club Record: Corby Town, Wellingborough Town, Rushden & Diamonds, Gloucester City, Rothwell Town +.
Note: Played for Gloucester City 1997/98.

KIRTON, J (IF)
1924/25 1 app 0 gls
1925/26 2 apps 2 gls
TOTAL 3 apps 2 gls

KNIGHT, ? (FB)
1946/47

KNIGHT, Keith (M)
b. 16/02/1969 Cheltenham, Glos.
1990/91 10 apps 1 sub 1 gl
1994/95 48 apps 2 subs 12 gls
1995/96 22 apps 2 subs 8 gls (4 nps)
1996/97 1 app 3 subs 0 gls
2003/04 30 apps 14 subs 2 gls
2004/05 17 apps 11 subs 4 gls (14 nps)
2005/06 8 apps 3 subs 0 gls (12 nps)
TOTAL 136 apps 36 subs 27 gls (30 nps)
Club Record: 1988-90 Reading (43-8), Gloucester City, Cheltenham Town (loan), BV Veendam (Holland), Trowbridge Town, Yeovil Town (loan), Gloucester City, Cheltenham Town (loan), Halesowen Town, Cheltenham Town, Worcester City, Witney Town, Clevedon Town, Swindon Supermarine, Cirencester Town, Gloucester City, Cinderford Town, Swindon Supermarine, Bishop's Cleeve, Cirencester Town +.

KNOTT, Alan (GK)
b. Qu1 1973 Cam, Glos.
1992/93 4 apps 0 gls
TOTAL 4 apps 0 gls
Club Record: Portsmouth (0), Birmingham City (loan) (0), West Bromwich Albion (loan) (0), Stoke City (loan) (0), Forest Green Rovers, Gloucester City, Carterton Town, Tuffley Rovers, Portsmouth (loan) (0), Slimbridge, Dursley Town +.

KNOX, Jimmy (W)
b. 1931
1957/58 29 apps 9 gls
TOTAL 29 apps 9 gls
Club Record: Greenock Morton (0), Gourock Juniors, Cheltenham Town, Gloucester City, Cinderford Town +.

KOTWICA, Jason Jozef (Sub)
b. Qu3 1977 Gloucester
1993/94

LACEY, Brian (FB)
b. Qu2 1938 Glossop, Lancs.
1958/59 2 apps 0 gls
1959/60 10 apps 0 gls
1960/61 29 apps 0 gls
1961/62 1 app 0 gls
TOTAL 42 apps 0 gls
Note: Brother of John Lacey.

LACEY, John (WH)
b. Qu1 1941 Blackburn, Lancs.
1960/61 1 app 0 gls
TOTAL 1 app 0 gls
Note: Brother of Brian Lacey.

LAMB, A (FB)
1903/04 1 app 0 gls
TOTAL 1 app 0 gls

LAMBE, W.H (FB)
1900/01 2 apps 0 gls
TOTAL 2 apps 0 gls

LAMBERT, Ben (GK)
1997/98 10 apps 0 gls
1998/99 2 apps 0 gls
TOTAL 12 apps 0 gls
Club Record: Viney Saint Swithins, Gloucester City +.

LANDELLS, James Marshall (IF) ++
b. 26/02/1914 Rothbury, Northumberland d. Qu2 2004 Northumberland Central
1939/40 19 apps 5 gls
TOTAL 19 apps 5 gls
Note: Brother of William Landells. Played for Gloucester City 1940/41.

LANDELLS, William (IF) ++
b. 28/10/1917 Rothbury, Northumberland d. Qu2 1985 Northumberland Central
1939/40 2 apps 0 gls
TOTAL 2 apps 0 gls
Note: Brother of James Landells.

LANDER, Martin T (D)
b. Qu3 1952 Kidderminster, Worcs.
1984/85 16 apps 0 gls
1985/86 49 apps 2 gls
1986/87 44 apps 1 sub 1 gl
1987/88 44 apps 2 subs 1 gl (1 nps)
1988/89 55 apps 3 gls
1989/90 42 apps 4 subs 0 gls (4 nps)
1990/91 7 apps 3 subs 0 gls (3 nps)
TOTAL 257 apps 10 subs 7 gls (8 nps)
Club Record: Aston Villa (0), Wolverhampton Wanderers (0), Kidderminster Harriers, Stourbridge, Gloucester City +.
Note: Club Player of the Year 1985/86.

LANE, Brian Hill (IF)
b. 1882 Gloucester d. ?
1898/99 6 apps 0 gls
TOTAL 6 apps 0 gls
Note: Brother of Lionel Lane and Herbert Lane.

LANE, Herbert (WH)
b. 1880 Gloucester d. ?
1898/99 10 apps 0 gls
1899/00 3 apps 1 gl
1900/01 2 apps 0 gls
TOTAL 15 apps 1 gl
Note: Brother of Lionel Lane and Brian Lane. Some sources have his name as Hubert.

LANE, John Baylis (HB)
b. Qu2 1891 Gloucester d. ?
1913/14 5 apps 0 gls
TOTAL 5 apps 0 gls

LANE, Lionel Alfred (W)
b. Qu2 1878 Gloucester d. ?
1897/98 2 apps 1 gl
1898/99 14 apps 5 gls
TOTAL 16 apps 6 gls
Club Record: Gloucester, Gloucester City Albions +.
Note: Club Secretary 1898-1899. Brother of Herbert Lane and Brian Lane. Some sources have his name as Alfred Lionel Lane.

LANE, S (M)
1987/88

LANGFORD, Melvyn J (F)
b. 09/12/1961 Bromsgrove, Worcs.
1984/85 38 apps 6 subs 10 gls (2 nps)
TOTAL 38 apps 6 subs 10 gls (2 nps)
Club Record: Coventry City (0), Bromsgrove Rovers, Worcester City, Evesham United, Gloucester City +.

LANGLEY, H.William (Bill) (FB/GK)
b. 1910 d. ?
1935/36 39 apps 0 gls
1936/37 36 apps 0 gls
1937/38 39 apps 0 gls
1938/39 5 apps 0 gls
1939/40 1 app 0 gls
TOTAL 120 apps 0 gls
Club Record: Watford, Bristol Rovers (0), Boston, Glastonbury, London Paper Mills, Gloucester City +.

LANGLEY, Mark (F)
1974/75 1 app 0 gls (6 nps)
TOTAL 1 app 0 gls (6 nps)

LANGLEY-SMITH, W (FB)
1899/00 2 apps 0 gls
TOTAL 2 apps 0 gls

LARDNER, E (WH) ++
1940/41
1941/42

LAUDER, ? (IF)
1959/60 6 apps 0 gls
TOTAL 6 apps 0 gls

LAURENCE, P (IF)
1927/28

LAWRENCE, Michael (W)
1954/55 9 apps 1 gl
TOTAL 9 apps 1 gl
Club Record: Ruardean, Gloucester City +.

LAWRENCE, Raymond Stanley (Ray) (CH) ++
b. 18/09/1911 Gainsborough, Lincs. d. 1987
1939/40 3 apps 0 gls
TOTAL 3 apps 0 gls
Club Record: Gainsborough Trinity, 1933-35 Hull City (34-1), 1936-38 Newport County (38-0), Gloucester City, Haarlem (Holland).

LAWSON, ? (IF) ++
1942/43 1 app 1 gl
TOTAL 1 app 1 gl

LAWSON, George (Jack) (FB)
b. 1923 Edinburgh, Scotland
1948/49 21 apps 0 gls
1949/50 51 apps 0 gls
1950/51 51 apps 0 gls
1951/52 48 apps 1 gl
TOTAL 171 apps 1 gl
Club Record: Polkemmet, 1946 Raith Rovers (11-2), Worcester City, Gloucester City, Hastings United +.

LAYCOCK, John (IF)
b. 1948
1971/72 23 apps 2 gls
TOTAL 23 apps 2 gls
Club Record: Bristol Rovers (0), Bath City, Gloucester City +.

LAYTON, John Henry (Johnny) (M)
b. 29/06/1951 Hereford, Herefordshire
1970/71 9 apps 0 gls
1971/72 13 apps 0 gls (2 nps)
1972/73 16 apps 0 gls
1980/81 29 apps 0 gls
1981/82 13 apps 1 gl
1982/83 22 apps 1 sub 0 gls
TOTAL 102 apps 1 sub 1 gl (2 nps)
Club Record: Hereford United, Gloucester City, Kidderminster Harriers, 1974-80 Hereford United (200-13), Gloucester City, Trowbridge Town, 1983 Newport County (1-0), 1984 Hereford United (0), Worcester City.
Note: Club Captain 1980-81. Club Manager Mar 1982- Oct 1982.

LEA, ? (HB)
1928/29

LEACH, Andy (Sub)
1983/84

LEACH, Harold (HB)
b. 1916 Churchdown, Gloucester
1934/35 8 apps 0 gls
1935/36 37 apps 4 gls
1936/37 11 apps 0 gls
1937/38 33 apps 0 gls
1938/39 38 apps 0 gls
1939/40 17 apps 0 gls
1941/42 1 app 0 gls
TOTAL 145 apps 4 gls
Club Record: Staverton, Parton Rovers, Gloucester City, Rotol AFC +.
Note: Played for Gloucester City 1940/41.

LEACH, Joe (WH)
b. 1929
1952/53 1 app 0 gls
TOTAL 1 app 0 gls
Note: Father of Wayne Leach.

LEACH, Wayne (D)
b. 1965
1980/81 1 app 0 gls (1 nps)
1981/82 2 apps 0 gls
TOTAL 3 apps 0 gls (1 nps)
Club Record: Cheltenham Town, Gloucester City +.
Note: Son of Joe Leach.

LEDBURY, Paul J (D)
b. 10/11/1961 Hereford, Herefordshire
1982/83 6 apps0 gls (3 nps)
TOTAL 6 apps 0 gls (3 nps)
Club Record: Ledbury Town, Gloucester City, Ledbury Town, Pegasus Juniors, Worcester City, Ledbury Town +.

LEE, E (HB)
1929/30 12 apps 0 gls
TOTAL 12 apps 0 gls

LEE, James William (CH)
b. Qu3 1897 Gloucester d. ?
1919/20

LEE, Justin (M)
b. 1975
1993/94 1 app 1 gl
TOTAL 1 app 1 gl
Club Record: Gloucester City, Thame United, Oxford City, Banbury United, Abingdon Town +.

LEITCH, Andrew Buchanan (Andy) (F)
b. 27/03/1950 Exeter, Devon
1983/84 5 apps 1 sub 0 gls
TOTAL 5 apps 1 sub 0 gls
Club Record: Bath City, Cadbury Heath, Paulton Rovers, 1975 Swansea City (17-6), Minehead, Weymouth, Bath City, Yeovil Town, Forest Green Rovers, Old Georgians, Gloucester City, Almondsbury Greenway, Dorchester Town.

LEONARD, P.S (GK)
1919/20

LESTER, Steve (D)
b. 1965
1994/95 41 apps 4 subs 1 gl (5 nps)
1995/96 19 apps 6 subs 0 gls (12 nps)
TOTAL 60 apps 10 subs 1 gl (17 nps)
Club Record: Long Ashton, Frome Town, Backwell United, Trowbridge Town, Mangotsfield United, Gloucester City, Clevedon Town, Nailsea Town +.

LEVEY, ? (CF) ++
1942/43 1 app 1 gl
TOTAL 1 app 1 gl
Club Record: Walthamstow Avenue, Gloucester City +.

LEWIS, ? (IF)
1903/04 1 app 1 gl
TOTAL 1 app 1 gl

LEWIS, David Dennis (Dave) (F)
b. 08/08/1951 Cheltenham, Glos.
1980/81 58 apps 35 gls
1981/82 43 apps 3 subs 26 gls (10 nps)
TOTAL 101 apps 3 subs 61 gls (10 nps)
Club Record: Cheltenham YMCA, Saint Marks, Cheltenham Town, Gloucester City, Cheltenham Town, Saint Marks, Bishop's Cleeve.

LEWIS, Keith (M)
1979/80 1 app 0 gls
TOTAL 1 app 0 gls

LEWIS, Lance Warren (F)
b. 23/10/1986 Gloucester
2005/06 2 apps 8 subs 0 gls
TOTAL 2 apps 8 subs 0 gls
Club Record: Swindon Town (0), Swindon Supermarine (loan), Gloucester City, Swindon Supermarine, Cirencester Town +.

LEWIS, Martin Barry (W)
b. Qu3 1872 Gloucester d. 27/02/1920 Winnipeg, Canada
1890/91
Note: Died of injuries sustained in WW1. Buried at Brookside Cemetery, Winnipeg, Canada.

LEWIS, Micky (W)
b. 26/08/1950
1972/73 4 apps 0 gls
1973/74 39 apps 1 sub 2 gls (1 nps)
1974/75 42 apps 1 sub 0 gls (7 nps)
TOTAL 85 apps 2 subs 2 gls (8 nps)
Club Record: Doncaster Rovers (0), Hereford United (0), Worcester City, Tamworth, Gloucester City +.

LEWIS, Rod (GK)
1978/79 1 app 0 gls
TOTAL 1 app 0 gls

LEWIS, W. H (CF)
1928/29 2 apps 1 gl
TOTAL 2 apps 1 gl
Club Record: Broadwell Amateurs, Gloucester City +.

LIBURO, Lincoln (F)
b. Jamaica
1986/87
Club Record: Coventry Sporting, Gloucester City +.

LIVINGSTONE, Ian (W)
b. 1940 Rutherglen, Glasgow, Scotland
1964/65 45 apps 6 gls
1965/66 17 apps 3 gls
TOTAL 62 apps 9 gls
Club Record: Heart of Midlothian (0), 1960 Berwick Rangers (22-1), 1961 Albion Rovers (31-5), Poole Town, Gloucester City, Melbourne Slavia (Australia) +.

LLEWELLYN, W (IF)
1899/00 1 app 1 gl
TOTAL 1 app 1 gl

LLOYD, Alan Christopher (IF)
b. 20/06/1938 Mumbles, Swansea, Wales
1957/58 3 apps 1 gl
TOTAL 3 apps 1 gl
Club Record: Llanelly, Grantham, Gloucester City, The Army, Bletchley Town, Clydach, Haverfordwest County, Milford United, South Wales Police.
Note: Awarded MBE in 2003 for services to life saving and to young people, Swansea.

LLOYD, J (Sub)
1983/84 0 apps 0 gls (1 nps)
TOTAL 0 apps 0 gls (1 nps)

LOBBAN, Brian (HB)
b. 1948
1972/73 12 apps 0 gls
1973/74 36 apps 3 gls (1 nps)
TOTAL 48 apps 3 gls (1 nps)
Club Record: Nuneaton Borough, Worcester City, Gloucester City +.

LOCKE, Paul (F)
b. 1963
1981/82 1 app 0 gls
TOTAL 1 app 0 gls

LONG, Neil (D)
2000/01
Club Record: Gloucester City (trial), Gloucester United +.

LONG, W (Nobby) (W)
1898/99 5 apps 0 gls
1899/00 5 apps 3 gls
TOTAL 10 apps 3 gls

LOOMES, Robin (Bob) (GK)
1971/72
Club Record: Frampton United, Gloucester City (loan) +.

LOSS, Colin Paul (M)
b. 15/08/1973 Brentwood, Essex
1997/98 2 apps 0 gls
TOTAL 2 apps 0 gls
Club Record: 1990 Norwich City (0), 1991 Derby County (0), Plymouth Argyle (0), Derry City, Gresley Rovers, 1994 Bristol City (5-0), Bath City (loan), Merthyr Tydfil (loan), Gloucester City, Barry Town, Carmarthen Town, Ebbw Vale, Merthyr Tydfil, Haverfordwest County.

LOUCH, L.A (IF)
b. 1910 d. ?
1933/34 9 apps 4 gls
1934/35 2 apps 0 gls
TOTAL 11 apps 4 gls
Club Record: Camberley, York Town, Gloucester City +.

LOWE, Derek (HB)
b. 1924
1949/50 43 apps 1 gl
1950/51 1 app 0 gls
TOTAL 44 apps 1 gl
Club Record: Hereford United, Gloucester City +.

LOWE, Gary Walter (M)
b. 25/09/1959 Manchester, Lancs.
1982/83 8 apps 1 gl (2 nps)
TOTAL 8 apps 1 gl (2 nps)
Club Record: 1976 Crystal Palace (0), 1979 Manchester City (0), 1980 Hereford United (9-0), Caroline Hill (Hong Kong), Gloucester City +.

LUCAS, Oliver James (IF)
b. Qu3 1887 Gloucester d. 28/04/1917 Etaples, France
1907/08 14 apps 5 gls
TOTAL 14 apps 5 gls
Note: Killed in action WW1.

LUCKMAN, M.R (W)
1896/97

LUKER, Frank (CH)
b. Qu2 1877 Gloucester d. ?
1897/98

MACAULEY, Robert (Bob) (D)
1984/85 12 apps 1 gl
1985/86 44 apps 1 sub 1 gl (1 nps)
TOTAL 56 apps 1 sub 2 gls (1 nps)
Club Record: Stourbridge, Kidderminster Harriers, Bridgnorth Town, Gloucester City +.

MACDONALD, Leslie (Les) (FB)
b. 02/04/1934 Newcastle-upon-Tyne, Northumberland
1967/68 44 apps 0 gls (1 nps)
TOTAL 44 apps 0 gls (1 nps)
Club Record: 1955 Portsmouth (0), 1957-65 Exeter City (294-0), Weymouth, Gloucester City, Waterlooville.

MACE, A (W)
1927/28 1 app 0 gls
TOTAL 1 app 0 gls
Club Record: Southgate, Tewkesbury Town, Gloucester City +.

MACFARLANE, Rev. A.B (FB)
1889/90 1 app 0 gls
TOTAL 1 app 0 gls
Note: Played for Gloucester 1890/91, 1891/92.

MACFARLANE, John Murray (FB)
b. 1895 d. 08/10/1915 Loos, France
1913/14 7 apps 0 gls
TOTAL 7 apps 0 gls
Note: Killed in action WW1.

MACKAY, ? (CH)
1895/96 1 app 0 gls
TOTAL 1 app 0 gls

MADDOCKS, ? (WH) ++
1942/43

MADGE, Mark (D)
1990/91 9 apps 0 gls
1991/92 12 apps 6 subs 0 gls (2 nps)
TOTAL 21 apps 6 subs 0 gls (2 nps)
Club Record: Bristol City (0), Gloucester City, Mangotsfield United, Bath City, Clevedon Town +.

MAIN, Ian Roy (GK)
b. 31/10/1959 Weston-Super-Mare, Somerset d. Qu3 1998 Exeter, Devon
1979/80 29 app 0 gls
TOTAL 29 apps 0 gls
Club Record: Bristol City (0), 1976 Stoke City (0), Gloucester City, 1978-81 Exeter City (78-0), Port Vale (trial) (0).

MAINWARING, Andrew John (Andy) (F)
b. 11/09/1973 Hereford, Herefordshire
1997/98 25 apps 18 gls
1998/99 23 apps 7 subs 8 gls (2 nps)
TOTAL 48 apps 7 subs 26 gls (2 nps)
Club Records: Everton (0), Inter Cardiff, Cwmbran Town, Bromsgrove Rovers, Gloucester City, Newport County, Clevedon Town, Merthyr Tydfil, Cwmbran Town, Merthyr Tydfil, Clevedon Town, Port Talbot, Cwmbran Town +.

MAISEY, J (W)
1935/36 1 app 0 gls
TOTAL 1 app 0 gls

MALLENDER, Kenneth (Ken) (CD)
b. 10/12/1943 Thrybergh, Nr. Rotherham, Yorks.
1978/79 3 apps 0 gls
TOTAL 3 apps 0 gls
Club Record: 1961-68 Sheffield United (143-2), 1968-70 Norwich City (46-1), 1972-73 Hereford United (72-1), Telford United, Gloucester City +.

MALPAS, Michael (Mike) (D)
b. 1961 Bristol
1987/88 23 apps 2 gls
1988/89 28 apps 5 gls (2 nps)
1990/91 6 apps 2 subs 0 gls (1 nps)
TOTAL 57 apps 2 subs 7 gls (3 nps)
Club Record: Bristol City (0) Minehead, Bristol Rovers (0), Bath City, Frome Town, Forest Green Rovers, Gloucester City +.
Note: Played for Gloucester City 1991/92.

MALPASS, A.S (IF)
1922/23 3 apps 0 gls
1923/24 2 apps 0 gls
TOTAL 5 apps 0 gls

MALPASS, J.L (W)
1923/24 7 apps 0 gls
1924/25 8 apps 0 gls
TOTAL 15 apps 0 gls

MALPASS, M (HB)
1925/26 4 apps 1 gl
TOTAL 4 apps 1 gl

MALPASS, Otho Roy (IF)
b. 07/07/1909 King's Stanley, Glos. d. Qu2 2003 Forest of Dean, Glos.
1933/34 4 apps 2 gls
TOTAL 4 apps 2 gls

MANDER, Norman Victor (FB)
b. 25/08/1906 Alcester, Warks. d. Qu2 1973 Gloucester
1929/30 28 apps 0 gls
1930/31 29 apps 0 gls
1931/32 1 app 0 gls
TOTAL 58 apps 0 gls
Club Record: Naunton Park, Gloucester City, Cheltenham Town +.

MANLEY, Darren (F)
1990/91
Club Record: Gloucester City, Ilminster Town +.

MANN, Ernest Walter (IF)
b.17/06/1912 Ashton-under-Lyne, Lancs. d. 9/2000 Gloucester
1931/32 1 app 0 gls
1932/33 1 app 0 gls
1933/34 1 app 2 gls
TOTAL 3 apps 2 gls

MANN, W (WH)
1932/33 1 app 0 gls
TOTAL 1 app 0 gls

MANNERS, ? (GK)
1936/37 3 apps 0 gls
TOTAL 3 apps 0 gls

MANSELL, Richard James (D)
b. 19/02/1986 Gloucester
2005/06 23 apps 9 subs 1 gl (5 nps)
TOTAL 23 apps 9 subs 1 gl (5 nps)
Club Record: Luton Town (0), Gloucester City, Bishop's Cleeve (loan), Bishop's Cleeve +.

MANSFIELD, ? (FB)
1894/95 1 app 0 gls
TOTAL 1 app 0 gls

MANSFIELD, C (W)
1931/32 1 app 0 gls
TOTAL 1 app 0 gls

MARDENBOROUGH, Stephen Alexander (Steve) (W)
b. 11/09/1964 Selly Oak, Warks.
1995/96 10 apps 1 gl (1 nps)
1996/97 5 apps 0 gls
TOTAL 15 apps 1 gl (1 nps)
Club Record: 1982 Coventry City (0), 1983 Wolverhampton Wanderers (9-1), 1983 Cambridge United (loan) (6-0), 1984 Swansea City (36-7), 1985-86 Newport County (64-11), 1986-87 Cardiff City (32-1), 1988 Hereford United (27-0), IFK Ostersund (Sweden), Cheltenham Town, 1990-92 Darlington (106-18), 1993 Lincoln City (21-2), 1994 Scarborough (1-0), Stafford Rangers, 1995 Colchester United (12-2), 1995 Swansea City (1-0), Merthyr Tydfil, Aberystwyth Town, Gloucester City.

MARLER, Leslie A (IF)
1926/27 13 apps 9 gls
1927/28 15 apps 3 gls
1928/29 19 apps 6 gls
1929/30 27 apps 10 gls
1930/31 23 apps 5 gls
1931/32 13 apps 4 gls
TOTAL 110 apps 37 gls
Club Record: Saltley College, Gloucester City, Cheltenham Town +.

MARSHALL, C (CH)
1919/20

MARSHALL, Gary Paul (M)
b. 09/08/1969 Stroud, Glos.
2000/01 38 apps 1 sub 6 gls (1 nps)
2001/02 33 apps 5 gls (3 nps)
2002/03 8 apps 19 subs 0 gls (15 nps)
TOTAL 79 apps 20 subs 11 gls (19 nps)
Club Record: Coventry City (0), Swindon Town (0), Shortwood United,
Cambridge United, Boston United (loan), Cheltenham Town, Forest Green
Rovers, Shortwood United, Forest Green Rovers, Evesham United (loan),
Cinderford Town, Yate Town, Melksham Town, Uplands United,
Cirencester Town, Newport County, Cirencester Town, Gloucester City,
Slimbridge +.

MARSHALL, Lee Andrew (M)
b. 20/05/1988 Bristol, Avon
2008/09 43 apps 7 subs 2 gls (2 nps)
TOTAL 43 apps 7 subs 2 gls (2 nps)
Club Record: Bristol Manor Farm, Paulton Rovers, Gloucester City +.
Note: Player's Player of the Season 2008/09.

MARTIN, Joe (Joey) (W)
b. 1925
1954/55 11 apps 0 gls
TOTAL 11 apps 0 gls
Club Record: 1946-51 Saint Mirren (100-3), Cheltenham Town, Gloucester
City +.

MARTYN, Stewart (GK)
b. 18/03/1962 Gloucester
1985/86 21 apps 0 gls
1986/87 26 apps 0 gls
1987/88 37 apps 0 gls
TOTAL 84 apps 0 gls
Club Record: Newent Town, Newport County, Cheltenham Town,
Gloucester City, Forest Green Rovers, Shortwood United +.

MASON, A.M (IF)
1893/94 2 apps 0 gls
TOTAL 2 apps 0 gls

MASON, W (IF)
1900/01 16 apps 9 gls
TOTAL 16 apps 9 gls

MASTERS, R (GK)
1923/24 1 app 0 gls
TOTAL 1 app 0 gls

MATCHWICK, Peter (F)
1974/75 2 apps 1 sub 0 gls
TOTAL 2 apps 1 sub 0 gls
Club Record: Wilton Rovers, Gloucester City, Cheltenham Town +.

MATTERS, ? (IF)
1927/28

MATTHEWS, A.A (WH)
1891/92 1 app 0 gls
TOTAL 1 app 0 gls

MATTHEWS, Lee Derek (GK)
b. 29/08/1988 Bristol, Avon
2006/07 1 app 0 gls (1 nps)
TOTAL 1 app 0 gls (1 nps)
Club Record: Bristol City (0), Burnley (0), Cambridge United, Forest
Green Rovers, Gloucester City, Swindon Supermarine, Yate Town +.

MATTHEWS, W.G (W)
1893/94 8 apps 2 gls
1894/95 2 apps 0 gls
TOTAL 10 apps 2 gls
Note: Played for Gloucester 1890/91, 1892/93.

MAY, E (IF)
1899/00 6 apps 3 gls
TOTAL 6 apps 3 gls

MAY, Harry (FB)
b. 15/10/1928 Glasgow, Scotland d. 2005
1957/58 31 apps 0 gls
TOTAL 31 apps 0 gls
Club Record: Thorniewood United, 1949 Cardiff City (1-0), 1950-51
Swindon Town (78-1), 1952-54 Barnsley (105-0), 1955 Southend United
(19-1), Gloucester City.
Note: Club Captain 1957-58.

MAY, R (CF)
1926/27 3 apps 2 gls
TOTAL 3 apps 2 gls

MAYO, T (IF)
1936/37 14 apps 6 gls
TOTAL 14 apps 6 gls
Note: Brother of WH Mayo.

MAYO, W.H (W)
1936/37 10 apps 2 gls
TOTAL 10 apps 2 gls
Note: Brother of T Mayo.

MAYSEY, Charles Henry (FB)
b. 25/03/1898 Gloucester d. Qu3 1988 Gloucester
1925/26 1 app 0 gls
1926/27 5 apps 0 gls
1927/28 2 apps 0 gls
TOTAL 8 apps 0 gls
Club Record: Gloucester Westgate, Gloucester YMCA +.

McADAM, ? (GK)
1949/50 1 app 0 gls
TOTAL 1 app 0 gls

McBEAN, Pete (F)
1986/87
Club Record: Coventry Sporting, Gloucester City +.

McCALL, John (WH)
1953/54 35 apps 0 gls
TOTAL 35 apps 0 gls
Club Record: Saint Johnstone (0), Gloucester City +.

McCLUSKEY, Darren Michael (D)
b. 03/09/1976 Swindon, Wilts.
1994/95 0 apps 0 gls (2 nps)
2001/02 31 apps 1 sub 4 gls
TOTAL 31 apps 1 sub 0 gls (2 nps)
Club Record: Gloucester City, Swindon Supermarine, Cinderford Town,
Witney Town, Yate Town, Salisbury City, Swindon Supermarine,
Shrivenham, Fairford Town +.
Note: Played for Gloucester City 1995/96.

McCLUSKEY, Ronald (Ronnie) (GK)
b. 03/11/1936 Johnstone, Scotland
1962/63 44 apps 0 gls
1963/64 37 apps 0 gls
1964/65 26 apps 0 gls
1965/66 47 apps 0 gls
TOTAL 154 apps 0 gls
Club Record: Rosyth Recreation, 1955-59 East Fife (48-0), 1960
Accrington Stanley (4-0), Gravesend & Northfleet, Gloucester City,
Cinderford Town, Biggleswade Town, Potton United, Kempston Rovers.

McCOOL, Robert (Bobby) (F)
b. 1948 Edinburgh, Scotland
1965/66 32 apps 12 gls
1966/67 18 apps 1 sub 3 gls (2 nps)
1967/68 39 apps 5 gls (6 nps)
1968/69 48 apps 8 gls (1 nps)
1969/70 54 apps 8 gls
1970/71 16 apps 2 subs 4 gls (2 nps)
1971/72 28 apps 7 gls (1 nps)
1972/73 23 apps 3 subs 6 gls (5 nps)
1973/74 23 apps 2 gls (5 nps)
1974/75 9 apps 2 gls (6 nps)
TOTAL 290 apps 6 subs 57 gls (28 nps)
Club Record: Ormiston Primrose, 1960 Third Lanark (3-0), Hamilton
Steelers (Canada), Cheltenham Town, Gloucester City.
Note: Club Player of the Season 1966/67, 1967/68.

McCOY, Dennis (D)
b. 1963 Wales
1983/84 33 apps 1 gl
1984/85 10 apps 2 subs 0 gls (5 nps)
TOTAL 43 apps 2 subs 1 gl (5 nps)
Club Record: Spencer Works (Newport), Gloucester City +.

McCREADIE, Martin (F)
1987/88 1 app 0 gls
TOTAL 1 app 0 gls

McDONOUGH, J (HB) ++
1939/40 18 apps 0 gls
1941/42 1 app 0 gls
TOTAL 19 apps 0 gls
Club Record: Northampton Town (0), Gloucester City +.
Note: Played for Gloucester City 1940/41.

McGRATH, John (D)
b. 20/12/1963
1996/97 26 apps 12 subs 1 gl (6 nps)
TOTAL 26 apps 12 subs 1 gl (6 nps)
Club Record: Shrewsbury Town (0), Worcester City, Kidderminster
Harriers, Worcester City, Gloucester City, Moor Green, Worcester City,
Pershore Town +.
Note: Played for Gloucester City 1998/99.

McINNES, ? (IF)
1968/69
Club Record: Cardiff City (0), Trowbridge Town, Gloucester City (trial) +.

McINTOSH, Alan (W)
b. 29/07/1939 Llandudno, Wales
1967/68
Club Record: Llandudno, 1961-63 Cardiff City (64-11), Gloucester City
(trial) +
International Record: Wales Amateur.

McINTOSH, John McGregor (Ian) (WH)
b. 14/09/1933 Glasgow, Scotland
1966/67 25 app 0 gls
1967/68 0 apps 0 gls (1 nps)
1968/69 47 apps 2 subs 1 gl (2 nps)
1969/70 11 apps 11 subs 0 gls (8 nps)
TOTAL 83 apps 13 subs 1 gl (11 nps)
Club Record: Campsie Black Watch, Petershill, 1953-57 Partick Thistle
(28-12), 1957-58 Bury (29-14), Weymouth, Oxford United, Hereford
United, Gloucester City.
Note: Club Manager Aug 1968- May 1970, Nov 1971 – Nov 1972.

McKEE, Francis Joseph (Frank) (HB)
b. 25/01/1923 Cowdenbeath, Scotland d. Qu3 1988 Slough, Berks.
1956/57 26 apps 1 gl
TOTAL 26 apps 1 gl
Club Record: Lochgelly Albert, Dundee United (0), 1948-50 Birmingham
City (22-0), 1952-54 Gillingham (53-0), Gloucester City.

McKEEVER, Mark Anthony (M)
b. 16/11/1978 Derry, Northern Ireland
2005/06 5 apps 1 gl
TOTAL 5 apps 1 gl
Club Record: Norwich City (0), 1996 Peterborough United (3-0), 1996-00
Sheffield Wednesday (5-0), 1998 Bristol Rovers (loan) (7-0), 1998 Reading
(loan) (7-2), 2000-02 Bristol Rovers (36-0), Kettering Town,
Weston-Super-Mare, Gloucester City (loan), Bath City, Mangotsfield
United (loan), Weston-Super-Mare +.
International Record: Eire U21 (4).

McKELLAR, Robert (Bobby) (W)
b. 1946
1966/67 1 app 0 gls (1 nps)
1967/68 1 app 0 gls
TOTAL 2 apps 0 gls (1 nps)

McKENZIE, John D (James) (IF)
b. 1914 Sudbrook, Wales
1934/35 48 apps 19 gls
TOTAL 48 apps 19 gls
Club Record: Chepstow Town, Gloucester City, Bristol Rovers (0),
Leicester City (0), 1935-38 Cardiff City (35-6), 1939 Notts County (1-1).

McKENZIE, Stainton L (D)
b. Qu3 1963 Birmingham, Warks.
1987/88 12 apps 1 sub 1 gl
TOTAL 12 apps 1 sub 1 gl
Club Record: Paget Rangers, Gloucester City, Bilston Town +.

McLAUGHLIN, James Charles (Jimmy) (W)
b. 10/12/1926 Stirling, Scotland d. 1981 Eastwood, Scotland
1954/55 24 apps 9 gls
TOTAL 24 apps 9 gls
Club Record: Torrance W, Falkirk (0), Alloa Athletic (0), 1953 Hartlepools
United (13-2), Gloucester City.

McLEAN, Ian (WH)
b. 1939
1960/61 20 apps 0 gls
TOTAL 20 apps 0 gls
Club Record: Arthurlie, Gloucester City +.

McLINTON, S (CF)
1892/93

McMILLAN, James (Jimmy/Mac) (FB)
b. 1931
1953/54 34 apps 0 gls
1954/55 4 apps 0 gls
1955/56 8 apps 0 gls
TOTAL 46 apps 0 gls
Club Record: Dundee United (0), Gloucester City +.

McMILLAN, William (Willy/Billy) (FB)
b. 1939 Scotland
1963/64 3 apps 0 gls
TOTAL 3 apps 0 gls
Club Record: Dalry Thistle, 1959 Dundee (6-0), 1962 Greenock Morton
(3-1), 1963 Raith Rovers (2-0), Gloucester City (trial), 1965-68 Montrose
(54-0) +.

McNEILL, Brian (D)
b. 01/04/1956 Newcastle-upon-Tyne, Northumberland
1982/83 13 apps 1 gl
TOTAL 13 apps 1 gl
Club Record: 1975-76 Bristol City (3-0), Los Angeles Aztecs (USA),
Portland Timbers (USA), 1978-80 Plymouth Argyle (47-0), 1981-82 Heart
of Midlothian (17-0), Gloucester City, San Diego Sockers (USA) +.

McNEILL, Thomas (Tommy) (IF)
b.1909 Lochgelly, Scotland d. 11/03/1943 At sea (SS Empire Lakeland)
North West of Rockall, Scotland
1937/38 41 apps 5 gls
TOTAL 41 apps 5 gls
Club Record: Lochgelly United, Cowdenbeath (0), 1927 Dunfermline
Athletic (4-0), King's Park, Liverpool (0), Rhyl, Yeovil & Petters United,
Gloucester City, Cheltenham Town
Note: Killed in action WW2.

McNIVEN, Donald (Don) (CF)
1957/58 8 apps 3 gls
1958/59 14 apps 4 gls
TOTAL 22 apps 7 gls
Club Record: Kilsyth Rangers, 1956 Cowdenbeath (4-1), Gloucester City +.

McPHERSON, Joseph Coulter (WH) ++
b. 1916 Livingston, Scotland
1941/42 8 apps 4 gls
TOTAL 8 apps 4 gls
Club Record: Armadale Thistle, 1935-38 Queen of the South (82-2), Aston
Villa (0), Gloucester City +.

McQUARRIE, Andrew (Andy) (IF)
b. 02/10/1939 Glasgow, Scotland
1968/69 34 apps 7 gls (1 nps)
1969/70 56 apps 3 gls
1972/73 46 apps 0 gls (1 nps)
TOTAL 136 apps 10 gls (2 nps)
Club Record: Largs Thistle, 1961-62 Albion Rovers (41-14), 1962-63
Chesterfield (38-12), 1964 Brighton & Hove Albion (2-1), Durban City
(South Africa), Cape Town City FC (South Africa), Gloucester City,
Worcester City, Gloucester City, Dowty Staverton, Longlevens +.
Note: Club Captain 1972-73.

McRAE, Duncan (F)
1987/88

McSHERRY, Ian George R (F)
b. Qu3 1981 Swindon, Wilts.
2006/07
Club Record: Swindon Town (0), Kidderminster Harriers, Witney Town,
Newbury Town, Highworth Town, Gloucester City (trial), Cirencester
United, Cirencester Town, Swindon Supermarine +.

MEACHAM, Jeff (F)
b. 06/02/1962 Bristol
1990/91 51 apps 2 subs 9 gls (1 nps)
1991/92 23 apps 1 sub 4 gls
1992/93 1 app 0 gls
TOTAL 75 apps 3 subs 13 gls (1 nps)
Club Record: Glastonbury, Almondsbury Greenway, Forest Green Rovers, Bath City, Trowbridge Town, 1986-87 Bristol Rovers (26-9), Weymouth, Bath City, Trowbridge Town, Gloucester City +.
Note: Player's Player of the Season 1990/91, Supporter's Player of the Season 1990/91.

MEADOWS, Donald Iver K (Don) (IF)
b. 14/02/1910 Gloucester d. 11/01/1984 Standish, Glos.
1931/32 1 app 0 gls
TOTAL 1 app 0 gls
Club Record: Bristol Tramways, Gloucester City +.
Note: Also played rugby for Gloucester RFC (Captain 1936).

MEADOWS, Joe (FB)
1972/73
Club Record: Gloucester YMCA, Gloucester City (trial) +.

MEADOWS, Jonathan (Johnny) (M)
b. 01/05/1975 Gloucester
2000/01 4 apps 7 subs 1 gl (4 nps)
TOTAL 4 apps 7 subs 1 gl (4 nps)
Club Record: Gloucester City, Gloucester United (loan), Tuffley Rovers, Slimbridge, Bishop's Cleeve +.

MEADOWS, W (W)
1936/37 2 apps 0 gls
1937/38 3 apps 0 gls
1938/39 2 apps 0 gls
TOTAL 7 apps 0 gls
Note: Played for Gloucester City 1940/41.

MEDCROFT, Geoffrey (Geoff) (CF)
b. Qu2 1947 Hucclecote, Gloucester
1964/65 14 apps 8 gls
1965/66 9 apps 4 gls
1967/68 11 apps 1 sub 4 gls
1976/77 10 apps 1 gl (3 nps)
1977/78 6 apps 0 gls
1981/82 1 app 0 gls
TOTAL 51 apps 1 sub 17 gls (3 nps)
Club Record: Gloucester City, Cinderford Town, Barry Town, Gloucester City, Sharpness, Forest Green Rovers +.
Note: Brother of Peter Medcroft and father of Scott Medcroft.

MEDCROFT, Peter D (IF)
b. Qu2 1941 Gloucester
1962/63 8 apps 1 gl
1963/64 3 apps 2 gls
TOTAL 11 apps 3 gls
Note: Brother of Geoff Medcroft and uncle of Scott Medcroft.

MEDCROFT, Scott (F)
1995/96 1 app 1 sub 0 gls (5 nps)
2000/01 7 apps 6 subs 1 gl (1 nps)
TOTAL 8 apps 7 subs 1 gl (6 nps)
Club Record: Gloucester City, Cinderford Town, Tuffley Rovers, Trowbridge Town +.
Note: Son of Geoff Medcroft and nephew of Peter Medcroft.

MEECHAM, Anthony (Tony) (M)
1980/81 1 app 0 gls
TOTAL 1 app 0 gls

MEEHAN, J (FB)
1931/32 1 app 0 gls
TOTAL 1 app 0 gls

MEEK, Donald (Don/Spot) (FB)
b. 1939
1956/57 23 apps 0 gls
1957/58 7 apps 0 gls
1960/61 19 apps 0 gls
TOTAL 49 apps 0 gls
Club Record: Harrow Hill, Gloucester City +.

MEEK, W (CH)
1931/32 17 apps 1 gl
1932/33 15 apps 0 gls
TOTAL 32 apps 1 gl

MEHEW, David Stephen (Boris) (M)
b. 29/10/1967 Camberley, Surrey
2006/07 0 apps 1 sub 0 gls (14 nps)
2007/08 0 apps 0 gls (8 nps)
2008/09 0 apps 1 sub 0 gls (16 nps)
TOTAL 0 apps 2 subs 0 gls (38 nps)
Club Record: Leeds United (0), 1985-92 Bristol Rovers (222-63), 1993 Exeter City (loan) (7-0), 1994 Walsall (13-0), Northampton Town (0), Yate Town, Bath City, Farnborough Town, Rushden & Diamonds, Forest Green Rovers, Bath City, Clevedon Town, Paulton Rovers, Brislington, Weston-Super-Mare, Bitton, Gloucester City.
Note: Team Manager Jun 2008 to date.

MEREDITH, Malcolm (W)
b. 1953
1971/72 9 apps 1 gl (4 nps)
TOTAL 9 apps 1 gl (4 nps)
Club Record: Arsenal (0), Gloucester City +.

MERRETT, ? (GK) ++
1939/40

MERRETT, J.H (HB)
1913/14 1 app 0 gls
TOTAL 1 app 0 gls

MERRICK, ? (IF)
1938/39 1 app 0 gls
TOTAL 1 app 0 gls

MERRICK, Geoffrey (Geoff) (D)
b. 29/04/1951 Bristol
1983/84 8 apps 0 gls
TOTAL 8 apps 0 gls
Club Record: 1967-81 Bristol City (367-10), Carolina Hills (Hong Kong), 1981 Bristol Rovers (0), Forest Green Rovers, Gloucester City, Bath City, Minehead +.

MERRIE, Alexander Breckinridge (Alex) (CF)
b. 20/05/1905 Saltcoats, Ayrshire, Scotland d. 1985 Saltcoats, Ayrshire, Scotland
1936/37 13 apps 5 gls
TOTAL 13 apps 5 gls
Club Record: Saltcoats Victoria, Nithsdale Wanderers, 1923 Saint Mirren (9-6), 1923 Saint Johnstone (loan), 1924 Alloa Athletic (loan), Stenhousemuir, 1925 Portsmouth (7-2), Nithsdale Wanderers, 1927-30 Aberdeen (32-26), 1930-33 Ayr United (81-48), 1933 Hull City (0), 1933 Clyde (5-2), 1934 Crewe Alexandra (32-11), 1935 Brechin City, unknown French Club, 1935 Aldershot (4-2), 1935 Ross County, 1935 Exeter City (4-2), 1935 Workington, Cork City (Eire), 1936 Leith Athletic, Gloucester City, Cheltenham Town, Evesham Town.

MERRY, W (W)
1899/00 2 apps 0 gls
TOTAL 2 apps 0 gls

MIDDLECOTE, ? (W)
b. 1916
1936/37 20 apps 2 gls
1937/38 2 apps 0 gls
TOTAL 22 apps 2 gls
Club Record: Cinderford Town, Gloucester City +.

MIDDLECOTE, R (CH)
1908/09

MIDWINTER, Thomas Henry (HB)
b. 27/04/1926 Cheltenham, Glos. d. Qu4 1990 Cheltenham, Glos.
1946/47 4 apps 1 gl
TOTAL 4 apps 1 gl
Club Record: Marines, Kassas XI (Ceylon), Gloucester City +.

MILBURN, Stanley (Stan) (FB)
b. 27/10/1926 Ashington, Northumberland
1954/55
Club Record: Ashington, 1946-51 Chesterfield (179-0), 1951-57 Leicester City (173-1), 1958-64 Rochdale (238-26).
International Record: England B.
Note: Played for Gloucester City as a guest in Frank Tredgett's benefit match. Brother of Jackie Milburn and uncle to Bobby and Jack Charlton.

PLAYERS' RECORDS

MILDENHALL, Stephen James (Steve) (GK)
b. 13/05/1978 Swindon, Wilts.
1996/97 8 app 0 gls
TOTAL 8 apps 0 gls
Club Record: 1995-00 Swindon Town (33-0), Gloucester City (loan), Worcester City (loan), Salisbury City (loan), 2001-04 Notts County (76-0), 2004 Oldham Athletic (6-0), 2005 Grimsby Town (46-0), 2006-07 Yeovil Town (75-0), 2008 Southend United (0) +.

MILES, Jeffrey M (Jeff) (GK)
b. 17/01/1949 Caldicot, Monmouth, Wales
1971/72 41 apps 0 gls
1972/73 48 apps 0 gls
1973/74 22 apps 0 gls
1974/75 30 apps 0 gls (1 nps)
1980/81 40 apps 0 gls
1981/82 2 apps 0 gls
TOTAL 183 apps 0 gls (1 nps)
Club Record: Chepstow Town, 1967-68 Newport County (4-0), Cheltenham Town, Hereford United (loan), Gloucester City, Cheltenham Town, Gloucester City +.
Note: Club Player of the Season 1971/72, 1972/73. Cousin of Ron and Mick Coltman.

MILLAR, James (Jim/Dusty) (CF)
b. 21/12/1927 Falkirk, Scotland d. 17/04/2002 Gloucester
1953/54 44 apps 16 gls
1954/55 10 apps 8 gls
1955/56 9 apps 4 gls
TOTAL 63 apps 28 gls
Club Record: East Stirlingshire (0), Arbroath (0), Sligo Rovers (Eire), Gloucester City, Worcester City, Abergavenny Thursdays, Deal Town, Crewe Alexandra (0).

MILLER, Jon (D/M)
b. 25/03/1980 Street, Somerset
2005/06 15 apps 2 gls
2006/07 14 apps 4 subs 0 gls (2 nps)
TOTAL 29 apps 4 subs 2 gls (2 nps)
Club Record: Yeovil Town, Street, Weston-Super-Mare, Street, Gloucester City, Street (loan) +.

MILLER, Kristian Alexander (Kris) (M)
b. Qu3 1990 Bristol, Avon
2008/09
Club Record: Bristol Rovers (0), Gloucester City (trial), Brislington +.

MILLER, William V (Bill) (CH)
b. Qu1 1920 Sculcoates, Hull, Yorks. d. ?
1946/47 36 apps 7 gls
1947/48 19 apps 1 gl
1950/51 1 app 0 gls
1951/52 1 app 0 gls
TOTAL 57 apps 8 gls
Club Record: Hull City (0), Crystal Palace (0), Gloucester City, Cheltenham Town, Gloucester City +.

MILLS, ? (CF)
1925/26 1 app 0 gls
TOTAL 1 app 0 gls

MILLS, F.L (HB)
1913/14 8 apps 0 gls
TOTAL 8 apps 0 gls
Note: Also played for Gloucester YMCA 1919/20, 1920/21.

MILLS, R (HB)
1934/35 1 app 0 gls
TOTAL 1 app 0 gls
Club Record: Cinderford Town, Gloucester City +.

MILLS, Timothy (Tim) (F)
1983/84 2 apps 0 gls
TOTAL 2 apps 0 gls

MILLYARD, Martin Richard (Sub)
b. Qu4 1957 Cheltenham, Glos. d. Qu 2 1975 Bristol, Avon
1974/75 0 apps 0 gls (1 nps)
TOTAL 0 apps 0 gls (1 nps)

MILNE, Maurice (W)
b. 21/10/1932 Dundee, Scotland d. 1998 Tayport, Fife, Scotland
1958/59 40 apps 12 gls
TOTAL 40 apps 12 gls
Club Record: Dundee St Joseph's, Dundee United (0), 1957 Norwich City (5-0), Gloucester City, Dunfermline Athletic (0), Brechin City (0), Forfar Athletic (0).

MILSOM, Paul Jason (F)
b. 05/10/1974 Bristol, Avon
1995/96 30 apps 2 subs 11 gls (2 nps)
1996/97 13 apps 13 subs 2 gls (1 nps)
1997/98 1 app 1 sub 0 gls
TOTAL 44 apps 16 subs 13 gls (3 nps)
Club Record: 1993 Bristol City (3-0), Clevedon Town (loan), 1994 Cardiff City (3-0), Stafford Rangers (loan), 1995 Oxford United (0), Gloucester City, Trowbridge Town, Clevedon Town, Forest Green Rovers (loan), Bath City, Tiverton Town, Mangotsfield United, Paulton Rovers +.

MINGS, Adrian Leon (Adie) (F)
b. 17/10/1968 Chippenham, Wilts.
1996/97 24 apps 14 subs 14 gls (5 nps)
1997/98 39 apps 4 subs 13 gls
1998/99 35 apps 6 subs 17 gls (2 nps)
2003/04 5 apps 1 gl
TOTAL 103 apps 24 subs 45 gls (7 nps)
Club Record: Melksham Town, Chippenham Town, Bath City, Worcester City (loan), Gloucester City, Forest Green Rovers, Yate Town (loan), Basingstoke Town, Chippenham Town, Gloucester City (loan), Weston-Super-Mare, Chippenham Town +.

MITCHELL, C (WH)
1890/91
Club Record: London Casuals, Gloucester +.

MITCHELL, David (Dave) (F)
b. 1966
1994/95 30 apps 5 subs 15 gls (3 nps)
TOTAL 30 apps 5 subs 15 gls (3 nps)
Club Record: Trowbridge Town, Westbury United, Trowbridge Town, Chippenham Town, Bristol Rovers (trial) (0), Trowbridge Town, Forest Green Rovers, Gloucester City, Trowbridge Town +.
Note: Played for Gloucester City 1995/96.

MITCHELL, E.J.D (CH)
1890/91

MOCKRIDGE, David C (Dave) (CH)
b. 15/01/1955 Bristol
1978/79 18 apps 2 gls
1979/80 49 apps 2 gls (1 nps)
TOTAL 67 apps 4 gls (1 nps)
Club Record: Bristol Saint George, Clevedon Town, Paulton Rovers, Gloucester City +.
Note: Brother of Gary Mockridge.

MOCKRIDGE, Gary D (WH)
b. 03/07/1951 Bristol
1977/78 4 apps 2 gls
1978/79 38 apps 7 gls (2 nps)
1979/80 54 apps 7 gls
1980/81 54 apps 1 sub 2 gls (1 nps)
1981/82 55 apps 1 gl (1 nps)
1983/84 0 apps 0 gls (1 nps)
TOTAL 205 apps 1 sub 19 gls (5 nps)
Club Record: Clevedon Town, Bristol Saint George, Bristol Rovers (0), Gloucester City, Forest Green Rovers +.
Note: Club Player of the Season 1978/79. Brother of Dave Mockridge.

MOGG, David J (Dave) (GK)
b. 11/02/1962 Bristol
1989/90 38 apps 0 gls
1990/91 43 apps 0 gls
1991/92 49 apps 0 gls
TOTAL 130 apps 0 gls
Club Record: Bristol City (0), Atvidaberg (Sweden), Bath City, Weymouth (loan), Cheltenham Town, Gloucester City, Bath City, Forest Green Rovers, Salisbury City (loan), Bristol City (0), Forest Green Rovers, Clevedon Town, Weston-Super-Mare, Chippenham Town, Clevedon Town, Taunton Town, Backwell United, Weston-Super-Mare, Hallen, Mangotsfield United +.
Note: Supporter's Player of the Season 1991/92.

[521]

MOKLER, Steve (GK)
1997/98 39 apps 0 gls
1998/99 30 apps 0 gls
TOTAL 69 apps 0 gls
Club Record: Luton Town (0), Thetford, Harwich & Parkeston, Newmarket, Harwich & Parkeston, Sudbury Town, Gloucester City, Moor Green (loan), Atherstone United +.

MOLLOY, George William (Billy) (W)
b. 28/08/1929 Coventry, Warks.
1952/53 13 apps 1 gl
TOTAL 13 apps 1 gl
Club Record: 1949 Southampton (1-0), Lockheed Leamington, 1950 Newport County (3-0), Lockheed Leamington, Gloucester City, Rugby Town +.

MOLLOY, Paul (M)
b. 23/02/1969
1998/99 0 apps 1 sub 0 gls (3 nps)
TOTAL 0 apps 1 sub 0 gls (3 nps)
Club Record: Stafford Rangers, Bromsgrove Rovers, Redditch United, Worcester City, Gloucester City +.

MONKS, E (IF)
1926/27 5 apps 2 gls
1927/28 17 apps 5 gls
TOTAL 22 apps 7 gls
Club Record: Hanham Athletic, Gloucester City +.

MOODY, Andrew Thomas (Sub)
b. 17/09/1986 Gloucester
2003/04 0 apps 1 sub 0 gls
TOTAL 0 apps 1 sub 0 gls

MOODY, John (GK)
b. Gloucester

MOORE, Graham (M)
b. abt. 1959
1986/87 7 apps 1 sub 0 gls (1 nps)
TOTAL 7 apps 1 sub 0 gls (1 nps)
Club Record: Newent Town, Gloucester City, Alvechurch, Racing Club Newent +.

MOORE, John William Michael (Johnny) (HB)
b. 25/09/1923 Chiswick, London
1948/49 52 apps 13 gls
TOTAL 52 apps 13 gls
Club Record: 1946-47 Brentford (4-0), Gloucester City, 1951 Colchester United (2-0), Staines Town.

MOORE, P (Sub)
1999/00

MOORE, Ray (IF)
b. 1921
1936/37 1 app 0 gls
TOTAL 1 app 0 gls
Note: Played for Gloucester City 1939/40.

MOORE, Richard (Rich) (D)
2000/01 25 apps 1 sub 2 gls
TOTAL 25 apps 1 sub 2 gls
Club Record: Forest Green Rovers, Shortwood United, Gloucester City, Slimbridge +.

MOREFIELD, William John Thomas (FB)
b. 26/10/1922 Gloucester d. 17/12/1997 Wakefield, Yorks.
1938/39 10 apps 0 gls
1939/40 1 app 0 gls
TOTAL 11 apps 0 gls
Club Record: Ipswich Town, Gloucester City, 1946-48 Halifax Town (65-0), Doncaster Rovers (0), Scunthorpe United (0).

MORETON, J.E (W)
1922/23 1 app 0 gls
TOTAL 1 app 0 gls

MORFORD, William Guy (Will) (F)
b. 28/04/1986 Ipswich, Suffolk
2007/08 25 apps 8 subs 12 gls (1 nps)
2008/09 31 apps 12 subs 8 gls (1 nps)
TOTAL 56 apps 20 subs 20 gls (2 nps)
Club Record: Staunton & Corse, Tuffley Rovers, Slimbridge, Gloucester City +.

MORGAN, ? (FB) ++
1942/43 6 apps 0 gls
TOTAL 6 apps 0 gls
Club Record: Old Centralians (Leeds), Gloucester City +.

MORGAN, ? (W)
1957/58

MORGAN, D (WH)
b. 1919
1936/37 1 app 0 gls
TOTAL 1 app 0 gls
Club Record: Viney Hill, Gloucester City +.

MORGAN, Darius Junior (F)
b. 07/12/1989 Gloucester
2007/08 1 app 3 subs 1 gl
TOTAL 1 app 3 subs 1 gl
Club Record: Cheltenham Town, Gloucester City +.

MORGAN, H (W)
1921/22 1 app 0 gls
TOTAL 1 app 0 gls

MORGAN, Jonathan Peter (Jon) (M)
b. 10/07/1970 Cardiff, Wales
1991/92 20 apps 2 subs 2 gls (2 nps)
TOTAL 20 apps 2 subs 2 gls (2 nps)
Club Record: 1988-90 Cardiff City (55-3), Merthyr Tydfil, Gloucester City, Inter Cardiff.

MORLEY, R.F (CH)
1899/00 1 app 0 gls
TOTAL 1 app 0 gls

MORRIS, ? (CF) ++
1942/43 2 apps 3 gls
TOTAL 2 apps 3 gls

MORRIS, ? (GK)
1992/93

MORRIS, F.M (FB)
1893/94 1 app 0 gls
1894/95 5 apps 1 gl
1895/96 1 app 0 gls
TOTAL 7 apps 1 gl
Note: Played for Gloucester 1889/90, 1891/92.

MORRIS, John/Mick (GK)
b. 1932
1953/54 1 app 0 gls
TOTAL 1 app 0 gls

MORRIS, L (W)
1931/32 7 apps 2 gls
TOTAL 7 apps 2 gls

MORRIS, Maldwyn Jones Gravell (Mal) (CF)
b. 03/08/1932 Swansea, Wales d. Qu3 2000 Haverfordwest, Dyfed, Wales
1958/59 51 apps 25 gls
1959/60 8 apps 4 gls
TOTAL 59 apps 29 gls
Club Record: Neyland AFC, Pembroke Borough, 1956-57 Swansea Town (14-6), Gloucester City.

MORRIS, Simon (GK)
2001/02 2 apps 0 gls
TOTAL 2 apps 0 gls
Club Record: Cinderford Town, Cheltenham Town, Shortwood United, Gloucester City, Tuffley Rovers +.

MORRISON, Gary Thomas (M)
b. Qu1 1986 Cheltenham, Glos.
2003/04 0 apps 0 gls (1 nps)
TOTAL 0 apps 0 gls (1 nps)
Club Record: Gloucester City, Gloucester United (loan), Chipping Norton Town +.

MORRISON, Lance (F)
b. 1959 Birmingham, Warks.
1987/88 11 apps 2 subs 2 gls (1 nps)
1988/89 34 apps 14 subs 14 gls (8 nps)
1989/90 47 apps 10 subs 13 gls
1990/91 13 apps 2 subs 8 gls
TOTAL 105 apps 28 subs 37 gls (9 nps)
Club Record: King's Heath, Nuneaton Borough, Moor Green, Alvechurch, Gloucester City +.
Note: Supporter's Player of the Season 1989/90.

MORRISON, William (Bill) (W)
1953/54 8 apps 1 gl
1954/55 2 apps 0 gls
TOTAL 10 apps 1 gl
Club Record: 1950-52 Falkirk (14-3), Gloucester City (loan) +.

MORSE, Jamie (GK)
b. 1989
2006/07 0 apps 0 gls (12 nps)
TOTAL 0 apps 0 gls (12 nps)
Club Record: Highworth Town, Cinderford Town, Gloucester City, Shrivenham +.

MORTIMER, Keith E.W (W)
b. 01/12/1946 Gloucester
1967/68 35 apps 5 gls (2 nps)
1976/77 29 apps 0 gls (2 nps)
1977/78 10 apps 1 sub 0 gls
TOTAL 74 apps 1 sub 5 gls (4 nps)
Club Record: Bristol Rovers (0), Cinderford Town, Melbourne Slavia (Australia), Gloucester City, Forest Green Rovers, Matson Athletic +.

MORTIMORE, K (FB)
1970s

MORTON, Geoffrey Dalgleish (Geoff) (GK)
b. 27/07/1924 Acton, Middlesex d. 28/01/2000 Malvern, Worcs.
1953/54 11 apps 0 gls
TOTAL 11 apps 0 gls
Club Record: Chelmsford City, 1948-51 Watford (107-0), 1951-52 Southend United (25-0), Gloucester City, 1953 Fulham (0), 1954 Exeter City (6-0) +.
Note: Also played cricket for Middlesex CCC 1950.

MOSCROP, Ronald J (Ron) (CF)
b.13/09/1928 Sunbury-on-Thames, Surrey
1947/48 1 app 0 gls
TOTAL 1 app 0 gls
Club Record: Tooting & Mitcham, Gloucester City, Cheltenham Town, Weymouth, Dorchester Town, Wareham, Portland.

MOUGHTON, Colin Edward (WH)
b. 30/12/1947 Harrow, London
1974/75 50 apps 0 gls (1 nps)
1975/76 15 apps 0 gls (1 nps)
TOTAL 65 apps 0 gls (2 nps)
Club Record: 1965-66 Queen's Park Rangers (6-0), 1968 Colchester United (4-0), Bedford Town, Cheltenham Town, Gloucester City +.

MOULE, D (WH)
b. 1921
1937/38 2 apps 0 gls
TOTAL 2 apps 0 gls

MOULSDALE, Colin B (WH)
b. 15/10/1948 Gloucester
1965/66 23 apps 1 gl
1966/67 50 apps 0 gls (1 nps)
1967/68 43 apps 0 gls (2 nps)
1975/76 42 apps 0 gls
1976/77 36 apps 1 gl
1977/78 23 apps 0 gls (4 nps)
TOTAL 217 apps 2 gls (7 nps)
Club Record: Parry Hall, Gloucester City, Banbury United, Gloucester City +.
Note: Player Manager May 1976–Nov 1977. Club Captain 1975-78. Brother of Ron Moulsdale and Uncle of Mike Moulsdale.

MOULSDALE, Michael C (Mike) (IF)
b. Qu4 1950 Cirencester, Glos.
1969/70 1 app 2 subs 1 gl
TOTAL 1 app 2 subs 1 gl
Club Record: Gloucester City, Stonehouse +.
Note: Son of Ron Moulsdale and nephew of Colin Moulsdale.

MOULSDALE, Ronald W (Ron) (IF)
b. Qu4 1931 Gloucester·
1954/55 2 apps 0 gls
TOTAL 2 apps 0 gls
Club Record: Stonehouse, Hoffman Athletic, Gloucester City +.
Note: Father of Mike Moulsdale and brother of Colin Moulsdale. Played for Gloucester City 1953/54.

MOUNTAIN, Patrick Douglas (Pat) (GK)
b. 01/08/1976 Pontypridd, Wales
1998/99 20 apps 0 gls
TOTAL 20 apps 0 gls
Club Record: Barry Town, 1996 Cardiff City (5-0), Barry Town, Yeovil Town, Gloucester City, Newport County +.
International Record: Wales U21 (2).
Note: Played for Gloucester City 1999/00.

MULLINS, F (W)
1921/22 3 apps 4 gls
1922/23 1 app 0 gls
TOTAL 4 apps 4 gls

MULRANEY, Michael Glyn (Mike) (F)
b. 13/05/1961 d. 11/12/2005 Gloucester
1983/84 1 app 0 gls
TOTAL 1 app 0 gls
Club Record: Spa Rangers, Churchdown Parish, Gloucester City +.

MUNRO, W (WH)
1889/90

MURCH, R (GK)
1889/90
Club Record: Gloucester, Clifton +.
Note: Stood in as Gloucester 'keeper when incumbent 'keeper failed to turn up. Was the groundsman at Clifton.

MURDIN, James Harold (W)
b. 1905 Manchester, Lancs. d. ?
1925/26 9 apps 1 gl
1926/27 1 app 0 gls
TOTAL 10 apps 1 gl

MURDOCK, Andrew Frances T (Andy) (HB)
b. 04/12/1903 Wheatenhurst, Glos. d. Qu3 1973 Gloucester
1923/24 8 apps 3 gls
1924/25 10 apps 0 gls
1925/26 15 apps 3 gls
1926/27 10 apps 0 gls
1927/28 17 apps 2 gls
1928/29 24 apps 0 gls
1929/30 32 apps 2 gls
1930/31 27 apps 1 gl
1931/32 20 apps 0 gls
1932/33 35 apps 1 gl
1933/34 34 apps 3 gls
TOTAL 232 apps 15 gls
Note: Club Captain 1931-33. Brother of Geoffrey Murdock.

MURDOCK, Geoffrey Amos S (Jock) (HB)
b. 31/07/1908 Wheatenhurst, Glos. d. Qu4 1975 Bristol, Avon
1928/29 1 app 0 gls
1929/30 13 apps 0 gls
1930/31 25 apps 2 gls
1931/32 1 app 0 gls
1934/35 41 apps 2 gls
1936/37 17 apps 0 gls
1937/38 3 apps 0 gls
TOTAL 101 apps 4 gls
Club Record: Gloucester City, Lister's Works +.
Note: Brother of Andrew Murdock.

MURDOCK, W (FB)
1932/33 1 app 0 gls
TOTAL 1 app 0 gls

MURNEY, Hugh Patrick ((IF)
b. 1939 Johnstone and Elderslie, Renfrewshire, Scotland
1963/64 3 apps 0 gls
TOTAL 3 app 0 gls
Club Record: Saint Johnstone (0), Gloucester City (trial) +.

MURPHY, Ricky (M)
1986/87 27 apps 4 gls
TOTAL 27 apps 4 gls
Club Record: Trowbridge Town, Forest Green Rovers, Gloucester City +.

MURRAY, ? (IF)
1946/47 1 app 0 gls
TOTAL 1 app 0 gls

MURRAY, C (GK)
1903/04 1 app 0 gls
TOTAL 1 app 0 gls

MUSKER, Russell (M)
b. 10/07/1962 Liverpool, Lancs.
1991/92 5 apps 2 subs 0 gls (1 nps)
TOTAL 5 apps 2 subs 0 gls (1 nps)
Club Record: 1980-83 Bristol City (46-1), Exeter City (loan) (6-0), 1983-85 Gillingham (64-7), 1986-87 Torquay United (45-0), Dawlish Town, 1990 Torquay United (21-1), 1991 Walsall (3-0), Gloucester City, Saltash United, Taunton Town.

MUSTOE, Neil John (M)
b. 05/11/1976 Gloucester
2002/03 33 apps 0 gls
2003/04 44 apps 4 subs 1 gl
2004/05 40 apps 2 gls
2005/06 27 apps 4 gls (1 nps)
2006/07 41 apps 4 subs 0 gls (3 nps)
2007/08 51 apps 0 gls
2008/09 43 apps 2 subs 2 gls (1 nps)
TOTAL 279 apps 10 subs 9 gls (5 nps)
Club Record: Robinswood, 1995-97 Manchester United (0), 1997 Wigan Athletic (0), 1998-02 Cambridge United (99-4), Cambridge City (loan), Gloucester City, Stevenage Borough, Yeovil Town, Gloucester City, Cirencester United (loan) +.
Note: Club Captain 2005-07. Joint Temporary Club Manager Jan 2006 (1 match). Player's Player of the Season 2007/08. Supporter's Player of the Season 2007/08.

MYATT, Greg (FB)
1972/73 27 apps 1 gl (1 nps)
TOTAL 27 apps 1 gl (1 nps)
Club Record: Bristol City (0), Gloucester City +.

MYERS, Stanley (Stan) (RH)
b. 19/03/1929 Whitehaven, Cumberland
1950/51 49 apps 7 gls
1951/52 48 apps 1 gl
1952/53 48 apps 1 gl
1953/54 40 apps 0 gls
1954/55 52 apps 2 gls
1955/56 49 apps 6 gls
1956/57 34 apps 6 gls
1957/58 11 apps 0 gls
1958/59 22 apps 0 gls
1959/60 34 apps 3 gls
1960/61 26 apps 0 gls
TOTAL 413 apps 26 gls
Club Record: Royal Air Force, Millwall (0), Gloucester City, Cinderford Town, Mitcheldean.
Note: Club Captain 1953-55. All-time record appearances in competitive games for Gloucester City.

NASH, Karl Philip (F)
b. 26/11/1988 Dursley, Glos.
2008/09 2 apps 1 sub 2 gls (2 nps)
TOTAL 2 apps 1 sub 2 gls (2 nps)
Club Record: Mangotsfield United, Berkeley Town, Gloucester City, Slimbridge +.

NEALE, F (FB)
1934/35 1 app 0 gls
TOTAL 1 app 0 gls

NEALE, Jim (GK/WH)
1937/38 19 apps 2 gls
1938/39 22 apps 0 gls
TOTAL 41 apps 2 gls
Club Record: Bristol City (0), Berkeley Town, Gloucester City +.

NEALE, Philip Anthony (Phil) (FB)
b. 05/06/1954 Scunthorpe, Lincs.
1986/87 9 apps 0 gls
TOTAL 9 apps 0 gls
Club Record: 1972 Scunthorpe United (0), 1974-84 Lincoln City (335-22), Worcester City, Gloucester City.
Note: Played cricket for Worcestershire CCC 1975-92. Awarded OBE in 2005 for services to cricket.

NEUMAN, ? (W)
1961/62 1 app 0 gls
TOTAL 1 app 0 gls

NEVILLE, John (CH)
b. 1942
1967/68 20 apps 0 subs 1 gl
1968/69 8 apps 1 sub 0 gls (1 nps)
TOTAL 28 apps 1 sub 1 gl (1 nps)
Club Record: Hereford United, Gloucester City +.

NEWCOMBE, Gordon (W)
1947/48 3 apps 0 gls
TOTAL 3 apps 0 gls
Club Record: Aberaman, Gloucester City +.

NEWLAND, ? (?)
1903/04

NEWLANDS, ? (WH)
1933/34 1 app 0 gls
TOTAL 1 app 0 gls

NEWLING, Vernon Henry (HB)
b. 11/02/1908 Farnham, Surrey d. 16/12/1984 Beckenham, Kent
1933/34 2 apps 0 gls
TOTAL 2 apps 0 gls
Club Record: Cardiff City (0), Gloucester City +.

NEWMAN, ? (WH)
1933/34 1 app 0 gls
TOTAL 1 app 0 gls

NEWMAN, ? (D)
1980/81 1 app 0 gls
TOTAL 1 app 0 gls

NEWMAN, A (GK)
1981/82

NEWMAN, Bradley (F)
b. abt. 1957
1977/78 4 apps 0 gls
TOTAL 4 apps 0 gls
Club Record: Taunton Town, Gloucester City +.

NEWMAN, James (Jimmy) (W)
b. 1921 d. 01/2008 Swindon, Wilts.
1949/50 41 apps 12 gls
TOTAL 41 apps 12 gls
Club Record: Swindon Town (trial) (0), Merthyr Tydfil, Gloucester City, Bath City, Chippenham Town.

NEWMAN, Richard (GK)
1997/98 1 app 0 gls
TOTAL 1 app 0 gls

NEWTON, A.E (HB)
1919/20

NEWTON, Jeremy John (F)
b. 23/01/1978 Bristol, Avon
1999/00 0 apps 1 sub 0 gls (2 nps)
TOTAL 0 apps 1 sub 0 gls (2 nps)
Club Record: Gloucester City, Wootton Bassett Town, AFC Newbury, Swindon Supermarine +.

NIBLETT, Nigel (D)
b. 12/08/1967 Stratford-Upon-Avon, Warks.
1998/99 20 apps 0 gls
1999/00 28 apps 1 sub 2 gls
TOTAL 48 apps 1 sub 2 gls
Club Record: Snitterfield Sports, Kidderminster Harriers, Hednesford Town, Telford United, Valley Sports Rugby, Stratford Town, Gloucester City, Rugby United, Redditch United.

NIBLETT, William Douglas (IF)
b. Qu1 1885 Horsley, Glos. d. ?
1906/07 5 apps 1 gl
TOTAL 5 apps 1 gl

NICHOLLS, David (F)
1997/98 2 apps 5 subs 0 gls (7 nps)
TOTAL 2 apps 5 subs 0 gls (7 nps)

NICHOLLS, Ernie (W)
b. abt. 1927
1950/51 3 apps 0 gls
1951/52 5 apps 1 gl
1952/53 1 app 0 gls
TOTAL 9 apps 1 gl

NICHOLLS, H (HB)
1899/00 1 app 0 gls
TOTAL 1 app 0 gls

NICHOLLS, Laurie B (GK)
b. 11/01/1959 Bristol
1978/79 13 apps 0 gls
TOTAL 13 apps 0 gls
Club Record: Cardiff City (0), Cheltenham Town, Worcester City, Gloucester City +.
Note: Son of Ron Nicholls former Gloucestershire Cricketer.

NICHOLLS, Walter Turner (W)
b. Qu3 1886 Gloucester d. ?
1906/07
Note: Brother of Wilfred Nicholls.

NICHOLLS, Wilfred Turner (IF)
b. Qu3 1884 Gloucester d. ?
1906/07 2 apps 1 gl
TOTAL 2 apps 1 gl
Note: Brother of Walter Nicholls.

"NIPPER, A" (W)
1928/29
Note: A pseudonym which cloaks the identity of a well-known figure in City football!

NOAKES, Michael Ian (M)
b. 12/04/1988 Gloucester
2004/05 1 app 3 subs 1 gl
2005/06 1 apps 2 subs 0 gls (2 nps)
2006/07 16 apps 3 subs 3 gls (7 nps)
2007/08 9 apps 0 gls (1 nps)
TOTAL 27 apps 8 subs 4 gls (10 nps)
Club Record: Gloucester City, Hardwicke +.

NOBLE, Wayne Ian (Bunter) (M)
b. 11/06/1967 Bristol
1988/89 58 apps 1 sub 11 gls (1 nps)
1989/90 56 apps 7 subs 9 gls
1990/91 46 apps 3 subs 7 gls (6 nps)
1991/92 44 apps 3 subs 6 gls
1992/93 43 apps 1 sub 6 gls (1 nps)
TOTAL 247 apps 15 subs 39 gls (8 nps)
Club Record: 1985-86 Bristol Rovers (22-1), Norwich City (0), Yeovil Town, Gloucester City, Bath City, Trowbridge Town, Cheltenham Town, Salisbury City, Cinderford Town, Weston-Super-Mare, Clevedon Town +.
Note: Chairman's Player of the Season 1990/91.

NORCOTT, Thomas Stanley (IF)
b. Qu3 1900 Gloucester d. ?
1922/23 17 apps 12 gls
TOTAL 17 apps 12 gls
Note: Played for Gloucester YMCA 1921/22.

NORMAN, Kenneth (Kenny) (D)
1980/81 20 apps 1 sub 0 gls (2 nps)
1985/86 40 apps 1 gl (1 nps)
1986/87 33 apps 1 sub 1 gl (1 nps)
1987/88 3 apps 4 subs 0 gls (4 nps)
TOTAL 96 apps 7 subs 2 gls (7 nps)
Club Record: Torquay United (0), Swindon Town (0), Gloucester City, Forest Green Rovers, Gloucester City +.

NORRINGTON, C.H (HB)
1893/94 2 apps 0 gls
TOTAL 2 apps 0 gls

NORRIS, Oliver P (Ollie) (CF)
b. 01/04/1929 Londonderry, Northern Ireland
1959/60 20 apps 7 gls
TOTAL 20 apps 7 gls
Club Record: 1951-53 Middlesbrough (12-2), Worcester City, 1955-58 Bournemouth & Boscombe Athletic (96-34), 1958 Northampton Town (14-1), Gloucester City, Ashford Town, 1960 Rochdale (2-1), Ashford Town, Sligo Rivers (Eire), Wilhelmina Melbourne (Australia), Melbourne Croatia (Australia).
Note: Club Manager Aug 1959 – Jan 1960.

NORRIS, Raymond George (Ray) (CH)
b. 15/07/1922 Bristol d. Qu2 1972 Bristol
1940s
Club Record: Bedminster Down, 1947 Bristol City (3-0), Gloucester City.

NORRIS, William Henry (Billy) (HB)
b. 22/12/1913 Blakeney, Glos. d. Qu4 1989 Gloucester
1935/36 3 apps 1 gl
1936/37 20 apps 0 gls
1937/38 5 apps 0 gls
TOTAL 28 apps 1 gl
Club Record: Blakeney, Newport County, Gloucester City +.

NORTHAM, Terry (IF)
1980/81 2 apps 0 gls
TOTAL 2 apps 0 gls
Club Record: Yate Town, Gloucester City +.

NORTHCOTT, George Edward (CH)
b. 07/05/1935 Torquay, Devon
1965/66 37 apps 1 gl
1966/67 39 apps 0 gls
TOTAL 76 apps 1 gl
Club Record: 1954-61 Torquay United (163-2), Cheltenham Town, 1963 Exeter City (1-0), Cheltenham Town, Gloucester City, Taunton Town.

NORTHOVER, Steve (M)
1978/79 1 app 1 sub 0 gls (1 nps)
TOTAL 1 app 1 sub 0 gls (1 nps)
Club Record: Brockworth Albion, Gloucester City +.

NUNEZ, Luis (IF)
b. Spain ?
1967/68 1 app 0 gls (2 nps)
TOTAL 1 app 0 gls (2 nps)
Club Record: Cheltenham Town, Gloucester City +.
Note: Played for Gloucester City 1970/71.

NUTT, ? (IF)
1947/48 6 apps 0 gls
TOTAL 6 apps 0 gls

OAKES, Michael Christian (Mike) (GK)
b. 30/10/1973 Northwich, Cheshire
1992/93 18 apps 0 gls
TOTAL 18 apps 0 gls
Club Record: 1991-99 Aston Villa (51-0), Gloucester City (loan), 1993 Scarborough (loan) (1-0), 1993 Tranmere Rovers (loan) (0), 1999-06 Wolverhampton Wanderers (199-0), 2007 Cardiff City (11-0) +.
International Record: England U21 (6).

OAKES, Thomas Frank (IR/OL/RH)
b. 1874 Cheltenham, Glos. d. ?
1900s
Club Record: Hereford Thistle, 1896-99 Small Heath (35-8), Gloucester City.
Note: Some sources have Thomas Oakes associated with Gloucester City. Thus far I have found nothing.

OAKEY, John Arthur (HB)
b. Qu1 1875 Gloucester d. Qu1 1963 Gloucester
1895/96 1 app 0 gls
1897/98 3 apps 1 gl
1898/99 13 apps 0 gls
1899/00 3 apps 1 gl
TOTAL 20 apps 2 gls
Club Record: Gloucester YMRIS, Gloucester, Gloucester Teachers, Gloucester +.
Note: Played for Gloucester 1896/97.

OAKLEY, ? (IF)
1890/91

O'BRIEN, Pat (HB)
1935/36 32 apps 0 gls
TOTAL 32 apps 0 gls
Club Record: Cheltenham Town, Gloucester City +.

O'GORMAN, ? (WH) ++
1942/43 6 apps 0 gls
TOTAL 6 apps 0 gls
Club Record: Glasgow Celtic (0), Gloucester City +.

O'HAGAN, Patrick (Pat) (GK)
1988/89 2 apps 0 gls
TOTAL 2 apps 0 gls

O'LAUGHLIN, T (?)
1955/56

OLDFIELD, Nigel (Sub)
b. 1963
1980/81 0 apps 0 gls (1 nps)
TOTAL 0 apps 0 gls (1 nps)

OLNER, Paul A (M)
b. 10/1965 Nuneaton, Warks.
1993/94 14 apps 1 gl
TOTAL 14 apps 1 gl
Club Record: Atherstone United, Gloucester City, Valley Sports Rugby, Sutton Coldfield Town, Hinckley United, Rugby United +.

0'REILLY, Christopher (Chris) (D)
b. 1963
1983/84 5 apps 1 gl (6 nps)
1984/85 21 apps 1 sub 0 gls (1 nps)
TOTAL 26 apps 1 sub 1 gl (7 nps)
Club Record: Newport County, Gloucester City +.

O'RIORDAN, Donald Joseph (Don) (CD)
b. 14/05/1957 Dublin, Eire
1996/97 1 app 1 sub 0 gls (1 nps)
TOTAL 1 app 1 sub 0 gls (1 nps)
Club Record: 1976-77 Derby County (6-1), 1977 Doncaster Rovers (loan) (2-0), Tulsa Roughnecks (USA), 1978 Preston North End (32-0), Tulsa Roughnecks (USA), 1979-82 Preston North End (126-8), 1983-84 Carlisle United (84-18), 1985 Middlesbrough (41-2), 1986-87 Grimsby Town (86-14), 1988-92 Notts County (109-5), 1989 Mansfield Town (loan) (6-0), 1992-95 Torquay United (79-3), 1995 Scarborough (1-0), Gloucester City, Dorchester Town (loan).
International Record: Eire U21 (1).

OVERSON, Richard John (CD)
b. 03/06/1959 Kettering, Northants.
1982/83 5 apps 0 gls
TOTAL 5 apps 0 gls
Club Record: 1977-79 Burnley (6-0), 1980-81 Hereford United (11-1), Gloucester City +.

OWEN, Steve (M)
1994/95
Club Record: Cheltenham Town, Gloucester City +.

OWNER, Alec Jesse (CH)
b. 06/07/1902 Gloucester d. 16/12/1970 Cheltenham, Glos.
1919/20

PAGE-JONES, Nigel (FB)
b. 04/05/1946 Bromyard, Herefordshire
1968/69 52 apps 1 gl
1969/70 56 apps 0 gls
TOTAL 108 apps 1 gl
Club Record: Hereford United, Gloucester City, Stade Brest (France), Saint Pol de Leon (France).
Note: Club Player of the Season 1969/70.

PALMER, C.E (CF)
1890/91

PALMER, Geoffrey (Geoff) (FB)
b. 12/11/1940 Barnsley, Yorks.
1962/63 36 apps 1 gl
1963/64 48 apps 0 gls
1964/65 48 apps 0 gls
1965/66 55 apps 0 gls
TOTAL 187 apps 1 gl
Club Record: 1957 Doncaster Rovers (0), 1961 Bristol City (1-0), Gloucester City, Weston-Super-Mare.

PALMER, James William (M)
b. 12/05/1988 Bristol, Avon
2008/09 5 apps 0 gls
TOTAL 5 apps 0 gls
Club Record: Bristol Rovers (0), Weston-Super-Mare, Gloucester City (loan) +.

PALMER, Karl Anthony (M)
b. 07/01/1986 Stroud, Glos.
2003/04 0 apps 3 subs 0 gls
2004/05 0 apps 0 gls (3 nps)
2007/08 3 apps 0 gls
TOTAL 3 apps 3 subs 0 gls (3 nps)
Club Record: Gloucester City, Tuffley Rovers (loan), Swindon Supermarine, Gloucester City (loan), Hardwicke +.

PALMER, Marcus James (F)
b. 06/01/1988 Gloucester
2007/08 4 apps 2 subs 5 gls
2008/09 1 app 2 subs 0 gls (1 nps)
TOTAL 5 apps 4 subs 5 gls (1 nps)
Club Record: Cheltenham Town, 2006-07 Hereford United (4-0), Cardiff City (trial) (0), Gloucester City (loan), Solihull Moors, Forest Green Rovers +.

PARKER, Albert (IF)
1902/03 9 apps 6 gls
1903/04 13 apps 5 gls
TOTAL 22 apps 11 gls

PARKER, D (Sub)
1999/00

PARKER, Grahame Wilshaw (FB)
b. 11/02/1912 Gloucester d. 11/11/1995 Sidmouth, Devon
1928/29 5 apps 0 gls
1929/30 26 apps 1 gl
1930/31 1 app 0 gls
TOTAL 32 apps 1 gl
Note: Son of Reginald Parker. Grahame Parker played rugby for Gloucester RFC, Cambridge University and Blackheath RFC and represented England 2 times. Also played cricket for Gloucestershire CCC 1932-1950 (Secretary 1968-77) and Cambridge University 1934-1935. Was awarded MBE for courage in the Italian Campaign during WW2. Played for Gloucester City 1946/47. Awarded OBE in 1962.

PARKER, J.M (HB)
1894/95 3 apps 0 gls
TOTAL 3 apps 0 gls

PARKER, Reginald Morton (FB)
b. Qu4 1885 Gloucester d. ?
1907/08 1 app 0 gls
1908/09 1 app 0 gls
TOTAL 2 apps 0 gls
Note: Father of Grahame Parker.

PARKES, Daryl (Sub)
b. 1960
1974/75 0 apps 0 gls (4 nps)
TOTAL 0 apps 0 gls (4 nps)
Club Record: Churchdown Panthers, Gloucester City +.

PARKS, ? (W)
1939/40 4 apps 1 gl
TOTAL 4 apps 1 gl

PARNELL, Matthew Kenneth (D)
b. 29/09/1979 Plymouth, Devon
2000/01 22 apps 1 gl (1 nps)
TOTAL 22 apps 1 gl (1 nps)
Club Record: Cheltenham Saracens, Gloucester City, AFC Totton, Bashley +.

PARRIS, John Edward (Eddie) (W)
b. 31/01/1911 Pwllmeyrick, Wales d. Qu1 1971 Gloucester
1939/40 19 apps 10 gls
1941/42 7 apps 10 gls
1942/43 19 apps 30 gls
1947/48 2 apps 0 gls
TOTAL 47 apps 50 gls
Club Record: Chepstow Town, 1928-33 Bradford Park Avenue (133-38), 1934-36 Bournemouth & Boscombe Athletic (100-23), 1936-37 Luton Town (7-2), 1937-38 Northampton Town (25-7), Cheltenham Town, Gloucester City.
International Record: Wales (1).
Note: Played for Gloucester City 1940/41. Club Captain 1941-42.

PARRISH, Robert (Bob) (W)
1963/64 1 app 0 gls
TOTAL 1 app 0 gls

PLAYERS' RECORDS

PARSONS, J.T (IF)
1909/10 8 apps 4 gls
1913/14 7 apps 0 gls
TOTAL 15 apps 4 gls
Club Record: Gloucester City, Gloucester YMCA +.
Note: Played for Gloucester City 1908/09 and Gloucester YMCA 1913/14.

PARSONS, Lindsay William (D)
b. 20/03/1946 Bristol
1980/81 26 apps 0 gls (1 nps)
1981/82 46 apps 0 gls
TOTAL 72 apps 0 gls (1 nps)
Club Record: 1963-76 Bristol Rovers (360-0), 1977-78 Torquay United (56-0), Taunton Town, Gloucester City, Cheltenham Town +.

PARSONS, Richard (M)
b. 1989
2005/06
Club Record: Bristol City (0), Gloucester City (trial) +.

PARTRIDGE, Brian (W)
1967/68 23 apps 7 gls
TOTAL 23 apps 7 gls
Club Record: Corby Town, Gloucester City +.

PATERSON, Terence J (Terry) (M)
b. 22/01/1955 Stroud, Glos.
1978/79 27 apps 13 gls
1979/80 52 apps 17 gls
1980/81 55 apps 1 sub 21 gls
1981/82 56 apps 1 subs 14 gls (1 nps)
1985/86 18 apps 5 subs 3 gls (4 nps)
TOTAL 208 app 7 subs 68 gls (5 nps)
Club Record: Forest Green Rovers, Cheltenham Town, Redditch United, Gloucester City, Cheltenham Town +.

PATTERSON, Nigel (D)
b. 1965 Bristol
1987/88 1 app 0 gls
TOTAL 1 app 0 gls

PAYNE, ? (W/FB)
1937/38 11 apps 3 gls
1939/40 2 apps 0 gls
TOTAL 13 apps 3 gls
Club Record: Cirencester Town, Gloucester City +.

PAYNE, David (F)
b. 1962
1988/89 2 apps 2 subs 0 gls (9 nps)
1989/90 39 apps 8 subs 12 gls (2 nps)
TOTAL 41 apps 10 subs 12 gls (11 nps)
Club Record: Robinsons, Bath City, Gloucester City, Bath City, Clevedon Town, Nailsea United, Brislington +.

PAYNE, Mark Ian (M)
b. 02/09/1966 Swindon, Wilts.
1986/87 32 apps 4 subs 2 gls (2 nps)
TOTAL 32 apps 4 subs 2 gls (2 nps)
Club Record: 1984 Swindon Town (3-0), Cheltenham Town, Gloucester City, Trowbridge Town, Salisbury City +.

PEACEY, Colin (M)
1994/95 1 app 2 subs 0 gls
TOTAL 1 app 2 subs 0 gls
Club Record: Cinderford Town, Stroud, Cinderford Town, unknown Belgian club, Bristol Rovers (0), Gloucester City, Cinderford Town, Cirencester Town (loan), Tuffley Rovers +.

PEACOCK, George (FB)
b. 10/02/1924 Pontypool, Wales d. Qu1 1984 Pontypool, Wales
1950/51 46 apps 0 gls
1951/52 43 apps 1 gl
TOTAL 89 apps 1 gl
Club Record: Pentwyn, Newport County, 1946 Bristol Rovers (7-0), Gloucester City.

PEACOCK, H (W)
1913/14

PEACOCK, Steve (FB)
b. 1952
1970/71 12 apps 0 gls (1 nps)
TOTAL 12 apps 0 gls (1 nps)
Club Record: Trowbridge Town, Cheltenham Town, Minehead, Gloucester City (trial) +.

PEARCE, F (IF)
1895/96 1 app 0 gls
TOTAL 1 app 0 gls

PEART, William Clarence (Bill) (CH)
b. 27/12/1904 Newport, Monmouth, Wales d. Qu2 1995 Doncaster, Yorks.
1935/36 4 apps 0 gls
1936/37 31 apps 1 gl
1937/38 23 apps 2 gls
1939/40 13 apps 0 gls
1941/42 1 app 0 gls
TOTAL 72 apps 3 gls
Club Record: Royal Navy, All Saints, Gloucester City +.
International Record: Wales Amateur (3), 1936 GB Olympic Team.
Note: Club Captain 1936-38. Played for Gloucester City 1940/41.

PECKOVER, L (CH)
1902/03 1 app 0 gls
TOTAL 1 app 0 gls
Note: Played for Gloucester City 1903/04.

PELLANT, Geoffrey A (Geoff) (GK)
b. 06/05/1947 Southampton, Hants.
1963/64 9 apps 0 gls
1964/65 22 apps 0 gls
1965/66 9 apps 0 gls
1966/67 4 apps 0 gls
1967/68 32 apps 0 gls
TOTAL 76 apps 0 gls
Club Record: Cheltenham Town, Gloucester City, Swindon Town (trial) (0), unknown Australian club, Cheltenham Town, Stonehouse.

PENDRICK, Steve (IF)
1966/67 2 apps 0 gls (1 nps)
TOTAL 2 apps 0 gls (1 nps)

PENFOLD, Robert S.V (FB)
b. 1871 Ruardean, Glos. d. ?
1892/93

PENNING, Phil (F)
1997/98
2001/02
Club Record: Gloucester City, Calne Town, Malmesbury Victoria, Pewsey Vale, Biddestone +.

PENNINGTON, ? (WH)
1893/94 1 app 0 gls
TOTAL 1 app 0 gls

PENNINGTON, ? (FB)
1946/47

PENNY, Shaun (F)
b. 24/09/1957 Bristol
1988/89 45 apps 4 subs 28 gls (2 nps)
1989/90 1 app 0 gls
1990/91 3 apps 6 subs 3 gls (7 nps)
1991/92 27 apps 10 subs 11 gls (9 nps)
1992/93 28 apps 7 subs 7 gls (3 nps)
TOTAL 104 apps 27 subs 49 gls (21 nps)
Club Record: 1974 Bristol City (0), 1979-81 Bristol Rovers (60-13), KTP Kotkan (Finland), Gloucester City, Stroud, Weston-Super-Mare, Bath City, Dorchester Town, Weymouth, Forest Green Rovers, Clevedon Town.

PEPWORTH, Richard (Dick) (CH)
b. 1952
1978/79 23 apps 2 gls
TOTAL 23 apps 2 gls
Club Record: Clevedon Town, Gloucester City +.

PERKINS, ? (IF)
1939/40 1 app 0 gls
TOTAL 1 app 0 gls

PERKINS, G.B (IF)
1889/90 2 apps 2 gls
1891/92 1 app 1 gl
TOTAL 3 apps 3 gls
Note: Played for Gloucester 1890/91.

PERKINS, Jim (IF)
1953/54 19 apps 3 gls
TOTAL 19 apps 3 gls
Club Record: Guildford City, Kidderminster Harriers, Gloucester City +.

PERKS, Reginald Henry (Harry) (IF)
b. 14/11/1901 Gloucester d. 28/11/1968 Cheltenham, Glos.
1925/26 29 apps 19 gls
1926/27 19 apps 18 gls
TOTAL 48 apps 37 gls
Club Record: Pope's Hill, Gloucester City, Lister's Works, Brimscombe +.
Note: Played for Gloucester City 1932/33.

PERRINS, J (FB)
1926/27 9 apps 1 gl
TOTAL 9 apps 1 gl

PERRIS, Michael John (Mike) (M)
b. Qu4 1975 Gloucester
1993/94 0 apps 0 gls (1 nps)
TOTAL 0 apps 0 gls (1 nps)
Club Record: Gloucester City, Tuffley Rovers, Longford, Gala Wilton FC +.

PERROTT, Ray (IF)
1946/47 3 apps 0 gls
TOTAL 3 apps 0 gls
Club Record: Royal Navy, Gloucester City +.

PERROTT, Robert (Bob) (FB)
b. 1954
1978/79 10 apps 0 gls (3 nps)
TOTAL 10 apps 0 gls (3 nps)
Club Record: Frome Town, Clevedon Town, Gloucester City +.

PERRY, Brian (M)
b. 1956
1978/79 19 apps 1 gl (1 nps)
TOTAL 19 apps 1 gl (1 nps)
Club Record: Clevedon Town, Melksham Town, Frome Town, Gloucester City, Clevedon Town +.
Note: Played for Gloucester City 1977/78.

PERRY, Ian (D)
b. 1957
1976/77 1 app 0 gls
1977/78 15 apps 1 sub 0 gls
TOTAL 16 apps 1 sub 0 gls
Club Record: Matson Athletic, Gloucester City, Wilton Rovers +.

PERRY, Richard (?)

PETTEY, C (IF)
1894/95 1 app 0 gls
1895/96 2 apps 1 gl
1897/98 1 app 0 gls
TOTAL 4 apps 1 gl

PETWORTH, Richard (Dick) (D)
1977/78
Club Record: Frome Town, Gloucester City +

PHILLIPS, G.R (WH)
1890/91

PHILLIPS, Marcus Stuart (W)
b. 17/10/1973 Bradford-on-Avon, Wilts.
1995/96 12 apps 3 subs 6 gls (4 nps)
TOTAL 12 apps 3 subs 6 gls (4 nps)
Club Record: 1993 Swindon Town (0), Gloucester City, FC Utrecht (Holland), 1996 Swindon (0), Witney Town, 1996 Oxford United (1-0), Cheltenham Town, Sydney United (Australia), Marconi Stallions (Australia), Olympic Sharks Sydney (Australia), Canberra Cosmos (Australia), Brunei (Malaysia), Northern Spirit (Australia), Brunei (Malaysia), Blacktown City (Australia) +.

PHILLIPS, Steven John (Steve) (GK)
b. 06/05/1978 Bath, Avon
1996/97 1 app 0 gls
TOTAL 1 app 0 gls
Club Record: Paulton Rovers, 1998-05 Bristol City (257-0), Gloucester City (loan), Evesham United (loan), Clevedon Town (loan), Worcester City (loan), 2006-08 Bristol Rovers (136-0), 2009 Shrewsbury Town (loan) (0) +.

PILLSWORTH, Eric William (GK)
b. Qu4 1897 Minchinhampton, Glos. d. ?
1925/26
Club Record: Dursley Town, Gloucester City +.

PINCOT, Frederick (Fred) (WH) ++
b. 19/03/1913 Bristol d. Qu1 2000 Winchester, Hants.
1939/40 1 app 0 gls
TOTAL 1 app 0 gls
Club Record: Bristol Victoria Albion, 1932 Wolverhampton Wanderers (2-0), 1934-39 Bournemouth & Boscombe Athletic (198-0), Gloucester City, Dartford, Gravesend United, 1947 Newport County (14-0), Bideford Town.

PINK, A (FB)
1889/90

PINNEGAR, Frederick John (FB)
b. Qu4 1876 Wotton-under-Edge, Glos. d. ?
1899/00 11 apps 0 gls
1900/01 4 apps 0 gls
TOTAL 15 apps 0 gls
Club Record: Gloucester, Saint Michael's +.

PITCHER, Jack (F)
b. 13/06/1983 Bristol, Avon
2007/08 40 apps 5 subs 22 gls (1 nps)
2008/09 37 apps 9 subs 13 gls (7 nps)
TOTAL 77 apps 14 subs 35 gls (8 nps)
Club Record: Winterbourne United, Mangotsfield United, Clevedon Town, Gloucester City +.

PITT, A. G (CF)
1923/24 8 apps 5 gls
1924/25 12 apps 6 gls
TOTAL 20 apps 11 gls
Club Record: Gloucester City Albion, Gloucester YMCA +.

PITT, William Thomas (CH)
b. 1875 Battersea, London d. ?
1894/95 5 apps 0 gls
1895/96 2 apps 0 gls
TOTAL 7 apps 0 gls
Club Record: Gloucester, Gloucester Post Office +.
Note: Played for Gloucester 1896/97.

PLATT, Edward (GK)
b. Qu2 1872 Gloucester d. ?
1889/90
Note: Brother of Francis Platt. Son of founders of Fielding & Platt.

PLATT, Francis James (FB)
b. Qu2 1869 Gloucester d. ?
1889/90
Note: Brother of Edward Platt. Son of founders of Fielding & Platt.

PLUMMER, Arthur Edward (RB)
b. Qu1 1907 Radstock, Somerset d. ?
1938/39 38 apps 1 gl
1939/40 7 apps 0 gls
TOTAL 45 apps 1 gl
Club Record: Bedminster Down Sports, 1927 Bristol City (0), Welton Rovers, Bath City, 1930-31 Coventry City (25-0), Boston Town, 1933 Walsall (3-0), Dundalk (Eire), Valenciennes (France), 1936 Bristol Rovers (0), Gloucester City.

POCOCK, Barrie (M)
b. 1957
1976/77 22 apps 1 gl (1 nps)
1977/78 2 apps 1 sub 0 gls (1 nps)
TOTAL 24 apps 1 sub 1 gl (2 nps)
Club Record: Fairford Town, Cirencester Town, Gloucester City, Cheltenham Town, Chippenham Town +.
Note: Brother of Fran Pocock.

POCOCK, Francis (Fran) (?)
b. bef. 1957
1970s
Club Record: Fairford Town, Cirencester Town, Cheltenham Town, Gloucester City +.
Note: Brother of Barrie Pocock.

POOLE, A (WH)
1891/92
Note: Could this be Edward Albert Poole (b. Qu3 1867, Cambridge) brother of Charles Poole and Percy Poole?

POOLE, Charles Frederick (IF)
b. 02/1860 Cambridge, Cambs. d. Jamaica
1889/90 3 apps 3 gls
TOTAL 3 apps 3 gls
Note: Brother of Percy Poole. Club Captain 1889-90.

POOLE, Percy Watson (WH)
b. Qu3 1870 Cambridge, Cambs. d. ?
1890/91
Note: Brother of Charles Poole.

PORTER, Christopher John (Chris) (M)
b. 30/04/1949 North Petherton, Somerset
1982/83 19 apps 5 gls (5 nps)
TOTAL 19 apps 5 gls (5 nps)
Club Record: Bridgwater Town, 1970-73 Swindon Town (35-4), Yeovil
Town, Bridgwater Town, Gloucester City, Chard Town, Taunton Town,
Frome Town.

PORTER, David (Dave) (D)
1993/94 6 apps 1 sub 2 gls
TOTAL 6 apps 1 sub 2 gls
Club Record: Gloucester City, Swindon Supermarine, Sutton United,
Swindon Supermarine +.

PORTER, Henry T (CF)
b. 1871 Bristol, Glos. d. ?
1895/96 1 app 0 gls
1897/98 7 apps 10 gls
1898/99 16 apps 6 gls
1899/00 20 apps 12 gls
1900/01 15 apps 3 gls
TOTAL 59 apps 31 gls
Club Record: Gloucester, Staple Hill, Gloucester +.
Note: Played for Gloucester City 1902/03.

PORTWAY, Steven Leonard (Steve) (F)
b. 21/08/1968 Stepney, London
1994/95 17 apps 3 subs 11 gls
1995/96 11 apps 1 sub 4 gls
TOTAL 28 apps 4 subs 15 gls
Club Record: Walthamstow Avenue, Brentwood, Bishop's Stortford,
Boreham Wood, Witham Town, Barking, Gravesend & Northfleet,
Gloucester City, Romford, Gravesend & Northfleet, Billericay, Chelmsford
City, Fisher Athletic, Tonbridge Angels, Erith & Belvedere, Heybridge
Swifts, Burnham Ramblers +.

POTTER-SMITH, Thomas (IL/IR/RH)
b. 07/06/1901 Newcastle-upon-Tyne, Northumberland d. Qu3 1978
Brighton, Sussex
1938/39 32 apps 2 gls
1939/40 6 apps 1 gl
TOTAL 38 apps 3 gls
Club Record: Saint Peter's Albion, 1922 Merthyr Town (18-6), 1923 Hull
City (8-2), 1924 Hartlepools United (30-7), 1925 Merthyr Town (14-4),
1925-28 Cardiff City (42-7), 1929-36 Brighton & Hove Albion (281-40),
1937 Crystal Palace (0), Gloucester City.
Note: Club Captain 1938-40.

POWELL, Cliff (F)
1984/85 1 app 0 gls
TOTAL 1 app 0 gls

POWELL, James O.T (CF)
b. 1874 Gloucester d. ?
1891/92 1 app 1 gl
1893/94 1 app 1 gl
1894/95 1 app 0 gls
TOTAL 3 apps 2 gls
Note: Played for Gloucester 1892/93. Brother of Trevor Powell.

POWELL, R.T (HB)
1935/36 2 apps 0 gls
TOTAL 2 apps 0 gls

POWELL, Steve (D)
1997/98 4 apps 5 subs 0 gls (5 nps)
TOTAL 4 apps 5 subs 0 gls (5 nps)

POWELL, Trevor Barrett (W)
b. Qu1 1871 Goodrich, Herefordshire d. ?
1889/90
1891/92
Note: Trevor Powell also played rugby for Gloucester RFC. Brother of
James Powell.

POXTON, James Harold (Jimmy) (IF) ++
b. 02/02/1904 Staveley, Derbys. d. Qu4 1971 Walsall, Staffs.
1940/41
Club Record: Staveley Town, 1926-27 West Bromwich Albion (9-1),
1927-28 Gillingham 43-8), 1929-33 Millwall (147-30), 1934 Watford
(23-9), 1935 Walsall (25-5), 1936 Bristol City (0), 1937 Reading (0),
Walthamstow Avenue, Royal Air Force, Gloucester City.

PRATT, David (WH)
1963/64 1 app 0 gls
TOTAL 1 app 0 gls
Club Record: Bristol City (0), Gloucester City +.

PREECE, Brian James (D)
b. 16/02/1957 Hereford, Herefordshire d. Qu3 1992 Malvern, Worcs.
1980/81 38 apps 5 gls (1 nps)
1982/83 1 app 0 gls (4 nps)
TOTAL 39 apps 5 gls (5 nps)
Club Record: Westfields, 1974-76 Hereford United (6-0), 1976-77 Newport
County (44-12), Trowbridge Town, Minehead, Gloucester City +.

PREECE, Callum John (D)
b. 16/03/1993 Gloucester
2007/08 0 apps 1 sub 0 gls
TOTAL 0 apps 1 sub 0 gls
Club Record: Gloucester City, Bristol City (0), Cirencester Town +.
Note: Became Gloucester City's youngest ever player coming on as sub on
15 April 2008.

PREECE, Mark (D)
b. 03/06/1987 Bristol, Avon
2005/06 15 apps 1 sub 1 gl
TOTAL 15 apps 1 sub 1 gl
Club Record: Bristol Rovers (0), Gloucester City (loan), Forest Green
Rovers, Weston-Super-Mare (loan) +.

PREEDY, Philip (Phil) (M)
b. 20/11/1975 Hereford, Herefordshire
1997/98 2 apps 4 subs 1 gl (2 nps)
TOTAL 2 apps 4 subs 1 gl (2 nps)
Club Record: 1993-96 Hereford United (51-4), Merthyr Tydfil (loan),
Gloucester City, Newport AFC, Evesham United, Ledbury Town, Malvern
Town +.

PREEST, Reg (W)
1958/59 10 apps 0 gls
TOTAL 10 apps 0 gls
Club Record: Coleford, Gloucester City +.

PRICE, J (IF)
1921/22 2 apps 2 gls
TOTAL 2 apps 2 gls

PRICE, Jamie Michael (M)
b. 22/07/1988 Hereford, Herefordshire
2007/08 7 apps 2 subs 0 gls
TOTAL 7 apps 2 subs 0 gls
Club Record: Cheltenham Town, Birmingham City, Tamworth (loan),
Gloucester City, Worcester City, Stourport Swifts +.

PRICE, Leonard Selby (GK/IF)
b. Qu4 1887 Gloucester d. ?
1919/20

PRICE, Peter (IF)
b. 26/02/1932 Tarbolton, Ayrshire, Scotland
1952/53 39 apps 8 gls
1953/54 5 apps 0 gls
TOTAL 44 apps 8 gls
Club Record: Craigmark Bruntonians, Glasgow Celtic (trial) (0), 1951
Saint Mirren (2-0), Gloucester City, 1953-54 Darlington (3-0), 1955-62 Ayr
United (199-173), Raith Rovers (0), 1962 Albion Rovers (13-4),
Gladesville (Australia).

PRICTOR, ? (D)
1980/81 1 app 0 gls
TOTAL 1 app 0 gls

PRIDAY, C (HB)
1919/20

PRINCE, Francis Anthony (Frankie) (M)
b. 01/12/1949 Penarth, Wales
1981/82 0 apps 1 sub 0 gls
TOTAL 0 apps 1 sub 0 gls
Club Record: 1967-79 Bristol Rovers (362-23), 1980-81 Exeter City (31-2), Gloucester City, Taunton Town.
International Record: Wales U23 (4).
Note: Was a sub in a full International against England in 1972, but never got off the bench.

PRINCE, Luke (M)
b. 10/08/1980 Oxford, Oxon.
2001/02 34 apps 3 gls
TOTAL 34 apps 3 gls
Club Record: Coventry City (0), Aston Villa (0), Wrexham (trials) (0), Saint Johnstone (trials) (0), Forest Green Rovers, Bath City, Gloucester City, Team Bath, Redditch United, Team Bath, Mangotsfield United, Salisbury City, Bath City (loan), Chippenham Town +.

PRINCE, T (FB)
1890/91

PRITCHARD, Justin (F)
b. 31/08/1977 Bristol, Avon
2005/06 2 apps 0 gls
TOTAL 2 apps 0 gls
Club Record: Bristol Rovers (0), Mangotsfield United, Clevedon Town, Bath City, Yate Town, Mangotsfield United, Merthyr Tydfil, Weston-Super-Mare, Yate Town, Weston-Super-Mare, Yate Town (loan), Gloucester City (loan), Bath City (loan), Taunton Town (loan), Yate Town, Hallen +.

PRITCHARD, Sidney (Sid) (GK)
1966/67 6 apps 0 gls
TOTAL 6 apps 0 gls
Club Record: Gloucester City, Stonehouse +.
Note: Played for Gloucester City 1967/68.

PRITCHETT, Mark Andrew (M)
b. 08/07/1988 Gloucester
2005/06 1 app 0 gls (3 nps)
TOTAL 1 app 0 gls (3 nps)
Club Record: Gloucester City, Slimbridge, Hardwicke, Cinderford Town +.

PROBYN, C (CF)
1919/20

PROCTOR, Hubert Sidney (HB)
b. 1905 Gloucester d. ?
1920/21
Note: Brother of William Proctor.

PROCTOR, William Victor (IF)
b. 09/02/1900 Gloucester d. Qu1 1984 Gloucester
1919/20
1921/22
Note: Brother of Hubert Proctor.

PROSSER, Ivor (WH)
b. 1937
1964/65 14 apps 1 gl
TOTAL 14 apps 1 gl
Club Record: Trowbridge Town, Swindon Town (0), Bath City, Trowbridge Town, Gloucester City +.

PROUDFOOT, Archibald Black (Archie) (FB)
b. 07/11/1923 Edinburgh, Scotland
1952/53 21 apps 0 gls
1953/54 27 apps 0 gls
1954/55 19 apps 0 gls
1955/56 14 apps 0 gls
1956/57 21 apps 0 gls
1957/58 16 apps 0 gls
TOTAL 118 apps 0 gls
Club Record: Edinburgh City, 1948-50 East Fife (23-0), Cowdenbeath (3-0), Linfield, Berwick Rangers (0), Gloucester City, Cinderford Town +.

PROUT, ? (WH) ++
1942/43 1 app 1 gl
TOTAL 1 app 1 gl
Club Record: Cheltenham Town, Gloucester City +.

PRUE, Kevin J (F)
b. Qu4 1956 Sodbury, Glos.
1980/81 22 apps 1 sub 5 gls (2 nps)
TOTAL 22 apps 1 sub 5 gls (2 nps)
Club Record: Forest Green Rovers, Paulton Rovers, Gloucester City, Yate Town +.

PUGSLEY, David (FB)
1966/67 8 apps 0 gls (1 nps)
TOTAL 8 apps 0 gls (1 nps)

PUGSLEY, David George (Dave) (GK)
b. 15/08/1931 Merthyr Tydfil, Wales
1950/51 2 apps 0 gls
1951/52 7 apps 0 gls
TOTAL 9 app 0 gls
Club Record: Gloucester City, 1952 Newport County (1-0), Aberdare Athletic, Gloucester City.

PULLEN, Walter Ernest (Wally) (IF)
b. 02/08/1919 Ripley, Surrey d. Qu3 1977 Luton, Beds.
1951/52 27 apps 9 gls
1952/53 41 apps 18 gls
TOTAL 68 apps 27 gls
Club Record: 1939 Fulham (0), 1946-50 Leyton Orient (117-37), Gloucester City.
Note: Club Captain 1952-53.

QUICK, S (FB)
1928/29 1 app 0 gls
TOTAL 1 app 0 gls

QUINLAN, Michael (Mike/Mick) (W/FB)
b. 04/12/1941 Barnsley, Yorks
1962/63 34 apps 0 gls
1963/64 43 apps 1 gl
TOTAL 77 apps 1 gl
Club Record: 1958 Doncaster Rovers (0), 1960 Bristol City (2-0), Cheltenham Town, Gloucester City, Welton Rovers +.

QUIXLEY, Frederick George Edmund (FB)
b. 20/06/1885 Luton, Beds. d. 19/01/1971 North Kesteven, Lincs.
1906/07 17 apps 0 gls
1907/08 14 apps 0 gls
1908/09 16 apps 0 gls
1909/10 4 apps 0 gls
TOTAL 51 apps 0 gls
Club Record: Gloucester City, Gloucester City Albion +.

RADCLIFFE, Tom (D)
2002/03 1 app 11 subs 0 gls (5 nps)
TOTAL 1 app 11 subs 0 gls (5 nps)
Club Record: Witney Town, Cirencester Town, Gloucester City, Slimbridge, Chipping Norton Town, Gloucester United +.

RADFORD, J (IF)
1894/95 2 apps 0 gls
1895/96 1 app 0 gls
TOTAL 3 apps 0 gls
Note: Played for Gloucester 1896/97.

RADFORD, Jason (?)
1990s

RADFORD, S (W)
1928/29 2 apps 0 gls
TOTAL 2 apps 0 gls

RANDALL, Lee (F)
b. 12/04/1978 Slough, Berks.
2001/02 1 app 0 gls
2004/05 11 apps 10 subs 1 gl
2005/06 2 apps 14 subs 1 gl (28 nps)
2006/07 1 app 4 subs 0 gls (13 nps)
TOTAL 15 apps 28 subs 2 gls (41 nps)
Club Record: Glasgow Celtic (0), Kilmarnock (0), Oldham Athletic (0), Slough Town, Chesham United, Harrow Borough, Windsor & Eton, Brockworth, Gloucester City, Brockworth Albion, Gloucester City, Cirencester United (loan), Cinderford Town, Brockworth Albion +.

RAVENHILL, J (GK) ++
1940/41

RAWLINGS, ? (GK) ++
1942/43

RAWLINS, Matthew Benjamin (Matt) (F)
b. 12/09/1975 Bristol, Avon
2000/01 20 apps 5 subs 13 gls
TOTAL 20 apps 5 subs 13 gls
Club Record: Arsenal (0), Wolverhampton Wanderers (0), AFC
Bournemouth (0), Cardiff City (0), Sligo Rovers (Eire), Mangotsfield
United, Weston-Super-Mare, Chippenham Town, Yate Town, Clevedon
Town, Gloucester City, Chippenham Town, Clevedon Town, Yate Town,
Taunton Town +.

REA, Gavin James (D)
b. Qu2 1984 Gloucester
2000/01 1 app 5 subs 0 gls (6 nps)
2001/02 4 apps 1 sub 0 gls (5 nps)
TOTAL 5 apps 6 subs 0 gls (11 nps)

REDWOOD, Douglas James (Doug) (W) ++
b. 24/10/1918 Ebbw Vale, Wales d. Qu1 1979 Walsall, Staffs,
1940/41
Club Record: Ebbw Vale, 1935-36 Cardiff City (13-0), 1937-38 Walsall
(27-6), 1939 Rochdale (0), Gloucester City +.

REEVES, J (FB/WH) ++
1939/40 2 apps 0 gls
1942/43 18 apps 7 gls
TOTAL 20 apps 7 gls
Note: Played for Gloucester City 1940/41.

REEVES, Neil (D)
1994/95 6 apps 0 gls
1995/96 29 apps 0 gls (2 nps)
TOTAL 35 apps 0 gls (2 nps)
Club Record: Bristol Rovers (0), Bath City, Trowbridge Town, Clevedon
Town, Gloucester City, Weston-Super-Mare +.

REEVES, Reg (FB)
1961/62 28 apps 0 gls
TOTAL 28 apps 0 gls

REFFOLD, Jimmy (W)
1969/70 1 app 0 gls
TOTAL 1 app 0 gls
Club Record: Aldershot (0), Gloucester City +.

REID, Jamie (M)
b. 20/04/1988 Gloucester
2004/05 3 apps 12 subs 0 gls (14 nps)
2005/06 12 apps 11 subs 3 gls (11 nps)
2006/07 36 apps 6 subs 5 gls (2 nps)
2007/08 40 apps 6 subs 6 gls (3 nps)
2008/09 0 apps 1 sub 0 gls
TOTAL 91 apps 36 subs 14 gls (30 nps)
Club Record: Hardwicke, Gloucester City, Almondsbury Town (loan),
Cirencester Town (loan) +.

REID, John (W)
1973/74 6 apps 0 gls
1977/78 0 apps 2 subs 0 gls (1 nps)
TOTAL 6 apps 2 subs 0 gls (1 nps)
Club Record: Bishop's Cleeve, Cheltenham Town, Gloucester City,
unknown Australian club, Gloucester City +.

REYNOLDS, David (Dave) (CF)
1960/61 1 app 0 gls
TOTAL 1 app 0 gls

REYNOLDS, Peter (Sub)
1968/69
Club Record: Merthyr Tydfil, Gloucester City (trial) +.

RHODES, J.H (GK)
1913/14 1 app 0 gls
TOTAL 1 app 0 gls

RICE, Selwyn (M)
b. 15/04/1949 Chulmleigh, Devon
1967/68 26 apps 3 gls (4 nps)
1968/69 37 apps 3 subs 9 gls (8 nps)
1969/70 23 apps 3 subs 5 gls (4 nps)
1970/71 46 apps 1 sub 1 gl (3 nps)
1978/79 14 apps 2 subs 1 gl
1979/80 21 apps 1 sub 0 gls (2 nps)
TOTAL 167 apps 10 subs 19 gls (21 nps)
Club Record: Exeter City (0), Weymouth, Gloucester City, Wimbledon,
Cheltenham Town, Cinderford Town, Dulwich Hamlet, Gloucester City,
Cheltenham Town, Barnstaple Town.

RICH, S.T (CF)
1899/00 1 app 0 gls
TOTAL 1 app 0 gls

RICHARDS, C (W)
1924/25 3 apps 0 gls
1925/26 1 app 0 gls
1926/27 6 apps 0 gls
TOTAL 10 apps 0 gls

RICHARDS, Marc (Ricco) (M/D)
b. 08/11/1981 Gloucester
2006/07 8 apps 1 sub 2 gls
2007/08 39 apps 4 subs 3 gls (1 nps)
2008/09 36 apps 3 subs 2 gls (1 nps)
TOTAL 83 apps 8 subs 7 gls (2 nps)
Club Record: Cheltenham Town, Cinderford Town, Weston-Super-Mare,
Swindon Supermarine, Cirencester Town, Gloucester City, Chippenham
Town, Gloucester City +.

RICHARDSON, Harold L (Harry) (IF)
b. 1873 Upton-on-Severn, Worcs. d. ?
1902/03 3 apps 0 gls
1903/04 2 apps 0 gls
TOTAL 5 apps 0 gls

RICHARDSON, Paul (M)
b. 25/10/1949 Selston, Notts.
1985/86 2 apps 1 sub 0 gls (1 nps)
TOTAL 2 apps 1 sub 0 gls (1 nps)
Club Record: 1967-76 Nottingham Forest (222-18), 1976 Chester (28-2),
1977-80 Stoke City (127-10), 1981-82 Sheffield United (36-2), 1982
Blackpool (loan) (4-0), 1983 Swindon Town (7-0), 1984 Swansea City
(12-0), Fairford Town, Gloucester City, Witney Town.
Note: Player Manager May 1985 - Nov 1985.

RICKELTON, ? (W)
1937/38 7 apps 2 gls
TOTAL 7 apps 2 gls

RICKS, B (W)
1926/27 1 app 0 gls
TOTAL 1 app 0 gls

RILEY, Joseph (Joe) (CF)
b. Qu2 1910 Sheffield, Yorks. d. ?
1938/39 36 apps 13 gls
TOTAL 36 apps 13 gls
Club Record: Conisborough Welfare, Denaby United, Goldthorpe United,
1931-32 Bristol Rovers (9-4), 1933-34 Bristol City (59-21), 1935-37
Bournemouth & Boscombe Athletic (93-57), 1937 Notts County (7-1),
Gloucester City, Cheltenham Town.

RIMMER, Colin (F)
b. 1956
1972/73
Club Record: Gloucester YMCA, Gloucester City (trial) +.

RIMMER, Edward (Eddie) (M)
b. 17/03/1988 Gloucester
2004/05 0 apps 4 subs 1 gl (4 nps)
2005/06 1 app 4 subs 0 gls (14 nps)
TOTAL 1 app 8 subs 1 gl (18 nps)
Club Record: Gloucester City, Hardwicke +.

RINGROSE, Sidney (IF)
1925/26 27 apps 17 gls
1926/27 10 apps 6 gls
1927/28 7 app 1 gl
1928/29 9 apps 3 gls
1929/30 1 app 0 gls
TOTAL 54 apps 27 gls
Club Record: Gloucester Westgate, Gloucester City +.

RIRREGAH, Serge (F)
b. France ?
2004/05

RISDALE, Steve (CF)
1979/80 8 apps 1 gl (2 nps)
TOTAL 8 apps 1 gl (2 nps)
Club Record: Minehead, Bath City, Gloucester City +.

ROBERTS, ? (W)
1946/47 4 apps 1 gl
1947/48 1 app 1 gl
1948/49 1 app 0 gls
TOTAL 6 apps 2 gls
Club Record: Royal Air Force, Gloucester City +.

ROBERTS, A (CF)
1896/97

ROBERTS, Christopher (Chris) (Sub)
2000/01

ROBERTS, Mills (CF)
1999/00

ROBERTS, Paul (GK)
1990/91 2 apps 0 gls (1 nps)
TOTAL 2 apps 0 gls (1 nps)

ROBERTS, R (W)
1934/35 1 app 0 gls
TOTAL 1 app 0 gls

ROBERTS, Trevor (GK)
1958/59 6 apps 0 gls
TOTAL 6 apps 0 gls
Club Record: Hereford United, Gloucester City (loan) +.

ROBERTSON, James (Jimmy) (W)
b. 1927 Scotland
1950/51 22 apps 14 gls
1951/52 14 apps 6 gls
TOTAL 36 apps 20 gls
Club Record: Stallcross Hearts (Falkirk), Plymouth Argyle (0), Gloucester City +.

ROBINS, H.T (IF/GK)
1891/92 1 app 1 gl
1892/93 3 app 2 gls
1893/94 15 apps 2 gls
1894/95 8 apps 2 gls
1895/96 3 apps 0 gls
1898/99 1 app 0 gls
TOTAL 31 apps 7 gls
Note: Played for Gloucester 1896/97. Club Secretary 1893-1897.

ROBISON, Darren (CD)
b. 19/05/1971 Plymouth, Devon
2006/07 1 app 0 gls (2 nps)
TOTAL 1 app 0 gls (2 nps)
Club Record: Millbrook, Falmouth Town, Truro City, Witney Town, Weston-Super-Mare, Trowbridge Town, Newport AFC, Cirencester Town, Merthyr Tydfil, Gloucester City, Cirencester United (loan), Carterton Town +.

ROBOTHAM, ? (CH)
1899/00 2 apps 0 gls
TOTAL 2 apps 0 gls

ROBSON, A.H (IF)
1896/97

ROCHE, S (FB)
1926/27 20 apps 0 gls
1929/30 1 app 0 gls
1930/31 1 app 0 gls
TOTAL 22 apps 0 gls
Club Record: Gloucester City, Pope's Hill +.

RODGERSON, Alan Ralph (Dodge) (IF)
b. 19/03/1939 Ashington, Northumberland
1968/69 45 apps 10 gls (2 nps)
1969/70 33 apps 2 subs 6 gls
TOTAL 78 apps 2 subs 16 gls (2 nps)
Club Record: Potters Bar, 1958-63 Middlesbrough (13-3), Cambridge United, Hereford United, Gloucester City +.

RODWAY, A (WH)
1897/98

RODWELL, J (WH)
1890/91

ROGERS, ? (FB) ++
1941/42
Club Record: Hull City (0), Gloucester City +.

ROGERS, Lee Martyn (D)
b. 08/04/1967 Bristol
1990/91 11 apps 0 gls
1991/92 23 apps 1 sub 0 gls (3 nps)
TOTAL 34 apps 1 sub 0 gls (3 nps)
Club Record: 1984-87 Bristol City (30-0), 1986 Hereford United (loan) (13-0), 1987 York City (7-0), 1988-90 Exeter City 78-0), Gloucester City, Weston-Super-Mare.

ROGERS, Martyn (Dodge) (FB)
b. 07/03/1955 Bristol
1987/88 14 apps 0 gls
TOTAL 14 apps 0 gls
Club Record: 1973 Bristol City (0), Bath City, 1979-84 Exeter City (132-5), Weymouth, Gloucester City, Tiverton Town +.
Note: Cousin of Peter Rogers.

ROGERS, Peter Philip (F)
b. 22/04/1953 Bristol
1987/88 14 apps 4 gls (1 nps)
TOTAL 14 apps 4 gls (1 nps)
Club Record: Minehead, Taunton Town, Bath City, 1978-83 Exeter City (205-39), Weymouth, Gloucester City, Tiverton Town +.
Note: Cousin of Martyn Rogers.

ROLES, Albert J (Albie) (FB)
b. 29/09/1921 Southampton, Hants.
1949/50 39 apps 0 gls
TOTAL 39 apps 0 gls
Club Record: 1948 Southampton (1-0), Gloucester City, Cowes +.

ROMANS, Francis Charles James (W)
b. Qu2 1882 Gloucester d. Qu4 1956 Gloucester
1902/03 9 apps 4 gls
TOTAL 9 apps 4 gls

ROSE, ? (WH) ++
1941/42 1 app 0 gls
TOTAL 1 app 0 gls

ROSE, Matthew Lee (M)
b. 03/05/1976 Cheltenham, Glos.
1999/00 32 apps 4 subs 4 gls
2007/08 41 apps 3 subs 3 gls (1 nps)
2008/09 45 apps 2 subs 1 gl
TOTAL 118 apps 9 subs 8 gls (1 nps)
Club Record: Cheltenham Town, Cirencester Town, Gloucester City, Newport County, Weston-Super-Mare, Gloucester City +.

ROSE, Paul (D)
1992/93
Club Record: Chippenham Town, Trowbridge Town, Westbury United, Gloucester City +.

ROSENIOR, Leroy De Graft (D/F)
b. 24/03/1964 Clapham, London
1995/96 1 app 2 subs 0 gls
1996/97 1 app 6 subs 1 gl (1 nps)
1997/98 5 apps 13 subs 1 gl (1 nps)
TOTAL 7 apps 21 subs 2 gls (2 nps)
Club Record: 1982-84 Fulham (54-15), 1985-86 Queen's Park Rangers (38-7), 1987 Fulham (34-20), 1987-91 West Ham United (53-15), 1990 Fulham (loan) (11-3), 1991Charlton Athletic (loan) (3-0), 1991-93 Bristol City (51-12), Fleet Town, Gloucester City.
International Record: Sierra Leone (1).
Note: Club Manager Mar 1996 – Oct 1998.

ROSS, Duncan (D)
1982/83 4 apps 1 sub 0 gls (1 nps)
TOTAL 4 apps 1 sub 0 gls (1 nps)
Club Record: Chelsea (0), Walsall (0), Gloucester City +.

ROSS, William Bernard (Bernie) (WH/IF)
b. 08/11/1924 Swansea, Wales d. Qu1 1999 Bangor, Wales
1953/54 32 apps 5 gls
TOTAL 32 apps 5 gls
Club Record: Towey United, 1946-47 Cardiff City (8-2), 1948 Sheffield United (3-1), 1949-50 Southport (47-13), Bangor City, Llanelli, Gloucester City, Llanelly, Haverfordwest, Caernarvon Town, Rhyl.

ROTHIN, Albert John (IF)
b. Qu1 1944 Cheltenham, Glos.
1961/62 3 apps 0 gls
1962/63 2 apps 0 gls
TOTAL 5 apps 0 gls
Club Record: Aston Villa (trial) (0), Gloucester City +.

ROUND, S (FB)
1928/29 1 app 0 gls
TOTAL 1 app 0 gls

ROUND, Stanley G (Stan) (F)
b. Qu3 1937 Wolverhampton, Staffs.
1970/71 15 apps 3 gls
TOTAL 15 apps 3 gls
Club Record: Wolverhampton Wanderers (0), Lye Town (loan), Hinckley Athletic, Burton Albion, Worcester City, Merthyr Tydfil, Hereford United, Kidderminster Harriers, Gloucester City.

ROUSE, Shaun (M)
b. 28/02/1972 Great Yarmouth, Norfolk
1995/96 45 apps 3 subs 3 gls (1 nps)
1996/97 0 apps 3 subs 0 gls (1 nps)
TOTAL 45 apps 6 subs 3 gls (2 nps)
Club Record: Glasgow Rangers (0), 1992 Bristol City (0), Weston-Super-Mare, 1993 Carlisle United (5-0), Gloucester City, Weston-Super-Mare, Trowbridge Town, Worcester City, Witney Town, Forest Green Rovers +.

ROWE, Mark (F)
b. 1957
1976/77 4 apps 0 gls
TOTAL 4 apps 0 gls
Club Record: Worcester City, AFC Bournemouth (0), Tamworth, Gloucester City +.

ROWNTREE, Martyn Edward (D)
b. 24/11/1978 East Staffs.
1997/98 7 apps 0 gls
TOTAL 7 apps 0 gls
Club Record: Derby County (0), Burton Albion, Gloucester City, Rocester, Scunthorpe United (0), Nuneaton Borough, Gresley Rovers +.

RUSHER, Barry (CH)
b. 1948
1967/68 7 apps 0 gls
TOTAL 7 apps 0 gls
Club Record: Reading (0), Crawley Town, Gloucester City +.

RUSHFORTH, ? (FB/CF) ++
1942/43 5 apps 2 gls
TOTAL 5 apps 2 gls

RUSSELL, ? (IF) ++
1941/42
Club Record: Cheltenham Town, Gloucester City +.

RUSSELL, K (Jack) (IF)
b. 1918
1936/37 31 apps 4 gls
TOTAL 31 apps 4 gls
Club Record: Halesowen Town, Gloucester City +.

RUST, Frederick James
b. 17/09/1856 Gloucester d. 14/09/1921 Gloucester
1883+
Note: The Citizen reported his death 16/09/1921 and indicated he played for Gloucester. He must have been a member of the original Gloucester team between 1883-1886. Father of Frederick and Thomas Rust.
Club Record: Gloucester, Gloucester City Albion +.

RUST, Frederick Thomas (IF)
b. Qu3 1879 Gloucester d. ?
1898/99 8 apps 4 gls
1899/00 20 apps 9 gls
1900/01 10 apps 7 gls
1902/03 12 apps 6 gls
1903/04 11 apps 15 gls
1906/07 1 app 0 gls
TOTAL 62 apps 41 gls
Club Record: Gloucester, Saint Michael's, Gloucester City, Gloucester Thursday +.
Note: Club Captain 1900-04. Son of Frederick Rust and brother of Thomas Rust.

RUST, Thomas Henry (Tom) (WH)
b. 03/03/1881 Gloucester d. 09/08/1962 Gloucester
1900/01 1 app 0 gls
1903/04 11 apps 1 gl
TOTAL 12 apps 1 gl
Club Record: Gloucester City, Gloucester Thursday +.
Note: Played for Gloucester City 1902/03. Played cricket for Gloucestershire CCC 1914. Son of Frederick Rust and brother of Frederick Rust.

RUTHERFORD, James Douglas Jamieson (Jim) (W)
b. 04/10/1930 Ladybank, Fife, Scotland d. 24/08//2008 Gloucester
1953/54 41 apps 10 gls
1954/55 44 apps 10 gls
1955/56 39 apps 9 gls
1956/57 32 apps 7 gls
1957/58 1 app 0 gls
1958/59 2 apps 0 gls
TOTAL 159 apps 36 gls
Club Record: Leslie Hearts, Dundonald Bluebell, East Fife (0), Gloucester City.
Note: Brother of Tom Rutherford.

RUTHERFORD, Thomas (Tom) (CF)
b. 26/01/1933 Thornton, Fife, Scotland d. 24/01/2009 Gloucester
1954/55 24 apps 10 gls
1955/56 1 app 0 gls
TOTAL 25 apps 10 gls
Club Record: Rose Street Boys Club, Thornton Hibs, Nairn Thistle, Birmingham City (trial) (0), West Bromwich Albion (trial) (0), Royal Air Force, Gloucester City, Abergavenny Thursdays, Cinderford Town.
Note: Brother of Jim Rutherford.

RUTTER, Thomas (Tommy) (F)
b. 25/03/1977 Stroud, Glos.
1998/99 5 apps 6 subs 0 gls (6 nps)
TOTAL 5 apps 6 subs 0 gls (6 nps)
Club Record: Swindon Town (0), Trowbridge Town, Gloucester City, Bishop's Cleeve, Shortwood United, Fram Reykjavik (Iceland), Wilmington Hammerheads (USA), Utah Blitz (USA), Harrisburg City Islanders (USA), Bishop's Cleeve +.
Note: Played for Gloucester City 1997/98.

RYAN, Nigel R (FB)
b. 1953 Bath, Somerset
1981/82 30 apps 1 sub 1 gl
TOTAL 30 apps 1 sub 1 gl
Club Record: Reading (0), AFC Bournemouth (0), Bath City, Trowbridge Town, Poole Town, Bath City, Yeovil Town, Gloucester City, Cheltenham Town, Forest Green Rovers +.

SABIN, J (CF)
1896/97

SADLER, O (FB)
1929/30 1 app 0 gls
TOTAL 1 app 0 gls

SALT, H (FB)
1921/22 4 apps 0 gls
TOTAL 4 apps 0 gls

SAMPSON, Raymond Victor (Ray) (IF)
b. 06/02/1935 Swindon, Wilts.
1961/62 21 apps 2 gls
TOTAL 21 app 2 gls
Club Record: 1953-58 Swindon Town (64-10), Trowbridge Town, Gloucester City +.

SAMPSON, T.G (FB)
1891/92 1 app 0 gls
TOTAL 1 app 0 gls

SAUNDERS, Frank Etheridge (HB)
b. 26/08/1864 Brighton, Sussex d. 14/05/1905 Tiverton, Devon
1890/91
Club Record: Cambridge University, Swifts, Corinthians, Gloucester, St Thomas Hospital +.
International Record: England (1).

SAUNDERS, G (F)
1897/98 1 app 1 gl
TOTAL 1 app 1 gl

SAUNDERS, Gordon (GK)
1933/34 34 apps 0 gls
1934/35 49 apps 0 gls
1935/36 39 apps 0 gls
1936/37 36 apps 0 gls
1937/38 24 app 0 gls
TOTAL 182 apps 0 gls

SAUNDERS, John (W)
b. 1950
1973/74 6 apps 0 gls
TOTAL 6 apps 0 gls
Club Record: King's Lynn, Cambridge United (0), Gloucester City +.

SAUNDERS, Mark A (Muttley) (D)
b. 21/03/1964 Cirencester, Glos.
1993/94 25 apps 0 gls
TOTAL 25 apps 0 gls
Club Record: Fairford Town, Devizes Town, Melksham Town, Cirencester Town, Moreton Town, Gloucester City, Swindon Supermarine +.

SAWYER, Kevin John (GK)
b. 14/04/1980 Swindon, Wilts.
2007/08 49 apps 0 gls (1 nps)
2008/09 52 apps 0 gls
TOTAL 101 apps 0 gls (1 nps)
Club Record: Cirencester Town, Salisbury City, Cirencester Town, Gloucester City, Weston-Super-Mare +.

SAYER, Donald (Don) (WH)
b. 25/06/1954 Gloucester d. Qu3 1975 Gloucester
1972/73 0 apps 1 sub 0 gls (1 nps)
TOTAL 0 apps 1 sub 0 gls (1 nps)
Club Record: York Road, Frampton United, Gloucester City (trial), Derby County (trial) (0) +.

SAYER, Victor Thomas (Vic) (W)
b. 13/05/1921 Bristol d. Qu2 1993 Shrewsbury, Shropshire
1947/48 1 app 0 gls
TOTAL 1 app 0 gls

SAYERS, ? (IF) ++
1942/43

SCANTLEBURY, Edward Hugh P (CH)
b. Qu4 1875 Aylesbury, Bucks. d. ?
1896/97

SCARROTT, Alan Richard (W)
b. 22/11/1944 Malmesbury, Wilts.
1970/71 10 apps 1 gl
TOTAL 10 apps 1 gl
Club Record: Chippenham Town, 1961 West Bromwich Albion (0), 1964 Bristol Rovers (0), 1965-67 Reading (90-7), Hereford United, Cheltenham Town, Gloucester City.

SCARROTT, Stephen W (Steve) (D/M)
b. 15/10/1955 Cheltenham, Glos.
1977/78 25 apps 0 gls
1978/79 24 apps 4 gls
1985/86 48 apps 4 gls (1 nps)
1986/87 32 apps 4 subs 0 gls (3 nps)
1987/88 14 apps 1 sub 0 gls
TOTAL 143 apps 5 subs 8 gls (4 nps)
Club Record: Dowty Rotol, Swindon Town (0), Bath City, Cheltenham Town, Gloucester City, Trowbridge Town, Cheltenham Town, Gloucester City, Forest Green Rovers +.
Note: Player Manager Nov 1985 – Jun 1987.

SCOTT, Herbert Harger (HB)
b. Qu1 1873 Stone, Glos. d. Qu1 1949 Nottingham, Notts
1891/92 1 app 0 gls
1892/93 3 app 0 gls
1893/94 15 apps 0 gls
1895/96 14 apps 0 gls
TOTAL 33 apps 0 gls
Club Record: Gloucester, Gloucester YMCA +.
Note: Club Captain 1895-96.

SEAFORTH, ? (FB) ++
1942/43 1 app 0 gls
TOTAL 1 app 0 gls
Club Record: Bristol Rovers (0), The Army, Gloucester City+.

SEARL, Adrian (D)
1997/98

SEARLES, H.E (IF)
1913/14 2 apps 0 gls
TOTAL 2 apps 0 gls

SEARLS, Anthony (Tony) (FB)
1973/74 2 apps 0 gls
TOTAL 2 apps 0 gls
Club Record: Stonehouse, Gloucester City +.

SEDDON, Elliot Jordan (GK)
b. Qu3 1989 Cheltenham, Glos.
2007/08 4 apps 0 gls (7 nps)
TOTAL 4 apps 0 gls (7 nps)
Club Record: Cheltenham Saracens, Purton, Bishop's Cleeve, Gloucester City, Hallen +.

SELKIRK, ? (W) ++
1941/42 3 apps 1 gl
TOTAL 3 apps 1 gl

SESSIONS, Walter (HB)
b. Qu4 1870 Gloucester d. 02/05/1948 Hempsted, Gloucester
1889/90 1 app 0 gls
1891/92 1 app 0 gls
1893/94 4 apps 2 gls
TOTAL 6 apps 2 gls
Club Record: Gloucester, Cardiff +.
Note: Played for Gloucester 1890/91, 1892/93. Club Captain 1890-92. Brother of Wilfred Sessions.

SESSIONS, Wilfred (F)
b. Qu4 1868 Gloucester d. ?
1892/93 2 app 3 gls
1893/94 2 apps 2 gls
TOTAL 4 apps 5 gls
Note: Played for Gloucester 1889/90, 1890/91, 1891/92. Brother of Walter Sessions.

SEWARD, Sidney Clifford (FB/CH)
b. 12/11/1915 d. Qu2 1999 South Glos.
1942/43 4 apps 0 gls
1946/47 28 apps 0 gls
1947/48 15 apps 0 gls
TOTAL 47 apps 0 gls
Club Record: Bristol Rovers (0), Gloucester City +.

SEWELL, Cyril Otto Hudson (IF)
b. 19/12/1874 Pietermaritzburg, South Africa d. 19/08/1951 Bexhill, Sussex
1895/96
Note: Played cricket for Gloucestershire CCC 1895-1919 (Captain 1913-14, Club Secretary 1912-14).

SEYMOUR, Geoff (F)
1982/83

SHADGETT, John Beecher (CH)
b. 06/01/1889 Gloucester d. Qu2 1973 Gloucester
1913/14 9 apps 0 gls
TOTAL 9 apps 0 gls

SHAKESPEARE, Adam (D)
b. 21/06/1982 Wolverhampton, Staffs.
2007/08
Club Record: Hednesford Town, Newtown, Pelsall Villa, Barry Town, Stourbridge, Gloucester City +.

SHANKS, Robert (Bob) (CH)
b. 14/12/1911 Sunniside, County Durham d. Qu41989 Swindon, Wilts.
1947/48 38 apps 0 gls
TOTAL 38 apps 0 gls
Club Record: 1934 Leeds United (0), 1935-36 Swindon Town (25-1), 1937-38 Crystal Palace (18-0), 1946 Swindon Town (1-0), Chippenham Town, Gloucester City, Trowbridge Town, Ilfracombe Town +.
Note: Club Captain 1947-48.

SHATFORD, Clive C (M)
b. 13/06/1958 Cheltenham, Glos.
1978/79 1 app 2 subs 1 gl (2 nps)
TOTAL 1 app 2 subs 1 gl (2 nps)
Club Record: Saint Marks CA, Cheltenham Town, Cinderford Town, Gloucester City, Moreton Town, Cheltenham Town, Dowty Dynamoes, Saint Marks CA +.

SHAW, John (GK)
b. 04/02/1954 Stirling, Scotland
1988/89 56 apps 0 gls
1989/90 12 apps 0 gls (3 nps)
TOTAL 68 apps 0 gls (3 nps)
Club Record: 1971-73 Leeds United (0), 1975-84 Bristol City (295-0),
1985-87 Exeter City (109-0), Gloucester City.

SHAW, W (IF)
1899/00 13 apps 17 gls
1900/01 11 apps 10 gls
TOTAL 24 apps 27 gls

SHAW, Wilfred (Wilf) (RB) ++
b. 21/04/1912 Rossington, Yorks. d. 20/02/1945 Germany
1941/42
Club Record: 1930-39 Doncaster Rovers (184-0), Gloucester City.
Note: Killed in action WW2.

SHAXTON, Matthew James (Matt) (M)
b. 07/06/1987 Bridgwater, Somerset
2006/07 3 apps 8 subs 1 gl (2 nps)
TOTAL 3 apps 8 subs 1 gl (2 nps)
Club Record: Bridgwater Town, Gloucester City, Cirencester Town +.

SHEARER, Mick (M)
1994/95 27 apps 1 gl
TOTAL 27 apps 1 gl
Club Record: Gloucester City, Halesowen Town +.

SHEEBY, ? (IF) ++
1939/40 1 app 0 gls
TOTAL 1 app 0 gls

SHELLEY, Albert (OR/OL/CF)
b. 02/02/1914 Aston, Birmingham, Warks. d. 10/04/1947 Gloucester
1935/36 37 apps 36 gls
1936/37 13 apps 7 gls
1939/40 2 apps 1 gl
TOTAL 52 apps 44 gls
Club Record: 1932 Birmingham (0), Oakengates Town, 1934 Southampton
(0), 1935 Bournemouth & Boscombe Athletic (0), Gloucester City, 1936
Sheffield Wednesday (3-2), 1937-38 Torquay United (36-10), Gloucester
City, Lovells Athletic.
Note: Grandson of Aston Villa and England International Joe Bache.

SHENTON, Alan (W)
1969/70 4 apps 0 gls
TOTAL 4 apps 0 gls
Note: Gloucester City (trial) +

SHENTON, F (GK)
1919/20

SHEPHERD, John Arthur (IF)
b. 20/09/1945 Maltby, Yorks.
1970/71 11 apps 1 gl (2 nps)
TOTAL 11 apps 1 gl (2 nps)
Club Record: 1965-67 Rotherham United (22-2), 1968 York City (5-0),
1969 Oxford United (11-1), Hereford United, Gloucester City, 1971
Reading (0), Cheltenham Town +.

SHERMAN, R (W)
1934/35 2 apps 0 gls
TOTAL 2 apps 0 gls
Club Record: Cam Mills, Gloucester City +.

SHERWOOD, Henry George (IF)
b. 1872 Stepney, London d. ?
1891/92 1 app 0 gls
1892/93 3 app 2 gls
1893/94 16 apps 5 gls
1894/95 20 apps 8 gls
1895/96 10 apps 3 gls
1897/98 4 apps 5 gls
1898/99 15 apps 9 gls
1899/00 2 apps 4 gls
TOTAL 71 apps 36 gls
Note: Joint Club Secretary 1902-1903.

SHERWOOD, Jeffrey (Jeff) (D)
b. 05/10/1959 Bristol
1990/91 33 apps 0 gls (1 nps)
1991/92 33 apps 1 sub 0 gls
TOTAL 66 apps 1 sub 0 gls (1 nps)
Club Record: Minehead, Taunton Town, Bath City, 1982 Bristol Rovers
(18-0), Bath City, Yeovil Town, Gloucester City, Merthyr Tydfil, Yeovil
Town, Clevedon Town, Bath City, Brislington, Trowbridge Town +.
Note: Club record fee of £15,000 paid to Yeovil Town 1990/91.

SHIPLEY, Paul (D)
b. 1967
1984/85 20 apps 0 gls (6 nps)
TOTAL 20 apps 0 gls (6 nps)
Club Record: Aston Villa (0), Gloucester City +.

SHORT, David (W)
b. 14/04/1941 St. Neots, Cambs.
1962/63 23 apps 3 gls
TOTAL 23 apps 3 gls
Club Record: St. Neots Town, Corby Town, 1958-59 Lincoln City (4-0),
Bedford Town, Gloucester City +.

SHORT, J (FB)
1934/35 2 apps 0 gls
TOTAL 2 apps 0 gls
Club Record: Minchinhampton, Gloucester City +.

SHORT, Rob (Sub)
b. 1957
1976/77 0 apps 1 sub 0 gls
TOTAL 0 apps 1 sub 0 gls

SIDES, C (CH)
1913/14 2 apps 0 gls
TOTAL 2 apps 0 gls

SILCOCKS, Leonard (Len) (GK)
b. abt. 1917
1947/48 37 apps 0 gls
TOTAL 37 apps 0 gls
Club Record: Peterborough United, Gloucester City, Cheltenham Town +.

SILLETT, Neil (M)
1983/84 4 apps 0 gls (4 nps)
TOTAL 4 apps 0 gls (4 nps)

SILVEY, ? (W)
1937/38 14 apps 1 gl
TOTAL 14 apps 1 gl
Club Record: Gloucester City, Rotol AFC +.

SIMCOCK, Peter (W)
1961/62 11 apps 1 gl
TOTAL 11 apps 1 gl
Club Record: The Army, Gloucester City +.

SIMKIN, Frederick G (IF)
b. 1938 Glasgow, Scotland
1960/61 2 apps 0 gls
TOTAL 2 apps 0 gls
Club Record: Strathclyde Juniors, Gloucester City +.

SIMPKINS, F (GK)
1919/20

SIMPSON, ? (GK)
1930/31 1 app 0 gls
TOTAL 1 app 0 gls

SIMPSON, E (W)
1908/09 8 apps 2 gls
TOTAL 8 apps 2 gls

SIMPSON, Robert Marcus (Rob) (W)
b. 19/12/1965 Cirencester, Glos.
1985/86 26 apps 3 subs 3 gls (3 nps)
TOTAL 26 apps 3 subs 3 gls (3 nps)
Club Record: Oxford United (0), Forest Green Rovers, Witney Town,
Gloucester City, Wycombe Wanderers, Fairford Town.

SIMPSON, Troy Michael (F)
b. Qu2 1988 Bristol, Avon
2006/07
2007/08
Club Record: Bristol Manor Farm, Gloucester City (trial) +.

SINKINSON, Arthur E (HB)
1931/32 12 apps 1 gl
TOTAL 12 apps 1 gl
Club Record: Cheltenham Town, Gloucester City, Cheltenham Town +.

SKIPP, R (W)
1927/28 2 apps 0 gls
TOTAL 2 apps 0 gls

SKULL, John (Johnny) (IF)
b. 25/08/1932 Swindon, Wilts.
1961/62 35 apps 11 gls
TOTAL 35 apps 11 gls
Club Record: 1949 Swindon Town (0), 1950 Wolverhampton Wanderers (0), Headington United, Banbury Spencer, 1957-58 Swindon Town (33-11), Trowbridge Town, Gloucester City +.

SLATTER, Neil John (FB)
b. 30/05/1964 Cardiff, Wales
1990/91 1 app 0 gls
TOTAL 1 app 0 gls
Club Record: 1980-84 Bristol Rovers (148-4), 1985-89 Oxford United (91-6), 1989 AFC Bournemouth (loan) (6-0), Gloucester City.

SLATTERY, Steve (M)
1985/86 6 apps 3 subs 0 gls (1 nps)
TOTAL 6 apps 3 subs 0 gls (1 nps)
Club Record: Gloucester City, Cheltenham Town +.

SLOAN, Thomas (Tommy) (CF)
b. 13/10/1925 Barrhead, Renfrewshire, Scotland
1957/58 16 apps 3 gls
TOTAL 16 apps 3 gls
Club Record: Arthurlie, 1946-51 Heart of Midlothian (110-24) , 1951-57 Motherwell (112-35), Gloucester City +.

SLY, Ron Roger (HB)
b. 1877 Calstock, Cornwall d. ?
1898/99 8 apps 0 gls
1899/00 21 apps 2 gls
1902/03 11 apps 1 gl
1903/04 5 apps 0 gls
TOTAL 45 apps 3 gls

SMALL, Sam (WH)
b. 1938
1961/62 15 apps 3 gls
1962/63 1 app 0 gls
TOTAL 16 apps 3 gls
Club Record: Birmingham City (0), Coventry City (0), Gloucester City +.

SMART, Gary Michael (M)
b. 08/12/1963 Bristol
1999/00 6 apps 0 gls
TOTAL 6 apps 0 gls
Club Record: Bristol Saint George, Mangotsfield United, , Devizes Town,1985-86 Bristol Rovers (19-4), Cheltenham Town, Bristol Manor Farm, Wokingham, Bath City, Mangotsfield United, Forest Green Rovers, Newport County, Gloucester City (loan), Paulton Rovers, Bath City.

SMITH, A.H (HB)
1906/07 16 apps 0 gls
1907/08 15 apps 2 gls
1908/09 16 apps 0 gls
1909/10 17 apps 2 gls
TOTAL 64 apps 4 gls

SMITH, Alan (CH)
1957/58 48 apps 1 gl
1958/59 52 apps 1 gl
1959/60 42 apps 8 gls
TOTAL 142 apps 10 gls
Club Record: Bromsgrove Rovers, 1956 Aston Villa (0), Gloucester City +.
Note: Club Captain 1959-60.

SMITH, Arthur Lloyd (Archie) (IF)
b. 07/08/1912 Blakeney, Glos. d. 02/2001 Gloucester
1934/35 3 apps 0 gls
1935/36 37 apps 20 gls
1936/37 16 apps 8 gls
TOTAL 56 apps 28 gls
Club Record: Blakeney, Gloucester City, Wolverhampton Wanderers (trial) (0) +.

SMITH, C (GK)
1920/21

SMITH, Christopher James (Chris) (W)
b. 28/03/1966 Fordinghambridge, Christchurch, Hants.
1990/91 2 apps 2 subs 0 gls
1991/92 5 apps 1 sub 0 gls
TOTAL 7 apps 3 subs 0 gls
Club Record: Cheltenham Town, 1983-84 Bristol Rovers (1-0), Cheltenham Town, Mangotsfield United, Bath City, Cinderford Town, Gloucester City, Trowbridge Town (loan), Cirencester Town (loan), Cinderford Town (loan), Moreton Town, Cinderford Town, Forest Green Rovers, Newport AFC, Forest Green Rovers.

SMITH, Dave (F)
1975/76 9 apps 2 gls (6 nps)
TOTAL 9 apps 2 gls (6 nps)
Club Record: Stonehouse, Cinderford Town, Gloucester City +.

SMITH, Dwayne (F)
1997/98 5 apps 11 subs 3 gls (6 nps)
TOTAL 5 apps 11 subs 3 gls (6 nps)
Club Record: Gloucester City, Yate Town +.

SMITH, F.E (IF)
b. abt. 1881 d. ?
1900/01 1 app 0 gls
TOTAL 1 app 0 gls

SMITH, F.G (IF)
1934/35 7 apps 0 gls
TOTAL 7 apps 0 gls
Club Record: Hereford United, Gloucester City +.

SMITH, Fred (HB)
1930/31 2 apps 3 gls
1931/32 15 apps 1 gl
1932/33 18 apps 1 gl
1933/34 33 apps 1 gl
1934/35 38 apps 0 gls
1935/36 2 apps 0 gls
TOTAL 108 apps 6 gls
Note: Played for Gloucester City 1940/41.

SMITH, G (IF)
1930/31

SMITH, Graham (M)
b. 1973
1993/94 4 apps 3 subs 0 gls (4 nps)
TOTAL 4 apps 3 subs 0 gls (4 nps)
Club Record: Bristol City (0), Weymouth, Ellwood, Gloucester City +.

SMITH, Harry (IF)
1906/07 12 apps 4 gls
TOTAL 12 apps 4 gls
Note: Played for Gloucester City 1907/08.

SMITH, James (Jim) (W)
b. 01/01/1920 Bolton, Lancs.
1948/49 1 app 0 gls
TOTAL 1 app 0 gls
Club Record: 1945 Burnley (0), 1946-47 Leyton Orient (22-3), Croydon Rovers, Gloucester City.

SMITH, James Hay (Jimmy) (F)
b. 22/11/1969 Johnstone, Renfrewshire, Scotland
1999/00 37 apps 4 subs 19 gls (2 nps)
TOTAL 37 apps 4 subs 19 gls (2 nps)
Club Record: Saint Mirren (0), 1987-89 Torquay United (44-5), Salisbury City, Cheltenham Town, Gloucester City, Salisbury City, Pollock, Kilburnie Ladeside, Brislington, Bishop's Cleeve +.

SMITH, James Scott (Jamie) (F)
b. 04/10/1981 Gloucester
1998/99 2 apps 4 subs 0 gls (1 nps)
2001/02 0 apps 6 subs 0 gls (1 nps)
TOTAL 2 apps 10 subs 0 gls (2 nps)
Club Record: Gloucester City, Aston Villa (trial) (0) +.
Note: Brother of Lee Smith.

SMITH, L (F)
1929/30 4 apps 0 gls
TOTAL 4 apps 0 gls
Note: Played for Gloucester City 1930/31.

SMITH, Lee Frank (Smudge) (M)
b. 08/09/1983 Gloucester
2000/01 6 apps 12 subs 1 gl
2001/02 19 apps 19 subs 2 gls (4 nps)
2002/03 40 apps 15 subs 10 gls
2003/04 48 apps 2 subs 8 gls
2004/05 44 apps 2 subs 8 gls
2007/08 44 apps 2 subs 6 gls (1 nps)
2008/09 48 apps 5 subs 15 gls
TOTAL 249 apps 57 subs 50 gls (5 nps)
Club Record: Gloucester City, Viney Saint Swithins (loan), Cirencester Town, Weston-Super-Mare, Gloucester City +.
Note: Supporter's Player of the Season 2004/05. Brother of Jamie Smith.

SMITH, Lloyd F (D)
b. Qu1 1958 Gloucester
1976/77 5 apps 0 gls (3 nps)
1977/78 1 app 0 gls (2 nps)
TOTAL 6 apps 0 gls (5 nps)
Club Record: Longlevens, Gloucester City, Shortwood United +.

SMITH, Matt (D)
b. 15/10/1982 Australia
2007/08
Club Record: Portsmouth (0), Palm Beach (Australia), Queensland Roar (Australia), Chichester City United, Cirencester Town, Swindon Supermarine, Gloucester City (trial) +.

SMITH, Nigel Keith (IF)
b. 12/01/1966 Bath, Somerset
1985/86 11 app 3 gls
TOTAL 11 app 3 gls
Club Record: 1982 Bristol City (2-0), 1984 Exeter City (loan) (1-0), Cheltenham Town, Gloucester City, unknown Belgian club +

SMITH, Phillip (WH)
b. 1949
1968/69 0 apps 2 subs 0 gls (4 nps)
TOTAL 0 apps 2 subs 0 gls (4 nps)
Club Record: Oxford United (0), Trowbridge Town, Gloucester City +.

SMITH, Robin (FB)
1963/64 1 app 0 gls
TOTAL 1 app 0 gls

SMITH, S.G (HB)
1931/32 1 app 0 gls
1935/36 1 app 0 gls
1936/37 1 app 0 gls
TOTAL 3 apps 0 gls
Club Record: Bristol City (0), Gloucester City +.

SMITH, Steve (GK)
1985/86 26 apps 0 gls
TOTAL 26 apps 0 gls

SMITH, W.H (HB/GK)
1919/20

SMITH, Wilfred (W)
1906/07 12 apps 2 gls
1908/09 13 apps 10 gls
1909/10 23 apps 7 gls
TOTAL 48 apps 19 gls
Club Record: Gloucester City, Cheltenham Town +.
Note: Played for Gloucester City 1903/04, 1907/08.

SNEDDON, William Cleland (Billy) (WH) ++
b. 01/04/1914 Wishaw, Lanarkshire, Scotland d. 01/04/1995 Bangor, Wales
1939/40 3 apps 0 gls
TOTAL 3 apps 0 gls
Club Record: Rutherglen Glencairn, 1936 Falkirk (36-8), 1937-38 Brentford (66-2), 1939-46 Swansea Town (5-0), Gloucester City, 1946 Newport County (18-0), Milford United.

SNELL, E.S (IF)
1893/94 1 app 0 gls
1894/95 3 apps 1 gl
1895/96 1 app 0 gls
TOTAL 5 apps 1 gl

SOCKETT, Dave (Sub)
1971/72
Club Record: Westfields, Gloucester City (trial) +.

SOMERVILLE, James Lawrence (FB)
b. 23/03/1868 Chorley, Lancs. d. Canada?
1892/93 3 apps 0 gls
1893/94 17 apps 1 gl
TOTAL 20 apps 1 gl
Note: Played for Gloucester 1891/92. Club Captain 1892-93. Emigrated to Canada.

SPAIGHT, W (W)
1934/35 14 apps 5 gls
TOTAL 14 apps 5 gls

SPECK, Albert Frederick (HB)
b. 15/05/1901 Aston, Birmingham, Warks. d. Qu1 1991 Gloucester
1926/27 2 apps 0 gls
TOTAL 2 apps 0 gls
Note: Son of John Speck. Nephew of George Speck and Walter Speck.

SPECK, George (GK)
b. Qu2 1862 Gloucester d. Qu3 1946 Bristol
1891/92 1 app 0 gls
1892/93 3 apps 0 gls
1894/95 21 apps 0 gls
1895/96 17 apps 0 gls
1897/98 8 apps 0 gls
1898/99 15 apps 0 gls
TOTAL 65 apps 0 gls
Club Record: Nelson Villa, Gloucester, Warmley, Bristol City (0), Gloucester, Gloucester United +.
Note: Played for Gloucester 1890/91. Brother of John Speck and Walter Speck. Uncle of Albert Speck.

SPECK, John (GK)
b. Qu1 1866 Gloucester d. Qu4 1925 Gloucester
1895/96 1 app 0 gls
TOTAL 1 app 0 gls
Club Record: Nelson Villa, Gloucester, Price Walkers +.
Note: Played for Gloucester 1890/91, 1891/92. Father of Albert Speck. Brother of George Speck and Walter Speck.

SPECK, Walter (W)
b. Qu4 1869 Gloucester d. ?
1889/90
Note: Brother of George Speck and John Speck. Uncle of Albert Speck.

SPEIGHT, Jamie (M)
b. 1975
1990s

SPENCE, Arthur (HB)
b. 1868 Frampton Cotterell, Glos. d. ?
1895/96 14 apps 0 gls
TOTAL 14 apps 0 gls

SPENCER, Dave (F)
1982/83 6 apps 2 gls
TOTAL 6 apps 2 gls

SPERTI, Francesco (Franco) (D)
b. 28/01/1955 Italy
1975/76 16 apps 1 gl
TOTAL 16 apps 1 gl
Club Record: 1973 Swindon Town (1-0), Gloucester City, Cheltenham Town +.

SPITTLE, Paul David (M)
b. 16/12/1964 Wolverhampton, Staffs.
1985/86 11 apps 4 gls
TOTAL 11 apps 4 gls
Club Record: 1982 Oxford United (0), 1983 Crewe Alexandra (6-1), Worcester City, Bromsgrove Rovers, Gloucester City, Trowbridge Town, Oxford City, Abingdon Town, Thame United, Brackley Town, Oxford City, Burnham, Chesham United, Ardley United, Bicester Town, Wantage Town.

SPRAGG, Gordon Robert (Sub)
b. 13/11/1957 Gloucester
2003/04
Note: City fan who arranged a friendly against Chalford and played 35 'quality' minutes at the age of 45 years 272 days.

SPRAGG, W (CF)
1929/30 1 app 0 gls
TOTAL 1 app 0 gls

SQUIER, Norman (CF)
b. Qu2 1888 Bulvan, Essex d. ?
1906/07 11 apps 12 gls
1907/08 15 apps 16 gls
1908/09 7 apps 5 gls
1909/10 4 apps 4 gls
TOTAL 37 apps 37 gls
Club Record: Chelmsford Town, Gloucester City +.

SQUIRES, ? (W)
1956/57 4 apps 0 gls
TOTAL 4 apps 0 gls
Club Record: Yeovil Town, Gloucester City +.

STAFFORD, ? (GK)
1900/01 1 app 0 gls
TOTAL 1 app 0 gls

STARLING, Leslie (Les) (W)
b. Qu4 1919 Peterborough, Northants.
1948/49 36 apps 7 gls
1949/50 6 apps 1 gl
TOTAL 42 apps 8 gls
Club Record: Peterborough United, Gloucester City +.

STARR, Fred (CF) ++
1941/42 5 apps 18 gls
TOTAL 5 apps 18 gls
Club Record: Queen's Park Rangers (0), Gloucester City +.
Note: Scored a record 9 goals in one match 1941/42.

STEADMAN, William Charles M (Will) (D/M)
b. 21/02/1980 Dagenham, London
1996/97 0 apps 1 sub 0 gls (1 nps)
1997/98 20 apps 12 subs 0 gls (5 nps)
1998/99 9 apps 2 subs 0 gls (9 nps)
1999/00 7 apps 0 gls
2000/01 29 apps 10 subs 1 gl (5 nps)
2001/02 34 apps 1 sub 0 gls (3 nps)
2002/03 41 apps 3 subs 1 gl (6 nps)
2003/04 1 app 3 subs 0 gls
TOTAL 141 apps 32 subs 2 gls (29 nps)
Club Record: Gloucester City, Cinderford Town, Gloucester City, Cinderford Town, Shortwood United +.

STEBBING, Edward Fisher (IF)
b. Qu3 1871 Massingham, Norfolk d. ?
1893/94 4 apps 2 gls
TOTAL 4 apps 2 gls
Note: Played for Gloucester 1890/91, 1891/92.

STEEL, Gregory R (Greg) (D)
b. 11/03/1959 Clevedon, Somerset
1979/80 29 apps 1 sub 0 gls (2 nps)
1988/89 47 apps 1 gl (1 nps)
1989/90 47 apps 2 gls (2 nps)
1990/91 2 apps 2 subs 0 gls (2 nps)
TOTAL 125 apps 3 subs 3 gls (7 nps)
Club Record: Clevedon Town, 1977 Newport County (3-0), Gloucester City, Forest Green Rovers, Gloucester City +.

STEELE, Hedley Verity (D)
b. 03/02/1954 Barnsley, Yorks.
1987/88 56 apps 7 gls
TOTAL 56 apps 7 gls
Club Record: Tiverton Town, 1974 Exeter City (7-1), Dorchester Town, Weymouth, Gloucester City, Tiverton Town, Willard Rovers, Cullompton.
Note: Club Captain 1987-88.

STENHOUSE, Mike (F)
1981/82
Club Record: Western League club, Gloucester City (trial) +.

STENTON, Edward Herbert (Eddie) (W)
b. Qu3 1928 Grimsby, Lincs. d. Qu3 2001 North East Lincs.
1946/47 18 apps 1 gl
TOTAL 18 apps 1 gl
Club Record: Hardy Rangers (Grimsby), Gloucester City, Grimsby Town (0) +.

STEPHENS, A.J (IF)
1897/98 2 apps 1 gl
TOTAL 2 apps 1 gl
Note: Played for Gloucester 1896/97.

STEPHENS, Eric James (Dick) (IF)
b. 23/03/1909 Gloucester d. 03/04/1983 Gloucester
1927/28 8 apps 4 gls
1930/31 1 app 1 gl
TOTAL 9 apps 5 gls
Club Record: Gloucester City, Hereford Town, Bristol Rovers (0).
Note: Played for Gloucester City 1926/27, 1935/36. Also played rugby for Gloucester RFC and cricket for Gloucestershire CCC 1927-1937.

STEPHENS, Kenneth John (Kenny) (W)
b. 14/11/1946 Bristol
1979/80 6 apps 0 gls
1980/81 29 apps 1 sub 5 gls (4 nps)
TOTAL 35 apps 1 sub 5 gls (4 nps)
Club Record: Phildown Rovers, 1966-68 West Bromwich Albion (22-2), 1968-69 Walsall (7-0), 1970-77 Bristol Rovers (225-13), 1977-79 Hereford United (60-2), Gloucester City, Hanham Athletic.
Note: Club record fee of £4,000 paid to Hereford United 1979/80.

STERRY, F (GK)
1938/39 10 apps 0 gls
1939/40 22 apps 0 gls
TOTAL 32 apps 0 gls
Club Record: Bristol Trams, Gloucester City, The Army +.
Note: Played for Gloucester City 1940/41.

STEVENS, John Miles (CF)
b. 21/08/1941 Hertford, Herts.
1967/68 11 apps 1 gl
1968/69 51 apps 34 gls
1969/70 44 apps 2 subs 16 gls
1971/72 16 apps 3 gls
1972/73 34 apps 2 subs 11 gls (7 nps)
TOTAL 156 apps 4 subs 65 gls (7 nps)
Club Record: 1958 Nottingham Forest (0), King's Lynn, Royal Air Force, 1962-63 Swindon Town (22-10), Guildford City, Cambridge City, Chelmsford City, Gloucester City, Salisbury City, Gloucester City, Pinehurst.
Note: Club Player of the Season 1968/69.

STEVENS, Mark (GK)
1987/88 9 apps 0 gls
TOTAL 9 apps 0 gls

STEVENS, S (IF)
1926/27

STEVENSON, ? (CH) ++
1941/42 26 apps 0 gls
1942/43 18 apps 0 gls
TOTAL 44 apps 0 gls
Club Record: Ards, Gloucester City +.

STIRLAND, Albert Victor (W)
b. 14/10/1897 Basford, Notts. d. 25/12/1976 Gloucester
1929/30 1 app 0 gls
TOTAL 1 app 0 gls
Note: Club Chairman 1934-38, 1958-59.

STIRLAND, Gary (F)
b. Qu1 1961 Middlesbrough, Yorks.
1982/83 13 apps 5 gls
TOTAL 13 apps 5 gls
Club Record: Aston Villa (0), Gloucester City +.

STOCK, J. W (W)
1898/99 1 app 0 gls
1899/00 12 apps 1 gl
TOTAL 13 apps 1 gl
Club Record: Saint Michael's, Gloucester +.

STOCKLEY, Nick (M)
b. 1984
2001/02 0 apps 6 subs 1 gl (3 nps)
TOTAL 0 apps 6 subs 1 gl (3 nps)
Club Record: Gloucester City, Staunton & Corse, Ledbury Town +.

STOKES, Wayne Darren (D)
b. 16/02/1965 Wolverhampton, Staffs.
1984/85 44 apps 1 sub 0 gls
TOTAL 44 apps 1 sub 0 gls
Club Record: 1981 Coventry City (0), 1982-83 Gillingham (3-0), Worcester City, Mariehamm (Finland), Aylesbury United, Gloucester City, 1986 Stockport County (18-1), 1987-89 Hartlepool United (62-1), Gateshead.

STOLES, Arthur William (IF)
b. 11/01/1918 Merthyr Tydfil, Wales d. Qu3 1984 Gloucester
1933/34 1 app 1 gl
1934/35 21 apps 5 gls
1935/36 12 apps 2 gls
1937/38 12 apps 1 gl
1938/39 12 apps 0 gls
1939/40 2 apps 0 gls
1941/42 26 apps 7 gls
1942/43 20 apps 5 gls
TOTAL 106 app 21 gls
Club Record: Gloucester City, Cheltenham Town +.
Note: Made his debut aged 15. Played for Gloucester City 1940/41.

STONE, E (IF)
1920/21

STONE, F (FB/HB)
1922/23 1 app 0 gls
TOTAL 1 app 0 gls
Note: Played for Gloucester YMCA 1920/21.

STONE, H (W)
1922/23 1 app 0 gls
TOTAL 1 app 0 gls

STONE, W.A (W)
1919/20

STONE, Walter (IF)
b. 1903 Elmore, Glos. d. ?
1926/27 1 app 5 gls
TOTAL 1 app 5 gls
Club Record: Old Plutonians, Gloucester City +.

STONEHOUSE, Paul (M)
b. 30/07/1987 Wegberg, West Germany
2005/06 7 apps 0 gls
2006/07 7 apps 0 gls
TOTAL 14 apps 0 gls
Club Record: Forest Green Rovers, Yate Town (loan), Cinderford Town (loan), Gloucester City (loan) +.

STOODLEY, ? (WH)
1934/35 1 app 0 gls
TOTAL 1 app 0 gls

STORER, G (IF)
1929/30 2 apps 0 gls
TOTAL 2 apps 0 gls

STOUT, Frank Moxon (HB)
b. 21/02/1877 Gloucester d. 30/05/1926 Storrington, Sussex
1893/94 14 apps 1 gl
1894/95 20 apps 0 gls
TOTAL 34 apps 1 gl
Note: Played for Gloucester 1891/92, 1892/93. Frank Stout also played rugby for Gloucester RFC and Richmond RFC and represented England 14 times (Captain 3 games 1905). Brother of James Stout and Percy Stout.

STOUT, James Temple (HB)
b. Qu2 1874 Gloucester d. Qu4 1931 Gloucester
1893/94 1 app 0 gls
TOTAL 1 app 0 gls
Note: Brother of Percy Stout and Frank Stout.

STOUT, Percy Wyford (F)
b. 20/11/1875 Gloucester d. 09/10/1937 Marylebone, London
1891/92 1 app 0 gls
1892/93 2 apps 0 gls
1893/94 17 apps 11 gls
1894/95 17 apps 20 gls
TOTAL 37 apps 31 gls
Club Record: Gloucester, Wotton-under-Edge, Bristol City (0) +.
Note: Percy Stout also played rugby for Gloucester RFC, Bristol RFC and Richmond RFC and represented England 5 times. Brother of James Stout and Frank Stout.

STOW, Angus Claude (Gus) (W)
b. 12/03/1928 Ipswich, Suffolk
1946/47 20 apps 8 gls
1947/48 25 apps 4 gls
1948/49 35 apps 5 gls
1949/50 13 apps 1 gl
1950/51 12 apps 7 gls
1951/52 14 apps 3 gls
TOTAL 119 apps 28 gls
Club Record: Ipswich Town (0), Royal Air Force, Gloucester City, Stonehouse, Lydbrook Athletic.
Note: Father of Rob Stow.

STOW, Robert T (Rob) (GK)
b. 27/03/1954 Gloucester
1973/74 25 apps 0 gls
1974/75 20 apps 0 gls
1975/76 44 apps 0 gls
1976/77 44 apps 0 gls
1977/78 17 apps 0 gls
TOTAL 150 apps 0 gls
Club Record: Derby County (trial) (0), Brighton & Hove Albion (0), Matson Athletic, Frampton United, Gloucester City, Cinderford Town +.
Note: Son of Gus Stow.

STRADLING, Adam John (D)
b. Qu4 1983 Bristol, Avon
2002/03 0 apps 1 sub 0 gls
TOTAL 0 apps 1 sub 0 gls
Club Record: Gloucester City, Ellwood, Hardwicke +.

STRICKLAND, William (GK) ++
1941/42 26 apps 0 gls
1942/43 21 apps 0 gls
TOTAL 47 apps 0 gls
Club Record: Bristol Aero, Lovells Athletic, Gloucester City +.
Note: Played for Gloucester City 1946/47.

STROUD, Vince (M)
1979/80 5 apps 0 gls (2nps)
TOTAL 5 apps 0 gls (2 nps)
Club Record: Swindon Town (0), Hereford United (0), Bath City, Trowbridge Town, Gloucester City +.

STYLES, Kenneth Simon S (Kenny) (D)
b. 22/01/1981 Hereford, Herefordshire
2004/05 2 apps 4 subs 0 gls
TOTAL 2 apps 4 subs 0 gls
Club Record: Westfields, Gloucester City, Wellington +.

SUMMERHAYES, D (GK)
b. 1929
1949/50 2 apps 0 gls
TOTAL 2 apps 0 gls

SUMMERS, L (GK)
1925/26 1 app 0 gls
TOTAL 1 app 0 gls

SUMPTER, Mark (GK)
b. 10/08/1967 Wrexham, Wales
1997/98 5 apps 1 sub 0 gls
TOTAL 5 apps 1 sub 0 gls
Club Record: Amesbury Town, Ballymena, Crewe United, Salisbury City, Kevelar (Germany), Venlo (Holland), Gloucester City, Tuffley Rovers +.

SURMAN, G (IF)
1921/22 3 apps 6 gls
1922/23 21 apps 15 gls
1923/24 20 apps 10 gls
1924/25 7 apps 2 gls
1925/26 1 app 1 gl
1926/27 12 apps 2 gls
TOTAL 64 apps 36 gls

SUTTON, Neil Francis (F)
b. 14/04/1958 Nether Stowey, Nr. Bridgwater, Somerset
1979/80 18 apps 6 gls
TOTAL 18 apps 6 gls
Club Record: Nether Stowey, Bridgwater Town, Gloucester City, Taunton Town +.

SWANKIE, Ian R (M)
b. Qu2 1956 Gloucester
1980/81 1 app 0 gls
TOTAL 1 app 0 gls
Club Record: Wilton Rovers, Gloucester City (loan), Hardwicke +.
Note: Son of Bob Swankie.

SWANKIE, Robert Beattie (Bob) (WH)
b. 25/02/1932 Arbroath, Scotland
1952/53 11 apps 1 gl
1954/55 10 apps 1 gl
TOTAL 21 apps 2 gls
Club Record: Arbroath Youth Club, 1950 Burnley (0), Gloucester City,
1953 Darlington (1-0), Gloucester City, Kidderminster Harriers, Cinderford
Town.
Note: Father of Ian Swankie.

SWEENEY, Gerald (Gerry) (IF)
b. 10/07/1945 Renfrew, Scotland
1982/83 17 apps 1 gl
1983/84 51 apps 3 gls
TOTAL 68 apps 4 gls
Club Record: Johnstone Burgh, Renfrew Juniors, 1966-70 Greenock
Morton (137-16), 1971-81 Bristol City (406-22), 1981 York City (12-0),
Gloucester City, Forest Green Rovers.
Note: Club Captain 1983-84.

SWEETING, Donald (IF)
1946/47 16 apps 3 gls
TOTAL 16 apps 3 gls

SYKES, Alexander Barrett (Alex/Syko) (M)
b. 02/04/1974 Newcastle-under-Lyme, Staffs.
2005/06 6 apps 0 gls
2006/07 41 apps 3 subs 14 gls
2007/08 42 apps 9 subs 17 gls
2008/09 37 apps 5 subs 27 gls (6 nps)
TOTAL 126 apps 17 subs 58 gls (6 nps)
Club Record: Westfields, Mansfield Town (0), Endsleigh, Forest Green
Rovers, Nuneaton Borough, Forest Green Rovers (loan), Bath City (loan),
Forest Green Rovers, Bath City, Gloucester City, Shortwood United (loan)
+.
International Record: England Futsal (38+).
Note: Supporter's Player of the Season 2008/09.

SYMINGTON, Andrew G.William (Andy/Willie) (W)
b. 1937 Edinburgh, Scotland
1959/60 39 apps 6 gls
1960/61 41 apps 11 gls
TOTAL 80 apps 17 gls
Club Record: Heart of Midlothian (0), Sunderland (trial) (0), Arsenal (trial)
(0), Falkirk (0), Dumbarton (0), Gloucester City +.

SYMONS, Michael Anthony (Mike) (F)
b. 22/06/1986 Bideford, Devon
2008/09 23 apps 1 sub 12 gls (1 nps)
TOTAL 23 apps 1 sub 12 gls (1 nps)
Club Record: Bristol City (0), Bideford Town, Barnstaple Town,
Cirencester Town, Clevedon Town, Forest Green Rovers (trial), Gloucester
City, Forest Green Rovers, Gloucester City +.

SYSUM, Matthew John (Matt) (M)
b. 29/09/1989 Gloucester
2007/08 8 apps 3 subs 0 gls (14 nps)
2008/09 16 apps 11 subs 2 gls (10 nps)
TOTAL 24 apps 14 subs 2 gls (24 nps)
Club Record: Hardwicke, Gloucester City, Cirencester Town (loan) +.

TABOR, Richard (Dick) (IF)
b. 1947
1966/67 6 apps 1 gl
TOTAL 6 apps 1 gl
Club Record: Swindon Town (0), Bournemouth & Boscombe Athletic (0),
Reading (0), Gloucester City, Cheltenham Town (trial), Morris Motors +.

TADMAN, Edgar Thomas Stuart (FB)
b. Qu3 1872 Maidstone, Kent d. ?
1893/94 3 apps 0 gls
1894/95 15 apps 0 gls
1895/96 12 apps 0 gls
TOTAL 30 apps 0 gls
Note: Club Captain 1894-95.

TALBOT, E.T (CF)
1896/97

TALBOYS, Steven John (Steve/Stixxy) (M)
b. 18/09/1966 Bristol
1987/88 28 apps 1 sub 11 gls
1988/89 29 apps 9 subs 9 gls (11 nps)
1989/90 52 apps 9 subs 24 gls (1 nps)
1990/91 38 apps 2 subs 14 gls (1 nps)
1991/92 28 apps 1 sub 8 gls
1999/00 1 app 0 gls
TOTAL 176 apps 22 subs 66 gls (13 nps)
Club Record: Forest Green Rovers, Mangotsfield United, Bath City,
Longwell Green, Trowbridge Town, Gloucester City, 1991-95 Wimbledon
(26-1), 1996-97 Watford (5-0), Kingstonian, Sutton United, Aldershot
Town, Paulton Rovers, Boreham Wood, Carshalton Athletic, Hampton &
Richmond, Gloucester City, Staines Town +.
Note: Player's Player of the Season 1989/90.

TANDY, Bernard Ivor (Sub)
b. 18/10/1938 Gloucester d. 04/08/1996 Cheltenham, Glos.
1971/72 0 apps 0 gls (1 nps)
1974/75 0 apps 0 gls (1 nps)
TOTAL 0 apps 0 gls (2 nps)
Note: Bernard's son Adrian Tandy succeeded his father as Club physio in
1996. Father of Daryl Tandy.

TANDY, Daryl Michael (GK)
b. 10/02/1969 Gloucester
1988/89 0 apps 0 gls (1 nps)
TOTAL 0 apps 0 gls (1 nps)
Note: Son of Bernard Tandy. Played for Gloucester City 1987/88, 1993/94,
1997/98.

TANNER, Keith (D)
b. 1958
1979/80 12 apps 0 gls
1982/83 32 apps 0 gls (4 nps)
1983/84 25 apps 2 gls (2 nps)
1984/85 27 apps 1 sub 0 gls
1985/86 0 apps 1 sub 0 gls (1 nps)
TOTAL 96 apps 2 subs 2 gls (7 nps)
Club Record: Gloucester City, Swindon Town (0), Trowbridge Town,
Gloucester City +.

TANNER, W.G (FB)
1927/28 1 app 0 gls
TOTAL 1 app 0 gls

TAYLOR, ? (CH)
1894/95 1 app 0 gls
TOTAL 1 app 0 gls

TAYLOR, ? (IF)
1909/10 1 app 0 gls
TOTAL 1 app 0 gls

TAYLOR, ? (CF)
1920/21

TAYLOR, A (IF)
1936/37 1 app 0 gls
1937/38 3 apps 0 gls
TOTAL 4 app 0 gls

TAYLOR, C (Sub)
1983/84 0 apps 0 gls (1 nps)
TOTAL 0 apps 0 gls (1 nps)

TAYLOR, F.E (FB)
b. abt. 1881 d. ?
1906/07 3 apps 0 gls
1908/09 1 app 0 gls
1909/10 1 app 0 gls
TOTAL 5 apps 0 gls

TAYLOR, Gareth Keith (D)
b. 25/02/1973 Weston-Super-Mare, Somerset
1991/92 2 apps 0 gls
TOTAL 2 apps 0 gls
Club Record: 1989 Southampton (0), 1991-95 Bristol Rovers (47-16),
Gloucester City (loan), Weymouth (loan), 1995 Crystal Palace (20-1),
1995-98 Sheffield United (84-25), 1998-99 Manchester City (43-9), 1999
Port Vale (4-0) (loan), 1999 Queen's Park Rangers (6-1) (loan), 2000-02
Burnley (95-36), 2003-05 Nottingham Forest (90-19), 2005 Crewe
Alexandra (loan) (15-4), 2006-07 Tranmere Rovers (60-10), 2007-08
Doncaster Rovers (29-1), Carlisle United (5-0) (loan), Wrexham +.
International Record: Wales (14), Wales U21 (7).

PLAYERS' RECORDS

TAYLOR, Greg (HB)
1989/90

TAYLOR, Jody Ross (F)
b. 06/08/1985 Gloucester
2007/08 0 apps 8 subs 0 gls (14 nps)
TOTAL 0 apps 8 subs 0 gls (14 nps)
Club Record: Mitcheldean, Ruardean Hill, Harrow Hill, Gloucester City, Shortwood United (loan), Cinderford Town, Gloucester City, Bishop's Cleeve, Hardwicke, Harrow Hill +.
Note: Played for Gloucester City 2008/09.

TAYLOR, John (D)
1980/81 8 apps 0 gls (7 nps)
TOTAL 8 apps 0 gls (7 nps)
Club Record: Monmouth Town, Gloucester City (trial) +.

TAYLOR, L (GK)
1933/34 4 apps 0 gls
TOTAL 4 apps 0 gls

TAYLOR, Matthew Adrian (Matt) (GK)
b. 02/02/1983 Ross-on-Wye, Herefordshire
2001/02 11 apps 0 gls
2002/03 3 apps 0 gls (2 nps)
TOTAL 14 apps 0 gls (2 nps)
Club Record: Northampton Town (0), Newport County, Gloucester City +.

TAYLOR, R (WH)
1926/27

TAYLOR, W (CF)
1929/30 30 apps 19 gls
1930/31 19 apps 19 gls
TOTAL 49 apps 38 gls
Club Record: Gloucester City, Tuffley YMCA +.

TAYNTON, A.G (WH)
1889/90

TEAGUE, William Edward (Bill) (GK)
b. 26/09/1937 Lydney, Glos. d. Qu3 1998 Gloucester
1956/57 28 apps 0 gls
1957/58 27 apps 0 gls
1958/59 6 apps 0 gls
1959/60 26 apps 0 gls
TOTAL 87 apps 0 gls
Club Record: Churchdown, Gloucester City, 1960-61 Swindon Town (3-0), 1961-62 Bristol City (0), Hereford United, Cheltenham Town.

TEASDALE, Mark (GK)
b. 11/11/1961 Consett, County Durham
1986/87 17 apps 0 gls
1987/88 12 apps 0 gls
TOTAL 29 apps 0 gls
Club Record: Saint Joseph's (Devizes), Devizes Town, Oxford City, Swindon Town (0), Gloucester City, Trowbridge Town, Bath City, Cheltenham Town +.

TEMPLE, Craig (D)
1997/98 1 app 0 gls (1 nps)
2001/02 18 apps 2 subs 0 gls (1 nps)
2002/03 2 apps 4 subs 0 gls (3 nps)
TOTAL 21 apps 6 subs 0 gls (5 nps)
Club Record: Brockworth, Gloucester City +.
Note: Brother of Mark Temple.

TEMPLE, Mark (M)
1999/00 2 apps 2 subs 0 gls (9 nps)
2001/02 0 apps 0 gls (2 nps)
TOTAL 2 apps 2 subs 0 gls (11 nps)
Club Record: Brockworth, Gloucester City +.
Note: Brother of Craig Temple.

THOMAS, ? (CH)
1920/21

THOMAS, ? (IF) ++
1941/42 1 app 0 gls
TOTAL 1 app 0 gls
Club Record: The Army, Gloucester City +.

THOMAS, ? (FB)
1947/48 4 apps 0 gls
TOTAL 4 apps 0 gls

THOMAS, Ashley John (Smash) (D)
b. 27/02/1982 Gloucester
2007/08 29 apps 2 subs 4 gls (1 nps)
2008/09 12 apps 5 subs 1 gl (5 nps)
TOTAL 41 apps 7 subs 5 gls (6 nps)
Club Record: Chalford, Shortwood United, Slimbridge, Shortwood United, Gloucester City, Shortwood United +.

THOMAS, Bradley (M)
b. 25/06/1973 Gloucester
2003/04
Club Record: Sharpness, Cinderford Town, Newport County, Forest Green Rovers, Newport County, Cinderford Town, Bath City, Weston-Super-Mare, Gloucester City, Slimbridge, Yate Town +.

THOMAS, Gareth (M)
b. 10/11/1989
Club Record: Hereford United (0), Gloucester City +.
2008/09

THOMAS, L.H (GK)
1919/20

THOMAS, Mel (W)
1962/63 14 apps 0 gls
TOTAL 14 apps 0 gls

THOMAS, Roderick John (Rod) (IF)
b. 11/01/1947 Glyncorrwg, Wales
1963/64 10 apps 3 gls
1982/83 0 apps 0 gls (1 nps)
TOTAL 10 apps 3 gls (1 nps)
Club Record: Gloucester City, 1965-73 Swindon Town (296-4), 1973-77 Derby County (89-2), 1977-81 Cardiff City (96-0), 1981 Newport County (3-0), Gloucester City (trial), Barry Town.
International Record: Wales (47), Wales U23 (6).

THOMPSON, Christopher David (Chris) (D/M)
b. 15/08/1982 Wroughton, Wilts.
2001/02 6 apps 0 gls
2002/03 49 apps 2 subs 10 gls
2003/04 49 apps 2 subs 1 gl (1 nps)
2004/05 46 apps 0 gls
2005/06 35 apps 1 sub 1 gl (1 nps)
2006/07 45 apps 2 subs 0 gls (2 nps)
2007/08 11 apps 0 gls (2 nps)
TOTAL 241 apps 7 subs 12 gls (6 nps)
Club Record: Brockworth, Gloucester City, Northampton Town (0) Gloucester City, Swindon Supermarine, Cirencester Town +.
Note: Club Captain 2005.

THOMPSON, Mark (M)
b. 1960
1983/84 3 apps 0 gls
TOTAL 3 apps 0 gls
Club Record: Swindon Town (0), Trowbridge Town, Gloucester City +.

THOMPSON, Martin (D)
1994/95

THOMPSON, Marvin Paul (D)
b. 15/10/1984 Gloucester
2003/04 3 apps 3 subs 1 gl (5 nps)
2004/05 32 apps 7 subs 1 gl (4 nps)
2005/06 14 apps 4 subs 0 gls (1 nps)
TOTAL 49 apps 14 subs 2 gls (10 nps)
Club Record: Cheltenham Town (0), Gloucester City, Cinderford Town, Cirencester Town +.

THOMPSON, Philip (IF)
1938/39 6 apps 3 gls
1939/40 5 apps 0 gls
TOTAL 11 apps 3 gls
Club Record: Wycombe Wanderers, Gloucester City +.

THOMPSON, Richard John (F)
b. 11/04/1969 Hawkesbury, Glos.
1989/90 2 apps 2 subs 0 gls (2 nps)
TOTAL 2 apps 2 subs 0 gls (2 nps)
Club Record: Yate Town, 1987-88 Newport County (13-2), 1988-89 Torquay United (15-4), Yeovil Town, Gloucester City, Trowbridge Town, Salisbury City, Yate Town, Forest Green Rovers, Mangotsfield United, Taunton Town, Tiverton Town, Taunton Town, Yate Town.

[541]

PLAYERS' RECORDS

THOMSON, Andrew John (Andy) (M)
b. 12/09/1988 Exeter, Devon
2007/08 0 apps 0 gls (1 nps)
TOTAL 0 apps 0 gls (1 nps)
Club Record: Exeter City, Forest Green Rovers, Gloucester City +

THONGER, T (FB)
1922/23 2 apps 0 gls
1923/24 1 app 0 gls
TOTAL 3 apps 0 gls

THORBURN, H (CF)
1922/23 3 apps 1 gl
TOTAL 3 apps 1 gl

THORNE, Gary Robert (D)
b. 22/03/1977 Swindon, Wilts.
1995/96 11 apps 0 gls
1996/97 49 apps 2 subs 0 gls
1997/98 59 apps 3 gls
1998/99 44 apps 2 subs 2 gls (1 nps)
1999/00 35 apps 2 gls
TOTAL 198 apps 4 subs 7 gls (1 nps)
Club Record: Swindon Town (0), Gloucester City, Newport County, Bath City, Merthyr Tydfil, Chippenham Town, Weston-Super-Mare, Mangotsfield United, Cirencester Town, Melksham Town +.
Note: Supporter's Player of the Season 1997/98. Brother of Wayne Thorne.

THORNE, Wayne Paul (M)
b. 28/07/1980 Swindon, Wilts.
1998/99 18 apps 2 subs 0 gls (3 nps)
1999/00 40 apps 3 subs 1 gl (1 nps)
2000/01 16 apps 3 subs 0 gls (2 nps)
TOTAL 74 apps 8 subs 1 gl (6 nps)
Club Record: Swindon Town (0), Gloucester City, Clevedon Town, Chippenham Town, Weston-Super-Mare (loan), Mangotsfield United, Melksham Town, Torrington , Melksham Town +.
Note: Supporter's Player of the Season 1999/2000. Brother of Gary Thorne.

TIBBITTS, J (W)
1948/49 5 apps 1 gl
TOTAL 5 apps 1 gl
Club Record: West Bromwich Albion (0), Gloucester City +.

TILLEY, Darren John (F)
b. 15/03/1967 Bristol
1993/94 4 apps 2 gls (1 nps)
TOTAL 4 apps 2 gls (1 nps)
Club Record: Yate Town, 1991-92 York City (21-0), Bath City, Gloucester City, Yate Town.

TILLING, Paul (GK)
b. 1963
1981/82 1 app 0 gls
TOTAL 1 app 0 gls

TILLION, J (WH) ++
1942/43 11 apps 0 gls
TOTAL 11 apps 0 gls

TIMMS, Peter N (FB)
b. Qu4 1944 Smethwick, Warks.
1971/72 19 apps 0 gls
TOTAL 19 apps 0 gls
Club Record: Wiggins Lads Club, Hereford United, Gloucester City, Wiggins, Lads Club.

TINGLE, Harold Clarence (IF)
b. Qu1 1901 East Dean, Glos. d. ?
1927/28 9 apps 6 gls
1928/29 15 apps 1 gl
1930/31 3 apps 0 gls
TOTAL 27 apps 7 gls
Club Record: Cinderford Town, Gloucester City +.

TOMKINS, Lyndon Philip (D)
b. 13/01/1979 Gloucester
2003/04 0 app 0 gls (5 nps)
2004/05 19 apps 1 sub 2 gls (5 nps)
2005/06 25 apps 1 sub 0 gls (6 nps)
2006/07 34 apps 4 gls
2007/08 11 apps 2 subs 0 gls (1 nps)
TOTAL 89 apps 4 subs 6 gls (17 nps)
Club Record: Gloucester City, Witney Town, Trowbridge Town, Cinderford Town, Gloucester City, Bishop's Cleeve (loan), Cinderford Town, Mitcheldean, Cirencester Town, Bishop's Cleeve, Gloucester City, Bishop's Cleeve +.
Note: Player's Player of the Season 2006/07, Supporter's Player of the Season 2006/07.

TOMLINSON, S.C (Tommy) (CH)
1921/22 11 apps 6 gls
1922/23 11 apps 7 gls
1923/24 12 apps 0 gls
1924/25 3 apps 0 gls
1925/26 29 apps 0 gls
1926/27 18 apps 0 gls
TOTAL 84 apps 13 gls
Note: Also played for Gloucester YMCA 1920/21. Club Captain 1921-23.

TOVEY, Luke (M)
b. 1983
2000/01 0 apps 0 gls (3 nps)
2001/02 0 apps 1 sub 0 gls (3 nps)
TOTAL 0 apps 1 sub 0 gls (6 nps)
Club Record: Gloucester City, Cheltenham Saracens, Bishop's Cleeve +.

TOWNSEND, Christopher Gordon (Chris) (F)
b. 30/03/1966 Caerleon, Wales
1988/89 31 apps 31 gls
1989/90 36 apps 3 subs 26 gls (2 nps)
1991/92 18 apps 3 subs 9 gls (1 nps)
TOTAL 85 apps 6 subs 66 gls (3 nps)
Club Record: 1983 Cardiff City (5-0), 1984 Southampton (0), Newport County, Forest Green Rovers, Cheltenham Town, Gloucester City, Dorchester Town, Bath City, Stroud (loan), Gloucester City, Ton Pentre, Chesham United +.
Note: Club record fee of £10,000 paid to Cheltenham Town 1988/89.

TOWNSEND, John (Johnny) (W)
1952/53 7 apps 1 gl
1953/54 2 apps 0 gls
1956/57 2 apps 0 gls
TOTAL 11 apps 1 gl
Club Record: Gloucester City, Cinderford Town +.

TOWNSEND, Michael (Mike/Rosy) (GK)
1973/74 2 apps 0 gls
TOTAL 2 apps 0 gls
Club Record: Charlton Kings, Cheltenham Town, Gloucester City +.

TOWNSEND, T (FB)
1929/30 1 app 0 gls
TOTAL 1 app 0 gls

TRAYNOR, W (W) ++
1940/41

TREDGETT, Kenneth Frank (CH)
b. 27/06/1927 Gloucester
1949/50 17 apps 0 gls
1950/51 47 apps 1 gl
1951/52 22 apps 0 gls
1952/53 43 apps 0 gls
1953/54 45 apps 0 gls
1954/55 52 apps 0 gls
1955/56 44 apps 0 gls
1956/57 49 apps 0 gls
1959/60 9 apps 1 gl
TOTAL 328 apps 2 gls
Club Record: Lonsdale United Boys Club, Cheltenham Town, Gloucester City, Toronto Hungarians (Canada), Gloucester City +.
Note: Player-Coach Jan 1960 – May 1960.

TREGALE, Steve (Sub)
1990/91 0 apps 0 gls (1 nps)
TOTAL 0 apps 0 gls (1 nps)
Club Record: Forest Green Rovers, Gloucester City +.

TREVARTHAN, Christopher (Chris) (GK)
1977/78 28 apps 0 gls
TOTAL 28 apps 0 gls
Club Record: Brockworth, Gloucester City, Stonehouse +.

TRIGG, Ian M (GK)
b. Qu4 1937 Gloucester
1960/61 3 apps 0 gls
1961/62 1 app 0 gls
TOTAL 4 apps 0 gls
Club Record: Darlington (0), Gloucester City +.

TRIPP, Nigel (D)
b. 1964
1991/92 1 app 0 gls
TOTAL 1 app 0 gls
Club Record: Chippenham Town, Trowbridge Town, Corsham Town, Melksham Town, Gloucester City, Mangotsfield United, Westbury United, Biddestone, Bradford Town.

TRUCHAN, Codie Pepperell (D)
b. 14/09/1991 Gloucester
2008/09

TRUEMAN, ? (FB)
1909/10 1 app 0 gls
TOTAL 1 app 0 gls

TRUEMAN, T (IF)
1903/04 5 apps 1 gl
TOTAL 5 apps 1 gl

TRUSWELL, Kevin (F)
b. 1962
1984/85 42 apps 3 subs 3 gls (1 nps)
1985/86 37 apps 2 subs 17 gls (4 nps)
1986/87 13 apps 5 subs 6 gls (1 nps)
1987/88 9 apps 3 subs 1 gl (1 nps)
TOTAL 101 apps 13 subs 27 gls (7 nps)
Club Record: Bromsgrove Rovers, Stourbridge, Gloucester City +.

TUCKER, Andrew (Andy) (D/M)
b. 13/06/1975 Cheltenham, Glos.
1995/96 12 apps 1 sub 0 gls
1996/97 20 apps 15 subs 2 gls (13 nps)
1997/98 46 apps 7 subs 4 gls (1 nps)
1998/99 33 apps 7 subs 3 gls (5 nps)
1999/00 32 apps 4 subs 0 gls
2000/01 43 apps 4 subs 2 gls
TOTAL 186 apps 37 subs 11 gls (19 nps)
Club Record: Cheltenham Town, Gloucester City, Bishop's Cleeve +.
Note: Joint Supporter's Player of the Season 2000/01.

TUCKER, C. H (IF)
1925/26 25 apps 15 gls
1926/27 22 apps 2 gls
1927/28 12 apps 8 gls
1928/29 11 apps 1 gl
TOTAL 70 apps 26 gls

TUCKER, Steve (Sub)
b. 1973 Swindon, Wilts.
1990/91 0 app 1 sub 0 gls (1 nps)
1991/92 0 apps 2 subs 0 gls (2 nps)
TOTAL 0 apps 3 subs 0 gls (3 nps)
Note: Played for Gloucester City 1993/94.

TURNER, E (W)
1926/27 5 apps 0 gls
1928/29 1 app 1 gl
TOTAL 6 apps 1 gl

TURNER, E.L (IF)
1894/95 1 app 0 gls
TOTAL 1 app 0 gls

TURNER, J (GK)
1919/20

TURNER, J.E (W)
1894/95

TURNER, John (IF)
b. 29/09/1950 Gloucester
1970/71 10 apps 2 gls
1974/75 5 apps 1 gl (1 nps)
1977/78 42 apps 12 gls
1978/79 46 apps 5 gls
1979/80 49 apps 9 gls
1980/81 7 apps 1 sub 1 gl (3 nps)
TOTAL 159 apps 1 sub 30 gls (4 nps)
Club Record: Matson Athletic, Bristol City (0), Brighton & Hove Albion (0), Gloucester City, Forest Green Rovers, Tuffley Rovers +.
Note: Club Captain 1979-80.

TURNER, Ronald (CF)
b. 19/06/1885 Gillingham, Kent d. 15/08/1915 Suvla Bay, Gallipoli Peninsula, Turkey
1907/08 6 apps 17 gls
TOTAL 6 apps 17 gls
Club Record: Millwall, Cambridge University, Gloucester City +.
International Record: England Amateur.
Note: Ronald Turner also played cricket for Gloucestershire CCC 1909. Killed in action WW1.

TURTON, J (FB) ++
1940/41
Club Record: Southend United (0), West Bromwich Albion (0), Gloucester City +.

TUSTAIN, Joseph Oliver (Joe) (F)
b. 24/02/1986 Cheltenham, Glos.
2006/07 7 apps 19 subs 2 gls (10 nps)
TOTAL 7 apps 19 subs 2 gls (10 nps)
Club Record: Bishop's Cleeve, Chipping Norton Town, Slimbridge, Gloucester City, Slimbridge (loan), Bishop's Cleeve, Cheltenham Saracens +.

TWEED, George Edward (LB/RB)
b. 04/12/1910 Newmarket, Suffolk d. Qu1 1971 Wells, Somerset
1946/47 8 apps 0 gls
TOTAL 8 apps 0 gls
Club Record: Newmarket Town, Bury Town, Newmarket Town, 1935 Coventry City (0), 1936-37 Bristol Rovers (25-0), 1937 Gillingham (31-0), Bath City, Gloucester City.

TWINNING, ? (W)
1920/21

TWINNING, ? (IF) ++
1942/43 1 app 2 gls
TOTAL 1 app 2 gls

TWYMAN, Jack Terence (F)
b. 17/09/1991 Chippenham, Wilts.
2008/09 1 app 3 subs 0 gls (7 nps)
TOTAL 1 app 3 subs 0 gls (7 nps)

TYLER, Simon (F)
b. 01/05/1962 Pontypool, Wales
1987/88 17 apps 8 gls
TOTAL 17 apps 8 gls
Club Record: Monmouth Town, Abergavenny Thursday, 1984-85 Newport County (4-0), Gloucester City, Ebbw Vale.
Note: Played for Gloucester City 1989/90.

ULLATHORNE, Simon (D)
b. 19/11/1971 Goole, Yorks.
1994/95 15 apps 3 gls (1 nps)
TOTAL 15 apps 3 gls (1 nps)
Club Record: Gravesend & Northfleet, Sittingbourne, Gloucester City, Hastings Town, King's Lynn, Crawley Town, Saint Albans City, Aldershot Town, Purfleet, Dover Athletic, Welling United, Slough Town, Eastbourne Borough, Horsham, Dagenham & Redbridge, Aveley, Tilbury +.
Note: Played for Gloucester City 1995/96.

UNDERHILL, Phil (D)
b. 1970
1991/92 18 apps 3 subs 0 gls (9 nps)
TOTAL 18 apps 3 subs 0 gls (9 nps)
Club Record: Torquay United (0), Bath City (loan), Bath City, Gloucester City, Forest Green Rovers.

UPCOTT, James Marcus (Jamie) (D)
b. 19/04/1990 Hereford, Herefordshire
2008/09 2 apps 1 sub 0 gls (4 nps)
TOTAL 2 apps 1 sub 0 gls (4 nps)
Club Record: Cardiff City (0), Gloucester City, Westfields +.

UTTERIDGE, Matt (GK)
1992/93 12 apps 0 gls
TOTAL 12 apps 0 gls
Club Record: Cheltenham Saracens, Bishop's Cleeve, Moreton Town, Gloucester City +.

VALE, Selwyn (FB)
b. 1942 West Bromwich, Staffs. d. Qu2 1988 Hereford, Herefordshire
1968/69 51 apps 1 gl
1969/70 56 apps 1 gl
1970/71 51 apps 5 gls
1971/72 30 apps 7 gls (4 nps)
1972/73 35 apps 1 sub 0 gls (8 nps)
1973/74 33 apps 2 gls (1 nps)
TOTAL 256 apps 1 sub 16 gls (13 nps)
Club Record: West Bromwich Albion (0), Hereford United, Gloucester City +.
Note: Club Captain 1969-70.

VANES, Michael (?)
Club Record: Bristol City (0) +.

VARNHAM, Andrew (Andy) (F)
b. 20/12/1986 Aldershot, Hants.
2004/05 3 apps 6 subs 0 gls (1 nps)
2005/06 1 apps 4 subs 0 gls (7 nps)
TOTAL 4 apps 10 subs 0 gls (8 nps)
Club Record: Gloucester City, Southside (loan), Slimbridge (loan), Slimbridge, Chipping Norton Town, Gloucester City, Chipping Norton Town, Cheltenham Saracens, Hardwicke +.

VASSALLO, Barrie Emmanuel (M)
b. 03/03/1956 Newport, Wales
1983/84 18 apps 1 gl
1984/85 45 apps 1 sub 0 gls
1985/86 29 apps 2 subs 4 gls (2 nps)
1986/87 3 apps 0 gls
TOTAL 95 apps 3 subs 5 gls (2 nps)
Club Record: 1973 Arsenal (0), 1974-75 Plymouth Argyle (13-2), 1975 Aldershot (0), Barnstaple, 1976-78 Torquay United (46-4), Bridgend Town, Kidderminster Harriers, Merthyr Tydfil, Gloucester City, Cinderford Town, Newport AFC.
Note: Club Captain 1984-86.

VASSELL, Robert Anthony (Rob) (FB)
b. 11/10/1972 Wolverhampton, Staffs.
1993/94 4 apps 1 sub 0 gls
TOTAL 4 apps 1 sub 0 gls
Club Record: Leicester City (0), Worcester City, Redditch United, Brierley Hill Town, Stafford Rangers, Moor Green, Dudley Town, Gloucester City, Bilston Town, Halesowen Harriers, Wednesfield, Rushall Olympic +.
Note: Any relation to England player Darius?

VAUGHAN, Charles Gilbert (FB)
b. 02/09/1868 Hewelsfield, Glos. d. 08/05/1952 McCammon, Idaho, USA
1894/95 3 apps 0 gls
TOTAL 3 apps 0 gls

VENN, J (GK) ++
1940/41
Club Record: Sunningend, Gloucester City +.

VERNON, Deion (F)
b. Bristol
1995/96 2 apps 3 subs 0 gls (4 nps)
TOTAL 2 apps 3 subs 0 gls (4 nps)
Club Record: Bristol City (0), Bath City, Gloucester City, Minehead, Bath City, Mangotsfield United, Welton Rovers, Clevedon Town +.
Note: Played for Gloucester City 1996/97.

VICK, ? (W)
1928/29 1 app 0 gls
TOTAL 1 app 0 gls
Club Record: Wycliffe College, Gloucester City +.

VICKERY, Thomas Frederick (HB)
b. 08/02/1892 Gloucester d. ?
1909/10 1 app 0 gls
TOTAL 1 app 0 gls
Note: Son of William H Vickery and brother of William C Vickery.

VICKERY, William C (GK)
b. 10/06/1886 Gloucester d. ?
1907/08 11 apps 0 gls
1908/09 16 apps 0 gls
1909/10 22 apps 0 gls
TOTAL 49 apps 0 gls
Note: Son of William H Vickery and brother of Thomas Vickery. Club Captain 1908-10.

VICKERY, William Henry (HB)
b. 19/07/1861 Birmingham, Warks. d. 19/11/1893 Gloucester
1889/90 2 apps 0 gls
TOTAL 2 apps 0 gls
Note: Father of William C Vickery and Thomas Vickery.

VIGNE, Percy George Aislebei (FB)
b. Qu4 1870 Exmouth, Devon d. ?
1892/93
1893/94

VILLARS, Anthony Keith (Tony) (W)
b. 24/01/1952 Cwmbran, Wales
1978/79
Club Record: 1967 Newport County (0), Panteg, Cwmbran Town, 1971-75 Cardiff City (73-4), 1976 Newport County (29-1), Gloucester City, Blaenavon Blues +.
International Record: Wales (3), Wales U23 (2).

VINSON, George Alfred (HB)
b. Qu3 1885 Gloucester d. ?
1906/07 15 apps 0 gls
1907/08 17 apps 1 gl
1908/09 16 apps 0 gls
1909/10 24 apps 0 gls
TOTAL 72 apps 1 gl
Club Record: Gloucester City, Cheltenham Town +.
Note: Brother of William Vinson.

VINSON, William Druce (FB)
b. Qu2 1882 Gloucester d. ?
1902/03 3 apps 0 gls
1906/07 4 apps 0 gls
1907/08 1 app 0 gls
1908/09 15 apps 0 gls
TOTAL 23 apps 0 gls
Club Record: Saint Michael's, Gloucester City, Saint Michael's +.
Note: Brother of George Vinson.

VITTLES, Jamie (D)
b. 15/10/1978 Sidmouth, Devon
1999/00
Club Record: Exeter City (0),Weymouth, Gloucester City +.

VOLPE, Keith Stuart (FB)
b. 21/01/1936 Hereford, Herefordshire d. Qu4 1987 Hereford, Herefordshire
1957/58 4 apps 0 gls
1958/59 9 apps 0 gls
1959/60 15 apps 0 gls
TOTAL 28 apps 0 gls
Club Record: Newport County (0), Hereford United, Gloucester City, Merthyr Tydfil +.

WADDLE, Alan Robert (F)
b. 09/06/1954 Wallsend, Northumberland
1982/83
Club Record: Wallsend Boys Club, 1971-72 Halifax Town (39-4), 1973-74 Liverpool (16-1), 1977 Leicester City (11-1), 1978-80 Swansea City (90-34), 1980-81 Newport County (27-8), Gloucester City, 1982 Mansfield Town (14-4), Happy Valley (Hong Kong), 1983 Hartlepool United (12-2), 1983-84 Peterborough United (36-12), 1984 Hartlepool United (4-0), 1984-85 Swansea City (40-10), unknown Finland club, Barry Town, Wakrah Sports (Qatar), Barry Town, Llanelli, Port Talbot, Maesteg Park, Bridgend Town, Llanelli.
Note: Cousin of England International Chris Waddle. Was on the bench for 1977 European Cup Final.

WADE, Rev. Reginald D (IF)
b. 1865 Marylebone, London d. ?
1889/90 3 apps 5 gls
TOTAL 3 apps 5 gls
Note: Played for Gloucester 1890/91, 1892/93.

PLAYERS' RECORDS

WADE-SMITH, Rev. Molineux (CH)
b. 01/1873 Burbage, Wilts. d. ?
1894/95 17 apps 0 gls
1895/96 9 apps 0 gls
TOTAL 26 apps 0 gls
Club Record: Gloucester, Clifton Athletic +.

WAITE, J (IF) ++
1940/41

WAITE, Mario (F)
1983/84 44 apps 14 gls (5 nps)
1984/85 25 apps 3 subs 6 gls (1 nps)
1985/86 6 apps 2 subs 3 gls
TOTAL 75 apps 5 subs 23 gls (6 nps)
Club Record: Pontllanfraith, Gloucester City +.
Note: Club Player of the Season 1983/84.

WAITE, Peter (GK)

WAKEFIELD, J (IF)
1899/00 8 apps 1 gl
1900/01 13 apps 6 gls
1902/03 7 apps 0 gls
1903/04 13 apps 3 gls
TOTAL 39 apps 10 gls

WAKEMAN, ? (W)
b. 1921
1938/39 1 app 0 gls
TOTAL 1 app 0 gls
Club Record: Brimscombe, Gloucester City +.

WALDEN, F (W) ++
1940/41

WALDER, Daniel Dwayne (Dan) (F)
b. 01/11/1985 Gloucester
2002/03

WALKER, ? (IF)
1960/61 1 app 0 gls
TOTAL 1 app 0 gls

WALKER, David (Dave) (FB)
b. 1949
1967/68 22 apps 0 gls
1968/69 1 app 0 gls (6 nps)
TOTAL 23 apps 0 gls (6 nps)
Club Record: Cheltenham Town, Gloucester City +.

WALKER, F (WH)
1891/92

WALKER, Shane (D)
b. 25/11/1957 Pontypool, Wales
1982/83 31 apps 3 gls
1983/84 41 apps 4 gls
TOTAL 72 apps 7 gls
Club Record: 1973 Arsenal (0), 1974 Bristol City (0), 1974-76 Hereford United (17-2), Sligo Rovers (Eire), 1977 Newport County (28-2), Gloucester City, Trowbridge Town, Caerloeon, Pontllanfraith, Forest Green Rovers, Ebbw Vale, Pontllanfraith, Ebbw Vale, Trinant, Newport County.

WALL, T (W)
1908/09
Club Record: Cheltenham Training College, Gloucester City +.

WALLACE, Ian (IF)
b. 1948
1967/68 2 apps 0 gls (1 nps)
TOTAL 2 apps 0 gls (1 nps)
Club Record: Wolverhampton Wanderers (0), Bristol Rovers (trial) (0), Gloucester City +.

WALSH, Matthew David (D)
b. 16/12/1989 Cardiff, Wales
2007/08 13 apps 2 gls
2008/09 2 apps 0 gls (1 nps)
TOTAL 15 apps 2 gls (1 nps)
Club Record: Cheltenham Town (0), Gloucester City, Clevedon Town, Port Talbot Town, Clevedon Town +.

WALTERS, ? (WH)
1890/91

WALTON, J (D)
2000/01

WALWIN, E (W)
1922/23

WARD, A (W)
1922/23 1 app 0 gls
TOTAL 1 app 0 gls

WARD, C (GK)
1948/49 2 apps 0 gls
TOTAL 2 apps 0 gls

WARD, G.S (WH)
1893/94 2 apps 0 gls
TOTAL 2 apps 0 gls
Note: Played for Gloucester 1889/90.

WARD, L (HB)
1923/24 3 apps 0 gls
1924/25 1 app 0 gls
TOTAL 4 apps 0 gls

WARD, Neil Stephen (D)
b. 10/05/1983 Bristol, Avon
2008/09 0 apps 3 subs 0 gls (1 nps)
TOTAL 0 apps 3 subs 0 gls (1 nps)
Club Record: Winterbourne United, Mangotsfield United, Tytherington Rocks, Winterbourne United, Gloucester City (loan), Yate Town +.

WARDLE, Bernard (W)
1967/68 1 app 0 gls
TOTAL 1 app 0 gls
Club Record: Cirencester Town, Gloucester City +.

WARNER, Ashley (F)
1995/96 2 apps 4 subs 1 gl (1 nps)
TOTAL 2 apps 4 subs 1 gl (1 nps)
Club Record: Peterborough United (0), Valley Sports Rugby, Telford United, Gloucester City, Corby Town, Rothwell Town, Oadby Town, Coalville Town +.

WARREN, Clive (Sub)
1979/80
Club Record: Taunton Town, Gloucester City +.

WASHBOURNE, James Gilbert (FB)
b. Qu4 1879 Hucclecote, Gloucester d. ?
1897/98 1 app 0 gls
1900/01 1 app 0 gls
TOTAL 2 apps 0 gls
Note: Played for Gloucester 1896/97. Club Secretary 1897-1898.

WATKINS, ? (FB)
1947/48 14 apps 0 gls
TOTAL 14 apps 0 gls
Note: Played for Gloucester City 1946/47.

WATKINS, Dale Allan (F)
b. 04/11/1971 Peterborough, Northants.
1996/97 51 apps 1 sub 35 gls
TOTAL 51 apps 1 sub 35 gls
Club Record: 1988 Sheffield United (0), 1988 Grimsby Town (0), 1989 Rotherham United (0), 1989-90 Peterborough United (5-0), Peterborough City, Wisbech Town, Grantham Town, Rushden & Diamonds, Gloucester City, 1999 Cheltenham Town (10-0), Kettering Town, Chelmsford City, Grantham Town (loan), King's Lynn (loan), Stamford, Yaxley (loan), Mirrlees Blackstone +.

WATKINS, Harold (Harry) (IF)
1935/36 1 app 0 gls
TOTAL 1 app 0 gls
Club Record: Broadhead Rovers, Gloucester City +.

WATKINS, James (Sub)
1994/95

WATKINS, L (IF)
1922/23 9 apps 4 gls
TOTAL 9 apps 4 gls

WATSON, G (HB)
1921/22 2 apps 0 gls
1922/23 2 apps 0 gls
TOTAL 4 apps 0 gls

WATSON, George Sutton (W)
b. 10/04/1907 Milton Regis, Kent d. 01/04/1974 Guildford, Surrey
1935/36 12 apps 5 gls
TOTAL 12 apps 5 gls
Club Record: Casuals, 1929 Charlton Athletic (14-2), Maidstone United, 1930 Crystal Palace (2-0), 1931 Clapton Orient (2-0), Nuneaton Town, Gloucester City.
International Record: England Amateur (2).
Note: Also played cricket for Kent CCC 1928-1929 and Leicestershire CCC 1934-1950.

WATSON, Ian (GK)
b. 05/02/1960 North Shields, Northumberland
1982/83 21 apps 0 gls
TOTAL 21 apps 0 gls
Club Record: 1978 Sunderland (1-0), 1979 Rochdale (loan) (33-0), York City (0), 1982 Newport County (0), Gloucester City (loan), 1983 Carlisle United (0), 1983-86 Berwick Rangers (83-1), 1987-88 Berwick Rangers (4-0) +.

WATSON, Sidney Melville (Sid) (CH)
b. 24/04/1935 Edinburgh, Scotland d. 22/10/1996 Gloucester
1956/57 2 apps 0 gls
1957/58 2 apps 0 gls
TOTAL 4 apps 0 gls

WATTS, A (IF)
1908/09 15 apps 7 gls
1909/10 21 apps 2 gls
TOTAL 36 apps 9 gls

WATTS, Anthony (Tony) (M)
1978/79 1 app 0 gls
1979/80 0 apps 1 sub 0 gls
TOTAL 1 app 1 sub 0 gls
Club Record: Gloucester City, Keynsham Town +.

WAYMAN, D (W) ++
1940/41

WAYMAN, Oliver Frederick (Ollie) (FB)
b. 30/01/1910 Westbury-on-Severn, Glos. d. Qu1 1996 Gloucester
1929/30 4 apps 0 gls
1932/33 2 apps 0 gls
1933/34 22 apps 1 gl
TOTAL 28 apps 1 gl
Club Record: Westbury United, Gloucester City, Pope's Hill +.

WEAVER, Reginald William (Reg) (CF/OR/IR)
b. 14/09/1905 Clutton, Somerset d. Qu3 1970 Gloucester
1937/38 39 apps 67 gls
1938/39 42 apps 33 gls
1946/47 3 apps 3 gls
TOTAL 84 apps 103 gls
Club Record: Llanhilleth United, 1926-27 Newport County (23-13), 1927-28 Wolverhampton Wanderers (50-29), 1928-31 Chelsea (20-8), 1932 Bradford City (8-3), 1932-33 Chesterfield (11-2), 1934 Newport County (29-8), Bath City, Gloucester City, Cheltenham Town, Gloucester City, Rotol AFC.
Note: Club record scorer in one season 1937-38.

WEBB, David (Spider) (GK)
1966/67 42 apps 0 gls
TOTAL 42 apps 0 gls
Club Record: Bristol Rovers (0), Chippenham Town, Gloucester City +.

WEBB, David Anthony (M)
b. 12/08/1966 Swindon, Wilts.
1990/91 26 apps 10 subs 6 gls (8 nps)
1993/94 17 apps 1 sub 2 gls (1 nps)
1995/96 44 apps 3 subs 7 gls (5 nps)
1996/97 40 apps 11 subs 14 gls (2 nps)
1997/98 26 apps 7 subs 4 gls
1998/99 35 apps 4 subs 3 gls (1 nps)
TOTAL 188 apps 36 subs 36 gls (17 nps)
Club Record: Swindon Supermarine, Wantage Town, Devizes Town, Stroud, Gloucester City, Trowbridge Town, Gloucester City, Highworth Town.
Note: Played for Gloucester City 1991/92, 1994/95.

WEBB, Robert (W) ++
b. ? d. 1970s
1942/43 18 apps 13 gls
TOTAL 18 apps 13 gls
Club Record: Luton Town (0), Gloucester City, Cinderford Town +.

WEBB, Robert (GK)
1987/88 2 apps 0 gls
1988/89 2 apps 0 gls
1989/90 3 apps 0 gls
TOTAL 7 apps 0 gls
Club Record: Gloucester City, Stroud +.

WEBB, Thomas Alan (Tom) (M)
b. 12/09/1984 Gloucester
2000/01 2 apps 2 subs 0 gls
2001/02 16 apps 10 subs 0 gls (5 nps)
2002/03 37 apps 18 subs 5 gls (2 nps)
2003/04 36 apps 8 subs 2 gls (1 nps)
2004/05 45 apps 2 gls (1 nps)
2005/06 47 apps 4 gls
2006/07 40 apps 5 subs 3 gls
2007/08 43 apps 6 subs 3 gls
2008/09 48 apps 3 subs 4 gls (1 nps)
TOTAL 314 apps 52 subs 23 gls (10 nps)
Club Record: Luton Town (0), Gloucester City, Viney Saint Swithins (loan), Highworth (loan), Yate Town (loan) +.
Note: Supporter's Player of the Season 2005/06.

WEBB, Victor James (M)
b. Qu4 1984 Gloucester
2004/05

WEBBER, Andrew (Andy) (D)
b. 1978
1995/96 1 app 4 subs 0 gls (8 nps)
TOTAL 1 app 4 subs 0 gls (8 nps)
Note: Played for Gloucester City 1996/97.

WEBSTER, Les (D)
1989/90 7 apps 0 gls
TOTAL 7 apps 0 gls
Club Record: Gloucester City, Nuneaton Borough (loan) +.

WELLS, Brian (Bomber) (IF)
b. 1940 Cheltenham, Glos.
1963/64 40 apps 14 gls
1964/65 38 apps 9 gls
1965/66 17 apps 3 gls
TOTAL 95 apps 26 gls
Club Record: Cheltenham Town, Worcester City, Gloucester City +.
Note: Brother of David Wells. No association with County cricketer with same nickname.

WELLS, David (IF)
1965/66 29 apps 15 gls
1966/67 3 apps 1 sub 1 gl (2 nps)
TOTAL 32 apps 1 sub 16 gls (2 nps)
Note: Brother of Brian Wells.

WELLS, F (CF)
1921/22 1 app 1 gl
TOTAL 1 app 1 gl

WELSH, Jason (F)
b. 08/02/1981 Cardiff, Wales
2006/07 30 apps 5 subs 13 gls
2007/08 6 apps 2 subs 1 gl (2 nps)
TOTAL 36 apps 7 subs 14 gls (2 nps)
Club Record: Taffs Well, Cwmbran Town, Merthyr Tydfil, Gloucester City, Swindon Supermarine, Port Talbot Town +.

WESTERBERG, Stephen A (Steve) (F)
b. Qu4 1961 Newport, Wales
1986/87 22 apps 2 subs 10 gls (1 nps)
TOTAL 22 apps 2 subs 10 gls (1 nps)
Club Record: Newport County, Merthyr Tydfil, Forest Green Rovers, Gloucester City +.

WESTLAKE, Mike (F)
1981/82 1 app 1 gl
TOTAL 1 app 1 gl

WESTON, James (Jimmy) (W)
b. 1937 Scotland
1956/57 25 apps 7 gls
1957/58 19 apps 7 gls
1958/59 38 apps 2 gls
1959/60 19 apps 0 gls
1960/61 39 apps 1 gl
1961/62 33 apps 5 gls
1962/63 20 apps 4 gls
TOTAL 202 apps 26 gls
Club Record: Greenock Morton (0), Gloucester City +.
Note: Club Captain 1960-61.

WESTON, L (WH)
1936/37 4 apps 0 gls
1937/38 7 apps 0 gls
TOTAL 11 apps 0 gls

WETSON, Robert Stephen (Bob) (IF)
b. 31/10/1951 Ledbury, Herefordshire d. Qu4 1973 Gloucester (Golden Valley)
1970/71 19 apps 1 sub 0 gls (3 nps)
TOTAL 19 apps 1 sub 0 gls (3 nps)
Club Record: Swindon Town (0), Gloucester City, Cheltenham Town +.
Note: Uncle of Shaun Wetson, Secretary 2007 to date.

WHEATON, N.F (CH)
1889/90

WHEELER, Martin (IF)
b. 1957 Bristol
1981/82 31 apps 1 sub 8 gls (3 nps)
TOTAL 31 apps 1 sub 8 gls (3 nps)
Club Record: Bristol Rovers (0), Clevedon Town, Bath City, Gloucester City, Forest Green Rovers, Bath City +.

WHISTON, R (W)
1932/33 8 apps 1 gl
TOTAL 8 apps 1 gl

WHITE, ? (IF) ++
1939/40 1 app 0 gls
TOTAL 1 app 0 gls

WHITE, C.F (HB)
1895/96 1 app 0 gls
TOTAL 1 app 0 gls
Note: Played for Gloucester 1892/93.

WHITE, G (GK)
1928/29 1 app 0 gls
TOTAL 1 app 0 gls

WHITEHOUSE, Jimmy (IF)
b. 1945
1972/73 19 apps 5 gls (1 nps)
1973/74 2 apps 1 sub 0 gls (2 nps)
TOTAL 21 apps 1 sub 5 gls (3 nps)
Club Record: Worcester City, Gloucester City +.
Note: Brother of Ken Whitehouse.

WHITEHOUSE, Ken (IF)
b. 1952
1972/73 17 apps 1 sub 6 gls (2 nps)
1973/74 1 app 0 gls
TOTAL 18 apps 1 subs 6 gls (2 nps)
Note: Brother of Jimmy Whitehouse.

WHITNEY, Henry (Harold) (CH)
b. 31/12/1910 Wheatenhurst, Glos. d. Qu4 1986 Cheltenham, Glos.
1930/31 15 apps 4 gls
1931/32 16 apps 0 gls
TOTAL 31 apps 4 gls
Club Record: Gloucester City, Cheltenham Town, Evesham Town, Gloucester City Albion +.
Note: Brother of William Whitney.

WHITNEY, William Frederick (FB)
b. 10/09/1908 Wheatenhurst, Glos. d. Qu2 1982 Gloucester
1930/31 3 apps 1 gl
1931/32 24 apps 0 gls
1932/33 3 apps 0 gls
1933/34 14 apps 0 gls
TOTAL 44 apps 1 gl
Note: Brother of Henry Whitney.

WHITTINGTON, Michael John (F)
b. 16/12/1986 Bristol, Avon
2005/06 8 apps 7 gls
2006/07 12 apps 6 gls
2007/08 10 apps 8 subs 2 gls (7 nps)
TOTAL 30 apps 8 subs 15 gls (7 nps)
Club Record: Cheltenham Town (0), Forest Green Rovers (loan), Gloucester City (loan), Gloucester City (loan), Weston-Super-Mare (loan), Mangotsfield United (loan), Gloucester City, Weston-Super-Mare, Yate Town, Paulton Rovers (loan) +.

WIFFILL, David Phillip (Dave) (F)
b. 19/04/1961 Bristol
1986/87 7 apps 1 sub 0 gls (3 nps)
TOTAL 7 apps 1 sub 0 gls (3 nps)
Club Record: Bath City, 1980 Manchester City (0), Happy Valley (Hong Kong), Thornbury Town, Gloucester City, Bath City, 1987 Bristol Rovers (2-0), Stroud.

WIGG, Nathan Marlow (M)
b. 27/09/1974 Cardiff, Wales
1999/00 15 apps 4 subs 0 gls (3 nps)
TOTAL 15 apps 4 subs 0 gls (3 nps)
Club Record: Swansea City (0), 1993-96 Cardiff City (58-1), Merthyr Tydfil (loan), Dundalk (Eire), Forest Green Rovers, Gloucester City, Cwmbran Town, Port Talbot Town, Clevedon Town, Risca United +.

WILBY, Paul (FB)
1973/74 4 apps 0 gls (2 nps)
TOTAL 4 apps 0 gls (2 nps)
Club Record: Worcester City, Gloucester City +.

WILKINS, Eric William J (W) ++
b. 02/02/1921 Gloucester d. Qu1 1993 Cheltenham, Glos.
1941/42 23 apps 23 gls
1942/43 8 apps 5 gls
TOTAL 31 apps 28 gls
Note: Played for Gloucester City 1939/40, 1940/41.

WILKINSON, David (Dave) (M)
b. 01/11/1983 Gloucester
2001/02 35 apps 3 subs 2 gls (1 nps)
2002/03 49 apps 2 subs 8 gls (1 nps)
2003/04 39 apps 9 subs 13 gls (4 nps)
2004/05 38 apps 1 sub 11 gls
2005/06 32 apps 4 subs 7 gls
2006/07 19 apps 12 subs 3 gls (4 nps)
2007/08 1 app 2 subs 0 gls (2 nps)
TOTAL 213 apps 33 subs 44 gls (12 nps)
Club Record: Gloucester City, Brockworth, Gloucester City, Cinderford Town +.

WILKINSON, Kenneth (Ken) (GK)
b. 1942
1958/59 1 app 0 gls
TOTAL 1 app 0 gls
Club Record: Bristol City (0), Gloucester City (loan) +.

WILLETTS, Harvey (GK)
b. Birmingham, Warks.
1990s
Club Record: Leeds United (0), Stockport County (0), Cape Cod Crusaders (USA), Stalybridge Celtic, Cheltenham Town, Newport AFC, Gloucester City, Evesham United, Trowbridge Town, Cape Cod Cardinals (USA), Evesham United, Bloxwich Town, Tamworth, Redditch United +.

WILLETTS, Kevin James (D/M)
b. 15/08/1962 Gloucester
1993/94 14 apps 0 gls
1994/95 31 apps 5 subs 1 gl (5 nps)
TOTAL 45 apps 5 subs 1 gl (5 nps)
Club Record: Sharpness, Worrall Hill, Cheltenham Town, Sharpness, Cheltenham Town, Forest Green Rovers (loan), Gloucester City, Weston-Super-Mare, Kidderminster Harriers, Worcester City, Witney Town.
Note: Played for Gloucester City 1989/90.

WILLETTS, W (GK)
1900/01 16 apps 0 gls
1902/03 11 apps 0 gls
1903/04 4 apps 0 gls
1906/07 18 apps 0 gls
TOTAL 49 apps 0 gls
Club Record: Gloucester, Saint Michael's, Gloucester City +.

PLAYERS' RECORDS

WILLIAMS, ? (WH)
1909/10 1 app 0 gls
TOTAL 1 app 0 gls
Note: Scored one goal which was taken away by a disciplinary committee along with two points deducted.

WILLIAMS, ? (WH)
1946/47

WILLIAMS, ?
1970s

WILLIAMS, Adrian (IF)
b. 04/08/1943 Bristol
1963/64 38 apps 21 gls
1964/65 36 apps 17 gls
1965/66 8 apps 0 gls
1966/67 5 apps 1 sub 1 gl (6 nps)
TOTAL 87 apps 1 sub 39 gls (6 nps)
Club Record: 1960 Bristol City (4-0), 1963 Exeter City (0), Gloucester City +.

WILLIAMS, Alan (CD)
b. 03/06/1938 Bristol
1973/74 25 apps 1 gl
TOTAL 25 apps 1 gl
Club Record: 1956-60 Bristol City (134-2), 1961-64 Oldham Athletic (172-9), 1965-66 Watford (43-4), 1966-68 Newport County (63-2), 1968-71 Swansea Town (143-7), Cheltenham Town, Gloucester City, Keynsham.
Note: Selected for England U23 game v Scotland in 1959 but game cancelled due to bad weather.

WILLIAMS, Colin (Sub)
1980/81 0 apps 0 gls (1 nps)
TOTAL 0 apps 0 gls (1 nps)
Club Record: Torquay United (0), Gloucester City +.

WILLIAMS, H (Sub)
1981/82 0 apps 0 gls (1 nps)
TOTAL 0 apps 0 gls (1 nps)

WILLIAMS, John (F)
b. 11/05/1968 Birmingham, Warks.
2006/07 1 app 0 gls
TOTAL 1 app 0 gls
Club Record: Cradley Town, 1991 Swansea City (39-11), 1992-94 Coventry City (80-11), 1994 Notts County (loan) (5-2), 1994 Stoke City (loan) (4-0), 1994 Swansea City (loan) (7-2), 1995-96 Wycombe Wanderers (48-9), 1996 Hereford United (11-3), 1997 Walsall (1-0), 1997 Exeter City (36-4), 1998 Cardiff City (43-12), 1999-00 York City (42-3), 2000 Darlington (24-5), 2001-02 Swansea City (68-5), 2003 Kidderminster Harriers (44-4), Bath City, Redditch United, Evesham United, Weston Super Mare, Gloucester City, Stourbridge.

WILLIAMS, Malcolm (IF)
b. 1951
1969/70 20 apps 2 subs 5 gls
1970/71 25 apps 1 sub 7 gls (1 nps)
TOTAL 45 apps 3 subs 12 gls (1 nps)
Club Record: Chelsea (0), Reading (0), Gloucester City, Cheltenham Town +.

WILLIAMS, Mark (M)
b. 17/09/1957 Hereford, Herefordshire
1981/82 0 apps 0 gls (1 nps)
1982/83 18 apps 3 gls (3 nps)
1993/94 0 apps 0 gls (1 nps)
TOTAL 18 apps 3 gls (5 nps)
Club Record: 1974 Arsenal (0), Bromsgrove Rovers, Kidderminster Harriers, 1976-78 Newport County (68-9), 1977 Hereford United (loan) (0), Telford United, Yeovil Town, Trowbridge Town, Gloucester City, Taunton Town (loan) +.

WILLIAMS, Martyn (Mazzer) (D)
b. 1966 Nottingham, Notts.
1987/88 19 apps 2 gls (1 nps)
1988/89 56 apps 3 gls
1989/90 54 apps 3 subs 4 gls (1 nps)
1990/91 3 apps 2 subs 1 gl (6 nps)
TOTAL 132 apps 5 subs 10 gls (8 nps)
Club Record: Sharpness, Forest Green Rovers, Gloucester City +.
Note: Player's Player of the Season 1988/89.

WILLIAMS, Mostyn Thomas Webb (FB)
b. 02/10/1928 Cwmfelinfach, Wales d. Qu2 1990 Newport, Monmouth, Wales
1952/53 19 apps 0 gls
TOTAL 19 apps 0 gls
Club Record: Ynysddu Welfare, 1949-51 Newport County (28-0), Gloucester City.

WILLIAMS, Paul (Sub)
1989/90 0 apps 0 gls (1 nps)
TOTAL 0 apps 0 gls (1 nps)

WILLIAMS, S (FB)
1926/27 16 apps 0 gls
1927/28 6 apps 1 gl
TOTAL 22 apps 1 gl
Note: S Williams also played rugby for Gloucester RFC.

WILLIAMS, Tudor (GK)
1952/53 10 apps 0 gls
TOTAL 10 apps 0 gls

WILLIAMSON, Andrew (Curly) ((IF)
1954/55 4 apps 2 gls
TOTAL 4 apps 2 gls
Club Record: Portadown, Gloucester City, Cheltenham Town +.

WILLMOTT, Ian Michael (D)
b. 10/07/1968 Bristol
1987/88 6 apps 0 gls (1 nps)
TOTAL 6 apps 0 gls (1 nps)
Club Record: Gloucester City, Weston-Super-Mare, 1989-91 Bristol Rovers (22-0), Yeovil Town (loan), Clevedon Town, Wycombe Wanderers, Taunton Town.

WILSON, Aaron Lewis (M)
b. 06/07/1986 Southampton, Hants.
2006/07 19 apps 10 subs 5 gls
TOTAL 19 apps 10 subs 5 gls
Club Record: Henbury Old Boys, Bristol Manor Farm, Gloucester City, Taunton Town, Weston-Super-Mare, Yate Town, Chippenham Town +.

WILSON, C (W)
1900/01 11 apps 2 gls
TOTAL 11 apps 2 gls

WILSON, F (FB) ++
1940/41

WILSON, M (FB)
1932/33 2 apps 0 gls
TOTAL 2 apps 0 gls

WILTON, Russell B (M)
b. Qu4 1962 Cheltenham, Glos.
1984/85 14 apps 1 sub 1 gl (1 nps)
1985/86 7 apps 1 sub 0 gls
TOTAL 21 apps 2 subs 1 gl (1 nps)
Club Record: Cheltenham Town, Moreton Town, Gloucester City, Witney Town, Forest Green Rovers, Cinderford Town +.

WINROW, Barry (FB)
b. 1954
1971/72 28 apps 0 gls (3 nps)
TOTAL 28 apps 0 gls (3 nps)
Club Record: Bury (0), Gloucester City +.

WISE, Charlie (W)
b. 1944
1964/65 3 apps 1 gl
1965/66 19 apps 4 gls
1966/67 32 apps 5 gls (8 nps)
1975/76 7 apps 0 gls (1 nps)
TOTAL 61 apps 10 gls (9 nps)
Club Record: Loughborough College, Gloucester City +.

WISE, S (W)
1919/20

WISE, S.R (HB)
1935/36 1 app 0 gls
TOTAL 1 app 0 gls

[548]

WITHEY, Graham Alfred (F)
b. 11/06/1960 Bristol
1989/90 20 apps 9 gls
1990/91 17 apps 3 subs 9 gls (2 nps)
TOTAL 37 apps 3 subs 18 gls (2 nps)
Club Record: Welton Rovers, Taunton Town, Weymouth, Bath City, 1982 Bristol Rovers (22-10), 1983 Coventry City (20-4), Seiko (Hong Kong), 1984 Coventry City (2-0), 1984-85 Cardiff City (27-7), Yeovil Town, Bath City, Cheltenham Town, 1988 Exeter City (7-2), Brisbane City (Australia), Gloucester City, Bath City, Trowbridge Town, Weston-Super-Mare.

WITHIN, ? (WH) ++
1939/40 1 app 0 gls
TOTAL 1 app 0 gls

WITT, Douglas (Doug) (CH/CF)
b. 1929
1950/51 5 apps 2 gls
1951/52 31 apps 4 gls
1952/53 13 apps 0 gls
TOTAL 49 apps 6 gls
Club Record: Salisbury City, Gloucester City +.

WIXEY, Daniel James (Dan) (D)
b. 21/01/1990 Gloucester
2007/08 0 apps 1 sub 0 gls (2 nps)
TOTAL 0 apps 1 sub 0 gls (2 nps)
Club Record: Gloucester City, UWIC Inter Cardiff, Gloucester City, Almondsbury Town (loan) +.
Note: Played for Gloucester City 2008/09.

WIXEY, Raymond (Ray) (FB)
b. 1947
1963/64 2 apps 0 gls
1964/65 13 apps 1 gl
1965/66 28 apps 2 gls
1966/67 29 apps 1 gl (2 nps)
1967/68 25 apps 0 gls (3 nps)
1972/73 47 apps 0 gls
1973/74 44 apps 1 gl
1974/75 50 apps 3 gls (1 nps)
1975/76 20 apps 0 gls (2 nps)
TOTAL 258 apps 8 gls (8 nps)
Club Record: Churchdown, Gloucester City, Sydney Croatia (Australia), Gloucester City +.
Note: Club Player of the Season 1973/74, 1974/75.

WOLLEN, Andrew (Andy) (D)
b. 1972
1995/96 2 apps 1 sub 0 gls (4 nps)
TOTAL 2 apps 1 sub 0 gls (4 nps)
Club Record: Swindon Town (0), Cheltenham Town, Andover, Newport (IOW), Gloucester City, Cirencester Town, Highworth Town +.

WOOD, ? (Sub)
1993/94

WOOD, Ben (M)
b. 1982
2004/05 0 apps 2 subs 0 gls (4 nps)
TOTAL 0 apps 2 subs 0 gls (4 nps)
Club Record: Gloucester City, Tuffley Rovers, Hardwicke +.

WOOD, Keith (F)
b. 10/05/1957 Surrey
1975/76 36 apps 1 sub 15 gls (5 nps)
1976/77 32 apps 4 subs 9 gls (9 nps)
1977/78 13 apps 2 gls (4 nps)
1978/79 0 apps 1 sub 0 gls
1979/80 0 apps 0 gls (1 nps)
TOTAL 81 apps 6 subs 26 gls (19 nps)
Club Record: Longford AFC, Gloucester City, Bristol Rovers (trial) (0) +.

WOOD, Lyndon B (Lyn) (GK)
b. Qu2 1942 Forest of Dean, Glos.
1960/61 2 apps 0 gls
1961/62 6 apps 0 gls
1963/64 2 apps 0 gls
TOTAL 10 apps 0 gls
Note: Played for Gloucester City 1964/65.

WOOD, S (W)
1892/93

WOOD, Troy Stephen (F)
b. 12/04/1988 Worcester, Worcs.
2006/07 3 apps 0 gls
TOTAL 3 apps 0 gls
Club Record: Worcester City, Gloucester City (loan), Evesham United (loan), Bromsgrove Rovers +.

WOODCOCK, V (GK)
1921/22 3 apps 0 gls
TOTAL 3 apps 0 gls

WOODGER, W.E (IF)
1921/22 4 apps 4 gls
TOTAL 4 apps 4 gls
Note: Also played for Gloucester YMCA 1920/21.

WOODRUFF, Robert W (Bobby) (M)
b. 09/11/1940 Highworth, Wilts.
1977/78 3 apps 0 gls
TOTAL 3 apps 0 gls
Club Record: 1958-63 Swindon Town (180-20), 1963-65 Wolverhampton Wanderers (63-18), 1966-69 Crystal Palace (125-48), 1969-73 Cardiff City (150-22), 1974-75 Newport County (52-7), Gloucester City, Everwarm (Bridgend).

WOODS, Mick (Sub)
1975/76

WOODWARD, G.H (WH)
1891/92
1892/93

WOODYER, H (FB)
1920/21

WOOKEY, David (D)
1982/83 1 app 0 gls
TOTAL 1 app 0 gls

WOOTTON, G (M)
1999/00

WRIGHT, A (CF)
1891/92

WRIGHT, Bernard Peter (Bernie) (F)
b. 17/09/1952 Birmingham, Warks
1985/86 38 apps 1 sub 13 gls
TOTAL 38 apps 1 sub 13 gls
Club Record: Paget Rangers, 1969 Birmingham City (0), 1971 Walsall (15-2), 1971-72 Everton (11-2), 1972-76 Walsall (152-38), 1976-77 Bradford City (66-13), 1978-79 Port Vale (76-23), Kidderminster Harriers, Trowbridge Town, Sutton Coldfield Town, Cheltenham Town, Worcester City, Burton Albion, Gloucester City.

WRIGHT, Brian (GK)
b. 1958
1975/76 5 apps 0 gls
1976/77 3 apps 0 gls
TOTAL 8 apps 0 gls
Club Record: Churchdown Panthers, Gloucester City +.

WRIGHT, Darren James (M)
b. 14/03/1968 West Bromwich, Staffs.
2000/01
Club Record: 1985 Wolverhampton Wanderers (1-0), 1986-89 Wrexham (110-4), Worcester City, Willenhall Town, Atherstone United, Cheltenham Town, Gloucester City (trial), Stafford Rangers, Halesowen Town +.

WRIGHT, E.C (CF)
1895/96

WRIGHT, Henry (F)
b. 15/02/1964
1996/97 0 apps 3 subs 0 gls (1 nps)
TOTAL 0 apps 3 subs 0 gls (1 nps)
Club Record: Hednesford Town, Worcester City (loan), Gloucester City (loan), Dudley Town +.

WRIGHT, Robert (Bob) (IF)
b. 1926 d. USA
1951/52 40 apps 6 gls
1952/53 23 apps 2 gls
TOTAL 63 apps 8 gls
Club Record: South Shields, Chelsea (0), Gloucester City, Worcester City +.

WYATT, Michael James (Mike) (M)
b. 12/09/1974 Bristol, Avon
1998/99 31 apps 7 subs 8 gls
1999/00 47 apps 1 sub 3 gls
TOTAL 78 apps 8 subs 11 gls
Club Record: 1993-94 Bristol City (13-0), 1995 Bristol Rovers (4-0), Forest Green Rovers, Bath City, Gloucester City, Worcester City, Bath City, Clevedon Town, Yate Town +.

WYNN, ? (FB)
1970/71

YATES, Luke (D)
1996/97 5 apps 0 gls
TOTAL 5 apps 0 gls
Club Record: Nottingham Forest (0), Halesowen Town, Sandwell Borough, Brierley Hill, Bilston Town, Hednesford Town, Gloucester City (loan), Nuneaton Borough, Stourbridge, Paget Rangers, Bromsgrove Rovers, Bloxwich, Racing Club Warwick, Oldbury United +.
Note: Played for Gloucester City 1994/95.

YEATES, W (IF)
1932/33 1 app 0 gls
1933/34 7 apps 5 gls
1934/35 4 apps 0 gls
TOTAL 12 apps 5 gls
Club Record: Sunningend, Gloucester City +.

YOUNG, Neil (Sub)
1986/87 0 apps 0 gls (1 nps)
1987/88 0 apps 2 subs 0 gls (7 nps)
TOTAL 0 apps 2 subs 0 gls (8 nps)

ADDITIONAL: NEW PLAYERS WHO FEATURED IN 2009-10
(Upto 04/09/2009. Not counted in figures above. Players in bold have played in competitive games)

BALDWIN, James Robert (D/M)
b. 14/05/1989 Gloucester
Club Record: Shortwood United, Forest Green Rovers, Gloucester City +.

BRYAN, Ashley Lloyd (GK)
b. Qu3 1988 Bristol, Avon
Club Record: Melbourn FC, Bristol Manor Farm, Cadbury Heath, Minehead, Gloucester City, Hanham Athletic +.

CUXAC, Julien (D)
b. France

HOLDCROFT, Daniel Thomas B (Danny) (GK)
b. 22/05/1978 Stoke-on-Trent, Staffs.
Club Record: Leek Town, Buckley Town, Caernarfon Town, TNS Llansantffraid, Bradford Town, Melksham Town, Almondsbury Town, Hungerford Town, Larkhall Athletic, Gloucester City +.

JONES, Edward (Eddie) (M)
b. 06/06/1991 Cheltenham, Glos.
Club Record: Forest Green Rovers, Gloucester City, Almondsbury Town (loan) +.

KITE, Alexandros (Alex) (D)
b. 07/03/1989 Chatham, Kent
Club Record: Bristol Rovers (0), Chippenham Town, Weston-Super-Mare (loan), Gloucester City (loan) +.

LIGHT, Neil (D)
Note: New Club Physio. Played second half against Gala Wilton.

PEARCE, Martin (GK)
Club Record: Shortwood United, Bishop's Cleeve, Gloucester City +.

ROBINSON, Samuel James (Sam) (M)
b. 02/09/1989 Kingston-upon-Thames, Surrey
Club Record: Woking, Metropolitan Police, Leatherhead, Corinthian Casuals, Gloucester City +.

RUSSELL, Curtis James (F)
b. Qu2 1992 Gloucester
Club Record: Bristol City (0), Viney Hill, Gloucester City +.

WALLINGTON, Daniel Luke (Danny) (M)
b. Qu2 1989 Gloucester
Club Record: Swindon Town (0), Cirencester Town, Highworth Town, Gloucester City +.

Between 1946/47 and possibly 1959/60 Public Trial Matches were held before the season started. The following players participated in these matches but never made the First XI competitively or in a friendly. These are not counted above.

BAKER, ? (W)
1949/50
Note: Played for the "Possibles" team.

BARNES, Trevor (CF)
1947/48
Note: Played for the "Possibles" team.

BARNETT, W (GK)
1946/47
Note: Played for the "Possibles" team.

BAUGH, M (?)
1955/56

BETHEL, ? (HB)
1947/48
Note: Played for the "Possibles" team.

BRADLEY, C.G
1948/49
Club Record: Walsall (0) +.
Note: Played for the "Red and White" team.

BRIDGE, ? (HB)
1947/48
Note: Played for the "Possibles" team.

CERRONE, Curly (HB)
1951/52

FURNESS, K (W)
1946/47
Note: Played for the "Possibles" team.

GORMAN, J (FB)
1948/49
Club Record: Halesowen Town +.
Note: Played for the "Red and White" team.

GRIFFITHS, A (FB)
1949/50
Club Record: Hereford United +.
Note: Played for the "Possibles" team.

HOOPER, L.R (IF)
1948/49
Club Record: Blackburn Rovers (0) +.
Note: Played for the "Red and White" team.

JENNINGS, Harold (GK)
1947/48
Club Record: Bournemouth & Boscombe Athletic (0) +.
Note: Played for the "Possibles" team.

MILLARD, ? (GK)
1950/51
Note: Played for the "Probables" team.

MOUNTSEY, Ken (GK)
1951/52
Club Record: Ipswich Town (0), Bedford Town +.

ROGERS, J (?)
1959/60
Note: Played for the "Possibles" team.

TAYLOR, Johnny (IF)
1951/52
Club Record: Pontypool +.

TRAVIS, K (?)
1955/56

WEBB, ? (GK)
1949/50
Note: Played for the "Possibles" team.

PLAYERS' RECORDS

On occasions, reserves to travel were added. The following never reached the First XI in either competitive or friendly games. I only add them for the sole reason that I noticed them. Patently, this is not complete and is not counted above.

BATTINSON, ?
1947/48
Note: Reserve for the "Possibles" team.

CUMMIN, P.J
1930/31

FOX, J ++
1940/41

GRANT, H. C
1926/27

JONES, P
1931/32

LIDGFORD, R
1928/29

LOVE, ? ++
1941/42

MALLENDER, F.N
1926/27

McALGER, J ++
1940/41

MIDDLECOTE, J
1926/27

MYNOTT, ? ++
1942/43

O'HARA, ? ++
1942/43
Club Record: Belfast Celtic +.

PRIDAY, F
1919/20

PROBYN, R
1919/20

RING, G
1931/32

RYDER, W
1926/27

SQUIRES, ? ++
1942/43

STROUD, E
1926/27

VALLENDER, H
1926/27

WATKINS, B
1923/24

GLOUCESTER BORN PLAYERS WHO GOT AWAY
The following were all born in Gloucester and went on to play League Football in Levels 1 to 4 but never donned the shirt of their birth city.

BIRD, David Alan (Dave) (M)
b. 26/12/1984
Club Record: Cinderford Town, 2001-08 Cheltenham Town (212-8) +.

BRADLEY, Shayne (F)
b. 08/12/1979
Club Record: 1998-99 Southampton (4-0), 1999 Swindon Town (loan) (7-0), 1999 Exeter City (loan) (8-1), 2000-01 Mansfield Town (42-10), Eastwood Town, 2002 Chesterfield (9-2), 2002 (loan) Lincoln City (3-1), Tuffley Rovers +.

COWE, Steven Mark (Steve) (F)
b. 29/09/1974
Club Record: 1993 Aston Villa (0), Hereford United, 1995-2000 Swindon Town (97-11), Newporrt County, Forest Green Rovers, Redditch United, Weston-Super-Mare, Cirencester Town, Cinderford Town.

FLEETWOOD, Stuart Keith (F)
b. 23/04/1986
Club Record: 2003-05 Cardiff City (8-0), 2006 Hereford United (27-3), 2007 Accrington Stanley (loan) (3-0), Forest Green Rovers, 2008 Charlton Athletic (0), 2008 Cheltenham Town (loan) (6-2), 2008 Brighton & Hove Albion (loan), (11-1), 2008 Exeter City (loan) (9-3) +.
International Record: Wales U21 (5).

HARDING, Daniel Andrew (Dan) (M)
b. 23/12/1983
Club Record: 2002-04 Brighton & Hove Albion (67-1), 2005 Leeds United (20-0), 2006-08 Ipswich Town (73-1), 2008 Southend United (loan) (19-1), 2008 Reading (loan) (3-0) +.
International Record: England U21 (4).

JOHNSON, David Nicholas Conrad (W)
b. 26/12/1962
Club Record: Redhill, 1981-83 Watford (7-0), 1984-85 Peterborough United (35-4), Bishop's Stortford.

LEONARD, John (Jack) (OR)
b. 1876 d. ?
Club Record: 1896 Saint Mirren (10-2), 1897 Derby County (1-1), 1897 Notts County (1-1), Eastville Rovers, 1899 Small Heath (7-1), Cheltenham Town.

MANSELL, Lee Richard Samuel (M)
b. 28/10/1982
Club Record: 2000-04 Luton Town (47-8), Nuneaton Borough (loan), 2005 Oxford United (44-1), 2006 Torquay United (45-4) +.
Note: Brother of Richard Mansell.

McKERNON, Craig Andrew (FB)
b. 23/02/1968
Club Record: 1984-89 Mansfield Town (93-0), 1990 Arsenal (0), Kettering Town.

SHARPE, Gerald Ralph (Gerry) (W)
b. 17/03/1946
Club Record: Longlevens, 1964-70 Bristol City (153-48).

SMITH, Timothy Carl (Tim) (M)
b. 19/04/1959
Club Record: 1976-77 Luton Town (2-0), Trowbridge Town, Cinderford Town.

THOMAS, Wayne Junior Robert (CD)
b. 17/05/1979
Club Record: 1995-99 Torquay United (123-5), 2000-04 Stoke City (189-7), 2005-07 Burnley (50-1), 2007-08 Southampton (30-0) +.

PLAYER AND TEAM STATISTICS

RECORDS IN COMPETITIVE MATCHES ONLY (upto 2008-09)
It has to be emphasised that these records are based on known information only and could be subject to change.

MOST APPEARANCES IN ALL MATCHES
(including playing subs appearances)

413	Stan Myers 1950-1960
368	Gary Kemp 1990-1999
366	Tom Webb 2000 to date
348	Rob Coldray 1954-1969
328	Frank Tredgett 1949-1959
315	Chris Burns 1996-2005
306	Lee Smith 2000 to date
296	Bobby McCool 1965-1974
289	Neil Mustoe 2002 to date
274	Neil Griffiths 1998-2005
271	Terry Hargreaves 1964-1976
267	Martin Lander 1984-1990
264	John Evans 1976-1982
264	Doug Foxwell 1972-1988
262	Wayne Noble 1988-1992
262	Adie Harris 1987 to date
258	Ray Wixey 1963-1975
257	Selwyn Vale 1968-1973
253	Matt Bath 2001-2006
252	Enos Drew 1931-1937

Most Appearances 1883-1914 – Arthur Fielding 102
George Vinson 72
Henry Sherwood 71
Other Appearances 1919-1942 – Sam Hamer 248
Andy Murdock 232

Note: I suspect Bobby McCool made over 300 appearances but non reporting of sub appearances during his time distort facts.

MOST PLAYING SUBSTITUTE APPEARANCES IN ALL MATCHES

74	Adie Harris 1987 to date
57	Lee Smith 2000 to date
52	Tom Webb 2000 to date
41	Karl Bayliss 1985-2004
37	Andy Tucker 1995-2000
36	David Webb 1990-1998
36	Keith Knight 1990-2005
36	Jimmy Cox 1999-2006
36	Jamie Reid 2004-2008
33	Dave Wilkinson 2001-2007
32	Will Steadman 1996-2003
31	Jody Bevan 2005-07

MOST NON PLAYING SUBSTITUTES IN ALL MATCHES
'They also serve who only stand and wait'

133	Adie Harris 1987 to date
41	Lee Randall 2001-2006
38	David Mehew 2006 to date
36	Karl Bayliss 1985-2004
30	Keith Knight 1990-2005
30	Jamie Reid 2004-2008
29	Will Steadman 1996-2003
28	Bobby McCool 1965-1974
24	Kenny Howard 2001-2003
24	Matt Sysum 2007 to date
23	Brian Hughes 1988-1999
22	Chris Burns 1996-2005
21	Selwyn Rice 1967-1979
21	Shaun Penny 1988-1992

MOST TIMES SELECTED IN ALL MATCHES
(This includes playing and non playing subs)

413	Stan Myers 1950-1960
395	Adie Harris 1987 to date
376	Tom Webb 2000 to date
374	Gary Kemp 1990-1999
349	Rob Coldray 1954-1969
328	Frank Tredgett 1949-1959
325	Chris Burns 1996-2005
324	Bobby McCool 1965-1974
311	Lee Smith 2000 to date
294	Neil Mustoe 2002 to date
288	Terry Hargreaves 1964-1976
280	Neil Griffiths 1998-2005
279	John Evans 1976-1982
279	Karl Bayliss 1985-2005
275	Martin Lander 1984-1990

270	Selwyn Vale 1968-1973
270	Doug Foxwell 1972-1988
270	Wayne Noble 1988-1992
266	Ray Wixey 1963-1975
265	Brian Hughes 1988-2000
258	Dave Wilkinson 2001-2007
257	Matt Bath 2001-2006
254	Chris Thompson 2001-2007
252	Enos Drew 1931-1937

MOST APPEARANCES IN LEAGUE MATCHES ONLY
(including playing subs appearances)

354	Stan Myers 1950-1960
302	Tom Webb 2000 to date
284	Rob Coldray 1954-1969
284	Gary Kemp 1990-1999
280	Frank Tredgett 1949-1959
247	Lee Smith 2000 to date
243	Bobby McCool 1965-1974
241	Chris Burns 1996-2005
236	Neil Mustoe 2002 to date
226	Ray Wixey 1963-1975
226	Neil Griffiths 1998-2005
225	Terry Hargreaves 1964-1976
220	Enos Drew 1931-1937
216	Selwyn Vale 1968-1973
214	Sam Hamer 1923-1934
211	John Evans 1976-1982
209	Matt Bath 2001-2006
208	Doug Foxwell 1972-1988
206	Dave Wilkinson 2001-2007
204	Chris Thompson 2001-2007
203	Ron Coltman 1952-1959

Most Appearances 1883-1914 – Arthur Fielding 92
Henry Sherwood 61
Henry Arkell 60
Other Appearances 1919-1942 – Andy Murdock 190

MOST APPEARANCES IN CUP MATCHES ONLY
(including playing subs appearances)

84	Gary Kemp 1990-1998
74	Martin Lander 1985-1989
74	Chris Burns 1996-2005
72	Wayne Noble 1988-1992
71	Brian Hughes 1988-1997
67	Adie Harris 1987 to date
64	Rob Coldray 1954-1965
64	Tom Webb 2001 to date
59	Stan Myers 1950-1960
59	Lee Smith 2000 to date
56	Doug Foxwell 1972-1988
54	Dave Webb 1990-1998
54	Karl Bayliss 1985-2004
53	Bobby McCool 1965-1974
53	John Evans 1976-1982
53	Steve Fergusson 1990-1999
53	Gary Thorne 1995-1999
53	Andy Tucker 1995-2000
53	Neil Mustoe 2002 to date

Most Appearances 1883-1914 – George Vinson 14
A.H. Smith 13
Frank Fielding 11
Most Appearances 1919-1942 – Andy Murdock 42
Sam Hamer 34
George Applin, Jerry Causon, Enos Drew 32

MOST APPEARANCES IN A SEASON IN ALL MATCHES

63	Wayne Noble 1989-1990
61	Bobby Brown 1981-1982
61	Steve Talboys 1989-1990
60	Brian Hughes 1989-1990
59	Wayne Noble 1988-1989
59	Chris Burns 1997-1998
59	Gary Thorne 1997-1998
58	Dave Lewis 1980-1981
58	Nicky Cornwell 1981-1982
58	Brian Hughes 1988-1989
57	Terry Paterson 1981-1982
57	Martyn Williams 1989-1990
57	Steve Fergusson 1997-1998

[552]

PLAYER AND TEAM STATISTICS

MOST SEASONS PLAYED

12	Sam Hamer 1923-1935
12	Doug Foxwell 1972-1989
11	Andy Murdock 1923-1934
11	Stan Myers 1950-1961
11	Rob Coldray 1954-1969
11	Karl Bayliss 1985-2005
10	Bobby McCool 1965-1975
10	Brian Hughes 1988-2000
10	Gary Kemp 1990-2000
10	Adie Harris 1987 to date

Note: Including friendly appearances Sam Hamer played 13 seasons (1923-40), Adie Harris 11 seasons and Arthur Fielding played 10 (1893-1904).

MOST PLAYERS USED IN ONE SEASON

43	1926/1927
42	2007/2008
41	1990/1991, 1991/1992
40	1939/1940, 2006/2007
39	1934/1935, 1980/1981
38	1982/1983, 1995/1996, 1997/1998, 1999/2000
37	2005/2006
36	1933/1934, 1936/1937, 1937/1938, 1941/1942, 1946/1947, 1993/1994, 2008/2009
35	1983/1984, 1987/1988
34	1929/1930, 1930/1931, 1932/1933
33	1909/1910, 1947/1948, 1981/1982, 2001/2002
32	1895/1896, 1928/1929, 1935/1936, 1977/1978, 1992/1993
31	1927/1928, 1961/1962, 1978/1979, 1979/1980,
30	1894/1895, 1931/1932, 1949/1950, 1959/1960, 1975/1976, 1986/1987

MOST YEARS BETWEEN FIRST AND LAST MATCH PLAYED

23 yrs 14 days	Bob Etheridge (11/10/1952 to 25/10/1975)
20 yrs 227 days	Adie Harris (22/08/1987 to 05/04/2008)
18 yrs 312 days	Karl Bayliss (11/11/1985 to 18/09/2004)
16 yrs 347 days	Geoff Medcroft (27/02/1965 to 09/02/1982)
16 yrs 86 days	Doug Foxwell (14/08/1972 to 08/11/1988)
15 yrs 128 days	Rob Coldray (25/12/1954 to 02/05/1970)
15 yrs 41 days	Keith Knight (16/10/1990 to 26/11/2005)
14 yrs 214 days	George Edwards (05/09/1925 to 06/04/1940)
14 yrs 24 days	Jason Eaton (17/11/1990 to 11/12/2004)
12 yrs 137 days	Steve Talboys (29/11/1987 to 15/04/2000)
12 yrs 125 days	Ivor Gwatkin (09/11/1935 to 13/03/1948)
12 yrs 118 days	Bert Ayland (26/12/1925 to 23/04/1938)
12 yrs 111 days	Selwyn Rice (19/08/1967 to 08/12/1979)
12 yrs 74 days	Colin Moulsdale (19/02/1966 to 04/05/1978)
12 yrs 44 days	Terry Hargreaves (12/12/1964 to 25/01/1977)
11 yrs 325 days	Ray Wixey (16/04/1964 to 06/03/1976)
11 yrs 129 days	Brian Hughes (20/08/1988 to 27/12/1999)
11 yrs 91 days	Greg Steel (18/08/1979 to 17/11/1990)
11 yrs 56 days	Sam Hamer (15/09/1923 to 10/11/1934)
11 yrs 28 days	Bob Cox (31/08/1935 to 28/09/1946)
11 yrs 5 days	Dick Etheridge (16/04/1955 to 21/04/1966)
10 yrs 374 days	Charlie Wise (24/10/1964 to 13/09/1975)
10 yrs 241 days	Stan Myers (19/08/1950 to 15/04/1961)
10 yrs 233 days	Frank Tredgett (14/09/1949 to 04/05/1960)
10 yrs 151 days	Steve Scarrott (26/11/1977 to 25/04/1988)
10 yrs 114 days	Eddie Bell (26/10/1957 to 17/02/1968)
10 yrs 100 days	Andy Murdock (19/01/1924 to 28/04/1934)
10 yrs 93 days	Ernest Allen (04/10/1913 to 05/01/1924)
10 yrs 71 days	Keith Mortimer (19/08/1967 to 29/10/1977)
10 yrs 3 days	John Turner (03/10/1970 to 06/10/1980)

Note: Sam Hamer did play in friendlies during the 1940/41 season as did George Edwards. Dick Etheridge played in a Benefit Match in the 1977/78 season. Rod Thomas spanned 1963/64 to 1982/83 but was a non playing sub in the latter season. Mark Williams spanned 1981/82 to 1993/94 but was a non playing sub in both these seasons. Karl Bayliss was a non playing sub 29/10/1985.

MOST GOALS IN ALL MATCHES

195	Jerry Causon 1930-1936
108	Rob Coldray 1954-1969
103	Reg Weaver 1937-1946
96	Jimmy Cox 1999 - 2006
92	Doug Foxwell 1972-1988
92	Karl Bayliss 1985-2004
85	John Evans 1976-1982
79	Enos Drew 1931-1938
74	Andy Hoskins 1997-2004
68	Terry Paterson 1978-1985
66	Gerry Horlick 1959-1963

66	Steve Talboys 1987-1991
66	Chris Townsend 1988-1991
65	John Stevens 1967-1972
61	Dave Lewis 1980-1981
60	Mike Bruton 1978-1983
58	Alex Sykes 2005 to date
57	Bobby McCool 1965-1974
50	Eddie Parris 1939-1947
50	Lee Smith 2000 to date

Most Goals 1883-1914 – Frank Fielding 46
Frederick Rust 41
Norman Squier 37

Note: I suspect Jerry Causon's tally exceeded 200 goals but unfortunately during his time many scorers not recorded.

MOST GOALS IN LEAGUE MATCHES ONLY

152	Jerry Causon 1930-1936
89	Reg Weaver 1937-1946
86	Rob Coldray 1954-1969
77	Karl Bayliss 1985-2004
77	Jimmy Cox 1999-2006
73	Doug Foxwell 1972-1988
71	John Evans 1976-1982
66	Enos Drew 1931-1938
58	Terry Paterson 1978-1985
57	John Stevens 1967-1972
57	Andy Hoskins 1997-2004
53	Gerry Horlick 1959-1963
53	Chris Townsend 1988-1991
51	Steve Talboys 1987-1991

Most Goals 1883-1914 – Frank Fielding 44
Frederick Rust 38
Henry Sherwood 35
Norman Squier 35

MOST GOALS IN CUP MATCHES ONLY

43	Jerry Causon 1930-1936
22	Rob Coldray 1954-1969
19	Dave Lewis 1980-1981
19	Doug Foxwell 1972-1988
19	Jimmy Cox 1999-2006
17	Mike Bruton 1978-1983
17	Andy Hoskins 1997-2004
15	Steve Talboys 1987-1991
15	Karl Bayliss 1985-2004

Most Goals 1883-1914 – Reginald Wade 5
C.M. Henderson 4
Francis Romans 4
Wilfred Smith 4
W.A. Jarman 4

Other goalscorers 1919-1942 – Reg Weaver 14
Harry Perks 13
Enos Drew 13

MOST GOALS IN A SEASON IN ALL MATCHES

67	Reg Weaver 1937-1938
49	Jerry Causon 1934-1935
47	Jerry Causon 1933-1934
37	Andy Hoskins 2003-2004
36	Albert Shelley 1935-1936
36	Kim Casey 1984-1985
35	Jerry Causon 1932-1933
35	Dave Lewis 1980-1981
35	Dale Watkins 1996-1997
34	John Stevens 1968-1969
33	Jerry Causon 1931-1932
33	Reg Weaver 1938-1939
31	Chris Townsend 1988-1989
30	Eddie Parris 1942-1943

Most Goals In A Season 1883-1914 – Percy Stout 20 1894/95

PLAYER AND TEAM STATISTICS

MOST HAT-TRICKS

25 Jerry Causon 1930-1936
12 Reg Weaver 1937-1946
7   Harry Perks 1925-1926
4   Ronald Turner 1907
4   W. Taylor 1929-1930
4   Eddie Parris 1939-1947
4   Rob Coldray 1954-1969
4   Gerry Horlick 1959-1963
4   Doug Foxwell 1972-1988
4   Kim Casey 1984
4   Chris Townsend 1988-1991
4   Andy Hoskins 1997-2004

MOST GOALS IN A MATCH

9 Fred Starr v RAF 'B' (H) 20/12/1941 (League)
7 Harry Perks v Fairford Town (H) 11/12/1926 (GNSAC1)
6 Jerry Causon v Forest Green Rovers (H) 28/11/1931 (League)
6 Fred Starr v Army 'G' (H) 06/12/1941 (League)
5 Percy Stout v Clevedon (H) 03/11/1894 (League)
5 W. Shaw v Forest Green Rovers (H) 13/01/1900 (League)
5 Frederick Rust v M & SWJR (A) 24/10/1903 (League)
5 Ronald Turner v Stroud (H) 23/11/1907 (League)
5 Ronald Turner v Linden Old Boys (H) 30/11/1907 (League)
5 Walter Stone v Woodchester (H) 11/09/26 (League)
5 Leslie Marler v Fairford Town (H) 11/12/1926 (GNSAC1)
5 Jerry Causon v Woodchester (A) 26/01/1935 (League)
5 Jerry Causon v Blakeney (A) 23/02/1935 (League)
5 Reg Weaver v Hinckley Athletic (H) 27/11/1937 (League)
5 Reg Weaver v Wolves 'A' (H) 02/04/1938 (League)
5 Eddie Parris v RAF 'D' (H) 30/01/1943 (GC2)
5 Mick Johnson v Merthyr Tydfil (H) 08/02/1958 (League)
5 Chris Townsend v Gosport Borough (H) 13/03/1990 (League)
5 Jack Pitcher v Yate Town (A) 14/09/2007 (FAC1Q)

MOST SUCCESSFUL PENALTY TAKER

19 Alex Sykes 2005 to date
12 Dave Lewis 1980-1981
11 Enos Drew 1931-1937
11 Jim Clark 1952-1961
10 Jimmy Canavan 1950-1952
10 Ian Fraser 1968-1970
9   Andy Hoskins 1997-2004
8   Steve Fergusson 1990-1999
8   Keith Knight 1990-2005
7   Johnny Moore 1948-1949
7   Mike Bruton 1978-1983
7   Chris Burns 1996-2005
7   Neil Mustoe 2002 to date
6   Doug Hunt 1948-1951
6   Doug Foxwell 1972-1988
6   Jon Holloway 1995-1998
5   George Edwards 1925-1939
5   Eddie Parris 1939-1947
5   Stan Myers 1950-1960
5   Dave Bruton 1981-1983
5   Steve Baddock 1986-1987
5   Karl Bayliss 1985-2004
5   Chris Townsend 1988-1991
5   Wayne Noble 1988-1992

OLDEST GOALSCORERS

41 yrs 315 days Adie Harris (5 Mar 1964/14 Jan 2006)
41 yrs 186 days George Edwards (14 Sep 1897/18 Mar 1939)
41 yrs 63 days Reg Weaver (14 Sep 1905/16 Nov 1946)
38 yrs 241 days Steve Fergusson (21 Apr 1961/18 Dec 1999)
38 yrs 227 days Vince Farrell (11 Sep 1908/26 Apr 1947)
38 yrs 192 days Thomas Potter-Smith (7 Jun 1901/16 Dec 1939)
38 yrs 166 days Jim Clark (1 May 1923/14 Oct 1961)
37 yrs 143 days Chris Burns (9 Nov 1967/2 Apr 2005)
36 yrs 311 days Doug Hunt (19 May 1914/26 Mar 1951)
36 yrs 207 days Karl Bayliss (24 Feb 1968/18 Sep 2004)
36 yrs 45 days Keith Knight (16 Feb 1969/2 Apr 2005)
36 yrs + -   Martin Lander (Qu3 1952/18 Mar 1989)
35 yrs 359 days Steve Abbley (19 Mar 1957/13 Mar 1993)
35 yrs 310 days Jason Eaton (29 Jan 1969/4 Dec 2004)
35 yrs 294 days Mark Boyland 30 Mar 1958/19 Jan 1994)
35 yrs 219 days Shaun Penny (24 Sep 1957/1 May 1993)
35 yrs 192 days Ian McIntosh (14 Sep 1933/25 Mar 1969)
35 yrs 190 days Harry Ferrier (20 May 1920/26 Nov 1955)
35 yrs 146 days Dave Gwyther (6 Dec 1948/30 Apr 1984)
35 yrs 126 days Adie Mings (17 Oct 1968/21 Feb 2004)

35 yrs 102 days Alan Williams (3 Jun 1938/13 Sep 1973)
35 yrs 72 days Rob Coldray (14 Jan 1935/27 Mar 1970)
35 yrs 16 days Alex Sykes (2 Apr 1974/18 Apr 2009)

YOUNGEST GOALSCORERS

15 yrs 349 days Arthur Stoles (11 Jan 1918/26 Dec 1933)
16 yrs 222 days Michael Noakes (12 Apr 1988/20 Nov 2004)
16 yrs 297 days Eddie Rimmer (17 Mar 1988/8 Jan 2005)
16 yrs 349 days Doug Foxwell (6 Oct 1955/14 Sep 1972)
16 yrs + -   Gordon Boseley (Qu3 1934/30 Mar 1951)
17 yrs 28 days Rod Thomas (11 Jan 1947/8 Feb 1964)
17 yrs 38 days Frank Stout (21 Feb 1877/31 Mar 1894)
17 yrs 160 days Colin Moulsdale (15 Oct 1948/24 Mar 1966)
17 yrs 171 days Jamie Reid (20 Apr 1988/8 Oct 2005)
17 yrs 232 days Lee Smith (8 Sep 1983/28 Apr 2001)
17 yrs 237 days Sam Ellis (10 Jan 1990/4 Sep 2007)
17 yrs 290 days Ben Ashford (1 Apr 1989/16 Jan 2007)
17 yrs 314 days Percy Stout (20 Nov 1875/30 Sep 1893)
17 yrs 325 days Dave Wilkinson (1 Nov 1983/22 Sep 2001)
17 yrs + -   Frank Fielding (Qu3 1872/9 Nov 1889)
17 yrs + -   Arthur Fielding (Qu1 1877/3 Nov 1894)
17 yrs + -   Eddie Bell (1941/26 Apr 1958)
17 yrs + -   Geoff Medcroft (Qu2 1947/6 Mar 1965)
17 yrs + -   Bobby McCool (1948/27 Nov 1965)
17 yrs + -   Kevin Bitchenor (Qu3 1958/22 Mar 1975)

RECORD LEAGUE VICTORY

16-0 v Army 'G' (H) 28/02/1942
14-2 v Army 'K' (H) 13/09/1941
12-1 v Bristol Saint George (H) 28/04/1934
12-2 v Army 'G' (H) 06/12/1941
11-1 v RAF 'B' (H) 20/12/1941
10-0 v Clevedon (H) 03/11/1894
10-0 v Forest Green Rovers (H) 13/01/1900
10-0 v Stroud (H) 23/11/1907
12-3 v RAF 'D' (H) 05/12/1942
10-1 v Stroud (A) 26/10/1907
10-1 v Linden Old Boys (H) 30/11/1907
10-1 v Cam Mills (A) 01/10/1927
10-1 v Army E (H) 02/01/1943
9-0 v Chalford (H) 06/04/1901
9-0 v RAF 'F' (H) 09/05/1942
9-0 v Gosport Borough (H) 13/03/1990
8-0 v Price Walkers (H) 04/02/1898
8-0 v Forest Green Rovers (H) 28/11/1931
8-0 v Lister's Works (H) 28/01/1933
8-0 v Mile Oak Rovers (H) 19/11/1988

RECORD LEAGUE DEFEAT

0-14 v Brimscombe (A) 27/01/1923
1-12 v Gillingham (A) 09/11/1946
0-11 v Bristol City Reserves (A) 26/11/1927
1-11 v Bristol Rovers Reserves (A) 16/01/1932
0-10 v Bexleyheath & Welling (A) 27/02/1960
1-10 v Tamworth (A) 01/05/1937
0-8 v Dursley Rovers (A) 10/03/1923
0-8 v Forest Green Rovers (A) 01/03/1924
0-8 v Broadwell Amateurs (A) 29/12/1928
0-8 v Viney Hill (A) 23/04/1929
0-8 v Merthyr Tydfil (H) 26/10/1946
0-8 v Colchester United (A) 06/09/1947
0-8 v Hereford United (A) 16/02/1957

RECORD CUP VICTORY

13-0 v Fairford Town (H) 11/12/1926 (GNSAC1)
13-1 v RAF 'D' (H) 30/01/1943 (GC2)
12-1 v Rotol AFC (H) 01/11/1941 (GC2)
10-0 v Clifton Association Reserves (H) 26/10/1889 (GJCC1)
10-0 v Sudbury Town (H) 17/10/1998 (FAC3Q)
9-0 v Tewkesbury Town (H) 05/01/1935 (GNSAC1)
8-0 v Clifton (H) 27/01/1894 (GSCC1)
8-0 v Stonehouse (H) 07/10/1933 (EAC1Q)
8-0 v Bristol Manor Farm (H) 09/09/1995 (FAC1Q)
8-1 v Rodborough Old Boys (H) 06/12/1930 (NSAC1)
8-1 v Stonehouse (H) 19/10/1961 (NSPCSF)
8-1 v Stourbridge (H) 25/08/1987 (SLC Gp13)
7-0 v Llanelli (H) 11/09/1979 (FATP)
7-0 v Westbury United (H) 29/08/1987 (FACP)

RECORD CUP DEFEAT

1-10 v Merthyr Tydfil (H) 24/01/1948 (SLC Gp2)
1-8 v Bath City (A) 28/08/1967 (SLC1-1)
0-7 v Leytonstone & Ilford (A) 10/01/1981 (FAT1)
1-7 v Brimscombe (A)10/01/1925 (GNSAC1)
1-7 v Merthyr Tydfil (A) 20/03/1948 (SLC Gp2)
1-7 v Cheltenham Town (A) 11/11/1985 (GSCCSF)
0-6 v Worcester City (A) 11/05/1939 (SLCWF-1)
0-6 v Andover (H) 30/08/1973 (SLC1-2)
0-6 v Merthyr Tydfil (A) 21/08/1976 (SLC1-1)
1-6 v Hereford United (A) 29/04/1948 (SLC Gp2)
1-6 v Merthyr Tydfil (A) 07/09/1960 (SLCQ-2)

MOST LEAGUE WINS IN ONE SEASON (Qual: 30 games)

28   1988-1989 Southern League Midland Division
25   1968-1969 Southern League Division 1
24   2003-2004 Southern League Western Division
23   1990-1991 Southern League Premier Division
22   1934-1935 Gloucestershire Northern Senior League
22   1994-1995 Southern League Premier Division
22   2002-2003 Southern League Western Division

MOST LEAGUE DRAWS IN ONE SEASON (Qual: 30 games)

17   2004-2005 Southern League Premier Division
15   1983-1984 Southern League Premier Division
14   1979-1980 Southern League Midland Division
14   1987-1988 Southern League Midland Division
14   1990-1991 Southern League Premier Division
14   1999-2000 Southern League Premier Division

MOST LEAGUE LOSSES IN ONE SEASON (Qual: 30 games)

28   1961-1962 Southern League Division 1
26   1960-1961 Southern League Division 1
26   1970-1971 Southern League Premier Division
26   1973-1974 Southern League Division 1 North
23   1946-1947 Southern League

LEAST LEAGUE WINS IN ONE SEASON (Qual: 30 games)

4   1924-1925 Gloucestershire Northern Senior League
5   1922-1923 Gloucestershire Northern Senior League
5   1923-1924 Gloucestershire Northern Senior League
6   1961-1962 Southern League Division 1
6   1970-1971 Southern League Premier Division

LEAST LEAGUE DRAWS IN ONE SEASON (Qual: 30 games)

1   1946-1947 Southern League
3   1922-1923 Gloucestershire Northern Senior League
4   1961-1962 Southern League Division 1
4   1963-1964 Southern League Division 1
4   1976-1977 Southern League Division 1 North

LEAST LEAGUE LOSSES IN ONE SEASON (Qual: 30 games)

3   1925-1926 Gloucestershire Northern Senior League
5   1990-1991 Southern League Premier Division
6   1988-1989 Southern League Midland Division
8   1968-1969 Southern League Division 1
9   1935-1936 Birmingham Combination
9   2003-2004 Southern League Western Division

MOST LEAGUE GOALS SCORED IN ONE SEASON

132+ 1941-1942 Gloucester City Hurran Cup League
104 1925-1926 Gloucestershire Northern Senior League
100 1968-1969 Southern League Division 1
99   1935-1936 Birmingham Combination
96   1937-1938 Birmingham Combination
95   1988-1989 Southern League Midland Division
92   1934-1935 Gloucestershire Northern Senior League
88   1963-1964 Southern League Division 1
87   2002-2003 Southern League Western Division
86   1987-1988 Southern League Midland Division
86   1990-1991 Southern League Premier Division

MOST LEAGUE GOALS CONCEDED IN ONE SEASON

120 1946-1947 Southern League
112 1922-1923 Gloucestershire Northern Senior League
104 1961-1962 Southern League Division 1
102 1960-1961 Southern League Division 1
101 1949-1950 Southern League
100 1948-1949 Southern League
98   1926-1927 Gloucestershire Northern Senior League
89   1963-1964 Southern League Division 1
86   2000-2001 Southern League Western Division
85   1937-1938 Birmingham Combination

LONGEST SEQUENCE OF UNBEATEN LEAGUE GAMES

26   15/02/1908 to 20/11/1909
24   18/03/1899 to 14/04/1900
22   05/11/1988 to 11/03/1989
18   20/12/2008 to 28/03/2009
17   18/10/1941 to 28/03/1942
15   15/03/1969 to 03/05/1969
14   22/11/1930 to 14/03/1931
14   03/12/1938 to 18/02/1939
14   19/03/1991 to 17/08/1991
12   13/11/1897 to 29/10/1898
12   20/02/1926 to 22/04/1926
12   03/04/1979 to 05/05/1979
12   15/02/1997 to 24/04/1997
11   27/09/1954 to 14/12/1954
11   27/10/2007 to 26/01/2008
10   09/05/1942 to 16/01/1943
10   24/04/1990 to 08/09/1990
10   01/01/1991 to 12/03/1991
10   23/01/1999 to 13/03/1999
10   06/09/2003 to 09/12/2003
10   28/02/2004 to 17/04/2004
10   04/02/2006 to 08/04/2006

LONGEST SEQUENCE WITHOUT A LEAGUE WIN

19   21/02/1948 to 06/11/1948
14   21/04/1923 to 22/12/1923
14   16/01/1936 to 03/04/1936
14   23/08/1960 to 19/11/1960
13   02/02/2000 to 22/04/2000
12   18/11/1922 to 03/02/1923
11   09/01/1960 to 02/04/1960
11   02/05/1970 to 03/10/1970
11   26/12/1970 to 10/03/1971
10   24/12/1966 to 15/02/1967
10   06/10/1973 to 08/12/1973

OLDEST PLAYER ON DEBUT

40 yrs 176 days Jeff Eckhardt (7 Oct 1965/1 Apr 2006)
38 yrs 360 days David Mehew (29 Oct 1967/24 Oct 2006)
38 yrs 213 days Vince Farrell (11 Sep 1908/12 Apr 1947)
38 yrs 177 days John Williams (11 May 1968/4 Nov 2006)
38 yrs 168 days Don O'Riordan (14 May 1957/29 Oct 1996)
37 yrs 88 days Thomas Potter-Smith (7 Jun 1901/3 Sep 1938)
37 yrs +-   Walter Beale (Qu2 1890/10 Sep 1927)
36 yrs 79 days Arthur Jepson (12 Jul 1915/29 Sep 1951)
36 yrs +-   Andy Cook (1965/25 Aug 2001)
35 yrs 270 days George Tweed (4 Dec 1910/31 Aug 1946)
35 yrs 222 days Sammy Collins (13 Jan 1923/23 Aug 1958)
35 yrs 257 days Bob Shanks (14 Dec 1911/28 Aug 1947)
35 yrs 144 days Mark Boyland (30 Mar 1958/21 Aug 1993)

TEAMS MOST GAMES PLAYED AGAINST IN TOTAL

211 Cheltenham Town
127 Merthyr Tydfil
89   Barry Town/Barry
89   Worcester City
66   Bath City
65   Trowbridge Town
60   Cinderford Town
60   Corby Town
58   Forest Green Rovers/Stroud
57   Banbury United/Banbury Spencer
56   Burton Albion
54   Gravesend & Northfleet
54   Bromsgrove Rovers
52   Chelmsford City
51   King's Lynn
51   Halesowen Town

TEAMS MOST GAMES PLAYED AGAINST IN LEAGUE FOOTBALL ONLY

118	Cheltenham Town
88	Merthyr Tydfil
68	Barry Town/Barry
64	Worcester City
60	Corby Town
55	Banbury United/Banbury Spencer
54	Bath City
54	Gravesend & Northfleet
50	Chelmsford City
50	King's Lynn
48	Burton Albion
48	Bromsgrove Rovers
48	Halesowen Town
46	Dartford
46	Kidderminster Harriers

TEAMS MOST GAMES PLAYED AGAINST IN CUP FOOTBALL ONLY

93	Cheltenham Town
39	Merthyr Tydfil
26	Cinderford Town
25	Worcester City
24	Forest Green Rovers/Stroud
21	Barry Town/Barry
19	Trowbridge Town
14	Stonehouse
13	Dorchester Town
12	Bath City
12	Witney Town
11	Ton Pentre
11	Yeovil Town
11	Redditch United
10	Salisbury

LONGEST FIXTURE ASSOCIATION

116 years	Clevedon/Clevedon Town 1893-2009
104	Cirencester Town 1904-2008
102	Trowbridge Town 1893-1995
101	Cheltenham Town 1898-1999
100	Forest Green Rovers/Stroud 1899-1999
82	Cinderford Town 1922-2004
82	Bristol City Reserves 1927-2009
78	Paulton Rovers 1927-2005
74	Bristol Rovers Reserves 1932-2006
74	Halesowen Town 1935-2009
74	Evesham Town/Evesham United 1935-2009
73	Stonehouse 1900-1973
73	Weston-Super-Mare 1930-2003
73	Bromsgrove Rovers 1935-2008
73	Banbury United/Banbury Spencer 1936-2009
72	Cheltenham Town Reserves 1932-2004

TOTAL NUMBER OF SEASONS AT EACH VENUE

26	The Ground, Cheltenham Road, Longlevens
22	Horton Road Stadium
21	Meadow Park, Hempsted
16	Budding's Field
7	Llanthony, Hempsted
6	Avenue Road Ground (Tuffley Avenue)
6	Sutgrove Park, Calton Road/Stroud Road
2	Bon Marche Ground, Estcourt Road
1	Co-operative Field, India Road, Tredworth (Groundshare)
1	The New Lawn, Forest Green, Nailsworth (Groundshare)
1	Corinium Stadium, Cirencester (Groundshare)

Note: Kingsholm Rugby Ground was also used on occasions between 1883 and 1900, Crypt School Ground, Friars' Orchard once 1891/92, Barnwood once 1907/08, Gloucester Old Boys Ground, Denmark Road once 1909/10, Whaddon Road, Cheltenham three times 1969/70, 1970/71 and 1974/75 and Supermarine Road, Swindon once 2005/06.

RECORD HOME ATTENDANCES

Budding's Field – 2,000 v Bedminster 25/02/1893 (GSCCSF)
Kingsholm – 700 v Eastville Rovers 11/11/1893 (League)
Avenue Road Ground – 1,200 v Chalford 06/04/1926 (League)
Co-operative Field – not known
Llanthony – not known
Sutgrove Park – not known
Bon Marche Ground – 2,500 v Frome Town 12/01/1935 (EAC1)
2,500 v Cheltenham Town 19/04/1935
(League)
Longlevens – 9,500 v Norwich City 26/11/1949 (FAC1)
Horton Road – 5,000 v Wimbledon 27/08/1964 (League)
Meadow Park – 4,000 v Dagenham & Redbridge 12/04/1997
(FATSF-2)
The New Lawn – 706 v Shortwood United 30/09/2007 (FAC2Q)
Corinium Stadium – 745 v Cambridge City 28/04/2009 (League Play-Off)
Note: Record attendance for the Avenue Road Ground was 2,000 v West Bromwich Albion 24/10/1925 (Friendly). Record attendance for Longlevens was 10,500 v Tottenham Hotspur 27/10/1952 (Friendly). Record attendance for Horton Road was 6,000 for a Combined City/Robins XI v Wolverhampton Wanderers 08/05/1975 (Memorial Match).

RECORD AWAY ATTENDANCES

17,058 at Bristol City 25/11/1950 (FAC1)
11,431 at Mansfield Town 27/11/1948 (FAC1)
10,000 at Gillingham 27/08/1949 (League)
10,000 at Colchester United 07/01/1950 (League)
8,500 at Merthyr Tydfil 11/09/1946 (League)
7,095 at Bath City 13/11/1948 (FAC4Q)
7,000 at Colchester United 25/12/1948 (League)
7,000 at Yeovil Town 26/08/1950 (League)
7,000 at Llanelly 16/09/1952 (FACPR)

BEST AVERAGE HOME ATTENDANCE

3,600	1956/57
3,554	1949/50
3,445	1951/52
3,427	1950/51
3,404	1954/55

WORST AVERAGE HOME ATTENDANCE

233	1973/74
243	1977/78
257	1979/80
259	1976/77
261	1978/79

OLDEST PLAYERS

44 yrs 31 days Adie Harris (5 Mar 1964/5 Apr 2008)
42 yrs 205 days George Edwards (14 Sep 1897/6 Apr 1940)
41 yrs 214 days Bob Etheridge (25 Mar 1934/25 Oct 1975)
41 yrs 58 days Reg Weaver (19 Sep 1905/16 Nov 1946)
41 yrs 48 days David Mehew (29 Oct 1967/16 Dec 2008)
40 yrs 204 days Jeff Eckhardt (7 Oct 1965/29 Apr 2006)
39 yrs 343 days Don O'Riordan (14 May 1957/22 Apr 1997)
39 yrs 4 days Jim Clark (1 May 1923/5 May 1962)
38 yrs 250 days Steve Fergusson (21 Apr 1961/27 Dec 1999)
38 yrs 241 days Vince Farrell (11 Sep 1908/10 May 1947)
38 yrs 201 days Thomas Potter-Smith (7 Jun 1901/25 Dec 1939)
38 yrs 177 days John Williams (11 May 1968/4 Nov 2006)
38 yrs 54 days Chris Burns (9 Nov 1967/2 Jan 2006)
38 yrs +- Martin Lander (1952/27 Oct 1990)
37 yrs 266 days Len Bond (12 Feb 1954/5 Nov 1991)
37 yrs 129 days Brian Hughes (20 Aug 1962/27 Dec 1999)
37 yrs 61 days Fred Bartlett (5 Mar 1913/6 May 1950)
37 yrs +- Walter Beale (Qu2 1890/19 Sep 1927)
37 yrs +- Bob Cox (1909/28 Sep 1946)
Note: Brian Godfrey non playing sub on 7 Apr 1990 at the age of 49 yrs 341 days, Adie Harris non playing sub 6 May 2009 at the age of 45 yrs 62 days, Bob Etheridge non playing sub on 13 Mar 1976 at the age of 41 yrs 353 days, David Mehew non playing sub 6 May 2009 aged 41 yrs 189 days and Andrew Cook non playing sub 10 Sep 2005 aged 40+.

YOUNGEST PLAYERS

15 yrs 30 days Callum Preece (16 Mar 1993/15 Apr 2008)
15 yrs 237 days Rod Thomas (11 Jan 1947/5 Sep 1962)
15 yrs 278 days Geoff Pellant (6 May 1947/8 Feb 1963)
15 yrs 349 days Arthur Stoles (11 Jan 1918/26 Dec 1933)
15 yrs +- Mike Emmerson (Qu3 1963/3 Apr 1979)
16 yrs 61 days William Morefield (26 Oct 1922/26 Dec 1938)
16 yrs 71 days Percy Stout (20 Nov 1875/30 Jan 1892)
16 yrs 154 days Jamie Reid (20 Apr 1988/21 Sep 2004)
16 yrs 188 days Eddie Rimmer (17 Mar 1988/21 Sep 2004)
16 yrs 216 days Michael Noakes (12 Apr 1988/20 Nov 2004)
16 yrs 221 days Tom Webb (12 Sep 1984/21 Apr 2001)
16 yrs 245 days Ivor Gwatkin (9 Mar 1919/9 Nov 1935)
16 yrs 252 days Grahame Parker (11 Feb 1912/20 Oct 1928)
16 yrs 305 days Frank Stout (21 Feb 1877/23 Dec 1893)

16 yrs 313 days Doug Foxwell (6 Oct 1955/14 Aug 1972)
16 yrs +-   Brian Lane (1882/8 Oct 1898)
16 yrs +-   Ray Moore (1921/13 Feb 1937)
16 yrs +-   D Moule (1921/29 Jan 1938)
16 yrs +-   Gordon Boseley (Qu3 1934/30 Mar 1951)
16 yrs +-   Michael Anderson (1945/9 Dec 1961)
16 yrs +-   Geoff Medcroft (Qu2 1947/26 Mar 1963)
16 yrs +-   Alistair Cameron (1955/01 Jan 1972)
16 yrs +-   Kevin Bitchenor (Qu3 1958/15 Mar 1975)
16 yrs +-   Wayne Leach (1965/25 Apr 1981)
16 yrs +-   Nick Gardner (Qu1 1966/09 Feb 1982)
16 yrs +-   Russell Elliott (1968/18 Aug 1984)
16 yrs +-   Steve Belfitt (Qu2 1975/7 Apr 1992)
16 yrs +-   Gavin Rea (Qu2 1984/27 Mar /2001)
16 yrs +-   Dan Avery (Qu11987/25 Nov 2003)
Note: Daryl Parkes was a non-playing sub 4 Jan 1975 aged 15 yrs +-.

MOST EXPERIENCED FOOTBALL LEAGUE PLAYER TO APPEAR FOR GLOUCESTER CITY

596 League App.   Dave Gwyther (51 apps. for Gloucester City)
572   Don O'Riordan (2)
570   Bobby Woodruff (3)
555   Alan Williams (25)
525   Jeff Eckhardt (6)
498   Gareth Taylor (2)
484   Rod Thomas (10)
480   Marcus Browning (18)
478   Phil Bater (2)
452   John Williams (1)
436   Paul Richardson (3)
418   Gerry Sweeney (68)
416   Lindsay Parsons (72)
411   John Delve (14)
404   John Shaw (71)

SENIOR INTERNATIONALS WHO PASSED THROUGH GLOUCESTER
(This list also includes players who were guests and played in friendlies only)

Frank Saunders (1890) – England (1 cap)
Ronald Turner (1907) – England Amateur
George Watson (1935) – England Amateur (2)
William Peart (1935-37, 1939-41) – Wales Amateur (3)
Eddie Parris (1939-47) – Wales (1)
Adolf Hanson (1941) – England War-Time (1)
Dai Jones (1942) – Wales (7)
Doug Hunt (1948-51) – England War-Time (1)
Arthur Evans (1950) – Wales Amateur
Stan Milburn (1954) – England B
Trevor Ford (1955) – Wales (38), Wales War-Time (1)
Rod Thomas (1962-63) – Wales (47), Wales U23 (6)
Tommy Casey (1963-64) - Northern Ireland (12)
Alan McIntosh (1967) – Wales Amateur
Tony Villars (1978) – Wales (3), Wales U23 (2)
Jeff Blockley (1981) – England (1), England U23 (10)
Frankie Prince (1981) – Wales U23 (4)
Peter Aitken (1982-83) – Wales U23 (3)
Don Gillies (1982-83) – Scotland U23 (1)
Chris Garland (1983) – England U23 (1)
Dave Gwyther (1983) – Wales U23 (2)
Tommy Hughes (1983) – Scotland U23 (2)
Ian Davies (1987) – Wales U21 (1)
Brian Godfrey (1988-89) – Wales (3), Wales U23 (1)
Kenny Hibbitt (1989) – England U23 (1)
Marcus Browning (1989-90) – Wales (5)
Phil Bater (1990) – Wales U21 (2)
Gareth Taylor (1991) – Wales (15), Wales U21 (7)
Mike Oakes (1992) – England U21 (6)
Leroy Rosenior (1995-97) – Sierra Leone (1)
Don O'Riordan (1996) – Eire U21 (1)
Dean Huggins (1997) – Wales U21 (1)
Pat Mountain (1998) – Wales U21 (2)
Mark McKeever (2005) – Eire U21 (4)
Dean Grubb (2008) – Wales U21 (1)

Other Sports
Frank Stout (1891-94) – England Rugby (14)
Percy Stout (1891-94) – England Rugby (5)
Gilbert Jessop (1895) – England Cricket (18)
Grahame Parker (1928-30) – England Rugby (2)
Arthur Jepson (1951-52) – Test Match Umpire (4)
Alex Sykes (2005-08) – England Futsal (38+)
Luke Ballinger (2008) – England Futsal (23+)

RELATIONS

Brothers who have been involved with Gloucester City
ADDIS – Chris and Daryl
ALDER – Walter*, Sammy and Percy
AVERY – Dan and Sam
BRINKWORTH – Trevor and Dick
BROWNING – William and Hubert
BRUTON – Dave and Mike
CASEY – Matt* and Ross
CHADBORN – Arthur*, William and Charles*
COLTMAN – Ron and Mick
COOPER – Jimmy and Tony
CRABTREE – Harold*, F Crabtree*, Percy*, Archibald* and James*
DANGERFIELD – John and David
ETHERIDGE – Bob and Dick
FIELDING – Frank, Arthur and Samuel
FORD – Leslie and Harry*
GARDNER – Chris, Phil and Nick
KIBBLE – Donald and Herbert
LACEY – Brian and John
LANDELLS – James and William
LANE – Lionel, Herbert and Brian
MAYO – T and WH
MEDCROFT – Peter and Geoff
MOCKRIDGE – Gary and Dave
MOULSDALE – Ron and Colin
MURDOCK – Andy and Jock
NICHOLLS – Wilfred and Walter*
PLATT – Francis* and Edward*
POCOCK – Fran* and Barrie
POOLE – Charles and Percy*
POWELL – Trevor* and James
PROCTOR – William* and Hubert*
RUST – Frederick and Tom
RUTHERFORD – Jim and Tom
SESSIONS – Wilfred and Walter
SMITH – Jamie and Lee
SPECK – George, John and Walter*
STOUT – James, Percy and Frank
TEMPLE – Craig and Mark
THORNE – Gary and Wayne
VICKERY – William and Thomas
VINSON – William and George
WELLS – Bomber and David
WHITEHOUSE – Jimmy and Ken
WHITNEY – William and Harold
* Indicates a brother who only played in a friendly

Father and Sons
ANDERSON – Don and Michael
BEATTIE – George and Andrew*
BOSELEY – Gordon and Steve
BURNS – Chris and Jake*
COX –Bob and Tony
DUDFIELD – James and Tim*
FOOTE – Ernest and Terry
HYDE – Chris and Cory
LEACH – Joe and Wayne
MEDCROFT – Geoff and Scott
MOULSDALE – Ron and Mike
PARKER – Reg and Grahame
RUST – Frederick* and Frederick and Thomas
SPECK – John and Albert
STOW – Gus and Rob
SWANKIE – Bob and Ian
TANDY – Bernard and Daryl
VICKERY – William and William and Thomas
*Indicates only played in a friendly

Grandfather and Grandson
BALLINGER – Brian and Luke

Uncle and Nephew
MEDCROFT – Peter to Scott
MOULSDALE – Colin to Mike
SPECK – George and Walter* to Albert
*Indicates only played in a friendly

Cousins
Mike and Ron COLTMAN to Jeff MILES
Martyn ROGERS to Peter ROGERS

PLAYER AND TEAM STATISTICS

CLUB CAPTAINS
Match reports indicated that the following have indeed held this position during the years indicated.

Charles F. Poole 1889-1890
Walter Sessions 1890-1892
James L. Somerville 1892-1893
Frank B. Fielding 1893-1894
Edgar T.S. Tadman 1894-1895
Herbert H. Scott 1895-1896
W.H. Godby 1896-1897
Arthur F. Fielding 1897-1900
Frederick T. Rust 1900-1904
Ernest F. Davy 1906-1908
William C. Vickery 1908-1910
Charles A. Bretherton 1913-1914
S.C. Tomlinson 1921-1923
Samuel Alder 1925-1926
George Edwards 1926-1928
Percy K. Alder 1929-1930
W. Richard Harrison 1930-1931
Andrew F.T. Murdock 1931-1933
Samuel C. Hamer 1933-1934
Enos W. Drew 1934-1935
William C. Peart 1936-1938
Thomas Potter-Smith 1938-1940
Roy Davis 1940-1941
Eddie Parris 1941-1942
Cyril G. Dean 1946-1947
Robert Shanks 1947-1948
Douglas A. Hunt 1948-1949
James Canavan 1950-1952
Walter E. Pullen 1952-1953
Stanley Myers 1953-1955
James D. Clark 1955-1957
Harry May 1957-1958
John Gallagher 1958-1959
Alan Smith 1959-1960
James Weston 1960-1961
David G. Head 1962-1963
Rob Coldray 1964-1966
James Ashall/Anthony Cottle 1966-1967
Robert Anderson 1968-1969
Selwyn Vale 1969-1970
Robert Anderson 1970-1972
Andrew McQuarrie 1972-1973
Ronnie Bird 1973-1974
Mick Hayden 1974-1975
Colin Moulsdale 1975-1978
Gary Bell 1978-1979
John Turner 1979-1980
John H. Layton 1980-1981
Jeff Blockley 1981
Dave Bruton 1981-1982
Don Gillies 1983
Gerald Sweeney 1983-1984
Barrie Vassallo 1984-1986
Hedley V. Steele 1987-1988
Brian D. Hughes 1988-1995
Gary Kemp 1995-1999
Christopher Burns 1999-2000
Neil Griffiths 2000-2005
Christopher D. Thompson 2005
Neil J. Mustoe 2005-to date

RECORD TRANSFER FEE PAID (incomplete)
Transfer fees are as quoted in various publications and are not official.

Steve Fergusson £25,000 to Worcester City 1990/91 *
David Holmes £25,000 to Gresley Rovers 1994/95
Steve Portway £17,500 to Gravesend & Northfleet 1994/95
Jeff Sherwood £15,000 to Yeovil Town 1990/91
Chris Townsend £10,000 to Cheltenham Town 1988/89
Jason Eaton £10,000 to Bristol City 1990/91
Dale Watkins £10,000 to Rushden & Diamonds 1996/97
Adie Mings £8,500 to Bath City 1996/97
Tony Cook £5,000 to Weymouth 1992/93
Deion Vernon £5000 to Bath City 1995/96
Kenny Stephens £4,000 to Hereford United 1979/80
Brian Hughes £4,000 to Cheltenham Town 1988/89
Gary Bradder £4,000 to Atherstone United 1988/89
Kim Casey £2,500 to AP Leamington 1984/85
Dave Mogg £2,500 to Cheltenham Town 1989/90
Brendan Hackett £2,500 to Worcester City 1990/91 *
Arthur Jepson £2,000 to Notts County 1951/52
George Beattie £2,000 to Tonbridge 1955/56

RECORD TRANSFER FEE RECEIVED (incomplete)
Transfer fees are as quoted in various publications and are not official.

Ian Hedges £25,000 from Bournemouth & BA 1989/90
Jason Eaton £20,000 from Cheltenham Town 1992/93
Darren Keeling £15,000 from Yeovil Town 1998/99
Chris Townsend £12,000 from Dorchester Town 1990/91
Steve Talboys £11,000 from Wimbledon 1991/92
Steve Fergusson £10,000 from Telford United 1991/92 *
Mike Bruton £6,000 from Newport County 1979/80
Gary Bradder £4,500 from Atherstone United 1989/90
Bob Etheridge £3,000 from Bristol City 1956/57
David Webb £3,000 from Trowbridge Town 1990/91
Alan Grubb/Gordon Boseley £2,500 from Tottenham Hotspur 1951/52
Kim Casey £2500 from Kidderminster Harriers 1985/86
Ray Baverstock £2,500 from Worcester City 1991/92
George Beattie £2,000 from Newport County 1950/51
Mike Bruton £2,000 from Oxford City 1980/81
Brendan Hackett £2,000 from Telford United 1991/92 *
Jackie Boyd £1,000 from Bristol City 1950/51
Charlie Cook £1,000 from Bristol City 1956/57
Albert Shelley £300 from Sheffield Wednesday 1936/37
* Combined fee.

CLUB PLAYER OF THE SEASON

1964/1965   Rob Coldray
1965/1966   Bobby Grant
1966/1967   Bobby McCool
1967/1968   Bobby McCool
1968/1969   John Stevens
1969/1970   Nigel Page-Jones
1970/1971   Bob Anderson
1971/1972   Jeff Miles
1972/1973   Jeff Miles
1973/1974   Ray Wixey
1974/1975   Ray Wixey
1975/1976   Alan Gough
1976/1977   John Evans
1977/1978   Doug Foxwell
1978/1979   Gary Mockridge
1979/1980   ?
1980/1981   ?
1981/1982   ?
1982/1983   Dave Bruton
1983/1984   Mario Waite
1984/1985   Kim Casey
1985/1986   Martin Lander

SUPPORTER'S PLAYER OF THE SEASON
From 2000/2001 the recipient presented with the 'Ken Selwyn Memorial Shield'

1986/1987   Steve Baddock
1987/1988   ?
1988/1989   Nigel Green
1989/1990   Lance Morrison
1990/1991   Jeff Meacham
1991/1992   Dave Mogg
1992/1993   Paul Bywater
1993/1994   Paul Bywater
1994/1995   Mark Hallam
1995/1996   Gary Kemp
1996/1997   Simon Cooper
1997/1998   Gary Thorne
1998/1999   Gary Kemp
1999/2000   Wayne Thorne
2000/2001   Jimmy Cox/Andy Tucker
2001/2002   Matt Bath
2002/2003   Adie Harris
2003/2004   Andy Hoskins
2004/2005   Lee Smith
2005/2006   Tom Webb
2006/2007   Lyndon Tomkins
2007/2008   Neil Mustoe
2008/2009   Alex Sykes

PLAYER'S PLAYER OF THE SEASON

1988/1989   Martyn Williams
1989/1990   Steve Talboys
1990/1991   Jeff Meacham
1991/1992 to 2005/2006   ?
2006/2007   Lyndon Tomkins
2007/2008   Neil Mustoe
2008/2009   Lee Marshall

[558]

PLAYER AND TEAM STATISTICS

CHAIRMAN'S PLAYER OF THE SEASON

1990/1991 Wayne Noble

KIT COLOURS

Upto 1905   Black Shirts with White Sleeves and Neckband, Black Shorts
1906 to 1908 Red and White Striped Shirts and White Shorts
1909 to 1910 Black Shirts with White Sleeves and Neckband, Black Shorts
1910 to 1913 Amber and Black Shirts
1913 to 1914 White Shirts
1919 to 1935 Red and White Striped Shirts and White Shorts
1935 to 1942 Red and White Quartered Shirts and Black Shorts
1946 to 1982 Red Shirts with White Sleeves and White Shorts
1982 to 1987 All Yellow
1987 to date Yellow and Black Striped Shirts and Black Shorts

SHIRT SPONSORS

1979-1980	Jaco
1980-1981 to 1990-1991	Westbury Homes
1991-1992	Port Services
1992-1993	Euroglaze
1993-1994	Jewson
1994-1995 to 1999-2000	Hartland Motors
2000-2001 to 2001-2002	no sponsor *
2002-2003 to 2007-2008	Keyway
2008-2009	SsangYong

*although no official sponsor Port Services shirts were worn 2001-2002.

APPLIED FOR FOOTBALL LEAGUE STATUS

Season ending:

1955/56: Crystal Palace 44 votes (re-elected), Swindon Town 42 (re-elected), Peterborough United 8, Boston United 1, **Gloucester City 1**, Bedford Town 0, Chelmsford City 0, Hastings United 0, Headington United 0, Hereford United 0, King's Lynn 0, Worcester City 0, Yeovil Town 0.

1957/58: Millwall 46 votes (re-elected), Exeter City 43 (re-elected), Southport 42 (re-elected), Crewe Alexandra 35 (re-elected), Peterborough United 15, Wigan Athletic 4, Hereford United 3, Bedford Town 2, Headington United 2, King's Lynn 2, Kettering Town 1, South Shields 1, Burton Albion 0, **Gloucester City 0**, Morecambe 0, Yeovil Town 0.

1958/59: Oldham Athletic 46 votes (re-elected), Southport 34 (re-elected), Barrow 32 (re-elected), Aldershot 31 (re-elected), Peterborough United 26, Headington United 7, Worcester City 7, Wigan Athletic 3, Cambridge City 2, **Gloucester City 1**, Kettering Town 1, Scarborough 1, South Shields 1, Bedford Town 0, Hereford United 0, King's Lynn 0, Morecambe 0, Yeovil Town 0.

1963/64: York City 48 votes (re-elected), Southport 45 (re-elected), Barrow 42 (re-elected), Hartlepools United 36 (re-elected), Wigan Athletic 5, Gateshead 4, Romford 4, Yeovil Town 3, Guildford City 2, New Brighton 2, South Shields 2, **Gloucester City 1**, Morecambe 1, Weymouth 1, Bexley United 0, Poole Town 0, Scarborough 0.

TOTAL NUMBER OF GAMES PLAYED IN LEAGUE COMPETITION

COMPETITION	SEASONS	FIRST	LAST	PLAYED	
BRISTOL & DISTRICT LEAGUE	2	1893/94	1894/95	40	Changed name to Western League 1895
WESTERN LEAGUE	1	1895/96		18	
GLOUCESTER & DISTRICT LEAGUE	7	1897/98	1906/07	66	
MID GLOUCESTERSHIRE LEAGUE	3	1898/99	1900/01	25	
CHELTENHAM & DISTRICT LEAGUE *	2	1906/07	1909/10	15.5	
NORTH GLOUCESTERSHIRE LEAGUE *	5	1907/08	1921/22	63.5	
GLOUCESTERSHIRE NORTHERN SENIOR LEAGUE	13	1922/23	1934/35	336	
BRISTOL CHARITY LEAGUE	6	1926/27	1934/35	62	
BIRMINGHAM COMBINATION	5	1935/36	1939/40	152	Inc. 1939/40 (2 games)
SOUTHERN LEAGUE	64	1939/40	2008/09	2604	Inc. 1939/40 (14 games)
					Inc. 1958/59 (8 games Inter Zone Comp.)
					Inc. 2008/09 (2 games Play-Off)
GLOUCESTER CITY HURRAN CUP LEAGUE	2	1941/42	1942/43	38	War-Time League
WESTERN FLOODLIGHT LEAGUE	4	1979/80	1982/83	11	
League matches expunged from records	-	1895/96	2003/04	11	
TOTAL				**3443**	

* In the 1909/1910 season permission was given for one fixture to count for both these leagues.

TOTAL NUMBER OF GAMES PLAYED IN CUP COMPETITION

COMPETITION	SEASONS	FIRST	LAST	PLAYED	
GLOS FA JUNIOR CUP	6	1885/86	1906/07	15	
GLOS FA SENIOR CUP	7	1891/92	1899/00	12	
ENGLISH AMATEUR CUP	12	1907/08	1934/35	29	
GLOS FA INTERMEDIATE CUP	3	1907/08	1909/10	5	
NORTH GLOUCESTERSHIRE MINOR CUP	1	1921/22		3	
GLOS FA NORTHERN SENIOR AMATEUR CUP	12	1922/23	1934/35	37	
FA CUP	67	1928/29	2008/09	178	
BIRMINGHAM SENIOR CUP	1	1935/36		2	
GLOS FA NORTHERN SENIOR PROFESSIONAL CUP	67	1936/37	2008/09	103	Inc. 1939/40 (2 games)
SOUTHERN LEAGUE CUP	64	1939/40	2008/09	235	Inc. 1939/40 (5 games)
GODSMAN CUP	2	1941/42	1942/43	6	War-Time Cup
CITY CUP	1	1942/43		4	War-Time Cup
WORCESTERSHIRE FA SENIOR CUP	4	1948/49	1984/85	7	
SOUTHERN LEAGUE CHAMPIONSHIP GAME	2	1956/57	1982/83	2	Champions v Cup Winners
WELSH FA CUP	1	1958/59		4	
FA TROPHY	40	1969/70	2008/09	126	
CLUBCALL CUP	1	1989/90		1	
PREMIER INTER LEAGUE CUP	1	1990/91		1	
TOTAL				**770**	

GRAND TOTAL OF COMPETITIVE GAMES = 4213

MANAGERS

The precise definition of 'manager' is at times an arbitrary one, particularly in the pre-1915 years. This means that 'secretaries' in the early years who did not have managerial responsibilities but had overall responsibility of the club are mentioned. The post of Manager of Gloucester City commenced 1935 at the time they turned semi-professional.

W.H. Clarke (Secretary 1883-1886)
Rev. Henry L. Brereton (Secretary 1889-1890)
W.H. Benfield (Secretary 1890–1893)
H.T. Robins (Secretary 1893-1897)
James G. Washbourne (Secretary 1897-1898)
Lionel A. Lane (Secretary 1898-1899)
Randolph Lewis (Secretary 1899-1902)
Henry W. Arkell/Henry Sherwood (Joint Secretaries 1902-1903)
Frank R. Crawley (Secretary 1903-1905)
J.E. Palmer (Secretary 1906-1909)
Oliver J.A. Carter (Secretary 1909-1910)
A.J. Hayward (Secretary 1910-1911)
H. Barry (Secretary 1911-1914)
Lemuel A. Beddis (Secretary-Manager 1919-1931)
Maurice Hukin (Secretary-Manager 1931-1935)
Maurice Hukin (Manager 1935-1938)
Capt. Albert Prince-Cox (Manager June 1938-1940)
William S. Blunn (Secretary 1940–1943)
Cyril Dean (Player-Manager 1946 - February 1948)
Jack F. Whiting/Bill Carver (Temporary February 1948 – November 1948)
Doug Hunt (Player-Manager November 1948 – July 1952)
Jimmy Buist (Player-Manager August 1952 - April 1954)
Harry Ferrier (Player-Manager April 1954 – May 1959)
Ollie Norris (Player-Manager August 1959 - January 1960)
Frank Tredgett (Player-Coach January 1960 - May 1960)
Phil Friel (Temporary Player-Coach August 1960 – September 1960)
Maurice Hukin (Manager September 1960 - May 1962)
Ron Humpston (Manager May 1962 - May 1963)
Tommy Casey (Player-Manager August 1963 - May1965)
Bob Grant (Player-Manager August 1965 –May 1966)
Cyril Williams (Manager June 1966 – March 1967)
Dick Etheridge (Caretaker March 1967 - June 1967)
Harold Fletcher (Coach June 1967 – May 1968)
Ian McIntosh (Player-Manager August 1968 – May 1970)
Rob Coldray (Manager May 1970 – October 1970)
Dick Etheridge (Caretaker October 1970 – November 1970)
John Preece (Manager November 1970 – November 1971)
Ian McIntosh (Manager November 1971 – November 1972) 2nd spell
Dick Etheridge (Manager December 1972 – November 1973)
Bobby Etheridge (Manager November 1973 – May 1976)
Colin Moulsdale (Player-Manager May 1976 – November 1977)
Bob Mursell (Manager November 1977 – September 1980)
Dick Etheridge (Caretaker September 1980 – October 1980)
Bobby Campbell (Manager October 1980 – March 1982)
Johnny Layton (Manager March 1982 - October 1982)
Bob Mursell (Manager October 1982 – April 1984) 2nd spell
Tony Freely (Manager May 1984 – March 1985)
Bobby Etheridge (Caretaker March 1985 – May 1985)
Paul Richardson (Player-Manager May 1985– November 1985)
Steve Scarrott (Manager November 1985 – June 1987)
Brian Godfrey (Manager June 1987–November 1991)
Steve Millard (Temporary November 1991 - February 1992)
Brian Godfrey (Manager February 1992 –March 1994) 2nd spell
Gary Goodwin/Brian Hughes (Temporary March 1994 – May 1994)
John Murphy (Manager May 1994 – March 1996)
Leroy Rosenior (Player-Manager March 1996 – October 1998)
Brian Hughes (Manager October 1998 – February 2000)
Tommy Callinan (Player-Manager February 2000 – June 2001)
Chris Burns (Player-Manager June 2001 – January 2006)
Neil Mustoe/Adie Harris (Temporary for 1 match January 2006)
Tim Harris (Manager January 2006 – June 2008)
Dave Mehew (Team Manager June 2008 to date)

LONGEST SERVING MANAGER (in calendar years)

13 Lemuel A. Beddis
11 Maurice Hukin
8   Brian Godfrey
7   Bob Mursell
6   Harry Ferrier
6   Chris Burns
5   H.T. Robins
5   Doug Hunt
5   Ian McIntosh
5   Dick Etheridge
5   Bobby Etheridge

MOST GAMES MANAGED

375 Maurice Hukin
370 Brian Godfrey
310 Lemuel Beddis
261 Harry Ferrier
232 Chris Burns
226 Bob Mursell
193 Doug Hunt
155 Ian McIntosh
148 Leroy Rosenior
143 Bob Etheridge
121 Tim Harris

OLDEST MANAGER

76 yrs 101 days Maurice Hukin (24 Jan 1886/5 May 1962)
59 yrs 258 days Bobby Campbell (28 Jun 1922/13 Mar 1982)
53 yrs 318 days Brian Godfrey (1 May 1940/15 Mar 1994)
51 yrs 42 days Bob Etheridge (25 Mar 1934/6 May 1985)
50 yrs +-   Capt. Albert Prince-Cox (Qu2 1890/18 May 1940)
48 yrs 192 days Tim Harris (17 Oct 1959/26 Apr 2008)
45 yrs 131 days Dick Etheridge (7 Jul 1935/15 Nov 1980)
41 yrs 308 days Adie Harris (5 Mar 1964/7 Jan 2006)
41 yrs 189 days David Mehew (29 Oct 1967/6 May 2009)
39 yrs 72 days Ian McIntosh (14 Sep 1933/25 Nov 1972)
38 yrs 347 days Harry Ferrier (20 May 1920/2 May 1959)
38 yrs 54 days Chris Burns (9 Nov 1967/2 Jan 2006)
38 yrs +-   Gary Goodwin (1956/7 May 1994)
37 yrs 350 days Doug Hunt (19 May 1914/3 May 1952)
37 yrs 176 days Brian Hughes (20 Aug 1962/12 Feb 2000)
36 yrs 17 days Paul Richardson (25 Oct 1949/11 Nov 1985)
35 yrs 314 days Jimmy Buist (19 Jun 1918/29 Apr 1954)
35 yrs 269 days Rob Coldray (14 Jan 1935/10 Oct 1970)
35 yrs 190 days Lemuel Beddis (3 Oct 1895/11 Apr 1931)
35 yrs 51 days Tommy Casey (11 Mar 1930/1 May 1965)

YOUNGEST MANAGER

17 yrs +-   James Washbourne (Qu4 1879/25 Sep 1897)
20 yrs +-   Lionel Lane (Qu2 1878/8 Oct 1898)
20 yrs +-   Frank Crawley (1883/24 Oct 1903)
24 yrs +-   Henry Arkell (Qu3 1878/1 Nov 1902)
24 yrs +-   Oliver Carter (Qu1 1885/25 Sep 1909)
25 yrs 287 days Rev. Henry Brereton (13 Jan 1864/26 Oct 1889)
25 yrs 330 days Bobby Grant (25 Sep1940/21 Aug 1965)
25 yrs 353 days Lemuel Beddis (3 Oct 1895/21 Sep 1921)
27 yrs 311 days Colin Moulsdale (15 Oct 1948/21 Aug 1976)
29 yrs 63 days Neil Mustoe (5 Nov 1976/7 Jan 2006)
30 yrs 143 days Ollie Norris (1 Apr 1929/22 Aug 1959)

MANAGERS AND CLUB OFFICIALS

* Also player with Gloucester City. See Players' Records for further details.

ARKELL, Henry Witcomb *
1902 to 1903
Title: Joint Secretary (with Henry Sherwood).
Total Games: 12

BARRY, H
1911 to 1914
Title: Secretary.
Total Games: 13

BEDDIS, Lemuel Archibald *
1919 to 1931
Title: Secretary-Manager.
Total Games: 310

BENFIELD, W.H *
1890 to 1893
Title: Secretary.
Total Games: 4

BLUNN, William S
1940 to 1943
Title: Secretary.
Total Games: 48

BRERETON, Rev. Henry Lloyd *
1889 to 1890
Title: Secretary.
Total Games: 3

BUIST, James Gibb (Jimmy) *
August 1952 to April 1954
Title: Player-Manager.
Total Games: 96

BURNS, Christopher (Chris) *
June 2001 to December 2005
Title: Player-Manager.
Total Games: 232

CALLINAN, Thomas Joseph (Tommy) *
February 2000 to June 2001
Title: Player-Manager.
Total Games: 66

CAMPBELL, Robert Inglis (Bobby)
b. 28/06/1922 Glasgow, Scotland d. 03/05/2009 Bristol
November 1980 to March 1982
Title: Manager.
Total Games: 83

CARTER, Oliver John Arthur (Olly) *
1909 to 1910
Title: Secretary.
Total Games: 26

CARVER, Bill
February 1948 to November 1948
Title: Joint Temporary Manager (with Jack Whiting).
Total Games: 33

CASEY, Thomas (Tommy) *
August 1963 to May 1965
Title: Player-Manager.
Total Games: 96

CLARKE, W.H
1883 to 1886
Title: Secretary.
Total Games: 2?

COLDRAY, Robert Alexander (Rob) *
May 1970 to October 1970
Title: Manager.
Total Games: 14

CRAWLEY, Frank R *
1903 to 1905
Title: Secretary.
Total Games: 13

DEAN, Cyril George *
1946 to February 1948
Title: Player-Manager.
Total Games: 66

ETHERIDGE, Richard Fredrick (Dick) *
March 1967 to June 1967 (13), October 1970 to November 1970 (5), December 1972 to November 1973 (48), September 1980 to November 1980 (12)
Title: Caretaker Manager 1967, 1970, Manager 1972-73, Caretaker Manager 1980.
Total Games: 78

ETHERIDGE, Robert James (Bob) *
November 1973 to May 1976 (128), March 1985 to May 1985 (15)
Title: Manager 1973-76, Caretaker Manager 1985.
Total Games: 143

FERRIER, Henry (Harry) *
April 1954 to May 1959
Title: Player-Manager.
Total Games: 261

FLETCHER, Harold
June 1967 to May 1968
Title: Coach.
Total Games: 47

FREELY, Tony
May 1984 to March 1985
Title: Manager.
Total Games: 41

FRIEL, Philip (Phil) *
August 1960 to September 1960
Title: Temporary Player-Coach.
Total Games: 8

GODFREY, Brian Cameron *
June 1987 to November 1991 (260), February 1992 to March 1994 (110)
Title: Manager.
Total Games: 370

GOODWIN, Gary *
March 1994 to May 1994
Title: Joint Temporary Manager (with Brian Hughes).
Total Games: 10

GRANT, Robert (Bobby) *
August 1965 to May 1966
Title: Player-Manager.
Total Games: 55

HARRIS, Adrian Gerald (Adie) *
January 2006
Title: Joint Temporary Manager (with Neil Mustoe).
Total Games: 1

HARRIS, Timothy (Tim) *
January 2006 to June 2008
Title: Manager.
Total Games: 121

HAYWARD, A.J
1910 to 1911
Title: Secretary.
Total Games: 0

HUGHES, Brian David *
March 1994 to May 1994 (10), October 1998 to February 2000 (77)
Title: Joint Temporary Manager (with Gary Goodwin), Manager 1998-2000.
Total Games: 87

HUKIN, Maurice Swain
b. 24/01/1886 Sheffield, Yorks. d. Qu3 1976 Gloucester
1931 to 1938 (293), September 1960 to May 1962 (82)
Title: Secretary-Manager 1931-35, Manager 1935-38, Manager 1960-62.
Total Games: 375

HUMPSTON, Ron
May 1962 to May 1963
Title: Manager.
Total Games: 44

HUNT, Douglas Arthur (Doug) *
November 1948 to July 1952
<u>Title:</u> Player-Manager.
<u>Total Games:</u> 193

LANE, Lionel Alfred *
1898 to 1899
<u>Title:</u> Secretary.
<u>Total Games:</u> 20

LAYTON, John Henry (Johnny) *
March 1982 to October 1982
<u>Title:</u> Manager.
<u>Total Games:</u> 28

LEWIS, Randolph
1899 to 1902
<u>Title:</u> Secretary.
<u>Total Games:</u> 40

McINTOSH, John McGregor (Ian) *
August 1968 to May 1970 (108), November 1971 to November 1972 (47)
<u>Title:</u> Player-Manager 1968-70, Manager 1971-72.
<u>Total Games:</u> 155

MEHEW, David Stephen (Dave) *
June 2008 to date
<u>Title:</u> Team Manager.
<u>Total Games:</u> 54

MILLARD, Steve (Ollie)
November 1991 to February 1992
<u>Title:</u> Temporary Manager.
<u>Total Games:</u> 18

MOULSDALE, Colin B *
May 1976 to November 1977
<u>Title:</u> Player-Manager.
<u>Total Games:</u> 64

MURPHY, John
May 1994 to March 1996
<u>Title:</u> Manager.
<u>Total Games:</u> 94

MURSELL, Robert (Bob)
November 1977 to September 1980 (136), October 1982 to April 1984 (90)
<u>Title:</u> Manager.
<u>Total Games:</u> 226

MUSTOE, Neil John *
January 2006
<u>Title:</u> Joint Temporary Manager (with Adie Harris).
<u>Total Games:</u> 1

NORRIS, Oliver P (Ollie) *
August 1959 to January 1960
<u>Title:</u> Player-Manager.
<u>Total Games:</u> 28

PALMER, J.E
1906 to 1909
<u>Title:</u> Secretary.
<u>Total Games:</u> 51

PREECE, John
November 1970 to November 1971
<u>Title:</u> Manager.
<u>Total Games:</u> 47

PRINCE-COX, Capt. Albert James
b. Qu3 1890 Portsea, Hants. d. ?
June 1938 to 1940
<u>Title:</u> Manager.
<u>Total Games:</u> 66

RICHARDSON, Paul *
May 1985 to Bovember 1985
<u>Title:</u> Player-Manager.
<u>Total Games:</u> 22

ROBINS, H.T *
1893 to 1897
<u>Title:</u> Secretary
<u>Total Games:</u> 65

ROSENIOR, Leroy De Graft *
March 1996 to October 1998
<u>Title:</u> Player-Manager.
<u>Total Games:</u> 148

SCARROTT, Stephen W (Steve) *
November 1985 to June 1987
<u>Title:</u> Manager.
<u>Total Games:</u> 80

SHERWOOD, Henry George *
1902 to 1903
<u>Title:</u> Joint Secretary (with Henry Arkell).
<u>Total Games:</u> 12

TREDGETT, Kenneth Frank *
January 1960 to May 1960
<u>Title:</u> Player-Coach.
<u>Total Games:</u> 20

WASHBOURNE, James Gilbert *
1897 to 1898
<u>Title:</u> Secretary.
<u>Total Games:</u> 10

WHITING, Jack F
February 1948 to November 1948
<u>Title:</u> Joint Temporary Manager (with Bill Carver).
<u>Total Games:</u> 33

WILLIAMS, Cyril
June 1966 to March 1967
<u>Title:</u> Manager.
<u>Total Games:</u> 39

Note: Total Games indicate number of competitive games managed. As actual dates of appointments and resignations not known with many these are approximate.

MANAGERS AND CLUB OFFICIALS

Gloucester information entered for following seasons:
1883/84, 1884/85, 1885/86, 1889/90, 1890/91, 1891/92, 1892/93, 1893/94, 1894/95, 1895/96, 1896/97, 1897/98, 1898/99, 1899/00, 1900/01, 1902/03, 1903/04, 1906/07, 1907/08, 1908/09, 1909/10, 1913/14, 1919/20, 1920/21, 1921/22, 1922/23, 1923/24, 1924/25, 1925/26, 1926/27, 1927/28, 1928/29, 1929/30, 1930/31, 1931/32, 1932/33, 1933/34, 1934/35, 1935/36, 1936/37, 1937/38, 1938/39, 1939/40, 1940/41, 1941/42, 1942/43, 1946/47, 1947/48, 1948/49, 1949/50, 1950/51, 1951/52, 1952/53, 1953/54, 1954/55, 1955/56, 1956/57, 1957/58, 1958/59, 1959/60, 1960/61, 1961/62, 1962/63, 1963/64, 1964/65, 1965/66, 1966/67, 1967/68, 1968/69, 1969/70, 1970/71, 1971/72, 1972/73, 1973/74, 1974/75, 1976/77, 1977/78, 1978/79, 1979/80, 1980/81, 1981/82, 1982/83, 1983/84, 1984/85, 1985/86, 1986/87, 1987/88, 1988/89, 1989/90, 1990/91, 1991/92, 1992/93, 1993/94, 1994/95, 1995/96, 1996/97, 1997/98, 1998/99, 1999/00, 2000/01, 2001/02, 2002/03, 2003/04, 2004/05, 2005/06, 2006/07, 2007/08, 2008/09 (108 seasons)

Main Sources:
Rob Kujawa Club Historian
Neil Phelps
Gloucester Citizen
Gloucester Journal
Gloucestershire Chronicle
Gloucestershire Echo
Tewkesbury Register
Dursley,Berkeley & Sharpness Gazette & Wotton-Under-Edge Advertiser
Gloucester Standard & Gloucestershire News
Stroud News & Gloucester County Advertiser
Stroud Journal
Dean Forest Mercury
Match Day Programmes 1937 to date (Home and Away).
Internet
Football League Players' Records 1888-1939 by Michael Joyce.
The PFA Premier And Football League Players' Records 1946-2005 Edited & Compiled by Barry J. Hugman.
Scottish League Player's Records Division One 1890/91 to 1938/39 by Steve Emms & Richard Wells.
Scottish League Players' Records Division One 1946/47 to 1974/75 by Richard Beal & Steve Emms.
Scottish League Players' Records Premier Division and Premier League 1975/76 to 1999/2000 by Steve Emms
The F.A. Cup Complete Results by Tony Brown
The Official Centenary History Of The Southern League 1894 to 1994 Compiled by Leigh Edwards.
Something To Shout About: The History Of Forest Green Rovers AFC by Tim Barnard
Town Score 100 +: The History Of Dursley Town FC by Colin Timbrell
The Who's Who Of Grantham Town Football Club by Jon Barnes
The Official History Of Worcester City FC by Bill Cook & Julian Pugh
Stars In Stripes: The Official History of Bath City Football Club by Kerry Miller
Gloucester City AFC Golden Jubilee Handbook, 1889-1939.
Gloucester City AFC Diamond Jubilee Handbook, 1889-1949.
Rothmans Football Yearbooks 1970 to 2002.
Sky Sports Football Yearbooks 2002 to date.

PROGRAMME

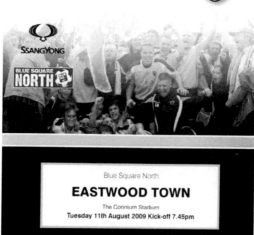

Blue Square North
EASTWOOD TOWN
The Corinium Stadium
Tuesday 11th August 2009 Kick-off 7.45pm

2009-2010

SUBSCRIBERS

Grateful thanks to the following who ordered a copy of this publication in advance.

1 Rob Kujawa
2 Mike Kujawa
3 Brian Hobbs
4 Karen & David Evans
5 Colin Timbrell, Gloucestershire
   FA Historian
6 Ian Clark
7 Tim Clark
8 Simon Clark
9 Phil Gough
10 Phil Warren
11 James Warren
12 John Warren
13 Andy Birchley (Shandy)
14 Nigel Dean
15 Adrian Stokes
16 David Stokes
17 Andrew Turner
18 Frances Turner
19 Dr. Bob Byrne
20 'Jake' Giddins
21 Terry Rodway
22 Robin Mogg
23 Tony Butt
24 Robert Gardiner
25 Trevor King
26 Graham Thomas (Egg)
27 Rob Coldray
28 Dave Collins
29 Paul Clark (Pablo)
30 Laurence G. Cook
31 Tim Batehup
32 Philip Grace
33 Bill Bulled
34 Andrew Bulled
35 Trevor Howard (aka Dr. Wart
   Hoover)
36 Dave Rey
37 Dick Etheridge
38 John Gamblin
39 Terry Foote
40 David Michael Woods
41 Graham Mitchell
42 David Staite
43 Parmjit Dhanda, M.P.
44 Jonathan Standen, Headmaster,
   The Crypt School
45 John Hammonds
46 Robbie Green
47 Raymond Elliott
48 Noreen & Liam Sadler
49 Marion & Padriac Duffy
50 Paul Caiden
51 Mike Caiden
52 Mike North-Bond
53 Adrian Harris
54 Neil Phelps
55 Montague Taynton

56 Richard Gittings
57 David Hammonds
58 Philip Keene
59 Mr. A. Moore
60 Jack Davis
61 Mrs.Thelma Rutherford
62 Sally & Gordon Pointer
63 A.W.S. Butler
64 John A. Cooper
65 Raymond Marshall
66 Mike Dunstan
67 Keith Dunstan
68 Matthew Gamston
69 David Peplow
70 Richard Peplow
71 David John Ashburner
72 Archie Paul Fox
73 Gerald Dwyer
74 Stan Myers
75 Steve Turk
76 David Hines
77 John Quinnell
78 Des Edwards
79 Mrs. Molly Hammonds
80 Martyn Ellis
81 Mr. R.D. Phillips
82 British International School,
   Belgrade, Serbia
83 Christopher D. Howie
84 Kevin S. Howie
85 Neil A. Howie
86 Stewart H. Howie
87 Mark Foote
88 Henry Lane
89 Keith Griffiths
90 Ray Millard
91 Mr. & Mrs. Archie Proudfoot
92 Judith & Derek Cooper
93 Mrs. Margaret Mackenzie
94 David Bush
95 Alan Lloyd, M.B.E.
96 Roy Fenner
97 Andrew Payne
98 Stephen Hyde
99 Pat Wetson
100 Shaun Wetson
101 Richard Joyce
102 Daryll Cox
103 Jimmy Cox
104 Derek Cox
105 Andy Clark
106 Andee Stevenson
107 Tony Gaze
108 James R.A. Nixon
109 Nigel Clarke
110 Simon R. Ellis
111 Mr. Matthew F. Phillips
112 Dr. Andrew C.G. Cook

113 Nick Gore
114 John Pugh
115 David Miller
116 Ade Tandy
117 Adam Lyons
118 Derek James
119 Ken Blackburn
120 Joe Green
121 Dave Phillips
122 Mark Witts
123 Rich Steele
124 Eric Hayward
125 Dave Hatton
126 Steve Searle
127 Derek Holmes
128 Rosemary Alder & Family
129 Matt 'Penalty' Bowman
130 Nigel Hughes
131 Matt Clift (Clifty)
132 Judith, John & Simon Evans
133 Marion Turner
134 Adam Parker
135 Haydn Hilton (Hilto)
136 Brian Wright
137 Jeffrey Neale
138 Antoni Proboszcz
139 B.E. Jones
140 David Carlile
141 Steve & Sean White
142 Gregory Turner
143 Derek Bowden
144 Paul Davis
145 Tarun Patel
146 John Bingle
147 Dan Bingle
148 Saul Hathaway
149 Paul Halford
150 Stephen Turner
151 Kevin Beedie
152 The Chase Family
153 Tim Harris
154 Sarah McGurk
155 Eamonn McGurk
156 Patrick McGurk
157 Erin McGurk
158 Ciara McGurk
159 Niamh McGurk
160 Lyndon Wood
161 Richard Wood
162 Paul Godfrey
163 Benjamin Spragg
164 Barrie Pope
165 John Vilimas
166 Paul Ackland
167 Mike Eaketts

Not Cheltenham, Forest Green,
City are the team for me;
We've got no money and we've got no ground but
We're City and we're proud.